Lecture Notes in Computer Science 13670

More information about this series at https://link.springer.com/bookseries/558

Shai Avidan · Gabriel Brostow ·
Moustapha Cissé · Giovanni Maria Farinella ·
Tal Hassner (Eds.)

Computer Vision – ECCV 2022

17th European Conference
Tel Aviv, Israel, October 23–27, 2022
Proceedings, Part X

 Springer

Editors
Shai Avidan
Tel Aviv University
Tel Aviv, Israel

Gabriel Brostow ⓘ
University College London
London, UK

Moustapha Cissé
Google AI
Accra, Ghana

Giovanni Maria Farinella ⓘ
University of Catania
Catania, Italy

Tal Hassner ⓘ
Facebook (United States)
Menlo Park, CA, USA

ISSN 0302-9743   ISSN 1611-3349 (electronic)
Lecture Notes in Computer Science
ISBN 978-3-031-20079-3   ISBN 978-3-031-20080-9 (eBook)
https://doi.org/10.1007/978-3-031-20080-9

This Springer imprint is published by the registered company Springer Nature Switzerland AG
The registered company address is: Gewerbestrasse 11, 6330 Cham, Switzerland

Foreword

Organizing the European Conference on Computer Vision (ECCV 2022) in Tel-Aviv during a global pandemic was no easy feat. The uncertainty level was extremely high, and decisions had to be postponed to the last minute. Still, we managed to plan things just in time for ECCV 2022 to be held in person. Participation in physical events is crucial to stimulating collaborations and nurturing the culture of the Computer Vision community.

There were many people who worked hard to ensure attendees enjoyed the best science at the 16th edition of ECCV. We are grateful to the Program Chairs Gabriel Brostow and Tal Hassner, who went above and beyond to ensure the ECCV reviewing process ran smoothly. The scientific program includes dozens of workshops and tutorials in addition to the main conference and we would like to thank Leonid Karlinsky and Tomer Michaeli for their hard work. Finally, special thanks to the web chairs Lorenzo Baraldi and Kosta Derpanis, who put in extra hours to transfer information fast and efficiently to the ECCV community.

We would like to express gratitude to our generous sponsors and the Industry Chairs, Dimosthenis Karatzas and Chen Sagiv, who oversaw industry relations and proposed new ways for academia-industry collaboration and technology transfer. It's great to see so much industrial interest in what we're doing!

Authors' draft versions of the papers appeared online with open access on both the Computer Vision Foundation (CVF) and the European Computer Vision Association (ECVA) websites as with previous ECCVs. Springer, the publisher of the proceedings, has arranged for archival publication. The final version of the papers is hosted by SpringerLink, with active references and supplementary materials. It benefits all potential readers that we offer both a free and citeable version for all researchers, as well as an authoritative, citeable version for SpringerLink readers. Our thanks go to Ronan Nugent from Springer, who helped us negotiate this agreement. Last but not least, we wish to thank Eric Mortensen, our publication chair, whose expertise made the process smooth.

October 2022

Rita Cucchiara
Jiří Matas
Amnon Shashua
Lihi Zelnik-Manor

Preface

Welcome to the proceedings of the European Conference on Computer Vision (ECCV 2022). This was a hybrid edition of ECCV as we made our way out of the COVID-19 pandemic. The conference received 5804 valid paper submissions, compared to 5150 submissions to ECCV 2020 (a 12.7% increase) and 2439 in ECCV 2018. 1645 submissions were accepted for publication (28%) and, of those, 157 (2.7% overall) as orals.

846 of the submissions were desk-rejected for various reasons. Many of them because they revealed author identity, thus violating the double-blind policy. This violation came in many forms: some had author names with the title, others added acknowledgments to specific grants, yet others had links to their github account where their name was visible. Tampering with the LaTeX template was another reason for automatic desk rejection.

ECCV 2022 used the traditional CMT system to manage the entire double-blind reviewing process. Authors did not know the names of the reviewers and vice versa. Each paper received at least 3 reviews (except 6 papers that received only 2 reviews), totalling more than 15,000 reviews.

Handling the review process at this scale was a significant challenge. To ensure that each submission received as fair and high-quality reviews as possible, we recruited more than 4719 reviewers (in the end, 4719 reviewers did at least one review). Similarly we recruited more than 276 area chairs (eventually, only 276 area chairs handled a batch of papers). The area chairs were selected based on their technical expertise and reputation, largely among people who served as area chairs in previous top computer vision and machine learning conferences (ECCV, ICCV, CVPR, NeurIPS, etc.).

Reviewers were similarly invited from previous conferences, and also from the pool of authors. We also encouraged experienced area chairs to suggest additional chairs and reviewers in the initial phase of recruiting. The median reviewer load was five papers per reviewer, while the average load was about four papers, because of the emergency reviewers. The area chair load was 35 papers, on average.

Conflicts of interest between authors, area chairs, and reviewers were handled largely automatically by the CMT platform, with some manual help from the Program Chairs. Reviewers were allowed to describe themselves as senior reviewer (load of 8 papers to review) or junior reviewers (load of 4 papers). Papers were matched to area chairs based on a subject-area affinity score computed in CMT and an affinity score computed by the Toronto Paper Matching System (TPMS). TPMS is based on the paper's full text. An area chair handling each submission would bid for preferred expert reviewers, and we balanced load and prevented conflicts.

The assignment of submissions to area chairs was relatively smooth, as was the assignment of submissions to reviewers. A small percentage of reviewers were not happy with their assignments in terms of subjects and self-reported expertise. This is an area for improvement, although it's interesting that many of these cases were reviewers hand-picked by AC's. We made a later round of reviewer recruiting, targeted at the list of authors of papers submitted to the conference, and had an excellent response which helped provide enough emergency reviewers. In the end, all but six papers received at least 3 reviews.

The challenges of the reviewing process are in line with past experiences at ECCV 2020. As the community grows, and the number of submissions increases, it becomes ever more challenging to recruit enough reviewers and ensure a high enough quality of reviews. Enlisting authors by default as reviewers might be one step to address this challenge.

Authors were given a week to rebut the initial reviews, and address reviewers' concerns. Each rebuttal was limited to a single pdf page with a fixed template.

The Area Chairs then led discussions with the reviewers on the merits of each submission. The goal was to reach consensus, but, ultimately, it was up to the Area Chair to make a decision. The decision was then discussed with a buddy Area Chair to make sure decisions were fair and informative. The entire process was conducted virtually with no in-person meetings taking place.

The Program Chairs were informed in cases where the Area Chairs overturned a decisive consensus reached by the reviewers, and pushed for the meta-reviews to contain details that explained the reasoning for such decisions. Obviously these were the most contentious cases, where reviewer inexperience was the most common reported factor.

Once the list of accepted papers was finalized and released, we went through the laborious process of plagiarism (including self-plagiarism) detection. A total of 4 accepted papers were rejected because of that.

Finally, we would like to thank our Technical Program Chair, Pavel Lifshits, who did tremendous work behind the scenes, and we thank the tireless CMT team.

October 2022

Gabriel Brostow
Giovanni Maria Farinella
Moustapha Cissé
Shai Avidan
Tal Hassner

Organization

General Chairs

Rita Cucchiara   University of Modena and Reggio Emilia, Italy
Jiří Matas   Czech Technical University in Prague, Czech Republic
Amnon Shashua   Hebrew University of Jerusalem, Israel
Lihi Zelnik-Manor   Technion – Israel Institute of Technology, Israel

Program Chairs

Shai Avidan   Tel-Aviv University, Israel
Gabriel Brostow   University College London, UK
Moustapha Cissé   Google AI, Ghana
Giovanni Maria Farinella   University of Catania, Italy
Tal Hassner   Facebook AI, USA

Program Technical Chair

Pavel Lifshits   Technion – Israel Institute of Technology, Israel

Workshops Chairs

Leonid Karlinsky   IBM Research, Israel
Tomer Michaeli   Technion – Israel Institute of Technology, Israel
Ko Nishino   Kyoto University, Japan

Tutorial Chairs

Thomas Pock   Graz University of Technology, Austria
Natalia Neverova   Facebook AI Research, UK

Demo Chair

Bohyung Han   Seoul National University, Korea

Social and Student Activities Chairs

Tatiana Tommasi   Italian Institute of Technology, Italy
Sagie Benaim   University of Copenhagen, Denmark

Diversity and Inclusion Chairs

Xi Yin   Facebook AI Research, USA
Bryan Russell   Adobe, USA

Communications Chairs

Lorenzo Baraldi   University of Modena and Reggio Emilia, Italy
Kosta Derpanis   York University & Samsung AI Centre Toronto,
                                Canada

Industrial Liaison Chairs

Dimosthenis Karatzas   Universitat Autònoma de Barcelona, Spain
Chen Sagiv   SagivTech, Israel

Finance Chair

Gerard Medioni   University of Southern California & Amazon,
                                USA

Publication Chair

Eric Mortensen   MiCROTEC, USA

Area Chairs

Lourdes Agapito   University College London, UK
Zeynep Akata   University of Tübingen, Germany
Naveed Akhtar   University of Western Australia, Australia
Karteek Alahari   Inria Grenoble Rhône-Alpes, France
Alexandre Alahi   École polytechnique fédérale de Lausanne,
                                Switzerland
Pablo Arbelaez   Universidad de Los Andes, Columbia
Antonis A. Argyros   University of Crete & Foundation for Research
                                and Technology-Hellas, Crete
Yuki M. Asano   University of Amsterdam, The Netherlands
Kalle Åström   Lund University, Sweden
Hadar Averbuch-Elor   Cornell University, USA

Hossein Azizpour	KTH Royal Institute of Technology, Sweden
Vineeth N. Balasubramanian	Indian Institute of Technology, Hyderabad, India
Lamberto Ballan	University of Padova, Italy
Adrien Bartoli	Université Clermont Auvergne, France
Horst Bischof	Graz University of Technology, Austria
Matthew B. Blaschko	KU Leuven, Belgium
Federica Bogo	Meta Reality Labs Research, Switzerland
Katherine Bouman	California Institute of Technology, USA
Edmond Boyer	Inria Grenoble Rhône-Alpes, France
Michael S. Brown	York University, Canada
Vittorio Caggiano	Meta AI Research, USA
Neill Campbell	University of Bath, UK
Octavia Camps	Northeastern University, USA
Duygu Ceylan	Adobe Research, USA
Ayan Chakrabarti	Google Research, USA
Tat-Jen Cham	Nanyang Technological University, Singapore
Antoni Chan	City University of Hong Kong, Hong Kong, China
Manmohan Chandraker	NEC Labs America, USA
Xinlei Chen	Facebook AI Research, USA
Xilin Chen	Institute of Computing Technology, Chinese Academy of Sciences, China
Dongdong Chen	Microsoft Cloud AI, USA
Chen Chen	University of Central Florida, USA
Ondrej Chum	Vision Recognition Group, Czech Technical University in Prague, Czech Republic
John Collomosse	Adobe Research & University of Surrey, UK
Camille Couprie	Facebook, France
David Crandall	Indiana University, USA
Daniel Cremers	Technical University of Munich, Germany
Marco Cristani	University of Verona, Italy
Canton Cristian	Facebook AI Research, USA
Dengxin Dai	ETH Zurich, Switzerland
Dima Damen	University of Bristol, UK
Kostas Daniilidis	University of Pennsylvania, USA
Trevor Darrell	University of California, Berkeley, USA
Andrew Davison	Imperial College London, UK
Tali Dekel	Weizmann Institute of Science, Israel
Alessio Del Bue	Istituto Italiano di Tecnologia, Italy
Weihong Deng	Beijing University of Posts and Telecommunications, China
Konstantinos Derpanis	Ryerson University, Canada
Carl Doersch	DeepMind, UK

Matthijs Douze	Facebook AI Research, USA
Mohamed Elhoseiny	King Abdullah University of Science and Technology, Saudi Arabia
Sergio Escalera	University of Barcelona, Spain
Yi Fang	New York University, USA
Ryan Farrell	Brigham Young University, USA
Alireza Fathi	Google, USA
Christoph Feichtenhofer	Facebook AI Research, USA
Basura Fernando	Agency for Science, Technology and Research (A*STAR), Singapore
Vittorio Ferrari	Google Research, Switzerland
Andrew W. Fitzgibbon	Graphcore, UK
David J. Fleet	University of Toronto, Canada
David Forsyth	University of Illinois at Urbana-Champaign, USA
David Fouhey	University of Michigan, USA
Katerina Fragkiadaki	Carnegie Mellon University, USA
Friedrich Fraundorfer	Graz University of Technology, Austria
Oren Freifeld	Ben-Gurion University, Israel
Thomas Funkhouser	Google Research & Princeton University, USA
Yasutaka Furukawa	Simon Fraser University, Canada
Fabio Galasso	Sapienza University of Rome, Italy
Jürgen Gall	University of Bonn, Germany
Chuang Gan	Massachusetts Institute of Technology, USA
Zhe Gan	Microsoft, USA
Animesh Garg	University of Toronto, Vector Institute, Nvidia, Canada
Efstratios Gavves	University of Amsterdam, The Netherlands
Peter Gehler	Amazon, Germany
Theo Gevers	University of Amsterdam, The Netherlands
Bernard Ghanem	King Abdullah University of Science and Technology, Saudi Arabia
Ross B. Girshick	Facebook AI Research, USA
Georgia Gkioxari	Facebook AI Research, USA
Albert Gordo	Facebook, USA
Stephen Gould	Australian National University, Australia
Venu Madhav Govindu	Indian Institute of Science, India
Kristen Grauman	Facebook AI Research & UT Austin, USA
Abhinav Gupta	Carnegie Mellon University & Facebook AI Research, USA
Mohit Gupta	University of Wisconsin-Madison, USA
Hu Han	Institute of Computing Technology, Chinese Academy of Sciences, China

Bohyung Han	Seoul National University, Korea
Tian Han	Stevens Institute of Technology, USA
Emily Hand	University of Nevada, Reno, USA
Bharath Hariharan	Cornell University, USA
Ran He	Institute of Automation, Chinese Academy of Sciences, China
Otmar Hilliges	ETH Zurich, Switzerland
Adrian Hilton	University of Surrey, UK
Minh Hoai	Stony Brook University, USA
Yedid Hoshen	Hebrew University of Jerusalem, Israel
Timothy Hospedales	University of Edinburgh, UK
Gang Hua	Wormpex AI Research, USA
Di Huang	Beihang University, China
Jing Huang	Facebook, USA
Jia-Bin Huang	Facebook, USA
Nathan Jacobs	Washington University in St. Louis, USA
C. V. Jawahar	International Institute of Information Technology, Hyderabad, India
Herve Jegou	Facebook AI Research, France
Neel Joshi	Microsoft Research, USA
Armand Joulin	Facebook AI Research, France
Frederic Jurie	University of Caen Normandie, France
Fredrik Kahl	Chalmers University of Technology, Sweden
Yannis Kalantidis	NAVER LABS Europe, France
Evangelos Kalogerakis	University of Massachusetts, Amherst, USA
Sing Bing Kang	Zillow Group, USA
Yosi Keller	Bar Ilan University, Israel
Margret Keuper	University of Mannheim, Germany
Tae-Kyun Kim	Imperial College London, UK
Benjamin Kimia	Brown University, USA
Alexander Kirillov	Facebook AI Research, USA
Kris Kitani	Carnegie Mellon University, USA
Iasonas Kokkinos	Snap Inc. & University College London, UK
Vladlen Koltun	Apple, USA
Nikos Komodakis	University of Crete, Crete
Piotr Koniusz	Australian National University, Australia
Philipp Kraehenbuehl	University of Texas at Austin, USA
Dilip Krishnan	Google, USA
Ajay Kumar	Hong Kong Polytechnic University, Hong Kong, China
Junseok Kwon	Chung-Ang University, Korea
Jean-Francois Lalonde	Université Laval, Canada

Ivan Laptev	Inria Paris, France
Laura Leal-Taixé	Technical University of Munich, Germany
Erik Learned-Miller	University of Massachusetts, Amherst, USA
Gim Hee Lee	National University of Singapore, Singapore
Seungyong Lee	Pohang University of Science and Technology, Korea
Zhen Lei	Institute of Automation, Chinese Academy of Sciences, China
Bastian Leibe	RWTH Aachen University, Germany
Hongdong Li	Australian National University, Australia
Fuxin Li	Oregon State University, USA
Bo Li	University of Illinois at Urbana-Champaign, USA
Yin Li	University of Wisconsin-Madison, USA
Ser-Nam Lim	Meta AI Research, USA
Joseph Lim	University of Southern California, USA
Stephen Lin	Microsoft Research Asia, China
Dahua Lin	The Chinese University of Hong Kong, Hong Kong, China
Si Liu	Beihang University, China
Xiaoming Liu	Michigan State University, USA
Ce Liu	Microsoft, USA
Zicheng Liu	Microsoft, USA
Yanxi Liu	Pennsylvania State University, USA
Feng Liu	Portland State University, USA
Yebin Liu	Tsinghua University, China
Chen Change Loy	Nanyang Technological University, Singapore
Huchuan Lu	Dalian University of Technology, China
Cewu Lu	Shanghai Jiao Tong University, China
Oisin Mac Aodha	University of Edinburgh, UK
Dhruv Mahajan	Facebook, USA
Subhransu Maji	University of Massachusetts, Amherst, USA
Atsuto Maki	KTH Royal Institute of Technology, Sweden
Arun Mallya	NVIDIA, USA
R. Manmatha	Amazon, USA
Iacopo Masi	Sapienza University of Rome, Italy
Dimitris N. Metaxas	Rutgers University, USA
Ajmal Mian	University of Western Australia, Australia
Christian Micheloni	University of Udine, Italy
Krystian Mikolajczyk	Imperial College London, UK
Anurag Mittal	Indian Institute of Technology, Madras, India
Philippos Mordohai	Stevens Institute of Technology, USA
Greg Mori	Simon Fraser University & Borealis AI, Canada

Vittorio Murino	Istituto Italiano di Tecnologia, Italy
P. J. Narayanan	International Institute of Information Technology, Hyderabad, India
Ram Nevatia	University of Southern California, USA
Natalia Neverova	Facebook AI Research, UK
Richard Newcombe	Facebook, USA
Cuong V. Nguyen	Florida International University, USA
Bingbing Ni	Shanghai Jiao Tong University, China
Juan Carlos Niebles	Salesforce & Stanford University, USA
Ko Nishino	Kyoto University, Japan
Jean-Marc Odobez	Idiap Research Institute, École polytechnique fédérale de Lausanne, Switzerland
Francesca Odone	University of Genova, Italy
Takayuki Okatani	Tohoku University & RIKEN Center for Advanced Intelligence Project, Japan
Manohar Paluri	Facebook, USA
Guan Pang	Facebook, USA
Maja Pantic	Imperial College London, UK
Sylvain Paris	Adobe Research, USA
Jaesik Park	Pohang University of Science and Technology, Korea
Hyun Soo Park	The University of Minnesota, USA
Omkar M. Parkhi	Facebook, USA
Deepak Pathak	Carnegie Mellon University, USA
Georgios Pavlakos	University of California, Berkeley, USA
Marcello Pelillo	University of Venice, Italy
Marc Pollefeys	ETH Zurich & Microsoft, Switzerland
Jean Ponce	Inria, France
Gerard Pons-Moll	University of Tübingen, Germany
Fatih Porikli	Qualcomm, USA
Victor Adrian Prisacariu	University of Oxford, UK
Petia Radeva	University of Barcelona, Spain
Ravi Ramamoorthi	University of California, San Diego, USA
Deva Ramanan	Carnegie Mellon University, USA
Vignesh Ramanathan	Facebook, USA
Nalini Ratha	State University of New York at Buffalo, USA
Tammy Riklin Raviv	Ben-Gurion University, Israel
Tobias Ritschel	University College London, UK
Emanuele Rodola	Sapienza University of Rome, Italy
Amit K. Roy-Chowdhury	University of California, Riverside, USA
Michael Rubinstein	Google, USA
Olga Russakovsky	Princeton University, USA

Mathieu Salzmann	École polytechnique fédérale de Lausanne, Switzerland
Dimitris Samaras	Stony Brook University, USA
Aswin Sankaranarayanan	Carnegie Mellon University, USA
Imari Sato	National Institute of Informatics, Japan
Yoichi Sato	University of Tokyo, Japan
Shin'ichi Satoh	National Institute of Informatics, Japan
Walter Scheirer	University of Notre Dame, USA
Bernt Schiele	Max Planck Institute for Informatics, Germany
Konrad Schindler	ETH Zurich, Switzerland
Cordelia Schmid	Inria & Google, France
Alexander Schwing	University of Illinois at Urbana-Champaign, USA
Nicu Sebe	University of Trento, Italy
Greg Shakhnarovich	Toyota Technological Institute at Chicago, USA
Eli Shechtman	Adobe Research, USA
Humphrey Shi	University of Oregon & University of Illinois at Urbana-Champaign & Picsart AI Research, USA
Jianbo Shi	University of Pennsylvania, USA
Roy Shilkrot	Massachusetts Institute of Technology, USA
Mike Zheng Shou	National University of Singapore, Singapore
Kaleem Siddiqi	McGill University, Canada
Richa Singh	Indian Institute of Technology Jodhpur, India
Greg Slabaugh	Queen Mary University of London, UK
Cees Snoek	University of Amsterdam, The Netherlands
Yale Song	Facebook AI Research, USA
Yi-Zhe Song	University of Surrey, UK
Bjorn Stenger	Rakuten Institute of Technology
Abby Stylianou	Saint Louis University, USA
Akihiro Sugimoto	National Institute of Informatics, Japan
Chen Sun	Brown University, USA
Deqing Sun	Google, USA
Kalyan Sunkavalli	Adobe Research, USA
Ying Tai	Tencent YouTu Lab, China
Ayellet Tal	Technion – Israel Institute of Technology, Israel
Ping Tan	Simon Fraser University, Canada
Siyu Tang	ETH Zurich, Switzerland
Chi-Keung Tang	Hong Kong University of Science and Technology, Hong Kong, China
Radu Timofte	University of Würzburg, Germany & ETH Zurich, Switzerland
Federico Tombari	Google, Switzerland & Technical University of Munich, Germany

James Tompkin	Brown University, USA
Lorenzo Torresani	Dartmouth College, USA
Alexander Toshev	Apple, USA
Du Tran	Facebook AI Research, USA
Anh T. Tran	VinAI, Vietnam
Zhuowen Tu	University of California, San Diego, USA
Georgios Tzimiropoulos	Queen Mary University of London, UK
Jasper Uijlings	Google Research, Switzerland
Jan C. van Gemert	Delft University of Technology, The Netherlands
Gul Varol	Ecole des Ponts ParisTech, France
Nuno Vasconcelos	University of California, San Diego, USA
Mayank Vatsa	Indian Institute of Technology Jodhpur, India
Ashok Veeraraghavan	Rice University, USA
Jakob Verbeek	Facebook AI Research, France
Carl Vondrick	Columbia University, USA
Ruiping Wang	Institute of Computing Technology, Chinese Academy of Sciences, China
Xinchao Wang	National University of Singapore, Singapore
Liwei Wang	The Chinese University of Hong Kong, Hong Kong, China
Chaohui Wang	Université Paris-Est, France
Xiaolong Wang	University of California, San Diego, USA
Christian Wolf	NAVER LABS Europe, France
Tao Xiang	University of Surrey, UK
Saining Xie	Facebook AI Research, USA
Cihang Xie	University of California, Santa Cruz, USA
Zeki Yalniz	Facebook, USA
Ming-Hsuan Yang	University of California, Merced, USA
Angela Yao	National University of Singapore, Singapore
Shaodi You	University of Amsterdam, The Netherlands
Stella X. Yu	University of California, Berkeley, USA
Junsong Yuan	State University of New York at Buffalo, USA
Stefanos Zafeiriou	Imperial College London, UK
Amir Zamir	École polytechnique fédérale de Lausanne, Switzerland
Lei Zhang	Alibaba & Hong Kong Polytechnic University, Hong Kong, China
Lei Zhang	International Digital Economy Academy (IDEA), China
Pengchuan Zhang	Meta AI, USA
Bolei Zhou	University of California, Los Angeles, USA
Yuke Zhu	University of Texas at Austin, USA

Todd Zickler   Harvard University, USA
Wangmeng Zuo   Harbin Institute of Technology, China

Technical Program Committee

Davide Abati
Soroush Abbasi
   Koohpayegani
Amos L. Abbott
Rameen Abdal
Rabab Abdelfattah
Sahar Abdelnabi
Hassan Abu Alhaija
Abulikemu Abuduweili
Ron Abutbul
Hanno Ackermann
Aikaterini Adam
Kamil Adamczewski
Ehsan Adeli
Vida Adeli
Donald Adjeroh
Arman Afrasiyabi
Akshay Agarwal
Sameer Agarwal
Abhinav Agarwalla
Vaibhav Aggarwal
Sara Aghajanzadeh
Susmit Agrawal
Antonio Agudo
Touqeer Ahmad
Sk Miraj Ahmed
Chaitanya Ahuja
Nilesh A. Ahuja
Abhishek Aich
Shubhra Aich
Noam Aigerman
Arash Akbarinia
Peri Akiva
Derya Akkaynak
Emre Aksan
Arjun R. Akula
Yuval Alaluf
Stephan Alaniz
Paul Albert
Cenek Albl

Filippo Aleotti
Konstantinos P.
   Alexandridis
Motasem Alfarra
Mohsen Ali
Thiemo Alldieck
Hadi Alzayer
Liang An
Shan An
Yi An
Zhulin An
Dongsheng An
Jie An
Xiang An
Saket Anand
Cosmin Ancuti
Juan Andrade-Cetto
Alexander Andreopoulos
Bjoern Andres
Jerone T. A. Andrews
Shivangi Aneja
Anelia Angelova
Dragomir Anguelov
Rushil Anirudh
Oron Anschel
Rao Muhammad Anwer
Djamila Aouada
Evlampios Apostolidis
Srikar Appalaraju
Nikita Araslanov
Andre Araujo
Eric Arazo
Dawit Mureja Argaw
Anurag Arnab
Aditya Arora
Chetan Arora
Sunpreet S. Arora
Alexey Artemov
Muhammad Asad
Kumar Ashutosh

Sinem Aslan
Vishal Asnani
Mahmoud Assran
Amir Atapour-Abarghouei
Nikos Athanasiou
Ali Athar
ShahRukh Athar
Sara Atito
Souhaib Attaiki
Matan Atzmon
Mathieu Aubry
Nicolas Audebert
Tristan T.
   Aumentado-Armstrong
Melinos Averkiou
Yannis Avrithis
Stephane Ayache
Mehmet Aygün
Seyed Mehdi
   Ayyoubzadeh
Hossein Azizpour
George Azzopardi
Mallikarjun B. R.
Yunhao Ba
Abhishek Badki
Seung-Hwan Bae
Seung-Hwan Baek
Seungryul Baek
Piyush Nitin Bagad
Shai Bagon
Gaetan Bahl
Shikhar Bahl
Sherwin Bahmani
Haoran Bai
Lei Bai
Jiawang Bai
Haoyue Bai
Jinbin Bai
Xiang Bai
Xuyang Bai

Yang Bai
Yuanchao Bai
Ziqian Bai
Sungyong Baik
Kevin Bailly
Max Bain
Federico Baldassarre
Wele Gedara Chaminda
    Bandara
Biplab Banerjee
Pratyay Banerjee
Sandipan Banerjee
Jihwan Bang
Antyanta Bangunharcana
Aayush Bansal
Ankan Bansal
Siddhant Bansal
Wentao Bao
Zhipeng Bao
Amir Bar
Manel Baradad Jurjo
Lorenzo Baraldi
Danny Barash
Daniel Barath
Connelly Barnes
Ioan Andrei Bârsan
Steven Basart
Dina Bashkirova
Chaim Baskin
Peyman Bateni
Anil Batra
Sebastiano Battiato
Ardhendu Behera
Harkirat Behl
Jens Behley
Vasileios Belagiannis
Boulbaba Ben Amor
Emanuel Ben Baruch
Abdessamad Ben Hamza
Gil Ben-Artzi
Assia Benbihi
Fabian Benitez-Quiroz
Guy Ben-Yosef
Philipp Benz
Alexander W. Bergman

Urs Bergmann
Jesus Bermudez-Cameo
Stefano Berretti
Gedas Bertasius
Zachary Bessinger
Petra Bevandić
Matthew Beveridge
Lucas Beyer
Yash Bhalgat
Suvaansh Bhambri
Samarth Bharadwaj
Gaurav Bharaj
Aparna Bharati
Bharat Lal Bhatnagar
Uttaran Bhattacharya
Apratim Bhattacharyya
Brojeshwar Bhowmick
Ankan Kumar Bhunia
Ayan Kumar Bhunia
Qi Bi
Sai Bi
Michael Bi Mi
Gui-Bin Bian
Jia-Wang Bian
Shaojun Bian
Pia Bideau
Mario Bijelic
Hakan Bilen
Guillaume-Alexandre
    Bilodeau
Alexander Binder
Tolga Birdal
Vighnesh N. Birodkar
Sandika Biswas
Andreas Blattmann
Janusz Bobulski
Giuseppe Boccignone
Vishnu Boddeti
Navaneeth Bodla
Moritz Böhle
Aleksei Bokhovkin
Sam Bond-Taylor
Vivek Boominathan
Shubhankar Borse
Mark Boss

Andrea Bottino
Adnane Boukhayma
Fadi Boutros
Nicolas C. Boutry
Richard S. Bowen
Ivaylo Boyadzhiev
Aidan Boyd
Yuri Boykov
Aljaz Bozic
Behzad Bozorgtabar
Eric Brachmann
Samarth Brahmbhatt
Gustav Bredell
Francois Bremond
Joel Brogan
Andrew Brown
Thomas Brox
Marcus A. Brubaker
Robert-Jan Bruintjes
Yuqi Bu
Anders G. Buch
Himanshu Buckchash
Mateusz Buda
Ignas Budvytis
José M. Buenaposada
Marcel C. Bühler
Tu Bui
Adrian Bulat
Hannah Bull
Evgeny Burnaev
Andrei Bursuc
Benjamin Busam
Sergey N. Buzykanov
Wonmin Byeon
Fabian Caba
Martin Cadik
Guanyu Cai
Minjie Cai
Qing Cai
Zhongang Cai
Qi Cai
Yancheng Cai
Shen Cai
Han Cai
Jiarui Cai

Bowen Cai
Mu Cai
Qin Cai
Ruojin Cai
Weidong Cai
Weiwei Cai
Yi Cai
Yujun Cai
Zhiping Cai
Akin Caliskan
Lilian Calvet
Baris Can Cam
Necati Cihan Camgoz
Tommaso Campari
Dylan Campbell
Ziang Cao
Ang Cao
Xu Cao
Zhiwen Cao
Shengcao Cao
Song Cao
Weipeng Cao
Xiangyong Cao
Xiaochun Cao
Yue Cao
Yunhao Cao
Zhangjie Cao
Jiale Cao
Yang Cao
Jiajiong Cao
Jie Cao
Jinkun Cao
Lele Cao
Yulong Cao
Zhiguo Cao
Chen Cao
Razvan Caramalau
Marlène Careil
Gustavo Carneiro
Joao Carreira
Dan Casas
Paola Cascante-Bonilla
Angela Castillo
Francisco M. Castro
Pedro Castro

Luca Cavalli
George J. Cazenavette
Oya Celiktutan
Hakan Cevikalp
Sri Harsha C. H.
Sungmin Cha
Geonho Cha
Menglei Chai
Lucy Chai
Yuning Chai
Zenghao Chai
Anirban Chakraborty
Deep Chakraborty
Rudrasis Chakraborty
Souradeep Chakraborty
Kelvin C. K. Chan
Chee Seng Chan
Paramanand Chandramouli
Arjun Chandrasekaran
Kenneth Chaney
Dongliang Chang
Huiwen Chang
Peng Chang
Xiaojun Chang
Jia-Ren Chang
Hyung Jin Chang
Hyun Sung Chang
Ju Yong Chang
Li-Jen Chang
Qi Chang
Wei-Yi Chang
Yi Chang
Nadine Chang
Hanqing Chao
Pradyumna Chari
Dibyadip Chatterjee
Chiranjoy Chattopadhyay
Siddhartha Chaudhuri
Zhengping Che
Gal Chechik
Lianggangxu Chen
Qi Alfred Chen
Brian Chen
Bor-Chun Chen
Bo-Hao Chen

Bohong Chen
Bin Chen
Ziliang Chen
Cheng Chen
Chen Chen
Chaofeng Chen
Xi Chen
Haoyu Chen
Xuanhong Chen
Wei Chen
Qiang Chen
Shi Chen
Xianyu Chen
Chang Chen
Changhuai Chen
Hao Chen
Jie Chen
Jianbo Chen
Jingjing Chen
Jun Chen
Kejiang Chen
Mingcai Chen
Nenglun Chen
Qifeng Chen
Ruoyu Chen
Shu-Yu Chen
Weidong Chen
Weijie Chen
Weikai Chen
Xiang Chen
Xiuyi Chen
Xingyu Chen
Yaofo Chen
Yueting Chen
Yu Chen
Yunjin Chen
Yuntao Chen
Yun Chen
Zhenfang Chen
Zhuangzhuang Chen
Chu-Song Chen
Xiangyu Chen
Zhuo Chen
Chaoqi Chen
Shizhe Chen

Xiaotong Chen
Xiaozhi Chen
Dian Chen
Defang Chen
Dingfan Chen
Ding-Jie Chen
Ee Heng Chen
Tao Chen
Yixin Chen
Wei-Ting Chen
Lin Chen
Guang Chen
Guangyi Chen
Guanying Chen
Guangyao Chen
Hwann-Tzong Chen
Junwen Chen
Jiacheng Chen
Jianxu Chen
Hui Chen
Kai Chen
Kan Chen
Kevin Chen
Kuan-Wen Chen
Weihua Chen
Zhang Chen
Liang-Chieh Chen
Lele Chen
Liang Chen
Fanglin Chen
Zehui Chen
Minghui Chen
Minghao Chen
Xiaokang Chen
Qian Chen
Jun-Cheng Chen
Qi Chen
Qingcai Chen
Richard J. Chen
Runnan Chen
Rui Chen
Shuo Chen
Sentao Chen
Shaoyu Chen
Shixing Chen

Shuai Chen
Shuya Chen
Sizhe Chen
Simin Chen
Shaoxiang Chen
Zitian Chen
Tianlong Chen
Tianshui Chen
Min-Hung Chen
Xiangning Chen
Xin Chen
Xinghao Chen
Xuejin Chen
Xu Chen
Xuxi Chen
Yunlu Chen
Yanbei Chen
Yuxiao Chen
Yun-Chun Chen
Yi-Ting Chen
Yi-Wen Chen
Yinbo Chen
Yiran Chen
Yuanhong Chen
Yubei Chen
Yuefeng Chen
Yuhua Chen
Yukang Chen
Zerui Chen
Zhaoyu Chen
Zhen Chen
Zhenyu Chen
Zhi Chen
Zhiwei Chen
Zhixiang Chen
Long Chen
Bowen Cheng
Jun Cheng
Yi Cheng
Jingchun Cheng
Lechao Cheng
Xi Cheng
Yuan Cheng
Ho Kei Cheng
Kevin Ho Man Cheng

Jiacheng Cheng
Kelvin B. Cheng
Li Cheng
Mengjun Cheng
Zhen Cheng
Qingrong Cheng
Tianheng Cheng
Harry Cheng
Yihua Cheng
Yu Cheng
Ziheng Cheng
Soon Yau Cheong
Anoop Cherian
Manuela Chessa
Zhixiang Chi
Naoki Chiba
Julian Chibane
Kashyap Chitta
Tai-Yin Chiu
Hsu-kuang Chiu
Wei-Chen Chiu
Sungmin Cho
Donghyeon Cho
Hyeon Cho
Yooshin Cho
Gyusang Cho
Jang Hyun Cho
Seungju Cho
Nam Ik Cho
Sunghyun Cho
Hanbyel Cho
Jaesung Choe
Jooyoung Choi
Chiho Choi
Changwoon Choi
Jongwon Choi
Myungsub Choi
Dooseop Choi
Jonghyun Choi
Jinwoo Choi
Jun Won Choi
Min-Kook Choi
Hongsuk Choi
Janghoon Choi
Yoon-Ho Choi

Yukyung Choi
Jaegul Choo
Ayush Chopra
Siddharth Choudhary
Subhabrata Choudhury
Vasileios Choutas
Ka-Ho Chow
Pinaki Nath Chowdhury
Sammy Christen
Anders Christensen
Grigorios Chrysos
Hang Chu
Wen-Hsuan Chu
Peng Chu
Qi Chu
Ruihang Chu
Wei-Ta Chu
Yung-Yu Chuang
Sanghyuk Chun
Se Young Chun
Antonio Cinà
Ramazan Gokberk Cinbis
Javier Civera
Albert Clapés
Ronald Clark
Brian S. Clipp
Felipe Codevilla
Daniel Coelho de Castro
Niv Cohen
Forrester Cole
Maxwell D. Collins
Robert T. Collins
Marc Comino Trinidad
Runmin Cong
Wenyan Cong
Maxime Cordy
Marcella Cornia
Enric Corona
Huseyin Coskun
Luca Cosmo
Dragos Costea
Davide Cozzolino
Arun C. S. Kumar
Aiyu Cui
Qiongjie Cui

Quan Cui
Shuhao Cui
Yiming Cui
Ying Cui
Zijun Cui
Jiali Cui
Jiequan Cui
Yawen Cui
Zhen Cui
Zhaopeng Cui
Jack Culpepper
Xiaodong Cun
Ross Cutler
Adam Czajka
Ali Dabouei
Konstantinos M. Dafnis
Manuel Dahnert
Tao Dai
Yuchao Dai
Bo Dai
Mengyu Dai
Hang Dai
Haixing Dai
Peng Dai
Pingyang Dai
Qi Dai
Qiyu Dai
Yutong Dai
Naser Damer
Zhiyuan Dang
Mohamed Daoudi
Ayan Das
Abir Das
Debasmit Das
Deepayan Das
Partha Das
Sagnik Das
Soumi Das
Srijan Das
Swagatam Das
Avijit Dasgupta
Jim Davis
Adrian K. Davison
Homa Davoudi
Laura Daza

Matthias De Lange
Shalini De Mello
Marco De Nadai
Christophe De
    Vleeschouwer
Alp Dener
Boyang Deng
Congyue Deng
Bailin Deng
Yong Deng
Ye Deng
Zhuo Deng
Zhijie Deng
Xiaoming Deng
Jiankang Deng
Jinhong Deng
Jingjing Deng
Liang-Jian Deng
Siqi Deng
Xiang Deng
Xueqing Deng
Zhongying Deng
Karan Desai
Jean-Emmanuel Deschaud
Aniket Anand Deshmukh
Neel Dey
Helisa Dhamo
Prithviraj Dhar
Amaya Dharmasiri
Yan Di
Xing Di
Ousmane A. Dia
Haiwen Diao
Xiaolei Diao
Gonçalo José Dias Pais
Abdallah Dib
Anastasios Dimou
Changxing Ding
Henghui Ding
Guodong Ding
Yaqing Ding
Shuangrui Ding
Yuhang Ding
Yikang Ding
Shouhong Ding

Haisong Ding
Hui Ding
Jiahao Ding
Jian Ding
Jian-Jiun Ding
Shuxiao Ding
Tianyu Ding
Wenhao Ding
Yuqi Ding
Yi Ding
Yuzhen Ding
Zhengming Ding
Tan Minh Dinh
Vu Dinh
Christos Diou
Mandar Dixit
Bao Gia Doan
Khoa D. Doan
Dzung Anh Doan
Debi Prosad Dogra
Nehal Doiphode
Chengdong Dong
Bowen Dong
Zhenxing Dong
Hang Dong
Xiaoyi Dong
Haoye Dong
Jiangxin Dong
Shichao Dong
Xuan Dong
Zhen Dong
Shuting Dong
Jing Dong
Li Dong
Ming Dong
Nanqing Dong
Qiulei Dong
Runpei Dong
Siyan Dong
Tian Dong
Wei Dong
Xiaomeng Dong
Xin Dong
Xingbo Dong
Yuan Dong

Samuel Dooley
Gianfranco Doretto
Michael Dorkenwald
Keval Doshi
Zhaopeng Dou
Xiaotian Dou
Hazel Doughty
Ahmad Droby
Iddo Drori
Jie Du
Yong Du
Dawei Du
Dong Du
Ruoyi Du
Yuntao Du
Xuefeng Du
Yilun Du
Yuming Du
Radhika Dua
Haodong Duan
Jiafei Duan
Kaiwen Duan
Peiqi Duan
Ye Duan
Haoran Duan
Jiali Duan
Amanda Duarte
Abhimanyu Dubey
Shiv Ram Dubey
Florian Dubost
Lukasz Dudziak
Shivam Duggal
Justin M. Dulay
Matteo Dunnhofer
Chi Nhan Duong
Thibaut Durand
Mihai Dusmanu
Ujjal Kr Dutta
Debidatta Dwibedi
Isht Dwivedi
Sai Kumar Dwivedi
Takeharu Eda
Mark Edmonds
Alexei A. Efros
Thibaud Ehret

Max Ehrlich
Mahsa Ehsanpour
Iván Eichhardt
Farshad Einabadi
Marvin Eisenberger
Hazim Kemal Ekenel
Mohamed El Banani
Ismail Elezi
Moshe Eliasof
Alaa El-Nouby
Ian Endres
Francis Engelmann
Deniz Engin
Chanho Eom
Dave Epstein
Maria C. Escobar
Victor A. Escorcia
Carlos Esteves
Sungmin Eum
Bernard J. E. Evans
Ivan Evtimov
Fevziye Irem Eyiokur
    Yaman
Matteo Fabbri
Sébastien Fabbro
Gabriele Facciolo
Masud Fahim
Bin Fan
Hehe Fan
Deng-Ping Fan
Aoxiang Fan
Chen-Chen Fan
Qi Fan
Zhaoxin Fan
Haoqi Fan
Heng Fan
Hongyi Fan
Linxi Fan
Baojie Fan
Jiayuan Fan
Lei Fan
Quanfu Fan
Yonghui Fan
Yingruo Fan
Zhiwen Fan

Zicong Fan
Sean Fanello
Jiansheng Fang
Chaowei Fang
Yuming Fang
Jianwu Fang
Jin Fang
Qi Fang
Shancheng Fang
Tian Fang
Xianyong Fang
Gongfan Fang
Zhen Fang
Hui Fang
Jiemin Fang
Le Fang
Pengfei Fang
Xiaolin Fang
Yuxin Fang
Zhaoyuan Fang
Ammarah Farooq
Azade Farshad
Zhengcong Fei
Michael Felsberg
Wei Feng
Chen Feng
Fan Feng
Andrew Feng
Xin Feng
Zheyun Feng
Ruicheng Feng
Mingtao Feng
Qianyu Feng
Shangbin Feng
Chun-Mei Feng
Zunlei Feng
Zhiyong Feng
Martin Fergie
Mustansar Fiaz
Marco Fiorucci
Michael Firman
Hamed Firooz
Volker Fischer
Corneliu O. Florea
Georgios Floros

Wolfgang Foerstner
Gianni Franchi
Jean-Sebastien Franco
Simone Frintrop
Anna Fruehstueck
Changhong Fu
Chaoyou Fu
Cheng-Yang Fu
Chi-Wing Fu
Deqing Fu
Huan Fu
Jun Fu
Kexue Fu
Ying Fu
Jianlong Fu
Jingjing Fu
Qichen Fu
Tsu-Jui Fu
Xueyang Fu
Yang Fu
Yanwei Fu
Yonggan Fu
Wolfgang Fuhl
Yasuhisa Fujii
Kent Fujiwara
Marco Fumero
Takuya Funatomi
Isabel Funke
Dario Fuoli
Antonino Furnari
Matheus A. Gadelha
Akshay Gadi Patil
Adrian Galdran
Guillermo Gallego
Silvano Galliani
Orazio Gallo
Leonardo Galteri
Matteo Gamba
Yiming Gan
Sujoy Ganguly
Harald Ganster
Boyan Gao
Changxin Gao
Daiheng Gao
Difei Gao

Chen Gao
Fei Gao
Lin Gao
Wei Gao
Yiming Gao
Junyu Gao
Guangyu Ryan Gao
Haichang Gao
Hongchang Gao
Jialin Gao
Jin Gao
Jun Gao
Katelyn Gao
Mingchen Gao
Mingfei Gao
Pan Gao
Shangqian Gao
Shanghua Gao
Xitong Gao
Yunhe Gao
Zhanning Gao
Elena Garces
Nuno Cruz Garcia
Noa Garcia
Guillermo
    Garcia-Hernando
Isha Garg
Rahul Garg
Sourav Garg
Quentin Garrido
Stefano Gasperini
Kent Gauen
Chandan Gautam
Shivam Gautam
Paul Gay
Chunjiang Ge
Shiming Ge
Wenhang Ge
Yanhao Ge
Zheng Ge
Songwei Ge
Weifeng Ge
Yixiao Ge
Yuying Ge
Shijie Geng

Zhengyang Geng
Kyle A. Genova
Georgios Georgakis
Markos Georgopoulos
Marcel Geppert
Shabnam Ghadar
Mina Ghadimi Atigh
Deepti Ghadiyaram
Maani Ghaffari Jadidi
Sedigh Ghamari
Zahra Gharaee
Michaël Gharbi
Golnaz Ghiasi
Reza Ghoddoosian
Soumya Suvra Ghosal
Adhiraj Ghosh
Arthita Ghosh
Pallabi Ghosh
Soumyadeep Ghosh
Andrew Gilbert
Igor Gilitschenski
Jhony H. Giraldo
Andreu Girbau Xalabarder
Rohit Girdhar
Sharath Girish
Xavier Giro-i-Nieto
Raja Giryes
Thomas Gittings
Nikolaos Gkanatsios
Ioannis Gkioulekas
Abhiram
  Gnanasambandam
Aurele T. Gnanha
Clement L. J. C. Godard
Arushi Goel
Vidit Goel
Shubham Goel
Zan Gojcic
Aaron K. Gokaslan
Tejas Gokhale
S. Alireza Golestaneh
Thiago L. Gomes
Nuno Goncalves
Boqing Gong
Chen Gong

Yuanhao Gong
Guoqiang Gong
Jingyu Gong
Rui Gong
Yu Gong
Mingming Gong
Neil Zhenqiang Gong
Xun Gong
Yunye Gong
Yihong Gong
Cristina I. González
Nithin Gopalakrishnan
  Nair
Gaurav Goswami
Jianping Gou
Shreyank N. Gowda
Ankit Goyal
Helmut Grabner
Patrick L. Grady
Ben Graham
Eric Granger
Douglas R. Gray
Matej Grcić
David Griffiths
Jinjin Gu
Yun Gu
Shuyang Gu
Jianyang Gu
Fuqiang Gu
Jiatao Gu
Jindong Gu
Jiaqi Gu
Jinwei Gu
Jiaxin Gu
Geonmo Gu
Xiao Gu
Xinqian Gu
Xiuye Gu
Yuming Gu
Zhangxuan Gu
Dayan Guan
Junfeng Guan
Qingji Guan
Tianrui Guan
Shanyan Guan

Denis A. Gudovskiy
Ricardo Guerrero
Pierre-Louis Guhur
Jie Gui
Liangyan Gui
Liangke Gui
Benoit Guillard
Erhan Gundogdu
Manuel Günther
Jingcai Guo
Yuanfang Guo
Junfeng Guo
Chenqi Guo
Dan Guo
Hongji Guo
Jia Guo
Jie Guo
Minghao Guo
Shi Guo
Yanhui Guo
Yangyang Guo
Yuan-Chen Guo
Yilu Guo
Yiluan Guo
Yong Guo
Guangyu Guo
Haiyun Guo
Jinyang Guo
Jianyuan Guo
Pengsheng Guo
Pengfei Guo
Shuxuan Guo
Song Guo
Tianyu Guo
Qing Guo
Qiushan Guo
Wen Guo
Xiefan Guo
Xiaohu Guo
Xiaoqing Guo
Yufei Guo
Yuhui Guo
Yuliang Guo
Yunhui Guo
Yanwen Guo

Akshita Gupta
Ankush Gupta
Kamal Gupta
Kartik Gupta
Ritwik Gupta
Rohit Gupta
Siddharth Gururani
Fredrik K. Gustafsson
Abner Guzman Rivera
Vladimir Guzov
Matthew A. Gwilliam
Jung-Woo Ha
Marc Habermann
Isma Hadji
Christian Haene
Martin Hahner
Levente Hajder
Alexandros Haliassos
Emanuela Haller
Bumsub Ham
Abdullah J. Hamdi
Shreyas Hampali
Dongyoon Han
Chunrui Han
Dong-Jun Han
Dong-Sig Han
Guangxing Han
Zhizhong Han
Ruize Han
Jiaming Han
Jin Han
Ligong Han
Xian-Hua Han
Xiaoguang Han
Yizeng Han
Zhi Han
Zhenjun Han
Zhongyi Han
Jungong Han
Junlin Han
Kai Han
Kun Han
Sungwon Han
Songfang Han
Wei Han

Xiao Han
Xintong Han
Xinzhe Han
Yahong Han
Yan Han
Zongbo Han
Nicolai Hani
Rana Hanocka
Niklas Hanselmann
Nicklas A. Hansen
Hong Hanyu
Fusheng Hao
Yanbin Hao
Shijie Hao
Udith Haputhanthri
Mehrtash Harandi
Josh Harguess
Adam Harley
David M. Hart
Atsushi Hashimoto
Ali Hassani
Mohammed Hassanin
Yana Hasson
Joakim Bruslund Haurum
Bo He
Kun He
Chen He
Xin He
Fazhi He
Gaoqi He
Hao He
Haoyu He
Jiangpeng He
Hongliang He
Qian He
Xiangteng He
Xuming He
Yannan He
Yuhang He
Yang He
Xiangyu He
Nanjun He
Pan He
Sen He
Shengfeng He

Songtao He
Tao He
Tong He
Wei He
Xuehai He
Xiaoxiao He
Ying He
Yisheng He
Ziwen He
Peter Hedman
Felix Heide
Yacov Hel-Or
Paul Henderson
Philipp Henzler
Byeongho Heo
Jae-Pil Heo
Miran Heo
Sachini A. Herath
Stephane Herbin
Pedro Hermosilla Casajus
Monica Hernandez
Charles Herrmann
Roei Herzig
Mauricio Hess-Flores
Carlos Hinojosa
Tobias Hinz
Tsubasa Hirakawa
Chih-Hui Ho
Lam Si Tung Ho
Jennifer Hobbs
Derek Hoiem
Yannick Hold-Geoffroy
Aleksander Holynski
Cheeun Hong
Fa-Ting Hong
Hanbin Hong
Guan Zhe Hong
Danfeng Hong
Lanqing Hong
Xiaopeng Hong
Xin Hong
Jie Hong
Seungbum Hong
Cheng-Yao Hong
Seunghoon Hong

Yi Hong
Yuan Hong
Yuchen Hong
Anthony Hoogs
Maxwell C. Horton
Kazuhiro Hotta
Qibin Hou
Tingbo Hou
Junhui Hou
Ji Hou
Qiqi Hou
Rui Hou
Ruibing Hou
Zhi Hou
Henry Howard-Jenkins
Lukas Hoyer
Wei-Lin Hsiao
Chiou-Ting Hsu
Anthony Hu
Brian Hu
Yusong Hu
Hexiang Hu
Haoji Hu
Di Hu
Hengtong Hu
Haigen Hu
Lianyu Hu
Hanzhe Hu
Jie Hu
Junlin Hu
Shizhe Hu
Jian Hu
Zhiming Hu
Juhua Hu
Peng Hu
Ping Hu
Ronghang Hu
MengShun Hu
Tao Hu
Vincent Tao Hu
Xiaoling Hu
Xinting Hu
Xiaolin Hu
Xuefeng Hu
Xiaowei Hu

Yang Hu
Yueyu Hu
Zeyu Hu
Zhongyun Hu
Binh-Son Hua
Guoliang Hua
Yi Hua
Linzhi Huang
Qiusheng Huang
Bo Huang
Chen Huang
Hsin-Ping Huang
Ye Huang
Shuangping Huang
Zeng Huang
Buzhen Huang
Cong Huang
Heng Huang
Hao Huang
Qidong Huang
Huaibo Huang
Chaoqin Huang
Feihu Huang
Jiahui Huang
Jingjia Huang
Kun Huang
Lei Huang
Sheng Huang
Shuaiyi Huang
Siyu Huang
Xiaoshui Huang
Xiaoyang Huang
Yan Huang
Yihao Huang
Ying Huang
Ziling Huang
Xiaoke Huang
Yifei Huang
Haiyang Huang
Zhewei Huang
Jin Huang
Haibin Huang
Jiaxing Huang
Junjie Huang
Keli Huang

Lang Huang
Lin Huang
Luojie Huang
Mingzhen Huang
Shijia Huang
Shengyu Huang
Siyuan Huang
He Huang
Xiuyu Huang
Lianghua Huang
Yue Huang
Yaping Huang
Yuge Huang
Zehao Huang
Zeyi Huang
Zhiqi Huang
Zhongzhan Huang
Zilong Huang
Ziyuan Huang
Tianrui Hui
Zhuo Hui
Le Hui
Jing Huo
Junhwa Hur
Shehzeen S. Hussain
Chuong Minh Huynh
Seunghyun Hwang
Jaehui Hwang
Jyh-Jing Hwang
Sukjun Hwang
Soonmin Hwang
Wonjun Hwang
Rakib Hyder
Sangeek Hyun
Sarah Ibrahimi
Tomoki Ichikawa
Yerlan Idelbayev
A. S. M. Iftekhar
Masaaki Iiyama
Satoshi Ikehata
Sunghoon Im
Atul N. Ingle
Eldar Insafutdinov
Yani A. Ioannou
Radu Tudor Ionescu

Umar Iqbal
Go Irie
Muhammad Zubair Irshad
Ahmet Iscen
Berivan Isik
Ashraful Islam
Md Amirul Islam
Syed Islam
Mariko Isogawa
Vamsi Krishna K. Ithapu
Boris Ivanovic
Darshan Iyer
Sarah Jabbour
Ayush Jain
Nishant Jain
Samyak Jain
Vidit Jain
Vineet Jain
Priyank Jaini
Tomas Jakab
Mohammad A. A. K.
    Jalwana
Muhammad Abdullah
    Jamal
Hadi Jamali-Rad
Stuart James
Varun Jampani
Young Kyun Jang
YeongJun Jang
Yunseok Jang
Ronnachai Jaroensri
Bhavan Jasani
Krishna Murthy
    Jatavallabhula
Mojan Javaheripi
Syed A. Javed
Guillaume Jeanneret
Pranav Jeevan
Herve Jegou
Rohit Jena
Tomas Jenicek
Porter Jenkins
Simon Jenni
Hae-Gon Jeon
Sangryul Jeon

Boseung Jeong
Yoonwoo Jeong
Seong-Gyun Jeong
Jisoo Jeong
Allan D. Jepson
Ankit Jha
Sumit K. Jha
I-Hong Jhuo
Ge-Peng Ji
Chaonan Ji
Deyi Ji
Jingwei Ji
Wei Ji
Zhong Ji
Jiayi Ji
Pengliang Ji
Hui Ji
Mingi Ji
Xiaopeng Ji
Yuzhu Ji
Baoxiong Jia
Songhao Jia
Dan Jia
Shan Jia
Xiaojun Jia
Xiuyi Jia
Xu Jia
Menglin Jia
Wenqi Jia
Boyuan Jiang
Wenhao Jiang
Huaizu Jiang
Hanwen Jiang
Haiyong Jiang
Hao Jiang
Huajie Jiang
Huiqin Jiang
Haojun Jiang
Haobo Jiang
Junjun Jiang
Xingyu Jiang
Yangbangyan Jiang
Yu Jiang
Jianmin Jiang
Jiaxi Jiang

Jing Jiang
Kui Jiang
Li Jiang
Liming Jiang
Chiyu Jiang
Meirui Jiang
Chen Jiang
Peng Jiang
Tai-Xiang Jiang
Wen Jiang
Xinyang Jiang
Yifan Jiang
Yuming Jiang
Yingying Jiang
Zeren Jiang
ZhengKai Jiang
Zhenyu Jiang
Shuming Jiao
Jianbo Jiao
Licheng Jiao
Dongkwon Jin
Yeying Jin
Cheng Jin
Linyi Jin
Qing Jin
Taisong Jin
Xiao Jin
Xin Jin
Sheng Jin
Kyong Hwan Jin
Ruibing Jin
SouYoung Jin
Yueming Jin
Chenchen Jing
Longlong Jing
Taotao Jing
Yongcheng Jing
Younghyun Jo
Joakim Johnander
Jeff Johnson
Michael J. Jones
R. Kenny Jones
Rico Jonschkowski
Ameya Joshi
Sunghun Joung

Felix Juefei-Xu
Claudio R. Jung
Steffen Jung
Hari Chandana K.
Rahul Vigneswaran K.
Prajwal K. R.
Abhishek Kadian
Jhony Kaesemodel Pontes
Kumara Kahatapitiya
Anmol Kalia
Sinan Kalkan
Tarun Kalluri
Jaewon Kam
Sandesh Kamath
Meina Kan
Menelaos Kanakis
Takuhiro Kaneko
Di Kang
Guoliang Kang
Hao Kang
Jaeyeon Kang
Kyoungkook Kang
Li-Wei Kang
MinGuk Kang
Suk-Ju Kang
Zhao Kang
Yash Mukund Kant
Yueying Kao
Aupendu Kar
Konstantinos Karantzalos
Sezer Karaoglu
Navid Kardan
Sanjay Kariyappa
Leonid Karlinsky
Animesh Karnewar
Shyamgopal Karthik
Hirak J. Kashyap
Marc A. Kastner
Hirokatsu Kataoka
Angelos Katharopoulos
Hiroharu Kato
Kai Katsumata
Manuel Kaufmann
Chaitanya Kaul
Prakhar Kaushik

Yuki Kawana
Lei Ke
Lipeng Ke
Tsung-Wei Ke
Wei Ke
Petr Kellnhofer
Aniruddha Kembhavi
John Kender
Corentin Kervadec
Leonid Keselman
Daniel Keysers
Nima Khademi Kalantari
Taras Khakhulin
Samir Khaki
Muhammad Haris Khan
Qadeer Khan
Salman Khan
Subash Khanal
Vaishnavi M. Khindkar
Rawal Khirodkar
Saeed Khorram
Pirazh Khorramshahi
Kourosh Khoshelham
Ansh Khurana
Benjamin Kiefer
Jae Myung Kim
Junho Kim
Boah Kim
Hyeonseong Kim
Dong-Jin Kim
Dongwan Kim
Donghyun Kim
Doyeon Kim
Yonghyun Kim
Hyung-Il Kim
Hyunwoo Kim
Hyeongwoo Kim
Hyo Jin Kim
Hyunwoo J. Kim
Taehoon Kim
Jaeha Kim
Jiwon Kim
Jung Uk Kim
Kangyeol Kim
Eunji Kim

Daeha Kim
Dongwon Kim
Kunhee Kim
Kyungmin Kim
Junsik Kim
Min H. Kim
Namil Kim
Kookhoi Kim
Sanghyun Kim
Seongyeop Kim
Seungryong Kim
Saehoon Kim
Euyoung Kim
Guisik Kim
Sungyeon Kim
Sunnie S. Y. Kim
Taehun Kim
Tae Oh Kim
Won Hwa Kim
Seungwook Kim
YoungBin Kim
Youngeun Kim
Akisato Kimura
Furkan Osman Kınlı
Zsolt Kira
Hedvig Kjellström
Florian Kleber
Jan P. Klopp
Florian Kluger
Laurent Kneip
Byungsoo Ko
Muhammed Kocabas
A. Sophia Koepke
Kevin Koeser
Nick Kolkin
Nikos Kolotouros
Wai-Kin Adams Kong
Deying Kong
Caihua Kong
Youyong Kong
Shuyu Kong
Shu Kong
Tao Kong
Yajing Kong
Yu Kong

Zishang Kong
Theodora Kontogianni
Anton S. Konushin
Julian F. P. Kooij
Bruno Korbar
Giorgos Kordopatis-Zilos
Jari Korhonen
Adam Kortylewski
Denis Korzhenkov
Divya Kothandaraman
Suraj Kothawade
Iuliia Kotseruba
Satwik Kottur
Shashank Kotyan
Alexandros Kouris
Petros Koutras
Anna Kreshuk
Ranjay Krishna
Dilip Krishnan
Andrey Kuehlkamp
Hilde Kuehne
Jason Kuen
David Kügler
Arjan Kuijper
Anna Kukleva
Sumith Kulal
Viveka Kulharia
Akshay R. Kulkarni
Nilesh Kulkarni
Dominik Kulon
Abhinav Kumar
Akash Kumar
Suryansh Kumar
B. V. K. Vijaya Kumar
Pulkit Kumar
Ratnesh Kumar
Sateesh Kumar
Satish Kumar
Vijay Kumar B. G.
Nupur Kumari
Sudhakar Kumawat
Jogendra Nath Kundu
Hsien-Kai Kuo
Meng-Yu Jennifer Kuo
Vinod Kumar Kurmi

Yusuke Kurose
Keerthy Kusumam
Alina Kuznetsova
Henry Kvinge
Ho Man Kwan
Hyeokjun Kweon
Heeseung Kwon
Gihyun Kwon
Myung-Joon Kwon
Taesung Kwon
YoungJoong Kwon
Christos Kyrkou
Jorma Laaksonen
Yann Labbe
Zorah Laehner
Florent Lafarge
Hamid Laga
Manuel Lagunas
Shenqi Lai
Jian-Huang Lai
Zihang Lai
Mohamed I. Lakhal
Mohit Lamba
Meng Lan
Loic Landrieu
Zhiqiang Lang
Natalie Lang
Dong Lao
Yizhen Lao
Yingjie Lao
Issam Hadj Laradji
Gustav Larsson
Viktor Larsson
Zakaria Laskar
Stéphane Lathuilière
Chun Pong Lau
Rynson W. H. Lau
Hei Law
Justin Lazarow
Verica Lazova
Eric-Tuan Le
Hieu Le
Trung-Nghia Le
Mathias Lechner
Byeong-Uk Lee

Chen-Yu Lee
Che-Rung Lee
Chul Lee
Hong Joo Lee
Dongsoo Lee
Jiyoung Lee
Eugene Eu Tzuan Lee
Daeun Lee
Saehyung Lee
Jewook Lee
Hyungtae Lee
Hyunmin Lee
Jungbeom Lee
Joon-Young Lee
Jong-Seok Lee
Joonseok Lee
Junha Lee
Kibok Lee
Byung-Kwan Lee
Jangwon Lee
Jinho Lee
Jongmin Lee
Seunghyun Lee
Sohyun Lee
Minsik Lee
Dogyoon Lee
Seungmin Lee
Min Jun Lee
Sangho Lee
Sangmin Lee
Seungeun Lee
Seon-Ho Lee
Sungmin Lee
Sungho Lee
Sangyoun Lee
Vincent C. S. S. Lee
Jaeseong Lee
Yong Jae Lee
Chenyang Lei
Chenyi Lei
Jiahui Lei
Xinyu Lei
Yinjie Lei
Jiaxu Leng
Luziwei Leng

Jan E. Lenssen
Vincent Lepetit
Thomas Leung
María Leyva-Vallina
Xin Li
Yikang Li
Baoxin Li
Bin Li
Bing Li
Bowen Li
Changlin Li
Chao Li
Chongyi Li
Guanyue Li
Shuai Li
Jin Li
Dingquan Li
Dongxu Li
Yiting Li
Gang Li
Dian Li
Guohao Li
Haoang Li
Haoliang Li
Haoran Li
Hengduo Li
Huafeng Li
Xiaoming Li
Hanao Li
Hongwei Li
Ziqiang Li
Jisheng Li
Jiacheng Li
Jia Li
Jiachen Li
Jiahao Li
Jianwei Li
Jiazhi Li
Jie Li
Jing Li
Jingjing Li
Jingtao Li
Jun Li
Junxuan Li
Kai Li

Kailin Li
Kenneth Li
Kun Li
Kunpeng Li
Aoxue Li
Chenglong Li
Chenglin Li
Changsheng Li
Zhichao Li
Qiang Li
Yanyu Li
Zuoyue Li
Xiang Li
Xuelong Li
Fangda Li
Ailin Li
Liang Li
Chun-Guang Li
Daiqing Li
Dong Li
Guanbin Li
Guorong Li
Haifeng Li
Jianan Li
Jianing Li
Jiaxin Li
Ke Li
Lei Li
Lincheng Li
Liulei Li
Lujun Li
Linjie Li
Lin Li
Pengyu Li
Ping Li
Qiufu Li
Qingyong Li
Rui Li
Siyuan Li
Wei Li
Wenbin Li
Xiangyang Li
Xinyu Li
Xiujun Li
Xiu Li

Xu Li
Ya-Li Li
Yao Li
Yongjie Li
Yijun Li
Yiming Li
Yuezun Li
Yu Li
Yunheng Li
Yuqi Li
Zhe Li
Zeming Li
Zhen Li
Zhengqin Li
Zhimin Li
Jiefeng Li
Jinpeng Li
Chengze Li
Jianwu Li
Lerenhan Li
Shan Li
Suichan Li
Xiangtai Li
Yanjie Li
Yandong Li
Zhuoling Li
Zhenqiang Li
Manyi Li
Maosen Li
Ji Li
Minjun Li
Mingrui Li
Mengtian Li
Junyi Li
Nianyi Li
Bo Li
Xiao Li
Peihua Li
Peike Li
Peizhao Li
Peiliang Li
Qi Li
Ren Li
Runze Li
Shile Li

Sheng Li
Shigang Li
Shiyu Li
Shuang Li
Shasha Li
Shichao Li
Tianye Li
Yuexiang Li
Wei-Hong Li
Wanhua Li
Weihao Li
Weiming Li
Weixin Li
Wenbo Li
Wenshuo Li
Weijian Li
Yunan Li
Xirong Li
Xianhang Li
Xiaoyu Li
Xueqian Li
Xuanlin Li
Xianzhi Li
Yunqiang Li
Yanjing Li
Yansheng Li
Yawei Li
Yi Li
Yong Li
Yong-Lu Li
Yuhang Li
Yu-Jhe Li
Yuxi Li
Yunsheng Li
Yanwei Li
Zechao Li
Zejian Li
Zeju Li
Zekun Li
Zhaowen Li
Zheng Li
Zhenyu Li
Zhiheng Li
Zhi Li
Zhong Li

Zhuowei Li
Zhuowan Li
Zhuohang Li
Zizhang Li
Chen Li
Yuan-Fang Li
Dongze Lian
Xiaochen Lian
Zhouhui Lian
Long Lian
Qing Lian
Jin Lianbao
Jinxiu S. Liang
Dingkang Liang
Jiahao Liang
Jianming Liang
Jingyun Liang
Kevin J. Liang
Kaizhao Liang
Chen Liang
Jie Liang
Senwei Liang
Ding Liang
Jiajun Liang
Jian Liang
Kongming Liang
Siyuan Liang
Yuanzhi Liang
Zhengfa Liang
Mingfu Liang
Xiaodan Liang
Xuefeng Liang
Yuxuan Liang
Kang Liao
Liang Liao
Hong-Yuan Mark Liao
Wentong Liao
Haofu Liao
Yue Liao
Minghui Liao
Shengcai Liao
Ting-Hsuan Liao
Xin Liao
Yinghong Liao
Teck Yian Lim

Che-Tsung Lin
Chung-Ching Lin
Chen-Hsuan Lin
Cheng Lin
Chuming Lin
Chunyu Lin
Dahua Lin
Wei Lin
Zheng Lin
Huaijia Lin
Jason Lin
Jierui Lin
Jiaying Lin
Jie Lin
Kai-En Lin
Kevin Lin
Guangfeng Lin
Jiehong Lin
Feng Lin
Hang Lin
Kwan-Yee Lin
Ke Lin
Luojun Lin
Qinghong Lin
Xiangbo Lin
Yi Lin
Zudi Lin
Shijie Lin
Yiqun Lin
Tzu-Heng Lin
Ming Lin
Shaohui Lin
SongNan Lin
Ji Lin
Tsung-Yu Lin
Xudong Lin
Yancong Lin
Yen-Chen Lin
Yiming Lin
Yuewei Lin
Zhiqiu Lin
Zinan Lin
Zhe Lin
David B. Lindell
Zhixin Ling

Zhan Ling
Alexander Liniger
Venice Erin B. Liong
Joey Litalien
Or Litany
Roee Litman
Ron Litman
Jim Little
Dor Litvak
Shaoteng Liu
Shuaicheng Liu
Andrew Liu
Xian Liu
Shaohui Liu
Bei Liu
Bo Liu
Yong Liu
Ming Liu
Yanbin Liu
Chenxi Liu
Daqi Liu
Di Liu
Difan Liu
Dong Liu
Dongfang Liu
Daizong Liu
Xiao Liu
Fangyi Liu
Fengbei Liu
Fenglin Liu
Bin Liu
Yuang Liu
Ao Liu
Hong Liu
Hongfu Liu
Huidong Liu
Ziyi Liu
Feng Liu
Hao Liu
Jie Liu
Jialun Liu
Jiang Liu
Jing Liu
Jingya Liu
Jiaming Liu

Jun Liu
Juncheng Liu
Jiawei Liu
Hongyu Liu
Chuanbin Liu
Haotian Liu
Lingqiao Liu
Chang Liu
Han Liu
Liu Liu
Min Liu
Yingqi Liu
Aishan Liu
Bingyu Liu
Benlin Liu
Boxiao Liu
Chenchen Liu
Chuanjian Liu
Daqing Liu
Huan Liu
Haozhe Liu
Jiaheng Liu
Wei Liu
Jingzhou Liu
Jiyuan Liu
Lingbo Liu
Nian Liu
Peiye Liu
Qiankun Liu
Shenglan Liu
Shilong Liu
Wen Liu
Wenyu Liu
Weifeng Liu
Wu Liu
Xiaolong Liu
Yang Liu
Yanwei Liu
Yingcheng Liu
Yongfei Liu
Yihao Liu
Yu Liu
Yunze Liu
Ze Liu
Zhenhua Liu

Zhenguang Liu
Lin Liu
Lihao Liu
Pengju Liu
Xinhai Liu
Yunfei Liu
Meng Liu
Minghua Liu
Mingyuan Liu
Miao Liu
Peirong Liu
Ping Liu
Qingjie Liu
Ruoshi Liu
Risheng Liu
Songtao Liu
Xing Liu
Shikun Liu
Shuming Liu
Sheng Liu
Songhua Liu
Tongliang Liu
Weibo Liu
Weide Liu
Weizhe Liu
Wenxi Liu
Weiyang Liu
Xin Liu
Xiaobin Liu
Xudong Liu
Xiaoyi Liu
Xihui Liu
Xinchen Liu
Xingtong Liu
Xinpeng Liu
Xinyu Liu
Xianpeng Liu
Xu Liu
Xingyu Liu
Yongtuo Liu
Yahui Liu
Yangxin Liu
Yaoyao Liu
Yaojie Liu
Yuliang Liu

Yongcheng Liu
Yuan Liu
Yufan Liu
Yu-Lun Liu
Yun Liu
Yunfan Liu
Yuanzhong Liu
Zhuoran Liu
Zhen Liu
Zheng Liu
Zhijian Liu
Zhisong Liu
Ziquan Liu
Ziyu Liu
Zhihua Liu
Zechun Liu
Zhaoyang Liu
Zhengzhe Liu
Stephan Liwicki
Shao-Yuan Lo
Sylvain Lobry
Suhas Lohit
Vishnu Suresh Lokhande
Vincenzo Lomonaco
Chengjiang Long
Guodong Long
Fuchen Long
Shangbang Long
Yang Long
Zijun Long
Vasco Lopes
Antonio M. Lopez
Roberto Javier
    Lopez-Sastre
Tobias Lorenz
Javier Lorenzo-Navarro
Yujing Lou
Qian Lou
Xiankai Lu
Changsheng Lu
Huimin Lu
Yongxi Lu
Hao Lu
Hong Lu
Jiasen Lu

Juwei Lu
Fan Lu
Guangming Lu
Jiwen Lu
Shun Lu
Tao Lu
Xiaonan Lu
Yang Lu
Yao Lu
Yongchun Lu
Zhiwu Lu
Cheng Lu
Liying Lu
Guo Lu
Xuequan Lu
Yanye Lu
Yantao Lu
Yuhang Lu
Fujun Luan
Jonathon Luiten
Jovita Lukasik
Alan Lukezic
Jonathan Samuel Lumentut
Mayank Lunayach
Ao Luo
Canjie Luo
Chong Luo
Xu Luo
Grace Luo
Jun Luo
Katie Z. Luo
Tao Luo
Cheng Luo
Fangzhou Luo
Gen Luo
Lei Luo
Sihui Luo
Weixin Luo
Yan Luo
Xiaoyan Luo
Yong Luo
Yadan Luo
Hao Luo
Ruotian Luo
Mi Luo

Tiange Luo
Wenjie Luo
Wenhan Luo
Xiao Luo
Zhiming Luo
Zhipeng Luo
Zhengyi Luo
Diogo C. Luvizon
Zhaoyang Lv
Gengyu Lyu
Lingjuan Lyu
Jun Lyu
Yuanyuan Lyu
Youwei Lyu
Yueming Lyu
Bingpeng Ma
Chao Ma
Chongyang Ma
Congbo Ma
Chih-Yao Ma
Fan Ma
Lin Ma
Haoyu Ma
Hengbo Ma
Jianqi Ma
Jiawei Ma
Jiayi Ma
Kede Ma
Kai Ma
Lingni Ma
Lei Ma
Xu Ma
Ning Ma
Benteng Ma
Cheng Ma
Andy J. Ma
Long Ma
Zhanyu Ma
Zhiheng Ma
Qianli Ma
Shiqiang Ma
Sizhuo Ma
Shiqing Ma
Xiaolong Ma
Xinzhu Ma

Gautam B. Machiraju
Spandan Madan
Mathew Magimai-Doss
Luca Magri
Behrooz Mahasseni
Upal Mahbub
Siddharth Mahendran
Paridhi Maheshwari
Rishabh Maheshwary
Mohammed Mahmoud
Shishira R. R. Maiya
Sylwia Majchrowska
Arjun Majumdar
Puspita Majumdar
Orchid Majumder
Sagnik Majumder
Ilya Makarov
Farkhod F.
    Makhmudkhujaev
Yasushi Makihara
Ankur Mali
Mateusz Malinowski
Utkarsh Mall
Srikanth Malla
Clement Mallet
Dimitrios Mallis
Yunze Man
Dipu Manandhar
Massimiliano Mancini
Murari Mandal
Raunak Manekar
Karttikeya Mangalam
Puneet Mangla
Fabian Manhardt
Sivabalan Manivasagam
Fahim Mannan
Chengzhi Mao
Hanzi Mao
Jiayuan Mao
Junhua Mao
Zhiyuan Mao
Jiageng Mao
Yunyao Mao
Zhendong Mao
Alberto Marchisio

Diego Marcos
Riccardo Marin
Aram Markosyan
Renaud Marlet
Ricardo Marques
Miquel Martí i Rabadán
Diego Martin Arroyo
Niki Martinel
Brais Martinez
Julieta Martinez
Marc Masana
Tomohiro Mashita
Timothée Masquelier
Minesh Mathew
Tetsu Matsukawa
Marwan Mattar
Bruce A. Maxwell
Christoph Mayer
Mantas Mazeika
Pratik Mazumder
Scott McCloskey
Steven McDonagh
Ishit Mehta
Jie Mei
Kangfu Mei
Jieru Mei
Xiaoguang Mei
Givi Meishvili
Luke Melas-Kyriazi
Iaroslav Melekhov
Andres Mendez-Vazquez
Heydi Mendez-Vazquez
Matias Mendieta
Ricardo A. Mendoza-León
Chenlin Meng
Depu Meng
Rang Meng
Zibo Meng
Qingjie Meng
Qier Meng
Yanda Meng
Zihang Meng
Thomas Mensink
Fabian Mentzer
Christopher Metzler

Gregory P. Meyer
Vasileios Mezaris
Liang Mi
Lu Mi
Bo Miao
Changtao Miao
Zichen Miao
Qiguang Miao
Xin Miao
Zhongqi Miao
Frank Michel
Simone Milani
Ben Mildenhall
Roy V. Miles
Juhong Min
Kyle Min
Hyun-Seok Min
Weiqing Min
Yuecong Min
Zhixiang Min
Qi Ming
David Minnen
Aymen Mir
Deepak Mishra
Anand Mishra
Shlok K. Mishra
Niluthpol Mithun
Gaurav Mittal
Trisha Mittal
Daisuke Miyazaki
Kaichun Mo
Hong Mo
Zhipeng Mo
Davide Modolo
Abduallah A. Mohamed
Mohamed Afham
    Mohamed Aflal
Ron Mokady
Pavlo Molchanov
Davide Moltisanti
Liliane Momeni
Gianluca Monaci
Pascal Monasse
Ajoy Mondal
Tom Monnier

Aron Monszpart
Gyeongsik Moon
Suhong Moon
Taesup Moon
Sean Moran
Daniel Moreira
Pietro Morerio
Alexandre Morgand
Lia Morra
Ali Mosleh
Inbar Mosseri
Sayed Mohammad
    Mostafavi Isfahani
Saman Motamed
Ramy A. Mounir
Fangzhou Mu
Jiteng Mu
Norman Mu
Yasuhiro Mukaigawa
Ryan Mukherjee
Tanmoy Mukherjee
Yusuke Mukuta
Ravi Teja Mullapudi
Lea Müller
Matthias Müller
Martin Mundt
Nils Murrugarra-Llerena
Damien Muselet
Armin Mustafa
Muhammad Ferjad Naeem
Sauradip Nag
Hajime Nagahara
Pravin Nagar
Rajendra Nagar
Naveen Shankar Nagaraja
Varun Nagaraja
Tushar Nagarajan
Seungjun Nah
Gaku Nakano
Yuta Nakashima
Giljoo Nam
Seonghyeon Nam
Liangliang Nan
Yuesong Nan
Yeshwanth Napolean

Dinesh Reddy
    Narapureddy
Medhini Narasimhan
Supreeth
    Narasimhaswamy
Sriram Narayanan
Erickson R. Nascimento
Varun Nasery
K. L. Navaneet
Pablo Navarrete Michelini
Shant Navasardyan
Shah Nawaz
Nihal Nayak
Farhood Negin
Lukáš Neumann
Alejandro Newell
Evonne Ng
Kam Woh Ng
Tony Ng
Anh Nguyen
Tuan Anh Nguyen
Cuong Cao Nguyen
Ngoc Cuong Nguyen
Thanh Nguyen
Khoi Nguyen
Phi Le Nguyen
Phong Ha Nguyen
Tam Nguyen
Truong Nguyen
Anh Tuan Nguyen
Rang Nguyen
Thao Thi Phuong Nguyen
Van Nguyen Nguyen
Zhen-Liang Ni
Yao Ni
Shijie Nie
Xuecheng Nie
Yongwei Nie
Weizhi Nie
Ying Nie
Yinyu Nie
Kshitij N. Nikhal
Simon Niklaus
Xuefei Ning
Jifeng Ning

Yotam Nitzan
Di Niu
Shuaicheng Niu
Li Niu
Wei Niu
Yulei Niu
Zhenxing Niu
Albert No
Shohei Nobuhara
Nicoletta Noceti
Junhyug Noh
Sotiris Nousias
Slawomir Nowaczyk
Ewa M. Nowara
Valsamis Ntouskos
Gilberto Ochoa-Ruiz
Ferda Ofli
Jihyong Oh
Sangyun Oh
Youngtaek Oh
Hiroki Ohashi
Takahiro Okabe
Kemal Oksuz
Fumio Okura
Daniel Olmeda Reino
Matthew Olson
Carl Olsson
Roy Or-El
Alessandro Ortis
Guillermo Ortiz-Jimenez
Magnus Oskarsson
Ahmed A. A. Osman
Martin R. Oswald
Mayu Otani
Naima Otberdout
Cheng Ouyang
Jiahong Ouyang
Wanli Ouyang
Andrew Owens
Poojan B. Oza
Mete Ozay
A. Cengiz Oztireli
Gautam Pai
Tomas Pajdla
Umapada Pal

Simone Palazzo
Luca Palmieri
Bowen Pan
Hao Pan
Lili Pan
Tai-Yu Pan
Liang Pan
Chengwei Pan
Yingwei Pan
Xuran Pan
Jinshan Pan
Xinyu Pan
Liyuan Pan
Xingang Pan
Xingjia Pan
Zhihong Pan
Zizheng Pan
Priyadarshini Panda
Rameswar Panda
Rohit Pandey
Kaiyue Pang
Bo Pang
Guansong Pang
Jiangmiao Pang
Meng Pang
Tianyu Pang
Ziqi Pang
Omiros Pantazis
Andreas Panteli
Maja Pantic
Marina Paolanti
Joao P. Papa
Samuele Papa
Mike Papadakis
Dim P. Papadopoulos
George Papandreou
Constantin Pape
Toufiq Parag
Chethan Parameshwara
Shaifali Parashar
Alejandro Pardo
Rishubh Parihar
Sarah Parisot
JaeYoo Park
Gyeong-Moon Park

Hyojin Park
Hyoungseob Park
Jongchan Park
Jae Sung Park
Kiru Park
Chunghyun Park
Kwanyong Park
Sunghyun Park
Sungrae Park
Seongsik Park
Sanghyun Park
Sungjune Park
Taesung Park
Gaurav Parmar
Paritosh Parmar
Alvaro Parra
Despoina Paschalidou
Or Patashnik
Shivansh Patel
Pushpak Pati
Prashant W. Patil
Vaishakh Patil
Suvam Patra
Jay Patravali
Badri Narayana Patro
Angshuman Paul
Sudipta Paul
Rémi Pautrat
Nick E. Pears
Adithya Pediredla
Wenjie Pei
Shmuel Peleg
Latha Pemula
Bo Peng
Houwen Peng
Yue Peng
Liangzu Peng
Baoyun Peng
Jun Peng
Pai Peng
Sida Peng
Xi Peng
Yuxin Peng
Songyou Peng
Wei Peng

Weiqi Peng
Wen-Hsiao Peng
Pramuditha Perera
Juan C. Perez
Eduardo Pérez Pellitero
Juan-Manuel Perez-Rua
Federico Pernici
Marco Pesavento
Stavros Petridis
Ilya A. Petrov
Vladan Petrovic
Mathis Petrovich
Suzanne Petryk
Hieu Pham
Quang Pham
Khoi Pham
Tung Pham
Huy Phan
Stephen Phillips
Cheng Perng Phoo
David Picard
Marco Piccirilli
Georg Pichler
A. J. Piergiovanni
Vipin Pillai
Silvia L. Pintea
Giovanni Pintore
Robinson Piramuthu
Fiora Pirri
Theodoros Pissas
Fabio Pizzati
Benjamin Planche
Bryan Plummer
Matteo Poggi
Ashwini Pokle
Georgy E. Ponimatkin
Adrian Popescu
Stefan Popov
Nikola Popović
Ronald Poppe
Angelo Porrello
Michael Potter
Charalambos Poullis
Hadi Pouransari
Omid Poursaeed

Shraman Pramanick
Mantini Pranav
Dilip K. Prasad
Meghshyam Prasad
B. H. Pawan Prasad
Shitala Prasad
Prateek Prasanna
Ekta Prashnani
Derek S. Prijatelj
Luke Y. Prince
Véronique Prinet
Victor Adrian Prisacariu
James Pritts
Thomas Probst
Sergey Prokudin
Rita Pucci
Chi-Man Pun
Matthew Purri
Haozhi Qi
Lu Qi
Lei Qi
Xianbiao Qi
Yonggang Qi
Yuankai Qi
Siyuan Qi
Guocheng Qian
Hangwei Qian
Qi Qian
Deheng Qian
Shengsheng Qian
Wen Qian
Rui Qian
Yiming Qian
Shengju Qian
Shengyi Qian
Xuelin Qian
Zhenxing Qian
Nan Qiao
Xiaotian Qiao
Jing Qin
Can Qin
Siyang Qin
Hongwei Qin
Jie Qin
Minghai Qin

Yipeng Qin
Yongqiang Qin
Wenda Qin
Xuebin Qin
Yuzhe Qin
Yao Qin
Zhenyue Qin
Zhiwu Qing
Heqian Qiu
Jiayan Qiu
Jielin Qiu
Yue Qiu
Jiaxiong Qiu
Zhongxi Qiu
Shi Qiu
Zhaofan Qiu
Zhongnan Qu
Yanyun Qu
Kha Gia Quach
Yuhui Quan
Ruijie Quan
Mike Rabbat
Rahul Shekhar Rade
Filip Radenovic
Gorjan Radevski
Bogdan Raducanu
Francesco Ragusa
Shafin Rahman
Md Mahfuzur Rahman
    Siddiquee
Hossein Rahmani
Kiran Raja
Sivaramakrishnan
    Rajaraman
Jathushan Rajasegaran
Adnan Siraj Rakin
Michaël Ramamonjisoa
Chirag A. Raman
Shanmuganathan Raman
Vignesh Ramanathan
Vasili Ramanishka
Vikram V. Ramaswamy
Merey Ramazanova
Jason Rambach
Sai Saketh Rambhatla

Clément Rambour
Ashwin Ramesh Babu
Adín Ramírez Rivera
Arianna Rampini
Haoxi Ran
Aakanksha Rana
Aayush Jung Bahadur
    Rana
Kanchana N. Ranasinghe
Aneesh Rangnekar
Samrudhdhi B. Rangrej
Harsh Rangwani
Viresh Ranjan
Anyi Rao
Yongming Rao
Carolina Raposo
Michalis Raptis
Amir Rasouli
Vivek Rathod
Adepu Ravi Sankar
Avinash Ravichandran
Bharadwaj Ravichandran
Dripta S. Raychaudhuri
Adria Recasens
Simon Reiß
Davis Rempe
Daxuan Ren
Jiawei Ren
Jimmy Ren
Sucheng Ren
Dayong Ren
Zhile Ren
Dongwei Ren
Qibing Ren
Pengfei Ren
Zhenwen Ren
Xuqian Ren
Yixuan Ren
Zhongzheng Ren
Ambareesh Revanur
Hamed Rezazadegan
    Tavakoli
Rafael S. Rezende
Wonjong Rhee
Alexander Richard

Christian Richardt
Stephan R. Richter
Benjamin Riggan
Dominik Rivoir
Mamshad Nayeem Rizve
Joshua D. Robinson
Joseph Robinson
Chris Rockwell
Ranga Rodrigo
Andres C. Rodriguez
Carlos Rodriguez-Pardo
Marcus Rohrbach
Gemma Roig
Yu Rong
David A. Ross
Mohammad Rostami
Edward Rosten
Karsten Roth
Anirban Roy
Debaditya Roy
Shuvendu Roy
Ahana Roy Choudhury
Aruni Roy Chowdhury
Denys Rozumnyi
Shulan Ruan
Wenjie Ruan
Patrick Ruhkamp
Danila Rukhovich
Anian Ruoss
Chris Russell
Dan Ruta
Dawid Damian Rymarczyk
DongHun Ryu
Hyeonggon Ryu
Kwonyoung Ryu
Balasubramanian S.
Alexandre Sablayrolles
Mohammad Sabokrou
Arka Sadhu
Aniruddha Saha
Oindrila Saha
Pritish Sahu
Aneeshan Sain
Nirat Saini
Saurabh Saini

Takeshi Saitoh
Christos Sakaridis
Fumihiko Sakaue
Dimitrios Sakkos
Ken Sakurada
Parikshit V. Sakurikar
Rohit Saluja
Nermin Samet
Leo Sampaio Ferraz
    Ribeiro
Jorge Sanchez
Enrique Sanchez
Shengtian Sang
Anush Sankaran
Soubhik Sanyal
Nikolaos Sarafianos
Vishwanath Saragadam
István Sárándi
Saquib Sarfraz
Mert Bulent Sariyildiz
Anindya Sarkar
Pritam Sarkar
Paul-Edouard Sarlin
Hiroshi Sasaki
Takami Sato
Torsten Sattler
Ravi Kumar Satzoda
Axel Sauer
Stefano Savian
Artem Savkin
Manolis Savva
Gerald Schaefer
Simone Schaub-Meyer
Yoni Schirris
Samuel Schulter
Katja Schwarz
Jesse Scott
Sinisa Segvic
Constantin Marc Seibold
Lorenzo Seidenari
Matan Sela
Fadime Sener
Paul Hongsuck Seo
Kwanggyoon Seo
Hongje Seong

Dario Serez
Francesco Setti
Bryan Seybold
Mohamad Shahbazi
Shima Shahfar
Xinxin Shan
Caifeng Shan
Dandan Shan
Shawn Shan
Wei Shang
Jinghuan Shang
Jiaxiang Shang
Lei Shang
Sukrit Shankar
Ken Shao
Rui Shao
Jie Shao
Mingwen Shao
Aashish Sharma
Gaurav Sharma
Vivek Sharma
Abhishek Sharma
Yoli Shavit
Shashank Shekhar
Sumit Shekhar
Zhijie Shen
Fengyi Shen
Furao Shen
Jialie Shen
Jingjing Shen
Ziyi Shen
Linlin Shen
Guangyu Shen
Biluo Shen
Falong Shen
Jiajun Shen
Qiu Shen
Qiuhong Shen
Shuai Shen
Wang Shen
Yiqing Shen
Yunhang Shen
Siqi Shen
Bin Shen
Tianwei Shen

Xi Shen
Yilin Shen
Yuming Shen
Yucong Shen
Zhiqiang Shen
Lu Sheng
Yichen Sheng
Shivanand Venkanna
    Sheshappanavar
Shelly Sheynin
Baifeng Shi
Ruoxi Shi
Botian Shi
Hailin Shi
Jia Shi
Jing Shi
Shaoshuai Shi
Baoguang Shi
Boxin Shi
Hengcan Shi
Tianyang Shi
Xiaodan Shi
Yongjie Shi
Zhensheng Shi
Yinghuan Shi
Weiqi Shi
Wu Shi
Xuepeng Shi
Xiaoshuang Shi
Yujiao Shi
Zenglin Shi
Zhenmei Shi
Takashi Shibata
Meng-Li Shih
Yichang Shih
Hyunjung Shim
Dongseok Shim
Soshi Shimada
Inkyu Shin
Jinwoo Shin
Seungjoo Shin
Seungjae Shin
Koichi Shinoda
Suprosanna Shit

Palaiahnakote
    Shivakumara
Eli Shlizerman
Gaurav Shrivastava
Xiao Shu
Xiangbo Shu
Xiujun Shu
Yang Shu
Tianmin Shu
Jun Shu
Zhixin Shu
Bing Shuai
Maria Shugrina
Ivan Shugurov
Satya Narayan Shukla
Pranjay Shyam
Jianlou Si
Yawar Siddiqui
Alberto Signoroni
Pedro Silva
Jae-Young Sim
Oriane Siméoni
Martin Simon
Andrea Simonelli
Abhishek Singh
Ashish Singh
Dinesh Singh
Gurkirt Singh
Krishna Kumar Singh
Mannat Singh
Pravendra Singh
Rajat Vikram Singh
Utkarsh Singhal
Dipika Singhania
Vasu Singla
Harsh Sinha
Sudipta Sinha
Josef Sivic
Elena Sizikova
Geri Skenderi
Ivan Skorokhodov
Dmitriy Smirnov
Cameron Y. Smith
James S. Smith
Patrick Snape

Mattia Soldan
Hyeongseok Son
Sanghyun Son
Chuanbiao Song
Chen Song
Chunfeng Song
Dan Song
Dongjin Song
Hwanjun Song
Guoxian Song
Jiaming Song
Jie Song
Liangchen Song
Ran Song
Luchuan Song
Xibin Song
Li Song
Fenglong Song
Guoli Song
Guanglu Song
Zhenbo Song
Lin Song
Xinhang Song
Yang Song
Yibing Song
Rajiv Soundararajan
Hossein Souri
Cristovao Sousa
Riccardo Spezialetti
Leonidas Spinoulas
Michael W. Spratling
Deepak Sridhar
Srinath Sridhar
Gaurang Sriramanan
Vinkle Kumar Srivastav
Themos Stafylakis
Serban Stan
Anastasis Stathopoulos
Markus Steinberger
Jan Steinbrener
Sinisa Stekovic
Alexandros Stergiou
Gleb Sterkin
Rainer Stiefelhagen
Pierre Stock

Ombretta Strafforello
Julian Straub
Yannick Strümpler
Joerg Stueckler
Hang Su
Weijie Su
Jong-Chyi Su
Bing Su
Haisheng Su
Jinming Su
Yiyang Su
Yukun Su
Yuxin Su
Zhuo Su
Zhaoqi Su
Xiu Su
Yu-Chuan Su
Zhixun Su
Arulkumar Subramaniam
Akshayvarun Subramanya
A. Subramanyam
Swathikiran Sudhakaran
Yusuke Sugano
Masanori Suganuma
Yumin Suh
Yang Sui
Baochen Sun
Cheng Sun
Long Sun
Guolei Sun
Haoliang Sun
Haomiao Sun
He Sun
Hanqing Sun
Hao Sun
Lichao Sun
Jiachen Sun
Jiaming Sun
Jian Sun
Jin Sun
Jennifer J. Sun
Tiancheng Sun
Libo Sun
Peize Sun
Qianru Sun

Shanlin Sun
Yu Sun
Zhun Sun
Che Sun
Lin Sun
Tao Sun
Yiyou Sun
Chunyi Sun
Chong Sun
Weiwei Sun
Weixuan Sun
Xiuyu Sun
Yanan Sun
Zeren Sun
Zhaodong Sun
Zhiqing Sun
Minhyuk Sung
Jinli Suo
Simon Suo
Abhijit Suprem
Anshuman Suri
Saksham Suri
Joshua M. Susskind
Roman Suvorov
Gurumurthy Swaminathan
Robin Swanson
Paul Swoboda
Tabish A. Syed
Richard Szeliski
Fariborz Taherkhani
Yu-Wing Tai
Keita Takahashi
Walter Talbott
Gary Tam
Masato Tamura
Feitong Tan
Fuwen Tan
Shuhan Tan
Andong Tan
Bin Tan
Cheng Tan
Jianchao Tan
Lei Tan
Mingxing Tan
Xin Tan

Zichang Tan
Zhentao Tan
Kenichiro Tanaka
Masayuki Tanaka
Yushun Tang
Hao Tang
Jingqun Tang
Jinhui Tang
Kaihua Tang
Luming Tang
Lv Tang
Sheyang Tang
Shitao Tang
Siliang Tang
Shixiang Tang
Yansong Tang
Keke Tang
Chang Tang
Chenwei Tang
Jie Tang
Junshu Tang
Ming Tang
Peng Tang
Xu Tang
Yao Tang
Chen Tang
Fan Tang
Haoran Tang
Shengeng Tang
Yehui Tang
Zhipeng Tang
Ugo Tanielian
Chaofan Tao
Jiale Tao
Junli Tao
Renshuai Tao
An Tao
Guanhong Tao
Zhiqiang Tao
Makarand Tapaswi
Jean-Philippe G. Tarel
Juan J. Tarrio
Enzo Tartaglione
Keisuke Tateno
Zachary Teed

Ajinkya B. Tejankar
Bugra Tekin
Purva Tendulkar
Damien Teney
Minggui Teng
Chris Tensmeyer
Andrew Beng Jin Teoh
Philipp Terhörst
Kartik Thakral
Nupur Thakur
Kevin Thandiackal
Spyridon Thermos
Diego Thomas
William Thong
Yuesong Tian
Guanzhong Tian
Lin Tian
Shiqi Tian
Kai Tian
Meng Tian
Tai-Peng Tian
Zhuotao Tian
Shangxuan Tian
Tian Tian
Yapeng Tian
Yu Tian
Yuxin Tian
Leslie Ching Ow Tiong
Praveen Tirupattur
Garvita Tiwari
George Toderici
Antoine Toisoul
Aysim Toker
Tatiana Tommasi
Zhan Tong
Alessio Tonioni
Alessandro Torcinovich
Fabio Tosi
Matteo Toso
Hugo Touvron
Quan Hung Tran
Son Tran
Hung Tran
Ngoc-Trung Tran
Vinh Tran

Phong Tran
Giovanni Trappolini
Edith Tretschk
Subarna Tripathi
Shubhendu Trivedi
Eduard Trulls
Prune Truong
Thanh-Dat Truong
Tomasz Trzcinski
Sam Tsai
Yi-Hsuan Tsai
Ethan Tseng
Yu-Chee Tseng
Shahar Tsiper
Stavros Tsogkas
Shikui Tu
Zhigang Tu
Zhengzhong Tu
Richard Tucker
Sergey Tulyakov
Cigdem Turan
Daniyar Turmukhambetov
Victor G. Turrisi da Costa
Bartlomiej Twardowski
Christopher D. Twigg
Radim Tylecek
Mostofa Rafid Uddin
Md. Zasim Uddin
Kohei Uehara
Nicolas Ugrinovic
Youngjung Uh
Norimichi Ukita
Anwaar Ulhaq
Devesh Upadhyay
Paul Upchurch
Yoshitaka Ushiku
Yuzuko Utsumi
Mikaela Angelina Uy
Mohit Vaishnav
Pratik Vaishnavi
Jeya Maria Jose Valanarasu
Matias A. Valdenegro Toro
Diego Valsesia
Wouter Van Gansbeke
Nanne van Noord

Simon Vandenhende
Farshid Varno
Cristina Vasconcelos
Francisco Vasconcelos
Alex Vasilescu
Subeesh Vasu
Arun Balajee Vasudevan
Kanav Vats
Vaibhav S. Vavilala
Sagar Vaze
Javier Vazquez-Corral
Andrea Vedaldi
Olga Veksler
Andreas Velten
Sai H. Vemprala
Raviteja Vemulapalli
Shashanka
    Venkataramanan
Dor Verbin
Luisa Verdoliva
Manisha Verma
Yashaswi Verma
Constantin Vertan
Eli Verwimp
Deepak Vijaykeerthy
Pablo Villanueva
Ruben Villegas
Markus Vincze
Vibhav Vineet
Minh P. Vo
Huy V. Vo
Duc Minh Vo
Tomas Vojir
Igor Vozniak
Nicholas Vretos
Vibashan VS
Tuan-Anh Vu
Thang Vu
Mårten Wadenbäck
Neal Wadhwa
Aaron T. Walsman
Steven Walton
Jin Wan
Alvin Wan
Jia Wan

Jun Wan
Xiaoyue Wan
Fang Wan
Guowei Wan
Renjie Wan
Zhiqiang Wan
Ziyu Wan
Bastian Wandt
Dongdong Wang
Limin Wang
Haiyang Wang
Xiaobing Wang
Angtian Wang
Angelina Wang
Bing Wang
Bo Wang
Boyu Wang
Binghui Wang
Chen Wang
Chien-Yi Wang
Congli Wang
Qi Wang
Chengrui Wang
Rui Wang
Yiqun Wang
Cong Wang
Wenjing Wang
Dongkai Wang
Di Wang
Xiaogang Wang
Kai Wang
Zhizhong Wang
Fangjinhua Wang
Feng Wang
Hang Wang
Gaoang Wang
Guoqing Wang
Guangcong Wang
Guangzhi Wang
Hanqing Wang
Hao Wang
Haohan Wang
Haoran Wang
Hong Wang
Haotao Wang

Hu Wang
Huan Wang
Hua Wang
Hui-Po Wang
Hengli Wang
Hanyu Wang
Hongxing Wang
Jingwen Wang
Jialiang Wang
Jian Wang
Jianyi Wang
Jiashun Wang
Jiahao Wang
Tsun-Hsuan Wang
Xiaoqian Wang
Jinqiao Wang
Jun Wang
Jianzong Wang
Kaihong Wang
Ke Wang
Lei Wang
Lingjing Wang
Linnan Wang
Lin Wang
Liansheng Wang
Mengjiao Wang
Manning Wang
Nannan Wang
Peihao Wang
Jiayun Wang
Pu Wang
Qiang Wang
Qiufeng Wang
Qilong Wang
Qiangchang Wang
Qin Wang
Qing Wang
Ruocheng Wang
Ruibin Wang
Ruisheng Wang
Ruizhe Wang
Runqi Wang
Runzhong Wang
Wenxuan Wang
Sen Wang

Shangfei Wang
Shaofei Wang
Shijie Wang
Shiqi Wang
Zhibo Wang
Song Wang
Xinjiang Wang
Tai Wang
Tao Wang
Teng Wang
Xiang Wang
Tianren Wang
Tiantian Wang
Tianyi Wang
Fengjiao Wang
Wei Wang
Miaohui Wang
Suchen Wang
Siyue Wang
Yaoming Wang
Xiao Wang
Ze Wang
Biao Wang
Chaofei Wang
Dong Wang
Gu Wang
Guangrun Wang
Guangming Wang
Guo-Hua Wang
Haoqing Wang
Hesheng Wang
Huafeng Wang
Jinghua Wang
Jingdong Wang
Jingjing Wang
Jingya Wang
Jingkang Wang
Jiakai Wang
Junke Wang
Kuo Wang
Lichen Wang
Lizhi Wang
Longguang Wang
Mang Wang
Mei Wang

Min Wang
Peng-Shuai Wang
Run Wang
Shaoru Wang
Shuhui Wang
Tan Wang
Tiancai Wang
Tianqi Wang
Wenhai Wang
Wenzhe Wang
Xiaobo Wang
Xiudong Wang
Xu Wang
Yajie Wang
Yan Wang
Yuan-Gen Wang
Yingqian Wang
Yizhi Wang
Yulin Wang
Yu Wang
Yujie Wang
Yunhe Wang
Yuxi Wang
Yaowei Wang
Yiwei Wang
Zezheng Wang
Hongzhi Wang
Zhiqiang Wang
Ziteng Wang
Ziwei Wang
Zheng Wang
Zhenyu Wang
Binglu Wang
Zhongdao Wang
Ce Wang
Weining Wang
Weiyao Wang
Wenbin Wang
Wenguan Wang
Guangting Wang
Haolin Wang
Haiyan Wang
Huiyu Wang
Naiyan Wang
Jingbo Wang

Jinpeng Wang
Jiaqi Wang
Liyuan Wang
Lizhen Wang
Ning Wang
Wenqian Wang
Sheng-Yu Wang
Weimin Wang
Xiaohan Wang
Yifan Wang
Yi Wang
Yongtao Wang
Yizhou Wang
Zhuo Wang
Zhe Wang
Xudong Wang
Xiaofang Wang
Xinggang Wang
Xiaosen Wang
Xiaosong Wang
Xiaoyang Wang
Lijun Wang
Xinlong Wang
Xuan Wang
Xue Wang
Yangang Wang
Yaohui Wang
Yu-Chiang Frank Wang
Yida Wang
Yilin Wang
Yi Ru Wang
Yali Wang
Yinglong Wang
Yufu Wang
Yujiang Wang
Yuwang Wang
Yuting Wang
Yang Wang
Yu-Xiong Wang
Yixu Wang
Ziqi Wang
Zhicheng Wang
Zeyu Wang
Zhaowen Wang
Zhenyi Wang

Zhenzhi Wang
Zhijie Wang
Zhiyong Wang
Zhongling Wang
Zhuowei Wang
Zian Wang
Zifu Wang
Zihao Wang
Zirui Wang
Ziyan Wang
Wenxiao Wang
Zhen Wang
Zhepeng Wang
Zi Wang
Zihao W. Wang
Steven L. Waslander
Olivia Watkins
Daniel Watson
Silvan Weder
Dongyoon Wee
Dongming Wei
Tianyi Wei
Jia Wei
Dong Wei
Fangyun Wei
Longhui Wei
Mingqiang Wei
Xinyue Wei
Chen Wei
Donglai Wei
Pengxu Wei
Xing Wei
Xiu-Shen Wei
Wenqi Wei
Guoqiang Wei
Wei Wei
XingKui Wei
Xian Wei
Xingxing Wei
Yake Wei
Yuxiang Wei
Yi Wei
Luca Weihs
Michael Weinmann
Martin Weinmann

Congcong Wen
Chuan Wen
Jie Wen
Sijia Wen
Song Wen
Chao Wen
Xiang Wen
Zeyi Wen
Xin Wen
Yilin Wen
Yijia Weng
Shuchen Weng
Junwu Weng
Wenming Weng
Renliang Weng
Zhenyu Weng
Xinshuo Weng
Nicholas J. Westlake
Gordon Wetzstein
Lena M. Widin Klasén
Rick Wildes
Bryan M. Williams
Williem Williem
Ole Winther
Scott Wisdom
Alex Wong
Chau-Wai Wong
Kwan-Yee K. Wong
Yongkang Wong
Scott Workman
Marcel Worring
Michael Wray
Safwan Wshah
Xiang Wu
Aming Wu
Chongruo Wu
Cho-Ying Wu
Chunpeng Wu
Chenyan Wu
Ziyi Wu
Fuxiang Wu
Gang Wu
Haiping Wu
Huisi Wu
Jane Wu

Jialian Wu
Jing Wu
Jinjian Wu
Jianlong Wu
Xian Wu
Lifang Wu
Lifan Wu
Minye Wu
Qianyi Wu
Rongliang Wu
Rui Wu
Shiqian Wu
Shuzhe Wu
Shangzhe Wu
Tsung-Han Wu
Tz-Ying Wu
Ting-Wei Wu
Jiannan Wu
Zhiliang Wu
Yu Wu
Chenyun Wu
Dayan Wu
Dongxian Wu
Fei Wu
Hefeng Wu
Jianxin Wu
Weibin Wu
Wenxuan Wu
Wenhao Wu
Xiao Wu
Yicheng Wu
Yuanwei Wu
Yu-Huan Wu
Zhenxin Wu
Zhenyu Wu
Wei Wu
Peng Wu
Xiaohe Wu
Xindi Wu
Xinxing Wu
Xinyi Wu
Xingjiao Wu
Xiongwei Wu
Yangzheng Wu
Yanzhao Wu

Yawen Wu
Yong Wu
Yi Wu
Ying Nian Wu
Zhenyao Wu
Zhonghua Wu
Zongze Wu
Zuxuan Wu
Stefanie Wuhrer
Teng Xi
Jianing Xi
Fei Xia
Haifeng Xia
Menghan Xia
Yuanqing Xia
Zhihua Xia
Xiaobo Xia
Weihao Xia
Shihong Xia
Yan Xia
Yong Xia
Zhaoyang Xia
Zhihao Xia
Chuhua Xian
Yongqin Xian
Wangmeng Xiang
Fanbo Xiang
Tiange Xiang
Tao Xiang
Liuyu Xiang
Xiaoyu Xiang
Zhiyu Xiang
Aoran Xiao
Chunxia Xiao
Fanyi Xiao
Jimin Xiao
Jun Xiao
Taihong Xiao
Anqi Xiao
Junfei Xiao
Jing Xiao
Liang Xiao
Yang Xiao
Yuting Xiao
Yijun Xiao

Yao Xiao
Zeyu Xiao
Zhisheng Xiao
Zihao Xiao
Binhui Xie
Christopher Xie
Haozhe Xie
Jin Xie
Guo-Sen Xie
Hongtao Xie
Ming-Kun Xie
Tingting Xie
Chaohao Xie
Weicheng Xie
Xudong Xie
Jiyang Xie
Xiaohua Xie
Yuan Xie
Zhenyu Xie
Ning Xie
Xianghui Xie
Xiufeng Xie
You Xie
Yutong Xie
Fuyong Xing
Yifan Xing
Zhen Xing
Yuanjun Xiong
Jinhui Xiong
Weihua Xiong
Hongkai Xiong
Zhitong Xiong
Yuanhao Xiong
Yunyang Xiong
Yuwen Xiong
Zhiwei Xiong
Yuliang Xiu
An Xu
Chang Xu
Chenliang Xu
Chengming Xu
Chenshu Xu
Xiang Xu
Huijuan Xu
Zhe Xu

Jie Xu
Jingyi Xu
Jiarui Xu
Yinghao Xu
Kele Xu
Ke Xu
Li Xu
Linchuan Xu
Linning Xu
Mengde Xu
Mengmeng Frost Xu
Min Xu
Mingye Xu
Jun Xu
Ning Xu
Peng Xu
Runsheng Xu
Sheng Xu
Wenqiang Xu
Xiaogang Xu
Renzhe Xu
Kaidi Xu
Yi Xu
Chi Xu
Qiuling Xu
Baobei Xu
Feng Xu
Haohang Xu
Haofei Xu
Lan Xu
Mingze Xu
Songcen Xu
Weipeng Xu
Wenjia Xu
Wenju Xu
Xiangyu Xu
Xin Xu
Yinshuang Xu
Yixing Xu
Yuting Xu
Yanyu Xu
Zhenbo Xu
Zhiliang Xu
Zhiyuan Xu
Xiaohao Xu

Yanwu Xu
Yan Xu
Yiran Xu
Yifan Xu
Yufei Xu
Yong Xu
Zichuan Xu
Zenglin Xu
Zexiang Xu
Zhan Xu
Zheng Xu
Zhiwei Xu
Ziyue Xu
Shiyu Xuan
Hanyu Xuan
Fei Xue
Jianru Xue
Mingfu Xue
Qinghan Xue
Tianfan Xue
Chao Xue
Chuhui Xue
Nan Xue
Zhou Xue
Xiangyang Xue
Yuan Xue
Abhay Yadav
Ravindra Yadav
Kota Yamaguchi
Toshihiko Yamasaki
Kohei Yamashita
Chaochao Yan
Feng Yan
Kun Yan
Qingsen Yan
Qixin Yan
Rui Yan
Siming Yan
Xinchen Yan
Yaping Yan
Bin Yan
Qingan Yan
Shen Yan
Shipeng Yan
Xu Yan

Yan Yan
Yichao Yan
Zhaoyi Yan
Zike Yan
Zhiqiang Yan
Hongliang Yan
Zizheng Yan
Jiewen Yang
Anqi Joyce Yang
Shan Yang
Anqi Yang
Antoine Yang
Bo Yang
Baoyao Yang
Chenhongyi Yang
Dingkang Yang
Dc-Nian Yang
Dong Yang
David Yang
Fan Yang
Fengyu Yang
Fengting Yang
Fei Yang
Gengshan Yang
Heng Yang
Han Yang
Huan Yang
Yibo Yang
Jiancheng Yang
Jihan Yang
Jiawei Yang
Jiayu Yang
Jie Yang
Jinfa Yang
Jingkang Yang
Jinyu Yang
Cheng-Fu Yang
Ji Yang
Jianyu Yang
Kailun Yang
Tian Yang
Luyu Yang
Liang Yang
Li Yang
Michael Ying Yang

Yang Yang
Muli Yang
Le Yang
Qiushi Yang
Ren Yang
Ruihan Yang
Shuang Yang
Siyuan Yang
Su Yang
Shiqi Yang
Taojiannan Yang
Tianyu Yang
Lei Yang
Wanzhao Yang
Shuai Yang
William Yang
Wei Yang
Xiaofeng Yang
Xiaoshan Yang
Xin Yang
Xuan Yang
Xu Yang
Xingyi Yang
Xitong Yang
Jing Yang
Yanchao Yang
Wenming Yang
Yujiu Yang
Herb Yang
Jianfei Yang
Jinhui Yang
Chuanguang Yang
Guanglei Yang
Haitao Yang
Kewei Yang
Linlin Yang
Lijin Yang
Longrong Yang
Meng Yang
MingKun Yang
Sibei Yang
Shicai Yang
Tong Yang
Wen Yang
Xi Yang

Xiaolong Yang
Xue Yang
Yubin Yang
Ze Yang
Ziyi Yang
Yi Yang
Linjie Yang
Yuzhe Yang
Yiding Yang
Zhenpei Yang
Zhaohui Yang
Zhengyuan Yang
Zhibo Yang
Zongxin Yang
Hantao Yao
Mingde Yao
Rui Yao
Taiping Yao
Ting Yao
Cong Yao
Qingsong Yao
Quanming Yao
Xu Yao
Yuan Yao
Yao Yao
Yazhou Yao
Jiawen Yao
Shunyu Yao
Pew-Thian Yap
Sudhir Yarram
Rajeev Yasarla
Peng Ye
Botao Ye
Mao Ye
Fei Ye
Hanrong Ye
Jingwen Ye
Jinwei Ye
Jiarong Ye
Mang Ye
Meng Ye
Qi Ye
Qian Ye
Qixiang Ye
Junjie Ye

Sheng Ye
Nanyang Ye
Yufei Ye
Xiaoqing Ye
Ruolin Ye
Yousef Yeganeh
Chun-Hsiao Yeh
Raymond A. Yeh
Yu-Ying Yeh
Kai Yi
Chang Yi
Renjiao Yi
Xinping Yi
Peng Yi
Alper Yilmaz
Junho Yim
Hui Yin
Bangjie Yin
Jia-Li Yin
Miao Yin
Wenzhe Yin
Xuwang Yin
Ming Yin
Yu Yin
Aoxiong Yin
Kangxue Yin
Tianwei Yin
Wei Yin
Xianghua Ying
Rio Yokota
Tatsuya Yokota
Naoto Yokoya
Ryo Yonetani
Ki Yoon Yoo
Jinsu Yoo
Sunjae Yoon
Jae Shin Yoon
Jihun Yoon
Sung-Hoon Yoon
Ryota Yoshihashi
Yusuke Yoshiyasu
Chenyu You
Haoran You
Haoxuan You
Yang You

Quanzeng You
Tackgeun You
Kaichao You
Shan You
Xinge You
Yurong You
Baosheng Yu
Bei Yu
Haichao Yu
Hao Yu
Chaohui Yu
Fisher Yu
Jin-Gang Yu
Jiyang Yu
Jason J. Yu
Jiashuo Yu
Hong-Xing Yu
Lei Yu
Mulin Yu
Ning Yu
Peilin Yu
Qi Yu
Qian Yu
Rui Yu
Shuzhi Yu
Gang Yu
Tan Yu
Weijiang Yu
Xin Yu
Bingyao Yu
Ye Yu
Hanchao Yu
Yingchen Yu
Tao Yu
Xiaotian Yu
Qing Yu
Houjian Yu
Changqian Yu
Jing Yu
Jun Yu
Shujian Yu
Xiang Yu
Zhaofei Yu
Zhenbo Yu
Yinfeng Yu

Zhuoran Yu
Zitong Yu
Bo Yuan
Jiangbo Yuan
Liangzhe Yuan
Weihao Yuan
Jianbo Yuan
Xiaoyun Yuan
Ye Yuan
Li Yuan
Geng Yuan
Jialin Yuan
Maoxun Yuan
Peng Yuan
Xin Yuan
Yuan Yuan
Yuhui Yuan
Yixuan Yuan
Zheng Yuan
Mehmet Kerim Yücel
Kaiyu Yue
Haixiao Yue
Heeseung Yun
Sangdoo Yun
Tian Yun
Mahmut Yurt
Ekim Yurtsever
Ahmet Yüzügüler
Edouard Yvinec
Eloi Zablocki
Christopher Zach
Muhammad Zaigham
    Zaheer
Pierluigi Zama Ramirez
Yuhang Zang
Pietro Zanuttigh
Alexey Zaytsev
Bernhard Zeisl
Haitian Zeng
Pengpeng Zeng
Jiabei Zeng
Runhao Zeng
Wei Zeng
Yawen Zeng
Yi Zeng

Yiming Zeng
Tieyong Zeng
Huanqiang Zeng
Dan Zeng
Yu Zeng
Wei Zhai
Yuanhao Zhai
Fangneng Zhan
Kun Zhan
Xiong Zhang
Jingdong Zhang
Jiangning Zhang
Zhilu Zhang
Gengwei Zhang
Dongsu Zhang
Hui Zhang
Binjie Zhang
Bo Zhang
Tianhao Zhang
Cecilia Zhang
Jing Zhang
Chaoning Zhang
Chenxu Zhang
Chi Zhang
Chris Zhang
Yabin Zhang
Zhao Zhang
Rufeng Zhang
Chaoyi Zhang
Zheng Zhang
Da Zhang
Yi Zhang
Edward Zhang
Xin Zhang
Feifei Zhang
Feilong Zhang
Yuqi Zhang
GuiXuan Zhang
Hanlin Zhang
Hanwang Zhang
Hanzhen Zhang
Haotian Zhang
He Zhang
Haokui Zhang
Hongyuan Zhang

Hengrui Zhang
Hongming Zhang
Mingfang Zhang
Jianpeng Zhang
Jiaming Zhang
Jichao Zhang
Jie Zhang
Jingfeng Zhang
Jingyi Zhang
Jinnian Zhang
David Junhao Zhang
Junjie Zhang
Junzhe Zhang
Jiawan Zhang
Jingyang Zhang
Kai Zhang
Lei Zhang
Lihua Zhang
Lu Zhang
Miao Zhang
Minjia Zhang
Mingjin Zhang
Qi Zhang
Qian Zhang
Qilong Zhang
Qiming Zhang
Qiang Zhang
Richard Zhang
Ruimao Zhang
Ruisi Zhang
Ruixin Zhang
Runze Zhang
Qilin Zhang
Shan Zhang
Shanshan Zhang
Xi Sheryl Zhang
Song-Hai Zhang
Chongyang Zhang
Kaihao Zhang
Songyang Zhang
Shu Zhang
Siwei Zhang
Shujian Zhang
Tianyun Zhang
Tong Zhang

Tao Zhang
Wenwei Zhang
Wenqiang Zhang
Wen Zhang
Xiaolin Zhang
Xingchen Zhang
Xingxuan Zhang
Xiuming Zhang
Xiaoshuai Zhang
Xuanmeng Zhang
Xuanyang Zhang
Xucong Zhang
Xingxing Zhang
Xikun Zhang
Xiaohan Zhang
Yahui Zhang
Yunhua Zhang
Yan Zhang
Yanghao Zhang
Yifei Zhang
Yifan Zhang
Yi-Fan Zhang
Yihao Zhang
Yingliang Zhang
Youshan Zhang
Yulun Zhang
Yushu Zhang
Yixiao Zhang
Yide Zhang
Zhongwen Zhang
Bowen Zhang
Chen-Lin Zhang
Zehua Zhang
Zekun Zhang
Zeyu Zhang
Xiaowei Zhang
Yifeng Zhang
Cheng Zhang
Hongguang Zhang
Yuexi Zhang
Fa Zhang
Guofeng Zhang
Hao Zhang
Haofeng Zhang
Hongwen Zhang

Hua Zhang
Jiaxin Zhang
Zhenyu Zhang
Jian Zhang
Jianfeng Zhang
Jiao Zhang
Jiakai Zhang
Lefei Zhang
Le Zhang
Mi Zhang
Min Zhang
Ning Zhang
Pan Zhang
Pu Zhang
Qing Zhang
Renrui Zhang
Shifeng Zhang
Shuo Zhang
Shaoxiong Zhang
Weizhong Zhang
Xi Zhang
Xiaomei Zhang
Xinyu Zhang
Yin Zhang
Zicheng Zhang
Zihao Zhang
Ziqi Zhang
Zhaoxiang Zhang
Zhen Zhang
Zhipeng Zhang
Zhixing Zhang
Zhizheng Zhang
Jiawei Zhang
Zhong Zhang
Pingping Zhang
Yixin Zhang
Kui Zhang
Lingzhi Zhang
Huaiwen Zhang
Quanshi Zhang
Zhoutong Zhang
Yuhang Zhang
Yuting Zhang
Zhang Zhang
Ziming Zhang

Zhizhong Zhang
Qilong Zhangli
Bingyin Zhao
Bin Zhao
Chenglong Zhao
Lei Zhao
Feng Zhao
Gangming Zhao
Haiyan Zhao
Hao Zhao
Handong Zhao
Hengshuang Zhao
Yinan Zhao
Jiaojiao Zhao
Jiaqi Zhao
Jing Zhao
Kaili Zhao
Haojie Zhao
Yucheng Zhao
Longjiao Zhao
Long Zhao
Qingsong Zhao
Qingyu Zhao
Rui Zhao
Rui-Wei Zhao
Sicheng Zhao
Shuang Zhao
Siyan Zhao
Zelin Zhao
Shiyu Zhao
Wang Zhao
Tiesong Zhao
Qian Zhao
Wangbo Zhao
Xi-Le Zhao
Xu Zhao
Yajie Zhao
Yang Zhao
Ying Zhao
Yin Zhao
Yizhou Zhao
Yunhan Zhao
Yuyang Zhao
Yue Zhao
Yuzhi Zhao

Bowen Zhao
Pu Zhao
Bingchen Zhao
Borui Zhao
Fuqiang Zhao
Hanbin Zhao
Jian Zhao
Mingyang Zhao
Na Zhao
Rongchang Zhao
Ruiqi Zhao
Shuai Zhao
Wenda Zhao
Wenliang Zhao
Xiangyun Zhao
Yifan Zhao
Yaping Zhao
Zhou Zhao
He Zhao
Jie Zhao
Xibin Zhao
Xiaoqi Zhao
Zhengyu Zhao
Jin Zhe
Chuanxia Zheng
Huan Zheng
Hao Zheng
Jia Zheng
Jian-Qing Zheng
Shuai Zheng
Meng Zheng
Mingkai Zheng
Qian Zheng
Qi Zheng
Wu Zheng
Yinqiang Zheng
Yufeng Zheng
Yutong Zheng
Yalin Zheng
Yu Zheng
Feng Zheng
Zhaoheng Zheng
Haitian Zheng
Kang Zheng
Bolun Zheng

Haiyong Zheng
Mingwu Zheng
Sipeng Zheng
Tu Zheng
Wenzhao Zheng
Xiawu Zheng
Yinglin Zheng
Zhuo Zheng
Zilong Zheng
Kecheng Zheng
Zerong Zheng
Shuaifeng Zhi
Tiancheng Zhi
Jia-Xing Zhong
Yiwu Zhong
Fangwei Zhong
Zhihang Zhong
Yaoyao Zhong
Yiran Zhong
Zhun Zhong
Zichun Zhong
Bo Zhou
Boyao Zhou
Brady Zhou
Mo Zhou
Chunluan Zhou
Dingfu Zhou
Fan Zhou
Jingkai Zhou
Honglu Zhou
Jiaming Zhou
Jiahuan Zhou
Jun Zhou
Kaiyang Zhou
Keyang Zhou
Kuangqi Zhou
Lei Zhou
Lihua Zhou
Man Zhou
Mingyi Zhou
Mingyuan Zhou
Ning Zhou
Peng Zhou
Penghao Zhou
Qianyi Zhou

Shuigeng Zhou
Shangchen Zhou
Huayi Zhou
Zhize Zhou
Sanping Zhou
Qin Zhou
Tao Zhou
Wenbo Zhou
Xiangdong Zhou
Xiao-Yun Zhou
Xiao Zhou
Yang Zhou
Yipin Zhou
Zhenyu Zhou
Hao Zhou
Chu Zhou
Daquan Zhou
Da-Wei Zhou
Hang Zhou
Kang Zhou
Qianyu Zhou
Sheng Zhou
Wenhui Zhou
Xingyi Zhou
Yan-Jie Zhou
Yiyi Zhou
Yu Zhou
Yuan Zhou
Yuqian Zhou
Yuxuan Zhou
Zixiang Zhou
Wengang Zhou
Shuchang Zhou
Tianfei Zhou
Yichao Zhou
Alex Zhu
Chenchen Zhu
Deyao Zhu
Xiatian Zhu
Guibo Zhu
Haidong Zhu
Hao Zhu
Hongzi Zhu
Rui Zhu
Jing Zhu

Jianke Zhu
Junchen Zhu
Lei Zhu
Lingyu Zhu
Luyang Zhu
Menglong Zhu
Peihao Zhu
Hui Zhu
Xiaofeng Zhu
Tyler (Lixuan) Zhu
Wentao Zhu
Xiangyu Zhu
Xinqi Zhu
Xinxin Zhu
Xinliang Zhu
Yangguang Zhu
Yichen Zhu
Yixin Zhu
Yanjun Zhu
Yousong Zhu
Yuhao Zhu
Ye Zhu
Feng Zhu
Zhen Zhu
Fangrui Zhu
Jinjing Zhu
Linchao Zhu
Pengfei Zhu
Sijie Zhu
Xiaobin Zhu
Xiaoguang Zhu
Zezhou Zhu
Zhenyao Zhu
Kai Zhu
Pengkai Zhu
Bingbing Zhuang
Chengyuan Zhuang
Liansheng Zhuang
Peiye Zhuang
Yixin Zhuang
Yihong Zhuang
Junbao Zhuo
Andrea Ziani
Bartosz Zieliński
Primo Zingaretti

Nikolaos Zioulis
Andrew Zisserman
Yael Ziv
Liu Ziyin
Xingxing Zou
Danping Zou
Qi Zou

Shihao Zou
Xueyan Zou
Yang Zou
Yuliang Zou
Zihang Zou
Chuhang Zou
Dongqing Zou

Xu Zou
Zhiming Zou
Maria A. Zuluaga
Xinxin Zuo
Zhiwen Zuo
Reyer Zwiggelaar

Contents – Part X

DFNet: Enhance Absolute Pose Regression with Direct Feature Matching

Shuai Chen[✉], Xinghui Li, Zirui Wang, and Victor A. Prisacariu

Active Vision Lab, University of Oxford, Oxford, England
shuaic@robots.ox.ac.uk

Abstract. We introduce a camera relocalization pipeline that combines absolute pose regression (APR) and direct feature matching. By incorporating exposure-adaptive novel view synthesis, our method successfully addresses photometric distortions in outdoor environments that existing photometric-based methods fail to handle. With domain-invariant feature matching, our solution improves pose regression accuracy using semi-supervised learning on unlabeled data. In particular, the pipeline consists of two components: Novel View Synthesizer and DFNet. The former synthesizes novel views compensating for changes in exposure and the latter regresses camera poses and extracts robust features that close the domain gap between real images and synthetic ones. Furthermore, we introduce an online synthetic data generation scheme. We show that these approaches effectively enhance camera pose estimation both in indoor and outdoor scenes. Hence, our method achieves a state-of-the-art accuracy by outperforming existing single-image APR methods by as much as 56%, comparable to 3D structure-based methods. (The code is available in https://code.active.vision.)

Keywords: Absolute pose regression · Feature matching · NeRF

1 Introduction

Estimating the position and orientation of cameras from images is essential in many applications, including virtual reality, augmented reality, and autonomous driving. While the problem can be approached via a geometric pipeline consisting of image retrieval, feature extraction and matching, and a robust Perspective-n-Points (PnP) algorithm, many challenges remain, such as invariance to appearance or the selection of the best set of method hyperparameters.

Learning-based methods have been used in traditional pipelines to improve robustness and accuracy, e.g. by generating neural network (NN)-based feature descriptors [7,15,16,24,25], combining feature extraction and matching into one network [29], or incorporating differentiable outlier filtering modules [1–3].

Supplementary Information The online version contains supplementary material available at https://doi.org/10.1007/978-3-031-20080-9_1.

S. Avidan et al. (Eds.): ECCV 2022, LNCS 13670, pp. 1–17, 2022.
https://doi.org/10.1007/978-3-031-20080-9_1

Although deep 3D-based solutions have demonstrated favorable results, many pre-requisites often remain, such as the need for an accurate 3D model of the scene and manual hyperparameter tuning of the remaining classical components.

The alternative end-to-end NN-based approach, termed absolute pose regression (APR), directly regresses the absolute pose of the camera from input images [13] without requiring prior knowledge about the 3D structure of the neighboring environment. Compared with deep 3D-based methods, APR methods can achieve at least one magnitude faster running speeds at the cost of inferior accuracy and longer training time. Although follow-up works such as MapNet [4] and Kendall *et al.* [12] attempt to improve APR methods by adding various constraints such as relative pose and scene geometry reprojection, a noticeable gap remains between APR and 3D-based methods.

Recently, Direct-PN [5] achieved state-of-the-art (SOTA) accuracy in indoor localization tasks among existing single-frame APR methods. As well as being supervised by ground-truth poses, the network directly matches the input image and a NeRF-rendered image at the predicted pose. However, it has two major limitations: (a) direct matching is very sensitive to photometric inconsistency, as images with different exposures could produce a high photometric error even from the same camera pose, which reduces the viability of photometric direct matching in environments with large photometric distortions, such as outdoor scenes; (b) there is a domain gap between real and rendered images caused by poor rendering quality or changes in content and appearance of the query scene.

In order to address these limitations, we propose a novel relocalization pipeline that combines APR and direct feature matching. First, we introduce a histogram-assisted variant of NeRF, which learns to control synthetic appearance via histograms of luminance information. This significantly reduces the gap between real and synthetic image appearance. Second, we propose a network *DFNet* that extracts domain invariant features and regresses camera poses, trained using a contrastive loss with a customized mining method. Matching these features instead of direct pixels colors boosts the performance of the direct dense matching further. Third, we improve generalizability by (i) applying a cheap Random View Synthesis (RVS) strategy to efficiently generate a synthetic training set by rendering novel views from randomly generated pseudo training poses and (ii) allow the use of unlabeled data. We show that our method outperforms existing single-frame APR methods by as much as 56% on both indoor 7-Scenes and outdoor Cambridge datasets. We summarize our main contributions as follows:

1. We introduce a direct feature matching method that offers better robustness than the prior photometric matching formulation, and devise a network DFNet that can effectively bridge the feature-level domain gap between real and synthetic images.
2. We introduce a histogram-assisted NeRF, which can scale the direct matching approach to scenes with large photometric distortions, *e.g.*, outdoor environments, and provide more accurate rendering appearance to unseen real data.

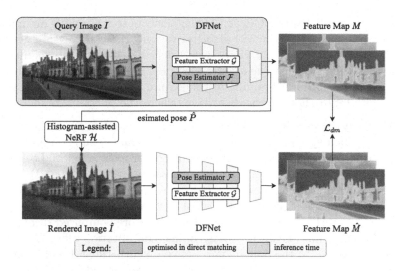

Fig. 1. Overview of the direct feature matching pipeline. Given an input image I, a pose regressor $\mathcal{F}$ estimates a camera pose $\hat{P}$, from which a luminance prior NVS system $\mathcal{H}$ renders a synthetic image $\hat{I}$. Domain invariant features of M and $\hat{M}$ are extracted using a feature extractor $\mathcal{G}$, supplying a feature-metric direct matching signal $\mathcal{L}_{dm}$ to optimize the pose regressor.

3. We show that a simpler synthetic data generation strategy such as RVS can improve pose regression performance.

2 Related Work

Absolute Pose Regression. Absolute pose regression aims to directly regress the 6-DOF camera pose from an image using Convolutional Neural Networks. The first practice in this area is introduced by PoseNet [13], which is a GoogLeNet-backbone network appended with an MLP regressor. Successors of PoseNet propose several variations in network architectures, such as adding LSTM layers [35], adapting an encoder-decoder backbone [18], splitting the network into position and orientation branches [37], or incorporating attentions using transformers [27,28]. Other methods propose different strategies to train APR. Bayesian PoseNet [14] inserts Monte Carlo dropout to a Bayesian CNN that estimates pose with uncertainty. Kendall *et al.* [12] proposes to balance the translation and rotation loss at training using learnable weights and reprojection error. MapNet [4] trains the network using both absolute pose loss and relative pose loss but can infer in a single-frame manner. Direct-PoseNet (Direct-PN) [5] adapts additional photometric loss by comparing the query image with NeRF synthesis on the predicted pose.

Semi-supervised Learning in APR. Several APR methods explore semi-supervised learning with additional images without ground-truth pose annotation to improve pose regression performance. To the best of our knowledge,

MapNet+ [4] and MapNet+PGO [4] are the pioneers to train APR on unlabeled video sequences using external VO algorithms [8,9]. Direct-PN+ [5] finetune on unlabeled data from arbitrary viewpoints solely based on its direct matching formulation. While the direct matching idea from Direct-PN+ inspires our proposed method, we focus on training in the feature space. Our solution can scale to scenes with large photometric distortion, where the previous method fails.

Novel View Synthesis in APR. Novel View Synthesis (NVS) can be beneficial to the visual relocalization task. For example, NVS can expand training space by generating extra synthetic data. Purkait *et al.* [23] propose a method to generate realistic synthetic training data for pose regression leveraging the 3D map and feature correspondences. LENS [21] deploys a NeRF-W [17] model to sample the scene boundaries and synthesize virtual views with uniformly generated virtual camera poses. However, Purkait *et al.* rely on a pre-computed reconstructed 3D map. LENS is limited by its costly offline computation efficiency and the lack of compensation to the domain gap between synthetic and real images, i.e., dynamic objects or artifacts. Another direction is to embed NVS into the pose estimation process. InLoc [31] verifies the predicted pose with view synthesis. Ng et al. [22] combine a multi-view stereo (MVS) model with a relative pose regressor (RPR). iNeRF [38], Wang *et al.* [36], and Direct-PN [5] utilize an inverted NeRF to optimize the camera pose. Our paper is the first to incorporate both strategies yet have major differences from the above methods. 1) we introduce an NVS method that can adapt to real exposure change in view synthesis. 2) we address the domain adaptation problem between the actual camera footage with synthetic images. 3) our synthetic data generation strategy is comparatively less constrained and can be deployed efficiently in online training.

3   Method

We illustrate our proposed direct feature matching pipeline in Fig. 1, which contains two primary components: 1) the DFNet network, which, given an input image I, uses a pose estimator $\mathcal{F}$ to predict a 6-DoF camera pose and a feature extractor $\mathcal{G}$ to compute a feature map M, and 2) a histogram-assisted NeRF $\mathcal{H}$, which compensates for high exposure fluctuation by providing luminance control when rendering a novel view given an arbitrary pose.

Training the direct feature matching pipeline can be split into two stages, (i) DFNet and the histogram-assisted NeRF, and (ii) direct feature matching. In stage one, we train the NVS module $\mathcal{H}$ like a standard NeRF, and the DFNet with a loss term $\mathcal{L}_{DFNet}$ in Eq. (5). In stage two, fixing the histogram-assisted NeRF and the feature extractor $\mathcal{G}$, we further optimize the main pose estimation module $\mathcal{F}$ via a direct feature matching signal between feature maps extracted from the real image and its synthetic counterpart $\hat{I}$, which is rendered from the predicted pose $\hat{P}$ of image I via the NVS module $\mathcal{H}$. At test time, only the pose estimator $\mathcal{F}$ is required given the query image, which ensures a rapid inference.

This section is organized as follows: the DFNet pipeline is detailed in Sect. 3.1, followed by a showcase of our histogram-assisted NeRF $\mathcal{H}$ in Sect. 3.2. To further

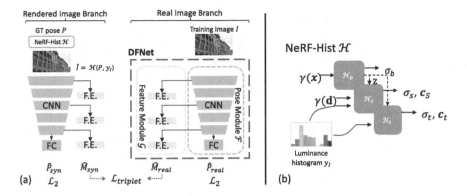

Fig. 2. (a) The training scheme for DFNet to close the domain gap between real images and rendered images. (b) The histogram-assisted NeRF architecture.

boost the pose estimation accuracy, an efficient Random View Synthesis (RVS) training strategy is introduced in Sect. 3.3.

3.1 Direct Feature Matching for Pose Estimation

This section aims to introduce: 1) the design of our main network DFNet, 2) the direct feature matching formulation that boosts pose estimation performance in a semi-supervised training manner, and 3) the contrastive-training scheme that closes the domain gap between real images and synthetic images.

DFNet Structure. The DFNet in our pipeline consists of two networks, a pose estimator $\mathcal{F}$ and a feature extractor $\mathcal{G}$. The pose estimator $\mathcal{F}$ in our DFNet is similar to an ordinary PoseNet, which predicts a 6-DoF camera pose $\hat{P} = \mathcal{F}(I)$ for an input image I, and can be supervised by an L_1 or L_2 loss between the pose estimation $\hat{P}$ and its ground truth pose P.

The feature extractor $\mathcal{G}$ in our DFNet takes as input feature maps extracted from various convolutional blocks in the pose estimator and pushes them through a few convolutional blocks, producing the final feature maps $M = \mathcal{G}(I)$, which are the key ingredients during feature-metric direct matching.

Two key properties of the feature extractor $\mathcal{G}$ that we seek to learn are 1) domain invariance, i.e., being invariant to the domain of real images and the domain of synthetic images and 2) transformation sensitive, i.e., being sensitive to the image difference that is caused by geometry transformations. With these properties learned, our feature extractor can extract domain-invariant features during feature-metric direct matching while preserving geometry-sensitive information for pose learning. We detail the way to train the DFNet in the *Closing the Domain Gap* section.

Direct Feature Matching. Direct matching in APR was first introduced by
Direct-PN [5], which minimizes the photometric difference between a real image
I and a synthetic image $\hat{I}$ rendered from the estimated pose $\hat{P}$ of the real image
I. Ideally, if the predicted pose $\hat{P}$ is close to its ground truth pose P, and the
novel view renderer produces realistic images, the rendered image $\hat{I}$ should be
indistinguishable from the real image.

In practice, we found the photometric-based supervision signal could be noisy
in direct matching, when part of scene content changes. For example, random
cars and pedestrians may appear through time or the NeRF rendering quality
is imperfect. Therefore, we propose to measure the distance between images in
feature space instead of in photometric space, given that the deep features are
usually more robust to appearance changes and imperfect renderings.

Specifically, for an input image I and its pose estimation $\hat{P} = \mathcal{F}(I)$, a synthetic image $\hat{I} = \mathcal{H}(\hat{P}, \mathbf{y}_I)$ can be rendered using the pose estimation $\hat{P}$ and
the histogram embedding $\mathbf{y}_I$ of the input image I. We then extract the feature
map $M \in \mathbb{R}^{H_M \times W_M \times C_M}$ and $\tilde{M} \in \mathbb{R}^{H_M \times W_M \times C_M}$ for image I and $\hat{I}$ respectively,
where H_M and W_M are the spatial dimensions and C_M is the channel dimension
of the feature maps. To measure the difference between two feature maps, we
compute a cosine similarity between feature $m_i \in \mathbb{R}^{C_M}$ and $\tilde{m}_i \in \mathbb{R}^{C_M}$ for each
feature location i:

$$\cos(m_i, \tilde{m}_i) = \frac{m_i \cdot \tilde{m}_i}{\|m_i\|_2 \cdot \|\tilde{m}_i\|_2}. \tag{1}$$

By minimizing the feature-metric direct matching loss $\mathcal{L}_{dm} = \sum_i (1 - \cos(m_i, \tilde{m}_i))$, the pose estimator $\mathcal{F}$ can be trained in a semi-supervised manner (note no ground truth label required for the input image I).

Our direct feature matching may optionally follow the procedure of semi-
supervised training proposed by MapNet+ [4] to improve pose estimation with
unlabeled sequences captured in the same scene. Unlike [4], which requires
sequential frames to enforce a relative geometric constraint using a VO algorithm, our feature-matching can be trained by images from arbitrary viewpoints
without ground truth pose annotation. Our method can be used at train time
with a batch of unlabeled images, or as a pose refiner for a single test image. In
the latter case, our direct matching can also be regarded as a post-processing
module. During the training stage, only the weights of the pose estimator will be
updated, whereas the feature extractor part remains frozen to back-propagation.

Closing the Domain Gap. We notice that synthetic images from NeRF are
imperfect due to rendering artifacts or lack of adaption of the dynamic content
of the scene, which leads to a domain gap between render and real images. This
domain gap poses difficulties to our feature extractor (Fig. 3), which we expect
to produce features far away if two views are from different poses and to produce
similar features between a rendered view and a real image from the same pose.

Intuitively, we could simply enforce the feature extractor to produce similar
features for a rendered image $\hat{I}$ and a real image I via a distance function
$d(\cdot)$ during training. However, this approach leads to model collapse [6], which

Fig. 3. A visual comparison of features before and after closing the domain gap. Ideally, a robust feature extractor shall produce indistinguishable features between real and rendered images from the same pose. Column 2/Column 3 are features trained without/with using our proposed $\mathcal{L}_{triplet}$ loss, where our method can effectively produce similar features across two domains.

motivates us to explore the original triplet loss:

$$\mathcal{L}_{triplet}^{ori} = \max\left\{ d(M_{real}^P, M_{syn}^P) - d(M_{real}^P, M_{syn}^{\bar{P}}) + \text{margin}, 0 \right\}, \qquad (2)$$

where M_{real}^P and M_{syn}^P, the feature maps of a real image and a synthetic image at pose P, compose a positive pair, and $M_{syn}^{\bar{P}}$ is a feature map of a synthetic image rendered at an arbitrary pose $\bar{P}$ other than the pose P.

With a closer look at the task of feature-metric direct matching, we implement a customized in-triplet mining which explores the minimum distances among negative pairs:

$$\mathcal{L}_{triplet} = \max\left\{ d(M_{real}^P, M_{syn}^P) - q_\ominus + \text{margin}, 0 \right\}, \qquad (3)$$

where the positive pair is as same as Eq. (2) and $q_\ominus$ is the minimum distance between four negative pairs:

$$q_\ominus = \min\left\{ d(M_{real}^P, M_{real}^{\bar{P}}), d(M_{real}^P, M_{syn}^{\bar{P}}), d(M_{syn}^P, M_{real}^{\bar{P}}), d(M_{syn}^P, M_{syn}^{\bar{P}}) \right\}, \qquad (4)$$

which essentially takes the hardest negative pair among all matching pairs between synthetic images and real images that are in different camera poses. The margin value is set to 1.0 in our implementation. Since finding the minimum of negative pairs is non-differentiable, we implement the in-triplet mining as a prior step before $\mathcal{L}_{triplet}$ is computed.

Overall, to train the pose estimator and to obtain domain invariant and transformation sensitive property, we adapt a siamese-style training scheme as illustrated in Fig. 2a. Given an input image I and its ground truth pose P, a synthetic image $\hat{I}$ can be rendered via the NVS module $\mathcal{H}$ (assumed pre-trained) using the ground truth pose P. We then present both the real image I and the synthetic image $\hat{I}$ to the pose estimator and the feature extractor, resulting in

(a) Ground Truth   (b) NeRF-W/15.20 dB   (c) Ours/ 18.22 dB

Fig. 4. Typically NeRF only renders views that reflect the appearance of its training sequences, as shown by NeRF-W's synthetic view (b). However, in relocalization tasks, the query set may have different appearances or exposures to the train set. The proposed histogram-assisted NeRF (c) can render a more accurate appearance to the unseen query set (a) in both quantitative (PSNR) and visual comparisons. We refer to the supplementary for more examples.

pose estimations $\hat{P}_{real}$ and $\hat{P}_{syn}$ and feature maps M_{real} and M_{syn} for the real image I and synthetic image $\hat{I}$, respectively. The training then is supervised via a combined loss function

$$\mathcal{L}_{DFNet} = \mathcal{L}_{triplet} + \mathcal{L}_{RVS} + \frac{1}{2}(\|P - \hat{P}_{real}\|_2 + \|P - \hat{P}_{syn}\|_2), \qquad (5)$$

where $\| \cdot \|$ denotes a L_2 loss and $\mathcal{L}_{RVS}$ is a supervision signal from our RVS training strategy, which we explain in Sect. 3.3.

3.2   Histogram-Assisted NeRF

The DFNet pipeline relies on an NVS module that renders a synthetic image from which we extract a feature map and compare it with a real image. Theoretically, while the NVS module in our pipeline can be in any form as long as it provides high-quality novel view renderings, in practice, we found that due to the presence of auto exposure during image capturing, it is necessary to have a renderer that can render images in a compensated exposure condition. Although employing direct matching in feature space could mediate the exposure issue to some extent, we find decoupling the exposure issue from the domain adaption issue leads to better pose estimation results.

One off-the-shelf option is a recent work NeRF-W [17], which offers the ability to control rendered appearance via an appearance embedding that is based on frame indices. However, in the context of direct matching, since we aim to compare a real image with its synthetic version, we desire a more fine-grained exposure control to render an image that matches the exposure condition of the real image, as illustrated in Fig. 4.

To this end, we propose a novel view renderer histogram-assisted NeRF (Fig. 2b) which renders an image $\hat{I} = \mathcal{H}(P, \mathbf{y}_I)$ that matches the exposure level of a query real image I via a histogram embedding $\mathbf{y}_I$ of the query image I at an arbitrary camera pose P. Specifically, our NeRF contains 3 components:

1. A base network $\mathcal{H}_b$ that provides a density estimation σ_b and a hidden state $\mathbf{z}$ for a coarse estimation: $[\sigma_b, \mathbf{z}] = \mathcal{H}_b(\gamma(\mathbf{x}))$.

2. A static network $\mathcal{H}_s$ to model density σ_s and radiance $\mathbf{c}_s$ for static structure and appearance: $[\sigma_s, \mathbf{c}_s] = \mathcal{H}_s(\mathbf{z}, \gamma(\mathbf{d}), \mathbf{y}_I)$.
3. A transient network $\mathcal{H}_t$ to model density σ_t, radiance $\mathbf{c}_t$ and an uncertainty estimation β for dynamic objects: $[\sigma_t, \mathbf{c}_t, \beta] = \mathcal{H}_t(\mathbf{z}, \mathbf{y}_I)$.

As for the input, $\mathbf{x}$ is a 3D point and $\mathbf{d}$ is a view angle that observes the 3D point, with both of them encoded by a positional encoding [10,19,34] operator $\gamma(\cdot)$ before injecting to each network.

During training, the coarse density estimation from the base network $\mathcal{H}_b$ provides a distribution where the other two networks could sample more 3D points near non-empty space accordingly. Both the static and the transient network are conditioned on a histogram-based embedding $\mathbf{y}_I \in \mathbb{R}^{C_y}$, which is mapped from a N_b bins histogram. The histogram is computed on the luma channel Y of a target image in YUV space. We found this approach works well in a direct matching context, not only in feature-metric space but also in photometric space.

We adopt a similar network structure and volumetric rendering method as in NeRF-W [17], to which we refer readers for more details.

3.3   Random View Synthesis

During the training of DFNet, we can generate training data by synthesis more views from randomly perturbed training poses. We refer this process as Random View Synthesis (RVS), and we use this data generation strategy to help the DFNet to better generalize to unseen views.

Specifically, given a training pose P, a perturbed pose P' can be generated around the training pose with a random translation noise of ψ meters and random rotation noise of ϕ degrees. A synthetic image $I' = \mathcal{H}(P', \mathbf{y}_{I_{nn}})$ is then rendered via histogram-assisted NeRF $\mathcal{H}$, with $\mathbf{y}_{I_{nn}}$ being the histogram embedding of the training image with the nearest training pose. The synthetic pose-image pair (P', I') is used as a training sample for the pose estimator to provide an additional supervision signal $\mathcal{L}_{RVS} = \|P' - \hat{P}'\|_2$, where $\hat{P}' = \mathcal{F}(I')$ is the pose estimation of the rendered image.

A key advantage of our method is efficiency in comparison with prior training sample generation methods. For example, LENS [21] generates high-resolution synthetic data with a maximum of 40 s/image and requires complicated parameter settings in finding candidate poses within scene volumes. In contrast, our RVS is a lightweight strategy that seamlessly fits our DFNet training at a much cheaper cost (12.2 fps) and with fewer constraints in pose generation while being able to reach similar performance. We refer to Sect. 4.5 for more discussion.

4   Experiments

4.1   Implementation

We introduce the implementation details for histogram-assisted NeRF, DFNet, and direct feature matching. We also provide more details in the supplementary.

Table 1. Pose regression results on 7-Scenes dataset. We compare DFNet and DFNet$_{dm}$ (DFNet with feature-metric direct matching) with prior single-frame APR methods and unlabeled training methods, in median translation error (m) and rotation error (°). Note that MapNet+ and MapNet+PGO are sequential methods with unlabeled training. Numbers in **bold** represent the best performance.

	Methods	Chess	Fire	Heads	Office	Pumpkin	Kitchen	Stairs	Average
1-frame APR	PoseNet(PN) [13]	0.32/8.12	0.47/14.4	0.29/12.0	0.48/7.68	0.47/8.42	0.59/8.64	0.47/13.8	0.44/10.4
	PN Learn σ^2 [12]	0.14/4.50	0.27/11.8	0.18/12.1	0.20/5.77	0.25/4.82	0.24/5.52	0.37/10.6	0.24/7.87
	geo. PN [12]	0.13/4.48	0.27/11.3	0.17/13.0	0.19/5.55	0.26/4.75	0.23/5.35	0.35/12.4	0.23/8.12
	LSTM PN [35]	0.24/5.77	0.34/11.9	0.21/13.7	0.30/8.08	0.33/7.00	0.37/8.83	0.40/13.7	0.31/9.85
	Hourglass PN [18]	0.15/6.17	0.27/10.8	0.19/11.6	0.21/8.48	0.25/7.0	0.27/10.2	0.29/12.5	0.23/9.53
	BranchNet [37]	0.18/5.17	0.34/8.99	0.20/14.2	0.30/7.05	0.27/5.10	0.33/7.40	0.38/10.3	0.29/8.30
	MapNet [4]	0.08/3.25	0.27/11.7	0.18/13.3	0.17/5.15	0.22/4.02	0.23/**4.93**	0.30/12.1	0.21/7.77
	Direct-PN [5]	0.10/3.52	0.27/8.66	0.17/13.1	0.16/5.96	0.19/3.85	0.22/5.13	0.32/10.6	0.20/7.26
	TransPoseNet [28]	0.08/5.68	0.24/10.6	0.13/12.7	0.17/6.34	0.17/5.6	0.19/6.75	0.30/7.02	0.18/7.78
	MS-Transformer [27]	0.11/4.66	0.24/9.60	0.14/12.2	0.17/5.66	0.18/4.44	**0.17**/5.94	0.17/5.94	0.18/7.28
	DFNet (ours)	**0.05/1.88**	**0.17/6.45**	**0.06/3.63**	**0.08/2.48**	**0.10/2.78**	0.22/5.45	**0.16/3.29**	**0.12/3.71**
UnlabelData	MapNet$_{+(seq.)}$ [4]	0.10/3.17	0.20/9.04	0.13/11.1	0.18/5.38	0.19/3.92	0.20/5.01	0.30/13.4	0.19/7.29
	MapNet$_{+PGO(seq.)}$ [4]	0.09/3.24	0.20/9.29	0.12/8.45	0.19/5.42	0.19/3.96	0.20/4.94	0.27/10.6	0.18/6.55
	Direct-PN+U [5]	0.09/2.77	0.16/4.87	0.10/6.64	0.17/5.04	0.19/3.59	0.19/4.79	0.24/8.52	0.16/5.17
	DFNet$_{dm}$ (ours)	**0.04/1.48**	**0.04/2.16**	**0.03/1.82**	**0.07/2.01**	**0.09/2.26**	**0.09/2.42**	**0.14/3.31**	**0.07/2.21**

NeRF. Our histogram-assisted NeRF model is trained with a re-aligned and re-centered pose in SE(3), similar to Mildenhall *et al.* [19]. The image histogram bin size is set to $N_b = 10$ and embedded with a vector dimension of 50 for the static model and 20 for the transient model. We train the model with a learning rate of 5×10^{-4} and an exponential decay of 5×10^{-4} for 600 epochs.

DFNet. Our DFNet adapts an ImageNet pre-trained VGG-16 [30] as the backbone, and an Adam optimizer with a learning rate of 1×10^{-4} is applied during training. For feature extraction, we extract $L = 3$ feature maps from the end of the encoder's first, third, and fifth blocks before pooling layers. All final feature outputs are upscaled to the same size as the input image $H \times W$ with bilinear upsampling. For pose regression, we regresses the SE(3) camera pose with a fully connected layer. A singular value decomposition (SVD) is applied to ensure the rotation component of $\hat{P}$ is normalized [5].

Direct Feature Matching. To validate our feature-metric direct matching formulation, we follow the same procedure from MapNet+ [4] and Direct-PN+U [5], which use a portion of validation images without the ground truth poses for finetuning. When finetuning DFNet, we optimize the pose regression module $\mathcal{F}$ solely based on the direct feature matching loss $\mathcal{L}_{dm}$. We set the batch size to 1 and the learning rate to 1×10^{-5}. For naming simplicity, we named our model trained with direct feature matching as DFNet$_{dm}$.

4.2   Evaluation on the 7-Scenes Dataset

We evaluate our method on an indoor camera localization dataset 7-Scenes [11,29]. The dataset consists of seven indoor scenes scaled from $1 \, \text{m}^3$ to $18, \text{m}^3$. Each scene contains 1000 to 7000 training sets and 1000 to 5000 validation sets.

Table 2. Single-frame APR results on Cambridge dataset. We report the median position and orientation errors in $m/°$ and the respective rankings over scene average as in [27,28]. The best results is highlighted in **bold**. For fair comparisons, we omit prior APR methods which did not publish results in Cambridge.

Methods	Kings	Hospital	Shop	Church	Average	Ranks	Final rank
PoseNet(PN) [13]	1.66/4.86	2.62/4.90	1.41/7.18	2.45/7.96	2.04/6.23	9/9	9
PN Learn σ^2 [12]	0.99/1.06	2.17/2.94	1.05/3.97	1.49/3.43	1.43/2.85	6/3	5
geo. PN [12]	0.88/1.04	3.20/3.29	0.88/3.78	1.57/3.32	1.63/2.86	7/4	6
LSTM PN [35]	0.99/3.65	1.51/4.29	1.18/7.44	1.52/6.68	1.30/5.51	5/8	7
MapNet [4]	1.07/1.89	1.94/3.91	1.49/4.22	2.00/4.53	1.63/3.64	7/7	8
TransPoseNet [28]	0.60/2.43	1.45/3.08	0.55/3.49	1.09/4.94	0.91/3.50	2/6	3
MS-Transformer [27]	0.83/1.47	1.81/2.39	0.86/3.07	1.62/3.99	1.28/2.73	4/2	2
DFNet (ours)	0.73/2.37	2.00/2.98	0.67/2.21	1.37/4.03	1.19/2.90	3/5	3
DFNet$_{dm}$ (ours)	**0.43/0.87**	**0.46/0.87**	**0.16/0.59**	**0.50/1.49**	**0.39/0.96**	1/1	1

Table 3. Comparison between our method and sequential-based APR methods and 3D structure-based methods.

	3D	Seq. APR					1-frame
Methods	AS [26]	MapNet +PGO [4]	CoordiNet [20]	CoordiNet+Lens [21]		VLocNet [33]	DFNet$_{dm}$
Chess	0.04/2.0	0.09/3.24	0.14/6.7	0.03/1.3		0.04/1.71	0.04/1.48
Fire	0.03/1.5	0.20/9.29	0.27/11.6	0.10/3.7		0.04/5.34	0.04/2.16
Heads	0.02/1.5	0.12/8.45	0.13/13.6	0.07/5.8		0.05/6.65	0.03/1.82
Office	0.09/3.6	0.19/5.42	0.21/8.6	0.07/1.9		0.04/1.95	0.07/2.01
Pumpkin	0.08/3.1	0.19/3.96	0.25/7.2	0.08/2.2		0.04/2.28	0.09/2.26
Kitchen	0.07/3.4	0.20/4.94	0.26/7.5	0.09/2.2		0.04/2.21	0.09/2.42
Stairs	0.03/2.2	0.27/10.6	0.28/12.9	0.14/3.6		0.10/6.48	0.14/3.31
Average	0.05/2.5	0.18/6.55	0.22/9.7	0.08/3.0		**0.05**/3.80	0.07/**2.21**
Kings	0.42/0.6	–	0.70/2.92	0.33/0.5		0.84/1.42	0.43/0.87
Hospital	0.44/1.0	–	0.97/2.08	0.44/0.9		1.08/2.41	0.46/0.87
Shop	0.12/0.4	–	0.73/4.69	0.27/1.6		0.59/3.53	0.16/0.59
Church	0.19/0.5	–	1.32/3.56	0.53/1.6		0.63/3.91	0.50/1.49
Average	0.29/0.63	–	0.92/2.58	**0.39**/1.15		0.78/2.82	**0.39/0.96**

Both histogram-assisted NeRF and DFNet use subsampled training data with a spacing window $d = 5$ for scenes containing ≤ 2000 frames and $d = 10$ otherwise. RVS poses are sampled on the training pose, and the DFNet parameters are $t_\psi = 0.2\,\mathrm{m}$, $r_\phi = 10°$, and $d_{max} = 0.2\,\mathrm{m}$. For fair comparison to other unlabeled training methods such as MapNet+ and Direct-PN, we finetune our DFNet$_{dm}$ using the same amount of unlabeled samples, which is 1/5 or 1/10 of the sequences based on the spacing window above to ensure our method is not overfitting to the entire test sequences.

We compared our method quantitatively with prior single-frame APR methods and unlabeled training APR methods in Table 1. The results show that both our DFNet and DFNet$_{dm}$ obtain superior accuracy, and DFNet$_{dm}$ achieves 56% and 57% improvement over averaged median translation and rotation errors compared to prior SOTA performance.

Table 4. (a) The effect of various level of features on DFNet$_{dm}$ result. Letter F, M, and C denote features extracted from fine, middle, and coarse levels in DFNet.**(b)** Ablation on DFNet (upper part) and histogram-assisted NeRF in photometric direct matching (lower part). DFM denotes Direct Feature Matching.

(b) Ablation

Method	Shop Facade
DFNet w/ $\mathcal{L}_{triplet}^{ori}$	1.49 m/5.80°
+RVS	0.86 m/4.05°
+$\mathcal{L}_{triplet}$	0.72 m/2.58°
+DFM (NeRF-W)	0.43 m/1.62°
+DFM (NeRF-Hist)	**0.15 m/0.65°**
Direct-PN	1.10 m/4.25°
Direct-PN+U	1.41 m/6.97°
+ NeRF-Hist	0.72 m/3.39°

(a) Featrue level vs. pose error

Feature Level	DFNet$_{dm}$ (ShopFacade)
F	**0.15m, 0.64**
F+M	0.19 m, 0.77
F+M+C	0.20 m, 0.77

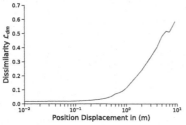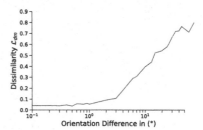

Fig. 5. Pose difference vs. feature dissimilarity. X-axis: camera position (**left**) and orientation difference (**right**) between a real image and a rendered image. Y-axis: feature dissimilarity $\mathcal{L}_{dm}$. Our direct feature matching loss $\mathcal{L}_{dm}$ is closely related to pose error, leading to effective training of the APR method.

4.3   Evaluation on Cambridge Dataset

We further compare our approach on four outdoor scenes from the Cambridge Landmarks [13] dataset, scaling from $875\,m^2$ to $5600\,m^2$. Each scene contains from 200+ to 1500 training samples. Our models are trained with 50% of training data, and DFNet's RVS are $t_\psi = 3\,m$, $r_\phi = 7.5°$, and $d_{max} = 1\,m$. For finetuning DFNet$_{dm}$ with unlabeled data, we use 50% of the unlabeled validation sequence since fewer validation sets are available than 7-Scenes. Table 2 shows a comparison between our approach and prior single-frame APR methods, which omits prior APR methods that did not report results in Cambridge. We observe that our DFNet$_{dm}$ outperforms other methods significantly (60%+ in scene average), which further proves the effectiveness of our approach.

4.4   Comparison to Sequential APR and 3D Approaches

Table 3 compares our method to other types of relocalization approaches, such as several state-of-the-art sequential-based APR approaches and 3D structure-based method Active Search [26]. We notice that our DFNet$_{dm}$ outperforms

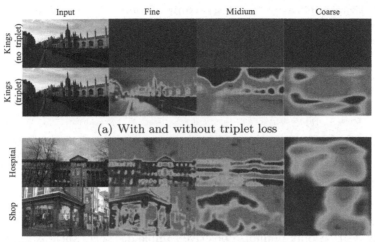

(a) With and without triplet loss

(b) More feature maps examples when trained with triplet loss

Fig. 6. (a) Top row: feature collapsing when training DFNet on Kings without using triplet loss. Bottom row: training DFNet with triplet loss can avoid the feature collapsing issue. (b) Feature maps of other scenes in Cambridge when training with triplet loss. We show that more refined level features consistently contain more meaningful details and, therefore more beneficial to use for direct feature matching.

most sequential-based APR methods except the translation error of VLocNet [33] on 7-Scenes in terms of the scene average performance. However, we still achieve superior accuracy than VLocNet in 7 out of 11 scenes. For the first time, the performance of single-image APR is comparable to 3D-structure methods. Our DFNet$_{dm}$ is slightly more accurate than Active Search [26] in average rotation error of 7-scenes. However, our method is still slightly behind in terms of translation error and Cambridge errors although by smaller margins.

4.5   Ablation Study

Effectiveness of Direct Feature Matching. We run a toy example of direct feature matching on Shop Facade using finest features and combinations of multi-level features, as in Table 4(a). We discover that finer-level features are more helpful for direct matching. We believe this to be due to their capability to preserve high frequency details and sharper contents, as shown in (Fig. 6(b)). This explains why we only use the finest feature in the feature-metric direct matching implementation. Furthermore, Fig. 5 shows how the direct matching loss $\mathcal{L}_{dm}$ successfully correlates the pose differences to the feature similarity between real images and rendered images.

Features Collapse. We demonstrate the difference when training DFNet's feature extractor with and without triplet loss in Fig. 6(a). We replace our triplet

Table 5. Data generation strategy comparison: RVS vs. LENS [21] on 7-Scenes. An EfficientNet backbone (as in LENS) is used in DFNet for a fair comparison. Our RVS strategy obtains a comparable results to LENS while using much less training data and rendering in much lower resolution, enabling online training.

Model	Backbone Top-1 Acc.	Pose error (m/degree)	Real data Quan-tity/Epoch	Synthetic data Quan-tity/Epoch	Synthetic reso-lution	Rendering cost	Generation mode
DFNet (VGG16)	71.59%	0.12/3.71	10–20%	10–20%	Low	Cheap	Online
DFNet (EB0)	76.3%	0.08/3.47	10–20%	10–20%	Low	Cheap	Online
LENS (EB3)	81.1%	0.08/3.00	71%–100%	710%–1000%	High	Expensive	Offline

loss with a mean square error (MSE) loss for the without triplet loss case. Intuitively, losses that only minimize positive sample distances such as MSE, L_2, or L_1 losses may lead to feature collapsing [6] since the feature extraction blocks in DFNet are likely to learn to cheat. On the other hand, using triplet loss supervised with additional negative samples works well for extracting dense domain invariant features.

Summary of Ablation. We break down our design decisions to show how each component contributes to the pose regression accuracy in Table 4(b). We start with training an DFNet model using with standard triplet loss without mining. The performance improves noticeably when we add the RVS. We also see around 16%/36% gain in translation and rotation errors when adding the customized triplet loss $\mathcal{L}_{triplet}$. We then validate our DFNet$_{dm}$'s direct feature matching (DFM), which further reduces error significantly. The DFM approach with histogram-assisted NeRF outperforms the NeRF-W one, which validates the effectiveness of our histogram embedding design. Finally, we attempt to train a Direct-PN+U model with our histogram-assisted NeRF modification. Our results show that the photometric direct matching-based method that can benefit from our new NVS method, though the pose estimation accuracy is worse than our feature-metric direct matching method.

Effectiveness of RVS. Table 5 shows a comparison between our online RVS strategy with another peer work LENS [21] that uses NeRF data generation for APR training. Although both data generation methods effectively improve APR performance, our RVS strategy is a much cheaper alternative requiring lower rendering resolution (80×60 vs. 320×240 [21]) and fewer data. We are able to reach similar performance with LENS when we replace our VGG16 backbone with an EfficientNet-B0 [32], which proves that a simpler data generation strategy could also effectively improves APR methods.

5   Conclusion

In summary, we introduce an Absolute Pose Regression (APR) pipeline for camera re-localization. Specifically: 1) we propose a histogram-assisted NeRF to compensate dramatic exposure variance in large scale scene with challenging exposure conditions. The histogram-assisted NeRF, serving as a novel view renderer, enables a direct matching training scheme; 2) we explore a direct matching scheme in feature space, leading to a more robust performance than the photometric approach, and address a domain gap issue that arises when matching real images with synthetic images via a contrastive learning scheme; 3) we devise an efficient data generation strategy, which proposes pseudo training poses around existing training trajectories, leading to better generalization capability to unseen data. As a result, our method achieves a state-of-the-art accuracy by outperforming existing single-image APR methods by as much as 56%, comparable to 3D structure-based methods.

Acknowledgment. The authors thank Michael Hobley, Theo Costain, Lixiong Chen, and Kejie Li for their thoughtful comments. Shuai Chen was supported by gift funding from Huawei.

References

1. Brachmann, E., et al.: DSAC - Differentiable RANSAC for Camera Localization. In: CVPR (2017)
2. Brachmann, E., Rother, C.: Learning less is more - 6D camera localization via 3D surface regression. In: CVPR (2018)
3. Brachmann, E., Rother, C.: Visual camera re-localization from RGB and RGB-D images using DSAC. arXiv (2020)
4. Brahmbhatt, S., Gu, J., Kim, K., Hays, J., Kautz, J.: Geometry-aware learning of maps for camera localization. In: IEEE Conference on Computer Vision and Pattern Recognition (CVPR) (2018)
5. Chen, S., Wang, Z., Prisacariu, V.: Direct-PoseNet: absolute pose regression with photometric consistency. In: 3DV (2021)
6. Chen, X., He, K.: Exploring simple siamese representation learning. In: CVPR (2021)
7. DeTone, D., Malisiewicz, T., Rabinovich, A.: Superpoint: self-supervised interest point detection and description. In: CVPRW (2018)
8. Engel, J., Koltun, V., Cremers, D.: DSO: direct sparse odometry. In: IEEE Transactions on Pattern Analysis and Machine Intelligence (TPAMI) (2017)
9. Engel, J., Schops, T., Cremers, D.: Semi-dense visual odometry for a monocular camera. In: In Proceedings of IEEE International Conference on Computer Vision (ICCV) (2013)
10. Gehring, J., Auli, M., Grangier, D., Yarats, D., Dauphin, Y.N.: Convolutional sequence to sequence learning. In: ICML (2017)
11. Glocker, B., Izadi, S., Shotton, J., Criminisi, A.: Real-time RGB-D camera relocalization. In: International Symposium on Mixed and Augmented Reality (ISMAR) (2013)

12. Kendall, A., Cipolla, R.: Geometric loss functions for camera pose regression with deep learning. In: IEEE Conference on Computer Vision and Pattern Recognition (CVPR) (2017)
13. Kendall, A., Grimes, M., Cipolla, R.: Posenet: a convolutional network for real-time 6-DOF camera relocalization. In: International Conference on Computer Vision (2015)
14. Kendall, A., Cipolla, R.: Modelling uncertainty in deep learning for camera relocalization. In: ICRA (2016)
15. Li, X., Han, K., Li, S., Prisacariu, V.: Dual-resolution correspondence networks. In: NeurIPS (2020)
16. Lindenberger, P., Sarlin, P.E., Larsson, V., Pollefeys, M.: Pixel-perfect structure-from-motion with featuremetric refinement. ICCV (2021)
17. Martin-Brualla, R., Radwan, N., Sajjadi, M.S.M., Barron, J.T., Dosovitskiy, A., Duckworth, D.: NeRF in the wild: neural radiance fields for unconstrained photo collections. In: CVPR (2021)
18. Melekhov, I., Ylioinas, J., Kannala, J., Rahtu, E.: Image-based localization using hourglass networks. In: ICCV Workshops (2017)
19. Mildenhall, B., Srinivasan, P.P., Tancik, M., Barron, J.T., Ramamoorthi, R., Ng, R.: NeRF: representing scenes as neural radiance fields for view synthesis. In: ECCV (2020)
20. Moreau, A., Piasco, N., Tsishkou, D., Stanciulescu, B., de La Fortelle, A.: CoordiNet: uncertainty-aware pose regressor for reliable vehicle localization. In: arxiv preprint, arxiv:2103.10796 (2021)
21. Moreau, A., Piasco, N., Tsishkou, D., Stanciulescu, B., de La Fortelle, A.: LENS: localization enhanced by nerf synthesis. In: CoRL (2021)
22. Ng, T., Lopez-Rodriguez, A., Balntas, V., Mikolajczyk, K.: Reassessing the limitations of CNN methods for camera pose regression. In: arXiv preprint arXiv:2108.07260 (2021)
23. Purkait, P., Zhao, C., Zach, C.: Synthetic view generation for absolute pose regression and image synthesis. In: BMVC (2018)
24. Sarlin, P.E., DeTone, D., Malisiewicz, T., Rabinovich, A.: Superglue: learning feature matching with graph neural networks. In: CVPR (2020)
25. Sarlin, P.E., et al.: Back to the feature: learning robust camera localization from pixels to pose. In: CVPR (2021)
26. Sattler, T., Leibe, B., Kobbelt, L.: Improving image-based localization by active correspondence search. In: Fitzgibbon, A., Lazebnik, S., Perona, P., Sato, Y., Schmid, C. (eds.) ECCV 2012. LNCS, vol. 7572, pp. 752–765. Springer, Heidelberg (2012). https://doi.org/10.1007/978-3-642-33718-5_54
27. Shavit, Y., Ferens, R., Keller, Y.: Learning multi-scene absolute pose regression with transformers. In: ICCV (2021)
28. Shavit, Y., Ferens, R., Keller, Y.: Paying attention to activation maps in camera pose regression. In: arXiv preprint arXiv:2103.11477 (2021)
29. Shotton, J., Glocker, B., Zach, C., Izadi, S., Criminisi, A., Fitzgibbon, A.: Scene coordinate regression forests for camera relocalization in RGB-D images. In: CVPR (2013)
30. Simonyan, K., Zisserman, A.: Very deep convolutional networks for large-scale image recognition. In: ICLR (2015)
31. Taira, H., et al.: InLoc: indoor visual localization with dense matching and view synthesis. CVPR (2018)
32. Tan, M., EfficientNet, Q.L.: EfficientNet: rethinking model scaling for convolutional neural networks. In: PMLR (2019)

33. Valada, A., Radwan, N., Burgard, W.: Deep auxiliary learning for visual localization and odometry. In: ICRA (2018)
34. Vaswani, A., .: Attention is all you need. In: NeurIPS (2017)
35. Walch, F., Hazirbas, C., Leal-Taixe, L., Sattler, T., Hilsenbeck, S., Cremers, D.: Image-based localization using LSTMs for structured feature correlation. In: International Conference on Computer Vision (2017)
36. Wang, Z., Wu, S., Xie, W., Chen, M., Prisacariu, V.A.: NeRF−: neural radiance fields without known camera parameters. arXiv preprint arXiv:2102.07064 (2021)
37. Wu, J., Ma, L., Hu, X.: Delving deeper into convolutional neural networks for camera relocalization. In: ICRA (2017)
38. Yen-Chen, L., Florence, P., Barron, J.T., Rodriguez, A., Isola, P., Lin, T.Y.: iNeRF: inverting neural radiance fields for pose estimation. In: arxiv arXiv:2012.05877 (2020)

Cornerformer: Purifying Instances for Corner-Based Detectors

Haoran Wei[1]($^\boxtimes$), Xin Chen[2], Lingxi Xie[2], and Qi Tian[2]

[1] University of Chinese Academy of Sciences, Beijing, China
weihaoran18@mails.ucas.ac.cn
[2] Huawei Inc., Shenzhen, China
tian.qi1@huawei.com

Abstract. Corner-based object detectors enjoy the potential of detecting arbitrarily-sized instances, yet the performance is mainly harmed by the accuracy of instance construction. Specifically, there are three factors, namely, 1) the corner keypoints are prone to false-positives; 2) incorrect matches emerge upon corner keypoint pull-push embeddings; and 3) the heuristic NMS cannot adjust the corners pull-push mechanism. Accordingly, this paper presents an elegant framework named Cornerformer that is composed of two factors. First, we build a Corner Transformer Encoder (CTE, a self-attention module) in a 2D-form to enhance the information aggregated by corner keypoints, offering stronger features for the pull-push loss to distinguish instances from each other. Second, we design an Attenuation-Auto-Adjusted NMS (A^3-NMS) to maximally leverage the semantic outputs and avoid true objects from being removed. Experiments on object detection and human pose estimation show the superior performance of Cornerformer in terms of accuracy and inference speed.

Keywords: Object detection · Corner-based · Corner Transformer Encoder · Attenuation-Auto-Adjusted NMS

1 Introduction

Object detection, which aims to localize and classify objects of interest in an image, is an active and fundamental research direction in computer vision. Current state-of-the-art detectors can be roughly classified into two categories, *i.e.*, anchor-based [3,13,14,23,26,31] and anchor-free. Recently, anchor-free detectors [9,11,20,37,42,43] have become a research hotspot due to its flexibility and efficiency, among which, corner-based detector (*e.g.*, CornerNet [20] and its variants [9,11]) is one of the most popular flowchats.

One key factor of corner-based detectors is how to construct instances from corner points. CornerNet [20] proposed a corner pooling module using a serial operation of maximize-and-merge operations to enhance corner features, and applied a grouping method upon pull-push loss [20,28] to formulate corner points

---

H. Wei—This work was done when the first author was interning at Huawei Inc.

S. Avidan et al. (Eds.): ECCV 2022, LNCS 13670, pp. 18–34, 2022.
https://doi.org/10.1007/978-3-031-20080-9_2

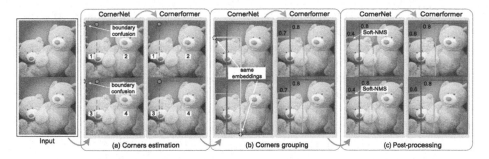

Fig. 1. Three problems of instance construction in corner-based detectors. (a) Bound-ries of nearby objects may coincide with each other, resulting in high-score false pos-itives that belong to no object (red "×" upon the top-left corner). (b) The pull-push mechanism is prone to confusing highly similar keypoints that belongs to different objects, so as to produce predictions across objects (red and yellow bounding boxes). Here we show an extreme case that objects are identical. (c) The commonly used Soft-NMS improperly decays lower-scored bounding box of two overlapped objects to be removed in visualization (lower than 0.5-score). (Color figure online)

into instances (bounding boxes), which minimize embedding distances of corner keypoints that belong to the same object and maximize those of different ones. To further enhance the correctness of corner grouping, CenterNet [11] introduced center points to filter false matched bounding boxes, while CentripetalNet [9] abandoned the 1D pull-push embeddings and presented a centripetal grouping method with a 2D-embedding form to better group paired corners.

As mentioned above, the correctness of corner grouping is one of the key factors in corner-based detectors. Although great progress has been made by previous methods [9,11,20] in corner matching, it is still an urgent demand to further improve the correctness and accuracy of instance construction of corner-based detectors. We believe the key factors that obstruct better instance con-struction lie in the following three aspects: 1) Corner keypoints are prone to false-positives due to boundary confusion that may largely disturb subsequent steps in the pipeline and produce inferior results (Fig. 1(a)). 2) Incorrect matches emerge upon corner keypoint pull-push embeddings, resulting in irregular detec-tion boxes, *e.g.*, boxes containing multiple objects (Fig. 1(b)). 3) The heuristic NMS cannot adjust the corners pull-push mechanism due to its fixed decay factor setting and thus falsely discarding overlapped instances (Fig. 1(c)).

Accordingly, we propose a Cornerformer framework that composed of two main modules, *i.e.,* a Corner Transformer Encoder (CTE, a self-attention mod-ule) and an Attenuation-Auto-Adjusted NMS (A^3-NMS), to efficiently address above stated drawbacks of corner-based detectors. Specifically, the CTE module is designed to be a 2D-Transformer, which can better capture nearby boundary information of a corner location with the help of self-attention mechanism, so as to effectively alleviate the boundary confusion problem and decrease false-positive keypoints. Additionally, we implant multiple positional encodings into

CTE, which makes CTE position-sensitive and dramatically enhance the distinguishing ability on similar keypoints from different objects. An A^3-NMS is a hyper-parameter-free Soft-NMS that can dynamically adjust attenuation weights of boxes to maximally leverage the semantic outputs and avoid true objects from being removed. Thus, the A^3-NMS is more suitable for the scenario of the corner pull-push mechanism than a vanilla Soft-NMS [2] that has a fixed decay weight.

Experimental results on MS-COCO [24] object detection, and both MS-COCO and CrowdPose [22] human pose estimation show that after equipping with the proposed Cornerformer, state-of-the-art corner-based detectors enjoy a consistent performance improvement in terms of accuracy and inference speed. Taking the classic CornerNet baseline as an example, after replacing corner pooling and Soft-NMS with CTE and A^3-NMS in Cornerformer, we obtain a satisfactory accuracy boosting of 3.0% in terms of AP and an inference speed lifting of 2.5 FPS.

2   Related Work

The success of deep neural networks (DNNs) [19,21] has largely promoted the development of object detection. Modern DNNs-based detectors can be simple divided into two categories: anchor-based [3,13,14,23,26,31] and anchor-free [9, 11,20,37,42,43].

2.1   Anchor-Based Detector

The anchor box is used to match a ground truth box and acts as a guidance for detectors to regress object bounding box. In Faster R-CNN [33], the design of anchor-based RPN made detectors end-to-end trainable. Later, anchor boxes were widely used in RPN-based two-stage detectors [3,13,14,27,33,41]. To further explore the efficiency of models, some anchor-based one-stage detectors [23,26,31,32,34,36] also appeared. They remove the RPN-stage and directly regress and classify anchor boxes. Despite the great success of the anchor mechanism, it also brings some drawbacks, e.g., excessively many hyper-parameters, unstable IoU-based (>0.7) positives selection strategy, and complex network structure. These drawbacks drive the community to study anchor-free detection methods.

2.2   Anchor-Free Detector

Anchor-free object detection is a very active research field in recent years. CornerNet [20] was the first keypoint-based approach, which predicted keypoints via generating and parsing heatmaps, and detected objects by predicting and grouping pairs of corner points. CenterNet [11] added a prediction branch of center points based on CornerNet settings, transforming corner matching into triplet matching. Upon CornerNet, CentripetalNet [9] proposed a new centripetal grouping algorithm and achieved state-of-the-art performance. Besides,

FCOS [37] proposed a dense regression anchor-free detector. It treats lots of pixels in bounding boxes as positive samples and directly regresses bounding boxes. Compared with anchor-based approaches, anchor-free methods enjoy flexibility and efficiency. However, the limitations of local modeling in CNN hinder its development.

Transformer is first proposed in natural language processing [38]. Compared with CNN, Transformer inplants self-attention mechanism into its basic operator, which is more suitable for capturing long-range contexts than convolution. Due to its superb ability, Transformers were introduced into computer vision [5,10,25,44] and soon leveraged in object detection. DETR [5] introduced Transformer [38] into object detection task for the first time, which eliminated many hand-craft modules (*e.g.,* anchor, NMS, and proposals) in previous detectors, and achieved on-par performance compared to classical CNN-based Faster R-CNN. Based on DETR, WB-DETR [25] replaced the ResNet [15] backbone with ViT [10] (a Transformer-based recognition system) to obtain a pure-Transformer detection system, making the detection pipeline neater.

Inspired by DETR, we explore how to integrate Transformer into keypoint-based detectors to improve the quality of instance construction.

3   Preliminary: The CornerNet Baseline

CornerNet utilizes heatmaps generated by the backbone to estimate corner keypoints and uses the pull-push loss to group embedding pairs. To refine corner coordinates extracted from heatmaps, CornerNet predict extra offsets. The pipeline of CornerNet is similar to the pipeline shown in Fig. 2, with a corner pooling module replacing the CTE module, and a Soft-NMS module replacing the A^3-NMS module.

CornerNet applies a modified pixel-level focal loss [23] as the training objective for heatmaps of paired corners. The backbone with output stride brings about discretization error in the process of remapping corner locations. To address this problem, CornerNet additionally regress offsets to refine corner coordinates.

The Associative Embedding [28] method is applied for paired corner matching. More specifically, the "pull" loss is leveraged to group paired corners and the "push" loss to separate irrelevant corners:

$$\mathcal{L}_{pull} = \frac{1}{N} \sum_{k=1}^{N} \left[(e_{t_k} - e_k)^2 + (e_{b_k} - e_k)^2 \right], \qquad (1)$$

$$\mathcal{L}_{push} = \frac{1}{N(N-1)} \sum_{k=1}^{N} \sum_{\substack{j=1 \\ j \neq k}}^{N} \max\left(0, \Delta - |e_k - e_j|\right), \qquad (2)$$

where e_k is the average of e_{t_k} and e_{b_k} and Δ is set to be 1. Pull-push loss is only applied at ground-truth corner locations [20].

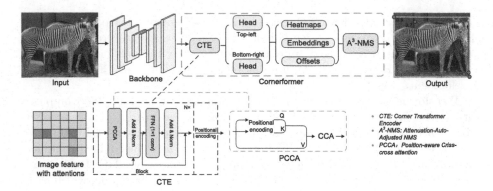

Fig. 2. The architecture of Cornerformer. A Cornerformer, composed of a CTE (Corner Transformer Encoder) module, keypoint grouping components, and an A^3-NMS module, takes image features extracted by the backbone as input, and generates predicted bounding boxes (paired corner keypoints) as output. The CTE, as a replacement of corner pooling module in CornerNet, captures contextual information and predicts corner keypoints (embeddings) more precisely from input feature maps. A^3-NMS is an improved NMS, which can maximally avoid true objects from being removed and is no longer restricted by manually set hyper-parameters.

Our Cornerformer is built upon the CornerNet baseline (or its variants, *i.e.*, CenterNet and CentripetalNet). In the rest of this paper, we apply the same settings used in corresponding baselines unless otherwise specified. For more details, please refer to the original papers [9,11,20].

4   Cornerformer

4.1   Towards Better Instance Construction

As stated in Sect. 1, there are three critical factors that hinder a better instance construction in corner-based object detection. Here we carry out a case analysis incorporating with Fig. 1 to further dissect them. 1) **Corner keypoints are prone to false-positives due to boundary confusion.** As shown in Fig. 1 (a). The top-most boundary of "teddy bear 2" and the left-most boundary of "teddy bear 1" coincides with each other, which will result in a high-score false estimation that neither belongs to "teddy bear 1" nor "teddy bear 2". Such needless keypoints will largely affect subsequent procedures and produce deteriorative predictions. 2) **Incorrect matches emerge upon corner keypoint pull-push embeddings.** The pull-push mechanism naturally lacks ability of distinguishing highly similar keypoints that belong to different objects, so that corner keypoints of different objects with similar appearances may be mistakenly grouped together. We show an extreme example that the input is generated by copy-and-paste the same image in Fig. 1 (b). The predicted bounding boxes (red and yellow) are unnaturally composed of two different instances. 3) **The**

heuristic NMS cannot adjust the corners pull-push mechanism. The commonly used Soft-NMS decays scores of overlapped bounding boxes with a fixed value, which may cause true detection boxes of overlapped objects being removed in visualization, as shown in Fig. 1 (c).

Accordingly, we propose Cornerformer to address above stated problems of corner-based detectors in instance construction. As shown in Fig. 2, Cornerformer is built upon a corner-based detector as baseline, e.g., CornerNet [20] or CenterNet [11]. A Cornerformer consists of two main components, i.e., a Corner Transformer Encoder (CTE) used to provide better corner features and lift the quality of pull-push embeddings, and an Attenuation-Auto-Adjusted NMS (A^3-NMS) used to maximally leverage the semantic outputs and avoid true objects from being removed. In the following, we delve into each part of Cornerformer and show how it helps a better instance construction.

4.2 Corner Transformer Encoder

Overview of the CTE. Corner Transformer Encoder (CTE) runs as a corner features enhancing module in Cornerformer. Corners often lay outside an object without explicit existent evidence, which needs feature enhancement via boundary contexts (the top-most, bottom-most, left-most, and right-most of an object). The CornerNet baseline applies a corner pooling module to enhance the visual reasoning of corners. However, corner pooling uses a serial operation of maximize-and-merge to extend corner information, suffering inefficient context around corner keypoints. As a special case, when a spatial location has similar boundary conditions, it is likely to be a high-score false corner estimation due to boundary confusion, as shown in Fig. 1 (a). In addition, there is no optimization for pull-push embeddings in corner pooling, so that the pull-push mechanism may gather wrong corner pairs that have highly similar corner embeddings, as shown in Fig. 1 (b). To this end, we propose CTE to better estimate and group target corners.

Position-Aware Criss-Cross Attention. To capture rich boundary contexts, the corner estimation module needs to look over information around potential corner keypoints, i.e., horizontal and vertical possible spatial locations related to boundaries. Thus, we naturally adopt the self-attention mechanism to capture rich information around potential corners. More specifically, for one query element q in image features, the corresponding keys (k) are sampled in the same row and column. It is notable that convolution can also capture information from a nearby area, but handling a larger area corresponding to a large object requires to stack more convolutional layers, which brings potential computational burdens.

As shown in Fig. 2, we adopt the Position-aware Criss-Cross Attention (PCCA) as the self-attention module, which is designed upon CCA [16] and enhanced with positional encoding. Vanilla CCA is used only to capture contextual information in horizontal and vertical directions for using light-weight computation and memory, which we find suitable for capturing boundary contextual information for corner keypoints. To further alleviate the false-positive

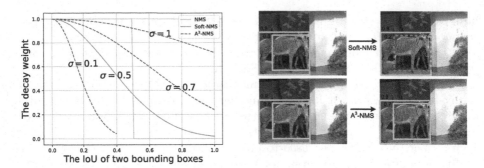

Fig. 3. Comparison of NMS, Soft-NMS, and A³-NMS. Soft-NMS uses a fixed decay weight value (σ) in both the scenario of decaying redundant boxes, where σ should be as large as possible to remove redundant boxes, and the scenario of overlapped objects, where σ should be as small as possible to retain bounding boxes of different objects. In contrast, our A³-NMS accomplishes an adaptive decay ratio upon embeddings to effectively address such scenarios.

problem of similar features, we equip a positional encoding [5] in "Q" and "K" of the original CCA to create a new Position-aware CCA. The positional encoding is as follows:

$$\begin{cases} \mathrm{PE}(pos, 2i) = \sin(pos/10000^{2i/d}) \\ \mathrm{PE}(pos, 2i+1) = \cos(pos/10000^{2i/d}), \end{cases} \tag{3}$$

where *pos* means the position, *i* indicates the channel ID, and *d* is 128 representing the total number of dimensions.

Settings of Transformer Blocks. One Transformer block in CTE is composed of a PCCA (as the self-attention module) and a 1×1 convolutional layer (as the feed forward network, FFN). Different from the vanilla 1D-Transformer block [5] that expects a sequence as input, the CTE is a 2D-form Transformer which can take 2D image features as input directly. We also find that multiple Transformer blocks in series can generate more robust features for corner estimation.

Optimizing Pull-Push Embeddings. We use the pull-push loss to group corner pairs, as mentioned in Sect. 3. The pull-push loss utilizes a self-supervised way to "pull" embeddings of corresponding corners and "push" irrelevant ones upon object features. When there are more than one objects with similar appearance in an image, as shown in Fig. 1 (b), the pull-push loss fails to distinguish different instances effectively. Thus, except for richer contexts embedded in corner keypoints, we further insert a global positional encoding after Transformer blocks to make CTE position-sensitive, so that the pull-push loss can better distinguish if a pair of corners that have similar feature responses belong to the same instance.

4.3 Attenuation-Auto-Adjusted NMS

Overview of the A^3-NMS. The heuristic Non-Maximum Suppression (NMS) has become the *de-facto* standard applied to suppress and filter out false-positives for detectors. The original NMS cannot solve the problem of largely overlapped objects. Soft-NMS addresses such problem by softening the suppression process with a score decay mechanism. The most commonly used decay function is as follows:

$$W_{iou(M,b_i)} = \exp(-\frac{iou(M,b_i)^2}{\sigma}) \tag{4}$$

where M is the highest score of box, b_i indicates the current box. σ is a hyper-parameter often set to be 0.5.

However, Soft-NMS still lacks flexibility because of its fixed σ value. As long as the IoU of two bounding boxes is the same, Soft-NMS decays the lower-scored one to the same score, whatever the scenario is overlapped instances or duplicated bounding boxes. To address such a limitation, we design the A^3-NMS that introduces adjustable attenuation and relies on no manually set hyper-parameters to flexibly handle both cases of duplicated boxes and overlapped instances.

Adjust Attenuation Upon Embeddings. To address the above problem, A^3-NMS applies a dynamic adjusted decay function as following:

$$W_{iou(M,b_i)} = \exp(-\frac{iou(M,b_i)^2}{f(|e_M - e_i|)}) \tag{5}$$

where e_M and e_i are embeddings of corresponding boxes. M represents the max-score box. f is a function to smooth embedding distance between e_M and e_i, and in this case we use the *tanh* function. We take mean value of paired corner embeddings as box embedding, *i.e.*, e_M or e_i. Thus, we can easily obtain distance of bounding boxes by calculating vector distance of their box embeddings. Since paired corners or boxes are grouped via the pull-push mechanism in corner-based detectors, the distance of box embeddings should be small if two boxes belong to the same instance, while it should be large if two boxes belong to different objects. The fixed σ in Eq. (4) becomes a dynamic value learned by the network in Eq. (5) so that the adjusted attenuation factor can well fit each situation. We plot curves of the decay function of different versions of NMS in Fig. 3, from which we can easily find that A^3-NMS can efficiently handle such scenarios.

More specifically, A^3-NMS runs in post-processing, and (e_M, e_i) are a pair of self-adjusted embeddings for the corresponding boxes, which belong to the side outputs of corner-based detectors. They contain useful information that measures the closeness of two detection boxes. That said, the smaller $f(|e_M - e_i|)$ is, the more similar b_i and b_M are, and thus the heavier b_i is suppressed. Compared to Soft-NMS that relies on a fixed factor σ, such a mechanism is more flexible and accurate.

Table 1. Performance comparison (%) with state-of-the-art detectors on MS COCO test-dev. DR and KB are abbreviations of dense regression and keypoint-based, respectively. ×2 means that two Corner Transformer Encoders without parameters sharing are used for the top-left and bottom-right corners, respectively. Blue up-arrows indicate the improved values compared with baselines. * indicates multi-scale testing. Input resolution represents training input size.

Method	Backbone	Input size	AP_{50}	AP_{75}	AP_S	AP_M	AP_L	AP	FPS
Two-stage:									
Cascade R-CNN [3]	ResNet-101	1333 × 800	62.1	46.3	23.7	45.5	55.2	42.8	–
Sparse R-CNN [35]	ResNeXt-101	1333 × 800	**66.3**	51.2	28.6	49.2	58.7	46.9	–
CPN [12]	Hourglass-104	1333 × 800	65.0	**51.0**	26.5	**50.2**	**60.7**	47.0	5.2
One-stage, anchor-based:									
RetinaNet [23]	ResNeXt-101	1333 × 800	61.1	44.1	24.1	44.2	51.2	40.8	5.4
YOLOv4 [1]	CSPDarkNet-53	608 × 608	65.7	47.3	26.7	46.7	53.3	43.5	–
ATSS [40] w/DCN [8]	ResNet-101	1333 × 800	64.7	50.4	27.7	49.8	58.4	46.3	8.4
One-stage, anchor-free (DR)									
FoveaBox [18]	ResNeXt-101	1333 × 800	61.9	45.2	24.9	46.8	55.6	42.1	5.1
FCOS [37]	ResNeXt-101	1333 × 800	62.1	45.2	25.6	44.9	52.0	42.1	7.3
Reppoints [39] w/DCN	ResNet-101	1333 × 800	66.1	49.0	26.6	48.6	57.5	45.0	8.7
One-stage, anchor-free (KB)									
ExtremeNet [43]	Hourglass-104	511 × 511	55.5	43.2	20.4	43.2	53.1	40.2	3.1
CenterNet [42]	Hourglass-104	512 × 512	61.1	45.9	24.1	45.5	52.8	42.1	7.8
CornerNet [20]	Hourglass-104	511 × 511	56.5	43.1	19.4	42.7	53.9	40.5	4.1
CornerNet w/Cornerformer	Hourglass-104	511 × 511	61.2	46.2	21.5	44.8	56.5	42.6 ↑ 2.1	7.4
CornerNet w/Cornerformer×2	Hourglass-104	511 × 511	61.7	46.8	22.3	45.6	57.1	43.5 ↑ 3.0	5.6
CenterNet [11]	Hourglass-104	511 × 511	62.4	48.1	25.6	47.4	57.4	44.9	3.3
CenterNet w/Cornerformer	Hourglass-104	511 × 511	63.0	49.7	26.0	48.6	59.3	46.1 ↑ 1.2	5.9
CenterNet w/Cornerformer×2	Hourglass-104	511 × 511	64.3	50.2	27.1	49.5	59.2	46.8 ↑ 1.9	4.8
CenterNet w/Cornerformer×2*	Hourglass-104	511 × 511	64.9	51.4	28.8	50.1	59.5	47.7	–
CentripetalNet [9]	Hourglass-104	511 × 511	63.1	49.7	25.3	48.7	59.2	46.1	3.4
CentripetalNet w/Cornerformer	Hourglass-104	511 × 511	64.5	50.3	26.2	49.4	59.6	47.1 ↑ 1.0	6.5
CentripetalNet w/Cornerformer×2	Hourglass-104	511 × 511	64.6	50.6	26.7	49.5	59.9	47.4 ↑ 1.3	5.0
CentripetalNet w/Cornerformer×2*	Hourglass-104	511 × 511	65.4	51.8	28.9	50.8	60.2	48.5	–

5   Experiments

5.1   Datasets, Metrics, and Implementation Details

Object Detection. We evaluate the effectiveness of the proposed Cornerformer on COCO [24] dataset. COCO is a large-scale and challenging benchmark in object detection, which contains 80 categories and more than 1.5 million object instances. We train all models on the train2017 and carry out all ablations with val2017. We compare with other state-of-the-art methods using the test-dev. Besides, there are few heavily occluded objects in MS-COCO.

Besides, to better support our claim, we conduct additional ablation experiments on Citypersons [7] (a pedestrian detection dataset). Citypersons contains six different labels, *i.e.,* ignore regions, pedestrians, riders, sitting persons, other persons with unusual postures, and group of people. We keep and merge the labels of pedestrians and riders that accounts a large proportion in vanilla data. There are 18204 persons in 2471 images on our processed training set. We show the performance of the proposed Cornerformer on the validation set that contains 439 images and 3666 persons.

Human Pose Estimation. To further test the generalization ability of the proposed CTE, we integrate it into the bottom-to-up human pose estimation model, HigherHRNet [6]. We evaluate the effectiveness of the CTE module on both COCO dataset, which contains $250k$ person instances labeled with 17 keypoints, and Crowdpose dataset [22], which contains more crowded scenes.

Metrics. We use the AP (average precision) metric to measure performance of both object detection and human pose estimation. AP in object detection (COCO) is computed over ten different IoU thresholds (*i.e.*, 0.5:0.05:0.95) and all categories, which is considered as the most important metric on the object detection task. For Citypersons, since the annotation (bounding box) is not as precise as COCO, the AP under a high IoU is meaningless, so we only test the AP with 0.5 IoU. Instead of IoU, the AP used in human pose estimation task is computed upon Object Keypoint Similarity (OKS): $\text{OKS} = \dfrac{\sum_i \exp(-d_i^2/2s^2k_i^2)\delta(v_i > 0)}{\sum_i \delta(v_i > 0)}$ Here, d_i represents the Euclidean distance between a detected keypoint and its corresponding ground truth, v_i is the visibility flag of the ground truth, s is the object scale, and k_i is a per-keypoint constant that controls falloff [6].

Training Details. We follow settings of corner-based models to train new detector equipped with the proposed Cornerformer on 16 NVIDIA RTX 3090 GPUs. Standard cropping, horizontal flipping, and color jittering are employed as data augmentation. All models are fine-tuned from the pre-trained Hourglass [20] backbone with randomly initialized Cornerformer layers for $250k$ iterations with a batch size of 64. The learning rate is set to $2.5e-4$ and dropped $10\times$ at $200k$ iteration. An Adam [17] optimizer is applied to optimize model parameters. For human pose estimation task, we choose the HigherHRNet [6] as baseline and follow its training settings.

Inference Details. We test inference speed of baseline models and their Cornerformer variants on a workstation with an NVIDIA Titan XP GPU. To guarantee a fair comparison with baselines, We strictly follow test settings of corresponding baselines.

5.2 Object Detection Results

We implant the proposed Cornerformer into several classical corner-based detectors, *e.g.*, CornerNet [20], CenterNet [11], and CentripetalNet [9], and evaluate the effectiveness of our design via performance comparisons, in terms of accuracy and inference speed.

Comparison on Accuracy. As shown in Table 1, CornerNet [20] with Cornerformer improved by 2.1% on AP (from 40.5% to 42.6%), which shows the advantage of the proposed Cornerformer on better construct instances. For large objects, AP_L increases from 53.9% to 56.5%, which is arguably owing to the feasibility of CTE to well capture long-range contexts. As shown in Fig. 4, the corners

CornerNet w/ corner pooling   CornerNet w/ CTE

Fig. 4. Corner estimation visualized comparison of corner pooling and the proposed Corner Transformer Encoder. Compared with corner pooling, CTE can reduce false-positive points which have confused boundary visual appearances.

estimated by Cornerformer are more precise. For CenterNet [11] baseline, Cornerformer also brings it a decent promotion of 1.2% on AP. For CentripetalNet [9] which does not use pull-push embeddings, we add a branch to obtain pull-push embeddings to apply the whole Cornerformer and harvest an improvement of 1.0%, proving our Cornerformer is very solid.

A single CTE in Cornerformer can capture both horizontal and vertical boundary information to enhance both top-left and bottom-right corners features. Under this setting, top-left and bottom-right corners share the same set of learned parameters, which may limit the representative power. To better distinguish different type of corners (top-left and bottom-right), we use two individual CTEs (represented as Cornerformer ($\times 2$)) to further test its ability. As we can see in Table 1, Cornerformer ($\times 2$), obtains improvements of 3.0%, 1.9%, and 1.3% upon CornerNet, CenterNet, and CentripetalNet baselines, respectively, further demonstrating the effectiveness of the proposed Cornerformer.

Comparison on Inference Speed. We also compare the inference speed of our method with baselines. As illustrated in Table 1, the inference speed of CornerNet with Cornerformer is 7.4 FPS, which is 3.3 FPS faster than the vanilla CornerNet using corner pooling. Besides, CenterNet with Cornerformer as well as CentripetalNet with Cornerformer is also more efficient than its baseline. It's worth noting that even if equipped with two CTEs, the inference speed is still faster than those corner pooling counterparts. The major speedup is brought by replacing corner pooling (a serial operation that requires a `for` loop) with CTE that is computed in parallel.

5.3   Pose Estimation Results

A Cornerformer is consisted of CTE and A^3-NMS, where CTE is used to enhance the corner features and improve the pull-push grouping as mentioned in Sect. 4.2. CTE is made up of multiple Transformer blocks and when stacking multiple

HigherHRNet   HigherHRNet w/ CTE

Fig. 5. Effectiveness of CTE in human pose estimation. Here we apply an extreme case – copy-and-paste the same object. HigherHRNet with CTE (right column) can distinguish local responses with similar visual appearances in different locations, making the pull-push grouping more reasonable, while the original HigherHRNet failed.

Table 2. Performance comparison of bottom-to-up human keypoint estimators on COCO test-dev. The CTE brings an improvement of 0.8% in terms of AP upon the HigherHRNet baseline.

Method	AP	AP_{50}	AP_{75}	AP_M	AP_L
OpenPose [4]	61.8	84.9	67.5	57.1	68.2
Hourglass [28]	65.5	86.8	72.3	60.6	72.6
SPM [29]	66.9	88.5	72.9	62.6	73.1
PersonLab [30]	68.7	89.0	75.4	64.1	75.5
HigherHRNet [6]	70.5	89.3	77.2	66.6	75.8
HigherHRNet w/CTE	71.3	90.1	78.0	67.2	76.9

blocks, a CTE is able to capture global contexts. Besides, CTE is designed to be position-sensitive and pull-push-enhanced, so that it can better distinguish between similar appearances from different locations. Accordingly, we apply CTE to bottom-to-up human keypoints estimator. To test this conjecture, we take HigherHRNet [6] as the baseline. As shown in Table 2 and 3, HigherHRNet with Cornerformer gains an improvement of 0.8% and 1.3% on COCO and Crowdpose, respectively. Such improvements show that Cornerformer is effective not only for the corner-based detectors, but also for human pose estimation tasks. As shown in Fig. 5, we copy-and-paste an image to visualize the effectiveness of Cornerformer on improving pull-push grouping. We can see that HigherHRNet cannot distinguish objects that have the same characteristics in different locations. CTE can overcome such problems, making the pull-push grouping more reasonable, further proving the position-sensitive CTE can make more accurate keypoint estimation.

5.4 Ablation Study

In this section, we conduct ablation analyses on COCO val2017 mainly for object detection and partially for human pose estimation. We mainly utilize CornerNet [20] as the baseline and use a single CTE for Cornerformer.

Table 3. Comparison on Crowdpose test dataset. Superscripts E, M, and H of AP stand for easy, medium and hard. The CTE brings an improvement of 1.3% in terms of AP upon the HigherHRNet.

Method	AP	AP_{50}	AP_{75}	AP_E	AP_M	AP_H
HigherHRNet [6]	67.6	87.4	72.6	75.8	68.1	58.9
HigherHRNet [6] w/CTE	68.9	88.9	73.5	77.2	69.6	60.3

Table 4. Effectiveness of Cornerformer. We compare the performance of CTE and A^3-NMS with the original corner pooling and Soft-NMS on COCO val split and Citypersons to validate the effectiveness of the proposed Cornerformer. CP represents corner pooling. AP_c means the AP gained on Citypersons.

CTE	CP	A^3-NMS	Soft-NMS	AP	AP_{50}	AP_{75}	AP_c
×	×	×	✓	36.9	52.2	38.9	–
×	✓	×	✓	39.1	54.4	40.1	29.1
✓	×	×	✓	40.8	56.5	43.6	40.3
✓	×	✓	×	41.3	57.2	44.1	45.4

Effectiveness of the Cornerformer. In this part, we compare CTE and A^3-NMS with corner pooling (presented as CP in Table 4) and Soft-NMS, respectively, to validate the effectiveness of components in Cornerformer. As shown in Table 4, CTE achieves a 1.7% improvement compared to corner pooling. Compared with corner pooling, CTE can distinguish different corner positions with similar boundary visual appearances, while corner pooling fails. When we utilize A^3-NMS to replace Soft-NMS, a consistent improvement of 0.5% on AP is obtained on COCO and 5.1% AP gains on Citypersons, which validates the effectiveness of A^3-NMS on preventing overlapped object boxes from being falsely decayed. Compared with the baseline (36.9% on COCO and 29.1% on Citypersons), the Cornerformer (CTE + A^3-NMS) counterpart improves detection performance by 4.4% and 16.3% respectively. Besides, for Citypersons, compared with commonly used benchmarks, *e.g.*, Faster-RCNN (25.0% on AP) and RetinaNet (27.9% on AP), CornerNet equipped with Cornerformer can obtain a large improvement (45.4% on AP), further demonstrating the effectiveness of the proposed Cornerformer firmly.

Positional Encoding in CTE. We embed positional encoding in self-attention module of CTE to help a model better distinguish corners with similar boundary features in the same row or column. Besides, to help the model "pull" or "push" corners better, we embed an additional positional encoding of full image in the output of CTE , as shown in Fig. 2. We conduct experiments to test if these designs are resultful. As shown in Table 5, PCCA (with a positional encoding upon CCA) is 0.8% higher than CCA. Further embedding an additional positional encoding (represented as PE) in the output of CTE brings another 0.7%

Table 5. Effectiveness of positional encoding. CCA is the original Criss-Cross attention [16]. PCCA is the proposed position-aware CCA. PE represents the positional encoding embedded in the output of Corner Transformer Encoder. All results are obtained with COCO val split.

CCA	PCCA	PE	AP	AP_{50}	AP_{75}	AP_S	AP_M	AP_L
✓	✗	✗	39.3	54.9	40.0	19.1	40.9	52.7
✗	✓	✗	40.1	55.6	42.9	19.4	41.5	53.0
✗	✓	✓	40.8	56.5	43.6	19.6	42.1	53.4

Table 6. Effects on number of CTE blocks. We verify that how many blocks of CTE are reasonable for different tasks on COCO val split.

Number of CTE Blocks	0	1	2	3	4
CornerNet [20] w/CTE (AP)	36.9	38.7	39.9	40.8	40.4
HigherHRNet [6] w/CTE (AP)	67.1	67.5	68.2	67.7	–

performance gain. The above results prove the significance of positional encoding for corner predicting and grouping.

Number of CTE Blocks. To validate the influence of the number of CTE blocks, we conduct experiments to test performance with different number of CTE blocks. As shown in Table 6, three CTE blocks is the best for object detection [20]. The reason that 4 CTE blocks brings slight performance drop compared to 3 may lie in insufficient training duration or data samples.

Besides, we further observe the performance on human pose estimation with respect to the number of CTE blocks. As shown in Table 6, two is the best choice for this task [6]. Three blocks CTE causes an AP drop, mainliy because an odd number of blocks leads to a focus on boundaries, which is ineffective for tasks with keypoints inside objects.

6   Conclusion

In this paper, we propose Cornerformer to address potential problems of corner-based detectors in instance construction. In Cornerformer, we design a 2D Corner Transformer Encoder to optimize corner estimation and pull-push grouping. Besides, upon the pull-push embeddings, we present an Attenuation-Auto-Adjusted NMS to further break limits of the heuristic NMS. Our research reveals that much room is left in constructing objects from mid-level visual cues. We hope that the simple and efficient design of Cornerformer will attract more attention to instance construction in corner-based detectors.

References

1. Bochkovskiy, A., Wang, C.Y., Liao, H.Y.M.: YOLOv4: optimal speed and accuracy of object detection. arXiv preprint arXiv:2004.10934 (2020)
2. Bodla, N., Singh, B., Chellappa, R., Davis, L.S.: Soft-NMS-improving object detection with one line of code. In: Proceedings of the IEEE International Conference on Computer Vision, pp. 5561–5569 (2017)
3. Cai, Z., Vasconcelos, N.: Cascade R-CNN: delving into high quality object detection. In: Proceedings of the IEEE Conference on Computer Vision and Pattern Recognition, pp. 6154–6162 (2018)
4. Cao, Z., Simon, T., Wei, S.E., Sheikh, Y.: Realtime multi-person 2D pose estimation using part affinity fields. In: Proceedings of the IEEE Conference on Computer Vision and Pattern Recognition, pp. 7291–7299 (2017)
5. Carion, N., Massa, F., Synnaeve, G., Usunier, N., Kirillov, A., Zagoruyko, S.: End-to-end object detection with transformers. In: Vedaldi, A., Bischof, H., Brox, T., Frahm, J.-M. (eds.) ECCV 2020. LNCS, vol. 12346, pp. 213–229. Springer, Cham (2020). https://doi.org/10.1007/978-3-030-58452-8_13
6. Cheng, B., Xiao, B., Wang, J., Shi, H., Huang, T.S., Zhang, L.: HigherhrNet: scale-aware representation learning for bottom-up human pose estimation. In: Proceedings of the IEEE/CVF Conference on Computer Vision and Pattern Recognition, pp. 5386–5395 (2020)
7. Cordts, M., et al.: The cityscapes dataset for semantic urban scene understanding. In: Proceedings of the IEEE Conference on Computer Vision and Pattern Recognition, pp. 3213–3223 (2016)
8. Dai, J., et al.: Deformable convolutional networks. In: Proceedings of the IEEE International Conference on Computer Vision, pp. 764–773 (2017)
9. Dong, Z., Li, G., Liao, Y., Wang, F., Ren, P., Qian, C.: CentripetalNet: pursuing high-quality keypoint pairs for object detection. In: Proceedings of the IEEE/CVF Conference on Computer Vision and Pattern Recognition, pp. 10519–10528 (2020)
10. Dosovitskiy, A., et al.: An image is worth 16x16 words: tansformers for image recognition at scale. arXiv preprint arXiv:2010.11929 (2020)
11. Duan, K., Bai, S., Xie, L., Qi, H., Huang, Q., Tian, Q.: CenterNet: keypoint triplets for object detection. In: Proceedings of the IEEE International Conference on Computer Vision, pp. 6569–6578 (2019)
12. Duan, K., Xie, L., Qi, H., Bai, S., Huang, Q., Tian, Q.: Corner proposal network for anchor-free, two-stage object detection. In: Vedaldi, A., Bischof, H., Brox, T., Frahm, J.-M. (eds.) ECCV 2020. LNCS, vol. 12348, pp. 399–416. Springer, Cham (2020). https://doi.org/10.1007/978-3-030-58580-8_24
13. Girshick, R.: Fast R-CNN. In: Proceedings of the IEEE International Conference on Computer Vision, pp. 1440–1448 (2015)
14. He, K., Gkioxari, G., Dollár, P., Girshick, R.: Mask R-CNN. In: Proceedings of the IEEE International Conference on Computer Vision, pp. 2961–2969 (2017)
15. He, K., Zhang, X., Ren, S., Sun, J.: Deep residual learning for image recognition. In: Proceedings of the IEEE Conference on Computer Vision and Pattern Recognition, pp. 770–778 (2016)
16. Huang, Z., Wang, X., Huang, L., Huang, C., Wei, Y., Liu, W.: CCNET: criss-cross attention for semantic segmentation. In: Proceedings of the IEEE International Conference on Computer Vision, pp. 603–612 (2019)
17. Kingma, D.P., Ba, J.: Adam: A method for stochastic optimization. arXiv preprint arXiv:1412.6980 (2014)

18. Kong, T., Sun, F., Liu, H., Jiang, Y., Li, L., Shi, J.: Foveabox: beyound anchor-based object detection. IEEE Trans. Image Process. **29**, 7389–7398 (2020)
19. Krizhevsky, A., Sutskever, I., Hinton, G.E.: ImageNet classification with deep convolutional neural networks. In: Advances in Neural Information Processing Systems, pp. 1097–1105 (2012)
20. Law, H., Deng, J.: CornerNet: detecting objects as paired keypoints. In: Proceedings of the European Conference on Computer Vision (ECCV), pp. 734–750 (2018)
21. LeCun, Y., Bottou, L., Bengio, Y., Haffner, P., et al.: Gradient-based learning applied to document recognition. Proc. IEEE **86**(11), 2278–2324 (1998)
22. Li, J., Wang, C., Zhu, H., Mao, Y., Fang, H.S., Lu, C.: CrowdPose: efficient crowded scenes pose estimation and a new benchmark. In: Proceedings of the IEEE/CVF Conference on Computer Vision and Pattern Recognition, pp. 10863–10872 (2019)
23. Lin, T.Y., Goyal, P., Girshick, R., He, K., Dollár, P.: Focal loss for dense object detection. In: Proceedings of the IEEE International Conference on Computer Vision, pp. 2980–2988 (2017)
24. Lin, T.-Y., et al.: Microsoft COCO: common objects in context. In: Fleet, D., Pajdla, T., Schiele, B., Tuytelaars, T. (eds.) ECCV 2014. LNCS, vol. 8693, pp. 740–755. Springer, Cham (2014). https://doi.org/10.1007/978-3-319-10602-1_48
25. Liu, F., Wei, H., Zhao, W., Li, G., Peng, J., Li, Z.: WB-DETR: transformer-based detector without backbone. In: Proceedings of the IEEE/CVF International Conference on Computer Vision, pp. 2979–2987 (2021)
26. Liu, W., et al.: SSD: single shot multibox detector. In: Leibe, B., Matas, J., Sebe, N., Welling, M. (eds.) ECCV 2016. LNCS, vol. 9905, pp. 21–37. Springer, Cham (2016). https://doi.org/10.1007/978-3-319-46448-0_2
27. Lu, X., Li, B., Yue, Y., Li, Q., Yan, J.: Grid R-CNN. In: Proceedings of the IEEE Conference on Computer Vision and Pattern Recognition, pp. 7363–7372 (2019)
28. Newell, A., Huang, Z., Deng, J.: Associative embedding: end-to-end learning for joint detection and grouping. In: Advances in Neural Information Processing Systems, pp. 2277–2287 (2017)
29. Nie, X., Feng, J., Zhang, J., Yan, S.: Single-stage multi-person pose machines. In: Proceedings of the IEEE/CVF International Conference on Computer Vision, pp. 6951–6960 (2019)
30. Papandreou, G., Zhu, T., Chen, L.C., Gidaris, S., Tompson, J., Murphy, K.: PersonLab: person pose estimation and instance segmentation with a bottom-up, part-based, geometric embedding model. In: Proceedings of the European Conference on Computer Vision (ECCV), pp. 269–286 (2018)
31. Redmon, J., Farhadi, A.: YOLO9000: better, faster, stronger. In: Proceedings of the IEEE Conference on Computer Vision and Pattern Recognition, pp. 7263–7271 (2017)
32. Redmon, J., Farhadi, A.: YOLOv3: an incremental improvement. arXiv preprint arXiv:1804.02767 (2018)
33. Ren, S., He, K., Girshick, R., Sun, J.: Faster R-CNN: towards real-time object detection with region proposal networks. In: Advances in Neural Information Processing Systems, pp. 91–99 (2015)
34. Sermanet, P., Eigen, D., Zhang, X., Mathieu, M., Fergus, R., LeCun, Y.: OverFeat: integrated recognition, localization and detection using convolutional networks. arXiv preprint arXiv:1312.6229 (2013)
35. Sun, P., et al.: Sparse R-CNN: end-to-end object detection with learnable proposals. In: Proceedings of the IEEE/CVF Conference on Computer Vision and Pattern Recognition, pp. 14454–14463 (2021)

36. Tan, M., Pang, R., Le, Q.V.: EfficientDet: scalable and efficient object detection. In: Proceedings of the IEEE/CVF Conference on Computer Vision and Pattern Recognition, pp. 10781–10790 (2020)
37. Tian, Z., Shen, C., Chen, H., He, T.: FCOS: fully convolutional one-stage object detection. In: Proceedings of the IEEE International Conference on Computer Vision, pp. 9627–9636 (2019)
38. Vaswani, A., et al.: Attention is all you need. arXiv preprint arXiv:1706.03762 (2017)
39. Yang, Z., Liu, S., Hu, H., Wang, L., Lin, S.: RepPoints: point set representation for object detection. In: Proceedings of the IEEE International Conference on Computer Vision, pp. 9657–9666 (2019)
40. Zhang, S., Chi, C., Yao, Y., Lei, Z., Li, S.Z.: Bridging the gap between anchor-based and anchor-free detection via adaptive training sample selection. In: Proceedings of the IEEE/CVF Conference on Computer Vision and Pattern Recognition, pp. 9759–9768 (2020)
41. Zhang, X., Wan, F., Liu, C., Ji, R., Ye, Q.: FreeAnchor: learning to match anchors for visual object detection. arXiv preprint arXiv:1909.02466 (2019)
42. Zhou, X., Wang, D., Krähenbühl, P.: Objects as points. arXiv preprint arXiv:1904.07850 (2019)
43. Zhou, X., Zhuo, J., Krahenbuhl, P.: Bottom-up object detection by grouping extreme and center points. In: Proceedings of the IEEE Conference on Computer Vision and Pattern Recognition, pp. 850–859 (2019)
44. Zhu, X., Su, W., Lu, L., Li, B., Wang, X., Dai, J.: Deformable DETR: deformable transformers for end-to-end object detection. arXiv preprint arXiv:2010.04159 (2020)

PillarNet: Real-Time and High-Performance Pillar-Based 3D Object Detection

Guangsheng Shi[1], Ruifeng Li[1(✉)], and Chao Ma[2(✉)]

[1] State Key Laboratory of Robotics and System,
Harbin Institute of Technology, Harbin, China
lrf100@hit.edu.cn
[2] MoE Key Lab of Artificial Intelligence, AI Institute,
Shanghai Jiao Tong University, Shanghai, China
chaoma@sjtu.edu.cn

Abstract. Real-time and high-performance 3D object detection is of critical importance for autonomous driving. Recent top-performing 3D object detectors mainly rely on point-based or 3D voxel-based convolutions, which are both computationally inefficient for onboard deployment. In contrast, pillar-based methods use solely 2D convolutions, which consume less computation resources, but they lag far behind their voxel-based counterparts in detection accuracy. In this paper, by examining the primary performance gap between pillar- and voxel-based detectors, we develop a real-time and high-performance pillar-based detector, dubbed PillarNet. The proposed PillarNet consists of a powerful encoder network for effective pillar feature learning, a neck network for spatial-semantic feature fusion and the commonly used detect head. Using only 2D convolutions, PillarNet is flexible to an optional pillar size and compatible with classical 2D CNN backbones, such as VGGNet and ResNet. Additionally, PillarNet benefits from our designed orientation-decoupled IoU regression loss along with the IoU-aware prediction branch. Extensive experimental results on the large-scale nuScenes Dataset and Waymo Open Dataset demonstrate that the proposed PillarNet performs well over state-of-the-art 3D detectors in terms of effectiveness and efficiency. Code is available at https://github.com/VISION-SJTU/PillarNet.

Keywords: 3D object detection · Point cloud · Autonomous driving

1 Introduction

With the success in point cloud representation learning using deep neural networks, LiDAR-based 3D object detection has made remarkable progress recently. However, the top-performing point cloud 3D object detectors on the large-scale

Work done while G. Shi visits the Vision and Learning Group at Shanghai Jiao Tong University.

S. Avidan et al. (Eds.): ECCV 2022, LNCS 13670, pp. 35–52, 2022.
https://doi.org/10.1007/978-3-031-20080-9_3

benchmark datasets, such as nuScenes Dataset [2] and Waymo Open Dataset [37], entail heavy computational load and large memory storage. Hence, it is desirable to develop a top-performing 3D detector with real-time speed for the onboard deployment on autonomous vehicles.

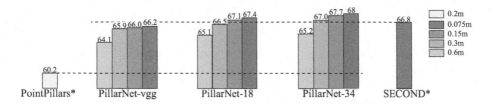

Fig. 1. Comparison between PillarNet variants along with different pillar sizes and two baselines on the nuScenes *val* set in nuScenes detection score (NDS). The reported results of these two baselines are from the latest CenterPoint [46]. All of our PillarNet variants use the same training schedules with CenterPoint-SECOND [46]. * denotes the reproduced two baselines using the center-based head from CenterPoint [46].

Existing point cloud 3D object detectors mainly use the grid-based representation over point cloud and can be broadly categorized into two groups, *i.e.*, 3D voxel-based and 2D pillar-based methods. Both of these two groups take the classical "encoder-neck-head" detection architecture [11,14,16,27,39,40,44,48,51]. Voxel-based methods [11,14,40,48,51] typically divide the input point cloud into regular 3D voxel grid. An encoder with sparse 3D convolutions [10] is then used to learn geometric representation across multiple levels. Following the encoder, a neck module with standard 2D CNNs fuses multi-scale features before feeding to the detection head. In contrast, pillar-based methods [16,27,39,44] project 3D point clouds into a 2D pseudo-image on the BEV plane, and then directly build the neck network upon the 2D CNN-based feature pyramid network (FPN) to fuse multi-scale features. For voxel-based methods, the effective voxel-wise feature learning powered by sparse 3D CNN delivers favorable detection performance. However, due to the 3D sparse convolution within the encoder, it is hard to aggregate multi-scale features with different resolutions on the BEV space. For pillar-based methods, a light encoder for pillar feature learning yields unsatisfied performance compared with their voxel-based counterparts. Moreover, the small sized pseudo-image and the large initial pillar further limit the detection performance. It is because a finer pillar leads to larger pseudo-image and more favorable performance but heavier computational load. Interestingly, both voxel- and pillar-based methods perform 3D detection using the aggregated multi-scale features on the BEV space (see Sect. 3.1)

We observe that previous pillar-based methods do not have powerful pillar feature encoding, which is the main cause of the unsatisfied performance. In addition, progressively downsampling pillar scales can help to decouple the output feature map size and the initial pseudo-image projection scale. As such, we design a real-time and high-performance pillar-based 3D detection method, dubbed PillarNet, that consists of an encoder for hierarchical deep pillar feature extraction, a neck module for multi-scale feature fusion, and the commonly-used center-based detect head. In our PillarNet, the powerful encoder network involves 5 stages. Stage 1 to 4 follow the same setting as the conventional 2D detection networks such as VGG [36] and ResNet [12] but substituted 2D convolutions with its sparse counterparts for resource savings. Stage 5 with standard 2D convolutions possesses a larger receptive field and feeds semantic features to the following neck network. The neck network exchanges sufficient information through stacked convolution layers between the further enriched high-level semantic feature from the encoder stage 5 and the low-level spatial feature from the encoder stage 4. For tuning the hard-balanced pillar size in previous pillar-based methods, PillarNet offers an effective solution by skillfully detaching the corresponding encoder stages for the chosen pillar scale. For example, to accommodate the input with 8 times pillar size ($0.075 * 8$ m in nuScenes Dataset), we can simply remove the $1\times$, $2\times$, and $4\times$ downsampled encoder stages.

As shown in Fig. 1, our PillarNet with variant configurations, *i.e.*, PillarNet-vgg/18/34, offer the scalability and flexibility for point cloud-based 3D object detection by using merely 2D convolutions. Our PillarNet significantly advances pillar-based 3D detectors and sheds new light on further research on point cloud object detection. Despite its simplicity, the proposed PillarNet achieves the state-of-the-art performance on two large-scale autonomous driving benchmarks [2, 37] and runs in real-time (see Sect. 4).

2   Related Works

2.1   Point Cloud 3D Object Detection

3D object detection with point cloud alone can mainly be summarized into two categories: point-based and grid-based methods.

Point-Based 3D Object Detectors. Powered by the pioneering PointNet [28,30], point-based methods directly process irregular point clouds and predict 3D bounding boxes. PointRCNN [33] proposes a point-based proposal generation paradigm directly from raw point clouds and then refines each proposal by devising an RoI pooling operation. STD [42] transforms point features inside of each proposal into compact voxel representation for RoI feature extraction. 3DSSD [23], as a one-stage 3D object detector, introduces F-FPS as a complement of existing D-FPS with set abstraction operation to benefit both regression and classification. These point-based methods naturally preserve accurate point location and enable flexible receptive fields with radius-based local feature aggregation. These methods, however, as summarized in [25], spend 90% of their runtime on organizing irregular point data rather than extracting features, and are not suitable for handling large-scale point clouds.

Grid-Based 3D Object Detectors. Most existing methods discrete the sparse and irregular point clouds into regular grids including 3D voxels and 2D pillars, and then capitalize on 2D/3D CNN to perform 3D object detection. The pioneering VoxelNet [51] divides point cloud into 3D voxels, and encodes scene feature using 3D convolutions. To tackle the empty voxels typically for the large outdoor space, SECOND [40] introduces 3D sparse convolution to accelerate VoxelNet [51] and improves the detection accuracy. Until now, 3D voxel-based methods dominate the majority of 3D detection benchmarks. For a long time, even with sparse 3D convolution, it was hard to balance between the fine resolution of 3D voxels and associated resource costs.

PointPillars [16] uses 2D voxelization on the ground plane with a PointNet [28] based per-pillar feature extractor. It can utilize 2D convolutions for deployment on embedded systems with limited costs. MVF [6] utilizes multi-view features to augment point-wise information before projecting raw points into 2D pseudo-image. HVNet [44] fuses different scales of pillar features at the point-wise level to achieve good accuracy and high inference speed. HVPR [27] cleverly keeps the efficiency of pillar-based detection while implicitly leveraging the voxel-based feature learning regime for better performance. Current Pillar-based advancements, however, focus on the sophisticated pillar feature projection or multi-scale aggregation strategies, to narrow the huge performance gap relative to their voxel-based counterparts. In contrast, we resort to a powerful backbone network to address the above issues and boost 3D detection performance.

2.2   Multi-Sensor Based 3D Object Detection

Most approaches expect the complementary information from multiple sensors, such as camera image and LiDAR, to achieve high performance 3D object detection. MV3D [6] designs 3D object anchors and generates proposals from BEV representations and refine them using features from LiDAR and camera. AVOD [15] instead fuses these features at the proposal generation stage and provides better detection results. ContFuse [19] learns to fuse image features with point cloud features onto BEV space. MMF [18] struggles for LiDAR-Camera feature fusion via proxy tasks including depth completion on RGB images and ground estimation from point clouds. 3D-CVF [47] tackles the multi-sensor registration issue for cross-view spatial feature fusion in the BEV domain. Almost all of these multi-modality frameworks rely on the intermediate BEV representation to perform 3D object detection. Our method extracts point cloud features on BEV space and may be promising to seamlessly integrate into existing multi-modality frameworks for advanced performance Fig. 2 .

3   PillarNet for 3D Object Detection

3.1   Preliminaries

The grid-based detectors perform 3D detection on BEV space, including 3D voxel-based detectors and 2D pillar-based detectors. Recent voxel-based detectors follow the SECOND [40] architecture with improved sparse 3D CNN for

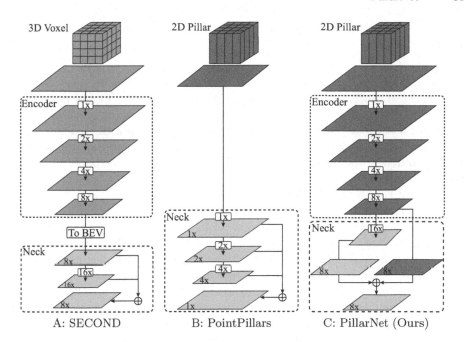

Fig. 2. Comparison of three types of architectures. The encoder uses sparse 3D CNN in SECOND [40] while sparse 2D CNN for PillarNet. The neck in all the three methods uses standard 2D CNN. On the nuScenes Dataset, the 3D voxel size in SECOND [40] is (0.075 m, 0.075 m, 0.2 m), and the 2D pillar size in PointPillars and our proposed PillarNet is (0.2 m, 0.2 m) and (0.075 m, 0.075 m) respectively.

effective voxel feature encoding over the pioneering VoxelNet [51]. Pillar-based detectors generally follow the pioneering PointPillars [16] architecture with only 2D CNN for multi-scale feature fusion. We first revisit these two representative point cloud detection architectures, which motivate us to construct the proposed PillarNet method.

SECOND. SECOND [40] is a typical voxel-based one-stage object detector, which lays the groundwork for succeeding voxel-based detectors with specialized sparse 3D convolutions [9,10]. It divides the unordered point cloud into regular 3D voxels and performs box prediction on BEV space. The entire 3D detection architecture contains three basic parts: (1) An encoder hierarchically encodes the input non-empty voxel features into 3D feature volumes with the $1\times$, $2\times$, $4\times$ and $8\times$ downsampled sizes. (2) A neck module further abstracts the flattened encoder output on the BEV space into multiple scales in a top-down manner. (3) A detect head performs box classification and regression using the fused multi-scale BEV features.

PointPillars. PointPillars [16] projects raw point cloud on the X-Y plane via a tiny PointNet [28], yielding a sparse 2D pseudo-image. PointPillars uses a 2D CNN-based top-down network to process the pseudo-image with stride $1\times$, $2\times$, and 4× convolution blocks and then concatenates the multi-scale features for the detect head.

Analysis. Despite the favorable runtime and memory efficiency, PointPillar [16] still lags far behind SECOND [40] on performance. Under the premise that sparse 3D convolutions possess the superior representation ability for point cloud learning, recent advanced pillar-based methods mainly focus on exploring attentive pillar feature extraction [24,44] from raw points or sophisticated multi-scale strategies [27,39,44]. These methods, on the other hand, suffer from unfavourable latency and still under-performs their 3D voxel-based counterparts by a large margin.

Alternatively, we take a different view by considering grid-based detectors as BEV-based detectors and revisit the entire point cloud learning architecture. We identify that the performance bottleneck of pillar-based methods mainly lies in the sparse encoder network for spatial feature learning and effective neck module for sufficient spatial-semantic features fusion. Specifically, PointPillars directly applies the feature pyramid network to fuse multi-scale features on the projected dense 2D pseudo-image, lacking the sparse encoder network for effective pillar feature encoding as in SECOND. On the other hand, PointPillars couples the size of the final output feature maps with the initial projected pillar scale, increasing the entire calculation and memory cost sharply as the pillar scale gets finer.

To resolve the above issues, we stand by the "encoder-neck-head" detection architecture on BEV space to improve the performance of pillar-based methods. Specifically, we explore the significant difference and respective function for the encoder and neck networks:

- We redesign the encoder in SECOND by substituting sparse 3D convolutions by its sparse 2D convolutions counterpart on loss-less pillar features from raw point clouds. It has been validated in the 3rd row of Table 4 that the sparse encoder process enhances 3D detection performance significantly.
- We formulate the neck module as the spatial-semantic feature fusion by inheriting the sparse spatial features from the sparse encoder output and further high-level semantic feature abstraction in low-resolution feature maps, as shown in the 6th row of Table 4, which is efficient and effective.

Finally, we build our PillarNet using the relatively heavyweight sparse encoder network for hierarchical pillar feature learning and the lightweight neck module for sufficient spatial-semantic feature fusion.

3.2   PillarNet Design for 3D Object Detection

In this subsection, we present the detailed structure of our PillarNet design. The overall architecture in Fig. 3 consists of three components: the encoder for deep pillar feature extraction, the neck module for spatial-semantic feature aggregation, and the 3D detect head. With the commonly used center-based detect head [46], we present the flexibility and scalability of our PillarNet.

Encoder Design. The encoder network aims to extract deep sparse pillar features hierarchically from the projected sparse 2D pillar features, where the

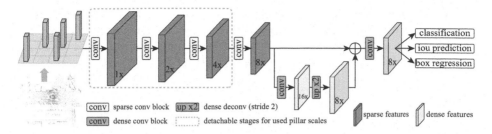

Fig. 3. The overall architecture of our proposed PillarNet. The input point clouds are first quantified into pillars to feed into the 2D sparse convolution-based encoder to learn multi-scale spatial features. Then the densified semantic feature is fused with the spatial feature in the neck module for the final 3D box regression, classification, and IoU prediction.

detachable stages from 1 to 4 progressively down-sample sparse pillar features using sparse 2D CNN. Compared to PointPillars [16], our designed encoder have two advantages:

(1) The sparse encoder network can take the progress on image-based 2D object detection, such as VGGNet [35] and ResNet [12]. The simple encoder for pillar feature learning can largely improve 3D detection performance.
(2) The hierarchically downsampling structure allows PillarNet to skillfully operate the sparse pillar features with different pillar sizes, which alleviates the limitation of coupling pillar size in previous pillar-based methods.

Our constructed PillarNet with variant backbones, PillarNet-vgg/18/34, with the similar complexities of VGGNet/ResNet-18/ResNet-34. The detailed network configurations can be found in the supplementary material.

Neck Design. The neck module, as in FPN [21], aims to fuse high-level abstract semantic features and low-level fine-grained spatial features for mainstream detect head (*i.e.*, anchor boxes or anchor points). The additional 16× downsampled dense feature maps further abstracts high-level semantic feature using a group of dense 2D CNNs, to enrich receptive field for large objects and populate object center-positioned features for center-based detect head. Equipped with spatial features from sparse encoder network, there are two alternative neck designs for the spatial-semantic feature fusion from the starting design in SECOND [40]:

(1) The naive design neckv1 (Fig. 4(A)) from SECOND [40] applies a top-down network to generate multi-scale features and concatenate multi-scale dense feature maps as the final output.
(2) The aggressive design neckv2 (Fig. 4(B)) considers sufficient information exchange between high-level semantic feature from additional 16× downsampled dense feature maps and low-level spatial feature from sparse encoder network using a group of convolution layers.

(3) The design neckv3 (Fig. 4(C)) further enriches the high-level semantic features on 16× downsampled dense feature maps through a group of convolution layers and fuses the spatial-semantic features with the other group of convolution layers for robust feature extraction.

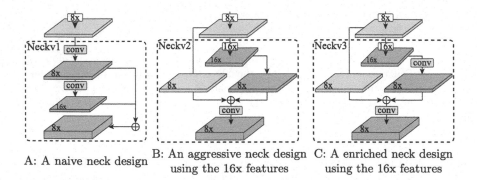

A: A naive neck design   B: An aggressive neck design   C: A enriched neck design
                          using the 16x features   using the 16x features

Fig. 4. Detailed structure of different neck designs. The neck A inherits directly from SECOND [40], while two alternative neck designs B and C introduce the spatial features from sparse encoder network and semantic features from the 16× dense feature maps.

3.3 Orientation-Decoupled IoU Regression Loss

In general, the IoU metric highly correlates with the localization quality and classification accuracy of the predicted 3D boxes. Previous methods [20] show that using the 3D IoU quality to re-weight the classification and supervise the box regression can achieve better localization accuracy.

For the classification branch, we follow previous methods [14,48] and use the IoU-rectification scheme to incorporate the IoU information into the confidence scores. The IoU-Aware rectification function [14] at the post-processing stage can be formulated as:

$$\hat{S} = S^{1-\beta} * W_{\text{IoU}}^{\beta} \tag{1}$$

where S indicates the classification score and W_{IoU} is the IoU score. β is a hyperparameter. For predicting the IoU score, we use L1 loss $\mathcal{L}_{iou}$ to supervise the IoU regression, where the target 3D IoU score W between the predicted 3D box and the ground truth box is encoded by $2 * (W - 0.5) \in [-1, 1]$.

For the regression branch, recent methods [20,49] extend the GIoU [31] loss or DIoU [50] loss from 2D detection to the 3D domain. However, the non-trivial 3D IoU computation slows down the training process. Furthermore, the coupled orientation for the IoU-related regression may negatively affect the training process. Figure 5 shows such an example. Given a typical 2D bounding box $[x, y, l, w, \theta] = [0, 0, 3.9, 1.6, 0]$, there exist cross-effects of orientation with center bias for x and y positions or of scale for width and length sizes during the optimization for IoU metric between biased box with ground-truth box as follows:

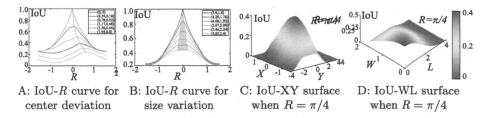

A: IoU-R curve for   B: IoU-R curve for   C: IoU-XY surface   D: IoU-WL surface
center deviation   size variation   when $R = \pi/4$ when $R = \pi/4$

Fig. 5. The IoU metric-based interplay of orientation (R) with center or size for a 2D rotated box [0, 0, 3.9, 1.6, 0]. A and B depict the effect of center variation and size oscillation on orientation regression separately. Red curve in A indicates the local optimum while red region in B for optimization plateau. C and D depict the effect of orientation bias $R = \pi/4$ on center and size regression separately (Color figure online).

- The effect of center deviation on orientation regression. The training phase easily settles into a local optimum, if the box center deviates far. See the red curve in Fig. 5(A).
- The effect of size variation on orientation regression. The training phase settles into the notorious optimization plateau, if box sizes change largely. See the red region in Fig. 5(B).
- The effect of orientation bias on center and size regression. The optimization direction remains consistent even if the orientation deviation is significant.

As a result, we present an alternative Orientation-Decoupled IoU-related regression loss by decoupling the orientation θ from the mutually-coupled seven parameters $(x, y, z, w, l, h, \theta)$. Specifically, we extend the IoU regression loss $\mathcal{L}_{od-iou}$ (OD-IoU/OD-GIoU/OD-DIoU) from the IoU loss [31], GIoU loss [31] and DIoU loss [50], respectively.

3.4   Overall Loss Function

Following [46], we apply the focal loss [22] for the heatmap classification $\mathcal{L}_{cls}$, and the L1 loss for localization offset $\mathcal{L}_{off}$, the z-axis location $\mathcal{L}_z$, 3D object size $\mathcal{L}_{size}$ and orientation $\mathcal{L}_{ori}$. The overall loss $\mathcal{L}_{total}$ is jointly optimized as follows:

$$\mathcal{L}_{total} = \mathcal{L}_{cls} + \mathcal{L}_{iou} + \lambda(\mathcal{L}_{od-iou} + \mathcal{L}_{off} + \mathcal{L}_z + \mathcal{L}_{size} + \mathcal{L}_{ori}) \qquad (2)$$

where the loss weight λ is empirically set parameter as in [46].

4   Experiments

nuScenes Dataset. nuScenes [2] contains 1000 driving sequences, with 700, 150, 150 sequences for training, validation, and testing, respectively. Each sequence is approximately 20-second long, with a LiDAR frequency of 20 FPS. nuScenes uses a 32 lanes LiDAR, which produces approximately 30k points per frame. The annotations include 10 classes with a long-tail distribution. The official evaluation metrics are mean Average Precision (mAP) and nuScenes detection score (NDS). We follow the convention to accumulate 10 LiDAR sweeps to densify the point clouds and report results by using the official evaluation protocol.

Waymo Open Dataset. Waymo Open Dataset [37] is currently the largest dataset with LiDAR point clouds for autonomous driving. There are total 798 training sequences with around 160k LiDAR samples, and 202 validation sequences with 40k LiDAR samples. It annotated the objects in the full 360° field. The evaluation metrics are calculated by the official evaluation tools, where the mean average precision (mAP) and the mean average precision weighted by heading (mAPH) are used for evaluation. The 3D IoU threshold is set as 0.7 for vehicle detection and 0.5 for pedestrian/cyclist detection.

Training and Inference Details. We use the same training schedules as prior CenterPoint-SECOND [46], where Adam optimizer is used with one-cycle learning rate policy, weight decay 0.01, and momentum 0.85 to 0.95 on 4 T V100 GPUs. We make runtime comparison with two baselines (*i.e., CenterPoint-SECOND and CenterPoint-PointPillars*) on desktop equipped with an i9 CPU and RTX 3090 GPU. To project raw point clouds into the pillar feature, we apply one-layer MLP-based PointNet associated with *atomic max*-based pooling on augmented point-wise feature of all inside points per pillar. We adopt the widely used data augmentation strategies as [46] during training, including the random scene flipping along, random rotation, random scene scaling, and random translation.

For nuScenes Dataset, we set the detection range to $[-54\,\text{m}, 54\,\text{m}]$ for the X and Y axis, and $[-5\,\text{m}, 3\,\text{m}]$ for the Z axis. We use $(0.075\,\text{m}, 0.075\,\text{m})$ as the basic pillar size for experiments. We train the PillarNet from scratch with batch size 16, max learning rate 1e-3 for 20 epochs. For the post-processing process during inference, following [46], we use class-agnostic NMS with the score threshold set to 0.1 and rectification factor β to 0.5 for all 10 classes. To compare on the nuScenes test set, we do not use any model ensembling except double-flip test-time augmentation as CenterPoint [46].

For Waymo Open Dataset, we set the detection range to $[-75.2\,\text{m}, 75.2\,\text{m}]$ for X and Y axes, and $[-2\,\text{m}, 4\,\text{m}]$ for Z axis. W use $(0.1\,\text{m}, 0.1\,\text{m})$ as the basic pillar size for experiments and train the PillarNet from scratch with batch size 16, max learning rate 3e-3 for 36 epochs. During inference, we simply follow [14] by using class-specific NMS with the IoU thresholds (0.8, 0.55, 0.55) and rectification factor β to (0.68, 0.71, 0.65) for vehicle, pedestrian and cyclist respectively.

4.1   Overall Results

Evaluation on nuScenes *test* set. We also compare our PillarNet variants with previous LiDAR-only non-ensemble methods on the nuScenes *test* set. As shown in Table 1, all our PillarNet-vgg/18/34 go beyond the stage-of-the-art methods by a large margin while running at a real-time speed of 14, 13 and 12

Table 1. The LiDAR-only non-ensemble 3D detection performance comparison on the nuScenes *test* set. The table is mainly sorted by nuScenes detection score (NDS) which is the official ranking metric.

Methods	Stages	NDS	mAP	Car	Truck	Bus	Trailer	Cons.Veh.	Ped.	Motor.	Bicycle	Tr.Cone	Barrier
WYSIWYG [13]	One	41.9	35.0	79.1	30.4	46.6	40.1	7.1	65.0	18.2	0.1	28.8	34.7
PointPillars [16]	One	45.3	30.5	68.4	23.0	28.2	23.4	4.1	59.7	27.4	1.1	30.8	38.9
3DVID [45]	One	53.1	45.4	79.7	33.6	47.1	43.1	18.1	76.5	40.7	7.9	58.8	48.8
3DSSD [41]	One	56.4	42.6	81.2	47.2	61.4	30.5	12.6	70.2	36.0	8.6	31.1	47.9
Cylinder3D [53]	One	61.6	50.6	–	–	–	–	–	–	–	–	–	–
CGBS [52]	One	63.3	52.8	81.1	48.5	54.9	42.9	10.5	80.1	51.5	22.3	70.9	65.7
CVCNet [3]	One	64.2	55.8	82.6	49.5	59.4	51.1	16.2	83.0	61.8	38.8	69.7	69.7
CenterPoint [46]	Two	65.5	58.0	84.6	51.0	60.2	53.2	17.5	83.4	53.7	28.7	76.7	70.9
HotSpotNet [4]	One	66.0	59.3	83.1	50.9	56.4	53.3	23.0	81.3	63.5	36.6	73.0	71.6
AFDetV2 [14]	One	68.5	62.4	86.3	54.2	62.5	58.9	26.7	85.8	63.8	34.3	80.1	71.0
PillarNet-vgg	One	69.6	63.3	86.9	56.0	62.2	62.0	28.6	86.3	62.6	33.5	79.6	75.6
PillarNet-18	One	70.8	65.0	87.4	56.7	60.9	61.8	**30.4**	87.2	67.4	40.3	82.1	76.0
PillarNet-34	One	**71.4**	**66.0**	**87.6**	**57.5**	**63.6**	**63.1**	27.9	**87.3**	**70.1**	**42.3**	**83.3**	**77.2**

Table 2. Single- (upper group) and multi-frame (lower group) LiDAR-only non-ensemble performance comparison on the Waymo Open Dataset *test* set. "L" and "LT" mean "all LiDARs" and "top-LiDAR only", respectively. † denotes the reported results from RSN [38].

Methods	Stages	Sensors	Frames	Vehicle (L1)		Vehicle (L2)		Ped. (L1)		Ped. (L2)		Cyc. (L1)		Cyc. (L2)	
				mAP	mAPH	mAP	mAPH	mAP	mAPH	mAP	mAPH	mAP	mAPH	mAP	mAPH
† PointPillars [16]	One	LT	1	68.60	68.10	60.50	60.10	68.00	55.50	61.40	50.10	–	–	–	–
RCD [1]	Two	–	1	71.97	71.59	65.06	64.70	–	–	–	–	–	–	–	–
CenterPoint [46]	Two	LT	1	80.20	79.70	72.20	71.80	78.30	72.10	72.20	66.40	–	–	–	–
AFDetV2 [14]	One	LT	1	80.49	80.43	72.98	72.55	79.76	**74.35**	73.71	**68.61**	**72.43**	**71.23**	**69.84**	**68.67**
PillarNet-vgg	One	LT	1	81.16	80.68	73.64	73.20	78.30	70.28	72.23	64.68	67.26	66.07	64.79	63.65
PillarNet-18	One	LT	1	81.85	81.40	74.46	74.03	79.97	72.68	73.95	67.09	67.98	66.80	65.50	64.36
PillarNet-34	One	LT	1	**82.47**	**82.03**	**75.07**	**74.65**	**80.82**	74.13	**74.83**	68.54	69.08	67.91	66.60	65.47
3D-MAN [43]	Multi	L	15	78.71	78.28	70.37	69.98	69.97	65.98	63.98	60.26	–	–	–	–
RSN [38]	Two	LT	3	80.70	80.30	71.90	71.60	78.90	75.60	70.70	67.80	–	–	–	–
CenterPoint [46]	Two	L	2	81.05	80.59	73.42	72.99	80.47	77.28	74.56	71.52	74.60	73.68	72.17	71.28
Pyramid R-CNN [26]	Two	L	2	81.77	81.32	74.87	74.43	–	–	–	–	–	–	–	–
AFDetV2 [14]	One	LT	2	81.65	81.22	74.30	73.89	81.26	78.05	75.47	72.41	**76.41**	**75.37**	**74.05**	**73.04**
PillarNet-vgg	One	LT	2	82.18	81.73	74.93	74.49	80.41	76.86	74.52	71.14	68.75	67.89	66.52	65.68
PillarNet-18	One	LT	2	82.68	82.25	75.53	75.12	81.71	78.29	75.91	**72.66**	70.19	69.30	68.01	67.15
PillarNet-34	One	LT	2	**83.23**	**82.80**	**76.09**	**75.69**	**82.38**	**79.02**	**76.66**	73.46	71.44	70.51	69.20	68.29

FPS, respectively. In addition, the promising results of PillarNet variants validate the good scalability of our PillarNet, where the performance behaves more favorably as the computational complexity rises. Typically, PillarNet-18 surprisingly surpasses the most advanced AFDetV2 by +2.3% NDS or +2.6% mAP. To the best of our knowledge, PillarNet-vgg/18/34 surpasses all the published LiDAR-only non-ensemble methods on the nuScenes Detection leaderboard on Mar 7, 2022. From this point on, PillarNet achieves new state-of-the-art performance using only 2D convolutions.

Evaluation on Waymo Open Dataset *test* set. We compare our PillarNet variants with previous methods on the Waymo Open Dataset *test* set. Table 2 contains two groups, where the upper group is single-frame LiDAR-only

Table 3. The single-frame LiDAR-only non-ensemble 3D AP/APH performance comparison on the Waymo Open Dataset *val* set. †: reported by [17].

Methods	Stages	Vehicle (L1)		Vehicle (L2)		Ped. (L1)		Ped. (L2)		Cyc. (L1)		Cyc. (L2)	
		mAP	mAPH	mAP	mAPH	mAP	mAPH	mAP	mAPH	mAP	mAPH	mAP	mAPH
MVF [6]	One	62.93	–	–	–	65.33	–	–	–	–	–	–	–
3D-MAN [43]	Multi	69.03	68.52	60.16	59.71	71.71	67.74	62.58	59.04	–	–	–	–
RCD [1]	Two	69.59	69.16	–	–	–	–	–	–	–	–	–	–
†SECOND [40]	One	72.27	71.69	63.85	63.33	68.70	58.18	60.72	51.31	60.62	59.28	58.34	57.05
†PointPillar [16]	One	56.62	–	–	–	59.25	–	–	–	–	–	–	–
LiDAR R-CNN [17]	Two	73.50	73.00	64.70	64.20	71.20	58.70	63.10	51.70	68.60	66.90	66.10	64.40
RangeDet [8]	One	72.85	–	–	–	75.94	–	–	–	65.80	–	–	–
MVF++ [29]	One	74.64	–	–	–	78.01	–	–	–	–	–	–	–
RSN [38]	Two	75.10	74.60	66.00	65.50	77.80	72.70	68.30	63.70	–	–	–	–
Voxel R-CNN [7]	Two	75.59	–	66.59	–	–	–	–	–	–	–	–	–
CenterPoint [46]	Two	76.70	76.20	68.80	68.30	79.00	72.90	71.00	65.30	–	–	–	–
Part-A² [34]	Two	77.05	76.51	68.47	67.97	75.24	66.87	66.18	58.62	68.60	67.36	66.13	64.93
PV-RCNN [32]	Two	77.51	76.89	68.98	68.41	75.01	65.65	66.04	57.61	67.81	66.35	65.39	63.98
AFDetV2 [14]	One	77.64	77.14	69.68	69.22	80.19	**74.62**	72.16	**66.95**	**73.72**	**72.74**	**71.06**	**70.12**
PillarNet-vgg	One	77.41	76.86	69.46	68.96	78.30	70.32	70.00	62.62	69.48	68.35	66.87	65.78
PillarNet-18	One	78.24	77.73	70.40	69.92	79.80	72.59	71.57	64.90	70.40	69.29	67.75	66.68
PillarNet-34	One	**79.09**	**78.59**	**70.92**	**70.46**	**80.59**	74.01	**72.28**	66.17	72.29	71.21	69.72	68.67
Two-frame 3D detection results of PillarNet variants for reference.													
PillarNet-vgg	One	78.26	77.73	70.56	70.07	80.88	77.53	72.73	69.58	67.72	66.88	65.54	64.72
PillarNet-18	One	79.59	79.06	71.56	71.08	82.11	78.82	74.49	71.35	70.41	69.57	68.27	67.46
PillarNet-34	One	79.98	79.47	72.00	71.53	82.52	79.33	75.00	71.95	70.51	69.69	68.38	67.58

non-ensemble methods and the bottom group is multi-frame LiDAR-only non-ensemble methods. Our PillarNet-34 outperforms all the previous single-frame and multi-frame LiDAR-only models for the vehicle and pedestrian categories while running at a speed of 19 FPS separately. Our lightweight PillarNet-vgg still achieves the comparable performance for the vehicle while running at a faster speed of 24 FPS. Using merely 2D convolutions, our real-time PillarNet variants are suitable for onboard deployment.

Evaluation on Waymo Open Dataset *val* set. We compare our PillarNet variants with all published single-frame LiDAR-only non-ensemble methods on Waymo *val* set in Table 3. We also present the performance of PillarNet variants using two-frame-merged LiDAR points for reference. Typically, PillarNet-18 achieves the state-of-the-art performance on the vehicle category, making it a viable replacement for previous state-of-the-art 3D voxel-based methods. Our PillarNet-34 outperforms previous state-of-the-art works with remarkable performance gains (+1.24 for the vehicle in terms of mAPH of LEVEL_2 difficulty). Excluding the latest voxel-based detector AFDetV2 with self-calibrated module and channel-wise and spatial-wise attention, PillarNet-34 outperforms the previous one-stage and two-stage 3D detectors for the vehicle and pedestrian detection while operating at super real-time speed. With the two-frame input, PillarNet on variant backbones consistently show the superior performance compared with their single-frame counterparts. However, for the cyclist detection, two-frame results are not the best. The reason may be the unbalanced sample distribution of three categories. The number of vehicles, pedestrians and cyclists scattered in the Waymo train set are 4352210, 2037627 and 49518 respectively. The training process using two frames aggravates the adverse effect, and this issue may be alleviated by addressing the unbalanced sample distribution.

Table 4. The analysis of each component of PillarNet with the same training schedules as SECOND and also comparison with the two baselines (*i.e.*, PointPillars and SECOND) on nuScenes *val* dataset. †: reported by used codebase.

Methods	FPS	mAP	NDS	mATE	mASE	mAOE	mAVE	mAAE
†CenterPoint-PointPillars [16]	31	50.26	60.22	31.32	25.94	39.50	32.54	19.79
†CenterPoint-SECOND [40]	8	59.56	66.76	29.22	25.51	30.24	25.91	19.34
PointPillars (0.075 m)[1]	9	48.63	59.51	30.70	26.35	35.81	35.52	19.70
PillarNet-18(neckv1)	17	57.87	66.16	29.88	26.05	27.86	25.78	18.14
PillarNet-18(neckv2)	16	58.53	66.41	29.82	26.05	29.56	24.53	18.65
PillarNet-18(neckv2-D)	16	59.40	66.96	29.07	25.86	29.61	24.69	18.17
PillarNet-18(neckv3)	16	59.48	67.15	29.03	25.83	27.54	24.54	18.90
PillarNet-18(OD-IoU)	16	59.51	67.09	28.51	25.57	29.31	24.63	18.64
PillarNet-18(OD-GIoU)	16	59.69	67.35	28.50	25.78	27.57	24.74	18.37
PillarNet-18(OD-DIoU)	16	59.72	67.39	28.40	25.81	27.38	24.67	18.41
PillarNet-18(IoU)	16	59.82	67.16	28.92	25.53	28.37	25.63	19.07
PillarNet-18	16	59.90	67.39	27.72	25.20	28.93	24.67	19.11

4.2 Ablation Studies

In this section, we investigate the individual components of the proposed Pillar-Net with extensive ablation experiments on the *val* set of nuScenes Dataset.

Analysis of PillarNet Improvements. The key contribution can be summarized into two parts: the designed PillarNet architecture (*i.e.*, encoder and neck networks) and the IoU-related modules (*i.e.*, Orientation-Decoupled IoU (OD-IoU) regression loss and IoU-Aware rectification). To analyze how our designed encoder and neck networks improve the 3D detection performance, we use the same hyper-parameters settings as CenterPoint-SECOND.

Encoder Network. Compared with CenterPoint-PointPillars [16] (1st row of Table 4), our newly introduced encoder network can significantly improve the detection performance by about +7.61% mAP and +5.94% NDS. Using the heavy encoder with extra stage 5 in 3rd to 6th rows can boost the 3D detection performance by a large margin. Therein, the enriched semantic features from encoder stage 5 in 4th to 5th rows perform better than the aggressive fusion strategy in 6th row.

Neck Network. Compared with the naive neck module neckv1, as shown in Table 4, our fusion design from 4th to 6th rows with a group of convolution layers

Table 5. The effect of different PillarNet variants by detaching two IoU-related modules.

Models	FPS	mAP	NDS
PillarNet-vgg	16	57.67	65.71
PillarNet-18	16	59.41	67.09
PillarNet-34	14	59.98	67.50

Table 6. The effect of different pillar sizes and its associated stages in PillarNet-18 encoder.

Pillar size	FPS	encoder stages	mAP	NDS
0.075 m	16	(1× 2× 4× 8× 16×)	59.48	67.15
0.075*2 m	16	(2× 4× 8× 16×)	58.70	66.56
0.075*4 m	16	(4× 8× 16×)	57.87	66.05
0.075*8 m	14	(8× 16×)	55.37	64.20

can improve detection performance by a large margin. The performance difference between neckv2 and neckv2-D shows that the dense convolutions enable stronger semantic abstraction at the object center than its sparse counterparts, due to LiDAR points sparsely scattering on the surface of the objects.

OD-IoU Regression Loss. All three types of losses (*i.e.*, OD-IoU, OD-GIoU and OD-DIoU) play a role in the critical positioning accuracy, while the OD-DIoU loss brings a maximum boost with +0.24% mAP or +0.24% NDS.

IoU-Aware Rectification. The IoU-Aware rectification alleviates the misalignment between localization confidence and classification score. Adding IoU-Aware rectification benefits the IoU-based mAP with +0.34% increase.

Analysis of Model Variants. We investigate PillarNet-vgg/18/34 with different model complexity by detaching IoU-related modules for a clean comparison. Table 5 shows that our PillarNet architecture can benefit from increasing model capacity with slightly more FLOPs and inference time. The good scalability can lead the pathway for deployment according to practical needs.

Analysis of Pillar Sizes. We investigate pillar size on detection performance by detaching IoU-related modules for a clean comparison. Specifically, we castrate the associated encoder stages to suit particular pillar scale, where a larger pillar size requires fewer encoder stages. From Table 6 and Fig 1, we can see that PillarNet benefit more from finer pillar scale and deeper pillar feature encoding. The much higher performance of PillarNet with 0.3 m and 0.6 m over PointPillars with 0.2 m manifests the effectiveness of our architectural design. Moreover, PointPillars [16] with 0.075 m in 3rd row of Table 4 performs slightly worse than that of 0.2 m. That is because the used lightweight encoder network hinders the gain from small pillar size. This also implies the importance of hierarchical pillar feature encoding of PillarNet for better performance with limited resource costs.

Runtime Analysis. We analyze inference runtime by fairly comparing with two baseline counterparts. our PillarNet-18 achieves a good speed-accuracy trade-off with 16 FPS than CenterPoint-SECOND of 8 FPS on nuScenes Dataset, and 21 FPS than CenterPoint-PointPillars of 19 FPS on Waymo Open Dataset. The slow inference speed for PillarNet with coarser pillar size and reduced encoder stages in Table 6 may be due to the fact that cuda *atomic max* operation struggles to handle more inside points per pillar based on global memory. This issue can be alleviated by the input point cloud sub-sampling or other efficient operation (*e.g.,* streaming pillarization as [5]).

5   Conclusions

In this work, we propose a real-time and high-performance one-stage 3D object detector. From the perspective of "encoder-neck-head" architecture design, PillarNet achieves the scalability and flexibility for the hard-balanced pillar size and model complexities. We expect that our findings will stimulate further research into pillar-based point cloud representation learning.

Acknowledgements. This work was supported in part by NSFC (61906119), and Shanghai Municipal Science and Technology Major Project (2021SHZDZX0102). We thank Huawei Noah's Ark Lab gratefully for sponsoring large-scale GPUs.

References

1. Bewley, A., Sun, P., Mensink, T., Anguelov, D., Sminchisescu, C.: Range conditioned dilated convolutions for scale invariant 3D object detection. In: Conference on Robot Learning (CoRL) (2020)
2. Caesar, H., et al.: nuScenes: a multimodal dataset for autonomous driving. In: Proceedings of the IEEE/CVF Conference on Computer Vision and Pattern Recognition, pp. 11621–11631 (2020)
3. Chen, Q., Sun, L., Cheung, E., Yuille, A.L.: Every view counts: cross-view consistency in 3D object detection with hybrid-cylindrical-spherical voxelization. In: Advances in Neural Information Processing Systems, vol. 33, pp. 21224–21235 (2020)
4. Chen, Q., Sun, L., Wang, Z., Jia, K., Yuille, A.: Object as hotspots: an anchor-free 3D object detection approach via firing of hotspots. In: Vedaldi, A., Bischof, H., Brox, T., Frahm, J.-M. (eds.) ECCV 2020. LNCS, vol. 12366, pp. 68–84. Springer, Cham (2020). https://doi.org/10.1007/978-3-030-58589-1_5
5. Chen, Q., Vora, S., Beijbom, O.: PolarStream: streaming lidar object detection and segmentation with polar pillars. arXiv preprint arXiv:2106.07545 (2021)
6. Chen, X., Ma, H., Wan, J., Li, B., Xia, T.: Multi-view 3D object detection network for autonomous driving. In: Proceedings of the IEEE conference on Computer Vision and Pattern Recognition, pp. 1907–1915 (2017)
7. Deng, J., Shi, S., Li, P., Zhou, W., Zhang, Y., Li, H.: Voxel R-CNN: towards high performance voxel-based 3D object detection. In: Proceedings of the AAAI Conference on Artificial Intelligence (2021)
8. Fan, L., Xiong, X., Wang, F., Wang, N., Zhang, Z.: RangeDet: in defense of range view for lidar-based 3D object detection. In: Proceedings of the IEEE/CVF International Conference on Computer Vision, pp. 2918–2927 (2021)
9. Graham, B., Engelcke, M., Van Der Maaten, L.: 3D semantic segmentation with submanifold sparse convolutional networks. In: Proceedings of the IEEE Conference on Computer Vision and Pattern Recognition, pp. 9224–9232 (2018)

10. Graham, B., van der Maaten, L.: Submanifold sparse convolutional networks. arXiv preprint arXiv:1706.01307 (2017)
11. He, C., Zeng, H., Huang, J., Hua, X.S., Zhang, L.: Structure aware single-stage 3D object detection from point cloud. In: Proceedings of the IEEE/CVF Conference on Computer Vision and Pattern Recognition, pp. 11873–11882 (2020)
12. He, K., Zhang, X., Ren, S., Sun, J.: Deep residual learning for image recognition. In: Proceedings of the IEEE Conference on Computer Vision and Pattern Recognition, pp. 770–778 (2016)
13. Hu, P., Ziglar, J., Held, D., Ramanan, D.: What you see is what you get: exploiting visibility for 3D object detection. In: Proceedings of the IEEE/CVF Conference on Computer Vision and Pattern Recognition, pp. 11001–11009 (2020)
14. Hu, Y., et al.: Afdetv2: rethinking the necessity of the second stage for object detection from point clouds (2021)
15. Ku, J., Mozifian, M., Lee, J., Harakeh, A., Waslander, S.L.: Joint 3D proposal generation and object detection from view aggregation. In: 2018 IEEE/RSJ International Conference on Intelligent Robots and Systems (IROS), pp. 1–8. IEEE (2018)
16. Lang, A.H., Vora, S., Caesar, H., Zhou, L., Yang, J., Beijbom, O.: Pointpillars: fast encoders for object detection from point clouds. In: Proceedings of the IEEE/CVF Conference on Computer Vision and Pattern Recognition, pp. 12697–12705 (2019)
17. Li, Z., Wang, F., Wang, N.: Lidar R-CNN: an efficient and universal 3D object detector. In: Proceedings of the IEEE/CVF Conference on Computer Vision and Pattern Recognition, pp. 7546–7555 (2021)
18. Liang, M., Yang, B., Chen, Y., Hu, R., Urtasun, R.: Multi-task multi-sensor fusion for 3D object detection. In: Proceedings of the IEEE/CVF Conference on Computer Vision and Pattern Recognition, pp. 7345–7353 (2019)
19. Liang, M., Yang, B., Wang, S., Urtasun, R.: Deep continuous fusion for multi-sensor 3D object detection. In: Proceedings of the European conference on computer vision (ECCV), pp. 641–656 (2018)
20. Liang, Z., Zhang, Z., Zhang, M., Zhao, X., Pu, S.: RangeIoUDet: range image based real-time 3D object detector optimized by intersection over union. In: Proceedings of the IEEE/CVF Conference on Computer Vision and Pattern Recognition, pp. 7140–7149 (2021)
21. Lin, T.Y., Dollár, P., Girshick, R., He, K., Hariharan, B., Belongie, S.: Feature pyramid networks for object detection. In: Proceedings of the IEEE Conference on Computer Vision and Pattern Recognition, pp. 2117–2125 (2017)
22. Lin, T.Y., Goyal, P., Girshick, R., He, K., Dollár, P.: Focal loss for dense object detection. In: Proceedings of the IEEE International Conference on Computer Vision, pp. 2980–2988 (2017)
23. Liu, W., et al.: SSD: single shot multibox detector. In: Leibe, B., Matas, J., Sebe, N., Welling, M. (eds.) ECCV 2016. LNCS, vol. 9905, pp. 21–37. Springer, Cham (2016). https://doi.org/10.1007/978-3-319-46448-0_2
24. Liu, Z., Zhao, X., Huang, T., Hu, R., Zhou, Y., Bai, X.: TANet: robust 3D object detection from point clouds with triple attention. In: Proceedings of the AAAI Conference on Artificial Intelligence, vol. 34, pp. 11677–11684 (2020)
25. Liu, Z., Tang, H., Lin, Y., Han, S.: Point-voxel CNN for efficient 3D deep learning. In: Advances in Neural Information Processing Systems, vol. 32 (2019)
26. Mao, J., Niu, M., Bai, H., Liang, X., Xu, H., Xu, C.: Pyramid R-CNN: towards better performance and adaptability for 3D object detection. In: Proceedings of the IEEE/CVF International Conference on Computer Vision, pp. 2723–2732 (2021)

27. Noh, J., Lee, S., Ham, B.: HVPR: hybrid voxel-point representation for single-stage 3D object detection. In: Proceedings of the IEEE/CVF Conference on Computer Vision and Pattern Recognition, pp. 14605–14614 (2021)
28. Qi, C.R., Su, H., Mo, K., Guibas, L.J.: PointNet: deep learning on point sets for 3D classification and segmentation. In: Proceedings of the IEEE Conference on Computer Vision and Pattern Recognition, pp. 652–660 (2017)
29. Qi, C.R., et al.: Offboard 3D object detection from point cloud sequences. In: Proceedings of the IEEE/CVF Conference on Computer Vision and Pattern Recognition, pp. 6134–6144 (2021)
30. Qi, C.R., Yi, L., Su, H., Guibas, L.J.: Pointnet++: deep hierarchical feature learning on point sets in a metric space. In: Advances in Neural Information Processing Systems, vol. 30 (2017)
31. Rezatofighi, H., Tsoi, N., Gwak, J., Sadeghian, A., Reid, I., Savarese, S.: Generalized intersection over union: a metric and a loss for bounding box regression. In: Proceedings of the IEEE/CVF Conference on Computer Vision and Pattern Recognition, pp. 658–666 (2019)
32. Shi, S., et al.: PV-RCNN: point-voxel feature set abstraction for 3D object detection. In: Proceedings of the IEEE/CVF Conference on Computer Vision and Pattern Recognition, pp. 10529–10538 (2020)
33. Shi, S., Wang, X., Li, H.: PointRCNN: 3d object proposal generation and detection from point cloud. In: Proceedings of the IEEE/CVF Conference on Computer Vision and Pattern Recognition, pp. 770–779 (2019)
34. Shi, S., Wang, Z., Shi, J., Wang, X., Li, H.: From points to parts: 3D object detection from point cloud with part-aware and part-aggregation network. IEEE Trans. Pattern Anal. Mach. Intell. **43**(8), 2647–2664 (2020)
35. Simonyan, K., Zisserman, A.: Two-stream convolutional networks for action recognition in videos. In: Advances in Neural Information Processing Systems, vol. 27 (2014)
36. Simonyan, K., Zisserman, A.: Very deep convolutional networks for large-scale image recognition. arXiv preprint arXiv:1409.1556 (2014)
37. Sun, P., et al.: Scalability in perception for autonomous driving: waymo open dataset. In: Proceedings of the IEEE/CVF Conference on Computer Vision and Pattern Recognition, pp. 2446–2454 (2020)
38. Sun, P., et al.: RSN: range sparse net for efficient, accurate lidar 3D object detection. In: Proceedings of the IEEE/CVF Conference on Computer Vision and Pattern Recognition, pp. 5725–5734 (2021)
39. Wang, B., An, J., Cao, J.: Voxel-FPN: multi-scale voxel feature aggregation in 3d object detection from point clouds. arXiv preprint arXiv:1907.05286 (2019)
40. Yan, Y., Mao, Y., Li, B.: Second: sparsely embedded convolutional detection. Sensors **18**(10), 3337 (2018)
41. Yang, Z., Sun, Y., Liu, S., Jia, J.: 3DSSD: point-based 3D single stage object detector. In: Proceedings of the IEEE/CVF Conference on Computer Vision and Pattern Recognition, pp. 11040–11048 (2020)
42. Yang, Z., Sun, Y., Liu, S., Shen, X., Jia, J.: STD: sparse-to-dense 3D object detector for point cloud. In: Proceedings of the IEEE/CVF International Conference on Computer Vision, pp. 1951–1960 (2019)
43. Yang, Z., Zhou, Y., Chen, Z., Ngiam, J.: 3D-man: 3D multi-frame attention network for object detection. In: Proceedings of the IEEE/CVF Conference on Computer Vision and Pattern Recognition, pp. 1863–1872 (2021)

44. Ye, M., Xu, S., Cao, T.: HVNet: hybrid voxel network for lidar based 3D object detection. In: Proceedings of the IEEE/CVF Conference on Computer Vision and Pattern Recognition, pp. 1631–1640 (2020)
45. Yin, J., Shen, J., Guan, C., Zhou, D., Yang, R.: Lidar-based online 3D video object detection with graph-based message passing and spatiotemporal transformer attention. In: Proceedings of the IEEE/CVF Conference on Computer Vision and Pattern Recognition, pp. 11495–11504 (2020)
46. Yin, T., Zhou, X., Krahenbuhl, P.: Center-based 3D object detection and tracking. In: Proceedings of the IEEE/CVF Conference on Computer Vision and Pattern Recognition, pp. 11784–11793 (2021)
47. Yoo, J.H., Kim, Y., Kim, J., Choi, J.W.: 3D-CVF: generating joint camera and lidar features using cross-view spatial feature fusion for 3D object detection. In: Vedaldi, A., Bischof, H., Brox, T., Frahm, J.-M. (eds.) ECCV 2020. LNCS, vol. 12372, pp. 720–736. Springer, Cham (2020). https://doi.org/10.1007/978-3-030-58583-9_43
48. Zheng, W., Tang, W., Chen, S., Jiang, L., Fu, C.W.: CIA-SSD: confident IoU-aware single-stage object detector from point cloud. In: AAAI (2021)
49. Zheng, W., Tang, W., Jiang, L., Fu, C.W.: SE-SSD: self-ensembling single-stage object detector from point cloud. In: Proceedings of the IEEE/CVF Conference on Computer Vision and Pattern Recognition, pp. 14494–14503 (2021)
50. Zheng, Z., Wang, P., Liu, W., Li, J., Ye, R., Ren, D.: Distance-IoU loss: faster and better learning for bounding box regression. In: Proceedings of the AAAI Conference on Artificial Intelligence, vol. 34, pp. 12993–13000 (2020)
51. Zhou, Y., Tuzel, O.: Voxelnet: end-to-end learning for point cloud based 3D object detection. In: Proceedings of the IEEE Conference on Computer Vision and Pattern Recognition, pp. 4490–4499 (2018)
52. Zhu, B., Jiang, Z., Zhou, X., Li, Z., Yu, G.: Class-balanced grouping and sampling for point cloud 3d object detection. arXiv preprint arXiv:1908.09492 (2019)
53. Zhu, X., et al.: Cylindrical and asymmetrical 3D convolution networks for lidar-based perception. IEEE Trans. Pattern Anal. Mach. Intell. **44**, 6807–6822 (2021)

Robust Object Detection with Inaccurate Bounding Boxes

Chengxin Liu[1], Kewei Wang[1], Hao Lu[1], Zhiguo Cao[1(✉)], and Ziming Zhang[2]

[1] School of Artificial Intelligence and Automation, Huazhong University of Science
and Technology, Wuhan, China
{cx_liu,zgcao}@hust.edu.cn
[2] Worcester Polytechnic Institute, Worcester, USA

Abstract. Learning accurate object detectors often requires large-scale
training data with precise object bounding boxes. However, labeling such
data is expensive and time-consuming. As the crowd-sourcing labeling
process and the ambiguities of the objects may raise noisy bounding box
annotations, the object detectors will suffer from the degenerated training data. In this work, we aim to address the challenge of learning robust
object detectors with inaccurate bounding boxes. Inspired by the fact
that localization precision suffers significantly from inaccurate bounding
boxes while classification accuracy is less affected, we propose leveraging classification as a guidance signal for refining localization results.
Specifically, by treating an object as a bag of instances, we introduce an
Object-Aware Multiple Instance Learning approach (OA-MIL), featured
with object-aware instance selection and object-aware instance extension. The former aims to select accurate instances for training, instead
of directly using inaccurate box annotations. The latter focuses on generating high-quality instances for selection. Extensive experiments on
synthetic noisy datasets (*i.e.*, noisy PASCAL VOC and MS-COCO) and
a real noisy wheat head dataset demonstrate the effectiveness of our
OA-MIL. Code is available at https://github.com/cxliu0/OA-MIL.

Keywords: Object detection · Inaccurate bounding boxes · Noisy
labels · Multiple instance learning

1 Introduction

Despite remarkable progress has been witnessed in the field of object detection
in recent years, the success of modern object detectors largely relies on large-
scale datasets like ImageNet [10] and MS-COCO [28]. However, acquiring precise
annotations is no easy task in professional and natural contexts. In practical
applications with professional backgrounds (*e.g.*, agricultural crop observation

Supplementary Information The online version contains supplementary material
available at https://doi.org/10.1007/978-3-031-20080-9_4.

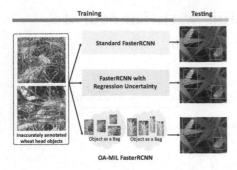

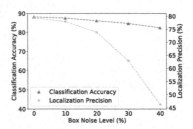

Fig. 1. Illustration of standard Faster-RCNN [34], FasterRCNN with regression uncertainty [20], and our OA-MIL FasterRCNN on the ECCV wheat head detection challenge dataset. Given inaccurately annotated objects, we aim to learn a robust object detector by treating each object as a bag of instances. The inaccurate ground-truth boxes are in red and the predictions are in green. (Color figure online)

Fig. 2. Classification accuracy and localization precision of FasterRCNN on the simulated "noisy" PASCAL VOC 2007 dataset [14], where box annotations are randomly perturbed. With the box noise level increases, *i.e.*, ground-truth box becomes more and more inaccurate, localization precision drops significantly while the classification still maintains high accuracy.

and medical image processing), domain knowledge is often required to annotate objects. This situation leads to a dilemma, *i.e.*, practitioners without computer vision background are not sure how to annotate high-quality boxes, while annotators without domain knowledge can also be difficult to annotate accurate object boxes. For example, recent wheat head detection challenge[1] that was hosted at the European Conference on Computer Vision (ECCV) workshop 2020 has shown that precise object bounding boxes are not easy to obtain, because in some domains the definition of the object is significantly different from generic objects in COCO, thus brings annotation ambiguities (Fig. 1). In these cases, there will be a demand calling for algorithms dealing with noisy bounding boxes. On the other hand, annotating a large amount of common objects in the natural context is expensive and time-consuming. To reduce the annotation cost [47], dataset producers may rely on social media platforms or crowd-sourcing platforms. Nevertheless, the above strategies would lead to low-quality annotations. Recent work [47] argues that the object detectors will suffer from the degenerated data. In addition, even large-scale datasets (*e.g.*, MS-COCO) are dedicated annotated, box ambiguities [20] still exist. Therefore, tackling noisy bounding boxes is a practical and meaningful task.

Recently, learning object detectors with noisy data have gained a surge of interest, several approaches [1,5,25,47] have made attempted to tackle noisy annotations. These approaches often assume that the noise occurs both on cat-

---

[1] https://www.kaggle.com/c/global-wheat-detection.

egory labels and bounding box annotations, and devise a disentangled architecture to learn object detectors. Different from previous work, we focus on object detection with noisy bounding box annotations. The reasons are two-fold: i) due to the ambiguities of the objects [20] and the crowd-sourcing labeling process, box noise commonly exists in the real world; ii) object detection datasets [23] often involve object class verification, thus we consider noisy category labels are less severe than inaccurate bounding boxes.

Motivated by the observation that localization precision suffers significantly from inaccurate bounding boxes while classification accuracy is less affected (Fig. 2), we propose leveraging classification as a guidance signal for localization. Specifically, we present an Object-Aware Multiple Instance Learning approach by treating each object as a bag of instances, where the concept of the object bag is illustrated in Fig. 1. The idea is to select accurate instances from the object bags for training, instead of using inaccurate box annotations. Our approach is featured with object-aware instance selection and object-aware instance extension. The former is designed to select accurate instances and the latter to generate high-quality instances for selection. The optimization process involves jointly training the instance selector, the instance classifier, and the instance generator. To validate the effectiveness of our approach, we experiment on both synthetic noisy datasets (*i.e.*, noisy PASCAL VOC 2007 [14] and MS-COCO [28]) and real noisy wheat head dataset [8,9]. The main contributions are as follows:

- We contribute a novel view for learning object detectors with inaccurate bounding boxes by treating an object as a bag of instances;
- We present an Object-Aware Multiple Instance Learning approach, featured by object-aware instance selection and object-aware instance extension;
- OA-MIL exhibits generality on off-the-shelf object detectors and obtains promising results on the synthetic and the real noisy datasets.

2   Related Work

Learning With Noisy Labels. Training accurate DNNs under noisy labels has been an active research area. A major line of research focuses on the classification task, and develops various techniques to deal with noisy labels, such as sample selection [18,21], label correction [32,37], and robust loss functions [16,50]. Recently, much effort [1,5,25,33,47] has been devoted to the object detection task. Simon *et al.* [5] first investigate the impact of different types of label noise on object detection, and propose a per-object co-teaching method to alleviate the effect of noisy labels. On the other hand, Li *et al.* [25] propose a learning framework that alternately performs noise correction and model training to tackle noisy annotations, where the noisy annotations consist of noisy category labels and noisy bounding boxes. Xu *et al.* [47] further introduce a meta-learning based approach to tackle noisy labels by leveraging a few clean samples.

In contrast to previous works, we emphasize learning object detectors with inaccurate bounding boxes and contribute a novel Object-Aware MIL view to addressing this problem. In addition, we do not assume the accessibility to clean box annotations as previous work [47] does.

Weakly-Supervised Object Detection (WSOD). WSOD refers to learning object detectors with only image-level labels. The majority of previous works formulate WSOD as a multiple instance learning (MIL) problem [13], where each image is considered as a "bag" of instances (instances are tentative object proposals) with image-level label. Under this formulation, the learning process alternates between detector training and object location estimation. Since MIL leads to a non-convex optimization problem, solvers may get stuck in local optima. Accordingly, much effort [2,7,11,35,36,38] has been made to help the solution escape from local optima. Recently, deep MIL methods [3] emerge. However, the non-convexity problem remains. To address this problem, various techniques have been developed, including spatial regularization [3,12,44], context information [22,46], and optimization strategy [12,24,39,44,45]. For example, Zhang *et al.* [48] tackle noisy initialized object locations in WSOD and propose a self-directed localization network to identify noisy object instances.

In this work, we tackle learning object detectors with noisy box annotations, which is different from WSOD where only image-level labels are given. Despite we also formulate object detection as a MIL problem, we remark that our formulation is significantly different from WSOD in two aspects: i) we establish the concept of the bag on the object instead of on the image, which encodes object-level information; ii) we dynamically construct the object bag instead of using a fixed one as in WSOD, yielding a higher performance upper bound.

Semi-Supervised Object Detection (SSOD). SSOD aims to train object detectors with a large scale of image-level annotations and a few box-level annotations. Some prior works [40–42] address SSOD by knowledge transfer, where the information is transferred from source classes with bounding-box labels to target classes with only image-level labels. Other than the knowledge transfer paradigm, a recent work [15] adopts a training-mining framework and proposes a noise-tolerant ensemble RCNN to eliminate the harm of noisy labels.

However, previous SSOD methods generally assume the availability of clean bounding box annotations. In contrast, we only assume the accessibility to noisy bounding box annotations.

3   Object-Aware Multiple Instance Learning

In this work, we aim to learn a robust object detector with inaccurate bounding box annotations. Motivated by the observation that classification maintains high accuracy under noisy box annotations (Fig. 2), we suggest leveraging classification to guide localization. Intuitively, instead of using the inaccurate ground-truth boxes, we expect the classification branch to select more precise boxes for training. This idea derives the concept of object bag, where each object is formulated as a bag of instances for selection. Build upon the object bag, we present an Object-Aware Multiple Instance Learning approach that features object-aware instance selection and object-aware instance extension. In the following, we first introduce some preliminaries about MIL. Then, we present our Object-Aware Multiple Instance Learning formulation. Finally, we show how to deploy our method on modern object detectors like FasterRCNN [34] and RetinaNet [27].

3.1 Preliminaries

Given image-level labels, an MIL method [7,45] in WSOD treats each image as a bag of instances, where instances are tentative object proposals. The learning process alternates between instance selection and instance classifier learning.

Formally, let $B_i \in \mathcal{B}$ denote the ith bag (image) and $\mathcal{B}$ denote the bag set (all training images). Each B_i is associated with a label $y_i \in \{1, -1\}$, where y_i indicates whether B_i contains positive instances. Also, let $\mathbf{b}_i^j$ denote the jth instance of bag B_i (i.e., $\mathbf{b}_i^j$ encodes the coordinates of an instance), where $j \in \{1, 2, \ldots, N_i\}$ and N_i is the number of instances in B_i. With the definitions above, the instance selector $f(\mathbf{b}_i^j, \omega_f)$ with parameter ω_f is applied to a positive bag B_i to select the most positive instance $\mathbf{b}_i^{j^*}$, the index j^* is obtained by:

$$j^* = \arg\max_j f(\mathbf{b}_i^j, \omega_f), \tag{1}$$

where the instance selector $f(\mathbf{b}_i^j, \omega_f)$ takes an instance $\mathbf{b}_i^j$ as input and outputs a confidence score that is in the range of $[-1, 1]$. Then, the selected instance $\mathbf{b}_i^{j^*}$ is used to train the instance classifier $g(\mathbf{b}_i^j, \omega_g)$ with parameter ω_g. The overall loss function is defined as:

$$L(\mathcal{B}, \omega_f, \omega_g) = \sum_i L_f(B_i, \omega_f) + L_g(B_i, \mathbf{b}_i^{j^*}, \omega_g), \tag{2}$$

where L_f and L_g are the loss of instance selector and instance classifier, respectively. Typically, L_f is defined as a standard hinge loss:

$$L_f(B_i, \omega_f) = \max(0, 1 - y_i \max_j f(\mathbf{b}_i^j, \omega_f)). \tag{3}$$

And the instance classifier loss L_g is defined as log-loss for classification.

3.2 Object-Aware MIL Formulation

Despite we formulate object detection as a MIL problem, we argue that the existing MIL paradigm in WSOD could not address the learning problem under noisy box annotations. First, since an image is defined as a bag in WSOD, the localization prior of objects is ignored. Second, the bags in WSOD are simply a collection of object proposals produced by off-the-shelf object proposal generators like selective search [43], which limits the detection performance.

Different from WSOD, in the context of our object bag, two challenges need to be solved: i) *how to select accurate instance in each object bag for training*; and ii) *how to generate high-quality instances for each object bag*.

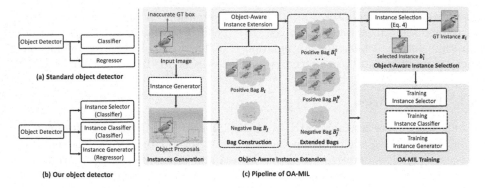

Fig. 3. An overview of our OA-MIL formulation. We augment the standard object detector (a) with an instance selector, forming our object detector (b). (c) illustrates the pipeline of OA-MIL. We first construct object bags based on the outputs of the instance generator (green and blue boxes), where the inaccurate ground-truth box (red box) is formulated as a positive bag B_i and the background box (blue box) is treated as a negative bag B_j. Then, object-aware instance extension is applied to obtain an extended bag set $\{B_i^0, B_i^1, \ldots, B_i^N, B_j\}$. Based on this bag set and the noisy ground-truth instance z_i, we adopt object-aware instance selection to select the best positive instance $\mathbf{b}_i^*$ for training object detector (including instance selector, instance classifier, and instance generator). (Color figure online)

To address the above challenges, we introduce an Object-Aware MIL formulation, which jointly optimizes the instance selector, the instance classifier, and the instance generator. In the following, we first give the definition of object bag. Then, we introduce object-aware instance selection and object-aware instance extension, where the former is designed to select the accurate instance, while the latter aims to produce a set of high-quality instances for selection. Finally, we describe how to train the instance selector, the instance classifier, and the instance generator. Figure 3 illustrates the pipeline of our OA-MIL formulation.

Bag Definition. We reuse the bag symbol in Sect. 3.1. But the definition of bag is different, *i.e.*, we treat each object as a bag. We denote $B_i \in \mathcal{B}$ as the ith bag (object), and $\mathcal{B}$ denotes the bag set (all objects in training images). A label $y_i \in \{1, -1\}$ is attached to each bag B_i. As illustrated in Fig. 3, we treat inaccurate ground-truth box as a positive bag B_i with $y_i = 1$, and the background box is treated as a negative bag B_j with $y_j = -1$. Suppose bag B_i contains N_i instances, we denote $\mathbf{b}_i^j$ as the jth instance of bag B_i, where $j \in \{1, \ldots, N_i\}$. With object bag defined above, we naturally introduce Eq. (3) to train the instance selector.

Object-Aware Instance Selection. Since we treat each inaccurate ground-truth box as a bag of instances, the quality of the selected instance is essential for training an accurate object detector. Intuitively, we expect the selected instance covers the actual object as tight as possible. However, as the instance selector has poor discriminative ability in the early stage of training, the instance classifier and instance generator will inevitably suffer from the low-quality positive instance. In some cases, poor instance initialization could render failure during training. As the inaccurate ground-truth box provides a strong prior of object localization, we jointly consider it and the selected instance to obtain a more suitable positive instance for training.

Specifically, we denote $\mathbf{z}_i$ as the inaccurate ground-truth instance. We perform object-aware instance selection by merging $\mathbf{z}_i$ and $\mathbf{b}_i^{j^*}$ as follows:

$$\mathbf{b}_i^* = \varphi(f(\mathbf{b}_i^{j^*}, \omega_f)) \cdot \mathbf{b}_i^{j^*} + (1 - \varphi(f(\mathbf{b}_i^{j^*}, \omega_f))) \cdot \mathbf{z}_i, \qquad (4)$$

where $\mathbf{b}_i^{j^*}$ is the most positive instance selected by the instance selector, and φ is a mapping function, which adaptively assigns the coefficient for $\mathbf{b}_i^{j^*}$ and $\mathbf{z}_i$.

Recall that our goal is to select high-quality positive instances for training, thus we expect $\varphi(\cdot)$ to satisfy two conditions. First, higher weights should be assigned to $\mathbf{b}_i^{j^*}$ when $f(\mathbf{b}_i^{j^*}, \omega_f)$ has large value, because it indicates the confidence of the positive instance $\mathbf{b}_i^{j^*}$. Second, $\varphi(\cdot)$ should balance the weights of $\mathbf{b}_i^{j^*}$ and $\mathbf{z}^i$ instead of relying on $\mathbf{b}_i^{j^*}$ when $f(\mathbf{b}_i^{j^*}, \omega_f)$ is close to 1. To satisfy the above conditions, we adopt a bounded exponential function as follows:

$$\varphi(x) = \min(x^\gamma, \theta), \qquad (5)$$

where γ and θ are hyper-parameters, and $x \in [0, 1]$. A key property of Eq. (5) is that the ascent speed and the upper bound of φ are controllable.

Object-Aware Instance Extension. The quality of instances is another factor that affects the training process. In our formulation, the bags are dynamically constructed based on the outputs of the instance generator. Thus, the quality of bag instances can not always be guaranteed. Fortunately, the instances inside a positive bag are homogeneous, *i.e.*, instances are closely related to each other both on spatial location and class information. Therefore, it is possible to promote the quality of a positive bag by extending the positive instances.

We present two strategies for instance extension. The first strategy is to obtain new positive instances by recursively constructing positive bags. Specifically, we first obtain the initial object bag based on the noisy ground-truth boxes, then we use the most positive instance selected by Eq. (4) to construct a new positive bag. The process repeats until reaching the termination condition. This strategy is generic and applicable to any existing object detectors. The second strategy is to refine the positive instances in a multi-stage manner [4], which is suitable for object detectors that feature with a bounding box refinement module (*e.g.*, FasterRCNN [34]). The extended object bags are subsequently used to train the instance selector. Note that we do not extend negative bags.

Suppose we have conducted N times of instance extension, which produces a set of extended positive bags $\{B_i^0, B_i^1, \ldots, B_i^N\}$, where B_i^0 denotes the initial object bag B_i (As shown in Fig. 3). We utilize the extended object bags to optimize the instance selector, the loss thus becomes:

$$L_f(\{B_i^k\}, \omega_f) = \sum_k L_f(B_i^k, \omega_f), \qquad (6)$$

where $k \in \{0, 1, \ldots, N\}$ only if B_i is a positive bag.

OA-MIL Training. Our OA-MIL involves jointly optimizing the instance selector, instance classifier, and the instance generator. The instance selector is trained using Eq. (6). As the instance classifier g (with parameter ω_g) is used to classify object, we adopt the binary-log-loss to train it:

$$L_g(B_i, \mathbf{b}_i^*, \omega_g) = -\sum_j \log(y_{i,j} \cdot (g(\mathbf{b}_i^j, \omega_g) - \frac{1}{2}) + \frac{1}{2}), \tag{7}$$

where $g(\mathbf{b}_i^j, \omega_g) \in (0, 1)$, which represents the probability of $\mathbf{b}_i^j$ contains objects with positive class. $y_{i,j}$ is defined as:

$$y_{i,j} = \begin{cases} +1, \text{ if } y_i = 1 \text{ and } \mathrm{IoU}(\mathbf{b}_i^j, \mathbf{b}_i^*) \geq 0.5 \\ -1, \text{ if } y_i = 1 \text{ and } \mathrm{IoU}(\mathbf{b}_i^j, \mathbf{b}_i^*) < 0.5 \\ -1, \text{ if } y_i = -1 \end{cases}, \tag{8}$$

where IoU denotes the Intersection over Union between two instances. Note that the loss of each instance becomes $\log(g(\mathbf{b}_i^j, \omega_g))$ when $y_{i,j} = 1$, and $\log(1 - g(\mathbf{b}_i^j, \omega_g))$ otherwise.

One major difference between our MIL and WSOD MIL is that we jointly train a learnable instance generator, which is crucial for dealing with inaccurate bounding boxes. The loss function of the instance generator is as follows:

$$L_\phi(\mathcal{B}, \omega_\phi) = \sum_i \mathbb{1}(B_i) \cdot L_{reg}(B_i, \mathbf{b}_i^*, \omega_\phi), \tag{9}$$

where ω_ϕ is the parameters of instance generator, $\mathbb{1}(B_i)$ equals 1 if B_i is a positive bag, otherwise $\mathbb{1}(B_i)$ is 0 because a negative bag does not correspond to any actual objects, and L_{reg} is defined as:

$$L_{reg}(B_i, \mathbf{b}_i^*, \omega_\phi) = \sum_j \delta(y_{i,j}) \cdot \ell_{reg}(\mathbf{b}_i^j, \mathbf{b}_i^*), \tag{10}$$

where $\delta(\cdot)$ is the unit-impulse function ($\delta(y_{i,j})$ equals to 1 when $y_{i,j}$ is 1, otherwise 0), and ℓ_{reg} is a regression loss like ℓ_1 loss or smooth ℓ_1 loss [34].

To summarize, the overall loss function is formulated as:

$$L(\mathcal{B}, \omega_f, \omega_g, \omega_\phi) = \lambda \sum_i \sum_k L_f(B_i^k, \omega_f) + \sum_i L_g(B_i^0, \mathbf{b}_i^*, \omega_g)$$
$$+ \sum_i \mathbb{1}(B_i^0) \cdot L_{reg}(B_i^0, \mathbf{b}_i^*, \omega_\phi), \tag{11}$$

where λ is a balance parameter, $\mathcal{B}$ is the extended object bags set, B_i^0 is the initial object bag, and $\mathbf{b}_i^*$ is selected by Eq. (4).

3.3   Deployment to Off-the-Shelf Object Detectors

We remark that our formulation is general and is not limited to specific object detectors. To demonstrate the generality of our method, we apply our method on a two-stage detector—FasterRCNN [34] and a one-stage detector—RetinaNet [27]. Here we introduce the deployment procedure on FasterRCNN.

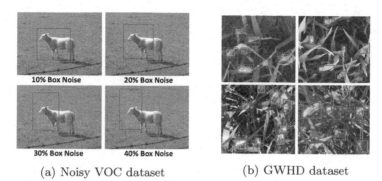

(a) Noisy VOC dataset   (b) GWHD dataset

Fig. 4. Examples of the inaccurate bounding boxes (red boxes) on VOC and GWHD dataset. The clean ground-truth boxes are in green. (Color figure online)

It includes two steps, the first step is to construct object bags and the second step is to apply OA-MIL on FasterRCNN. More details can be found in the supplementary.

Bag Construction. We construct object bags based on the outputs of the second stage of FasterRCNN. Specifically, we treat each inaccurately annotated object as a positive bag, where instances are positive anchors (object proposals) corresponding to a specific object.

OA-MIL Deployment. The instance selector and the instance classifier share the same classifier. The regressor in the second stage is treated as the instance generator. We perform object-aware instance extension by multi-stage refinement, which produces a set of extended object bags $\{B_i^0, B_i^1, \ldots, B_i^N\}$. Then, object-aware instance selection is applied to select the best instance $\mathbf{b}_i^*$, where $\mathbf{b}_i^*$ is used to train the instance generator (regressor), the instance selector (classifier), and the object detector (classifier). We follow Eq. (11) to train the second stage of FasterRCNN. Note that the training objective of RPN is the same as [34].

Implementation Details. We implement our method on FasterRCNN [34] with ResNet50-FPN [19,26] backbone. Following common practices [17], the model is trained with "1×" schedule. The hyper parameters are set as $\gamma = 7.5$, $\theta = 0.85$, $N = 4$, and λ is selected from $\{0.01, 0.1\}$ (depending on datasets and noise levels). Our implementation is based on MMDetection toolbox [6].

4 Results and Discussions

4.1 Datasets and Evaluation Metrics

Synthetic Noisy Dataset. Modern object detection datasets are delicately annotated and contain few inaccurate bounding boxes. Thus, we simulate noisy bounding boxes by perturbing the clean ones on two object detection datasets, including PASCAL VOC 2007 [14] and MS-COCO [28].

Table 1. Performance comparison on the PASCAL VOC 2007 test set. The evaluation metric is mAP@0.5 (%). The best performance is in **boldface**.

Model	Method	Box noise level			
		10%	20%	30%	40%
FasterRCNN	Noisy-FasterRCNN	76.3	71.2	60.1	42.5
	KL loss [20]	75.8	72.7	64.6	48.6
	Co-teaching [18]	75.4	70.6	60.9	43.7
	SD-LocNet [48]	75.7	71.5	60.8	43.9
	Ours	**77.4**	**74.3**	**70.6**	**63.8**
RetinaNet	Noisy-RetinaNet	71.5	67.5	57.9	45.0
	FreeAnchor [49]	73.0	67.5	56.2	41.6
	Ours	**73.1**	**69.1**	**62.9**	**53.4**
Clean model	Clean-FasterRCNN	77.2	77.2	77.2	77.2
	Clean-RetinaNet	73.5	73.5	73.5	73.5

Box Noise Simulation. We simulate noisy bounding boxes by perturbing clean boxes. Specifically, let (cx, cy, w, h) denote the center x coordinate, center y coordinate, width, and height of an object. We simulate an inaccurate bounding box by randomly shifting and scaling the box as follows:

$$\begin{cases} \hat{cx} = cx + \Delta_x \cdot w, & \hat{cy} = cy + \Delta_y \cdot h, \\ \hat{w} = (1 + \Delta_w) \cdot w, & \hat{h} = (1 + \Delta_h) \cdot h, \end{cases} \tag{12}$$

where Δ_x, Δ_y, Δ_w, and Δ_h follow the uniform distribution $U(-r, r)$, r is the box noise level. We simulate various box noise levels ranging from 10% to 40%. For example, when $r = 40\%$, Δ_x, Δ_y, Δ_w, and Δ_h are in the range of $(-0.4, 0.4)$. Note that Eq. (12) is performed on **every bounding box** in the training data. Figure 4a shows examples of the synthetic inaccurate bounding boxes under different box noise level r's on the VOC dataset, where r ranges from 10% to 40%.

Real Noisy Dataset. We also evaluate our approach on the Global Wheat Head Detection (GWHD) dataset [8,9]. This dataset includes 3.6K training images, 1.4K validation images, and 1.3K test images. It has two versions of training data, the first "noisy" challenge version (see footnote 1) (inaccurate bounding box annotations) and the second "clean" version (calibrated clean annotations). Specifically, the "noisy" version contains around 20% noisy ground-truth boxes and the rest 80% boxes are the same as the "clean" version. We separately train on the "noisy" and "clean" training data to validate our approach. Figure 4b shows some examples of the real inaccurate bounding boxes and the calibrated clean boxes.

Evaluation Metric. For VOC and COCO, we use mean average precision (mAP@.5) and mAP@[.5,.95] as evaluation metrics. Regarding GWHD dataset,

Table 2. Performance comparison on the MS-COCO dataset.

Method	20% box noise level						40% box noise level					
	AP	AP^{50}	AP^{75}	AP^S	AP^M	AP^L	AP	AP^{50}	AP^{75}	AP^S	AP^M	AP^L
FasterRCNN												
Clean-FasterRCNN	37.9	58.1	40.9	21.6	41.6	48.7	37.9	58.1	40.9	21.6	41.6	48.7
Noisy-FasterRCNN	30.4	54.3	31.4	17.4	33.9	38.7	10.3	28.9	3.3	5.7	11.8	15.1
KL loss [20]	31.0	54.3	32.4	18.0	34.9	39.5	12.1	36.7	3.7	6.2	13.0	17.4
Co-teaching [18]	30.5	54.9	30.5	17.3	34.0	39.1	11.5	31.4	4.2	6.4	13.1	16.4
SD-LocNet [48]	30.0	54.5	30.3	17.5	33.6	38.7	11.3	30.3	4.3	6.0	12.7	16.6
Ours	**32.1**	**55.3**	**33.2**	**18.1**	**35.8**	**41.6**	**18.6**	**42.6**	**12.9**	**9.2**	**19.9**	**26.5**
RetinaNet												
Clean-RetinaNet	36.7	56.1	39.0	21.6	40.4	47.4	36.7	56.1	39.0	21.6	40.4	47.4
Noisy-RetinaNet	30.0	53.1	30.8	17.9	33.7	38.2	13.3	33.6	5.7	8.4	15.9	18.0
FreeAnchor [49]	28.6	53.1	28.5	16.6	32.2	37.0	10.4	28.9	3.3	5.8	12.1	14.9
Ours	**30.9**	**54.0**	**32.3**	**18.5**	**34.9**	**39.6**	**19.2**	**45.2**	**12.0**	**11.3**	**23.0**	**24.9**

we follow the GWHD Challenge 2021[2] to use Average Domain Accuracy (ADA) as the evaluation metric.

4.2 Comparison with State of the Art

We compare our method with several state-of-the-art approaches [18, 20, 48] on PASCAL VOC 2007 [14], MS-COCO [28], and GWHD [8, 9] datasets. Note that, we denote Clean-FasterRCNN and Noisy-FasterRCNN as FasterRCNN models trained under clean and noisy training data with the default setting, respectively. Similarly, Clean-RetinaNet and Noisy-RetinaNet denote RetinaNet models trained under clean and noisy training data, respectively.

Results on the VOC 2007 Dataset. Table 1 shows the comparison results on the VOC 2007 test set. For FasterRCNN, we observe that inaccurate bounding box annotations significantly deteriorate the detection performance of the vanilla model. On the contrary, our approach is more robust to noisy bounding boxes and outperforms other methods by a large margin under high box noise levels, *e.g.*, 30% and 40% box noise. In addition, Co-teaching and SD-LocNet only slightly improve the detection performance, which indicates that small-loss sample selection and sample weight assignment can not well tackle noisy box annotations. For RetinaNet, we compare our approach with the vanilla RetinaNet model and FreeAnchor [49]. As shown in Table 1, our approach still achieves consistent improvement over the vanilla model, which indicates that our approach is effective on both two-stage and one-stage detectors.

Results on the MS-COCO Dataset. The comparison results on the MS-COCO dataset are reported in Table 2. For FasterRCNN, our approach achieves considerable improvements over the vanilla model and performs favorably against

---

[2] https://www.aicrowd.com/challenges/global-wheat-challenge-2021.

Table 3. Comparison results on the GWHD validation and test set, where models are trained on "noisy" and "clean" training data, respectively. The evaluation metric is ADA. FRCNN denotes FasterRCNN.

Model	Method	Trained on "Noisy" GWHD		Trained on "Clean" GWHD	
		Val ADA	Test ADA	Val ADA	Test ADA
FRCNN	Vanilla FRCNN	0.608	0.509	0.632	0.511
	KL Loss [20]	0.607	0.496	0.631	0.507
	Co-teaching [18]	0.624	0.491	0.631	0.504
	SD-LocNet [48]	0.621	0.498	0.626	0.512
	Ours	**0.639**	**0.526**	**0.658**	**0.530**
RetinaNet	Vanilla RetinaNet	0.607	0.494	0.622	0.503
	FreeAnchor [49]	0.619	**0.517**	0.635	0.525
	Ours	**0.621**	0.516	**0.640**	**0.527**

state-of-the-art methods. For example, under 40% box noise, the vanilla model suffers from catastrophic performance drop, *e.g.*, AP^{50} drops from 58.1 to 28.9. On the other hand, our approach significantly boosts the detection performance across all metrics, achieving 8.3%, 13.7%, and 9.6% improvements on AP, AP^{50}, and AP^{75}, respectively. Co-teaching and SD-LocNet, however, still can not well address inaccurate bounding box annotations, but KL Loss slightly improves the performance under 20% and 40% box noise. In addition, we observe that objects with different sizes suffer similarly under different noise levels. For RetinaNet, our approach also obtains consistent improvements. For example, our approach improves the performance of the vanilla RetinaNet by 5.9%, 11.6%, and 6.3% on AP, AP^{50}, and AP^{75} under 40% box noise, respectively.

Results on the GWHD Dataset. Here we report the results on both noisy and clean training data.

Results on the "Noisy" GWHD Dataset. Table 3 shows the comparison results. Deploying our method on FasterRCNN boosts the Val ADA of the vanilla model from 0.608 to 0.639 and Test ADA from 0.509 to 0.526. Interestingly, our approach even performs better than the vanilla model that trained on clean training data (0.639 vs. 0.632 on Val ADA, 0.526 vs. 0.511 on Test ADA). In addition, Co-teaching and SD-LocNet improve the Val ADA but deteriorate the Test ADA, we infer that the large domain gap between validation and test data leads to the controversy. For RetinaNet, our approach obtains moderate improvements and performs favorably against FreeAnchor. Note that FreeAnchor performs well on "Noisy" GWHD because the clean ground-truth boxes dominate this dataset (around 80% boxes are clean), which is different from the synthetic VOC and COCO datasets where noisy ground-truth boxes are the majority.

Results on the "Clean" GWHD Dataset. Table 3 shows that our approach can further improve the detection performance when trained on clean data. The reason may be that our OA-MIL exploits the information between object instances,

Table 4. Ablation study on the VOC 2007 test set and COCO validation set. The evaluation metric is mAP@0.5 (%).

No.	Method	IS Loss	OA-IS	OA-IE	VOC 2007				COCO	
					10%	20%	30%	40%	20%	40%
B1	Vanilla FasterRCNN				76.3	71.2	60.1	42.5	54.3	28.9
B2	OA-MIL FasterRCNN	✓			77.1	73.3	66.9	56.0	54.6	32.6
B3		✓	✓		77.2	74.2	70.2	63.3	55.2	39.8
B4		✓	✓	✓	77.4	74.3	70.6	63.8	55.3	42.6

thus strengthening the discriminative capability of the detection model. Specifically, we advance the performance of the vanilla FasterRCNN by 2.6% and 1.7% on Val ADA and Test ADA, respectively. Regarding RetinaNet, our approach outperforms the vanilla model by 1.8% on Val ADA and 2.4% on Test ADA, respectively. In addition, our approach can also cooperate with the runner-up solution [29,30] of the GWHD2021 challenge (see footnote 2), which adopts the idea of dynamic network [31] to improve wheat head detection.

4.3 Ablation Study

Here we investigate the effectiveness of each component in our approach, including: (i) our object bag formulation, *i.e.*, training object detector with instance selection loss (IS Loss), where the loss is computed based on object bag; (ii) object-aware instance selection (OA-IS); (iii) object-aware instance extension (OA-IE). Table 4 shows the results. B1 is the performance of the vanilla Faster-RCNN trained under different box noise levels. From B2 to B4, we gradually add IS Loss, OA-IS, and OA-IE into training. In addition, the analysis of parameter sensitivity (*e.g.*, γ and θ in Eq. (5)) can be found in the supplementary.

Effectiveness of Object Bag Formulation. Interestingly, simply training under our object bag formulation significantly boosts the mAP performance of FasterRCNN on the VOC 2007 dataset across several box noise levels. For instance, our object bag formulation achieves 6.8% and 13.5% improvements under 30% and 40% box noise level, respectively. As for the COCO dataset, we still obtains moderate improvements. An intuitive explanation is that the instance selector is forced to select high-quality instances (*e.g.*, instance that covers the actual object more tightly) to minimize the loss function. As a consequence, the object detector benefits from the joint optimization process.

Effectiveness of OA-IS. Applying OA-IS further improves the detection performance on the VOC and COCO datasets, especially under high box noise levels. For example, under 40% box noise level, OA-IS boosts the performance from 56.0 to 63.3 on the VOC dataset and from 32.6 to 39.8 on the COCO dataset. To understand OA-IS more intuitively, we visualize the instances selected by OA-IS in Fig. 5. It is clear that the selected instances cover the objects more tightly than

Fig. 5. Examples of the selected instances (red boxes). Noisy ground-truth boxes are in yellow and the clean ground-truth boxes are in green. (Color figure online)

    (a) Qualitative results   (b) Failure cases

Fig. 6. (a) Qualitative results of OA-MIL FasterRCNN (red boxes) and vanilla Faster-RCNN (yellow boxes) on the COCO dataset. The ground-truth boxes are in green. (b) Failure cases, *e.g.*, missing detections on small/overlapped objects. (Color figure online)

the noisy ground-truth boxes. Although the selected instances are not perfect, they provide more precise supervision signals for training the instance classifier and the instance generator.

Effectiveness of OA-IE. OA-IE is designed to improve the quality of the bag instances. We observe that the impact of OA-IE is minor under low box noise levels. The reason is likely that the quality of bag instances is relatively high under low box noise situations. Nevertheless, OA-IE still brings improvement under high noise levels. For example, it improves the detection performance from 39.8 to 42.6 on the COCO dataset under 40% box noise.

Qualitative Results. Figure 6a illustrates the qualitative results of the COCO dataset. The vanilla FasterRCNN tends to predict bounding boxes that cover object parts or include background areas. Instead, our method can predict more accurate bounding boxes. In addition, some failure cases are shown in Fig. 6b. Our approach may suffer from overlapped objects or small objects.

5   Conclusion

In this work, we tackle learning robust object detectors with inaccurate bounding boxes. By treating an object as a bag of instances, we present an Object-Aware Multiple Instance Learning method featured with object-aware instance selection and object-aware instance extension. Our approach is general and can easily cooperate with modern object detectors. Extensive experiments on the synthetic noisy datasets and real noisy GWHD dataset demonstrate that OA-MIL can obtain promising results with inaccurate bounding box annotations.

For future work, we plan to incorporate the attributes of the objects to address the limitation of OA-MIL.

Acknowledgement. This work was supported by the National Natural Science Foundation of China under Grant No. 61876211, No. U1913602, and No. 62106080.

References

1. Bernhard, M., Schubert, M.: Correcting imprecise object locations for training object detectors in remote sensing applications. Remote Sens. **13**(24), 4962 (2021)
2. Bilen, H., Pedersoli, M., Tuytelaars, T.: Weakly supervised object detection with convex clustering. In: CVPR, pp. 1081–1089 (2015)
3. Bilen, H., Vedaldi, A.: Weakly supervised deep detection networks. In: CVPR, pp. 2846–2854 (2016)
4. Cai, Z., Vasconcelos, N.: Cascade R-CNN: delving into high quality object detection. In: CVPR, pp. 6154–6162 (2018)
5. Chadwick, S., Newman, P.: Training object detectors with noisy data. In: Proceedings of the IEEE Intelligent Vehicles Symposium (IV), pp. 1319–1325 (2019)
6. Chen, K., et al.: MMDetection: open MMLab detection toolbox and benchmark. arXiv (2019)
7. Cinbis, R.G., Verbeek, J., Schmid, C.: Multi-fold mil training for weakly supervised object localization. In: CVPR, pp. 2409–2416 (2014)
8. David, E., et al.: Global wheat head detection (GWHD) dataset: a large and diverse dataset of high-resolution RGB-labelled images to develop and benchmark wheat head detection methods. Plant Phenomics **2020** (2020)
9. David, E., et al.: Global wheat head detection 2021: an improved dataset for benchmarking wheat head detection methods. Plant Phenomics **2021** (2021)
10. Deng, J., Dong, W., Socher, R., Li, L., Li, K., Fei-Fei, L.: Imagenet: a large-scale hierarchical image database. In: CVPR, pp. 248–255 (2009)
11. Deselaers, T., Alexe, B., Ferrari, V.: Localizing objects while learning their appearance. In: Daniilidis, K., Maragos, P., Paragios, N. (eds.) ECCV 2010. LNCS, vol. 6314, pp. 452–466. Springer, Heidelberg (2010). https://doi.org/10.1007/978-3-642-15561-1_33
12. Diba, A., Sharma, V., Pazandeh, A., Pirsiavash, H., Van Gool, L.: Weakly supervised cascaded convolutional networks. In: CVPR, pp. 5131–5139 (2017)
13. Dietterich, T., Lathrop, R., Lozano-Pérez, T.: Solving the multiple instance problem with axis-parallel rectangles. Artif. Intell. **89**, 31–71 (1997)
14. Everingham, M., Van Gool, L., Williams, C.K.I., Winn, J., Zisserman, A.: The pascal visual object classes (VOC) challenge. IJCV **88**(2), 303–338 (2010)
15. Gao, J., Wang, J., Dai, S., Li, L., Nevatia, R.: Note-RCNN: noise tolerant ensemble RCNN for semi-supervised object detection. In: CVPR, pp. 9507–9516 (2019)
16. Ghosh, A., Kumar, H., Sastry, P.S.: Robust loss functions under label noise for deep neural networks. In: AAAI, pp. 1919–1925 (2017)
17. Girshick, R., Radosavovic, I., Gkioxari, G., Dollár, P., He, K.: Detectron (2018). https://github.com/facebookresearch/detectron
18. Han, B., et al.: Co-teaching: robust training of deep neural networks with extremely noisy labels. In: NeurIPS, pp. 8536–8546 (2018)
19. He, K., Zhang, X., Ren, S., Sun, J.: Deep residual learning for image recognition. In: CVPR, pp. 770–778 (2016)

20. He, Y., Zhu, C., Wang, J., Savvides, M., Zhang, X.: Bounding box regression with uncertainty for accurate object detection. In: CVPR, pp. 2883–2892 (2019)
21. Jiang, L., Zhou, Z., Leung, T., Li, L., Fei-Fei, L.: Mentornet: learning data-driven curriculum for very deep neural networks on corrupted labels. In: ICML, pp. 2309–2318 (2018)
22. Kantorov, V., Oquab, M., Cho, M., Laptev, I.: ContextLocNet: context-aware deep network models for weakly supervised localization. In: Leibe, B., Matas, J., Sebe, N., Welling, M. (eds.) ECCV 2016. LNCS, vol. 9909, pp. 350–365. Springer, Cham (2016). https://doi.org/10.1007/978-3-319-46454-1_22
23. Kuznetsova, A., et al.: The open images dataset V4. IJCV **128**(7), 1956–1981 (2020)
24. Li, D., Huang, J., Li, Y., Wang, S., Yang, M.: Weakly supervised object localization with progressive domain adaptation. In: CVPR, pp. 3512–3520 (2016)
25. Li, J., Xiong, C., Socher, R., Hoi, S.C.H.: Towards noise-resistant object detection with noisy annotations. arXiv abs/2003.01285 (2020)
26. Lin, T., Dollár, P., Girshick, R., He, K., Hariharan, B., Belongie, S.: Feature pyramid networks for object detection. In: CVPR, pp. 936–944 (2017)
27. Lin, T.Y., Goyal, P., Girshick, R., He, K., Dollár, P.: Focal loss for dense object detection. In: ICCV, pp. 2999–3007 (2017)
28. Lin, T.-Y., et al.: Microsoft COCO: common objects in context. In: Fleet, D., Pajdla, T., Schiele, B., Tuytelaars, T. (eds.) ECCV 2014. LNCS, vol. 8693, pp. 740–755. Springer, Cham (2014). https://doi.org/10.1007/978-3-319-10602-1_48
29. Liu, C., Wang, K., Lu, H., Cao, Z.: Dynamic color transform for wheat head detection. In: ICCVW, pp. 1278–1283 (2021)
30. Liu, C., Wang, K., Lu, H., Cao, Z.: Dynamic color transform networks for wheat head detection. Plant Phenomics **2022** (2022)
31. Lu, H., Dai, Y., Shen, C., Xu, S.: Index networks. IEEE TPAMI **44**(1), 242–255 (2022)
32. Ma, X., et al.: Dimensionality-driven learning with noisy labels. In: ICML, pp. 3355–3364 (2018)
33. Mao, J., Yu, Q., Aizawa, K.: Noisy localization annotation refinement for object detection. In: ICIP, pp. 2006–2010 (2020)
34. Ren, S., He, K., Girshick, R., Sun, J.: Faster R-CNN: towards real-time object detection with region proposal networks. IEEE TPAMI **39**(6), 1137–1149 (2017)
35. Siva, P., Xiang, T.: Weakly supervised object detector learning with model drift detection. In: ICCV, pp. 343–350 (2011)
36. Siva, P., Russell, C., Xiang, T.: In defence of negative mining for annotating weakly labelled data. In: Fitzgibbon, A., Lazebnik, S., Perona, P., Sato, Y., Schmid, C. (eds.) ECCV 2012. LNCS, vol. 7574, pp. 594–608. Springer, Heidelberg (2012). https://doi.org/10.1007/978-3-642-33712-3_43
37. Song, H., Kim, M., Lee, J.G.: SELFIE: refurbishing unclean samples for robust deep learning. In: ICML, pp. 5907–5915 (2019)
38. Song, H.O., Lee, Y.J., Jegelka, S., Darrell, T.: Weakly-supervised discovery of visual pattern configurations. In: NeurIPS, pp. 1637–1645 (2014)
39. Tang, P., Wang, X., Bai, X., Liu, W.: Multiple instance detection network with online instance classifier refinement. In: CVPR, pp. 3059–3067 (2017)
40. Tang, Y., Wang, J., Gao, B., Dellandréa, E., Gaizauskas, R., Chen, L.: Large scale semi-supervised object detection using visual and semantic knowledge transfer. In: CVPR, pp. 2119–2128 (2016)
41. Tang, Y., et al.: Visual and semantic knowledge transfer for large scale semi-supervised object detection. IEEE TPAMI **40**(12), 3045–3058 (2018)

42. Uijlings, J.R.R., Popov, S., Ferrari, V.: Revisiting knowledge transfer for training object class detectors. In: CVPR, pp. 1101–1110 (2018)
43. Uijlings, J.R.R., van de Sande, K.E.A., Gevers, T., Smeulders, A.W.M.: Selective search for object recognition. IJCV **104**(2), 154–171 (2013)
44. Wan, F., Wei, P., Jiao, J., Han, Z., Ye, Q.: Min-entropy latent model for weakly supervised object detection. In: CVPR, pp. 1297–1306 (2018)
45. Wan, F., Liu, C., Ke, W., Ji, X., Jiao, J., Ye, Q.: C-MIL: continuation multiple instance learning for weakly supervised object detection. In: CVPR, pp. 2199–2208 (2019)
46. Wei, Y., et al.: TS2C: tight box mining with surrounding segmentation context for weakly supervised object detection. In: ECCV, pp. 454–470 (2018)
47. Xu, Y., Zhu, L., Yang, Y., Wu, F.: Training robust object detectors from noisy category labels and imprecise bounding boxes. IEEE TIP **30**, 5782–5792 (2021)
48. Zhang, X., Yang, Y., Feng, J.: Learning to localize objects with noisy labeled instances. In: AAAI, pp. 9219–9226 (2019)
49. Zhang, X., Wan, F., Liu, C., Ji, R., Ye, Q.: Freeanchor: learning to match anchors for visual object detection. In: NeurIPS, pp. 147–155 (2019)
50. Zhang, Z., Sabuncu, M.R.: Generalized cross entropy loss for training deep neural networks with noisy labels. In: NeurIPS, pp. 8792–8802 (2018)

Efficient Decoder-Free Object Detection
with Transformers

Peixian Chen[1], Mengdan Zhang[1], Yunhang Shen[1], Kekai Sheng[1], Yuting Gao[1], Xing Sun[1], Ke Li[1(✉)], and Chunhua Shen[2]

[1] Tencent Youtu Lab, Shanghai, China
{peixianchen,davinazhang,saulsheng,yutinggao,tristanli}@tencent.com,
winfred.sun@gmail.com
[2] Zhejiang University, Hangzhou, China

Abstract. Vision transformers (ViTs) are changing the landscape of object detection approaches. A natural usage of ViTs in detection is to replace the CNN-based backbone with a transformer-based backbone, which is straightforward and effective, with the price of bringing considerable computation burden for inference. More subtle usage is the DETR family, which eliminates the need for many hand-designed components in object detection but introduces a decoder demanding an extra-long time to converge. As a result, transformer-based object detection can not prevail in large-scale applications. To overcome these issues, we propose a novel decoder-free fully transformer-based (DFFT) object detector, achieving high efficiency in both training and inference stages, for the first time. We simplify objection detection into an encoder-only single-level anchor-based dense prediction problem by centering around two entry points: 1) Eliminate the training-inefficient decoder and leverage two strong encoders to preserve the accuracy of single-level feature map prediction; 2) Explore low-level semantic features for the detection task with limited computational resources. In particular, we design a novel lightweight detection-oriented transformer backbone that efficiently captures low-level features with rich semantics based on a well-conceived ablation study. Extensive experiments on the MS COCO benchmark demonstrate that DFFT$_{SMALL}$ outperforms DETR by 2.5% AP with 28% computation cost reduction and more than 10× fewer training epochs. Compared with the cutting-edge anchor-based detector RetinaNet, DFFT$_{SMALL}$ obtains over 5.5% AP gain while cutting down 70% computation cost. The code is available at https://github.com/peixianchen/DFFT.

Keywords: Object detector · Transformers · Efficient network

1 Introduction

Object detection is a classic computer vision task aiming to locate and recognize objects in natural images. Recently, vision transformers [5,10,24,30] have

---

P. Chen and M. Zhang—Equal Contribution.

Supplementary Information The online version contains supplementary material available at https://doi.org/10.1007/978-3-031-20080-9_5.

S. Avidan et al. (Eds.): ECCV 2022, LNCS 13670, pp. 70–86, 2022.
https://doi.org/10.1007/978-3-031-20080-9_5

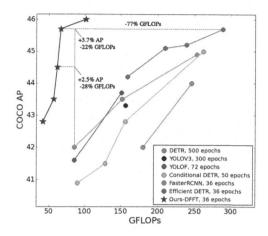

Fig. 1. The trade-off between performance (AP) and efficiency (Epochs & GFLOPs) for detection methods. With a lightweight detection-oriented backbone and a decoder-free single-level dense prediction module, DFFT$_{MEDIUM}$ gets 22% faster inference, more than 10× fewer training epochs and 3.7% higher AP than DETR, cuts down the 77% GFLOPs from Efficient DETR.

been widely developed as powerful backbones in traditional detection frameworks such as Faster RCNN [26], Mask RCNN [17], and RetinaNet [20]. However, these transformer-based detectors achieve high precision at the expense of computational efficiency (*e.g.*, at least 200 GFLOPs), which precludes their use in real-world applications with limited resources. DETR [2] is a pioneering work that addresses this issue by using an encoder-decoder transformer design that reduces object detection to an end-to-end set prediction problem. DETR's novel decoder helps object queries attend to diverse regions of interest on single-level representation, considerably boosting inference efficiency (ranging from 86 to 253 GFLOPs). Unfortunately, this enhancement comes at the expense of around 10 × to 20 × slower training convergence. As a result, it remains open whether transformer-based detectors can attain high precision without losing efficiency in training and inference stages.

Recent work in the DETR family has mainly focused on improving the delayed convergence induced by the decoder. They augment object queries in the decoder with explicit spatial priors such as reference points [36], anchor points [28,31], RPN proposals [26,34], and conditional spatial embeddings [13,25]. However, introducing spatial priors to the decoder stage sacrifices the detector's inference efficiency, consuming more than 1.5 × GFLOPs. It also raises the question whether the above efficient yet accurate transformer-based detector inevitably needs a decoder.

In this paper, we build a novel detection architecture named DFFT: **D**ecoder-**F**ree **F**ully **T**ransformer-based object detector, which achieves both higher accuracy and better training-inference efficiency across a spectrum of low resource constraints (*e.g.*, from 40 to 100 GFLOPs) as shown in Fig. 1. Based on a well-conceived analysis of how different transformer architectures (*e.g.*, attention components' type, position and linkage) involved in the backbone, feature fusion, and class/box network, impact the trade-off between detection performance and efficiency, DFFT simplifies the whole object detection pipeline to an encoder-only single-level anchor-based dense prediction task. Specifically, our design of DFFT centers around two entry points:

Entry Point 1: Eliminate the training-inefficient decoder and leverage two strong encoders to preserve the accuracy of single-level feature map prediction. To design a light-weight detection pipeline comparable to DETR and maintain high training efficiency, we eliminate the training-inefficient decoder and propose two strong transformer encoders in the feature fusion and class/box network to avoid performance decline after trimming the decoder. Benefiting from two strong encoders, DFFT conducts anchor-based dense prediction only on a single-level feature map, ensuring training and inference efficiency while maintaining high accuracy. (1) The *scale-aggregated encoder* summarizes multi-scale cues to one feature map by progressively analyzing global spatial and semantic relations of two consecutive feature maps. Thus, instances of various scales are easily detected on the single feature map, avoiding exhaustive search across network layers. (2) The *task-aligned encoder* enables DFFT to conduct classification and regression simultaneously in a coupled head. By taking advantage of group channel-wise attention, it resolves the learning conflicts from the two tasks and provides consistent predictions [6,27].

Entry Point 2: Explore low-level semantic features as much as possible for the detection task with limited computational resources. We design a strong and efficient detection-oriented transformer backbone after an in-depth study on different characteristics of transformer attention components (e.g., spatial-wise attention and channel-wise attention). Furthermore, we propose to incorporate semantic-augmented attention modules into several stages of the backbone to capture rich low-level semantics. Low-level semantics from different stages help the detector distinguish distractors in detail. Such design is quite different from common backbones [10,24,30] that are dedicated to learn final high-level semantics for the classification task.

Finally, we conduct comprehensive experiments to verify the superiority of DFFT as well as the effectiveness of all the above designs. Compared to the foundation work deformable DETR [36], DFFT achieves 61% inference acceleration, 28% training acceleration, and 1.9% AP gain.

2   Related Work

2.1   One-Stage and Two-Stage Detectors

Mainstream detectors exploit two types of anchors: anchor boxes [20,26] and anchor points [9,29]. Anchors are generated at the center of each sliding-window position to offer candidates for objects. Typical one-stage detectors [4,9,15,20, 29] directly predict categories and offsets of anchors for the whole feature maps, while two-stage detectors [1,17,26] first generate region proposals from dense anchor boxes by a Region Proposal Network (RPN) [26] and then refine the detection for each proposed region afterward.

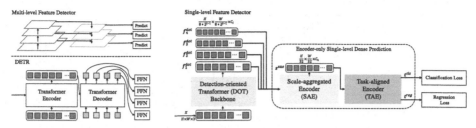

(a) Overview of existing detection methods.

(b) Overview of our proposed DFFT.

Fig. 2. Overview of existing detection methods and our proposed Decoder-Free Fully Transformer-based (DFFT) detector. **(a)** Existing methods either rely on multi-level feature detectors [20] or adopt the DETR framework [2]. **(b)** Our DFFT simplifies object detection to an encoder-only single-level dense prediction framework. The proposed two strong encoders enables us to conduct fast but accurate inference on a single-level feature map, outperforming existing multi-level feature detectors. The design also trims the training-inefficient decoder for more than 10× training acceleration over DETR. We also propose a novel lightweight detection-oriented transformer backbone to capture richer low-level semantic features and further boost object detection.

One main challenge in object detection is to represent objects at vastly different scales effectively. Both one-stage and two-stage detectors overcome it with multi-scale features and multi-level predictions. FPN [19] is widely used in these detectors [17,20,29], which builds feature pyramid by sequentially combining two adjacent layers in feature hierarchy in backbone model with top-down and lateral connections. Later CNN-based designs on cross-scale connections use bottom-up paths [23], U-shape modules [35], and the neural architecture search [16,32]. YOLOF [4] provides an alternative solution, which exploits dilated encoder to detect all objects on single-level features. In contrast, our DFFT introduces large receptive fields to cover large objects based on the transformer's global relation modeling, and meanwhile, aggregates low-level semantics through the scale-aggregated encoder. Such designs enable DFFT to achieve superior detection performance.

Recently, transformer-based backbones [5,10,24,30] have shown superior performance in object detection based on standard frameworks such as MaskR-CNN [1,17] and RetinaNet [20]. However, these backbones are usually directly plugged into the framework without regard for the effects of replacing CNN with transformers. These methods typically consume enormous computation costs (e.g., over 300 GFLOPs for MobileFormer [5]). DFFT is the first method to explore efficient and fully transformer-based detection.

2.2 End-to-End Detectors

End-to-end detectors [2,11,13,25,36] remove the complicated post-processing like NMS and achieve one-to-one matching between the target and the candidate by the Hungarian algorithm. DETR [2] uses an encoder-decoder transformer

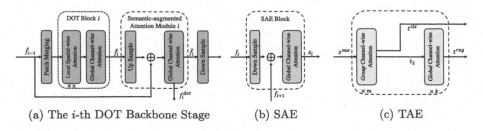

(a) The i-th DOT Backbone Stage   (b) SAE   (c) TAE

Fig. 3. Illustration of the three major modules in our proposed DFFT. DFFT contains a light-weight **D**etection-**O**riented **T**ransformer backbone with four DOT stages to extract features with rich semantic information, a **S**cale-**A**ggregated **E**ncoder (SAE) with three SAE blocks to aggregate multi-scale features into one feature map for efficiency, and a **T**ask-**A**ligned **E**ncoder (TAE) to resolve conflicts between classification and regression tasks in the coupled detection head.

framework. The transformer encoder processes the flattened deep features from the CNN backbone. The non-autoregressive decoder takes the encoder's outputs and a set of learned object query vectors as the input, and predicts the category labels and bounding boxes accordingly. The decoder's cross-attention module attend to different locations in the image for different object queries, which requires high-quality content embeddings and thus training costs. DETR needs a long training process (500 epochs) and is not suitable for small objects. Deformable DETR [36] accelerates the convergence via learnable sparse sampling and multi-scale deformable encoders. It generates a reference point for each object query and uses deformable attention to make each reference point only focus on a small fixed set of sampling points. Anchor DETR [31] exploits anchor points to accelerate training. Conventional designs such as RPN [34], RCNN, and FCOS [28] are also used to optimize the DETR framework. Although better performance and fast convergence are achieved, the computation cost increases significantly (e.g., 2× GFLOPs in deformable DETR) due to multi-scale feature encoding [28,36]. Moreover, dense priors such as reference points [36], anchor points [28,31], proposals [28], and conditional spatial embedding [25] are introduced to optimize the DETR pipeline for fast convergence. It shows that DETR is not the only solution for efficient, fully transformer-based detectors. Compared with them, DFFT trims the decoder, also ensures both fast training convergence and inference while maintains comparable performance.

3   Method

In this section, we introduce DFFT, an efficient Decoder-Free Fully Transformer-based object detector. An overview of DFFT is illustrated in Fig. 2b. The Detection-oriented Transformer backbone F extracts features at four scales and sends them to the following encoder-only single-level dense prediction module. The prediction module first aggregates the multi-scale feature into a single feature map through the Scale-Aggregated Encoder S. Then we use the Task-

Aligned Encoder T to align the feature for classification and regression tasks simultaneously for higher inference efficiency.

3.1 Detection-Oriented Transformer Backbone

Detection-oriented transformer (DOT) backbone aims to extract multi-scale features with strong semantics. As shown in Fig. 3a, it hierarchically stacks one embedding module and four DOT stages, where a novel semantic-augmented attention module aggregates the low-level semantic information of every two consecutive DOT stages. For each input image $x \in \mathbb{R}^{H \times W \times 3}$, the DOT backbone extracts features at four different scales:

$$f_1^{\text{dot}}, f_2^{\text{dot}}, f_3^{\text{dot}}, f_4^{\text{dot}} = F(x), \tag{1}$$

where $f_i^{\text{dot}} \in \mathbb{R}^{\frac{H}{8 \cdot 2^{i-1}} \times \frac{W}{8 \cdot 2^{i-1}} \times C_i}$ is the i-th feature with C_i channels for $i \in \{1, 2, 3, 4\}$. In what follows, we expand the formalization of the DOT backbone function F.

Embedding Module. For an input image $x \in \mathbb{R}^{H \times W \times 3}$, we first divide it into $\frac{H \times W}{8 \times 8}$ patches and feed these patches to a linear projection to obtain patch embeddings $\hat{f}_0$ of size $\frac{H}{8} \times \frac{W}{8} \times C_1$, written as

$$\hat{f}_0 = F_{\text{embed}}(x) \in \mathbb{R}^{\frac{H}{8} \times \frac{W}{8} \times C_1}, \tag{2}$$

where F_{embed} is the embedding module described above.

DOT Block. Each DOT stage contains one DOT block F_{block}, designed to efficiently capture both the local spatial and the global semantic relations at each scale. When processing high-resolution feature maps in dense prediction, conventional transformer blocks reduce computational costs by replacing the multi-head self-attention (MSA) layer with the local spatial-wise attention layer, such as spatial-reduction attention (SRA) [30] and shifted window-based multi-head self-attention (SW-MSA) [24]. However, this design sacrifices detection performance as it only extracts multi-scale features with limited low-level semantics.

To mitigate this shortcoming, our DOT block includes multiple SW-MSA blocks [24] and one global channel-wise attention block [10], as illustrated in the first part of Fig. 3a. Note that each attention block contains an attention layer and an FFN layer, and we omit the FFN layer in each attention block of Fig. 2 to simplify the illustration. We denote by $\hat{f}_i$ the DOT block's output feature at the i-th DOT stage. We find that placing a lightweight channel-wise attention layer behind consecutive local spatial-wise attention layers can benefit deducing object semantics at each scale.

Semantic-Augmented Attention. While the DOT block has enhanced the semantic information in low-level features through the global channel-wise attention, semantics can be improved even further to benefit the detection task. Thus, we propose a novel *semantic-augmented attention* (SAA) module $F_{\text{se-att}}$, which exchanges semantic information between two consecutive scale levels and augments their features. SAA consists of an up-sampling layer and a global channel-wise attention block. We incorporate SAA into every two consecutive DOT blocks, as illustrated in the second part of Fig. 3a. Formally, SAA takes the outputs from the current DOT block and the former DOT stage, and then returns the semantic augmented feature, which is sent to the next DOT stage and also contributes to the final multi-scale feature f_i^{dot}. We denote by $\widehat{f}_i$ SAA's output feature at the i-th DOT stage.

DOT Stage. The final DOT backbone contains four DOT stages F_{stage} where each stage consists of one DOT block and one SAA module (except the first stage). Specifically, the first stage contains one DOT block and no SAA module, because the inputs of the SAA module are from two consecutive DOT stages. Each of the remaining three stages contains a patch merging module to reduce the number of patches similar to [24], a DOT block, and a SAA module followed by a down-sampling layer to recover the input dimension, as shown in Fig. 3a. Thus, the formulation of the DOT block in the i-th stage can be defined as

$$\hat{f}_i = \begin{cases} F_{\mathrm{block}}(\hat{f}_{i-1}), & i = 1, 2 \\ F_{\mathrm{block}}(\mathrm{down}(\widetilde{f}_{i-1})), & i = 3, 4 \end{cases} \tag{3}$$

where down denotes the downsampling function.

The i-th stage's SAA module can be defined as

$$\widetilde{f}_i = \begin{cases} F_{\mathrm{se\text{-}att}}\Big(\mathrm{up}(\hat{f}_i) + \hat{f}_{i-1}\Big), & i = 2 \\ F_{\mathrm{se\text{-}att}}\Big(\mathrm{up}(\hat{f}_i) + \widetilde{f}_{i-1}\Big), & i = 3, 4 \end{cases} \tag{4}$$

where up denotes the upsampling function.

The final multi-scale feature from the DOT backbone can be written as

$$f_i^{\mathrm{dot}} = \begin{cases} \widetilde{f}_{i+1}, & i = 1, 2, 3 \\ \hat{f}_i, & i = 4 \end{cases} \tag{5}$$

3.2   Encoder-Only Single-Level Dense Prediction

This module is designed to improve both the inference and training efficiency of the fully transformer-based object detector with two novel encoders. It first uses the *scale-aggregated* encoder (SAE) to aggregate the multi-scale features f_i^{dot} from the DOT backbone into one feature map s^{sae}. After that, it uses the *task-aligned* encoder (TAE) to generate aligned classification feature t^{cls} and regression feature t^{reg} simultaneously in a single head.

Scale-Aggregated Encoder. We design this encoder with three SAE blocks, as illustrated in Fig. 3b. Each SAE block takes two features as the input and aggregates the features step by step across all SAE blocks. We set the scale of final aggregated feature to $\frac{H}{32} \times \frac{W}{32}$ to balance the detection precision and computational costs. For this purpose, the last SAE block will up-sample the input feature to $\frac{H}{32} \times \frac{W}{32}$ before aggregation. This procedure can be described as

$$
\begin{aligned}
s_0 &= f_1^{\text{dot}}, \\
s_1 &= S_{\text{att}}\left(\text{down}(s_0) + f_2^{\text{dot}}\right), \\
s_2 &= S_{\text{att}}\left(\text{down}(s_1) + f_3^{\text{dot}}\right), \\
s_3 &= S_{\text{att}}\left(s_2 + \text{up}(f_4^{\text{dot}})\right),
\end{aligned}
\tag{6}
$$

where S_{att} is the global channel-wise attention block and $s^{\text{sae}} = s_3$ is the final aggregated feature map.

Task-Aligned Encoder. Recent one-stage detectors [4,29] perform object classification and localization independently with two separate branches (e.g., decoupled head). This two-branch design omits the interaction between two tasks and leads to inconsistent predictions [12,14]. Meanwhile, feature learning for two tasks in a coupled head usually exists conflicts [7,27]. We propose the task-aligned encoder which offers a better balance between learning task-interactive and task-specific features via stacking *group* channel-wise attention blocks in a coupled head.

As shown in Fig. 3c, this encoder consists of two kinds of channel-wise attention blocks. First, the stacked *group* channel-wise attention blocks T_{group} align and finally split the aggregated feature s^{sae} into two parts. Second, the *global* channel-wise attention blocks T_{global} further encode one of the two split features for the subsequent regression task. This procedure can be described as

$$
\begin{aligned}
t_1, t_2 &= T_{\text{group}}(s^{\text{sae}}), \\
t^{\text{cls}} &= t_1, \\
t^{\text{reg}} &= T_{\text{global}}(t_2),
\end{aligned}
\tag{7}
$$

where $t_1, t_2 \in \mathbb{R}^{\frac{H}{32} \times \frac{W}{32} \times 256}$ are the split features, and $t^{\text{cls}} \in \mathbb{R}^{\frac{H}{32} \times \frac{W}{32} \times 256}$ and $t^{\text{reg}} \in \mathbb{R}^{\frac{H}{32} \times \frac{W}{32} \times 512}$ are the final features for the classification and regression tasks, respectively.

Specifically, the differences between the *group* channel-wise attention block and the *global* channel-wise attention block lie in that all the linear projections except the projections for key/query/value embeddings in the *group* channel-wise attention block are conducted in two groups. Thus, features interact in attention operations while deduced separately in output projections.

3.3   Miscellaneous

Since DFFT conducts the single-level dense prediction on a single feature map, the pre-defined anchors are sparse. Applying the Max-IoU matching [20] based on the sparse anchors will cause an imbalance problem for positive anchors, making detectors pay attention to large ground-truth boxes while ignoring the small ones when training. To overcome this problem, we use the uniform matching strategy

Table 1. The definition and performance of DFFT models with different magnitudes. In the backbone setting, we list the output feature's number of channels C_i and the number of SA blocks in all four backbone stages. In the effectiveness evaluation, we report the accuracy of the pre-trained backbone on ImageNet and the detection AP of DFFT after training on the MS COCO dataset.

Models	Backbone settings		Effectiveness (%)		Efficiency (GFLOPs)	
	Value of C_i	Number of SA	Accuracy	AP	Backbone	DFFT
$DFFT_{NANO}$	$(3, 3, 6, 9)$	$(2, 2, 6, 2)$	80.0	42.8	26	42
$DFFT_{TINY}$	$(4, 4, 8, 12)$	$(1, 1, 5, 1)$	81.1	43.5	39	57
$DFFT_{SMALL}$	$(4, 4, 8, 12)$	$(2, 2, 6, 2)$	82.1	44.5	44	62
$DFFT_{MEDIUM}$	$(4, 4, 7, 12)$	$(2, 2, 18, 2)$	82.7	45.7	48	67
$DFFT_{LARGE}$	$(6, 6, 8, 12)$	$(2, 2, 18, 2)$	83.1	46.0	83	101

proposed by YOLOF [4] to ensure that all ground-truth boxes uniformly match with the same number of positive anchors regardless of their sizes. Similar to the setting of most conventional detection methods [4,20,29], our loss function consists of a focal loss for classification and a generalized IOU loss for regression. At the inference stage, we conduct object detection efficiently based on the final aggregated feature map s^{sae} with a single pass.

4   Experiments

We evaluate our proposed DFFT on the challenging MS COCO benchmark [21] following the commonly used setting. It contains around 160K images of 80 categories. We compare DFFT with conventional one-stage/two-stage detection methods and DETR-based methods. We also provide a comprehensive ablation study to quantitatively analyze the effectiveness of each module in DFFT. The standard mean average precision (AP) metric is used to measure detection under different IoU thresholds and object scales.

4.1   Settings

The DOT backbone is pre-trained on ImageNet [8] with the same setting as [24]. We train DFFT with the standard 1× (12 epochs) and 3× (36 epochs) training configurations as introduced in [24]. We use the AdamW [18] optimizer with a batch size of 32, an initial learning rate of $1e - 4$ and weight decay of 0.05. The learning rate is stepped down by a factor of 0.1 at the 67% and 89% of training epochs. We conduct all experiments on 8 V100 GPUs.

   We implemented models with different magnitudes. The settings and performance of these backbones are shown in Table 1, where C_i denotes the number of channels of the i-th DOT stage's output feature, and the number of SA blocks within each DOT stage is also provided. Only one global channel-wise attention block is added to the end of each stage. For each model, accuracy refers to the

Table 2. Comparison of our DFFT and modern detection methods on the MS COCO benchmark [21]. The table is divided into four sections from top to bottom: (1) anchor-based methods, (2) DFFT trained for 12 epochs, (3) DETR-based methods, and (4) DFFT trained for 36 epochs. DFFT achieves competitive precision with significantly fewer training epochs and inference GFLOPs.

Methods	Epochs	AP (%)	AP$_{50}$ (%)	AP$_{75}$ (%)	AP$_S$ (%)	AP$_M$ (%)	AP$_L$ (%)	GFLOPs
Faster RCNN-FPN-R50 [26]	36	40.2	61.0	43.8	24.2	43.5	52.0	180
RetinaNet [20]	12	35.9	55.7	38.5	19.4	39.5	48.2	201
YOLOF-R50 [4]	12	37.7	56.9	40.6	19.1	42.5	53.2	86
Swin-Tiny-RetinaNet [24]	12	42.0	–	–	–	–	–	245
Focal-Tiny-RetinaNet [33]	12	43.7	–	–	–	–	–	265
Mobile-Former [5]	12	34.2	53.4	36.0	19.9	36.8	45.3	322
DFFT$_{NANO}$	12	39.1	58.3	41.7	19.0	42.9	51.2	42
DFFT$_{SMALL}$	12	41.4	60.9	44.5	20.1	45.4	58.9	62
DFFT$_{MEDIUM}$	12	42.6	62.5	45.5	22.6	46.7	61.4	67
DETR-R50 [2]	500	42.0	62.4	44.2	20.5	45.8	61.1	86
WB-DETR [22]	500	39.6	58.4	43.8	18.2	42.7	54.9	62
YOLOS [11]	150	37.6	–	–	–	–	–	172
Deformable DETR [36]	50	43.8	62.6	47.7	26.4	47.1	58.0	173
SMCA-R50 [13]	50	43.7	63.6	47.2	24.2	47.0	60.4	152
Anchor DETR-DC5-R50 [31]	50	44.2	64.7	47.5	24.7	48.2	60.6	151
Conditional DETR-R50 [25]	50	40.9	61.8	43.3	20.8	44.6	59.2	90
TSP-FCOS-R50 [28]	36	43.1	62.3	47.0	26.6	46.8	55.9	189
Efficient DETR-R50 [34]	36	44.2	62.2	48.0	**28.4**	47.5	56.6	159
DFFT$_{NANO}$	36	42.8	61.9	46.2	23.4	46.8	59.7	42
DFFT$_{SMALL}$	36	44.5	63.6	48.0	24.5	49.0	60.7	62
DFFT$_{MEDIUM}$	36	**45.7**	**64.8**	**49.7**	25.5	**50.4**	**63.1**	67

backbone's accuracy on ImageNet and AP refers to the precision after training on the MS COCO dataset. All GFLOPs are obtained on the MS COCO dataset.

4.2   Main Results

Compare with Two-Stage/One-Stage Detection Methods. The performance of conventional two-stage/one-stage detection methods is shown in the first part of Table 2. Overall, anchor-based methods converge fast within only 12 epochs, and the transformer-based methods generally outperform CNN-based methods. For instance, Focal-Tiny-RetinaNet [33] achieves 7.8% higher AP than the original RetinaNet [20]. However, such good performance comes at the expense of high computational costs; most of these methods need 170 GFLOPs at the minimum. Even the more efficient single-level feature detection method YOLOF [4] needs 86 GFLOPs when using ResNet-50 as the backbone.

The performance of our proposed DFFT with 12 epochs is shown in the second part of Table 2. In contrast to the above methods that endure an obvious trade-off between detection precision and inference efficiency, our DFFT can improve these two metrics simultaneously. For example, DFFT$_{NANO}$ decreases 51% GFLOPs of YOLOF while still increasing 1.4% AP, and DFFT$_{MEDIUM}$

achieves 42.6% AP with only 67 GFLOPs. Furthermore, DFFT reduces 200 GFLOPs from the best-performed Focal-Tiny-RetinaNet [33] at the cost of merely 1% lower AP. These comparisons indicate that our DFFT can effectively reduce the computational cost of the inference stage without sacrificing the detection precision.

Compare with DETR-Based Methods. The performance of DETR-based methods is shown in the third part of Table 2. We observe that DETR-based methods can achieve better performance and inference efficiency but converges slower. For instance, DETR only needs 86 GFLOPs at the inference stage to achieve 42.0% AP, but it requires as large as 500 epochs to converge. WB-DETR [22] can only achieve 39.6% AP if given the same training epochs. Subsequent optimized DETR-based methods improve the convergence speed but at the cost of inference efficiency. For example, while Deformable DETR [36] and Condition DETR [25] need 50 epochs to converge and TSP-FOCS [28] and Efficient DETR [34] need only 36 epochs to converge, their GFLOPs are around 4%–120% larger than DETR.

The performance of our DFFT with 36 epochs is listed in the fourth part of Table 2. In contrast to the DETR-based methods that endure a hard-to-optimize trade-off between the convergence and inference efficiency, our DFFT can achieve state-of-the-art detection prevision without sacrificing neither of these two metrics. Compared with DETR [36], our DFFT$_{NANO}$ model improves 13× convergence speed and decreases 51% GFLOPs while achieving significant detection precision (42.0% vs. 42.8%). Compared with Efficient DETR [34] under the same number of training epochs, our model achieves state-of-the-art 45.7% AP with only 67 GFLOPs (57% lower). We further demonstrate the convergence curves

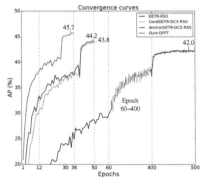

Fig. 4. The convergence curves of DFFT and DETR-based methods on the COCO 2017 validation set. Our DFFT converges significantly faster than the counterparts.

of DFFT and DETR-based methods in Fig. 4. DFFT reduces 28%–92% training epochs of state-of-the-art methods.

These comparisons verify that our DFFT can effectively optimize training and inference efficiency while achieving competitive and even state-of-the-art detection precision.

4.3   Ablation Study

We provide a comprehensive ablation study of all designs in our DFFT: the detection-oriented transformer (DOT) backbone, scale-aggregated encoder (SAE), and task-aligned encoder (TAE). The ablation study starts with the major components in DFFT, followed by the specific design of each component.

We conduct all the experiments on $DFFT_{SMALL}$ model that is trained for 12 epochs.

Major Components. We first evaluate the efficacy of the major components in DFFT. We disable each component by replacing it with a vanilla method as they are not easily removable from our detection framework. Specifically, we (1) replace the DOT backbone (line 1) with Swin-Transformer [24] with the similar GFLOPs; (2) disable the SAE module (lines 1, 2, 4) by directly upsampling the last stage's outputs to $\frac{H}{32} \times \frac{W}{32}$ and feed them to TAE; and (3) replace the TAE module (lines 1–3) with YOLOF's head. The results are shown in Table 3.

Firstly, the DOT backbone promotes the precision from 33.8% to 37.9%, indicating that it can obtain better semantic features that are more suitable for the detection task. Even without the SAE, it gets competitive precisions with only the last stage's outputs. This also suggests that the SAA can capture multi-scale information when aggregating semantic information.

Table 3. Ablation study of the three major modules in DFFT.

DOT	SAE	TAE	AP (%)	GFLOPs
–	–	–	33.8	45
✔	–	–	37.9	47
✔	✔	–	39.9	58
✔	–	✔	39.8	51
✔	✔	✔	41.4	62

Secondly, SAE further improves the precision to 39.9% by aggregating multi-scale features into one feature map. Yet, disabling SAE would decrease the precision by 1.6%.

Finally, disabling TAE would decrease the prevision by 1.5%. It verifies the necessity of using TAE to align and encode both the classification and regression features.

Detection-Oriented Transformer (DOT) Block. Table 4 studies how the global channel-wise attention (GCA) and semantic-augmented attention (SAA) contributes to DOT's performance. We only modify the backbone network without disabling the SAE and TAE modules. Lines 1 and 2 show that switching from SW-MSA to our global

Table 4. Ablation study of the DOT backbone. GCA means adding a global channel-wise attention at the end of each DOT block. In the third line, we replace SAA with GCA.

GCA	SAA	AP (%)	GFLOPs
–	–	39.0	48.59
✔	–	40.1	48.97
✔	GCA	40.4	58.65
✔	✔	41.4	62.23

channel-wise attention can improve 1.1% precision without significant impact on FLOPs. Lines 2 and 3 show that adding one GCA block costs 11 GFLOPs yet only gains 0.3% AP. Once we replace the GCA block with the SAA module (so that the two settings have the same number of attention nodes), the precision increases from 40.1% to 41.4%. These two observations suggest that SAA can enhance performance, and having more attention nodes is not the primary cause.

We further visualize the feature maps from each backbone stage of $DFFT_{MEDIUM}$ trained 12 epochs in Fig. 5. In the first two stages, our DOT backbone can obtain low-level features with sufficient semantic information to capture small objects. The third stage then focuses on medium and large objects. Finally, the last stage only responds to large objects. These observations verify

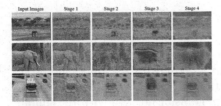

Fig. 5. Visualization of the feature map obtained by each DOT backbone stage. The first two stages focus on small objects while the third stage focuses on medium or larger objects. The last stage only responses to large objects.

Fig. 6. Illustration of detection results from the best anchors for classification (red) and localization (orange). Ground-truth is indicated by blue boxes and centers. Our TAE helps provide consistency in predictions of classification and localization. (Color figure online)

that our DOT backbone can enhance semantic information in low-level features and thus boosting the detection precision.

Semantic-Augmented Attention (SAA). SAA obtains richer low-level semantic features for object detection task by augmenting the semantic information from high-level features to the low-level ones, sharing a similar effect as FPN [19]. For a fair comparison with FPN, we disable the two encoders and directly feed features from the backbone to RetinaNet's head, which is a multi-level feature head that accepts four-scale features. The results are shown in Table 5. While both SAA and FPN improves the precision, SAA obtains 0.5% higher AP with 9 fewer GFLOPs than FPN. Thus, the global channel-wise attention suits the transformer better than FPN. Including SAA within the forward pass can obtain an even stronger model.

Scale-Aggregated Encoder (SAE). SAE aggregates multi-scale features into one feature map to reduce the inference stage's computational costs. We compare SAE with a similar design in YOLOF, which exploits a dilated encoder to convert features from multiple scales. Table 6 shows that SAE improves 1.1% AP from the dilated encoder of YOLOF. When compared with a vanilla concatenation operation, SAE gets 1.8% higher precision. Overall, SAE can achieve better performance with low computational costs.

Task-Aligned Encoder (TAE). Benefiting from the group channel-wise attention's capability of modeling semantic relations, TAE handles task conflicts in a coupled head and further generates task-aligned predictions in a single pass. As shown in the first row of Fig. 6, after replacing TAE with YOLOF's head in the baseline model, the best anchors for classification (red) and localization (orange) are distant from each other. That is because YOLOF [4] uses a task-unaligned decoupled head that leads to inconsistent predictions of classification and localization. Comparatively, our TAE provides aligned predictions with both high classification and IOU scores (*e.g.*, person, zebra and cat in Fig. 6).

Table 5. Analysis of SAA. We disable the two encoders and uses the RetinaNet's head, which is a multi-level feature head accepting four-scale features.

SAA	FPN	AP (%)	GFLOPs
–	–	37.4	319
✔	–	38.9	332
-	✔	38.4	341

Table 6. Analysis of SAE. CON-CAT: the direct concatenation of multiple features. YOLOF: exploiting a dilated encoder to convert features.

Method	AP (%)	GFLOPs
CONCAT	39.6	56
YOLOF	40.3	58
DFFT	41.4	62

Table 7. Analysis of how the output feature's number of channels C_i and the number of attention blocks impact GFLOPs and FPS. All the results are measured on the same machine with a V100 GPU using mmdetection [3].

Models	Backbone settings		AP	GFLOPs	FPS
	Value of C_i	Number of SA			
DETR-R50	–	–	42.0	86	24
Deformable DETR	–	–	43.8	173	14
DFFT$_{NANO}$	$(3,3,6,9)$	$(3,3,7,3)$	42.8	42	22
DFFT$_{TINY}$	$(4,4,8,12)$	$(2,2,6,2)$	43.5	57	24
DFFT$_{SMALL}$	$(4,4,8,12)$	$(3,3,7,3)$	44.5	62	22
DFFT$_{MEDIUM}$	$(4,4,7,12)$	$(3,3,19,3)$	45.7	67	17
DFFT$_{LARGE}$	$(6,6,8,12)$	$(3,3,19,3)$	46.0	101	17

Analysis of the Impact on GFLOPs and FPS. We compare the performance of different models in terms of prediction AP and inference GFLOPs and FPS in Table 7. For computational performance, GFLOPs and FPS are sensitive to the number of channels and the number of attention blocks, respectively. For example, compared with DFFT$_{NANO}$, DFFT$_{TINY}$ increases 15 GFLOPs but has a better FPS due to fewer attention blocks, and DFFT$_{SMALL}$ increases 20 GFLOPs but gets a similar FPS. Overall, we achieve better AP and inference efficiency than deformable DETR; at the same FPS, our DFFT has better accuracy and GFLOPS than DETR. Lastly, although we designed the network architecture mainly to reduce GFLOPs, we note that the above observations can also be used to redesign our network and optimize for FPS in the future.

5   Conclusion

In this work, we discover a trade-off between training and inference efficiency that hinders transformer-based object detection in large-scale applications. Rather than porting transformers directly to the conventional framework or optimizing the DETR framework, we propose DFFT, a novel design of fully transformer-based object detectors. It enables efficiency in both the training and inference stages for the first time without sacrificing noticeable detection precision. Extensive evaluation reveals our DFFT's unique advantages in capturing low-level semantic features in object detection, as well as its ability to preserve detection precision while trimming the training-inefficient decoders in DETR. Finally, DFFT achieves state-of-the-art performance while using only half the GFLOPs of previous approaches, indicating a promising future work on the large-scale application of transformers in object detection.

References

1. Cai, Z., Vasconcelos, N.: Cascade R-CNN: delving into high quality object detection. In: Proceedings of the IEEE Conference on Computer Vision and Pattern Recognition, pp. 6154–6162 (2018)
2. Carion, N., Massa, F., Synnaeve, G., Usunier, N., Kirillov, A., Zagoruyko, S.: End-to-end object detection with transformers. In: Vedaldi, A., Bischof, H., Brox, T., Frahm, J.-M. (eds.) ECCV 2020. LNCS, vol. 12346, pp. 213–229. Springer, Cham (2020). https://doi.org/10.1007/978-3-030-58452-8_13
3. Chen, K., et al.: MMDetection: open MMLAB detection toolbox and benchmark. arXiv (2019)
4. Chen, Q., Wang, Y., Yang, T., Zhang, X., Cheng, J., Sun, J.: You only look one-level feature. In: Proceedings of the IEEE/CVF Conference on Computer Vision and Pattern Recognition, pp. 13039–13048 (2021)
5. Chen, Y., et al.: Mobile-former: bridging MobileNet and transformer. arXiv (2021)
6. Cheng, B., Wei, Y., Shi, H., Feris, R., Xiong, J., Huang, T.: Revisiting RCNN: on awakening the classification power of faster RCNN. In: Ferrari, V., Hebert, M., Sminchisescu, C., Weiss, Y. (eds.) ECCV 2018. LNCS, vol. 11219, pp. 473–490. Springer, Cham (2018). https://doi.org/10.1007/978-3-030-01267-0_28
7. Dai, X., et al.: Dynamic head: unifying object detection heads with attentions. In: Proceedings of the IEEE/CVF Conference on Computer Vision and Pattern Recognition, pp. 7373–7382 (2021)
8. Deng, J., Dong, W., Socher, R., Li, L.J., Li, K., Fei-Fei, L.: ImageNet: a large-scale hierarchical image database. In: 2009 IEEE Conference on Computer Vision and Pattern Recognition, pp. 248–255. IEEE (2009)
9. Duan, K., Bai, S., Xie, L., Qi, H., Huang, Q., Tian, Q.: CenterNet: keypoint triplets for object detection. In: Proceedings of the IEEE/CVF International Conference on Computer Vision, pp. 6569–6578 (2019)
10. El-Nouby, A., et al.: XCiT: cross-covariance image transformers. arXiv (2021)
11. Fang, Y., et al.: You only look at one sequence: rethinking transformer in vision through object detection. arXiv (2021)
12. Feng, C., Zhong, Y., Gao, Y., Scott, M.R., Huang, W.: TOOD: task-aligned one-stage object detection. In: Proceedings of the IEEE/CVF International Conference on Computer Vision, pp. 3510–3519 (2021)
13. Gao, P., Zheng, M., Wang, X., Dai, J., Li, H.: Fast convergence of DETR with spatially modulated co-attention. arXiv (2021)
14. Gao, Z., Wang, L., Wu, G.: Mutual supervision for dense object detection. In: Proceedings of the IEEE/CVF International Conference on Computer Vision, pp. 3641–3650 (2021)

15. Ge, Z., Liu, S., Wang, F., Li, Z., Sun, J.: YOLOX: exceeding YOLO series in 2021. arXiv (2021)
16. Ghiasi, G., Lin, T.Y., Le, Q.V.: NAS-FPN: learning scalable feature pyramid architecture for object detection. In: Proceedings of the IEEE/CVF Conference on Computer Vision and Pattern Recognition, pp. 7036–7045 (2019)
17. He, K., Gkioxari, G., Dollár, P., Girshick, R.: Mask R-CNN. In: Proceedings of the IEEE International Conference On Computer Vision, pp. 2961–2969 (2017)
18. Kingma, D.P., Ba, J.: Adam: a method for stochastic optimization. arXiv (2014)
19. Lin, T.Y., Dollár, P., Girshick, R., He, K., Hariharan, B., Belongie, S.: Feature pyramid networks for object detection. In: Proceedings of the IEEE Conference on Computer Vision and Pattern Recognition, pp. 2117–2125 (2017)
20. Lin, T.Y., Goyal, P., Girshick, R., He, K., Dollár, P.: Focal loss for dense object detection. In: Proceedings of the IEEE International Conference on Computer Vision, pp. 2980–2988 (2017)
21. Lin, T.-Y., et al.: Microsoft COCO: common objects in context. In: Fleet, D., Pajdla, T., Schiele, B., Tuytelaars, T. (eds.) ECCV 2014. LNCS, vol. 8693, pp. 740–755. Springer, Cham (2014). https://doi.org/10.1007/978-3-319-10602-1_48
22. Liu, F., Wei, H., Zhao, W., Li, G., Peng, J., Li, Z.: WB-DETR: transformer-based detector without backbone. In: Proceedings of the IEEE/CVF International Conference on Computer Vision, pp. 2979–2987 (2021)
23. Liu, S., Qi, L., Qin, H., Shi, J., Jia, J.: Path aggregation network for instance segmentation. In: Proceedings of the IEEE Conference on Computer Vision and Pattern Recognition, pp. 8759–8768 (2018)
24. Liu, Z., et al.: Swin transformer: hierarchical vision transformer using shifted windows. arXiv (2021)
25. Meng, D., et al.: Conditional DETR for fast training convergence. In: Proceedings of the IEEE/CVF International Conference on Computer Vision, pp. 3651–3660 (2021)
26. Ren, S., He, K., Girshick, R., Sun, J.: Faster R-CNN: towards real-time object detection with region proposal networks. Adv. Neural. Inf. Process. Syst. **28**, 91–99 (2015)
27. Song, G., Liu, Y., Wang, X.: Revisiting the sibling head in object detector. In: Proceedings of the IEEE/CVF Conference on Computer Vision and Pattern Recognition, pp. 11563–11572 (2020)
28. Sun, Z., Cao, S., Yang, Y., Kitani, K.M.: Rethinking transformer-based set prediction for object detection. In: Proceedings of the IEEE/CVF International Conference on Computer Vision, pp. 3611–3620 (2021)
29. Tian, Z., Shen, C., Chen, H., He, T.: FCOS: fully convolutional one-stage object detection. In: Proceedings of the IEEE/CVF International Conference on Computer Vision, pp. 9627–9636 (2019)
30. Wang, W., et al.: Pyramid vision transformer: a versatile backbone for dense prediction without convolutions. arXiv (2021)
31. Wang, Y., Zhang, X., Yang, T., Sun, J.: Anchor DETR: query design for transformer-based detector. arXiv (2021)
32. Xu, H., Yao, L., Zhang, W., Liang, X., Li, Z.: Auto-FPN: automatic network architecture adaptation for object detection beyond classification. In: Proceedings of the IEEE/CVF International Conference on Computer Vision, pp. 6649–6658 (2019)
33. Yang, J., et al.: Focal self-attention for local-global interactions in vision transformers. arXiv (2021)

34. Yao, Z., Ai, J., Li, B., Zhang, C.: Efficient DETR: improving end-to-end object detector with dense prior. arXiv (2021)
35. Zhao, Q., et al.: M2Det: a single-shot object detector based on multi-level feature pyramid network. In: Proceedings of the AAAI, vol. 33, pp. 9259–9266 (2019)
36. Zhu, X., Su, W., Lu, L., Li, B., Wang, X., Dai, J.: Deformable DETR: deformable transformers for end-to-end object detection. arXiv (2020)

Cross-Modality Knowledge Distillation Network for Monocular 3D Object Detection

Yu Hong[1], Hang Dai[2(✉)], and Yong Ding[1(✉)]

[1] Zhejiang University, Zhejiang, China
yuhong_1999@zju.edu.cn, dingy@vlsi.zju.edu.cn
[2] MBZUAI, Abu Dhabi, UAE
hang.dai@mbzuai.ac.ae

Abstract. Leveraging LiDAR-based detectors or real LiDAR point data to guide monocular 3D detection has brought significant improvement, e.g., Pseudo-LiDAR methods. However, the existing methods usually apply non-end-to-end training strategies and insufficiently leverage the LiDAR information, where the rich potential of the LiDAR data has not been well exploited. In this paper, we propose the **C**ross-**M**odality **K**nowledge **D**istillation (CMKD) network for monocular 3D detection to efficiently and directly transfer the knowledge from LiDAR modality to image modality on both features and responses. Moreover, we further extend CMKD as a semi-supervised training framework by distilling knowledge from large-scale unlabeled data and significantly boost the performance. Until submission, CMKD ranks 1st among the monocular 3D detectors with publications on both KITTI *test* set and Waymo *val* set with significant performance gains compared to previous state-of-the-art methods. Our code will be released at https://github.com/Cc-Hy/CMKD.

1 Introduction

Detecting objects in 3D space is crucial to a wide range of applications, such as augmented reality, robotics and autonomous driving. The 3D detectors are to generate 3D bounding boxes with size, location, orientation and category parameters to localize and classify the detected objects, enabling the system to perceive and understand the surrounding environment. In autonomous driving [2,12,16], 3D object detectors can be categorized into LiDAR point cloud based [9,52,53], stereo image based [26,32,56], monocular image based [22,39,49,54] and multi-modality based methods [23,43] according to the input resources. Compared with LiDAR sensors, monocular cameras have many unique advantages such as low price, colored information and dense perception, and monocular 3D object

---

Supplementary Information The online version contains supplementary material available at https://doi.org/10.1007/978-3-031-20080-9_6.

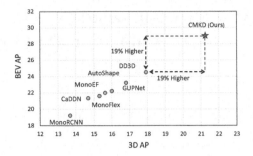

Fig. 1. Comparison between top-ranking monocular 3D detectors and CMKD (Ours) on KITTI leaderboard [16] for Car with $3D\ AP$ and $BEV\ AP$ metrics. Higher is better.

detection has become an active research area. However, there exists a large performance gap between LiDAR-based 3D detectors and monocular 3D detectors due to the lack of precise 3D information in monocular images. Thus, monocular 3D object detection is an extremely challenging task.

Recently, leveraging LiDAR-based detectors or real LiDAR point data to guide monocular 3D detection has brought significant improvement. For example, Pseudo-LiDAR methods [41,58,59] transform the 2D images into 3D pseudo points via depth estimation networks [13,27], and use a LiDAR-based detector [24,46] to perform 3D detection. Many methods [41,44,50,58,59], including most of the Pseudo-LiDAR methods, use real LiDAR point data to provide accurate 3D supervision during training, e.g., projecting the LiDAR points onto the image plane for a sparse ground truth depth map for depth supervision.

However, there is still room for improvement in this pattern. These methods only mimic the LiDAR data representation and extract some plain information from the LiDAR data like depth maps, but do not consider further exploiting deeper information such as high-dimensional features. To transfer the useful knowledge from the LiDAR data more efficiently and directly, we propose a novel cross-modality knowledge distillation network to mitigate the gap between the image modality and the LiDAR modality on both features and responses. Specifically, we use a LiDAR-based detector as the teacher model to provide the Bird's-Eye-View (BEV) feature map which inherits accurate 3D information from LiDAR points as the feature guidance. And we use the predictions of the teacher model with the awareness of soft label quality as the response guidance. We then transform the knowledge from the LiDAR-based teacher model to the image-based student model in both feature and response level via distillation, thus more fully exploiting the beneficial information of the LiDAR data.

Additionally, the unlabeled data, e.g., raw images and LiDAR points without ground truth 3D labels, is widely used by monocular 3D detectors [41,44,58, 62,63], but only for a sub-task like depth pre-training, and the potential of the unlabeled data has not been well exploited for the main detection task. To this end, we further extend CMKD as a semi-supervised training framework to technically better leverage the unlabeled data. Given a relatively small number

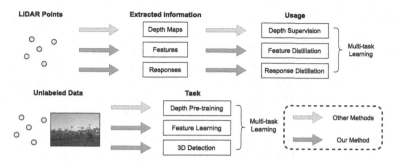

Fig. 2. Comparison between other methods and CMKD (Ours). For the LiDAR points, CMKD performs knowledge distillation by extracting features and responses from them, not only the depth maps. For the unlabeled data, CMKD can directly use it for multi-task training including feature learning and 3D detection, not only the depth pre-training sub-task.

of labeled samples to train the LiDAR-based teacher model, we can directly train CMKD on unlabeled data with the teacher model extracting beneficial information and transferring it to the student model. Unlike the existing methods who only use the unlabeled data for depth pre-training, CMKD can directly perform the multi-task training with unlabeled data in an end-to-end manner. Meanwhile, our semi-supervised training pipeline generalizes the application of CMKD in real-world scenes, where we only need to label a small portion of the data and can use the whole set for training, thus significantly reducing the annotation cost. We show the major difference between CMKD and the existing methods using LiDAR point information and unlabeled data in Fig. 2.

We summarize our contributions in three-fold: **i**) We propose a novel cross-modality knowledge distillation network to directly and efficiently transfer the knowledge from LiDAR modality to image modality on both features and responses, digging deeper in cross-modality knowledge transfer and significantly improving monocular 3D detection accuracy (Fig. 1). **ii**) We propose to distill the unlabeled data with our CMKD framework in a semi-supervised manner. With a relatively small amount of annotated data, CMKD can be trained end-to-end on the unlabeled data, which enables it to be trained with state-of-the-art performance while significantly reducing annotation cost. **iii**) CMKD ranks 1st among the monocular 3D detectors with publications on KITTI *test* set [16] and Waymo *val* set [12] with remarkable performance gains.

2 Related Works

LiDAR-Based 3D Detection. LiDAR-based 3D detection [28–31, 47, 52, 53, 66] has been developing rapidly in recent years. LiDAR sensors capture precise 3D measurement information from the surroundings in the form of unordered 3D points $(x, y, z, \cdots)$, where x, y, z are the absolute 3D coordinates of each point and the others could be additional information such as reflection intensity.

Point-based methods, e.g., PointNet [47], PointNet++ [48] take the raw point clouds as input, and extract point-wise features through structures like multi-layer perceptron for 3D object detection. Voxel-based methods, e.g., VoxelNet [66], SECOND [61] extend the representation of 2D image as pixels into 3D space by dividing 3D space into voxels. Thanks to the precise 3D information provided by point clouds, LiDAR-based methods have achieved relatively high accuracy on different 3D object detection benchmarks [2,12,16].

Pseudo-LiDAR Based 3D Detection. Pseudo-LiDAR based 3D detectors [6,41,58,59,63] benefit from both mimicking the LiDAR data representation and the accurate 3D information provided by the LiDAR data. These methods first transform the 2D images into intermediate 3D representations like pseudo point clouds via depth estimators [13,27], and then perform LiDAR-based methods on them. In this work, we take advantage of the LiDAR data by extracting features and responses, thus further exploiting the potential of the LiDAR data.

Leveraging Unlabeled Data. Leveraging large-scale unlabeled data has been very popular among monocular 3D detectors especially for depth estimation pre-training. Pseudo-LiDAR [58] and many extension works [41,55,62] use an off-the-shelf depth estimator like DORN [13] that is well-trained on the unlabeled KITTI Raw for depth estimation. DD3D [44] leverages extra super-large scale unlabeled data DDAD15M for depth pre-training which leads to significant performance improvements for monocular 3D detection. A major improvement is that CMKD can directly use the unlabeled data to perform multi-task training in an end-to-end manner, not only the depth pre-training sub-task.

Knowledge Distillation. The standard knowledge distillation [8,14,20,21,37,60] is performed between different models on the same modality. Usually, a well-trained heavy teacher model is applied on the input to obtain informative representations and then supervise the features or the output logits of a simple student model, compressing the model yet maintaining high accuracy. In this work, we use the cross-modality knowledge distillation between the LiDAR modality and monocular image modality for monocular 3D detection.

Difference Between CMKD and Similar Methods. The general idea of knowledge distillation has been explored by some existing works, and we explain the difference. LIGA-Stereo [18] focuses on the feature distillation only, and it is proposed for the stereo 3D detection task. MonoDistill [7] converts the representation of LiDAR modality to image modality, while CMKD converts the representation of image modality to LiDAR modality. LPCG [45] uses a LiDAR-based detector to generate pseudo labels without considering the intermediate high-dimensional features. Moreover, LPCG applies a one-size-fits-all method to use the soft labels, while we further take the soft label quality into account and use the quality-aware confidence scores to adaptively penalize the contribution of each soft label. DA-3d [62] applies non-end-to-end training strategies with fixed 2D detector and depth estimator, and only the trainable feature extractor is optimized for the feature distillation. But the monocular detector in CMKD is fully differentiable and can be trained end-to-end with all components jointly

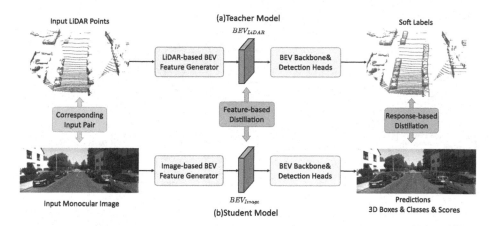

Fig. 3. Overview of the cross-modality knowledge distillation (CMKD) network for monocular 3D detection. (a) A pre-trained LiDAR-based 3D detector as the teacher model that extracts beneficial information from the LiDAR point data as soft guidance. (b) A trainable monocular 3D detector as the student model with the feature-based and response-based knowledge distillation.

optimized. Overall, CMKD jointly uses feature and response distillation for the monocular 3D detection task in an end-to-end manner. With the novel design of using totally soft guidance, CMKD can further handle large-scale unlabeled data which is easy to collect for autonomous driving cars, extending its application in real-world scenarios and boosting the performance. Apart from the general idea of knowledge distillation, CMKD is also different in the way to perform distillation with novel explorations in each distillation module, achieving new state-of-the-art performance on KITTI and Waymo benchmarks.

3   Method

3.1   Framework Overview

Figure 3 illustrates the overview of the cross-modality knowledge distillation network for monocular 3D object detection. The general idea is simple and straightforward. The key is to extract the same type of feature and response representations from both input LiDAR points and input monocular images, and perform knowledge distillation between the two modalities. Our framework includes a pre-trained LiDAR-based 3D detector as the teacher model, which extracts information from LiDAR points as soft guidance in the training stage, a trainable monocular 3D detector as the student model, and the cross-modality knowledge distillation on both features and responses.

Training. In the training stage, we take the monocular image and the corresponding LiDAR points as the input pair. The pre-trained teacher model is inferred only from input LiDAR points to provide the BEV feature maps that

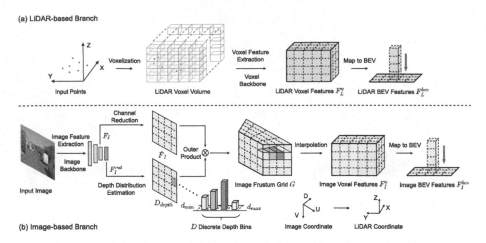

Fig. 4. BEV feature map generation. (a) The LiDAR-based branch. (b) The image-based branch.

inherit accurate 3D information from LiDAR points as the feature guidance, and the predictions with 3D bounding boxes, object classes and their corresponding confidence scores as the response guidance. The student model is trainable to generate BEV feature maps and 3D object detection results from monocular images, and uses the soft guidance in both feature level and response level from the teacher model for useful knowledge transfer.

Inference. In the inference stage, we use the student model alone to perform 3D object detection with monocular images as input only.

3.2 BEV Feature Learning

LiDAR-Based. We use SECOND [61], a simple LiDAR-based baseline as the teacher model to extract the BEV features from LiDAR points. The input points are subdivided into 3D voxels, which are fed to a voxel backbone to extract voxel features $F_L^v \in \mathbb{R}^{X \times Y \times Z \times C}$, where X, Y, Z are the width, length and height of the voxel feature volume, and C is the number of feature channels. Then, the voxel features F_L^v are collapsed to a LiDAR BEV feature map with features $F_L^{bev} \in \mathbb{R}^{X \times Y \times Z*C}$ by stacking the height dimension. When pre-training the teacher model, we use Intersection over Unions (IoUs) as the continuous quality labels with the Quality Focal Loss [33] instead of the original one-hot labels in the classification head. Thus, the predicted confidence scores are more IoU-aware to represent the 'quality' of the predictions.

Image-Based. For the image-based model, we use the architecture in CaDDN [50] to obtain the BEV features from the monocular image $I \in \mathbb{R}^{W \times H \times 3}$. We use an image backbone, e.g., ResNet [19] to extract image features $\hat{F}_I \in \mathbb{R}^{W_I \times H_I \times C}$, and a depth distribution estimation network, e.g., DeepLabV3 [4] to predict the

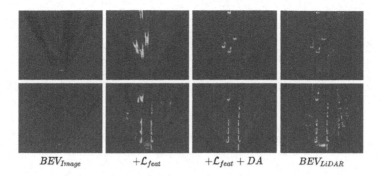

BEV_{Image} $+\mathcal{L}_{feat}$ $+\mathcal{L}_{feat}+DA$ BEV_{LiDAR}

Fig. 5. Illustration of BEV feature maps: the initial BEV feature map from image (1st column), with feature distillation loss $\mathcal{L}_{feat}$ (2nd column), with $\mathcal{L}_{feat}$ and DA module (3rd column), and the corresponding LiDAR BEV feature map (4th column).

pixel-wise depth distribution $D_{depth} \in \mathbb{R}^{W_I \times H_I \times D}$. We use the image features together with the estimated depth distributions to construct a frustum grid G with features $F_G \in \mathbb{R}^{W_I \times H_I \times D \times C}$, where D is the number of discrete depth bins, and C is the number of the feature channels. Then, the frustum volume is converted to a cuboid volume in LiDAR coordinate via interpolation operation with known calibration parameters, and we obtain the image voxel features $F_I^v \in \mathbb{R}^{X_I \times Y_I \times Z_I \times C}$. The voxel features are collapsed to a BEV feature map with features $\tilde{F}_I^{bev} \in \mathbb{R}^{X_I \times Y_I \times Z_I * C}$, which then goes through a channel compression network to obtain the image BEV feature map with features $F_I^{bev} \in \mathbb{R}^{X_I \times Y_I \times C}$.

We visualize the BEV feature map generation process in Fig. 4. More details can be found in the *Supplementary Materials*.

3.3 Domain Adaptation via Self-calibration

The image BEV features F_I^{bev} are different from LiDAR BEV features F_L^{bev} in spatial-wise and channel-wise feature distribution due to the fact that they come from different input modalities with different backbones. We employ a domain adaptation (DA) module to align the feature distribution of F_I^{bev} to that of F_L^{bev} and enhance F_I^{bev} at the meantime. Specifically, we stack five Self-Calibrated Blocks [36] after F_I^{bev} to apply spatial-wise and channel-wise transformations:

$$\hat{F}_I^{bev} = DA(F_I^{bev}) \tag{1}$$

where $\hat{F}_I^{bev} \in \mathbb{R}^{X_I \times Y_I \times C}$ are the enhanced BEV features after the DA module. More details can be found in the *Supplementary Materials*.

3.4 Feature-Based Knowledge Distillation

We use the BEV features F_L^{bev} from LiDAR points as the intermediate high-dimensional feature distillation guidance for $\hat{F}_I^{bev}$. We use the mean square error (MSE) to calculate the feature distillation loss:

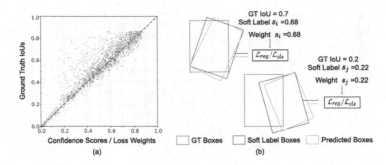

Fig. 6. (a) The IoU confidence scores of soft labels are trained to be positively correlated with the ground truth IoUs. (b) We use the IoU confidence score of the soft label box to indicate its 'quality' and weight the loss $\mathcal{L}_{reg}/\mathcal{L}_{cls}$ in response distillation.

$$\mathcal{L}_{feat} = MSE(\hat{F}_I^{bev}, F_L^{bev}) \tag{2}$$

Our monocular 3D detector benefits from the feature-based knowledge distillation due to the following aspects. Firstly, F_L^{bev} contains accurate 3D information directly extracted from LiDAR points, e.g., depth and geometry. And the feature representation of F_L^{bev} is well-trained for 3D object detection from point clouds which is more robust to diverse scenarios such as low-light condition and weather changing. We can distill such patterns from F_L^{bev} and transfer them to $\hat{F}_I^{bev}$. As shown in Fig. 5, after feature-based knowledge distillation with the proposed DA module, the object features are highlighted and the patterns of the image BEV features are close to the LiDAR BEV features, which are the key information to detect 3D objects. Besides, an intermediate feature guidance can ease the condition of over-fitting with high-dimensional information as the regularization term in the overall loss function [17,51].

3.5   Response-Based Knowledge Distillation

The predictions of the teacher model are in form of $(x, y, z, h, w, l, \theta, c, s)$, where (x, y, z) is the center of the 3D bounding box, (h, w, l) is the size of the 3D bounding box, θ is the rotation angle, c is the predicted category and s is the confidence score. And we use the predictions as the response guidance for the student model. Compared with the hard labels, the soft labels contain more information per training sample [20,65]. Moreover, the teacher model can act as a sample filter for the training samples, e.g., samples which are very difficult to detect for the teacher model tend to be eliminated or assigned with low confidence scores, and the stable samples are assigned with high confidence scores.

Quality-Aware Distillation. The loss for response-based distillation includes the regression loss $\mathcal{L}_{reg}$ for 3D bounding boxes and the classification loss $\mathcal{L}_{cls}$ for object classes following the teacher model [61]:

$$\mathcal{L}_{res} = \mathcal{L}_{reg} + \mathcal{L}_{cls} \tag{3}$$

For the i-th anchor, we use the Smooth L1 loss as the regression loss which is penalized by the IoU confidence score of the soft label:

$$\mathcal{L}_{reg} = Smooth\,L1(a_i^{soft}, a_i^{pred}) \times s_i \qquad (4)$$

where a_i^{soft} and a_i^{pred} are the bounding box parameters of the soft label and the prediction, and s_i is the IoU confidence score of the soft label box predicted by the teacher model to indicate its 'quality'. Similarly, we use the Quality Focal Loss (QFL) [33] that is penalized by s_i for classification:

$$\mathcal{L}_{cls} = QFL(C_i^{soft}, C_i^{pred}) \times s_i \qquad (5)$$

where C_i^{soft} and C_i^{pred} are the classification parameters of the soft label and the prediction. As shown in Fig. 6, the IoU confidence scores of the soft labels are trained to be positively correlated with their ground truth IoUs, which serve to weight the loss produced by each prediction of the student model. Thus, our quality-aware distillation can provide more meaningful and flexible guidance.

3.6   Loss Function

Teacher Model. We train the teacher model with the regression loss $\mathcal{L}_{reg}$ and the classification loss $\mathcal{L}_{cls}$ inherited from SECOND [61] except for replacing the Focal Loss [34] with the Quality Focal Loss [33]:

$$\mathcal{L}_{teacher} = \mathcal{L}_{reg} + \mathcal{L}_{cls} \qquad (6)$$

Backbone Pre-training. As with other methods discussed in this paper, we use the depth pre-trained backbone to make the network depth-aware, also, we initialize the backbone with the weights pre-trained on COCO [35] before pre-training. We inherit the depth loss from CaDDN [50] for backbone pre-training:

$$\mathcal{L}_{pre} = \mathcal{L}_{depth} \qquad (7)$$

Student Model. The loss function for the student model is defined as the combination of the feature-based and the response-based distillation loss:

$$\mathcal{L}_{student} = \mathcal{L}_{feat} + \mathcal{L}_{res} \qquad (8)$$

3.7   Extension: Distilling Unlabeled Data

After the teacher model is pre-trained with the labeled samples, every loss term in the overall loss function for the student model $\mathcal{L}_{student}$ in Eq. (8) does not use any information from manual hard labels. Thus, we can easily and naturally extend CMKD as a semi-supervised training framework with large-scale unlabeled data that is easy to collect for autonomous driving cars. With the teacher model

Table 1. Results for Car on KITTI *test* set. The best results are in **bold** and the second best results are underlined. We present the results for two experimental setups, CMKD and CMKD*. CMKD is trained with the official training set KITTI *trainval* (∼ 7.5k) and CMKD* is trained with the unlabeled KITTI Raw (∼ 42k).

Methods	Reference	3D AP				BEV AP			
		Easy	Moderate	Hard	Average	Easy	Moderate	Hard	Average
M3D-PRN [1]	ICCV 2019	14.76	9.71	7.42	10.63	21.02	13.67	10.23	14.97
AM3D [41]	ICCV 2019	16.50	10.74	9.52	12.25	25.03	17.32	14.91	19.08
PatchNet [40]	ECCV 2020	15.68	11.12	10.17	12.32	22.97	16.86	14.97	18.27
DA-3d [62]	ECCV2020	16.80	11.50	8.90	12.40	–	–	–	–
D4LCN [10]	CVPR 2020	16.65	11.72	9.51	12.63	22.51	16.02	12.55	17.03
Monodle [42]	CVPR 2021	17.23	12.26	10.29	13.26	24.79	18.89	16.00	19.89
MonoRUn [3]	CVPR 2021	19.65	12.30	10.58	14.18	27.94	17.34	15.24	20.17
MonoRCNN [54]	ICCV 2021	18.36	12.65	10.03	13.68	25.48	18.11	14.10	19.23
PCT [57]	NIPS 2021	21.00	13.37	11.31	15.23	29.65	19.03	15.92	21.53
DFR-Net [67]	ICCV 2021	19.40	13.63	10.35	14.46	28.17	19.17	14.84	20.73
CaDDN [50]	CVPR 2021	19.17	13.41	11.46	14.68	27.94	18.91	17.19	21.35
GUPNet [38]	ICCV 2021	22.26	15.02	13.12	16.80	30.29	21.19	18.20	23.23
DD3D [44]	ICCV 2021	23.22	16.34	14.20	17.92	30.98	22.56	20.03	24.52
CMKD	–	**25.09**	**16.99**	**15.30**	**19.13**	**33.69**	**23.10**	**20.67**	**25.82**
Improvement	–	+1.87	+0.65	+1.10	+1.21	+2.71	+0.54	+0.64	+1.30
CMKD*	–	**28.55**	**18.69**	**16.77**	**21.34**	**38.98**	**25.82**	**22.80**	**29.20**
Improvement	–	+5.33	+2.35	+2.57	+3.42	+8.00	+3.26	+2.77	+4.68

extracting beneficial information and transferring it to the student model as the soft guidance, we can use the partial labeled samples and train the model with the whole unlabeled set. This extended ability of CMKD to handle unlabeled data significantly reduces the annotation cost and brings performance improvements, which generalizes the application of CMKD in real-world scenarios.

Note that, the utilization of unlabeled data is not new for monocular 3D detection task, especially for Pseudo-LiDAR methods. Our contribution is to improve the utilization of unlabeled data with our cross-modality knowledge distillation network. The main difference is that other methods use unlabeled data only for the depth pre-training, a sub-task, but we further use it for knowledge distillation with all components of the network jointly optimized.

4 Experiments

4.1 Datasets

KITTI 3D. KITTI 3D [16] is the most widely used benchmark for 3D object detection consisting of 7481 training images and 7518 testing images as well as the corresponding point clouds, which are denoted as KITTI *trainval* and KITTI *test* respectively. The training set is commonly divided into training split with 3712 samples and validation split with 3769 samples following [5], which are denoted as KITTI *train* and KITTI *val* respectively. The official evaluation

Table 2. Results for Cyclist and Pedestrian on KITTI *test* set. The best results are in **bold** and the second best results are <u>underlined</u>. We present two setup results, CMKD and CMKD*. CMKD is trained with the official training set KITTI *trainval* ($\sim 7.5\,k$) and CMKD* is trained with the unlabeled KITTI Raw ($\sim 42\,k$).

Methods	Cyclist 3D AP/BEV AP			Pedestrian 3D AP/BEV AP		
	Easy	Moderate	Hard	Easy	Moderate	Hard
DFR-Net [67]	5.69/5.99	3.58/4.00	3.10/3.95	6.09/6.66	3.62/4.52	3.39/3.71
MonoFlex [64]	4.17/4.41	2.35/2.67	2.04/2.50	9.43/10.36	6.31/7.36	5.26/6.29
CaDDN [50]	7.00/9.67	3.41/5.38	3.30/<u>4.75</u>	12.87/14.72	8.14/9.41	6.76/8.17
MonoPSR [25]	<u>8.37</u>/<u>9.87</u>	<u>4.74</u>/<u>5.78</u>	<u>3.68</u>/4.57	8.37/9.87	4.74/5.78	3.68/4.57
GUPNet [38]	5.58/6.94	3.21/3.85	2.66/3.64	<u>14.95</u>/15.62	<u>9.76</u>/10.37	<u>8.41</u>/8.79
DD3D [44]	2.39/3.20	1.52/1.99	1.31/1.79	13.91/<u>15.90</u>	9.30/<u>10.85</u>	8.05/<u>9.41</u>
CMKD	**9.60/12.53**	**5.24/7.24**	**4.50/6.21**	**17.79/20.42**	**11.69/13.47**	**10.09/11.64**
Improvement	+1.23/+2.66	+0.50/+1.46	+0.72/+1.46	+2.84/+4.52	+1.93/+2.62	+1.68/+2.23
CMKD*	**12.52/14.66**	**6.67/8.15**	**6.34/7.23**	13.94/16.03	8.79/10.28	7.42/8.85
Improvement	+4.15/+4.79	+1.93/+2.37	+2.66/+2.48	–1.01/+0.13	–0.97/–0.57	–0.99/–0.56

metrics are 3D IoU and BEV IoU with the average precision metric, which we denote as *3D AP* and *BEV AP* respectively.

KITTI Raw. KITTI Raw [15] is a raw dataset with $\sim 42k$ unlabeled samples in sequence form. And KITTI 3D is a subset of KITTI Raw chosen with high-quality samples for 3D object detection. Moreover, KITTI Raw is the official depth prediction training set where the training samples are commonly divided into *Eigen* splits [11]. However, there is an overlap [55,58] between *Eigen train* and KITTI *val*. To avoid this, we use the *Eigen clean* split from DD3D [44] that filters out KITTI *val* from *Eigen train* for the validation experiments.

Waymo Open Dataset. The Waymo Open Dataset [12] is a more recently released dataset with 798 training sequences and 202 validation sequences which consist of about $200k$ samples in total, and we denote them as Waymo *train* and Waymo *val* respectively. CaDDN [50] is the first monocular detector reporting the performance on Waymo *val* set using samples from the front-camera only, and we follow the same settings for a fair comparison. The official evaluation metrics are 3D IoU with mean average precision and mean average precision weighted by heading, which are denoted as *3D mAP* and *3D mAPH* respectively.

4.2 Experiment Settings

KITTI. We pre-train the teacher model SECOND [61] on KITTI *trainval* for 80 epochs. For ablation studies, we train CMKD on KITTI *train* for 80 epochs or KITTI *train* and *Eigen clean* for 30 epochs according to different experiment settings, and report the performance for Car on KITTI *val*. The image backbone uses depth pre-training on KITTI *train* for 40 epochs. For comparisons on KITTI *test*, we present two experiment setups, CMKD and CMKD*. CMKD is trained with the official training set KITTI *trainval* ($\sim 7.5k$) for 80 epochs, and CMKD* is trained with the unlabeled KITTI Raw ($\sim 42k$) for 30 epochs. Following

Table 3. Results for vehicle on Waymo *val* set. The best results are in **bold**.

Difficulty	Method	3D mAP				3D mAPH			
		Overall	0–30 m	30–50 m	50 m-∞	Overall	0–30 m	30–50 m	50 m-∞
LEVEL 1	M3D-RPN [1]	0.35	1.12	0.18	0.02	0.34	1.10	0.18	0.02
	CaDNN [50]	5.03	14.54	1.47	0.10	4.99	14.43	1.45	0.10
	CMKD	**12.95**	**33.45**	**6.84**	**0.74**	**12.82**	**33.21**	**6.79**	**0.73**
	Improvement	**+7.92**	**+18.91**	**+5.37**	**+0.64**	**+7.83**	**+18.78**	**+5.34**	**+0.63**
LEVEL 2	M3D-RPN [1]	0.33	1.12	0.18	0.02	0.33	1.10	0.17	0.02
	CaDNN [50]	4.49	14.50	1.42	0.09	4.45	14.38	1.41	0.09
	CMKD	**11.44**	**33.04**	**6.22**	**0.58**	**11.33**	**32.80**	**6.17**	**0.57**
	Improvement	**+7.45**	**+18.54**	**+4.80**	**+0.49**	**+6.88**	**+18.42**	**+4.76**	**+0.48**

Table 4. Effectiveness of both distillation and the extension to handle unlabeled data. *Pre.* denotes using depth pre-trained backbone. *Feat.* denotes feature distillation. *Res.* denotes response distillation. *Un.* denotes distilling additional unlabeled data.

Pre.	Feat.	Res.	Un.	3D AP		
				Easy	Moderate	Hard
×	×	×	×	11.88	8.52	7.40
✓	×	×	×	17.60	13.48	11.81
✓	×	✓	×	18.81	14.49	12.16
✓	✓	×	×	22.20	15.46	13.47
✓	✓	✓	×	23.53	16.33	14.44
✓	✓	✓	✓	**30.17**	**21.54**	**19.44**

DD3D [44], the image backbone uses depth pre-training on *eigen clean* split for 10 epochs. We report the performance for all classes on KITTI *test*.

Waymo. We pre-train SECOND [61] on Waymo *train* for 10 epochs with a sampling interval 10. We train CMKD on Waymo *train* for 10 epochs with a sampling interval 5 and report the performance for Vehicle on Waymo *val*. The input image is resized to [960×640]. We do not use depth pre-training on Waymo.

4.3   Results on KITTI Test Set

We show the results on KITTI *test* in Table 1 and Table 2. Until submission, for all the three classes, either CMKD or CMKD* achieves new state-of-the-art results with significant improvements on KITTI *test*. With the official KITTI *trainval*, CMKD significantly surpasses the top ranking methods. With additional unlabeled data from KITTI Raw and our semi-supervised training framework, CMKD* achieves further boosted performance with significant improvements for Car and Cyclist. This implies that the extension to a semi-supervised framework is efficient in distilling beneficial information from massive unlabeled data and improves the performance. However, the performance for Pedestrian

Table 5. Effectiveness of components in feature distillation. $\mathcal{L}_{feat}$ denotes the feature distillation loss. DA denotes the domain adaptation module.

KITTI *train*					KITTI *train* + *Eigen clean*				
$\mathcal{L}_{feat}$	DA	3D AP			$\mathcal{L}_{feat}$	DA	3D AP		
		Easy	Moderate	Hard			Easy	Moderate	Hard
✗	✗	18.81	14.49	12.16	✗	✗	26.07	19.17	17.45
✓	✗	21.72	15.24	12.93	✓	✗	28.52	20.74	18.73
✓	✓	**23.53**	**16.33**	**14.44**	✓	✓	**30.17**	**21.54**	**19.44**

Table 6. Effectiveness of components in response distillation. $\mathcal{L}_{res}$ denotes the response distillation loss. $Conf.$ denotes the IoU-aware confidence scores of soft labels used to perform weighted supervision.

KITTI *train*					KITTI *train* + *Eigen clean*				
$\mathcal{L}_{res}$	$Conf.$	3D AP			$\mathcal{L}_{res}$	$Conf.$	3D AP		
		Easy	Moderate	Hard			Easy	Moderate	Hard
✗	✗	20.20	13.46	11.47	✗	✗	27.24	19.56	17.67
✓	✗	22.78	15.69	13.97	✓	✗	28.16	20.67	18.97
✓	✓	**23.53**	**16.33**	**14.44**	✓	✓	**30.17**	**21.54**	**19.44**

becomes worse with additional unlabeled data, and we conduct extra experiments to explore the reasons for this observation. This lies in the fact that the soft labels provided by the teacher model for Pedestrian are of insufficient quality, which can not provide good guidance for the student model. Detailed experiments and discussions can be found in the *Supplementary Materials*.

Note that DD3D [44], the top method before ours, uses large-scale extra dataset DDAD15M with $\sim 15M$ samples for depth training besides KITTI, while CMKD/CMKD* uses only KITTI and surpasses DD3D by a large margin. Also, other top methods like DD3D [44] or GUPNet [38], works well for Car and Pedestrian but poor for Cyclist, while CMKD works well for all three object classes, which demonstrates its good generalization performance across different object classes. We visualize some prediction results in Fig. 7.

4.4   Results on Waymo Open Dataset

We show the results for Vehicle on Waymo *val* in Table 3. With fewer training samples and lower image resolution than that in M3D-RPN [1] and CaDDN [50], CMKD achieves significant improvements on the two difficulty levels considering different distance ranges. We visualize some prediction results in Fig. 7.

4.5   Ablation Studies

Effectiveness of Both Distillation. As discussed earlier in this paper, existing Pseudo-LiDAR methods [41,58,59,63] leverage the LiDAR data via depth pre-training, while we further exploit the LiDAR data via knowledge distillation. As can be seen in Table 4, when using the depth pre-trained image backbone, the performance significantly improves against the baseline, indicating that the accurate depth information provided by LiDAR points is helpful for the task. And when each of our distillation module is applied, the performance is further significantly improved, indicating that our novel utilization of the LiDAR data via distillation can more fully exploit the potential of the LiDAR data and further improve the performance of the monocular 3D detector.

Effectiveness of Distilling Unlabeled Data. In Sect. 3.7, we introduced the improved utilization of unlabeled data in a semi-supervised manner. As shown in Table 4, the performance of CMKD is further improved when unlabeled data is added to distillation pipeline, indicating that our method is efficient in extracting beneficial information from massive unlabeled data and improves the performance. Specifically, we use $\sim 18k$ samples for training with $\sim 3.7k$ labeled and we reduce about 80% annotation cost. Also, we conducted experiments on the impact of different amounts of unlabeled data on the performance. Detailed experiments and discussions can be found in the *Supplementary Materials*.

Apart from jointly applying both distillation, we present novel designs in each distillation module, e.g., the DA module and the quality-aware supervision. We conduct experiments to show that the novel components are helpful for the task.

Effectiveness of Components in Feature Distillation. Here, the baseline is the full version of CMKD without the feature distillation loss $\mathcal{L}_{feat}$ and the DA module. As shown in Table 5, the performance improves significantly with the two components in the feature distillation. As can be seen from Fig. 5, the BEV feature map shows more clear patterns with highlighted object features when $\mathcal{L}_{feat}$ is added, and avoids smearing effects with aligned BEV features when DA is added. This shows that the components are effective in transferring the knowledge between the two modalities in the feature space.

Effectiveness of Components in Response Distillation. Here, the baseline is the full version of CMKD without the response distillation loss $\mathcal{L}_{res}$ and the quality-aware penalization weights. As shown in Table 6, the performance improves with the response distillation loss, and achieves further improvements with the awareness of soft label quality, i.e., with the adaptive supervision. This shows that the components are effective in transferring the knowledge between the two modalities in the response space.

Fig. 7. Qualitative results on KITTI *test* (top line) and Waymo *val* (bottom line). None of the samples were seen during training.

5   Conclusion

In this work, we propose the cross-modality knowledge distillation (CMKD) network to directly and efficiently transfer the knowledge from LiDAR modality to image modality on both features and responses, and significantly improve monocular 3D detection accuracy. Moreover, we extend CMKD as a semi-supervised training framework to distill useful knowledge from large-scale unlabeled data, further boosting the performance while reducing the annotation cost. CMKD achieves new state-of-the-art performance on both KITTI and Waymo benchmarks for monocular 3D object detection with significant performance gains compared to other methods, which shows its great effectiveness.

Broader Impact. Our CMKD framework opens up a new perspective in monocular 3D detection. We believe the effective distillation of unlabeled data demonstrates the potential of CMKD to generalize its application in real-world scenarios, where the unlabeled data is easy to collect for autonomous driving cars.

Acknowledgement. This work was supported by the National Key Research and Development Program of China (Grant No. 2018YFE0183900) and the YUNJI Technology Co. Ltd.

References

1. Brazil, G., Liu, X.: M3d-rpn: Monocular 3d region proposal network for object detection. In: ICCV (2019)
2. Caesar, H., Bankiti, V., Lang, A.H., et al.: Nuscenes: a multimodal dataset for autonomous driving. In: CVPR (2020)
3. Chen, H., Huang, Y., Tian, W., et al.: Monorun: monocular 3d object detection by reconstruction and uncertainty propagation. In: CVPR (2021)
4. Chen, L., Papandreou, G., Schroff, F., et al.: Rethinking atrous convolution for semantic image segmentation. CoRR abs/1706.05587 (2017)
5. Chen, X., Kundu, K., Zhu, Y., et al.: 3d object proposals for accurate object class detection. In: NIPS (2015)

6. Chen, Y.N., Dai, H., Ding, Y.: Pseudo-stereo for monocular 3d object detection in autonomous driving. In: Proceedings of the IEEE/CVF Conference on Computer Vision and Pattern Recognition, pp. 887–897 (2022)
7. Chong, Z., Ma, X., Zhang, H., Yue, Y., Li, H., Wang, Z., Ouyang, W.: Monodistill: learning spatial features for monocular 3d object detection (2022)
8. Dai, X., Jiang, Z., Wu, Z., et al.: General instance distillation for object detection. In: CVPR (2021)
9. Deng, J., Shi, S., Li, P., et al.: Voxel r-cnn: towards high performance voxel-based 3d object detection. In: AAAI (2021)
10. Ding, M., Huo, Y., Yi, H., et al.: Learning depth-guided convolutions for monocular 3d object detection. In: CVPR (2020)
11. Eigen, D., Puhrsch, C., Fergus, R.: Depth map prediction from a single image using a multi-scale deep network. In: NIPS (2014)
12. Ettinger, S., Cheng, S., Caine, B., et al.: Large scale interactive motion forecasting for autonomous driving: the waymo open motion dataset. CoRR abs/2104.10133 (2021)
13. Fu, H., Gong, M., Wang, C., et al.: Deep ordinal regression network for monocular depth estimation. In: CVPR (2018)
14. Furlanello, T., Lipton, Z.C., Tschannen, M., et al.: Born-again neural networks. In: Proceedings of International Conference on Machine Learning (ICML) (2018)
15. Geiger, A., Lenz, P., Stiller, C., Urtasun, R.: Vision meets robotics: the kitti dataset. In: International Journal of Robotics Research (IJRR) (2013)
16. Geiger, A., Lenz, P., Urtasun, R.: Are we ready for autonomous driving? the kitti vision benchmark suite. In: CVPR (2012)
17. Gülçehre, Ç., Bengio, Y.: Knowledge matters: importance of prior information for optimization. In: ICLR (2013)
18. Guo, X., Shi, S., et al.: Liga:learning lidar geometry aware representations for stereo-based 3d detector. In: ICCV (2021)
19. He, K., Zhang, X., Ren, S., et al.: Deep residual learning for image recognition. In: CVPR (2016)
20. Hinton, G.E., Vinyals, O., Dean, J.: Distilling the knowledge in a neural network. CoRR abs/1503.02531 (2015)
21. Huang, Z., Wang, N.: Like what you like: Knowledge distill via neuron selectivity transfer. CoRR abs/1707.01219 (2017)
22. Jörgensen, E., Zach, C., Kahl, F.: Monocular 3d object detection and box fitting trained end-to-end using intersection-over-union loss. CoRR abs/1906.08070
23. Ku, J., Mozifian, M., Lee, J., Harakeh, A., Waslander, S.L.: Joint 3d proposal generation and object detection from view aggregation. In: IROS (2018)
24. Ku, J., Mozifian, M., Lee, J., et al.: Joint 3d proposal generation and object detection from view aggregation. In: IEEE/RSJ International Conference on Intelligent Robots and Systems (IROS) (2018)
25. Ku, J., Pon, A.D., Waslander, S.L.: Monocular 3d object detection leveraging accurate proposals and shape reconstruction. In: CVPR (2019)
26. Königshof, H., Salscheider, N.O., Stiller, C.: Realtime 3D object detection for automated driving using stereo vision and semantic information. In: Proceedings of the IEEE Intelligent Transportation Systems Conference (2019)
27. Lee, J.H., Han, M.K., Ko, D.W., et al.: From big to small: multi-scale local planar guidance for monocular depth estimation (2019)
28. Li, J., Dai, H., Shao, L., Ding, Y.: Anchor-free 3d single stage detector with mask-guided attention for point cloud. In: Proceedings of the 29th ACM International Conference on Multimedia, pp. 553–562 (2021)

29. Li, J., Dai, H., Shao, L., Ding, Y.: From voxel to point: Iou-guided 3d object detection for point cloud with voxel-to-point decoder. In: Proceedings of the 29th ACM International Conference on Multimedia, pp. 4622–4631 (2021)
30. Li, J., et al.: 3d iou-net: Iou guided 3d object detector for point clouds. arXiv preprint. arXiv:2004.04962 (2020)
31. Li, J., et al.: P2v-rcnn: point to voxel feature learning for 3d object detection from point clouds. IEEE Access **9**, 98249–98260 (2021)
32. Li, P., Chen, X., Shen, S.: Stereo r-cnn based 3d object detection for autonomous driving. In: CVPR (2019)
33. Li, X., Wang, W., Wu, L., et al.: Generalized focal loss: Learning qualified and distributed bounding boxes for dense object detection. In: NIPS (2020)
34. Lin, T.Y., Goyal, P., Girshick, R., He, K., Dollár, P.: Focal loss for dense object detection. In: Proceedings of the IEEE International Conference on Computer Vision, pp. 2980–2988 (2017)
35. Lin, T.Y., et al.: Microsoft COCO: common objects in context. In: Fleet, D., Pajdla, T., Schiele, B., Tuytelaars, T. (eds.) ECCV 2014. LNCS, vol. 8693, pp. 740–755. Springer, Cham (2014). https://doi.org/10.1007/978-3-319-10602-1_48
36. Liu, J., Hou, Q., Cheng, M., et al.: Improving convolutional networks with self-calibrated convolutions. In: CVPR (2020)
37. Lu, X., Li, Q., Li, B., Yan, J.: MimicDet: bridging the gap between one-stage and two-stage object detection. In: Vedaldi, A., Bischof, H., Brox, T., Frahm, J.-M. (eds.) ECCV 2020. LNCS, vol. 12359, pp. 541–557. Springer, Cham (2020). https://doi.org/10.1007/978-3-030-58568-6_32
38. Lu, Y., Ma, X., Y ang, L., et al.: Geometry uncertainty projection network for monocular 3d object detection. arXiv preprint. arXiv:2107.13774 (2021)
39. Luo, S., Dai, H., Shao, L., Ding, Y.: M3dssd: Monocular 3d single stage object detector. In: Proceedings of the IEEE/CVF Conference on Computer Vision and Pattern Recognition, pp. 6145–6154 (2021)
40. Ma, X., Liu, S., Xia, Z., Zhang, H., Zeng, X., Ouyang, W.: Rethinking pseudo-lidar representation. In: Vedaldi, A., Bischof, H., Brox, T., Frahm, J.-M. (eds.) ECCV 2020. LNCS, vol. 12358, pp. 311–327. Springer, Cham (2020). https://doi.org/10.1007/978-3-030-58601-0_19
41. Ma, X., Wang, Z., Li, H., et al.: Accurate monocular 3d object detection via color-embedded 3d reconstruction for autonomous driving. In: ICCV (2019)
42. Ma, X., Zhang, Y., Xu, D., et al.: Delving into localization errors for monocular 3d object detection. In: CVPR (2021)
43. Pang, S., Morris, D.D., Radha, H.: Clocs: camera-lidar object candidates fusion for 3d object detection. In: IROS (2020)
44. Park, D., Ambrus, R., Guizilini, V.O.: Is pseudo-lidar needed for monocular 3d object detection? In: ICCV (2021)
45. Peng, L., Liu, F., Yu, Z., et al.: Lidar point cloud guided monocular 3d object detection. CoRR (2021)
46. Qi, C.R., Wei, L., Wu, C., et al.: Frustum pointnets for 3d object detection from rgb-d data. In: CVPR (2018)
47. Qi, C.R., Su, H., Mo, K., et al.: Pointnet: deep learning on point sets for 3d classification and segmentation. In: CVPR (2017)
48. Qi, C.R., Yi, L., Su, H., et al.: Pointnet++: deep hierarchical feature learning on point sets in a metric space. In: NIPS (2017)
49. Qin, Z., Wang, J., Lu, Y.: Monogrnet: a geometric reasoning network for 3d object localization. In: AAAI (2019)

50. Reading, C., Harakeh, A., Chae, J., Waslander, S.L.: Categorical depth distribution network for monocular 3d object detection. In: CVPR (2021)
51. Romero, A., Ballas, N., Kahou, S.E., et al.: Fitnets: hints for thin deep nets. In: ICLR (2015)
52. Shi, S., Guo, C., Jiang, L., et al.: Pv-rcnn: point-voxel feature set abstraction for 3d object detection. In: CVPR (2020)
53. Shi, S., Wang, X., Li, H.: Pointrcnn: 3d object proposal generation and detection from point cloud. In: CVPR (2019)
54. Shi, X., Ye, Q., Chen, X., et al.: Geometry-based distance decomposition for monocular 3d object detection. In: ICCV (2021)
55. Simonelli, A., Bulò, S.R., Porzi, L., et al.: Demystifying pseudo-lidar for monocular 3d object detection. CoRR abs/2012.05796 (2020)
56. Sun, J., Chen, L., Xie, Y., et al.: Disp r-cnn: stereo 3d object detection via shape prior guided instance disparity estimation. In: CVPR (2020)
57. Wang, L., Zhang, L., Zhu, Y., et al.: Progressive coordinate transforms for monocular 3d object detection. In: NIPS (2021)
58. Wang, Y., Chao, W.L., Garg, D., et al.: Pseudo-lidar from visual depth estimation: bridging the gap in 3d object detection for autonomous driving. In: CVPR (2019)
59. Weng, X., Kitani, K.: Monocular 3D Object Detection with Pseudo-LiDAR Point Cloud. arXiv:1903.09847 (2019)
60. Xu, Z., Hsu, Y., et al.: Training shallow and thin networks for acceleration via knowledge distillation with conditional adversarial networks. In: ICLR (2018)
61. Yan, Y., Mao, Y., Li, B.: SECOND: sparsely embedded convolutional detection. Sensors **18**(10), 3337 (2018)
62. Ye, X., et al.: Monocular 3D object detection via feature domain adaptation. In: Vedaldi, A., Bischof, H., Brox, T., Frahm, J.-M. (eds.) ECCV 2020. LNCS, vol. 12354, pp. 17–34. Springer, Cham (2020). https://doi.org/10.1007/978-3-030-58545-7_2
63. You, Y., Wang, Y., Chao, W.L., et al.: Pseudo-lidar++: accurate depth for 3d object detection in autonomous driving. In: ICLR (2020)
64. Zhang, Y., Lu, J., Zhou, J.: Objects are different: flexible monocular 3d object detection. In: CVPR (2021)
65. Zheng, W., Tang, W., Jiang, L., et al.: Se-ssd: self-ensembling single-stage object detector from point cloud. In: CVPR (2021)
66. Zhou, Y., Tuzel, O.: Voxelnet: end-to-end learning for point cloud based 3d object detection. CoRR abs/1711.06396 (2017)
67. Zou, Z., Ye, X., Du, L., et al.: The devil is in the task: exploiting reciprocal appearance-localization features for monocular 3d object detection. In: ICCV (2021)

ReAct: Temporal Action Detection with Relational Queries

Dingfeng Shi[1], Yujie Zhong[2], Qiong Cao[3(✉)], Jing Zhang[4], Lin Ma[2],
Jia Li[1(✉)], and Dacheng Tao[3,4]

[1] State Key Laboratory of Virtual Reality Technology and Systems, School of
Computer Science and Engineering, Beihang University, Beijing, China
jiali@buaa.edu.cn
[2] Meituan Inc, Beijing, China
[3] JD Explore Academy, Beijing, China
mathqiong2012@gmail.com
[4] The University of Sydney, Camperdown, Australia

Abstract. This work aims at advancing temporal action detection
(TAD) using an encoder-decoder framework with action queries, similar to DETR, which has shown great success in object detection. However, the framework suffers from several problems if directly applied to
TAD: the insufficient exploration of inter-query relation in the decoder,
the inadequate classification training due to a limited number of training
samples, and the unreliable classification scores at inference. To this end,
we first propose a relational attention mechanism in the decoder, which
guides the attention among queries based on their relations. Moreover,
we propose two losses to facilitate and stabilize the training of action classification. Lastly, we propose to predict the localization quality of each
action query at inference in order to distinguish high-quality queries.
The proposed method, named ReAct, achieves the state-of-the-art performance on THUMOS14, with much lower computational costs than
previous methods. Besides, extensive ablation studies are conducted to
verify the effectiveness of each proposed component. The code is available
at https://github.com/sssste/React.

1 Introduction

Temporal action detection (TAD) has been actively studied because of the deep
learning era. Inspired by the advance of one-stage object detectors [10,21,31],
many recent works focus on one-stage action detectors [17], which show excellent performance while having a relatively simple structure. On the other hand,
DETR [4], which tackles object detection in a Transformer encoder-decoder
framework, attracted considerable attention. In this work, we propose a novel

---

D. Shi—This work is done during an internship at JD Explore Academy.

Supplementary Information The online version contains supplementary material
available at https://doi.org/10.1007/978-3-031-20080-9_7.

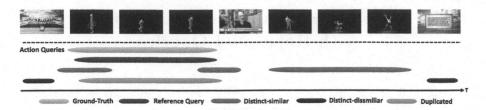

Fig. 1. The relation of queries. We choose the green one as the reference query, and the queries in a different relation to it are labeled with different colors. Only the Distinct-similar pair (Blue ones) will be kept for attention computation. (Color figure online)

one-stage action detector ReAct that is based on such a learning paradigm. Inspired by DETR, ReAct models action instances as a set of learnable action queries. These action queries are fed into the decoder as inputs, and they iteratively attend to the output features of the encoder as well as update their predictions. The action classification and localization are then predicted by two simple feedforward neural nets.

However, the DETR-like methods suffer from several problems when applied to TAD task. First, the inter-query relations are not fully explored by the self-attention in the decoder, which is performed densely over all the queries. Second, DETR-like methods may suffer from the inadequate training of action classification since the number of positive training samples for the classifier is relatively small compared to anchor-based/free methods. Moreover, when multiple queries fire for the same action instance at inference, queries with higher classification scores may not necessarily have better temporal localization. In the following, we elaborate on these problems and introduce the proposed methods to alleviate them in three aspects: attention mechanism, training losses, and inference.

The decoder in DETR-like methods applies the self-attention over the action queries to capture their relations, which can not fully explore the complex relations among queries. In this work, we denote the action queries that are responsible for localizing different action instances of similar or same action classes as *distinct-similar* queries, and those detecting different action classes as *distinct-dissimilar* queries. For the queries that fire for the same action instance, we regard them as *duplicate* queries. In this work, we propose a novel **attention mechanism**, named Relational Attention with IoU Decay (RAID), to explicitly handle these three types of query relations in the decoder. As Fig. 1 shows, RAID focuses on the communication among distinct-similar queries (since they are expected to provide more informative signals) and blocks the attention between distinct-dissimilar and duplicate queries. Furthermore, the proposed IoU decay encourages the duplicate queries to be slightly different from each other to enable a more diverse prediction.

Another problem is that a DETR-like approach may have a relatively low classification accuracy due to inadequate classification training. This is because the positive training samples for the classification of DETR-like methods are much fewer than those of the anchor-free methods. Namely, for DETR-like methods, the number of positives per input clip is only the same as the ground truth actions because of the bipartite-matching-based label assignment. To address this problem, we propose two **training losses**, codenamed Action Classification Enhancement (ACE) losses, to facilitate the classification learning. The first loss ACE-*enc* is applied to the input features of the encoder and is designed to reduce the intra-class variance and inter-class similarity of action instances. This loss explicitly improves the discriminability of video features regarding acting classes, thus benefiting the classification. Meanwhile, a ACE-*dec* loss is proposed as the classification loss in the decoder, which considers both the predicted segments and the ground-truth segments for action classification. It increases the training samples and generates a stable learning signal for the classifier.

Lastly, the action queries are redundant by design compared to the actual action instances. At inference, it is a common situation where multiple actions queries fire for the same action instance. Hence, it is important to focus on precise action localization queries. Nonetheless, the classification score is deficient in measuring the temporal localization quality. As a result, we propose a Segment Quality to predict the localization quality of each action query **at inference**, such that the more high-quality queries can be distinguished.

To summarize, we make the following contributions in this work:

- We approach temporal action detection using a DETR-like framework and identify three limitations of such method when directly applied to TAD.
- We propose the relational attention with IoU decay, the action classification enhancement losses, and the segment quality prediction, which alleviate the identified problems from the perspectives of attention mechanism, training losses, and network inference, respectively.
- Experiments on two action detection benchmarks demonstrate the superiority of ReAct: it achieves the state-of-the-art performance on THUMOS14, with much lower computational costs than previous methods. Extensive ablation studies are conducted to verify the effectiveness of each component.

2   Related Work

Temporal Action Detection. Temporal action detection (TAD) aims to detect all the start and end timestamps and the corresponding action types based on the video stream information. The existing methods can be roughly divided into two categories: two-stage methods and one-stage methods. Two-stage methods [11,12,16,18,20,27,35,40] split the detection task into two subtasks: proposal generation and proposal classification. Concretely, some methods [16,18,20] generate the proposals by predicting the probability of the start point and endpoint of the action and then selecting the proposal segments according to prediction score. In addition, PGCN [40] considers the relationship between proposals, then refines and classifies the proposals by Graph Convolutional Network. These two-stage methods can perform better by combining proposal generation networks and proposal classification networks. However, they can not be trained in an end-to-end manner and are computationally inefficient. To solve the above problems, some one-stage methods [6,17,19,25,34] are proposed. Some works [6,17,37] try to adapt to the high variance of the action duration by constructing a temporal feature pyramid, while Liu *et al.* [22] propose to dynamically sample temporal features by learnable parameters. These one-stage methods reduce the complexity of the models, which are more computationally friendly. In this work, we mainly follow the one-stage fashion and the deformable convolution design [9,22,44] to build a efficient action detector, which will be detailed in the Sect. 3.

Attention-Based Model. Attention-based models [32] have achieved great success in machine translation and been extended to the field of computer vision [1,8,23,24,36,41] in recent years. The attention module computes a soft weight dynamically for a set of points at runtime. Concretely, DETR [4] proposes a Transformer-based image detection paradigm. It learns decoder input features shared by all input videos and detects a fixed number of outputs. Deformable DETR [44] improves DETR by reducing the number of pairs to be computed in the attention module with learnable spatial offsets. Liu *et al.* [22] propose an end-to-end framework for TAD based on Deformable DETR. This type of training paradigm is highly efficient and fast in prediction. However, there is still a performance gap between these methods and the latest methods in TAD [22,40]. Our work is built on DETR-like workflows. In contrast to the above work, our approach suppresses the flow of invalid information by constricting a computational subset for the attention module, which improves performance effectively.

Contrastive Learning. Contrastive learning [7] is a method that has been widely used in unsupervised learning. NCE [13] mines data features by distinguishing between data and noise. Info-NCE [26] is proposed to extract representations from high-dimensional data with a probabilistic contrastive loss. Lin *et al.* [17] leverage contrastive learning to help network identify action boundaries. Inspired by these works, we use contrastive learning to extract a global common representation of action categories and enlarge the feature distance between action segments and noise segments.

3   Method

Problem Definition. This work focuses on the problem of temporal action detection (TAD). Specifically, given a set of untrimmed videos $\mathcal{D} = \{\mathcal{V}_i\}_{i=1}^n$. A set of $\{X_i, Y_i\}$ can be extracted from each video $\mathcal{V}_i$, where $X_i = \{x_t\}_{t=1}^T$ corresponds to the image (and optical flow) features of T snippets and $Y_i = \{m_k, d_k, c_k\}_{k=1}^{K_i}$ is K_i segment labels for the video V_i with the action segment midpoint time m_k, the action duration d_k and the corresponding action category c_k. Temporal action detection aims at predicting all segments Y_i based on the input feature X_i.

Method Overview. Motivated by DETR [4], we approach the problem of TAD by an encoder-decoder framework based on the transformer network. As Fig. 3

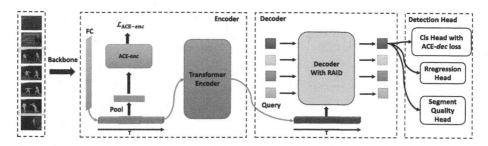

Fig. 2. Illustration of the proposed framework. The video feature is extracted by a pretrained backbone, followed by a fully-connected layer to project the feature, and is additionally supervised by the AEC-Enc loss. After enhancement by the Transformer encoder, the features are fed into the decoder and attended by L_q action queries in the decoder. The classification head is trained with the proposed ACE-Dec loss.

shows, the overall architecture of ReAct contains three parts: a video feature extractor, an action encoder, and an action decoder. First, video clip features are extracted from each RGB frame by using the widely-used 3D-CNN (*e.g.*, TSN [33] or I3D [5]). The optical flow features are also extracted using TVL1 optical flow algorithm [39]. Following that, a 1-D conv layer is used to modify the feature dimension of the clip features. The output features are then passed to the action encoder, which is a L_E-layer transformer network. The encoded clip features serve as one of the inputs to the action decoder. The decoder is a L_D-layer transformer, and it differs from the encoder in two aspects. It has action queries (which are learnable embeddings) as inputs, and the queries attend the encoder outputs in each layer of the decoder, known as Cross-attention. Essentially, ReAct maps action instances as a set of action queries. The action queries are transformed by the decoder into output embeddings which are used for both action classification and temporal localization by separate feed-forward neural nets. The details of the encoder structure are provided in the appendix.

At training, following previous works [4,22,44], the Hungarian Algorithm [15] is applied to assign labels to the action queries. The edge weight is defined by the summation of the segment IoU, the probability of classification, and the L1 norm between two coordinates. Based on the matching, ReAct applies several losses to the action queries, including the action classification loss and temporal segment regression loss.

Limitations of DETR-Like Methods for TAD. DETR-like methods may suffer from several problems when applied to TAD task. First, the decoder performs the self-attention densely over all the queries, which causes the inter-query relations not to be sufficiently explored. Second, compared with anchor-based/free methods, DETR-like methods may have issues in deficit training of action classification attributed to relatively smaller number of positive training samples for the classifier. Third, queries with higher classification scores may not be reliable due to multiple queries firing for the same action instance at inference.

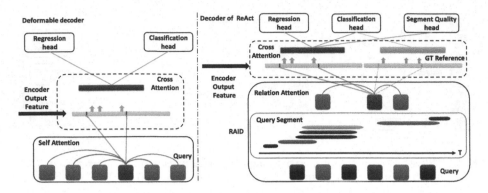

Fig. 3. Illustration of our decoder. **Left:** plain deformable decoder. Each query performs the attention operation with all other query features and sample segment features from the encoder output. **Right:** decoder of ReAct. Each query only attends to specific queries based on the inter-query relation. Besides, the ground-truth segment provides an additional loss to further supervise the classification head. Note that for clarity, the LayerNorm, FFN, and residual connection are not shown in the figure (see appendix for detailed network structure).

In this work, we mitigate these problems in three aspects: (1) We propose the Relational Attention with IoU Decay which allows each action query to attend to others in the decoder based on their relations; (2) We design two Action Classification Enhancement losses to enhance the action classification learning at the encoder and decoder, respectively; (3) We introduce a Segment Quality to predict the localization quality of each action query at inference to compensate the deficiency of classification score at inference. We elaborate on these three aspects in the following.

3.1   Relational Attention with IoU Decay

To better explore the inter-query relation in the decoder, we present the Relational Attention with IoU Decay (RAID) which replaces the self-attention in the transformer decoder. Below, we describe the proposed method in detail.

Relational Attention. As a recap, we define three types of queries with respect to an action query q_i, which are differentiated by their relations to q_i. *Distinct-similar* queries are the queries that try to detect different action instances but of similar (or same) action class to q_i. *Distinct-dissimilar* queries are those which try to detect different action instances and of dissimilar action class to q_i. *Duplicate* queries are the queries that try to detect the same action instance as q_i. Intuitively, we anticipate that attending to distinct-dissimilar queries does not provide informative signals to q_i, since they focus on different action classes, and the relation between action classes may not be a reliable cue for detecting actions. On the contrary, attending to distinct-similar queries can benefit the query q by gathering some background information and cues around q_i. For example, some actions may occur multiple times in a clip, and attending to each other can increase the confidence of the detection. Moreover, duplicate queries only repeat the prediction as q_i, so they bring no extra information and should be ignored in the attention for q_i.

To find the distinct-similar queries for a query q_i, we consider two properties, namely, high context similarity and low temporal overlap. To measure context similarity, we compute a similarity matrix $A \in \mathbb{R}^{L_q \times L_q}$ (L_q is the number of queries) based on the query features, where each element represents the cosine similarity of two queries. Then the query-pair set $\mathcal{E}_{sim}$ is constructed by

$$\mathcal{E}_{sim} = \{(i,j)|A[i,j] - \gamma > 0\}, \tag{1}$$

where $\gamma \in [-1,1]$ is a preset similarity threshold. To identify the queries having low temporal overlap with q, a natural strategy is using the Interaction of Union (IoU) in the time domain, which measures the overlap between two temporal segments. Therefore, we compute a pair-wise IoU matrix $B \in \mathbb{R}^{L_q \times L_q}$ for the reference segments and construct a query-pair set $\mathcal{E}_{IoU}$ as follows:

$$\mathcal{E}_{IoU} = \{(i,j)|B[i,j] - \tau < 0\}, \tag{2}$$

where i and j denote the i-th and j-th queries respectively, and $\tau \in [0,1]$ is a preset IoU threshold. As shown in Fig. 3, this simple strategy removes the segments which have large temporal overlap. We can then define the distinct-similar query-pair set $\mathcal{E}$ by combining $\mathcal{E}_{sim}$, $\mathcal{E}_{IoU}$ and the query itself $\mathcal{E}_s$. The definition is given as follow:

$$\mathcal{E} = (\mathcal{E}_{IoU} \setminus \mathcal{E}_{sim}) \cup \mathcal{E}_s. \tag{3}$$

For a query q_i and its distinct query-pair set $\mathcal{E}_i$, the key and value features can be written as $K_i = concatenate(\{k_j|(i,j) \in \mathcal{E}_i\})$ and $V_i = concatenate(\{v_j|(i,j) \in \mathcal{E}_i\})$. Then, the query features q_i are updated by

$$q_i' = a_i V_i^T, \tag{4}$$

where the attention weight a_i is

$$a_i = Softmax_K(q_i K_i^T). \tag{5}$$

Note that by considering both the context similarity and temporal overlap, the proposed relational attention successfully preserves the communication between q_i and useful queries while blocking that between uninformative ones.

IoU Decay. Apart from relational attention, we introduce a further improvement by handling duplicate queries. Namely, we propose a regularization, termed as IoU decay, which is added to the network optimization. It is given as

$$\omega_d = \frac{1}{2} \sum_{i=1}^{L_q} \sum_{j=1}^{L_q} IoU(s_i, s_j). \tag{6}$$

During the detector training, it penalizes the IoU between queries, such that duplicate queries can be diversified and different from each other, which can increase the probability of obtaining a more precise localization for the target action instance.

3.2   Action Classification Enhancement

To combat the issue of the inadequate learning of classification when applying the DETR-like methods to TAD, we propose two Action Classification Enhancement (ACE) losses to boost the classification performance.

ACE-*enc* Loss. We aim to enhance the features with respect to action classification in the phase of encoder by enlarging the similarity of inter-class action instances and reducing the variance between intra-class action instances. We posit that explicitly increasing the discriminability of the features on the action detection dataset in an early stage can also benefit the final action classification. Specifically, we optimize the input features of the encoder using contrastive loss.

The positive and negative action instance pairs are constructed as follows. For a given ground-truth action segment s_g and its category c_g in a video v_i, we choose its positive instances by sampling the action segments of the same category c_g from either the same or different videos. As for its negative instances, we choose them from two different sources: (1) segments of action categories different from c_g and (2) segments that are completely inside the ground-truth segment, but their IoU is less than a specific threshold ξ.

For a given segment s, we denote $x \in \mathbb{R}^{T \times D'}$ and $\widetilde{x} \in \mathbb{R}^{T \times D}$ as the pre-trained video feature and feature further projected by a fully-connected layer l (i.e. $\widetilde{x} = l(x)$), respectively. Then, the segment feature after temporal RoI pooling [35] can be denoted as $f = RoI(\widetilde{x}, s) \in \mathbb{R}^D$. The loss is given by

$$\mathcal{L}_{ACE-enc} = -\log \frac{\exp(f^T f_p)}{\sum_{j \in \mathcal{D}} \exp(f^T f_j)}, \tag{7}$$

where f_p is a positive segment of f and $\mathcal{D}$ is the index of k random negative instances as well as a positive instance.

ACE-*dec* Loss. Anchor-based/free methods treat all (or multiple) the temporal locations within the ground truth action segment as positives (*i.e.*, belonging to an action class rather than backgrounds) for training the action classifiers, whereas DETR-like methods have much fewer positives due to the bipartite matching at label assignment. We, therefore, propose the ACE-*dec* loss to train the action classifiers.

As Fig. 3 (right) shows, in the training phase, an additional positive training sample is fed to the action classifiers for each query segment (*i.e.*, the green one) matched with a ground-truth action instance. The additional positive is obtained by feeding the ground-truth segment (*i.e.*, the yellow one) as a normal query segment to the cross-attention layer. The details of the cross-attention layer are described in the supplementary material.

Concretely, every decoder layer is attached a ACE-*dec* loss which is given by

$$\mathcal{L}_{ACE-dec} = \mathcal{L}^q_{foc} + \mathbb{1}_{y \neq \emptyset}[\mathcal{L}^{gt}_{foc}], \tag{8}$$

where $\mathcal{L}^q_{foc}$ and $\mathcal{L}^{gt}_{foc}$ is the sigmoid Focal Loss [21] for the query and ground-truth classification loss respectively. Note that, only the queries that are matched to ground-truth segments will contribute the ground-truth classification loss.

3.3   Segment Quality Prediction

To remedy the problem that classification score is unreliable for selecting the best query among a set of duplicate queries, we propose a Segment Quality to predict the localization quality of each action query at inference for distinguishing high-quality queries. The proposed segment quality prediction considers both the midpoint of the segment as well as its temporal coverage on the action instance. Concretely, given a predicted segment s_q and its query feature f_q, we define $(\zeta_1, \zeta_2) = \phi(f_q)$, where ϕ is a single fully-connected layer and $\zeta_1, \zeta_2 \in [0, 1]$. Then, a final quality value ζ is defined by $\zeta = \zeta_1 \cdot \zeta_2$. Segment Quality is supervised by a two-dimensional vector composing of the offset of the predicted midpoint and its ground truth for localizing the midpoint precisely, and the IoU between the predicted segment and its closest ground-truth segment for accurate temporal localization and coverage. The overall loss is given by

$$\mathcal{L}_\zeta = \sum \left| \phi(f_q) - (\exp(-\frac{1}{l_{gt}}|m_q - m_{gt}|), IoU(s_q, s_{gt})) \right|_1, \tag{9}$$

where m_q is the midpoint of the predicted segment, and m_{gt}, l_{gt} are the midpoint and length of the ground-truth segment, respectively. At inference, ζ is multiplied with the classification score of the segment.

3.4   Training Losses

At training, based on the label assignment by the Hungarian Algorithm, ReAct is trained by the total loss as follow:

$$\mathcal{L} = \mathcal{L}_{ACE-enc} + \mathcal{L}_{ACE-dec} + \mathcal{L}_\zeta + \mathcal{L}_{reg}. \tag{10}$$

Here, $\mathcal{L}_{reg}$ is the commonly used regression loss for TAD which regresses the midpoint and the duration of the detected segments using the summation of L1 distance and the generalized IoU distance [28] for the matched pair. We define each objective as follows:

$$\begin{aligned}
\mathcal{L}_{reg} &= \frac{1}{N_{c_{gt} \neq \emptyset}} \sum_{j \in L_q} \mathbb{1}_{c^{(j)}_{gt} \neq \emptyset} [\gamma_1 \mathcal{L}^{(j)}_{L1} + \gamma_2 \mathcal{L}^{(j)}_{gIoU}], \\
\mathcal{L}^{(j)}_{L1} &= |m^{(j)}_{gt} - m^{(j)}| + |d^{(j)}_{gt} - d^{(j)}|, \\
\mathcal{L}^{(j)}_{gIoU} &= 1 - gIoU(s^{(j)}_{gt}, s^{(j)}),
\end{aligned} \tag{11}$$

where $s^{(j)} = (m^{(j)}, d^{(j)})$ is j-th detected segment represented by midpoint and the duration. $c_{gt}^{(j)}$ is a set of the ground-truth segments that s^j is matched and $N_{c_{gt} \neq \emptyset}$ is the number of segments in $c_{gt}^{(j)}$. $s_{gt}^{(j)} = (m_{gt}^{(j)}, d_{gt}^{(j)})$ is the matched ground-truth segment of s^j and $s_{gt}^{(j)} \in c_{gt}^{(j)}$. In addition, we follow the segment refinement fashion [22, 44] to predict detections in each decoder layer, each of which will be updated by summing with the upper layer segment and renormalizing it. In this way, each layer provides auxiliary classification loss $\mathcal{L}'_{cls}$ and regression loss $\mathcal{L}'_{reg}$, which further helps the network training.

4   Experiment

We conduct experiments on two challenging datasets: THUMOS14 [14] and ActivityNet-1.3 [3].

4.1   Implementation Details

Architecture Details. For THUMOS14, we set $L_q = 40$, $L_E = 2$, $L_D = 4$ for the number of queries, encoder layer and decoder layer, respectively. Each deformable attention module samples 4 temporal offsets for computing the attention. The hidden layer dimension of the feedforward network is set to 1024, and the other hidden feature dimension in the intermediate of the network is all set to 256. The pair-wise IoU threshold τ and feature similarity threshold γ in ACE module are set to 0.2 and 0.2, respectively. For ActivityNet-1.3, we set $L_q = 60$, $L_E = 3$, $L_D = 4$, $\tau = 0.9$, $\gamma = -0.2$. We sample 4 temporal offsets for the deformable module. For more implementation details including feature extraction and training details, please refer to the supplementary material.

Optimization Parameters and Inference. We train the ReAct with AdamW optimizer with a batch size of 16. The learning rate is set to 2×10^{-4} and 1×10^{-4} for THUMOS14 and ActivityNet-1.3 respectively. ReAct is trained for 15 epochs on THUMOS14 and 35 epochs on ActivityNet-1.3. At inference, the classification head output is activated by sigmoid. Then all the predictions will be processed with Soft-NMS [2] to remove the redundant and low-quality segments.

4.2   Main Results

On THUMOS14 (see Table 1), our ReAct achieves superior performance and suppresses the state-of-the-art one-stage and two-stage methods in mAP at different thresholds. In particular, ReAct achieves 55.0% in the average mAP, which outperforms TadTR by a large margin, namely about the 9.4% absolute improvement. Besides, we compare the computational performance during testing. We adopt Floating-point operations per second (FLOPs) per clip following the previous works. [22, 45]. We can see that our model has FLOPS of 0.68 G, which is 0.06 G lower than TadTr and much lower than all the other methods. Note that

Table 1. Comparison with the state-of-the-art methods on THUMOS14 dataset. We report the mean Average Precision (mAP) in different thresholds and the floating-point operations (FLOPs, G).

Type	Method	0.3	0.4	0.5	0.6	0.7	Avg.	FLOPs
Two-stage	BSN [20]	53.5	45.0	36.9	28.4	20.0	36.8	3.4
	BMN [18]	56.0	47.4	38.8	29.7	20.5	38.5	171.0
	G-TAD [35]	54.5	47.6	40.3	30.8	23.4	39.3	639.8
	TAL [6]	53.2	48.5	42.8	33.8	20.8	39.8	–
	TCANet [27]	60.6	53.2	44.6	36.8	26.7	44.3	–
	CSA+BMN [29]	64.4	58.0	49.2	38.2	27.8	47.5	–
	P-GCN [40]	63.6	57.8	49.1	–	–	–	4.4
	RTD-Net [30]	68.3	62.3	51.9	38.8	23.7	49.0	–
	VSGN [42]	66.7	60.4	52.4	41.0	30.4	50.2	–
	ContextLoc [45]	68.3	63.8	54.3	41.8	26.2	50.9	3.1
One-stage	SSAD [19]	43.0	35.0	24.6	–	–	–	–
	SSN [38]	51.9	41.0	29.9	–	–	–	–
	A2Net [37]	58.6	54.1	45.5	32.5	17.2	41.6	30.4
	AFSD [17]	67.3	62.4	55.5	43.7	31.1	52.0	5.1
	TadTr [22]	62.4	57.4	49.2	37.8	26.3	46.6	0.75
	ReAct	**69.2**	**65.0**	**57.1**	**47.8**	**35.6**	**55.0**	**0.68**

the FLOPS we report in the table does not include the computation of video feature extraction with backbone. For methods like AFSD, which fine-tunes the backbone and does feature extraction during testing, we ignore the computation of feature extraction and only report the FLOPs afterward.

On ActivityNet-1.3, our method achieves comparable results to the state-of-the-art (See Table 2). The ReAct outperforms the other DETR-based methods while enjoying a low computational cost (*e.g.*, 0.38 G). The Actioness and Anchor-based methods tend to have higher performance compared with the DETR-based methods. One possible reason is that the DETR-based methods take learnable query embedding as input, which is video-agnostic and only keeps statistical information. For a dataset with a large variance in action time, a query feature has to take both long and short action into account (See appendix for more details) and is prone to conflicts.

4.3   Ablation Study

In this section, we conduct the ablation studies on the THUMOS14 dataset.

Main Components. We demonstrate the effectiveness of three proposed components in ReAct: RAID, ACE, and Segment Quality. From Table 3 (row 2 and

Table 2. Comparison with the state-of-the-art methods on ActivityNet-1.3 dataset.

Type	Method	0.5	0.75	0.95	Avg.	FLOPs(G)
Actioness	BSN [20]	46.5	30.0	8.0	28.2	–
	SSN [38]	43.2	28.7	5.6	28.3	–
	BMN [18]	50.1	34.8	8.3	33.9	45.6
	G-TAD [35]	50.4	34.6	9.0	34.1	45.7
	BU-TAL [43]	43.5	33.9	**9.2**	34.3	–
	VSGN [42]	**52.3**	**35.2**	8.3	**34.7**	–
Anchor-based	TAL [6]	38.2	18.3	1.3	20.2	–
	PGCN [40]	48.3	33.2	3.3	31.1	5.0
	TCANet [27]	52.3	**36.7**	**6.9**	**35.5**	–
	AFSD [17]	**52.4**	35.2	6.5	34.3	15.3
DETR-based	RTD-Net [30]	47.2	30.7	**8.6**	30.8	–
	TadTr [22]	49.1	32.6	8.5	32.3	**0.38**
	ReAct	**49.6**	**33.0**	8.6	**32.6**	**0.38**

Table 3. Ablation study on three main components.

Method	RAID	ACE	SQ	0.3	0.4	0.5	0.6	0.7	Avg.
Our Base				66.6	59.2	49.7	38.0	25.0	47.7
		√	√	66.6	61.5	53.7	43.4	31.2	51.3
	√		√	67.0	62.6	54.4	44.0	32.2	52.1
	√	√		69.1	63.3	54.2	43.5	31.0	52.2
	√	√	√	**69.2**	**65.0**	**57.1**	**47.8**	**35.6**	**55.0**

row 5), we can see that compared with the plain deformable decoder layer, our RAID brings about a 3.7% absolute improvement in the average mAP, proving the effectiveness of the module by introducing the relational attention based on the defined distinct-similar, distinct-dissimilar and duplicated queries. Besides, from rows 4 and 5 of the Table, we see our ACE improves the average mAP performance by 2.9%, which shows its effectiveness by designing new losses to enhance classification learning. Finally, from rows 3 and 5, the proposed Segment Quality achieves 2.8% improvements in average mAP, which effectively estimates the predicted segments' quality at inference.

Analysis of RAID. We study the effect of two hyperparameters γ and τ in Sect. 3.1 for thresholding the similarity scores and IoU values when constructing the distinct similar and dissimilar query sets. First, we set $\tau = 1$ and plot the average mAP when varying γ. From Fig. 5(a) we see that as γ increases, the mAP exhibits an increase followed by a decrease, with a peak at $\tau = 0.2$. Besides, we observe that the detection performance shows greater volatility as τ decreases

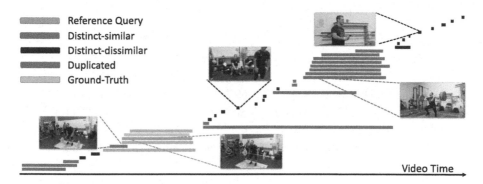

Fig. 4. Visualization of the queries for a test video in THUMOS14. Some example frames are shown for the queries, and we can see that many distinct-dissimilar queries correspond to noises (i.e. not actions).

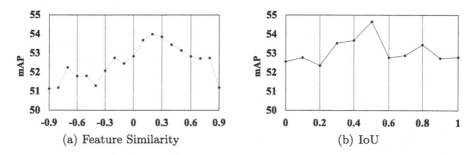

Fig. 5. (a) is visualization of the choice of the hyperparameter γ, with $\tau = 1$; (b) is visualization of the choice of the hyperparameter τ, with $\gamma = 0.2$

further (*i.e.*, $\tau < -0.1$). Intuitively, smaller τ leads to more irrelevant query pairs communicating, thus introducing greater uncertainty. Next, we study the effect of the choice of τ by fixing $\gamma = 0.2$. From Fig. 5(b) we observe a similar trend with the figure for similarity as τ changes, and the optimal value is obtained at 0.5. Notice that the smaller τ is, the more queries will be excluded, and when $\tau = 0$, only those that do not overlap will be retained. Intuitively, partially overlapped queries tend to be in the vicinity of the target query, which helps to perceive the information near the boundary. A visualized example of the queries is presented in Fig. 4 to illustrate the work of RAID.

Analysis of ACE. We analyze the effect of ACE-enc loss in the following aspects: the construction of contrastive pairs, where to apply ACE-*enc* loss and training losses. First, we study how contrastive pairs affect performance. In particular, to form the positive segment pairs, we randomly choose segments of the same category from either the same video or different videos, denoted by **S1** and **S2**, respectively. As for negative pairs, there are two ways: segment pairs belonging to different action classes (denoted by **N1**), and segment pairs that

Table 4. Comparison of different settings of ACE module.

Module	Setting	0.3	0.4	0.5	0.6	0.7	Avg.
ACE-*enc*	No contrastive	68.1	63.4	55.0	46.0	32.8	53.1
	{S1, S2} + {N1}	68.3	63.4	55.4	**46.2**	33.9	53.4
	{S1, S2} + {N2}	69.7	64.6	55.7	45.6	33.8	53.9
	{S1, S2} + {N1, N2}	**69.7**	**64.5**	**56.6**	45.9	**34.7**	**54.3**
	{S1} + {N1, N2}	69.1	64.4	56.3	**46.2**	34.6	54.1
	Before transformer enc.	**69.7**	**64.3**	**56.1**	46.4	**34.2**	**54.1**
	After transformer enc.	66.4	61.2	53.3	43.4	32.0	51.2
ACE-*dec*	$\mathcal{L}_{foc}^{q}$ Only	67.5	62.6	53.9	43.3	33.2	52.1
	$\mathcal{L}_{foc}^{gt}$ Only	66.1	61.1	53.6	44.2	30.9	51.2
	$\mathcal{L}_{foc}^{q} + \mathcal{L}_{foc}^{gt}$	**68.3**	**63.4**	**55.4**	**46.2**	**33.9**	**53.4**

one completely includes the other, but their IoU is less than a threshold (denoted by **N2**), as described in 3.2. Table 4 presents the results using different combinations of positive and negative pairs. In Table 4, we see that **N2** play a more important role in training than **N1** (*e.g.*, average mAP 53.9 versus 53.4), and merging them can gain further promotion (*i.e.*, 54.3).

Secondly, we study the effect of where to apply ACE-*enc* loss. We mainly consider two positions: before the transformer encoder and after it. We train a single fully connected layer for the former to enhance the video features. For the latter, we use the encoder output. The experimental results show that a single fully connected layer is much better than a complex transformer encoder. Intuitively, after encoder processing, the features on each frame already contain local temporal information, therefore, the pooled segment features can not represent the action precisely, leading to inaccurate convergence.

Finally, to go deeper into the ACE-*dec* loss, we conducted three experiments: query classification loss only, ground-truth classification loss only, and the complete ACE-*dec* loss. For the case of the ground-truth classification loss only, we still predict and match the ground-truth segment with the input query feature, which provides the matched query position and reference ground-truth segment. However, we only update the network with ground-truth classification loss $\mathcal{L}_{foc}^{gt}$. From the Table 4, neither $\mathcal{L}_{foc}^{q}$ nor $\mathcal{L}_{foc}^{gt}$ can perform well, but when we combine them together, the result are significantly better (*e.g.*, 53.4 versus 51.2).

5 Conclusion

In this work, we consider the task of temporal action detection and propose a novel one-stage action detector ReAct based on a DETR-like learning framework. Three limitations of such a method when directly applied to TAD are identified. We propose the relational attention with IoU decay, the action classification enhancement losses, and the segment quality prediction and handle those issues from three aspects: attention mechanism, training losses, and network inference, respectively. ReAct achieves the state-of-the-art performance with much lower computational costs than previous methods on THUMOS14. Extensive ablation studies are also conducted to demonstrate the effectiveness of each proposed component. In the future, we plan to include the video feature extractor in the action detection training to improve the performance further.

Acknowledgement. This work is supported by the Major Science and Technology Innovation 2030 "New Generation Artificial Intelligence" key project (No. 2021ZD0111700), National Natural Science Foundation of China under Grant 62132002, Grant 61922006 and Grant 62102206.

References

1. Arnab, A., Dehghani, M., Heigold, G., Sun, C., Lučić, M., Schmid, C.: Vivit: a video vision transformer. In: Proceedings of the IEEE/CVF International Conference on Computer Vision, pp. 6836–6846 (2021)
2. Bodla, N., Singh, B., Chellappa, R., Davis, L.S.: Soft-nms-improving object detection with one line of code. In: Proceedings of the IEEE International Conference on Computer vision, pp. 5561–5569 (2017)
3. Caba Heilbron, F., Escorcia, V., Ghanem, B., Carlos Niebles, J.: Activitynet: A large-scale video benchmark for human activity understanding. In: Proceedings of the IEEE Conference on Computer Vision and Pattern Recognition, pp. 961–970 (2015)
4. Carion, N., Massa, F., Synnaeve, G., Usunier, N., Kirillov, A., Zagoruyko, S.: End-to-End object detection with transformers. In: Vedaldi, A., Bischof, H., Brox, T., Frahm, J.-M. (eds.) ECCV 2020. LNCS, vol. 12346, pp. 213–229. Springer, Cham (2020). https://doi.org/10.1007/978-3-030-58452-8_13
5. Carreira, J., Zisserman, A.: Quo vadis, action recognition? a new model and the kinetics dataset. In: proceedings of the IEEE Conference on Computer Vision and Pattern Recognition, pp. 6299–6308 (2017)
6. Chao, Y.W., Vijayanarasimhan, S., Seybold, B., Ross, D.A., Deng, J., Sukthankar, R.: Rethinking the faster r-cnn architecture for temporal action localization. In: Proceedings of the IEEE Conference on Computer Vision and Pattern Recognition, pp. 1130–1139 (2018)
7. Chen, T., Kornblith, S., Norouzi, M., Hinton, G.: A simple framework for contrastive learning of visual representations. In: International Conference on Machine Learning, pp. 1597–1607. PMLR (2020)
8. Chen, X., Cao, Q., Zhong, Y., Zhang, J., Gao, S., Tao, D.: Dearkd: data-efficient early knowledge distillation for vision transformers. In: Proceedings of the IEEE/CVF Conference on Computer Vision and Pattern Recognition, pp. 12052–12062 (2022)
9. Dai, J., Qi, H., Xiong, Y., Li, Y., Zhang, G., Hu, H., Wei, Y.: Deformable convolutional networks. In: Proceedings of the IEEE International Conference on Computer Vision, pp. 764–773 (2017)
10. Feng, C., Zhong, Y., Gao, Y., Scott, M.R., Huang, W.: Tood: task-aligned one-stage object detection. arXiv preprint. arXiv:2108.07755 (2021)

11. Gao, J., Chen, K., Nevatia, R.: CTAP: complementary temporal action proposal generation. In: Ferrari, V., Hebert, M., Sminchisescu, C., Weiss, Y. (eds.) ECCV 2018. LNCS, vol. 11206, pp. 70–85. Springer, Cham (2018). https://doi.org/10.1007/978-3-030-01216-8_5

12. Gao, J., Yang, Z., Chen, K., Sun, C., Nevatia, R.: Turn tap: temporal unit regression network for temporal action proposals. In: Proceedings of the IEEE International Conference on Computer Vision, pp. 3628–3636 (2017)

13. Gutmann, M., Hyvärinen, A.: Noise-contrastive estimation: a new estimation principle for unnormalized statistical models. In: Proceedings of the 13th International Conference on Artificial Intelligence and Statistics, pp. 297–304. JMLR Workshop and Conference Proceedings (2010)

14. Jiang, Y.G., et al.: THUMOS challenge: action recognition with a large number of classes (2014)

15. Kuhn, H.W.: The hungarian method for the assignment problem. Naval Res. Logistics Q. **2**(1–2), 83–97 (1955)

16. Lin, C., et al.: Fast learning of temporal action proposal via dense boundary generator. In: Proceedings of the AAAI Conference on Artificial Intelligence, vol. 34, pp. 11499–11506 (2020)

17. Lin, C., et al.: Learning salient boundary feature for anchor-free temporal action localization. In: Proceedings of the IEEE/CVF Conference on Computer Vision and Pattern Recognition, pp. 3320–3329 (2021)

18. Lin, T., Liu, X., Li, X., Ding, E., Wen, S.: Bmn: boundary-matching network for temporal action proposal generation. In: Proceedings of the IEEE/CVF International Conference on Computer Vision, pp. 3889–3898 (2019)

19. Lin, T., Zhao, X., Shou, Z.: Single shot temporal action detection. In: Proceedings of the 25th ACM international conference on Multimedia, pp. 988–996 (2017)

20. Lin, T., Zhao, X., Su, H., Wang, C., Yang, M.: BSN: boundary sensitive network for temporal action proposal generation. In: Ferrari, V., Hebert, M., Sminchisescu, C., Weiss, Y. (eds.) ECCV 2018. LNCS, vol. 11208, pp. 3–21. Springer, Cham (2018). https://doi.org/10.1007/978-3-030-01225-0_1

21. Lin, T.Y., Goyal, P., Girshick, R., He, K., Dollár, P.: Focal loss for dense object detection. In: Proceedings of the IEEE International Conference on Computer Vision, pp. 2980–2988 (2017)

22. Liu, X., Wang, Q., Hu, Y., Tang, X., Bai, S., Bai, X.: End-to-end temporal action detection with transformer. arXiv preprint. arXiv:2106.10271 (2021)

23. Liu, Z., et al.: Swin transformer: Hierarchical vision transformer using shifted windows. In: Proceedings of the IEEE/CVF International Conference on Computer Vision, pp. 10012–10022 (2021)

24. Liu, Z., et al.: Video swin transformer. arXiv preprint. arXiv:2106.13230 (2021)

25. Long, F., Yao, T., Qiu, Z., Tian, X., Luo, J., Mei, T.: Gaussian temporal awareness networks for action localization. In: Proceedings of the IEEE/CVF Conference on Computer Vision and Pattern Recognition, pp. 344–353 (2019)

26. Van den Oord, A., Li, Y., Vinyals, O.: Representation learning with contrastive predictive coding. arXiv e-prints, pp. arXiv-1807 (2018)

27. Qing, Z., et al.: Temporal context aggregation network for temporal action proposal refinement. In: Proceedings of the IEEE/CVF Conference on Computer Vision and Pattern Recognition, pp. 485–494 (2021)

28. Rezatofighi, H., Tsoi, N., Gwak, J., Sadeghian, A., Reid, I., Savarese, S.: Generalized intersection over union: a metric and a loss for bounding box regression. In: Proceedings of the IEEE/CVF Conference on Computer Vision and Pattern Recognition, pp. 658–666 (2019)

29. Sridhar, D., Quader, N., Muralidharan, S., Li, Y., Dai, P., Lu, J.: Class semantics-based attention for action detection. In: Proceedings of the IEEE/CVF International Conference on Computer Vision, pp. 13739–13748 (2021)
30. Tan, J., Tang, J., Wang, L., Wu, G.: Relaxed transformer decoders for direct action proposal generation. In: Proceedings of the IEEE/CVF International Conference on Computer Vision, pp. 13526–13535 (2021)
31. Tian, Z., Shen, C., Chen, H., He, T.: Fcos: fully convolutional one-stage object detection. In: Proceedings of the IEEE International Conference on Computer Vision, pp. 9627–9636 (2019)
32. Vaswani, A., et al.: Attention is all you need. In: Advances in Neural Information Processing Systems, vol. 30 (2017)
33. Wang, L., Xiong, Y., Wang, Z., Qiao, Y., Lin, D., Tang, X., Van Gool, L.: Temporal segment networks for action recognition in videos. IEEE Trans. Pattern Anal. Mach. Intell. **41**(11), 2740–2755 (2018)
34. Xu, H., Das, A., Saenko, K.: R-c3d: region convolutional 3d network for temporal activity detection. In: Proceedings of the IEEE International Conference on Computer Vision, pp. 5783–5792 (2017)
35. Xu, M., Zhao, C., Rojas, D.S., Thabet, A., Ghanem, B.: G-tad: sub-graph localization for temporal action detection. In: Proceedings of the IEEE/CVF Conference on Computer Vision and Pattern Recognition, pp. 10156–10165 (2020)
36. Xu, Y., Zhang, Q., Zhang, J., Tao, D.: Vitae: vision transformer advanced by exploring intrinsic inductive bias. In: Advances in Neural Information Processing Systems, vol. 34 (2021)
37. Yang, L., Peng, H., Zhang, D., Fu, J., Han, J.: Revisiting anchor mechanisms for temporal action localization. IEEE Trans. Image Process. **29**, 8535–8548 (2020)
38. Yu, T., Ren, Z., Li, Y., Yan, E., Xu, N., Yuan, J.: Temporal structure mining for weakly supervised action detection. In: Proceedings of the IEEE/CVF International Conference on Computer Vision, pp. 5522–5531 (2019)
39. Zach, C., Pock, T., Bischof, H.: A duality based approach for realtime TV-L^1 optical flow. In: Hamprecht, F.A., Schnörr, C., Jähne, B. (eds.) DAGM 2007. LNCS, vol. 4713, pp. 214–223. Springer, Heidelberg (2007). https://doi.org/10.1007/978-3-540-74936-3_22
40. Zeng, R., et al.: Graph convolutional networks for temporal action localization. In: Proceedings of the IEEE/CVF International Conference on Computer Vision, pp. 7094–7103 (2019)
41. Zhang, Q., Xu, Y., Zhang, J., Tao, D.: Vitaev2: vision transformer advanced by exploring inductive bias for image recognition and beyond. arXiv preprint. arXiv:2202.10108 (2022)
42. Zhao, C., Thabet, A.K., Ghanem, B.: Video self-stitching graph network for temporal action localization. In: Proceedings of the IEEE/CVF International Conference on Computer Vision, pp. 13658–13667 (2021)
43. Zhao, P., Xie, L., Ju, C., Zhang, Y., Wang, Y., Tian, Q.: Bottom-up temporal action localization with mutual regularization. In: Vedaldi, A., Bischof, H., Brox, T., Frahm, J.-M. (eds.) ECCV 2020. LNCS, vol. 12353, pp. 539–555. Springer, Cham (2020). https://doi.org/10.1007/978-3-030-58598-3_32
44. Zhu, X., Su, W., Lu, L., Li, B., Wang, X., Dai, J.: Deformable detr: deformable transformers for end-to-end object detection. arXiv preprint. arXiv:2010.04159 (2020)
45. Zhu, Z., Tang, W., Wang, L., Zheng, N., Hua, G.: Enriching local and global contexts for temporal action localization. In: Proceedings of the IEEE/CVF International Conference on Computer Vision, pp. 13516–13525 (2021)

Towards Accurate Active Camera Localization

Qihang Fang[1], Yingda Yin[2], Qingnan Fan[3(✉)], Fei Xia[4], Siyan Dong[1],
Sheng Wang[5], Jue Wang[3], Leonidas J. Guibas[4], and Baoquan Chen[2(✉)]

[1] Shandong University, Jinan, China
[2] Peking University, Beijing, China
baoquan@pku.edu.cn
[3] Tencent AI Lab, Shenzhen, China
fqnchina@gmail.com
[4] Stanford University, Stanford, USA
[5] 3vjia, Guangzhou, China

Abstract. In this work, we tackle the problem of active camera localization, which controls the camera movements actively to achieve an accurate camera pose. The past solutions are mostly based on Markov Localization, which reduces the position-wise camera uncertainty for localization. These approaches localize the camera in the discrete pose space and are agnostic to the localization-driven scene property, which restricts the camera pose accuracy in the coarse scale. We propose to overcome these limitations via a novel active camera localization algorithm, composed of a passive and an active localization module. The former optimizes the camera pose in the continuous pose space by establishing point-wise camera-world correspondences. The latter explicitly models the scene and camera uncertainty components to plan the right path for accurate camera pose estimation. We validate our algorithm on the challenging localization scenarios from both synthetic and scanned real-world indoor scenes. Experimental results demonstrate that our algorithm outperforms both the state-of-the-art Markov Localization based approach and other compared approaches on the fine-scale camera pose accuracy. Code and data are released at https://github.com/qhFang/AccurateACL.

1 Introduction

The problem of camera localization is to estimate the accurate camera pose in a known environment. Such a problem is of great importance in many computer vision and robotics applications [27,50–52]. The research efforts in the past decades have been mostly devoted to camera localization in a passive

---

Q. Fang and Y. Yin—Equal contribution.

Supplementary Information The online version contains supplementary material available at https://doi.org/10.1007/978-3-031-20080-9_8.

S. Avidan et al. (Eds.): ECCV 2022, LNCS 13670, pp. 122–139, 2022.
https://doi.org/10.1007/978-3-031-20080-9_8

manner [4,5,10,11,29,40,45,48], which predicts the camera pose from the provided RGB/RGB-D frame. However, the passive localization approaches become unstable and fragile when they run into many well-known localization challenges, such as repetitive objects [23] and textureless regions [8].

To resolve the aforementioned issues, the ability of active camera movement has been deployed in a set of works [15,21,24,28], also known as *active camera localization*. Three critical questions need to be answered to solve such a problem: 1) How to locate: how to localize the camera for the most accurate camera pose. 2) Where to go: the camera is initialized at an unknown position in the environment, where it should move for accurate active localization. As there are numerous localizable positions in the continuous camera pose space, the problem of active localization becomes highly ambiguous and difficult to solve. 3) When to stop: the agent is unaware of its ground truth camera pose, hence when it should decide to stop the camera movement.

Due to the difficulties raised by these questions, there has been very little research in this field. Most active localization works are inspired by Markov Localization [9], a passive localization approach that takes random actions to reduce camera uncertainty within a 2D discrete belief map by Bayesian filtering. To decide camera movements, the early research of active localization [21] handcrafts greedy heuristics to minimize the camera uncertainty in the coming step, while the recent work [15] deploys a policy network to directly estimate the camera movement for higher localization accuracy via reinforcement learning. These approaches have dominated the active localization field in the past few decades. However, they still suffer from a few drawbacks that make them prohibitive for practical applications: 1) *Camera localization in the coarse-scale discrete pose space*. The localization accuracy relies on the predefined resolution of the 2D discrete belief map (40 cm, 90° [15]), which is usually unsatisfactory for many practical applications. Pursuing fine-scale accuracy (5 cm, 5°) would result in significantly increased state space, which is both memory and computation inefficient, and not scalable to large environments and continuous camera pose space. 2) *Camera movement agnostic to localization-driven scene uncertainty*. The past approaches control the actions mainly based on the camera uncertainty, without considering the localization-driven scene uncertainty information much. Scene uncertainty is an intrinsic scene property, which is small for geometry- and texture- rich regions and large for repetitive and textureless regions (common localization challenges). Scene uncertainty serves as the important guidance for camera movements towards the localizable scene region, and ignorance of such information limits the localization accuracy.

To overcome the limitations exhibited in the existing approaches, we propose a novel active camera localization algorithm solved by reinforcement learning for accurate camera localization. Our algorithm consists of two functional modules, the *passive localization* module and the *active localization* module. The former passive module answers the "How to locate" question, and estimates the step-wise camera pose in the entire episode. It abandons localization in the discrete pose space, instead learns to predict the world coordinates from the single RGB-D frame, and optimizes the instant camera pose in the continuous pose space via the established camera-world coordinate correspondences. The latter active module consists of the scene uncertainty and camera uncertainty components that answer the "Where to go" and "When to stop" questions separately. The scene uncertainty component explicitly models the localization-driven scene properties and instant localization estimations in the scene, hence it aims to guide the camera movement towards the localizable region. The camera uncertainty component explicitly models the quality of camera pose estimations, and determines the adaptive stop condition for the camera movement.

We validate our algorithm on both the synthetic and scanned real-world indoor scenes. Experimental results demonstrate that our proposed algorithm is able to achieve very high fine-scale camera pose accuracy (5 cm, 5°) compared to the Markov Localization based approach and other baselines. Benefited from the proposed scene uncertainty and camera uncertainty components, our algorithm learns various intelligent behaviors.

2   Related Work

Passive Localization. The past camera localization approaches are mostly passive. They can be separated into two categories, which mainly differ in the input that comes from a single frame or a sequence of frames.

For single-frame camera localization, one trend focuses on direct camera pose estimations by retrieving the most similar database image for the pose approximation of a reference image [2,35,36,41] or directly regressing the camera pose through neural networks [7,25,26,46]. The other trend is indirect pose estimation that employs a two-step procedure, where the first step is to regress the 3D scene coordinates from the input RGB/RGB-D observation, and the second step takes a RANSAC based optimization to produce the final camera pose. The popular scene coordinate regression approaches are implemented as a decision tree [10,11,29,40,45] or a convolution neural network [4,5,48]. These approaches builds structure-based knowledge in a more explicit way, and performs better than image retrieval on small- or middle- scale environments.

For temporal camera localization, one trend focuses on extending PoseNet to the time domain [16,32,43,47], whose performance is however limited by the image retrieval nature of PoseNet, as pointed out by [37]. The other more popular trend assumes a uniform belief of the current camera pose, and leverages Bayesian filtering to iteratively maximize the belief until a certain stop condition is reached. According to the representations of the belief, these approaches can be separated into Kalman Filter [17,34,53], Markov Localization [20,22] and Monte-Carlo localization [18,42]. Most active localization approaches are developed based on Markov Localization, which characterizes the belief as a 2D discrete map grid and the belief is maximized when the camera randomly navigates in the environment. However, Markov Localization suffers from expensive computation due to the huge state space for step-wise comparison.

Active Localization. The pioneering work in active localization is active Markov Localization [9], which adopts the greedy strategy for action selection to reduce the camera pose uncertainty. This work inspires a few followups [24,28]. However, as the problem of active localization is highly ambiguous, the traditional approaches mostly fall into shortsighted solutions. Thanks to the rapid development of reinforcement learning, active neural localization (ANL) [15] firstly learns a policy model to seek a more accurate solution from visual observations. All the above approaches benefit from Markov Localization, yet also suffer from the limited discrete camera pose space and ignorance of scene-specific localization knowledge, as discussed in the Introduction session.

Navigation. Visual navigation [1,14,38] aims at reaching *a specific target* with the guidance of points (PointNav), images (ImageNav), semantics (ObjNav), etc. In contrast, active visual localization targets reaching an accurate camera pose. As there are *numerous localizable poses*, the problem becomes highly ambiguous and more difficult to solve [15]. On the other hand, localization is an essential module in a navigation system, where active localization algorithms could be adopted in a navigation pipeline to further improve its performance.

3 Approach

3.1 Task Setup

Initializing the camera at an unknown position and orientation in an environment, the problem of *active camera localization* is to control the camera movement actively towards a better place to obtain an accurate camera pose. Such a task provides us with two inputs. 1) A sequence of RGB-D frames along with the corresponding ground truth camera poses, denoted as $\{I_{\text{basis}}^{(i)}, C_{\text{basis}}^{(i)}\}_{i=1}^m$, where m is the number of frames, following previous works [10,11,29,40,45]. Such a posed RGB-D stream can be easily obtained by the SLAM system [30] with visual odometry and loop closure and roughly covers the scene. It provides the basis for both passive and active localization. 2) The instant RGB-D frame $I^{(t)}$ obtained during active localization.

The entire procedure of our framework is as follows. With the initial RGB-D frame $I^{(0)}$, the passive localization module estimates the current camera pose $\hat{C}^{(0)}$, and the active localization module estimates the next action for camera movement and then obtains a new RGB-D frame. Such a process is iterated until the active localization module decides to stop the movement, and the final camera pose is chosen as the estimated camera pose at the last step. The entire framework is shown in Fig. 1. We also refer readers to Algorithm 1 in the supplementary material for the entire procedure.

3.2 Passive Localization Module

The passive localization module answers the "How to locate" question. Instead of localizing the camera in the discrete pose space within a grid-based map as previous approaches [15,21], we propose to optimize the camera pose in the continuous pose space through a passive localizer. We adopt the state-of-the-art

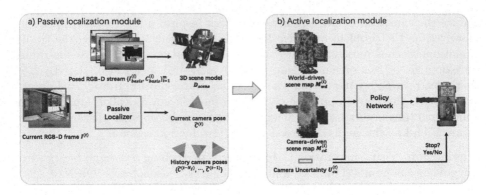

Fig. 1. The full pipeline of our algorithm. a) Given the current RGB-D frame, the passive localizer estimates its camera pose, then b) the policy network takes the scene and camera uncertainty component to estimate the next action for camera movement, and the camera uncertainty component determines when to stop the movement. The 3D scene model is fused from the posed RGB-D stream, and further combined with the estimated current and history camera poses to construct the camera and scene uncertainty components.

approach, decision tree [11], to achieve this purpose thanks to its online adaption ability in novel scenes. We briefly describe it below[1].

A decision tree, denoted as DT, takes a 2D image pixel $I_j^{(t)}$ sampled from the captured RGB-D frame $I^{(t)}$ as input, and performs hierarchical routing to estimate the index of one leaf node $DT(i)$, which consists of a set of 3D scene points $\{P_{dt,k}\}_{k \in \Omega_{dt,DT(i)}}$, where $\Omega_{dt,DT(i)}$ is the index set of 3D points belonging to the leaf node $DT(i)$ and $P_{dt,k}$ is back-projected in the world space with the posed RGB-D stream $\{I_{\text{basis}}^{(t)}, C_{\text{basis}}^{(t)}\}_{t=1}^m$. Then it randomly samples a 3D scene point from the distribution fitted from $\{P_{dt,k}\}_{k \in \Omega_{dt,DT(i)}}$ to establish the 2D-3D correspondence between the camera and world space. With correspondences obtained for many such input pixels, it infers the ranked camera pose hypotheses via pose optimization over the correspondences, and determines the camera pose $\hat{C}^{(t)}$ for the input frame $I^{(t)}$ by iteratively discarding the worse pose hypotheses until the last one left. The parameters of the decision tree lie in the split node determining the routing strategy. They are pre-trained on the 7-Scenes dataset [40] and require no further finetuning. In novel scenes, only the leaf nodes are adaptively refilled online with the posed RGB-D stream[2]. The 3D scene model D_{scene} is further constructed by fusing the posed RGB-D stream and the basis to generate the camera and scene uncertainty component for the active localization module.

3.3 Active Localization Module

In the vast literature of passive camera localization, two important factors have been studied widely for accurate localization. The first is *camera uncertainty*,

---

[1] Note we do not consider the implementation of passive localizer as our technical contribution, yet focus on how to make the best use of it for the entire task.

[2] Please refer to [11] for more implementation details of the decision tree.

which indicates the confidence of camera pose estimations, and determines which camera pose to keep for localization [6,11,40]. The second is *scene uncertainty*, which refers to the effectiveness of each scene region for accurate localization. For example, the passive localization approaches are able to achieve almost 100% camera pose accuracy (5 cm, 5°) in scenes with small uncertainties, such as the texture- and geometry- rich scenes [40,44], yet underperform when there exhibit the scene regions with large uncertainties, such as textureless regions and repetitive objects [8], which are all the common localization challenges. We consider that both camera uncertainty and scene uncertainty are also necessary for accurate active localization, while the focus of most active localization works lies in camera uncertainty. Our active localization module consists of the scene uncertainty and camera uncertainty components, which answer the "Where to go" and "When to stop" questions separately.

Scene Uncertainty Component. Scene uncertainty is an intrinsic localization-driven scene property, and we describe such property from two perspectives, *where the camera is located* and *what underlying part of the scene is observed are more effective for accurate localization*. To model the above information, we propose the camera-driven scene map and world-driven scene map. They answer the "Where to go" question, and guide the camera movement towards scene regions with smaller uncertainties by combining the scene uncertainty property and the estimated camera properties (pose/world coordinate). The scene uncertainty property is purely determined by the scene model D_{scene} and the passive localization module, hence pre-computed and invariant to the active localization process, while the estimated camera properties are instantly computed from the captured RGB-D frame during the camera movements.

Camera-Driven Scene Map: The camera-driven scene map $M_{cd}^{(t)}$ at time step t is represented in the form of the 2D top-view orthographic projection of the 3D scene model D_{scene}, and visualized in Fig. 2. It consists of three components, position-wise uncertainty value U_{cd}, camera pose estimations of the current and history frames $F_{cd\_c}^{(t)}, F_{cd\_h}^{(t)}$. The scene map $M_{cd}^{(t)}$ is computed as the position-wise concatenation of the three components and thus of size $X \times Y \times 3$, where X, Y are the map size,

$$M_{cd}^{(t)} = \text{Concat}\{U_{cd}, F_{cd\_c}^{(t)}, F_{cd\_h}^{(t)}\} \tag{1}$$

To filter out the invalid camera positions, we initialize all the map channels as the binary traversable map where the traversable and obstacle positions are filled with 0 and -1 separately, and only update the values at traversable positions.

The uncertainty channel U_{cd} describes the probability of successful passive localization at each valid camera position in the scene map. To be specific, for each valid camera position, we render RGB-D frames along N_{cd} uniformly sampled camera directions with the scene model D_{scene}, and estimate the corresponding camera poses via the passive localization module. The position-wise uncertainty value $U_{cd,i}$ is inversely proportional to the camera pose accuracy

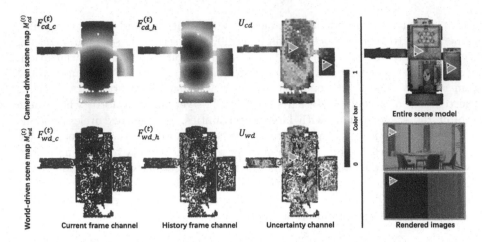

Fig. 2. Left: visualization of the different channels in both the camera-driven and world-driven scene maps. The value range of $F_{cd\_c}^{(t)}$ and $F_{cd\_h}^{(t)}$ is scaled into $[0,1]$ for better visualization with the color bar. Right: we render two first-view images with rich (green camera) or poor (blue camera) geometry and texture details, which are consistent with the uncertainty values shown in U_{cd} and U_{wd}. (Color figure online)

(within λ_{cd} cm, λ_{cd} degrees) averaged over all the rendered RGB-D frames,

$$U_{cd,i} = 1 - \frac{1}{N_{cd}} \sum_{j \in [1, N_{cd}]} A^{(j)} \tag{2}$$

where $A^{(j)}$ is the binary camera pose accuracy for the jth frame.

The current camera pose estimation channel $F_{cd\_c}^{(t)}$ indicates where the camera is located in the scene map estimated from the current RGB-D frame $I^{(t)}$. As the camera pose is estimated in the orientation-aware continuous space, and not compatible with the orientation-agnostic discrete scene map, to minimize this gap, we simply discretize the camera pose and project it onto the 2D scene map by only considering its translation on the horizontal plane. However, the estimated camera pose formulated in this way is nothing but a single point shown in the scene map, and tends to be overwhelmed by its blank neighborhood via the common convolution operations. To highlight the importance of the camera pose information in the 2D map, we draw a distance map centered on the discretized camera position via distance transform [3] as $F_{cd\_c}^{(t)}$. For the history camera pose estimation channel, we obtain the estimated camera positions in the 2D scene map for the last N_f frames $(I^{(t-N_f)}, ..., I^{(t-1)})$ same as the current channel, and draw a distance map centered on the history camera positions via distance transform as $F_{cd\_h}^{(t)}$.

World-Driven Scene Map: The world-driven scene map $M_{wd}^{(t)}$ at time step t is represented in the form of the 3D point cloud sampled from the scene model D_{scene}, and visualized in Fig. 2 from the top view for better comparison with the camera-driven scene map. It consists of four components, the x, y, z world coordinates of the scene points P_{wd}, point-wise uncertainty value U_{wd}, world coordinate estimations of the current and history frames $F_{wd\_c}^{(t)}$, $F_{wd\_h}^{(t)}$. The scene map $M_{wd}^{(t)}$ is computed as the point-wise concatenation of the four components and thus of size $N_{wd\_p} \times 6$ (with N_{wd_p} points and 6 channels),

$$M_{wd}^{(t)} = \text{Concat}\{P_{wd}, U_{wd}, F_{wd\_c}^{(t)}, F_{wd\_h}^{(t)}\} \tag{3}$$

The uncertainty channel U_{wd} describes the effectiveness of each observable scene point to the successful passive localization, and the point-wise uncertainty value is highly related to the viewpoint where the scene point is observed. To compute the uncertainty value, we first render N_{wd_r} RGB-D frames that are randomly positioned and oriented within the traversable region. We associate each 3D scene point $P_{wd,i}$ with an index set of 2D image pixels $\Omega_{wd,i}$ that can be back-projected to it as follows,

$$\Omega_{wd,i} = \{j | \forall j \in \Omega_{wd\_r}, \|P_{wd\_r,j} - P_{wd,i}\| < \lambda_{wd}\} \tag{4}$$

where Ω_{wd_r} is the index set of all the image pixels in the N_{wd_r} rendered frames, $P_{wd\_r,j}$ is the 3D point in the world space back-projected from the pixel j in Ω_{wd_r}, and λ_{wd} is a threshold and measured in centimeters.

Then for each 2D pixel, we evaluate its uncertainty value $U_{wd\_r,j}$ as the estimation quality of the passive localizer, which in our case is the routing quality of the decision tree and adapted from the common measurement for the camera pose evaluation [10,40]. To be specific, $U_{wd\_r,j}$ is computed as a binary value that judges if its back-projected 3D point $P_{wd\_r,j}$ is close to any 3D point in its routed leaf node of the decision tree,

$$U_{wd\_r,j} = \begin{cases} 0 & (\min_{k \in \Omega_{dt,DT(j)}} \|P_{wd\_r,j} - P_{dt,k}\|) < \lambda_{wd} \\ 1 & \text{otherwise} \end{cases} \tag{5}$$

where $\Omega_{dt,DT(j)}$ is the index set of the 3D points $P_{dt,k}$ in the leaf node $DT(j)$ where the pixel j is routed. Then the uncertainty value of each 3D scene point $U_{wd,i}$ is averaged over the ones of its associated 2D pixels,

$$U_{wd,i} = \frac{1}{N_{wd,i}} \sum_{j \in \Omega_{wd,i}} U_{wd\_r,j} \tag{6}$$

where $N_{wd,i}$ is the size of the index set $\Omega_{wd,i}$.

The current world coordinate estimation channel indicates where the world coordinates back-projected from the current RGB-D frame using the estimated camera pose are located on the scene point cloud, hence is computed as the point-wise binary value that describes if each scene point is occupied by at least one back-projected world coordinates. To be specific, for each scene point $P_{wd,i}$, its binary value $F_{wd\_c,i}^{(t)}$ is outputted by an indicator function based on the unidirectional Chamfer distance from the estimated world coordinates to the scene point,

$$F^{(t)}_{wd\_c,i} = \begin{cases} 0 & (\min_{l \in \Omega_f^{(t)}} \|P_{wd,i} - P_{f,l}^{(t)}\|_2^2) < \lambda_{wd} \\ 1 & \text{otherwise} \end{cases} \tag{7}$$

where $\Omega_f^{(t)}$ is the index set of 3D points $P_{f,l}^{(t)}$ back-projected from the current frame $I^{(t)}$ with the estimated camera pose $\hat{C}^{(t)}$.

The history world coordinate estimation channel is simply averaged over the last N_f frames. Specifically, $F^{(t)}_{wd\_h,i}$ is computed as,

$$F^{(t)}_{wd\_h,i} = \frac{1}{N_f} \sum_{t' \in [1, N_f]} F^{(t-t')}_{wd\_c,i} \tag{8}$$

Analysis of Scene Uncertainty: We visualize the computed uncertainty channel in both the camera-driven and world-driven scene maps in Fig. 2. The uncertainty value denotes how much the valid camera positions and observable scene points are uncertain to successful camera localization. For a better understanding of the computed uncertainty values, we also render two first-view images with the green and blue cameras separately in the scene. The blue camera captures an image with poor texture and geometry, which is a common localization challenge, correspondingly, its camera position and observed scene points in the uncertainty channel all contain very large uncertainties. On the other hand, The green camera observes an image with rich texture and geometry, which is usually easy for accurate localization, correspondingly, its camera position and observed scene points mostly contain small uncertainties. The above observation further validates the design of the proposed scene uncertainty component.

Camera Uncertainty Component. Camera uncertainty is an intrinsic camera property, which represents the quality of the current camera pose estimation during camera movements. The camera uncertainty component answers the "When to stop" question, and hence determines the adaptive stop condition for active movements. Ideally, the camera uncertainty value should be computed by directly comparing the estimated camera pose with the ground truth camera pose, which is however absent during active movements. To alleviate the above difficulty, instead of directly dealing with the camera pose, we propose to calculate the camera uncertainty value by comparing the captured depth observation that represents the ground truth camera pose and the depth image projected from the 3D scene model D_{scene} with the estimated camera pose $\hat{C}^{(t)}$. To be specific, given the observed depth and projected depth images, we first back-project the two images into the point clouds in the camera space with the known camera intrinsic parameters. Then we leverage the recent colored point cloud registration approach (Colored ICP) [31] to register the two point clouds and estimate the relative camera pose between them. When the two point clouds are roughly aligned, the adopted ICP approach is able to achieve very tight point cloud alignment. Therefore, the estimated relative pose indicates how far the current camera pose estimation $\hat{C}^{(t)}$ is to the ground truth, and is treated as the camera uncertainty component $U_{cu}^{(t)} \in \mathbb{R}^2$.

To ease policy learning, many previous works fix the episode length [9,15,24] for camera movements, which is inefficient in implementation. In this work, we propose to adaptively stop the camera movement based on the proposed camera uncertainty component. To be specific, we consider a successful localization to stop the camera movement when the camera uncertainty component is within λ_{cu} cm, λ_{cu} degrees.

Analysis of Camera Uncertainty: To justify the effectiveness of the camera uncertainty component, we evaluate how close the estimated relative pose is to the ground truth in Fig. 3, which contains 4500 samples randomly collected in the indoor scenes introduced in Sect. 4.1. We can observe that most samples lie on diagonal lines, which means the relative pose estimations are accurate in general.

To be specific, when the estimated relative poses are within 5 cm, 5° (2362 samples), most samples (94.14% = 2362/2509) are truly within 5 cm, 5° compared to the ground truth (2509 samples). It means the adaptive stop condition judged by the camera uncertainty component is trustworthy.

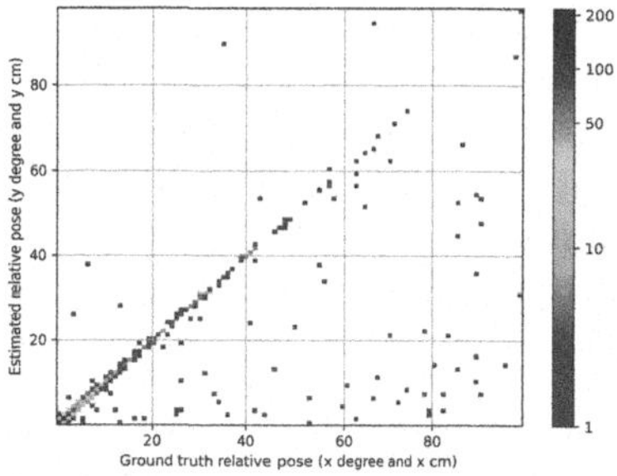

Fig. 3. Justification of the camera uncertainty component. The color bar indicates the sample number.

Reinforcement Learning Formulation. We optimize the policy with the off-policy learning method Proximal Policy Optimization (PPO) [39] by maximizing the accumulated reward in the entire episode. The policy network is detailed in the supplementary material.

Reward Function: We design the reward $\mathcal{R}$, consisting of a slack reward $\mathcal{R}_s$ and an exploration reward $\mathcal{R}_e$. The slack reward punishes unnecessary steps and is defined as $\mathcal{R}_s = -0.1$, which gives a negative reward for every action performed. The exploration reward $\mathcal{R}_e$ awards the agent for visiting the unseen cells to avoid repeated traversal among the same region following [33,49]. To achieve this, we maintain a 2D occupancy map with the same map size as the camera-driven scene map, and each cell is filled with the visit count from the episode initialization. Then $\mathcal{R}_e = 0.1/v$, where v is the visit count in the currently occupied cell, whose position is obtained from the ground truth as the reward is only employed during training. The final reward is the summation of both rewards, $\mathcal{R} = \mathcal{R}_s + \mathcal{R}_e$.

Policy Input: The input of the policy should encode the knowledge of the sensor input and the scene, and have positive guidance for the agents to move towards more localizable regions acknowledged by the passive localization module. In order to achieve this goal, the policy takes the scene uncertainty and camera uncertainty components at time step t as input $\{M_{cd}^{(t)}, M_{wd}^{(t)}, U_{cu}^{(t)}\}$.

Action Space: Following the previous active localization setting [15,21], we assume that the agent (camera) moves with the 3-DoF (Degree of Freedom) action space within the 1-meter high 2D plane parallel to the ground. The agent is capable of performing three actions, *move forward*, *turn left* and *turn right*. The agent moves forward by 20 cm, and turns left/right by 30°. We further disturb the actions with Gaussian noises as introduced in the supplementary material.

4 Experiments

4.1 Experimental Setup

Data Processing: We evaluate our algorithm on both the synthetic and scanned real-world indoor scenes. To alleviate the difficulty of creating the common localization challenges in the synthetic data, we collect 35 high-quality indoor scenes with an average area of $40.9m^2$, that feature textureless walls, repetitive pillows/drawings, *etc*, by design, and provide a train/test split of the scenes (train/test: 15/20 scenes). For the scanned real-world data, we collect 5 indoor scenes with an average area of $64.8m^2$ from the public Matterpot3D dataset [12] only for evaluation. For each indoor scene, we provide a list of data as follows:

- A sequence of <RGB-D image, camera pose> pairs $\{I_{\text{basis}}^{(t)}, C_{\text{basis}}^{(t)}\}_{t=1}^m$ that provides the basis for localization and roughly covers the scene.
- Instant RGB-D frame $I^{(t)}$ obtained during active localization.
- 100 test images in each test scene. They are randomly sampled in the scene region of large uncertainties to increase the localization difficulty (1 m away from the positions of $U_{cd,i} \leq 0.5$).

We name the synthetic dataset ACL-synthetic, and the real-world dataset ACL-real. Our algorithm is trained only on the train split of the ACL-synthetic dataset, and evaluated on both the test split of the ACL-synthetic dataset and the entire ACL-real dataset. During training, the camera is initialized randomly in the scene. During evaluation, the camera is initialized with one of the 100 test images. More details about both datasets[3] are in the supplementary material.

Training Setting: The passive localizer is adapted online in novel scenes with the posed RGB-D stream as mentioned in Sect. 3.2, hence only the policy network needs to be trained in our algorithm. Following the popular camera pose accuracy measured by 5 cm, 5° [4,5,10,11,29,40,45,48], we set $\lambda_{cd} = \lambda_{wd} = \lambda_{cu} = 5$. It means we encourage the agent to move to the scene region where the camera pose estimated from the passive localization module is within 5 cm, 5° to the

---

[3] Note we do not claim the contribution of the collected indoor scenes, which can be replaced with any ones in public indoor scene datasets.

Table 1. Numerical results evaluated with the fine-scale 5 cm, 5° accuracy.

Methods	ACL-synthetic		ACL-real	
	Acc (%)	#steps	Acc (%)	#steps
ANL [15]	3.25	100	3.20	100
No-movement (DecisionTree)	9.35	0	6.80	0
No-movement (DSAC)	14.90	0	7.80	0
Turn-around	25.00	12	35.20	12
Camera-descent (t+1)	61.55	22.90	61.40	26.85
Camera-descent (t+2)	55.30	22.60	59.20	25.78
Scene-descent	57.65	18.56	54.20	16.87
Ours (w/o $\mathcal{R}_e \& M_{cd}^{(t)}$)	67.65	17.40	70.60	19.71
Ours (w/o $\mathcal{R}_e \& M_{wd}^{(t)}$)	66.40	16.27	67.40	18.63
Ours (w/o $\mathcal{R}_e$)	72.50	18.57	73.00	20.72
Ours	**83.05**	17.33	**82.40**	17.90

ground truth, and stop the camera movement when it believes the estimated camera pose is within 5 cm, 5° to the ground truth.

Evaluation Metrics: The major goal of active camera localization lies in achieving higher camera pose accuracy. We evaluate the accuracy (%) as the proportion of successful localization episodes whose translation and rotation error for the final camera pose is within 5 cm, 5° by default, a fine-scale measurement compared to 40 cm, 90° adopted in ANL [15]. We further compute the number of steps (#steps) taken to finish the successful localization acknowledged by the accuracy measure. It is only a complementary metric, while we value the accuracy most. We limit all the approaches with a maximum step length of 100.

4.2 Compared Approaches

We detail the compared approaches below.

- **No-movement.** It only uses the passive localization module to estimate the camera pose for the initial test frame. We adopt two passive localizers for comparison, the default decision tree [11] (No-movement (DecisionTree)) and the popular CNN-based passive localizer [4] (No-movement (DSAC)).
- **Turn-around.** This baseline works by turning a circle along the vertical axis for 12 uniformly-sampled directions without any forward movement, and stopping at the camera pose with the smallest camera uncertainty value.
- **Camera-descent.** It iterates over all the possible actions in the future steps and selects the one with the smallest camera uncertainty value as the following path, hence it moves along the camera uncertainty descent direction. It stops when it triggers our adaptive stop condition. Depending on the number of explored future steps (1/2 steps), we derive two baselines, Camera-descent

Table 2. Numerical results evaluated with the coarse-scale 20 cm, 90° accuracy.

Methods	ACL-synthetic		ACL-real	
	Acc (%)	#steps	Acc (%)	#steps
Markov Loc. [20]	44.70	100	39.20	100
Active Markov Loc. [21]	44.10	100	40.00	100
ANL [15]	87.30	100	84.20	100
Ours	**88.75**	17.09	**85.20**	17.88

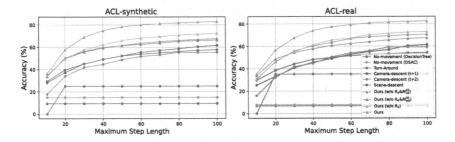

Fig. 4. Plot of the localization accuracy that varies with different maximum step lengths.

(t+1/t+2). We adopt beam search to implement Camera-descent (t+2) for memory efficiency.

– **Scene-descent**. It assumes the estimated camera pose is roughly correct, and computes the shortest path from the estimated camera pose to the more localizable region ($U_{cd,i} \leq 0.5$) in the camera-driven uncertainty channel. Therefore, it moves along the scene uncertainty descent direction. It stops when it finishes the traversal over the shortest path.

– **ANL**. Active neural localization (ANL) [15] is a state-of-the-art active localization approach derived from the Markov localization. Due to the significant requirement of memory and computation resources, its camera pose is limited at the resolution of 20 cm, 90° with Nvidia Tesla V100 of 32 G memory in our implementation (40 cm, 90° in [15]).

4.3   Results

Comparison with Baselines: The comparison is shown in Table 1. We analyze the results in the synthetic indoor scenes (ACL-synthetic) first. The No-movement baselines achieve upmost 14.90% accuracy, indicating the fact that passive localization is not sufficient in our challenging localization scenarios. By enabling the rotation actions, the accuracy of the Turn-around heuristic is only 25.00% at most, which suggests the importance of active camera movements. The Camera-descent and Scene-descent baselines contain smarter designs based on our proposed camera uncertainty and scene uncertainty components, and also

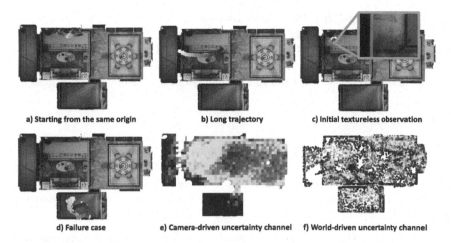

a) Starting from the same origin   b) Long trajectory   c) Initial textureless observation

d) Failure case   e) Camera-driven uncertainty channel   f) World-driven uncertainty channel

Fig. 5. Qualitative results. White arrow: start position; Green arrow: end position (successfully localized); The dots with color gradient indicate the path the agent takes. Intelligent behaviors: **a)** Starting from the same location, the agent travels to various regions for localization. **b)** The agent is able to travel along a long trajectory for accurate localization. **c)** Initialized with a textureless image, the agent emerges the turn around behavior for localization. Failure case: **d)** The agent fail to get out of a small room. Uncertainty visualization: **e)** The camera-driven uncertainty channel. **f)** The world-driven uncertainty channel.

significantly improve the accuracy. Our algorithm outperforms all the approaches in the camera pose accuracy (83.05%) with limited steps being taken. Similar phenomenons can also be observed in the scanned real-world indoor scenes (ACL-real). We further visualize the accuracy that progresses along the increasing maximum step length in Fig. 4, where our algorithm is consistently better than all the others.

Comparison with ANL: ANL is trained on the discrete belief map of resolution 20 cm, 90°, which is almost the upper bound of the camera pose scale it can achieve. Therefore, it performs poorly on the finer-scale accuracy (5 cm, 5°) as expected. Furthermore, we evaluate both ANL and our method on the coarse-scale 20 cm, 90° accuracy where ANL is good at, shown in Table 2. We can see that ANL achieves significantly better results on the coarser-scale accuracy, while our method still achieves comparable localization accuracy, with much fewer moving steps. We also compare with Markov localization [20] and Active Markov Localization [21] on the coarse-scale 20 cm, 90° accuracy following [15].

Ablation Study: We justify our algorithm by ablating three components, the exploration reward $\mathcal{R}_e$, camera-driven scene map $M_{cd}^{(t)}$ and world-driven scene map $M_{wd}^{(t)}$. Experimentally, we observe that our algorithm benefits from all three components.

Time analysis and Intelligent Behavior: It takes only 9.59 s to adapt the passive localizer in a novel scene, and 0.87 s to evaluate our entire algorithm for a single step, where the bottleneck comes from the CPU-based implementation of ICP [54] (0.59 s), which can be further improved with more efficient GPU implementation. Our learned intelligent behaviors are visualized in Fig. 5.

5   Conclusion

In this paper, we propose a novel active camera localization algorithm, consisting of a passive and an active localization module. The former one estimates the accurate camera pose in the continuous pose space. The latter one learns a reinforcement learning policy from the explicitly modeled camera and scene uncertainty component for accurate camera localization.

Limitation and Future Work: Figure 5 e) demonstrates a failure case, where the agent is initialized in a room with a small exit and large scene uncertainties. It fails to leave the room before reaching the maximum step length. Although we already employ a naive exploration reward to avoid repeated traversal in the same region, a smarter design, such as frontier-based exploration [19] and long-term goal planning [13], can be incorporated in the future for further improvement.

Acknowledgments. We thank the anonymous reviewers for the insightful feedback. This work was supported in part by NSFC Projects of International Cooperation and Exchanges (62161146002), NSF grant IIS-1763268, a Vannevar Bush Faculty Fellowship, and a gift from the Amazon Research Awards program.

References

1. Anderson, P., et al.: On evaluation of embodied navigation agents. arXiv preprint. arXiv:1807.06757 (2018)
2. Arandjelovic, R., Gronat, P., Torii, A., Pajdla, T., Sivic, J.: Netvlad: cnn architecture for weakly supervised place recognition. In: Proceedings of the IEEE Conference on Computer Vision and Pattern Recognition, pp. 5297–5307 (2016)
3. Borgefors, G.: Distance transformations in digital images. Comput. Vis. Graphi. Image Process. **34**(3), 344–371 (1986)
4. Brachmann, E., et al.: Dsac-differentiable ransac for camera localization. In: Proceedings of the IEEE Conference on Computer Vision and Pattern Recognition, pp. 6684–6692 (2017)
5. Brachmann, E., Rother, C.: Learning less is more-6d camera localization via 3d surface regression. In: Proceedings of the IEEE Conference on Computer Vision and Pattern Recognition, pp. 4654–4662 (2018)
6. Brachmann, E., Rother, C.: Neural-guided ransac: learning where to sample model hypotheses. In: Proceedings of the IEEE International Conference on Computer Vision, pp. 4322–4331 (2019)
7. Brahmbhatt, S., Gu, J., Kim, K., Hays, J., Kautz, J.: Geometry-aware learning of maps for camera localization. In: Proceedings of the IEEE Conference on Computer Vision and Pattern Recognition, pp. 2616–2625 (2018)

8. Bui, M., et al.: 6D camera relocalization in ambiguous scenes via continuous multi-modal inference. In: Vedaldi, A., Bischof, H., Brox, T., Frahm, J.-M. (eds.) ECCV 2020. LNCS, vol. 12363, pp. 139–157. Springer, Cham (2020). https://doi.org/10.1007/978-3-030-58523-5_9

9. Cassandra, A.R., Kaelbling, L.P., Kurien, J.A.: Acting under uncertainty: discrete bayesian models for mobile-robot navigation. In: Proceedings of IEEE/RSJ International Conference on Intelligent Robots and Systems. IROS'96, vol. 2, pp. 963–972. IEEE (1996)

10. Cavallari, T., et al.: Real-time RGB-D camera pose estimation in novel scenes using a relocalisation cascade. In: IEEE Transactions on Pattern Analysis and Machine intelligence (2019)

11. Cavallari, T., Golodetz, S., Lord, N.A., Valentin, J., Di Stefano, L., Torr, P.H.: On-the-fly adaptation of regression forests for online camera relocalisation. In: Proceedings of the IEEE Conference on Computer Vision and Pattern Recognition, pp. 4457–4466 (2017)

12. Chang, A., et al.: Matterport3d: learning from RGB-D data in indoor environments. arXiv preprint. arXiv:1709.06158 (2017)

13. Chaplot, D.S., Gandhi, D., Gupta, S., Gupta, A., Salakhutdinov, R.: Learning to explore using active neural slam. In: International Conference on Learning Representations (ICLR) (2020)

14. Chaplot, D.S., Gandhi, D.P., Gupta, A., Salakhutdinov, R.R.: Object goal navigation using goal-oriented semantic exploration. In: Advances in Neural Information Processing Systems, vol. 33, pp. 4247–4258 (2020)

15. Chaplot, D.S., Parisotto, E., Salakhutdinov, R.: Active neural localization. In: International Conference on Learning Representations (2018)

16. Clark, R., Wang, S., Markham, A., Trigoni, N., Wen, H.: Vidloc: a deep spatio-temporal model for 6-dof video-clip relocalization. In: Proceedings of the IEEE Conference on Computer Vision and Pattern Recognition, pp. 6856–6864 (2017)

17. Cox, I.J., Leonard, J.J.: Modeling a dynamic environment using a bayesian multiple hypothesis approach. Artif. Intell. 66(2), 311–344 (1994)

18. Dellaert, F., Fox, D., Burgard, W., Thrun, S.: Monte carlo localization for mobile robots. In: Proceedings 1999 IEEE International Conference on Robotics and Automation (Cat. No. 99CH36288C), vol. 2, pp. 1322–1328. IEEE (1999)

19. Dornhege, C., Kleiner, A.: A frontier-void-based approach for autonomous exploration in 3d. Adv. Robot. 27(6), 459–468 (2013)

20. Fox, D.: Markov localization-a probabilistic framework for mobile robot localization and navigation. Ph.D. thesis, Universität Bonn (1998)

21. Fox, D., Burgard, W., Thrun, S.: Active markov localization for mobile robots. Robot. Auton. Syst. 25(3), 195–208 (1998)

22. Fox, D., Burgard, W., Thrun, S.: Markov localization for mobile robots in dynamic environments. J. Artif. Intell. Res. 11, 391–427 (1999)

23. Halber, M., Shi, Y., Xu, K., Funkhouser, T.: Rescan: inductive instance segmentation for indoor rgbd scans. In: Proceedings of the IEEE/CVF International Conference on Computer Vision, pp. 2541–2550 (2019)

24. Jensfelt, P., Kristensen, S.: Active global localization for a mobile robot using multiple hypothesis tracking. IEEE Trans. Robot. Autom. 17(5), 748–760 (2001)

25. Kendall, A., Cipolla, R.: Geometric loss functions for camera pose regression with deep learning. In: Proceedings of the IEEE Conference on Computer Vision and Pattern Recognition, pp. 5974–5983 (2017)

26. Kendall, A., Grimes, M., Cipolla, R.: Posenet: a convolutional network for real-time 6-dof camera relocalization. In: Proceedings of the IEEE International Conference on Computer Vision, pp. 2938–2946 (2015)
27. Luo, W., Sun, P., Zhong, F., Liu, W., Zhang, T., Wang, Y.: End-to-end active object tracking and its real-world deployment via reinforcement learning. IEEE Trans. Pattern Anal. Mach. Intell. 42(6), 1317–1332 (2019)
28. Mariottini, G.L., Roumeliotis, S.I.: Active vision-based robot localization and navigation in a visual memory. In: 2011 IEEE International Conference on Robotics and Automation, pp. 6192–6198. IEEE (2011)
29. Meng, L., Tung, F., Little, J.J., Valentin, J., de Silva, C.W.: Exploiting points and lines in regression forests for RGB-D camera relocalization. In: 2018 IEEE/RSJ International Conference on Intelligent Robots and Systems (IROS), pp. 6827–6834. IEEE (2018)
30. Mur-Artal, R., Tardós, J.D.: Orb-slam2: an open-source slam system for monocular, stereo, and rgb-d cameras. IEEE Trans. Rob. 33(5), 1255–1262 (2017)
31. Park, J., Zhou, Q.Y., Koltun, V.: Colored point cloud registration revisited. In: Proceedings of the IEEE International Conference on Computer Vision, pp. 143–152 (2017)
32. Radwan, N., Valada, A., Burgard, W.: Vlocnet++: deep multitask learning for semantic visual localization and odometry. IEEE Robot. Autom. Lett. 3(4), 4407–4414 (2018)
33. Ramakrishnan, S.K., Jayaraman, D., Grauman, K.: An exploration of embodied visual exploration. Int. J. Comput. Vis. 129(5), 1616–1649 (2021)
34. Roumeliotis, S.I., Bekey, G.A.: Bayesian estimation and kalman filtering: a unified framework for mobile robot localization. In: Proceedings 2000 ICRA. Millennium Conference. IEEE International Conference on Robotics and Automation. Symposia Proceedings (Cat. No. 00CH37065), vol. 3, pp. 2985–2992. IEEE (2000)
35. Sarlin, P.E., Cadena, C., Siegwart, R., Dymczyk, M.: From coarse to fine: robust hierarchical localization at large scale. In: Proceedings of the IEEE Conference on Computer Vision and Pattern Recognition, pp. 12716–12725 (2019)
36. Sattler, T., Leibe, B., Kobbelt, L.: Fast image-based localization using direct 2d-to-3d matching. In: 2011 International Conference on Computer Vision, pp. 667–674. IEEE (2011)
37. Sattler, T., Zhou, Q., Pollefeys, M., Leal-Taixe, L.: Understanding the limitations of cnn-based absolute camera pose regression. In: Proceedings of the IEEE Conference on Computer Vision and Pattern Recognition, pp. 3302–3312 (2019)
38. Savva, M., et al.: Habitat: a platform for embodied ai research. In: Proceedings of the IEEE/CVF International Conference on Computer Vision, pp. 9339–9347 (2019)
39. Schulman, J., Wolski, F., Dhariwal, P., Radford, A., Klimov, O.: Proximal policy optimization algorithms. arXiv preprint. arXiv:1707.06347 (2017)
40. Shotton, J., Glocker, B., Zach, C., Izadi, S., Criminisi, A., Fitzgibbon, A.: Scene coordinate regression forests for camera relocalization in RGB-D images. In: Proceedings of the IEEE Conference on Computer Vision and Pattern Recognition, pp. 2930–2937 (2013)
41. Taira, H., et al.: Inloc: indoor visual localization with dense matching and view synthesis. In: Proceedings of the IEEE Conference on Computer Vision and Pattern Recognition, pp. 7199–7209 (2018)
42. Thrun, S., Fox, D., Burgard, W., Dellaert, F.: Robust monte carlo localization for mobile robots. Artif. Intell. 128(1–2), 99–141 (2001)

43. Valada, A., Radwan, N., Burgard, W.: Deep auxiliary learning for visual localization and odometry. In: 2018 IEEE International Conference on Robotics and Automation (ICRA), pp. 6939–6946. IEEE (2018)
44. Valentin, J., et al.: Learning to navigate the energy landscape. In: 2016 Fourth International Conference on 3D Vision (3DV), pp. 323–332. IEEE (2016)
45. Valentin, J., Nießner, M., Shotton, J., Fitzgibbon, A., Izadi, S., Torr, P.H.: Exploiting uncertainty in regression forests for accurate camera relocalization. In: Proceedings of the IEEE Conference on Computer Vision and Pattern Recognition, pp. 4400–4408 (2015)
46. Wang, B., Chen, C., Lu, C.X., Zhao, P., Trigoni, N., Markham, A.: Atloc: attention guided camera localization (2020)
47. Xue, F., Wang, X., Yan, Z., Wang, Q., Wang, J., Zha, H.: Local supports global: deep camera relocalization with sequence enhancement. In: Proceedings of the IEEE/CVF International Conference on Computer Vision, pp. 2841–2850 (2019)
48. Yang, L., Bai, Z., Tang, C., Li, H., Furukawa, Y., Tan, P.: Sanet: scene agnostic network for camera localization. In: Proceedings of the IEEE International Conference on Computer Vision, pp. 42–51 (2019)
49. Ye, J., Batra, D., Das, A., Wijmans, E.: Auxiliary tasks and exploration enable objectgoal navigation. In: Proceedings of the IEEE/CVF International Conference on Computer Vision, pp. 16117–16126 (2021)
50. Ye, K., et al.: Multi-robot active mapping via neural bipartite graph matching. In: Proceedings of the IEEE/CVF Conference on Computer Vision and Pattern Recognition, pp. 14839–14848 (2022)
51. Zhong, F., Sun, P., Luo, W., Yan, T., Wang, Y.: Ad-vat+: an asymmetric dueling mechanism for learning and understanding visual active tracking. IEEE Trans. Pattern Anal. Mach. Intell. **43**(5), 1467–1482 (2019)
52. Zhong, F., Sun, P., Luo, W., Yan, T., Wang, Y.: Towards distraction-robust active visual tracking. In: International Conference on Machine Learning, pp. 12782–12792. PMLR (2021)
53. Zhou, L., et al.: Kfnet: learning temporal camera relocalization using kalman filtering. In: Proceedings of the IEEE/CVF Conference on Computer Vision and Pattern Recognition, pp. 4919–4928 (2020)
54. Zhou, Q.Y., Park, J., Koltun, V.: Open3d: a modern library for 3d data processing. arXiv preprint. arXiv:1801.09847 (2018)

Camera Pose Auto-encoders
for Improving Pose Regression

Yoli Shavit and Yosi Keller[(✉)]

Bar-Ilan University, Ramat Gan, Israel
{yolisha,yosi.keller}@gmail.com

Abstract. Absolute pose regressor (APR) networks are trained to estimate the pose of the camera given a captured image. They compute
latent image representations from which the camera position and orientation are regressed. APRs provide a different tradeoff between localization accuracy, runtime, and memory, compared to structure-based localization schemes that provide state-of-the-art accuracy. In this work, we
introduce Camera Pose Auto-Encoders (PAEs), multilayer perceptrons
that are trained via a Teacher-Student approach to encode camera poses
using APRs as their teachers. We show that the resulting latent pose representations can closely reproduce APR performance and demonstrate
their effectiveness for related tasks. Specifically, we propose a light-weight
test-time optimization in which the closest train poses are encoded and
used to refine camera position estimation. This procedure achieves a new
state-of-the-art position accuracy for APRs, on both the Cambridge-
Landmarks and 7Scenes benchmarks. We also show that train images
can be reconstructed from the learned pose encoding, paving the way for
integrating visual information from the train set at a low memory cost.
Our code and pre-trained models are available at https://github.com/
yolish/camera-pose-auto-encoders.

1 Introduction

Estimating the position and orientation of a camera given a query image is a fundamental problem in computer vision. It has applications in multiple domains,
such as virtual and augmented reality, indoor navigation, autonomous driving,
to name a few. Contemporary state-of-the-art camera localization methods are
based on matching pixels in the query image to 3D world coordinates. Such
2D-3D correspondences are obtained either through scene coordinate regression
[3–5] or by extracting and matching deep features in the query and reference
images, for which 3D information is available [10,23,28,36]. The resulting correspondences are used to estimate the camera pose with Perspective-N-Point
(PnP) and RANSAC [11]. Consequently, both approaches require the intrinsic

---

Supplementary Information The online version contains supplementary material
available at https://doi.org/10.1007/978-3-031-20080-9_9.

parameters of the query camera, which might not be available or accurate. In addition, matching the query and reference images typically involves storing visual and 3D information on a remote server or the end device.

An alternative approach is to directly regress the camera pose from the query image [16] with absolute pose regressors (APRs). With these methods, the query image is first encoded into a latent representation using a convolutional backbone [7,18,21,33,42–44] or Transformers encoders [34]. The latent image representation is then used to regress the position and orientation with one or more multi-layer perceptron heads. APRs are typically optimized through a supervision of the ground truth poses [15,16,32] and can be trained per scene, or as more recently proposed, in a multi-scene manner (training a single model for multiple scenes) [2,34]. While being less accurate than state-of-the-art (SOTA) structure-based localization approaches [3,4], APRs offer a different trade-off between accuracy versus runtime and memory, by being faster and simpler. In addition, they do not require the intrinsic parameters of the query camera as an input. A related body of work focuses on regressing the relative motion between a pair of images. When the camera pose of a reference image is known, its relative motion to the query can be used to estimate its pose by simple matrix inversion and multiplication. By harnessing relative pose regression for camera pose estimation, relative pose regressors (RPRs) can offer better generalization and accuracy [9] but require images or their model-specific high-dimensional encoding to be available at inference time (supplementary Sect. 1.1). Although RPRs can also be coupled with a sequential acquisition, we are mainly interested in scenarios where only a single query image is provided at a time.

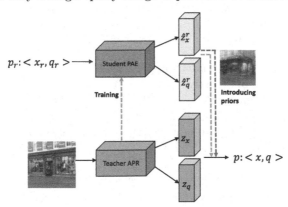

Fig. 1. A camera pose auto-encoder (PAE) is trained using a teacher-student approach, to generate the same pose encoding as the one computed by a teacher APR, enabling the teacher to perform accurate pose regression. The trained student PAE allows to introduce prior information and improve the teacher APR localization accuracy.

In this work, we propose to make the geometric and visual information of reference images (training set) available during inference time, without incurring significant memory or runtime costs. Our motivation is to maintain the attractive properties of APRs (fast, lightweight, and standalone) while improving their localization accuracy using prior information. For this purpose, we propose the Camera Pose Auto-Encoder (PAE) shown in Fig. 1: an MLP that is trained to encode camera poses into latent representations learned by APRs from the respective images. We train PAEs using a Teacher-Student approach, where given a latent representation of an image, obtained with a pretrained teacher APR, the student PAE learns to generate the same encoding for the respective camera pose. The pose encoding is optimized to be as similar as possible to the latent image representation and to enable accurate pose regression with the teacher APR. The proposed training scheme uses multiple images acquired from similar poses with varying appearances, but the PAE is applied without using the reference image as input. Thus, the resulting PAE-based pose encoding is robust to appearance. Once a PAE is trained, we can use it to introduce prior information and improve the APR localization accuracy.

We evaluate our approach on the Cambridge Landmarks and 7Scenes datasets, which provide various outdoor and indoor localization challenges. We first show that student PAEs can closely reproduce the performance of their teacher APRs across datasets, APR and PAE architectures. We then provide examples for using PAEs to improve camera pose regression. We describe a lightweight test-time optimization method, where given an initial pose estimate, the nearest poses in the train set can be encoded and used to derive an improved *position* estimation. This simple procedure achieves a new state-of-the-art localization accuracy compared to current APR solutions across datasets. We further show that images can be reconstructed from camera pose encoding, allowing for performing relative pose regression without the need to store the actual images or their model-specific encodings. This in turn results in competitive position estimation and improves the initial estimate of the teacher APR.

In summary, our main contributions are as follows:

- We introduce a Teacher-Student approach for learning to encode poses into appearance-robust informative latent representations, and show that the trained student Camera Pose Auto Encoders (PAEs) effectively reproduce their teacher APRs.
- We propose a fast and lightweight test-time optimization procedure which utilizes PAEs and achieves a new state-of-the-art position accuracy for absolute pose regression.
- We show that the learned camera pose encoding can be used for image reconstruction, paving the way for coupling relative and absolute pose regression and improving pose estimation, without the typical memory burden of RPRs.

2   Related Work

2.1   Structure-Based Pose Estimation

Structure-based pose estimation methods detect or estimate either 2D or 3D feature points that are matched to a set of reference 3D coordinates. PnP approaches are then applied to estimate the camera pose based on 2D-to-3D matches [36]. The 3D scene model is commonly acquired using SfM [30], or a depth sensor [8]. Such approaches achieve SOTA localization accuracy but require the ground truth poses and 3D coordinates of a set of reference images and their respective local features, as well as the intrinsics parameters of the query and reference cameras. They also need to store the image descriptors for retrieving the reference images that will be matched and the 3D coordinates of their local features. The required memory can be reduced by product quantization of the 3D point descriptors [39], or using only a subset of all 3D points [19,30]. This subset can be obtained, for example, by a prioritized matching step that first considers features more likely to yield valid 2D-to-3D matches [30]. Recently, Sarlin et al. [29] proposed a CNN to detect multilevel invariant visual features, with pixel-wise confidence for query and reference images. Levenberg-Marquardt optimization was applied in a coarse-to-fine manner, to match the corresponding features using their confidence, and the training was supervised by the predicted pose. Instead of retrieving reference images and matching local features to obtain 2D-to-3D correspondences, some approaches regress the 3D scene coordinates directly from the query image [35]. The resulting matches between 2D pixels and 3D coordinates regressed from the query image are used to estimate the pose with PnP-RANSAC. Brachmann and Rother [3,4] extended this approach by training an end-to-end trainable network. A CNN was used to estimate the 3D locations corresponding to the pixels in the query image, and the 2D-to-3D correspondences were used by a differentiable PnP-RANSAC to estimate the camera pose. Such approaches achieve state-of-the-art accuracy, but similarly to other structure-based pose estimation methods, require the intrinsics of the query camera.

2.2 Regression-Based Pose Estimation

Kendall et al. [16] were the first to apply convolutional backbones to absolute pose regression, where the camera pose is directly regressed from the query image. Specifically, an MLP head was attached to a GoogLeNet backbone, to regress the camera's position and orientation. Regression-based approaches are far less accurate than SOTA structure-based localization [3,4], but allow pose estimation with a single forward pass in just a few milliseconds and without requiring the camera intrinsics, which might be inaccurate and unavailable. Some APR formulations proposed using different CNN backbones [18,21,33,44] and deeper architectures for the MLP head [21,44]. Other works tried to reduce overfitting by averaging predictions from models with randomly dropped activations [17] or by reducing the dimensionality of the global image encoding with Long-Short-Term-Memory (LSTM) layers [42]. Multimodality fusion (for example, with inertial sensors) was also suggested as a means of improving accuracy [6]. Attention-based schemes and Transformers were more recently shown to boost the performance of APRs. Wang et al. suggested to use attention to guide the regression process [43]. Dot product self-attention was applied to the output of the CNN backbone and updated with the new representation based on attention (by summation). The pose was then regressed with an MLP head.

A transformer-based approach to multiscene absolute pose regression was proposed by Shavit et al. [34]. In their work, the authors used a shared backbone to encode multiple scenes using a full transformer. The scheme was shown to provide SOTA multi-scene pose accuracy compared to current APRs. One of the main challenges in APR is weighing the position and orientation losses. Kendall et al. [15] learn the trade-off between the losses to improve the localization accuracy. Although this approach was adopted by many pose regressors, it requires manually tuning the parameters' initialization for different datasets [41]. To reduce the need for additional parameters while maintaining comparable accuracy, Shavit et al. [33], trained separate models for position and orientation. Other orientation formulations were proposed to improve the pose loss balance and stability [6,44].

The relative motion between the query image and a reference image, for which the ground truth pose is known, has also been employed to estimate the absolute camera pose in a similar, yet separate subclass of works. Thus, learning such RPR models focuses on regressing the relative pose given a pair of images [1,9]. These methods generalize better since the model is not restricted to an absolute reference scene, but require a pose-labeled database of anchors at inference time. Combining relative and absolute regression has been shown to achieve impressive accuracy [9,25], but requires the encoding of the train images or localization with more than a single query image. As graph neural networks (GNNs) allow exchanging information between non-consecutive frames of a video clip, researchers were motivated to use them for learning multi-image RPR for absolute pose estimation. Xue et al. [45] introduced the GL-Net GNN for multiframe learning, where an estimate of the relative pose loss is applied to regularize the APR. Turkoglu et al. [40] also applied GNN to multi-frame relative localization. In both the training and testing phases, NetVLAD embeddings are used to retrieve the most similar images. A GNN is applied to the retrieved images, and message passing is used to estimate the pose of the camera. Visual landmarks were used by Saha et al. in the AnchorPoint localization approach [27]. With this method, anchor points are distributed uniformly throughout the environment to allow the network to predict, when presented with a query image, which anchor points will be the most relevant in addition to where they are located in relation to the query image.

The inversion of the neural radiation field (NeRF) was recently proposed for test-time optimization of camera poses [46]. In the proposed scheme, the appearance deviation between the input query and the rendered image was used to optimize the camera pose, without requiring an explicit 3D scene representation (as NeRFs can be estimated directly from images). While offering a novel and innovative approach to camera pose estimation, this procedure is relatively slow compared to structure and regression-based localization methods. In this work, we focus on absolute pose regression with a single image. We aim at maintaining the low memory and runtime requirements, while improving accuracy through encoding of pose priors.

3   Absolute Pose Regression Using Pose Auto-encoders

A camera pose $\mathbf{p}$, can be represented with the tuple $< \mathbf{x}, \mathbf{q} >$ where $\mathbf{x} \in \mathbb{R}^3$ is the position of the camera in world coordinates and $\mathbf{q} \in \mathbb{S}^3$ is a unit quaternion encoding its spatial orientation. An APR $\mathbf{A}$ [15,16,32] can be decomposed into the encoders $\mathbf{E_x}$ and $\mathbf{E_q}$, which encode the *query image* into respective latent representations $\mathbf{z_x} \in \mathbb{R}^d$ and $\mathbf{z_q} \in \mathbb{R}^d$, and the heads $\mathbf{R_x}$ and $\mathbf{R_q}$, which regress $\mathbf{x}$ and $\mathbf{q}$ from $\mathbf{z_x}$ and $\mathbf{z_q}$, respectively. In this work we propose the *camera pose auto-encoder* (PAE) $\mathbf{f}$, which encodes *the pose* $< \mathbf{x}, \mathbf{q} >$ to the high-dimensional latent encodings, $\hat{\mathbf{z}}_\mathbf{x} \in \mathbb{R}^d$ and $\hat{\mathbf{z}}_\mathbf{q} \in \mathbb{R}^d$, respectively. We would like $\hat{\mathbf{z}}_\mathbf{x}$ and $\hat{\mathbf{z}}_\mathbf{q}$ to encode geometric and visual information such that an APR's heads $\mathbf{R_x}$ and $\mathbf{R_q}$ can decode back $< \mathbf{x}, \mathbf{q} >$. We show that PAE can be applied to single- and multi-scene APRs.

3.1   Training Camera Pose Auto-encoders

An APR $\mathbf{A}$ plays a dual role in training $\mathbf{f}$, both as a teacher and as a decoder. Specifically, the PAE $\mathbf{f}$ can be considered as a student of $\mathbf{A}$, such that $\mathbf{A}$'s outputs $\mathbf{z_x}$ and $\mathbf{z_q}$ are used to train the PAE by minimizing the loss:

$$L_\mathbf{f} = ||\mathbf{z_x} - \hat{\mathbf{z}}_\mathbf{x}||_2 + ||\mathbf{z_q} - \hat{\mathbf{z}}_\mathbf{q}||_2 + L_\mathbf{p}, \tag{1}$$

where $\hat{\mathbf{z}}_\mathbf{x}$ and $\hat{\mathbf{z}}_\mathbf{q}$ are the outputs of the PAE. We require $\hat{\mathbf{z}}_\mathbf{x}$ and $\hat{\mathbf{z}}_\mathbf{q}$ to allow an accurate *decoding* of the pose $< \mathbf{x}, \mathbf{q} >$ using the respective regressors $\mathbf{R_x}$ and $\mathbf{R_q}$, minimizing the loss of camera pose [15], given by:

$$L_\mathbf{p} = L_\mathbf{x} \exp(-s_\mathbf{x}) + s_\mathbf{x} + L_\mathbf{q} \exp(-s_\mathbf{q}) + s_\mathbf{q} \tag{2}$$

where s_x and s_q are learned parameters representing the uncertainty associated with position and orientation estimation, respectively, [15] and $L_\mathbf{x}$ and $L_\mathbf{q}$ are the position and orientation losses, with respect to a ground truth pose $\mathbf{p}_0 =< \mathbf{x}_0, \mathbf{q}_0 >$:

$$L_\mathbf{x} = ||\mathbf{x}_0 - \mathbf{x}||_2 \tag{3}$$

and

$$L_\mathbf{q} = ||\mathbf{q}_0 - \frac{\mathbf{q}}{||\mathbf{q}||}||_2. \tag{4}$$

Following previous works [15,16,34], we normalize $\mathbf{q}$ to a unit norm quaternion to map it to a valid spatial rotation. The training and formulation of $\mathbf{f}$ can be extended to multi-scene APR by additionally encoding the scene index $\mathbf{s}$, given as input. Figure 2 illustrates the training process of PAEs.

3.2   Network Architecture

In this work, we implement a camera pose auto-encoder $\mathbf{f}$ using two MLPs encoding $\mathbf{x}$ and $\mathbf{q}$, respectively. Following the observations of [26,38] that high

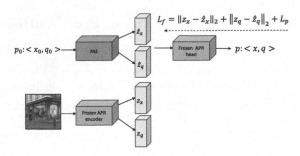

Fig. 2. A teacher-student approach for training PAEs. A trained APR teacher network is used to train the student PAE network.

frequency functions can help in learning low-dimensional signals (and in particularly camera poses [20]), we first embed $\mathbf{x}$ and $\mathbf{q}$ in a higher dimensional space using Fourier Features . We use the formulation and implementation of [20], and apply the following function:

$$\gamma(p) = \left(\sin\left(2^0\pi p\right), \cos\left(2^0\pi p\right), \cdots, \sin\left(2^{-1}\pi p\right), \cos\left(2^{-1}\pi p\right)\right), \qquad (5)$$

γ maps $\mathbb{R}$ into a higher dimensional space $\mathbb{R}^{2L}$, and is separately applied to each coordinate of $\mathbf{x}$ and $\mathbf{q}$, respectively. We also concatenate the original input so that the final dimension of the encoding is $2L + d_0$, d_0 being the dimension of the embedded input. The corresponding MLP head is then applied on the resulting representation to compute $\mathbf{e_x} \in \mathbb{R}^d$ and $\mathbf{e_q} \in \mathbb{R}^d$. In a multi-scene scenario with n_s encoded scenes, a scene index $s = 0, ..., n_s - 1$ is encoded using Fourier Features as in Eq. 5, similarly to $\mathbf{x}$ and $\mathbf{q}$, and then concatenated to their encoding before applying the respective MLP head.

3.3   Applications of Camera Pose Auto-encoders

PAEs allow us to introduce prior information (i.e., localization parameters of the training set's poses) at a low memory and run-time cost to improve the localization accuracy of APRs. We demonstrate this idea through two example applications: Test-time Position Refinement and Virtual Relative Pose Regression.

Test-Time Position Refinement. Given a pre-trained APR $\mathbf{A}$ and a query image, we first compute the latent representations $\mathbf{z_x}$ and $\mathbf{z_q}$ and a pose estimate $\mathbf{p} :< \mathbf{x}, \mathbf{q} >$. Using $\mathbf{p}$, we can get k poses of images from the training set, whose *poses* are the closest to the *pose* of the query image. This requires only to store the pose information $< \mathbf{x}, \mathbf{q} > \in \mathbb{R}^7$, and not the images themselves. Given a pre-trained pose auto-encoder $\mathbf{f}$, we encode each of the k train reference poses, $\{p_r^i\}_{i=0}^{k-1}$, into latent representations: $\{\hat{\mathbf{z}}_\mathbf{x}^i, \hat{\mathbf{z}}_\mathbf{q}^i\}_{i=0}^{k-1}$. Using the simple test-time optimization shown in Fig. 3, we can estimate $\mathbf{x}$ as an affine combination of train positions:

$$\mathbf{x} = \sum_{i=0}^{k-1} a_i x_r^i, \ s.t. \sum a_i = 1. \tag{6}$$

The weight vector $\mathbf{a}$ is calculated by optimizing an MLP regressor for an affine combination of train pose encodings that are closest to the latent encoding of the image

$$\mathbf{a} = \arg\min_{\mathbf{a}} ||\mathbf{z_p} - \sum_{i=0}^{k-1} a_i \hat{\mathbf{z}}_{\mathbf{p_r}}^{\mathbf{i}}||_2,$$

$$s.t. \sum a_i = 1, \ \mathbf{z_p} = \begin{bmatrix} \mathbf{z_x} \\ \mathbf{z_q} \end{bmatrix}$$

A similar test-time optimization was shown to perform well for estimating the camera pose from the nearest image descriptors [31]. However, as opposed to poses, image descriptors mostly encode the image appearance and are thus encoder dependent.

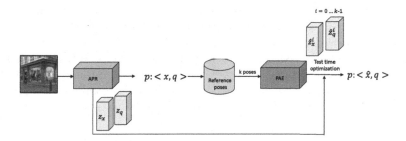

Fig. 3. Test-time optimization of position estimation with PAEs.

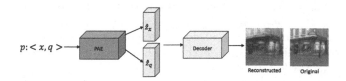

Fig. 4. Decoding images from learned camera pose encoding.

Virtual Relative Pose Regression. The proposed pose embedding encodes both visual and geometric information, allowing to reconstruct the respective image given *only* the input pose $\mathbf{p} :< \mathbf{x}, \mathbf{q} >$. This can be achieved by training a simple MLP decoder $\mathbf{D}$ to minimize the $\mathbb{L}_1$ loss between the original and

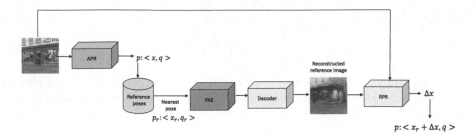

Fig. 5. Virtual relative pose regression for position estimation.

reconstructed images, as illustrated in Fig. 4. The ability to reconstruct images from pose encoding paves the way for performing *virtual* relative pose regression. While in regression-based RPR, the images are encoded by a CNN, we propose to encode only the localization parameters using the PAE. Specifically, as opposed to common relative pose regression, where the relative motion is regressed from latent image encoding of the query and nearest images, here we can encode reconstructed images 'on-the-fly'. We can further exploit the *virtual* pose regression to improve the localization of APR (Fig. 5). Similarly to our test-time optimization procedure, we start by computing the pose estimate $\mathbf{p} :< \mathbf{x}, \mathbf{q} >$ from the query image using an APR $\mathbf{A}$. We then retrieve the closest train reference pose, encode it with a pre-trained pose auto-encoder $\mathbf{f}$ and reconstruct the image with a pre-trained decoder $\mathbf{D}$. Given the query image and the reconstructed train image, a pretrained RPR can be applied to regress the relative translation from which a refined position estimate can be obtained.

3.4   Implementation Details

The proposed PAE consists of two MLP heads, each with four fully connected (FC) layers with ReLU non-linearity, expanding the initial Fourier Feature dimension to 64, 128, 256 and d, the APR latent dimension, respectively. In our experiments, we set $d = 256$, for all APR architectures. We apply Eq. 5 with $L = 6$ for encoding x, q as well as the scene index s for multiscene PAEs. For training and evaluation, we consider different single- and multi- scene APR teachers: a PoseNet-like [16] architecture with different convolutional backbones (MobileNet [14], ResNet50 [13] and EfficientNet-B0 [37]), and a recent state-of-the-art transformer-based APR (MS-Transformer [34]). We implement PoseNet-like APRs using a convolutional backbone of choice and an additional two FC layers and ReLU nonlinearity to map the backbone dimension to d and generate the respective latent representations for $\mathbf{x}$ and $\mathbf{q}$. The regressor head consist of two FC layers to regress $\mathbf{x}$ and $\mathbf{q}$, respectively. For MS-Transformer, we used the pretrained implementation provided by the authors. Our test-time optimization is implemented with $k = 3$ nearest neighbors and $n = 3$ iterations. For image reconstruction we use a four-layer MLP decoder with ReLU non-linearity, increasing the initial encoding dimension d to 512, 1024, 2048 and $3hw^2$, where

h and w, the height and width of the reconstructed image, are set to 64. In order to perform virtual relative pose regression, we apply a Siamese network with a similar architecture to our PoseNet-like APRs. We use Efficient-B0 for the convolutional backbone and apply it twice. The resulting flattened activation maps are concatenated and then used to regress $\mathbf{x}$ and $\mathbf{q}$ as in PoseNet-like APRs (the only difference is in the first FC layer, which maps from twice the backbone dimension to d). We implement all the models and the proposed procedures in PyTorch [24]. Training and inference were performed on an NVIDIA GeForce GTX 1080 GPU with 8 Gb. In order to support easy reproduction of the reported results, we provide the implementation of all the architectures and procedures described in this paper and make our code and pre-trained models publicly available.

4   Experimental Results

4.1   Experimental Setup

Datasets. The proposed PAE scheme is evaluated using the 7Scenes [12] and the Cambridge Landmarks [16] datasets, which are commonly benchmarked in contemporary pose regression works [15,16,34]. The 7Scenes dataset consists of seven small-scale scenes $(-1 - 10\,m^2)$ depicting an indoor office environment. There are six scenes in the Cambridge Landmark dataset $(-900 - 5500\,m^2)$ captured at outdoor urban locations, out of which four scenes were considered for our comparative analysis as they are typically used for evaluating APRs.

Training Details. We optimize the single-scene APR teachers using Adam, with $\beta_1 = 0.9$, $\beta_2 = 0.999$ and $\epsilon = 10^{-10}$. We minimize the learned pose loss (Eq. 2) and initialize its parameters as in [41]. Each APR is trained for 300 epochs, with a batch size of 32 and an initial learning rate of 10^{-3}. For the MS-Transformer teacher, we use the provided pretrained models [34] for the CambridgeLandmarks and 7Scenes datasets. The PAEs are trained using the same training configuration as their teachers when optimizing the loss in Eq. 1. Our test-time optimization is performed with AdamW and a learning rate of 10^{-3}. We applied Adam to optimize our decoder and relative pose regressor, with initial learning rates of 10^{-2} and 10^{-3}, respectively. Additional augmentation and training details are provided in the supplementary materials (suppl. materials).

4.2   Evaluation of Camera Pose Auto-encoders (PAEs)

We evaluate the proposed PAEs by comparing the original localization error of the teacher APR and the error observed when using the APR's head to regress the pose from the PAE encoding. We report the results for the CambridgeLandmarks (Table 1) and 7Scenes (Table 2) datasets, respectively, using the MS-Transformer as the teacher APR. The student auto-encoder obtains an accuracy similar to the teacher APR, across both datasets. While in most cases,

Table 1. Median position/orientation error in meters/degrees, when learning from images and when decoding a latent pose encoding from a student PAE. We use MS-Transformer [34], pre-trained on the CambridgeLandmarks dataset, as our teacher APR.

Method	K. College	Old Hospital	Shop Facade	St. Mary
Teacher APR	0.83/1.47	1.81/2.39	0.86/ 3.07	1.62/ 3.99
Student PAE	0.90/1.49	2.07/2.58	0.99/ 3.88	1.64/ 4.16

Table 2. Median position/orientation error in meters/degrees, when learning from images and when decoding a latent pose encoding from a student PAE (S. PAE). We use MS-Transformer[34], pre-trained on the 7Scenes dataset, as our teacher APR (T. APR).

Method	Chess	Fire	Heads	Office	Pumpkin	Kitchen	Stairs
T. APR	0.11/4.66	0.24 /9.60	0.14/12.2	0.17/5.66	0.18/4.44	0.17/5.94	0.26/8.45
S. PAE	0.12/4.95	0.24/ 9.31	0.14/12.5	0.19/5.79	0.18/4.89	0.18/6.19	0.25/8.74

the student accuracy is still inferior with respect to the teacher, in some cases (e.g., the orientation error for the Fire scene), the student provides a better estimation.

4.3   Ablation Study

We further carry out different ablations to assess the proposed PAE architecture and the robustness of the proposed concept in different teacher APRs. Table 3 shows the median position and orientation errors for the KingsCollege scene from the CambridgeLandmarks dataset, obtained with three different PAE architectures: 2-layers MLP, 4-layers MLP and a 4-layers MLP applied in conjunction with Fourier Features (selected architecture). Although all three variants achieve similar performance, the latter achieves the best trade-off between position and orientation. Additional ablation study of the dimensionality of Fourier Features (the effect of L) is provided in our suppl. materials (suppl. section 1.3).

Since PAEs are not limited to a particular APR teacher, we further evaluate several single- and multi- scene APR teacher architectures: three PoseNet variants with different convolutional backbones and MS-Transformer. Table 4 shows the results for the KingsCollege scene. The student auto-encoder is able to closely reproduce its teacher's performance, regardless of the specific architecture used.

Learning to encode camera poses allows us to leverage available prior information at a potentially low cost. We report the runtime and memory requirements associated with using a PAE and with retrieving and storing reference poses (Table 5). Applying a multi-scene PAE requires an additional runtime of 1.22 ms and < 1 Mb for the model's weights. Storing all poses from the CambridgeLandmarks and 7Scenes datasets incurs a total of 2.15 Mb with an average retrieval runtime of 0.16 ms.

Table 3. Ablations of the PAE architecture. We compare the median position and orientation errors when using shallow and deep MLP architectures with and without Fourier Features (position encoding). The performance is reported for the KingsCollege scene (CambridgeLandmarks dataset). The Teacher is a PoseNet APR with a MobileNet architecture.

Auto Encoder Architecture	Position [m]	Orientation [deg]
2-Layers MLP	1.27	**3.41**
4-Layers MLP	1.26	3.54
Fourier Features + 4-Layers MLP	**1.15**	3.58

Table 4. Ablations of the teacher (single/multi-scene) APR architecture. We compare the median position and orientation errors when training on images and when decoding from a student auto-encoder. The performance is reported for the KingsCollege scene (CambridgeLandmarks dataset).

APR Architecture	Teacher APR [m/deg]	Student PAE [m/deg]
PoseNet+MobileNet	1.24/3.45	1.15/3.58
PoseNet+ResNet50	1.56/3.79	1.50/3.77
PoseNet+EfficientNet	0.88/2.91	**0.83**/2.97
MS-Transformer	**0.83/1.47**	0.90/**1.49**

4.4 Refining Position Estimation with Encoded Poses

We evaluate the proposed use of PAEs (Sect. 3.3) for position refinement and image reconstruction. Tables 6 and 7 show the average of median position/orientation errors in meters/degrees obtained for the CambridgeLandmarks and 7Scenes datasets, respectively. We report the results of single-scene and multi-scene APRs and the result when refining the position with our test-time optimization procedure for MS-Transformer (orientation is estimated with MS- Transformer without refinement). Using camera pose encoding of the train images achieves a new SOTA accuracy for absolute pose regression on both datasets. Specifically, we improve the average position error of the current SOTA

Table 5. Additional runtime and memory required for using a PAE, and retrieving and storing reference poses.

Requirement	Runtime [ms]	Memory [Mb]
Components		
Camera Pose Auto-Encoder	1.22	0.89
Retrieving and Storing Poses	0.16	2.15

Table 6. Localization results for the Cambridge Landmarks dataset. We report the average of median position/orientation errors in meters/degrees. The best results are highlighted in bold.

APR Architecture	Average [m/deg]
PoseNet [16]	2.09/6.84
BayesianPN [17]	1.92/6.28
LSTM-PN [42]	1.30/5.52
SVS-Pose [21]	1.33/5.17
GPoseNet [7]	2.08/4.59
PoseNet-Learnable [15]	1.43/2.85
GeoPoseNet [15]	1.63/2.86
MapNet [6]	1.63/3.64
IRPNet [33]	1.42/3.45
MSPN [2]	2.47/5.34
MS-Transformer [34]	1.28/ **2.73**
MS-Transformer + Optimized Position (Ours)	**0.96/2.73**

APR (MS-Transformer) from 1.28 m to a sub-meter error (0.96 m) for the CambridgeLandmarks dataset and reduce it by 17% for the 7Scenes dataset (0.15 versus 018, respectively). We report additional results for single-scene APRs with position refinement as well as verification results obtained when starting from an initial guess of the pose, sampled around the ground truth pose, in our suppl. materials (suppl. section 1.4). Our test-time optimization achieves a consistent trend of improvement regardless of the specific APR architecture used and across scenes and datasets. The total additional runtime required for the proposed test-time optimization (retrieving poses, encoding them and computing the weights of the affine transformation) is 7.51 ms.

We further explore the application of camera pose encoding for image reconstruction and virtual relative pose regression. Figure 6 shows the original and reconstructed images from the Shop Facade (Cambridge Landmarks dataset) and the Heads (7Scenes dataset) scenes. Our simple MLP decoder learns to decode images at a 64×64 resolution. Although the reconstructed images are blurry, their main visually identifying features are clearly visible. In the context of our work, image reconstruction aims to serve virtual relative pose regression for refining the position of APRs. Table 8 reports the median position error for the ShopFacade and Heads scenes, for single scene and multi-scene APRs, and when refining the position through image reconstruction and relative pose regression (section 3.3). For both scenes, the proposed procedure improves the position accuracy of the teacher APR's initial estimation and achieves a new SOTA position accuracy for absolute pose regression. The total run time required for this procedure (retrieving the closest pose, encoding it, decoding the image, applying the regressor, and computing the new position) is 15.31 ms.

Table 7. Localization results for the 7Scenes dataset. We report the average of median position/orientation errors in meters/degrees. The best results are highlighted in bold.

APR Architecture	Average [m/deg]
PoseNet [16]	0.44/10.4
BayesianPN [17]	0.47/9.81
LSTM-PN [42]	0.31/9.86
GPoseNet [7]	0.31/9.95
PoseNet-Learnable [15]	0.24/7.87
GeoPoseNet [15]	0.23/8.12
MapNet [6]	0.21/7.78
IRPNet [33]	0.23/8.49
AttLoc [43]	0.20/7.56
MSPN [2]	0.20/8.41
MS-Transformer [34]	0.18/ **7.28**
MS-Transformer+Optimized Position (Ours)	**0.15**/ **7.28**

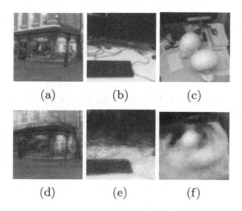

Fig. 6. Images reconstructed from learned camera pose encoding. (a)-(c) Original images from the Shop Facade and Heads scenes at a 64×64 resolution. (d)-(e) Corresponding reconstructed images.

4.5   Limitations and Future Research

Although our work demonstrates useful applications of the proposed PAEs for advancing APR accuracy, they focus on position estimation and image reconstruction. Our preliminary experiments show that for orientation estimation, the proposed encoding can provide a reasonable estimate but does not advance SOTA APR accuracy (suppl. section 1.5). Further research into orientation-optimized encoding, as well as different architecture choices for our decoder and relative pose regressor, are directions for further improvements. Another interesting aspect is the ability of camera PAEs to increase the resolution of the training set by encoding virtual unseen poses, which can enrich existing datasets with a minimal cost. We also note that APRs are a family of methods within a larger body of localization works (Sect. 2). Although our work focuses on advancing

Table 8. Median position error with/without virtual relative pose regression for the ShopFacdade and Heads scenes (orientation error remains fixed).

APR Architecture	Shop Facade [m]	Heads [m]
PoseNet [16]	1.46	0.29
BayesianPN [17]	1.25	0.31
LSTM-PN [42]	1.18	0.21
SVS-Pose [22]	0.63	--
GPoseNet [7]	1.14	0.21
PoseNet-Learnable [15]	1.05	0.18
GeoPoseNet [15]	0.88	0.17
MapNet [6]	1.49	0.18
IRPNet [33]	0.72	0.15
AttLoc [43]	--	0.61
MSPN [2]	2.92	0.16
MS-Transformer [32]	0.86	0.14
MS-Transformer + Virtual RPR (ours)	**0.62**	**0.10**

the accuracy of APRs and extending them to use prior information, while maintaining its advantages (lightweight, fast, and robust to query camera intrinsics), it is still inferior to structure-based methods in terms of accuracy. We provide a comparison of different representative localization schemes to show the current gaps and advancements made (suppl. section 1.6).

5   Conclusions

In this paper, we proposed Camera Pose Auto-Encoders for encoding camera poses into latent representations that can be used for absolute and relative pose regression. Encoding camera poses paves the way for introducing visual and geometric priors with relatively minor runtime and memory costs, and is shown to improve position estimation and achieve a new SOTA absolute pose regression accuracy across contemporary outdoor and indoor benchmarks.

References

1. Balntas, V., Li, S., Prisacariu, V.: RelocNet: continuous metric learning relocalisation using neural nets. In: Ferrari, V., Hebert, M., Sminchisescu, C., Weiss, Y. (eds.) Computer Vision – ECCV 2018. LNCS, vol. 11218, pp. 782–799. Springer, Cham (2018). https://doi.org/10.1007/978-3-030-01264-9_46
2. Blanton, H., Greenwell, C., Workman, S., Jacobs, N.: Extending absolute pose regression to multiple scenes. In: Proceedings of the IEEE/CVF Conference on Computer Vision and Pattern Recognition Workshops, pp. 38–39 (2020)

3. Brachmann, E., et al.: Dsac - differentiable ransac for camera localization. In: 2017 IEEE Conference on Computer Vision and Pattern Recognition (CVPR), pp. 2492–2500. IEEE Computer Society, Los Alamitos, CA, USA (2017). https://doi.org/10.1109/CVPR.2017.267, https://doi.ieeecomputersociety.org/10.1109/CVPR.2017.267

4. Brachmann, E., Rother, C.: Learning less is more - 6d camera localization via 3d surface regression. In: 2018 IEEE/CVF Conference on Computer Vision and Pattern Recognition, pp. 4654–4662 (2018). https://doi.org/10.1109/CVPR.2018.00489

5. Brachmann, E., Rother, C.: Visual camera re-localization from RGB and RGB-D images using DSAC. IEEE Trans. Pattern Anal. Mach. Intell. (01), 1 (2021)

6. Brahmbhatt, S., Gu, J., Kim, K., Hays, J., Kautz, J.: Geometry-aware learning of maps for camera localization. In: IEEE Conference on Computer Vision and Pattern Recognition (CVPR) (2018)

7. Cai, M., Shen, C., Reid, I.: A hybrid probabilistic model for camera relocalization (2019)

8. Cavallari, T., Golodetz, S., Lord, N.A., Valentin, J.P.C., di Stefano, L., Torr, P.H.S.: On-the-fly adaptation of regression forests for online camera relocalisation. In: 2017 IEEE Conference on Computer Vision and Pattern Recognition, CVPR 2017, Honolulu, HI, USA, 21–26 July 2017, pp. 218–227. IEEE Computer Society (2017)

9. Ding, M., Wang, Z., Sun, J., Shi, J., Luo, P.: Camnet: coarse-to-fine retrieval for camera re-localization. In: Proceedings of the IEEE/CVF International Conference on Computer Vision (ICCV) (2019)

10. Dusmanu, M., et al.: D2-net: a trainable cnn for joint description and detection of local features. In: 2019 IEEE/CVF Conference on Computer Vision and Pattern Recognition (CVPR), pp. 8084–8093 (2019). https://doi.org/10.1109/CVPR.2019.00828

11. Fischler, M.A., Bolles, R.C.: Random sample consensus: a paradigm for model fitting with applications to image analysis and automated cartography. Commun. ACM **24**(6), 381–395 (1981)

12. Glocker, B., Izadi, S., Shotton, J., Criminisi, A.: Real-time RGB-D camera relocalization. In: 2013 IEEE International Symposium on Mixed and Augmented Reality (ISMAR), pp. 173–179 (2013). https://doi.org/10.1109/ISMAR.2013.6671777

13. He, K., Zhang, X., Ren, S., Sun, J.: Deep residual learning for image recognition. In: 2016 IEEE Conference on Computer Vision and Pattern Recognition (CVPR), pp. 770–778 (2016). https://doi.org/10.1109/CVPR.2016.90

14. Howard, A.G., et al.: Mobilenets: efficient convolutional neural networks for mobile vision applications. arXiv preprint. arXiv:1704.04861 (2017)

15. Kendall, A., Cipolla, R.: Geometric loss functions for camera pose regression with deep learning. In: 2017 IEEE Conference on Computer Vision and Pattern Recognition (CVPR), pp. 6555–6564 (2017). https://doi.org/10.1109/CVPR.2017.694

16. Kendall, A., Grimes, M., Cipolla, R.: Posenet: A convolutional network for real-time 6-DOF camera relocalization. In: 2015 IEEE International Conference on Computer Vision (ICCV), pp. 2938–2946 (2015). https://doi.org/10.1109/ICCV.2015.336

17. Kendall, A., Cipolla, R.: Modelling uncertainty in deep learning for camera relocalization. In: Proceedings of the International Conference on Robotics and Automation (ICRA) (2016)

18. Melekhov, I., Ylioinas, J., Kannala, J., Rahtu, E.: Image-based localization using hourglass networks. In: 2017 IEEE International Conference on Computer Vision Workshops, ICCV Workshops 2017, Venice, Italy, 22–29 October 2017, pp. 870–877. IEEE Computer Society (2017). https://doi.org/10.1109/ICCVW.2017.107

19. Mera-Trujillo, M., Smith, B., Fragoso, V.: Efficient scene compression for visual-based localization. In: 2020 International Conference on 3D Vision (3DV), pp. 1–10. IEEE Computer Society, Los Alamitos, CA, USA (nov 2020). https://doi.org/10.1109/3DV50981.2020.00111, https://doi.ieeecomputersociety.org/10.1109/3DV50981.2020.00111

20. Mildenhall, B., Srinivasan, P.P., Tancik, M., Barron, J.T., Ramamoorthi, R., Ng, R.: NeRF: representing scenes as neural radiance fields for view synthesis. In: Vedaldi, A., Bischof, H., Brox, T., Frahm, J.-M. (eds.) ECCV 2020. LNCS, vol. 12346, pp. 405–421. Springer, Cham (2020). https://doi.org/10.1007/978-3-030-58452-8_24

21. Naseer, T., Burgard, W.: Deep regression for monocular camera-based 6-DoF global localization in outdoor environments. 2017 IEEE/RSJ International Conference on Intelligent Robots and Systems (IROS), pp. 1525–1530 (2017)

22. Naseer, T., Burgard, W.: Deep regression for monocular camera-based 6-DoF global localization in outdoor environments. In: IROS (2017)

23. Noh, H., Araujo, A., Sim, J., Weyand, T., Han, B.: Large-scale image retrieval with attentive deep local features. In: 2017 IEEE International Conference on Computer Vision (ICCV), pp. 3476–3485 (2017). https://doi.org/10.1109/ICCV.2017.374

24. Paszke, A., et al.: Pytorch: an imperative style, high-performance deep learning library. In: Wallach, H., Larochelle, H., Beygelzimer, A., Alche-Buc, F., Fox, E., Garnett, R. (eds.) Advances in Neural Information Processing Systems. vol. 32, pp. 8026–8037. Curran Associates, Inc. (2019)

25. Radwan, N., Valada, A., Burgard, W.: Vlocnet++: deep multitask learning for semantic visual localization and odometry. IEEE Rob. Autom. Lett. 3(4), 4407–4414 (2018). https://doi.org/10.1109/LRA.2018.2869640

26. Rahaman, N., et al.: On the spectral bias of deep neural networks (2018)

27. Saha, S., Varma, G., Jawahar, C.V.: Improved visual relocalization by discovering anchor points. In: British Machine Vision Conference 2018, BMVC 2018, Newcastle, UK, 3–6 September 2018, p. 164. BMVA Press (2018)

28. Sarlin, P., Cadena, C., Siegwart, R., Dymczyk, M.: From coarse to fine: Robust hierarchical localization at large scale. In: 2019 IEEE/CVF Conference on Computer Vision and Pattern Recognition (CVPR), pp. 12708–12717 (2019). https://doi.org/10.1109/CVPR.2019.01300

29. Sarlin, P.E., et al.: Back to the feature: learning robust camera localization from pixels to pose. In: CVPR (2021)

30. Sattler, T., Leibe, B., Kobbelt, L.: Efficient & effective prioritized matching for large-scale image-based localization. IEEE Trans. Pattern Anal. Mach. Intell. 39(9), 1744–1756 (2017). https://doi.org/10.1109/TPAMI.2016.2611662

31. Sattler, T., Zhou, Q., Pollefeys, M., Leal-Taixé, L.: Understanding the limitations of cnn-based absolute camera pose regression. In: 2019 IEEE/CVF Conference on Computer Vision and Pattern Recognition (CVPR), pp. 3297–3307 (2019). https://doi.org/10.1109/CVPR.2019.00342

32. Shavit, Y., Ferens, R.: Introduction to camera pose estimation with deep learning (2019)

33. Shavit, Y., Ferens, R.: Do we really need scene-specific pose encoders. In: To Appear in 2021 IEEE International Conference on Pattern Recognition (ICPR) (2021)

34. Shavit, Y., Ferens, R., Keller, Y.: Learning multi-scene absolute pose regression with transformers. In: 2021 IEEE International Conference on Computer Vision (ICCV) (2021)
35. Shotton, J., Glocker, B., Zach, C., Izadi, S., Criminisi, A., Fitzgibbon, A.: Scene coordinate regression forests for camera relocalization in rgb-d images. In: Proceedings of the Computer Vision and Pattern Recognition (CVPR). IEEE (2013)
36. Taira, H., et al.: Inloc: indoor visual localization with dense matching and view synthesis. In: IEEE Transactions on Pattern Analysis and Machine Intelligence, pp. 1–1 (2019). https://doi.org/10.1109/TPAMI.2019.2952114
37. Tan, M., Le, Q.: EfficientNet: rethinking model scaling for convolutional neural networks. In: Proceedings of Machine Learning Research, vol. 97, pp. 6105–6114. PMLR, Long Beach, California, USA (09–15 Jun 2019)
38. Tancik, M., et al.: Fourier features let networks learn high frequency functions in low dimensional domains. In: Advances in Neural Information Processing Systems, vol. 33, pp. 7537–7547 (2020)
39. Torii, A., Arandjelovic, R., Sivic, J., Okutomi, M., Pajdla, T.: 24/7 place recognition by view synthesis. IEEE Trans. Pattern Anal. Mach. Intell. 40(2), 257–271 (2018)
40. Turkoglu, M., Brachmann, E., Schindler, K., Brostow, G.J., Monszpart, A.: Visual camera re-localization using graph neural networks and relative pose supervision. In: 2021 International Conference on 3D Vision (3DV), pp. 145–155. Los Alamitos, CA, USA (2021)
41. Valada, A., Radwan, N., Burgard, W.: Deep auxiliary learning for visual localization and odometry. ICRA, pp. 6939–6946 (2018)
42. Walch, F., Hazirbas, C., Leal-Taixé, L., Sattler, T., Hilsenbeck, S., Cremers, D.: Image-based localization using lstms for structured feature correlation. In: 2017 IEEE International Conference on Computer Vision (ICCV), pp. 627–637 (2017). https://doi.org/10.1109/ICCV.2017.75
43. Wang, B., Chen, C., Lu, C.X., Zhao, P., Trigoni, N., Markham, A.: Atloc: attention guided camera localization. In: Proceedings of the AAAI Conference on Artificial Intelligence, vol. 34, pp. 10393–10401 (2020)
44. Wu, J., Ma, L., Hu, X.: Delving deeper into convolutional neural networks for camera relocalization. In: 2017 IEEE International Conference on Robotics and Automation (ICRA), pp. 5644–5651 (2017). https://doi.org/10.1109/ICRA.2017.7989663
45. Xue, F., Wu, X., Cai, S., Wang, J.: Learning multi-view camera relocalization with graph neural networks. In: 2020 IEEE/CVF Conference on Computer Vision and Pattern Recognition (CVPR), pp. 11372–11381 (2020). https://doi.org/10.1109/CVPR42600.2020.01139
46. Yen-Chen, L., Florence, P., Barron, J.T., Rodriguez, A., Isola, P., Lin, T.Y.: iNeRF: inverting neural radiance fields for pose estimation. In: IEEE/RSJ International Conference on Intelligent Robots and Systems (IROS) (2021)

Improving the Intra-class Long-Tail in 3D Detection via Rare Example Mining

Chiyu Max Jiang$^{(\boxtimes)}$, Mahyar Najibi, Charles R. Qi, Yin Zhou, and Dragomir Anguelov

Waymo LLC., Mountain View, CA 94043, USA
{maxjiang,najibi,rqi,yinzhou,dragomir}@waymo.com

Abstract. Continued improvements in deep learning architectures have steadily advanced the overall performance of 3D object detectors to levels on par with humans for certain tasks and datasets, where the overall performance is mostly driven by common examples. However, even the best performing models suffer from the most naive mistakes when it comes to rare examples that do not appear frequently in the training data, such as vehicles with irregular geometries. Most studies in the long-tail literature focus on class-imbalanced classification problems with known imbalanced label counts per class, but they are not directly applicable to the intra-class long-tail examples in problems with large intra-class variations such as 3D object detection, where instances with the same class label can have drastically varied properties such as shapes and sizes. Other works propose to mitigate this problem using active learning based on the criteria of uncertainty, difficulty, or diversity. In this study, we identify a new conceptual dimension - rareness - to mine new data for improving the long-tail performance of models. We show that rareness, as opposed to difficulty, is the key to data-centric improvements for 3D detectors, since rareness is the result of a lack in data support while difficulty is related to the fundamental ambiguity in the problem. We propose a general and effective method to identify the rareness of objects based on density estimation in the feature space using flow models, and propose a principled cost-aware formulation for mining rare object tracks, which improves overall model performance, but more importantly - significantly improves the performance for rare objects (by 30.97%).

Keywords: Intra-class long tail · Rare example · Active learning

1 Introduction

Long-tail learning is a challenging yet important topic in applied machine learning, particularly for safety-critical applications such as autonomous driving or

Supplementary Information The online version contains supplementary material available at https://doi.org/10.1007/978-3-031-20080-9_10.

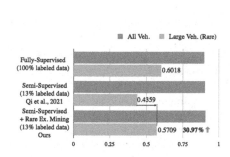

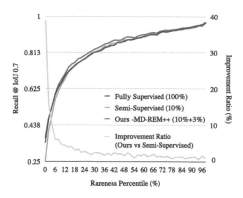

Fig. 1. Vehicle 3D object detection Average Precision (AP) on the Waymo Open Dataset with fully-/semi-supervised learning. While standard semi-supervised learning (with a strong auto labeling teacher model [40]) can achieve on par results with fully supervised method on the common cases, the performance gap on rare objects (e.g. large vehicles) is significant (60.18 v.s. 43.59). Our method is able to close this gap using rare example mining.

Fig. 2. Correlation between inferred rareness percentile (lower is more rare) and model performance for subsets of ground truth, indicated by recall. In all models (from fully-supervised to semi-supervised), model performance is strongly correlated to the rareness measure obtained from the log probability inferred by the flow model. By mining a mere 3% of remaining data, our model significantly improves upon the semi-supervised detector, with big gains in the rare intra-class long-tail.

medical diagnostics. However, even though imbalanced classification problems have been heavily studied in the literature, we have limited tools in defining, identifying, and improving on intra-class rare instances, such as irregularly shaped vehicles or pedestrians in Halloween costumes, since they come from a diverse open set of anything but common objects. Inspired by Leo Tolstoy's famous quote, we observe: "Common objects are all alike; Every rare object is rare in its own way".

We refer to the spectrum of such rare instances as the *intra-class long-tail*, where we do not have the luxury of prespecified class-frequency-based rareness measurements. Objects of the intra-class long-tail can be of particular importance in 3D detection due to its safety relevance. While overall performance for modern 3D detectors can be quite high, we note that even fully supervised models perform significantly worse on rare subsets of the data, such as large vehicles (Fig. 1). The problem is exacerbated by semi-supervised learning, a popular and cost-efficient approach to quickly scale models on larger datasets where average model performance have been shown to be on par with fully-supervised counterparts using a fraction of the labeled data.

Several challenges make it difficult for targeted improvement on the intra-class long-tail for 3D detection. First, as box regression is an important aspect of object detection, conventional long-tail learning approaches utilizing class fre-

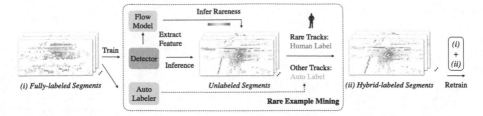

Fig. 3. Overview of the rare example mining (REM) pipeline. Our detector, bootstrap-trained on a smaller pool of fully labeled segments, extracts features for a flow model to infer the log probability of every detected instance, which is a strong indicator of rareness. The rare tracks in the unlabeled segments are sent for human labeling while all remaining tracks are labeled using an offboard auto-labeler. The combined datasets is then used for retraining the detector, resulting in an overall performance boost, particularly on rare examples.

quencies, or active learning approaches utilizing entropy or margin uncertainties that depend on classification output distributions are not applicable. Second, since labeling cost given a run segment is proportional to the number of labeled instance tracks, not frames, we require a more granular mining approach that gracefully handles missing labels for objects in the scene. Last but not least, unlike long-tail problems for imbalanced classification tasks, it is challenging to define which examples belongs to the intra-class long-tail, which leads to difficulty in evaluating and mining additional data to improve the long-tail performance of these models.

In light of these challenges, we propose a generalizable yet effective way to measure and define rareness as the density of instances in the latent feature space. We discover that normalizing flow models are highly effective for feature density estimation and robust for anomaly detection, contrary to negative results on anomaly detection using normalizing flows directly on high dimensional image inputs, as reported by prior work [38]. We present a cost-aware formulation for track-level data-mining and active learning using the rareness criteria, as 3D object labeling cost is often proportional to the number of unique tracks in each run segment. We do this in conjunction with a powerful offboard 3D auto-labeler [40,58] for filling in missing data, and show stronger model improvement compared to difficulty, uncertainty, or heuristics based active learning baselines, particularly for objects in the tail distributions.

Furthermore, we investigate rareness as a novel data-mining criterion, in relation to the conventional uncertainty or error-based mining methods. Though models tend to perform poorly on either rare or hard examples, we note a clear distinction between the concept of rare versus hard. In this discussion, "rare" maps to epistemic uncertainty (reducible error) where the model is uncertain due to a lack of data support in the training set, while "hard" maps to aleatoric uncertainty (irreducible error), where the model is uncertain due to the fundamental ambiguity and uncertainty of the given problem, for example, if the target object is heavily occluded. We further illustrate that while conventional uncertainty estimates (such as ensembling methods) will uncover both hard and rare objects, filtering out hard examples will result in a significantly higher concentration of rare examples which significantly improves active learning performance, underscoring the importance of rare examples in active learning.

In summary, the main contributions of this work are:

- We identify rareness as a novel criterion for data mining and active learning, for improving model performance for problems with large intra-class variations such as 3D detection.
- We propose an effective way of identifying rare objects by estimating latent feature densities using a flow model, and demonstrate a strong correlation between estimated log probabilities, known rare subcategories, and model performance.
- We propose a fine-grained, cost-aware, track level mining methodology for 3D detection that utilizes a powerful offboard 3D auto-labeler for annotating unlabeled objects in partially labeled frames, resulting in a strong performance boost (30.97%) on intra-class long-tail subcategories compared to convetional semi-supervised baselines.

2   Related Work

Long-Tail Visual Recognition. Long-tail is conventionally defined as an imbalance in a multinomial distribution between various different class labels, either in the image classification context [8,24,26,27,36,55,62,64], dense segmentation problems [20,23,52,53,56,59], or between foreground / background labels in object detection problems [33,34,50,51,60]. Existing approaches for addressing class-imbalanced problems include resampling (oversampling tail classes or head classes), reweighitng (using inverse class frequency, effective number of samples [8]), novel loss function design [1,34,50–52,63], meta learning for head-to-tail knowlege transfer [7,27,35,55], distillation [32,57] and mixture of experts [54].

However, there is little work targeting improvements for the intra-class long-tail in datasets with inherently large intra-class variations, or for regression problems. Zhu et al. [66] studies the long-tail problem for subcategories, but assumes given subcategory labels. Dong et al. [12] studies imbalance between fine-grained attribute labels in clothing or facial datasets. To the best of our knowledge, our work is among the first to address the intra-class long-tail in 3D object detection.

Active Learning: In this work we mainly address pool-based active learning [45], where we assume an existing smaller pool of fully-labeled data along with a larger pool of unlabeled data, from which we actively select samples for human labeling. Existing active learning methods mainly fall under two categories, uncertainty-based and diversity-based methods. Uncertainty-based methods select new labeling targets based on criteria such as ensemble variance [2] or classification output distribution such as entropy, margin or confidence

[6,14,21,22,25,41] in the case of classification outputs. More similar to our approach are diversity-based approaches, that aim at balancing the distribution of training data while mining from the unlabeled pool [18,19,39,44]. Gudovskiy et al. [18] further targets unbalanced datasets. However, these methods are developed for classification problems and are not directly applicable to the intra-class long-tail for detection tasks. Similar to our approach, Sinha et al. [47] proposes to learn data distributions in the latent space, though they employ a discriminator in a variational setting that does not directly estimate the density of each data sample. Segal et al. [43] investigated fine-grained active learning in the context self-driving vehicles using region-based selection with a focus on joint perception and prediction. Similar to our approach, Elezi et al. [13] uses auto-labeling to improve active learning performances for 2D detection tasks.

Flow Models: Normalizing flow models are a class of generative models that can approximate probability distributions and efficiently and exactly estimate the densities of high dimensional data [4,10,11,17,28,30,42]. Various studies have reported unsuccessful attempts at using density estimations estimated by normalizing flows for detecting out-of-distribution data by directly learning to map from the high dimensional pixel space of images to the latent space of flow models [5,38,61], assigning higher probability to out-of-distribution data. However, similar to our finding, Kirichenko et al. [29] find that the issue can be easily mitigated by training a flow model on the features extracted by a pretrained model such as an EfficientNet pretrained on ImageNet [9], rather than directly learning on the input pixel space. This allows the model to better measure density in a semantically relevant space. We are among the first to use densities estimated by normalizing flows for identifying long-tail examples.

3   Methods

In this section, we present a general and effective method for mining rare examples based on density estimations from the data, which we refer to as data-centric rare example mining (REM). To offer further insights to rareness in relation to difficulty, we propose another conceptually simple yet effective method for mining rare examples by simply filtering out hard examples from overall uncertain examples. In Sect. 4.2, we show that combining both approaches can further improve long-tail performance. Last but not least, we propose a cost-aware, fine-grained track-level active learning method that aggregates per-track rareness as a selection criteria for requesting human annotation, and utilize a powerful off-board 3D auto-labeler for populating unmined, unlabeled tracks to maximize the utility of all data when retraining the model.

3.1   Rare Example Mining

Data-Centric Rare Example Mining (D-REM). The main intuition behind data-centric REM is that we measure the density of every sample in a learned feature embedding space as an indicator for rareness.

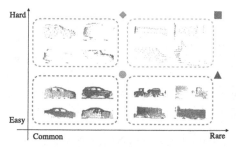

Mining Method	Mined Data	
Random Mining	◆ + ■ + ▲ + ●	
Hard Example Mining	◆ + ■	
Ensemble Mining	◆ + ■ + ▲	
Data-centric Rare Example	■ + ▲	} *Ours*
Model-centric Rare Example	▲	
M+D Rare Example Mining	▲	

Fig. 4. Hard (aleatoric uncertainty) is a fundamentally different dimension compared to rare (epistemic uncertainty). Our REM method directly targets rare subsets of the data. Our Data-centric REM method directly estimates rareness based on inferred probabilities by a normalizing flow model trained on learned feature vectors, while our Model-centric REM method performs hard example filtering on top of generic uncertain objects mined by the ensemble mining approach. We further combine the two approaches (MD-REM) by performing hard example filtering on top of D-REM to increase easy-rare examples.

The full data-centric REM workflow (see Fig. 3) consists of the following steps. First, we pretrain the detection model on an existing source pool of fully-labeled data that might be underrepresenting long-tail examples. Second, we use the pretrained task model to run inference over the source pool along with a large unlabeled pool of data, and extract per-instance raw feature vectors via Region-of-interest (ROI) pooling, followed by PCA dimensionality reduction and normalization. We then train a normalizing flow model over the feature vectors to estimate per-instance rareness (negative log probability) for data mining.

Object Feature Extraction: As previously mentioned, one major difference between our proposed approach for estimating rare examples, compared with earlier works in the literature that were not successful in using normalizing flow for out-of-distribution detection [5,38,61], is that we propose to estimate the probability density of each example in the latent feature space of pretrained models to leverage the semantic similarity between objects for distinguishing rare instances. As observed by Kirichenko et al. [29], normalizing flow directly trained on high dimensional raw input features tend to focus more on local pixel correlations rather than semantics as it doesn't leverage high-level embeddings.

We extract per-object feature embeddings from the final Birds-Eye-View (BEV) feature map of a 3D object detector via region of interest (ROI) max-pooling [16] by cropping the feature map with the prediction boxes. We mainly apply this for our implementation of the state-of-the-art MVF [40,65] 3D detector, though the process is generally applicable to majority of detectors that produce intermediate feature maps [31,37,49].

We further perform principal component analysis (PCA) for dimensionality reduction for improved computational efficiency, followed by normalization on the set of raw feature vectors $X_{\mathrm{roi}} \in \mathbb{R}^{n \times d}$ obtained via ROI pooling

$$X_{\text{pca}} = (X_{\text{roi}} - mean(X_{\text{roi}}))W_{\text{pca}}^T \tag{1}$$
$$X_{\text{norm}} = X_{\text{pca}} \; / \; std(X_{\text{pca}}) \tag{2}$$

where $W_{\text{pca}} \in \mathbb{R}^{k \times d}$ is a weight matrix consisting of the top-k PCA components, $mean(\cdot) : \mathbb{R}^{n \times d} \mapsto \mathbb{R}^d$, $std(\cdot) : \mathbb{R}^{n \times d} \mapsto \mathbb{R}^d$ are the mean and standard deviation operators along the first dimension.

In summary, the training dataset for our flow model consists of normalized feature vectors after PCA-transformation obtained via ROI max-pooling the final feature map of 3D detectors using predicted bounding boxes.

$$\mathcal{D}_x = \{X_{\text{norm}}[i], \forall i \in [0, n)\} \tag{3}$$

Rareness Estimation Using Normalizing Flow: We use the continuous normalizing flow models for directly estimating the log probability of each example represented as a feature vector x. We present a quick review of normalizing flows below.

Typical normalizing flow models [28] consist of two main components: a base distribution $p(z)$, and a learned invertible function $f_\theta(x)$, also known as a bijector, where θ are the learnable parameters of the bijector, $f_\theta(x)$ is the forward method and $f_\theta^{-1}(x)$ is the inverse method. The base distribution is generally chosen to be an analytically tractable distribution whose probability density function (PDF) can be easily computed, such as a spherical multivariate Gaussian distribution, where $p(z) = \mathcal{N}(z; 0, I)$. A learnable bijector function can take many forms, popular choices include masked scale and shift functions such as RealNVP [11,28] or continuous bijectors utilizing learned ordinary differential equation (ODE) dynamics [4,17].

The use of normalizing flows as generative models has been heavily studied in the literature [28], where new in-distribution samples can be generated via passing a randomly sampled latent vector through the forward bijector:

$$x = f_\theta(z), \quad \text{where } z \sim p(z) \tag{4}$$

However, in this work, we are more interested in using normalizing flows for estimating the exact probabilities of each data example. The latent variable corresponding to a data example can be inferred via $z = f_\theta(x)$. Under a change-of-variables formula, the log probability of a data sample can be estimated as:

$$\log p_\theta(x) = \log p(f_\theta(x)) + \log |\det(df_\theta(x)/dx)| \tag{5}$$
$$= \log p(z) + \log |\det(dz/dx)| \tag{6}$$

The first term, $\log p(z)$, can be efficiently computed from the PDF of the base distribution, whereas the computation of the log determinant of the Jacobian: $\log |\det(df_\theta(x)/dx)|$ vary based on the bijector type.

The training process can be described as a simple maximization of the expected log probability of the data (or equivalently minimization of the expected negative log likelihood of the parameters) from the training data $\mathcal{D}_x$ and can be learned via batch stochastic gradient descent:

$$\arg\min_{\theta} \; \mathbb{E}_{x \sim \mathcal{D}_x} [-\log p_\theta(x)] \tag{7}$$

In our experiments, we choose the base distribution $p(z)$ to be a spherical multivariate Gaussian $\mathcal{N}(z; 0, I)$, and we use the FFJORD [17] bijector.

For the final rare example scoring function for the i-th object, r_i, we have:

$$r_i = -\log p_\theta(x_i) \tag{8}$$

Model-Centric Rare Example Mining (M-REM). We present an alternative model-centric formulation for REM that is conceptually easy and effective, yet illustrative of the dichotomy between rare and hard examples. Different from the data-centric REM perspective, model-centric REM leverages the divergence among an ensemble of detectors as a measurement of total uncertainty.

Different from methods that directly use ensemble divergence as a mining critera for active learning [2], our key insight is that while ensemble divergence is a good measurement of the overall uncertainties for an instance, it could be either due to the problem being fundamentally difficult and ambiguous (i.e., hard), or due to the problem being uncommon and lack training support for the model (i.e., rare). In the case of 3D object detection, a leading reason for an object being physically hard to detect is occlusion and low number of LiDAR points from the object. Conceptually, adding more hard examples such as faraway and heavily occluded objects with very few visible LiDAR points would not be helpful, as these cases are fundamentally ambiguous and cannot be improved upon simply with increased data support.

A simple approach for obtaining rare examples, hence, is to filter out hard examples from the set of overall uncertain examples. In practice, a simple combination of two filters: (i) low number of LiDAR points per detection example, or (ii) a large distance between the detection example and the LiDAR source, proves to be surprisingly effective for improving model performance through data mining and active learning.

We implement model-centric REM as follows. Let $\mathcal{M} = \{M_1, M_2, \cdots, M_N\}$ be a set of N independently trained detectors with identical architecture and training configurations, but different model initialization. Denote detection score for the i-th object by the j-th detector as s_i^j. s_i^j is set to zero if there is a missed detection. The detection variance for the i-th object by the model ensemble $\mathcal{M}$ is defined as:

$$v_i = \frac{1}{N} \sum_{j=1}^{N} (s_i^j - \frac{1}{N} \sum_{k=1}^{N} s_i^k)^2 \tag{9}$$

For hard example filtering, denote the number of LiDAR points within the i-th object as p_i, and the distance of the i-th object from the LiDAR source as d_i. A simple hard example filter function can be defined as:

$$h_i = 1 \text{ if } (p_i > \tilde{p}) \text{ \& } (d_i < \tilde{d}) \text{ else } 0 \tag{10}$$

where $\tilde{p}, \tilde{d}$ are the respective point threshold and distance thresholds. In our experiments, we have $N = 5, \tilde{p} = 200, \tilde{d} = 50$ (meters).

The final rare example scoring function for the i-th object, r_i, can be given as:

$$r_i = h_i * v_i \tag{11}$$

3.2   Track-Level REM for Active Learning

To apply our REM method towards active learning as a principled way of collecting rare instances from a large unlabeled pool in a cost-effective manner, we propose a novel track-level mining and targeted annotation strategy in conjunction with a high-performance offboard 3D auto-labeler for infilling missing labels. We choose to mine at the track-level because labeling tools are optimized to label entire object tracks, which is cheaper than labeling per frame. Please refer to Fig. 3 for an overview of the active learning pipeline and Algorithm 1 for a detailed breakdown of the mining process.

First, starting with a labeling budget of K tracks, we score each detected object from the unlabeled dataset using one of the rare example scoring functions above (Eq. (8, 11)). Starting from the detection object with the highest rareness score, we sequentially route each example to human labelers for labeling the entire track T corresponding to the object and add the track to the set of mined and human-labeled tracks $\mathcal{S}_h$. Then all model detections that intersect with T (> 0 IoU) are removed. This procedure is iteratively performed until the number of tracks in $\mathcal{S}_h$ reaches the budget of K. All auto-labeled tracks $\mathcal{S}_a$ that intersect with $\mathcal{S}_h$ are removed, and the two sets of tracks are merged into a hybrid, fully-labeled dataset $\mathcal{S} = \mathcal{S}_a \cup \mathcal{S}_h$.

4   Experiments

We use the Waymo Open Dataset [48] as the main dataset for our investigations due to its unparalleled diversity based on geographical coverage, compared with other camera+LiDAR datasets available [3,15], as well as its large industry-level scale. The Waymo Open Dataset consists of 1150 scenes that span 20 s, recorded across a range of weather conditions in multiple cities.

In the experiments below, we seek to answer three questions: (1) Does model performance correlate with our rareness measurement for intra-class long-tail (Sect. 4.1), (2) Can our proposed rare example mining methodology successfully find and retrieve more rare examples (Sect. 4.1), and (3) Does adding rare data to our existing training data in an active learning setting improve overall model performance, in particular for the long-tail (Sect. 4.2).

4.1   Rare Example Mining Analysis

In this section, we investigate the ability of the normalizing flow model in our data-centric REM method for detecting intra-class long-tail examples.

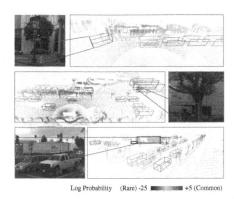

Log Probability   (Rare) -25 ▮▮▮▮ +5 (Common)

Fig. 5. Visualization of the rarest object tracks in the Waymo Open Dataset based on log probability inferred by the data-centric REM algorithm, where low log probability indicates rareness. The most rare instances include incorrectly labeled ground truth boxes, motorcycle underneath a trailer, and large vehicles.

Input

Model detections $\mathcal{D}_b = b_1, b_2, \cdots, b_n$
(sort by descending rareness score)
Auto-labeled tracks
$\mathcal{S}_a = \{T_1', T_2', \cdots, T_m'\}$
Labeling budget K

Output

Fully labeled tracks
$\mathcal{S} = \mathcal{S}_h \cup (\mathcal{S}_a - (\mathcal{S}_h \cap \mathcal{S}_a))$

1: **procedure** TRACKMINING
2:     $\mathcal{S}_h \leftarrow \{\varnothing\}$
3:     **while** $|\mathcal{S}_h| < K$ **do**
4:         $b \leftarrow \mathcal{D}_b.pop(0)$
5:         **if** HumanCheckExists(b) **then**
6:             $T =$HumanLabelTrackFromBox(b)
7:             $\mathcal{S}_h.push(T)$
8:             $\mathcal{D}_b \leftarrow$ DiscardIntersectingBoxes($\mathcal{D}_b, T$)
9:         **end if**
10:     **end while**
11:     $\mathcal{S}_a \leftarrow \mathcal{S}_a - (\mathcal{S}_h \cap \mathcal{S}_a)$
12: **return** $\mathcal{S} = \mathcal{S}_a \cup \mathcal{S}_h$
13: **end procedure**

Algorithm 1: Track-level REM

Correlation: Rareness and Performance. We investigate the correlation between the rareness metric (as indicated by low inferred log probability score on ground-truth labels), and the associated model performance on these examples, as measured by recall on GT examples grouped by rareness. We present the results in Fig. 2. All ground-truth examples are grouped by sorting along their inferred log probability (from an MVF and flow model trained on 100% data) into 2% bins. Recall metric for different experiments are computed for each bin. More details on our active learning experiment will be presented in Sect. 4.2.

We derive two main conclusions: (1) the performance for all models are strongly correlated with our proposed rareness measurement, indicating our flow probability-based estimation of rareness is highly effective. (2) Our proposed rare example mining method achieves significant performance improvement on rare examples compared to the original semi-supervised baseline using a small fraction of additional human-labeled data.

Visualizing Rare Examples: We visualize the rarest ground-truth examples from the Waymo Open Dataset as determined by the estimated log probability of every instance. We aggregate the rareness score for every track by taking the mean log probability of the objects from different frames in each track. We then rank the objects by descending average log probability. See Fig. 5 for a visualization of the rarest objects in the dataset.

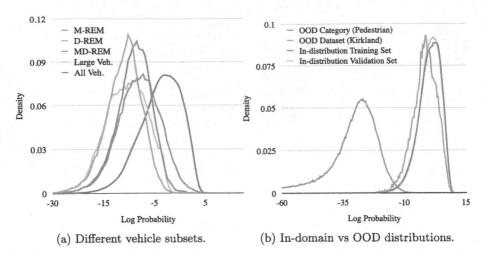

(a) Different vehicle subsets.   (b) In-domain vs OOD distributions.

Fig. 6. Distributional sensitivity of the flow model trained on the vehicle class of the Waymo Open Dataset [48]. (a) Log probability distribution of different vehicle subsets (size subsets and REM mined subsets). (b) Log probability distribution of in-/out-of-distribution examples.

The rarest ground-truth objects include boxes around vehicle parts (protruding ducts, truck loading ramp) and oversized or irregularly shaped vehicles (trucks, flatbed trailers), which match our intuition regarding rare vehicles. Moreover we discover a small number of mislabeled ground-truth instances among the rarest examples. This illustrates that rare example detection is an out-of-distribution detection problem. Intra-class long-tail examples, in one sense, can be defined as in-category, out-of-distribution examples.

Distributional Sensitivity of the Flow Model: In-light of the observation that rare example mining is inherently an out-of-distribution detection problem, we seek to perform a more quantitative analysis of the model's sensitivity to out-of-distribution instances. See Fig. 6 for a detailed breakdown of the analysis. In Fig. 6a, we compare the flow model's inferred log probability distributions between vehicle boxes of different sizes. Vehicle size is defined as the max between box length, width and height. We perform a simple partition for all vehicle examples along the size dimension: regular vehicles as size $\in [3, 7)$ (m), and large vehicles as size $\in [7, \infty)$ (m). Our flow model assigns significantly higher overall log probability for the subset of regular-sized vehicles (96.18% of total), compared to rare subsets such as large vehicles. Note that we leverage vehicle size as an sanity check for the general REM method to distinguish between known rare and common distribution.

Furthermore, we validate that the flow model is effective at detecting out-of-distribution examples (Fig. 6b). The flow model infers almost-identical log probability distributions between the training and validation sets, while assigning lower probabilities to vehicles from an out-of-distribution set (the Kirkland set

Table 1. Composition of mined tracks. We use the ratio of large (> 7 m) objects as a reference for measuring the ratio of rare tracks mined by different approaches. REM is able to mine a higher proportion of rare instances.

Mining criteria	Ratio of large
Random uniform	2.60%
Ensemble [2]	13.72%
Model-centric REM	24.61%
Data-centric REM	30.60%
Model+Data-centric REM	**31.86%**

Table 2. Impact of mining budget on model performance. With a small increase in mining budget (6%), we (MD-REM++) can match the performance of a fully-supervised model on both ends of the spectrum.

Experiment	Human labels	All	Regular	Large
Fully supervised	100%; 0%	0.895	0.900	0.602
Ours	10%; 3%	0.904	**0.904**	0.571
Ours	10%; 6%	0.904	0.903	**0.612**
Our	10%; 9%	**0.905**	**0.904**	0.606

from the Waymo Open Dataset, collected from a different geographical region with mostly rainy weather condition). Moreover, the model assigns significantly lower probabilities on OOD categories (Pedestrian) if we perform ROI pooling using the pedestrian ground-truth boxes to extract pedestrian feature vectors from the vehicle model and query the log probability distribution against the flow model.

4.2 Rare Example Mining for Active Learning

To demonstrate the applicability of the REM approach for targeted improvement of the model's performance in the intra-class long-tail, we utilize track-level REM for active learning, as detailed in Sect. 3.2.

Experiment Setup. Our experiment setup is as follows. Following Qi et al. [40], we perform a random split on the main training set of the Waymo Open Dataset [48] into a 10% fully-labeled source pool, and a remaining 90% as a larger "unlabeled" pool, from which we withhold ground-truth labels. We first train our main model on the fully-labeled source pool, and perform track-level data mining on the remaining unlabeled pool using various methods, including our proposed data-centric and model-centric REM approaches. For all active learning baseline experiments, we mine for a fixed budget of 1268 tracks, amounting to ∼ 3% of all remaining tracks.

Our main model consists of a single-frame MVF detector [40,65]. While in all baseline experiments we utilize the main model for self-labeling unlabeled tracks in the unlabeled pool, we demonstrate that using a strong offboard 3D auto-labeler [40] trained on the same existing data can further boost the overall performance of our REM approach.

Composition of Mined Tracks. We first analyze the composition of the mined tracks, in all cases 1268 tracks obtained using various mining approaches (see Table 1).

We derive three main findings from the composition analysis: (1) Data-centric REM is able to effectively retrieve known rare subsets, upsampling large objects

Table 3. Active learning experiment results. Our method significantly improves model performance across the spectrum, particularly significantly on rare subsets. We denote human label ratio as $(\%s, \%t)$ to indicate the model being trained with $\%s$ of full-labeled run segments, along with $\%t$ of the remaining tracks that is mined and labeled.

(a) Reference experiments w/o active learning.

Experiment	Human labels	All	Regular	Large
Partial-supervised	10%; 0%	0.845	0.853	0.378
Semi-supervised (SL)	10%; 0%	0.854	0.864	0.350
Semi-supervised (AL)	10%; 0%	0.902	0.910	0.419
Fully-supervised	100%; 0%	0.895	0.900	0.602

(b) Oracle active learning experiments.

	Human labels	All	Regular	Large
Oracle Hard [46]	10%; 3%	0.865	0.875	0.341
Oracle Size	10%; 3%	0.869	0.875	0.583

(c) Main active learning experiments.

Experiment	Human Labels	All	Regular	Large
Partial-supervised	10%; 0%	0.845	0.853	0.378
Random	10%; 3%	0.873	0.881	0.355
Predict Size	10%; 3%	0.865	0.871	0.498
Ensemble [2]	10%; 3%	0.869	0.879	0.353
Ours (M-REM)	10%; 3%	0.886	0.893	0.478
Ours (D-REM)	10%; 3%	0.882	0.888	0.483
Ours (D-REM++)	10%; 3%	**0.906**	**0.913**	0.533
Ours (MD-REM++)	10%; 3%	0.904	0.909	**0.571**

by as much as 1214%. (2) Comparing model-centric REM to ensemble mining method, a simple hard example filtering operator leads to drastically upsampled rare instances, signifying the dichotomy of rare and hard. By using a hard example filter we can significantly increase the ratio of rare examples among mined tracks. (3) Combining model and data-centric REM (by further performing hard example filtering from instanced mined by data-centric REM) further boosts the ratio of large vehicles.

Active Learning Experiment. We present our active learning experiments in Table 3. Results are on vehicles from the Waymo Open Dataset [48], reported as AP at IoU 0.5. We compute subset metrics on all vehicles ("All"), regular vehicles ("Regular") of size within $3 - 7$ m, large vehicles ("Large") of size > 7 m. "Regular" subset is a proxy of the common vehicles, while "Large" subset is a proxy for rare.

In Table 3a, we present performances of the single-frame MVF model trained on different compositions of the data. We denote semi-supervised method using self-labeled segments as "SL" and auto-labeled segments as "AL". The main observation is that although auto-labeling can significantly improve overall model performance, in particular for common (regular-sized) vehicles, the resulting model performance is significantly weaker for rare subsets, motivating our REM approach.

For the active learning experiments, we first compare two oracle-based approaches (Table 3b) that utilize 100% ground-truth knowledge for the mining process. "Oracle Hard" is an error-driven mining method inspired by [46], that ranks tracks by $s = \mathrm{IoU}(\mathrm{GT}, \mathrm{Pred}) * \mathrm{Probability\_Score}(\mathrm{Pred})$ to mine tracks which either the base model made a wrong prediction on, or made an inconfident prediction. "Oracle Size" explicitly mines 3% of ground-truth tracks whose box size is $> 7m$. The main observation is that error-based mining favors difficult examples which do not help improve model performance. Though size-based mining can effectively improve large vehicle performance, it solely improves large vehicles and does not help on regular vehicles.

We then compare across a suite of active learning baselines and our proposed REM methods (Table 3c). "Random" mines the tracks via randomized selection, "Predict Size" mines tracks associated with the largest predicted boxes, and "Ensemble" mines the tracks with highest ensemble variance (Eq. (9)). For our proposed REM methods, we prefix model-centric REM approaches with "M-", data-centric approaches with "D-", and a hybrid approach leveraging hard-example filtering on top of data-centric approaches with "MD-". To further illustrate the importance of a strong offboard auto-labeler, we add auto-labeler to our method, denoting the experiments with "++".

The active learning experiments show that: (1) Both data-centric and model-centric approaches significantly help to improve performance on the rare subset, and a combination of the two can further boost the long-tail performance, (2) While heuristics based mining methods ("Predict Size") can achieved targeted improvement for large vehicles, it likely fails to capture other degrees of rareness, resulting in lower overall performance.

5   Ablation Studies

We further study the impact of increasing mining budget on our REM approach (Table 2). With a small increase of mining budget (6%), we can match the performance of a fully-supervised model for both common and rare subsets.

6   Discussions and Future Work

In this work, we illustrate the limitations of learned detectors with respect to rare examples in problems with large intra-class variations, such as 3D detection. We propose an active learning approach based on data-centric and model-centric rare example mining which is effective at discovering rare objects in unlabled data. Our active learning approach, combined with a state-of-the-art semi-supervised method can achieve full parity with a fully-supervised model on both common and rare examples, utilizing as little as 16% of human labels.

A limitation of this study is the scale of the existing datasets for active learning, where data mining beyond the scale of available datasets is limited. Results on a larger dataset will be more informative. Our work shares the same risks and opportunities for the society as other works in 3D detection.

Future work includes extending the REM approach beyond 3D detection, including other topics in self-driving such as trajectory prediction and planning.

Acknowledgements. We thank Marshall Tappen, Zhao Chen, Tim Yang, Abhishek Sinh and Luna Yue Huang for helpful discussions, Mingxing Tan for proofreading and constructive feedback, and anonymous reviews for in-depth discussions and feedback.

References

1. Abdelkarim, S., Achlioptas, P., Huang, J., Li, B., Church, K., Elhoseiny, M.: Long-tail visual relationship recognition with a visiolinguistic hubless loss (2020)
2. Beluch, W.H., Genewein, T., Nürnberger, A., Köhler, J.M.: The power of ensembles for active learning in image classification. In: Proceedings of the IEEE Conference on Computer Vision and Pattern Recognition, pp. 9368–9377 (2018)
3. Caesar, H., et al.: nuscenes: a multimodal dataset for autonomous driving. In: Proceedings of the IEEE/CVF Conference on Computer Vision and Pattern Recognition, pp. 11621–11631 (2020)
4. Chen, R.T., Rubanova, Y., Bettencourt, J., Duvenaud, D.: Neural ordinary differential equations. arXiv preprint. arXiv:1806.07366 (2018)
5. Choi, H., Jang, E., Alemi, A.A.: Waic, but why? generative ensembles for robust anomaly detection. arXiv preprint. arXiv:1810.01392 (2018)
6. Choi, J., Elezi, I., Lee, H.J., Farabet, C., Alvarez, J.M.: Active learning for deep object detection via probabilistic modeling. arXiv preprint. arXiv:2103.16130 (2021)
7. Chu, P., Bian, X., Liu, S., Ling, H.: Feature space augmentation for long-tailed data. In: Vedaldi, A., Bischof, H., Brox, T., Frahm, J.-M. (eds.) ECCV 2020. LNCS, vol. 12374, pp. 694–710. Springer, Cham (2020). https://doi.org/10.1007/978-3-030-58526-6_41
8. Cui, Y., Jia, M., Lin, T.Y., Song, Y., Belongie, S.: Class-balanced loss based on effective number of samples. In: Proceedings of the IEEE/CVF Conference on Computer Vision and Pattern Recognition, pp. 9268–9277 (2019)
9. Deng, J., et al.: Imagenet: a large-scale hierarchical image database. In: 2009 IEEE Conference on Computer Vision and Pattern Recognition, pp. 248–255. IEEE (2009)
10. Dinh, L., Krueger, D., Bengio, Y.: Nice: Non-linear independent components estimation. arXiv preprint. arXiv:1410.8516 (2014)
11. Dinh, L., Sohl-Dickstein, J., Bengio, S.: Density estimation using real nvp. arXiv preprint. arXiv:1605.08803 (2016)
12. Dong, Q., Gong, S., Zhu, X.: Class rectification hard mining for imbalanced deep learning. In: Proceedings of the IEEE International Conference on Computer Vision, pp. 1851–1860 (2017)
13. Elezi, I., Yu, Z., Anandkumar, A., Leal-Taixe, L., Alvarez, J.M.: Not all labels are equal: Rationalizing the labeling costs for training object detection. In: Proceedings of the IEEE/CVF Conference on Computer Vision and Pattern Recognition, pp. 14492–14501 (2022)
14. Gal, Y., Islam, R., Ghahramani, Z.: Deep bayesian active learning with image data. In: International Conference on Machine Learning, pp. 1183–1192. PMLR (2017)
15. Geiger, A., Lenz, P., Stiller, C., Urtasun, R.: Vision meets robotics: the kitti dataset. Int. J. Rob. Res. **32**(11), 1231–1237 (2013)
16. Girshick, R., Donahue, J., Darrell, T., Malik, J.: Rich feature hierarchies for accurate object detection and semantic segmentation. In: Proceedings of the IEEE Conference on Computer Vision and Pattern Recognition, pp. 580–587 (2014)
17. Grathwohl, W., Chen, R.T., Bettencourt, J., Sutskever, I., Duvenaud, D.: Ffjord: free-form continuous dynamics for scalable reversible generative models. In: ICLR (2018)
18. Gudovskiy, D., Hodgkinson, A., Yamaguchi, T., Tsukizawa, S.: Deep active learning for biased datasets via fisher kernel self-supervision. In: Proceedings of the

IEEE/CVF Conference on Computer Vision and Pattern Recognition, pp. 9041–9049 (2020)

19. Guo, Y.: Active instance sampling via matrix partition. In: NIPS, pp. 802–810 (2010)

20. Gupta, A., Dollar, P., Girshick, R.: Lvis: A dataset for large vocabulary instance segmentation. In: Proceedings of the IEEE/CVF Conference on Computer Vision and Pattern Recognition, pp. 5356–5364 (2019)

21. Harakeh, A., Smart, M., Waslander, S.L.: Bayesod: A bayesian approach for uncertainty estimation in deep object detectors. In: 2020 IEEE International Conference on Robotics and Automation (ICRA), pp. 87–93. IEEE (2020)

22. Holub, A., Perona, P., Burl, M.C.: Entropy-based active learning for object recognition. In: 2008 IEEE Computer Society Conference on Computer Vision and Pattern Recognition Workshops, pp. 1–8. IEEE (2008)

23. Hsieh, T.I., Robb, E., Chen, H.T., Huang, J.B.: Droploss for long-tail instance segmentation. arXiv preprint. arXiv:2104.06402 (2021)

24. Jamal, M.A., Brown, M., Yang, M.H., Wang, L., Gong, B.: Rethinking class-balanced methods for long-tailed visual recognition from a domain adaptation perspective. In: Proceedings of the IEEE/CVF Conference on Computer Vision and Pattern Recognition, pp. 7610–7619 (2020)

25. Joshi, A.J., Porikli, F., Papanikolopoulos, N.: Multi-class active learning for image classification. In: 2009 IEEE Conference on Computer Vision and Pattern Recognition, pp. 2372–2379. IEEE (2009)

26. Kang, B., et al.: Decoupling representation and classifier for long-tailed recognition. arXiv preprint. arXiv:1910.09217 (2019)

27. Kim, J., Jeong, J., Shin, J.: M2m: imbalanced classification via major-to-minor translation. In: Proceedings of the IEEE/CVF Conference on Computer Vision and Pattern Recognition, pp. 13896–13905 (2020)

28. Kingma, D.P., Dhariwal, P.: Glow: generative flow with invertible 1x1 convolutions. arXiv preprint. arXiv:1807.03039 (2018)

29. Kirichenko, P., Izmailov, P., Wilson, A.G.: Why normalizing flows fail to detect out-of-distribution data. In: NIPS (2020)

30. Kobyzev, I., Prince, S., Brubaker, M.: Normalizing flows: an introduction and review of current methods. In: IEEE Transactions on Pattern Analysis and Machine Intelligence (2020)

31. Lang, A.H., Vora, S., Caesar, H., Zhou, L., Yang, J., Beijbom, O.: Pointpillars: fast encoders for object detection from point clouds. In: Proceedings of the IEEE/CVF Conference on Computer Vision and Pattern Recognition, pp. 12697–12705 (2019)

32. Li, T., Wang, L., Wu, G.: Self supervision to distillation for long-tailed visual recognition. In: Proceedings of the IEEE/CVF International Conference on Computer Vision, pp. 630–639 (2021)

33. Li, Y., et al.: Overcoming classifier imbalance for long-tail object detection with balanced group softmax. In: Proceedings of the IEEE/CVF Conference on Computer Vision and Pattern Recognition, pp. 10991–11000 (2020)

34. Lin, T.Y., Goyal, P., Girshick, R., He, K., Dollár, P.: Focal loss for dense object detection. In: Proceedings of the IEEE International Conference on Computer Vision, pp. 2980–2988 (2017)

35. Liu, B., Li, H., Kang, H., Hua, G., Vasconcelos, N.: Gistnet: a geometric structure transfer network for long-tailed recognition. arXiv preprint. arXiv:2105.00131 (2021)

36. Liu, Z., Miao, Z., Zhan, X., Wang, J., Gong, B., Yu, S.X.: Large-scale long-tailed recognition in an open world. In: Proceedings of the IEEE/CVF Conference on Computer Vision and Pattern Recognition, pp. 2537–2546 (2019)
37. Meyer, G.P., Laddha, A., Kee, E., Vallespi-Gonzalez, C., Wellington, C.K.: Lasernet: an efficient probabilistic 3d object detector for autonomous driving. In: Proceedings of the IEEE/CVF Conference on Computer Vision and Pattern Recognition, pp. 12677–12686 (2019)
38. Nalisnick, E., Matsukawa, A., Teh, Y.W., Gorur, D., Lakshminarayanan, B.: Do deep generative models know what they don't know? In: International Conference on Learning Representations (2018). https://openreview.net/forum?id=H1xwNhCcYm
39. Nguyen, H.T., Smeulders, A.: Active learning using pre-clustering. In: Proceedings of the twenty-first international conference on Machine learning, p. 79 (2004)
40. Qi, C.R., et al.: Offboard 3d object detection from point cloud sequences. In: Proceedings of the IEEE/CVF Conference on Computer Vision and Pattern Recognition, pp. 6134–6144 (2021)
41. Qi, G.J., Hua, X.S., Rui, Y., Tang, J., Zhang, H.J.: Two-dimensional active learning for image classification. In: 2008 IEEE Conference on Computer Vision and Pattern Recognition, pp. 1–8. IEEE (2008)
42. Rezende, D., Mohamed, S.: Variational inference with normalizing flows. In: International Conference on Machine Learning, pp. 1530–1538. PMLR (2015)
43. Segal, S., et al.: Just label what you need: fine-grained active selection for perception and prediction through partially labeled scenes. arXiv preprint arXiv:2104.03956 (2021)
44. Sener, O., Savarese, S.: Active learning for convolutional neural networks: a core-set approach (2017)
45. Settles, B.: Active learning literature survey (2009)
46. Shrivastava, A., Gupta, A., Girshick, R.: Training region-based object detectors with online hard example mining. In: Proceedings of the IEEE Conference on Computer Vision and Pattern Recognition, pp. 761–769 (2016)
47. Sinha, S., Ebrahimi, S., Darrell, T.: Variational adversarial active learning. In: Proceedings of the IEEE/CVF International Conference on Computer Vision, pp. 5972–5981 (2019)
48. Sun, P., et al.: Scalability in perception for autonomous driving: waymo open dataset. In: Proceedings of the IEEE/CVF Conference on Computer Vision and Pattern Recognition, pp. 2446–2454 (2020)
49. Sun, P., et al.: Rsn: range sparse net for efficient, accurate lidar 3d object detection. In: Proceedings of the IEEE/CVF Conference on Computer Vision and Pattern Recognition, pp. 5725–5734 (2021)
50. Tan, J., Lu, X., Zhang, G., Yin, C., Li, Q.: Equalization loss v2: a new gradient balance approach for long-tailed object detection. arXiv preprint. arXiv:2012.08548 (2020)
51. Tan, J., et al.: Equalization loss for long-tailed object recognition. In: Proceedings of the IEEE/CVF Conference on Computer Vision and Pattern Recognition, pp. 11662–11671 (2020)
52. Wang, J., et al.: Seesaw loss for long-tailed instance segmentation. arXiv preprint. arXiv:2008.10032 (2020)
53. Wang, T., et al.: Classification calibration for long-tail instance segmentation. arXiv preprint. arXiv:1910.13081 (2019)

54. Wang, X., Lian, L., Miao, Z., Liu, Z., Yu, S.X.: Long-tailed recognition by routing diverse distribution-aware experts. In: International Conference on Learning Representations (2021). https://openreview.net/forum?id=D9I3drBz4UC
55. Wang, Y.X., Ramanan, D., Hebert, M.: Learning to model the tail. In: Proceedings of the 31st International Conference on Neural Information Processing Systems, pp. 7032–7042 (2017)
56. Wu, J., Song, L., Wang, T., Zhang, Q., Yuan, J.: Forest r-cnn: large-vocabulary long-tailed object detection and instance segmentation. In: Proceedings of the 28th ACM International Conference on Multimedia, pp. 1570–1578 (2020)
57. Xiang, L., Ding, G., Han, J.: Learning from multiple experts: self-paced knowledge distillation for long-tailed classification. In: Vedaldi, A., Bischof, H., Brox, T., Frahm, J.-M. (eds.) ECCV 2020. LNCS, vol. 12350, pp. 247–263. Springer, Cham (2020). https://doi.org/10.1007/978-3-030-58558-7_15
58. Yang, B., Bai, M., Liang, M., Zeng, W., Urtasun, R.: Auto4d: learning to label 4d objects from sequential point clouds. arXiv preprint. arXiv:2101.06586 (2021)
59. Zang, Y., Huang, C., Loy, C.C.: Fasa: Feature augmentation and sampling adaptation for long-tailed instance segmentation. arXiv preprint. arXiv:2102.12867 (2021)
60. Zhang, C. et al.: A simple and effective use of object-centric images for long-tailed object detection. arXiv e-prints, pp. arXiv-2102 (2021)
61. Zhang, L., Goldstein, M., Ranganath, R.: Understanding failures in out-of-distribution detection with deep generative models. In: International Conference on Machine Learning, pp. 12427–12436. PMLR (2021)
62. Zhao, Y., et al.: Improving long-tailed classification from instance level. arXiv preprint. arXiv:2104.06094 (2021)
63. Zheng, Y., Pal, D.K., Savvides, M.: Ring loss: convex feature normalization for face recognition. In: Proceedings of the IEEE Conference on Computer Vision and Pattern Recognition, pp. 5089–5097 (2018)
64. Zhong, Z., Cui, J., Liu, S., Jia, J.: Improving calibration for long-tailed recognition. arXiv preprint. arXiv:2104.00466 (2021)
65. Zhou, Y., et al.: End-to-end multi-view fusion for 3d object detection in lidar point clouds. In: Conference on Robot Learning, pp. 923–932. PMLR (2020)
66. Zhu, X., Anguelov, D., Ramanan, D.: Capturing long-tail distributions of object subcategories. In: Proceedings of the IEEE Conference on Computer Vision and Pattern Recognition, pp. 915–922 (2014)

Bagging Regional Classification Activation Maps for Weakly Supervised Object Localization

Lei Zhu[1,2,3], Qian Chen[1,2,3], Lujia Jin[1,2,3], Yunfei You[1,2,3], and Yanye Lu[1,2,3(✉)]

[1] Institute of Medical University, Peking University, Beijing, China
zhulei@stu.pku.edu.cn, yanye.lu@pku.edu.cn
[2] Department of Biomedical Engineering, Peking University, Beijing, China
[3] Institute of Biomedical Engineering, Peking University Shenzhen Graduate School, Beijing, China

Abstract. Classification activation map (CAM), utilizing the classification structure to generate pixel-wise localization maps, is a crucial mechanism for weakly supervised object localization (WSOL). However, CAM directly uses the classifier trained on image-level features to locate objects, making it prefers to discern global discriminative factors rather than regional object cues. Thus only the discriminative locations are activated when feeding pixel-level features into this classifier. To solve this issue, this paper elaborates a plug-and-play mechanism called BagCAMs to better project a well-trained classifier for the localization task without refining or re-training the baseline structure. Our BagCAMs adopts a proposed regional localizer generation (RLG) strategy to define a set of regional localizers and then derive them from a well-trained classifier. These regional localizers can be viewed as the base learner that only discerns region-wise object factors for localization tasks, and their results can be effectively weighted by our BagCAMs to form the final localization map. Experiments indicate that adopting our proposed BagCAMs can improve the performance of baseline WSOL methods to a great extent and obtains state-of-the-art performance on three WSOL benchmarks. Code are released at https://github.com/zh460045050/BagCAMs.

Keywords: Weakly supervised learning · Object localization

1 Introduction

Weakly supervised learning, using coarse annotations as supervision during model learning, has attracted extensive attention in recent years, especially for localization relevant vision tasks, such as image segmentation [4,9,13] and object

Supplementary Information The online version contains supplementary material available at https://doi.org/10.1007/978-3-031-20080-9_11.

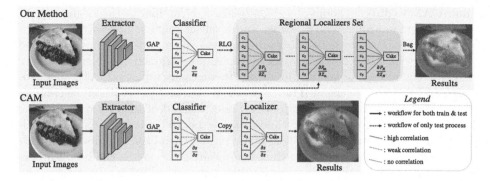

Fig. 1. Comparison between our BagCAMs and CAM. Our BagCAMs (upper part) derives regional localizers from the classifier with the RLG strategy, while CAM (bottom part) only copies the globally-learned classifier to locate objects.

detection [10,27]. Typically, weakly supervised object localization (WSOL) releases the requirements of bounding boxes or even the densely-annotated pixel-level localization masks by only learning the localization model with image-level annotations, *i.e.*, the class of images, which effectively saves human resources for the annotation process. The majority of WSOL methods adopt the mechanism of classification activation map (CAM) [38], utilizing the global average pooling (GAP) to spatially average the pixel-level features into image-level to learn an image classifier with the image-level supervision. Except for generating the classification results, this image classifier also serves as an object localizer that acts on pixel-level features to produce the localization map in the test process.

Though CAM provides an efficient tool for learning a localization model with weak supervision, it directly adopts the classifier as the localizer without considering the difference between them. In detail, the classifier is only learned based on the image-level features, which are spatially aggregated and contain sufficient object features to be discerned. Catching some discriminative factors is enough for the classifier to discern the class of objects. However, the object localizer focuses on discerning the class of all regional positions based on the pixel-level features, where discriminative factors may not be well-aggregated, *i.e.*, insufficient to activate the globally-learned classifier. Thus, the classifier of CAM will only catch the most discriminative parts rather than the whole object locations when directly adopting it to locate objects for pixel-level features.

To solve this issue, a series of methods have been proposed to force the classifier discerning object features more comprehensively, for example, developing augmentation strategies to enrich the global features [17,25,32], aligning the feature distribution between image-level and pixel-level [35,39], adopting multi-classifier to synergistically localize the object [16,30,31,34], or refining the classifier to catch class-agnostic object features [11,37]. Though these strategies show some effect, adopting them requires re-training or revising the baseline structure, enhancing the complexity of the training process. Moreover, they still follow CAM to directly adopt the globally-learned classifier as the localizer, indicating that the gap between classifier and localizer remains unresolved.

Unlike the above methods, our work proposes a plug-and-play approach called BagCAMs, which can better project an image-level trained classifier to comply with the requirement of localization tasks. It can easily replace the classifier projection of CAM and be engaged into existing WSOL methods without re-training the network structure. As visualized in Fig. 1, instead of directly adopting the globally-learned classifier, our method focuses on deriving a set of regional localizers from this well-trained classifier. Those regional localizers can discern object-related factors with respect to each spatial position, acting as the base learners of ensemble learning. With those regional localizers, the final localization results can be obtained by integrating their effect. Experiments show that the proposed BagCAMs significantly improves the performance of the baseline methods and achieves state-of-the-art performance on three WSOL benchmarks.

2   Related Work

Existing WSOLs can be categorized into multi-stage methods [6,11,18–20,33] and one-stage methods [25,31,35–37,39]. The former requires training additional structures upon the classification structure to generate class-agnostic localization results. Our method belongs to the latter, which produces the localization score by projecting the image-classifier back to the pixel-level feature based on CAM, so we just review representative one-stage methods.

To force the classifier to discern some indistinguishable features of objects, Singh et al. [17] proposed hide-and-seek (HAS) augmentation that randomly hides the patches of images in the training process. However, hiding patches also causes information loss. Yun et al. [32] elaborated a CutMix strategy to solve this issue, which replaces the hidden regions with a patch of another image. Babar [1] adopts the siamese neural network to align location maps of two images that contain complementary patches of the input. Instead of developing augmentation strategies, some one-stage methods also focus on fusing the localization maps of multiple classifiers to comprehensively catch object parts. Typically, Zhang et al. [34] suggested learning two classifiers to discern features of objects in a complementary way. Kou et al. [16] added an additional classifier to adaptively produce the auxiliary pixel-level mask, which is then utilized by a metric learning loss for supervision. To consider hierarchical cues, Xue et al. [30] elaborated the DANet by learning multiple classifiers based on hierarchical features, and Tan et al. [25] proposed a pixel-level class selection (PCS) strategy to generalize CAM for hierarchical features. Seunghun et al. [31] fused localization maps of different classes with non-local block [29,40] to help catch locations that correlated to multiple classes. Compared with them, our BagCAMs generates multiple localizers for each spatial position by degrading a well-trained classifier with efficient post-processing like CAM, rather than re-training the extractor or additional classifiers, increasing the complexity of the training process.

Beyond the community of WSOL, some methods also improved CAM for the visual explanation of convolutional neural networks, i.e., explaining why CNN makes specific decisions. To engage CAM into CNN without the GAP operator, Selvaraju et al. [23] proposed the GradCAM that summarizes the gradient as the importance of neurons to aggregate feature maps. Aditya et al. [5] further improved the GradCAM by elaborating a spatial weighing strategy when summarizing the gradient. Recently, Wang et al. [28] and Desai [22] explored obtaining neuron importance through forward passing to avoid the gradient calculation. Unlike these methods that aim to better activate the discriminative locations, our method focuses on complying CAM mechanism with the purpose of WSOL, activating object locations as many as possible.

3   Methodology

This section first formally overviews our proposed method that localizes objects with a series of regional localizers. Then, the regional localizer generation (RLG) strategy is illustrated, helping generate these regional localizers for the localization task. Finally, the BagCAMs is proposed to derive these localizers from a well-trained image classifier and produce the final localization map.

3.1   Problem Definition

Given an input image represented by $\boldsymbol{X} \in \mathbb{R}^{3 \times N^I}$, WSOL aims to approximate the localization map $\boldsymbol{Y} \in \mathbb{R}^{K \times N^I}$ by a localization model learned only with the image-level classification mask $\boldsymbol{y} \in \mathbb{R}^{K \times 1}$, where K and N^I are the numbers of classes of interest and pixels, respectively. To learn the localization model with $\boldsymbol{y}$, a backbone network, i.e., ResNet [12] or InceptionV3 [24], is firstly adopted as the feature extractor $e(\cdot)$ to extract pixel-level features $\boldsymbol{Z} = e(\boldsymbol{X}) \in \mathbb{R}^{C \times N}$, where C is the channels of the features with the spatial resolution N. These pixel-level features are fed into the GAP layer to generate the image-level feature $\boldsymbol{z} \in \mathbb{R}^{C \times 1}$. Finally, the classifier $c(\cdot)$ implemented as the fully-connected layer with weight $\mathbf{W} \in \mathbb{R}^{K \times C}$ is acted on the image-level feature to generate the classification result $\boldsymbol{s}$:

$$s_k = c(\boldsymbol{z})_k = (\mathbf{W}\boldsymbol{z})_k = \sum_c \mathbf{W}_{k,c} \boldsymbol{z}_c, \tag{1}$$

where k and c are the index of class and channel, respectively. This classification score $\boldsymbol{s}$ is supervised by the cross-entropy $\mathcal{L}_{ce}(\boldsymbol{y}, \boldsymbol{s})$ to learn the extractor $e(\cdot)$ and the classifier $c(\cdot)$ in the training process.

In the test process, except for generating the classification score $\boldsymbol{s}$, CAM-based methods also utilize the classifier $c(\cdot)$ as a localizer $f(\cdot)$ that acts onto the pixel-level features $\boldsymbol{Z}$ to obtain the localization maps $\boldsymbol{P} \in \mathbb{R}^{K \times N}$:

$$\boldsymbol{P}_{k,i} = f(\boldsymbol{Z})_{k,i} = c(\boldsymbol{Z}_{:,i})_k = \sum_c \mathbf{W}_{k,c} \boldsymbol{Z}_{c,i}. \tag{2}$$

As discussed in Sect. 1, the classifier $c(\cdot)$ is only learned based on the image-level feature $\boldsymbol{z}$, which aggregates the object features on all the positions of $\boldsymbol{Z}$.

This makes the classifier $c(\cdot)$ only discern the most discriminative feature rather than all features that are correlated to the objects. When directly projecting the classifier $c(\cdot)$ as the localizer $f(\cdot)$ that acts on the pixel-level features, some indistinguishable parts, $i.e.$, the body of animals, will not be activated on the output localization maps $\boldsymbol{P}$. Thus, our method adopts the proposed RLG strategy to generate a base localizer set $\mathcal{F} = \{f_1, f_2, ..., f_n\}$ to comprehensively discern the feature of objects. Then, the proposed BagCAMs can implement the base localizer set $\mathcal{F}$ based on the image-classifier $c(\cdot)$ and generate a series of localization maps $\mathcal{P} = \{\boldsymbol{P}_1, \boldsymbol{P}_2, ..., \boldsymbol{P}_n\}$. Finally, these maps are integrated with co-efficient $\{\lambda_1, \lambda_2, ..., \lambda_n\}$ to form the final localization map $\boldsymbol{P}^*$ that determines $\boldsymbol{Y}$:

$$\boldsymbol{P}^* = \sum_n \lambda_n f_n(\boldsymbol{Z}). \tag{3}$$

3.2   Regional Localizers Generation Strategy

The proposed RLG strategy utilizes localization scores and pixel-level feature maps to generate a set of regional localizers, which focuses more on the regional features rather than only discerning the global features as the classifier of the classification task. To better illustrate the proposed RLG strategy, we firstly design the regional localizer inspired by the property of an image classifier. In detail, by differentiating from Eq. 1, the weight $\mathbf{W}$ of the global classifier $c(\cdot)$ can be reformulated [25]:

$$\mathbf{W} = \frac{\partial c(z)}{\partial z} = (\frac{\partial \boldsymbol{s}}{\partial z})^\top. \tag{4}$$

Taking it into the Eq. 1, a equivalency of the classifier $c(\cdot)$ can be obtained [25]:

$$c(z) = \mathbf{W}z = (\frac{\partial \boldsymbol{s}}{\partial z})^\top z. \tag{5}$$

Equation 5 indicates that an image classifier $c(\cdot)$ can be represented by the transposition of the partial derivative between the image classification score $\boldsymbol{s}$ and the image feature z [25]. Analogizing this property to the localization task, the regional localizer can be simulated with the following definition.

Definition 1. *Assuming $f(\cdot)$ is a localizer that generates the classification score $\boldsymbol{p}$ on a specific spatial location based on the pixel-level features $\boldsymbol{Z} \in \mathbb{R}^{C \times N}$, i.e., $\boldsymbol{p} = f(\boldsymbol{Z})$, the localizer $f(\cdot)$ can be simulated by a function set $\mathcal{F}$ that contains the partial derivative between this regional classification score $\boldsymbol{p}$ and each regional position of pixel-level features $\boldsymbol{Z}$:*

$$\mathcal{F} = \{f_1, ..., f_n, ..., f_N\} = \{(\frac{\partial \boldsymbol{p}}{\partial \boldsymbol{Z}_{:,1}})^\top, ..., (\frac{\partial \boldsymbol{p}}{\partial \boldsymbol{Z}_{:,n}})^\top, ..., (\frac{\partial \boldsymbol{p}}{\partial \boldsymbol{Z}_{:,N}})^\top\}, \tag{6}$$

where $f_n(\cdot) = (\frac{\partial \boldsymbol{p}}{\partial \boldsymbol{Z}_{:,i}})^\top (\cdot)$ is the regional localizer that catches the relation between regional score $\boldsymbol{p}$ and the pixel-level feature of a specific regional position $\boldsymbol{Z}_{:,i}$.

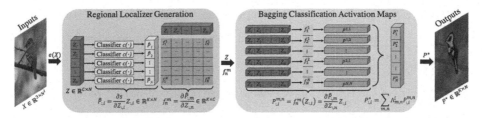

Fig. 2. Workflow of our method, where the RLG strategy (orange) generates a set of classifiers and the BagCAMs (green) weights their effect to produce localization maps. (Color figure online)

Based on Definition 1, each row vector $P_{:,i}$ of a given localization map $P \in \mathbb{R}^{K \times N}$ can be viewed as a regional classification score p that defines N regional localizers based on the pixel-level feature Z. Thus, as indicated in Fig. 2, our RLG strategy (noted by orange) can simulate $N*N$ regional localizers based on the correlation between each vector pair of P and Z:

$$f_n^m(x) = (\frac{\partial P_{:,m}}{\partial Z_{:,n}})^\top (x) \quad \longrightarrow \quad f_n^m(x)_k = \sum_c \frac{\partial P_{k,m}}{\partial Z_{c,n}} x_c, \qquad (7)$$

where $f_n^m(\cdot)_k$ represents the regional localizer of class k and $x \in \mathbb{R}^{C \times 1}$ is a variable that represents a feature vector. With this extension, a localizer set $\mathcal{F}^*$ that contains $N*N$ regional localizer can be defined based on P and Z, i.e., $\mathcal{F}^* = \{f_1^1, ..., f_n^m, ..., f_N^N\}$. Compared with the global classifier $(\frac{\partial s}{\partial z})^\top$ used by CAM, our regional localizer set $\mathcal{F}^*$ contains sufficient localizers that catch the regional correlation between scores and features on each position, which helps comprehensively discern features of the objects.

3.3 Bagging Regional Classification Activation Maps

The proposed RLG strategy provides an efficient mechanism to generate a localizer set $\mathcal{F}^*$ based on the localization map P. When implementing P as a coarse localization map $\hat{P} \in \mathbb{R}^{K \times N}$, those regional localizers f_n^m can be viewed as the base learners that can be integrated as a strong learner to locate objects. For this purpose, our BagCAMs is proposed as shown in Fig. 2 (noted by green), which generates the base localizers based on a coarse localization map $\hat{P}$ and then weights their localization results as the final localization score:

$$P_{k,i}^* = \sum_m \sum_n \Lambda_{m,n}^i f_n^m(Z_{:,i})_k = \sum_m \sum_n \Lambda_{m,n}^i \sum_c \frac{\partial \hat{P}_{k,m}}{\partial Z_{c,n}} Z_{c,i}, \qquad (8)$$

where P^* is the localization map of our proposed BagCAMs whose element $P_{k,i}^*$ represents the score on class k at position i. Λ^i is a matrix, and its element $\Lambda_{m,n}^i$ means the co-efficient of regional localizer f_n^m at position i. In detail, PCS

Table 1. Summary of degrading the proposed BagCAMs into other methods

	Initial score $\hat{P}_{k,m}$	Co-efficient matrix Λ^i	Localization score $P^*_{k,i}$
CAM	s_k	$\Lambda^i = \frac{1}{N}\mathbf{I}$	$\sum_c \frac{\partial s_k}{\partial z_c} Z_{c,i}$
GradCAM	s_k	$\Lambda^i = \frac{1}{N}\mathbf{I}$	$\frac{1}{N}\sum_{n,c} \frac{\partial s_k}{\partial Z_{c,n}} Z_{c,i}$
GradCAM++	s_k	$\Lambda^i = diag(\alpha)$	$\sum_{n,c} \alpha_m \frac{\partial s_k}{\partial Z_{c,n}} Z_{c,i}$
PCS	s_k	$\Lambda^i_{m,n} = \begin{cases} 1, & i=n \\ 0, & i \neq n \end{cases}$	$\sum_c \frac{\partial s_k}{\partial Z_{c,i}} Z_{c,i}$
Ours	$\sum_c \frac{\partial s_k}{\partial Z_{c,m}} Z_{c,m}$	$\Lambda^i_{m,n} = \begin{cases} 1, & i=n \\ 0, & i \neq n \end{cases}$	$\sum_{m,c_2} \frac{\partial(\sum_{c_1} \frac{\partial s_k}{\partial Z_{c_1,m}} Z_{c_1,m})}{\partial Z_{c_2,i}} Z_{c_2,i}$

strategy [25] is adopted to initialize the coarse localization map $\hat{P}_{k,m}$ to pursue the convenience of calculation and performance on intermediate feature maps:

$$\hat{P}_{k,m} = \sum_c \frac{\partial s_k}{\partial Z_{c,m}} Z_{c,m}. \tag{9}$$

With this initialization coarse localization map $\hat{P}_{k,m}$ and defining $\bar{s} = log(s)$, the formulation of our base localizer generated by our RLG derivatives into the following, whose proof are given in Appendix B:

$$f^m_n(\boldsymbol{x})_k = \sum_{c_1} s_k (1 + \frac{\partial \bar{s}_k}{\partial Z_{c_1,m}} Z_{c_1,m}) \sum_{c_2} (\frac{\partial \bar{s}_k}{\partial Z_{c_2,n}} \boldsymbol{x}_{c_2}). \tag{10}$$

As for the weight matrix Λ^i, the grouping strategy of PCS [25] is also adopted for consistency, assuming $(\frac{\partial p}{\partial Z_{:,i}})^\top$ is the localizer specifically for the position i:

$$\Lambda^i_{m,n} = \begin{cases} 1, & i=n \\ 0, & i \neq n \end{cases}. \tag{11}$$

This setting assigns the $N * N$ regional localizers into N groups, each applied specifically to position i. Note that Λ^i can also be implemented with other mechanisms, for example, spatial average [23] or spatial attention [5], but we find the grouping strategy performs the best due to lesser noise. Finally, taking Eq. 10 and Eq. 11 into Eq. 8, an executable formulation of BagCAMs is obtained:

$$P^*_{k,i} = \sum_m \sum_{c_1} s_k (1 + \frac{\partial \bar{s}_k}{\partial Z_{c_1,m}} Z_{c_1,m})(\sum_{c_2} \frac{\partial \bar{s}_k}{\partial Z_{c_2,i}} Z_{c_2,i}). \tag{12}$$

As indicated in Eq. 12, the computation of our BagCAMs only relies on the gradients $\frac{\partial \bar{s}}{\partial Z}$, which can be calculated by backward propagating gradients on the logarithm of the classification score s. Thus, our BagCAMs can be projected onto the intermediate layer of CNN and retain similar computation complexity as gradient-based CAM mechanisms [5,23,25]. Moreover, Table 1 also shows PCS [25] and other CAM mechanisms [5,23,38] can also be generalized by our

BagCAMs with the assumption that the initial localization result of each position i are all equal to s_k, i.e., $\forall \hat{P}_{k,m} = s_k$. However, this assumption is obviously invalid for the localization task because the background locations of the image should not have the same score as the object locations. Compared with them, our BagCAMs generates a specific initial score $\hat{P}_{k,m} \in \mathbb{R}^{K \times N}$ for each position to obtain more valid base localizers to generate high-quality localization maps, rather than defining the localizer only based on the global score $s \in \mathbb{R}^{K \times 1}$. This makes our BagCAMs perform much better than these mechanisms when engaged into WSOL.

The proposed BagCAMs can easily replace CAM step of WSOL methods to generate the localization maps. Algorithm 1 and Fig. 2 show the workflow of localizing objects for an input image X based on a trained WSOL model that contains a feature extractor $e(\cdot)$ and a classifier $c(\cdot)$. Specifically, the input image X is firstly fed into the feature extractor $e(\cdot)$ to generate the pixel-level feature $Z = e(X)$. Then, Z is aggregated into image-level feature z, which is fed into the classifier to produce the classification score s determining the object class $k = \arg\max(s)$. Next, backward propagation is adopted for $\bar{s}_k$ to calculate $\frac{\partial \bar{s}_k}{\partial Z}$ that is crucial for defining the base localizer. Finally, the localization map Y is obtained by weighing the localization scores of base localizers as in Eq. 12.

Algorithm 1. Workflow of BagCAMs for a Given WSOL Model

Input: Input image X, Classifier $c(\cdot)$, Extractor $e(\cdot)$.
  1: Calculating pixel-level feature Z of input image X with extractor $e(X)$.
  2: Obtaining image-level feature z with GAP or other aggregation mechanisms.
  3: Generating image classification score s with classifier $c(z)$.
  4: Calculating classification results $k = \arg\max(s)$.
  5: Backward propagating $\bar{s} = \log(s)_k$ to obtain the gradient $\frac{\partial \bar{s}_k}{\partial Z}$.
  6: Generating BagCAMs localization map $P_{k,:}^{*}$ by Eq. 12 and upsampling it as Y.
Output: Localization Score Y, Classification Score s.

---

4   Experiments

This section first introduces the setting of experiments. Then, results of our BagCAMs are shown to compare with SOTA methods on three datasets. Finally, we investigate different settings of our BagCAMs to further reflect its validity.

4.1   Settings

The proposed BagCAMs can be engaged into a well-trained WSOL model by simply replacing CAM in the test process. Thus, we reproduced five WSOL methods as the baseline methods to train them with their optimal settings, including CAM [38], HAS [17], CutMix [32], ADL [6], and DAOL [39]. In detail, the ResNet-50, removing the down-sample layer of Res_4, was used as the feature extractor. When using InceptionV3 as the extractor, we follow existing works [20, 25,34,35] that add two additional layers at the end of the original structure. The classifier is implemented as a fully-connected layer, whose outputs are supervised by the cross entropy based on the image-level annotation in the training process. Except for the method-specific strategy [6,17,32], the random resize with size 256×256 and random horizontal flip crop with size 224×224 were adopted as the augmentation. SGD with weight decay 10^{-4} and momentum 0.9 was set as the optimizer. Note that the learning rate and the method-specific hyper-parameters for all datasets were adopted as the released optimal settings [7,39]. In the test process, our BagCAMs replaced the CAM step of these methods to project the learned classifier as the localizer based on features outputted by Res_3 of the ResNet (Mix_{6e} for the InceptionV3). All experiments were implemented with Pytorch toolbox [21] on an Intel Core i9 CPU and an NVIDIA RTX 3090 GPU.

Three standard benchmarks were utilized to evaluate our methods:

- **CUB-200 dataset** [26] contains 11,788 images that are fine-grained anno-tated for 200 classes of birds. We follow the official training/test split to use 5,944 images as the training set that only utilizes image-level annotation to supervise WSOL methods. Other 5,794 images, given additional bounding boxes and pixel-level masks, serve as the test set to evaluate the performance.
- **ILSVRC dataset** [8] contains 1.3 million images that include 1000 classes of objects. Among them, 50,000 images, whose bounding boxes annotation is provided, are adopted as the test set to report the localization performance.
- **OpenImages dataset** [3,7] contains 37,319 images of 100 classes, where 29,819 images serve as the training set. Following the split released by Jun-suk [7], the rest 7,500 images, annotated by pixel-level localization mask, are divided into the validation set (2,500 images) and test set (5,000 images).

Note that our BagCAMs does not contain any hyper-parameters, thus only the test images of these dataset are utilized for comparison. The Top-1 local-ization accuracy (T-Loc) [17], ground-truth known localization accuracy (G-Loc) [17], and the recently proposed MaxBoxAccV2 [7] (B-Loc) were adopted to evaluate the performance based on bounding box annotations. As for pixel-level localization masks, the peak intersection over union (pIOU) [37] and the pixel average precision (PxAP) [7] were calculated as the metrics.

4.2   Comparison with State-of-the-Arts

Table 2 illustrates the results of SOTA methods and our BagCAMs on the three standard WSOL benchmarks. It shows that adopting our proposed BagCAMs improves the performance of baseline methods to a great extent, especially on the CUB-200 dataset. This is because the CUB-200 dataset is a fine-graining dataset that only contains birds, making the classifier more likely to catch discrimina-tive parts rather than the common parts of birds. As discussed in Sect. 3, this situation basically causes unsatisfactory performance when directly using the

Table 2. Comparison with SOTA methods with ResNet50 (**border** means the best).

	CUB-200					ILSVRC			OpenImages	
	T-Loc	G-Loc	B-Loc	pIoU	PxAP	T-Loc	G-Loc	B-Loc	pIoU	PxAP
DGL [25]	60.82	76.65	–	–	–	53.41	66.52	–	–	–
CAAM [1]	64.70	77.35	–	–	–	52.36	67.89	–	–	–
DANet [30]	61.10	–	–	–	–	–	–	–	–	–
ICLCA [14]	56.10	72.79	63.20	–	–	48.40	67.62	65.15	–	–
PAS [2]	59.53	77.58	66.38	–	–	49.42	62.20	64.72	–	60.90
IVR [15]	–	–	71.23	–	–	–	–	65.57	–	58.90
PSOL [33]	70.68	–	–	–	–	53.98	65.54	–	–	–
SEM [37]	–	–	–	–	–	53.84	67.00	–	–	–
FAM [19]	**73.74**	85.73	–	–	–	**54.46**	64.56	–	–	–
CAM [38]	55.31	66.06	59.21	46.70	65.94	49.93	67.30	62.69	43.13	57.88
+Ours	70.89	87.44	76.22	64.40	84.38	52.14	70.78	69.13	47.92	62.52
HAS [17]	54.48	72.55	66.25	51.00	71.87	50.80	66.91	64.67	42.28	55.83
+Ours	65.93	89.65	84.45	70.24	88.94	53.32	70.67	69.17	47.71	62.45
CutMix [32]	56.27	64.13	59.08	44.21	65.23	50.17	65.84	63.73	42.85	57.97
+Ours	72.96	87.44	79.67	64.93	85.36	53.02	69.92	68.53	46.67	60.16
ADL [6]	52.13	66.75	59.31	45.40	59.49	50.40	66.88	64.50	42.29	56.21
+Ours	64.41	86.06	74.48	60.46	81.07	53.05	70.51	68.97	47.04	61.76
DAOL [39]	62.40	81.83	69.87	56.18	74.70	43.26	70.27	68.23	49.68	65.42
+Ours	69.67	**94.01**	**84.88**	**74.51**	**90.38**	44.24	**72.08**	**69.97**	**52.17**	**67.68**

Table 3. Comparison with SOTA methods with InceptionV3 (**border** means the best).

Method	CUB-200					ILSVRC			OpenImages	
	T-Loc	G-Loc	B-Loc	pIoU	PxAP	T-Loc	G-Loc	B-Loc	pIoU	PxAP
DGL [25]	50.50	67.64	–	–	–	52.23	68.08	–	–	–
SPG [35]	56.64	–	–	–	–	49.60	64.69	–	–	–
I^2C [36]	55.99	72.60	–	–	–	53.11	68.50	–	–	–
ICLCA [14]	56.10	67.93	–	–	–	49.30	65.21	–	–	–
PAS [2]	69.96	73.65	–	–	–	50.56	64.44	–	–	63.30
IVR [15]	–	–	61.74	–	–	–	–	66.04	–	64.08
UPSP [20]	53.38	72.14	–	–	–	52.73	68.33	–	–	–
PSOL [33]	65.51	–	–	–	–	54.82	65.21	–	–	–
GCNet [18]	–	–	–	–	–	49.06	–	–	–	–
FAM [19]	**70.67**	87.25	–	–	–	**55.24**	68.62	–	–	–
CAM [38]	48.96	63.44	57.14	49.28	70.95	50.75	66.16	63.61	47.51	63.31
+Ours	54.75	74.75	65.65	60.34	81.49	52.22	68.84	66.46	49.98	65.91
HAS [17]	52.68	70.89	62.39	52.78	74.07	51.00	66.99	64.26	42.87	59.50
+Ours	57.93	79.44	69.65	61.75	83.03	52.22	69.20	66.89	48.44	64.37
CutMix [32]	51.86	66.62	59.44	51.40	74.19	50.72	66.96	64.44	46.30	62.12
+Ours	58.48	79.58	68.09	**62.44**	**83.15**	52.60	70.57	**68.04**	49.28	65.23
ADL [6]	49.10	62.62	57.01	49.72	70.06	50.20	66.30	63.66	47.03	63.42
+Ours	54.75	74.34	64.87	60.09	81.41	51.63	68.81	66.42	49.22	65.31
DAOL [39]	56.29	80.03	68.01	51.80	71.03	52.70	69.11	64.75	48.01	64.46
+Ours	60.07	**89.78**	**76.94**	58.05	72.97	53.87	**71.02**	66.93	**50.79**	**66.89**

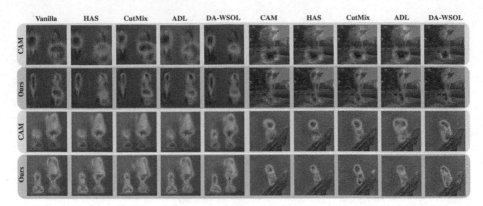

Fig. 3. Visualization on replacing CAM into BagCAMs for different WSOL methods.

classifier to localize objects as CAM. By adopting our BagCAMs to project the classifier into a set of regional localizers, the regional factors of the class of bird can be better concerned, improving nearly 21.38% in G-Loc than the baseline method. Additionally, when more finely evaluated by the pixel-level mask, the improvements of our method are still remarkable, achieving 64.40% pIoU and 84.38% PxAP, which are 17.70% and 18.44% higher than CAM, respectively. As for the larger scale dataset ILSVRC, directly replacing CAM into our BagCAMs in the test process also achieves 3.48% higher performance in G-Loc metric, *i.e.*, correcting the localization of nearly 1,740 images without any fine-tuning process or structure modification. In addition, even using the most recently proposed DAOL [39] that achieves the SOTA performance on the OpenImages dataset, adopting our method can still obviously improve its performance about 2.49% and 2.26%, respectively in the pIOU and PxAP.

Except for the five reproduced methods, the other nine SOTA methods were also used for comparison in Table 2, whose scores are cited from corresponding papers. Our BagCAMs outperforms SOTA methods for nearly all metrics on all three datasets even though engaged in the vanilla WSOL structure, *i.e.*, "CAM + Ours". Only the T-Loc metric of our BagCAMs is lower than the methods that generate class-agnostic localization results and adopt addition stages for classification (noted by underline style) [19,33,37]. This is because our Bag-CAMs is only adopted in the test process to enhance the localization results, and our classification accuracy is directly determined by the baseline WSOL methods. Moreover, Table 3 also shows the comparison of using InceptionV3 as the feature extractor for WSOL methods to indicate our generalization for the backbone other than ResNet. The results are in accordance with utilizing ResNet, improving the performance on all baseline methods, for example, 11.31% and 9.38% G-Loc improvement for the vanilla structure (CAM) and DAOL on the CUB-200 dataset, respectively. Moreover, our BagCAMs still outperforms other SOTA methods with InceptionV3 on nearly all metric for these three datasets.

Localization maps generated by WSOL methods with our BagCAMs are also visualized in Fig. 3. For localization maps of the vanilla structure, only the most discriminative locations are activated, *e.g.*, the pedestal of the toy, both ends of the pillar, the shade of the lamp, and the head of the bird. Though existing WSOL methods catch more positions of objects, they only enlarge or refine the activation of regions that near the discriminative parts rather than catching more parts of the object. This also visually verifies that the mechanism of CAM limits the performance of these WSOL methods, making the localizer only concern global cues. Profited by the utilization of our base localizer set, more object parts are effectively activated when adopting our BagCAMs to replace CAM for those methods, for example, the head of the toy, the pedestal of the lamp, and the body of the pillar/bird. Moreover, our BagCAMs can generate the localization map on intermediate layers that contains more fining cues such as pixels near the edge of objects, which also contributes to our high performance (Table 6).

Table 4. The best scores of different CAMs on layers of ResNet for CUB-200 dataset

	T-Loc	G-Loc	B-Loc	pIoU	PxAP
CAM	55.31	66.06	59.21	46.70	65.94
PCS	60.27	73.93	65.24	52.05	72.06
Grad	56.68	69.93	61.70	49.51	68.69
Grad++	61.10	73.79	69.14	53.61	76.33
Ours	**70.89**	**87.44**	**76.22**	**64.40**	**84.38**
HAS	54.48	72.55	66.25	51.00	71.87
PCS	53.65	73.24	67.9	54.87	76.72
Grad	56.82	77.79	69.37	55.64	76.77
Grad++	55.31	76.82	70.29	53.34	75.54
Ours	**65.93**	**89.65**	**84.45**	**70.24**	**88.94**
CutMix	56.27	64.13	59.08	44.21	65.23
PCS	57.65	68.13	61.51	48.19	68.74
Grad	60.96	72.68	64.50	52.10	71.49
Grad++	63.17	77.10	67.67	53.77	74.78
Ours	**72.96**	**87.44**	**79.67**	**64.93**	**85.36**
ADL	52.13	66.75	59.31	45.40	59.49
PCS	52.13	66.75	59.31	45.40	59.49
Grad	52.13	66.75	59.31	45.40	59.49
Grad++	53.65	70.89	61.19	44.72	61.14
Ours	**64.41**	**86.06**	**74.48**	**60.46**	**81.07**
DAOL	62.40	81.83	69.87	56.18	74.70
PCS	63.30	84.57	71.49	58.94	76.81
Grad	63.30	84.57	71.49	58.94	76.81
Grad++	66.13	89.60	75.71	63.08	80.23
Ours	**69.67**	**94.01**	**84.88**	**74.51**	**90.38**

Table 5. PxAP on layers of ResNet

Method	Res_1	Res_2	Res_3	Res_4
PCS	42.01	51.36	72.96	65.94
Grad	15.05	19.61	68.69	65.94
Grad++	13.16	32.01	76.33	71.49
Ours	**71.35**	**78.71**	**84.38**	**72.98**

Table 6. PxAP on layers of Inception

Method	Mix_{6b}	Mix_{6c}	Mix_{6d}	Mix_{6e}
PCS	41.42	61.37	75.36	76.32
Grad	28.91	46.62	65.41	76.19
Grad++	26.77	43.26	65.41	68.00
Ours	**78.14**	**81.46**	**82.80**	**81.49**

Table 7. Efficiency (fps) of CAMs

Method	Res_1	Res_2	Res_3	Res_4
PCS	**90.88**	90.40	**91.86**	**91.04**
Grad	89.72	**91.04**	90.94	90.75
Grad++	90.61	89.25	90.62	89.67
Ours	88.44	86.40	87.02	87.77

Table 8. Different weight strategy

	T-Loc	G-Loc	B-Loc	PxAP
CAM	55.31	66.06	59.21	65.94
Ours$_1$	66.75	82.34	74.80	77.29
Ours$_2$	70.20	86.20	74.16	81.79
Ours$_3$	70.89	87.44	76.22	84.38

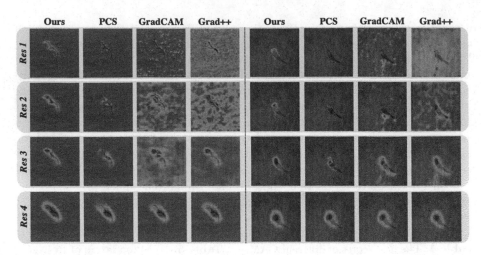

Fig. 4. Localization map generated by the features of different ResNet layer by CAMs.

4.3 Discussion

To deeply investigate the effectiveness of our BagCAMs, we also conducted experiments to compare it with methods that generalize or enhance CAM on GAP-free structures or intermediate layers of CNN, *e.g.*, GradCAM (Grad) [23], GradCAM++ (Grad++) [5], PCS [25]. We adopted the same trained checkpoint for these methods and utilized them to project the classifier in the test process. Except for the original CAM, other methods can be added onto the intermediate layers of the feature extractor. Thus, we generated localization maps on each layer and chose the best performance to report.

Corresponding results are illustrated in Table 4 where the baseline methods, *i.e.*, CAM, HAS, ADL, CutMix, and DAOL, represent directly adopting the classifier for localization as CAM. It shows that for all baseline WSOL methods, our BagCAMs achieves the highest improvement compared with other CAM mechanisms. This is because other CAMs methods all initialize $\hat{P}$ with the global classification results s for all positions as discussed in Sect. 3.3, resulting in their lower improvement. Unlike them, our BagCAMs adopts $\hat{P}_{:,m}$ to distribute a specific initial localization score for each position m, which helps generate valid localizers and contributes to our outstanding improvement, *e.g.*, 15.68% higher PxAP than using the original CAM for the DAOL.

In addition, our BagCAMs can also achieve satisfactory performance when localizing objects based on features of intermediate layers, which may inspire generating localization maps with higher resolution to consider more details. Table 5 illustrates the PxAP metric for generating localization maps based on the feature of Res_1 ($256 \times 56 \times 56$), Res_2 ($512 \times 28 \times 28$), Res_3 ($1024 \times 28 \times 28$), and Res_4 ($2048 \times 28 \times 28$). Note that the original CAM can only adopt to the last layer before GAP due to the difference between the number of channels in W and the intermediate features, thus we did not include the original CAM in this Table 5. It can be seen that GradCAM and GradCAM++ have great performance drops when projected to the prior intermediate layers, $i.e.$, Res_1 and Res_2. Though the PCS, proposed for generating localization results on intermediate layers, slightly decelerates this decline, its PxAP of Res_1 is still 30.97% lower than Res_4. Compared with them, our BagCAMs generates the localization map by bagging the performance of $N \times N$ base localizers, where N is the spatial resolution of the feature map. Thus, for the previous layers with higher resolution, more basic localizers can be defined for bagging, $i.e.$, 3,136 for Res_1. This makes our BagCAMs achieve 29.34% higher PxAP compared with the best of others, when projected on the feature of Res_1.

Figure 4 also qualitatively visualizes the localization maps generated on the intermediate features. It can be seen that localization maps of GradCAM and GradCAM++ contain more noise on Res_1 and Res_2, and the PCS only activates a few discriminative locations. Compared with them, though our BagCAMs suffers from the grid effect caused by the down-sampling, our localization map can cover more object parts even for Res_1. Finally, the efficiencies of different CAMs are also shown in Table 7, where their mean frame per second (fps) for inferring CUB-200 test are reported. It can be seen that, though considering multiple regional localizers rather than only the global one, the complexity of our Bag-CAMs is only a bit higher than other methods. This indicates that our method can balance the localization performance and efficiency well.

Except for comparing with other CAM mechanisms, the choice of different weighting strategies, $i.e.$, various settings of the weight matrix Λ, were also explored on the CUB-200 dataset. Specifically, we designed three types of Bag-CAMs: (1) Ours$_1$ that only averages the scores generated by localizers f_n^m, $i.e.$, $\Lambda^i = \frac{1}{N}\mathbf{I}$. (2) Ours$_2$ that aggregates the scores with the spatially weighting mechanism of GradCAM++ [5], $i.e.$, $\Lambda^i = diag(\alpha)$. (3) Ours$_3$, the mechanism we used in our paper as defined in Eq. 9, which only selects specific localizers for each position like PCS [25]. Corresponding results are shown in Table 8. It can be seen that using these three weighting mechanisms can all enhance the performance of the baseline methods, profited by adopting the regional localizer set rather than the globally defined classifier. Specifically, when simply averaging the localization scores of the regional localizers (Ours$_1$), the performance improves about 11.35% on the PxAP metric. Adopting the spatial weighting strategy to consider the effect based on each spatial position will bring an additional 4.5% improvement. When grouping the $N * N$ localizers into N clusters that are specifically used for each spatial position to reduce noise as PCS [25], the performance hits the highest, $i.e.$, about 84.38% PxAP. Thus, we suggest adopting this grouping strategy to weight the effect of the regional localizers.

4.4   Conclusion

This paper proposes a novel mechanism called BagCAMs for WSOL to replace CAM [38] when projecting an image-level trained classifier as the localizer to locate objects. Our BagCAMs can be engaged in existing WSOL methods to improve their performance without re-training the baseline structure. Experiments show that our method achieves SOTA performance on three WSOL benchmarks.

Acknowledgements. This work was supported in part by the Beijing Natural Science Foundation under Grant Z210008; in part by the Shenzhen Science and Technology Program under Grant KQTD20180412181221912 and Grant JCYJ20200109140603831.

References

1. Babar, S., Das, S.: Where to look?: Mining complementary image regions for weakly supervised object localization. In: 2021 IEEE Winter Conference on Applications of Computer Vision (WACV) (2021)
2. Bae, W., Noh, J., Kim, G.: Rethinking class activation mapping for weakly supervised object localization. In: Vedaldi, A., Bischof, H., Brox, T., Frahm, J.-M. (eds.) ECCV 2020. LNCS, vol. 12360, pp. 618–634. Springer, Cham (2020). https://doi.org/10.1007/978-3-030-58555-6_37
3. Benenson, R., Popov, S., Ferrari, V.: Large-scale interactive object segmentation with human annotators. In: Proceedings of the IEEE/CVF Conference on Computer Vision and Pattern Recognition (CVPR), pp. 11700–11709 (2019)
4. Chang, Y.T., Wang, Q., Hung, W.C., Piramuthu, R., Tsai, Y.H., Yang, M.H.: Weakly-supervised semantic segmentation via sub-category exploration. In: Proceedings of the IEEE/CVF Conference on Computer Vision and Pattern Recognition (CVPR), pp. 8991–9000 (2020)
5. Chattopadhay, A., Sarkar, A., Howlader, P., Balasubramanian, V.N.: Grad-CAM++: generalized gradient-based visual explanations for deep convolutional networks. In: 2018 IEEE Winter Conference on Applications of Computer Vision (WACV), pp. 839–847. IEEE (2018)
6. Choe, J., Lee, S., Shim, H.: Attention-based dropout layer for weakly supervised single object localization and semantic segmentation. IEEE Trans. Pattern Anal. Mach. Intell. (TPAMI) **43**(12), 4256–4271 (2020)
7. Choe, J., Oh, S.J., Lee, S., Chun, S., Akata, Z., Shim, H.: Evaluating weakly supervised object localization methods right. In: Proceedings of the IEEE/CVF Conference on Computer Vision and Pattern Recognition (CVPR), pp. 3133–3142 (2020)
8. Deng, J., Dong, W., Socher, R., Li, L.J., Li, K., Fei-Fei, L.: ImageNet: a large-scale hierarchical image database. In: IEEE Conference on Computer Vision and Pattern Recognition (CVPR), pp. 248–255. IEEE (2009)
9. Fan, J., Zhang, Z., Tan, T., Song, C., Xiao, J.: CIAN: cross-image affinity net for weakly supervised semantic segmentation. In: Proceedings of the AAAI Conference on Artificial Intelligence (AAAI), vol. 34, pp. 10762–10769 (2020)
10. Fang, L., Xu, H., Liu, Z., Parisot, S., Li, Z.: EHSOD: CAM-guided end-to-end hybrid-supervised object detection with cascade refinement. In: Proceedings of the AAAI Conference on Artificial Intelligence (AAAI), vol. 34, pp. 10778–10785 (2020)
11. Guo, G., Han, J., Wan, F., Zhang, D.: Strengthen learning tolerance for weakly supervised object localization. In: Proceedings of the IEEE/CVF Conference on Computer Vision and Pattern Recognition (CVPR), pp. 7403–7412 (2021)
12. He, K., Zhang, X., Ren, S., Sun, J.: Deep residual learning for image recognition. In: Proceedings of the IEEE/CVF Conference on Computer Vision and Pattern Recognition (CVPR), pp. 770–778 (2016)

13. Hsu, C.C., Hsu, K.J., Tsai, C.C., Lin, Y.Y., Chuang, Y.Y.: Weakly supervised instance segmentation using the bounding box tightness prior. In: Advances in Neural Information Processing Systems (NeurIPS), vol. 32, pp. 6586–6597 (2019)
14. Ki, M., Uh, Y., Lee, W., Byun, H.: In-sample contrastive learning and consistent attention for weakly supervised object localization. In: Proceedings of the Asian Conference on Computer Vision (ACCV) (2020)
15. Kim, J., Choe, J., Yun, S., Kwak, N.: Normalization matters in weakly supervised object localization. In: Proceedings of the IEEE/CVF International Conference on Computer Vision (ICCV), pp. 3427–3436 (2021)
16. Kou, Z., Cui, G., Wang, S., Zhao, W., Xu, C.: Improve CAM with auto-adapted segmentation and co-supervised augmentation. In: 2021 IEEE Winter Conference on Applications of Computer Vision (WACV) (2021)
17. Kumar Singh, K., Jae Lee, Y.: Hide-and-Seek: forcing a network to be meticulous for weakly-supervised object and action localization. In: Proceedings of the IEEE/CVF International Conference on Computer Vision (ICCV), pp. 3524–3533 (2017)
18. Lu, W., Jia, X., Xie, W., Shen, L., Zhou, Y., Duan, J.: Geometry constrained weakly supervised object localization. In: Vedaldi, A., Bischof, H., Brox, T., Frahm, J.-M. (eds.) ECCV 2020. LNCS, vol. 12371, pp. 481–496. Springer, Cham (2020). https://doi.org/10.1007/978-3-030-58574-7_29
19. Meng, M., Zhang, T., Tian, Q., Zhang, Y., Wu, F.: Foreground activation maps for weakly supervised object localization. In: Proceedings of the IEEE/CVF International Conference on Computer Vision (ICCV), pp. 3385–3395 (2021)
20. Pan, X., et al.: Unveiling the potential of structure preserving for weakly supervised object localization. In: Proceedings of the IEEE/CVF Conference on Computer Vision and Pattern Recognition (CVPR), pp. 11642–11651 (2021)
21. Paszke, A., et al.: PyTorch: an imperative style, high-performance deep learning library. In: Advances in Neural Information Processing Systems (NeurIPS), pp. 8024–8035 (2019)
22. Ramaswamy, H.G., et al.: Ablation-CAM: visual explanations for deep convolutional network via gradient-free localization. In: Proceedings of the IEEE/CVF Winter Conference on Applications of Computer Vision, pp. 983–991 (2020)
23. Selvaraju, R.R., Cogswell, M., Das, A., Vedantam, R., Parikh, D., Batra, D.: Grad-CAM: visual explanations from deep networks via gradient-based localization. In: Proceedings of the IEEE/CVF International Conference on Computer Vision (ICCV), pp. 618–626 (2017)
24. Szegedy, C., Vanhoucke, V., Ioffe, S., Shlens, J., Wojna, Z.: Rethinking the inception architecture for computer vision. In: Proceedings of the IEEE/CVF Conference on Computer Vision and Pattern Recognition (CVPR), pp. 2818–2826 (2016)
25. Tan, C., Gu, G., Ruan, T., Wei, S., Zhao, Y.: Dual-gradients localization framework for weakly supervised object localization. In: Proceedings of the 28th ACM International Conference on Multimedia, pp. 1976–1984 (2020)
26. Wah, C., Branson, S., Welinder, P., Perona, P., Belongie, S.: The Caltech-UCSD Birds-200-2011 dataset (2011)
27. Wan, F., Liu, C., Ke, W., Ji, X., Jiao, J., Ye, Q.: C-MIL: continuation multiple instance learning for weakly supervised object detection. In: Proceedings of the IEEE/CVF Conference on Computer Vision and Pattern Recognition (CVPR), pp. 2199–2208 (2019)
28. Wang, H., et al.: Score-CAM: score-weighted visual explanations for convolutional neural networks. In: Proceedings of the IEEE/CVF Conference on Computer Vision and Pattern Recognition Workshops, pp. 24–25 (2020)

29. Wang, X., Girshick, R., Gupta, A., He, K.: Non-local neural networks. In: IEEE Conference on Computer Vision and Pattern Recognition (CVPR), pp. 7794–7803 (2018)
30. Xue, H., Liu, C., Wan, F., Jiao, J., Ji, X., Ye, Q.: DANet: divergent activation for weakly supervised object localization. In: Proceedings of the IEEE/CVF International Conference on Computer Vision (ICCV), pp. 6589–6598 (2019)
31. Yang, S., Kim, Y., Kim, Y., Kim, C.: Combinational class activation maps for weakly supervised object localization. In: Proceedings of the IEEE/CVF Winter Conference on Applications of Computer Vision (WACV), pp. 2941–2949 (2020)
32. Yun, S., Han, D., Oh, S.J., Chun, S., Choe, J., Yoo, Y.: CutMix: regularization strategy to train strong classifiers with localizable features. In: Proceedings of the IEEE/CVF International Conference on Computer Vision (ICCV), pp. 6023–6032 (2019)
33. Zhang, C.L., Cao, Y.H., Wu, J.: Rethinking the route towards weakly supervised object localization. In: Proceedings of the IEEE/CVF Conference on Computer Vision and Pattern Recognition (CVPR), pp. 13460–13469 (2020)
34. Zhang, X., Wei, Y., Feng, J., Yang, Y., Huang, T.S.: Adversarial complementary learning for weakly supervised object localization. In: Proceedings of the IEEE/CVF Conference on Computer Vision and Pattern Recognition (CVPR), pp. 1325–1334 (2018)
35. Zhang, X., Wei, Y., Kang, G., Yang, Y., Huang, T.: Self-produced guidance for weakly-supervised object localization. In: Ferrari, V., Hebert, M., Sminchisescu, C., Weiss, Y. (eds.) ECCV 2018. LNCS, vol. 11216, pp. 610–625. Springer, Cham (2018). https://doi.org/10.1007/978-3-030-01258-8_37
36. Zhang, X., Wei, Y., Yang, Y.: Inter-image communication for weakly supervised localization. In: Vedaldi, A., Bischof, H., Brox, T., Frahm, J.-M. (eds.) ECCV 2020. LNCS, vol. 12364, pp. 271–287. Springer, Cham (2020). https://doi.org/10.1007/978-3-030-58529-7_17
37. Zhang, X., Wei, Y., Yang, Y., Wu, F.: Rethinking localization map: towards accurate object perception with self-enhancement maps. arXiv preprint arXiv:2006.05220 (2020)
38. Zhou, B., Khosla, A., Lapedriza, A., Oliva, A., Torralba, A.: Learning deep features for discriminative localization. In: Proceedings of the IEEE/CVF Conference on Computer Vision and Pattern Recognition (CVPR), pp. 2921–2929 (2016)
39. Zhu, L., She, Q., Chen, Q., You, Y., Wang, B., Lu, Y.: Weakly supervised object localization as domain adaption. In: Proceedings of the IEEE/CVF Conference on Computer Vision and Pattern Recognition, pp. 14637–14646 (2022)
40. Zhu, L., et al.: Unifying nonlocal blocks for neural networks. In: Proceedings of the IEEE/CVF International Conference on Computer Vision, pp. 12292–12301 (2021)

UC-OWOD: Unknown-Classified Open World Object Detection

Zhiheng Wu[1,2], Yue Lu[1,2], Xingyu Chen[3], Zhengxing Wu[1,2(✉)],
Liwen Kang[1,2], and Junzhi Yu[1,4]

[1] Institute of Automation, Chinese Academy of Sciences, Beijing, China
{wuzhiheng2020,luyue2018,zhengxing.wu,kangliwen2020,junzhi.yu}@ia.ac.cn
[2] School of Artificial Intelligence, University of Chinese Academy of Sciences,
Beijing, China
[3] Xiaobing.AI, Beijing, China
chenxingyu@xiaobing.ai
[4] Peking University, Beijing, China

Abstract. Open World Object Detection (OWOD) is a challenging computer vision problem that requires detecting unknown objects and gradually learning the identified unknown classes. However, it cannot distinguish unknown instances as multiple unknown classes. In this work, we propose a novel OWOD problem called Unknown-Classified Open World Object Detection (UC-OWOD). UC-OWOD aims to detect unknown instances and classify them into different unknown classes. Besides, we formulate the problem and devise a two-stage object detector to solve UC-OWOD. First, unknown label-aware proposal and unknown-discriminative classification head are used to detect known and unknown objects. Then, similarity-based unknown classification and unknown clustering refinement modules are constructed to distinguish multiple unknown classes. Moreover, two novel evaluation protocols are designed to evaluate unknown-class detection. Abundant experiments and visualizations prove the effectiveness of the proposed method. Code is available at https://github.com/JohnWuzh/UC-OWOD.

Keywords: OWOD · UC-OWOD · Object detection · Clustering

1 Introduction

Nowadays, deep learning methods have achieved great success in object detection [8,10,20,31,35,47]. Traditional object detection methods are developed under a closed-world assumption, so they can only detect known (labeled) categories [17,46,62]. However, the real world contains many unknown (unlabeled) classes that can hardly be properly handled by conventional detection. Therefore, studying the Open World Object Detection (OWOD) problem for detecting unknown instances is of great significance to facilitate the practical application.

Supplementary Information The online version contains supplementary material available at https://doi.org/10.1007/978-3-031-20080-9_12.

Fig. 1. The comparison between OWOD and UC-OWOD. They can both learn the newly annotated classes by human annotators without forgetting in the next task. (a) OWOD detects unknown objects as a same class. (b) UC-OWOD can detect unknown objects as different classes.

The OWOD problem was pioneered by [24], as shown in Fig. 1(a). OWOD contains multiple incremental tasks. In each task, OWOD is able to identify all unknown instances as *unknown*. Then, human annotators can gradually assign labels to classes of interest, and the model learns these classes incrementally in the next task. However, beyond distinguishing unknown classes, we also need to determine whether multiple unknown instances belong to the same category. Therefore, there is still a huge difficulty when using OWOD for real-world tasks. For example, in practical applications in robotics [16,28] and self-driving cars [7, 53], it is necessary to explore the unknown environment and adopt different strategies for different unknown classes, which requires detection algorithms to confidently localize unknown instances and classify them into different unknown classes.

Most existing open-world detectors are designed for OWOD problem. For example, Open World Object Detector (ORE) [24] can detect unknown classes, but it does not consider the case of classifying unknown objects. More specifically, ORE used pseudo-label supervised training to detect unknown instances. Since pseudo-labels can only be marked as *unknown*, the ORE model cannot be directly used to solve the problem of detecting unknown classes as different classes. Similarly, existing OWOD methods models such as [18,60] follow ORE's spirit, and we are not aware of any previous work that can distinguish multiple unknown classes.

Another difficulty in studying unknown object classification problems is the immature evaluation criterion. Existing metrics only evaluate the degree of confusion between unknown and known classes. They cannot evaluate the situation where two unknown objects of different classes are detected as the same class. But these problems cannot be ignored because they may cause the model to misclassify unknown objects. Therefore, a more reasonable evaluation metric is urgently needed to evaluate the detection accuracy of multiple unknown classes.

Considering the above issues, we propose a novel OWOD problem that is closer to the real-world setting, namely, Unknown-Classified Open World Object Detection (UC-OWOD), which can detect unknown objects as different unknown classes (see Fig. 1(b)). Meanwhile, we propose a novel framework based on the two-stage detection pipeline to solve this problem. In particular, we design the unknown label-aware proposal (ULP) to construct unknown object ground-truth, the unknown-discriminative classification head (UCH) to mine unknown objects, the similarity-based unknown classification (SUC) to detect unknown objects as different classes, and the unknown clustering refinement (UCR) to refine the classification of unknown objects. To more accurately evaluate the UC-OWOD problem, we propose novel metrics to evaluate the classification and localization performance of unknown instances. A maximum matching is used to assign ground-truth to unknown objects more reasonably. Ultimately, our model achieves the best performance in both existing evaluation metrics and new evaluation metrics. Our main contributions are as follows:

- We introduce a new problem setting, i.e., unknown-classified open world object detection, to inspire future research on real-world object detection.
- We propose a method to solve the UC-OWOD problem based on the unknown label-aware proposal, the unknown-discriminative classification head, the similarity-based unknown classification, and the unknown clustering refinement.
- Novel evaluation metrics for UC-OWOD are proposed, which can evaluate the localization and classification of unknown objects. Extensive experiments are conducted, and the results demonstrate the effectiveness of our method and new metrics for the UC-OWOD problem.

2   Related Work

Open Set Recognition and Detection. Open Set Recognition was first defined as a constrained minimization problem [51], and it can submit unknown classes to the algorithm during the testing phase. It was developed to a multi-class classifier by [23,50]. Liu et al. considered a long-tailed recognition environment and developed a metric learning framework to identify unseen classes as unknown classes [33]. Self-supervised learning [41] and unsupervised learning with reconstruction [58] have also been used for open-set recognition. Yue et al. provided a theoretical ground for balancing and improving the seen/unseen classification imbalance [59]. Bendale and Boult proposed a method to adapt deep networks to Open Set Recognition, using OpenMax layers to estimate the probability that the input is from an unknown class [6]. Dhamija et al. first proposed the open-set object detection protocol and formalized the open-set object detection problem [11]. Miller et al. improved object detection performance by extracting label uncertainty under open conditions commonly encountered in robot vision [40]. Some follow-up work also exploited measures of (spatial and semantic) uncertainty in object detectors to reject unknown categories [19].

Miller et al. found that the correct choice of affinity clustering combinations can greatly improve the effectiveness of classification, spatial uncertainty estimation, and the resulting object detection performance [39]. However, these methods cannot gradually adjust their knowledge in a dynamic world. By contrast, our model can dynamically update known classes based on human-annotated labels.

Open World Recognition and Detection. Compared to open set problems, open world problem has dynamic datasets and can continuously add new known classes like continuous learning [13,26,42,48,54]. Bendale et al. first proposed Open World Recognition and presented a protocol for the evaluation of open world recognition systems [5]. Xu et al. proposed a meta-learning approach to the open world learning problem that uses only examples of instantly seen classes (including newly added classes) for classification and rejection [57]. Joseph et al. presented a new computer vision problem called OWOD [24]. The ORE proposed by them can classify proposals between known and unknown classes, but it relies on a holdout validation set with weak unknown supervision to learn the energy distributions of known and unknown classes. The open-world detection transformer (OW-DETR) improved performance using multi-scale self-attention and deformable receptive fields [18]. Zhao et al. further proposed an OWOD framework including an auxiliary proposal advisor and a class-specific expelling classifier [60]. None of these methods implements the classification of unknown classes. Our work mainly studies the classification of unknown objects.

Constrained Clustering. Constrained clustering is a semi-supervised learning method that involves prior knowledge to assist clustering. The proposed methods for constrained clustering can be divided into three types, i.e., search-based (also known as constraint-based), distance-based (also known as similarity-based), and hybrid (also known as search-and-distance-based) methods [61]. A common technique in search-based methods is to modify the objective function by adding penalty terms for unsatisfied constraints. In distance-based methods, existing clustering methods are usually used, but the distance metric of this method is modified according to prior knowledge. Hybrid methods integrate search-based and distance-based methods. They benefit from the strengths of both and generally perform better than separate methods [12]. Basu et al. allowed the constraints to be violated with violation cost, while optimizing the distance metric [4]. Hsu et al. designed a new loss function to normalize classification with constrained clustering losses, while using other similarity prediction models as pairwise constraints in the clustering process [22]. Lin et al. took pairwise constraints as prior knowledge to guide the clustering process [30]. We use pairwise constraints to optimize the unknown object classification in the model.

3   Unknown-Classified Open World Object Detection

3.1   Problem Formulation

The UC-OWOD problem is defined as follows. There are a set of tasks $\mathcal{T} = \{T_1, T_2, ...\}$. In task T_t, we have a known class set $\mathcal{K}^t = \{1, 2, ..., C\}$ and unknown

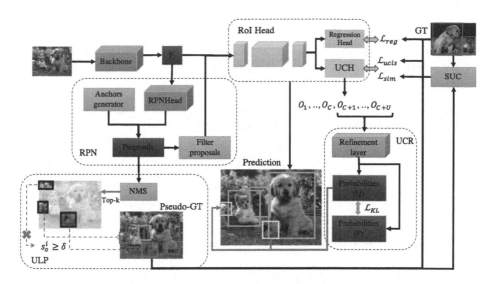

Fig. 2. The architecture of our model. Pseudo-label candidate boxes are filtered according to whether their score s_o^i is greater than the threshold δ. During the training, ULP constructs Pseudo-GT for unknown objects based on the proposals of RPN. According to the regression head and UCH of the model, $\mathcal{L}_{reg}$ and $\mathcal{L}_{ucls}$ are calculated respectively, and $\mathcal{L}_{sim}$ is got by SUC. During the refining, the unknown objects $\{O_{C+1}, ..., O_{C+U}\}$ obtained by UCH are input to UCR to refine clustering, where U is the number of unknown classes.

class set $\mathcal{U}^t = \{C + 1, C + 2, ...\}$, where C is the number of known classes. The known class set in task T_{t+1} contains that in task T_t, i.e., $\mathcal{K}^t \subset \mathcal{K}^{t+1}$. The label of the k-th object of the known class dataset $\mathcal{D}^t = \{\mathbf{X}^t, \mathbf{Y}^t\}$ is $\mathbf{y}_k = [l_k, x_k, y_k, w_k, h_k]$, where the class label $l_k \in \mathcal{K}^t$ and x_k, y_k, w_k, h_k denote the bounding box centre coordinates, width and height, respectively. $\mathbf{X}^t$ and $\mathbf{Y}^t$ are the input images and labels, respectively. Instances of unknown classes do not have labels. The object detector $\mathcal{M}_C$ is able to identify test instances belonging to any known class, and can also detect the new or unseen class instances as different unknown classes. Human users can identify u new classes of interest from the unknown set of instances $\mathbf{U}^t$ and provide the corresponding training examples. Update known class set $\mathcal{K}^{t+1} = \mathcal{K}^t \cup \{C+1, ..., C+u\}$. By incrementally adding u new classes in the next task, the learner creates an updated model $\mathcal{M}_{C+u}$ without the need to retrain the model on the entire dataset.

3.2 Overall Architecture

Figure 2 shows the overall architecture of the proposed method for UC-OWOD. We use Faster R-CNN [47] as the base detector. We introduce (1) ULP and UCH to solve the problem of discovering unknown classes from the background, (2) SUC to detect unknown objects as different classes, and (3) UCR to refine the classification of unknown objects and enhance the robustness of the algorithm.

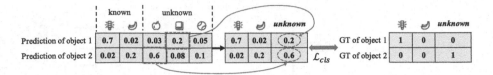

Fig. 3. The diagram of UCH. Traffic light and banana are known classes. Apple, book, and baseball are unknown classes. The unknown class only selects the value with the highest score when calculating the loss.

In order to model the differences between unknown objects, we propose a new classification loss. Details will be discussed in the following subsections.

3.3   Detection of Unknown Objects

Unknown Label-Aware Proposal. Since unknown instances are not labeled, pseudo-labels need to be constructed to train the model's ability to detect unknown classes. We adopt a novel pseudo-labeling strategy, which has better generalization and applicability in detection with multiple unknown classes, as shown in the bottom left of Fig. 2. Based on the fact that the Region Proposal Network (RPN) is class-agnostic, we construct pseudo-labels with bounding box proposals generated by RPN and corresponding objectness scores. First, all proposals are filtered by Non-Maximum Suppression (NMS) to avoid partial overlap between pseudo-labels. Second, we select the filtered top-k background proposals as candidates, which are sorted by their objectness scores. Third, in order to avoid marking the real background regions proposals as *unknown* and make the training results more robust, among the candidates, the proposals with objectness score s_o greater than the threshold δ are used as pseudo-labels, i.e., $\mathbf{y}_{unk} = [\text{unknown}, x_i, y_i, w_i, h_i]$ serves as the unknown label-aware proposal.

Unknown-Discriminative Classification Head. To enable the model to locate and classify unknown classes, we introduce multiple unknown classes in the original classification head: $F_{cls} : \mathbb{R}^D \rightarrow \mathbb{R}^{C+U}$, where U is the number of unknown classes. In the training phase, the pseudo-labels are all marked as *unknown*. The original classification strategy cannot classify a variety of unknown objects, so we modify the original classification loss. As shown in Fig. 3, the classification loss of unknown classes is computed by using pseudo labels and the maximum probabilities that are predicted by multiple unknown classes. The new classification loss is constructed as

$$\mathcal{L}_{ucls} = -\frac{1}{N} \sum_{i=1}^{N} (\sum_{j=1}^{C} l_{i,j} \log(p_{i,j}) - l_i^* \log(\max\{p_{i,C+1}, ..., p_{i,C+U}\})), \quad (1)$$

where N is the number of instances, l is the label of the known class, l^* is the pseudo-label of the unknown class, and p is the predicted probability.

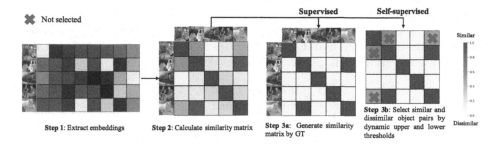

Fig. 4. Build of similarity matrix of embeddings, using supervised method for known classes and self-supervised method for unknown classes.

3.4 Similarity-Based Unknown Classification

Clustering unknown classes allow the model to distinguish between different unknown classes. We adopt a pairwise classification loss to measure the similarity between samples. By determining whether pairs of samples are similar, our model can classify unknown classes. The outputs E of the UCH, which can represent category information, are used to compute the similarity matrix S:

$$S_{ij} = \frac{E_i E_j^T}{||E_i||||E_j||}, \tag{2}$$

where $|| \cdot ||$ is L2 norm and $i, j \in \{1, \ldots, n\}$, and n represents the number of proposals. S_{ij} represents the similarity between the i-th proposal and the j-th proposal. As shown in Fig. 4, we use supervised and self-supervised methods successively to optimize the model.

Supervised Method. We treat labeled data as prior knowledge and use it to guide similar relationships between different unknown instances. In supervised methods, since the relationship between unknown instances is not known, we only use known-known instance pairs, unknown-known instance pairs, known-background instance pairs, and unknown-background instance pairs. We can construct the label matrix M as

$$M_{ij} = \begin{cases} 1, & \text{if } l_i = l_j \text{ and } l_i, l_j \notin \mathcal{U}, \\ 0, & \text{if } l_i \neq l_j, \\ \text{Not selected,} & \text{otherwise,} \end{cases} \tag{3}$$

where l_i is the class label of the i-th instance, $i, j \in \{1, \ldots, n\}$, and $\mathcal{U}$ is the set of unknown classes. Known instances with ground-truth are utilized to reduce errors. Therefore, we construct a similarity loss $\mathcal{L}_{sim}$ with labels M and similarity S as

$$\mathcal{L}_{sim}(M_{ij}, S_{ij}) = -M_{ij} \log(S_{ij}) - (1 - M_{ij}) \log(1 - S_{ij}). \tag{4}$$

Self-supervised Method. We use thresholds to determine whether unknown instance pairs are similar. $TH(\lambda)$ and $TL(\lambda)$ are dynamic upper and lower thresholds applied to the similarity matrix S to obtain the self-labeled matrix $\tilde{M}$, where λ is an adaptive parameter that controls sample selection. Those unknown instance pairs that have similarities between $TH(\lambda)$ and $TL(\lambda)$ are excluded from the training phase. $\tilde{M}$ is defined as follows:

$$\tilde{M}_{ij} = \begin{cases} 1, & \text{if } l_i, l_j \in \mathcal{U} \text{ and } S_{ij} > TH(\lambda), \\ -1, & \text{if } l_i, l_j \in \mathcal{U} \text{ and } S_{ij} < TL(\lambda), \\ 0, & \text{otherwise.} \end{cases} \tag{5}$$

Then, we construct the label matrix $\hat{M}$ with the self-labeled matrix $\tilde{M}$ and the class labels l as

$$\hat{M}_{ij} = \begin{cases} 1, & \text{if } l_i = l_j \text{ and } l_i, l_j \notin \mathcal{U}, \text{ or } \tilde{M}_{ij} > 0, \\ 0, & \text{if } l_i \neq l_j \text{ or } \tilde{M}_{ij} < 0, \\ \text{Not selected, otherwise.} \end{cases} \tag{6}$$

The similarity loss $\hat{\mathcal{L}}_{sim}$ is computed by the similarity matrix S and the label matrix $\hat{M}$:

$$\hat{\mathcal{L}}_{sim}(\hat{M}_{ij}, S_{ij}) = -\hat{M}_{ij} \log(S_{ij}) - (1 - \hat{M}_{ij}) \log(1 - S_{ij}) + \mathcal{L}_{ul}(\lambda), \tag{7}$$

where the penalty term $\mathcal{L}_{ul}(\lambda)$ for the number of samples is given as

$$\mathcal{L}_{ul}(\lambda) = TH(\lambda) - TL(\lambda). \tag{8}$$

The adaptive parameter λ updated by:

$$\lambda := \lambda - \eta \cdot \frac{\partial \mathcal{L}_{ul}(\lambda)}{\partial \lambda}, \tag{9}$$

where η is the learning rate of λ. More and more instance pairs participate in the training phase as λ is updating. To obtain clustering-friendly representations, we train the model from easily classified unknown instance pairs to hardly classified unknown instance pairs iteratively as the thresholds change. The iterative process is terminated when $TH(\lambda) \leq TL(\lambda)$.

3.5   Unknown Clustering Refinement

To enhance the robustness of the proposed algorithm, we apply the soft assignment method [56] to improve the unknown classification based on the previous network output. UCR uses clustering to improve the separability of unknown objects. In the first step, according to the output of UCH, the embedding E of the unknown class and the cluster centroid Φ of the unknown class are obtained. And we compute a soft assignment between E_i and Φ_j saved in the refinement layer while using the Student's t-distribution [36] as the kernel:

$$P_{ij} = \frac{(1 + ||E_i - \Phi_j||^2)^{-1}}{\sum_k (1 + ||E_i - \Phi_k||^2)^{-1}}, \tag{10}$$

where P_{ij} can be interpreted as the probability (soft assignment) of assigning instance i to cluster j. In the second step, the auxiliary target distribution Q is used to refine the clusters based on their high confidence assignments:

$$Q_{ij} = \frac{P_{ij}^2/F_i}{\sum_k P_{ik}^2/F_k}, \tag{11}$$

where $F_i = \sum_i P_{ij}$ is soft cluster frequencies. The quadratic term of the auxiliary target distribution can emphasize high confidence assignments. Therefore, with the assistance of the auxiliary target distribution, the model can gradually learn good clustering structure and improve clustering purity. Then, we minimize the Kullback-Leibler (KL) divergence loss between the soft assignments P and the auxiliary distribution Q to refine clustering:

$$\mathcal{L}_{KL} = \mathrm{KL}(Q\|P) = \sum_i \sum_j Q_{ij} \log \frac{Q_{ij}}{P_{ij}}. \tag{12}$$

3.6   Training and Refining

Training. Our model is trained end-to-end with the following loss function:

$$\mathcal{L}_{tra} = \alpha_1 \mathcal{L}_{rpn} + \alpha_2 \mathcal{L}_{ucls} + \alpha_3 \mathcal{L}_{reg} + \alpha_4 \mathcal{L}_{sim}, \tag{13}$$

where $\mathcal{L}_{rpn}$ and $\mathcal{L}_{reg}$ denote the loss terms for RPN and bounding box regression, respectively. In detail, $\mathcal{L}_{rpn}$ is formulated using the standard RPN loss [47], $\mathcal{L}_{reg}$ is the standard ℓ_1 regression loss. $\alpha_1, \alpha_2, \alpha_3, \alpha_4$ denote weight factors. When the model is only trained with the current class of task T_t, it will catastrophically forget the information learned in the previous task [15,38]. Comparing existing solutions, i.e. parameter regularization [2,29], exemplar replay [9,45], dynamically expanding networks [37,49,52], and meta-learning [25,44], we choose a relatively simple few-example replay method [24,43,55]. The model is finetuned using a set of stored examples for each known class after learning the task T_t.

Refining. In the clustering refinement stage for unknown objects, the main purpose is to improve the classification of unknown objects. We only use the KL divergence loss for training on unknown objects:

$$\mathcal{L}_{ref} = \mathcal{L}_{KL}. \tag{14}$$

4   Experiments

4.1   Preparation

Datasets. We evaluate our model for the UC-OWOD problem on the set of tasks $\mathcal{T} = \{T_1, T_2, \cdots\}$. Classes in T_λ are introduced when $t = \lambda$. For the task T_t, all

Table 1. Datasets for each task. Table shows the semantics and the number of images and instances each task contains.

Task	Task 1	Task 2	Task 3	Task 4
Semantic split	VOC classes	Outdoor, accessories appliance, truck	Sports food	Electronic, indoor kitchen, furniture
Training images	16551	45520	39402	40260
Training instances	47223	113741	114452	138996
Test images	10246			
Test instances	61707			

introduced classes in $\{T_\tau : \tau \leq t\}$ are *known* and classes in $\{T_\tau : \tau > t\}$ are *unknown*. As shown in Table 1, we construct 4 tasks with 20 classes in each task using the Pascal VOC [14] and MS-COCO [32] datasets. The task T_1 consists of all VOC classes and data, which do not contain any information about unknown instances. This allows the model to be tested without any *unknown* information during the training phase. The remaining 60 classes of MS-COCO are divided into three parts, i.e., T_2, T_3, and T_4. Although the training images in T_2 and T_3 do not have labels of unknown instances, they contain unknown instances, which can test the effect of the model in this situation. In every task, the evaluation data consists of Pascal VOC test split and MS-COCO validation split.

Evaluation Metrics. For the overall evaluation of unknown classes, we use two evaluation metrics, i.e., Absolute Open-Set Error (A-OSE) [24,40] and Wilderness Impact (WI) [11,24]. A-OSE is the number of unknown objects misclassified into *known*. WI is calculated by true positive proposals $TP_\mathcal{K}$ and false positive proposals $FP_\mathcal{K}$ of current *known*:

$$\text{WI} = \frac{\text{A-OSE}}{TP_\mathcal{K} + FP_\mathcal{K}}. \tag{15}$$

For the refinement of unknown classes, there is no label-prediction pair, so mean average precision (mAP) does not work. We are also not aware of any other metric that can handle the evaluate multiple unknown categories. Inspired by the clustering evaluation metric, i.e., clustering accuracy [1], we introduce a novel evaluation metric, unknown mean average precision (UC-mAP), to evaluate the detection of unknown classes. Therefore, UC-mAP is the mAP with automatic category matching:

$$\text{UC-mAP}(\mathcal{Y}_{gt}, \mathcal{Y}_{pre}) = \max_{perm \in \mathcal{P}} \text{mAP}(perm(\mathcal{Y}_{pre}), \mathcal{Y}_{gt}), \tag{16}$$

where $\mathcal{P}$ is the set of all permutations in of 1 to U, U is the number of unknown classes, $\mathcal{Y}_{pre}$ is the predicted value, and $\mathcal{Y}_{gt}$ is the ground-truth. The best match uses the Hungarian algorithm [27] for fast computation. The model is also better if it can detect some new instances which are unlabeled in the MS-COCO dataset, but traditional mAP metrics are very sensitive to missing annotations and treat such detections as false positives. Therefore, we also use the unknown class Recall [3,18,34] after maximum matching as the evaluation metric, i.e., UC-Recall.

☐ GT of *unknown*-1

☐ GT of *unknown*-2

☐ Predictions of *known*

☐ Predictions of *unknown*-1

☐ Predictions of *unknown*-2

WI: 1, A-OSE: 1, U-Recall: 66.67   WI: 1, A-OSE: 1, U-Recall: 66.67
UC-Recall: 25.00, UC-mAP: 25.00   UC-Recall: 75.00, UC-mAP: 75.00

Fig. 5. *Car* is *unknown*-1 and *giraffe* is *unknown*-2. Both images mis-detect the car on the right as *known*, and the left image mis-detects the giraffe as *unknown*-1.

Table 2. Validation results of UC-mAP and UC-Recall. Label-free UC-mAP can achieve the same evaluation results as label-based mAP, as does Recall.

	Task 1	Task 2	Task 3	Task 4
mAP/Recall	56.43/75.40	46.14/68.02	28.03/53.26	26.72/50.88
UC-mAP/UC-Recall	56.43/75.40	46.14/68.02	28.03/53.26	26.72/50.88

Implementation Details. Our model is based on the standard Faster R-CNN [47] object detector with ResNet-50 [21] backbone. We set the total number of unknown and known classes to 80, which corresponds to the MS-COCO dataset. As described earlier, in the classification loss, we only learn the unknown class with the highest prediction probability. This is achieved by setting the logits of the invisible classes to a large negative value (v) so that their contribution to the softmax is negligible ($e^{-v} \rightarrow 0$). We set $TH(\lambda) = 0.95 - \lambda$, $TL(\lambda) = 0.455 + 0.1\lambda$, $\alpha_1 = \alpha_2 = \alpha_3 = 1, \alpha_4 = 0.5$, and learning rate is 0.01. When refining, we fix the layers before the refinement layer and use a learning rate of 0.1. The initial cluster centroids of unknown classes are obtained using K-means. Because the refinement phase relies on the unknown object information in the training set, we only use UCR for task 2 and task 3.

Validity of UC-mAP and UC-Recall. We analyze the evaluation results of WI, A-OSE, U-Recall, UC-Recall and UC-mAP in different situations (see Fig. 5). All metrics reflect the situation where unknown objects are misclassified

Table 3. The performance of our model on known classes. PK means the mAP of previously known instances and CK means the mAP of current known instances.

	Task 1	Task 2	Task 3	Task 4
PK (↑)/CK (↑)	−/50.66	33.13/30.54	28.80/16.34	25.57/15.88

Table 4. The performance of our model on UC-OWOD. WI, A-OSE, UC-mAP and UC-Recall quantify how the model handles unknown classes.

Task 1	Oracle	Faster-RCNN	Faster-RCNN+Finetuning	ORE	Ours	Ours+UCR
UC-mAP (↑)	0	0	–	0.0133	**0.1344**	–
WI (↓)	–	0.0188	–	0.0155	**0.0136**	–
A-OSE (↓)	–	13300	–	10672	**9294**	–
UC-Recall (↑)	–	0	–	0.7772	**2.3915**	–
Task 2	Oracle	Faster-RCNN	Faster-RCNN+Finetuning	ORE	Ours	Ours+UCR
UC-mAP (↑)	15.50	0	0	0.0065	0.0862	**0.1694**
WI (↓)	0.0022	0.0069	0.0140	0.0153	0.0116	0.0117
A-OSE (↓)	6050	4582	7169	10376	5602	5602
UC-Recall (↑)	40.45	0	0	0.0371	2.6926	**3.4431**
Task 3	Oracle	Faster-RCNN	Faster-RCNN+Finetuning	ORE	Ours	Ours+UCR
UC-mAP (↑)	10.61	0	0	0.0070	0.0249	**0.0744**
WI (↓)	0.0042	0.0241	0.0099	0.0086	0.0073	**0.0073**
A-OSE (↓)	4857	4841	9181	7544	3801	**3801**
UC-Recall (↑)	28.54	0	0	0.8833	4.8077	**8.7303**

as known. WI, A-OSE, and U-Recall [18] cannot determine whether *unknown*-1 and *unknown*-2 are wrongly classified into the same class, but UC-Recall and UC-mAP may result in higher scores under correct detection. UC-Recall and UC-mAP are further evaluated with known classes of *Oracle* detectors, which can access to all known and unknown labels at any task (see Table 2). We can see that UC-mAP/UC-Recall are equivalent to mAP/Recall when the model is trained with the corresponding labels.

4.2 Results and Analysis

As shown in Table 3, our model is able to avoid catastrophic forgetting of previous classes. To better analyze the performance on the UC-OWOD problem, we compare our model with Faster-RCNN and ORE, whose performance on unknown object detection is shown in Table 4. Due to limited space, full experimental data are given in Supplementary Materials. WI and A-OSE metrics are used to quantify the degree of confusion between unknown instances and any known classes. The UC-Recall metric is used to quantify the ability of the model to retrieve unknown object instances. The UC-mAP metric is used to quantify the average level of detection of all unknown classes by the model. Under

Fig. 6. Qualitative results of our model. *unknown_x* represents an unknown object of the *x*-th class. Our model detects the *house* as *unknown*-11 and is able to distinguish it from other unknown classes in the same image. This means that our model cannot only detect the categories annotated in the MS-COCO dataset, but also mine new categories and distinguish them from other categories. Some other unknown classes are also shown, i.e., *toilet* as *unknown*-24, *knife* as *unknown*-39 and so on. The last column shows a failure case that misclassify *surfboard* as *unknown*-38 which was actually *cake*. The Supplementary Materials contain more visualised results.

Table 5. Ablation experimental results of our model.

ID	UCH	SUC	WI (↓)	A-OSE (↓)	UC-Recall (↑)	UC-mAP (↑)
1	✗	✗	0.0213	16453	0	0
2	✗	✔	0.0247	16667	0	0
3	✔	✗	0.0155	**9185**	1.4796	0.0176
4	✔	✔	**0.0136**	9294	**2.3915**	**0.1343**

the setting of UC-OWOD, Faster-RCNN and Faster-RCNN +Finetuning do not have the ability to detect unknown instances, and finetuning will result in lower scores for WI and A-OSE. In all tasks, we achieve better results than ORE on measures about unknown classes. The ability of the model to detect unknown objects is significantly improved after adding UCR. Figure 6 and Supplementary Materials show qualitative results on example images.

4.3   Ablation Study

Ablation of Components. We design ablation experiments to study the contributions of UCH and SUC in the model (see Table 5). When UCH and SUC (row 1 and row 2) are missing, the model loses its ability to detect unknown classes. Adding only SUC (row 2) will not improve the model's ability to detect unknown classes. Only the absence of SUC (row 3) affects the classification ability for unknown classes, but the model performs best at the detection of known classes. Hence, the scores of WI, UC-Recall, and UC-mAP are worse than those that have both UCH and SUC (row 4). Therefore, the best performance is achieved when both components are present.

Table 6. Sensitivity analysis on hyperparameters.

ID	NMS threshold	δ	Number of pseudo-GT	WI ($\downarrow$)	A-OSE ($\downarrow$)	UC-Recall ($\uparrow$)	UC-mAP ($\uparrow$)
1	0.3	0.3	1	0.0146	12649	0.9314	0.0375
2	0.3	0.3	5	0.0136	**9294**	**2.3915**	**0.1343**
3	0.3	0.7	1	**0.0101**	11323	1.9017	0.0995
4	0.3	0.7	5	0.0143	10161	1.6730	0.1212
5	0.7	0.3	1	0.0203	12243	0.7222	0.0037
6	0.7	0.3	5	0.0202	12780	0.7923	0.0120
7	0.7	0.7	1	0.0240	13032	0.1399	0.0004
8	0.7	0.7	5	0.0141	12156	0.8827	0.0026

Sensitivity Analysis on Hyperparameters. As shown in Table 6, we analyze the detection performance of the model under different hyperparameter settings. When the NMS threshold is large, the recall rate for unknown classes is low, because the model may set the region with a high degree of coincidence with the known class label as a pseudo label. The model can only locate known instance regions, but cannot locate unknown instance regions. When the value of δ is large, the model tends to label fewer unknown classes, resulting in poorer detection performance of the model for unknown classes. Similarly, when the Number of pseudo-GT is set to 1, the model will be less effective due to fewer unknown classes being labeled. We chose the hyperparameter settings with the better scores for WI, A-OSE, UC-Recall, and UC-mAP, i.e., NMS threshold is 0.3, δ is 0.3, and Number of pseudo-GT is 5.

5   Conclusions and Future Work

In this work, we have proposed a novel problem UC-OWOD on the basis of OWOD, which is closer to the real world. The UC-OWOD requires detecting unknown objects as different unknown classes. We also establish evaluation protocols for this issue. In addition, we propose a new method including ULP, UCH, SUC, and UCR. Abundant experiments demonstrate the effectiveness of our method on the UC-OWOD problem and also verify the rationality of our metrics. In future work, we hope to apply our method to some real-world online tasks and achieve open-world automatic annotation.

Acknowledgements. This work was supported in part by the National Key Research and Development Program of China under Grant 2019YFB1310300 and in part by the National Natural Science Foundation of China under Grant 62022090.

References

1. Ahmadinejad, N., Liu, L.: J-Score: a robust measure of clustering accuracy. arXiv preprint arXiv:2109.01306 (2021)

2. Aljundi, R., Babiloni, F., Elhoseiny, M., Rohrbach, M., Tuytelaars, T.: Memory aware synapses: learning what (not) to forget. In: Ferrari, V., Hebert, M., Sminchisescu, C., Weiss, Y. (eds.) ECCV 2018. LNCS, vol. 11207, pp. 144–161. Springer, Cham (2018). https://doi.org/10.1007/978-3-030-01219-9_9

3. Bansal, A., Sikka, K., Sharma, G., Chellappa, R., Divakaran, A.: Zero-shot object detection. In: Ferrari, V., Hebert, M., Sminchisescu, C., Weiss, Y. (eds.) ECCV 2018. LNCS, vol. 11205, pp. 397–414. Springer, Cham (2018). https://doi.org/10.1007/978-3-030-01246-5_24

4. Basu, S., Banerjee, A., Mooney, R.J.: Active semi-supervision for pairwise constrained clustering. In: Proceedings of the 2004 SIAM International Conference on Data Mining, pp. 333–344 (2004)

5. Bendale, A., Boult, T.: Towards open world recognition. In: Proceedings of the IEEE/CVF Conference on Computer Vision and Pattern Recognition (CVPR), pp. 1893–1902 (2015)

6. Bendale, A., Boult, T.E.: Towards open set deep networks. In: Proceedings of the IEEE/CVF Conference on Computer Vision and Pattern Recognition (CVPR), pp. 1563–1572 (2016)

7. Caesar, H., et al.: nuScenes: a multimodal dataset for autonomous driving. In: Proceedings of the IEEE/CVF Conference on Computer Vision and Pattern Recognition (CVPR), pp. 11621–11631 (2020)

8. Cao, J., Cholakkal, H., Anwer, R.M., Khan, F.S., Pang, Y., Shao, L.: D2Det: towards high quality object detection and instance segmentation. In: Proceedings of the IEEE/CVF Conference on Computer Vision and Pattern Recognition (CVPR) (2020)

9. Castro, F.M., Marín-Jiménez, M.J., Guil, N., Schmid, C., Alahari, K.: End-to-end incremental learning. In: Ferrari, V., Hebert, M., Sminchisescu, C., Weiss, Y. (eds.) ECCV 2018. LNCS, vol. 11216, pp. 241–257. Springer, Cham (2018). https://doi.org/10.1007/978-3-030-01258-8_15

10. Chen, X., Yu, J., Kong, S., Wu, Z., Wen, L.: Joint anchor-feature refinement for real-time accurate object detection in images and videos. IEEE Trans. Circ. Syst. Video Technol. **31**(2), 594–607 (2020)

11. Dhamija, A., Gunther, M., Ventura, J., Boult, T.: The overlooked elephant of object detection: open set. In: Proceedings of the IEEE/CVF Winter Conference on Applications of Computer Vision (WACV), pp. 1021–1030 (2020)

12. Dinler, D., Tural, M.K.: A survey of constrained clustering. In: Celebi, M.E., Aydin, K. (eds.) Unsupervised Learning Algorithms, pp. 207–235. Springer, Cham (2016). https://doi.org/10.1007/978-3-319-24211-8_9

13. Dong, N., Zhang, Y., Ding, M., Lee, G.H.: Bridging non co-occurrence with unlabeled in-the-wild data for incremental object detection. In: Proceedings of Advances in Neural Information Processing Systems (NeurIPS), pp. 30492–30503 (2021)

14. Everingham, M., Van Gool, L., Williams, C.K., Winn, J., Zisserman, A.: The Pascal visual object classes (VOC) challenge. Int. J. Comput. Vis. (IJCV) **88**(2), 303–338 (2010). https://doi.org/10.1007/s11263-009-0275-4

15. French, R.M.: Catastrophic forgetting in connectionist networks. Trends Cogn. Sci. **3**(4), 128–135 (1999)

16. Geiger, A., Lenz, P., Stiller, C., Urtasun, R.: Vision meets robotics: the KITTI dataset. Int. J. Robot. Res. **32**(11), 1231–1237 (2013)

17. Girshick, R.B.: Fast R-CNN. In: Proceedings of the IEEE/CVF International Conference on Computer Vision (ICCV), pp. 1440–1448 (2015)

18. Gupta, A., Narayan, S., Joseph, K., Khan, S., Khan, F.S., Shah, M.: OW-DETR: open-world detection transformer. In: Proceedings of the IEEE/CVF Conference on Computer Vision and Pattern Recognition (CVPR), pp. 9235–9244 (2022)
19. Hall, D., et al.: Probabilistic object detection: definition and evaluation. In: Proceedings of the IEEE/CVF Winter Conference on Applications of Computer Vision (WACV), pp. 1031–1040 (2020)
20. He, K., Gkioxari, G., Dollár, P., Girshick, R.: Mask R-CNN. In: Proceedings of the IEEE/CVF International Conference on Computer Vision (ICCV), pp. 2961–2969 (2017)
21. He, K., Zhang, X., Ren, S., Sun, J.: Deep residual learning for image recognition. In: Proceedings of the IEEE/CVF Conference on Computer Vision and Pattern Recognition (CVPR), pp. 770–778 (2016)
22. Hsu, Y.C., Lv, Z., Kira, Z.: Learning to cluster in order to transfer across domains and tasks. In: Proceedings of International Conference on Learning Representations (ICLR) (2018)
23. Jain, L.P., Scheirer, W.J., Boult, T.E.: Multi-class open set recognition using probability of inclusion. In: Fleet, D., Pajdla, T., Schiele, B., Tuytelaars, T. (eds.) ECCV 2014. LNCS, vol. 8691, pp. 393–409. Springer, Cham (2014). https://doi.org/10.1007/978-3-319-10578-9_26
24. Joseph, K., Khan, S., Khan, F.S., Balasubramanian, V.N.: Towards open world object detection. In: Proceedings of the IEEE/CVF Conference on Computer Vision and Pattern Recognition (CVPR), pp. 5830–5840 (2021)
25. Joseph, K.J., Balasubramanian, V.N.: Meta-consolidation for continual learning. In: Proceedings of the Advances in Neural Information Processing Systems (NeurIPS), pp. 14374–14386 (2020)
26. Kj, J., Rajasegaran, J., Khan, S., Khan, F.S., Balasubramanian, V.N.: Incremental object detection via meta-learning. IEEE Trans. Pattern Anal. Mach. Intell. (PAMI), early access (2021). https://doi.org/10.1109/TPAMI.2021.3124133
27. Kuhn, H.W.: The Hungarian method for the assignment problem. Nav. Res. Logist. Q. $\mathbf{2}$(1–2), 83–97 (1955)
28. Lenz, I., Lee, H., Saxena, A.: Deep learning for detecting robotic grasps. Int. J. Robot. Res. $\mathbf{34}$(4–5), 705–724 (2015)
29. Li, Z., Hoiem, D.: Learning without forgetting. IEEE Trans. Pattern Anal. Mach. Intell. (PAMI) $\mathbf{40}$(12), 2935–2947 (2018)
30. Lin, T.E., Xu, H., Zhang, H.: Discovering new intents via constrained deep adaptive clustering with cluster refinement. In: Proceedings of the AAAI Conference on Artificial Intelligence (AAAI), pp. 8360–8367 (2020)
31. Lin, T.Y., Goyal, P., Girshick, R., He, K., Dollár, P.: Focal loss for dense object detection. In: Proceedings of the IEEE/CVF International Conference on Computer Vision (ICCV), pp. 2980–2988 (2017)
32. Lin, T.-Y., et al.: Microsoft COCO: common objects in context. In: Fleet, D., Pajdla, T., Schiele, B., Tuytelaars, T. (eds.) ECCV 2014. LNCS, vol. 8693, pp. 740–755. Springer, Cham (2014). https://doi.org/10.1007/978-3-319-10602-1_48
33. Liu, Z., Miao, Z., Zhan, X., Wang, J., Gong, B., Yu, S.X.: Large-scale long-tailed recognition in an open world. In: Proceedings of the IEEE/CVF Conference on Computer Vision and Pattern Recognition (CVPR), pp. 2537–2546 (2019)
34. Lu, C., Krishna, R., Bernstein, M., Fei-Fei, L.: Visual relationship detection with language priors. In: Leibe, B., Matas, J., Sebe, N., Welling, M. (eds.) ECCV 2016. LNCS, vol. 9905, pp. 852–869. Springer, Cham (2016). https://doi.org/10.1007/978-3-319-46448-0_51

35. Lu, Y., Chen, X., Wu, Z., Yu, J.: Decoupled metric network for single-stage few-shot object detection. IEEE Trans. Cybern. early access, 1–12 (2022). https://doi.org/10.1109/TCYB.2022.3149825
36. Van der Maaten, L., Hinton, G.: Visualizing data using t-SNE. J. Mach. Learn. Res. (JMLR) **9**(11), 2579–2605 (2008)
37. Mallya, A., Lazebnik, S.: PackNet: adding multiple tasks to a single network by iterative pruning. In: Proceedings of the IEEE/CVF Conference on Computer Vision and Pattern Recognition (CVPR), pp. 7765–7773 (2018)
38. McCloskey, M., Cohen, N.: Catastrophic interference in connectionist networks: the sequential learning problem. Psychol. Learn. Motiv. **24**, 109–165 (1989)
39. Miller, D., Dayoub, F., Milford, M., Sünderhauf, N.: Evaluating merging strategies for sampling-based uncertainty techniques in object detection. In: Proceedings of the IEEE International Conference on Robotics and Automation (ICRA), pp. 2348–2354 (2019)
40. Miller, D., Nicholson, L., Dayoub, F., Sünderhauf, N.: Dropout sampling for robust object detection in open-set conditions. In: Proceedings of the IEEE International Conference on Robotics and Automation (ICRA), pp. 3243–3249 (2018)
41. Perera, P., et al.: Generative-discriminative feature representations for open-set recognition. In: Proceedings of the IEEE/CVF Conference on Computer Vision and Pattern Recognition (CVPR), pp. 11814–11823 (2020)
42. Perez-Rua, J.M., Zhu, X., Hospedales, T.M., Xiang, T.: Incremental few-shot object detection. In: Proceedings of the IEEE/CVF Conference on Computer Vision and Pattern Recognition (CVPR), pp. 13846–13855 (2020)
43. Prabhu, A., Torr, P.H.S., Dokania, P.K.: GDumb: a simple approach that questions our progress in continual learning. In: Vedaldi, A., Bischof, H., Brox, T., Frahm, J.-M. (eds.) ECCV 2020. LNCS, vol. 12347, pp. 524–540. Springer, Cham (2020). https://doi.org/10.1007/978-3-030-58536-5_31
44. Rajasegaran, J., Khan, S., Hayat, M., Khan, F.S., Shah, M.: iTAML: an incremental task-agnostic meta-learning approach. In: Proceedings of the IEEE/CVF Conference on Computer Vision and Pattern Recognition (CVPR), pp. 13588–13597 (2020)
45. Rebuffi, S.A., Kolesnikov, A., Sperl, G., Lampert, C.H.: iCaRL: incremental classifier and representation learning. In: Proceedings of the IEEE/CVF Conference on Computer Vision and Pattern Recognition (CVPR), pp. 2001–2010 (2017)
46. Redmon, J., Divvala, S., Girshick, R., Farhadi, A.: You only look once: unified, real-time object detection. In: Proceedings of IEEE Conference on Computer Vision and Pattern Recognition (CVPR), pp. 779–788 (2016)
47. Ren, S., He, K., Girshick, R., Sun, J.: Faster R-CNN: towards real-time object detection with region proposal networks. In: Proceedings of Advances in Neural Information Processing Systems (NeurIPS), pp. 91–99 (2015)
48. Rostami, M., Spinoulas, L., Hussein, M., Mathai, J., Abd-Almageed, W.: Detection and continual learning of novel face presentation attacks. In: Proceedings of the IEEE/CVF International Conference on Computer Vision (ICCV), pp. 14851–14860 (2021)
49. Rusu, A.A., et al.: Progressive neural networks. arXiv preprint arXiv:1606.04671 (2016)
50. Scheirer, W.J., Jain, L.P., Boult, T.E.: Probability models for open set recognition. IEEE Trans. Pattern Anal. Mach. Intell. (PAMI) **36**(11), 2317–2324 (2014)
51. Scheirer, W.J., de Rezende Rocha, A., Sapkota, A., Boult, T.E.: Toward open set recognition. IEEE Trans. Pattern Anal. Mach. Intell. (PAMI) **35**(7), 1757–1772 (2013)

52. Serra, J., Suris, D., Miron, M., Karatzoglou, A.: Overcoming catastrophic forgetting with hard attention to the task. In: Proceedings of International Conference on Machine Learning (ICML), pp. 4548–4557 (2018)
53. Sun, P., et al.: Scalability in perception for autonomous driving: Waymo open dataset. In: Proceedings of the IEEE/CVF Conference on Computer Vision and Pattern Recognition (CVPR), pp. 2446–2454 (2020)
54. Wang, J., Wang, X., Shang-Guan, Y., Gupta, A.: Wanderlust: online continual object detection in the real world. In: Proceedings of the IEEE/CVF International Conference on Computer Vision (ICCV), pp. 10829–10838 (2021)
55. Wang, X., Huang, T.E., Gonzalez, J., Darrell, T., Yu, F.: Frustratingly simple few-shot object detection. In: Proceedings of the International Conference on Machine Learning (ICML), pp. 9919–9928 (2020)
56. Xie, J., Girshick, R., Farhadi, A.: Unsupervised deep embedding for clustering analysis. In: Proceedings of International Conference on Machine Learning (ICML), pp. 478–487 (2016)
57. Xu, H., Liu, B., Shu, L., Yu, P.: Open-world learning and application to product classification. In: Proceedings of the World Wide Web Conference (WWW), pp. 3413–3419 (2019)
58. Yoshihashi, R., Shao, W., Kawakami, R., You, S., Iida, M., Naemura, T.: Classification-reconstruction learning for open-set recognition. In: Proceedings of the IEEE/CVF Conference on Computer Vision and Pattern Recognition (CVPR), pp. 4016–4025 (2019)
59. Yue, Z., Wang, T., Sun, Q., Hua, X.S., Zhang, H.: Counterfactual zero-shot and open-set visual recognition. In: Proceedings of the IEEE/CVF Conference on Computer Vision and Pattern Recognition (CVPR), pp. 15404–15414 (2021)
60. Zhao, X., Liu, X., Shen, Y., Ma, Y., Qiao, Y., Wang, D.: Revisiting open world object detection. arXiv preprint arXiv:2201.00471 (2022)
61. Zhigang, C., Xuan, L., Fan, Y.: Constrained k-means with external information. In: Proceedings of 2013 8th International Conference on Computer Science & Education, pp. 490–493 (2013)
62. Zhu, X., Su, W., Lu, L., Li, B., Wang, X., Dai, J.: Deformable DETR: deformable transformers for end-to-end object detection. In: Proceedings of International Conference on Learning Representations (ICLR) (2021)

RayTran: 3D Pose Estimation and Shape Reconstruction of Multiple Objects from Videos with Ray-Traced Transformers

Michał J. Tyszkiewicz[2], Kevis-Kokitsi Maninis[1(✉)], Stefan Popov[1], and Vittorio Ferrari[1]

[1] Google Research, Wallisellen, Switzerland
kmaninis@google.com
[2] EPFL, Lausanne, Switzerland

Abstract. We propose a transformer-based neural network architecture for multi-object 3D reconstruction from RGB videos. It relies on two alternative ways to represent its knowledge: as a global 3D grid of features and an array of view-specific 2D grids. We progressively exchange information between the two with a dedicated bidirectional attention mechanism. We exploit knowledge about the image formation process to significantly sparsify the attention weight matrix, making our architecture feasible on current hardware, both in terms of memory and computation. We attach a DETR-style head [9] on top of the 3D feature grid in order to detect the objects in the scene and to predict their 3D pose and 3D shape. Compared to previous methods, our architecture is single stage, end-to-end trainable, and it can reason holistically about a scene from multiple video frames without needing a brittle tracking step. We evaluate our method on the challenging Scan2CAD dataset [3], where we outperform (1) state-of-the-art methods [15,34,35,39] for 3D object pose estimation from RGB videos; and (2) a strong alternative method combining Multi-View Stereo [17] with RGB-D CAD alignment [4].

1 Introduction

Detecting and reconstructing objects in 3D is a challenging task with multiple applications in computer vision, robotics, and AR/VR that require semantic 3D understanding of the world. In this paper we propose RayTran, a transformer-based [59] neural network architecture for reconstructing multiple objects in 3D given an RGB video as input. Our key new element is a backbone which infers a global representation of the 3D volume of the scene. We attach a DETR-style head [9] on top of it, which detects objects in the 3D representation and predicts their 3D pose and shape (Fig. 1).

M. J. Tyszkiewicz—Work done while at Google Research.

Supplementary Information The online version contains supplementary material available at https://doi.org/10.1007/978-3-031-20080-9_13.

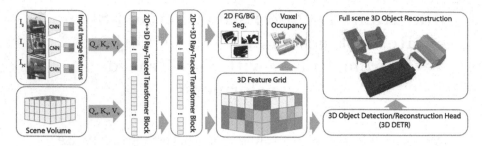

Fig. 1. Overview of our method: The RayTran backbone processes information in two parallel network streams. The first one (2D) works on features extracted on the multiple input frames. The second one (3D) starts from an empty volumetric feature representation of the scene. The 2D stream gradually consolidates features on the 3D volume and visa-versa with repeated blocks of ray-traced transformers. The backbone outputs a 3D feature grid which offers a global representation of the 3D volume of the scene. We attach a DETR-style head [9] to this representation, to detect all objects in 3D and to predict their 3D pose and 3D shape. We further help training with two auxiliary tasks: predicting 3D coarse binary occupancy for all objects together, and predicting amodal 2D foreground-background masks.

The backbone inputs multiple video frames showing different views of the same static scene. Its task is to jointly analyze all views and to consolidate the extracted information into a global 3D representation. Internally, the backbone maintains two alternative scene representations. The first is three-dimensional and describes the volume of the scene. The second is two-dimensional and describes the volume from the perspective of the individual views. We connect these two representations with a bidirectional attention mechanism to exchange information between them, allowing the 3D representation to progressively accumulate view-specific features, while at the same time the 2D representation accumulates global 3D features.

Processing videos with transformers is notoriously resource-consuming [2,7]. Our case is no exception: if we relied on attention between all elements in the 2D and 3D representations, the attention matrix would have infeasible memory requirements (and it would also be computationally very expensive). To overcome this, we propose a *sparse ray-traced attention* mechanism. Given the camera parameters for each view, we exploit the image formation process to identify pairs of 2D and 3D elements that are unlikely to interact. We omit these pairs and store the attention matrix in a sparse format. This greatly reduces its computational and memory complexity, by a factor of $O(|V|^{\frac{2}{3}})$, where $|V|$ is the number of voxels in the 3D representation.

We attach a DETR-style head [9] on top of the 3D representation produced by the backbone. This head detects objects and predicts their class, 3D shape, and 3D pose (translation, rotation, scale). We represent object shapes with a voxel grid and then extract meshes using marching cubes [33]. We also predict coarse binary volumetric occupancy for all objects together, using a 3D convolutional layer on top of the global 3D representation. This provides an auxiliary task that teaches the network about the scene's geometry, and is essential for training.

As a second auxiliary task, we add an additional network head that predicts the 2D amodal foreground-background binary masks of all objects in the scene. Besides enabling this task, this head also helps training the backbone as it closes the loop between images and the 3D representation.

Several recent works [34,39,52] tackle 3D scene reconstruction from videos in the same setting. They rely on a 3-step pipeline: (1) object detection in individual 2D frames, along with estimating properties such as 3D rotation, parts of 3D scale, and 3D shape (either as a parametric surface [34] or by retrieving a CAD model from a database [39]); (2) tracking-by-detection [1,6,8], to associate 2D detections across frames; (3) multi-view optimization to integrate the per-frame predictions. This completes all 3D pose parameters, resolving the scale-depth ambiguities, and places all objects in a common, global 3D coordinate frame.

Our method was inspired by these works and addresses several of their shortcomings. The pipelines are composed of heterogeneous steps, which are trained separately and require manual tuning to work well together. The pipelines are complicated and over-engineered due to the intricate nature of the full-scene object reconstruction task. The tracking step is especially brittle. Objects often go out of view and re-appear later, and occlude each other over time. This poses a major challenge and leads to objects broken into multiple tracks, as well as tracks mixing multiple objects. These tracking errors harm the quality of the final 3D reconstructions.

In contrast, our method is end-to-end trainable. It is built from well understood neural network modules and it has a simple, modular architecture in comparison. Importantly, *we avoid tracking altogether*. Furthermore, our method does not rely on any notion of time sequence, so it is also applicable to sparse multi-view inputs (in addition to video).

We evaluate RayTran on the challenging Scan2CAD [3] dataset, featuring videos of complex indoor scenes with multiple objects. Through extensive comparisons we show that RayTran outperforms several works: (1) two baselines that process frames individually, defined in [39] as extensions of Mask2CAD [31]. This illustrates the value of jointly processing multiple frames in RayTran; (2) four recent multi-frame methods Vid2CAD [39], ODAM [34], MOLTR [35], ImVoxNet [15]. Besides performing better, RayTran also offers a much simpler design than [34,35,39], with an end-to-end trainable, unified architecture which does not require a tracking module; (3) a strong alternative method that combines the state-of-the-art Multi-View Stereo [17] and RGB-D CAD alignment [4] methods.

2 Related Work

3D from Multiple Views. Classic SfM/SLAM works cast 3D reconstruction as estimation of 3D points from multiple views based on keypoint correspondences [18,43,49,54,61]. However, the output point cloud is not organized into objects instances with their classes, 3D shapes, or poses. A line of works detect and localize objects in 3D using multi-view projection constraints, by approximating the object shapes with 3D boxes [64] and ellipsoids [45]. ODAM [34] goes a step further to creates a scene representation out of superquadrics, by using a graph neural network as core architecture for object association in time. FroDO [52] and MO-LTR [35] rely on both 2D image cues and the sparse 3D point clouds from SfM/SLAM to reconstruct objects in the scene. Qian et al. [51] produce volumetric reconstructions of multiple objects in a synthetically generated scene. Vid2CAD [39] integrates the single-view predictions of Mask2CAD [31] across time, to place objects from a CAD database into the 3D scene.

A common caveat of multi-view methods for 3D object reconstruction is that their architectures are overly complex, they cannot be trained end-to-end due to their heterogeneity, and they often rely on a brittle tracking-by-detection step. Instead, our proposed method provides a light-weight end-to-end architecture for the task, while we completely avoid tracking.

Similar to RayTran, the concurrent ImVoxelNet [15] keeps its 3D knowledge in a global 3D representation and does not require tracking. It uses a hand-crafted unidirectional mechanism to project and consolidate image features onto it. In contrast, our ray-traced transformers learn the optimal way to consolidate features. They are also bidirectional, which enables 2D supervision through reprojection as well as additional tasks, like novel-view synthesis. Moreover, RayTran reconstructs the 3D shapes of the detected objects, going beyond detecting 3D boxes.

Transformer Architectures for Computer Vision. Several recent works use attention-based architectures (transformers) [59] for computer vision tasks. ViT [16] replaces the traditional convolutional backbones with attention among patches for image classification. The same idea has been incorporated into network designs for semantic segmentation [12,57,65], object detection [9], and panoptic segmentation [12]. Transformers have been introduced recently also for video processing. TrackFormer [40] uses a transformer architecture for multi-object tracking. ViViT [2] and TimeSFormer [7] use ViT-like patches from multiple frames for video classification.

The main bottleneck of these approaches are the prohibitive memory requirements. TrackFormer [40] can only process 2 images at a time, which prevents end-to-end training on the whole video. Similarly, the all-to-all patch attention, which is the cornerstone of [2,7], comes with often infeasible memory requirements. ViViT [2] needs the combined memory of 32 TPU accelerators to process a single batch of 128 frames. Our work overcomes these limitations by using sparse attention between 2D and 3D features. The sparsity is achieved by using image formation constraints directly from the poses of the cameras, which significantly reduces the memory requirements. For reference, RayTran processes up to 96 frames of a video and reconstructs all instances on a single 16 GB GPU.

3D Using a Dedicated Depth Sensor. Our work draws inspiration from several 3D object reconstruction methods that directly work on point clouds obtained by fusing RGB-D video frames. Early works use known pre-scanned objects [53], hand-crafted features [21,36,44,56], and human intervention [56]. Recent works use deep networks to directly align shapes on the dense point clouds [3–5,28,55]. Fei et al. [20] align a known set of shapes on a video in 4 DoF, by using a camera with an inertial sensor.

Using an additional sensor reduces the search-space required to accurately re-construct an object in 3D. Both the depth and the inertial sensors eliminate the depth-scale ambiguity, and compared to re-constructing from pure RGB, RGB-D sensors provide cleaner, much more realistic results. Our work does not require the intermediate step of point-based reconstruction, does not use the extra depth sensor, and can directly reconstruct objects in a posed RGB video.

3D Detection and Reconstruction from a Single Image. Pioneering works in this area process a single image to either infer the pose of an object as an oriented 3D bounding box [38,42], or to also predict the 3D shape of the object [11,13,22,41,47,60,62,63]. Works that are able to predict an output for multiple object instances, typically first detect them in the 2D image, and then reconstruct their 3D pose and/or shape [19,23,24,26,27,29–32,46,50,58].

3D predictions from single images tend to be inaccurate due to scale-depth ambiguity, and often methods of this category compensate for it in a variety of ways, e.g., based on estimating an approximate pixel-wise depth map from the input image [27], by requiring manually provided objects' depth and/or scale [23,31,32] at test time, or by estimating the position of a planar floor in the scene and assuming that all objects rest on it [29]. Some works [46,50,58] attempt to predict object depth and scale directly based on image appearance. Our proposed approach processes multiple frames simultaneously, and implicitly compensates for the scale-depth ambiguity by using many different view-points of the objects appearing in the scene.

3   Proposed Approach

Our method takes multiple views (video frames) of a scene and their camera parameters as input. Each view captures a different part of the same 3D scene. It outputs the 3D pose (rotation, translation, scale), the class, and the 3D shape of all objects in the scene.

We achieve this with a single, end-to-end trainable, neural network model. We propose a transformer-based backbone that processes the input views and infers a global 3D volume representation for the entire scene. We use this representation to predict the object shapes, poses, and classes, by attaching a DETR-style [9] head to it. In addition, we perform two additional auxiliary tasks: 3D occupancy, where we predict coarse binary volumetric occupancy for all objects together, and 2D foreground-background amodal segmentation. The overview of our architecture is illustrated in Fig. 1.

3.1   The RayTran Backbone

We propose a neural network architecture that operates on two alternative representations in parallel. The first one is three-dimensional and describes the 3D

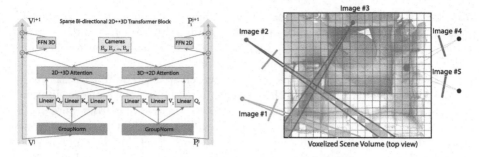

Fig. 2. $2D \Leftrightarrow 3D$ **ray-traced transformer block (left).** Each block uses two parallel residual network streams that exchange information by attention. They consist of two layers of ray-traced sparse attention (2D→3D and 3D→2D) followed by a feed-forward network (FFN) composed of 3D and 2D convolutions, respectively. The voxel features (3D) inform the image features (2D) at each stage of the backbone. The 3D reconstruction head uses the voxel features (output of left stream), whereas the 2D foreground-background segmentation head uses the pixel grid (output of right stream). **Intertwining 3D voxel- with 2D image features (right):** Multiple voxels can project on the same pixel, and multiple pixels from multiple cameras can look at the same voxel. The proposed attention layer models this interaction in an intuitive way.

space that the scene occupies. We use a voxel grid V with *global* features that coincides with this space. The second one is two-dimensional and describes the scene from the perspective of the individual views. For each view $i = 1..N$, we use a pixel grid P_i of *image* features that coincides with the view's image.

The two representations are connected implicitly through the image formation process. We model this as a sequence of $2D \Leftrightarrow 3D$ neural network transformer blocks (Fig. 2, left). The j-th block takes all views $P_{1...N}^j$ and the volume V^j as input, mixes their features, and outputs a pair of new representations ($P_{1...N}^{j+1}$ and V^{j+1}). This allows the global 3D representations to be progressively populated by local features from the different views, while at same time the 2D representations progressively accumulate global features in different depths of the network.

The output of the RayTran backbone is a 3D feature representation of the scene, derived from the input views. In order to compute the initial 2D representation P_i^0, we embed ResNet-18 [25] in our backbone (pre-trained on ImageNet). We run ResNet-18 over the input views i and we take the output of its penultimate block for each view. To initialize the 3D volume representation V^0, we cast a ray (un-project) from all the pixels P_i^0 onto the 3D volume. We then average the image features that fall into each voxel of V^0.

Block Operation. The 2D⇔3D blocks of RayTran consist of two parallel network streams, as shown in Fig. 2 (left). The first one ($2D \Rightarrow 3D$), mixes features from P_i^j into V^j and outputs V^{j+1}. The second one ($3D \Rightarrow 2D$) from V^j into P_i^j, resulting in P_i^{j+1}. We propose to build both networks using the multi-headed attention mechanism [59].

The attention mechanism can translate an input vector (1D array of features) from a source domain into a differently-sized vector in a target domain. To do this, the mechanism computes a *key* vector that describes each position in the source domain and a *query* vector that describes each position in the target domain. It then computes a matrix describing the relation between source and target positions, by storing the dot product between the features at position i in the *key* and position j in the *query* at (i, j) in the matrix. Finally, the mechanism computes a *value* vector from the input vector and multiplies this with the attention matrix in order to obtain the output. The *key* and the *value* depend on the input vector (from the source domain), while the *query* depends on a vector from the target domain. The goal of the attention mechanism is to learn the dependencies between the two domains.

The attention mechanism is intrinsically well suited to model the connection between pixels and voxels. Multiple pixels from multiple cameras can look at the same voxel, as shown in Fig. 2 (right). We need a mechanism to consolidate their features in the voxel. Similarly, multiple voxels can project onto the same pixel and we need to consolidate their features. The matrix-*value* multiplication in the attention mechanism naturally achieves the desired effect.

For $2D \Rightarrow 3D$ attention, we derive the *key* and the *value* from all pixels from all views of P_i^j and the *query* from all voxels of V^j. For $3D \Rightarrow 2D$ attention, conversely, from V^j and P_i^j. We introduce skip connections in both networks, by adding the inputs of the attention mechanism to its outputs. We then post-process with a feed-forward network, built with 3D and 2D convolution layers respectively (Fig. 2).

Ray-Traced Attention Layers. In a realistic setting, the attention layer has infeasible memory requirements. Our backbone operates on multiple frames simultaneously, 20 during training and 96 at inference time, each using a 2D feature grid of 40×30 for the 2D features P_i. We use a voxel grid with resolution $48 \times 48 \times 16$ to model a $9\,m \times 9\,m \times 3.5\,m$ volume, corresponding to voxel dimensions of approximately $19\,cm \times 19\,cm \times 22\,cm$. We use 256 features in both the 2d and 3d representations and 8 heads in the attention layers. Given the above numbers, the attention matrices in each $2D \Leftrightarrow 3D$ block alone would require $\approx 52\,GB$ of memory with 20 frames, which is prohibitive.

To overcome this, we embed knowledge about the image formation process into the architecture (Fig. 3). A pixel and a voxel can interact with each other directly only if there is a camera ray that passes through both of them. If no such ray exists, the two are unlikely to interact, and we set the corresponding entry in the attention matrix to zero. This is mathematically equivalent to the masking mechanism employed in autoregressive transformers to enforce causality [59], but crucially allows us to store the matrix in sparse form and significantly reduce memory consumption. A pixel can only interact with $O(\sqrt[3]{|V|})$ voxels, where $|V|$ is the number of voxels in V, since any ray can only pass through at most this many voxels. We thus need $O(|V|^{\frac{2}{3}})$ times less memory to store the matrix. In sparse coordinate format, which encodes each matrix entry with 3 numbers (row, column, value), the matrix from our example above would consume 270 times

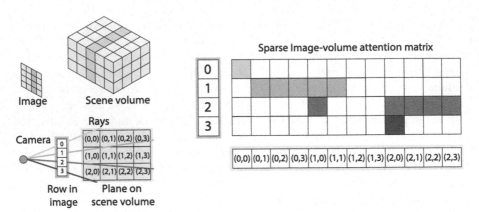

Fig. 3. Ray-traced sparse attention. A pixel and a voxel are likely to interact only if a ray passes through both of them. We exploit this to significantly reduce the memory requirements of our 2D ⇔ 3D blocks, by sparsifying the attention matrices. If no ray passes though a pixel/voxel pair, the two are unlikely to interact and we omit the corresponding value in the matrix.

less memory (3×64.4 MB instead of 52 GB). We call multi-headed attention based on such sparse matrices *ray-traced sparse attention.*

We use the camera parameters to determine which pixel-voxel pairs interact with each other. In turn, the camera parameters can be computed with off-the-shelf pipelines such as COLMAP [54]. To make full use of the limited volume that our backbone can focus on, we center the camera positions within it.

3.2   Task-Specific Heads on Top of the Backbone

3D Pose Estimation and Shape Reconstruction. For our main task, we predict the 3D pose, and reconstruct the shape of all objects seen in the video. We use a DETR-style [9] architecture, with multi-headed attention between 64 object query slots and the voxels in the backbone output. In each slot, we predict the object's class, its shape in canonical pose, 3D center, 3D anisotropic scale, and 3D rotation. We use a special *padding* class to indicate that a query slot does not contain a valid object. We encode the shape as a $63 \times 63 \times 63$ voxel grid, which we predict with a sequence of transposed 3D convolution layers from the query's embedding. We use Marching Cubes [33] to convert the voxel grid to a mesh. We only predict rotation around the 'up'-axis of each object (as one angle), as most objects in our dataset are only rotated along this axis.

We use cross entropy for predicting the class, binary cross entropy for the shape's voxels, soft L_1 loss for the object center, L_1 loss over the logarithm of the scales, and a soft L_1 loss for the rotation angles. Finally, we match predictions to ground-truth objects in DETR using a linear combination of all losses except the voxel one, which we exclude for performance reasons. As in [9], we supervise at all intermediate layers.

Table 1. Quantitative results on the Scan2CAD [3] dataset using the original Scan2CAD metrics. Results for Mask2CAD variants, MVS+RGB-D fitter, and Vid2CAD are as reported in [39]. ODAM originally reports in another metric (Table 2). We re-evaluate in the Scan2CAD metrics based on model outputs provided to us by the authors. Note that ODAM was not trained to predict the 'other' class. When excluding it from the metrics, ODAM achieves class avg. of 28.8% and global avg. of 33.5%.

Family	Method	Class avg.	Global avg.	Bathtub	Bookshelf	Cabinet	Chair	Display	Sofa	Table	Trashbin	Other
Single-frame baselines	Mask2CAD [31] +avg	2.5	3.5	0.0	1.9	1.5	6.8	3.7	2.7	1.4	3.0	1.2
	Mask2CAD [31] +pred	11.6	16.0	8.3	3.8	5.4	30.9	17.3	5.3	7.1	25.9	0.5
Multi-frame methods	MVS [17] + RGB-D fitter [4]	18.8	21.7	15.8	8.5	17.3	34.3	25.7	15.0	10.9	35.8	6.1
	ODAM [34]	25.6	29.2	24.2	12.3	13.1.	42.8	36.6	28.3	31.1	42.2	0.0
	Vid2CAD [39]	30.7	38.6	28.3	12.3	23.8	64.6	37.7	26.5	28.9	47.8	6.6
	RayTran	**36.2**	**43.0**	19.2	34.4	36.2	59.3	30.4	44.2	42.5	31.5	27.8

3D Occupancy Prediction. As an auxiliary task, we also predict the binary 3D occupancy of all objects for the whole scene on a coarse voxel grid. We use one 3D convolution layer on top of the backbone output, and we supervise with binary-cross-entropy. We run occupancy prediction as an auxiliary task, to directly teach the network about the combined object geometry. This is crucial for the 3D object reconstruction task, as the DETR-style head fails to pick up any training signal if the network is trained without it.

2D Foreground-Background (FG/BG) Segmentation. As a second auxiliary task, we predict a 2D *amodal* segmentation mask in each view, for all objects together. A pixel belongs to the mask if it lies on any object in the view, regardless of occlusion. We use transposed convolutions, combined with non-linearities and normalization layers, to up-sample the pixel stream output P_i^n of the last 2D ⇔ 3D block to the original input resolution (16-fold). We supervise using the binary cross entropy loss. We create the amodal masks by rasterizing the combined geometry of all ground-truth 3D objects into each view. Predicting amodal masks enhances the backbone's 3D understanding of the world. In general, the amodal mask is ill-defined for occluded regions in a single image. It becomes well defined with multiple views however, if some of them observe the object behind the occluder. Hence, this FG/BG task pushes our network to reason about geometric relations across multiple views.

Novel View Synthesis. While we focus on multi-object 3D reconstruction, our backbone and the scene-level representation it outputs can be used for other 3D tasks as well. In the supplemental material, we provide qualitative results for Novel View Synthesis, which builds upon RayTran's backbone.

Table 2. Quantitative results on Scan2CAD using the ODAM [34] metrics. To evaluate RayTran, we derive an oriented 3D box by using the 3D transformations predicted by the model. RayTran outperforms all other works, especially at the stricter IoU threshold (@IoU> 0.5), showing it produces particularly accurate object poses. Note that for Vid2CAD we report the updated results from https://github.com/likojack/ODAM (which match exactly the Vid2CAD paper [39]). Also note that ImVoxelNet outputs axis-aligned boxes, which hinders its performance at high IoU thresholds. Finally, results for MOLTR and ODAM are as reported in [34].

Prec./Rec./F1	MOLTR [35]	ODAM [34]	Vid2CAD [39]	ImVoxelNet [15]	RayTran
@IoU> 0.25	54.2/55.8/55.0	64.7/58.6/61.5	56.9/55.7/56.3	52.9/53.2/53.0	**65.4/61.8/63.6**
@IoU> 0.5	15.2/17.1/16.0	31.2/28.3/29.7	34.2/33.5/33.9	17.0/17.1/17.0	**41.9/39.6/40.7**

4   Experiments

Datasets and Evaluation Metrics. We evaluate our method on Scan 2CAD [3], following their protocol and evaluation metrics. Concretely, we use videos from ScanNet [14], 3D CAD models from ShapeNetCore [10], and annotations that connect the two from Scan2CAD [3]. ScanNet provides videos of rich indoor scenes with multiple objects in complex spatial arrangements. ShapeNet-Core provides CAD models from 55 object classes, in a canonical orientation within a class. Scan2CAD provides manual 9-DoF alignments of ShapeNetCore models onto ScanNet scenes for 9 super-classes.

We use these datasets both for training and evaluation. During training, we consider all ScanNet videos in the official train split whose scenes have Scan2CAD annotations (1194 videos). We evaluate on the 306 videos of the validation set, containing a total of 3184 aligned 3D objects. We quantify performance using the original Scan2CAD metrics [3] and the metrics introduced in ODAM [34]. In the Scan2CAD metrics, a ground-truth 3D object is considered accurately detected if one of the objects output by the model matches its class and pose alignment (passing three error thresholds at the same time: 20% scale, 20° rotation, 20 cm translation). We report accuracy averaged over classes ('class avg.') as well as over all object instances ('global avg'). In the metrics of [34], an object is considered accurately detected if the Intersection-over-Union (IoU) of its oriented 3D bounding box to a ground-truth box of the same class is above a predefined threshold. We report precision, recall, and F1 score. Finally, the dataset also provides dense 3D meshes for the scene produced using a dedicated depth sensor. We ignore this data, both at training and test time (in contrast to some previous works which rely on it [3–5,28,55]).

Training Details. We implement our model in PyTorch [48]. We train on 20 frames per video, using 16-bit float arithmetic. This allows us to fit one video on a GPU with 16 GB of memory. We use 8 GPUs in total, resulting in a batch size of 8. We train RayTran in three stages. We first train just the backbone for 224k steps (1500 epochs) on the task of predicting 3D occupancy (Sect. 3.2). We then enable all other tasks except the shape predictor and we train for another 239k

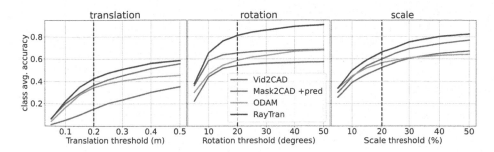

Fig. 4. Transformation type ablation: Class-avg accuracy as a function of the evaluation threshold (the vertical dotted line shows the default value, used in Table 1). We examine each transformation type separately. RayTran achieves better accuracy than Vid2CAD, ODAM, and 'Mask2CAD +pred' on all transformation types.

steps (1604 epochs). Finally, we train just the shape predictor for another 5k steps (17 epochs), after freezing the rest of the network parameters. We use the AdamW [37] optimizer, with a learning rate of 10^{-4} and weight decay $5 \cdot 10^{-2}$.

Compared Methods. We compare RayTran against Vid2CAD [39], ODAM [34], MOLTR [35], and ImVoxelNet [15], four recent methods for 3D object pose estimation and detection from RGB videos.

We further compare to two baselines that process frames individually, defined by [39]. These extend Mask2CAD [31], which in its original form does not predict the 3D depth nor the scale of the object. The first baseline, 'Mask2CAD +avg', estimates an object's depth and scale by taking the average over its class instances in the training set. The second baseline, 'Mask2CAD +pred', predicts the scale of the actual object in the image (and then derives its depth from it). Both baselines aggregate 3D object predictions across all video frames and remove duplicates that occupy the same volume in 3D.

Several previous methods report strong results on Scan2CAD by using a dedicated RGB-D depth sensor to acquire a dense 3D point-cloud of the scene. Those methods have an intrinsic advantage and operate by directly fitting CAD models on the scene's 3D point cloud [3–5, 28]. Instead, our method only uses the RGB frames. Hence, we compare to a strong alternative method, defined in [39], that replaces the input of the best RGB-D fitting method [4] with 3D point-clouds generated by the state-of-the-art multi-view stereo method DVMVS [17]. We train DVMVS on ScanNet, and re-train [4] on its output.

Main Results. Table 1 shows the results in the Scan2CAD metrics. RayTran outperforms both single-frame baselines as well as the 'MVS + RGBD fitter' combination by a wide margin (+33.7%, +24.6%, +17.4% class avg. accuracy respectively). RayTran also outperforms both competitors that align CAD model to RGB videos but rely on tracking: Vid2CAD [39] (+5.5%) and ODAM [34] (+10.6%). Importantly, RayTran is also much simper in design, as [34,39] consist of multiple disjoint steps (object detection, tracking, multi-view optimization). Figure 5 and Fig. 6 illustrate qualitative results for our method.

Table 3. Effects of object segmentation in RayTran. Without FG/BG segmentation as an auxiliary task, the network performs worse (first two rows). If we grant the model the ground-truth segmentation masks as input, results substantially improve, highlighting how future progress on automatic 2D segmentation will benefit our work too (last row). In all cases, the model is trained with the main 3D object pose/shape estimation loss (Sect. 3.2), in addition to the auxiliary losses listed here.

Method	Extra input	Auxiliary tasks	Class avg.	Global avg.
RayTran	–	3D occupancy + 2D FG/BG seg	36.2	43.0
RayTran w/o FG/BG	–	3D occupancy	33.8	40.1
RayTran + GT masks	2D GT masks	3D occupancy + 2D FG/BG seg	47.6	52.5

Looking at individual categories, we obtain the best result on 5 out of 9, and in particular on the "other" category, which is hard for methods based on retrieving CAD models [3,4,39]. Our method instead predicts 3D shapes as voxel grids which helps to generalize better and to adapt to the large variety of object shapes in this catch-all category. On 'trashbin' we do moderately worse, possibly because of the relatively coarse voxel resolution of the backbone representation.

For completeness, we also compare to methods [3,4] in their original form, i.e. fitting CAD models to high-quality dense RGB-D scans. Surprisingly, RayTran (36.2%/43.0%) improves over [3] (35.6%/31.7%), despite using only RGB video as input. While the state-of-the-art [4] performs even better (44.6%/50.7%), this family of methods are limited to videos acquired by RGB-D sensors.

Figure 4 reports accuracy for each transformation type separately (translation, rotation, and scales). Our method predicts all transformation types better than Vid2CAD, ODAM, and the best single-frame baseline Mask2CAD+pred. As objects are considered accurately detected only when passing all 3 thresholds *simultaneously*, improving translation is the biggest avenue for improving our overall quantitative results (Table 1).

Table 2 reports results in the ODAM metrics, which allow us to compare to MOLTR [35] and ImVoxelNet [15]. We choose an object score threshold to maximize the F1 score on the val set for methods that predict object scores (RayTran, Vid2CAD, ImVoxelNet), following the practice of [34]. RayTran outperforms all four methods [15,34,35,39] at both IoU thresholds. ImVoxelNet [15] reports results on ScanNet, not on Scan2CAD. To compare properly we use their publicly available source code and re-train on Scan2CAD. The original code only outputs axis-aligned object boxes on ScanNet (and hence on Scan2CAD, which is derived from it). This prevents comparison on the Scan2CAD metrics, as we cannot compute precise rotation and scale components. Finally, predicting box rotation could potentially improve the results in the ODAM metrics.

Ablation: 2D FG/BG Segmentation as Auxiliary Task. Our model predicts amodal masks, which reinforces the backbone's 3D understanding. Pixels where the object is occluded can only be predicted correctly in 2D as part of the amodal mask by relying on signal from other frames, via the global 3D representation. To support this claim, we trained a version of our model where we

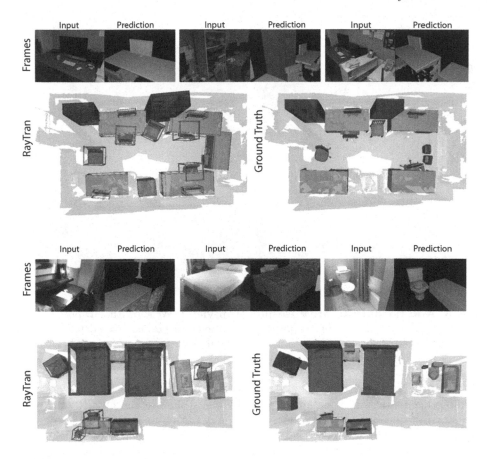

Fig. 5. Qualitative Results (top-view, with frame overlays): We show the 3D pose estimation (as oriented boxes) and shape reconstruction outputs of RayTran against the ground truth, from the top and from the viewpoint of the images. The objects are colored by class. We are able to reconstruct complex scenes in a single pass.

disabled the 2D FG/BG segmentation auxiliary task of Sect. 3.2. This reduces class-avg accuracy by −2.4% (36.2% vs. 33.8 first two rows of Table 3).

Ablation: Perfect Segmentation. Our model performs both 2D and 3D analysis. The main challenge in the 2D analysis is pixelwise segmentation in the input frames. We explore here what would happen if our model were granted perfect object segmentation as input. We train a model which inputs a binary mask as a 4th channel, in addition to RGB. A pixel in the mask is on if it belongs to any object of the 9 classes annotated in Scan2CAD, and 0 otherwise. This augmented model improves class-avg accuracy by +11.4% (reaching 47.6%), and global-avg by +9.5% (reaching 52.5%, Table 3 last row). Hence, as research on 2D segmentation improves, so will our model's 3D scene understanding ability.

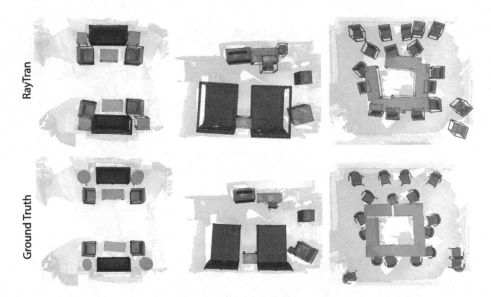

Fig. 6. Additional qualitative Results (top-view): We show the 3D pose estimation and shape reconstruction outputs for 3 additional scenes. For each detected object we visualize its 3D oriented bounding box, as well as its reconstructed mesh.

Ablation: Number of Objects in the Scene. By design, our network cannot predict more object instances than the query slots in the DETR head (64). Moreover, typically only about 30% of all query slots bind to an actual object [9] in scenes containing many objects. This limits recall on such scenes, which sometimes do occur in Scan2CAD. Carion et al. [9] believe that query slots tend to bind to fixed spatial regions, regardless of the content of a test image, causing this limitation. We operate in 3D, which likely exacerbates it because we need many more queries to cover the 3D space.

To understand the effect of this phenomenon on our model's performance, we evaluate here on 3 subsets of Scan2CAD's val split, containing scenes with *at most* 10, 20, and 30 objects respectively. This reduces the number of objects undetected by the fixed 64 query slots in our DETR head.

The class-avg accuracy of RayTran indeed improves in scenes containing fewer objects (from 36.2% in all scenes, up to 37.4% in scenes with <10 objects). The accuracy of the best previous method Vid2CAD instead remains constant. In scenes with at most 10 objects, we outperform Vid2CAD by 6.7% (37.4% vs. 30.7%), which is a larger difference than on all scenes (5.5%: 36.2% vs. 30.7%). Hence, DETR's limitation is affecting our model as well and improving upon it will improve our overall performance.

Ablation: Number of Input Frames. Our model can process a variable number of input frames per video. We use 20 frames at training time to limit memory requirements. In all experiments so far, we used 96 frames at inference time, as using more frames improves coverage of the 3D volume of the scene and hence accuracy of the output. To support this claim, we now reduce the number of frames at inference time. With 48 frames class-avg. falls by -0.4%. Worse yet, if inference were constrained to 20 frames as during training, then performance would drop by -3.3%. This highlights the value of our model's ability to input a variable number of frames.

5   Conclusions

We presented RayTran, a novel backbone architecture for 3D scene reconstruction from RGB video frames, that uses transformers for unprojecting 2D features and consolidating them into a global 3D representation. We introduced the ray-traced sparse transformer block, which enables feature sharing between the 2D and 3D network streams, in a computationally feasible way on current hardware. We use this architecture to perform 3D object reconstruction for the full scene by combining it with a DETR-style network head. Our architecture can reconstruct the whole scene in a single pass, is end-to-end trainable, and does not rely on tracking. We perform experiments on the Scan2CAD benchmark, where RayTran outperforms (1) recent state-of-the-art methods [15,34,35,39] for 3D object pose estimation from RGB videos; and (2) a strong alternative method combining Multi-view Stereo [17] with RGB-D CAD alignment [4].

References

1. Andriluka, M., Roth, S., Schiele, B.: People-tracking-by-detection and people-detection-by-tracking. In: CVPR (2008)
2. Arnab, A., Dehghani, M., Heigold, G., Sun, C., Lučić, M., Schmid, C.: ViViT: a video vision transformer. In: CVPR (2021)
3. Avetisyan, A., Dahnert, M., Dai, A., Savva, M., Chang, A.X., Nießner, M.: Scan2CAD: learning CAD model alignment in RGB-D scans. In: CVPR (2019)
4. Avetisyan, A., Dai, A., Nießner, M.: End-to-end CAD model retrieval and 9DoF alignment in 3D scans. In: ICCV (2019)
5. Avetisyan, A., Khanova, T., Choy, C., Dash, D., Dai, A., Nießner, M.: SceneCAD: predicting object alignments and layouts in RGB-D scans. In: Vedaldi, A., Bischof, H., Brox, T., Frahm, J.-M. (eds.) ECCV 2020. LNCS, vol. 12367, pp. 596–612. Springer, Cham (2020). https://doi.org/10.1007/978-3-030-58542-6_36
6. Bergmann, P., Meinhardt, T., Leal-Taixe, L.: Tracking without bells and whistles. In: ICCV (2019)
7. Bertasius, G., Wang, H., Torresani, L.: Is space-time attention all you need for video understanding? In: ICML (2021)
8. Breitenstein, M.D., Reichlin, F., Leibe, B., Koller-Meier, E., Van Gool, L.: Robust tracking-by-detection using a detector confidence particle filter. In: ICCV (2009)
9. Carion, N., Massa, F., Synnaeve, G., Usunier, N., Kirillov, A., Zagoruyko, S.: End-to-end object detection with transformers. In: Vedaldi, A., Bischof, H., Brox, T., Frahm, J.-M. (eds.) ECCV 2020. LNCS, vol. 12346, pp. 213–229. Springer, Cham (2020). https://doi.org/10.1007/978-3-030-58452-8_13

10. Chang, A.X., et al.: ShapeNet: an information-rich 3D model repository. arXiv:1512.03012 (2015)
11. Chen, Z., Tagliasacchi, A., Zhang, H.: BSP-Net: generating compact meshes via binary space partitioning. In: CVPR (2020)
12. Cheng, B., Schwing, A.G., Kirillov, A.: Per-pixel classification is not all you need for semantic segmentation. In: NeurIPS (2021)
13. Choy, C.B., Xu, D., Gwak, J.Y., Chen, K., Savarese, S.: 3D-R2N2: a unified approach for single and multi-view 3D object reconstruction. In: Leibe, B., Matas, J., Sebe, N., Welling, M. (eds.) ECCV 2016. LNCS, vol. 9912, pp. 628–644. Springer, Cham (2016). https://doi.org/10.1007/978-3-319-46484-8_38
14. Dai, A., Chang, A.X., Savva, M., Halber, M., Funkhouser, T., Nießner, M.: ScanNet: richly-annotated 3D reconstructions of indoor scenes. In: CVPR (2017)
15. Rukhovich, D., Vorontsova, A., Konushin, A.: ImVoxelNet: image to voxels projection for monocular and multi-view general-purpose 3D object detection. In: WACV (2022)
16. Dosovitskiy, A., et al.: An image is worth 16×16 words: transformers for image recognition at scale. In: ICLR (2020)
17. Duzceker, A., Galliani, S., Vogel, C., Speciale, P., Dusmanu, M., Pollefeys, M.: DeepVideoMVS: multi-view stereo on video with recurrent spatio-temporal fusion. In: CVPR (2021)
18. Engel, J., Koltun, V., Cremers, D.: Direct sparse odometry. TPAMI **40**(3), 611–625 (2017)
19. Engelmann, F., Rematas, K., Leibe, B., Ferrari, V.: From points to multi-object 3D reconstruction. In: Proceedings of the IEEE/CVF Conference on Computer Vision and Pattern Recognition, pp. 4588–4597 (2021)
20. Fei, X., Soatto, S.: Visual-inertial object detection and mapping. In: Ferrari, V., Hebert, M., Sminchisescu, C., Weiss, Y. (eds.) ECCV 2018. LNCS, vol. 11215, pp. 318–334. Springer, Cham (2018). https://doi.org/10.1007/978-3-030-01252-6_19
21. Frome, A., Huber, D., Kolluri, R., Bülow, T., Malik, J.: Recognizing objects in range data using regional point descriptors. In: Pajdla, T., Matas, J. (eds.) ECCV 2004. LNCS, vol. 3023, pp. 224–237. Springer, Heidelberg (2004). https://doi.org/10.1007/978-3-540-24672-5_18
22. Girdhar, R., Fouhey, D.F., Rodriguez, M., Gupta, A.: Learning a predictable and generative vector representation for objects. In: Leibe, B., Matas, J., Sebe, N., Welling, M. (eds.) ECCV 2016. LNCS, vol. 9910, pp. 484–499. Springer, Cham (2016). https://doi.org/10.1007/978-3-319-46466-4_29
23. Gkioxari, G., Malik, J., Johnson, J.: Mesh R-CNN. In: ICCV (2019)
24. Gümeli, C., Dai, A., Nießner, M.: ROCA: robust CAD model retrieval and alignment from a single image. arXiv:2112.01988 (2021)
25. He, K., Zhang, X., Ren, S., Sun, J.: Deep residual learning for image recognition. In: CVPR (2016)
26. Hu, H.N., et al.: Joint monocular 3D vehicle detection and tracking. In: ICCV (2019)
27. Huang, S., Qi, S., Zhu, Y., Xiao, Y., Xu, Y., Zhu, S.-C.: Holistic 3D scene parsing and reconstruction from a single RGB image. In: Ferrari, V., Hebert, M., Sminchisescu, C., Weiss, Y. (eds.) ECCV 2018. LNCS, vol. 11211, pp. 194–211. Springer, Cham (2018). https://doi.org/10.1007/978-3-030-01234-2_12
28. Izadinia, H., Seitz, S.M.: Scene recomposition by learning-based ICP. In: CVPR (2020)
29. Izadinia, H., Shan, Q., Seitz, S.M.: Im2CAD. In: CVPR (2017)

30. Kundu, A., Li, Y., Rehg, J.M.: 3D-RCNN: instance-level 3D object reconstruction via render-and-compare. In: CVPR (2018)
31. Kuo, W., Angelova, A., Lin, T.-Y., Dai, A.: Mask2CAD: 3D shape prediction by learning to segment and retrieve. In: Vedaldi, A., Bischof, H., Brox, T., Frahm, J.-M. (eds.) ECCV 2020. LNCS, vol. 12348, pp. 260–277. Springer, Cham (2020). https://doi.org/10.1007/978-3-030-58580-8_16
32. Kuo, W., Angelova, A., Lin, T.Y., Dai, A.: Patch2CAD: patchwise embedding learning for in-the-wild shape retrieval from a single image. In: ICCV (2021)
33. Lewiner, T., Lopes, H., Vieira, A.W., Tavares, G.: Efficient implementation of marching cubes' cases with topological guarantees. J. Graph. Tools **8**(2), 1–15 (2003)
34. Li, K., et al.: ODAM: object detection, association, and mapping using posed RGB video. In: ICCV (2021)
35. Li, K., Rezatofighi, H., Reid, I.: MOLTR: multiple object localization, tracking and reconstruction from monocular RGB videos. IEEE Robot. Autom. Lett. **6**(2), 3341–3348 (2021)
36. Li, Y., Dai, A., Guibas, L., Nießner, M.: Database-assisted object retrieval for real-time 3D reconstruction. In: Computer Graphics Forum, vol. 34. Wiley Online Library (2015)
37. Loshchilov, I., Hutter, F.: Decoupled weight decay regularization. arXiv preprint arXiv:1711.05101 (2017)
38. Mahendran, S., Ali, H., Vidal, R.: A mixed classification-regression framework for 3D pose estimation from 2D images. arXiv:1805.03225 (2018)
39. Maninis, K.K., Popov, S., Niesser, M., Ferrari, V.: Vid2CAD: CAD model alignment using multi-view constraints from videos. IEEE Trans. Pattern Anal. Mach. Intell. (2022)
40. Meinhardt, T., Kirillov, A., Leal-Taixe, L., Feichtenhofer, C.: TrackFormer: multi-object tracking with transformers. arXiv (2021)
41. Mescheder, L., Oechsle, M., Niemeyer, M., Nowozin, S., Geiger, A.: Occupancy networks: learning 3D reconstruction in function space. In: CVPR (2019)
42. Mousavian, A., Anguelov, D., Flynn, J., Kosecka, J.: 3D bounding box estimation using deep learning and geometry. In: CVPR (2017)
43. Mur-Artal, R., Montiel, J.M.M., Tardos, J.D.: ORB-SLAM: a versatile and accurate monocular SLAM system. IEEE Trans. Robot. **31**(5), 1147–1163 (2015)
44. Nan, L., Xie, K., Sharf, A.: A search-classify approach for cluttered indoor scene understanding. ACM Trans. Graph. (TOG) **31**(6), 1–10 (2012)
45. Nicholson, L., Milford, M., Sünderhauf, N.: QuadricSLAM: dual quadrics from object detections as landmarks in object-oriented SLAM. RA-L **4**(1), 1–8 (2018)
46. Nie, Y., Han, X., Guo, S., Zheng, Y., Chang, J., Zhang, J.J.: Total3DUnderstanding: joint layout, object pose and mesh reconstruction for indoor scenes from a single image. In: CVPR (2020)
47. Park, J.J., Florence, P., Straub, J., Newcombe, R., Lovegrove, S.: DeepSDF: learning continuous signed distance functions for shape representation. In: CVPR (2019)
48. Paszke, A., et al.: PyTorch: an imperative style, high-performance deep learning library. In: Wallach, H., Larochelle, H., Beygelzimer, A., d'Alché-Buc, F., Fox, E., Garnett, R. (eds.) Advances in Neural Information Processing Systems, vol. 32, pp. 8024–8035. Curran Associates, Inc. (2019). http://papers.neurips.cc/paper/9015-pytorch-an-imperative-style-high-performance-deep-learning-library.pdf
49. Pollefeys, M., Koch, R., Van Gool, L.: Self-calibration and metric reconstruction inspite of varying and unknown intrinsic camera parameters. IJCV **32**(1), 7–25 (1999). https://doi.org/10.1023/A:1008109111715

50. Popov, S., Bauszat, P., Ferrari, V.: CoReNet: coherent 3D scene reconstruction from a single RGB image. In: Vedaldi, A., Bischof, H., Brox, T., Frahm, J.-M. (eds.) ECCV 2020. LNCS, vol. 12347, pp. 366–383. Springer, Cham (2020). https://doi.org/10.1007/978-3-030-58536-5_22

51. Qian, S., Jin, L., Fouhey, D.F.: Associative3D: volumetric reconstruction from sparse views. In: Vedaldi, A., Bischof, H., Brox, T., Frahm, J.-M. (eds.) ECCV 2020. LNCS, vol. 12360, pp. 140–157. Springer, Cham (2020). https://doi.org/10.1007/978-3-030-58555-6_9

52. Runz, M., et al.: FroDO: from detections to 3D objects. In: CVPR (2020)

53. Salas-Moreno, R.F., Newcombe, R.A., Strasdat, H., Kelly, P.H., Davison, A.J.: SLAM++: simultaneous localisation and mapping at the level of objects. In: CVPR (2013)

54. Schönberger, J.L., Frahm, J.M.: Structure-from-motion revisited. In: CVPR (2016)

55. Shan, M., Feng, Q., Jau, Y.Y., Atanasov, N.: ELLIPSDF: joint object pose and shape optimization with a bi-level ellipsoid and signed distance function description. In: ICCV (2021)

56. Shao, T., Xu, W., Zhou, K., Wang, J., Li, D., Guo, B.: An interactive approach to semantic modeling of indoor scenes with an RGBD camera. ACM Trans. Graph. (TOG) 31(6), 1–11 (2012)

57. Strudel, R., Garcia, R., Laptev, I., Schmid, C.: Segmenter: transformer for semantic segmentation. In: ICCV (2021)

58. Tulsiani, S., Gupta, S., Fouhey, D., Efros, A.A., Malik, J.: Factoring shape, pose, and layout from the 2D image of a 3D scene. In: CVPR (2018)

59. Vaswani, A., et al.: Attention is all you need. In: NeurIPS (2017)

60. Wang, N., Zhang, Y., Li, Z., Fu, Y., Liu, W., Jiang, Y.-G.: Pixel2Mesh: generating 3D mesh models from single RGB images. In: Ferrari, V., Hebert, M., Sminchisescu, C., Weiss, Y. (eds.) ECCV 2018. LNCS, vol. 11215, pp. 55–71. Springer, Cham (2018). https://doi.org/10.1007/978-3-030-01252-6_4

61. Wu, C.: Towards linear-time incremental structure from motion. In: 3DV (2013)

62. Wu, J., Zhang, C., Xue, T., Freeman, W.T., Tenenbaum, J.B.: Learning a probabilistic latent space of object shapes via 3D generative-adversarial modeling. In: NIPS (2016)

63. Xie, H., Yao, H., Zhang, S., Zhou, S., Sun, W.: Pix2Vox++: multi-scale context-aware 3D object reconstruction from single and multiple images. IJCV 128(12), 2919–2935 (2020). https://doi.org/10.1007/s11263-020-01347-6

64. Yang, S., Scherer, S.: CubeSLAM: monocular 3-D object SLAM. IEEE Trans. Robot. 35(4), 925–938 (2019)

65. Zheng, S., et al.: Rethinking semantic segmentation from a sequence-to-sequence perspective with transformers. In: CVPR (2021)

GTCaR: Graph Transformer for Camera Re-localization

Xinyi Li[1] and Haibin Ling[2]([✉])

[1] Magic Leap, Sunnyvale, CA, USA
xinli@magicleap.com
[2] Stony Brook University, Stony Brook, NY, USA
hling@cs.stonybrook.edu

Abstract. Camera re-localization or absolute pose regression is the centerpiece in numerous computer vision tasks such as visual odometry, structure from motion (SfM) and SLAM. In this paper we propose a neural network approach with a graph Transformer backbone, namely **GTCaR** (**G**raph **T**ransformer for **Ca**mera **R**e-localization), to address the multi-view camera re-localization problem. In contrast with prior work where the pose regression is mainly guided by photometric consistency, GTCaR effectively fuses the image features, camera pose information and inter-frame relative camera motions into encoded graph attributes. Moreover, GTCaR is trained towards the graph consistency and pose accuracy combined instead, yielding significantly higher computational efficiency. By leveraging graph Transformer layers with edge features and enabling the adjacency tensor, GTCaR dynamically captures the global attention and thus endows the pose graph with evolving structures to achieve improved robustness and accuracy. In addition, optional temporal Transformer layers actively enhance the spatiotemporal inter-frame relation for sequential inputs. Evaluation of the proposed network on various public benchmarks demonstrates that GTCaR outperforms state-of-the-art approaches.

1 Introduction

The past decade has witnessed surging research interest in developing camera pose regression methods, benefiting various computer vision applications including robot navigation, autonomous driving and AR/VR technologies. *Camera re-localization* is an absolute pose regression (APR) process to localize query images against a known 3D environment. Conventional approaches solving the camera pose estimation problem involve extensive implementations of Perspective-n-Point (PnP) [19] followed by optimization steps of bundle adjustment (BA) [37], which is the iterative process of joint optimization of the 3D scene points and the 6-DoF camera pose parameters, aided by numerical solvers. The formulation yields a non-linear high-dimensional system and is thus computationally challenging to solve [36,44].

Supplementary Information The online version contains supplementary material available at https://doi.org/10.1007/978-3-031-20080-9_14.

With the prevalence of deep neural networks, many recent studies have steered research attentions towards leveraging deep learning techniques to re-formulate the camera pose estimation problem as a pose regression network, *i.e.*, the network is trained with training images and the ground-truth camera poses such that it can learn to regress the camera pose(s) given single or multiple images. Among these studies, PoseNet [22] pioneers in incorporating neural networks into camera pose regression frameworks, where the CNN-based network is trained to directly estimate the camera pose from individual images without explicit feature processing. As multi-view APR methods can preserve more inter-frame information (*e.g.*, temporal/global pose consistency) beyond those achieved solely from single image retrieval, they yield higher accuracy and robustness [26,28,29,31,48]. Later work adopts sophisticated networks to address the task, *e.g.*, in VidLoc [6] a CNN-RNN joint model is presented to leverage the temporal consistency of the sequential images. Recently, GNNs have been exploited in camera pose regression [48], where the message passing scheme embraces the inter-frame dependency.

Lately, the development of Transformers [39] has empowered massively successful applications in natural language processing (NLP), computer vision [3,12] and many other fields. Specifically, the adoption of the self-attention mechanisms enables Transformers to effectively capture the global spatiotemporal consistency of sequential information. Additionally, while graph-based networks such as GNNs have been widely proven to be efficient in modeling arbitrarily structured inputs, it is generally computationally challenging to have the networks update the graph structure dynamically [40,46,50,51], limiting its performance on downstream tasks where high amounts of noise or missing information are present.

Inspired by the aforementioned observations, in this work we propose a neural network fused with a graph Transformer backbone, namely *GTCaR*, to tackle the camera re-localization problem. In GTCaR, the view graph is constructed by a novel graph embedding mechanism, where the nodes are encoded with image features and 6-DoF absolute camera pose of the image frame, while the edge attributes consist of the relative inter-frame camera motions. Moreover, our proposed network introduces an *adjacency tensor* that stores the correlation on both the feature level and the frame level. In particular, the feature correspondences between the frames are encoded into the elements in the adjacency matrix, where the element value is based on the normalized feature correspondence score and thus falls into the range of [0, 1]. The adjacency matrix is updated through the graph Transformer layers to reflect the evolving graph structure, *e.g.*, redundant/noisy edge pruning, newly-added edges according to high correlations between a new image and some previous image, *etc*. GTCaR is trained end-to-end, guided by the loss function that integrates the graph consistency [1] such that to localize multiple query images simultaneously. Additionally, the temporal Transformer layers are utilized to obtain the temporal graph attention for consecutive images.

The architecture overview of GTCaR is given in Fig. 1. The design of the proposed network is favorable for camera re-localization tasks in three aspects. First, it is efficient to exploit the intra- and inter-frame structure information and

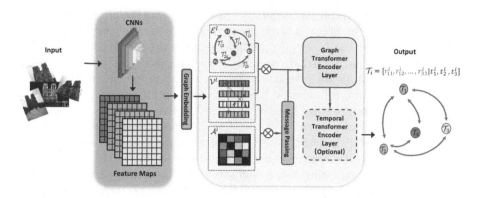

Fig. 1. Overview of the proposed GTCaR architecture for camera re-localization. The network takes query images as input and then models the corresponding camera poses, image features and the pair-wise relative camera motions into a graph $\mathcal{G}(\mathcal{V}, \mathcal{E})$. Then, the adjacency tensor $\mathcal{A}$ and nodes are fed into the message passing layers, before passing through the graph Transformer encoder layers ("l" indicates the l-th layer). For consecutive image sequences, the graph will be passed through additional temporal Transformer encoder layers. The global camera poses are embedded into the node information in the final output.

correlation with the utilization of graphs; Second, the self-attention mechanism can effectively capture the spatiotemporal consistency in arbitrarily long-term periods, achieving high global pose accuracy; Third, with the adjacency matrix being dynamically updated, the network can quickly adjust according to the changing graph structure, further reducing the negative effects caused by erroneous feature matching.

To the best of our knowledge, our proposed network is the first to exploit graph Transformer for camera re-localization. Our contributions can be summarized as:

- We propose a novel framework with the Transformer backbone for the multiple camera re-localization task. By encoding the image features, intra- and inter-frame relative camera poses into a graph, the proposed network is trained efficiently towards both the pose accuracy and the graph consistency.
- We design an adjacency tensor to dynamically capture the global attention, so as to endow the pose-graph with an evolving structure to achieve boosted robustness and accuracy.
- We exploit optional temporal Transformer layers to obtain the temporal graph attention for consecutive images, such that the proposed model can work with both unordered and sequential data.

2   Related Work

Graph Transformers. By virtue of its powerful yet agile data representation, GNNs [23, 32, 40] have achieved exceptional performances on numerous computer vision tasks. In [10], Graph-BERT enables pre-training on the original graphs and adopts a subgraph batching scheme for parallelized learning. However, Graph-BERT assumes that the subgraphs are linkless, thus not suitable for tasks where global connectivity is important. Recently with the success of Transformers [39], several studies [5,13,43,50] have attempted to develop graph Transformers which can leverage the powerful message passing scheme on graphs while utilizing the multi-head self attention mechanism in Transformers. Among which the approach proposed in [43] is capable of transforming the heterogeneous graphs into homogeneous graphs such that the Transformer can be exploited. GTNs proposed in [50] also addresses the heterogeneous graphs, where the proposed network is capable of generating new graph structures by defining meta-paths with arbitrary edge types. In [13], a generalized graph form of Transformers is proposed with the edge features addressed. Despite their successes, straightforward adoptions of GNNs in modeling camera re-localization task is not applicable due to GNN's vulnerability against noisy graphs [15,30,38,46,52].

Camera Pose Regression Networks. It was not until recently that research interests began to focus on incorporating deep neural networks into SfM pipelines and camera pose regression tasks [2,11,14,22,24,36,41,47]. As one of the earliest work adopting neural networks for camera pose regression, the deep convolutional neural network pose regressor proposed in [22] is trained according to a loss function embedding the absolute camera pose prediction error. While [22] pioneers in fusing the power of neural networks into pose regression frameworks, it does not take the intra-frame constraints or connectivity of the view-graph into optimization and thus barely over-performs conventional counterparts on accuracy, as improved later in [6,31,48]. Other work exploits the algebraic or geometric relations among the given images and train the networks to predict to locate the images [4,6,38,41], among which [6] leverages temporal consistency of the sequential images by equipping bi-directional LSTMs [18] with a CNN-RNN model such that temporal regularity can provide more pose information in the regression. The approach in [4] trains DNNs model with the pair-wise geometric constraints between frames, by leveraging additional sensor measurements.

Recent work [48] is the first study to leverage GNNs in a full absolute camera pose regression framework, where the authors model the view-graph with CNN-feature nodes. Later study [26] proposes a pose-graph optimization framework with GNNs, guided by the multiple rotation averaging scheme. In [33], a multi-scene absolute camera pose regression framework with Transformers is proposed. While GNNs are capable of effectively capturing the topological neighborhood information of each individual node (*i.e.*, the featured frame in such task), they are rather prone to noise; Moreover, co-visibility graphs in real-world camera relocalization tasks are often quite dense, causing either noise removal or 'edge-dropping' further entangled [13,26,44,51]. Leveraging graph Transformers in relocalization tasks facilitates the noise handling by virtue of the attention mechanism in (original) Transformers. Our work differs from [33] on: 1) we model the pose regression with a graph structure; 2) we train one end-to-end graph Transformer network while in [33] two separate Transformers are adopted for rotation and translation regression respectively; 3) we leverage rotation averaging addressing both the graph consistency and pose accuracy to guide the training, whereas only camera pose loss is exploited in the training of [33].

3 Problem Formulation

Given a set of 2D image frames and a known 3D scene, *camera re-localization* seeks a consistent set of optimized camera rigid motions, aiming to recover the locations and orientations of the camera aligned with the scene coordinate. Formally, let $\mathbf{R}_i \in \mathbb{SO}(3)$ and $\mathbf{t}_i \in \mathbb{R}^3$ denote the camera orientation and the camera translation for the ith image frame respectively, the absolute camera pose is denoted by $\mathcal{T}_i = [\mathbf{R}_i | \mathbf{t}_i]$. Then the camera re-localization task can be formulated into the following pose regression objective

$$\arg\min_{\mathcal{T}_i} \sum_i \rho\big(d(\mathcal{T}_i, \overline{\mathcal{T}_i})\big), \tag{1}$$

where $\rho(\cdot)$ is a robust cost function, $d(\cdot, \cdot)$ is a distance metric and $\overline{\mathcal{T}_i} = [\overline{\mathbf{R}_i} | \overline{\mathbf{t}_i}]$ denotes the groundtruth camera poses. Accordingly, let $\mathcal{T}_{ij} = [\mathbf{R}_{ij} | \mathbf{t}_{ij}]$ denote the relative camera motion between the ith and j^{th} image frames. In our formulation, we leverage multiple rotation averaging [25, 26, 29, 34, 49] and introduce the *graph-level consistency* term into the objective, that is

$$\arg\min_{\mathbf{R}_i, \mathbf{R}_j} \sum_{(i,j)} \rho\big(d(\mathbf{R}_{ij}, \mathbf{R}_j \mathbf{R}_i^{-1})\big). \tag{2}$$

In detail, given the camera relative orientations $\{\mathbf{R}_{ij}\}$, the optimization process involves minimizing a cost function that penalizes the discrepancy between the camera relative orientations achieved from image retrieval and those inferred from the solved absolute camera poses. We argue that low costs in Eq. 2 indicate high global consistency of the solution set, and thus fuse the cost into the loss function as the *global consistency loss*. Therefore, given the ground truth camera poses, the objective function is assembled as

$$\arg\min_{\mathbf{R}_i, \mathbf{R}_j} \sum_{(i,j)} \rho\big(d_{\mathbf{R}}(\mathbf{R}_{ij}, \mathbf{R}_j \mathbf{R}_i^{-1})\big)$$
$$+ \arg\min_{\mathbf{R}_i} \sum_i \rho'\big(d_{\mathbf{R}}(\mathbf{R}_i, \overline{\mathbf{R}_i})\big) + \arg\min_{\mathbf{t}_i} \sum_i \rho''\big(d_{\mathbf{t}}(\mathbf{t}_i, \overline{\mathbf{t}_i})\big), \tag{3}$$

where ρ' and ρ'' are robust cost functions, $d_{\mathbf{R}} : \mathbb{SO}(3) \times \mathbb{SO}(3) \to \mathbb{R}_+$ and $d_{\mathbf{t}} : \mathbb{R}^3 \times \mathbb{R}^3 \to \mathbb{R}_+$ are the distance metrics for rotations and translations respectively. Specifically, the first term measures the global consistency, *i.e.*, it should be zero if the relative transformations on the edges align perfectly with the absolute transformations on the nodes for the whole graph. The other two terms depict the rotation and translation prediction errors respectively, echoing Eq. 1. Details on the loss function formulation are given in Sect. 4.4.

In the design of our proposed network, we model the multi-view camera re-localization problem as graphs and embed the 2D image features and the camera absolute pose $\mathcal{T}_i$ as the corresponding latent node information, whereas the inter-frame camera relative motions $\mathcal{T}_{ij}$ are encoded as the edge attributes, as introduced in Sect. 4.2.

4 GTCaR Architecture

In this section we detail the network architecture of the proposed GTCaR. First we provide the architecture overview in Sect. 4.1, followed by the elaboration of feature embedding and graph embedding in Sect. 4.2. We then emphasize the structure of the spatiotemporal graph Transformer layers in Sect. 4.3, followed by the graph update and the proposed graph loss function illustrated in Sect. 4.4.

4.1 Architecture Overview

As shown in Fig. 1, the proposed network takes query RGB images as input. The images are first fed into a pre-trained CNN-type [17] feature network, then the output feature maps are embedded in an initial view-graph such that the nodes encode the visual information of the images, and the edges encode inter-frame correlations. Additionally, the local feature matching information and the aggregated image matching score are combined and arranged into a tensorized adjacency matrix, namely the adjacency tensor.

After assembling the images into a graph, the adjacency tensor and the hidden node features are first passed into MPNN [16] layers such that, for each node, the neighboring node features are aggregated efficiently with the implicit attention information embedded in the adjacency tensor. Then the aggregated node features are fed into graph Transformer encoder layers, where the self attention mechanism are equipped with edge features such that the camera relative transformations encoded on the edges can be exploited to generate the attention weights. Additionally, the temporal Transformer encoder layers capture the self-attention for the sequential input. The global camera poses, as node attributes, are updated through the network and are embedded in the final output as the localized camera poses.

4.2 Graph Embedding

We propose to model the input query images, the corresponding camera poses and the pair-wise camera transformations into a graph based on the construction of conventional pose graph, i.e., each node represents an image frame and the edges connecting two nodes represent the inter-frame image relations. In detail, consider a graph $\mathcal{G} = (\mathcal{V}, \mathcal{E})$ where $\mathcal{V} = \{v_i\}$ denotes the set of the images and $\mathcal{E} = \{(i, j) | v_i, v_j \in \mathcal{V}\}$ represents the pair-wise feature-base connectivity between frames. Additionally, let $\mathcal{A}_{\mathcal{G}}$ denote the adjacency matrix of $\mathcal{G}$ such

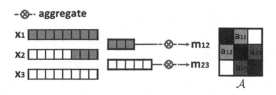

Fig. 2. Each element a_{ij} of the adjacency tensor $\mathcal{A}$ embeds the feature correspondences and the normalized aggregated value. $m_{ij} = 0$ if there exists none co-visible feature between image i and image j. Note that $\mathcal{A}$ is symmetric.

that $\mathcal{A}_{\mathcal{G}}(i,j) = 0$ if $(i,j) \notin \mathcal{E}$ and vice versa. For simplicity of notation, we will use $\mathcal{A}$ for $\mathcal{A}_{\mathcal{G}}$ in the following discussion.

Node Attributes. Consider an image $\mathbf{I}_i$, let $\mathbf{x}_i$ denote the feature vector as the output of the CNN-type feature sub-network, and denote $\mathbf{p}_i \in \mathbb{R}^7$ as the camera absolute pose vector, where $\mathbf{p}_i$ consists of the 4-dimensional quaternion ω_i representing the camera orientation and the 3-dimensional t_i representing the camera translation. That is, the vector embedding of each node v_i contains the information part which encodes the image latent feature and the learning part which embeds the camera pose. It is noteworthy to mention that, in contrast with NLP tasks where the word positions or text orders are crucial, the camera absolute poses are invariant to node positions as we leverage the graph structure to model the problem. We believe that topological position (vertex degree, local neighborhood structure, global connectivity, etc.) plays a significant role in the proposed graph-based framework, therefore we skip the positional encoding in the original Transformer model [39] and embed the 'relative position' or 'relative distance' as the image matching vector into the adjacency tensor instead.

Adjacency Tensor. Let a_{ij} be the element at (i,j) of the adjacency matrix with self-connections $\mathcal{A}$, by convention $a_{ij} = 1$ if there exists an edge connecting v_i and v_j and $a_{ij} = 0$ otherwise. To capture and maintain the pair-wise relation, we introduce the adjacency tensor where a_{ij} represents the vector feature correspondence index between the ith and j^{th} image frames.

Specifically, consider $a_{ij} \in \mathcal{A}$ and let $\mathbf{x}_i$ and $\mathbf{x}_j$ be the corresponding feature vectors, and assume that there exists some feature correspondences between image i and image j. Then a_{ij}^k, *i.e.*, the kth element of a_{ij} portraying the kth feature correspondence, is a tuple with the feature index in $\mathbf{x}_i$ and $\mathbf{x}_j$ respectively. That is, $\mathbf{x}_i(a_{ij}^k(1)) \sim \mathbf{x}_j(a_{ij}^k(2))$. Additionally, each vector a_{ij} is aggregated into an initial meta-feature $\mathbf{m}_{ij}$ as the normalized feature correspondence score with range $[0,1]$, which measures the edge credibility evaluation and the image matching result between the two connected nodes. The adjacency tensor encodes pixel-wise and image-wise correspondence, depicting the edge weights and is updated through the network while interacting spatiotemporally with the whole evolving graph. Illustration of the adjacency tensor is given in Fig. 2.

Edge Attributes. Similar with the 7-dimensional pose feature embedded on the nodes, the camera relative transformation is encoded on the edge connecting

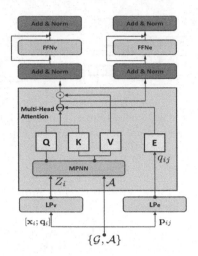

Fig. 3. The graph Transformer encoder layer structure. Q, K and V are compliant with the original Transformer, E represents the edge attention module.

v_i and v_j as $\mathbf{p}_{ij} = \langle \omega_{ij}, t_{ij} \rangle$. During the graph embedding, only nodes with matched features are connected with edges with initialized edge feature (unit quaternion translation and zero vector translation). In our modeling of the graph we consider the edge features as node-symmetric according to the nature of pose graph construction. As we aim to keep the graph lightweight, the edges do not contain any low-level correspondence information between the connected nodes. Instead, the inter-node dependency is implicitly arranged into the adjacency tensor $\mathcal{A}$.

4.3 Graph Transformer Layer

Now we have constructed the graph embedding the node and edge features as the input into the graph Transformer layer. Our proposed network adopts the encoder layer structure in the original Transformer [39] and transforms the initial source graph to the target graph with evolved structural edge information and derived pose values on the nodes. Specifically, the graph Transformer layer exploits the multi-head attention mechanism to generate the sptiotemporal relation between nodes, such that 1) the edges connecting two nodes where high amounts of common features (pair-wise co-visible visual features) are equipped with high attention weights and 2) the edges carrying abundant or noisy image matching yield low attention weights or get removed from the graph. The emerging adjacency tensor progressively interacts with the whole graph and propagates the update over the nodes and the edges.

Message Passing. Before passing the graph into the graph Transformer encoder layer, the neighboring node features are aggregated along with the adjacency tensor for each node. Specifically, consider the graph at the lth layer and let

Z^l denote the hidden feature tensor of the nodes, let $\mathcal{A}^l$ denote the adjacency tensor. Then after the message passing layers the node tensor is thus

$$\hat{Z}^l = Z^l \mathbin{+\!\!+} [\phi(\mathcal{A}^l, Z^l) \otimes Z^l], \tag{4}$$

where $\mathbin{+\!\!+}$ denotes the concatenation operation, $\phi(,)$ denotes the message aggregation, $\otimes$ denotes the tensor product. We adopt the mean function as the aggregation operation in this work. Precisely, Z^l embeds the node information while the latter term embeds the edge information over the neighborhood. The adjacency tensor is exploited here instead of the edges as $\mathcal{A}$ has collected the local attention information such that the message passing is more efficient.

Graph Transformer Encoder Layer. We leverage the multi-head self attention mechanism in the graph Transformer encoder layer with edge features. Borrowing notations from the original Transformer network, let $Q_k^l, K_k^l, V_k^l \in \mathbb{R}^{d_k \times d}$, where $k = 1$ to N is the number of the attention heads, d_k denotes the query dimension. Consider the attention weight for the kth head on the edge connecting the source node i and the target node j, that is

$$w_{ij} = \text{softmax}_j(Q_k^l \hat{Z}_i^l \odot K_k^l \hat{Z}_j^l), \tag{5}$$

where $\odot$ denotes the Hadamard product. Following [13], we add the edge features into generating the attention. Let E_k^l be in the same dimension space with Q_k^l, K_k^l, V_k^l and let q_{ij} denote the hidden edge features, then the attention weight with edge feature is thus

$$w_{ij}^e = \text{softmax}_j \Theta(Q_k^l \hat{Z}_i^l, K_k^l \hat{Z}_j^l, E_k^l q_{ij}^l), \tag{6}$$

where Θ denotes the consecutive dot product operation. Then the update function for nodes and edges are thus

$$Z_i^{l+1} = \mathbin{+\!\!+}_k (w_{ij}^e V_k^l \hat{Z}_j^l) \otimes O_Z^l, \tag{7}$$

$$q_{ij}^{l+1} = \mathbin{+\!\!+}_k (w_{ij}^e) \otimes O_e^l, \tag{8}$$

where $O_Z^l, O_e^l \in \mathbb{R}^{d \times d}$, d is the dimension of the hidden space of nodes and edges, $\mathbin{+\!\!+}_k$ denotes multihead (k heads) concatenation. Illustration is given in Fig. 3.

Temporal Transformer Encoder Layer. The temporal inter-frame relation contains high amounts of useful information especially when the input is sequential images or video clips. In the proposed network we address the temporal dependencies for consecutive camera re-localization tasks by equipping the network with an optional temporal Transformer encoder layer. The temporal Transformer encoder layer exploits the standard Transformer network structure, takes the graph embedding as input and generates intra-graph temporal dependencies between nodes by constructing temporal attention.

4.4   Graph Loss and Update

GTCaR is trained end-to-end, guided by the joint loss function representing both the graph consistency and the accuracy of the predicted camera poses. Recalling the objective function Eq. 3, the loss function is thus assembled as follows

$$
\mathcal{L} = \alpha \sum_{i,j} \rho(d_{\mathbf{R}}(\omega_{ij}, \omega_j \omega_i^{-1})) + \alpha' \sum_{i,j} \rho'(d_{\mathbf{t}}(t_{ij}, d_{\mathbf{t}}(t_i, t_j)))
$$
$$
+ \beta \sum_i \rho(d_{\mathbf{R}}(\omega_i, \overline{\omega_i})) + \beta' \sum_i \rho'(d_{\mathbf{t}}(t_i, \overline{t_i})), \tag{9}
$$

where $\alpha, \alpha', \beta, \beta' \in \mathbb{R}$ are the loss parameters, $\overline{\omega_i}, \overline{t_i}$ are the ground truth camera orientations and translations. The graph loss function can be seen as a joint optimization regarding both the graph consistency and the prediction accuracy.

Specifically, during the training the nodes are updated according to a) edge updates which reflect both relative transformation updates and graph connectivity updates (first two terms in Eq. 9), and b) node updates according to the absolute pose loss (last two terms in Eq. 9). Therefore the graph evolves in terms of 1) message passing aggregates attention with the pose information embedded into the nodes and the local connectivity embedded by the adjacency tensor, then 2) attention mechanism assists to update attention weights on the edges, followed by 3) node and edge features (absolute and relative poses) are updated according to the attention, represented in Eq. 7 and Eq. 8. The graph is therefore evolving with nodes, edges, and adjacency updated.

5   Experimental Results

The proposed network is evaluated on three public benchmarks: 7-Scenes [35], the Cambridge dataset [22] and the Oxford Robotcar dataset [27]. We first elaborate the datasets, metrics, baselines and implementation details we conduct the experiments with (Sect. 5.1), followed by the evaluation results (Sect. 5.2), we then conduct the ablation study on the spatiotemporal mechanism of the proposed network (Sect. 5.3) and discuss the limitations (Sect. 5.4).

5.1   Experiment Setting

Implementation Details. The proposed network is implemented in PyTorch on a machine with Intel(R) i7-7700 3.6 GHz processors with 8 threads and 64 GB memory and a single Nvidia GeForce 3060Ti GPU with 8 GB memory. For training we adopt standard SGD optimizer with no dropout, the learning rate is annealed geometrically starting at 1e−3 and decreases to 1e−5.

We adopt ResNet [17] pretrained on ImageNet [9] for the feature handling. The input RGB images are scaled to 341×256 pixels, normalized by the subtraction of mean pixel values. The proposed network is pre-trained end-to-end on ScanNet [7], an RGB-D video sequence dataset which contains 2.5 million

Table 1. Experiment results on the 7—Scenes Dataset [35]. Results are cited directly, the best results are **highlighted**.

Scene Scene scale	Chess 3 × 2 m²	Fire 2.5 × 1 m²	Heads 2 × 0.5 m²	Office 2.5 × 2 m²	Pumpkin 2.5 × 2 m²	Kitchen 4 × 3 m²	Stairs 2.5 × 2 m²	Avg.
RelocNet [2]	0.12 m, 4.14°	0.26 m, 10.4°	0.14 m, 10.5°	0.18 m, 5.32°	0.26 m, 4.17°	0.23 m, 5.08°	0.28 m, 7.53°	0.21 m, 6.73°
LsG [47]	0.09 m, 3.28°	0.26 m, 10.92°	0.17 m, 12.70°	0.18 m, 5.45°	0.20 m, 3.69°	0.23 m, 4.92°	0.23 m, 11.3°	0.19 m, 7.47°
MapNet [4]	0.08 m, 3.25°	0.27 m, 11.69°	0.18 m, 13.25°	0.17 m, 5.15°	0.22 m, 4.02°	0.23 m, 4.93°	0.30 m, 12.08°	0.21 m, 7.77°
MapNet+ [4]	0.10 m, 3.17°	**0.20 m**, 9.04°	0.13 m, 11.13°	0.18 m, 5.38°	0.19 m, 3.92°	0.20 m, 5.01°	0.30 m, 13.37°	0.19 m, 7.29°
MapNet(pgo) [4]	0.09 m, 3.24°	**0.20 m**, 9.29°	**0.12 m, 8.45°**	0.19 m, 5.42°	0.19 m, 3.96°	0.20 m, 4.94°	0.27 m, 10.57°	0.18 m, 6.55°
PoseNet15 [22]	0.32 m, 8.12°	0.47 m, 14.4°	0.29 m, 12.0°	0.48 m, 7.68°	0.47 m, 8.42°	0.59 m, 8.64°	0.47 m, 13.8°	0.44 m, 10.4°
PoseNet16 [20]	0.37 m, 7.24°	0.43 m, 13.7°	0.31 m, 12.0°	0.48 m, 8.04°	0.61 m, 7.08°	0.58 m, 7.54°	0.48 m, 13.1°	0.47 m, 9.81°
PoseNet17 [21]	0.14 m, 4.50°	0.27 m, 11.80°	0.18 m, 12.10°	0.20 m, 5.77°	0.25 m, 4.82°	0.24 m, 5.52°	0.37 m, 10.60°	0.24 m, 7.87°
PoseNet17+ [21]	0.13 m, 4.48°	0.27 m, 11.30°	0.17 m, 13.00°	0.19 m, 5.55°	0.26 m, 4.75°	0.23 m, 5.35°	0.35 m, 12.40°	0.23 m, 8.12°
LSTM+Pose [42]	0.24 m, 5.77°	0.34 m, 11.9°	0.21 m, 13.7°	0.30 m, 8.08°	0.33 m, 7.00°	0.37 m, 8.83°	0.40 m, 13.7°	0.31 m, 9.85°
Hourglass [28]	0.15 m, 6.17°	0.27 m, 10.84°	0.19 m, 11.63°	0.21 m, 8.48°	0.25 m, 7.01°	0.27 m, 10.15°	0.29 m, 12.46°	0.23 m, 9.53°
BranchNet [45]	0.18 m, 5.17°	0.34 m, 8.99°	0.20 m, 14.15°	0.30 m, 7.05°	0.27 m, 5.10°	0.33 m, 7.40°	0.38 m, 10.26°	0.29 m, 8.30°
VidLoc [6]	0.18 m, —	0.26 m, —	0.14 m, —	0.26 m, —	0.36 m, —	0.31 m, —	0.26 m, —	0.25 m, —
CNN+GNN [48]	**0.08 m**, 2.82°	0.26 m, 8.94°	0.17 m, 11.41°	0.18 m, 5.08°	**0.15 m**, 2.77°	0.25 m, 4.48°	**0.23 m**, 8.78°	0.19 m, 6.33°
MS-Trans. [33]	0.11 m, 4.66°	0.24 m, 9.6°	0.14 m, 12.19°	0.17 m, 5.66°	0.18 m, 4.44°	**0.17 m**, 5.94°	0.26 m, 8.45°	0.18 m, 7.28°
GTCaR (ours)	0.09 m, **1.94°**	0.27 m, **8.45°**	**0.12 m**, 9.34°	**0.12 m, 2.41°**	**0.15 m, 2.13°**	0.21 m, **2.73°**	0.26 m, 8.92°	**0.17 m, 5.13°**

views in over 1500 indoor scans, we only use the RGB monocular images and the ground truth camera pose values are given by [8]. The node poses (absolute pose) and edge poses (relative pose) are initialized as unit orientations and zero translations. We fix the input query size to be 32 though we have observed that the proposed network is capable of taking large input size up to 128. In all the experiments, the image frames are fed sequentially from the test set, analogous to existing work [6, 47, 48] for a fair comparison.

Datasets and Metrics. We conduct extensive experiments on datasets with different scales and report the median errors of camera orientation (°) and translation (m). The *7-Scenes dataset* [35] consists of RGB-D video sequences covering seven small indoor scenes, captured by hand-held Kinect camera. In some of the scenes, many texture-less surfaces and repetitive patterns are present, thus making the dataset challenging in spite of its relatively small size containing less than 10K images. The *Cambridge dataset* is a large-scale dataset containing six outdoor scene scans outside the Cambridge University, the dataset consists of around 12K images and the corresponding camera pose ground truth.

The *Oxford RobotCar dataset* contains image sequences taken through driving in Oxford with different weathers, traffic conditions and lighting, the total trajectory is over 10km and is very challenging for camera re-localization. Following [4, 47, 48], we conduct experiments on the LOOP route (1120 m) and FULL route (9562 m) to evaluate the performance of the proposed network on long consecutive sequences. In all the experiments, we comply with the train/test split provided in the original 7-Scenes and Cambridge benchmarks, and that given in MapNet [4] for fair comparisons.

Baselines. The proposed network is evaluated against recent state-of-the-art camera re-localization networks, including single image-based absolute camera pose regression network PoseNet and its variants [20–22, 42] among which, LSTM+Pose [42] along with MapNet and its variants [4], LsG [47] and VidLoc [6] have utilized temporal inter-frame relations in the network. CNN+GNN [48]

Table 2. Experiment results on the Cambridge Dataset [22]. Evaluation with Map-Net [4] is cited from [31], other results are cited directly. The average is taken on the first four datasets. The best results are **highlighted**.

Scene Scene scale	College $5.6 \times 10^3\,\mathrm{m}^2$	Shop $8.8 \times 10^3\,\mathrm{m}^2$	Church $4.8 \times 10^3\,\mathrm{m}^2$	Hospital $2.0 \times 10^3\,\mathrm{m}^2$	Court $8.0 \times 10^3\,\mathrm{m}^2$	Street $5.0 \times 10^3\,\mathrm{m}^2$	Avg.
MapNet [4]	1.07 m, 1.89°	1.49 m, 4.22°	2.00 m, 4.53°	1.94 m, 3.91°	7.85 m, 3.76°	22.23 m, 27.55°	1.63 m, 3.64°
PoseNet15 [22]	1.66 m, 4.86°	1.41 m, 7.18°	2.45 m, 7.96°	2.62 m, 4.90°	-	-	2.04 m, 6.23°
PoseNet16 [20]	1.74 m, 4.06°	1.25 m, 7.54°	2.11 m, 8.38°	2.57 m, 5.14°	-	-	1.92 m, 6.28°
LSTM+Pose [42]	0.99 m, 3.65°	1.18 m, 7.44°	**1.52 m**, 6.68°	1.51 m, 4.29°	-	-	1.30 m, 5.52°
PoseNet17 [21]	0.99 m, 1.06°	1.05 m, 3.97°	1.49 m, 3.43°	2.17 m, 2.94°	7.00 m, 3.65°	20.70 m, 25.70°	1.43 m, 2.85°
PoseNet17+ [21]	0.88 m, 1.04°	0.88 m, 3.78°	1.57 m, 3.32°	3.20 m, 3.29°	6.83 m, 3.47°	20.30 m, 25.50°	1.63 m, 2.86°
CNN+GNN [48]	0.59 m 0.65°	0.50 m, 2.87°	1.90 m, 3.29°	1.88 m, 2.78°	6.67 m, 2.79°	14.72 m, 22.44°	1.12 m, 2.40°
MS-Trans. [33]	0.83 m 1.47°	0.86 m, 3.07°	1.62, 3.99°	1.81 m, 2.39°	-	-	1.28 m, 2.73°
GTCaR (ours)	**0.42 m, 0.52°**	**0.64 m, 1.56°**	1.55 m, **2.56°**	**1.32 m, 1.97°**	**5.62 m, 2.17°**	**10.27 m, 19.88°**	**0.98 m, 1.65°**

models the multi-view camera pose regression with a graph and leverages GNNs on the task. Other approaches include RelocNet [2], Hourglass [28] and Branch-Net [45].

5.2 Performance Evaluation

7-Scenes. We first evaluate GTCaR on the 7-Scenes dataset against recent state-of-the-art approaches, the experiment results are given in Table 1. It can be observed that our proposed network overperforms the other approaches on most of the scenes. Among the approaches, LsG [47], MapNet [4] and VidLoc [6] rely heavily on the temporal information of the input, *i.e.*, the approaches can handle consecutive sequences more efficiently but tend to lose the spatial inter-frame correlation especially for large-scale datasets or over long camera trajectories. Additionally, PoseNet [22] and its variants conduct absolute pose regression from single images, such that the networks perform poorly on the scene where repetitive patterns or texture-less surfaces are present (Table 2).

Similar to our proposed network, CNN+GNN [48] leverages graphs to model the multi-view camera re-localization with message passing among the image-embedded nodes. However, the network does not exploit temporal information in sequential images, and enforces a maximum value of neighbors of each node. As a result, it tends to miss the temporal correlation for consecutive frames or discard useful inter-frame spatial correlation. It is also noteworthy that the proposed approach achieves real-time performance for all the experiments, as we have observed the average runtime ranging from 12 ms to 23 ms per frame with the batch size set to be 32, while [48] records 8-batch performance with unknown runtime efficiency.

Cambridge. We demonstrate the capability to handle large-scale dataset of GTCaR by evaluating the network on the Cambridge dataset, where the proposed network outperforms the baselines on most of the scenes. Among the scenes, 'Court' and 'Street' are the largest datasets in size and cover long complex trajectories and huge outdoor areas, as challenging to handle with single image-based regression networks like PoseNet15, PoseNet16 and even LSTM+Pose

Table 3. Experiment results on the Oxford Robotcar Dataset [27]. Evaluation with PoseNet [22] is cited from [4], other results are cited directly, the best results are **highlighted**.

Scene Scene scale	LOOP 1120 m	FULL 9562 m
MapNet [4]	9.84 m, 3.96°	41.4 m, 12.5°
MapNet+ [4]	8.17 m, 2.62°	30.3 m, 7.8°
MapNet(pgo) [4]	6.73 m, 2.23°	29.5 m, 7.8°
PoseNet [22]	25.29 m, 17.45°	125.6 m, 27.1°
LsG [47]	9.19 m, 3.52°	31.65 m, 4.51°
CNN+GNN [48]	8.15 m, 2.57°	17.35 m, **3.47°**
GTCaR (ours)	**5.46 m, 1.98°**	**14.37 m**, 3.68°

with additional LSTM units, the aforementioned networks have not reported the results on these two datasets. It can be observed that GTCaR demonstrates great improvements over approaches solely relying on temporal relation or spatial relation on datasets with long camera trajectories.

RobotCar. The RobotCar dataset is especially challenging for the presence of weather variations, dynamic objects/pedestrians, occlusions, *etc.* Following [4, 22,47,48], we conduct experiments on the two subsets from the dataset. The LOOP route covers 1120 m and the FULL route has a total length of 9562 m.

As PoseNet [22] conducts camera pose regression with heavy reliance on the visual information from singe images, large amounts of outliers are produced with insufficient inter-frame correlations, thus yielding low accuracy. MapNet [4] utilizes inputs from other sensors like GPS and IMU and fuses the measurements to aid the camera re-localization. Specifically, MapNet(pgo) acquires the relative camera pose from VO and acts in a sliding-window manner to predict the absolute poses. Compared with GNN-based approach [48], the proposed network shows major improvement as it efficiently models the spatiotemporal relation for sequential images, whereas the former network mainly relies on the spatial inter-frame dependencies (Table 3).

Additionally, we report the cumulative distributions of the translation and rotation prediction errors on the two datasets against prior work in the *supplementary*. The baselines include PoseNet [22], MapNet [4], LsG [47] and CNN+GNN [48]. It can be observed that the proposed network outperforms the baselines on all the datasets.

5.3 Ablation Study

We conduct ablation study to investigate the significance of different modules of the proposed network. We show the ablation results on 'Pumpkin' scene from 7-Scenes dataset, 'Court' from the Cambridge and LOOP from the RobotCar

Table 4. Ablations on Pumpkin, Court and LOOP.

Configuration	Pumpkin	Court	LOOP
GTCaR	**0.15 m, 2.13°**	**5.62 m, 2.17°**	**5.46 m, 1.98°**
GTCaR [temporal]	0.31 m, 3.26°	6.95 m, 2.95°	8.25 m, 3.48°
GTCaR [graph]	0.17 m, 2.28°	7.34 m, 4.84°	9.03 m, 3.55°
GTCaR [MPNN]	0.20 m, **2.13°**	5.98 m, 2.38°	7.95 m, 2.64°

dataset, to cover scenes of different scales and lengths. The results are given in Table 4. The comprehensive ablation experiments are given in the *supplementary*.

We first evaluate GTCaR without the MPNN layers, such that the graph is directly fed into the graph Transformer layers without the node information aggregation aided by the adjacency tensor. It can be observed that the performance of the network is significantly worse on the 'Court' dataset. The reason is that the simple linear projection of the node features cannot preserve much information, compared with the message aggregated node features in the original network, where the neighboring node information is efficiently preserved. For the 'Pumpkin' scene, high amounts of repetitive patterns are present such that the graph is densely connected; For the LOOP route, the images are highly consecutive such that temporal Transformer can capture the neighboring node information along the temporal dimension. We then study the effects of the individual Transformer modules, *i.e.*, the experiments are conducted with GTCaR without graph Transformer layers (GTCaR[temporal]) and without temporal Transformer layers (GTCaR[graph]). It can be observed that the accuracy of GTCaR[temporal] decreases harshly on 'Court' and 'Pumpkin' without the spatial correlation. Indeed, GTCaR can be seen as a GNN+RNN type of camera re-localization network, which can only preserve inter-frame dependencies over short period of time but tend to yield a overly sparse graph. On the other hand, the performance of GTCaR[graph] is slightly worse than the original network on all the datasets without significant decreased accuracy.

5.4   Discussions and Limitations

Generalizability. By virtue of utilizing the underlying geometric constraints implicitly, the proposed network can deliver higher accuracy and better robustness compared to its single-view APR counterparts. Nonetheless we have observed that the network generalizability to vastly different scenes is still limited, *i.e.*, the best performance is achieved by training the network on sets of similar scenes regarding indoor/outdoor, scale and lighting, *etc.*

Computational Cost. From the experiments and the ablation study, we have observed that the output graphs are mostly dense according to the spatiotemporal dependencies. The high density brings in high amounts of unnecessary computations, especially in the case where the scene scale is small and the camera motion is slow. Equipping more GNN layers after the Transformer layers can remove the unnecessary edges but tends to introduce over-fitting and graph memory overhead to the network.

6   Conclusion

In this paper we propose a neural network approach with a graph Transformer backbone, namely GTCaR, to address the multi-view camera re-localization problem. We model the multi-view camera pose regression problem with graph embedding, where the image features, camera poses and pair-wise camera transformations are fused into graph attributes. With the introduction of a novel adjacency tensor, the proposed network can effectively capture the local node connection information. By leveraging graph Transformer layers with edge features and enabling temporal Transformer to generate the spatiotemporal dependencies between the frames, GTCaR can actively gain the graph attention and achieves state-of-the-art robustness, accuracy and efficiency.

Acknowledgement. We thank all reviewers for valuable comments and suggestions. Ling was supported in part by US National Science Foundation Grants 2006665, 2128350 and 1814745.

References

1. Arrigoni, F., Fusiello, A., Ricci, E., Pajdla, T.: Viewing graph solvability via cycle consistency. In: Proceedings of the IEEE/CVF International Conference on Computer Vision (ICCV) (2021)
2. Balntas, V., Li, S., Prisacariu, V.: RelocNet: continuous metric learning relocalisation using neural nets. In: Ferrari, V., Hebert, M., Sminchisescu, C., Weiss, Y. (eds.) Computer Vision – ECCV 2018. LNCS, vol. 11218, pp. 782–799. Springer, Cham (2018). https://doi.org/10.1007/978-3-030-01264-9_46
3. Bertasius, G., Wang, H., Torresani, L.: Is space-time attention all you need for video understanding? In: Proceedings of the IEEE Conference on Computer Vision and Pattern Recognition (CVPR) (2021)
4. Brahmbhatt, S., Gu, J., Kim, K., Hays, J., Kautz, J.: Geometry-aware learning of maps for camera localization. In: Proceedings of the IEEE Conference on Computer Vision and Pattern Recognition (CVPR) (2018)
5. Chu, P., Wang, J., You, Q., Ling, H., Liu, Z.: TransMOT: spatial-temporal graph transformer for multiple object tracking. arXiv abs/2104.00194 (2021). https://arxiv.org/abs/2104.00194
6. Clark, R., Wang, S., Markham, A., Trigoni, N., Wen, H.: VidLoc: a deep spatiotemporal model for 6-DoF video-clip relocalization. In: Proceedings of the IEEE Computer Society Conference on Computer Vision and Pattern Recognition (CVPR) (2017)
7. Dai, A., Chang, A.X., Savva, M., Halber, M., Funkhouser, T., Nießner, M.: ScanNet: Richly-annotated 3D reconstructions of indoor scenes. In: Proceedings of the IEEE Conference on Computer Vision and Pattern Recognition (CVPR) (2017)
8. Dai, A., Nießner, M., Zollhöfer, M., Izadi, S., Theobalt, C.: BundleFusion: real-time globally consistent 3d reconstruction using on-the-fly surface reintegration. ACM Trans. Graph. (ToG) **36**(4), 1 (2017)

9. Deng, J., Dong, W., Socher, R., Li, L.J., Li, K., Fei-Fei, L.: ImageNet: a large-scale hierarchical image database. In: IEEE Conference on Computer Vision and Pattern Recognition (CVPR). IEEE (2009)

10. Devlin, J., Chang, M.W., Lee, K., Toutanova, K.: BERT: pre-training of deep bidirectional transformers for language understanding. NAACL (2019)

11. Ding, M., Wang, Z., Sun, J., Shi, J., Luo, P.: CamNet: coarse-to-fine retrieval for camera re-localization. In: Proceedings of the IEEE International Conference on Computer Vision (ICCV) (2019)

12. Dosovitskiy, A., et al.: An image is worth 16 × 16 words: transformers for image recognition at scale. In: International Conference on Learning Representations (ICLR) (2021)

13. Dwivedi, V.P., Bresson, X.: A generalization of transformer networks to graphs. In: DLG-AAAI (2021)

14. Garg, R., B.G., V.K., Carneiro, G., Reid, I.: Unsupervised CNN for single view depth estimation: geometry to the rescue. In: Leibe, B., Matas, J., Sebe, N., Welling, M. (eds.) ECCV 2016. LNCS, vol. 9912, pp. 740–756. Springer, Cham (2016). https://doi.org/10.1007/978-3-319-46484-8_45

15. Gidaris, S., Komodakis, N.: Generating classification weights with GNN denoising autoencoders for few-shot learning. In: Proceedings of the IEEE Computer Society Conference on Computer Vision and Pattern Recognition (CVPR) (2019)

16. Gilmer, J., Schoenholz, S.S., Riley, P.F., Vinyals, O., Dahl, G.E.: Neural message passing for quantum chemistry. In: International Conference on Machine Learning (ICML) (2017)

17. He, K., Zhang, X., Ren, S., Sun, J.: Deep residual learning for image recognition. In: Proceedings of the IEEE Conference on Computer Vision and Pattern Recognition (CVPR) (2016)

18. Hochreiter, S., Schmidhuber, J.: Long short-term memory. Neural Comput. **9**, 1735–1780 (1997)

19. Horn, B.K.: Closed-form solution of absolute orientation using unit quaternions. Josa a (1987)

20. Kendall, A., Cipolla, R.: Modelling uncertainty in deep learning for camera relocalization. In: IEEE International Conference on Robotics and Automation (ICRA). IEEE (2016)

21. Kendall, A., Cipolla, R.: Geometric loss functions for camera pose regression with deep learning. In: Proceedings of the IEEE Conference on Computer Vision and Pattern Recognition (CVPR) (2017)

22. Kendall, A., Grimes, M., Cipolla, R.: PoseNet: a convolutional network for real-time 6-DoF camera relocalization. In: Proceedings of the IEEE International Conference on Computer Vision (ICCV) (2015)

23. Kipf, T.N., Welling, M.: Semi-supervised classification with graph convolutional networks. In: International Conference on Learning Representations (ICLR) (2017)

24. Klodt, M., Vedaldi, A.: Supervising the new with the old: learning SFM from SFM. In: Ferrari, V., Hebert, M., Sminchisescu, C., Weiss, Y. (eds.) ECCV 2018. LNCS, vol. 11214, pp. 713–728. Springer, Cham (2018). https://doi.org/10.1007/978-3-030-01249-6_43

25. Lerman, G., Shi, Y.: Robust group synchronization via cycle-edge message passing. Found. Comput. Math. (2021)

26. Li, X., Ling, H.: PoGO-Net: pose graph optimization with graph neural networks. In: Proceedings of the IEEE International Conference on Computer Vision (ICCV) (2021)

27. Maddern, W., Pascoe, G., Linegar, C., Newman, P.: 1 Year, 1000 km: the Oxford RobotCar dataset. Int. J. Robot. Res. (IJRR) **36**(1), 3–15 (2017)
28. Melekhov, I., Ylioinas, J., Kannala, J., Rahtu, E.: Image-based localization using hourglass networks. In: Proceedings of the IEEE International Conference on Computer Vision Workshops (ICCV Workshops) (2017)
29. Purkait, P., Chin, T.-J., Reid, I.: NeuRoRA: neural robust rotation averaging. In: Vedaldi, A., Bischof, H., Brox, T., Frahm, J.-M. (eds.) ECCV 2020. LNCS, vol. 12369, pp. 137–154. Springer, Cham (2020). https://doi.org/10.1007/978-3-030-58586-0_9
30. Rong, Y., Huang, W., Xu, T., Huang, J.: DropEdge: towards deep graph convolutional networks on node classification. In: International Conference on Learning Representations (ICLR) (2020)
31. Sattler, T., Zhou, Q., Pollefeys, M., Leal-Taixe, L.: Understanding the limitations of CNN-based absolute camera pose regression. In: Proceedings of the IEEE Computer Society Conference on Computer Vision and Pattern Recognition (CVPR) (2019)
32. Scarselli, F., Gori, M., Tsoi, A.C., Hagenbuchner, M., Monfardini, G.: The graph neural network model. IEEE Trans. Neural Netw. **20**(1), 61–80 (2008)
33. Shavit, Y., Ferens, R., Keller, Y.: Learning multi-scene absolute pose regression with transformers. In: Proceedings of the IEEE International Conference on Computer Vision (ICCV) (2021)
34. Shi, Y., Lerman, G.: Message passing least squares framework and its application to rotation synchronization. In: International Conference on Machine Learning (ICML) (2020)
35. Shotton, J., Glocker, B., Zach, C., Izadi, S., Criminisi, A., Fitzgibbon, A.: Scene coordinate regression forests for camera relocalization in RGB-D images. In: Proceedings of the IEEE Conference on Computer Vision and Pattern Recognition (CVPR) (2013)
36. Tang, C., Tan, P.: BA-Net: dense bundle adjustment networks. In: International Conference on Learning Representations (ICLR) (2018)
37. Triggs, B., McLauchlan, P.F., Hartley, R.I., Fitzgibbon, A.W.: Bundle adjustment—a modern synthesis. In: Triggs, B., Zisserman, A., Szeliski, R. (eds.) IWVA 1999. LNCS, vol. 1883, pp. 298–372. Springer, Heidelberg (2000). https://doi.org/10.1007/3-540-44480-7_21
38. Valada, A., Radwan, N., Burgard, W.: Deep auxiliary learning for visual localization and odometry. In: Proceedings of the IEEE International Conference on Robotics and Automation (ICRA) (2018)
39. Vaswani, A., et al.: Attention is all you need. In: Conference on Neural Information Processing Systems (NeurIPS) (2017)
40. Veličković, P., Cucurull, G., Casanova, A., Romero, A., Lio, P., Bengio, Y.: Graph attention networks. In: International Conference on Learning Representations (ICLR) (2018)
41. Vijayanarasimhan, S., Ricco, S., Schmid, C., Sukthankar, R., Fragkiadaki, K.: SFM-Net: learning of structure and motion from video. arXiv preprint arXiv:1704.07804 (2017)
42. Walch, F., Hazirbas, C., Leal-Taixe, L., Sattler, T., Hilsenbeck, S., Cremers, D.: Image-based localization using LSTMs for structured feature correlation. In: Proceedings of the IEEE International Conference on Computer Vision (ICCV) (2017)
43. Wang, X., et al.: Heterogeneous graph attention network. In: The World Wide Web Conference (WWW) (2019)

44. Wu, C., et al.: VisualSFM: a visual structure from motion system (2011)
45. Wu, J., Ma, L., Hu, X.: Delving deeper into convolutional neural networks for camera relocalization. In: IEEE International Conference on Robotics and Automation (ICRA). IEEE (2017)
46. Xu, K., Hu, W., Leskovec, J., Jegelka, S.: How powerful are graph neural networks? In: International Conference on Learning Representations (ICLR) (2019)
47. Xue, F., Wang, X., Yan, Z., Wang, Q., Wang, J., Zha, H.: Local supports global: deep camera relocalization with sequence enhancement. In: Proceedings of the IEEE International Conference on Computer Vision (ICCV) (2019)
48. Xue, F., Wu, X., Cai, S., Wang, J.: Learning multi-view camera relocalization with graph neural networks. In: Proceedings of the IEEE Computer Society Conference on Computer Vision and Pattern Recognition (CVPR) (2020)
49. Yang, L., Li, H., Rahim, J.A., Cui, Z., Tan, P.: End-to-end rotation averaging with multi-source propagation. In: Proceedings of the IEEE Conference on Computer Vision and Pattern Recognition (CVPR) (2021)
50. Yun, S., Jeong, M., Kim, R., Kang, J., Kim, H.J.: Graph transformer networks. In: Conference on Neural Information Processing Systems (NeurIPS) (2019)
51. Zhang, J., Zhang, H., Xia, C., Sun, L.: Graph-BERT: only attention is needed for learning graph representations. arXiv preprint arXiv:2001.05140 (2020)
52. Zhao, L., Akoglu, L.: PairNorm: tackling oversmoothing in GNNs. In: International Conference on Learning Representations (ICLR) (2019)

3D Object Detection with a Self-supervised Lidar Scene Flow Backbone

Emeç Erçelik[1]([✉])[ID], Ekim Yurtsever[2][ID], Mingyu Liu[1,3][ID], Zhijie Yang[1],
Hanzhen Zhang[1], Pınar Topçam[1], Maximilian Listl[1], Yılmaz Kaan Çaylı[1],
and Alois Knoll[1][ID]

[1] Chair of Robotics, Artificial Intelligence and Real-Time Systems,
Technical University of Munich, 85748 Garching, Germany
{emec.ercelik,mingyu.liu,zhijie.yang,hanzhen.zhang,
pinar.topcam,maximilian.listl,kaan.cayl}@tum.de, knoll@in.tum.de
[2] Ohio State University, Columbus, OH 43212, USA
yurtsever.2@osu.edu
[3] Tongji University, Shanghai 201804, China

Abstract. State-of-the-art lidar-based 3D object detection methods rely on supervised learning and large labeled datasets. However, annotating lidar data is resource-consuming, and depending only on supervised learning limits the applicability of trained models. Self-supervised training strategies can alleviate these issues by learning a general point cloud backbone model for downstream 3D vision tasks. Against this backdrop, we show the relationship between self-supervised multi-frame flow representations and single-frame 3D detection hypotheses. Our main contribution leverages learned flow and motion representations and combines a self-supervised backbone with a supervised 3D detection head. First, a self-supervised scene flow estimation model is trained with cycle consistency. Then, the point cloud encoder of this model is used as the backbone of a single-frame 3D object detection head model. This second 3D object detection model learns to utilize motion representations to distinguish dynamic objects exhibiting different movement patterns. Experiments on KITTI and nuScenes benchmarks show that the proposed self-supervised pre-training increases 3D detection performance significantly. https://github.com/emecercelik/ssl-3d-detection.git.

Keywords: 3D detection · Self-supervised learning · Scene flow · Lidar point clouds

1 Introduction

Lidar promises accurate distance measurement, which is crucial for real-time systems such as 3D perception modules of automated vehicles. Supervised learning methods have dominated benchmarks created for challenging downstream

---

E. Erçelik and E. Yurtsever—These authors contributed equally.

Supplementary Information The online version contains supplementary material available at https://doi.org/10.1007/978-3-031-20080-9_15.

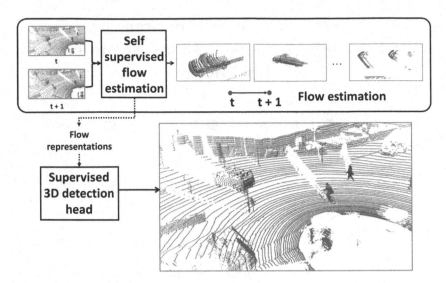

Fig. 1. This study shows the relationship between self-supervised flow representations and supervised 3D detection hypotheses. We illustrate the importance of defining 3D objects-of-interest hypotheses in a spatio-temporal context. For example, a car should not just be defined by its shape but also by its capability to move in space and time. To this end, a scene flow estimation network is trained with cycle consistency in a self-supervised manner. Then, the backbone of this pre-trained model is used to feed a supervised 3D object detection head. The proposed strategy improves detection performance significantly compared to baselines when the amount of labeled data is less for supervised learning.

3D vision tasks [5,9,12,40]. However, high-performing models need a copious amount of labeled data for training. Annotating lidar data is labor-intensive and is a bottleneck for real-world deployment.

Recent work showed the importance of self-supervised learning to build large backbones by exploiting the structure of data. For example, the temporal contextual changes in videos can be exploited in contrastive learning strategies [41]. Contrastive methods have also been used with data augmentation [31] for similar purposes. MoCo [16] classifies images in binary form as positive and negative to learn useful representations. Another approach is to quantize representations from a teacher network [1,6]. However, these works focus solely on the RGB image domain. Not much work focuses on unsupervised or self-supervised 3D object detection. Point cloud sparsity poses additional challenges, as the structure of data is significantly different from denser modalities.

The main body of state-of-the-art 3D object detection with point cloud literature comprises supervised learning methods [10,15,22,37–39,55–58,62].

Point cloud scene flow is another important 3D vision task. Initially, supervised learning was shown to be superior for the task [14,25,26,32,45,51,52].

More recently, self-supervised and unsupervised 3D scene flow and stereo flow methods have been introduced [2,7,13,19,21,28,34,49,50,60,64]. However, these developments have not been utilized for the 3D object detection task up until now.

We propose to employ a scene flow backbone trained in a self-supervised fashion to learn useful representations that other downstream head models can utilize after fine-tuning, such as a 3D object detection head (Fig. 1). First, we follow the cycle-consistency approach [30] to train a FlowNet3D-based [25] scene-flow backbone using self-supervised learning. We introduce architectural changes to the FlowNet3D module to incorporate a point cloud backbone that can also be utilized with a detection head. We explore several training and loss strategies, including auxiliary training, to find the best layout. Empirical evidence obtained from KITTI [12] and nuScenes [5] datasets show that the proposed strategy increases 3D detection performance significantly.

Our method differs from [30] in two important ways. To the best of our knowledge, lidar point cloud-based 3D object detection has not been successfully achieved with a self-supervised backbone up until now. Our modifications to the FlowNet3D [25] architecture enables the integration of point-level temporal changes with 3D detection. Secondly, our combined auxiliary training cycle consistency and supervised 3D detection losses lead to learning more general representations as well as motion representations, which identify objects based on their contextual motion patterns.

A summary of our main contributions is as follows:

– Employing self-supervised point cloud scene flow estimation to learn motion representations for 3D object detection in tandem with supervised fine-tuning
– We show that auxiliary training is the best strategy for using self-supervised cycle-consistency loss along with supervised 3D detection loss.
– The proposed strategy is especially effective with a lesser amount of supervised data. We obtained a significant performance boost when only a smaller part of supervised training data was used for the 3D detection task.

2   Related Work

Scene Flow. Scene flow was first introduced as an extension of optical flow in the third dimension and was estimated with a linear computation algorithm [42]. Stereo cameras [18,43] and RGB-D were also [36] utilized to derive scene flow. Current state-of-the-art uses lidar point clouds and deep neural networks to estimate scene flow with supervised learning [14,25,51]. Most commonly, two subsequent lidar frames are used to estimate the flow vectors of each point in the scene. Building ground truth for such vectors is labor-intensive. As such, synthetic datasets are more popular for scene flow benchmarking [32].

Self-supervised Scene Flow Estimation. Self-supervised scene flow estimation is a relatively understudied angle. A recently proposed solution [30] is to use cycle-consistency and nearest neighbors losses to train an estimation network. Several other distance metrics and regularization techniques such as using chamfer distance, smoothing, and regularization [53] have also been employed for the same task. A more recent study showed that self-supervised scene flow could also be combined with motion segmentation [3].

Self-supervised 3D Object Detection. A monocular 3D object detection model has been trained with self-supervised learning using shape priors and 2D instance masks [4]. Another monocular 3D object detection model with weak supervision has been trained using shape priors [48]. [35] generates random synthetic point cloud scenes for pre-training to learn useful representations from CAD models. [17,23,54] mainly use contrastive pre-training to learn geometrical point cloud representations with different views of the same scene. However, there is not much work focusing on self-supervised 3D object detection considering motion representations with point clouds. We aim to fill this gap in the literature.

3   Method

Backbone of a 3D object detector is mainly used to extract point, voxel, or region features to detect possible objects in that vicinity. Due to the limitation in labelled dataset sizes, we aim to train the backbone on a large unlabelled dataset using self-supervision to obtain good motion-aware point representations. Afterwards, it is possible to use the pre-trained backbone for the 3D detection supervised training with a smaller dataset. Thus, the 3D detection network can benefit from the initialized point motion representations to distinguish objects based on movement patterns. We summarize our method in Fig. 2.

3.1   Problem Definition

Given two subsequent lidar point cloud frames $\mathcal{P}_t = \{\mathbf{p}_i\}_M, \mathbf{p}_i \in \mathbb{R}^3$ and $\mathcal{P}_{t+1} \in \mathbb{R}^{N \times 3}$, we are first interested in estimating the scene flow $\mathcal{F}_{t \to t+1} = \{d_i\}_M$, where $\mathbf{d}_i = \mathbf{p}'_i - \mathbf{p}_i$. $\mathbf{p}'_i$ denotes the new position at time $t + 1$ of point i in the first point cloud $\mathcal{P}_t$. It should be noted that the second point cloud may or may not contain a point corresponding to $\mathbf{p}'_i$ due to sparsity. The second objective is to map $\mathcal{P} \to \{T_j\}_U$, where T_j is the 3D object detection tuple containing class id and bounding box shape and coordinates, using previously-learned spatio-temporal representations. U is the total number of objects in the point cloud frame.

We aim to benefit from the point motion representations learned by the 3D feature extractor, g, during self-supervised scene flow training $\mathcal{F}_{t \to t+1} = s(g(\mathcal{P}_t, \mathcal{P}_{t+1}))$, where s is the scene flow head. In this way, the 3D detection head, h, can use the spatio-temporal motion representations learned in g to better identify complex object point patterns for meaningful detection results such that $\{T_j\}_U = h(g(\mathcal{P}))$.

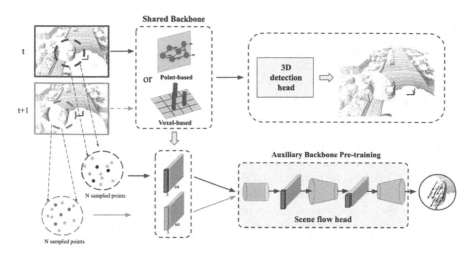

Fig. 2. Our self-supervised 3D object detection pre-training: The auxiliary scene flow head is used to train the 3D detection backbone (point- or voxel-based) for motion-aware point cloud representations with self-supervised cycle consistency loss [30]. The motion representations learned without labelled data can help distinguish objects based on their motion patterns for a 3D downstream task. Then, we further train the pre-trained backbone and a 3D detection head for 3D detection with labelled data.

3.2 Self-supervised Scene Flow

Backbone: We first follow the cycle-consistency approach [30] to train a scene flow estimator. We use a 3D detector's backbone to extract local features of sampled points from two consecutive frames. This allows the self-supervised scene flow gradients to be backpropagated through the backbone. Hence, the backbone learns point representations encoding object movement patterns. The learned spatio-temporal features can be further used to distinguish objects from the background and other objects for the 3D perception task.

Scene Flow Head: The scene flow head based on FlowNet3D [25] generates flow embeddings from local point features provided by the 3D backbone. The shape of input points, $\mathcal{P}_t$, is reconstructed by applying *set upconv layers* to local flow embeddings for the final scene flow estimations $\mathcal{F}_{t \to t+1}$.

Training with Cycle Consistency: We use 3D detection backbone as the feature extractor for the scene flow head. Both the backbone and the scene flow head are trained with the self-supervised cycle consistency loss given in [30]. For the cycle consistency, the scene flow is calculated in forward and backward directions, meaning $\mathcal{F}_{t \to t+1}$ and $\mathcal{F}_{t+1 \to t}$. The $\mathcal{F}_{t+1 \to t}$ makes use of the new positions of the propagated points $\mathbf{p}'_i$ to close the cycle. The $\mathbf{p}''_i$ is the estimated positions of the $\mathbf{p}_i$ in the backward direction with the $\mathcal{F}_{t+1 \to t}$. The mismatch between the $\mathbf{p}_i$ and the $\mathbf{p}''_i$ at frame t allows training of the backbone in a self-supervised way. With the self-supervised training, 3D backbone learns to generate regional flow and motion features from the given set of point clouds.

3.3   Downstream Task: 3D Object Detection

We are interested in the 3D object detection as the 3D downstream task. The scene flow head, s, and the 3D object detection head, h, use the same backbone, g, as seen in Fig. 2. Also, point- or voxel-based 3D backbone encodings can be used. We initialize 3D detector's backbone weights with the pre-trained weights from the auxiliary self-supervised scene flow training. In this way, we assume that the pre-trained backbone from scene flow can already provide good geometry- and motion-aware point features. The 3D detection head takes distinguishable spatio-temporal point cloud features based on different object motion patterns. Hence, the 3D detection network can detect objects more accurately even after supervised training with a smaller labelled dataset. We show the efficacy of our approach in Sect. 5. Note that the scene flow head is for the auxiliary scene flow training and is not used during the 3D detection training and inference.

4   Implementation Details

Our self-supervised auxiliary backbone pre-training approach can be used with different 3D detector architectures. We evaluate our method with mainly three different 3D detectors, Point-GNN[1] [39], CenterPoint[2] [59], and PointPillars (See Footnote 2) [22], which are point-, voxel-based approaches. For the self-supervised scene flow task, we add the modified FlowNet3D as well as the cycle-consistency loss[3] [30] to 3D detectors' training pipelines.

4.1   Pre-training with Self-supervised Scene Flow

The FlowNet3D takes a set of points from two successive frames as input and estimates the flow vectors. The network extracts the point features with two cascaded *PointNet Set Abstraction* modules, each with a 3-layer MLP. We remove the first *PointNet Set Abstraction* module and feed in the point features from 3D detector's backbone to the second *PointNet Set Abstraction* module.

Point Cloud Backbone: We use Point-GNN, PointPillars, and CenterPoint backbones for our main and ablation results. The CenterPoint and PointPillars backbones have the same architecture as we use mmdetection3d [8] implementations. Point-GNN extracts keypoint features from a 3-level graph network used as a backbone, from which we obtain keypoint features of two consecutive point clouds. After sampling N points from each frame, we apply bilinear interpolation to get features of the sampled points from keypoint features according to their positions. We use the settings provided for the best performing Point-GNN with $T = 3$, which represents the number of graph levels. For the CenterPoint and

---

[1] https://github.com/WeijingShi/Point-GNN.
[2] https://github.com/open-mmlab/mmdetection3d/.
[3] https://github.com/HimangiM/Just-Go-with-the-Flow-Self-Supervised-Scene-Flow-Estimation.

PointPillars detectors, we follow a similar approach and use their voxel encoders to obtain features of the sampled points from two consecutive frames without making any changes to the 3D detector's architecture.

Scene Flow Head: Scene flow head is responsible for estimating 3D motion of the points between two sequential frames. The FlowNet3D's scene flow head consists of *flow embedding, set conv layers*, and *set upconv layers* followed by fully-connected layers for estimating point flow vectors. The scene flow head takes the local point features as inputs. We remove only the final *set upconv layer* that takes skip connections from the first *PointNet Set Abstraction* module, which we replace with the 3D detector's backbone.

Training Strategy: We train the point cloud backbone and scene flow head end-to-end using the self-supervised scene flow loss. For the scene flow training on Point-GNN backbone, we initialize our scene flow head weights with the pre-trained FlowNet3D weights on the supervised FlyingThings3D [29] simulation data, we use Stochastic Gradient Descent (SGD) optimizer with 6.25×10^{-5} learning rate. We train the scene flow network for 80k steps on the KITTI tracking dataset without using any labels. The model is trained on a single Nvidia Tesla V100 GPU. We train the PointPillars scene flow network on KITTI tracking dataset using optimizer AdamW with 0.001 learning rate. The training is done with batch size 2 on one Nvidia RTX 2080 GPU for 10 epochs. For the PointPillars- and CenterPoint-based scene flow training on nuScenes dataset, we use AdamW optimizer using the voxel encoders as the bakcbone with a 0.001 learning rate. Our batch size is 2. We train the network for 4 epochs on one Nvidia RTX 3090 GPU. For all networks, we sample $N = 2048$ points per frame.

4.2   3D Detection Fine-tuning

3D Detection Heads: We use Point-GNN, CenterPoint, and PointPillars as the 3D detectors for our results to show the efficacy of our self-supervised scene flow pre-training approach. We initialize detectors' backbone weights with the pre-trained backbone weights from the auxiliary scene flow task for a better point feature representation.

Training Strategy: After initializing weights of the 3D detector backbone from the scene flow task, we further train the backbone and the 3D detection heads with the 3D detection loss. We apply an alternating training strategy between the self-supervised scene flow and supervised 3D detection trainings: **(i)** Train the backbone and the scene flow head for self-supervised scene flow, **(ii)** train the pre-trained backbone and the detection head with 3D detection training, **(iii)** train the backbone from step (ii) and the scene flow head from step (i) for the scene flow, and finally **(iv)** train the backbone from step (iii) and the detection head from step (ii) for 3D detection.

We train the Point-GNN baseline for $1400k$ steps using the SGD optimizer with a learning rate of 0.125 as done in the Point-GNN paper. For the training in step **(ii)** and step **(iv)**, we use SGD with a learning rate of 0.1. The trainings took place on an Nvidia Tesla V100 GPU. We use batch size 4 for all Point-GNN trainings. All the PointPillars and CenterPoint detectors training are on one RTX3090 GPU. For PointPillars on KITTI, we set batch size 18 using AdamW as optimizer with learning rate 0.001. The PointPillars detector on nuScenes is trained for 24 epochs with a learning rate of 0.001 using AdamW optimizer. We use batch size 4 for the detection training. The training of CenterPoint detector is trained for 20 epochs with batch size 20 and the learning rate of 0.001 using the AdamW optimizer.

4.3   Datasets

We use KITTI 3D Object Detection, KITTI Multi-object Tracking datasets [12] as well as nuScenes dataset [5] for the self-supervised scene flow and the supervised 3D detection training and validation.

KITTI 3D Object Detection: KITTI 3D Object Detection dataset consists of 7481 training frames sampled from different drives. Since the provided frames are not sequential, we use lidar point clouds only for 3D object detection training. Only objects visible in the camera-view are annotated. We utilize the common train-val split with 3712 training and 3769 validation samples. For the evaluation, the KITTI average precision (AP) metric is used for three different difficulty levels with $IoU = 0.7$ for the car class.

KITTI Multi-object Tracking: This dataset contains 21 training and 29 testing drives, each of which consists of several sequential frames. We use the tracking dataset only for the self-supervised scene flow training without using any annotations. Therefore, we combine all the training and testing drive data for training except the training drives 11, 15, 16, and 18, which are used for observing cycle consistency validation loss. This gives us 11902 frames for self-supervised scene flow training.

nuScenes: nuScenes is also an autonomous driving dataset, which consists of 700 training and 150 validation drives. The annotations are provided 2 Hz for 360-degree objects and the lidar sweeps are collected 20 Hz. nuScenes is a larger dataset than KITTI and it is collected from denser and more challenging environments. There are 10 classes annotated in the nuScenes dataset. The main metrics are the average precision (AP) per class, mean average precision (mAP) among all classes, and the nuScenes detection score (NDS). Since the provided data contains sequential lidar point clouds, we use this dataset for both self-supervised scene flow and 3D detection trainings.

4.4   Loss

For the 3D object detection training, we keep the same loss functions used for the 3D detectors.

Point-GNN [39]: Point-GNN combines localization, classification, and regularization losses. Classification loss is calculated with the average cross-entropy loss among four classes, which are *background*, horizontal and vertical anchor box classes, and a *don't care* class. The network regresses 7 bounding box parameters for the center, size, and orientation. The Huber loss and $L1$ regularization are used as regression and regularization losses, respectively. We use the original loss coefficients for the total loss.

PointPillars [22]: Similarly, PointPillars regresses the 7 bounding box parameters and utilizes the Huber loss as a regression loss. The orientation is predicted from a set of discrete bins, for which the softmax classification loss is utilized. The focal loss is used as a classification loss for the object classes. All the loss values are combined with respective coefficients for the total loss and we use the default values given in the *mmdetection3d* [8] repository.

CenterPoint [59]: CenterPoint is trained with the focal loss for the heatmap-based classification and the binary cross entropy loss for the IoU-based confidence score. Huber loss is used for the regression of box parameters. We keep the default values given in the *mmdetection3d* [8] repository.

Self-supervised Scene Flow Loss: We utilize the self-supervised loss used in [30] for training the 3D detector backbone and the scene flow head. The loss consists of the nearest neighbor and the cycle consistency losses. The nearest neighbor loss calculates the Euclidean distance of the point $\mathbf{p}'_i$ to its nearest neighbor in frame $t + 1$. $\mathbf{p}'_i$ is the point transformed from frame t to $t + 1$. For the cycle consistency loss calculation the flow is applied in the forward $(\mathcal{F}_{t \to t+1})$ and the backward $(\mathcal{F}_{t+1 \to t})$ directions. The distance between the resulting $\mathbf{p}''_i$ point and its anchor $\mathbf{p}_i$ is used for the cycle consistency loss. Both losses are summed up for the total loss and only this loss is used for the training of the backbone and the scene flow head.

4.5   Experiments

We conduct several experiments to show the efficacy of our self-supervised pre-training method on 3D object detection using Point-GNN, PointPillars, Center-Point, and SSN [63] 3D detectors. First, we compare our self-supervised pre-trained Point-GNN, CenterPoint, and PointPillars with their baselines trained with 100% of the annotated 3D detection data. We show our results on KITTI and nuScenes validation and test sets. Then, we check the performance of our self-supervised detectors and their baselines in the low-data regime by training detectors using only a smaller part of the annotated data in the ablation study. We also report detection accuracy of self-supervised detectors trained with and without alternating training strategy to justify our alternating self-supervised scene flow and supervised 3D detection scheme. Finally, we compare our self-supervised scene flow pre-training method against other self-supervised learning methods.

5   Results and Discussion

In this section, we provide our main results obtained using our scene flow-based self-supervised training with Point-GNN, CenterPoint, and PointPillars 3D detectors on KITTI and nuScenes validation and test sets.

Fig. 3. Qualitative Results: Three different scenes from the KITTI 3D Detection validation set in the columns. Blue and green bounding boxes are for our approach and the baseline Point-GNN [39], respectively. Our method can detect a distant hard object (left-most column) and a moving distant car (middle column) while the baseline misses it. Our method also performs better in a denser environment (right-most column). (Color figure online)

Table 1. Self-supervised Point-GNN & PointPillars compared with the baseline on KITTI val. set for car class. (*Reproduced baseline results for $AP_{R_{40}}$.)

Car (IoU = 0.7)	3D $AP_{R_{40}}$			BEV $AP_{R_{40}}$		
Method	Easy	Mod	Hard	Easy	Mod	Hard
Point-GNN* [39]	90.44	82.12	77.70	93.03	89.31	86.86
Self-supervised Point-GNN	**91.43**	**82.85**	**80.12**	**93.55**	**89.79**	**87.23**
Improvement	+0.99	+0.73	+2.42	+0.52	+0.48	+0.37
PointPillars	85.41	73.98	67.76	89.93	86.57	85.20
Self-supervised PointPillars	**85.92**	**76.33**	**74.32**	**89.96**	**87.44**	**85.53**
Improvement	+0.51	+2.36	+6.56	+0.03	+0.87	+0.33

5.1   Point-GNN

The self-supervised Point-GNN is pre-trained on the scene flow task with cycle consistency loss using KITTI Tracking dataset without any annotations. Following, it is trained with the annotated KITTI 3D detection dataset using the proposed alternating training scheme. The baseline is trained using the same configuration and hyper-parameters. The only difference is that the baseline network weights are initialized randomly. Table 1 shows the 3D and BEV $AP_{R_{40}}$ scores of the baseline and self-supervised Point-GNN on KITTI validation set, where our method outperforms the baseline in all difficulty levels and especially with a large margin in hard difficulty level (2.5%). Similarly, our self-supervised Point-GNN outperforms its baseline on the KITTI test set on hard difficulty level with a 2% improvement. In supplementary material, we also include the same comparison with $AP_{R_{11}}$ metric using the reported Point-GNN results, where our

Table 2. Self-supervised PointPillars compared with the baseline on KITTI test set for car class using 3D $AP_{R_{40}}$ metric.

Car (IoU = 0.7)	3D $AP_{R_{40}}$			BEV $AP_{R_{40}}$		
Method	Easy	Mod	Hard	Easy	Mod	Hard
AVOD [20]	76.39	66.47	60.23	89.75	84.95	78.32
F-PointNet [33]	82.19	69.79	60.59	91.17	84.67	74.77
TANet [27]	84.39	75.94	68.82	91.58	86.54	81.19
Associate-3Ddet [11]	85.99	77.40	70.53	91.40	88.09	82.96
UBER-ATG-MMF [24]	88.40	77.43	70.22	93.67	88.21	81.99
CenterNet3D [46]	86.20	77.90	73.03	91.80	88.46	83.62
SECOND [55]	87.44	79.46	73.97	92.01	88.98	83.67
SERCNN [61]	87.74	78.96	74.30	94.11	88.10	83.43
PointPillars	80.51	68.57	61.79	**90.74**	84.98	79.63
Self-supervised PointPillars	**82.54**	**72.99**	**67.54**	88.92	**85.73**	**80.33**
Improvement	+2.03	+4.42	+5.75	−1.82	+0.75	+0.7

method outperforms the original Point-GNN. These results show that motion-related point representations help distinguish even difficult objects that reflect only a small number of points.

The Fig. 3 shows our qualitative results on KITTI 3D Object Detection scenes. The blue bounding boxes and green bounding boxes indicate results of our approach and the baseline, respectively. We show the bird's eye view and front-view lidar visualizations at the top and middle rows. At the bottom, we show the projected 3D bounding boxes on the image plane. Our approach can detect distant objects (left-most column) better as well as distant and moving objects (middle column). In addition, as seen in the right-most column of Fig. 3, our approach can provide better detection results in a denser scene.

5.2 CenterPoint

Our self-supervised CenterPoint also outperforms the CenterPoint baseline on nuScenes validation and test sets as the mAP and NDS results given in Tables 3 and 4, respectively. We obtained the baseline scores with the best-performing *mmdetection3d* CenterPoint checkpoint [8] for both evaluation sets.

5.3 PointPillars

We also report results of our self-supervised pre-training method using Point-Pillars [22] 3D detector on the nuScenes and KITTI datasets. We pre-train the PointPillars voxel encoder with the self-supervised scene flow task without annotations. Following, the entire PointPillars network is trained on the annotated 3D detection data using our alternating training strategy. We compare our self-supervised PointPillars with its baseline on the KITTI validation and test sets as

Table 3. Self-supervised PointPillars and CenterPoint results on nuScenes validation set. (* mmdetection3d PointPillars checkpoint results, on which we built our work.)

Method	mAP	NDS	Car	Ped	Bus	Barrier	T. C.	Truck	Trailer	Moto.
SECOND [55]	27.12	–	75.53	59.86	29.04	32.21	22.49	21.88	12.96	16.89
PointPillars* [22]	40.02	53.29	80.60	72.40	46.30	52.60	33.60	35.10	26.20	38.40
Self-supervised PointPillars	**42.06**	**55.02**	**81.10**	**74.50**	**49.50**	**54.70**	**34.70**	**38.40**	**29.70**	**38.80**
CenterPoint* [59]	49.13	59.73	83.70	77.40	**61.90**	59.40	**52.90**	50.20	35.00	**44.40**
Self-supervised CenterPoint	**49.94**	**60.06**	**84.10**	**77.90**	61.50	**61.00**	52.50	**51.00**	**35.20**	44.10

given in Tables 1 and 2, respectively. Consistent with the previously-introduced results, our method improves the baseline results with a large margin for the 3D detection task. The increment is the most obvious for 3D AP moderate and hard difficulty levels with 2.4% and 6.6% for the validation set and with 4.4% and 5.8% for the test set.

In Table 3, we compare our self-supervised PointPillars with the baseline on nuScenes validation set. The baseline results are obtained from the best checkpoint given in the well-known mmdetection3d repository [8]. Our self-supervised PointPillars outperforms the baseline with a large increment on mAP and NDS metrics (2%) as well as for all class scores. Moreover, we provide results of our self-supervised PointPillars on nuScenes test set in Table 4 comparing to the previously-submitted PointPillars versions from the nuScenes leaderboard.

Table 4. Self-supervised PointPillars and CenterPoint results on nuScenes test set comparing with other PointPillars-based detector and CenterPoint baseline submissions from the nuScenes leaderboard. The CenterPoint baseline is from mmdetection3d.

Method	mAP	NDS	Car	Ped	Bus	Barrier	T. C.	Truck	Trailer	Moto.
PointPillars [22]	30.50	45.30	68.40	59.70	28.20	38.90	30.80	23.00	23.40	27.40
InfoFocus [47]	39.50	39.50	77.90	63.40	**44.80**	47.80	46.50	31.40	37.30	29.00
PointPillars+ [44]	40.10	55.00	76.00	64.00	32.10	56.40	45.60	31.00	36.60	34.20
Self-supervised PointPillars	**43.63**	**56.28**	**81.00**	**73.10**	37.10	**58.20**	**47.80**	**36.10**	**41.80**	**35.40**
CenterPoint [44]	49.54	59.64	83.40	76.10	54.20	62.40	62.40	44.40	**48.90**	37.80
Self-supervised CenterPoint	**51.42**	**60.92**	**83.80**	**77.00**	**56.80**	**65.10**	**63.90**	**46.30**	48.50	**41.10**

5.4   Ablation Study

We conduct two types of ablation studies to further justify the effectiveness of our self-supervised pre-training approach: (i) performance after training with

Table 5. Self-supervised (SSL) Point-GNN trained with a percentage (1%, 5%, and 20%) of labelled 3D detection data. 3D $AP_{R_{40}}$ results for car class on KITTI val. set.

Training data size	1%			5%			20%		
Car AP (IoU = 0.7)	Easy	Mod	Hard	Easy	Mod	Hard	Easy	Mod	Hard
Point-GNN	63.34	50.92	44.05	81.26	71.27	65.05	88.47	77.20	74.20
SSL Point-GNN	**66.47**	**51.42**	**44.63**	**84.04**	**72.69**	**65.93**	**88.65**	**79.52**	**74.87**
Improvement	+3.13	+0.50	+0.58	+2.78	+1.42	+0.88	+0.18	+2.32	+0.67

limited annotated data and (ii) performance with and without alternating training strategy. Datasets with 3D annotations are mostly limited for the real-world scenarios due to expense and difficulty of requiring expert knowledge for the annotation process. To show our method's enhancement over the baseline using the self-supervised pre-training, we train our self-supervised 3D detectors and baselines with a percentage of the annotated datasets.

In Table 5, we show the performance of self-supervised Point-GNN and the baseline trained with 1%, 5%, and 20% of the KITTI train split. Our method consistently outperforms the baseline for all difficulty levels on KITTI validation set. We note that all self-supervised 3D detector ablation results are obtained without alternating training except the alternating training ablation. We conduct the same experiment for PointPillars, CenterPoint, and SSN 3D detectors on nuScenes validation set and report the results in the supplementary material. Similarly, self-supervised 3D detectors outperform their baselines with large margins. Overall, our results suggest that the self-supervised scene flow pre-training can help learn more representative point-wise features in the lack of labelled training data.

In addition, we conduct an ablation study to justify our alternating training strategy. The alternating training enhances the hard difficulty 3D AP with 2.32% increment for Point-GNN. We think that this improvement is due to the repeated motion-awareness of the backbone brought by the first 3D detection fine-tuning. The detailed 3D and BEV AP results for Point-GNN are provided in the supplementary material. Similarly, the alternating training results for PointPillars, CenterPoint, and SSN 3D detectors reported in the supplementary material support our argument.

5.5   Comparison with Other Self-supervised Learning Methods

Our method is the first study that shows the relation between the self-supervised scene flow and 3D detection representations. Our experiments show that the self-supervised scene flow pre-training provides useful point representations for the supervised 3D detection training. In addition, we compare our CenterPoint-based self-supervised scene flow pre-training against other state-of-the-art self-supervised learning methods in Table 6. Our method performs better than other CenterPoint-based self-supervised methods in the low-data regime on the nuScenes validation set.

Table 6. Comparison against other self-supervised learning methods on nuScenes validation set. GCC3D and PointContrast results are taken from [23].

Approach	Model	5%		10%	
		mAP	NDS	mAP	NDS
PointContrast [54]	CenterPoint [59]	30.79	41.57	38.25	50.1
GCC3D [23]		32.75	44.2	39.14	50.48
Ours		**36.04**	**48.28**	**41.29**	**51.35**

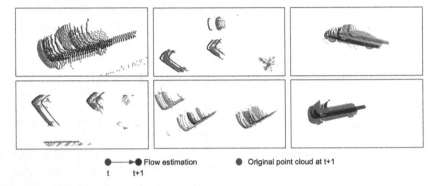

Flow estimation   Original point cloud at t+1
t   t+1

Fig. 4. Sparse scene flow estimation on the sampled KITTI lidar points. Gray points are from the full point clouds at frame $t+1$, red points are sampled points at frame t, and green ones are the propagated points to the frame $t+1$ using scene flow estimation. (Color figure online)

5.6   Sparse Scene Flow Estimations

Figure 4 shows visualized sparse scene flow estimations on the sampled KITTI lidar point clouds obtained using Point-GNN backbone. Red points are the sparsely-sampled points at frame t, which are propagated to the frame $t+1$ using the estimated flow vectors as shown with the green points. The green points closely match the gray points, which are the original point cloud at frame $t+1$. The network is trained with the cycle consistency loss followed by a 100 epoch fine-tuning on the KITTI Scene Flow Dataset following [30]. This suggests that our scene flow network learns useful point features and therefore the point cloud motion patterns, which improves the 3D object detection accuracy.

6   Conclusion

In this study, we propose a self-supervised backbone training approach for 3D object detection. We utilize large unlabelled datasets for self-supervised training of the 3D detection backbone. The scene flow task is used for the self-supervision using the cycle consistency, which helps the backbone learning the point cloud data structure. We show that our approach can improve the detection results of different 3D detectors comparing to their baselines on KITTI and nuScenes datasets. We also show that self-supervised pre-training is especially helpful with the lack of data. Our approach is flexible and can be combined with different point- and voxel-based 3D detectors.

References

1. Asano, Y.M., Rupprecht, C., Vedaldi, A.: Self-labelling via simultaneous clustering and representation learning. arXiv preprint arXiv:1911.05371 (2019)
2. Basha, T., Moses, Y., Kiryati, N.: Multi-view scene flow estimation: a view centered variational approach. Int. J. Comput. Vis. **101**(1), 6–21 (2013). https://doi.org/10.1007/s11263-012-0542-7
3. Baur, S.A., Emmerichs, D.J., Moosmann, F., Pinggera, P., Ommer, B., Geiger, A.: SLIM: self-supervised LiDAR scene flow and motion segmentation. In: Proceedings of the IEEE/CVF International Conference on Computer Vision, pp. 13126–13136 (2021)
4. Beker, D., et al.: Monocular differentiable rendering for self-supervised 3D object detection. In: Vedaldi, A., Bischof, H., Brox, T., Frahm, J.-M. (eds.) ECCV 2020. LNCS, vol. 12366, pp. 514–529. Springer, Cham (2020). https://doi.org/10.1007/978-3-030-58589-1_31
5. Caesar, H., et al.: nuScenes: a multimodal dataset for autonomous driving. In: Proceedings of the IEEE/CVF Conference on Computer Vision and Pattern Recognition, pp. 11621–11631 (2020)
6. Caron, M., Misra, I., Mairal, J., Goyal, P., Bojanowski, P., Joulin, A.: Unsupervised learning of visual features by contrasting cluster assignments. arXiv preprint arXiv:2006.09882 (2020)
7. Chen, Y., Schmid, C., Sminchisescu, C.: Self-supervised learning with geometric constraints in monocular video: connecting flow, depth, and camera. In: Proceedings of the IEEE/CVF International Conference on Computer Vision, pp. 7063–7072 (2019)
8. MMDetection3D Contributors: MMDetection3D: OpenMMLab next-generation platform for general 3D object detection (2020). https://github.com/open-mmlab/mmdetection3d
9. Creß, C., et al.: A9-Dataset: multi-sensor infrastructure-based dataset for mobility research. arXiv preprint arXiv:2204.06527 (2022)
10. Deng, J., Shi, S., Li, P., Zhou, W., Zhang, Y., Li, H.: Voxel R-CNN: towards high performance voxel-based 3D object detection. In: Proceedings of the AAAI Conference on Artificial Intelligence, vol. 35, pp. 1201–1209 (2021)
11. Du, L., et al.: Associate-3Ddet: perceptual-to-conceptual association for 3D point cloud object detection. In: Proceedings of the IEEE/CVF Conference on Computer Vision and Pattern Recognition, pp. 13329–13338 (2020)
12. Geiger, A., Lenz, P., Urtasun, R.: Are we ready for autonomous driving? The KITTI vision benchmark suite. In: 2012 IEEE Conference on Computer Vision and Pattern Recognition, pp. 3354–3361. IEEE (2012)
13. Godard, C., Mac Aodha, O., Firman, M., Brostow, G.J.: Digging into self-supervised monocular depth estimation. In: Proceedings of the IEEE/CVF International Conference on Computer Vision, pp. 3828–3838 (2019)

14. Gu, X., Wang, Y., Wu, C., Lee, Y.J., Wang, P.: HPLFlowNet: hierarchical permutohedral lattice flownet for scene flow estimation on large-scale point clouds. In: Proceedings of the IEEE/CVF Conference on Computer Vision and Pattern Recognition, pp. 3254–3263 (2019)
15. He, C., Zeng, H., Huang, J., Hua, X.S., Zhang, L.: Structure aware single-stage 3D object detection from point cloud. In: Proceedings of the IEEE/CVF Conference on Computer Vision and Pattern Recognition, pp. 11873–11882 (2020)
16. He, K., Fan, H., Wu, Y., Xie, S., Girshick, R.: Momentum contrast for unsupervised visual representation learning. In: Proceedings of the IEEE/CVF Conference on Computer Vision and Pattern Recognition, pp. 9729–9738 (2020)
17. Hou, J., Graham, B., Nießner, M., Xie, S.: Exploring data-efficient 3D scene understanding with contrastive scene contexts. In: Proceedings of the IEEE/CVF Conference on Computer Vision and Pattern Recognition, pp. 15587–15597 (2021)
18. Huguet, F., Devernay, F.: A variational method for scene flow estimation from stereo sequences. In: 2007 IEEE 11th International Conference on Computer Vision, pp. 1–7. IEEE (2007)
19. Hur, J., Roth, S.: Self-supervised monocular scene flow estimation. In: Proceedings of the IEEE/CVF Conference on Computer Vision and Pattern Recognition, pp. 7396–7405 (2020)
20. Ku, J., Mozifian, M., Lee, J., Harakeh, A., Waslander, S.L.: Joint 3D proposal generation and object detection from view aggregation. In: 2018 IEEE/RSJ International Conference on Intelligent Robots and Systems (IROS), pp. 1–8. IEEE (2018)
21. Lai, H.Y., Tsai, Y.H., Chiu, W.C.: Bridging stereo matching and optical flow via spatiotemporal correspondence. In: Proceedings of the IEEE/CVF Conference on Computer Vision and Pattern Recognition, pp. 1890–1899 (2019)
22. Lang, A.H., Vora, S., Caesar, H., Zhou, L., Yang, J., Beijbom, O.: PointPillars: fast encoders for object detection from point clouds. In: Proceedings of the IEEE/CVF Conference on Computer Vision and Pattern Recognition, pp. 12697–12705 (2019)
23. Liang, H., et al.: Exploring geometry-aware contrast and clustering harmonization for self-supervised 3D object detection. In: Proceedings of the IEEE/CVF International Conference on Computer Vision, pp. 3293–3302 (2021)
24. Liang, M., Yang, B., Chen, Y., Hu, R., Urtasun, R.: Multi-task multi-sensor fusion for 3D object detection. In: Proceedings of the IEEE/CVF Conference on Computer Vision and Pattern Recognition, pp. 7345–7353 (2019)
25. Liu, X., Qi, C.R., Guibas, L.J.: FlowNet3D: learning scene flow in 3D point clouds. In: Proceedings of the IEEE/CVF Conference on Computer Vision and Pattern Recognition, pp. 529–537 (2019)
26. Liu, X., Yan, M., Bohg, J.: MeteorNet: deep learning on dynamic 3D point cloud sequences. In: Proceedings of the IEEE/CVF International Conference on Computer Vision, pp. 9246–9255 (2019)
27. Liu, Z., Zhao, X., Huang, T., Hu, R., Zhou, Y., Bai, X.: TANet: robust 3D object detection from point clouds with triple attention. In: Proceedings of the AAAI Conference on Artificial Intelligence, vol. 34, pp. 11677–11684 (2020)
28. Luo, C., et al.: Every Pixel Counts++: joint learning of geometry and motion with 3D holistic understanding. IEEE Trans. Pattern Anal. Mach. Intell. **42**(10), 2624–2641 (2019)
29. Mayer, N., et al.: A large dataset to train convolutional networks for disparity, optical flow, and scene flow estimation. In: Proceedings of the IEEE Conference on Computer Vision and Pattern Recognition, pp. 4040–4048 (2016)

30. Mittal, H., Okorn, B., Held, D.: Just go with the flow: self-supervised scene flow estimation. In: Proceedings of the IEEE/CVF Conference on Computer Vision and Pattern Recognition, pp. 11177–11185 (2020)
31. Purushwalkam, S., Gupta, A.: Demystifying contrastive self-supervised learning: invariances, augmentations and dataset biases. In: Advances in Neural Information Processing Systems, vol. 33 (2020)
32. Puy, G., Boulch, A., Marlet, R.: FLOT: scene flow on point clouds guided by optimal transport. In: Vedaldi, A., Bischof, H., Brox, T., Frahm, J.-M. (eds.) ECCV 2020. LNCS, vol. 12373, pp. 527–544. Springer, Cham (2020). https://doi.org/10.1007/978-3-030-58604-1_32
33. Qi, C.R., Liu, W., Wu, C., Su, H., Guibas, L.J.: Frustum PointNets for 3D object detection from RGB-D data. In: Proceedings of the IEEE Conference on Computer Vision and Pattern Recognition, pp. 918–927 (2018)
34. Ranjan, A., et al.: Competitive collaboration: joint unsupervised learning of depth, camera motion, optical flow and motion segmentation. In: Proceedings of the IEEE/CVF Conference on Computer Vision and Pattern Recognition, pp. 12240–12249 (2019)
35. Rao, Y., Liu, B., Wei, Y., Lu, J., Hsieh, C.J., Zhou, J.: RandomRooms: unsupervised pre-training from synthetic shapes and randomized layouts for 3D object detection. In: Proceedings of the IEEE/CVF International Conference on Computer Vision, pp. 3283–3292 (2021)
36. Shao, L., Shah, P., Dwaracherla, V., Bohg, J.: Motion-based object segmentation based on dense RGB-D scene flow. IEEE Robot. Autom. Lett. **3**(4), 3797–3804 (2018)
37. Shi, S., Guo, C., Jiang, L., Wang, Z., Shi, J., Wang, X., Li, H.: PV-RCNN: point-voxel feature set abstraction for 3D object detection. In: Proceedings of the IEEE/CVF Conference on Computer Vision and Pattern Recognition, pp. 10529–10538 (2020)
38. Shi, S., Wang, X., Li, H.: PointRCNN: 3D object proposal generation and detection from point cloud. In: Proceedings of the IEEE/CVF Conference on Computer Vision and Pattern Recognition, pp. 770–779 (2019)
39. Shi, W., Rajkumar, R.: Point-GNN: graph neural network for 3D object detection in a point cloud. In: Proceedings of the IEEE/CVF Conference on Computer Vision and Pattern Recognition, pp. 1711–1719 (2020)
40. Sun, P., et al.: Scalability in perception for autonomous driving: Waymo open dataset. In: Proceedings of the IEEE/CVF Conference on Computer Vision and Pattern Recognition, pp. 2446–2454 (2020)
41. Tschannen, M., et al.: Self-supervised learning of video-induced visual invariances. In: Proceedings of the IEEE/CVF Conference on Computer Vision and Pattern Recognition, pp. 13806–13815 (2020)
42. Vedula, S., Rander, P., Collins, R., Kanade, T.: Three-dimensional scene flow. IEEE Trans. Pattern Anal. Mach. Intell. **27**(3), 475–480 (2005)
43. Vogel, C., Schindler, K., Roth, S.: 3D scene flow estimation with a piecewise rigid scene model. Int. J. Comput. Vis. **115**(1), 1–28 (2015). https://doi.org/10.1007/s11263-015-0806-0
44. Vora, S., Lang, A.H., Helou, B., Beijbom, O.: PointPainting: sequential fusion for 3D object detection. In: Proceedings of the IEEE/CVF Conference on Computer Vision and Pattern Recognition, pp. 4604–4612 (2020)
45. Wang, G., Wu, X., Liu, Z., Wang, H.: Hierarchical attention learning of scene flow in 3D point clouds. IEEE Trans. Image Process. **30**, 5168–5181 (2021)

46. Wang, G., Tian, B., Ai, Y., Xu, T., Chen, L., Cao, D.: CenterNet3D: an anchor free object detector for autonomous driving. arXiv preprint arXiv:2007.07214 (2020)
47. Wang, J., Lan, S., Gao, M., Davis, L.S.: InfoFocus: 3D object detection for autonomous driving with dynamic information modeling. In: Vedaldi, A., Bischof, H., Brox, T., Frahm, J.-M. (eds.) ECCV 2020. LNCS, vol. 12355, pp. 405–420. Springer, Cham (2020). https://doi.org/10.1007/978-3-030-58607-2_24
48. Wang, R., Yang, N., Stückler, J., Cremers, D.: DirectShape: direct photometric alignment of shape priors for visual vehicle pose and shape estimation. In: 2020 IEEE International Conference on Robotics and Automation (ICRA), pp. 11067–11073. IEEE (2020)
49. Wang, X., Gupta, A.: Unsupervised learning of visual representations using videos. In: Proceedings of the IEEE International Conference on Computer Vision, pp. 2794–2802 (2015)
50. Wang, X., Jabri, A., Efros, A.A.: Learning correspondence from the cycle-consistency of time. In: Proceedings of the IEEE/CVF Conference on Computer Vision and Pattern Recognition, pp. 2566–2576 (2019)
51. Wang, Z., Li, S., Howard-Jenkins, H., Prisacariu, V., Chen, M.: FlowNet3D++: geometric losses for deep scene flow estimation. In: Proceedings of the IEEE/CVF Winter Conference on Applications of Computer Vision, pp. 91–98 (2020)
52. Wei, Y., Wang, Z., Rao, Y., Lu, J., Zhou, J.: PV-RAFT: point-voxel correlation fields for scene flow estimation of point clouds. In: Proceedings of the IEEE/CVF Conference on Computer Vision and Pattern Recognition, pp. 6954–6963 (2021)
53. Wu, W., Wang, Z., Li, Z., Liu, W., Fuxin, L.: PointPWC-Net: a coarse-to-fine network for supervised and self-supervised scene flow estimation on 3D point clouds. arXiv preprint arXiv:1911.12408 (2019)
54. Xie, S., Gu, J., Guo, D., Qi, C.R., Guibas, L., Litany, O.: PointContrast: unsupervised pre-training for 3D point cloud understanding. In: Vedaldi, A., Bischof, H., Brox, T., Frahm, J.-M. (eds.) ECCV 2020. LNCS, vol. 12348, pp. 574–591. Springer, Cham (2020). https://doi.org/10.1007/978-3-030-58580-8_34
55. Yan, Y., Mao, Y., Li, B.: Second: sparsely embedded convolutional detection. Sensors **18**(10), 3337 (2018)
56. Yang, Z., Sun, Y., Liu, S., Jia, J.: 3DSSD: point-based 3D single stage object detector. In: Proceedings of the IEEE/CVF Conference on Computer Vision and Pattern Recognition, pp. 11040–11048 (2020)
57. Yang, Z., Sun, Y., Liu, S., Shen, X., Jia, J.: STD: sparse-to-dense 3D object detector for point cloud. In: Proceedings of the IEEE/CVF International Conference on Computer Vision, pp. 1951–1960 (2019)
58. Ye, M., Xu, S., Cao, T.: HVNet: hybrid voxel network for LiDAR based 3D object detection. In: Proceedings of the IEEE/CVF Conference on Computer Vision and Pattern Recognition, pp. 1631–1640 (2020)
59. Yin, T., Zhou, X., Krahenbuhl, P.: Center-based 3D object detection and tracking. In: Proceedings of the IEEE/CVF Conference on Computer Vision and Pattern Recognition, pp. 11784–11793 (2021)
60. Yin, Z., Shi, J.: GeoNet: unsupervised learning of dense depth, optical flow and camera pose. In: Proceedings of the IEEE Conference on Computer Vision and Pattern Recognition, pp. 1983–1992 (2018)
61. Zhou, D., et al.: Joint 3D instance segmentation and object detection for autonomous driving. In: Proceedings of the IEEE/CVF Conference on Computer Vision and Pattern Recognition, pp. 1839–1849 (2020)

62. Zhou, Y., Tuzel, O.: VoxelNet: end-to-end learning for point cloud based 3D object detection. In: Proceedings of the IEEE Conference on Computer Vision and Pattern Recognition, pp. 4490–4499 (2018)

63. Zhu, X., Ma, Y., Wang, T., Xu, Y., Shi, J., Lin, D.: SSN: shape signature networks for multi-class object detection from point clouds. In: Vedaldi, A., Bischof, H., Brox, T., Frahm, J.-M. (eds.) ECCV 2020. LNCS, vol. 12370, pp. 581–597. Springer, Cham (2020). https://doi.org/10.1007/978-3-030-58595-2_35

64. Zou, Y., Luo, Z., Huang, J.-B.: DF-Net: unsupervised joint learning of depth and flow using cross-task consistency. In: Ferrari, V., Hebert, M., Sminchisescu, C., Weiss, Y. (eds.) ECCV 2018. LNCS, vol. 11209, pp. 38–55. Springer, Cham (2018). https://doi.org/10.1007/978-3-030-01228-1_3

Open Vocabulary Object Detection with Pseudo Bounding-Box Labels

Mingfei Gao$^{(\boxtimes)}$, Chen Xing, Juan Carlos Niebles, Junnan Li, Ran Xu, Wenhao Liu, and Caiming Xiong

Salesforce Research, Palo Alto, USA
{mingfei.gao,cxing,jniebles,junnan.li,ran.xu,wenhao.liu, cxiong}@salesforce.com

Abstract. Despite great progress in object detection, most existing methods work only on a limited set of object categories, due to the tremendous human effort needed for bounding-box annotations of training data. To alleviate the problem, recent open vocabulary and zero-shot detection methods attempt to detect novel object categories beyond those seen during training. They achieve this goal by training on a pre-defined base categories to induce generalization to novel objects. However, their potential is still constrained by the small set of base categories available for training. To enlarge the set of base classes, we propose a method to automatically generate pseudo bounding-box annotations of diverse objects from large-scale image-caption pairs. Our method leverages the localization ability of pre-trained vision-language models to generate pseudo bounding-box labels and then directly uses them for training object detectors. Experimental results show that our method outperforms the state-of-the-art open vocabulary detector by 8% AP on COCO novel categories, by 6.3% AP on PASCAL VOC, by 2.3% AP on Objects365 and by 2.8% AP on LVIS. *Code is available here.*

Keywords: Open vocabulary detection · Pseudo bounding-box labels

1 Introduction

Object detection [11,19,20,27] is a core task in computer vision that has considerably advanced with the adoption of deep learning and continues to attract significant research effort [26,31,33]. Current deep object detection methods achieve astonishing performance when learning a pre-defined set of object categories that have been annotated in a large number of training images (PASCAL VOC [6], COCO [17]). Unfortunately, their success is still limited to detecting

---

M.Gao and C. Xing contributed equally.

Supplementary Information The online version contains supplementary material available at https://doi.org/10.1007/978-3-031-20080-9_16.

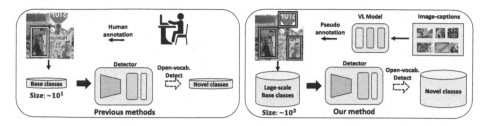

Fig. 1. Previous methods (left) rely on human-provided box-level annotations of pre-defined base classes during training and attempt to generalize to objects of novel classes during inference. Our method (right) generates pseudo bounding-box annotations from large-scale image-caption pairs by leveraging the localization ability of pre-trained vision-language (VL) models. Then, we utilize them to improve our open vocabulary object detector. Compared to the human annotations of a fixed/small set of base classes, our pseudo bounding-box label generator easily scales to a large set of diverse objects from the large-scale image-caption dataset, thus is able to achieve better detection performance on novel objects compared to previous methods

a small number of object categories (e.g., 80 categories in COCO). One reason is that most detection methods rely on supervision in the form of instance-level bounding-box annotations, hence requiring very expensive human labeling efforts to build training datasets. Furthermore, when we need to detect objects from a new category, one has to further annotate a large number of bounding-boxes in images for this new object category.

Two families of recent work have attempted to reduce the need of annotating new object categories: zero-shot object detection and open vocabulary object detection. In zero-shot detection methods [1,22], object detection models are trained on *base* object categories with human-provided bounding box annotations to promote their generalization ability on *novel* object categories, by exploiting correlations between base and novel categories. These methods can alleviate the need for large amounts of human labeled data to some extent. Building on top of such methods, open vocabulary object detection [34] aims to improve the detection performance of novel objects with the help of image captions. However, the potential of existing zero-shot and open vocabulary methods is constrained by the small size of the base category set at training, due to the high cost of acquiring large-scale bounding-box annotations of diverse objects. As a result, it is still challenging for them to generalize well to diverse objects of novel categories in practice.

A potential avenue for improvement is to enable open vocabulary detection models to utilize a larger set of base classes of diverse objects by reducing the requirement of manual annotations. In this paper we ask: can we automatically generate bounding-box annotations for objects at scale using existing resources? Can we use these generated annotations to improve open vocabulary detection? The most recent progress on vision-language pre-training gives us some hope. Vision-language models [12,15,16,21,28] are pre-trained with large scale image-caption pairs from the web. They show amazing zero-shot performance on image classification, as well as promising results on tasks related to text-visual region alignment, such as referring expressions, which implies strong localization ability.

Motivated by these observations, we improve open vocabulary object detection using pseudo bounding-box annotations generated from large-scale image-caption pairs, by taking advantage of the localization ability of pre-trained vision-language models. As shown in Fig. 1, we design a pseudo bounding-box label generation strategy to automatically obtain pseudo box annotations of a diverse set of objects from existing image-caption datasets. Specifically, given a pre-trained vision-language model and an image-caption pair, we compute an activation map (Grad-CAM [24]) in the image that corresponds to an object of interest mentioned in the caption. We then convert the activation map into a pseudo bounding-box label for the corresponding object category. Our open vocabulary detector is then directly trained with supervision of these pseudo labels. Our detector can also be fine-tuned with human-provided bounding boxes if they are available. Since our method for generating pseudo bounding-box labels is fully automated with no manual intervention, the size and diversity of the training data, including the number of training object categories, can be largely increased. This enables our approach to outperform existing zero-shot/open vocabulary detection methods that are trained with a limited set of base categories.

We evaluate the effectiveness of our method by comparing with the state-of-the-art (SOTA) zero-shot and open vocabulary object detectors on four widely used datasets: COCO, PASCAL VOC, Objects365 and LVIS. Experimental results show that our method outperforms the best open vocabulary detection method by 8% mAP on novel objects on COCO, when both of the methods are fine-tuned with COCO base categories. Moreover, we surprisingly find that even when not fine-tuned with COCO base categories, our method can still outperform fine-tuned SOTA baseline by 3% mAP. We also evaluate the generalization performance of our method to other datasets. Experimental results show that under this setting, our method outperforms existing approaches by 6.3%, 2.3% and 2.8% on PASCAL VOC, Objects365 and LVIS, respectively.

Our contributions are summarized as follows: (1) We propose an open vocabulary object detection method that can train detectors with pseudo bounding-box annotations generated from large-scale image-caption pairs. To the best of our knowledge, this is the first work which enables open vocabulary object detection using pseudo labels during training. (2) We introduce a pseudo label generation strategy using the existing pre-trained vision-language models. (3) With the help of pseudo labels, our method largely outperforms the SOTA methods. Moreover, when trained with only pseudo labels, our method achieves higher performance than the SOTA that rely on training with manual bounding-box annotations.

2   Related Work

Object detection aims at localizing objects in images. Traditional detection methods are supervised using human-provided bounding box annotations. Two-stage detection methods [8,11,23] are one of the most popular frameworks. These methods generate object proposals in the first stage and classify these proposals to different categories in the second stage. Weakly supervised object detectors seek to relieve such heavy human annotation burden by using image-level labels such as image-level object categories [2,29], captions [32] and object counts [7] for training. Although these approaches show promising performance, they only support objects in a fixed set of categories. Whenever one needs to detect objects from a new category, they have to collect and manually annotate instances from the new category and retrain the detector.

Open vocabulary and zero-shot object detection target at training an object detector with annotations on base object classes to generalize to novel object classes during inference. Most zero-shot detection methods achieve this level of generalization by aligning the visual and the text representation spaces for objects from base classes during training [1,22,36], and inferring novel objects during inference by exploiting correlation between base and novel objects. Recent methods encourage the visual-semantic alignment for novel objects by different strategies such as synthesizing visual representations of novel classes [35,36] or utilizing existing object names semantically similar to their names [22]. Joseph et al. introduce OREO [13] to incrementally learn unknown objects based on contrastive clustering and energy based unknown identification. To further improve the zero-shot performance on novel object categories, Zareian et al. [34] propose open vocabulary object detection that transfers knowledge from a pre-trained vision-language model by initializing their detector with parameters of the image encoder of the vision-language model. This strategy improves the state-of-the-art by a large margin. Gu et al. [9] propose ViLD which achieves good zero-shot performance by distilling knowledge from a large-scale vision-language model (CLIP [21]). However, all these methods are trained with a small set of base categories that have bounding-box labels since acquiring bounding-box annotations of diverse objects in large-scale training data is expensive. In practice, if a novel category at inference is very different from base categories, it is still challenging for these methods to generalize well to such novel objects. In contrast, our method generates pseudo box labels for diverse objects from large-scale image-caption pairs and use them to train the detector. When human-provided box annotations are available, our framework has the flexibility to utilize them.

Vision-language pre-training models are trained with large-scale image-caption pairs. They have been successful not only in image-language tasks such as image retrieval, VQA and referring expression [12,15,16,28], but also in pure image tasks such as zero-shot image classification [21]. Recent methods typically utilize a multi-modal module to encourage the interaction between the vision and language modalities [15,16,28], which may implicitly encode the word-to-region localization information inside the model. We take advantage of their localization ability and design a strategy to obtain pseudo bounding-box labels of a large and diverse set of objects from the large-scale image-caption datasets. With this strategy, we largely improve open vocabulary object detection.

3   Our Approach

Our framework contains two components: a pseudo bounding-box label generator and an open vocabulary object detector. Our pseudo label generator automatically generates bounding-box labels for a diverse set of objects by leveraging a pre-trained vision-language model. We then train our detector directly with the generated pseudo labels. For fair comparison with existing open vocabulary detection methods, when base object categories with human annotated bounding-boxes are available, we can also fine-tune our trained detector with such data.

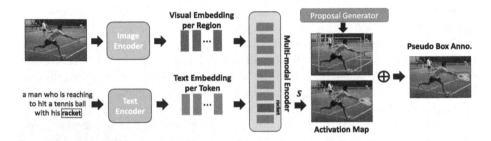

Fig. 2. Illustration of our pseudo box label generation process. The input to the system is an image-caption pair. We use image and text encoders to extract the visual and text embeddings of the image and its corresponding caption. We then obtain multi-modal features by image-text interaction via cross-attention. We maintain objects of interest in our pre-defined object vocabulary. For each object of interest embedded in the caption (for example, *racket* in this figure), we use Grad-CAM to visualize its activation map in the image. This map indicates the contribution of the image regions to the final representation of the object word. Finally, we determine the pseudo bounding-box label of the object by selecting the object proposal that has the largest overlap with the activation

3.1   Generating Pseudo Box Labels

Figure 2 illustrates the overall procedure of our pseudo label generation. Our goal is to generate pseudo bounding-box annotations for objects of interest in an image, by leveraging the implicit alignment between regions in the image and words in its corresponding caption in a pre-trained vision-language model. Before diving into our method, we first briefly introduce the general structure of the recent vision-language models.

An image $\mathbf{I}$ and its corresponding caption, $\mathbf{X} = \{x_1, x_2, \ldots, x_{N_T}\}$, are the inputs to the model, where N_T is the number of words in the caption (including [CLS] and [SEP]). An image encoder is used to extract image features $\mathbf{V} \in \mathbb{R}^{N_V \times d}$ and a text encoder is utilized to get text representations $\mathbf{T} \in \mathbb{R}^{N_T \times d}$. N_V is the number of region representations of the image. Moreover, a multi-modal encoder with L consecutive cross-attention layers is often employed to fuse the information from both image and text encoders. In the l-th cross-attention layer, the interaction of an object of interest x_t in the caption with the image regions is shown in Eqs. 1 and 2, where $\mathbf{A}_t^l$ denotes the corresponding visual attention scores at the l-th cross-attention layer. $\mathbf{h}_t^{l-1}$ indicates the hidden representations obtained from the previous $(l-1)$-th cross-attention layer and $\mathbf{h}_t^0$ is the representation of x_t from the text encoder.

$$\mathbf{A}_t^l = \text{Softmax}(\frac{\mathbf{h}_t^{l-1}\mathbf{V}^T}{\sqrt{d}}), \tag{1}$$

$$\mathbf{h}_t^l = \mathbf{A}_t^l \cdot \mathbf{V}. \tag{2}$$

From these equations, a cross-attention layer measures the relevance of the visual region representations with respect to a token in the input caption, and calculates the weighted average of all visual region representations accordingly. As a result, the visual attention scores $\mathbf{A}_t^l$ can directly reflect how important different visual regions are to token x_t. Therefore, we visualize the activation maps based on the attention scores to locate an object in an image given its name in the caption.

We use Grad-CAM [24] as the visualization method and follow its original setting to take the final output s from the multi-modal encoder, and calculate its gradient with respect to the attention scores. s is a scalar that represents the similarity between the image and its caption. Specifically, the final activation map $\mathbf{\Phi}_t$ of the image given an object name x_t is calculated as

$$\mathbf{\Phi}_t = \mathbf{A}_t^l \cdot \max(\frac{\partial s}{\partial \mathbf{A}_t^l}, 0). \tag{3}$$

If there are multiple attention heads in a cross-attention layer, we average the activation map $\mathbf{\Phi}_t$ from all heads as the final activation map.

After we get an activation map of an object of interest in the caption using this strategy, we draw a bounding box covering the activated region as the pseudo label of the category. We adopt existing proposal generators, e.g., [11,30] to generate proposal candidates $\mathbf{B} = \{b_1, b_2, \ldots, b_K\}$ and select the one overlapping the most with $\mathbf{\Phi}_t$:

$$\hat{b} = \arg\max_i \frac{\sum_{b_i} \mathbf{\Phi}_t(b_i)}{\sqrt{|b_i|}}, \tag{4}$$

where $\sum_{b_i} \mathbf{\Phi}_t(b_i)$ indicates summation of the activation map within a box proposal and $|b_i|$ indicates the proposal area. In practice, we maintain a list of objects of interest (referred as object vocabulary) during training and get pseudo bounding-box annotations for all objects in the training vocabulary (see Sect. 4.1 for details). Figure 4 shows some examples of the activation maps. As we can see, the activated regions correspond well with the relevant regions. The generated bounding boxes are of good quality. When they are directly used to train an open vocabulary object detector, the object detector significantly outperforms the current SOTA open-vocabulary/zero-shot object detectors.

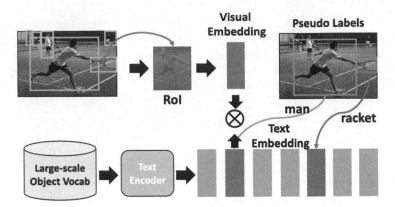

Fig. 3. Illustration of our detector. An image is processed by a feature extractor followed by a region proposal network. Region-based features are then calculated by applying RoI pooling/RoI align over region proposals and the corresponding visual embeddings are obtained. Similarity of the visual and text embeddings of the same object are encouraged during training

3.2 Open Vocabulary Object Detection with Pseudo Labels

After we get pseudo bounding-box labels, we can use them to train an object detector. Since our pseudo-label generation is disentangled from detector training process, our framework can accommodate detectors with any architecture. In this work, we focus on the open vocabulary scenario where a detector aims at detecting arbitrary objects during inference.

A general open vocabulary detection system [34] is shown in Fig. 3. A feature map is extracted from an input image using a feature extractor based on which object proposals are generated. Then, region-based visual embeddings, $\mathbf{R} = \{\mathbf{r}_1, \mathbf{r}_2, \ldots, \mathbf{r}_{N_r}\}$, are obtained by RoI pooling/RoI align [11] followed by a fully connected layer, where N_r denotes the number of regions. In the meanwhile, text embeddings, $\mathbf{C} = \{\mathbf{bg}, \mathbf{c}_1, \mathbf{c}_2, \ldots, \mathbf{c}_{N_c}\}$, of object candidates from the object vocabulary are acquired by a pre-trained text encoder, where N_c is the training object vocabulary size and $\mathbf{bg}$ indicates "background" that matches irrelevant visual regions. The goal of the open vocabulary object detector is to pull close the visual and text embeddings of the same objects and push away those of different objects. The probability of $\mathbf{r}_i$ matches $\mathbf{c}_j$ is calculated as

$$p(\mathbf{r}_i \text{ matches } \mathbf{c}_j) = \frac{\exp\left(\mathbf{r}_i \cdot \mathbf{c}_j\right)}{\exp(\mathbf{r}_i \cdot \mathbf{bg}) + \sum_k \exp\left(\mathbf{r}_i \cdot \mathbf{c}_k\right)}, \tag{5}$$

where text embeddings $\mathbf{C}$ is fixed during training. The cross entropy loss is used to encourage the matching of positive pairs and discourage the negative ones.

During inference, given a group of object classes of interest, a region proposal will be matched to the object class if its text embedding has the smallest distance to the visual embedding of the region compared to all object names in the vocabulary. This strategy is similar to other zero-shot/open vocabulary detection methods. To perform a fair comparison to prior work, we also adopt Mask-RCNN as the base of our open vocabulary detector. We set **bg=0** and include objectness classification, objectness box regression and class-agnostic box regression losses following [34].

4   Experiments

4.1   Datasets and Object Vocabulary for Training

Training Datasets. In our method, we generate pseudo bounding-box annotations of diverse objects from a combination of existing image-caption datasets including COCO Caption [3], Visual-Genome [14], and SBU Caption [18]. Our final dataset for pseudo label generation and detector training contains about one million images.

Object Vocabulary. When we generate pseudo labels for object categories from the aforementioned dataset, our default object vocabulary is constructed by the union of all the object names in COCO, PASCAL VOC, Objects365 and LVIS, resulting in 1,582 categories. We would also like to note that since our method doesn't require extra human annotation efforts, our training object vocabulary can be easily augmented.

4.2   Evaluation Benchmarks

Baselines. We compare with recent zero-shot and open vocabulary methods [1,22,34,36]. Among the baselines, *Zareian et al.* [34] is the SOTA method, thus, is treated as our major baseline.

Generalized Setting in COCO. Most existing methods are evaluated under this setting proposed in [1]. COCO detection training set is split to base set containing 48 base/seen classes and target set including 17 novel/unseen classes. Base classes are used for training. During inference, models predict object categories from the union of base and novel classes. The performance of models is evaluated using the mean average precision over the novel classes.

Our method can be trained using the large-scale dataset with the generated pseudo labels. To perform a fair comparison with baselines, we fine-tune our detector using COCO base categories following their setup. Moreover, we also report our method's performance without fine-tuning on COCO base categories.

Generalization Ability to Other Datasets. We are interested in measuring the generalization ability of a model to other datasets that the model is not trained on. Therefore, we evaluate our method and the strongest baseline (both are fine-tuned using COCO base classes) on PASCAL VOC [5] test set, Objects365 v2 [25] validation set and LVIS [10] validation set[1]. PASCAL VOC

---

[1] We use LVIS v0.5, since the validation set of LVIS v1.0 contains images from *COCO train 2017* which our method may finetune on in some experiments.

Table 1. Performance on COCO dataset. Our method outperforms all the previous approaches when all models are fine-tuned on COCO base categories. When our method is not fine-tuned, it still outperforms other fine-tuned baselines

Method	Fine-tuned with Box Anno. on COCO **Base** categories	Generalized setting		
		Novel AP	Base AP	Overall AP
Bansal et al. [1]	Yes	0.3	29.2	24.9
Zhu et al. [36]	Yes	3.4	13.8	13.0
Rahman et al. [22]	Yes	4.1	35.9	27.9
Zareian et al. [34]	Yes	22.8	46.0	39.9
Our method	Yes	**30.8**	46.1	42.1
Our method	No	**25.8**	–	–

Table 2. Generalization performances to other datasets. Our method has better generalization performance to other datasets compared to *Zareian et al.*

Method	Fine-tuned on COCO **Base** categories	PASCAL VOC	Objects365	LVIS
Zareian [34]	Yes	52.9	4.6	5.2
Our method	Yes	**59.2**	**6.9**	**8.0**
Our method	No	44.4	**5.1**	**6.5**

is a widely used dataset by traditional object detection methods which contains 20 object categories. Objects365 and LVIS are datasets include 365 and 1,203 object categories, respectively, which makes them very challenging. When evaluating on each of these datasets (PASCAL VOC, Objects365 and LVIS), visual regions will be matched to one of the object categories (including background) of each dataset during inference.

Evaluation Metric. Following prior work [34], we use the standard metric in object detection tasks, i.e., mean average precision over classes, and set the IoU threshold to 0.5.

4.3   Implementation Details

In our main experiment, we use the ALBEF model pre-trained with 14M data[2] as our vision-language model for pseudo label generation. We follow the default setting of ALBEF, unless otherwise noted. The cross-attention layer used for Grad-CAM visualization is set to $l = 8$ in Eq. 3. We conduct our main experiments using ALBEF because of its good performance in object grounding when image captions are present. Note that other pre-trained vision-language models

---

[2] https://github.com/salesforce/ALBEF (BSD-3-Clause License).

Table 3. Effect of proposal quality. All models are fine-tuned on COCO base classes. Better proposals lead to better detection performance

Method	Proposal generator	Generalized COCO novel	PASCAL VOC	Objects365	LVIS
Zareian et al. [34]	–	22.8	52.9	4.6	5.2
Our method	Selective Search	**28.5**	**53.0**	**5.5**	**5.9**
	Mask-RCNN	**30.8**	**59.2**	**6.9**	**8.0**

Table 4. Effect of different vision-language models. All models are fine-tuned on COCO base classes. Better VL model leads to better detection performance

Method	VL model	Generalized COCO novel	PASCAL VOC	Objects365	LVIS
Zareian et al. [34]	–	22.8	52.9	4.6	5.2
Our method	LXMERT [28]	**27.0**	**56.5**	**5.5**	**6.4**
	ALBEF [15]	**30.8**	**59.2**	**6.9**	**8.0**

can also fit our framework without major modifications or adding additional constraints on detector training. We conduct an ablation study to show our method's performance when another pre-trained vision-language model (LXMERT [28]) is employed in Sect. 4.5. As a default option, we use a off-the-shelf Mask-RCNN with ResNet-50 trained on COCO 2017 train set as our proposal generator. To ensure there is no labels of novel categories leaking to our model, we have excluded the novel categories when training the proposal generator. We also show our results with an unsupervised proposal generator, selective search [30], in Sect. 4.5.

We use Mask-RCNN with ResNet-50 as the base of our open vocabulary detector and keep following the default settings here[3]. We utilize the pre-trained CLIP (ViT-B/32) text encoder to extract text embeddings of objects in our vocabulary and use the text prompts provided in [9] to ensemble the text representation. We use a batch size of 64 with learning rate of 0.02 when training the open vocabulary detector using our large-scale dataset with pseudo bounding-box labels, and a batch size of 8 with base learning rate of 0.0005 when optionally fine-tuning on COCO base classes. Models are optimized using SGD. The weight decay is set to 0.0001. The maximum iteration number is 150,000 and the learning rate is updated by a decreasing factor of 0.1 at 60,000 and 120,000 iterations.

4.4 Experimental Results

As shown in Table 1, when fine-tuned using COCO base categories same as our baselines, our method outperforms our strongest baseline (*Zareian et al.*) largely

---

[3] https://github.com/alirezazareian/ovr-cnn (MIT License).

Table 5. Performance of our method when using vocabularies of different sizes for pseudo label generation. $\mathbb{V}^-$ and $\mathbb{V}$ contain 65 and 1.5k+ categories, respectively

Methods	Vocabulary	Generalized setting		
		Novel AP (17)	Base AP (48)	Overall AP (65)
Zareian et al. [34]	–	22.8	46.0	39.9
Our method	$\mathbb{V}^-$(65)	**29.7**	44.3	40.4
	$\mathbb{V}$ (1.5k+)	**30.8**	46.1	42.1

Table 6. Performance of our method when trained with pseudo labels generated from different amounts of data. All models are fine-tuned using COCO base categories. Our performance improves when trained with pseudo labels of more data

Methods	Data of pseudo label generation	Generalized setting		
		Novel AP (17)	Base AP (48)	Overall AP (65)
Zareian et al. [34]	–	22.8	46.0	39.9
Our method	COCO Cap	**29.1**	44.4	40.4
	COCO Cap, VG, SBU	**30.8**	46.1	42.1

by 8%. When not fine-tuned using COCO base categories and only trained with generated pseudo labels, our method achieves 25.8% AP on the novel categories, which still significantly outperforms the SOTA method (*Zareian et al.*) by 3%.

Generalization ability to a wide range of datasets is also important for an open vocabulary object detector, since it makes a detector directly usable as an out-of-the-box method in the wild. Table 2 shows the generalization performance of detectors to different datasets, where both our method and our baseline are not trained using these datasets. Since objects365 and LVIS have a large set of diverse object categories, evaluation results on these datasets would be more representative to demonstrate the generalization ability. Results show that our method achieves better performance than *Zareian et al.* on all three datasets when both of the methods are fine-tuned with COCO base categories. Our method improves the results of our baseline by 2.3% in Objects365 and 2.8% on LVIS. Besides, our fine-tuned method beats the SOTA largely by 6.3% on PASCAL VOC. When not fine-tuned with COCO base categories, the performance of our method still outperforms *Zareian et al.* (fine-tuned with COCO base categories) on Objects365 and LVIS. When not fine-tuned, our method's underperforms our fine-tuned baseline on PASCAL VOC. It is very likely because of that there is a large semantic overlap between the COCO base categories and PASCAL VOC object categories. Therefore, fine-tuning on COCO base set helps the model's transfer ability to PASCAL VOC.

4.5 Ablation Study

How Does the Quality of Bounding-Box Proposals Affect Performance? Our pseudo label generator combines object proposals and the acti-

Table 7. Performance of our method with different text encoders

Method	Text encoder	Generalized setting		
		Novel AP	Base AP	Overall AP
Zareian et al. [34]	Bert	22.8	46.0	39.9
Our method	Bert	**28.8**	45.1	40.9
	CLIP	**30.8**	46.1	42.1

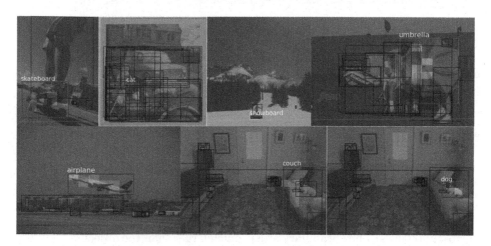

Fig. 4. Visualization of some activation maps. Colorful blocks indicate values of Grad-CAM activation map in the corresponding regions. We zero out blocks with values smaller than half of the max value in the map so the main focus is highlighted. Black boxes indicate object proposals and read boxes indicate the final selected pseudo bounding-box labels (Color figure online)

vation map to select boxes. Generally, the better the proposals are, the more accurate our pseudo bounding-box annotations would be. The default proposal generator in our main experiments is a Mask-RCNN trained with COCO detection category excluding the novel categories. To analyze the effect of proposal quality, we also run experiments with an unsupervised proposal generator, Selective Search [30] and summarize results in Table 3. The results show that our method with Selective Search outperforms *Zareian et al.* with a clear margin. This demonstrates the effectiveness of our method even with an unsupervised proposal generator.

What Is the Effect of Different Pre-trained Vision-Language Models? Besides the utilization of ALBEF in our main experiment, we also experiment with LXMERT [28], which is an earlier vision-language model that also fuses information from both the vision and language modalities. Specifically, we generate pseudo labels based on the activation map in the last layer of the (text-to-vision) cross-attention module. Results are shown in Table 4. It shows that

Fig. 5. Visualization of our generated pseudo bounding-box annotations on COCO. The red boxes indicate successful cases and the yellow one denote failure case. Our pseudo label generator can generate objects (slippers, pot and pie) that are not covered by COCO's category list. The generator cannot capture an object if it is not shown in the caption (e.g. the car in the last column) (Color figure online)

with LXMERT, our method's performance is slightly worse compared with our method using ALBEF. This may due to the fact that LXMERT employs less image-caption data for training. While compared with *Zareian et al.*, our method with LXMERT still performs significantly better.

What Is the Effect of Our Object Vocabulary Size? We utilize an object vocabulary containing over 1.5k object categories ($\mathbb{V}$) by default when generating our pseudo labels. The vocabulary size is much larger than the object vocabulary of any dataset we evaluated on, such as base and novel object categories in COCO ($\mathbb{V}^-$). A natural question is, for performance of COCO novel categories, for example, would it be better if we just use $\mathbb{V}^-$ for pseudo-box generation and detector training? To answer the question, we conduct experiments using these two scales of vocabularies. Experimental results in Table 5 show that $\mathbb{V}$ leads to better performance than $\mathbb{V}^-$ on COCO novel categories. The results suggest that adding additional object categories outside the COCO categories during pre-training will benefit our model performance. Besides, using the larger vocabulary improves model's generalization ability to datasets that include a large set of object categories, i.e., Objects365 and LVIS. We observe that using $\mathbb{V}$ improves results of $\mathbb{V}^-$ by 2.3% in Objects365 and by 2.7% in LVIS.

Does More Data for Pseudo Label Generation Help? Our pseudo labels are generated from image-caption pairs. Intuitively, the more data is used for pseudo label generation, the larger amount of diverse objects will be utilized for training our open vocabulary detector. As a result, our model performance should be improved. We show the performance of our method using pseudo labels with different amounts of image-caption pairs in Table 6. Results show that our method can benefit from a larger dataset. Our performance is improved by ∼2% on the target set when using more data. Moreover, our method still outperforms the baseline significantly even when pre-trained with *COCO Cap* only.

What Is the Effect of Different Text Encoders? Besides our default choice of text encoder (CLIP), we implement our method with another encoder, i.e.,

Fig. 6. Some example results of our open vocabulary detector. The shown categories are from novel categories in COCO (Color figure online)

Bert (base) [4] which is a widely used language model that is trained using text data only. Our main baseline *Zareian et al.* uses Bert as their text encoder as well. The comparison results are shown in Table 7. The results suggest that with Bert encoder, our method's performance is slightly worse on COCO target set compared with our method using CLIP text encoder. This may due to the fact that CLIP text encoder is trained using image-caption pairs which results in better generalization performance for image-related tasks. While our method with Bert encoder still outperforms *Zareian et al.* by 6% AP on novel categories. It indicates that the performance improvement of our method doesn't mainly come from a better text encoder, but from training with large-scale pseudo bounding-box labels.

Qualitative Visualization. We visualize examples of our generated pseudo bounding boxes in Fig. 4 and Fig. 5. As we can see, the generated pseudo labels show promising performance (see red boxes) in grounding objects and are able to cover categories, e.g., pot, slippers and pie (Fig. 5), that are not in the original object list of COCO's ground-truth annotations. We also observe that some background objects will be missed when it is not mentioned in the caption (see the yellow box in the last column of Fig. 5). Nevertheless, instances of the same object category may show up in other image-caption pairs in the large-scale dataset and our method could generate pseudo box labels for those cases. Therefore, our detector can still recognize this object after training. We also show some examples of our detection results in Fig. 6. They are all from COCO novel categories which are not covered by COCO base annotations. The results demonstrate promising generalization ability of our method to novel objects.

5 Closing Remarks

We propose a novel framework that trains an open vocabulary object detector with pseudo bounding-box labels generated from large-scale image-caption pairs. We introduce a pseudo label generator that leverages the localization ability of pre-trained vision-language models to generate pseudo bounding-box annotations for diverse objects embedded in image captions. The generated pseudo labels can be used to improve open vocabulary object detection. Experimental results show that our method outperforms the state-of-the-art zero-shot and open vocabulary object detection methods by a large margin.

Potential Negative Societal Impact. Our method generates pseudo bounding box labels to alleviate human labeling efforts. Since our pseudo label generator mines annotations of objects from the input captions without human intervention, our pseudo labels might be biased because of the bias embedded in the language descriptions. Manually filtering out the biased object names in the vocabulary could be an effective solution.

References

1. Bansal, A., Sikka, K., Sharma, G., Chellappa, R., Divakaran, A.: Zero-shot object detection. In: Ferrari, V., Hebert, M., Sminchisescu, C., Weiss, Y. (eds.) ECCV 2018. LNCS, vol. 11205, pp. 397–414. Springer, Cham (2018). https://doi.org/10.1007/978-3-030-01246-5_24
2. Bilen, H., Vedaldi, A.: Weakly supervised deep detection networks. In: CVPR, pp. 2846–2854 (2016)
3. Chen, X., et al.: Microsoft COCO captions: data collection and evaluation server. arXiv preprint arXiv:1504.00325 (2015)
4. Devlin, J., Chang, M.W., Lee, K., Toutanova, K.: BERT: pre-training of deep bidirectional transformers for language understanding. arXiv preprint arXiv:1810.04805 (2018)
5. Everingham, M.: The pascal visual object classes challenge, (voc2007) results (2007). http://pascallin.ecs.soton.ac.uk/challenges/VOC/voc2007/index.html
6. Everingham, M., Eslami, S.A., Van Gool, L., Williams, C.K., Winn, J., Zisserman, A.: The pascal visual object classes challenge: a retrospective. Int. J. Comput. Vis. 111(1), 98–136 (2015)
7. Gao, M., Li, A., Yu, R., Morariu, V.I., Davis, L.S.: C-WSL: count-guided weakly supervised localization. In: Ferrari, V., Hebert, M., Sminchisescu, C., Weiss, Y. (eds.) ECCV 2018. LNCS, vol. 11205, pp. 155–171. Springer, Cham (2018). https://doi.org/10.1007/978-3-030-01246-5_10
8. Girshick, R.: Fast R-CNN. In: Proceedings of the IEEE International Conference on Computer Vision, pp. 1440–1448 (2015)
9. Gu, X., Lin, T.Y., Kuo, W., Cui, Y.: Zero-shot detection via vision and language knowledge distillation. arXiv preprint arXiv:2104.13921 (2021)
10. Gupta, A., Dollar, P., Girshick, R.: LVIS: a dataset for large vocabulary instance segmentation. In: Proceedings of the IEEE Conference on Computer Vision and Pattern Recognition (2019)
11. He, K., Gkioxari, G., Dollár, P., Girshick, R.: Mask R-CNN. In: Proceedings of the IEEE International Conference on Computer Vision, pp. 2961–2969 (2017)

12. Jia, C., et al.: Scaling up visual and vision-language representation learning with noisy text supervision. arXiv preprint arXiv:2102.05918 (2021)

13. Joseph, K., Khan, S., Khan, F.S., Balasubramanian, V.N.: Towards open world object detection. In: Proceedings of the IEEE/CVF Conference on Computer Vision and Pattern Recognition, pp. 5830–5840 (2021)

14. Krishna, R., et al.: Visual genome: connecting language and vision using crowd-sourced dense image annotations. Int. J. Comput. Vis. **123**(1), 32–73 (2017)

15. Li, J., Selvaraju, R.R., Gotmare, A.D., Joty, S., Xiong, C., Hoi, S.: Align before fuse: vision and language representation learning with momentum distillation. In: NeurIPS (2021)

16. Li, L.H., Yatskar, M., Yin, D., Hsieh, C.J., Chang, K.W.: VisualBERT: a simple and performant baseline for vision and language. arXiv preprint arXiv:1908.03557 (2019)

17. Lin, T.-Y., et al.: Microsoft COCO: common objects in context. In: Fleet, D., Pajdla, T., Schiele, B., Tuytelaars, T. (eds.) ECCV 2014. LNCS, vol. 8693, pp. 740–755. Springer, Cham (2014). https://doi.org/10.1007/978-3-319-10602-1_48

18. Ordonez, V., Kulkarni, G., Berg, T.: Im2Text: describing images using 1 million captioned photographs. Adv. Neural. Inf. Process. Syst. **24**, 1143–1151 (2011)

19. Papageorgiou, C., Poggio, T.: A trainable system for object detection. Int. J. Comput. Vis. **38**(1), 15–33 (2000)

20. Papageorgiou, C.P., Oren, M., Poggio, T.: A general framework for object detection. In: Sixth International Conference on Computer Vision (IEEE Cat. No. 98CH36271), pp. 555–562. IEEE (1998)

21. Radford, A., et al.: Learning transferable visual models from natural language supervision. arXiv preprint arXiv:2103.00020 (2021)

22. Rahman, S., Khan, S., Barnes, N.: Improved visual-semantic alignment for zero-shot object detection. In: AAAI, pp. 11932–11939 (2020)

23. Ren, S., He, K., Girshick, R., Sun, J.: Faster R-CNN: towards real-time object detection with region proposal networks. Adv. Neural. Inf. Process. Syst. **28**, 91–99 (2015)

24. Selvaraju, R.R., Cogswell, M., Das, A., Vedantam, R., Parikh, D., Batra, D.: Grad-CAM: visual explanations from deep networks via gradient-based localization. In: Proceedings of the IEEE International Conference on Computer Vision, pp. 618–626 (2017)

25. Shao, S., et al.: Objects365: a large-scale, high-quality dataset for object detection. In: Proceedings of the IEEE/CVF International Conference on Computer Vision, pp. 8430–8439 (2019)

26. Sun, P., et al.: Sparse R-CNN: end-to-end object detection with learnable proposals. In: Proceedings of the IEEE/CVF Conference on Computer Vision and Pattern Recognition, pp. 14454–14463 (2021)

27. Szegedy, C., Toshev, A., Erhan, D.: Deep neural networks for object detection (2013)

28. Tan, H., Bansal, M.: LXMERT: learning cross-modality encoder representations from transformers. arXiv preprint arXiv:1908.07490 (2019)

29. Tang, P., et al.: PCL: proposal cluster learning for weakly supervised object detection. IEEE Trans. Pattern Anal. Mach. Intell. **42**(1), 176–191 (2018)

30. Uijlings, J.R., Van De Sande, K.E., Gevers, T., Smeulders, A.W.: Selective search for object recognition. IJCV **104**(2), 154–171 (2013)

31. Xie, E., et al.: DetCo: unsupervised contrastive learning for object detection. In: Proceedings of the IEEE/CVF International Conference on Computer Vision, pp. 8392–8401 (2021)

32. Ye, K., Zhang, M., Kovashka, A., Li, W., Qin, D., Berent, J.: Cap2Det: learning to amplify weak caption supervision for object detection. In: ICCV, pp. 9686–9695 (2019)
33. Yin, T., Zhou, X., Krahenbuhl, P.: Center-based 3D object detection and tracking. In: Proceedings of the IEEE/CVF Conference on Computer Vision and Pattern Recognition, pp. 11784–11793 (2021)
34. Zareian, A., Rosa, K.D., Hu, D.H., Chang, S.F.: Open-vocabulary object detection using captions. In: CVPR, pp. 14393–14402 (2021)
35. Zhu, P., Wang, H., Saligrama, V.: Zero shot detection. IEEE Trans. Circuits Syst. Video Technol. 30(4), 998–1010 (2019)
36. Zhu, P., Wang, H., Saligrama, V.: Don't even look once: synthesizing features for zero-shot detection. In: CVPR, pp. 11693–11702 (2020)

Few-Shot Object Detection by Knowledge Distillation Using Bag-of-Visual-Words Representations

Wenjie Pei[2], Shuang Wu[2], Dianwen Mei[2], Fanglin Chen[2], Jiandong Tian[3], and Guangming Lu[1,2(✉)]

[1] Guangdong Provincial Key Laboratory of Novel Security Intelligence Technologies, Shenzhen, China
[2] Harbin Institute of Technology, Shenzhen, China
luguangm@hit.edu.cn
[3] Shenyang Institute of Automation, Chinese Academy of Sciences, Shenyang, China

Abstract. While fine-tuning based methods for few-shot object detection have achieved remarkable progress, a crucial challenge that has not been addressed well is the potential class-specific overfitting on base classes and sample-specific overfitting on novel classes. In this work we design a novel knowledge distillation framework to guide the learning of the object detector and thereby restrain the overfitting in both the pre-training stage on base classes and fine-tuning stage on novel classes. To be specific, we first present a novel Position-Aware Bag-of-Visual-Words model for learning a representative bag of visual words ($BoVW$) from a limited size of image set, which is used to encode general images based on the similarities between the learned visual words and an image. Then we perform knowledge distillation based on the fact that an image should have consistent $BoVW$ representations in two different feature spaces. To this end, we pre-learn a feature space independently from the object detection, and encode images using $BoVW$ in this space. The obtained $BoVW$ representation for an image can be considered as distilled knowledge to guide the learning of object detector: the extracted features by the object detector for the same image are expected to derive the consistent $BoVW$ representations with the distilled knowledge. Extensive experiments validate the effectiveness of our method and demonstrate the superiority over other state-of-the-art methods.

Keywords: Few-shot object detection · Bag of visual words · Knowledge distillation

---

W. Pei and S. Wu—Equal contribution.

Supplementary Information The online version contains supplementary material available at https://doi.org/10.1007/978-3-031-20080-9_17.

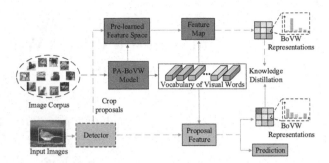

Fig. 1. We learn a representative bag of visual words (*BoVW*) using the proposed *PA-BoVW* model. For an extracted positive proposal, we encode it with *BoVW* in a pre-learned feature space and the feature space of the object detector, respectively. Then we perform knowledge distillation by matching two *BoVW* representations to guide the learning of the object detector.

1   Introduction

Few-shot object detection aims to learn effective object detectors on a set of base classes with sufficient samples, which can be generalized efficiently to novel classes with only a few samples available. Thus, few-shot object detection eliminates exhaustive label annotation of massive data on novel classes. Compared to general object detection [27,31,32,40], few-shot object detection [3,19] is much more challenging due to the difficulty of learning generalizable features that can be transferred from base classes to novel classes.

A classical type of methods for few-shot object detection is fine-tuning based methods [1,9,26,30,38,44,48,49,57], which first train the object detector using the samples from base classes, then fine-tune the model on novel classes. A prominent example is TFA [44], which first adopts such two-stage training strategy to transfer knowledge from base classes to novel classes. Based on such fine-tuning framework, many methods are proposed to deal with various challenges of few-shot object detection. Typical methods include FSCE [38] aiming to facilitate the separability among similar classes, MPSR [49] which seeks to rectify the sample distribution for novel classes, and HallucFsDet [57] which is designed to tackle the problem of data scarcity.

A crucial challenge of fine-tuning based framework for few-shot object detection is the potential class-specific overfitting on base classes and sample-specific overfitting on novel classes. On the one hand, although sufficient samples are provided for base classes, the object detector is still prone to overfitting on base classes during the first stage of training process. In this case, the detector learns the class-specific features instead of the class-agnostic features, which cannot be transferred to novel classes and would adversely affect object detection for novel classes. On the other hand, owing to the scarcity of training samples for novel classes in the fine-tuning stage, the object detector tends to be overfitting on these individual samples and thus learns sample-specific features that cannot be generalized across different samples for a same novel class.

To address above limitation, we propose to perform knowledge distillation to guide the learning process of few-shot object detection and thus restrain the potential overfitting on both base classes and novel classes. As shown in Fig. 1, we propose the novel Position-Aware Bag-of-Visual-Words (*PA-BoVW*) model, which is able to learn a bag of visual words (*BoVW*) from a limited size of image set. The learned visual words are representative and comprehensive to be capable of encoding general images based on the similarities between the learned visual words and an image. Then we can perform knowledge distillation based on the intuition that an image should have consistent *BoVW* representations in two different feature spaces, provided that the image is encoded properly, namely not overfitted, in both feature spaces. Concretely, we first pre-learn a feature space and derive a *BoVW* representation for an image in this space. The obtained *BoVW* representation can be considered as distilled knowledge to guide the learning of object detector: the extracted features by the object detector for the same image are expected to derive the consistent *BoVW* representation with the distilled knowledge.

Unlike typical way that identifies visual words as the clustering centroids in the deep feature space [11,18], we learn visual words as learnable vectorial embeddings. To be specific, our proposed *PA-BoVW* model first constructs an effective deep embedding space for learning the visual words by training a backbone network in a self-supervised way. Then the visual words is learned in this embedding space in a supervised way employing image classification as a pretext task. Besides, we employ DeCov loss [5] as an auxiliary loss to reduce the inter-word redundancy and encourage the diversity of visual words. As a result, the *PA-BoVW* model is learned in an independent way from the task of object detection. Thus the encoded *BoVW* representation in its embedding space can be used as distilled knowledge, which can be transferred to the learning process of the detector to restrain potential overfitting on both base and novel classes.

To conclude, we make following contributions: 1) We propose the novel *PA-BoVW* model, which constructs an effective embedding space to learn a representative vocabulary of visual words; 2) Based on the *PA-BoVW* model, we design a knowledge distillation framework to guide the learning of the object detector and thereby restrain the potential overfitting on both base classes and novel classes; 3) Extensive experiments validate the effectiveness of our method and demonstrate the advantages of our method over state-of-the-art methods for few-shot object detection.

2   Related Work

Few-Shot Learning. Early works of few-shot learning focus on the task of image classification. Metric-based methods learn a suitable embedding space, where samples can be categorized correctly via a nearest neighbor classifier with Euclidean distance [37], cosine similarity [4,41] or graph distance [21,36,53]. Initialization-based methods aim to learn good initialization so that the model can adapt to novel tasks by a few optimization steps [10,23]. Hallucination-based methods alleviate data scarcity issue via learning generators to augment novel classes [14, 45]. However, these approaches could not be directly applied to few-shot object detection which requires both classification and localization.

Few-Shot Object Detection. Few-shot object detection aims to detect objects with few annotated training examples provided. There are several early methods adopting the idea of meta-learning [8, 13, 17, 19, 24, 50, 52, 56]. FSRW [19] is a novel few-shot detector based on YOLOv2 [31], which re-weights the features with channel-wise attention and leverages these features to detect novel objects. Meta R-CNN [52] applies similar feature re-weighting scheme to Faster R-CNN [32] and performs meta-learning over RoI features. These methods usually suffer from a complicated training process and fail to learn generalizable features that can be transferred from base classes to novel classes. Recently, several fine-tuning based methods [1, 9, 26, 30, 38, 44, 48, 49, 57] achieve higher performance compared to meta-learning based methods. TFA [44] performs a simple two-stage fine-tuning approach which fine-tunes only the last layer on novel classes. MPSR [49] proposes to generate multi-scale positive samples to solve the problem of scale variations. FSCE [38] provides a strong baseline which fine-tunes feature extractors during the fine-tuning stage and employs a contrastive branch to rescue misclassifications. However, all these fine-tuning based methods suffer from overfitting on both base classes and novel classes. In this work, we design a novel knowledge distillation framework to tackle the problem.

Bag of Visual Words. Bag-of-Visual-Words is a popular technique for image recognition. Many variants of *BoVW* have been proposed in the past [6, 22, 42] and they continue to be widely used in recent deep learning approaches [11, 12, 18, 34]. VWE [34] designs a visual words learning module to generate CAMs [58] for weakly-supervised semantic segmentation. BoWNet [11] and OBOW [12] apply *BoVW* to self-supervised learning. QuEST [18] introduces to distill the quantized feature maps from the teacher to the student. In this work, we learn a *BoVW* model via a self-supervised task and image classification task.

Knowledge Distillation for Object Detection. Knowledge distillation [16] is an effective way to transfer knowledge acquired in teacher network to student network. Early works focus on the task of image classification [33, 39, 55]. Recently, there are several works which propose to transfer knowledge for object detection. Chen et al. [2] distill knowledge from the teacher detector to the student detector in all components (i.e., feature extraction, RPN, classification and regression networks). Wang et al. [43] design a fine-grained feature imitation method which distills the features from foreground area. In this work, we propose a novel knowledge distillation method which transfers knowledge from a *BoVW* model to a few-shot object detector, aiming to suppress potential overfitting on both base and novel classes.

3   Method

To deal with the potential overfitting in few-shot object detection based on deep learning networks, we propose to perform knowledge distillation to guide the

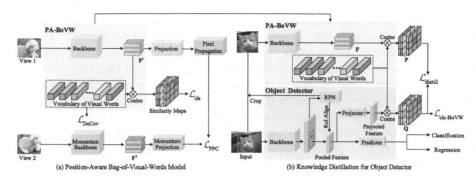

Fig. 2. The overall architecture of our method. We first train the proposed *PA-BoVW* model for learning a bag of visual words (*BoVW*) via two pretext tasks: pixel-to-propagation consistency [51] and base-class recognition task. During the training procedure of the detector, given a positive region proposal, we crop it from original images and fed it into our pre-learned *PA-BoVW* model to obtain the *BoVW* representation. Then we use the obtained *BoVW* representation as distilled knowledge to guide the learning of the detector.

learning process of few-shot object detection. Specifically, we learn a bag of visual words (*BoVW*) for encoding images. The learned visual words are presumably representative, hence an image should have consistent *BoVW* representations in two independent feature spaces. We first pre-learn a feature space and the derived *BoVW* representation in this space can be considered as distilled knowledge that is transferred to the learning of the few-shot object detector. The extracted features by the object detector for each positive proposal are expected to derive consistent *BoVW* representation with the distilled knowledge, thereby avoiding overfitting during supervised learning.

In this section, we will first elaborate on the proposed Position-Aware Bag-of-Visual-Words model (*PA-BoVW*) for learning a bag of visual words and encoding images based on these visual words. Then we will show how to perform knowledge distillation to guide the learning of few-shot object detection.

3.1 Position-Aware Bag-of-Visual-Words Model

A typical way of constructing a bag of visual words from an image corpus is to cluster the image patches in the corpus in deep feature space and select the clustering centroids as the visual words [11,18]. While such an unsupervised method is straightforward and feasible given a sufficiently large image corpus, it shows limited effectiveness when the size of image corpus is limited. This is mainly because such a method tends to focus on the statistically frequent image patches which may not be semantically representative.

In this work we present a novel Position-Aware Bag-of-visual-Words (*PA-BoVW*) model, which is able to learn a representative vocabulary of visual words from a limited size of image set. As shown in Fig. 2 (a), we view each visual word as a learnable embedding and learn the parameters of all word embeddings in a supervised way based on two pretext tasks. The first pretext task is Pixel-to-Propagation Consistency [51], which trains the backbone network to construct the embedding space for learning visual words in a self-supervised learning framework. Then we perform image classification on the representations encoded by our *PA-BoVW* model. Hence, the task of image classification serves as the second pretext task for optimizing the parameter learning of both the word embeddings and the backbone network. To this end, we first construct an iconic-object image dataset $\mathcal{D}$ as image corpus by extracting all base class objects from the detection dataset according to their ground-truth bounding boxes and labels. We then train our *PA-BoVW* model on $\mathcal{D}$.

Learnable Word Embeddings. Unlike the typical way that identifies visual words as the clustering centroids in the deep feature space, we learn visual words as learnable vectorial embeddings. A prominent benefit of such way is that the visual words do not necessarily correspond to image patches in the corpus. Instead, our model can learn an effective vocabulary of word embeddings freely from the whole embedding space under the optimization of the designed supervision (i.e., the classification pretext-task in our case).

Self-supervised Learning of Embedding Space via Pixel-to-Propagation Consistency. To construct an effective embedding space for learning visual words, we employ a backbone network to encode the input image into a latent feature space and optimize the backbone network using Pixel-to-Propagation Consistency (PPC) [51] in a self-supervised way. PPC optimizes the backbone to make each pixel distinguishable from other pixels in the embedding space.

Formally, given an image corpus $\mathcal{D}$, for an image $I \in \mathcal{D}$, two views (I^1, I^2) are generated by typical data augmentations (random cropping, color distortion, etc.). They are then fed into a self-supervised framework including a regular encoding network and a paired momentum encoding network to extract features respectively, as shown in Fig. 2(a). The encoding network consists of a backbone network and a projection network. The features which pass the backbone networks are denoted as $(\mathbf{F}^1, \mathbf{F}^2)$. Then the projection networks convert them to $(\mathbf{E}^1, \mathbf{E}^2)$. Each pixel in the feature maps that pass the regular encoding network are processed by a pixel propagation module [51] to enrich its feature by attending to all other pixels in the same view according to their similarities, for instance, the pixel $\mathbf{x}_i^1$ in $\mathbf{E}^1$ is processed as:

$$q(\mathbf{x}_i^1) = \sum_{j \in \mathbf{E}^1} \max\left(\frac{(\mathbf{x}_i^1)^\top \cdot \mathbf{x}_j^1}{\|\mathbf{x}_i^1\|_2 \|\mathbf{x}_j^1\|_2}, 0\right)^2 \cdot \Psi(\mathbf{x}_j^1), \forall \mathbf{x}_i^1 \in \mathbf{E}^1. \tag{1}$$

$\Psi(\cdot)$ is a feature transformation module comprising 2 convolution layers with a batch normalization layer and a ReLU layer. The obtained feature $q(\mathbf{x}_i^1)$ is then used to maximize its cosine similarities with its corresponding pixel $\mathbf{x}_i^2$ in the other view $\mathbf{E}^2$ passing the momentum backbone:

$$\mathcal{L}_{\text{PPC}} = 2 - \frac{q(\mathbf{x}_i^1)^\top \cdot \mathbf{x}_i^2}{\|q(\mathbf{x}_i^1)\|_2 \|\mathbf{x}_i^2\|_2} - \frac{q(\mathbf{x}_i^2)^\top \cdot \mathbf{x}_i^1}{\|q(\mathbf{x}_i^2)\|_2 \|\mathbf{x}_i^1\|_2}. \tag{2}$$

Note that $\mathbf{x}_i^1$ and $\mathbf{x}_i^2$ are the corresponding pixels in two views $(\mathbf{E}^1, \mathbf{E}^2)$, but they could have different positional coordinates. Since only the feature maps going through the regular backbone are processed by PPC [51], both views have chance to go through the regular backbone and the momentum backbone respectively.

Since the embedding space is constructed independently from the learning of the object detector, the embedding space and the feature space of the object detector are two different feature spaces. Thus, the constructed embedding space can be used to not only learn the vocabulary of visual words, but encode *BoVW* representations based on the learned visual words for an image as distilled knowledge. Such distilled knowledge is further used to guide the learning of the object detector.

Position-Aware Encoding of *BoVW* Representation. Typical way of representing images using the visual words is to divide an image into patches and calculate the histogram over the visual words [22]. However, such encoding scheme loses the position information which is crucial for object detection. To address this limitation, we encode an image using the vocabulary of visual words by calculating the Cosine similarity between each pixel of the image and each visual word in the embedding space while retaining the positional relationship among pixels. Formally, given an image I, its features which pass the backbone network are denoted as $\mathbf{F} \in \mathbb{R}^{C \times H \times W}$ with C feature maps of size $H \times W$. The learned vocabulary of visual words are denoted as $\mathbf{V} \in \mathbb{R}^{K \times D}$ in which K is the number of visual words and D is the feature dimension for each word. The Cosine similarity between the pixel (h, w) in $\mathbf{F}$ and the j-th word in $\mathbf{V}$ is calculated as:

$$\mathbf{P}_{j,h,w} = \frac{\mathbf{V}_j^\top \cdot \mathcal{F}_{\mathrm{conv}}(\mathbf{F}_{h,w})}{\left\|\mathbf{V}_j^\top\right\|_2 \left\|\mathcal{F}_{\mathrm{conv}}(\mathbf{F}_{h,w})\right\|_2}, \tag{3}$$

where $\mathcal{F}_{\mathrm{conv}}$ is a transformation function implemented by a convolutional layer to project $\mathbf{F}$ from C channels to D channels. Consequently, we obtain a similarity map $\mathbf{P} \in \mathbb{R}^{K \times H \times W}$ as the encoded *BoVW* representation for the image I, which retains the position information for each pixel.

Supervised Learning of Visual Words by the Pretext Task of Image Classification. We employ image classification as a pretext task to guide the learning of the visual words based on two considerations: 1) the visual words should be discriminative for object recognition in that our goal is object detection; 2) the learned visual words should have well generalizability and can be used for knowledge distillation to restrain potential overfitting for object detection, thus the pretext task should be independent of the task of object detection.

Given an image $I \in \mathcal{D}$, we first encode it with *BoVW*. Then the obtained *BoVW* representation is fed into a simple classification head consisting of a pooling layer and a fully-connected layer. Formally, we perform average pooling over the *BoVW* representation of I, namely the similarity map $\mathbf{P}$, along the H and W dimension and thus achieve a vectorial representation whose dimension is equal to the size of the vocabulary $\mathbf{V}$:

$$\mathbf{P}_{\mathrm{avg}} = \frac{1}{HW} \sum_{h=1}^{H} \sum_{w=1}^{W} \mathbf{P}_{j,h,w}. \tag{4}$$

The obtained $\mathbf{P}_{\mathrm{avg}}$ are further fed into a fully-connected layer $\mathcal{F}_{\mathrm{fc}}$ and Softmax function $\mathcal{F}_{\mathrm{softmax}}$ for classification prediction. Cross Entropy (CE) loss is used for optimization:

$$\mathcal{L}_{\mathrm{cls}} = \mathrm{CE}(y_I, \mathcal{F}_{\mathrm{softmax}}(\mathcal{F}_{\mathrm{fc}}(\mathbf{P}_{\mathrm{avg}}))), \tag{5}$$

where y_I is the groundtruth label for image I.

Reducing Inter-Word Correlation. To encourage the diversity of visual words and reduce the redundancy among words, we add DeCov loss [5] as an auxiliary loss to minimize the correlation between different visual words:

$$\mathcal{L}_{\mathrm{DeCov}} = \frac{1}{2}(\|\Sigma(\mathbf{V})\|_F^2 - \|\mathrm{diag}(\Sigma(\mathbf{V}))\|_2^2), \tag{6}$$

where $\Sigma(\cdot)$ denotes the covariance matrix and $\mathrm{diag}(\cdot)$ extracts the diagonal elements of a matrix.

The whole Bag-of-Visual-Words model can be trained under the supervision by above three loss functions jointly:

$$\mathcal{L}_{\mathrm{BoVW}} = \mathcal{L}_{\mathrm{PPC}} + \mathcal{L}_{\mathrm{cls}} + \mathcal{L}_{\mathrm{DeCov}}, \tag{7}$$

Note that although our *PA-BoVW* model is learned independently from the object detector in an extra step, it can be trained quite efficiently due to small size of object images and relatively simple supervision tasks compared to the task of object detection.

3.2   Knowledge Distillation for Object Detection

Our Position-Aware Bag-of-Visual-Words (*PA-BoVW*) model learns the embedding space for visual words using PPC [51] as the pretext task, and learns the vocabulary of visual words based on the pretext task of image classification. Thus, our *PA-BoVW* model is optimized in a completely independent way from the task of object detection. As a result, the encoded *BoVW* representation in the embedding space of the *PA-BoVW* model for an image can be viewed as distilled knowledge, which can be transferred to the learning process of few-shot object detection to suppress potential overfitting on this image. The rationale behind this design is that a well learned (non-overfitting) feature representation for an object by a detector should bear consistent similarity distribution over the learned visual words with the corresponding *BoVW* representation by our *PA-BoVW* model. Thus, we can derive consistent *BoVW* representations from the learned features by the object detector and our *PA-BoVW* model, respectively.

As shown in Fig. 2(b), we adopt the typical object detection framework, which is built upon Faster R-CNN [32]. Actually, our proposed method of knowledge distillation can be readily integrated into any classical object detection framework. Given a positive region proposal r generated by RPN (Region Proposal Network), which is assigned with one of the ground-truth labels and bounding boxes during training, we crop the corresponding region from the original input image and resize it to a fixed size by bilinear interpolation, then fed it into our

PA-BoVW model to obtain its *BoVW* representation $\mathbf{P}(r) \in \mathbb{R}^{K \times H \times W}$ by Eq. 3. Meanwhile, we calculate the Cosine similarities between the features $\mathbf{G}(r)$ for r, obtained from the RoI pooling layer of the object detector, and the vocabulary of visual words $\mathbf{V}$. Note that $\mathbf{G}(r)$ and the visual words are not learned in the same feature space, thus we project them into the same feature space first and then compute the Cosine similarities in the same way as Eq. 3:

$$\mathbf{Q}_{j,h,w}(r) = \frac{g(\mathbf{V}_j)^{\top} \cdot \phi(\mathbf{G}_{h,w}(r))}{\|g(\mathbf{V}_j)\|_2 \, \|\phi(\mathbf{G}_{h,w}(r))\|_2}, \tag{8}$$

$$j = 1, \ldots, K, h = 1, \ldots, H, w = 1, \ldots, W.$$

Herein, $g(\cdot)$ is the project function implemented as a fully connected layer for $\mathbf{V}$, while $\phi(\cdot)$ denotes the project function for features $\mathbf{G}(r)$, which is formulated as a 1×1 convolutional layer. K, H, W are the size of the vocabulary $\mathbf{V}$, the height and the width of $\mathbf{G}(r)$, respectively.

The obtained $\mathbf{Q}(r) \in \mathbb{R}^{K \times H \times W}$ is equivalent to the *BoVW* representation encoded on the learned features $\mathbf{G}$ of the object detector. If $\mathbf{G}(r)$ is learned well and not overfitting on the input data, it should result in consistent *BoVW* representation as our pre-trained *PA-BoVW* model. Thus, we minimize the L1-norm distance between these two *BoVW* representations to guide the learning process of the object detector:

$$L_{\text{distill}} = \frac{1}{RHW} \sum_{r=1}^{R} \sum_{h=1}^{H} \sum_{w=1}^{W} \|\mathbf{P}_{h,w}(r) - \mathbf{Q}_{h,w}(r)\|_1, \tag{9}$$

where R is the number of positive proposals.

Knowledge Distillation on Both Base Classes and Novel Classes. As most fine-tuning based methods [30,38,44,49] do, we first train the object detector on base classes and then fine-tune the model on the novel classes. We perform the knowledge distillation process in both training stages to restrain the potential overfitting on base classes and novel classes, respectively.

Collaborative Object Detection with *BoVW* Representations. The obtained *BoVW* representation $\mathbf{Q}(r)$ can also be used for object classification for the region proposal r. Thus, we perform classification by fusing the predicted scores from $\mathbf{Q}(r)$ and the original features respectively:

$$p = \eta \cdot p_{\text{orig}} + (1 - \eta) \cdot p',$$
$$p' = \mathcal{F}_{\text{softmax}}(\mathcal{F}_{\text{fc}}(\mathbf{Q}(r))), \tag{10}$$

where p_{orig} and p' are predicted scores from the original features and from the *BoVW* representation respectively. Here p' is obtained by performing a linear transformation $\mathcal{F}_{\text{fc}}$ and softmax function on $\mathbf{Q}(r)$. η is a hyper-parameter to fuse two scores. During training, Cross Entropy loss is used as an auxiliary loss to guide the optimization:

$$\mathcal{L}_{\text{cls-BoVW}} = \text{CE}(y, p'), \tag{11}$$

where y is the groundtruth label for the region proposal r.

Consequently, the object detector is trained under the supervision of three losses jointly:

$$\mathcal{L}_{\text{obj}} = \mathcal{L}_{\text{det}} + \mathcal{L}_{\text{distill}} + \mathcal{L}_{\text{cls-BoVW}}, \tag{12}$$

where $\mathcal{L}_{det}$ corresponds to the standard Faster R-CNN [32] losses for object detection, including the losses for RPN, classification and box regression.

4   Experiments

4.1   Experimental Setup

Benchmarks. We evaluate our approach on PASCAL VOC [7] dataset and MS COCO [28] dataset. We follow the previous work [19] for data construction to have a fair comparison. PASCAL VOC comprises 15 base classes and 5 novel classes. We utilize the same three class splits introduced in [19], where each novel class has $k = 1, 2, 3, 5, 10$ instances sampled from the combination of VOC 2007 and VOC 2012 trainval sets. VOC 2007 test set is used for evaluation. As for MS COCO, the 60 categories disjoint with PASCAL VOC are selected as base classes, and the remaining 20 categories are used as novel classes with $K = 10, 30$. For evaluation metrics, we report AP50 of novel classes (nAP50) for PASCAL VOC and COCO-style AP of the novel classes for MS COCO.

Implementation Details. We evaluate our approach by building it upon two state-of-the-art methods: TFA++ [38] and DeFRCN [30]. TFA++ [38] is a strong baseline which jointly fine-tunes the feature extractors and box predictors during the fine-tuning stage. DeFRCN [30] is a simple yet effective architecture which is the current state of the art.

For *PA-BoVW* model, we use an ImageNet [35] pre-trained ResNet101 [15] as the backbone. The input size is 224×224. The feature dimension of visual word is 512. The number of visual words is set to 256 for PASCAL VOC and 1024 for MS COCO. We follow the same data augmentation strategy in PPC [51], where two random patches of an image are independently sampled, followed by random horizontal flip, color distortion, gaussian blur, and solarization. We use AdamW optimizer to optimize the *PA-BoVW* model with the initial learning rate of 1e−4 for 24 epochs. We decay the learning rate by ratio 0.1 at epoch 18 and 22. The total batch size is set to 256. The object detector is trained on 8 GPUs with a batch size of 16. The η is uniformly set to 0.5. All other training settings are the same as that in TFA++ [38] and DeFRCN [30].

4.2   Comparison with State-of-the-Art Methods

Results on PASCAL VOC. Table 1 presents the results on PASCAL VOC, which show that our approach improves the performance of TFA++ [38] by a large margin in all cases including different numbers of training shots in different splits. Particularly, for the 2-shot case of Novel Split 1, 5-shot case of Novel Split 2 and 2-shot case of Novel Split 3, our approach is 8.1%, 6.5%, 5.5% higher

Table 1. Comparison with existing few-shot object detection methods using nAP50 as evaluation metric on three PASCAL VOC Novel Split sets. 'Ours (KD-TFA++)' denotes our method using TFA++ [38] as the baseline. † indicates that model is evaluated using the released code.

Method/Shots	Novel Split 1					Novel Split 2					Novel Split 3				
	1	2	3	5	10	1	2	3	5	10	1	2	3	5	10
LSTD [3]	8.2	1.0	12.4	29.1	38.5	11.4	3.8	5.0	15.7	31.0	12.6	8.5	15.0	27.3	36.3
MetaDet [46]	18.9	20.6	30.2	36.8	49.6	21.8	23.1	27.8	31.7	43.0	20.6	23.9	29.4	43.9	44.1
Meta R-CNN [52]	19.9	25.5	35.0	45.7	51.5	10.4	19.4	29.6	34.8	45.4	14.3	18.2	27.5	41.2	48.1
FSRW [19]	14.8	15.5	26.7	33.9	47.2	15.7	15.3	22.7	30.1	40.5	21.3	25.6	28.4	42.8	45.9
RepMet [20]	26.1	32.9	34.4	38.6	41.3	17.2	22.1	23.4	28.3	35.8	27.5	31.1	31.5	34.4	37.2
NP-RepMet [54]	37.8	40.3	41.7	47.3	49.4	**41.6**	43.0	43.4	47.4	49.1	33.3	38.0	39.8	41.5	44.8
MPSR [49]	41.7	-	51.4	55.2	61.8	24.4	-	39.2	39.9	47.8	35.6	-	42.3	48.0	49.7
TFA w/cos [44]	39.8	36.1	44.7	55.7	56.0	23.5	26.9	34.1	35.1	39.1	30.8	34.8	42.8	49.5	49.8
HallucFsDet [57]	47.0	44.9	46.5	54.7	54.7	26.3	31.8	37.4	37.4	41.2	40.4	42.1	43.3	51.4	49.6
Retentive R-CNN[9]	42.4	45.8	45.9	53.7	56.1	21.7	27.8	35.2	37.0	40.3	30.2	37.6	43.0	49.7	50.1
FSCE [38]	44.2	43.8	51.4	61.9	63.4	27.3	29.5	43.5	44.2	50.2	37.2	41.9	47.5	54.6	58.5
FADI [1]	50.3	54.8	54.2	59.3	63.2	30.6	35.0	40.3	42.8	48.0	45.7	49.7	49.1	55.0	59.6
CME [25]	41.5	47.5	50.4	58.2	60.9	27.2	30.2	41.4	42.5	46.8	34.3	39.6	45.1	48.3	51.5
UP-FSOD [47]	43.8	47.8	50.3	55.4	61.7	31.2	30.5	41.2	42.2	48.3	35.5	39.7	43.9	50.6	53.3
QA-FewDet [13]	42.4	51.9	55.7	62.6	63.4	25.9	37.8	46.6	48.9	51.1	35.2	42.9	47.8	54.8	53.5
TFA++† [38]	43.4	42.1	47.3	57.2	60.8	24.3	27.7	42.0	42.0	48.5	38.0	41.0	45.8	54.0	56.2
Ours (KD-TFA++)	47.0	50.2	52.5	62.1	64.2	29.7	32.9	45.9	48.5	51.1	42.6	46.5	48.8	56.8	57.4
DeFRCN [30]	57.0	58.6	64.3	67.8	67.0	35.8	42.7	51.0	54.5	52.9	52.5	56.6	55.8	60.7	**62.5**
Ours (KD-DeFRCN)	**58.2**	**62.5**	**65.1**	**68.2**	**67.4**	37.6	**45.6**	**52.0**	**54.6**	**53.2**	**53.8**	**57.7**	**58.0**	**62.4**	62.2

than the baseline. When applying our approach to DeFRCN [30], which is the current state of the art, our method still improves the performance in most cases, especially in the extremely-few-shot regimes such as 1-shot and 2-shot.

Results on MS COCO. Table 2 shows the results on MS COCO. Applying our approach to two baselines achieves 1.1% and 0.3% nAP performance gain for 10-shot, 0.6% and 0.1% in terms of novel AP performance gain for 30-shot, respectively. There is no as large performance gain as on PASCAL VOC, which is probably because MS COCO has much more training images and thus has a lower risk of overfitting. To validate this speculation, we further evaluate our method by only using a small subset of base-class data for training. Specifically, we randomly select 10% samples from base classes to form a training set. For novel classes, we keep the same setting in standard few-shot object detection. Table 3 shows that the performance gains are larger than using all training data.

4.3 Ablation Studies

In this section, we conduct ablation studies on the Novel Split 1 of PASCAL VOC using TFA++ [38] as the baseline.

Table 2. Few-shot object detection performance on MS COCO.

Method	nAP		nAP75	
	10	30	10	30
LSTD [3]	3.2	6.7	2.1	5.1
MetaDet [46]	7.1	11.3	6.1	8.1
Meta R-CNN [52]	8.7	12.4	6.6	10.8
FSRW [19]	5.6	9.1	4.6	7.6
TFA w/cos [44]	10.0	13.7	9.3	13.4
MPSR [49]	9.8	14.1	9.7	14.2
SRR-FSD [59]	11.3	14.7	9.8	13.5
Retentive R-CNN [9]	10.5	13.8	–	–
FSCE [38]	11.9	16.4	10.5	16.2
FADI [1]	12.2	16.1	11.9	15.8
CME [25]	15.1	16.9	16.4	17.8
UP-FSOD [47]	11.0	15.6	10.7	15.7
QA-FewDet [13]	11.6	16.5	9.8	15.5
TFA++† [38]	11.7	16.0	10.3	15.3
Ours (KD-TFA++)	12.8	16.6	11.5	16.1
DeFRCN [30]	18.6	22.5	17.6	22.3
Ours (KD-DeFRCN)	**18.9**	**22.6**	**17.8**	**22.6**

Table 3. Results on MS COCO with 10% labeled base-class samples.

Method	nAP		nAP75	
	10	30	10	30
DeFRCN [30]	12.1	14.9	8.5	11.5
Ours (KD-DeFRCN)	**13.0**	**16.0**	**9.7**	**12.6**

Table 4. Effect of each loss function.

L_{DeCov}	$L_{distill}$	$L_{cls\text{-}BoVW}$	3-shot	5-shot	10-shot
✓			47.3	57.2	60.8
✓	✓		51.2	59.9	62.6
	✓	✓	50.8	60.1	61.3
✓	✓	✓	**51.6**	**60.6**	**63.1**

Effect of Each Functional Component. Table 5 shows the efficacy of each functional components for few-shot object detection on novel classes, including distillation on base classes, novel classes and score fusion for classification in Eq. 10. With the knowledge distillation for base classes, the performance gain is 4.2%/2.5%/1.9% for 3/5/10-shot, respectively. By performing distillation on novel class during the fine-tuning stage, the performance gain increases 0.1%/0.9%/0.4% respectively, which indicates the improved generalization ability on novel classes by our method. Finally, fusing the predicted scores from the original features and from the BoVW representation for classification yields the extra performance gain by 0.9%/1.5%/1.1%.

Effect of Each Loss Function. Table 4 shows the effect of each loss function. Both the distillation loss $L_{distill}$ and collaborative detection loss $\mathcal{L}_{cls\text{-}BoVW}$ improve the performance distinctly. Comparing the results in the last two rows, the $\mathcal{L}_{DeCov}$ which is designed to encourage the diversity of visual words and reduce the redundancy among words, also improves the performance.

Quantification for the Overfitting on Base Classes. Fine-tuning training strategy tends to make models overfit on base classes. Since most parameters of the feature extractors are frozen or just fine-tuned slightly during the fine-tuning stage, most model capacity is allocated to fitting the base samples. To quantify such overfitting on base classes, we perform three experiments: 1) Using fine-tuning training strategy, we first pre-train the baseline TFA++ on base classes, then fine-tune it with sufficient novel-class samples instead of k shot per class, which is denoted as two-stage training mode; 2) Similar to the setting in 1), we fine-tune our model with sufficient novel-class samples after pre-training; 3) we train the baseline using sufficient samples for both base and novel classes together

Table 5. Ablation studies of key components.

Baseline	Distillation for base	Distillation for novel	Score fusion	nAP50		
				3-shot	5-shot	10-shot
✓				47.3	57.2	60.8
✓	✓			51.5	59.7	62.7
✓	✓	✓		51.6	60.6	63.1
✓	✓	✓	✓	**52.5**	**62.1**	**64.2**

Table 6. Quantification for the overfitting.

Methods	nAP50	Misclassified cases (novel → base)
TFA++ (two-stage)	73.2	1021
Ours (KD-TFA++) (two-stage)	76.7	723
TFA++ (one-stage)	85.8	631

Table 7. Effect of different pretext tasks.

Pretext tasks	nAP50		
	3	5	10
w/o distillation	47.3	57.2	60.8
Cluster	49.6	57.4	61.1
Cls	52.3	60.8	63.6
Cls + PPC	**52.5**	**62.1**	**64.2**

Table 8. Distillation on deep features vs on *BoVW* representations.

Distillation methods	nAP50				
	1	2	3	5	10
Baseline	43.4	42.1	47.3	57.2	60.8
On deep features	33.2	37.9	36.5	47.1	48.3
On BoVW	**47.0**	**50.2**	**52.5**	**62.1**	**64.2**

in one-stage mode. We compare both nAP50 and the number of misclassified samples from novel to base classes to measure the overfitting. The results in Table 6 show that 1) the baseline trained in two-stage mode performs much worse than training itself in one-stage mode and has a larger number of misclassified samples, indicating that the model is heavily biased towards base classes; 2) using the same two-stage training mode, our method achieves 3.5% of performance gain than baseline and substantially decreases misclassified cases, which demonstrates the effectiveness of our method for suppressing the overfitting on base classes.

Effect of Different Pretext Tasks for Learning *BoVW* Models. We conduct experiments to compare our *PA-BoVW* model and the typical method for learning the visual words (denoted as *'Cluster'*), which trains a classification network on base classes and selects the clustering centroids of the feature vectors as visual words. Then we evaluate the performance our *PA-BoVW* optimized using only the image classification as the pretext task (denoted as *'Cls'*). Table 7 shows that the performance gains from *'Cluster'* is smaller than that of our *PA-BoVW* using only the pretext task of image classification. Using the pretext task of PPC further boosts the performance substantially, which implies the importance of learning the embedding space by PPC in a self-supervised way.

Distillation on Deep Features vs on *BoVW* Representations. A classical way to perform knowledge distillation is to learn an independent feature space

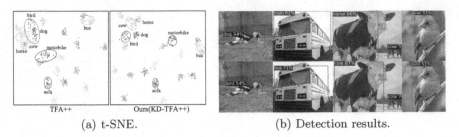

(a) t-SNE.   (b) Detection results.

Fig. 3. (a) The t-SNE visualization of proposal embeddings of baseline with and without distillation. (b) Detection results based on the 10-shot case. The first row shows the results of the baseline and the second row shows the results of our approach.

and perform distillation between two feature spaces. We conduct such experiment to compare between distillation on deep features and on *BoVW* representations. Specifically, we directly distill the pooled deep features in our trained *PA-BoVW* model to the feature space of the detector. The results of such method shown in Table 8 are much worse than our method. This is reasonable since distillation between feature space relies heavily on 1) the quality of the referenced features from which the distillation is performed and 2) well modeling of mapping between two feature space. By contrast, our method distills knowledge based on the similarity distribution over learned visual words, which benefits from similar merits of feature representations as Bag-of-Word representations used in NLP.

Qualitative Evaluation. Figure 3(a) shows the t-SNE [29] visualization of proposal embeddings from randomly selected 30 instance bounding boxes per category. The baseline (TFA++ [38]) tends to misclassify some samples of novel classes as similar base classes. For instance, the samples from novel classes 'bird' and 'cow' cannot be clearly separated from other base classes like 'dog' and 'horse'. In contrast, applying our approach to the baseline model leads to more accurate boundaries. Figure 3(b) shows the detection results of the baseline and our approach. We can observe that our method can successfully detect the novel objects while the baseline tends to misclassify these objects as base classes.

5   Conclusion

To solve the potential overfitting in few-shot object detection, we propose a knowledge distillation framework. We first learn a *PA-BoVW* model using two pretext tasks, namely Pixel-to-Propagation Consistency and image classification. Based on the *PA-BoVW* model, then we perform distillation to guide the learning of detector. As an orthogonal component, our approach can be easily combined with other methods and significantly improve the performance.

Acknowledgements. This work was supported in part by the NSFC fund (U2013210, 62006060, 62176077), in part by the Guangdong Basic and Applied Basic Research Foundation under Grant (2019Bl515120055, 2021A1515012528, 2022A1515010306), in part by the Shenzhen Key Technical Project under Grant 2020N046, in part by the Shenzhen Fundamental Research Fund under Grant (JCYJ20210324132210025), in part by the Shenzhen Stable Support Plan Fund for Universities (GXWD20201230155427003-20200824125730001, GXWD202012 30155427003-20200824164357001), in part by the Medical Biometrics Perception and Analysis Engineering Laboratory, Shenzhen, China, and in part by the Guangdong Provincial Key Laboratory of Novel Security Intelligence Technologies (2022B1212010005).

References

1. Cao, Y., et al.: Few-shot object detection via association and discrimination. In: NeurIPS (2021)
2. Chen, G., Choi, W., Yu, X., Han, T., Chandraker, M.: Learning efficient object detection models with knowledge distillation. In: NeurIPS (2017)
3. Chen, H., Wang, Y., Wang, G., Qiao, Y.: LSTD: a low-shot transfer detector for object detection. In: AAAI (2018)
4. Chen, W.Y., Liu, Y.C., Kira, Z., Wang, Y.C.F., Huang, J.B.: A closer look at few-shot classification. In: ICLR (2018)
5. Cogswell, M., Ahmed, F., Girshick, R., Zitnick, L., Batra, D.: Reducing overfitting in deep networks by decorrelating representations. arXiv preprint arXiv:1511.06068 (2015)
6. Csurka, G., Dance, C., Fan, L., Willamowski, J., Bray, C.: Visual categorization with bags of keypoints. In: ECCVW (2004)
7. Everingham, M., Van Gool, L., Williams, C.K., Winn, J., Zisserman, A.: The pascal visual object classes (VOC) challenge. Int. J. Comput. Vis. **88**(2), 303–338 (2010)
8. Fan, Q., Zhuo, W., Tang, C.K., Tai, Y.W.: Few-shot object detection with attention-RPN and multi-relation detector. In: CVPR (2020)
9. Fan, Z., Ma, Y., Li, Z., Sun, J.: Generalized few-shot object detection without forgetting. In: CVPR (2021)
10. Finn, C., Abbeel, P., Levine, S.: Model-agnostic meta-learning for fast adaptation of deep networks. In: ICML (2017)
11. Gidaris, S., Bursuc, A., Komodakis, N., Pérez, P., Cord, M.: Learning representations by predicting bags of visual words. In: CVPR (2020)
12. Gidaris, S., Bursuc, A., Puy, G., Komodakis, N., Cord, M., Perez, P.: OBoW: online bag-of-visual-words generation for self-supervised learning. In: CVPR (2021)
13. Han, G., He, Y., Huang, S., Ma, J., Chang, S.F.: Query adaptive few-shot object detection with heterogeneous graph convolutional networks. In: ICCV (2021)
14. Hariharan, B., Girshick, R.B.: Low-shot visual recognition by shrinking and hallucinating features. In: ICCV (2017)
15. He, K., Zhang, X., Ren, S., Sun, J.: Deep residual learning for image recognition. In: CVPR (2016)
16. Hinton, G., Vinyals, O., Dean, J.: Distilling the knowledge in a neural network. arXiv preprint arXiv:1503.02531 (2015)
17. Hu, H., Bai, S., Li, A., Cui, J., Wang, L.: Dense relation distillation with context-aware aggregation for few-shot object detection. In: CVPR (2021)
18. Jain, H., Gidaris, S., Komodakis, N., Pérez, P., Cord, M.: QuEST: quantized embedding space for transferring knowledge. In: Vedaldi, A., Bischof, H., Brox, T., Frahm, J.-M. (eds.) ECCV 2020. LNCS, vol. 12366, pp. 173–189. Springer, Cham (2020). https://doi.org/10.1007/978-3-030-58589-1_11

19. Kang, B., Liu, Z., Wang, X., Yu, F., Feng, J., Darrell, T.: Few-shot object detection via feature reweighting. In: ICCV (2019)
20. Karlinsky, L., et al.: RepMet: representative-based metric learning for classification and few-shot object detection. In: CVPR (2019)
21. Kim, J., Kim, T., Kim, S., Yoo, C.D.: Edge-labeling graph neural network for few-shot learning. In: CVPR (2019)
22. Lazebnik, S., Schmid, C., Ponce, J.: Beyond bags of features: Spatial pyramid matching for recognizing natural scene categories. In: CVPR (2006)
23. Lee, K., Maji, S., Ravichandran, A., Soatto, S.: Meta-learning with differentiable convex optimization. In: CVPR (2019)
24. Li, A., Li, Z.: Transformation invariant few-shot object detection. In: CVPR (2021)
25. Li, B., Yang, B., Liu, C., Liu, F., Ji, R., Ye, Q.: Beyond max-margin: class margin equilibrium for few-shot object detection. In: CVPR (2021)
26. Li, Y., et al.: Few-shot object detection via classification refinement and distractor retreatment. In: CVPR (2021)
27. Lin, T.Y., Goyal, P., Girshick, R., He, K., Dollár, P.: Focal loss for dense object detection. In: ICCV (2017)
28. Lin, T.-Y., et al.: Microsoft COCO: common objects in context. In: Fleet, D., Pajdla, T., Schiele, B., Tuytelaars, T. (eds.) ECCV 2014. LNCS, vol. 8693, pp. 740–755. Springer, Cham (2014). https://doi.org/10.1007/978-3-319-10602-1_48
29. Van der Maaten, L., Hinton, G.: Visualizing data using t-SNE. J. M. Learn. Res. 9(11), 2579–2605 (2008)
30. Qiao, L., Zhao, Y., Li, Z., Qiu, X., Wu, J., Zhang, C.: DeFRCN: decoupled faster R-CNN for few-shot object detection. In: ICCV (2021)
31. Redmon, J., Farhadi, A.: YOLO9000: better, faster, stronger. In: CVPR (2017)
32. Ren, S., He, K., Girshick, R., Sun, J.: Faster R-CNN: towards real-time object detection with region proposal networks. In: NeurIPS (2015)
33. Romero, A., Ballas, N., Kahou, S.E., Chassang, A., Gatta, C., Bengio, Y.: FitNets: hints for thin deep nets. arXiv preprint arXiv:1412.6550 (2014)
34. Ru, L., Du, B., Zhan, Y., Wu, C.: Weakly-supervised semantic segmentation with visual words learning and hybrid pooling. Int. J. Comput. Vis. 130(4), 1127–1144 (2022)
35. Russakovsky, O., et al.: ImageNet large scale visual recognition challenge. Int. J. Comput. Vis. 115(3), 211–252 (2015)
36. Satorras, V.G., Estrach, J.B.: Few-shot learning with graph neural networks. In: ICLR (2018)
37. Snell, J., Swersky, K., Zemel, R.S.: Prototypical networks for few-shot learning. In: NeurIPS (2017)
38. Sun, B., Li, B., Cai, S., Yuan, Y., Zhang, C.: FSCE: few-shot object detection via contrastive proposal encoding. In: CVPR (2021)
39. Tian, Y., Krishnan, D., Isola, P.: Contrastive representation distillation. In: ICLR (2019)
40. Tian, Z., Shen, C., Chen, H., He, T.: FCOS: fully convolutional one-stage object detection. In: ICCV (2019)
41. Vinyals, O., Blundell, C., Lillicrap, T., Kavukcuoglu, K., Wierstra, D.: Matching networks for one shot learning. In: NeurIPS (2016)
42. Wang, J., Yang, J., Yu, K., Lv, F., Huang, T., Gong, Y.: Locality-constrained linear coding for image classification. In: CVPR (2010)
43. Wang, T., Yuan, L., Zhang, X., Feng, J.: Distilling object detectors with fine-grained feature imitation. In: CVPR (2019)

44. Wang, X., Huang, T., Gonzalez, J., Darrell, T., Yu, F.: Frustratingly simple few-shot object detection. In: ICML (2020)
45. Wang, Y.X., Girshick, R.B., Hebert, M., Hariharan, B.: Low-shot learning from imaginary data. In: CVPR (2018)
46. Wang, Y.X., Ramanan, D., Hebert, M.: Meta-learning to detect rare objects. In: ICCV (2019)
47. Wu, A., Han, Y., Zhu, L., Yang, Y.: Universal-prototype enhancing for few-shot object detection. In: ICCV (2021)
48. Wu, A., Zhao, S., Deng, C., Liu, W.: Generalized and discriminative few-shot object detection via SVD-dictionary enhancement. In: NeurIPS (2021)
49. Wu, J., Liu, S., Huang, D., Wang, Y.: Multi-scale positive sample refinement for few-shot object detection. In: Vedaldi, A., Bischof, H., Brox, T., Frahm, J.-M. (eds.) ECCV 2020. LNCS, vol. 12361, pp. 456–472. Springer, Cham (2020). https://doi.org/10.1007/978-3-030-58517-4_27
50. Xiao, Y., Marlet, R.: Few-shot object detection and viewpoint estimation for objects in the wild. In: Vedaldi, A., Bischof, H., Brox, T., Frahm, J.-M. (eds.) ECCV 2020. LNCS, vol. 12362, pp. 192–210. Springer, Cham (2020). https://doi.org/10.1007/978-3-030-58520-4_12
51. Xie, Z., Lin, Y., Zhang, Z., Cao, Y., Lin, S., Hu, H.: Propagate yourself: exploring pixel-level consistency for unsupervised visual representation learning. In: CVPR (2021)
52. Yan, X., Chen, Z., Xu, A., Wang, X., Liang, X., Lin, L.: Meta R-CNN: towards general solver for instance-level low-shot learning. In: ICCV (2019)
53. Yang, L., Li, L., Zhang, Z., Zhou, X., Zhou, E., Liu, Y.: DPGN: distribution propagation graph network for few-shot learning. In: CVPR (2020)
54. Yang, Y., Wei, F., Shi, M., Li, G.: Restoring negative information in few-shot object detection. In: NeurIPS (2020)
55. Yim, J., Joo, D., Bae, J., Kim, J.: A gift from knowledge distillation: fast optimization, network minimization and transfer learning. In: CVPR (2017)
56. Zhang, L., Zhou, S., Guan, J., Zhang, J.: Accurate few-shot object detection with support-query mutual guidance and hybrid loss. In: CVPR (2021)
57. Zhang, W., Wang, Y.X.: Hallucination improves few-shot object detection. In: CVPR (2021)
58. Zhou, B., Khosla, A., Lapedriza, A., Oliva, A., Torralba, A.: Learning deep features for discriminative localization. In: CVPR (2016)
59. Zhu, C., Chen, F., Ahmed, U., Shen, Z., Savvides, M.: Semantic relation reasoning for shot-stable few-shot object detection. In: CVPR (2021)

SALISA: Saliency-Based Input Sampling for Efficient Video Object Detection

Babak Ehteshami Bejnordi[1][✉], Amirhossein Habibian[1], Fatih Porikli[2], and Amir Ghodrati[1]

[1] Qualcomm AI Research, Amsterdam, The Netherlands
{behtesha,ahabibia,ghodrati}@qti.qualcomm.com
[2] Qualcomm AI Research, San Diego, USA
fporikli@qti.qualcomm.com

Abstract. High-resolution images are widely adopted for high-performance object detection in videos. However, processing high-resolution inputs comes with high computation costs, and naive down-sampling of the input to reduce the computation costs quickly degrades the detection performance. In this paper, we propose SALISA, a novel non-uniform SALiency-based Input SAmpling technique for video object detection that allows for heavy down-sampling of unimportant background regions while preserving the fine-grained details of a high-resolution image. The resulting image is spatially smaller, leading to reduced computational costs while enabling a performance comparable to a high-resolution input. To achieve this, we propose a differentiable resampling module based on a thin plate spline spatial transformer network (TPS-STN). This module is regularized by a novel loss to provide an explicit supervision signal to learn to "magnify" salient regions. We report state-of-the-art results in the low compute regime on the ImageNet-VID and UA-DETRAC video object detection datasets. We demonstrate that on both datasets, the mAP of an EfficientDet-D1 (EfficientDet-D2) gets on par with EfficientDet-D2 (EfficientDet-D3) at a much lower computational cost. We also show that SALISA significantly improves the detection of small objects. In particular, SALISA with an EfficientDet-D1 detector improves the detection of small objects by 77%, and remarkably also outperforms EfficientDet-D3 baseline.

Keywords: Video object detection · Saliency · Resampling · Efficient object detection · Spatial transformer

1 Introduction

The rise in the quality of image capturing devices such as 4K cameras has enabled AI solutions to discover the most detailed video contents and, therefore, allowed them to be widely adopted for high-performance object detection in videos. However, the increased recognition performance resulting from this higher resolution signal comes

---

Qualcomm AI Research is an initiative of Qualcomm Technologies, Inc.

Supplementary Information The online version contains supplementary material available at https://doi.org/10.1007/978-3-031-20080-9_18.

with increased computational costs. This limits the application of state-of-the-art video object detectors on resource-constrained devices. As such, designing efficient object detection methods for processing high-resolution video streams becomes crucial for a wide range of real-world applications such as autonomous driving, augmented reality, and video surveillance.

To enable efficient video object detection, a large body of works has been focusing on reducing feature computation on visually-similar adjacent video frames [4,9,17, 22,23,40,41]. This is achieved by interleaving heavy and light feature extractors [17], limiting the computation to a local window [4,9], or extrapolating features from a key frame to subsequent frames using a light optical flow predictor [40,41]. However, these approaches either suffer from feature misalignment resulting from two different feature extractors, or inefficiency in dealing with frequent global scene changes.

An alternative approach to efficient object detection is to focus on designing lightweight yet highly accurate architectures such as EfficientDet [33]. Recent astounding advances in developing such models have deemed some of the above efficient approaches no longer applicable. For instance, flow-based feature extrapolation might no longer be a proper substitute for existing efficient feature extractors [32,33], as the cost of flow computation is no longer negligible. To be more specific, EfficientDet-D0 [33]

Fig. 1. An illustration of a non-uniform detail-preserving downsampling of input by SALISAleading to improved detection results.

costs only 2.5 GFLOPs per frame, while estimating flow by FlowNet-Inception [5] alone costs 1.8 GFLOPs, translating to 72% of the backbone itself [23]. However, such efficient architectures may still be expensive when applied to high-resolution video frames. On the other hand, naive down-sampling of the input to reduce the computation costs quickly degrades the performance [33,42]. For example, the performance of EfficientDet-D6 on COCO [15] degrades from 52.6% to 47.6% when the input is down-sampled by a factor of two [33].

In this work, we propose SALISA, a novel non-uniform input sampling technique that retains the fine-grained details of a high-resolution image while allowing for heavy down-sampling of unimportant background regions (see Fig. 1). The resulting detail-preserved image is spatially smaller, leading to reduced computational cost but at the same time enabling a performance comparable to a high-resolution input. Given a sequence of video frames, we first apply a high performing detection model on a high-resolution input at $T = 1$ (without resampling). We then generate a saliency map from the detection output to guide the detailed-preserving resampling for the next high-resolution frame. This is achieved via a resampling module that applies a thin plate spline (TPS) [6] transformation to warp the high-resolution input to a down-scaled, detail-preserved one. The resulting resampled frame is then fed to the detector, which consequently has an easier job detecting objects at a lower computational cost.

Our resampling module is based on a thin plate spline spatial transformer network (TPS-STN) [10]. TPS-STN was originally proposed for image classification and used the task loss to train the parameters of STN for digit recognition in MNIST and SVHN.

However, adapting this training scheme to object detection in natural images is nontrivial as STN cannot learn to "magnify" salient regions without an explicit supervision signal. To address this, we propose a loss term that imposes STN to mimic a content-aware up-sampler. In particular, we use a weighted ℓ_2-loss between the sampling grid generated by our TPS-STN and the non-parametric attention-based sampler [38] designed for preserving details. Unlike the non-parametric approaches such as attention-based sampler [38] or classical seam carving techniques [1, 29], our regularized sampling module is fully differentiable, computationally inexpensive, and generates distortion-free outputs.

Our contributions are as follows:

- We propose a novel efficient framework for video object detection. Using a saliency map obtained from a previous frame, we perform a non-uniform detail-preserving down-sampling of the current frame, enabling an accurate prediction at a lower computational cost.
- To perform the resampling, we develop a fully differentiable resampling module based on a thin plate spline spatial transformer network. We propose a new regularization technique that enables a more effective transformation of the input.
- We report state-of-the-art results in the low compute regime on the ImageNet-VID and UA-DETRAC video object detection datasets. In particular, we demonstrate that on both datasets, the mAP of an EfficientDet-D1 (EfficientDet-D2) gets on par with EfficientDet-D2 (EfficientDet-D3) at a much lower computational cost.

2   Related Work

Efficient Video Object Detection. A straightforward approach to efficient video object detection is to apply existing efficient object detectors [2, 3, 18, 27, 33, 42] on a per-frame basis. However, such an approach does not take the temporal redundancy into account and therefore is computationally sub-optimal for video object detection. In this paper, we specifically use the state-of-the-art cost-effective detection model EfficientDet [33] as our baseline and further extend it for video object detection.

Several methods are proposed to leverage temporal coherency between adjacent frames by tracking previous object detections to skip current detection [19, 22], using template matching to learn patchwise correlation features in adjacent frames [23], limiting the feature computation by processing only a small sub-window of the frames [4, 9], using heavy and light networks in an interleaving manner [17], or efficiently propagating features via a light FlowNet [40, 41]. However, these methods might suffer from tracking errors, misalignments between features, or finding a suitable sub-window. Moreover, with existing efficient backbones [32], one may find out flow-based techniques no longer yield significant speed-ups, as the cost of flow computation is not negligible. As an alternative, we propose to resample the frame such that it retains the fine-grained details while allowing for heavy downsampling of background areas. The resulting image is spatially smaller, leading to a reduction in computation cost while enabling a performance comparable to a high-resolution input.

Adaptive Spatial Sampling. One of the major challenges in object detection is to represent and detect fine-grained details in high-resolution images efficiently. One way to tackle this problem is to use hierarchical representations. [8, 12, 30, 36] introduce hierarchical methods to refine the processing of a high-resolution image by adaptively zooming into their proper scales. However, such a hierarchical processing approach makes these methods less suitable for real-time applications.

An alternative approach is to adaptively transform the input such that important fine-grained details are better preserved [7, 10, 26, 38]. The pioneering work of Spatial Transformer Networks (STN) [10] proposes a differentiable module that enables a generic class of input transformations such as affine, projective, and thin plate spline transformations. While STN works well for MNIST and SVHN datasets, without explicit supervision, it has a hard job of learning effective transformations for complex recognition tasks. Learning-to-zoom [26] uses saliency maps generated by a CNN as guidance to performing a nonuniform sampling that magnifies small details. However, this method causes substantial deformation in the vicinity of the magnified regions, which is particularly harmful when objects overlap or positioned next to each other. Trilinear attention sampling network [38] aims to learn subtle feature representations from hundreds of part proposals for fine-grained image recognition. This technique overcomes the undesirable deformations observed in [26]. However, it is computationally more expensive, non-differentiable, and may still generate undesirable deformations in the background or lower saliency regions. Our method is based on a thin plate spline STN and employs [38] to supervise the STN, allowing it to work on complex datasets while largely eliminating the undesirable distortions caused by [38].

The adaptive spatial sampling techniques discussed above were primarily designed for image classification tasks. However, optimizing these techniques for downstream tasks such as object detection and semantic segmentation is more challenging. In particular, an undesirable deformation on a non-salient region is unlikely to harm the output prediction of a classification network. At the same time, it can deteriorate the performance of object detection or semantic segmentation model. Jin et al. [11] have proposed to use the learning-to-zoom approach [26] for adaptive downsampling of the input for semantic segmentation. To discourage the network from a naive sampling of easy-to-segment regions like background, the authors add an edge loss introduced in [24]. Recently, [34] has proposed a magnification layer based on learning-to-zoom [26] to resample pixels such that background pixels make room for salient pixels of interest. While the major focus of [26] is on improving object detection accuracy on small objects, we concentrate on increasing efficiency and at the same time improving the performance.

3 SALISA

Given a set of high-resolution video frames and their labels $\{\mathbf{f}_i, \mathbf{y}_i\}_{i=1}^N$, we aim to detect the bounding box and category of objects in each frame. Figure 2 presents an overview of our proposed SALiency-based Input SAmpling (SALISA) framework for efficient video object detection. SALISA consists of $i)$ two off-the-shelf object detection models $\mathcal{D}_{\text{key}}$ and $\mathcal{D}$, where $\text{FLOPs}_{\mathcal{D}} \ll \text{FLOPs}_{\mathcal{D}_{\text{key}}}$, $ii)$ a saliency map generator, $iii)$ a resampling module, and $iv)$ an inverse transformation module. At inference, in the first step, we pass the first high-resolution frame $\mathbf{f}_i$ (key frame) to a high-performing detection model $\mathcal{D}_{\text{key}}$. The bounding boxes generated by this model and their corresponding

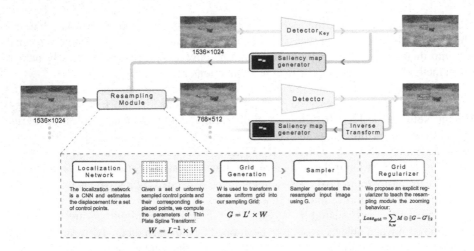

Fig. 2. Overview of SALISA. The first frame, from a set of high-resolution frames, is passed to a high performing detector ($\mathcal{D}_{\text{key}}$). The saliency map generator uses the prediction output to generate a saliency map. This map and the second high-resolution frame are passed to our resampling module to perform a detail-preserving down-sampling operation. The output of this module is passed to a light detector ($\mathcal{D}$) which is able to perform on par with $\mathcal{D}_{\text{key}}$ at a much lower computational cost. The output of $\mathcal{D}$ undergoes an inverse transformation to get back to the original image grid before being fed to the saliency map generation for the next frame. This process is continued for processing subsequent frames.

scores are then passed to a saliency map generator to build a global saliency map. This map and the second high-resolution frame $\mathbf{f}_{i+1}$ are then passed to our resampling module. The output of the resampling module is a down-sampled detail-preserving image $\mathbf{f}'_{i+1}$ which is fed to the light detector $\mathcal{D}$. Due to the nature of this down-sampled image, $\mathcal{D}$ is able to perform on par with $\mathcal{D}_{\text{key}}$ at a lower computational cost. For each of the following frames $\mathbf{f}_j$, we generate the saliency map from the detection output of frame $\mathbf{f}_{j-1}$ using $\mathcal{D}$. To avoid propagating errors over time, we update the detection output using the strong detector $\mathcal{D}_{\text{key}}$ at every S frames. In the following sections, we describe the different components of SALISA in details.

3.1 Saliency Map Generator

The saliency map generator is a non-parametric detection-to-mask generator, outputting a map corresponding to salient pixels that need to be preserved during resampling. We generate this mask from all the bounding box detections with a score above τ. The objects with an area $\alpha < 0.5\%$ of the image area are assigned a label of 1 and the ones with a larger area are assigned a label of 0.5 (we performed an ablation study on the area parameter α in Sect. 4.3). This will allow our resampling module to focus more on preserving the resolution of smaller objects. The background pixels are labeled as 0. Note that the saliency values of 0.5 and 1 are chosen to make a distinction between large and small objects and the exact choice of saliency values are not critical for performance. We down-sample this saliency map to 128×128 before passing it to the resampling module.

3.2   Resampling Module

Our resampling module is based on a thin plate spline spatial transformer [10]. TPS-STN has three main components: *i)* The localization network, *ii)* The grid generator, and *iii)* the sampler.

Localization Network. Our localization network is a VGG-style [31] architecture consisting of 10 convolutional and 2 fully connected layers (0.06 GFLOPs and 739k parameters). This network gets the saliency map as input and estimates the displacement of a set of $N = 256$ control points defined on a 16×16 grid in a Euclidean plane.

Grid Generator. The grid generator is responsible for producing the sampling grid and works as follows. Given a set of N control points sampled uniformly on a 2D grid $\dot{P} \in \mathbb{R}^{N \times 2}$ and their corresponding displaced control points $\dot{V} \in \mathbb{R}^{N \times 2}$ provided by the localization network, we solve a linear system to derive the parameter $W \in \mathbb{R}^{(N+3) \times 2}$ of TPS as follows:

$$W = \underbrace{\begin{bmatrix} K & P \\ P^T & O \end{bmatrix}^{-1}}_{L} \times V, \qquad P = [\mathbf{1}, \dot{P}], \qquad V = \begin{bmatrix} \dot{V} \\ \mathbf{0} \end{bmatrix} \tag{1}$$

where the submatrix $K \in \mathbb{R}^{N \times N}$ is defined as $K_{ij} = U(\|\mathbf{p}_i, \mathbf{p}_j\|)$ where $\mathbf{p} \in \dot{P}$ and $U(r) = r^2 log(r)$ is the radial basis kernel. $O \in \mathbb{R}^{3 \times 3}$, and $\mathbf{0} \in \mathbb{R}^{3 \times 2}$ are submatrices of zeros and $\mathbf{1} \in \mathbb{R}^{N \times 1}$ is submatrix of ones. Note that one can precompute $L \in \mathbb{R}^{(N+3) \times (N+3)}$ and its inverse. We refer the reader to the **Appendix** for the detailed overview of the algebraic crux of the thin plate method.

   Once we estimate W, we can conveniently apply the deformation to a dense uniform grid to obtain the sampling grid G, as follows:

$$G = L' \times W, \tag{2}$$

where L' is computed similarly to L but with dense points.

Sampler. In the final step, the sampler takes the sampling grid G, along with the input image $\mathbf{f}_{i+1}$ to produce the detail-preserving resampled image $\mathbf{f}'_{i+1}$. Figure 3 shows the deformation field obtained from G and the resampling results for two example images.

Regularization. Learning the parameters of the localization network, without direct guidance on where to magnify, results in inhomogeneous distortions and may not preserve the desired detail. To address this, we propose to regularize the sampling grid

Fig. 3. Deformation field of TPS transformation. Left shows the deformation field overlaid on original images. Right shows the resampled images.

G through a non-parametric attention-based sampling method [38]. This resampling method takes as input a saliency map and generates a sampling grid that preserves the salient regions in the map. We propose to use the sampling grid generated by this method as a supervision signal for our sampling module to learn an explicit zooming effect. However, despite obtaining superior sampling results compared to alternative methods [13,26], this approach [38] is non-differentiable, computationally expensive, and may generate undesirable deformations when multiple objects with various saliency levels appear in the same image. This method decomposes the saliency map into two marginal distributions over x and y axes. Unfortunately, this marginalization leads to undesirable distortions for low saliency regions located on the same row/column as an object with a higher saliency level. More concretely, if the coordinates (i, j) and (i', j') in the saliency map have high values, the resulting sampling grid is not only dense at (i, j) and (i', j'), but also at (i, j') and (i', j) regardless of its saliency level. This error can be problematic when there are multiple objects with different saliency levels in the image. While our resampling module is fully differentiable and computationally inexpensive, getting an unmediated supervision from [38] may carry the same undesirable artifacts to our sampler. To address this issue, we design the following weighted ℓ_2-loss function:

$$Loss_{\text{grid}} = \sum_{h,w} M \odot \|G - G'\|_2, \tag{3}$$

where G is a grid generated by our resampling module, G' is the grid generated by the attention-based sampling method [38], and M is a weighted mask with the spatial dimension of $h \times w$. The weighted mask gets assigned different values for the small objects (O_s), large objects (O_l), and background (bg). Categorising the objects as small or large is based on the area parameter α. If the saliency map generated in Step 3.1 only contains small objects or only large objects we set (O_s, O_l, bg) to $(1, 0, \gamma)$ and $(0, 1, \gamma)$, respectively. Otherwise if it contains both small and large objects to $(1, 0, 0)$. Intuitively, when the saliency map is composed of a single saliency level (e.g., multiple small objects), [38] generates plausible zooming effects for all the objects and, therefore, we can get full supervision for the entire grid. In contrast, when the saliency map is composed of multiple saliency levels (e.g., a combination of small and large objects), the method [38] may distort objects with lower saliency. Therefore, we choose not to get supervision in those regions by masking them to zero. Note that having a down-weighted supervision (soft) in these regions did not lead to any improvements.

We train our network end-to-end by adding $Loss_{\text{grid}}$ to the detection loss. As can be seen in Fig. 4, our resampling module generally generates similar zooming effects to [38] yet largely eliminates its distortions (see the flying jets and the median barrier separating the cars).

3.3   Inverse Transformation Module

Given the bounding box outputs of the detector D for a resampled image, we apply an inverse transformation to bring the bounding boxes coordinates back to the original image grid. This is achieved by subtracting the grid displacement offset from the bounding box coordinates. As the bounding box coordinates are floating point values, for each bounding box coordinate, we obtain the exact original coordinate by linearly interpolating the displacements corresponding to its two closest cells on the deformation grid.

4 Experiments

To demonstrate the efficacy of SALISA, we conduct experiments on two large-scale video object detection datasets ImageNet-VID [28] and UA-DETRAC [20,21,35] as described in Sect. 4.1. We provide comparisons to state-of-the-art video object detection models and demonstrate that SALISA outperforms the state of the art while significantly reducing computational costs in Sect. 4.2. Additionally, to demonstrate the efficacy of our regularized sampling module, we compare our method with other competing sampling approaches. Finally, we present several ablation studies to discuss the effect of several design choices on the performance of our method in Sect. 4.3.

4.1 Experimental Setup

Datasets. We evaluate our method on two large video object detection datasets: ImageNet-VID [28] and UA-DETRAC [20,21,35]. ImageNet-VID contains 30 object categories with 3862 training and 555 validation videos. Following the protocols in [17,41], during training, we also use a subset of ImageNet-DET training images, which contain the same 30 categories. We report standard mean average precision (mAP) at IoU = 0.5 on the validation set, similar to [17,41]. UA-DETRAC consists of 10 h of video (about $140k$ frames in total) captured from 100 real-world traffic scenes. The scenes include urban highways, traffic crossings, T-junctions, etc., and the bounding box annotations are provided for vehicles. The dataset comes with a partitioning of 60 and 40 videos as train and test data, respectively. Following [9], average precision (AP), averaged over multiple IoU thresholds varying from 0.5 to 0.95 with a step size of 0.05 is reported on the test data.

Implementation Details. We use different variants of EfficientDet [33], namely D0-D4, as detectors in our video object detection framework. SALISA has two separate object detectors, one for the key frame ($\mathcal{D}_{key}$) and another for all succeeding frames ($\mathcal{D}$). In our experiments, we use two successive scaled-up variants of EfficientDet, for example, EfficientDet-D3 and EfficientDet-D2, where the heavier model is applied to the key frame and the lighter one to the rest of the frames. In this particular example, we refer to our model as SALISA with EfficientDet-D2. We follow the same procedure, for baseline EfficientDet models without resampling.

We first trained the resampling module independently from the detection network using the regularization loss described in Sect. 3.2. For both datasets, we then trained the EfficientDet networks, pre-trained on MS-COCO [15], in an image-based fashion. In the final step, we fine-tuned the resampling module and the object detection networks end-to-end. The complete details for training are provided in the **Appendix**.

During inference, key frames are picked once every S frames ($S = 2 \sim 32$ frames) and passed to $\mathcal{D}_{key}$ while the succeeding $S - 1$ frames are processed by $\mathcal{D}$. For ImageNet-VID and UA-DETRAC experiments, we set S to 16 and 32, respectively. We set the parameter of the saliency map generator τ to 0.5. We set γ controlling the

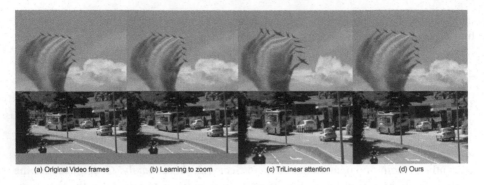

(a) Original Video frames   (b) Learning to zoom   (c) TriLinear attention   (d) Ours

Fig. 4. Comparison of different input resampling methods. (a) shows example video frames from ImageNet-VID dataset. (b), (c), and (d) show the result of resampling using learning to zoom [26], TriLinear attention [38], and our proposed resampling module, respectively. Our resampling module effectively preserves the spatial resolution of salient objects and despite being regularized by [38], does not generate artifacts in background regions. This is evident from the resampled images (see the flying jets and the median barrier separating the cars).

weight of the regularizer in background regions to 0.5. We report the average per-frame computation cost of our model by considering the FLOPs of $\mathcal{D}_{key}$, $\mathcal{D}$, and resampling module. In our experiments, unless otherwise specified, for both baseline models and SALISA, predictions are made for odd frames f_i where $i \in \{1, 3, 5, \ldots, N - 1\}$ and propagated to the next frame f_{i+1} without further processing. For SALISA, this means propagating the saliency maps every other frame. For both baseline and SALISA, this setup yields up to 50% reduction in FLOPs with only a small drop in the accuracy. To achieve the highest performance on each benchmark, we still apply our model densely to all frames and explicitly mention dense prediction if that is the case.

4.2 Results

Comparison to State of the Art: UA-DETRAC. We compare SALISA to several image and video object detectors on the UA-DETRAC dataset: EfficientDet [33] as the state of the art in efficient object detection in images and the main baseline for SALISA, Deep Feature Flow (DFF) [41] as a seminal work on efficient object detection, and Spot-Net [25] as the highest performing method on the UA-DETRAC benchmark. Figure 5 presents accuracy vs. computations trade-off curves for SALISA and the baseline EfficientDet models (D0-D3) for video object detection in UA-DETRAC. As can be seen, our method consistently outperforms the baseline EfficientDet models. Importantly, SALISA with EfficientDet-D2 (61.2%) outperforms EfficientDet-D3 model (60.3%) at lower than half the computational cost. In the low-compute regime, SALISA with EfficientDet-D0 outperforms the baseline EfficientDet-D0 model by 2.9%. The comparison with competing methods is shown in Table 1. We outperform DFF [41] both in terms of computational costs and accuracy. When densely applied to all frames, SAL-ISA with EfficientDet-D3 achieves state-of-the-art mAP of 62.9% on UA-DETRAC at a much lower computational cost than SpotNet (972 VS. 40 GFlops).

Table 1. Comparison with state of the art on UA-DETRAC.

Method	Backbone	mAP (%)	FLOPs (G)
DFF [41]	ResNet-50	52.6	75.3
SpotNet [25]	CenterNet [39]	62.8	972.0
EfficientDet [33]	EfficientNet-B2	59.4	5.9
EfficientDet [33]	EfficientNet-B3	60.3	13.4
SALISA(Ours)	EfficientNet-B2	61.2	5.9
SALISA(Ours)	EfficientNet-B3	62.4	13.4
EfficientDet [33]	EfficientNet-B0	51.3	1.36
EfficientDet [33]	EfficientNet-B1	56.9	3.20
SALISA(Ours)	EfficientNet-B0	54.2	1.39
SALISA(Ours)	EfficientNet-B1	59.1	3.23

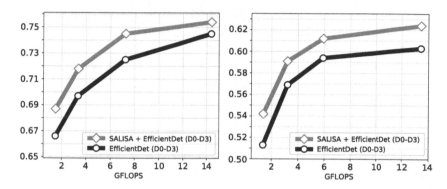

Fig. 5. Performance comparison of baseline EfficientDet [33] and corresponding SAL-ISA+EfficientDet models on ImageNet-VID (left) and UA-DETRAC (Right).

Finally, the results presented in Fig. 6 show some challenging object detection scenes from the test set. For example, the frame in the first row shows a crowded scene with many vehicles which makes zooming particularly challenging. Our model has squeezed the right side of the road to increase the resolution of the salient objects. This has enabled SALISA with EfficientDet-D1 to detect new cars which were neither detected by the baseline EfficientDet-D1 nor by the heavier keyframe detector EfficientDet-D2.

Comparison to State of the Art: ImageNet-VID. The experimental results of SAL-ISA on the ImageNet-VID dataset are presented in Table 2. We compare our method to PatchNet [23], PatchWork [4], TSM [14], DFF [41], Mobile-DFF [41], Mobile-SSD, TAFM [16], SkipConv [9], and finally EfficientDet [33] as our baseline. DFF and Mobile-DFF are flow-based methods, PatchNet is a tracking method, TAFM is an LSTM-based recurrent method, PatchWork and SkipConv conditionally limit feature computation, and TSM reduces the computation by shifting features across time. In Table 2, these methods are categorized as low compute and extremely low com-

Table 2. Comparison with state of the art on ImageNet-VID. * indicates that the model has been applied every three frames.

Method	Backbone	mAP (%)	FLOPs (G)
DFF (R-FCN) [41]	ResNet-101	72.5	34.9
PatchNet (R-FCN) [23]	ResNet-101	73.1	34.2
TSM [14]	ResNext101 [37]	76.3	169
SkipConv [9]	EfficientNet-B2	72.3	9.2
SkipConv [9]	EfficientNet-B3	75.2	22.4
EfficientDet [33]	EfficientNet-B2	72.5	7.2
EfficientDet [33]	EfficientNet-B3	74.5	14.4
SALISA(Ours)	EfficientNet-B2	74.5	7.2
SALISA(Ours)	EfficientNet-B3	75.4	14.4
Mobile-SSD	MobileNet-V2	54.7	2.0
PatchWork [4]	MobileNet-V2	57.4	0.97
PatchNet (EfficientDet) [23]	EfficientNet-B0	58.9	0.73
Mobile-DFF [41]	MobileNet	62.8	0.71
TAFM (SSDLite) [16]	MobileNet-V2	64.1	1.18
SkipConv [9]	EfficientNet-B0	66.2	0.98
SkipConv [9]	EfficientNet-B1	70.5	2.90
EfficientDet [33]	EfficientNet-B0	66.6	1.48
EfficientDet [33]	EfficientNet-B1	69.7	3.35
SALISA(Ours)	EfficientNet-B0*	67.4	0.86
SALISA(Ours)	EfficientNet-B0	68.7	1.50
SALISA(Ours)	EfficientNet-B1	71.8	3.38

pute. The results show that among the extremely low compute methods, SALISA with EfficientDet-D0 significantly outperforms Mobile-SSD, PatchWork [4], TAFM [16], and SkipConv [9] at a lower computational cost. While PatchNet [23] and Mobile-DFF [41] have roughly 0.15 lower GFLOPs than our lightest model, they show a significant drop in mAP ($\sim$10%) compared to SALISA. In general, template matching techniques offer significant computational saving without improving accuracy while SALISA can provide gains in both aspects. See **Appendix** for additional comparison with tracking baselines.

Among the low compute methods, SALISA with EfficientDet-D3 outperforms DFF and PatchNet by 2.9% and 2.3%, respectively at roughly 40% of their computational cost. TSM is the highest performing competitor that achieves an mAP of 76.3% at the cost of 169 GFLOPs. When densely applied to all frames, SALISA with EfficientDet-D3, obtains an mAP of 76.4% at 40 GFLOPs. Figure 5 presents accuracy vs. computations trade-off curves for SALISA and EfficientDet baseline models (D0-D3) for video object detection in ImageNet-VID. SALISA consistently boosts the performance of EfficientDet variants by adaptively resampling the input. Finally, SALISA with

Table 3. Performance comparison (mAP) across different object sizes on UA-DETRAC.

Table 4. Impact of input sampling method on UA-DETRAC (upper part) and ImageNet-VID (bottom part).

Model	Small	Medium	Large
EfficientDet-D0	6.4	47.8	72.1
EfficientDet-D1	8.4	54.8	75.7
EfficientDet-D2	12.3	58.1	77.1
EfficientDet-D3	12.5	59.1	78.5
SALISA-D0	7.4	53.1	73.0
SALISA-D1	14.9	58.2	76.6
SALISA-D2	15.3	59.4	77.7
SALISA-D3	16.6	60.1	78.0

Resampling method	D0	D1	D2
TPS-STN [10]	51.7	57.6	60.8
Learning to zoom [26]	39.2	47.7	52.1
Trilinear attention [38]	53.6	58.7	61.5
Our resampling module	**55.6**	**61.4**	**62.7**
TPS-STN [10]	69.1	71.1	73.7
Learning to zoom [26]	69.0	71.3	74.9
Trilinear attention [38]	69.4	71.5	74.8
Our resampling module	**69.7**	**72.4**	**75.2**

EfficientDet-D2 matches the mAP of the baseline EfficientDet-D3 at half the computational cost.

Performance Across Different Object Sizes. To demonstrate the efficacy of SALISA for detecting small objects, we report the mAP scores for different object sizes using the COCO framework [15]. As shown in Table 3, SALISA significantly improves small object detection compared to the baseline EfficientDet models. In particular, SALISA with EfficientDet-D1, improves the accuracy of small object detection by 77% (8.4% to 14.9%). Surprisingly, this is even higher than 12.5% mAP of EfficientDet-D3 baseline for small objects.

The mAP of medium-sized object detection increases from 54.8 to 58.2. There is no significant change in the performance of large object sizes as the base model can also effectively detect them. That is why lighter models with smaller inputs benefit more compared to heavier models that already receive a high resolution input.

Comparison to Different Sampling Approaches. In this experiment, we compare the performance of various sampling approaches [10, 26, 38] for a detail-preserving downsampling on both ImageNet-VID and UA-DETRAC datasets. To this end, we substitute our resampling module with these methods and use the same training protocol discussed in Sect. 4.1. The results are presented in Table 4. We first compare our resampling module to TPS-STN [10]. As can be seen, our regularization scheme is crucial for improving the results. TPS-STN without our regularizer, barely improves upon the baseline EfficientDet models. Our resampling module also yields a higher accuracy compared to [26] and [38] on both ImageNet-VID and UA-DETRAC datasets. While the gap in performance in different resampling methods is small on the ImageNet-VID dataset, SALISA greatly benefits from our resampling module on UA-DETRAC with a gap of more than 2% mAP. The videos in the ImageNet-VID dataset are mostly comprising one or two objects. The videos in the UA-DETRAC dataset, in contrast, include mostly crowded scenes with many objects in each frame. We conjecture that, in such multi-object wild videos the undesirable deformations induced by [26] and [38] can lower their benefits. Overall, our resampling module consistently outperforms competitors in all settings.

Wall-Clock Timing. We report the wall-clock timing (msec) of SALISA and the baseline EfficientDet models using Nvidia Tesla-V100 32GB. The inference time of Effi-

(a) Original Video frames   (b) EfficientDet-D2   (c) EfficientDet-D1   (d) SALISA (EfficientDet-D1)

Fig. 6. Detection results on the UA-DETRAC test set. Yellow boxes indicate true detections, red indicates false positive detections, and green boxes refer to new detections produced by our method as a result of input resampling. (a) shows the original video frames from UA-DETRAC dataset, (b), (c), and (d) show detection results generated by EfficientDet-D2 ($\mathcal{D}_{key}$), the baseline EfficientDet-D1 detector, and SALISA with EfficientDet-D1, respectively. As can be seen from the detections in the first and third row of *(c)*, the right side of the road in the first image and the vegetation in the third image have been pushed to the side to enable magnifying salient objects. This detail-preserving down-sampling has allowed for discovery of new objects that were otherwise missed by the baseline object detector. (Color figure online)

cientDet and SALISA for a batch size of one are as follows: **D0:** 49.4 vs 50.2, **D1:** 91.0 vs 95.4, **D2:** 152.7 vs 159.4, and **D3:** 304.8 vs 313.4. The overhead of our sampler (0.06 GFLOPs) is very small primarily because of its small input size.

4.3   Ablation Study

Number of Control Points in TPS. Estimating the parameters of TPS relies on defining correspondences between a set of control points and their displacements. Increasing the number of control points generally increases the flexibility of TPS. While we observe a reduction in $loss_{grid}$ when we increase the number of control points from 256 to 1024, we also notice more fluctuations and artifacts in the resulting resampled images as shown in Fig. 7. By increasing the number of control points from 256 to 1024, the mAP of SALISA with EfficientDet-D0 on UA-DETRAC drops from 54.2 to 45.7, and for EfficientDet-D1 from 59.1 to 49.5. As defining 256 control points gives better detection results, we set the number of TPS control points to 256.

Robustness to Keyframe Detector. In this ablation, we analyze different combination possibilities for the keyframe detector ($\mathcal{D}_{key}$) and the main detector ($\mathcal{D}$) to examine the robustness of SALISA for different key detectors. The results are presented in Table 5 for different object size categories. As can be seen, there is no extra gain in medium- and large-sized object detection when combining the main detector with more expensive

Table 5. Various combinations of keyframe detector $\mathcal{D}_{key}$ (rows) and the main detector $\mathcal{D}$ (columns). (a-c) shows the mAP of various combinations for small, medium, and large object detection, respectively. (d) shows the computational costs in GFLOPs.

	D0	D1	D2		D0	D1	D2		D0	D1	D2		D0	D1	D2
D1	7.4	–	–	D1	53.1	–	–	D1	73.0	–	–	D1	1.39	–	–
D2	7.4	14.9	–	D2	53.2	58.2	–	D2	73.0	76.6	–	D2	1.54	3.23	–
D3	7.8	15.3	15.3	D3	53.2	58.2	59.4	D3	73.0	76.6	77.7	D3	1.98	3.67	5.96

(a) Small (mAP)	(b) Medium (mAP)	(c) Large (mAP)	(d) GFLOPs

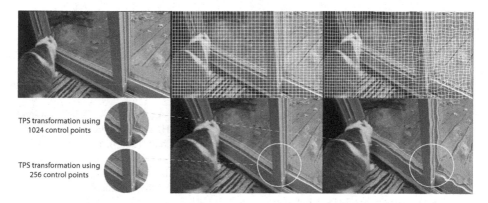

Fig. 7. Effect of the number of control points on TPS transformation. The top row shows the grid deformations produced by TPS with 256 (middle column) and 1024 control points (right column). The bottom row shows the corresponding resampled images.

key frame detectors. This indicates the robustness of SALISA to the choice of keyframe detector. Note that although the mAP of small object detection improves, the additional costs of heavier networks undermine the extra gained accuracy.

Analysis of the Area Threshold. The resampling module gives extra focus in preserving the resolution of small object. The area threshold α determines which objects should be considered as small. Generally, we observe that a smaller value of α improves small object detection. See **Appendix** for detailed results.

5   Discussion and Conclusion

In this paper, we proposed SALISA, a saliency-based input sampling technique for efficient video object detection. SALISA performs a nonuniform downsampling of the input by retaining the fine-grained details of a high-resolution image while allowing for heavy downsampling of background areas. The resulting image is spatially smaller, leading to a reduction in computation costs, but preserves the important details enabling a performance comparable to a high-resolution input. We propose a novel and fully differentiable resampling module based on thin plate spline spatial transformers that generates artifact-free resampled images. SALISA achieves state-of-the-art accuracy on the

ImageNet-VID and UA-DETRAC video object detection datasets in the low compute regime. In particular, it offers significant improvements in the detection of small- and medium-sized objects. A limitation of our model is that, it preserves high-resolution details by downsampling background regions more aggressively. However, when the scene is fully covered with objects, e.g. in a heavy traffic scene, proper zooming is less achievable as there is less background pixels to sub-sample.

Acknowledgements. We thank Michael Hofmann, Haitam Ben Yahia, Mohsen Ghafoorian, and Ilia Karmanov for their feedback and discussions.

References

1. Avidan, S., Shamir, A.: Seam carving for content-aware image resizing. In: ACM SIGGRAPH 2007 Papers, p. 10-es (2007)
2. Bochkovskiy, A., Wang, C.Y., Liao, H.Y.M.: YOLOv4: optimal speed and accuracy of object detection. arXiv preprint arXiv:2004.10934 (2020)
3. Carion, N., Massa, F., Synnaeve, G., Usunier, N., Kirillov, A., Zagoruyko, S.: End-to-end object detection with transformers. In: Vedaldi, A., Bischof, H., Brox, T., Frahm, J.-M. (eds.) ECCV 2020. LNCS, vol. 12346, pp. 213–229. Springer, Cham (2020). https://doi.org/10.1007/978-3-030-58452-8_13
4. Chai, Y.: Patchwork: a patch-wise attention network for efficient object detection and segmentation in video streams. In: Proceedings of the IEEE/CVF International Conference on Computer Vision, pp. 3415–3424 (2019)
5. Dosovitskiy, A., et al.: FlowNet: learning optical flow with convolutional networks. In: Proceedings of the IEEE International Conference on Computer Vision, pp. 2758–2766 (2015)
6. Duchon, J.: Splines minimizing rotation-invariant semi-norms in Sobolev spaces. In: Schempp, W., Zeller, K. (eds.) Constructive Theory of Functions of Several Variables. LNM, pp. 85–100. Springer, Heidelberg (1977). https://doi.org/10.1007/BFb0086566
7. Gao, J., Wang, Z., Xuan, J., Fidler, S.: Beyond fixed grid: learning geometric image representation with a deformable grid. In: Vedaldi, A., Bischof, H., Brox, T., Frahm, J.-M. (eds.) ECCV 2020. LNCS, vol. 12354, pp. 108–125. Springer, Cham (2020). https://doi.org/10.1007/978-3-030-58545-7_7
8. Gao, M., Yu, R., Li, A., Morariu, V.I., Davis, L.S.: Dynamic zoom-in network for fast object detection in large images. In: Proceedings of the IEEE Conference on Computer Vision and Pattern Recognition, pp. 6926–6935 (2018)
9. Habibian, A., Abati, D., Cohen, T.S., Bejnordi, B.E.: Skip-convolutions for efficient video processing. In: Proceedings of the IEEE/CVF Conference on Computer Vision and Pattern Recognition, pp. 2695–2704 (2021)
10. Jaderberg, M., Simonyan, K., Zisserman, A., et al.: Spatial transformer networks. Adv. Neural. Inf. Process. Syst. **28**, 2017–2025 (2015)
11. Jin, C., Tanno, R., Mertzanidou, T., Panagiotaki, E., Alexander, D.C.: Learning to downsample for segmentation of ultra-high resolution images. arXiv preprint arXiv:2109.11071 (2021)
12. Katharopoulos, A., Fleuret, F.: Processing megapixel images with deep attention-sampling models. In: International Conference on Machine Learning, pp. 3282–3291. PMLR (2019)
13. Li, Z., Yang, Y., Liu, X., Zhou, F., Wen, S., Xu, W.: Dynamic computational time for visual attention. In: Proceedings of the IEEE International Conference on Computer Vision Workshops, pp. 1199–1209 (2017)

14. Lin, J., Gan, C., Han, S.: TSM: temporal shift module for efficient video understanding. In: Proceedings of the IEEE/CVF International Conference on Computer Vision, pp. 7083–7093 (2019)

15. Lin, T.-Y., et al.: Microsoft COCO: common objects in context. In: Fleet, D., Pajdla, T., Schiele, B., Tuytelaars, T. (eds.) ECCV 2014. LNCS, vol. 8693, pp. 740–755. Springer, Cham (2014). https://doi.org/10.1007/978-3-319-10602-1_48

16. Liu, M., Zhu, M.: Mobile video object detection with temporally-aware feature maps. In: Proceedings of the IEEE Conference on Computer Vision and Pattern Recognition, pp. 5686–5695 (2018)

17. Liu, M., Zhu, M., White, M., Li, Y., Kalenichenko, D.: Looking fast and slow: memory-guided mobile video object detection. arXiv preprint arXiv:1903.10172 (2019)

18. Liu, W., et al.: SSD: single shot MultiBox detector. In: Leibe, B., Matas, J., Sebe, N., Welling, M. (eds.) ECCV 2016. LNCS, vol. 9905, pp. 21–37. Springer, Cham (2016). https://doi.org/10.1007/978-3-319-46448-0_2

19. Luo, H., Xie, W., Wang, X., Zeng, W.: Detect or track: towards cost-effective video object detection/tracking. In: AAAI (2019)

20. Lyu, S., et al.: UA-DETRAC 2018: report of AVSS2018 & IWT4S challenge on advanced traffic monitoring. In: 2018 15th IEEE International Conference on Advanced Video and Signal Based Surveillance (AVSS), pp. 1–6. IEEE (2018)

21. Lyu, S., et al.: UA-DETRAC 2017: report of AVSS2017 & IWT4S challenge on advanced traffic monitoring. In: 2017 14th IEEE International Conference on Advanced Video and Signal Based Surveillance (AVSS), pp. 1–7. IEEE (2017)

22. Mao, H., Kong, T., Dally, W.J.: CaTDet: cascaded tracked detector for efficient object detection from video. arXiv preprint arXiv:1810.00434 (2018)

23. Mao, H., Zhu, S., Han, S., Dally, W.J.: PatchNet-short-range template matching for efficient video processing. arXiv preprint arXiv:2103.07371 (2021)

24. Marin, D., et al.: Efficient segmentation: learning downsampling near semantic boundaries. In: Proceedings of the IEEE/CVF International Conference on Computer Vision, pp. 2131–2141 (2019)

25. Perreault, H., Bilodeau, G.A., Saunier, N., Héritier, M.: SpotNet: self-attention multi-task network for object detection. In: CRV (2020)

26. Recasens, A., Kellnhofer, P., Stent, S., Matusik, W., Torralba, A.: Learning to zoom: a saliency-based sampling layer for neural networks. In: Ferrari, V., Hebert, M., Sminchisescu, C., Weiss, Y. (eds.) ECCV 2018. LNCS, vol. 11213, pp. 52–67. Springer, Cham (2018). https://doi.org/10.1007/978-3-030-01240-3_4

27. Ren, S., He, K., Girshick, R., Sun, J.: Faster R-CNN: towards real-time object detection with region proposal networks. Adv. Neural. Inf. Process. Syst. **28**, 91–99 (2015)

28. Russakovsky, O., et al.: ImageNet large scale visual recognition challenge. Int. J. Comput. Vis. **115**(3), 211–252 (2015)

29. Setlur, V., Takagi, S., Raskar, R., Gleicher, M., Gooch, B.: Automatic image retargeting. In: Proceedings of the 4th International Conference on Mobile and Ubiquitous Multimedia, pp. 59–68 (2005)

30. Shen, Y., et al.: Globally-aware multiple instance classifier for breast cancer screening. In: Suk, H.-I., Liu, M., Yan, P., Lian, C. (eds.) MLMI 2019. LNCS, vol. 11861, pp. 18–26. Springer, Cham (2019). https://doi.org/10.1007/978-3-030-32692-0_3

31. Simonyan, K., Zisserman, A.: Very deep convolutional networks for large-scale image recognition. arXiv preprint arXiv:1409.1556 (2014)

32. Tan, M., Le, Q.: EfficientNet: rethinking model scaling for convolutional neural networks. In: International Conference on Machine Learning, pp. 6105–6114. PMLR (2019)

33. Tan, M., Pang, R., Le, Q.V.: EfficientDet: scalable and efficient object detection. In: Proceedings of the IEEE/CVF Conference on Computer Vision and Pattern Recognition, pp. 10781–10790 (2020)
34. Thavamani, C., Li, M., Cebron, N., Ramanan, D.: FOVEA: foveated image magnification for autonomous navigation. In: Proceedings of the IEEE/CVF International Conference on Computer Vision, pp. 15539–15548 (2021)
35. Wen, L., et al.: UA-DETRAC: a new benchmark and protocol for multi-object detection and tracking. Comput. Vis. Image Underst. **193**, 102907 (2020)
36. Xia, F., Wang, P., Chen, L.-C., Yuille, A.L.: Zoom better to see clearer: human and object parsing with hierarchical auto-zoom net. In: Leibe, B., Matas, J., Sebe, N., Welling, M. (eds.) ECCV 2016. LNCS, vol. 9909, pp. 648–663. Springer, Cham (2016). https://doi.org/10.1007/978-3-319-46454-1_39
37. Xie, S., Girshick, R., Dollár, P., Tu, Z., He, K.: Aggregated residual transformations for deep neural networks. In: Proceedings of the IEEE Conference on Computer Vision and Pattern Recognition, pp. 1492–1500 (2017)
38. Zheng, H., Fu, J., Zha, Z.J., Luo, J.: Looking for the devil in the details: learning trilinear attention sampling network for fine-grained image recognition. In: Proceedings of the IEEE/CVF Conference on Computer Vision and Pattern Recognition, pp. 5012–5021 (2019)
39. Zhou, X., Wang, D., Krähenbühl, P.: Objects as points. arXiv preprint arXiv:1904.07850 (2019)
40. Zhu, X., Dai, J., Yuan, L., Wei, Y.: Towards high performance video object detection. In: Proceedings of the IEEE Conference on Computer Vision and Pattern Recognition, pp. 7210–7218 (2018)
41. Zhu, X., Xiong, Y., Dai, J., Yuan, L., Wei, Y.: Deep feature flow for video recognition. In: Proceedings of the IEEE Conference on Computer Vision and Pattern Recognition, pp. 2349–2358 (2017)
42. Zoph, B., Cubuk, E.D., Ghiasi, G., Lin, T.-Y., Shlens, J., Le, Q.V.: Learning data augmentation strategies for object detection. In: Vedaldi, A., Bischof, H., Brox, T., Frahm, J.-M. (eds.) ECCV 2020. LNCS, vol. 12372, pp. 566–583. Springer, Cham (2020). https://doi.org/10.1007/978-3-030-58583-9_34

ECO-TR: Efficient Correspondences Finding via Coarse-to-Fine Refinement

Dongli Tan[1,3], Jiang-Jiang Liu[2,3], Xingyu Chen[3], Chao Chen[3],
Ruixin Zhang[3], Yunhang Shen[3], Shouhong Ding[3], and Rongrong Ji[1,4(✉)]

[1] Media Analytics and Computing Lab, School of Informatics, Xiamen University,
Xiamen, China
rrji@xmu.edu.cn
[2] TMCC, CS, Nankai University, Tianjin, China
[3] Youtu Lab, Tencent Technology (Shanghai) Co., Ltd., Shanghai, China
{harleychen,ruixinzhang,ericshding}@tencent.com
[4] Institute of Artificial Intelligence, Xiamen University, Xiamen, China

Abstract. Modeling sparse and dense image matching within a unified functional correspondence model has recently attracted increasing research interest. However, existing efforts mainly focus on improving matching accuracy while ignoring its efficiency, which is crucial for real-world applications. In this paper, we propose an efficient structure named Efficient Correspondence Transformer (**ECO-TR**) by finding correspondences in a coarse-to-fine manner, which significantly improves the efficiency of functional correspondence model. To achieve this, multiple transformer blocks are stage-wisely connected to gradually refine the predicted coordinates upon a shared multi-scale feature extraction network. Given a pair of images and for arbitrary query coordinates, all the correspondences are predicted within a single feed-forward pass. We further propose an adaptive query-clustering strategy and an uncertainty-based outlier detection module to cooperate with the proposed framework for faster and better predictions. Experiments on various sparse and dense matching tasks demonstrate the superiority of our method in both efficiency and effectiveness against existing state-of-the-arts. Project page: https://dltan7.github.io/ecotr/.

Keywords: Image matching · Correspondence · Transformer · Functional method · Coarse-to-fine

1 Introduction

As a fundamental research direction in computer vision, finding the correspondences among pairs of images has been widely utilized in plenty of down-stream

---

D. Tan and J.-J. Liu—Authors contributed equally.

Supplementary Information The online version contains supplementary material available at https://doi.org/10.1007/978-3-031-20080-9_19.

S. Avidan et al. (Eds.): ECCV 2022, LNCS 13670, pp. 317–334, 2022.
https://doi.org/10.1007/978-3-031-20080-9_19

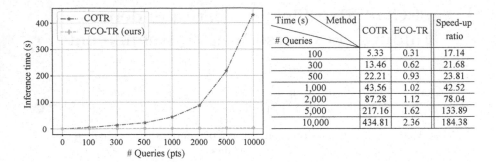

Fig. 1. Comparison of the inference time between the proposed ECO-TR and COTR [14]. The query numbers are set from 100 to 10,000. As we can see, the time-consuming of COTR increases linearly as the number of points increases, while our method basically does not change.

tasks, including optical flow estimation [8,19,53], visual localization [32,34,46], camera position calibration [15,41], 3D reconstruction [5,11], and visual tracking [30]. Given a pair of images, according to how the queries and correspondences are determined, the applications mentioned above can be generally categorized into sparse matching and dense matching. The former focuses on two sets of keypoints being sparsely and respectively extracted from both images and matched to minimize a pre-defined alignment error [15,21,34]; the latter treats all pixels in the first image as queries which are densely mapped to the other image for correspondences [19,37,51,59].

The above two kinds of applications were studied independently for a long time, and various optimizations were designed separately. Recently, COTR [14] claims that these two applications can be naturally modeled within a unified framework since the only difference between the sparse and dense matching is the number of points to query. It proposes to recursively apply a transformer-based [4,7,52] model at multiple scales in a gradually zooming-in manner to obtain accurate correspondences. Though impressive performance has been achieved, its complex off-line pipeline and slow inference speed seriously limit its practicality in real-world applications.

We argue that there are three main reasons leading to the unsatisfactory COTR. The first is the recursive zoom-in refinement framework, which must re-extract the corresponding features in the next local patch matching. In the case of many queries, these features are likely to overlap, which means plenty of repeated and redundant calculations. The second is switching the role of the queries and correspondences to filter out the mismatched queries, which double the overall computation. The third is that the staged training strategy leads to unstable training convergence which needs to be carefully fine-tuned.

Instead of sacrificing speed for performance, in this work, we present an efficient correspondence transformer network (ECO-TR), showing that both efficiency and effectiveness can be achieved within a single feed-forward pass.

Specifically, we propose to complete the coarse-to-fine refinement process of the found correspondences in a stage-by-stage manner. Our framework consists of a bottom-up convolutional neural network (CNN) for multi-scale feature extraction and several top-down transformer blocks corresponding to different matching accuracies. During the coarse-to-fine refinement process, rather than cropping image patches of different positions and sizes according to the coarsely predicted coordinates and recursively re-feeding them into CNN to obtain the corresponding feature maps, we obtain the multi-scale feature maps $w.r.t.$ the input image at one time by taking advantages of the pyramid and translation invariance nature of modern CNNs, and directly crop on the collected feature maps. The proposed feature-level cropping method can effectively avoid repeated calculations. To a certain extent, the inference speed of the model does not increase linearly with the increase of query points.

To further improve the efficiency of our framework, an Adaptive Query-Clustering (AQC) module is proposed to gather similar queries into a cluster, which speeds up the inference. Moreover, we propose an uncertainty module to estimate the confidence of the predicted correspondences, which achieves good performance on outlier detection nearly for free. As illustrated in Table 1, our approach can process 1000 queries within one second on a single NVIDIA Telsa V100 GPU for a pair of images with size 800 × 800, which is around **40 times** faster than COTR under the same conditions.

To evaluate the performance of the proposed approach, we report the results on multiple challenging datasets covering both sparse and dense correspondence finding tasks. Experimental results demonstrate that our method surpasses COTR in performance and speed by a large margin. In addition, we conduct extensive ablation experiments to better understand the impact of each component in our framework. The contributions are summarized below:

- We propose a new coarse-to-fine framework for finding correspondence that can be applied to both sparse and dense matching tasks. Our method can be optimized end-to-end and evaluate an arbitrary number of queries within a single feed-forward.
- We design an adaptive query-clustering strategy and an uncertainty-based outlier filtering module to achieve a better balance between efficiency and effectiveness.
- Our method significantly outperforms the existing best-performing functional method in speed and still achieves comparable performance in sparse correspondence tasks and better in dense correspondence tasks.

2   Related Work

Sparse Methods. The most common paradigm for sparse image matching pipelines consists of three stages: keypoint detection, keypoint description, and feature matching. In terms of the detection stage, a sparse set of repeatable and matchable keypoints are selected by the detection methods [2,31,35,50], which are robust against viewpoint changes and different lighting conditions.

Then, the keypoints are described by patch-level input or image-level input. Patch-based description methods [10,24,44,45] take cropped patches as inputs and are usually trained by metric learning. Image-based description methods such as [6,9,22,27,43] take a full image as input and apply fully-convolutional neural networks [20] to generate dense descriptors. This kind of method usually combines detector and descriptor, which share the same backbone in training and yield better performance on both tasks.

Traditional feature matching methods use Nearest Neighbor (NN) search to find potential matches. Recently, many approaches [3,40,54–56] filter outliers by heuristics or learned priors. SuperGlue [33] uses an attentional graph neural network and optimal transport method to obtain state-of-the-art performance on sparse matching tasks. Unlike the method mentioned above, given some keypoints as queries, COTR [14] refines the matches in the other image recursively by correspondence neural network. Following COTR, we design an end-to-end model to accelerate this scheme.

Dense Methods. The main purpose of dense matching is to estimate the optical flow. NC-Net [29] represents all keypoints and possible correspondences as a 4D correspondence volume restricted to low-resolution images. Sparse NC-Net [28] applies sparse correlation layers instead of all possible correspondences to mitigate this restriction, whereby higher resolution images can be tackled. DRC-Net [17] reduces the computational cost and promotes performance by using coarse-resolution and fine-resolution feature maps of different layers. GLU-Net [48] finds pixel-wise correspondences by global and local features extracted from images with different resolutions. GOCor [47] disambiguates features in similar regions via an improved feature correlation layer. PDC-Net [49] excludes incorrect dense matches in occluded and homogeneous regions by estimating an uncertainty map and filtering the inaccurate correspondences. Patch2Pix [58] replaces pixel-level matches with patch-level match proposals and later refines them by regression layers. LoFTR [39] establishes accurate semi-dense matches with linear transformers in a coarse-to-fine manner. For COTR, the dense matching result is generated by interpolating sufficient sparse queries' results. Same with COTR, our method can give dense matching results by interpolation, too.

Functional Methods. The functional method in image matching. COTR is the first one that obtains matches by a functional correspondence finding architecture. Given a pair of images and coordinates of one query, COTR regresses the possible match in the other image via a transformer-based correspondence finding network. Each query is processed independently, and dense correspondences are estimated by interpolating sparse correspondences using Delaunay triangulation of the queries. However, being a recursive method, it will be extremely time-consuming when many keypoints are queried. We mitigate this problem in an end-to-end manner, which runs dozens of times faster than COTR and achieves comparable or superior performance.

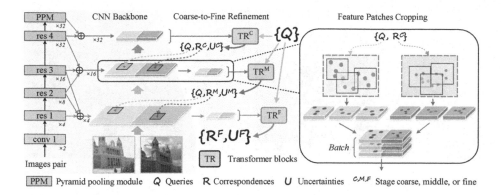

Fig. 2. The pipeline of our proposed framework. It takes a pair of images (bottom-left) and a set of queries ($\{Q\}$) of arbitrary numbers as input and outputs the correspondences ($\{R^F\}$) and uncertainty scores ($\{U^F\}$), respectively. The right part illustrates the feature patches cropping process during each prediction refinement stage. (Color figure online)

3 Coarse-to-Fine Refinement Network

This section describes the proposed end-to-end framework that can find the correspondences for arbitrary queries given a pair of images within a single feedforward pass in detail.

3.1 Overall Pipeline

We show a schematic diagram of the overall pipeline of the proposed framework in Fig. 2. It mainly consists of a bottom-up multi-scale feature extraction pathway based on the CNN and a top-down coarse-to-fine prediction refinement pathway based on the transformer. Given a pair of images I^A and I^B, we first resize them to the same spatial resolution ($B \times C \times H \times W$, B is the 'batch' dimension) and feed them into the CNN backbone to obtain multi-scale features. After that, the collected multi-scale features are used along with the input queries to predict the correspondences in a coarse-to-fine, gradually refining manner in the top-down pathway. We also predict an uncertainty score w.r.t. each correspondence representing how confident the network is of its prediction, which can be utilized to filter out the outliers nearly for free. Since it could be a bunch of queries to be processed in one feed-forward, we further introduce an adaptive query-clustering strategy to better balance efficiency and effectiveness. The following subsections describe the above-mentioned components in detail.

3.2 Efficient Feature Extraction

To obtain correspondence locations precisely, existing work usually crops image patches around potential matching regions and iteratively feeds them back into

Fig. 3. Illustration of the uncertainty estimation branch. Green and red points indicate matches with low uncertainties and high uncertainties, respectively. ECO-TR gives ambiguous predictions in textureless regions and the border area with high uncertainties. (Color figure online)

the network in a progressively enlarged manner. The main drawbacks of the aforementioned practice are: 1) the input image is cropped and resized into patches multiple times with different zoom-in factors around each query position. Each patch generated is then fed into the network, which involves many redundant computations. 2) Image patches for each query are cropped and processed by the network independently, which usually means serial processing and inefficient use of computational resources. We found that the main cause of these two shortcomings can be attributed to the setting of cropping patches at different spatial levels directly on the image.

Considering the pyramid and translation invariance nature of modern CNNs, we propose to alleviate the drawbacks mentioned above by deferring the cropping operation after the feature extraction step. Specifically, we first obtain the multi-scale feature maps w.r.t. each input image at one time and then directly crop on the collected feature maps to get feature patches at any position and scale. We take the ResNet-50 [26] network as our backbone for multi-scale feature extraction without loss of generality. Following the previous success in generating more powerful and representative features, we attach a pyramid pooling module (PPM) [57] to capture more global information at the top of ResNet-50. The output of PPM and the side-outputs at `res1-4` stages of the ResNet-50 network are collected to build a hierarchical multi-scale feature integration structure. As shown in the left part of Fig. 2, to meet the needs of the subsequent top-down pathway which has three refinement stages (*i.e.*, coarse, middle, and fine), we choose to combine the intermediate outputs of {PPM, res4}, {res2-4} and {res1-3} stages, respectively. The integrated three sets of features (denoted as $\{\mathbb{F}^C, \mathbb{F}^M, \mathbb{F}^F\}$) are then resized to 1/32, 1/16, and 1/4 spatial resolutions w.r.t. the input stitched images pair, respectively.

3.3   Coarse-to-Fine Prediction Refinement

The schematic pipeline of the coarse-to-fine prediction refinement process is shown in the middle part (light orange parallelogram background) of Fig. 2. Generally speaking, it consists of three successively connected stages: coarse, middle, and fine, respectively responsible for predicting correspondences with different precision. Each stage is a transformer building block of three encoders and three decoders. The coarse stage (TR^C) takes a set of queries $\mathbb{Q}$ of arbitrary numbers and the entire previously combined features $\mathbb{F}^C$ as input. It outputs the coarsely predicted correspondences set $\mathbb{R}^C$ along with their uncertainty scores. With the guidance of the coordinates in $\mathbb{Q}$ and $\mathbb{R}^C$, we crop square patches centered at them on the previously collected middle-level features $\mathbb{F}^M$ with a fixed window size of w^M, as illustrated by the dashed arrows in the middle left of Fig. 2. The cropped feature patches are then re-arranged into a new batch along with the input queries $\mathbb{Q}$ (normalized based on the cropping centers and window sizes) being forwarded to the next stage (i.e., the middle stage (TR^M)). The fine stage shares similar procedures with the middle stage. After the fine stage, we obtain the final outputs of the proposed framework: the finest correspondences $\mathbb{R}^F$ and their uncertainty scores $\mathbb{U}^F$.

For each stage, concatenated backbone features are supplemented by 2D linear positional encoding in the sinusoidal format and flattened before being fed into the transformer encoder. During the decode stage, coordinates of queries with positional encoding attend to the output of the transformer encoder. Here, we disallow self-attention among the query points, for queries are independent of each other. COTR computes the cycle consistency errors and rejects matches whose errors are greater than a specified threshold to filter out uncertain matches, which doubles the computational cost. To further accelerate our framework, we introduce an uncertainty estimation branch. Two FFN branches follow the outputs of the last transformer decoder. One is employed to regress the corresponding relative coordinates of each query, and the other is to predict the uncertainties of these coordinates. Unreliable predictions with high uncertainties will be filtered during the inference stage.

Having predicted matches $\mathbb{R}^i$ and their uncertainties $\mathbb{U}^i$ of level i, loss $\mathbb{L}^i$ is calculated by:

$$\mathbb{L}^i = \left\|\mathbb{R}^i - \mathbb{R}^i_{gt}\right\| \cdot (1 - \mathbb{U}^i) + \lambda^i \cdot \mathbb{U}^i, \tag{1}$$

where $\mathbb{R}^i_{gt}$ is ground truth matches coordinates of queries and λ^i is the threshold of level i, where $i \in \{C, M, F\}$ represents stages coarse, middle, and fine. We set $\lambda^C = 0.1$, $\lambda^M = 0.05$, $\lambda^F = 0.01$ during training.

All three stages are supervised during training at the same time. Specifically, the final loss $\mathbb{L}$ is defined as

$$\mathbb{L} = \mathbb{L}^C + \mathbb{L}^M + \mathbb{L}^F. \tag{2}$$

Experiments show that the mid- and fine-level supervision during training provides predictions for corresponding stages and gives distinctive back-propagation signals to the CNN backbone, which is beneficial to the prediction of coarse-level. More details are provided in Sect. 4.5.

Algorithm 1: Adaptive Query-Clustering Algorithm

    Input: Coordinates of queries Q; Matches of Q predicted by previous stage R;
             Iteration number t; K-means class number K_{num}; Distance threshold Th
    Output: All patch pairs and corresponding matches in these patches

1 **for** $i = 1$ *to* t **do**
2   Divide Q to K_{num} clusters by K-means algorithm, and assign class labels to
        every pair in (Q, R) ;
3   **for** *each class j* **do**
4   Set (Q', R') = all pairs labeled j ;
5   Set c_q = the center coordinates of Q' ;
6   Set c_r = the center coordinates of R' ;
7   **for** *each pair (q, r) in (Q', R')* **do**
8   **if** $\|q - c_q\| > Th$ or $\|r - c_r\| > Th$
9   Set the class label of $(q, r) = -1$
10   **end**
11   Crop patches centered at c_q and c_r and assign pairs labeled j to these
          patches
12   **end**
13   Set (Q, R) = all pairs labeled -1
14 **end**
15 **for** *each pair (q, r) labeled -1 in (Q, R)* **do**
16   Crop patches centered at q and r, and assign pair (q, r) to these patches
17 **end**

3.4 Adaptive Query-Clustering

The transformer structure is capable of processing many queries in one forward propagation. To improve efficiency, each patch should contain as many queries as possible. A straightforward practice is to directly slice the input images pair into two sets of grids according to the pre-defined window sizes and strides (usually, the stride is set equal to the corresponding window size). By densely coupling the patches between these two sets, any query-correspondence pair can be assigned to one of the patch pairs. We denote the above way of point-to-patch assignment as GRID for simplicity. However, we observe that an inevitable drawback of the query-correspondence independent kind of assignment strategies is that some matches will always exist around the patches' borders, which usually got suboptimal matching results. We attribute this unsatisfying phenomenon to the lack of sufficient contextual information around the border area.

    To achieve a better trade-off between efficiency and effectiveness, we propose an Adaptive Query-Clustering (AQC) algorithm to automatically and dynamically assign images patches for all query-correspondence pairs, as illustrated in Algorithm 1. To demonstrate the superiority of AQC, we compare it with GRID in Sect. 4.5. Experiments show that clustering by AQC gives better performance than GRID.

Table 1. Quantitative results on HPatches. Average End Point Error (AEPE) and Percentage of Correct Keypoints (PCK) are reported here. For each method, different thresholds (1px, 3px and 5px) of PCK are used. For a fair comparison of PCK, we report the reproduced results of COTR under the same image size.

Method	AEPE ↓	PCK-1px ↑	PCK-3px ↑	PCK-5px ↑
LiteFlowNet [13]	118.85	13.91	–	31.64
PWC-Net [38]	96.14	13.14	–	37.14
GLU-Net [48]	25.05	39.55	71.52	78.54
GLU-Net+GOCor [47]	20.16	**41.55**	–	81.43
COTR+Interp (reproduce) [14]	3.83	36.64	76.65	87.42
ECO-TR+Interp	**2.67**	40.19	**79.89**	**90.24**
COTR (reproduce) [14]	3.62	**38.72**	**80.90**	**90.85**
ECO-TR	**2.52**	38.02	79.79	90.71

3.5 Implementation Details

We implemented our model in PyTorch [25]. The local feature CNN uses a modified version of ResNet-50 as a backbone without pretraining. For coarse-to-fine refinement modules, we set the crop window size $w^M = 17$, $w^F = 13$. For the AQC module, we set $t = 1$, $K_{num} = 128$. The distance threshold Th is set to 0.8 times of the corresponding side of patches during training and 0.6 times during inference. More details can be found in the supplementary material.

4   Experiments

We evaluate our method across several datasets. We do not retrain or fine-tune our model on any other dataset for a fair comparison. Experiments are arranged as follows:

1. Dense matching tasks are evaluated on HPatches [1], KITTI [12], and ETH [36] datasets. Following COTR's evaluation protocol, we evaluate the results of sampled matches and interpolated dense optical flow.
2. We evaluate the pose estimation task on the same scene as COTR from Megadepth [18] dataset for sparse matching.
3. For ablations studies, we evaluate the impact of each proposed contribution using the ETH3D dataset.

4.1   Results on HPatches Dataset

We evaluate ECO-TR on the HPatches dataset for dense matching tasks in the first experiment. HPatches dataset contains 116 scenes, with 57 scenes changing in viewpoint and 59 scenes changing in lighting conditions. Following COTR,

Table 2. Quantitative results on KITTI. Average End Point Error (AEPE) and flow outlier ratio (Fl) on KITTI-2012 and KITTI-2015 are reported below. COTR† means we evaluated it with DenseMatching tools provided by the authors of GLU-Net.

Method	KITTI-2012		KITTI-2015	
	AEPE ↓	Fl.[%] ↓	AEPE ↓	Fl.[%] ↓
LiteFlowNet [13]	4.00	17.47	10.39	28.50
PWC-Net [38]	4.14	20.28	10.35	33.67
DGC-Net [23]	8.50	32.28	14.97	50.98
GLU-Net [48]	3.34	18.93	9.79	37.52
RAFT [42]	–	–	5.04	17.8
GLU-Net+GOCor [47]	2.68	15.43	6.68	27.57
PDC-Net [49]	2.08	7.98	5.22	15.13
COTR† + Interp. [14]	1.47	8.79	3.65	13.65
ECO-TR + Interp.	**1.46**	**6.64**	**3.16**	**12.10**
COTR† [14]	1.15	6.98	2.06	9.14
ECO-TR	**0.96**	**3.77**	**1.40**	**6.39**

we evaluate the dense matching results on viewpoint-changing splits. Same with GLU-Net, we resize the reference image during our evaluation, while COTR is evaluated under the original scale in its experiments, which is not comparable in PCK value. Therefore, we reproduce the number of COTR under fair settings. For each method, we find a maximum of 1,000 matches from each pair. Then, we interpolate correspondences on the Delaunay triangulation map of the queries and get the dense correspondences. The results are reported in Table 1.

For the dense matching task, ECO-TR achieves better performance than COTR under all metrics. For the matching accuracy, COTR is a little better than ECO-TR evaluated by PCK. We attribute this gap to the difference in image resolution. COTR can utilize high-resolution images via four recursive zoom-ins, which is unmanageable for ECO-TR due to its end-to-end architecture. The average endpoint error (AEPE) for ECO-TR is lower than COTR.

4.2 Results on KITTI Dataset

We use the KITTI dataset to evaluate the performance of our method under real road scenes. KITTI2012 dataset contains static scenes only, while the KITTI2015 dataset has more challenging dynamic scenes. Following [14,42,47], we use the training split, which has ground truth of camera intrinsics, poses, and depth maps collected by LIDAR. All methods above-mentioned were trained on other datasets and evaluated on this training split. In line with previous works[DGC, GLU, GOC, COTR], We employ the Average End-point Error (AEPE) and percentage of optical flow outliers (Fl) as evaluation metrics. Here, inliers are

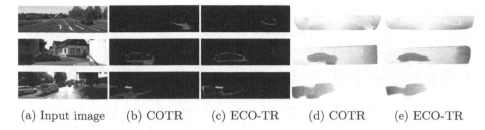

(a) Input image   (b) COTR   (c) ECO-TR   (d) COTR   (e) ECO-TR

Fig. 4. Qualitative results on KITTI – We show the error map (Columns (b, c)) and optical flow (Columns (d, e)) for three pairs from KITTI-2015. ECO-TR provided clearer outlines of moving objects.

Table 3. Results on ETH3D. We evaluated our method over pairs of ETH3D images sampled from different frame intervals. Average End Point Error (AEPE) are reported here. Lower AEPE is better.

Method	AEPE ↓						
	Rate = 3	Rate = 5	Rate = 7	Rate = 9	Rate = 11	Rate = 13	Rate = 15
LiteFlowNet [13]	1.66	2.58	6.05	12.95	29.67	52.41	74.96
PWC-Net [38]	1.75	2.10	3.21	5.59	14.35	27.49	43.41
DGC-Net [23]	2.49	3.28	4.18	5.35	6.78	9.02	12.23
GLU-Net [48]	1.98	2.54	3.49	4.24	5.61	7.55	10.78
COTR+Interp. [14]	1.71	1.92	2.16	2.47	2.85	3.23	3.76
ECO-TR+Interp.	**1.52**	**1.70**	**1.87**	**2.06**	**2.21**	**2.44**	**2.69**
COTR [14]	1.66	1.82	1.97	2.13	2.27	2.41	2.61
ECO-TR	**1.48**	**1.61**	**1.72**	**1.81**	**1.89**	**1.97**	**2.06**

defined as AEPE < 3 pixels or < 5%. Same with COTR, We sample 40,000 points for a fair comparison.

As shown in Table 2, our method outperforms all others on these two datasets. For example, our method achieves AEPE = 1.09 and 1.70 on KITTI-2012 and KITTI-2015, respectively, which is 30% higher than COTR on average. The interpolated results are slightly worse than the sparse results, yet still better than the other dense methods by a large margin, including PDC-Net, which estimates dense correspondence and excludes unreliable matches, too. Qualitative examples on KITTI dataset are illustrated in Fig. 4.

4.3   Results on ETH3D Dataset

ETH3D dataset contains ten image sequences of indoor and outdoor scenes and provides ground truth sparse correspondences under different frame intervals. Following COTR, we report the performance of our method under pairs with seven different intervals, from 3 to 15, respectively. The results in Table 3 show that our proposal outperforms other competitors under all rates, especially when matching pairs with large geometric transformations, *i.e.* pairs with a higher rate.

Fig. 5. Qualitative results on MegaDepth dataset. We set queries on left images and obtain matches in right images. We estimate the relative pose between image pairs and the angular errors in rotation and translation are reported in the upper-left corner. The number of inliers evaluated by epipolar distance is shown as well.

Table 4. Quantitative results on MegaDepth. We evaluated our method against COTR with different numbers of predicted matches. Mean average accuracy (mAA) at a $5^c irc$ and $10^c irc$ error threshold are reported here.

Method	N = 2048		N = 1024		N = 512		N = 300		N = 100	
#Matches	@5	@10	@5	@10	@5	@10	@5	@10	@5	@10
COTR	0.443	0.660	0.448	**0.665**	0.434	0.650	**0.434**	**0.654**	0.410	0.626
ECO-TR	**0.453**	**0.661**	**0.452**	0.664	**0.447**	**0.656**	0.430	0.652	**0.418**	**0.636**

4.4 Results on Megadepth Dataset

MegaDepth [18] images show extreme viewpoint and appearance variations. The poses of images are generated via structure-from-motion and multi-view stereo (MVS) methods, which can be used as ground truth during evaluation. We choose St. Paul's Cathedral as our test scene. We sample 900 pairs of images that have commonly visible regions. Mean average accuracy (mAA) at a 5° and 10° error threshold are reported here, where the error is defined as the maximum of angular error in rotation and translation. For COTR, we follow the strategy used in its paper and evaluate the performance under different numbers of matches. For ECO-TR, we estimate the scale of buildings in pairs first. We sample sparse points in one image as queries and predict their correspondences by coarse-stage ECO-TR. Then, we crop original images and obtain patches that share regions of two images. We resize cropped patches and feed them to the model again, and take random points in one image as queries and find reliable matches with low uncertainty in the other image. To further improve performance, a cycle consistency check is applied here. To compare the performance under the same number of matches, we drop some matches randomly. For a fair comparison, other settings except the matching method are fixed for two methods. The results in Table 4 show that ECO-TR gives a comparable performance, while our pipeline is significantly faster than COTR. Qualitative examples of MegaDepth are illustrated in Fig. 5.

Table 5. Detailed inference time (sec.) of each component.

# points	Pre- and post-process	Backbone	TR^C	TR^M	TR^F
0.1 k	0.036	0.064	0.012	0.120	0.081
10 k	0.037	0.062	0.026	0.480	1.740

Table 6. Detailed comparison of inference time (sec.) with COTR.

Method	# points	Backbone	Transformer	Pre- and post-process	Sum
COTR	0.1 k	0.67	3.74	1.03	5.44
ECO-TR	0.1 k	0.06	0.21	0.04	0.31
COTR	10 k	92.55	60.71	280.27	433.53
ECO-TR	10 k	0.06	2.24	0.05	2.35

4.5 Ablation Studies

In this section, we will conduct several ablation experiments on ETH3D dataset to discuss the efficiency and effectiveness of our method. More ablations on KITTI dataset are provided in the supplementary material.

Analysis of Inference Time. Table 5 reports the time cost of each component of ECO-TR. Table 6 further compares the runtimes of the corresponding components between ECO-TR and COTR with similar GPU memory costs (about 8192 MB). As can be seen, all components in ECO-TR are more efficient than COTR's, where the end-to-end framework (pre- and post-process in an end-to-end manner) contributes most to the efficiency.

Analysis of Multistage Zoom-Ins. First, we analyze the effect of multistage zoom-ins architecture. As shown in Table 7, we evaluate the result of ECO-TR without middle- and fine-stage inference (E_C). It leads to substantially worse results. Adding middle-stage inference benefits the results (E_{CM}) but is still less effective than three stages version (E_{CMF}). We can see that the design of three-stage refinement is essential for good performance. Furthermore, instead of training with the supervision of all three branches, we detach the middle-stage and fine-stage branches during training ($E_{C'}$). The result shows that it leads to worse results, which indicates that deeply supervised models give more distinctive features which yield better performance.

Analysis of Clustering Method. We test the performance of our pipeline with different clustering methods mentioned in Sect. 3.4. GRID and AQC are evaluated under the same distance threshold Th for a fair comparison. The results of AQC and GRID clustering are provided in E_{AQC} and E_{GRID} in Table 7, respectively. The result shows that our Adaptive Query-Clustering

Table 7. Ablations on ETH3D. We evaluate the impact of each component of our method over image pairs from the ETH3D dataset. Pairs are sampled from 3 different frame intervals, which indicate varying difficulty levels. Average End Point Error (AEPE) is reported here. Lower AEPE is better.

AEPE ↓	E_C	$E_{C'}$	E_{CM}	E_{CMF}	E_{AQC}	E_{GRID}	E_{fully}	E_{linear}	E_{cyc}	E_{unc}	$E_{cyc+unc}$
rate = 3	5.21	5.63	2.47	1.53	1.53	1.64	1.53	1.55	1.53	1.48	1.48
rate = 9	7.17	7.50	3.09	2.11	2.11	2.32	2.11	2.12	2.00	1.82	1.81
rate = 15	9.19	9.53	3.83	2.72	2.72	3.10	2.72	2.74	2.45	2.08	2.06

yields better performance than GRID clustering. The gap between the two strategies gradually increases as the difficulty of test pairs increases.

Analysis of Transformer Type. We replace the full attention transformer block in our middle- and fine-stage model with the linear substitution [16] used in LoFTR, and the corresponding results are shown in E_{linear}. Compared with full attention result in E_{fully}, the AEPE of pairs with rate = 3 increases by 0.02 and pairs with rate=3,5 increase by 0.01, while still better than other methods in Table 3 by a large margin. Furthermore, the average inference time of ECO-TR is reduced by 20 percent when the linear transformer is applied, but this generally leads to a slight degradation in performance. It shows our pipeline has the potential to be further accelerated at a small cost.

Analysis of Outlier Filtering Method. We compare the effectiveness of the uncertainty-based outlier filtering algorithm in Table 7. We run ECO-TR with different filtering strategies. E_{cyc} employs cycle consistency check as a filter, and E_{unc} employs uncertainty estimation as a filter. The result shows that filtering by uncertainty estimation gives better performance than filtering by cycle consistency check method. Additionally, $E_{cyc+unc}$ employs uncertainty estimation and cycle consistency checks together. Results show that by further using these two strategies together, ECO-TR achieves better performance.

5   Conclusions

This paper introduces an efficient coarse-to-fine transformer-based network for local feature matching. The main improvement is from three sides: 1) We propose an efficient network structure in a coarse-to-fine manner, fully utilizing the information from different layers and can be trained integrally. 2) We design an adaptive query-clustering (AQC) module that gathers similar query points in the same patch and achieves a better balance between efficiency and effectiveness. 3) An uncertainty-based outlier detection module is proposed to filter out the queries without correspondence. Our method significantly improves the speed of functional matching and achieves comparable or better performance both on sparse and dense matching tasks.

Limitations. The main limitation is that the training of ECO-TR requires a large amount of GPU computing resources. In addition, simple interpolation and refinement techniques limit the performance of dense estimates. We leave these for the future work.

Acknowledgments. This work was supported by the National Science Fund for Distinguished Young Scholars (No. 62025603), the National Natural Science Foundation of China (No. U21B2037, No. 62176222, No. 62176223, No. 62176226, No. 62072386, No. 62072387, No. 62072389, and No. 62002305), Guangdong Basic and Applied Basic Research Foundation (No. 2019B1515120049), and the Natural Science Foundation of Fujian Province of China (No. 2021J01002).

References

1. Balntas, V., Lenc, K., Vedaldi, A., Mikolajczyk, K.: HPatches: a benchmark and evaluation of handcrafted and learned local descriptors. In: Proceedings of the IEEE Conference on Computer Vision and Pattern Recognition, pp. 5173–5182 (2017)
2. Barroso-Laguna, A., Riba, E., Ponsa, D., Mikolajczyk, K.: Key.Net: keypoint detection by handcrafted and learned CNN filters. In: Proceedings of the IEEE/CVF International Conference on Computer Vision, pp. 5836–5844 (2019)
3. Bian, J., Lin, W.Y., Matsushita, Y., Yeung, S.K., Nguyen, T.D., Cheng, M.M.: GMS: grid-based motion statistics for fast, ultra-robust feature correspondence. In: Proceedings of the IEEE Conference on Computer Vision and Pattern Recognition, pp. 4181–4190 (2017)
4. Carion, N., Massa, F., Synnaeve, G., Usunier, N., Kirillov, A., Zagoruyko, S.: End-to-end object detection with transformers. In: Vedaldi, A., Bischof, H., Brox, T., Frahm, J.-M. (eds.) ECCV 2020. LNCS, vol. 12346, pp. 213–229. Springer, Cham (2020). https://doi.org/10.1007/978-3-030-58452-8_13
5. Cheng, J., Leng, C., Wu, J., Cui, H., Lu, H.: Fast and accurate image matching with cascade hashing for 3D reconstruction. In: Proceedings of the IEEE Conference on Computer Vision and Pattern Recognition, pp. 1–8 (2014)
6. DeTone, D., Malisiewicz, T., Rabinovich, A.: SuperPoint: self-supervised interest point detection and description. In: Proceedings of the IEEE Conference on Computer Vision and Pattern Recognition Workshops, pp. 224–236 (2018)
7. Dosovitskiy, A., et al.: An image is worth 16x16 words: transformers for image recognition at scale. arXiv preprint arXiv:2010.11929 (2020)
8. Dosovitskiy, A., et al.: FlowNet: learning optical flow with convolutional networks. In: Proceedings of the IEEE International Conference on Computer Vision, pp. 2758–2766 (2015)
9. Dusmanu, M., et al.: D2-Net: a trainable CNN for joint description and detection of local features. In: Proceedings of the IEEE/CVF Conference on Computer Vision and Pattern Recognition, pp. 8092–8101 (2019)
10. Ebel, P., Mishchuk, A., Yi, K.M., Fua, P., Trulls, E.: Beyond Cartesian representations for local descriptors. In: Proceedings of the IEEE/CVF International Conference on Computer Vision, pp. 253–262 (2019)
11. Fan, B., et al.: A performance evaluation of local features for image-based 3D reconstruction. IEEE Trans. Image Process. **28**(10), 4774–4789 (2019)

12. Geiger, A., Lenz, P., Stiller, C., Urtasun, R.: Vision meets robotics: the KITTI dataset. Int. J. Robot. Res. **32**(11), 1231–1237 (2013)
13. Hui, T.W., Tang, X., Loy, C.C.: LiteFlowNet: a lightweight convolutional neural network for optical flow estimation. In: Proceedings of the IEEE Conference on Computer Vision and Pattern Recognition, pp. 8981–8989 (2018)
14. Jiang, W., Trulls, E., Hosang, J., Tagliasacchi, A., Yi, K.M.: COTR: correspondence transformer for matching across images. In: Proceedings of the IEEE/CVF International Conference on Computer Vision, pp. 6207–6217 (2021)
15. Jin, Y., et al.: Image matching across wide baselines: from paper to practice. Int. J. Comput. Vis. **129**(2), 517–547 (2021)
16. Katharopoulos, A., Vyas, A., Pappas, N., Fleuret, F.: Transformers are RNNs: fast autoregressive transformers with linear attention. In: International Conference on Machine Learning, pp. 5156–5165. PMLR (2020)
17. Li, X., Han, K., Li, S., Prisacariu, V.: Dual-resolution correspondence networks. Adv. Neural. Inf. Process. Syst. **33**, 17346–17357 (2020)
18. Li, Z., Snavely, N.: MegaDepth: learning single-view depth prediction from internet photos. In: Proceedings of the IEEE Conference on Computer Vision and Pattern Recognition, pp. 2041–2050 (2018)
19. Liu, C., Yuen, J., Torralba, A.: SIFT flow: dense correspondence across scenes and its applications. IEEE Trans. Pattern Anal. Mach. Intell. **33**(5), 978–994 (2010)
20. Long, J., Shelhamer, E., Darrell, T.: Fully convolutional networks for semantic segmentation. In: Proceedings of the IEEE Conference on Computer Vision and Pattern Recognition, pp. 3431–3440 (2015)
21. Lowe, D.G.: Distinctive image features from scale-invariant keypoints. Int. J. Comput. Vis. **60**(2), 91–110 (2004)
22. Luo, Z., et al.: ASLFeat: learning local features of accurate shape and localization. In: Proceedings of the IEEE/CVF Conference on Computer Vision and Pattern Recognition, pp. 6589–6598 (2020)
23. Melekhov, I., Tiulpin, A., Sattler, T., Pollefeys, M., Rahtu, E., Kannala, J.: DGC-Net: dense geometric correspondence network. In: 2019 IEEE Winter Conference on Applications of Computer Vision (WACV), pp. 1034–1042. IEEE (2019)
24. Mishchuk, A., Mishkin, D., Radenovic, F., Matas, J.: Working hard to know your neighbor's margins: local descriptor learning loss. Adv. Neural Inf. Process. Syst. **30** (2017)
25. Paszke, A., et al.: PyTorch: an imperative style, high-performance deep learning library. Adv. Neural Inf. Process. Syst. **32** (2019)
26. Ren, S., He, K., Girshick, R., Sun, J.: Faster R-CNN: towards real-time object detection with region proposal networks. Adv. Neural Inf. Process. Syst. **28** (2015)
27. Revaud, J., et al.: R2D2: repeatable and reliable detector and descriptor. arXiv preprint arXiv:1906.06195 (2019)
28. Rocco, I., Arandjelović, R., Sivic, J.: Efficient neighbourhood consensus networks via submanifold sparse convolutions. In: Vedaldi, A., Bischof, H., Brox, T., Frahm, J.-M. (eds.) ECCV 2020. LNCS, vol. 12354, pp. 605–621. Springer, Cham (2020). https://doi.org/10.1007/978-3-030-58545-7_35
29. Rocco, I., Cimpoi, M., Arandjelović, R., Torii, A., Pajdla, T., Sivic, J.: Neighbourhood consensus networks. Adv. Neural Inf. Process. Syst. **31** (2018)
30. Rosten, E., Drummond, T.: Fusing points and lines for high performance tracking. In: Tenth IEEE International Conference on Computer Vision (ICCV 2005), vol. 2, pp. 1508–1515. IEEE (2005)

31. Rosten, E., Drummond, T.: Machine learning for high-speed corner detection. In: Leonardis, A., Bischof, H., Pinz, A. (eds.) ECCV 2006. LNCS, vol. 3951, pp. 430–443. Springer, Heidelberg (2006). https://doi.org/10.1007/11744023_34

32. Sarlin, P.E., Cadena, C., Siegwart, R., Dymczyk, M.: From coarse to fine: robust hierarchical localization at large scale. In: Proceedings of the IEEE/CVF Conference on Computer Vision and Pattern Recognition, pp. 12716–12725 (2019)

33. Sarlin, P.E., DeTone, D., Malisiewicz, T., Rabinovich, A.: SuperGlue: learning feature matching with graph neural networks. In: Proceedings of the IEEE/CVF Conference on Computer Vision and Pattern Recognition, pp. 4938–4947 (2020)

34. Sattler, T., Leibe, B., Kobbelt, L.: Improving image-based localization by active correspondence search. In: Fitzgibbon, A., Lazebnik, S., Perona, P., Sato, Y., Schmid, C. (eds.) ECCV 2012. LNCS, vol. 7572, pp. 752–765. Springer, Heidelberg (2012). https://doi.org/10.1007/978-3-642-33718-5_54

35. Savinov, N., Seki, A., Ladicky, L., Sattler, T., Pollefeys, M.: Quad-networks: unsupervised learning to rank for interest point detection. In: Proceedings of the IEEE Conference on Computer Vision and Pattern Recognition, pp. 1822–1830 (2017)

36. Schops, T., et al.: A multi-view stereo benchmark with high-resolution images and multi-camera videos. In: Proceedings of the IEEE Conference on Computer Vision and Pattern Recognition, pp. 3260–3269 (2017)

37. Sun, D., Roth, S., Black, M.J.: A quantitative analysis of current practices in optical flow estimation and the principles behind them. Int. J. Comput. Vis. 106(2), 115–137 (2014). https://doi.org/10.1007/s11263-013-0644-x

38. Sun, D., Yang, X., Liu, M.Y., Kautz, J.: PWC-Net: CNNs for optical flow using pyramid, warping, and cost volume. In: Proceedings of the IEEE Conference on Computer Vision and Pattern Recognition, pp. 8934–8943 (2018)

39. Sun, J., Shen, Z., Wang, Y., Bao, H., Zhou, X.: LoFTR: detector-free local feature matching with transformers. In: Proceedings of the IEEE/CVF Conference on Computer Vision and Pattern Recognition, pp. 8922–8931 (2021)

40. Sun, W., Jiang, W., Trulls, E., Tagliasacchi, A., Yi, K.M.: ACNe: attentive context normalization for robust permutation-equivariant learning. In: Proceedings of the IEEE/CVF Conference on Computer Vision and Pattern Recognition, pp. 11286–11295 (2020)

41. Svärm, L., Enqvist, O., Kahl, F., Oskarsson, M.: City-scale localization for cameras with known vertical direction. IEEE Trans. Pattern Anal. Mach. Intell. 39(7), 1455–1461 (2016)

42. Teed, Z., Deng, J.: RAFT: recurrent all-pairs field transforms for optical flow. In: Vedaldi, A., Bischof, H., Brox, T., Frahm, J.-M. (eds.) ECCV 2020. LNCS, vol. 12347, pp. 402–419. Springer, Cham (2020). https://doi.org/10.1007/978-3-030-58536-5_24

43. Tian, Y., Balntas, V., Ng, T., Barroso-Laguna, A., Demiris, Y., Mikolajczyk, K.: D2D: keypoint extraction with describe to detect approach. In: Proceedings of the Asian Conference on Computer Vision (2020)

44. Tian, Y., Fan, B., Wu, F.: L2-Net: deep learning of discriminative patch descriptor in Euclidean space. In: Proceedings of the IEEE Conference on Computer Vision and Pattern Recognition, pp. 661–669 (2017)

45. Tian, Y., Yu, X., Fan, B., Wu, F., Heijnen, H., Balntas, V.: SOSNet: second order similarity regularization for local descriptor learning. In: Proceedings of the IEEE/CVF Conference on Computer Vision and Pattern Recognition, pp. 11016–11025 (2019)

46. Toft, C., et al.: Semantic match consistency for long-term visual localization. In: Ferrari, V., Hebert, M., Sminchisescu, C., Weiss, Y. (eds.) ECCV 2018. LNCS, vol. 11206, pp. 391–408. Springer, Cham (2018). https://doi.org/10.1007/978-3-030-01216-8_24

47. Truong, P., Danelljan, M., Gool, L.V., Timofte, R.: GOCor: bringing globally optimized correspondence volumes into your neural network. Adv. Neural. Inf. Process. Syst. **33**, 14278–14290 (2020)

48. Truong, P., Danelljan, M., Timofte, R.: GLU-Net: global-local universal network for dense flow and correspondences. In: Proceedings of the IEEE/CVF Conference on Computer Vision and Pattern Recognition, pp. 6258–6268 (2020)

49. Truong, P., Danelljan, M., Van Gool, L., Timofte, R.: Learning accurate dense correspondences and when to trust them. In: Proceedings of the IEEE/CVF Conference on Computer Vision and Pattern Recognition, pp. 5714–5724 (2021)

50. Tyszkiewicz, M., Fua, P., Trulls, E.: DISK: learning local features with policy gradient. Adv. Neural. Inf. Process. Syst. **33**, 14254–14265 (2020)

51. Ummenhofer, B., et al.: DeMoN: depth and motion network for learning monocular stereo. In: Proceedings of the IEEE Conference on Computer Vision and Pattern Recognition, pp. 5038–5047 (2017)

52. Vaswani, A., et al.: Attention is all you need. Adv. Neural Inf. Process. Syst. **30** (2017)

53. Weinzaepfel, P., Revaud, J., Harchaoui, Z., Schmid, C.: DeepFlow: large displacement optical flow with deep matching. In: Proceedings of the IEEE International Conference on Computer Vision, pp. 1385–1392 (2013)

54. Yi, K.M., Trulls, E., Ono, Y., Lepetit, V., Salzmann, M., Fua, P.: Learning to find good correspondences. In: Proceedings of the IEEE Conference on Computer Vision and Pattern Recognition, pp. 2666–2674 (2018)

55. Zhang, J., et al.: Learning two-view correspondences and geometry using order-aware network. In: Proceedings of the IEEE/CVF International Conference on Computer Vision, pp. 5845–5854 (2019)

56. Zhao, C., Cao, Z., Li, C., Li, X., Yang, J.: NM-Net: mining reliable neighbors for robust feature correspondences. In: Proceedings of the IEEE/CVF Conference on Computer Vision and Pattern Recognition, pp. 215–224 (2019)

57. Zhao, H., Shi, J., Qi, X., Wang, X., Jia, J.: Pyramid scene parsing network. In: Proceedings of the IEEE Conference on Computer Vision and Pattern Recognition, pp. 2881–2890 (2017)

58. Zhou, Q., Sattler, T., Leal-Taixe, L.: Patch2Pix: epipolar-guided pixel-level correspondences. In: Proceedings of the IEEE/CVF Conference on Computer Vision and Pattern Recognition, pp. 4669–4678 (2021)

59. Zhou, T., Brown, M., Snavely, N., Lowe, D.G.: Unsupervised learning of depth and ego-motion from video. In: Proceedings of the IEEE Conference on Computer Vision and Pattern Recognition, pp. 1851–1858 (2017)

Vote from the Center: 6 DoF Pose Estimation in RGB-D Images by Radial Keypoint Voting

Yangzheng Wu$^{(\boxtimes)}$(ID), Mohsen Zand(ID), Ali Etemad(ID), and Michael Greenspan(ID)

Department of Electrical and Computer Engineering, Ingenuity Labs Research Institute, Queen's University, Kingston, ON, Canada
y.wu@queensu.ca

Abstract. We propose a novel keypoint voting scheme based on intersecting spheres, that is more accurate than existing schemes and allows for fewer, more disperse keypoints. The scheme is based upon the distance between points, which as a 1D quantity can be regressed more accurately than the 2D and 3D vector and offset quantities regressed in previous work, yielding more accurate keypoint localization. The scheme forms the basis of the proposed RCVPose method for 6 DoF pose estimation of 3D objects in RGB-D data, which is particularly effective at handling occlusions. A CNN is trained to estimate the distance between the 3D point corresponding to the depth mode of each RGB pixel, and a set of 3 disperse keypoints defined in the object frame. At inference, a sphere centered at each 3D point is generated, of radius equal to this estimated distance. The surfaces of these spheres vote to increment a 3D accumulator space, the peaks of which indicate keypoint locations. The proposed radial voting scheme is more accurate than previous vector or offset schemes, and is robust to disperse keypoints. Experiments demonstrate RCVPose to be highly accurate and competitive, achieving state-of-the-art results on the LINEMOD (99.7%) and YCB-Video (97.2%) datasets, notably scoring +4.9% higher (71.1%) than previous methods on the challenging Occlusion LINEMOD dataset, and on average outperforming all other published results from the BOP benchmark for these 3 datasets. Our code is available at http://www.github.com/aaronwool/rcvpose.

Keywords: 6 DoF pose estimation · Keypoint voting

1 Introduction

Object pose estimation is an enabling technology for many applications including robot manipulation, human-robot interaction, augmented reality, and

Supplementary Information The online version contains supplementary material available at https://doi.org/10.1007/978-3-031-20080-9_20.

S. Avidan et al. (Eds.): ECCV 2022, LNCS 13670, pp. 335–352, 2022.
https://doi.org/10.1007/978-3-031-20080-9_20

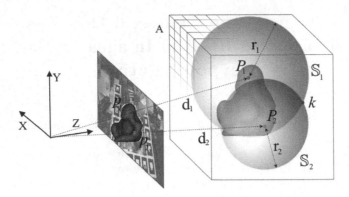

Fig. 1. Radial voting scheme: 3D scene point P_i at depth d_i projects to 2D image pixel p_i. The network estimates radial distance r_i from p_i. Sphere S_i is centered at P_i with radius r_i, and all accumulator space A voxels on the surface of S_i are incremented. Keypoint k lies at the intersection of $S_1 \cap S_2$, and all other S_i.

autonomous driving [35,36,45]. It is challenging due to background clutter, occlusions, sensor noise, varying lighting conditions, and object symmetries. Traditional methods have tackled the problem by establishing correspondences between a known 3D model and image features [15,40]. They have generally relied on hand-crafted features and therefore fail when objects are featureless or when scenes are very cluttered and occluded [18,36]. Recent methods use deep learning and train end-to-end networks to directly regress an input image to a 6 DoF pose [19,49]. For example, CNN-based techniques have been proposed which regress 2D keypoints and use Perspective-n-Point (PnP) to estimate the 6 DoF pose parameters [35,43]. As an alternate to directly regressing keypoint coordinates, methods which *vote* for keypoints have been shown to be highly effective [18,36,37,49], especially when objects are partially occluded. These schemes regress a distinct geometric quantity that relates positions of 2D pixels to 3D keypoints, and for each pixel casts this quantity into an accumulator space. As votes accumulate independently per pixel, these methods perform especially well in challenging occluded scenes.

While recent voting methods have shown great promise and leading performance, they require the regression of either a 2-channel (for 2D voting) [36] or 3-channel (for 3D voting) [14] activation map where voting quantities are accumulated in order to vote for keypoints. The activation map is the image shaped tensor where voting quantities are saved. The dimensionality of the activation map follows from the formulation of the geometric quantity being regressed, and the estimation errors in each channel tend to compound. This leads to reduced localization accuracy for higher dimensional activation maps when voting for keypoints. This observation has motivated our novel radial voting scheme, which regresses a one dimensional activation map for RGB-D data, leading to more accurate localization. The increase in keypoint localization accuracy also allows us to disperse our keypoint set farther, which increases the accuracy of transformation estimation, and ultimately that of 6 DoF pose estimation.

Our proposed method, *RCVPose*, trains a CNN to estimate the distance between a 3D keypoint, and the 3D scene point corresponding to each 2D RGB pixel. At inference, this distance is estimated for each 2D scene pixel, which is a 1D quantity and therefore has the potential to be more accurate than higher-dimension quantities regressed in previous methods. For each pixel, a sphere of radius equal to this regressed distance is centered at each corresponding 3D scene point. Those 3D accumulator space cells (*voxels*) that intersect with the surface of these spheres are incremented, and peaks indicate keypoint locations, as illustrated in Fig. 1. Executing this for minimally 3 keypoints allows the unique recovery of the 6 DoF object pose.

Our main contribution is a novel *radial voting scheme* (based on a 1D regression) which we experimentally show to be more accurate than previous voting schemes (which are based on 2D and 3D regressions). Based on our radial voting scheme, a further contribution is a novel 6 DoF pose estimation method, called RCVPose. Notably, RCVPose requires only 3 keypoints per object, which is fewer than existing methods that use 4 or more keypoints [14,36,37]. We experimentally characterize the performance of RCVPose on 3 standard datasets, and show that it outperforms previous peer-reviewed methods, performing especially well in highly occluded scenes. We also conduct experiments to justify certain design decisions and hyperparameter settings.

2   Related Work

Estimating 6 DoF pose has been extensively addressed in the literature [3,15, 26,49]. Recent deep learning-based methods use CNNs to generate pose and can be generally classified into the three categories of *viewpoint-based* [15], *keypoint-based* [49], and *voting-based* methods [37].

Viewpoint-based methods predict 6 DoF poses by matching 3D or projected 2D templates. In [33], a generative auto-encoder architecture used a GAN to convert RGB images into 3D coordinates, similar to the image-to-image translation task. Generated pixel-wise predictions were used in multiple stages to form 2D to 3D correspondences to estimate poses with RANSAC-based PnP. Manhardt *et al.* [27] proposed predicting several 6 DoF poses for each object instance to estimate the pose distribution generated by symmetries and repetitive textures. Each predicted hypothesis corresponded to a single 3D translation and rotation, and estimated hypotheses collapsed onto the same valid pose when the object appearance was unique. Recent variations include Trabelsi *et al.* [44], who used a multi-task CNN-based encoder/multi-decoder network, and Wang *et al.* [47] and [20,34,42], who used a rendering method by a self-supervised model on unannotated real RGB-D data to find an optimal alignment.

Keypoint-based methods detect specified object-centric keypoints and apply PnP for final pose estimation. Hu *et al.* [18] proposed a segmentation-driven 6

DoF pose estimation method which used the visible parts of objects for local pose prediction from 2D keypoint locations. They then used the output confidence scores of a YOLO-based [39] network to establish 2D to 3D correspondences between the image and the object's 3D model. Zakharov *et al.* [50] proposed a dense pose object detector to estimate dense 2D to 3D correspondence maps between an input image and available 3D models, recovering 6 DoF pose using PnP and RANSAC. In addition to RGB data, depth information was used in [14] to detect 3D keypoints with a Deep Hough Voting network, with the 6 DoF pose parameters then fit with a least-squares method.

Voting-based methods have a long history in pose estimation. Before artificial intelligence became widespread, first the Hough Transform [8] and RANSAC [10] and subsequently methods such as pose clustering [32] , image retrieval [4,41] and geometric hashing [21] were widely used to localize simple geometric shapes, objects in images and full 6 DoF object pose. Hough Forests [11], while learning-based, still required hand-crafted feature descriptors. Voting was also extended to 3D point cloud images, such as 4PCS [1] and its variations [29,30], to estimate affine-invariant poses.

Following the advent of CNNs, hybrid methods emerged combining aspects of both data-driven and classical voting approaches. Both [18] and [36] conclude with RANSAC-based keypoint voting, whereas Deep Hough Voting [37] proposed a complete MLP pipeline of keypoint localization using a series of convolutional layers as the voting module. To estimate keypoints, two different deep learning-based voting schemes have appeared [18,36,37,49], the proposed scheme introducing a third. At training, all voting schemes regress a distinct quantity that relates positions of pixels to keypoints. At inference, this quantity is estimated for each pixel, and is cast into an accumulator space in a voting process. Accumulator spaces can cover the 2D [18,37,49] image space, or more recently the 3D [36] camera reference frame. After voting, peaks in accumulator space indicate positions of keypoints in the 2D image or 3D camera frame.

While only a few hybrid voting-based methods exist for 6 DoF pose estimation, they have outstanding performance, which has motivated us to develop RCVPose as a further advance of this class of hybrid method. Specifically, our method is inspired by PVNet [36], and is most closely related to the recently proposed PVN3D of He *et al.* [14], which combined PVNet and Deep Hough Voting [37] with a 3D accumulator space, utilizing the offset voting scheme of [49].

3 Methodology

3.1 Keypoint Voting Scheme Alternatives

The three keypoint voting schemes are illustrated in 2D in Fig. 2a, for image pixel p and keypoint k to be estimated. The grid represents the (initially empty) accumulator space bins, which are the voxel space elements where votes are cast. In *offset* voting, the values of Δx and Δy are estimated from forward inference through the network. These values are used to offset p to reference

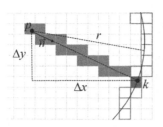
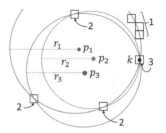

(a) Votes cast (in 2D) for offset, vector, and radial voting

(b) Accumulator space values after radial voting for 3 points

Fig. 2. Keypoint Voting Schemes in 2D: a) Pixel p casts votes for keypoint k at blue bin (offset and vector voting), green bins (vector voting), and red bins (radial voting). b) Radial votes cast for pixels p_1, p_2, and p_3 result in bin peaks at the intersection of the circles, with the peak occuring at keypoint k. (Color figure online)

that accumulator bin (shown in blue) containing k, the value of which is then incremented. Alternately, in *vector* voting, the direction $\vec{n}$ is estimated, and all bins (shown in green and blue) that intersect with $\vec{n}$ are incremented. Finally, in *radial* voting, the scalar r is estimated, and all bins (shown outlined in red) are incremented that intersect with the perimeter of the circle of radius r centered at p. When repeated for all image pixels, the bin containing k will contain the maximum accumulator space value, irrespective of which scheme is used, so long as the quantities estimated by network inference are sufficiently accurate. In Fig. 2b, circles generated by radial voting are illustrated for three image pixels. Each bin contains a count of the number of circle perimeters that it intersects, such that the peak value of 3 indicates the location of keypoint k. The above three voting schemes extend directly to 3D space, in which the accumulator space is a grid of voxels, the offset scheme contains an additional Δz component, $\vec{n}$ is a 3-dimensional vector, and the radial scheme casts votes on the surfaces of 3D spheres rather than 2D circles.

Formally, let p_i be pixel from RGB-D image I with 2D image coordinate (u_i, v_i) and corresponding 3D camera frame coordinate (x_i, y_i, z_i). Further let $k_j^\theta = (x_j, y_j, z_j)$ denote the camera frame coordinate of the jth keypoint of an object located at 6 DoF pose θ. The quantity $\mathbf{m_o}$ regressed in the first *offset* scheme [18,37] is the displacement between the two 3D points, denoted as $\mathbf{m_o} = (\Delta x, \Delta y, \Delta z) = (x_i - x_j,\ y_i - y_j,\ z_i - z_j)$. Alternately, the 3D quantity $\mathbf{m_v}$ from the second *vector* scheme [36,49] is the unit vector pointing to k_j^θ from p_i, denoted as $\mathbf{m_v} = (dx, dy, dz) = \frac{\mathbf{m_o}}{\|\mathbf{m_o}\|}$. The 3D vector scheme can alternately be parametrized into a 2D *polar* scheme, denoted as $\mathbf{m_p} = (\phi, \psi) = (\cos^{-1} dz, \tan^{-1} \frac{dy}{dx})$. Finally, the 1D quantity $\mathbf{m_r}$ from the *radial* scheme proposed here is simply the Euclidean distance between the points, i.e. $\mathbf{m_r} = \|\mathbf{m_o}\|$.

The above quantities encode different information about the relationship between p_i and k_j^θ. For example, $\mathbf{m_v}$, $\mathbf{m_p}$, and $\mathbf{m_r}$ can be derived directly from

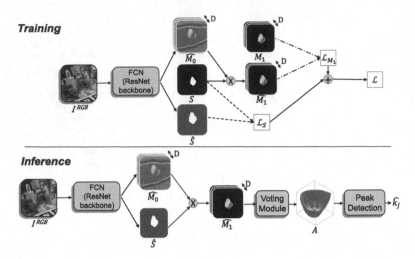

Fig. 3. RCVPose training and inference. $\widehat{M}_0$, $\widehat{M}_1$, and M_1 have channel depth $D = 1$ for radial, $D = 2$ for polar, or $D = 3$ for offset or vector voting schemes.

$\mathbf{m_o}$, whereas $\mathbf{m_o}$ cannot be derived from the others. Also, $\mathbf{m_r}$ and $\mathbf{m_v}$ (and $\mathbf{m_p}$) are independent of one another. This difference in geometric information leads to their different dimensionality, and ultimately the greater accuracy of radial voting, as discussed in Sect. 4.4.

3.2 Keypoint Estimation Pipeline

The above described voting schemes can be used interchangeably within a keypoint estimation pipeline. The training inputs (Fig. 3) are: RGB fields I^{RGB} of image I; ground truth binary segmented image S of the foreground object at pose θ; ground truth keypoint coordinate k_j^θ, and; the ground truth voting scheme values (i.e. one of $\mathbf{m_o}$, $\mathbf{m_v}$, $\mathbf{m_p}$ or $\mathbf{m_r}$) for each pixel in S, represented by matrix M_1. M_1 is calculated for a given k_j^θ using one of the voting scheme values, and has either channel depth $D = 3$ for $\mathbf{m_o}$ or $\mathbf{m_v}$, $D = 2$ for $\mathbf{m_p}$, or $D = 1$ for $\mathbf{m_r}$. Both S and M_1 are assessed to compute the loss $\mathcal{L}$ as:

$$\mathcal{L} = \mathcal{L}_S + \mathcal{L}_{M_1}, \tag{1}$$

$$\mathcal{L}_S = \frac{1}{N} \sum_{i=1}^{N} \left| \widehat{S}_i - S_i \right|, \tag{2}$$

$$\mathcal{L}_{M_1} = \frac{1}{N} \sum_{i=1}^{N} \left(|\widehat{M}_{1i} - M_{1i}| \right), \tag{3}$$

with summations over all N pixels. The network output is estimate $\widehat{S}$ of S, and (unsegmented) estimate $\widehat{M}_0$ of M_1.

At inference (Fig. 3), I^{RGB} is fed to the network which returns estimates $\widehat{S}$ and $\widehat{M_0}$, the element-wise multiplication of which yields segmented estimate $\widehat{M_1}$. Each pixel (u_i, v_i) of $\widehat{M_1}$, with corresponding 3D coordinate (x_i, y_i, z_i) drawn from the depth field I^D of I, then independently casts a vote through the voting module into the initially empty 3D accumulator space A.

Vote casting is performed for each (u_i, v_i), and is distinct for each voting scheme. In *offset* voting, accumulator space A bin $A[x_i + \widehat{M_1}[u_i, v_i, 0], \ y_i + \widehat{M_1}[u_i, v_i, 1], z_i + \widehat{M_1}[u_i, v_i, 2]]$ is incremented, thereby voting for the specific bin of A that contains keypoint k_j^θ. In *vector* and *polar* voting, every A bin is incremented that intersects with the ray $\alpha(x_i + \widehat{M_1}[u_i, v_i, 0], \ y_i + \widehat{M_1}[u_i, v_i, 1], \ z_i + \widehat{M_1}[u_i, v_i, 2])$, for $\alpha > 0$, thereby casting a vote for every bin along the ray that intersects with (x_i, y_i, z_i) and k_j^θ. Finally, in *radial* voting, every A bin is incremented that intersects with the sphere of radius $\widehat{M_1}[u_i, v_i]$ centered at (x_i, y_i, z_i), thereby voting for every bin that lies on the surface of a sphere upon which k_j^θ resides. Whichever scheme is used, at the conclusion of vote casting for all (u_i, v_i), a global peak will exist in the A bin containing k_j^θ, and a simple peak detection operation is then sufficient to estimate keypoint position $\widehat{k}_j^\theta$, within the precision of A. The radial voting scheme has been shown to be more accurate than the other schemes at keypoint estimation, as shown in the experiments in Sect. 4.4.

3.3   RCVPose

The above keypoint voting method formed the core of RCVPose. Radial voting was used, based on its superior accuracy as demonstrated in Sect. 4.4. The network of Fig. 3 was used with ResNet-152 as the FCN-ResNet module. The minimal $K = 3$ keypoints were used for each object, selected from the corners of each object's bounding box. Based on Sect. 4.5, keypoints were scaled to lie beyond the surface of each object, ~ 2 object radius units from its centroid.

The network structure was based on a Fully Convolutional ResNet-152 [12], similar to PVNet [36], albeit with two main differences. First, we replaced LeakyReLU with ReLU as the activation function. This was because our radial voting scheme only includes positive values, in contrast to the vector voting scheme of PVNet which also admits negative values. Second, we increased the number of skip connections linking the downsampling and upsampling layers from three to five, to include extra local features when upsampling [24].

All voxels were initialized to zero, with their values incremented as votes were cast. The voting process is similar to 3D sphere rendering, wherein those voxels that intersect with the sphere surface have their values incremented. The process is based on Andre's circle rendering algorithm [2]. We generate a series of 2D slices of A parallel to the x-y plane, that fall within the sphere radius from the sphere center in both directions of the z-axis. For each slice, the radius of the circle formed by the intersection of the sphere and that slice is calculated, and all voxels that intersect with this circumference are incremented. The algorithm is accurate and efficient, requiring that only a small portion of the voxels be visited for each sphere rendering. It was implemented in Python and parallelized at the thread level, and executes with an efficiency similar to forward network inference.

Once the $K = 3$ keypoint locations are estimated for an image, it is straightforward to determine the object's 6 DoF rigid transformation θ, from the corresponding estimated scene and ground truth object keypoint coordinates [17,25]. This is analogous to the approach of [14], and is efficient compared to previous pure RGB approaches [36] which employ an iterative PnP method.

4   Experiments

4.1   Datasets

The **LINEMOD** dataset [15] includes 1200 images per object. The training set contains only 180 training samples using the standard 15%/85% training/testing split [5,14,18,36,49]. We augmented the dataset by rendering the objects with a random rotation and translation, transposed using the BOP rendering kit [16] onto a background image drawn from the MSCOCO dataset [23]. An additional 1300 augmented images were generated for each object in this way, inflating the training set to 1480 images per object.

The LINEMOD depth images have an offset compared to the ground-truth pose values, for unknown reasons [28]. To reduce the impact of this offset, we regenerated the depth field for each training image from the ground truth pose, by reprojecting the depth value drawn from the object pose at each 2D pixel coordinate. The majority (1300) of the resulting training set were in this way purely synthetic images, and the minority (180) comprised real RGB and synthetic depth. All test images were original, real and unaltered.

Occlusion LINEMOD [3] is a re-annotation of LINEMOD comprising a subset of 1215 challenging test images of partially occluded objects. The protocol is to train using LINEMOD images only, and then test on Occlusion LINEMOD to verify robustness.

YCB-Video [49] is a much larger dataset, containing 130 K key frames of 21 objects over 92 videos. We split 113 K frames for training and 27 K frames for testing, following PVN3D [14]. For data augmentation, YCB-Video provides 80 K synthetic images with random object poses, rendered on a black background. We repeated here the process described above, by rendering random MSCOCO images as background. The complete training dataset therefore comprised 113 K real + 80 K synthetic = 193 K images.

4.2   Implementation Details

Prior to training, each RGB image is shifted and scaled to adhere to the ImageNet mean and standard deviation [6]. The 3D coordinates were calculated from the image depth fields and represented in decimeter units, as all LINEMOD and YCB-Video objects are at most 1.5 dm in diameter and the backbone network can estimate better when the output is within a normalized range. The loss functions of Eqs. 1-3 were used with an Adam optimizer, with initial learning rate lr = 1e−4. The lr was adjusted on a fixed schedule, re-scaled by a factor of 0.1 every 70 epochs. The network trained for 300 and 500 epochs for each object in the LINEMOD and YCB-Video datasets respectively, with batch size 32.

The accumulator space A is represented as a flat 3D integer array, i.e. an axis-aligned grid of voxel cubes. The size of A was set for each test image to the bounding box of the 3D data. The voxel resolution was set to 5 mm, which was found to be a good tradeoff between memory expense and keypoint localization accuracy (see Supplementary Material Sect. S.4.5).

For each object, 3 instances of the network were trained, one for each keypoint. We also implemented a version in which all 3 keypoints were trained simultaneously, within a single network. In this version, the $\hat{M}_0$, $\hat{M}_1$, and M_1 representations of Fig. 3 are replicated 3 times, and the FCN-ResNet weights are shared. Our experiments (detailed in the supplementary material) showed that the accuracy was poorer for this version, than when using separate networks for each keypoint. The only two methods that have used a combined network for all keypoints and all objects are GDRNet [48] and SOPose [7], against which our performance compares favourably (see Sect. 4.6).

4.3   Evaluation Metrics

We follow the ADD(s) metric defined by [15] to evaluate LINEMOD, whereas YCB-Video is evaluated based on both ADD(s) and AUC as proposed by [49]. All metrics are based on the distances between corresponding points as objects are transformed by the ground truth and estimated transformations. ADD measures the average distance between corresponding points, whereas ADDs averages the minimum distance between closest points, and is more forgiving for symmetric objects. A pose is considered correct if its ADD(s) falls within 10% of the object radius. AUC applies the ADD(s) values to determine the success of an estimated transformation, integrating these results over a varying 0 to 100 mm threshold.

4.4   Comparison of Keypoint Voting Schemes

We first conducted an experiment to evaluate the relative accuracies of the four voting schemes at keypoint localization, using the process from Sect. 3.2. Each scheme used the same 15%/85% train/test split of a subset of objects from the LINEMOD dataset. All four schemes used the exact same backbone network and hyperparameters. Specifically, they all used a fully convolutional ResNet-18 [24], batch size 48, initial learning rate 1e−3, and Adam optimizer, with accumulator space resolution of 1 mm. They were all trained with a fixed learning rate reduction schedule, which reduced the rate by a factor of 10 following every 70 epochs, and all trials trained until they fully converged.

The only difference between trials, other than the selective use of either $\mathbf{m_o}, \mathbf{m_v}, \mathbf{m_p}$ or $\mathbf{m_r}$ in training $\widehat{M}_1$, was a slight variation in the loss functions. For $\mathbf{m_o}$ and $\mathbf{m_r}$, the L1 loss from Eqs. 1–3 was used, identical to the offset

Table 1. Keypoint localization error $\bar{\epsilon}$, for surface (FPS) and disperse keypoints: mean μ and standard deviation σ for 4 voting schemes $\{v, o, p, r\}$, with $\bar{r}$ = mean keypoint distance to object centroid

| | | | $\bar{\epsilon}$ [mm] | | | | | | | |
| | | | vector (3D) | | offset (3D) | | polar (2D) | | radial (1D) | |
		$\bar{r}$ [mm]	μ_v	σ_v	μ_o	σ_o	μ_p	σ_p	μ_r	σ_r
Ape	FPS	61.2	10.0	5.8	5.8	2.6	5.6	2.4	**1.3**	**0.7**
Driller		129.4	10.0	2.3	6.5	4.7	5.3	2.5	**2.2**	**1.0**
Eggbox		82.5	11.8	5.3	5.2	2.7	4.9	1.9	**2.0**	**0.7**
ape	Disperse	142.1	12.5	7.6	10.4	5.3	5.7	2.5	**1.8**	**0.8**
Driller		318.8	11.3	8.2	9.5	3.5	5.2	2.6	**2.7**	**0.8**
Eggbox		197.3	13.7	8.5	11.4	4.7	7.2	3.4	**2.4**	**1.2**

voting in PVN3D [14]. Alternately, for $\mathbf{m_v}$ and $\mathbf{m_p}$, the Smooth L1 equivalents of Eqs. 2 and 3 (with $\beta = 1$) were used, as in PVNet [36] (albeit therein using a 2D accumulator space).

Surface Keypoints: Sets of size $K=4$ surface keypoints were selected for each object tested, using the Farthest Point Sampling (*FPS*) method [9]. FPS selects points on the surface of an object which are well separated, and is a popular keypoint generation strategy [14,36–38]. Following training, each keypoint's location $\widehat{k}_j^{\theta_i}$ was estimated by passing each test image I_i through the network, as in Fig. 3. The error $\epsilon_{i,j}$ for each estimate was its Euclidean distance from its ground truth location, i.e. $\epsilon_{i,j} = \|\widehat{k}_j^{\theta_i} - k_j^{\theta_i}\|$. The average of $\epsilon_{i,j}$ for an object over all test images and keypoints was the *keypoint estimation error*, denoted as $\bar{\epsilon}$.

Each voting scheme was implemented with care, so that they were numerically accurate and equivalent. To test the correctness of voting in isolation, ground truth values of M_1 calculated for each object and voting scheme were passed directly into the voting module, effectively replacing $\widehat{M}_1$ with M_1 in the inference stage of Fig. 3. For each voting scheme, the average $\bar{\epsilon}$ for all objects was similar and less than the accumulator space resolution of 1 mm, indicating that the implementations were correct and accurate.

The $\bar{\epsilon}$ values were evaluated for the four voting schemes for the ape, driller and eggbox LINEMOD objects as summarized in Table 1. These three particular objects were chosen as the ape is the smallest and the driller the largest of the objects, whereas the eggbox includes a rotational symmetry. Table 1 includes a measure of the average distance $\bar{r}$ of the ground truth keypoints to each object centroid. Radial voting is seen to be the most accurate method, with a mean value 1.9–4.3x more accurate than the next most accurate polar voting, with smaller standard deviations. Notably, the ordinal relationship between the four schemes remains consistent across the scheme dimensionality, which indicates that dimensionality impacts keypoint localization error.

Disperse Keypoints: We repeated this experiment for keypoints selected from the corners of each object's bounding box, which was first scaled by a factor of 2 so that the keypoints were dispersed to fall outside of the object's surface. The results in Table 1 indicate that radial voting still outperforms the other two schemes by a large margin. Whereas the other two methods decrease in accuracy sharply as the mean keypoint distance $\bar{r}$ increases, radial voting accuracy degrades more gracefully. For example, for the ape, the 232% increase in $\bar{r}$ from 61.2 to 142.1 mm, reduced accuracy for offset voting by 80% (from 5.8 to 10.4 mm), but only by 23% (from 2.2 to 2.7 mm) for radial voting.

The improved accuracy of radial voting is likely due to the fact that the radial scheme regresses a 1D quantity, compared with the 2D polar, and the 3D offset and vector scheme quantities. It seems likely that the errors in each independent dimension compound during voting. This is further supported by the recognition that the polar scheme is simply a reduced dimensionality parametrization of the vector scheme, and yet its performance is far superior, with between 1.7–2.4x greater accuracy. Radial voting also has a degree of resilience to rotations, which is lacking in the other schemes. Specifically, the three voting quantities $\mathbf{m_o}$, $\mathbf{m_v}$, and $\mathbf{m_p}$ are all sensitive to object in-plane rotations, whereas only radius scheme $\mathbf{m_r}$ is invariant to in-plane rotations.

4.5   Keypoint Dispersion

Impact on Transformation Estimation: It was suggested in [36] that 6 DoF pose estimation accuracy is improved by selecting keypoints that lie on the object surface, rather than the bounding box corners which lie just beyond the object surface. This may be the case when keypoint localization error increases signficantly with keypoint disperson, as occurs with vector and offset voting. There is, however, an advantage to dispersing the keypoints farther apart when using radial voting, which has a lower estimation error.

To demonstrate this, we conducted an experiment in which the keypoint locations were dispersed to varying degrees under a constant keypoint estimation error, with the impact measured on the accuracy of the resulting estimated transformation. We first selected a set $\mathcal{K} = \{k_j\}_{j=1}^{4}$ keypoints on the surface of an object, using the FPS strategy. This set was then rigidly transformed by T, comprising a random rotation (within $0°$ to $360°$ for each axis) and a random translation (within $1/2$ of the object radius), to form keypoint set $\mathcal{K}_T$. Each keypoint in $\mathcal{K}_T$ was then independently pertubed by a magnitude of 1.5 mm in a random direction, to simulate the keypoint estimation error of the radial voting scheme, resulting in (estimated) keypoint set $\widetilde{\mathcal{K}}_{\widetilde{T}}$.

Next, the estimated transformation $\widetilde{T}$ between $\widetilde{\mathcal{K}}_{\widetilde{T}}$ and the original (ground truth) keypoint set $\mathcal{K}$ was calculated using the Horn method [17]. This process simulates the pose estimation that would occur between estimated keypoint

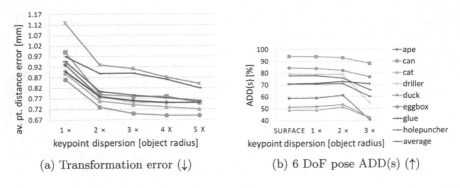

(a) Transformation error (↓)   (b) 6 DoF pose ADD(s) (↑)

Fig. 4. Impact of keypoint dispersion on (a) Transformation estimation error, and (b) 6 DoF pose estimation ADD(s).

locations, each with some error, and their corresponding ground truth model keypoints. The surface points of the object were then transformed by both the ground truth T and the estimated $\tilde{T}$ transformations, and the distances separating corresponding transformed surface points were compared, as a measure of the accuracy of the estimated transformation.

The above process was repeated for versions of $\mathcal{K}$ that were dispersed by scaling an integral factor of the object radius from the object centroid. The exact same error perturbations (i.e. magnitudes and directions) were applied to each keypoint for each new scale value. The scaled trials therefore represented keypoints that were dispersed more distant from the object centroid, albeit with the exact same localization error.

This process was executed for all Occlusion LINEMOD objects, with 100 trials for each scale factor value from 1 to 5. The means of the corresponding point distances (i.e. the ADD metric as defined in [15]) are plotted in Fig. 4a. It can be seen that ADD decreases for the first few scale factor increments for all objects, indicating an improved transformation estimation accuracy for larger keypoint dispersions. This increase in accuracy stems from improved rotational estimates, as the same positional perturbation error of a keypoint under a larger moment arm will result in a smaller angular error. The translational component of the transformation is not impacted by the scaling, as the Horn method starts by centering the two point clouds. After a certain increase in scale factor of 3 or 4, the unaffected translational error dominates, and the error plateaus.

This experiment shows that the transformation estimate from corresponding ground truth and estimated keypoints will be more accurate, when the keypoints are dispersed further (∼1 object radius, i.e. a scale of 2x) from the object's surface, when keypoint estimation error itself remains small (∼1.5 cm).

Impact on 6 DoF Pose Estimation: The above result can be leveraged to further improve the accuracy of 6 DoF pose estimation when using radial voting. An experiment was executed for all Occlusion LINEMOD objects for

Table 2. LINEMOD and Occlusion LINEMOD accuracy results

Mode	Method	ADD(s) [%]	
		LM	O-LM
RGB	SSD6D [19]	9.1	–
	Oberweger [31]	–	27.1
	Hu et al. [18]	–	30.4
	Pix2Pose [33]	72.4	32.0
	DPOD [50]	83.0	32.8
	PVNet [36]	86.3	40.8
	DeepIM [22]	88.6	–
	PPRN [44]	93.9	58.4
	GDR-Net [48]	93.7	62.2
	SO-Pose [7]	96.0	62.3
RGB +D ref	YOLO6D [43]	56.0	6.4
	SSD6D+ref [19]	34.1	27.5
	PoseCNN [49]	–	24.9
	DPOD+ref [50]	95.2	47.3
RGB-D	DenseFusion [46]	94.3	–
	PVN3D [14]	99.4	63.2
	PR-GCN [51]	99.6	65.0
	FFB6D [13]	**99.7**	66.2
	RCVPose	99.4	70.2
	RCVPose+ICP	**99.7**	**71.1**

Table 3. YCB-Video accuracy results

D ref?	Method	ADD(s)	AUC
No	PoseCNN [49]	59.9	75.8
	DF (per-pixel) [46]	82.9	91.2
	SO-Pose [7]	56.8	90.9
	GDR-Net [48]	60.1	91.6
	PVN3D [14]	91.8	95.5
	PR-GCN [51]	–	95.8
	FFB6D [13]	92.7	**96.6**
	RCVPose	**95.2**	**96.6**
Yes	PoseCNN [49]	85.4	93.0
	DF (iterative) [46]	86.1	93.2
	PVN3D [14]+ICP	92.3	96.1
	FFB6D [13]+ICP	93.1	97.0
	RCVPose+ICP	**95.9**	**97.2**

varying keypoint dispersions. The keypoints were first selected to lie on the surface of each object using FPS, and the complete RCVPose inference pipeline was executed, yielding an ADD(s) value for each trial image. The keypoints were then projected outward from each object's centroid to a distance of 1, 2 and 3 object radius values, and RCVPose inference was once again executed and ADD(s) recalculated.

The results are plotted in Fig. 4b. Of the 8 objects, 4 had a higher ADD(s) value at a dispersion of 2x, as did the average over all objects. It seems that the decreased transformation estimation error (Fig. 4a) at 2x radius dispersion more than compensates for the gradual increase in keypoint localization error exhibited by radial voting.

4.6   Comparison with SOTA

We next compared RCVPose against other recent competitive methods in the literature. We achieved state-of-art results on all three datasets, under a moderate

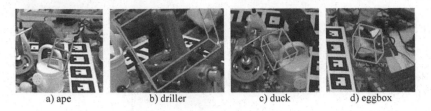

a) ape   b) driller   c) duck   d) eggbox

Fig. 5. RCVPose sample Occlusion LINEMOD results: Blue box = ground truth, green box = estimate. RCVPose shows robustness to (even severe) occlusion. (Color figure online)

training effort (i.e. hyper-parameter adjustment). The most challenging dataset was Occlusion LINEMOD, with results in Table 2. RCVPose+ICP outperformed all other methods on average, achieving 71.1% mean accuracy, exceeding the next closest method PVN3D by 7.9%. It achieved the top performance on all objects except duck, where PVNet had the best result. Even without ICP refinement, RCVPose achieved close to the same results at 70.2% mean accuracy.

One strength of RCVPose is scale tolerance. Unlike most other methods whose performance reduced with smaller objects, our method was not impacted much. Significantly, accuracy improved over FFB6D from 47.2%, 45.7% to 61.3%, 51.2% for the ape and cat, respectively. Another advantage is that it accumulates votes independently for each pixel and is therefore robust to partial occlusions, capable of recognizing objects that undergo up to 70% occlusion (see Fig. 5). The LINEMOD dataset is less challenging, as objects are unoccluded. As listed in Table 2, RCVPose+ICP still achieved the highest mean accuracy of 99.7%, slightly exceeding the tie between RCVPose (without ICP) and PVN3D. RCV-Pose+ICP was the only method to achieve 100% accuracy for more than one object. Again the RGB-D methods outperformed all other data modes, and the top RGB method that included depth refinement [33] outperformed the best pure RGB method [27], supporting the benefits of the added depth mode.

The YCB-Video results in Table 3 list AUC and ADD(s), with and without depth refinement. RCVPose is the top performing method, achieving from 95.2% to 95.9% ADD(s) and from 96.6% to 97.2% AUC accuracy, outperforming the next best method FFB6D by 2.8% ADD(s) and 0.2% AUC. Notably, RCVPose increased ADD(s) of the relatively small tuna fish can by a full 6% compared to the second best PVN3D. We also evaluated RCVPose on the BOP challenge benchmark [16], which is a standardized split of a number of datasets. Our results on their LINEMOD, Occlusion LINEMOD, and YCB-Video splits showed that RCVPose outperformed all other published results tested on this benchmark, when averaged over all 3 datasets (see Supplementary Material Sect. S.3). RCV-Pose runs at 18 fps on a server with an Intel Xeon 2.3 GHz CPU and RTX8000 GPU for a 640 × 480 image input. This compares well to other voting-based methods, such as PVNet at 25 fps, and PVN3D at 5 fps. The backbone network forward path, radial voting process, and Horn transformation solver take approximately 10, 41, and 4 msecs. per image respectively at inference time.

5 Conclusion

We have proposed RCVPose, a hybrid 6 DoF pose estimator with a ResNet-based radial estimator and a novel keypoint radial voting scheme. Our radial voting scheme is shown to be more accurate than previous schemes, especially when the keypoints are more dispersed, which leads to more accurate pose estimation requiring only 3 keypoints. We achieved state-of-the-art results on three popular benchmark datasets, YCB-Video, LINEMOD and the challenging Occlusion LINEMOD, ranking high on the BOP Benchmark, with an 18 fps runtime. A limitation is that training and inference are executed separately for each object and keypoint (also true for other recent competitive approaches) and that the 3D voting space is memory intensive, which will be the focus of future work.

Acknowledgements. Thanks to Bluewrist Inc. and NSERC for their support of this work.

References

1. Aiger, D., Mitra, N.J., Cohen-Or, D.: 4-points congruent sets for robust surface registration. ACM Trans. Graph. **27**(3), 1–10 (2008), #85
2. Andres, E.: Discrete circles, rings and spheres. Comput. Graph. **18**(5), 695–706 (1994)
3. Brachmann, E., Krull, A., Michel, F., Gumhold, S., Shotton, J., Rother, C.: Learning 6D object pose estimation using 3D object coordinates. In: Fleet, D., Pajdla, T., Schiele, B., Tuytelaars, T. (eds.) ECCV 2014. LNCS, vol. 8690, pp. 536–551. Springer, Cham (2014). https://doi.org/10.1007/978-3-319-10605-2_35
4. Brogan, J., et al.: Fast local spatial verification for feature-agnostic large-scale image retrieval. IEEE Trans. Image Process. **30**, 6892–6905 (2021)
5. Bukschat, Y., Vetter, M.: Efficientpose-an efficient, accurate and scalable end-to-end 6d multi object pose estimation approach. arXiv preprint arXiv:2011.04307 (2020)
6. Deng, J., Dong, W., Socher, R., Li, L., Li, K., Fei-Fei, L.: Imagenet: a large-scale hierarchical image database. In: 2009 IEEE Conference on Computer Vision and Pattern Recognition, pp. 248–255 (2009). https://doi.org/10.1109/CVPR.2009.5206848
7. Di, Y., Manhardt, F., Wang, G., Ji, X., Navab, N., Tombari, F.: So-pose: exploiting self-occlusion for direct 6d pose estimation. In: Proceedings of the IEEE/CVF International Conference on Computer Vision, pp. 12396–12405 (2021)
8. Duda, R.O., Hart, P.E.: Use of the hough transformation to detect lines and curves in pictures. Commun. ACM **15**(1), 11–15 (1972)
9. Eldar, Y., Lindenbaum, M., Porat, M., Zeevi, Y.Y.: The farthest point strategy for progressive image sampling. IEEE Trans. Image Process. **6**(9), 1305–1315 (1997)
10. Fischler, M.A., Bolles, R.C.: Random sample consensus: a paradigm for model fitting with applications to image analysis and automated cartography. Commun. ACM **24**(6), 381–395 (1981)
11. Gall, J., Yao, A., Razavi, N., Van Gool, L., Lempitsky, V.: Hough forests for object detection, tracking, and action recognition. IEEE Trans. Pattern Anal. Mach. Intell. **33**(11), 2188–2202 (2011). https://doi.org/10.1109/TPAMI.2011.70

12. He, K., Zhang, X., Ren, S., Sun, J.: Deep residual learning for image recognition. In: Proceedings of the IEEE Conference on Computer Vision and Pattern Recognition, pp. 770–778 (2016)
13. He, Y., Huang, H., Fan, H., Chen, Q., Sun, J.: Ffb6d: a full flow bidirectional fusion network for 6d pose estimation. In: Proceedings of the IEEE/CVF Conference on Computer Vision and Pattern Recognition, pp. 3003–3013 (2021)
14. He, Y., Sun, W., Huang, H., Liu, J., Fan, H., Sun, J.: Pvn3d: a deep point-wise 3d keypoints voting network for 6dof pose estimation. In: Proceedings of the IEEE/CVF Conference on Computer Vision and Pattern Recognition (CVPR) (2020)
15. Hinterstoisser, S., et al.: Model based training, detection and pose estimation of texture-less 3D objects in heavily cluttered scenes. In: Lee, K.M., Matsushita, Y., Rehg, J.M., Hu, Z. (eds.) ACCV 2012. LNCS, vol. 7724, pp. 548–562. Springer, Heidelberg (2013). https://doi.org/10.1007/978-3-642-37331-2_42
16. Hodaň, T., et al.: BOP challenge 2020 on 6D object localization. In: Bartoli, A., Fusiello, A. (eds.) ECCV 2020. LNCS, vol. 12536, pp. 577–594. Springer, Cham (2020). https://doi.org/10.1007/978-3-030-66096-3_39
17. Horn, B.K.P., Hilden, H.M., Negahdaripour, S.: Closed-form solution of absolute orientation using orthonormal matrices. J. Opt. Soc. Am. A 5(7), 1127–1135 (1988)
18. Hu, Y., Hugonot, J., Fua, P., Salzmann, M.: Segmentation-driven 6d object pose estimation. In: Proceedings of the IEEE/CVF Conference on Computer Vision and Pattern Recognition, pp. 3385–3394 (2019)
19. Kehl, W., Manhardt, F., Tombari, F., Ilic, S., Navab, N.: Ssd-6d: making rgb-based 3d detection and 6d pose estimation great again. In: Proceedings of the IEEE International Conference on Computer Vision, pp. 1521–1529 (2017)
20. Labbé, Y., Carpentier, J., Aubry, M., Sivic, J.: CosyPose: consistent multi-view multi-object 6D pose estimation. In: Vedaldi, A., Bischof, H., Brox, T., Frahm, J.-M. (eds.) ECCV 2020. LNCS, vol. 12362, pp. 574–591. Springer, Cham (2020). https://doi.org/10.1007/978-3-030-58520-4_34
21. Lamdan, Y., Wolfson, H.J.: Geometric hashing: a general and efficient model-based recognition scheme. In: [1988 Proceedings] Second International Conference on Computer Vision, pp. 238–249 (1988). https://doi.org/10.1109/CCV.1988.589995
22. Li, Y., Wang, G., Ji, X., Xiang, Y., Fox, D.: Deepim: deep iterative matching for 6d pose estimation. In: Proceedings of the European Conference on Computer Vision (ECCV), pp. 683–698 (2018)
23. Lin, T.-Y., et al.: Microsoft COCO: common objects in context. In: Fleet, D., Pajdla, T., Schiele, B., Tuytelaars, T. (eds.) ECCV 2014. LNCS, vol. 8693, pp. 740–755. Springer, Cham (2014). https://doi.org/10.1007/978-3-319-10602-1_48
24. Long, J., Shelhamer, E., Darrell, T.: Fully convolutional networks for semantic segmentation. In: Proceedings of the IEEE Conference on Computer Vision and Pattern Recognition, pp. 3431–3440 (2015)
25. Lorusso, A., Eggert, D.W., Fisher, R.B.: A comparison of four algorithms for estimating 3-D rigid transformations. Citeseer (1995)
26. Lowe, D.G.: Object recognition from local scale-invariant features. In: Proceedings of the Seventh IEEE International Conference on Computer Vision, vol. 2, pp. 1150–1157. IEEE (1999)
27. Manhardt, F., et al.: Explaining the ambiguity of object detection and 6d pose from visual data. In: Proceedings of the IEEE/CVF International Conference on Computer Vision (ICCV) (2019)

28. Manhardt, F., Kehl, W., Navab, N., Tombari, F.: Deep model-based 6d pose refinement in rgb. In: Proceedings of the European Conference on Computer Vision (ECCV), pp. 800–815 (2018)
29. Mohamad, M., Ahmed, M.T., Rappaport, D., Greenspan, M.: Super generalized 4pcs for 3d registration. In: 2015 International Conference on 3D Vision, pp. 598–606 (2015). https://doi.org/10.1109/3DV.2015.74
30. Mohamad, M., Rappaport, D., Greenspan, M.: Generalized 4-points congruent sets for 3d registration. In: 2014 2nd International Conference on 3D Vision, vol. 1, pp. 83–90 (2014). https://doi.org/10.1109/3DV.2014.21
31. Oberweger, M., Rad, M., Lepetit, V.: Making deep heatmaps robust to partial occlusions for 3d object pose estimation. In: Proceedings of the European Conference on Computer Vision (ECCV), pp. 119–134 (2018)
32. Olson, C.F.: Efficient pose clustering using a randomized algorithm (1997). https://doi.org/10.1023/A:1007906812782
33. Park, K., Patten, T., Vincze, M.: Pix2pose: pixel-wise coordinate regression of objects for 6d pose estimation. In: Proceedings of the IEEE/CVF International Conference on Computer Vision, pp. 7668–7677 (2019)
34. Park, K., Patten, T., Vincze, M.: Neural object learning for 6d pose estimation using a few cluttered images. In: Vedaldi, A., Bischof, H., Brox, T., Frahm, J.M. (eds.) Computer Vision - ECCV 2020, pp. 656–673. Springer International Publishing, Cham (2020). https://doi.org/10.1007/978-3-030-58548-8_38
35. Pavlakos, G., Zhou, X., Chan, A., Derpanis, K.G., Daniilidis, K.: 6-dof object pose from semantic keypoints. In: 2017 IEEE international conference on robotics and automation (ICRA), pp. 2011–2018. IEEE (2017)
36. Peng, S., Liu, Y., Huang, Q., Zhou, X., Bao, H.: Pvnet: pixel-wise voting network for 6dof pose estimation. In: Proceedings of the IEEE/CVF Conference on Computer Vision and Pattern Recognition, pp. 4561–4570 (2019)
37. Qi, C.R., Litany, O., He, K., Guibas, L.J.: Deep hough voting for 3d object detection in point clouds. In: Proceedings of the IEEE/CVF International Conference on Computer Vision (ICCV) (2019)
38. Qi, C.R., Yi, L., Su, H., Guibas, L.J.: Pointnet++: deep hierarchical feature learning on point sets in a metric space. arXiv preprint arXiv:1706.02413 (2017)
39. Redmon, J., Farhadi, A.: Yolov3: an incremental improvement. arXiv preprint arXiv:1804.02767 (2018)
40. Rothganger, F., Lazebnik, S., Schmid, C., Ponce, J.: 3d object modeling and recognition using local affine-invariant image descriptors and multi-view spatial constraints. Int. J. Comput. Vis. 66(3), 231–259 (2006)
41. Schönberger, J.L., Price, T., Sattler, T., Frahm, J.-M., Pollefeys, M.: A vote-and-verify strategy for fast spatial verification in image retrieval. In: Lai, S.-H., Lepetit, V., Nishino, K., Sato, Y. (eds.) ACCV 2016. LNCS, vol. 10111, pp. 321–337. Springer, Cham (2017). https://doi.org/10.1007/978-3-319-54181-5_21
42. Shao, J., Jiang, Y., Wang, G., Li, Z., Ji, X.: Pfrl: pose-free reinforcement learning for 6d pose estimation. In: IEEE/CVF Conference on Computer Vision and Pattern Recognition (CVPR) (2020)
43. Tekin, B., Sinha, S.N., Fua, P.: Real-time seamless single shot 6d object pose prediction. In: Proceedings of the IEEE Conference on Computer Vision and Pattern Recognition, pp. 292–301 (2018)
44. Trabelsi, A., Chaabane, M., Blanchard, N., Beveridge, R.: A pose proposal and refinement network for better 6d object pose estimation. In: Proceedings of the IEEE/CVF Winter Conference on Applications of Computer Vision, pp. 2382–2391 (2021)

45. Tremblay, J., To, T., Sundaralingam, B., Xiang, Y., Fox, D., Birchfield, S.: Deep object pose estimation for semantic robotic grasping of household objects. arXiv preprint arXiv:1809.10790 (2018)
46. Wang, C., et al.: Densefusion: 6d object pose estimation by iterative dense fusion. In: Proceedings of the IEEE/CVF Conference on Computer Vision and Pattern Recognition, pp. 3343–3352 (2019)
47. Wang, G., Manhardt, F., Shao, J., Ji, X., Navab, N., Tombari, F.: Self6D: self-supervised monocular 6D object pose estimation. In: Vedaldi, A., Bischof, H., Brox, T., Frahm, J.-M. (eds.) ECCV 2020. LNCS, vol. 12346, pp. 108–125. Springer, Cham (2020). https://doi.org/10.1007/978-3-030-58452-8_7
48. Wang, G., Manhardt, F., Tombari, F., Ji, X.: Gdr-net: geometry-guided direct regression network for monocular 6d object pose estimation. In: Proceedings of the IEEE/CVF Conference on Computer Vision and Pattern Recognition, pp. 16611–16621 (2021)
49. Xiang, Y., Schmidt, T., Narayanan, V., Fox, D.: Posecnn: a convolutional neural network for 6d object pose estimation in cluttered scenes (2018)
50. Zakharov, S., Shugurov, I., Ilic, S.: Dpod: 6d pose object detector and refiner. In: Proceedings of the IEEE/CVF International Conference on Computer Vision, pp. 1941–1950 (2019)
51. Zhou, G., Wang, H., Chen, J., Huang, D.: Pr-gcn: a deep graph convolutional network with point refinement for 6d pose estimation. In: Proceedings of the IEEE/CVF International Conference on Computer Vision, pp. 2793–2802 (2021)

Long-Tailed Instance Segmentation Using Gumbel Optimized Loss

Konstantinos Panagiotis Alexandridis[1,2]([envelope]) [ID], Jiankang Deng[3] [ID],
Anh Nguyen[2] [ID], and Shan Luo[1,2] [ID]

[1] King's College London, London WC2R 2LS, UK
{konstantinos.alexandridis,shan.luo}@kcl.ac.uk
[2] University of Liverpool, Liverpool L69 3BX, UK
{konsa15,anguyen,shan.luo}@liverpool.ac.uk
[3] Imperial College London, London SW7 2AZ, UK
j.deng16@imperial.ac.uk

Abstract. Major advancements have been made in the field of object
detection and segmentation recently. However, when it comes to rare
categories, the state-of-the-art methods fail to detect them, resulting in
a significant performance gap between rare and frequent categories. In
this paper, we identify that Sigmoid or Softmax functions used in deep
detectors are a major reason for low performance and are sub-optimal
for long-tailed detection and segmentation. To address this, we develop a
Gumbel Optimized Loss (*GOL*), for long-tailed detection and segmentation. It aligns with the Gumbel distribution of rare classes in imbalanced
datasets, considering the fact that most classes in long-tailed detection
have low expected probability. The proposed *GOL* significantly outperforms the best state-of-the-art method by 1.1% on *AP*, and boosts the
overall segmentation by 9.0% and detection by 8.0%, particularly improving detection of rare classes by 20.3%, compared to Mask-RCNN, on LVIS
dataset. Code available at: https://github.com/kostas1515/GOL.

Keywords: Long-tailed distribution · Long-tailed instance
segmentation · Gumbel activation

1 Introduction

There have been astonishing advancements in the fields of image classification, object detection and segmentation recently. They have been made possible
by using curated and balanced datasets, e.g., CIFAR [20], ImageNet [9] and
COCO [22] and by using deep Convolutional Neural Networks (CNNs). Despite
that, all these advancements could be in vain if they are not usable in real-world
applications. For example, the performance of classifiers in ImageNet is similar

Supplementary Information The online version contains supplementary material
available at https://doi.org/10.1007/978-3-031-20080-9_21.

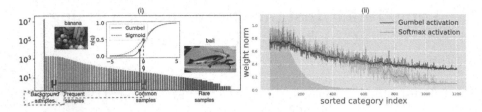

Fig. 1. (i) Gumbel activation function (blue) is asymmetric and it aligns better with the long-tailed instance segmentation distribution due to the extreme background and foreground class imbalance, whereas Sigmoid activation (red) is symmetric and more appropriate for balanced distributions. (ii) Gumbel activation (blue) produces more balanced weight norms in comparison to Softmax activation (orange) in the LVIS [11] dataset using Mask-RCNN [12]. (Color figure online)

to humans, however, ImageNet pretrained detectors still struggle as they suffer from various sources of imbalance [27]. Moreover, existing instance segmentation models [2,5,12] fail to generalize for long-tailed datasets and their performance significantly decreases for the rare categories [11]. As a result, it is difficult to exploit the advancements in image classification and transfer them to applications like object detection and segmentation due to the imbalance problem. Furthermore, there is a significant gap in performance between frequent (head) and infrequent (tail) classes in long-tailed datasets, as the state-of-the-art (SOTA) methods only detect the frequent classes [21,36]. All such problems may deteriorate the reliability of autonomous systems that rely on object detection and segmentation and raise concerns.

One possible solution for improving the long-tailed instance segmentation performance is to gather more samples for rare classes, as it is known that CNNs can achieve better results by using more data. Unfortunately, data collection will be not only costly but also intractable. The physical world contains objects that follow the Zipfian distribution [23]. This means that by increasing the distinct classes of a dataset, it is unavoidable that some will be frequent while others will be rare.

The main reason for the low performance of instance segmentation in long-tailed datasets is class imbalance. As discussed in [24,33,35], head classes dominate during training and they cause large discouraging gradients for tail classes. Since tail classes have fewer training samples, the amount of positive feedback is scarce and in the end, the model is trained effectively only for the head classes. It is also reflected by the norms of the classifier's weights [16]: classifiers trained under the long-tailed paradigm have classification weights whose norms are larger for head classes and lower for tail classes. As larger weights produce larger probabilities, the classifiers are therefore biased towards head classes. For these reasons, many prior works focus on balancing either the weight norms or the gradients caused by head and tail classes or performing two-stage training where the model is first trained for all classes and then fine-tuned for tail categories.

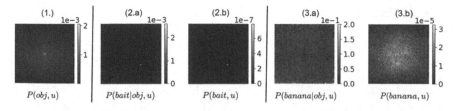

Fig. 2. Object distributions in the LVIS long-tailed object detection dataset [11]. (1): The distribution of objects $P(obj, u)$ in the dataset (irrespective of their class); (2.a): the class probability conditioned on object and its location $P(y|obj, u)$, and (2.b): the expected class distribution $P(y, u)$, for the tail class *bait*; (3.a): the class probability conditioned on object and its location $P(y|obj, u)$, and (3.b): the expected class distribution $P(y, u)$, for the head class *banana*. As shown in the figures, the distributions of objects in a long-tailed object dataset have a normal distribution as a whole and also for the head classes, whereas follows a Gumbel distribution for tail classes.

In contrast, we argue that the low performance in long-tailed instance segmentation is partially due to the use of sub-optimal activation functions in bounding box classification. Most classes in this long-tailed distribution have extremely low expected probabilities due to imbalance [27], making the widely used activation functions such as Sigmoid and Softmax unsuitable. For this reason, we develop a new activation function, namely Gumbel activation and a new Gumbel loss function to model the long-tailed distribution in instance segmentation. Gumbel activation is an asymmetric function that aligns better with the long-tailed instance segmentation distribution as shown in Fig. 1(i). Moreover, Gumbel loss allows the gradient of positive samples to grow exponentially while suppressing the gradient of negative samples. This is especially useful for rare category learning, in which positive feedback is scarce. At the same time, it produces more balanced classification weight norms in comparison to Softmax as shown in Fig. 1(ii), suppressing the classification bias. Both head and tail categories can benefit from Gumbel loss, without the need of gradient re-balancing, exhausting parameter tuning, weight normalization or complex two-stage training. Furthermore, Gumbel is agnostic to frameworks, it can be used alongside with other loss functions and datasets, which makes it widely applicable. Based on the proposed Gumbel loss, we have developed Gumbel optimized methods, that outperform the state-of-the-art instance segmentation methods on the LVIS [11] dataset. We list our contributions as follows:

- We identify the problem of activation functions in long-tailed instance segmentation for the first time, via extensive experiments;
- We propose a new loss, i.e., Gumbel Optimized Loss (*GOL*), for long-tailed instance segmentation;
- We have validated the effectiveness of *GOL* on real-world long-tailed instance segmentation datasets, outperforming the SOTA methods by a large margin.

2   Related Works

Long-Tailed Object Classification. It has been a hot topic to address the imbalance problem in object classification. Long-tailed object classification datasets of CIFAR10, CIFAR100 and ImageNet have been investigated to tackle imbalanced classification using techniques such as data re-sampling [4,24,31,42], Cost Sensitive Learning (CSL) [8,17], margin adjustment [3,18,25,30] and two stage training [16,36]. Data re-sampling methods re-sample the rare classes and have been most widely used and investigated [4,24,31,42]. However, such methods cost more training effort and pose the risk of overfitting for rare classes, while under-sampling under-fits heads class and deteriorates the overall performance. The CSL methods construct a cost matrix so that the cost function can be more sensitive to the rare classes [8,17], so as to exploit the data available. But CSL methods are dependent on the dataset and require careful calibration to avoid exploding gradients caused by excessive costs. Margin adjustment techniques change the decision boundary of the classifiers by either normalizing the classifier weight norms, engineering appropriate losses or modifying the classification prediction a-posteriori [3,18,25,30], which do not cost additional training time. Their drawback is that the margins are difficult to compute, and they are based on dataset statistics.

Long-Tailed Object Detection. Some methods addressing the long-tailed image classification could be applied in long-tailed object detection [16,30,33,35]. However, many SOTA long-tailed classification methods obtain low performance for tasks that include the special *background* class [26]. Under this realistic scenario, the performance drop is caused by the extreme imbalance between the dominant *background* class and other foreground classes. The same applies in long-tailed object detection where the imbalance factor is ∼ 1000 larger than the imbalance factor in image classification. For this reason, not all long-tailed classification methods are transferable to long-tailed instance segmentation. Instead, many methods are developed to tackle long-tailed object detection, directly. Some of them include the creation of specialized loss functions that balance the gradient contribution of positive and negative samples [29,32,33,35,37]. Others construct hierarchical groups [21,38], enforce margins in the classifier's prediction [10,30,34] or use two-stage strategies [16,36,40]. These methods have produced promising results but they suffer from limitations: Two-stage methods are complex and laborious; hierarchical methods require pre-processing and careful grouping; loss engineering methods have many hyper-parameters that need tuning. All these methods use Sigmoid or Softmax as their activation function, which is not close to the target distribution and not a good choice as we discuss in Sect. 3.

To the best of our knowledge, we are the first to tackle long-tailed segmentation by using Gumbel loss function. The most related work is [1], where they used the general extreme value distribution to classify Covid-19 cases. In contrast, we develop Gumbel for long-tailed instance segmentation.

3   Problem Formulation

Assume a dataset $X = \{x_i, y_i\}, i \in \{1, ..., N\}$, where x_i, y_i are images and annotations respectively and N is the total number of training images. We can train
a convolutional neural network $f(X, \theta) = z$, where z is the latent representation
and θ is the network's weight parameters. To calculate the prediction $\bar{y}$, one first
can use a fully connected layer $q(z) = W^T z + b$, where W is the classification
weights and b is the bias term, to calculate the score q_i. Then $\bar{p}_i = \eta(q_i)$ is used
to transform the score q_i into probability $\bar{p}_i$, using the activation function $\eta(\cdot)$
and finally the prediction $\bar{y}$ is calculated using $\bar{y} = \arg\max_i(\bar{p}_i)$.

In image classification and instance segmentation, the Sigmoid activation,
i.e., $\eta_{\text{sigmoid}}(q_i) = \frac{1}{1+e^{-q_i}}$, or the Softmax activation, i.e., $\eta_{\text{softmax}}(q_i) = \frac{e^{q_i}}{\sum e^{q_j}}$,
has been commonly used. For the binary case, it assumes that $\bar{p}_i$ follows a
Bernoulli distribution as the score $q_i = \log\frac{\bar{p}_i}{1-\bar{p}_i}$ and it can be interpreted as
the odds-ratio of the event $\bar{p}_i$, i.e., how many times an event happens $\bar{p}_i$ divided
by how many times it does not happen $1 - \bar{p}_i$ in a log scale.

It would be reasonable to use the Sigmoid or Softmax activation function for
image classification, where the expected probability distribution $\mathbb{P}$ is a Bernoulli
distribution and all classes are mutually exclusive, thus one can use Sigmoid or
Softmax to effectively model the data. However, we argue that it would not be
well suitable to use these activation functions for long-tailed instance segmentation as the expected distribution of objects is not the same as the expected
image distribution in classification. Object distribution is more complex as it is
affected by class imbalance and location imbalance.

3.1   Object Distribution

To make this clear, we first calculate the ground truth object distribution. To
this end, we calculate the expected number of objects $P(obj, u)$ whose centers
fall inside the cell $u = [i, j]$ of the normalized grid as follows:

$$P(obj, u) = \frac{\sum_{x=1}^{x=N} \mathbb{1}(obj, x)\mathbb{1}(obj, u)}{M} \tag{1}$$

where obj is the object occurrence, $\mathbb{1}$ is the indicator function and M is the
total number of objects in the dataset. Next, we calculate the class membership
$P(y|obj, u)$ for each location u, which summarizes the uncertainty of an object
belonging to each class y in the dataset for the specific location u (i.e., it holds
that $\sum_{y=1}^{y=C} P(y|obj, u) = 1$). Finally, we calculate $P(y, u)$[1] as:

$$P(y, u) = P(y|obj, u)P(obj, u) \tag{2}$$

The final target distribution is a distribution that we aim to estimate by
minimizing the cross entropy between the target and the data distribution.

---

[1] Here we omit obj for simplicity since $P(y, obj, u) = P(y, u)$ due to that y shows there
is object occurrence obj.

In Fig. 2, we visualize $P(obj, u)$, $P(y|obj, u)$ and $P(y, u)$ for one head class and one tail class of LVIS dataset. The probability of detection for a head class i.e., *banana* in the example, is low in each location and varies in different locations of the image. For a tail class, i.e., *bait* in the example, is even lower and zero for most locations. This is different from long-tailed image classification, in which the expected class probabilities are not affected by location imbalance, only by class imbalance. On the other hand, in long-tailed instance segmentation, classes have even lower expected probabilities as they are affected by both location imbalance and class imbalance. For example, even head classes like *banana* have even lower expectation for locations far away from the center of the image, making the long-tailed segmentation more challenging for both head and tail classes. This highlights the magnitude of imbalance in long-tailed segmentation and motivates us to develop Gumbel activation.

Using Gumbel, we assume that the target distribution follows Gumbel distribution and this is a better choice than using Sigmoid or Softmax because the expected classification probabilities are minuscule. In fact, by using any activation function, one assumes how the ground truth is distributed. It is a common practice to use Sigmoid or Softmax and this assumes that the target distribution is Bernoulli. While this is a rational choice for image classification, it is unrealistic for long-tailed instance segmentation as the expected classification probabilities are infinitesimal. For this reason, we assume that the target distribution is Gumbel and we use Gumbel activation. We further explain why choosing an activation, that implicitly assumes the target distribution, below.

3.2   Activations as Priors

To understand why choosing an activation implicitly assumes the target distribution, we consider an example of binary classification, however, it can be extended to multi-class classification easily. In a binary classification problem, the true variable y relates with the representations z as follows:

$$y = \begin{cases} 1, & \text{if } W^T z + b + \epsilon > 0 \\ 0, & \text{otherwise} \end{cases} \tag{3}$$

where ϵ is the error that is a random variable. The classification boundary is set to 0, but it could be any other value as it is adjusted by the bias term b in optimization. We are interested in the probability $P(y = 1)$ and this is calculated as:

$$P(y = 1) = P(W^T z + b + \epsilon > 0)$$
$$P(\epsilon > -W^T z - b) = 1 - F(-q) \tag{4}$$

where F is the cumulative distribution function. Many practitioners use Sigmoid to activate q and estimate $P(y = 1)$ and this means that:

$$P(y = 1) = \eta_{\text{sigmoid}}(q) = \frac{1}{1 + e^{-q}}$$
$$\eta_{\text{sigmoid}}(q) = F_{\text{logistic}}(q; 0, 1) \tag{5}$$
$$P(y = 1) = 1 - F_{\text{logistic}}(-q; 0, 1)$$

By comparing Eq. 4 and the last expression of Eq. 5, it is understood that by using Sigmoid activation, one assumes that the error term ϵ follows the standard logistic distribution (with $\mu = 0$ and $\sigma = 1$), as one chooses F to be logistic. In practice, when any activation function $\eta(q)$ is applied, it is implicitly assumed how ϵ is distributed and as a result the target distribution $y \sim \mathbb{P}$ is assumed. For example, if a Sigmoid function is used, the variable q is transformed into a binomial probability distribution, which implies that it has a success rate $\bar{p}$ and a failure rate $1 - \bar{p}$, like a coin toss. In this case, it is assumed that y follows Bernoulli Distribution and the error ϵ follows Logistic Distribution. Finally, the training of the model is to minimize the discrepancy between the target distribution $\mathbb{P}$ and the predicted distribution $\mathbb{Q}$ using Cross Entropy:

$$H(\mathbb{P}(x), \mathbb{Q}(x)) = - \sum_{x \in X} \mathbb{P}(x) \log(\mathbb{Q}(x)) \tag{6}$$

In training, as Stochastic Gradient Descent is an iterative algorithm, the starting conditions play a significant role. This suggests that it is preferable to have a good starting prior so that the initial estimation of $\mathbb{P}$ is reasonable and the choice of the activation function will facilitate the initial estimation. This has a similar concept to the prior distribution in Bayesian Inference, where it is important to choose a suitable prior for optimal results.

Hypothesis. In long-tailed instance segmentation, the expected classification probabilities are significantly low due to imbalance problems as mentioned by [27] and explained in Eq. 2. For this reason, we hypothesize that Gumbel activation will produce superior results as it models the data using Gumbel Distribution which is closer to the real object distribution.

In conclusion, long-tailed instance segmentation is far more challenging than image classification and naive usage of Sigmoid or Softmax activation infringes on the underlying assumptions. Nevertheless, one can use Cross Entropy to minimize the discrepancy between the target distribution $\mathbb{P}$ and the predicted distribution $\mathbb{Q}$ but if the prior guess is significantly different than the actual distribution $\mathbb{P}$ then the results might be sub-optimal. By choosing the activation function, one guesses how the target $\mathbb{P}$ is distributed. For Sigmoid or Softmax, one believes that $\mathbb{P}$ is Bernoulli distribution and while this is reasonable for image classification, we argue that in long-tailed instance segmentation it is not optimal and we empirically show that Gumbel can produce superior results.

4   Gumbel Activation for Long-Tailed Detection

4.1   Sigmoid Activation for Object Classification

It is useful to remind the readers about Sigmoid activation as we can make clear distinctions between this and our suggested activation. The formula is $\eta_\sigma(q_i) = \frac{1}{1+\exp(-q_i)}$. If one encodes the ground truth y as a one-hot vector then the gradient using Eq. 6 is $\frac{dL(\eta_\sigma(q_i),y_i)}{dq_i} = y_i(\eta_\sigma(q_i) - 1) + (1 - y_i)\eta_\sigma(q_i)$.

Sigmoid is a symmetric activation function: the positive gradient (i.e., when $y = 1$) takes values from $(-1, 0)$, while the negative gradient (i.e., when $y = 0$) takes values from $(0, 1)$ and the response value grows with the same rate for both positive and negative input, as shown in Fig. 3(i).

4.2   Gumbel Activation for Rare-Class Segmentation

We notice that $P(y, u)$ has infinitesimal probabilities. For tail classes it has a maximum value in the scale of $1e$–7, for head classes it has a maximum $1e$–5 and for both cases, it has even lower probabilities for edge locations in the image. This motivates us to model $P(y, u)$ using the extreme value distribution Gumbel. Gumbel is useful for modelling extreme events, i.e., those with very low probabilities. For example, Gumbel can be used to predict the next great earthquake because this has a much lower probability than regular earthquakes. Other applications of Gumbel can be found in finance and biology and the readers are referred to this work [19] for more information on extreme value distribution. In long-tailed instance segmentation, one can use the cumulative density function of the standard Gumbel distribution as the activation function (we further study the choice of non-standard Gumbel activation in supplementary material):

$$\eta_\gamma(q_i) = F_{\text{Gumbel}}(q; 0, 1) = \exp(-\exp(-q_i)) \tag{7}$$

Combining Eq. 6 and Gumbel activation we derive Gumbel Loss (GL) as:

$$GL(\eta_\gamma(q_i), y_i) = \begin{cases} -\log(\eta_\gamma(q_i)), & if \ \ y_i = 1 \\ -\log(1 - \eta_\gamma(q_i)), & if \ \ y_i = 0 \end{cases} \tag{8}$$

The gradient of Eq. 8 is:

$$\frac{dL(\eta_\gamma(q_i), y_i)}{dq_i} = \begin{cases} -\exp(-q_i), & if \ \ y_i = 1 \\ \frac{\exp(-q_i)}{\exp(\exp(-q_i))-1}, & if \ \ y_i = 0 \end{cases} \tag{9}$$

The Gumbel activation is asymmetric as illustrated in Fig. 3(i). This means that the positive gradients (i.e., when $y = 1$) will take values from $(-\infty, 0)$ while the negative gradients (i.e., when $y = 0$) will take values from $(0, 1)$. This is a beneficial property that allows the positive feedback to grow exponentially while it suppresses the negative feedback. It is especially useful in long-tailed segmentation as the positive feedback for rare categories is scarce. With Gumbel activation, positive gradients can grow faster than by using Sigmoid activation as shown in Fig. 3(ii) and this can boost the performance of rare classes.

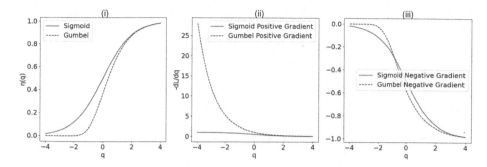

Fig. 3. Activation properties for Gumbel (blue dashed lines), Sigmoid (red solid lines) activation functions. Their activation behaviours are illustrated in (i). The Gumbel activation is asymmetric, whereas Sigmoid is symmetric. Their positive gradients and negative gradients are illustrated in (ii) and (iii) respectively, using inverted y-axis $\frac{-dL}{dq}$. The positive gradients of the Gumbel activation (i.e., when $y = 1$) ranges in $(-\infty, 0)$, while the negative gradients (i.e., when $y = 0$) ranges in $(0, 1)$. (Color figure online)

4.3 Gumbel Optimised Loss

Gumbel activation can be used not only with Cross Entropy loss but with other state-of-the-art loss functions as well. We select the recently proposed Droploss [14] as the loss function of our enhanced Gumbel-based model, other loss functions are shown in Fig. 4(ii). Using Gumbel activation and Droploss we propose Gumbel Optimised Loss GOL as follows:

$$\mathcal{L}_{GOL} = -\sum_{j=1}^{C} \log(w_j^{Drop}\bar{p}_j), \quad \bar{p}_j = \begin{cases} \eta_\gamma(q_i), & if \ y_j = 1 \\ 1 - \eta_\gamma(q_i), & if \ y_j = 0 \end{cases} \tag{10}$$

where w_j^{Drop} are class specific weights proposed by DropLoss [14]. We show the full equation in supplementary material due to space limitations.

5 Experimental Setup

Dataset and Evaluation Metrics. For our experiments on long-tailed instance segmentation, we use LVIS (Large Vocabulary Instance Segmentation) dataset [11]. We mainly use version 1 which contains 100k images for training and 19.8k images for validation. LVISv1 dataset contains $1,203$ categories that are grouped according to their image frequency: *rare* categories (those with 1–10 images in the dataset), *common* categories (11 to 100 images in the dataset) and *frequent* categories (those with > 100 images in the dataset.) Some previous methods use the LVISv0.5 dataset, which has 1230 classes instead of 1203. For fairness, we also show results in this dataset. We report our results using average segmentation performance AP, average box performance AP^b and average segmentation performance for rare AP^r, common AP^c and frequent categories AP^f.

Table 1. Comparative results for LVISv1 using schedule 1x, random sampler (left) and RFS [11] sampler (right). Gumbel activation is superior than Softmax, especially for the case of random sampling when the distribution is unaltered.

Sampler	Random					RFS [11]					
Method	AP	AP^r	AP^c	AP^f	AP^b	Method	AP	AP^r	AP^c	AP^f	AP^b
Sigmoid	16.4	0.8	12.7	27.3	17.2	Sigmoid	22.0	11.4	20.9	27.9	**23.0**
Softmax	15.2	0.0	10.6	26.9	16.1	Softmax	21.5	9.7	20.7	27.6	22.4
Gumbel (ours)	**19.0**	**4.9**	**16.8**	**27.6**	**19.1**	Gumbel (ours)	**22.7**	**12.2**	**21.2**	**28.0**	22.9

Implementation Details. For our experiments, we use 4 V100 GPUs, a total batch size of 16 images, a learning rate of 0.02, weight decay of 0.0001, Stochastic Gradient Descent and momentum of 0.9. We use random horizontal flipping and multi-scaling as data augmentations for training, following the conventions of the community. We train our models using the *mmdetection* framework [6] and during inference, we use score threshold of 0.0001 as in [11].

For our intermediate experiments, we use Gumbel activation and a plethora of architectures, backbones, loss functions and sampling strategies using the 1x schedule. For our enhanced *GOL* model, we use Mask-RCNN [12], the 2x schedule, Normalised Mask [35], RFS sampler [11] and a stricter Non-Maximum Suppression threshold that is 0.3. When using Gumbel activation, we initialize the weights of the classifier to 0.001 and the bias terms to -2.0, to enable stable training. More implementation details, design choices and results are discussed in our supplementary material.

6   Results

6.1   Results with Different Sampling Strategies

We compare activations when using a random sampler and 1x schedule. Under this configuration, the target distribution is unaltered and the probability of sampling is equal to the dataset's class probability. As Table 1 suggests, the best activation function using a random sampler is Gumbel which largely outperforms Sigmoid and Softmax. It increases overall AP by 2.6%, AP^r and AP^c by 4.1% and AP^b by 1.9% compared to Sigmoid and AP by 3.8%, AP^r by 4.9%, AP^c by 6.2% and AP^b by 3.0% compared to Softmax. Noticeably, the gap in mask and box performance is smaller with Gumbel activation at 19.0% and 19.1% respectively, while other activations have larger gaps between box and segmentation performance. This suggests that Gumbel is more suitable for long-tailed segmentation than other activation functions.

We apply the state-of-the-art RFS [11] method, which is an oversampling method and report the results in Table 1. With RFS, images containing rare categories are up-sampled, thus the original distribution is distorted. Under this scenario, Gumbel activation does not boost the performance as much as before,

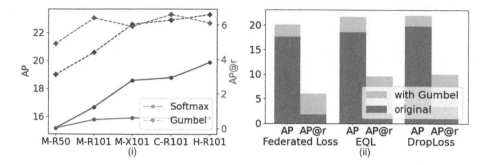

Fig. 4. (i): Comparison of Softmax against Gumbel activation using common instance segmentation frameworks. (ii): Comparison of Sigmoid-based SOTA losses against the Gumbel-based alternatives. All models use 1x schedule and random sampling.

as the object distribution becomes more balanced with oversampling. Nevertheless, Gumbel improves overall performance by a respective margin of 0.7% in overall segmentation and by 0.8% AP^r which is attributed to the fact that firstly, there are still classes in the dataset that suffer from imbalance after using RFS, thus Gumbel can model them better than Sigmoid or Softmax; secondly, Gumbel activation has a lower gap in bounding box and segmentation performance than Sigmoid or Softmax, which results in higher segmentation performance (i.e., 0.7% increase) given similar box performance.

6.2   Integrating Gumbel Activation

We conduct experiments using training schedule 1x with larger backbones, i.e., Resnet101 [13] and ResNeXt101 [39] and architectures i.e., Cascade Mask RCNN [2] and Hybrid Task Cascade [5] to determine if the proposed activation generalizes for deeper models. As shown in Fig. 4 (i), Gumbel activation is a better choice than the Softmax activation function as it achieves better overall AP and AP in rare categories.

Next, we examine the behavior of the Gumbel activation function using SOTA loss functions Equalization loss (EQL) [33], DropLoss [14] and Federated Loss [41]. For EQL and DropLoss, we use the hyperparameter $\lambda = 0.0011$ which is more appropriate for LVISv1 as described in [32] and we change only the activation function from Sigmoid to Gumbel. For Federated Loss, we use the same hyper-parameters as described in [41] changing only the activation from Sigmoid to Gumbel. As Fig. 4 (ii) indicates, Gumbel significantly boosts the performance of all models in both overall AP and rare category AP and this highlights its applicability and efficacy. We show more detailed results in our supplementary material.

Table 2. Ablation study, using Mask-RCNN, Resnet50 and training schedule 2x.

RFS	EQL	Gumbel	Enh	DropLoss	AP	AP^r	AP^c	AP^f	AP^b
					18.7	1.1	16.2	29.2	19.5
✓					23.7	13.3	23.0	29.0	24.7
✓	✓				25.3	17.4	24.9	29.2	26.0
✓	✓	✓			26.1	18.4	25.9	29.8	26.8
✓	✓	✓	✓		26.9	18.1	26.5	**31.3**	26.8
✓		✓	✓	✓	**27.7**	**21.4**	**27.7**	30.4	**27.5**

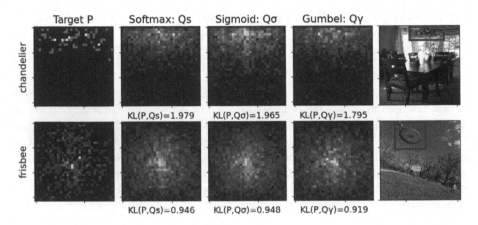

Fig. 5. Comparison of two object distributions in LVIS validation set, using Softmax (second column), Sigmoid (third column) and Gumbel (fourth column). Gumbel predicts distributions that have smaller KL divergence than Sigmoid or Softmax.

6.3   GOL Components

We conduct an ablation study using a 2x-schedule and we report the most significant findings, a more detailed ablation study is provided in our supplementary material. We use the standard Mask-RCNN, EQL [33] and RFS [11] as the basis and examine the behavior of Gumbel. As shown in Table 2, Gumbel can significantly boost the performance of this pipeline by 0.8%. To further boost the performance, we use a stricter Non-Maximum Suppression threshold that is 0.3 and Mask normalization, we denote these enhancements in the Table as (Enh). Next, we adopt DropLoss which is a recent improvement in the loss function of EQL, proposed by [14]. Finally, the best performance is achieved using RFS, Gumbel, Enh and DropLoss, we codename this as pipeline GOL.

Total Performance. In the end, our GOL method significantly improves the vanilla Mask-RCNN AP by 9.0%, and it largely improves AP^r by 20.3%, AP^c by 11.5%, AP^f by 1.2% and AP^b by 8.0%.

Table 3. Comparison against SOTA on the LVIS dataset.

Method	Dataset	Framework	AP	AP^r	AP^c	AP^f	AP^b
RFS [11]	LVIS v0.5	Mask-RCNN R50-FPN	25.4	16.3	25.7	28.7	25.4
DropLoss [14]			26.4	17.3	28.7	27.2	25.8
BAGS [21]			26.2	18.0	26.9	28.7	25.8
BALMS [30]			27.0	19.6	28.9	27.5	27.6
Forest-RCNN [38]			25.6	18.3	26.4	27.6	25.9
EQLv2 [32]			27.1	18.6	27.6	29.9	27.0
LOCE [10]			28.4	22.0	29.0	30.2	**28.2**
DisAlign [40]			27.9	16.2	29.3	**30.8**	27.6
GOL (ours)			**29.5**	**22.5**	**31.3**	30.1	**28.2**
RFS [11]	LVIS v1.0	Mask-RCNN R50-FPN	23.7	13.3	23.0	29.0	24.7
EQLv2 [32]			25.5	17.7	24.3	30.2	26.1
LOCE [10]			26.6	18.5	26.2	**30.7**	27.4
NorCal with RFS [28]			25.2	19.3	24.2	29.0	26.1
Seesaw [35]			26.4	19.5	26.1	29.7	**27.6**
GOL (ours)			**27.7**	**21.4**	**27.7**	30.4	27.5
RFS [11]	LVIS v1.0	Mask-RCNN R101-FPN	25.7	17.5	24.6	30.6	27.0
EQLv2 [32]			27.2	20.6	25.9	31.4	27.9
LOCE [10]			28.0	19.5	27.8	**32.0**	29.0
NorCal with RFS [28]			27.3	20.8	26.5	31.0	28.1
Seesaw [35]			28.1	20.0	28.0	31.8	28.9
GOL(ours)			**29.0**	**22.8**	**29.0**	31.7	**29.2**

Comparison with Other Methods. As shown in Table 3, *GOL* significantly surpasses the state-of-the-art in LVIS Dataset using the standard Mask-RCNN benchmark. In detail, in LVISv0.5, *GOL* achieves 29.5% *AP*, surpassing RFS [11] by 4.1% and the best state-of-art LOCE [10] by 1.1% in *AP*. Moreover, our method achieves the best performance at rare and common categories and it consistently surpasses many other recent works. In LVISv1, *GOL* achieves 27.7% overall *AP*, surpassing RFS [11] by 4.0%, LOCE by 1.1%, Seesaw Loss [35] by 1.3% and EQLv2 [32] by 2.2% using ResNet50 backbone. It also achieves the best *AP*, which is at least 0.9% higher than other methods, using the larger ResNet101 backbone. Finally, it consistently outperforms all other methods for rare and common categories in both Resnet50 and Resnet101 backbones.

6.4   Model Analysis

We analyze the behavior of Mask-RCNN using Gumbel Loss. In detail, we visualize Mask-RCNN predicted object distributions in the validation set, for two random classes *chandelier* and *frisbee*. We compare, the predicted distributions $\mathbb{Q}$ of Softmax, Sigmoid and Gumbel against the ground truth $\mathbb{P}$ using the Kullback Leibler divergence.

As Fig. 5 suggests, Gumbel produces object distributions that are closer to the target distribution, as they have smaller Kullback-Leibler (KL) divergence.

Moreover, as [16] has suggested, there is a positive correlation between the weight norms of the classifier and the image frequency of categories, which results in classification bias. In our case, we visualize the weight norms of the Mask-RCNN classifier trained with Softmax (baseline model), and Gumbel respectively. As Fig. 1 (ii) suggests, the weight norm distribution of the Mask-RCNN classifier trained with Gumbel is more uniform than the distribution of vanilla Mask-RCNN. This suggests that the classifier norms are more balanced when using Gumbel loss which validates its efficacy.

6.5 Long-Tailed Image Classification

We further test Gumbel activation in long-tailed image classification benchmarks. For all classification experiments, we use random sampling and decoupled strategy. In decoupled strategy, the model is first trained with Softmax activation and then only the classifier is re-trained with Gumbel activation.

CIFAR100-LT [3]. We train a ResNet32 for 240 epochs using Auto-Augment [7], SGD, weight decay 0.0002, batch size 64 and learning rate 0.1 that decays at epoch 200 and 220 by 0.01. In the second stage, we retrain the classifier using a learning rate of 1e−4 for 15 epochs.

ImageNet-LT, Places-LT [23]. For ImageNet-LT, we train ResNet50 with and without Squeeze and Excite [15] modules for 200 epochs using Auto-Augment. For Places-LT, we finetune an ImageNet pretrained ResNet152 for 30 epochs. For both datasets, we use SGD, weight decay 0.0005, batch size 256, and learning rate 0.2 with cosine scheduler. In the second stage, we retrain the classifier using a learning rate of 1e−5 for 10 epochs.

Table 4. Top-1 accuracy on long-tailed classification datasets.

Dataset	CIFAR100-LT			ImageNet-LT		Places-LT
Imbalance factor	50	100	200	256		996
Model		ResNet-32		ResNet-50	SE-ResNet-50	ResNet-152
Softmax	46.2	42.4	38.3	45.2	45.9	28.7
Gumbel	**49.0**	**45.5**	**41.5**	**48.2**	**48.5**	**30.0**

As Table 4 indicates, Gumbel activation can boost the classification performance of all models in all datasets consistently.

7   Conclusion and Discussions

We hypothesize that real-world long-tailed detection and segmentation data follows a distribution that is closer to Gumbel distribution and not Bernoulli. For this reason, we propose to use Gumbel activation instead of Sigmoid or Softmax. We validate the superiority of Gumbel against Sigmoid and Softmax under different sampling strategies, deeper models and loss functions and we develop the *GOL* method based on Gumbel activation that significantly outperforms the state-of-the-art. Our extensive experiments validate that Gumbel is a superior activation function that can be used as a component with both off-the-shelf methods and state-of-the-art models to further increase their performance.

We have also tested Gumbel activation in long-tailed classification benchmarks and saw consistent improvements when Gumbel is used as a decoupled method. Finally, Gumbel could also be used for dense object detection and we have seen a 0.4% increase in AP when using RetinaNet on COCO and 1x schedule. Currently, Gumbel cannot be used with Softmax-based loss functions and it does not take full advantage of oversampling methods. In the future, we will develop a custom loss function and sampling mechanism tailored to Gumbel activation.

Acknowledgments. This work was supported by the Engineering and Physical Sciences Research Council (EPSRC) Centre for Doctoral Training in Distributed Algorithms [EP/S023445/1]; EPSRC ViTac project (EP/T033517/1); King's College London NMESFS PhD Studentship; the University of Liverpool and Vision4ce. It also made use of the facilities of the N8 Centre of Excellence in Computationally Intensive Research provided and funded by the N8 research partnership and EPSRC [EP/T022167/1].

References

1. Bridge, J., et al.: Introducing the GEV activation function for highly unbalanced data to develop COVID-19 diagnostic models. IEEE J. Biomed. Health Inform. **24**(10), 2776–2786 (2020)
2. Cai, Z., Vasconcelos, N.: Cascade R-CNN: high quality object detection and instance segmentation. IEEE Trans. Pattern Anal. Mach. Intell. **43**(5), 1483–1498 (2019)
3. Cao, K., Wei, C., Gaidon, A., Arechiga, N., Ma, T.: Learning imbalanced datasets with label-distribution-aware margin loss. In: Advances in Neural Information Processing Systems (2019)
4. Chawla, N.V., Bowyer, K.W., Hall, L.O., Kegelmeyer, W.P.: SMOTE: synthetic minority over-sampling technique. J. Artif. Intell. Res. **16**, 321–357 (2002)
5. Chen, K., et al.: Hybrid task cascade for instance segmentation. In: Proceedings of the IEEE/CVF Conference on Computer Vision and Pattern Recognition, pp. 4974–4983 (2019)
6. Chen, K., et al.: MMDetection: open MMLab detection toolbox and benchmark. arXiv preprint arXiv:1906.07155 (2019)
7. Cubuk, E.D., Zoph, B., Mane, D., Vasudevan, V., Le, Q.V.: Autoaugment: learning augmentation strategies from data. In: Proceedings of the IEEE/CVF Conference on Computer Vision and Pattern Recognition, pp. 113–123 (2019)
8. Cui, Y., Jia, M., Lin, T.Y., Song, Y., Belongie, S.: Class-balanced loss based on effective number of samples. In: Proceedings of the IEEE/CVF Conference on Computer Vision and Pattern Recognition, pp. 9268–9277 (2019)

9. Deng, J., Dong, W., Socher, R., Li, L.J., Li, K., Fei-Fei, L.: ImageNet: a large-scale hierarchical image database. In: 2009 IEEE Conference on Computer Vision and Pattern Recognition, pp. 248–255. IEEE (2009)
10. Feng, C., Zhong, Y., Huang, W.: Exploring classification equilibrium in long-tailed object detection. In: Proceedings of the IEEE/CVF International Conference on Computer Vision, pp. 3417–3426 (2021)
11. Gupta, A., Dollar, P., Girshick, R.: LVIS: a dataset for large vocabulary instance segmentation. In: Proceedings of the IEEE/CVF Conference on Computer Vision and Pattern Recognition, pp. 5356–5364 (2019)
12. He, K., Gkioxari, G., Dollár, P., Girshick, R.: Mask R-CNN. In: Proceedings of the IEEE International Conference on Computer Vision, pp. 2961–2969 (2017)
13. He, K., Zhang, X., Ren, S., Sun, J.: Deep residual learning for image recognition. In: Proceedings of the IEEE Conference on Computer Vision and Pattern Recognition, pp. 770–778 (2016)
14. Hsieh, T.I., Robb, E., Chen, H.T., Huang, J.B.: Droploss for long-tail instance segmentation. In: Proceedings of the AAAI Conference on Artificial Intelligence, vol. 35, pp. 1549–1557 (2021)
15. Hu, J., Shen, L., Sun, G.: Squeeze-and-excitation networks. In: Proceedings of the IEEE Conference on Computer Vision and Pattern Recognition, pp. 7132–7141 (2018)
16. Kang, B., et al.: Decoupling representation and classifier for long-tailed recognition. In: Eighth International Conference on Learning Representations (ICLR) (2020)
17. Khan, S.H., Hayat, M., Bennamoun, M., Sohel, F.A., Togneri, R.: Cost-sensitive learning of deep feature representations from imbalanced data. IEEE Trans. Neural Netw. Learn. Syst. **29**(8), 3573–3587 (2017)
18. Kim, B., Kim, J.: Adjusting decision boundary for class imbalanced learning. IEEE Access **8**, 81674–81685 (2020)
19. Kotz, S., Nadarajah, S.: Extreme Value Distributions: Theory and Applications. World Scientific, Singapore (2000)
20. Krizhevsky, A., Hinton, G., et al.: Learning multiple layers of features from tiny images (2009)
21. Li, Y., et al.: Overcoming classifier imbalance for long-tail object detection with balanced group softmax. In: Proceedings of the IEEE/CVF Conference on Computer Vision and Pattern Recognition, pp. 10991–11000 (2020)
22. Lin, T.-Y., et al.: Microsoft COCO: common objects in context. In: Fleet, D., Pajdla, T., Schiele, B., Tuytelaars, T. (eds.) ECCV 2014. LNCS, vol. 8693, pp. 740–755. Springer, Cham (2014). https://doi.org/10.1007/978-3-319-10602-1_48
23. Liu, Z., Miao, Z., Zhan, X., Wang, J., Gong, B., Yu, S.X.: Large-scale long-tailed recognition in an open world. In: Proceedings of the IEEE/CVF Conference on Computer Vision and Pattern Recognition, pp. 2537–2546 (2019)
24. Mahajan, D., et al.: Exploring the limits of weakly supervised pretraining. In: Proceedings of the European Conference on Computer Vision (ECCV), pp. 181–196 (2018)
25. Menon, A.K., Jayasumana, S., Rawat, A.S., Jain, H., Veit, A., Kumar, S.: Long-tail learning via logit adjustment. In: International Conference on Learning Representations (2021). https://openreview.net/forum?id=37nvvqkCo5
26. Mullapudi, R.T., Poms, F., Mark, W.R., Ramanan, D., Fatahalian, K.: Background splitting: finding rare classes in a sea of background. In: Proceedings of the IEEE/CVF Conference on Computer Vision and Pattern Recognition, pp. 8043–8052 (2021)

27. Oksuz, K., Cam, B.C., Kalkan, S., Akbas, E.: Imbalance problems in object detection: a review. IEEE Trans. Pattern Anal. Mach. Intell. **43**(10), 3388–3415 (2020)
28. Pan, T.Y., et al.: On model calibration for long-tailed object detection and instance segmentation. In: Advances in Neural Information Processing Systems, vol. 34 (2021)
29. Peng, J., Bu, X., Sun, M., Zhang, Z., Tan, T., Yan, J.: Large-scale object detection in the wild from imbalanced multi-labels. In: Proceedings of the IEEE/CVF Conference on Computer Vision and Pattern Recognition, pp. 9709–9718 (2020)
30. Ren, J., et al.: Balanced meta-softmax for long-tailed visual recognition. In: Proceedings of Neural Information Processing Systems(NeurIPS) (2020)
31. Shen, L., Lin, Z., Huang, Q.: Relay backpropagation for effective learning of deep convolutional neural networks. In: Leibe, B., Matas, J., Sebe, N., Welling, M. (eds.) ECCV 2016. LNCS, vol. 9911, pp. 467–482. Springer, Cham (2016). https://doi.org/10.1007/978-3-319-46478-7_29
32. Tan, J., Lu, X., Zhang, G., Yin, C., Li, Q.: Equalization loss v2: a new gradient balance approach for long-tailed object detection. In: Proceedings of the IEEE/CVF Conference on Computer Vision and Pattern Recognition, pp. 1685–1694 (2021)
33. Tan, J., et al.: Equalization loss for long-tailed object recognition. In: Proceedings of the IEEE/CVF Conference on Computer Vision and Pattern Recognition, pp. 11662–11671 (2020)
34. Tang, K., Huang, J., Zhang, H.: Long-tailed classification by keeping the good and removing the bad momentum causal effect. Adv. Neural. Inf. Process. Syst. **33**, 1513–1524 (2020)
35. Wang, J., et al.: Seesaw loss for long-tailed instance segmentation. In: Proceedings of the IEEE/CVF Conference on Computer Vision and Pattern Recognition, pp. 9695–9704 (2021)
36. Wang, T., et al.: The devil is in classification: a simple framework for long-tail instance segmentation. In: Vedaldi, A., Bischof, H., Brox, T., Frahm, J.-M. (eds.) ECCV 2020. LNCS, vol. 12359, pp. 728–744. Springer, Cham (2020). https://doi.org/10.1007/978-3-030-58568-6_43
37. Wang, T., Zhu, Y., Zhao, C., Zeng, W., Wang, J., Tang, M.: Adaptive class suppression loss for long-tail object detection. In: Proceedings of the IEEE/CVF Conference on Computer Vision and Pattern Recognition, pp. 3103–3112 (2021)
38. Wu, J., Song, L., Wang, T., Zhang, Q., Yuan, J.: Forest R-CNN: large-vocabulary long-tailed object detection and instance segmentation. In: Proceedings of the 28th ACM International Conference on Multimedia, pp. 1570–1578 (2020)
39. Xie, S., Girshick, R., Dollár, P., Tu, Z., He, K.: Aggregated residual transformations for deep neural networks. In: Proceedings of the IEEE Conference on Computer Vision and Pattern Recognition, pp. 1492–1500 (2017)
40. Zhang, S., Li, Z., Yan, S., He, X., Sun, J.: Distribution alignment: a unified framework for long-tail visual recognition. In: Proceedings of the IEEE/CVF Conference on Computer Vision and Pattern Recognition, pp. 2361–2370 (2021)
41. Zhou, X., Koltun, V., Krähenbühl, P.: Probabilistic two-stage detection. arXiv preprint arXiv:2103.07461 (2021)
42. Zou, Y., Yu, Z., Kumar, B., Wang, J.: Unsupervised domain adaptation for semantic segmentation via class-balanced self-training. In: Proceedings of the European Conference on Computer Vision (ECCV), pp. 289–305 (2018)

DetMatch: Two Teachers are Better than One for Joint 2D and 3D Semi-Supervised Object Detection

Jinhyung Park[1] , Chenfeng Xu[2(✉)] , Yiyang Zhou[2], Masayoshi Tomizuka[2], and Wei Zhan[2]

[1] Carnegie Mellon University, Pittsburgh, PA 15213, USA
jinhyun1@andrew.cmu.edu
[2] University of California, Berkeley, CA 94720, USA
{xuchenfeng,yiyang.zhou,tomizuka,wzhan}@berkeley.edu

Abstract. While numerous 3D detection works leverage the complementary relationship between RGB images and point clouds, developments in the broader framework of semi-supervised object recognition remain uninfluenced by multi-modal fusion. Current methods develop independent pipelines for 2D and 3D semi-supervised learning despite the availability of paired image and point cloud frames. Observing that the distinct characteristics of each sensor cause them to be biased towards detecting different objects, we propose DetMatch, a flexible framework for joint semi-supervised learning on 2D and 3D modalities. By identifying objects detected in both sensors, our pipeline generates a cleaner, more robust set of pseudo-labels that both demonstrates stronger performance and stymies single-modality error propagation. Further, we leverage the richer semantics of RGB images to rectify incorrect 3D class predictions and improve localization of 3D boxes. Evaluating our method on the challenging KITTI and Waymo datasets, we improve upon strong semi-supervised learning methods and observe higher quality pseudo-labels. Code will be released here: https://github.com/Divadi/DetMatch.

Keywords: Semi-Supervised Learning · Multi-modal learning · Object detection

1 Introduction

Recent advances in Semi-Supervised Learning (SSL) for object recognition focus on the single-modality setting, demonstrating improvements in either 2D or 3D

J. Park—Work conducted during visit to University of California, Berkeley.

Supplementary Information The online version contains supplementary material available at https://doi.org/10.1007/978-3-031-20080-9_22.

Fig. 1. Matching 2D and 3D detections, DetMatch removes false negatives and positives to generate cleaner pseudo-labels. Points are colored for visualization.

detection when leveraging unlabeled samples of that modality. However, SSL works rarely study the combination of 2D and 3D sensors. In recently published datasets, autonomous vehicles are equipped with a comprehensive collection of sensors that yields multi-modal observations of each scene. Among these devices, 2D RGB cameras and 3D LiDARs have emerged as two independently useful but also mutually complementary modalities. Thus, it is important for SSL methods to utilize both 2D and 3D modalities for autonomous driving applications.

We propose a novel multi-modal SSL framework, **DetMatch**, that leverages paired but unlabeled data of multiple modalities to train stronger single-modality object detectors. Our pipeline is agnostic to the designs of the detectors, allowing for flexible usage in conjunction with perpendicular advancements in architectures. Further, by yielding single-modality models, DetMatch does not constrain the trained detectors to the multi-modal or even the autonomous driving setting.

We observe that differences in modality characteristics between RGB images and point clouds cause them to each be better at detecting different types of objects as illustrated in Fig. 1. 3D point clouds are sparse, and their lack of color causes structurally similar objects to be indistinguishable. On the other hand, 2D RGB images contain a dense array of color information, allowing for easier discrimination of similarly shaped classes and better detection of objects with few 3D points captured. However, unlike point clouds, RGB images lack depth values. Each point in the 3D point cloud represents an exact, observed location in 3D space, making objects spatially separable - this facilitates 3D detection of objects that have overlapping, similar-colored projections in 2D. These factors support our intuition that not only are RGB images and point clouds mutually beneficial, but that their detection results are strongly complementary.

To leverage this relationship for SSL while keeping each detection model single-modal, we associate 2D and 3D results at the detection level. Since 2D and 3D have their own strengths, we use predictions in each modality that have a corresponding detection in the other modality to generate a cleaner subset of box predictions that is used to pseudo-label the unlabeled data for that modality. We find that such pseudo-labels chosen using multiple modalities outperform single-modality generated pseudo-labels. Although this method exploits the advantages of each modality to generate stronger pseudo-labels, it insufficiently utilizes the RGB images' unique rich semantics. In the previous pipeline, a correctly localized & classified 2D detection cannot directly rectify a poor 3D detection. To remedy this gap, we additionally enforce box and class consistency between matched 2D pseudo-labels and 3D predictions and observe improved performance.

Our main contributions are as follows:

- We observe that differences in characteristics between 2D and 3D modalities allow objects of high occlusion to be better detected in 3D, and objects of similar shape but different class to be better identified and localized in 2D.
- Our SSL framework leverages the mutually beneficial relationship between multiple modalities during training to yield stronger single-modality models.
- We extensively validate DetMatch the difficult KITTI [12] and Waymo [57] datasets, notably achieving around 10 mAP absolute improvement over labeled-only 3D baseline on the 1% and 2% KITTI settings and a 10.6 AP improvement for Pedestrians in 3D on the 1% Waymo setting.

2   Related Work

Semi-Supervised Learning. SSL methods either use consistency regularization [1,24,43,47,60] or pseudo-labeling [2,3,25,53,77]. The former forces noised predictions on unlabeled images to be consistent. The seminal work [1] enforces consistency over dropout, Temporal Ensembling [24] stores exponential moving averages (EMA) of past predictions, and Mean Teacher [60] enforces consistency between "student" and "teacher" models, the latter an EMA of the former.

Pseudo-labeling methods explicitly generate labels on unlabeled data and train on them in lieu of ground truth. MixMatch [3] ensembles over augmentations, ReMixMatch [2] uses weak augmentations for labeling and strong augmentations for training, and FixMatch [53] uses a confidence threshold to generate labels. Our method builds on intuitions from Mean Teacher [60] and asymmetric augmentations [3,27,33,53] to ensure the teacher model can correctly supervise the student by maintaining an advantage over the student.

SSL for Object Detection. 2D detection models [5,29,32,44,45,61] consist of a feature extraction backbone [14], a region proposal network [32,45], and optionally, a second-stage proposal refinement module [5,45]. 3D object detection methods [13,28,48,72,82] follow a similar structure, instead using voxel [9,11,13,50,72] or point [39,41,49,70,74] representations instead of 2D modules. Our proposed DetMatch is agnostic to the single-modality detectors used.

Some 2D SSL object detection methods [19,59] enforce consistency over augmentations, STAC [54] generates pseudo-labels offline, and Instant-Teaching [81] uses Mosaic [4] and MixUp [78]. A line of work [26,71] improves thresholding, and others use EMA for predictions [73] and teacher models [33,59]. Similarly, for 3D SSL, SESS [80] trains consistency over asymmetric augmentations and 3DIoUMatch [64] thresholds on predicted IoU. Compared to 2D, more 3D methods use offline labeling [6,42,65], with some [42,65] using ensembling and multiple timesteps to refine detections. Improvements in multi-frame fusion are perpendicular to our work, as our DetMatch generates cleaner per-frame pseudo-labels that can be used for downstream multi-timestep aggregation and refinement. Unlike these single-modality SSL methods, our pipeline jointly leverages the unique characteristics of RGB and point clouds to improve SSL for each modality.

2D-3D Multi-modal Learning. Many works have explored 2D-3D fusion for detection and segmentation. Some methods [23,40,66] constrain the 3D search space through 2D detection, while others fuse 2D and 3D features [16,52,63, 76,79] or predictions [37,38,62,68,75]. Some works have explored cross modal distillation [8], contrastive pretraining [34–36], or directly transferring 2D model into 3D [69]. Most relevant to our work is xMUDA [18], which proposes a cross-modality loss for semantic segmentation domain adaptation. Their 3D model is supervised by 2D segmentation results and vice versa. However, unlike pixels and points on which segmentation is done, detections in 2D and 3D do not have a directly calculable bijective mapping, making cross-modal supervision in object detection a less constrained problem. Further, training box regression requires extra consideration. We address these difficulties in our framework.

3   Method

3.1   Problem Definition

In semi-supervised object detection, we have a small set of labeled data $\{(\mathbf{x}_i^l, \mathbf{y}_i^l)\}_{i=1}^{N_l}$ and a larger set of unlabeled data $\{\mathbf{x}_i^u\}_{i=1}^{N_u}$, where N_l and N_u are the number of labeled and unlabeled frames, respectively. We typically have $N_u >> N_l$. We omit the scripts on $\mathbf{x}_i^l$ when they are clear from context. In autonomous driving [12,57] and indoor scene understanding [10,17,51,56,67], a single input sample is a multi-modal tuple $\mathbf{x} = (\mathbf{x}_{2D}, \mathbf{x}_{3D})$. $\mathbf{x}_{2D}$ is a 2D RGB image and $\mathbf{x}_{3D}$ is a 3D point cloud. Similarly, each ground truth annotation is a tuple of 2D and 3D labels, which in turn are each a set of boxes and classification labels:

$$\mathbf{y} = \left(\mathbf{y}_{2D} = \left\{(\mathbf{b}_{2D}, \mathbf{c}_{2D})^{(j)}\right\}, \mathbf{y}_{3D} = \left\{(\mathbf{b}_{3D}, \mathbf{c}_{3D})^{(j)}\right\}\right)$$

$\mathbf{b}_{2D} \in \mathbb{R}^4$ is a 2D box, $\mathbf{b}_{3D} \in \mathbb{R}^7$ is a 3D box, and $\mathbf{c} \in \{0,1\}^C$ is a one-hot label indicating one of C classes. To reduce the labeling burden for training, we generate $\mathbf{y}_{2D}$ from $\mathbf{y}_{3D}$ by projecting $\mathbf{b}_{3D}$ to 2D to get $\mathbf{b}_{2D}$ using camera parameters. Thus, our pipeline requires no 2D labels for the target dataset.

3.2   Teacher-Student Framework

We use a student model $\mathbf{S}$ and a teacher model $\mathbf{T}$ of the same architecture. At a high level, the teacher $\mathbf{T}$ generates pseudo-labels on the unlabeled data that the student $\mathbf{S}$ trains on. For the teacher to correctly and stably supervise the student, the teacher must maintain an advantage over the student in terms of the performance. We accomplish this by iteratively updating and improving the teacher model through training via exponential moving average (EMA) accumulation:

$$\theta_{\mathbf{T}} \leftarrow \alpha\theta_{\mathbf{T}} + (1 - \alpha)\theta_{\mathbf{S}} \tag{1}$$

where α is the EMA momentum, and the θ are the model parameters. Unlike methods that pseudo-label offline [6,42,54], our student and its EMA teacher allow for continuous improvement of pseudo-labels throughout training.

3.3   Single-Modality Semi-supervised Learning

Overview. In this section, we outline a straightforward teacher-student, single-modality SSL approach based on the state-of-the-art 2D SSL method Unbiased Teacher [33]. We find that with a well-tuned confidence threshold, this simple baseline compares favorably against more complicated approaches in 3D such as 3DIoUMatch [64]. We omit modality indicators $2D$ and $3D$ for this section, because this SSL baseline is applicable to any detection model.

Pre-training. For the teacher to reasonably guide the student from the start, we first pre-train the student model on the labeled data. Let $\mathbf{T}(\mathbf{x}) = \hat{\mathbf{y}}_{\mathbf{T}} = \left\{(\hat{\mathbf{b}}_{\mathbf{T}}, \hat{\mathbf{c}}_{\mathbf{T}})^{(j)}\right\}$ and $\mathbf{S}(\mathbf{x}) = \hat{\mathbf{y}}_{\mathbf{S}} = \left\{(\hat{\mathbf{b}}_{\mathbf{S}}, \hat{\mathbf{c}}_{\mathbf{S}})^{(j)}\right\}$ denote the predictions of the teacher and the student models respectively, with each consisting of a set of bounding boxes and classification probabilities. The loss on labeled samples is:

$$\mathcal{L}^l = \mathcal{L}_{loc}\left(\hat{\mathbf{y}}_{\mathbf{S}}^l, \left\{\mathbf{b}^{l^{(j)}}\right\}\right) + \mathcal{L}_{cls}\left(\hat{\mathbf{y}}_{\mathbf{S}}^l, \left\{\mathbf{c}^{l^{(j)}}\right\}\right) \tag{2}$$

where $\mathcal{L}_{loc}$ and $\mathcal{L}_{cls}$ represent the localization and classification losses, respectively. After the student is pre-trained to convergence, the teacher is initialized with the student weights before the SSL training begins.

Semi-supervised Training. To retain representations learned from the labeled data, we train using an equal number of labeled and unlabeled samples per batch:

$$\mathcal{L} = \mathcal{L}^l + \lambda\mathcal{L}^u \tag{3}$$

where $\mathcal{L}^l$ is as defined in Eq. 2, $\mathcal{L}^u$ is the loss on unlabeled samples and λ is a weighting hyperparameter. To train on unlabeled data, we get box predictions from the teacher and only keep the ones with maximum classification confidence above a threshold τ as pseudo-labels. We can write the teacher's generated pseudo-labels on the unlabeled data as:

$$\hat{\mathbf{y}}_{\mathbf{T}}^{(>\tau)} = \left\{(\hat{\mathbf{b}}_{\mathbf{T}}, \hat{\mathbf{c}}_{\mathbf{T}})^{(j)}\right\}^{(>\tau)} = \left\{\left(\hat{\mathbf{b}}_{\mathbf{T}}^{(j)}, \hat{\mathbf{c}}_{\mathbf{T}}^{(j)}\right) \mid \max(\hat{\mathbf{c}}_{\mathbf{T}}^{(j)}) > \tau\right\} \tag{4}$$

giving us the unlabeled loss:

$$\mathcal{L}^u = \mathcal{L}_{loc}\left(\hat{\mathbf{y}}_{\mathbf{S}}^u, \left\{\mathbf{b}_{\mathbf{T}}^{(j)}\right\}^{(>\tau)}\right) + \mathcal{L}_{cls}\left(\hat{\mathbf{y}}_{\mathbf{S}}^u, \left\{\text{argmax}(\mathbf{c}_{\mathbf{T}}^{(j)})\right\}^{(>\tau)}\right) \tag{5}$$

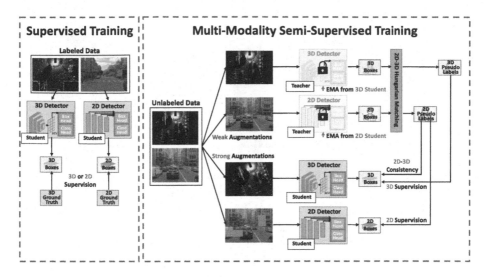

Fig. 2. The proposed DetMatch. We have a teacher and student for each modality and match 2D and 3D teacher predictions to supervise the students. The 2D teacher also directly supervises the 3D student through 2D-3D Consistency.

After SSL training, we take the teacher as our final model for more stability.

Asymmetric Data Augmentation. Although EMA makes the teacher more stable than the student, EMA alone does not give the teacher a large enough advantage in performance. To further decouple their predictions, we adopt asymmetric data augmentation on the inputs of the teacher and the student. We use weak augmentation $\mathcal{A}_{weak}(\mathbf{x})$ for the teacher and strong augmentation $\mathcal{A}_{strong}(\mathbf{x})$ for the student. We find that this single-modality SSL framework outperforms 3DIoUMatch on driving datasets, so we adopt it as our baseline for comparison.

3.4 Multi-modality Semi-supervised Learning

Overview. Although this single-modality SSL framework improves over labeled-only training, it has several disadvantages. Firstly, it does not leverage the paired 2D and 3D inputs, leading to sub-optimal single-modality results. Secondly, classification confidence is a poor measure of box localization performance as noted by prior work [20,55]. Finally, we find that single-modality self-training is prone to error propagation, leading to decreased performance in some cases.

To address these problems, we present our multi-modal semi-supervised framework shown in Fig. 2. DetMatch jointly maintains a teacher and a student for each modality and matches 2D and 3D teacher predictions to generate a cleaner set of pseudo-labels. Furthermore, to leverage the unique advantages of dense, colorful 2D RGB images, we propose a 2D-3D consistency module that

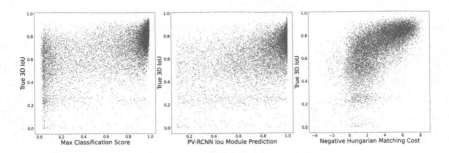

Fig. 3. Comparison between boxes' true 3D ground-truth IoU and various methods of assessing box quality on KITTI 1% unlabeled data.

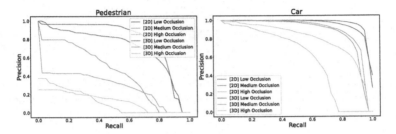

Fig. 4. 2D and 3D model performance at various occlusion levels.

forces 3D student predictions to be similar to 2D teacher boxes. Our multi-modal framework also performs pre-training and keeps labeled losses $\mathcal{L}_{2D}^l, \mathcal{L}_{3D}^l$ during SSL training for each modality as in Sect. 3.3. As the pseudo-label generation changes, our unlabeled losses $\mathcal{L}_{2D}^u, \mathcal{L}_{3D}^u$ are different from Eq. 5. We also introduce an additional $\mathcal{L}_{consistency}$ loss. The overall loss for our DetMatch is:

$$\mathcal{L} = (\mathcal{L}_{2D}^l + \mathcal{L}_{3D}^l) + (\mathcal{L}_{2D}^u + \mathcal{L}_{3D}^u) + \mathcal{L}_{consistency} \qquad (6)$$

2D-3D Hungarian Matching & Supervision. A drawback of the pipeline in Sect. 3.3 is its use of classification confidence to determine pseudo-labels. We visualize this issue in the left plot of Fig. 3, which shows that many 3D boxes with a low max score are highly overlapped with a ground truth box. Moreover, although scoring modules directly supervised by true IoU [48,64] are better than max classification score as shown in the middle plot, this IoU prediction module is unable to differentiate among high IoU values 0.6–0.9 as evidenced by the vertical cluster on the right side. As such, pseudo-labels generated using these single-modality measures of box quality prediction remain noisy.

We first examine the pros and cons of the 2D and 3D modalities. We plot in Fig. 4 the P/R curves of 2D and 3D detections for Pedestrian and Car classes on the KITTI validation dataset, with a separate curve for ground truth objects labeled as low, medium, and high occlusion. We find that at the same occlusion level, 2D better detects and localizes Pedestrians when compared to 3D. Due

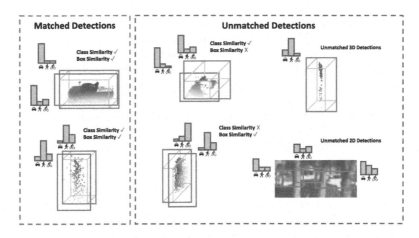

Fig. 5. Illustration of the 2D-3D Hungarian matching algorithm.

to the sparsity of point clouds and their lack of color information, Pedestrians are often confused with poles and trees of similar shape in 3D. However, such ambiguous objects are clearly identifiable in the dense 2D RGB image.

On the other hand, 2D detection struggles with highly overlapping objects due to its lack of depth information - when viewed in the 3D point cloud, such overlapping objects are clearly separated. This trend is especially clear when viewing the P/R curves for the Car class. Although 2D outperforms 3D for objects of low occlusion, we see a clear reversal for highly occluded objects. These observations clearly demonstrate that 2D and 3D modalities are complementary at the detection level - a relationship we propose to leverage for SSL by choosing as pseudo-labels detections with a corresponding match in the other modality.

More specifically, as shown in Fig. 5, we compute an optimal bipartite matching between 2D and 3D teacher predictions using the Hungarian Algorithm [22] and consider pairs with a matching cost below a threshold τ_{hung} "matched". The algorithm for matched pairs generation can be written as:

$$\left\{ \left((\hat{\mathbf{b}}_{\mathbf{T}}, \hat{\mathbf{c}}_{\mathbf{T}})^{2D}, (\hat{\mathbf{b}}_{\mathbf{T}}, \hat{\mathbf{c}}_{\mathbf{T}})^{3D} \right)^{(j)} \right\}^{(<\tau_{hung})} = Hungarian_{2D\text{-}3D}^{\tau_{hung}}(\hat{\mathbf{y}}_{\mathbf{T}}^{2D}, \hat{\mathbf{y}}_{\mathbf{T}}^{3D}) \quad (7)$$

We omit notation for the matching algorithm and thresholding for brevity. Inspired by recent works [7,58] on detection using learnable queries, our matching cost between a pair of 2D and 3D box predictions has three components:

$$\mathcal{L}_{match} \left((\hat{\mathbf{b}}_{\mathbf{T}}, \hat{\mathbf{c}}_{\mathbf{T}})^{2D}, (\hat{\mathbf{b}}_{\mathbf{T}}, \hat{\mathbf{c}}_{\mathbf{T}})^{3D} \right) = \lambda_{L1}\mathcal{L}_{L1} + \lambda_{iou}\mathcal{L}_{iou} + \lambda_{d\text{-}focal}\mathcal{L}_{d\text{-}focal} \quad (8)$$

Note that unlike classification score, a *lower* cost indicates a stronger match.

$\mathcal{L}_{L1}$ and $\mathcal{L}_{iou}$ are box consistency costs between the projected 3D box and the 2D box. To get the former, we project the 8 corners of the 3D box to the image and compute a tightly fitted 2D box. $\mathcal{L}_{L1}$ calculates l_1 loss between the

2D box parameters and $\mathcal{L}_{iou}$ calculates generalized IoU loss [46]. These costs force paired 2D and 3D pseudo-labels to refer to the same object agree on its localization. Unlike single-modality box localization confidence methods that suffer from modality-specific drawbacks and self-confidence bias, our multi-modal box consistency cost gives us a natural way to assess box quality.

$\mathcal{L}_{d\text{-}focal}$ calculates class prediction consistency between the 2D and 3D predictions. We formulate a double-sided version of FocalLoss [30]:

$$\mathcal{L}_{d\text{-}focal} = FocalLoss\left(\hat{\mathbf{c}}_{\mathbf{T}}^{2D}, \mathrm{argmax}(\hat{\mathbf{c}}_{\mathbf{T}}^{3D})\right) + FocalLoss\left(\hat{\mathbf{c}}_{\mathbf{T}}^{3D}, \mathrm{argmax}(\hat{\mathbf{c}}_{\mathbf{T}}^{2D})\right) \tag{9}$$

Note that this double-sided FocalLoss allows for a smooth trade-off between 2D and 3D confidence. A low-confidence 3D box *can still be chosen as a pseudo-label* if its matched 2D box has high confidence. Intuitively, high-confidence predictions of one modality can "promote" low-confidence predictions of the other modality, a dynamic selection not possible with simple confidence thresholding. Further, although this formulation of $\mathcal{L}_{focal}$ does prefer higher-confidence boxes, its motivation is different from that of confidence thresholding - $\mathcal{L}_{focal}$ considers *consistency* between classification predictions in 2D and 3D. If both modalities agree on the semantic class of a region, they will have a lower matching cost.

Our proposed 2D-3D matching cost is a remarkably more accurate measure of box localization quality as shown in the rightmost plot of Fig. 3. We then use the matched and thresholded pairs of 2D and 3D teacher boxes as pseudo-labels to supervise the 2D and 3D students on the unlabeled data:

$$\mathcal{L}_{modal}^{u} = \mathcal{L}_{loc}\left(\hat{\mathbf{y}}_{\mathbf{S}}^{modal}, \left\{(\mathbf{b}_{\mathbf{T}}^{modal})^{(j)}\right\}^{(<\tau_{hung})}\right) \tag{10}$$

$$+ \mathcal{L}_{cls}\left(\hat{\mathbf{y}}_{\mathbf{S}}^{modal}, \left\{\mathrm{argmax}\left((\mathbf{c}_{\mathbf{T}}^{modal})^{(j)}\right)\right\}^{(<\tau_{hung})}\right)$$

$$\text{for } modal \in \{2D, 3D\}$$

2D-3D Consistency. Through our 2D-3D Hungarian Matching, we generated a cleaner set of pseudo-labels to supervise each student. However, although we have leveraged the advantages 3D can provide 2D, we have not fully exploited the benefits 3D can get from 2D. We have fulfilled the former because although a core advantage of 3D is detection of highly occluded or visually unclear boxes, we need to differentiate these beneficial 3D teacher boxes from the false positives 3D detection is especially prone to. So, it is necessary to first match 3D boxes with 2D teacher boxes to filter noisy boxes while retaining the beneficial boxes.

On the other hand, the semantically rich format of 2D RGB images make class confusion less likely and instead enables better localization of non-heavily occluded objects as shown in Fig. 4. So, high-confidence 2D boxes can provide an additional strong supervision for the 3D student. However, in our previous pipeline, 2D teacher boxes can only supervise 3D indirectly through 3D teacher boxes that are potentially worse than 2D in terms of classification and localization. We propose to directly match 2D pseudo-labels and 3D student boxes and

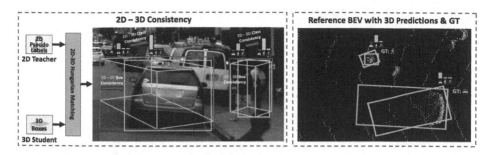

Fig. 6. The box and class consistency between the 2D teacher and the 3D student.

enforce box and class consistency between them as shown in Fig. 6. Applying Hungarian Matching and thresholding as in Eq. 7:

$$\left\{ \left((\hat{\mathbf{b}}_\mathbf{T}, \hat{\mathbf{c}}_\mathbf{T})^{2D}, (\hat{\mathbf{b}}_\mathbf{S}, \hat{\mathbf{c}}_\mathbf{S})^{3D} \right)^{(j)} \right\}^{(<\tau_{hung})} = Hungarian_{2D\text{-}3D}^{\tau_{hung}}(\hat{\mathbf{y}}_\mathbf{T}^{2D}, \hat{\mathbf{y}}_\mathbf{S}^{3D}) \quad (11)$$

Then, the 2D-3D consistency loss between matched 2D and 3D pairs is:

$$\mathcal{L}_{consistency} = \lambda_{L1}\mathcal{L}_{L1} + \lambda_{iou}\mathcal{L}_{iou} + \lambda_{focal}\mathcal{L}_{focal} \quad (12)$$

Losses $\mathcal{L}_{L1}$ and $\mathcal{L}_{iou}$ are identical to the box consistency costs in Eq. 8. $\mathcal{L}_{focal}$ is FocalLoss with 3D student probabilities supervised by the 2D teacher box class. This final 2D-3D consistency loss fully utilizes the strengths of RGB.

4   Experiments

4.1   Datasets and Evaluation Metrics

KITTI. We follow 3DIoUMatch and evaluate on the same 1% and 2% labeled frames sampled from 3712 training frames, and we also evaluate on 20% of driving *sequences*. We average over three splits for each % setting. We report for both 2D and 3D the moderate mAP for the Car, Pedestrian, and Cyclist classes.

Waymo Open Dataset. We also evaluate on the large-scale Waymo dataset, which has 158361 training frames. Each frame has 360°C LiDAR and 5 RGB cameras, with the cameras only capturing 240°C. This limitation, coupled with the complex and diverse urban setting, makes multi-modal training especially difficult on Waymo. We validate our framework on the 1% labeled data setting, sampling 1% of the 798 sequences, which results in around 1.4k frames. Due to the sheer scale of the Waymo dataset and the observation that even this 1% split has four times the cars and eight times the pedestrians as the full KITTI dataset, we validate on a single Waymo split. We report mAP and mAPH at both LEVEL 1 and LEVEL 2 difficulties for Car and Pedestrian.

Table 1. 3D detection performance comparison on KITTI. Training on the labeled samples to convergence, we observe slightly better labeled-only performance than 3DIouMatch. Improvement is increase from labeled-only results.

Method	1%				2%				20%			
	mAP	Car	Ped	Cyc	mAP	Car	Ped	Cyc	mAP	Car	Ped	Cyc
Labeled-Only (3DIoUMatch Reported)	43.5	73.5	28.7	28.4	54.3	76.6	40.8	45.5	–	–	–	–
3DIoUMatch	48.0	76.0	31.7	36.4	61.0	78.7	48.2	56.2	–	–	–	–
Improvement	+4.5	+2.5	+3.0	+8.0	+6.7	+2.1	+7.4	+10.7	–	–	–	–
Labeled-Only (Reproduced by Us)	45.9	73.8	30.4	33.4	55.8	76.1	44.9	46.4	61.3	77.9	47.1	58.9
Confidence Thresholding	54.4	75.9	42.7	44.6	63.3	76.5	50.0	63.4	68.1	77.8	58.0	68.6
Improvement	+8.5	+2.1	+12.3	+11.2	+7.5	+0.4	+5.1	+17.0	+6.8	−0.1	+10.9	+9.7
Ours	59.0	77.5	57.3	42.3	65.6	78.2	54.1	64.7	68.7	78.7	57.6	69.6
Improvement	+13.1	+3.7	+26.9	+8.9	+9.8	+2.1	+9.2	+18.3	+7.4	+0.8	+10.5	+10.7

Table 2. 2D detection performance comparison on KITTI. Note that although we train with projected 3D boxes, we evaluate with annotated 2D boxes.

Method	1%				2%				20%			
	mAP	Car	Ped	Cyc	mAP	Car	Ped	Cyc	mAP	Car	Ped	Cyc
Labeled-Only	65.3	86.6	68.6	40.8	68.9	87.4	70.7	48.3	63.9	87.5	64.5	39.8
Confidence Thresholding	60.4	86.1	69.2	25.8	65.5	87.6	71.5	37.2	66.2	88.8	70.0	39.7
Improvement	−4.9	−0.5	+0.6	−15.0	−3.4	+0.2	+0.8	−11.1	+2.3	+1.3	+5.5	−0.1
Soft-Teacher [71]	67.3	88.3	68.9	44.7	70.5	88.7	70.8	52.1	67.2	89.0	69.2	43.4
Improvement	+2.0	+1.7	+0.3	+3.9	+1.6	+1.3	+0.1	+3.8	+3.3	+1.5	+4.7	+3.6
Ours	71.4	88.8	73.9	51.7	74.5	89.0	74.6	59.9	72.8	89.1	71.6	57.7
Improvement	+6.1	+2.2	+5.3	+10.9	+5.6	+1.6	+3.9	+11.6	+8.9	+1.6	+7.1	+17.9

4.2   Implementation Details

We use PV-RCNN [48] for 3D detection and Faster-RCNN [45] with FPN [29] and ResNet50 [14] for 2D detection. To reduce labeling costs specifically for autonomous driving, we follow multi-modality methods [40,52,62] and pre-train the 2D detector on COCO [31]. This is a reasonable setting because labeling costs associated with annotating autonomous driving frames in 3D for specific applications do not preclude the existence of publicly available 2D detection datasets in another domain. Further, we find in Table 7 that DetMatch still dramatically improves over SSL baselines even without COCO pre-training.

We set $\tau_{3D} = 0.3$, $\tau_{2D} = 0.7$, and $\tau_{hung} = -1.5$, and use the same τ_{hung} threshold for both applications of Hungarian Matching. For KITTI, we train for 5k iterations with a batch size of 24; for Waymo, we train for 12k iterations with a batch size of 12. Additional details can be found in the supplementary.

4.3   Results on KITTI

We evaluate our model on 2D and 3D object detection on KITTI, comparing with 3DIoUMatch and our SSL baseline, which is equivalent to Unbiased Teacher [33] in 2D. The results are shown in Tables 1 and 2. First, we find that with a well-tuned 3D confidence threshold, our 3D-only confidence threshold-

Table 3. Performance comparison on the validation set of the Waymo Dataset.

1% Data	3D								2D			
	Car L1		Car L2		Ped L1		Ped L2		Car		Ped	
	mAP	mAPH	mAP	mAPH	mAP	mAPH	mAP	mAPH	L1	L2	L1	L2
Labeled-Only	47.3	45.6	43.6	42.0	28.9	15.6	26.2	14.1	42.3	39.5	50.8	47.0
Confidence Thresholding	52.6	51.6	48.4	47.5	35.2	16.7	32.0	15.2	44.4	41.3	48.7	45.1
Improvement	**+5.3**	**+6.0**	**+4.8**	**+5.5**	+6.3	+1.1	+5.8	+1.1	+2.1	+1.8	−2.1	−1.9
Ours	52.2	51.1	48.1	47.2	39.5	18.9	35.8	17.1	47.8	44.4	50.6	46.8
Improvement	+4.9	+5.5	+4.5	+5.2	**+10.6**	**+3.3**	**+9.6**	**+3.0**	**+5.5**	**+4.9**	−0.2	−0.2

ing baseline is able to outperform 3DIoUMatch in both mAP absolute performance and improvement. However, we note that for the Car class, 3DIoUMatch outperforms the 3D SSL baseline which struggles to improve performance over labeled-only training in 2% and 20% settings. This is because Car is the most common class and is already well-trained just from the labeled data, making further improvements difficult. Our proposed DetMatch, leveraging both 2D and 3D detections, consistently outperforms all methods. Notably, we find that in the 1% setting, we observe a remarkable **26.9%** boost in AP, far outperforming 3DIoUMatch, which achieves a 3% improvement, and our 3D SSL baseline, which achieves a 12.3% improvement. This gap can be attributed to the ambiguity of pedestrians in 3D and the relative clarity of this class when viewed in the RGB image.

For 2D detection, we see that the Unbiased Teacher baseline suffers from a drop in performance through SSL training for 1% and 2% settings despite our hyperparameter search. Soft-Teacher [71] is able to improve performance, but only by a small margin. We attribute this to two factors. First, SSL on autonomous driving datasets is a more difficult setting than SSL on COCO because driving datasets like KITTI have less image diversity, making it more susceptible to over-fitting. Indeed, as the amount of labeled data increases for KITTI, 2D SSL improves. We note that even the limited 1% setting on COCO has 1171 images, each in a completely different scene. On the other hand, KITTI 1% only has 37 images, and even the larger 20% setting, due to its constraint of sampling driving sequences, has comparatively lower scene diversity. These factors, coupled with pre-training on COCO which strengthens the original model, make improving on the labeled-only baseline difficult. Second, single-modality training is far more susceptible to self-training error propagation. Although the asymmetric augmentation and EMA work to decouple the student from the teacher, their predictions are still highly correlated, causing the student to over-fit to its own predictions, including its own errors. Our results show that the proposed DetMatch is more robust to these factors, demonstrating substantial performance gains over the labeled-only and 2D SSL baselines. Notably, we find that detection of Cyclists, a rare category, declines by 15% mAP under Unbiased Teacher in KITTI 1% but improves by 10.9% mAP with DetMatch, a gap of 25.9% mAP.

Table 4. 3D effect of τ_{hung}.

3D Eval	mAP	Car	Ped	Cyc
Labeled-Only	45.9	73.8	30.4	33.4
$\tau_{hung} = -1$	54.2	76.1	49.3	37.2
$\tau_{hung} = -1.5$	**57.9**	76.7	**55.0**	**42.0**
$\tau_{hung} = -2$	52.4	**76.9**	43.7	36.7

Table 5. 2D effect of τ_{hung}.

2D Eval	mAP	Car	Ped	Cyc
Labeled-Only	65.3	86.6	68.6	40.8
$\tau_{hung} = -1$	69.3	87.9	70.4	49.5
$\tau_{hung} = -1.5$	**70.2**	88.7	**72.1**	**49.9**
$\tau_{hung} = -2$	56.5	**89.5**	52.3	27.7

Table 6. Ablation of DetMatch Modules.

1% Data	3D				2D			
	mAP	Car	Ped	Cyc	mAP	Car	Ped	Cyc
Labeled-Only	45.9	73.8	30.4	33.4	65.3	86.6	68.6	40.8
+Confidence Thresholding	54.4	75.9	42.7	44.6	60.4	86.1	69.2	25.8
+ 2D-3D Teacher Matching	57.9	76.7	55.0	42.0	70.2	88.7	72.1	49.9
+ 2D Teacher & 3D Student Box Consistency	59.4	77.4	56.5	44.4	69.8	88.5	71.9	49.0
+ 2D Teacher & 3D Student Class Consistency	59.0	77.5	57.3	42.3	71.4	88.8	73.9	51.7
+ 2D Teacher & 3D Student MSE instead of Focal	58.2	77.6	57.7	39.3	68.1	88.6	72.0	50.8

4.4 Results on Waymo Open Dataset

To test the robustness of our framework, we additionally benchmark DetMatch on the difficult Waymo dataset. Because Waymo's 2D cameras have a combined FOV of 240 °C, we use the 3D SSL pseudo-labels for the remaining 120°C when training DetMatch. We keep hyperparameters of DetMatch, which were tuned on KITTI, the same for Waymo and find that they are generally applicable. Our 3D and 2D results are summarized in Table 3. We find that the confidence thresholding baseline is strong, consistently demonstrating improvements of 5% or 6% on the mAP metric for 3D. For 2D, we see a smaller improvement and even observe the performance on pedestrian drop by two points. We attribute this to the same factors that caused a drop in KITTI - although Waymo dataset is larger, its 1% labeled data diversity less than that of COCO.

DetMatch slightly drops in performance for Cars in 3D compared to the SSL baseline. However, it improves on the SSL baseline by a substantial 4.3 mAP for Pedestrian L1. Further, DetMatch achieves a large boost of 3.4 mAP for Car L1 in 2D over single-modality SSL, and although it does not boost performance for 2D Pedestrian, DetMatch stymies the decline from Unbiased Teacher.

Overall, compared to the labeled-only and SSL baselines, our method significantly boosts performance for Pedestrian on 3D and Car on 2D while largely maintaining other settings' performance. We attribute the large Pedestrian 3D improvement to DetMatch's effective use of RGB images' advantage in identifying and localizing this class. On the other hand, the Car 2D boost stems from the 2D detector benefiting from 3D's stronger detection of Cars, which are often highly occluded in the urban streets captured in Waymo. Thus, although our DetMatch does not uniformly boost all classes, perhaps due to Faster-RCNN with ResNet50 being an older and weaker model in 2D compared to PV-RCNN in 3D, the remarkable boost regardless in Pedestrian 3D detection and Car 2D

Table 7. Impact of COCO Pre-training.

1% Data		3D				2D			
		mAP	Car	Ped	Cyc	mAP	Car	Ped	Cyc
w/ COCO Pre-training	Labeled-Only	45.9	73.8	30.4	33.4	65.3	86.6	68.6	40.8
	Ours	59.0	77.5	57.3	42.3	71.4	88.8	73.9	51.7
w/o COCO Pre-training	Labeled-Only	45.9	73.8	30.4	33.4	46.2	77.6	47.1	13.9
	Ours	57.1	77.7	55.3	38.3	59.1	85.9	59.0	30.7

detection demonstrate that our pipeline is effective in exploiting the unique advantages of each sensor to improve detections of the other modality.

4.5   Ablation Studies and Discussion

Here, we focus on quantitative results; visualizations are in the supplementary.

Threshold for DetMatch. Results for KITTI 1% at various τ_{hung} on Det-Match with just the 2D-3D Teacher Matching pseudo-labeling module are shown in Tables 4 and 5. Ablations on single-modality thresholds τ_{3D} and τ_{2D} are in the supplementary. We find that Car prefers a more stringent (lower) cost threshold. Further, we observe that 2D and 3D mAP both peak at the *same* $\tau_{hung} = -1.5$, which shows that improvements in one modality strongly benefit the other.

Ablation of Multi-Modal Components. Next, we study the effect of each module of DetMatch in Table 6. Components not part of our final model are in gray. We focus on the Car and Pedestrian classes for this fine-grained comparison as Cyclist results vary by up to 3 AP even on 100% labeled data runs. Replacing the single-modality thresholding with our 2D-3D teacher matched pseudo-labels results in a large improvement. This shows us that pseudo-labeling with objects consistently detected in both modalities better supervises the student.

Enforcing box consistency between the 2D teacher and 3D student improves substantially improves the 3D performance with a small 0.2 point drop in Car and Pedestrian 2D performance. We attribute this boost to the 3D student now generating boxes that better fit objects in the dense 2D image. FocalLoss class consistency boosts 3D and 2D Pedestrian performance by 0.8 and 2 points, respectively. This is in-line with our observations that Pedestrian is difficult to detect in 3D - by rectifying class prediction of under-confident or incorrect 3D detections using 2D, the 3D model improves. Further, the 2D performance improves because 2D pseudo-labels are tied with 3D teacher predictions. By training the 3D model to generate more accurate 3D Pedestrian detections, the 2D model is better supervised as well. This improvement demonstrates the mutually beneficial relationship between improvements in the 2D and 3D models.

We try replacing FocalLoss in class consistency with MSE following Mean Teacher [60]. That this decreases performance gives us more insight into the purpose of class consistency. MSE encourages logit matching [21,60], which is closely related to knowledge distillation [15], where, by imitating class similarities predicted by a teacher, the student learns the underlying function of the teacher. In our setting, the teacher and student are of different modalities and consume data of very different representations, inhibiting such mimicking. As such, what our consistency module does is directly interpretable - it rectifies 3D student box and class predictions using the 2D teacher outputs.

Without COCO Pre-training. We also evaluate our pipeline without COCO pre-training, as shown in Table 7. We find that although COCO pre-training is important for 2D performance, we still achieve strong 3D performance without it, notably maintaining a substantial 24.9% AP improvement for Pedestrian. This shows that DetMatch does not need COCO, instead benefiting more from the multi-modal interaction. Further, improvements from using COCO shows that our framework is a unique and effective way of transferring benefits from 2D labels, which are easier to annotate than 3D labels, to the 3D detection task.

5   Conclusion

In this work, we proposed DetMatch, a flexible multi-modal SSL framework for object detection that obtains state-of-the-art performance on various limited labeled data settings on KITTI and Waymo. We demonstrate that pseudo-labels generated by matching 2D and 3D detections allow each modality to benefit from the other's advantages and improvements. Further, by enforcing consistency between 3D student and 2D teacher boxes, we leverage the unique advantages that the dense RGB image gives the 2D detector in detecting ambiguous objects. As our pipeline achieves improved performance on 3D detection by using a COCO pre-trained 2D detector, our method also shows potential in leveraging cheaper or publicly available 2D annotations to lower 3D data requirements.

Acknowledgements. Co-authors from UC Berkeley were sponsored by Berkeley Deep Drive (BDD).

References

1. Bachman, P., Alsharif, O., Precup, D.: Learning with pseudo-ensembles. Adv. Neural Inf. Proc. Syst. **27** (2014)
2. Berthelot, D., et al.: Remixmatch: semi-supervised learning with distribution matching and augmentation anchoring. In: ICLR (2020)
3. Berthelot, D., Carlini, N., Goodfellow, I., Papernot, N., Oliver, A., Raffel, C.A.: Mixmatch: a holistic approach to semi-supervised learning. Adv. Neural Inf. Proc. Syst. **32** (2019)
4. Bochkovskiy, A., Wang, C.Y., Liao, H.Y.M.: Yolov4: optimal speed and accuracy of object detection. ArXiv arXiv:2004.10934 (2020)
5. Cai, Z., Vasconcelos, N.: Cascade R-CNN: delving into high quality object detection. 2018 IEEE/CVF Conference on Computer Vision and Pattern Recognition, pp. 6154–6162 (2018)
6. Caine, B., et al.: Pseudo-labeling for scalable 3D object detection. ArXiv arXiv:2103.02093 (2021)

7. Carion, N., Massa, F., Synnaeve, G., Usunier, N., Kirillov, A., Zagoruyko, S.: End-to-end object detection with transformers. In: Vedaldi, A., Bischof, H., Brox, T., Frahm, J.-M. (eds.) ECCV 2020. LNCS, vol. 12346, pp. 213–229. Springer, Cham (2020). https://doi.org/10.1007/978-3-030-58452-8_13

8. Chong, Z., et al.: Monodistill: learning spatial features for monocular 3D object detection. ArXiv arXiv:2201.10830 (2022)

9. Choy, C., Gwak, J., Savarese, S.: 4D spatio-temporal convnets: minkowski convolutional neural networks. In: 2019 IEEE/CVF Conference on Computer Vision and Pattern Recognition (CVPR), pp. 3070–3079 (2019)

10. Dai, A., Chang, A.X., Savva, M., Halber, M., Funkhouser, T., Nießner, M.: Scannet: richly-annotated 3D reconstructions of indoor scenes. In: 2017 IEEE Conference on Computer Vision and Pattern Recognition (CVPR), pp. 2432–2443 (2017)

11. Feng, D., Zhou, Y., Xu, C., Tomizuka, M., Zhan, W.: A simple and efficient multi-task network for 3D object detection and road understanding. In: 2021 IEEE/RSJ International Conference on Intelligent Robots and Systems (IROS), pp. 7067–7074. IEEE (2021)

12. Geiger, A., Lenz, P., Urtasun, R.: Are we ready for autonomous driving? the kitti vision benchmark suite. In: 2012 IEEE Conference on Computer Vision and Pattern Recognition, pp. 3354–3361 (2012)

13. Graham, B., Engelcke, M., Maaten, L.V.D.: 3D semantic segmentation with sub-manifold sparse convolutional networks. In: 2018 IEEE/CVF Conference on Computer Vision and Pattern Recognition, pp. 9224–9232 (2018)

14. He, K., Zhang, X., Ren, S., Sun, J.: Deep residual learning for image recognition. In: 2016 IEEE Conference on Computer Vision and Pattern Recognition (CVPR), pp. 770–778 (2016)

15. Hinton, G., Vinyals, O., Dean, J., et al.: Distilling the knowledge in a neural network. arXiv preprint arXiv:1503.02531 2(7) (2015)

16. Huang, T., Liu, Z., Chen, X., Bai, X.: EPNet: enhancing point features with image semantics for 3D object detection. In: Vedaldi, A., Bischof, H., Brox, T., Frahm, J.-M. (eds.) ECCV 2020. LNCS, vol. 12360, pp. 35–52. Springer, Cham (2020). https://doi.org/10.1007/978-3-030-58555-6_3

17. Janoch, A., et al.: A category-level 3-D object dataset: Putting the Kinect to work. In: ICCV Workshops (2011)

18. Jaritz, M., Vu, T.H., de Charette, R., Wirbel, É., Pérez, P.: xMUDA: cross-modal unsupervised domain adaptation for 3D semantic segmentation. In: 2020 IEEE/CVF Conference on Computer Vision and Pattern Recognition (CVPR), pp. 12602–12611 (2020)

19. Jeong, J., Lee, S., Kim, J., Kwak, N.: Consistency-based semi-supervised learning for object detection. In: NeurIPS (2019)

20. Jiang, B., Luo, R., Mao, J., Xiao, T., Jiang, Y.: Acquisition of localization confidence for accurate object detection. In: Proceedings of the European conference on computer vision (ECCV), pp. 784–799 (2018)

21. Kim, T., Oh, J., Kim, N., Cho, S., Yun, S.Y.: Comparing Kullback-Leibler divergence and mean squared error loss in knowledge distillation. In: IJCAI (2021)

22. Kuhn, H.W.: The hungarian method for the assignment problem. Naval Res. Logist. Quart. **2**, 83–97 (1955)

23. Lahoud, J., Ghanem, B.: 2D-driven 3D object detection in RGB-D images. In: 2017 IEEE International Conference on Computer Vision (ICCV), pp. 4632–4640 (2017)

24. Laine, S., Aila, T.: Temporal ensembling for semi-supervised learning. In: ICLR (2017)

25. Lee, D.H., et al.: Pseudo-label: the simple and efficient semi-supervised learning method for deep neural networks. In: Workshop on Challenges in Representation Learning, ICML, vol. 3, p. 896 (2013)
26. Li, H., Wu, Z., Shrivastava, A., Davis, L.S.: Rethinking pseudo labels for semi-supervised object detection. In: Proceedings of the AAAI Conference on Artificial Intelligence, vol. 36, pp. 1314–1322 (2022)
27. Li, Y.J., Park, J., O'Toole, M., Kitani, K.: Modality-agnostic learning for radar-lidar fusion in vehicle detection. In: Proceedings of the IEEE/CVF Conference on Computer Vision and Pattern Recognition, pp. 918–927 (2022)
28. Liang, Z., Zhang, M., Zhang, Z., Zhao, X., Pu, S.: Rangercnn: towards fast and accurate 3D object detection with range image representation. ArXiv arXiv:2009.00206 (2020)
29. Lin, T.Y., Dollár, P., Girshick, R.B., He, K., Hariharan, B., Belongie, S.J.: Feature pyramid networks for object detection. In: 2017 IEEE Conference on Computer Vision and Pattern Recognition (CVPR), pp. 936–944 (2017)
30. Lin, T.Y., Goyal, P., Girshick, R.B., He, K., Dollár, P.: Focal loss for dense object detection. IEEE Trans. Pattern Anal. Mach. Intell. **42**, 318–327 (2020)
31. Lin, T.Y., et al.: Microsoft COCO: common objects in context. In: Fleet, D., Pajdla, T., Schiele, B., Tuytelaars, T. (eds.) ECCV 2014. Lecture Notes in Computer Science, vol. 8693, pp. 740–755. Springer, Cham (2014). https://doi.org/10.1007/978-3-319-10602-1_48
32. Liu, W., et al.: SSD: single shot multibox detector. In: Leibe, B., Matas, J., Sebe, N., Welling, M. (eds.) ECCV 2016. LNCS, vol. 9905, pp. 21–37. Springer, Cham (2016). https://doi.org/10.1007/978-3-319-46448-0_2
33. Liu, Y.C., et al.: Unbiased teacher for semi-supervised object detection. In: ICLR (2021)
34. Liu, Y.C., et al.: Learning from 2D: Pixel-to-point knowledge transfer for 3D pre-training. ArXiv arXiv:2104.04687 (2021)
35. Liu, Y., Yi, L., Zhang, S., Fan, Q., Funkhouser, T.A., Dong, H.: P4contrast: contrastive learning with pairs of point-pixel pairs for RGB-D scene understanding. ArXiv arXiv:2012.13089 (2020)
36. Liu, Z., Qi, X., Fu, C.W.: 3D-to-2D distillation for indoor scene parsing. In: 2021 IEEE/CVF Conference on Computer Vision and Pattern Recognition (CVPR), pp. 4462–4472 (2021)
37. Park, J.D., Weng, X., Man, Y., Kitani, K.: Multi-modality task cascade for 3D object detection. In: BMVC (2021)
38. Qi, C., Chen, X., Litany, O., Guibas, L.: Imvotenet: boosting 3D object detection in point clouds with image votes. In: 2020 IEEE/CVF Conference on Computer Vision and Pattern Recognition (CVPR), pp. 4403–4412 (2020)
39. Qi, C., Litany, O., He, K., Guibas, L.: Deep hough voting for 3D object detection in point clouds. In: 2019 IEEE/CVF International Conference on Computer Vision (ICCV), pp. 9276–9285 (2019)
40. Qi, C., Liu, W., Wu, C., Su, H., Guibas, L.: Frustum pointnets for 3D object detection from RGB-D data. In: 2018 IEEE/CVF Conference on Computer Vision and Pattern Recognition, pp. 918–927 (2018)
41. Qi, C., Yi, L., Su, H., Guibas, L.: Pointnet++: deep hierarchical feature learning on point sets in a metric space. In: NIPS (2017)
42. Qi, C., et al.: Offboard 3D object detection from point cloud sequences. In: 2021 IEEE/CVF Conference on Computer Vision and Pattern Recognition (CVPR), pp. 6130–6140 (2021)

43. Rasmus, A., Berglund, M., Honkala, M., Valpola, H., Raiko, T.: Semi-supervised learning with ladder networks. Adv. Neural Inf. Process. Syst. **28** (2015)

44. Redmon, J., Divvala, S.K., Girshick, R.B., Farhadi, A.: You only look once: unified, real-time object detection. In: 2016 IEEE Conference on Computer Vision and Pattern Recognition (CVPR), pp. 779–788 (2016)

45. Ren, S., He, K., Girshick, R.B., Sun, J.: Faster R-CNN: towards real-time object detection with region proposal networks. IEEE Trans. Pattern Anal. Mach. Intell. **39**, 1137–1149 (2015)

46. Rezatofighi, S.H., Tsoi, N., Gwak, J., Sadeghian, A., Reid, I.D., Savarese, S.: Generalized intersection over union: a metric and a loss for bounding box regression. In: 2019 IEEE/CVF Conference on Computer Vision and Pattern Recognition (CVPR), pp. 658–666 (2019)

47. Sajjadi, M., Javanmardi, M., Tasdizen, T.: Regularization with stochastic transformations and perturbations for deep semi-supervised learning. Adv. Neural Inf. Process. Syst. 29 (2016)

48. Shi, S., et al.: PV-RCNN: point-voxel feature set abstraction for 3d object detection. In: 2020 IEEE/CVF Conference on Computer Vision and Pattern Recognition (CVPR), pp. 10526–10535 (2020)

49. Shi, S., Wang, X., Li, H.: Pointrcnn: 3D object proposal generation and detection from point cloud. In: 2019 IEEE/CVF Conference on Computer Vision and Pattern Recognition (CVPR), pp. 770–779 (2019)

50. Shi, S., Wang, Z., Shi, J., Wang, X., Li, H.: From points to parts: 3D object detection from point cloud with part-aware and part-aggregation network. IEEE Trans. Pattern Anal. Mach. Intell. (2020)

51. Silberman, N., Hoiem, D., Kohli, P., Fergus, R.: Indoor segmentation and support inference from RGBD images. In: Fitzgibbon, A., Lazebnik, S., Perona, P., Sato, Y., Schmid, C. (eds.) ECCV 2012. LNCS, vol. 7576, pp. 746–760. Springer, Heidelberg (2012). https://doi.org/10.1007/978-3-642-33715-4_54

52. Sindagi, V., Zhou, Y., Tuzel, O.: Mvx-net: multimodal voxelnet for 3D object detection. In: 2019 International Conference on Robotics and Automation (ICRA), pp. 7276–7282 (2019)

53. Sohn, K., et al.: Fixmatch: simplifying semi-supervised learning with consistency and confidence. Adv. Neural. Inf. Process. Syst. **33**, 596–608 (2020)

54. Sohn, K., Zhang, Z., Li, C.L., Zhang, H., Lee, C.Y., Pfister, T.: A simple semi-supervised learning framework for object detection. ArXiv arXiv:2005.04757 (2020)

55. Song, G., Liu, Y., Wang, X.: Revisiting the sibling head in object detector. In: 2020 IEEE/CVF Conference on Computer Vision and Pattern Recognition (CVPR), pp. 11560–11569 (2020)

56. Song, S., Lichtenberg, S.P., Xiao, J.: Sun RGB-D: a RGB-D scene understanding benchmark suite. In: 2015 IEEE Conference on Computer Vision and Pattern Recognition (CVPR), pp. 567–576 (2015)

57. Sun, P., et al.: Scalability in perception for autonomous driving: waymo open dataset. In: 2020 IEEE/CVF Conference on Computer Vision and Pattern Recognition (CVPR), pp. 2443–2451 (2020)

58. Sun, P., et al.: Sparse R-CNN: end-to-end object detection with learnable proposals. In: 2021 IEEE/CVF Conference on Computer Vision and Pattern Recognition (CVPR), pp. 14449–14458 (2021)

59. Tang, Y., Chen, W., Luo, Y., Zhang, Y.: Humble teachers teach better students for semi-supervised object detection. In: 2021 IEEE/CVF Conference on Computer Vision and Pattern Recognition (CVPR), pp. 3131–3140 (2021)

60. Tarvainen, A., Valpola, H.: Mean teachers are better role models: Weight-averaged consistency targets improve semi-supervised deep learning results. Adv. Neural Inf. Process. Syst. **30** (2017)
61. Tian, Z., Shen, C., Chen, H., He, T.: FCOS: fully convolutional one-stage object detection. In: 2019 IEEE/CVF International Conference on Computer Vision (ICCV), pp. 9626–9635 (2019)
62. Vora, S., Lang, A.H., Helou, B., Beijbom, O.: Pointpainting: sequential fusion for 3d object detection. In: 2020 IEEE/CVF Conference on Computer Vision and Pattern Recognition (CVPR), pp. 4603–4611 (2020)
63. Wang, C.H., Chen, H.W., Fu, L.C.: Vpfnet: voxel-pixel fusion network for multi-class 3D object detection. ArXiv arXiv:2111.00966 (2021)
64. Wang, H., Cong, Y., Litany, O., Gao, Y., Guibas, L.J.: 3dioumatch: leveraging IOU prediction for semi-supervised 3D object detection. In: 2021 IEEE/CVF Conference on Computer Vision and Pattern Recognition (CVPR), pp. 14610–14619 (2021)
65. Wang, J., Gang, H., Ancha, S., Chen, Y.T., Held, D.: Semi-supervised 3D object detection via temporal graph neural networks. In: 2021 International Conference on 3D Vision (3DV), pp. 413–422 (2021)
66. Wang, Z., Jia, K.: Frustum convnet: sliding frustums to aggregate local point-wise features for amodal. In: 2019 IEEE/RSJ International Conference on Intelligent Robots and Systems (IROS), pp. 1742–1749 (2019)
67. Xiao, J., Owens, A., Torralba, A.: Sun3d: a database of big spaces reconstructed using sfm and object labels. In: 2013 IEEE International Conference on Computer Vision, pp. 1625–1632 (2013)
68. Xie, L., Xiang, C., Yu, Z., Xu, G., Yang, Z., Cai, D., He, X.: Pi-RCNN: an efficient multi-sensor 3D object detector with point-based attentive cont-conv fusion module. AAAI arXiv:1911.06084 (2020)
69. Xu, C., et al.: Image2point: 3D point-cloud understanding with pretrained 2D convnets. arXiv preprint arXiv:2106.04180 (2021)
70. Xu, C., et al.: You only group once: efficient point-cloud processing with token representation and relation inference module. In: 2021 IEEE/RSJ International Conference on Intelligent Robots and Systems (IROS), pp. 4589–4596. IEEE (2021)
71. Xu, M., et al.: End-to-end semi-supervised object detection with soft teacher. In: 2021 IEEE/CVF International Conference on Computer Vision (ICCV), pp. 3040–3049 (2021)
72. Yan, Y., Mao, Y., Li, B.: Second: sparsely embedded convolutional detection. Sensors (Basel, Switzerland) **18** (2018)
73. Yang, Q., Wei, X., Wang, B., Hua, X., Zhang, L.: Interactive self-training with mean teachers for semi-supervised object detection. In: 2021 IEEE/CVF Conference on Computer Vision and Pattern Recognition (CVPR), pp. 5937–5946 (2021)
74. Yang, Z., Sun, Y., Liu, S., Jia, J.: 3DSSD: point-based 3D single stage object detector. In: 2020 IEEE/CVF Conference on Computer Vision and Pattern Recognition (CVPR), pp. 11037–11045 (2020)
75. Yin, T., Zhou, X., Krähenbühl, P.: Multimodal virtual point 3D detection. In: NeurIPS (2021)
76. Yoo, J.H., Kim, Y., Kim, J., Choi, J.W.: 3D-CVF: generating joint camera and LiDAR features using cross-view spatial feature fusion for 3D object detection. In: Vedaldi, A., Bischof, H., Brox, T., Frahm, J.-M. (eds.) ECCV 2020. LNCS, vol. 12372, pp. 720–736. Springer, Cham (2020). https://doi.org/10.1007/978-3-030-58583-9_43

77. Zhang, B., et al.: Flexmatch: boosting semi-supervised learning with curriculum pseudo labeling. Adv. Neural. Inf. Process. Syst. **34**, 18408–18419 (2021)
78. Zhang, H., Cissé, M., Dauphin, Y., Lopez-Paz, D.: mixup: beyond empirical risk minimization. In: ICLR (2018)
79. Zhao, L., Zhou, H., Zhu, X., Song, X., Li, H., Tao, W.: LIF-SEG: lidar and camera image fusion for 3d lidar semantic segmentation. ArXiv arXiv:2108.07511 (2021)
80. Zhao, N., Chua, T.S., Lee, G.H.: SESS: self-ensembling semi-supervised 3D object detection. In: 2020 IEEE/CVF Conference on Computer Vision and Pattern Recognition (CVPR), pp. 11076–11084 (2020)
81. feng Zhou, Q., Yu, C., Wang, Z., Qian, Q., Li, H.: Instant-teaching: an end-to-end semi-supervised object detection framework. In: 2021 IEEE/CVF Conference on Computer Vision and Pattern Recognition (CVPR), pp. 4079–4088 (2021)
82. Zhou, Y., Tuzel, O.: Voxelnet: end-to-end learning for point cloud based 3D object detection. In: 2018 IEEE/CVF Conference on Computer Vision and Pattern Recognition, pp. 4490–4499 (2018)

ObjectBox: From Centers to Boxes for Anchor-Free Object Detection

Mohsen Zand$^{(\boxtimes)}$, Ali Etemad , and Michael Greenspan

Department of Electrical and Computer Engineering, Ingenuity Labs Research Institute, Queen's University, Kingston, ON, Canada
m.zand@queensu.ca

Abstract. We present ObjectBox, a novel single-stage anchor-free and highly generalizable object detection approach. As opposed to both existing anchor-based and anchor-free detectors, which are more biased toward specific object scales in their label assignments, we use only object center locations as positive samples and treat all objects equally in different feature levels regardless of the objects' sizes or shapes. Specifically, our label assignment strategy considers the object center locations as shape- and size-agnostic anchors in an anchor-free fashion, and allows learning to occur at all scales for every object. To support this, we define new regression targets as the distances from two corners of the center cell location to the four sides of the bounding box. Moreover, to handle scale-variant objects, we propose a tailored IoU loss to deal with boxes with different sizes. As a result, our proposed object detector does not need any dataset-dependent hyperparameters to be tuned across datasets. We evaluate our method on MS-COCO 2017 and PASCAL VOC 2012 datasets, and compare our results to state-of-the-art methods. We observe that ObjectBox performs favorably in comparison to prior works. Furthermore, we perform rigorous ablation experiments to evaluate different components of our method. Our code is available at: https://github.com/MohsenZand/ObjectBox.

Keywords: Object detection · Anchor-free · Object center · MS-COCO 2017 · PASCAL VOC 2012

1 Introduction

Current state-of-the-art object detection methods, regardless of whether they are a two-stage [2,7,8] or a one-stage method [24,29,38], hypothesize bounding boxes, extract features for each box, and label the object class. They both conduct bounding box localization and classification tasks on the shared local features. A common strategy is to use hand-crafted dense anchors on convolutional

---

Supplementary Information The online version contains supplementary material available at https://doi.org/10.1007/978-3-031-20080-9_23.

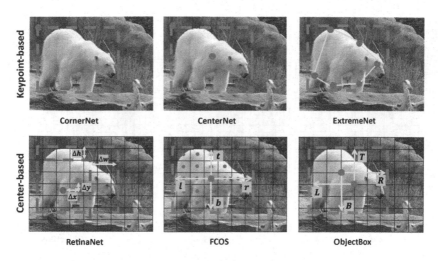

Fig. 1. The first row shows keypoint-based anchor-free methods which use different combinations of keypoints and then group them for bounding box prediction. A pair of corners, a triplet of keypoints, and extreme points on the object are respectively used in CornerNet [16], CenterNet [4], and ExtremeNet [41]. The second row shows center-based methods, which can be anchor-based (such as RetinaNet [18]) or anchor-free (such as FCOS [29]). As opposed to FCOS which employs all the locations inside the bounding box, ObjectBox only uses 2 corners of the central cell location for bounding box regression.

feature maps to generate rich candidates for shared local features [12,32]. These anchors generate a consistent distribution of bounding box sizes and aspect ratios, which are assigned based on the Intersection over Union (IoU) between objects and anchors.

Object detection has been dominated by anchor-based methods [18,24] due to their great success. They however suffer from a number of common and serious drawbacks. First, using predefined anchors introduces additional hyperparameters to specify their sizes and aspect ratios, which impairs generalization to other datasets. Second, anchors must densely cover the image to maximize the recall rate. A small number of anchors however overlap with most ground truth boxes, leading to a huge imbalance between positive and negative anchor boxes and adds extra computational cost, which slows down training and inference [3,16]. Third, anchor boxes must be designed carefully in terms of their number, scales, and aspect ratios, as varying these parameters impacts performance.

In response to these challenges, a number of anchor-free object detectors [11,16,22,29,35,40,41] have been recently developed, which can be categorized into keypoint-based [16,22,40,41] and center-based methods [11,29,35]. In keypoint-based methods, multiple object points, such as center and corner points, are located using a standard keypoint estimation network (e.g., HourglassNet [21]), and grouped to bound the spatial extent of objects. They however require a complicated combinatorial grouping algorithm after keypoint detection. In contrast, center-based methods are more similar to anchor-based approaches

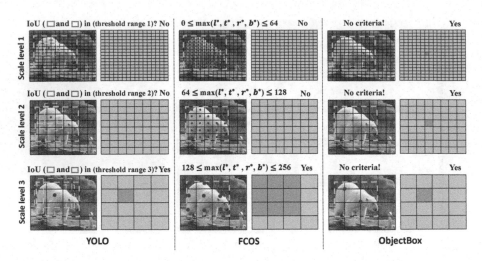

Fig. 2. ObjectBox treats the target boxes at all scales as positive (orange) samples, while target boxes at some scales are discarded as negatives (gray) in other methods (both anchor-based and anchor-free). For instance, YOLO utilizes the IoU scores to threshold out negative samples and FCOS uses range constraints to select positive samples. (Color figure online)

as they use the object region of interest or central locations to define positive samples. While anchor-based methods use anchor boxes as predefined reference boxes on these central locations, anchor-free methods instead directly regress the bounding boxes at these locations (see Fig. 1).

It is shown in [37] that the main difference between anchor-based and anchor-free methods in center-based approaches is the definition of positive and negative training samples, which leads to a performance gap. To distinguish between positive and negative samples, anchor-based methods use IoU to select positives in spatial and scale dimension simultaneously, whereas anchor-free methods use some spatial and scale constraints to first find candidate positives in the spatial dimension, then select final positives in the scale dimension. Nevertheless, both static strategies impose constraint thresholds to determine the boundaries between positive and negative samples, ignoring the fact that for objects with different sizes, shapes or occlusion conditions, the optimal boundaries may vary [6]. Many dynamic assignment mechanisms have been developed in response to this issue [6,13,37]. For instance, in [37], the division boundary is proposed to be set for each target based on some statistical criterions.

In this paper, we propose to relax all constraints imposed by static or dynamic assignment strategies and, thus, treat all objects in all scales equally. To learn the classification labels and regression offsets regardless of the object shape or size, we only regress from object central locations which are treated as shape- and size- agnostic anchors [40]. To support this, we define new regression targets as the distances from two corners of the grid cell that contains the object center, to the bounding box boundaries (L, R, B, and T in Fig. 1). As illustrated in

Fig. 2, we use no criteria compared to other methods in different scale levels. We therefore expand the positive samples without any bells and whistles. To learn these positive samples from all scales, we propose a new scale-invariant criteria as an IoU measure which penalizes the error between target and predicted object boxes with different sizes at different scale levels.

In summary, our contribution is the proposal of a novel anchor-free object detector, ObjectBox, which is better equipped to handle the label assignment issue, and performs favorably in comparison to the state-of-the-art. Moreover, our method is plug-and-play and can be easily applied across various datasets without the need for any hyperparameter tuning. Our method is therefore more robust and generalizable, and achieves state-of-the-art results. Lastly, we will make our code implementation publicly available upon publication of this paper.

2   Related Work

2.1   Anchor-Based Object Detectors

To localize objects at different scales with various aspect ratios, Faster R-CNN introduced *anchor boxes* as fixed sized bounding box proposals. The rationale behind anchor boxes is to use a set of predefined shapes (i.e. sizes and aspect ratios) as bounding box proposals, an idea which has become common in other object detection methods [1,18,20,24].

Early anchor-based methods include two stages for region proposal generation and object detection, which make them unsuitable for real-time applications. To achieve real-time performance, single-shot detectors [18,20,24,34] used anchors without relying on RPNs. They directly predicted bounding boxes and class probabilities from the entire image in a single evaluation. The most representative single-shot detectors are SSD [20], RetinaNet [18], and YOLO [1,24]. Several other techniques used different variations of anchor boxes. For example, a multiple anchor learning approach was proposed in [12] to construct anchor bags and select the most representative anchors from each bag.

2.2   Anchor-Free Object Detectors

A limitation of anchor-based methods is that they require predefined hyperparameters to specify the sizes and aspect ratios of the anchor boxes. Specifying these hyperparameters requires heuristic tuning and several empirical tricks, and is dependent on the dataset and therefore lacks generality. Anchor-free detectors have been recently proposed to overcome the drawbacks of anchor boxes. They can be categorized as *keypoint-based* and *center-based* approaches.

Keypoint-based methods detect specific object points, such as center and corner points, and group them for bounding box prediction. Although they show improved performance over anchor-based methods, the grouping procedure is time-consuming, and they usually result in a low recall rate. Some representative examples include CornerNet [16], ExtremeNet [41], CenterNet [4,40], and CentripetalNet [3].

Center-based methods use an object region of interest or central locations to determine positive samples, which makes them more comparable to anchor-based approaches. FCOS [29], for instance, considered all locations within the object bounding box to be candidate positives and found the final positives in each scale dimension. It computed the distances from these positive locations to the four sides of the bounding box. It however generated many low-quality predicted bounding boxes from locations far from the object center. To suppress these predictions, it used a *centerness* score to down-weight the scores of low-quality bounding boxes. Moreover, it utilized a 5-level FPN (Feature Pyramid Network) [17] to detect objects with different sizes at different levels of feature maps. FoveaBox [14] predicted both the locations where the object center is likely to exist, and the bounding box for each positive location. FSAF (Feature Selective Anchor-Free) [42] attached an anchor-free branch to each level of the feature pyramid in RetinaNet [18].

2.3   Label Assignment

It is shown in [37] that anchor-based and anchor-free methods achieve similar results if they use the same *label assignment* strategy. In label assignment, each feature map point is labeled positive or negative based on the object ground-truth and the assignment strategy. Some anchor-free methods such as FCOS [29] utilize static constraints to define positives, while a proper constraint may vary based on the objects' sizes and shapes.

Many other label assignment strategies have been recently proposed. ATSS [37] (Adaptive Training Sample Selection), for example, proposed a dynamic strategy based on statistical features of the objects. In [13], the anchor assignment is modeled as a probabilistic procedure by calculating anchor scores from a detector model and maximizing the likelihood of these scores for a probability distribution. OTA [6] (Optimal Transport Assignment) proposed to formulate label assignment as an optimal transport problem, which is a variant of linear programming in optimization theory. It characterized each ground-truth as a *supplier* of a particular number of labels, and defines each anchor as a *demander* that requires one unit label. If an anchor obtains a large enough number of positive labels from a given ground-truth, it is treated as one positive anchor for that ground-truth.

These strategies, however, do not maintain *equality between different objects*, and they tend to assign more positive samples for larger objects. This can be alleviated by assigning the same number of positive samples and allowing learning to occur at all scales for every object regardless of its size.

3   ObjectBox

Let a training image $X \in \mathbb{R}^{W \times H \times 3}$ contain n objects with ground-truth $\{b_i, c_i\}_{i=1}^n$, where b_i and c_i respectively denote the bounding box and the object class label for the ith object. Each bounding box $b = \{x, y, w, h\}$ is represented by its center

 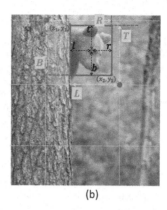

(a)   (b)

Fig. 3. ObjectBox computes the distances from two corners of the center cell to the bounding box boundaries. A large and small object are respectively shown in (a) and (b). In (b), the small object lies completely within a cell, which usually occurs in larger strides (e.g., $s_i = 32$). ObjectBox however does not discard these cases as it regresses to four sides of the bounding box for all objects with varying scales.

(x, y), width w and height h. Our goal is to locate these boxes in an image and assign their class labels.

3.1 Label Assignment Based on Object Central Locations

The bounding box b with center (x, y) in the input image can be defined using its corner points as $\{(x_1^{(i)}, y_1^{(i)}), (x_2^{(i)}, y_2^{(i)})\}$, where $(x_1^{(i)}, y_1^{(i)})$ and $(x_2^{(i)}, y_2^{(i)})$ denote the respective coordinates of the top-left and bottom-right corners at scale i. Our method predicts bounding boxes at 3 different scales to handle object scale variations. Hence, different sizes of objects can be detected on 3 feature maps corresponding to these scales. We specifically choose strides $s = \{8, 16, 32\}$ and map each bounding box center to certain locations on these embeddings.

We map the center (x, y) to the center location (i.e., the orange cell in Fig. 3(a)) in the embedding for scale i, and separately compute the distances from its top-left and bottom-right corners (red circles) each respectively from two boundaries of the bounding box. Specifically, as shown in Fig. 3, we compute the distances from the bottom-right corner to the left and top boundaries (L and T), and the distances from the top-left corner to the right and bottom boundaries (R and B) as follows:

$$
\begin{cases}
L^{(i)^*} = (\lfloor \frac{x}{s_i} \rfloor + 1) - (x_1^{(i)}/s_i) \\
T^{(i)^*} = (\lfloor \frac{y}{s_i} \rfloor + 1) - (y_1^{(i)}/s_i) \\
R^{(i)^*} = (x_2^{(i)}/s_i) - \lfloor \frac{x}{s_i} \rfloor \\
B^{(i)^*} = (y_2^{(i)}/s_i) - \lfloor \frac{y}{s_i} \rfloor
\end{cases}
\tag{1}
$$

where $(L^{(i)^*}, T^{(i)^*}, R^{(i)^*}, B^{(i)^*})$ represent the regression targets at scale i, and $(\lfloor \frac{x}{s_i} \rfloor, \lfloor \frac{y}{s_i} \rfloor)$ and $(\lfloor \frac{x}{s_i} \rfloor + 1, \lfloor \frac{y}{s_i} \rfloor + 1)$ denote the respective coordinates of the top-left and the bottom-right corners of the center location. It should be noted that $L^{(i)^*} + R^{(i)^*} = w^{(i)} + 1$ and $T^{(i)^*} + B^{(i)^*} = h^{(i)} + 1$, where $w^{(i)} = w/s_i$ and $h^i = h/s_i$ denote the width and height of the bounding box b at scale i, respectively. The predictions corresponding to these distances are as follows:

$$\begin{cases} L^{(i)} = (2 \times \sigma(p_0))^2 * 2^i \\ T^{(i)} = (2 \times \sigma(p_1))^2 * 2^i \\ R^{(i)} = (2 \times \sigma(p_2))^2 * 2^i \\ B^{(i)} = (2 \times \sigma(p_3))^2 * 2^i \end{cases} \qquad (2)$$

where σ stands for the logistic sigmoid function, and (p_0, p_1, p_2, p_3) denote the network predictions for distance values, which we enforce by sigmoid, to be in the range of 0 and 1. Multiplying by 2 allows detected values to cover a slightly larger range. With $()^2$, the output is stably initialized with around zero gradient. We differentiate between different scales by multiplying to a constant scale gain, i.e., $2^i, i = 1, 2, 4$. The overall network outputs include one prediction per location per scale, each of which comprises the above-mentioned distance values, as well as an objectness score and a class label for each bounding box.

Our formulation ensures that all the distances being regressed remain positive under different conditions. As illustrated in Fig. 3(b), the 4 distances can be computed as positive values even for a small object which is contained completely within a cell at a larger stride. More importantly, we treat all the objects as positive samples at different scales. This is in contrast to existing center-based approaches (i.e., both anchor-based and anchor-free methods). In the anchor-based methods, for instance, each center location in a certain scale is seen as the center of multiple anchor boxes, and if the IoUs of the target box and these anchor boxers are not within the threshold ranges, then it is considered as a negative sample. Similarly, anchor-free methods discard some target boxes as being negative samples based on different spatial and scale constraints. FCOS [29], for example, defines a set of maximum distance values that limit the range of object sizes that can be detected at each feature level. As another example, FoveaBox [14] controls the scale range for each pyramid level by an empirically-learned parameter, while in [42], a set of constant scale factors is used to define positive and negative boxes. As seen in Fig. 2, ObjectBox however treats all target boxes at all scales as positive samples. It therefore learns from all scales regardless of the object size to achieve more reliable regressions from multiple levels. As ObjectBox considers only central locations for each object, the number of positive samples per object is independent of object size.

As the geometric center of the box might lie near a boundary of the center cell, we augment the center with its neighboring cells. For example, the above location is used in addition to the center cell when the center of the bounding box is on the upper half of the cell.

Our method detects the objects from their central regions. If two boxes overlap, their centers are less likely to overlap given that it is quite rare for two box centers to be situated at the same location. In MS-COCO [19] and PASCAL VOC 2012 [5], we found no cases where centers of overlapping objects overlap.

Fig. 4. The areas in SDIoU loss for box regression.

Our augmented center locations, however, can be useful in dealing with these boxes. In our experiments (Sect. 4.2), we show that adding more points in addition to the central locations hurts the detection performance.

Our strategy implicitly harnesses the intuition behind anchor boxes, which are usually created by clustering the dimensions of the ground truth boxes in the dataset [23]. Their dimensions are obtained as estimates of the most common shapes in different sizes. For instance, Faster R-CNN [25] and YOLO [1,24] use three scales and three aspect ratios, yielding 9 anchors at each position. Our method however uses the central locations of the bounding boxes at each scale to generate multiple predictions for each object. Our method is also more effective than other anchor-free methods such as FCOS [29] which leverage additional levels of FPN (i.e., a total of 5 layers) to handle the overlapping bounding boxes.

3.2 Box Regression

As $\{L^{(i)}, T^{(i)}, R^{(i)}, B^{(i)}\}$ are distances, they can be treated independently and Mean Square Error (MSE) can be used to perform regression on these values individually. Nevertheless, such a strategy would disregard the integrity of the object bounding box. IoU (Intersection over Union or Jaccard index) loss has already been proposed to take the coverage of the predicted and ground-truth bounding box areas into consideration. IoU is a widely-used similarity metric between two shapes, which due to its appealing feature of being differentiable, can be directly used as an objective function for optimization [26,31,35,39]. In object detection, IoU can encode the width, height, and location of each bounding box into a normalized measure. The IoU loss ($\mathcal{L}_{IoU} = 1 - IoU$) thus allows a bounding box to be recognized as a single entity, and jointly regresses the four coordinate points of the bounding box.

IoU loss has been recently improved upon by considering different cases. For example, GIoU (Generalized IoU) loss [26] included the shape and orientation of the object in addition to the coverage area. It can find the smallest area that can simultaneously cover the predicted and ground-truth bounding boxes, and use it as the denominator to replace the original denominator used in IoU loss. DIoU (Distance IoU) loss [39] additionally emphasized the distance between the centers of the predicted and ground-truth boxes. CIoU (Complete IoU) loss [39] simultaneously included the overlapping area, the distance between center points, and the aspect ratio.

In our case, we are interested in minimizing the distance between two boxes which are each given by four distance values. As we learn from different scales for objects with different sizes (*i.e.*, we do not differentiate between scale levels), our bounding box regression loss function should be scale-invariant. Nevertheless, ℓ_n-based losses grow as the scales of the bounding boxes become larger [27]. As opposed to the original IoU loss and its variants, our loss does not require the bounding box locations to be matched, since the localization task is already embedded in the process. Moreover, the predicted and ground-truth boxes share at least one point in the worst case (i.e., overlap ≥ 0). This is because $\{L^{(i)}, T^{(i)}, R^{(i)}, B^{(i)}\} \geq 0$ for each box. In this work, we propose an IoU-based loss tailored for our object detection method, which can be used to improve other anchor-free detectors as well (the experiments are provided in the supplementary materials). Our proposed loss, called SDIoU which stands for scale-invariant distance-based IoU, is directly applied on the network outputs which are distance values from the object center to top-left and bottom-right corners. Other IoU-based losses, however, work on the object center and object width and height. As SDIoU is based on the Euclidean distances between corresponding offsets of the predicted and ground-truth boxes, it can keep the box integrity and score the overlapping area in all 4 directions.

Similar to CIoU [39] and scale balanced loss [27], we consider non-overlapping areas, overlapping or intersection area, and smallest box that covers both boxes. We first compute the non-overlapping area, S, by summing the squares of all the Euclidean distances between corresponding distance values as:

$$S = (L^* - L)^2 + (T^* - T)^2 + (R^* - R)^2 + (B^* - B)^2, \tag{3}$$

where $\{L, T, R, B\}$ and $\{L^*, T^*, R^*, B^*\}$ are the predicted and ground-truth distances, respectively. (We omit here the scale i, for better readability.) Intuitively, computing the squared Euclidean distances between different distance values can effectively consider the predicted and ground-truth distances at 4 directions.

We obtain the intersection area, I, by computing the square of the length of the intersection area's diagonal as:

$$I = (w^I)^2 + (h^I)^2, \tag{4}$$

where w^I and h^I are the width and height of the intersection area, respectively, and are computed as:

$$\begin{aligned} w^I &= min(L^*, L) + min(R^*, R) - 1 \\ h^I &= min(T^*, T) + min(B^*, B) - 1. \end{aligned} \tag{5}$$

The smallest area that covers both predicted and ground-truth boxes, C, is calculated by the square of its length as:

$$C = (w^C)^2 + (h^C)^2, \tag{6}$$

where w^C and h^C respectively denote C's width and height, which are computed as:

$$w^C = max(L^*, L) + max(R^*, R) - 1$$
$$h^C = max(T^*, T) + max(B^*, B) - 1. \tag{7}$$

By minimizing C, the predicted box can move towards the ground-truth box at 4 directions. We finally compute the SDIoU as:

$$SDIoU = \frac{(I - \rho S)}{C}, \tag{8}$$

where ρ denotes a positive trade-off value that favors the overlap area (we however set $\rho = 1$ in all the experiments). We use both I and $(-S)$ in the numerator to score the intersection area as well as penalizing the non-overlapping area. The predicted 4 distance values are thus enforced to faster match the ground-truth distances. The SDIoU loss is eventually defined as $\mathcal{L}_{IoU} = 1 - IoU$. Figure 4 illustrates the areas considered in our SDIoU loss.

4   Experiments

Datasets. Two common challenging datasets, MS-COCO [19] and PASCAL VOC 2012 [5], which are widely-used benchmarks for natural scene object detection, were selected to evaluate the proposed ObjectBox method and compare it against current state-of-the-art methods. MS-COCO is a challenging dataset that includes a large number of objects labeled in 80 object categories. We used the trainval35k split containing 115k images for training our network, and reported the results on the test-dev split with 20k images. The PASCAL VOC 2012 dataset consists of complex scene images of 20 diverse object classes. We trained our model using the VOC 2012 and VOC 2007 trainval splits (17k images) and tested it on the VOC 2012 test split (16k images). Experimental results on the PASCAL VOC 2012 [5] can be found in the supplementary materials (Sec. S.2).

Implementation Details. We implemented our method on two different backbones, *i.e.*, ResNet-101 and CSPDarknet [1, 10, 33]. We use ResNet-101 which is a widely-used backbone in many object detectors to provide a fair comparison with other state-of-the-art methods. We also utilized CSPDarknet and add SPP (Spatial Pyramid Pooling) [1, 9, 24] over the backbone to increase the receptive field of the extracted features. CSPDarknet has the potential to enhance the learning abilities of the CNNs and reduce the memory cost [1].

The training hyperparameters were set to an initial learning rate of 0.01, momentum of 0.937, weight decay of 0.0005, warm-up epochs of 3, and warm-up

Table 1. Performance comparison with the state-of-the-art methods on the MS-COCO dataset in single-model and single-scale results. The bold and underlined numbers respectively indicate the best and second best results in each column.

Method	Backbone	Avg. Precision, IoU			Avg. Precision, Area			Avg. Recall, # Dets			Avg. Recall, Area		
		AP	AP_{50}	AP_{75}	AP_S	AP_M	AP_L	AR_1	AR_{10}	AR_{100}	AR_S	AR_M	AR_L
SSD513 [20]	ResNet-101	31.2	50.4	33.3	10.2	34.5	49.8	28.3	42.1	44.4	17.6	49.2	65.8
DeNet [30]	ResNet-101	33.8	53.4	36.1	12.3	36.1	50.8	29.6	42.6	43.5	19.2	46.9	64.3
F-RCNN w/ FPN [17]	ResNet-101	36.2	59.1	39.0	18.2	39.0	48.2	-	-	-	-	-	-
YOLOv2 [23]	DarkNet-19	21.6	44.0	19.2	5.0	22.4	35.5	20.7	31.6	33.3	9.8	36.5	54.4
RetinaNet [18]	ResNet-101	39.1	59.1	42.3	21.8	42.7	50.2	-	-	-	-	-	-
YOLOv3 [24]	DarkNet-53	33.0	57.9	34.4	18.3	35.4	41.9	-	-	-	-	-	-
CornerNet [16]	Hourglass-104	40.6	56.4	43.2	19.1	42.8	54.3	35.3	54.7	59.4	37.4	62.4	**77.2**
CenterNet [4]	Hourglass-52	41.6	59.4	44.2	22.5	43.1	54.1	34.8	55.7	60.1	38.6	63.3	76.9
ExtremeNet [41]	Hourglass-104	40.2	55.5	43.2	20.4	43.2	53.1	-	-	-	-	-	-
FCOS [29]	ResNeXt-101	42.1	62.1	45.2	25.6	44.9	52.0	-	-	-	-	-	-
ASSD513 [34]	ResNet101	34.5	55.5	36.6	15.4	39.2	51.0	29.9	45.6	47.6	22.8	52.2	67.9
SaccadeNet [15]	DLA-34-DCN	40.4	57.6	43.5	20.4	43.8	52.8	-	-	-	-	-	-
YOLOv4 [1]	CSPDarknet	43.5	65.7	47.3	26.7	46.7	53.3	-	-	-	-	-	-
FoveaBox [14]	ResNeXt-101	43.9	63.5	47.7	26.8	46.9	55.6	-	-	-	-	-	-
RetinaNet+CBAF [28]	ResNet-101	43.0	63.2	46.3	25.9	45.6	51.4	-	-	-	-	-	-
ATSS [37]	ResNet-101	43.6	62.1	47.4	26.1	47.0	53.6	-	-	-	-	-	-
PAA [13]	ResNet-101	44.8	63.3	48.7	26.5	48.8	56.3	-	-	-	-	-	-
OTA [6]	ResNet-101	45.3	63.5	49.3	26.9	48.8	56.1	-	-	-	-	-	-
VarifocalNet [36]	ResNet-101	46.0	64.2	**50.0**	**27.5**	49.4	56.9	-	-	-	-	-	-
ObjectBox	ResNet-101	46.1	65.0	48.3	26.0	48.7	57.3	35.3	57.1	60.5	39.2	**65.0**	76.9
ObjectBox	CSPDarknet	**46.8**	**65.9**	49.5	26.8	**49.5**	**57.6**	**36.0**	**57.5**	**60.7**	**39.4**	65.2	77.0

momentum of 0.8. The initial learning rate was multiplied with a factor 0.1 at 400,000 steps, and then again at 450,000 steps. We set the batch size to 24 and used SGD optimization. We trained our models to a maximum of 300 epochs with early stopping patience of 30 epochs. The experiments were executed on a single Titan RTX GPU. The NMS (Non-Maximum Suppression) threshold was also set as 0.6 in all experiments.

We used CutMix and Mosaic data augmentation during training [1]. They both mix different contexts to facilitate detection of objects outside their normal context. CutMix mixes 2 input images, while Mosaic mixes 4 training images. For each scale level s, we use a multitask loss as:

$$\ell^s = \ell^s_{cls} + \ell^s_{obj} + \ell^s_{box} \tag{9}$$

where ℓ^s_{cls}, ℓ^s_{obj}, and ℓ^s_{box} respectively denote the classification loss, a binary cross entropy loss, and the regression loss for box offsets at scale s. We use the binary cross entropy between the target classes and the predicted probabilities as our classification loss and the binary confidence score. We employ SDIoU loss as the regression loss between the proposed targets and the predicted ones. The losses are computed for each scale and are summed as $\mathcal{L} = \sum_s \ell^s$.

4.1   MS-COCO Object Detection

Table 1 shows the evaluation results on the MS-COCO dataset. Compared to the baseline methods, ObjectBox is considerably more accurate, achieving the best AP performance of 46.8% with a CSPDarknet backbone. Our method also achieves the second-best performance of 46.1% with a ResNet-101 backbone. The relative improvement of AP (which is averaged over 10 IoU thresholds of 0.5 to 0.95) indicates that ObjectBox generates more accurate boxes with better localization. With the CSPDarknet backbone, the improvements are also achieved over 8 other metrics including AP_{50}, AP_M, AP_L, AR_1, AR_{10}, AR_{100}, AR_S, and AR_M. Notably, ObjectBox with ResNet-101 obtains the second-best performance over 7 different metrics. These improvements over both anchor-based and anchor-free methods are mainly due to our strategy to learn object features in different scales fairly. Nonetheless, this is not possible without regressing from the object central locations, which can be seen as shape- and size-agnostic anchors.

The relative improvement in AR_S indicates that our method can detect more small objects (which are more likely to overlap and generally harder to detect). The performance boost is also evident for AP_L when detection of larger objects can benefit from all feature maps at 3 scale levels. This is another major difference with other detectors which learn from all points in the objects. To maintain the relative equality between different objects, they consider the larger objects as positive samples only for embeddings with larger strides.

The second best performing method, VarifocalNet [36], replaces the classification score of the ground-truth class with a new IoU-aware classification score. It is built on an ATSS [37] version of FCOS [29]. In ATSS, the Adaptive Training Sample Selection (ATSS) mechanism is used to define positive and negative points on the feature pyramids during training. FoveaBox [14], which is also an anchor-free detector and concentrates on the object center, achieves $AP = 43.9$. It however separates samples as positives and negatives at each scale. Improvements over FCOS [29] (+4%) shows that central regions of the objects include enough recognizable visual patterns to detect the objects if we consider positive samples from all scales, and therefore, learning all the pixels inside the bounding box is not required for a general object detection method.

It is also interesting to note that ObjectBox does not use any data-dependent hyperparameters. Other anchor-free methods which tend to address the generalization issue often use a number of such hyperparameters. FCOS [29], for example, defines a hyperparameter for thresholding the object sizes at different scales, while FoveaBox [14] defines a hyperparameter to control the scale range.

4.2   Ablation Study

To verify the effectiveness of our method, we performed several experiments with different settings on the MS-COCO dataset. We utilized ObjectBox with a CSPDarknet backbone in all ablation experiments.

Box Regression Locations. Table 2 part A shows the impact of regression from different locations by choosing the boxes to be regressed from different

Table 2. The ablation study of ObjectBox with CSPDarknet on MS-COCO. We investigate the influence of box regression from different locations (A), number of predictions per location per scale (B), and imposing constraints based on the object size (C).

	Experiment	Method	Avg. Precision, IoU			Avg. Precision, Area		
			AP	AP_{50}	AP_{75}	AP_S	AP_M	AP_L
A	Regression locations	(1) center	33.1	56.8	36.0	17.5	35.2	42.1
		(2) aug. center (ObjectBox)	46.8	65.9	49.5	26.8	49.5	57.6
		(3) h-centers	42.3	56.9	46.5	24.1	45.3	54.2
		(4) aug. center + h-centers	41.7	58.2	45.2	23.6	43.3	54.5
		(5) 4 corners	28.2	51.5	35.6	16.0	33.9	41.3
		(6) 4 corners + center	37.4	57.8	43.0	20.4	39.7	45.5
B	#Pred	1 prediction (ObjectBox)	46.8	65.9	49.5	26.8	49.5	57.6
		4 predictions	37.3	58.3	41.9	19.5	41.6	48.0
C	Scale constraints	$m = \{0, 32, 64, \infty\}$	29.6	45.8	30.4	17.0	31.8	40.6
		$m = \{0, 64, 128, \infty\}$	35.8	58.0	36.8	19.2	39.1	46.5
		$m = \{0, 128, 256, \infty\}$	30.4	49.2	32.0	16.8	33.5	43.5
		$m = \{0, 256, 512, \infty\}$	27.3	43.5	29.6	14.7	30.4	38.1

locations. We defined 6 cases: (1) only one location at the center (referred to as 'center'), (2) center location augmented with its neighboring locations (as done in ObjectBox, denoted by 'aug. center'), (3) the centers of the connecting lines between the box center and two top-left and bottom-right box corner points (referred to as 'h-centers'), (4) central locations in (2) plus all locations in (3) (denoted by 'aug. center + h-centers'), (5) four corners of the bounding box, and (6) corner points in (5) plus the center location. The results show that using only the center cell is not sufficient for box regression. Another important point is that (3) outperforms (1), meaning that selection of two other points close to the center is better than only center point. Removing these two locations and considering only central locations in (2) even brings further improvements. Interestingly, in (4), no improvement is seen over (3). This indicates not only that considering locations other than the central locations does not add valuable information, but also that doing so can actually degrade detection performance. The worst case occurs when we use only the corner points of the bounding box. While the performance is improved by the addition of one center location to the points in (5), the results are still far from those in (2), (3), and (4), where box regression is obtained only from points that are closer to the center locations.

Number of Predicted Boxes. We analyzed the influence of the number of predictions per location, and reported the results in Table 2 part B. In this experiment, we assigned 4 predictions to each location based on the offset of the object center in that location. Specifically, each location was divided into four equal finer locations, with one prediction given to each of them. When we predict 4 boxes at each location, surprisingly the performance degrades, confirming that our strategy of returning just one prediction per scale level is indeed beneficial.

Specialized Feature Maps. To show the impact of imposing constraints on the feature maps at different scales, we chose four sets of thresholds: (1) $m = \{0, 32, 64, \infty\}$, (2) $m = \{0, 64, 128, \infty\}$, (3) $m = \{0, 128, 256, \infty\}$, and (4)

Table 3. The influence of different loss functions on ObjectBox.

Method	Avg. Precision, IoU			Avg. Precision, Area		
	AP	AP_{50}	AP_{75}	AP_S	AP_M	AP_L
MSE	22.6	44.1	19.4	12.5	18.3	35.7
Adopted GIoU	27.4	46.9	28.2	23.8	30.2	41.8
Adopted CIoU	27.1	46.5	28.1	24.0	30.5	41.0
SDIoU	46.8	65.9	49.5	26.8	49.5	57.6

$m = \{0, 256, 512, \infty\}$. An object at scale i is considered as a negative sample if $\{w, h\} < m_{i-1}$ or $\{w, h\} > m_i$ for $i \doteq 1, 2, 3$. The negative boxes thus are not regressed. This is similar to both anchor-based and anchor-free detectors. Specifically, anchor-free methods like YOLO [1,24] assign anchor boxes with different sizes to different feature levels, and anchor-free methods such as FCOS [29] directly limit the range of box regression for each level. The results in Table 2 part C show the high sensitivity of the performance to these thresholds. Moreover, this experiment verifies our choice of considering embeddings in all scale levels for all objects, as thresholding the feature maps drastically hurts the results.

Loss Functions. To show the effectiveness of our SDIoU loss for box regression, we replaced it with three other common losses in three different experiments. We first used MSE (Mean Square Error) loss on all 4 distances separately. In the second and third experiments, we converted the 4 distances to $\{x, y, w, h\}$ and used the GIoU [26] and CIoU losses [39]. As observed in Table 3, these losses are not suitable in anchor-free detectors like ObjectBox. More importantly, the benefit of our IoU loss is evident from these experiments.

We provide more experiments in the supplemental materials (Sec. S.4) to verify the effectiveness of SDIoU in other anchor-free approaches like FCOS [29].

5   Conclusion

ObjectBox, an anchor-free object detector, is presented without the need for any hyperparameter tuning. It uses object central locations and employs a new regression target for bounding box regression. Moreover, by relaxing the label assignment constraints, it treats all objects equally in all feature levels. A tailored IoU loss also minimizes the distance between the new regression targets and the predicted ones. It was demonstrated that using existing backbone architectures such as CSPDarknet and ResNet-101, ObjectBox compares favorably to other anchor-based and anchor-free methods.

Acknowledgments. Thanks to Geotab Inc., the City of Kingston, and the Natural Sciences and Engineering Research Council of Canada (NSERC) for their support of this work.

References

1. Bochkovskiy, A., Wang, C.Y., Liao, H.Y.M.: YOLOv4: optimal speed and accuracy of object detection. arXiv preprint arXiv:2004.10934 (2020)
2. Cai, Z., Vasconcelos, N.: Cascade R-CNN: delving into high quality object detection. In: Proceedings of the IEEE Conference on Computer Vision and Pattern Recognition, pp. 6154–6162 (2018)
3. Dong, Z., Li, G., Liao, Y., Wang, F., Ren, P., Qian, C.: CentripetalNet: pursuing high-quality keypoint pairs for object detection. In: Proceedings of the IEEE/CVF Conference on Computer Vision and Pattern Recognition, pp. 10519–10528 (2020)
4. Duan, K., Bai, S., Xie, L., Qi, H., Huang, Q., Tian, Q.: CenterNet: keypoint triplets for object detection. In: Proceedings of the IEEE International Conference on Computer Vision, pp. 6569–6578 (2019)
5. Everingham, M., Eslami, S.A., Van Gool, L., Williams, C.K., Winn, J., Zisserman, A.: The pascal visual object classes challenge: a retrospective. Int. J. Comput. Vis. **111**(1), 98–136 (2015)
6. Ge, Z., Liu, S., Li, Z., Yoshie, O., Sun, J.: OTA: optimal transport assignment for object detection. In: Proceedings of the IEEE/CVF Conference on Computer Vision and Pattern Recognition, pp. 303–312 (2021)
7. Girshick, R.: Fast R-CNN. In: Proceedings of the IEEE International Conference on Computer Vision, pp. 1440–1448 (2015)
8. He, K., Gkioxari, G., Dollár, P., Girshick, R.: Mask R-CNN. In: Proceedings of the IEEE International Conference on Computer Vision, pp. 2961–2969 (2017)
9. He, K., Zhang, X., Ren, S., Sun, J.: Spatial pyramid pooling in deep convolutional networks for visual recognition. IEEE Trans. Pattern Anal. Mach. Intell. **37**(9), 1904–1916 (2015)
10. Huang, G., Liu, Z., Van Der Maaten, L., Weinberger, K.Q.: Densely connected convolutional networks. In: Proceedings of the IEEE Conference on Computer Vision and Pattern Recognition, pp. 4700–4708 (2017)
11. Huang, L., Yang, Y., Deng, Y., Yu, Y.: DenseBox: unifying landmark localization with end to end object detection. arXiv preprint arXiv:1509.04874 (2015)
12. Ke, W., Zhang, T., Huang, Z., Ye, Q., Liu, J., Huang, D.: Multiple anchor learning for visual object detection. In: Proceedings of the IEEE/CVF Conference on Computer Vision and Pattern Recognition, pp. 10206–10215 (2020)
13. Kim, K., Lee, H.S.: Probabilistic anchor assignment with IoU prediction for object detection. In: Vedaldi, A., Bischof, H., Brox, T., Frahm, J.-M. (eds.) ECCV 2020. LNCS, vol. 12370, pp. 355–371. Springer, Cham (2020). https://doi.org/10.1007/978-3-030-58595-2_22
14. Kong, T., Sun, F., Liu, H., Jiang, Y., Li, L., Shi, J.: FoveaBox: beyound anchor-based object detection. IEEE Trans. Image Process. **29**, 7389–7398 (2020)
15. Lan, S., Ren, Z., Wu, Y., Davis, L.S., Hua, G.: SaccadeNet: a fast and accurate object detector. In: Proceedings of the IEEE/CVF Conference on Computer Vision and Pattern Recognition, pp. 10397–10406 (2020)
16. Law, H., Deng, J.: CornerNet: detecting objects as paired keypoints. In: Proceedings of the European Conference on Computer Vision (ECCV), pp. 734–750 (2018)
17. Lin, T.Y., Dollár, P., Girshick, R., He, K., Hariharan, B., Belongie, S.: Feature pyramid networks for object detection. In: Proceedings of the IEEE Conference on Computer Vision and Pattern Recognition, pp. 2117–2125 (2017)
18. Lin, T.Y., Goyal, P., Girshick, R., He, K., Dollár, P.: Focal loss for dense object detection. In: Proceedings of the IEEE International Conference on Computer Vision, pp. 2980–2988 (2017)

19. Lin, T.-Y., et al.: Microsoft COCO: common objects in context. In: Fleet, D., Pajdla, T., Schiele, B., Tuytelaars, T. (eds.) ECCV 2014. LNCS, vol. 8693, pp. 740–755. Springer, Cham (2014). https://doi.org/10.1007/978-3-319-10602-1_48
20. Liu, W., et al.: SSD: single shot multibox detector. In: Leibe,.B., Matas, J., Sebe, N., Welling, M. (eds.) ECCV 2016. LNCS, vol. 9905, pp. 21–37. Springer, Cham (2016). https://doi.org/10.1007/978-3-319-46448-0_2
21. Newell, A., Yang, K., Deng, J.: Stacked hourglass networks for human pose estimation. In: Leibe, B., Matas, J., Sebe, N., Welling, M. (eds.) ECCV 2016. LNCS, vol. 9912, pp. 483–499. Springer, Cham (2016). https://doi.org/10.1007/978-3-319-46484-8_29
22. Redmon, J., Divvala, S., Girshick, R., Farhadi, A.: You only look once: unified, real-time object detection. In: Proceedings of the IEEE Conference on Computer Vision and Pattern Recognition, pp. 779–788 (2016)
23. Redmon, J., Farhadi, A.: YOLO9000: better, faster, stronger. In: Proceedings of the IEEE Conference on Computer Vision and Pattern Recognition, pp. 7263–7271 (2017)
24. Redmon, J., Farhadi, A.: YOLOv3: an incremental improvement. arXiv preprint arXiv:1804.02767 (2018)
25. Ren, S., He, K., Girshick, R., Sun, J.: Faster R-CNN: towards real-time object detection with region proposal networks. In: Advances in Neural Information Processing Systems, pp. 91–99 (2015)
26. Rezatofighi, H., Tsoi, N., Gwak, J., Sadeghian, A., Reid, I., Savarese, S.: Generalized intersection over union: a metric and a loss for bounding box regression. In: Proceedings of the IEEE Conference on Computer Vision and Pattern Recognition, pp. 658–666 (2019)
27. Sun, D., et al.: A scale balanced loss for bounding box regression. IEEE Access **8**, 108438–108448 (2020)
28. Tang, Z., Yang, J., Pei, Z., Song, X.: Coordinate-based anchor-free module for object detection. Appl. Intell. **51**(12), 9066–9080 (2021). https://doi.org/10.1007/s10489-021-02373-8
29. Tian, Z., Shen, C., Chen, H., He, T.: FCOS: fully convolutional one-stage object detection. In: Proceedings of the IEEE International Conference on Computer Vision, pp. 9627–9636 (2019)
30. Tychsen-Smith, L., Petersson, L.: DeNet: scalable real-time object detection with directed sparse sampling. In: Proceedings of the IEEE International Conference on Computer Vision, pp. 428–436 (2017)
31. Tychsen-Smith, L., Petersson, L.: Improving object localization with fitness NMS and bounded IoU loss. In: Proceedings of the IEEE Conference on Computer Vision and Pattern Recognition, pp. 6877–6885 (2018)
32. Uzkent, B., Yeh, C., Ermon, S.: Efficient object detection in large images using deep reinforcement learning. In: The IEEE Winter Conference on Applications of Computer Vision, pp. 1824–1833 (2020)
33. Wang, C.Y., Mark Liao, H.Y., Wu, Y.H., Chen, P.Y., Hsieh, J.W., Yeh, I.H.: CSPNet: a new backbone that can enhance learning capability of CNN. In: Proceedings of the IEEE/CVF Conference on Computer Vision and Pattern Recognition Workshops, pp. 390–391 (2020)
34. Yi, J., Wu, P., Metaxas, D.N.: ASSD: attentive single shot multibox detector. Comput. Vis. Image Underst. **189**, 102827 (2019)
35. Yu, J., Jiang, Y., Wang, Z., Cao, Z., Huang, T.: UnitBox: an advanced object detection network. In: Proceedings of the 24th ACM International Conference on Multimedia, pp. 516–520 (2016)

36. Zhang, H., Wang, Y., Dayoub, F., Sunderhauf, N.: VarifocalNet: an IoU-aware dense object detector. In: Proceedings of the IEEE/CVF Conference on Computer Vision and Pattern Recognition, pp. 8514–8523 (2021)
37. Zhang, S., Chi, C., Yao, Y., Lei, Z., Li, S.Z.: Bridging the gap between anchor-based and anchor-free detection via adaptive training sample selection. In: Proceedings of the IEEE/CVF Conference on Computer Vision and Pattern Recognition, pp. 9759–9768 (2020)
38. Zhang, X., Wan, F., Liu, C., Ji, R., Ye, Q.: FreeAnchor: learning to match anchors for visual object detection. In: Advances in Neural Information Processing Systems, vol. 32 (2019)
39. Zheng, Z., Wang, P., Liu, W., Li, J., Ye, R., Ren, D.: Distance-IoU loss: faster and better learning for bounding box regression. In: AAAI, pp. 12993–13000 (2020)
40. Zhou, X., Wang, D., Krähenbühl, P.: Objects as points. arXiv preprint arXiv:1904.07850 (2019)
41. Zhou, X., Zhuo, J., Krahenbuhl, P.: Bottom-up object detection by grouping extreme and center points. In: Proceedings of the IEEE Conference on Computer Vision and Pattern Recognition, pp. 850–859 (2019)
42. Zhu, C., He, Y., Savvides, M.: Feature selective anchor-free module for single-shot object detection. In: Proceedings of the IEEE/CVF Conference on Computer Vision and Pattern Recognition, pp. 840–849 (2019)

Is Geometry Enough for Matching in Visual Localization?

Qunjie Zhou[1]([envelope])(iD), Sérgio Agostinho[2](iD), Aljoša Ošep[1](iD),
and Laura Leal-Taixé[1](iD)

[1] Technical University of Munich, Munich, Germany
{qunjie.zhou,aljosa.osep,leal.taixe}@tum.de
[2] Universidade de Lisboa, Lisbon, Portugal
sergio.agostinho@tecnico.ulisboa.pt
https://github.com/dvl-tum/gomatch

Abstract. In this paper, we propose to go beyond the well-established approach to vision-based localization that relies on visual descriptor matching between a query image and a 3D point cloud. While matching keypoints via visual descriptors makes localization highly accurate, it has significant storage demands, raises privacy concerns and requires update to the descriptors in the long-term. To elegantly address those practical challenges for large-scale localization, we present GoMatch, an alternative to *visual-based matching* that solely relies on geometric information for matching image keypoints to maps, represented as sets of bearing vectors. Our novel bearing vectors representation of 3D points, significantly relieves the cross-modal challenge in *geometric-based matching* that prevented prior work to tackle localization in a realistic environment. With additional careful architecture design, GoMatch improves over prior geometric-based matching work with a reduction of $(10.67\,\text{m}, 95.7°)$ and $(1.43\,\text{m}, 34.7°)$ in average median pose errors on Cambridge Landmarks and 7-Scenes, while requiring as little as $1.5/1.7\%$ of storage capacity in comparison to the best visual-based matching methods. This confirms its potential and feasibility for real-world localization and opens the door to future efforts in advancing city-scale visual localization methods that do not require storing visual descriptors.

1 Introduction

In this paper we tackle scalable, data-driven visual localization. The ability to localize a query image within a 3D map based representation of the environment is vital in many applications, ranging from robotics to virtual and augmented reality. In past years, researchers have made a significant progress in

---

Q. Zhou and S. Agostinho—Equal contribution.

Supplementary Information The online version contains supplementary material available at https://doi.org/10.1007/978-3-031-20080-9_24.

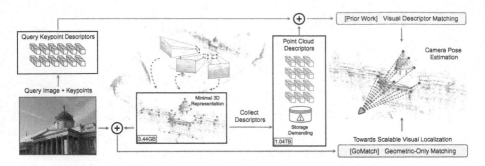

Fig. 1. In this work, we propose GoMatch to tackle visual localization w.r.t. a scene represented as a 3D point cloud. By relying only on geometric information for matching, GoMatch allows structure-based methods to achieve localization solely through the use of keypoints, sidestepping the need to store visual descriptors for matching. Keeping only the minimal representation of a 3D model, *i.e.*, its coordinates, leads to a more scalable pipeline towards large-scale localization that bypasses privacy concerns and is easy to maintain.

vision-based localisation [20,25,30,42,46,51,54,65,72,74]. The majority of methods [25,51,65,67,72] rely on a pre-built 3D representation of the environment, typically obtained using structure-from-motion (SfM) techniques [57,59]. Such 3D maps store 3D points and D-dimensional visual feature descriptors [55]. To determine the pose of a query image, *i.e.*, its 3D position and orientation, these methods match visual descriptors, obtained from the query image, with the ones stored in the point cloud. Once image-to-point-cloud matches are established, a Perspective-n-Point (PnP) solver [27,36] is used to estimate the camera pose. While working well in practice, this approach suffers from several drawbacks. First, we need to explicitly store per-point visual descriptors for point clouds, which hinders its applicability to large-scale environments due to the expensive storage requirement. Second, this limits the applicability to point clouds with specific descriptors, which increases the 3D map descriptor maintenance effort – maps need to be re-built or updated to be used in conjunction with newly developed descriptors [24]. Third, this approach in practice necessitates a visual descriptor exchange between the server (storing the 3D model and descriptors) and an online feature extractor. This is a point of privacy vulnerability, as human identities and personal information can be recovered from visual descriptors intercepted during the transmission [16,22,23,26,28,29,48,63]. The aforementioned issues lead to the main question we pose in this paper: *can we localize an image without relying on visual descriptors?* This would significantly reduce the map storage demands and get rid of descriptor maintenance. Recently, Campbell *et al.* [10,40] showed that it is feasible to directly match 2D image keypoints with a 3D point cloud using only geometrical cues. However, this is limited to ideal scenarios where outliers are not present. This assumption does not hold in real-world scenes and is not directly applicable to challenging visual localization. This is not surprising, as relying only on geometrical cues is a significantly more challenging compared to matching visual descriptors. In contrast to a single 2D/3D point coordinate, a visual descriptor provides a rich visual context, since it is commonly extracted from the local image patch centered around a keypoint [20,25,42,72] (Fig. 1).

In this paper, we achieve significant progress in making keypoints-to-point cloud direct matching ready for real-world visual localization. To cope with noisy images, point clouds, and inevitably keypoint outliers, we present **GoMatch**, a novel neural network architecture that relies on **G**eometrical information only. GoMatch leverages self- and cross- attention mechanisms to establish initial correspondences between image keypoints and point clouds, and further improves the matching robustness by filtering match outliers using a classifier. To the best of our knowledge, GoMatch is the first approach that is applicable to visual localization *in the wild* and does not rely on storage-demanding visual descriptors. In particular, compared to its prior work on geometric matching-based localization, GoMatch leads to a reduction of $(10.67\,\text{m}, 95.7°)$ and $(1.43\,\text{m}, 34.7°)$ in average median pose errors on Cambridge Landmarks dataset [35] and 7-Scenes dataset [61], confirming its potential in real-world visual localization.

We summarize our contributions as the following: (i) we develop a novel method to match query keypoints to a point cloud relying only on geometrical information; (ii) We bridge the difference in data modalities between a 2D image keypoint to a 3D point by representing it with its bearing vectors projected into co-visible reference views and show this is remarkably more robust compared to direct cross-modal matching; (iii) Our extensive evaluation shows that our method significantly outperforms prior work, effectively enabling real-world visual localization based on geometric-only matching; (iv) Finally, we thoroughly compare our method to the well-established visual localization baselines and discuss advantages and disadvantages of each approach. With this analysis, we hope to open the door for future progress towards more general and scalable structure-based methods for visual localization, which do not critically rely on storing visual descriptors, thereby reducing storage, relieving privacy concerns and eliminating the need for descriptor maintenance.

2   Related Work

Structure-Based Localization. Methods of this kind [5,50,53,58,66] commonly establish explicit correspondences between the query image pixels and the 3D points of the environment to compute the query image pose from the established matches using PnP solvers [27,36]. Keypoint correspondences are made by computing and matching visual descriptors for each keypoint from a query and database images [20,25,30,42,51,65,72]. Another recent work [52] iteratively optimizes a camera pose by minimizing visual descriptor distances between the 3D points observed in the query and the reference images. While it does not establish matches, it relies on visual descriptors extracted from a neural network and requires 3D points. Structure-based localization methods achieve impressive localization accuracy and state-of-the-art performance [20,50,51] in the long-term localization benchmark [54,67].

Table 1. On the challenges of large-scale structure-based localization. Analysis is performed on the MegaDepth [39] composed of many landmarks (similar to city districts), acting as an example of a city-scale dataset. We compare visual-based matching (VM) and geometric-based matching (GM) methods by analysing their storage requirement and considering whether a method requires to maintain map descriptors as well as provides privacy protection (*c.f.* the supplementary for more details.) For structured-based localization, scene coordinates (3D) and camera metadata (Cameras) are stored to obtain 2D-3D correspondences. In contrast to VM methods that need to additionally store visual descriptors or extract descriptors on-the-fly from the raw images, we show that using GM instead of VM, significantly reduces storage requirements, safeguards user privacy and bypasses the need for descriptor maintenance [24].

	Method	Desc. Maintenance	Privacy	Database Storage (GB, ↓)				Total
				Cameras (MB)	3D	Raw Ims	Descs	
VM	SIFT [41]	✗	✗	15.73	3.44	✗	130.10 (uint8)	133.33
	SuperPoint [20]	✗	✗	15.73	3.44	✗	1040.76 (fp32)	1044.21
	Extract on-the-fly	✗	✗	15.73	3.44	157.84	✗	161.29
Geometric-based Matching		✓	✓	15.73	3.44	✗	✗	**3.45**

Practical Challenges in Structure-Based Localization. Despite being highly accurate, modern localization solutions encounter practical challenges when deployed onto real-life applications, spanning city-level scale. The challenges are threefold: i) Relying on visual descriptors [20,25,42,72] makes the system demanding in storage[1] as shown in Table 1. To reduce storage requirement of the 3D scene representation, compression can be done by keeping a subset of the 3D points [13,14,43] and quantising [13,17,69] the descriptors associated with the 3D points. HybridSC [13] stands out among the existing work, with its extreme compression rate and minimal accuracy loss.   ii) Localization methods following a server-client model need to transmit visual descriptors between the server and client, which exposes the model to a risk of a privacy breach [16,22,23,48]. To mitigate this issue, recent work [26,47] developed descriptors that are more robust against privacy attacks with slightly lower accuracy. iii) With the ongoing advancements in local features methods [20,25,26,42,47,72], continuously updating scene descriptors is a foreseeable demand [24] for visual-based matching methods. However, such an update requires either re-building the map with new descriptors or transforming the existing descriptors [24] to new ones. In this paper, we propose an *orthogonal* direction to address the storage, privacy and descriptor maintenance challenges in structure-based localization by relying solely on more lightweight geometric information for matching.

End-to-End Learned Localization. A recent trend of methods leverage data-driven techniques to learn to localize in an end-to-end manner, without relying on point clouds. This is achieved by either regressing scene coordinates, regressing the camera's absolute pose or regressing its relative pose w.r.t. to a database image. Scene coordinate regression methods [3,5,6,8,15,38,73] directly regress

---

[1] *Storage* as in non-volatile preservation of data, in contrast to volatile *memory*.

dense 3D scene coordinates from 2D images. However, they need to be re-trained for every new scene due to their lack of generalization [5–7,15]. In certain cases, multiple instances of the same network are trained on sub-regions of the scene, due to the limited capacity of a single network [7]. Therefore, it is unclear how to scale these methods [3,5,6,8,15,38,73], that are traditionally evaluated only on small indoor rooms, to large-scale scenes. Absolute pose regression (APR) methods implicitly encode the scene representation inside the network and directly regress the pose from the query image [33–35,49,71]. While earlier methods required training a model per scene and have been shown to overfit to the viewpoints and appearance of the training images [56], recent work in multi-scene APR [4,60] loosened the per-scene training requirements. Compared to multi-scene APR, our method generalizes across scenes as other structure-based localization methods (*c.f.* Sect. 5.5) while addressing its aforementioned practical challenges. Another related approach that sidesteps maintaining a 3D model with visual descriptors, is to regress relative camera poses [2,21,37,75] from a query image to its relevant database images. However, directly regressing the geometric transformations in general leads to limited generalization [56,75].

Direct Geometric Keypoint Matching. Matching image keypoints directly to 3D point clouds while jointly estimating pose has been widely investigated under relatively constrained environments [9–12,19,40,45]. Some require pose initialization [19] or pose distribution priors [45], while others, based on globally optimal estimators, have prohibitive runtime requirements in order to produce accurate estimates [9,11,12]. In contrast, the recent state-of-the-art, data-driven, geometric matching approaches [10,40] strike a good compromise between pose accuracy and time required to produce an accurate estimate. Despite not producing globally optimal solutions, BPnPNet [10] is able to estimate a reliable pose in a fraction of a second. Given a set of 2D keypoints in the query image and a set of 3D points in the scene point cloud, BPnPNet jointly estimates matches between these two sets *purely* based on geometric information. However, this approach was shown to work in idealistic scenarios assuming no outlier keypoints and, as we experimentally demonstrate, the matching performance degrades significantly once outliers are introduced. The outlier-free assumption clearly does not hold for challenging real-world localization scenarios as map building and keypoint detection are all challenging tasks, prone to errors and noise. In our work, we build upon BPnPNet and design a geometric matching module that is robust against keypoint outliers. We show in Sect. 5.3 that our approach significantly outperforms BPnPNet in matching keypoints with noisy outliers, effectively enabling the applicability of geometric-based matching to real-world visual localization.

3   Task Definition

Structure-Based Localization Pipeline. Structure-based methods assume as input a query image, a 3D point cloud of the scene, and database images with known poses. These methods first retrieve a set of database images that

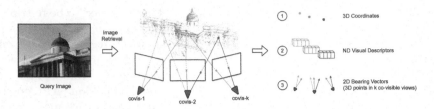

Fig. 2. Co-visible views & keypoint representations. Retrieving co-visible reference images (views) of a query image, narrows the matching against a full 3D point cloud to a subset of points that are more likely to be visible to the query image. Each 3D point can be represented differently by: 1) its 3D coordinate; 2) a visual descriptor that incorporates local appearance; or 3) a bearing vector that represents the direction from the reference camera origin to a 3D point in normalized coordinates. In this paper, we explore keypoint matching using representations 1) and 3).

are co-visible with the query image, *i.e.*, have a visual overlap, as illustrated in Fig. 2. Next, after narrowing down the search space, they establish 2D-3D correspondences between the query image keypoints and a (retrieved) subset of the 3D point cloud. This set of correspondences can be used to estimate the query image pose using a PnP solver [27,32]. The majority of prior work [20, 25,30,42,50,51,72] rely on storage-consuming visual descriptors, stored together with the point cloud, to establish 2D-3D matches. The key challenge we address is how to establish those correspondences *without* visual descriptors.

Problem Formulation. We assume two point sets, one with 2D keypoint coordinates in the image plane $p_i \in \mathbb{R}^2$, and the second containing 3D point coordinates $q_j \in \mathbb{R}^3$. We seek the matching set $\mathcal{M} := \{(i,j)|p_i = \pi(q_j; \mathtt{K}, \mathtt{R}, t)\}$, *i.e.*, the set of index pairs i and j, for which if the j-th 3D keypoint is projected to the image plane, it matches the coordinates specified by the corresponding i-th 2D point. The camera intrinsic matrix $\mathtt{K} \in \mathbb{R}^{3 \times 3}$ is assumed to be known, and the operator $\pi(\cdot)$ represents the camera projection function, which transforms 3D points onto the camera's frame of reference and projects them to the image plane according to the camera's intrinsics. Our goal is to find the correct 2D-3D keypoint matches for accurate pose estimation.

Keypoint Representation. We represent 2D pixels using 2D coordinates $(u, v) \in \mathbb{R}^2$ in the image plane. To learn a matching function that is agnostic to different camera models, we uplift those 2D points into a bearing vector representation $b \in \mathbb{R}^2$, effectively removing the effect of the camera intrinsics. Bearing vectors encode the direction (or bearing) of points in a camera's frame of reference. We compute bearing vectors from image pixels as: $[b^\top \ 1]^\top \propto \mathtt{K}^{-1}[u\,v\,1]^\top$. For a 3D point, we consider two different representations (see Fig. 2): (i) as 3D coordinates $(x, y, z) \in \mathbb{R}^3$ w.r.t. a 3D world reference/origin; and (ii) as a bearing vector w.r.t. a reference database image. The bearing vector representation allows bringing both 2D pixels and 3D points to the same data modality. Given a 3D point $p \in \mathbb{R}^3$ and transformation $(\mathtt{R}, t)$ from the world to the database image's frame of reference, we compute the corresponding bearing vector as:

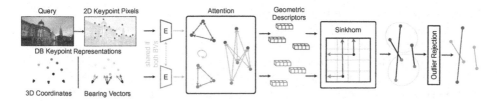

Fig. 3. GoMatch components overview. The query image and database keypoints first undergo a feature encoder **E** to generate per-point features. We share encoders in the query and database branch when database points are represented as bearing vectors otherwise not. These features are refined in the attention layer and then used in the Sinkhorn matching stage to establish an initial set of candidate matches, from which erroneous matches are filtered with an outlier rejection layer.

$$p' = \mathrm{R}p + t, \quad [b^\top\ 1]^\top = p'/p'_z, \tag{1}$$

where p' represents p in the camera's frame of reference, and p'_z represents its z coordinate. As shown in Table 1, these geometric-based point representations require significantly lower storage compared to visual descriptor based ones, *e.g.*, as low as 3% compared to the storage of modern descriptors.

4   Geometric-Only Matching

BPnPNet in a Nutshell. BPnPNet [10] made great progress towards establishing correspondence between the query keypoints and 3D point cloud in the absence of visual descriptors. It proposes an end-to-end trainable, differentiable matcher that performs 2D to 3D cross modal matching without relying on appearance information. While this is a step in the right direction, we show in Sect. 5.3 that it does not scale to the real-world visual localization scenarios where outliers, *i.e.* points without a match, are pervasive. Direct 2D-3D matching of sparse keypoints is a challenging problem due to low amount of discriminative data, *i.e.* points no longer have a local visual appearance, and its cross-modal nature. In a nutshell, BPnPNet (i) encodes points to obtain per point features, (ii) establishes matches using the Sinkhorn algorithm [18,62], which finds the optimal assignment between geometrical features, and finally, (iii) leverages a differentiable PnP solver that imposes an additional pose supervision on the network. In the following, we build on the observation that the lightweight geometric feature encoder does not possess the necessary representational power to produce features that generalize simultaneously to situations with and without outliers.

4.1   GoMatch: Embracing Outliers

In GoMatch we (i) propose architectural changes that enable resilience to outliers and (ii) cast the *cross-modal* nature of 2D-3D matching to an *intra-modal* setting through the use of bearing vectors. Below, we explain the details of these contributions, which are experimentally validated to be all necessary and critical to outlier-robust geometric matching in Sect. 5.3. We refer to Fig. 3 for a visual overview of the entire network. Furthermore, we add an outlier rejection layer to retain only quality matches from the Sinkhorn outputs. While we introduce the novel network components in the following paragraphs, we refer the reader to the supplementary material for an in-depth description of all network components.

Feature Refinement Through Attention. In BPnPNet, each keypoint node is processed in parallel with an MLP-style encoder to extract features directly for matching, and information exchange happens only in the Sinkhorn matching stage. This might lead to a learned feature representation which lacks context information within each 2D/3D modality and cross modality. Based on this assumption, we explore adding information exchange prior to matching. To enhance the context information within each modality, we apply *self-attention* to the raw encoded features where a graph neural network [31] refines features of every keypoint by exchanging the information with a fixed number of closest neighbors in coordinate space. This is followed by *cross-attention* [70], where every keypoint from one modality will interact with all keypoints from the other modality through a sequence of multi-head attention layers. By stacking several blocks of such self-/cross-attention layers, we are able to learn more representative features, which allows Sinkhorn to identify significantly better outlier matches.

Outlier Rejection. After Sinkhorn matching, the estimated corresponding pairs may still contain outlier matches. To filter those, we follow [44] and add a classifier that takes in the concatenated geometric features from the query and database keypoints, and predicts confidence scores for all matches. Estimated correspondences with confidence below a threshold (0.5 in practice) are rejected.

Matching with Bearing Vectors. Directly matching 2D keypoints to cross-modal 3D coordinates is challenging because it requires the network to learn features that have to consider not only the relationship between keypoints, but also the influence of different camera poses. Furthermore, the different distributions of 3D point clouds between datasets, *e.g.*, different scene sizes or different gravity directions, are particularly challenging for a single encoder to learn. Based on this observation, we propose to leverage the *bearing vector* representation of the database points to sidestep the difference in data modalities. In addition to nullifying the effects of the camera intrinsics, projecting 3D points as bearing vectors onto a "covisible" frame that is closer to the query frame (compared to the world reference frame), effectively mitigates the influence of the camera pose (viewpoint changes) during matching, albeit dependent on the quality of retrieval. Finally, bearing vectors provide a common modality between query and database keypoints, eliminating the need for a separate encoder. As we demonstrate in our experimental section, the change in input type has a substantial positive effect.

4.2   Training GoMatch

All of our models are trained to learn feature matching and outlier filtering jointly, using a matching loss and an outlier rejection loss.

Matching Loss. The Sinkhorn matching layer is trained to output a discrete joint probability distribution of two sets of keypoints being matched. We denote this distribution as $\tilde{P} \in \mathbb{R}_+^{M+1 \times N+1}$, such that $\sum_{i=1}^{M+1} \sum_{j=1}^{N+1} \tilde{P}_{ij} = 1$, i.e., is a valid probability distribution. Here, M and N denote the total number of query and database keypoints considered during the matching. We include an extra row and column to allow keypoints not to be matched. We employ a negative log loss to the joint discrete probability distribution. Consider the set of all ground truth matches $\mathcal{M}$, as well as the set of unmatched query keypoints $\mathcal{U}_q$ and database keypoints $\mathcal{U}_d$. The matching loss is of the form:

$$L_{\text{match}} = -\frac{1}{N_m} \left(\sum_{(i,j) \in \mathcal{M}} \log \tilde{P}_{ij} + \sum_{i \in \mathcal{U}_q} \log \tilde{P}_{i(N+1)} + \sum_{j \in \mathcal{U}_d} \log \tilde{P}_{(M+1)j} \right), \quad (2)$$

where $N_m = |\mathcal{M}| + |\mathcal{U}_q| + |\mathcal{U}_d|$.

Outlier Rejection Loss. For the outlier rejection layer we employ a mean weighted binary cross-entropy loss:

$$L_{\text{or}} = -\frac{1}{N_c} \sum_{i=1}^{N_c} w_i \left(y_i \log p_i + (1 - y_i) \log(1 - p_i) \right), \quad (3)$$

where N_c denotes the total number of correspondences supplied to the outlier rejection layer. The term p_i denotes the classifier output probability for each correspondence, while y_i denotes the correspondence target label, and w_i is the weight balancing the negative and positive samples. Our final loss balances both terms equally, i.e., $L_{\text{total}} = L_{\text{match}} + L_{\text{or}}$. We present implementation details about training and testing process in our supplementary material.

5   Experimental Evaluation

In this section, we thoroughly study the potential of using our proposed geometric-based matching for the task of real-world visual localization. We start our experiments by testing the robustness of BPnPNet [10] and GoMatch with keypoint outliers. Next, we verify our technical contribution of successfully diagnosing the missing components leading to robust geometric matching and enabling geometry-based visual localization. Furthermore, we position gemetric-based localization among other state-of-the-art visual localization approaches by comprehensively analysing each method in terms of localization accuracy, descriptor maintenance effort [24], privacy risk, and storage demands (Sect. 5.4). Finally, we present a generalization study (Sect. 5.5) to highlight that our proposed method generalizes across different types of datasets and keypoint detectors. We hope that our in-depth study serves as a starting point of this rarely explored new direction, and inspires new work to advance scalable visual localization through geometric-only matching in the future.

5.1   Datasets

We use MegaDepth [39] for training and ablations, given its large scale. It consists of images captured in-the-wild from 196 outdoor landmarks. We adopt the original test set proposed in [39], and split the remaining sequences into training and validation sets. After verifying our best models on Megadepth, we evaluate them on the popular Cambridge Landmarks [35] (Cambridge) dataset which consists of 4 outdoor scenes of different scales. It allows for convenient comparison to other localization approaches. We use the reconstructions released by [52]. In addition, we evaluate on the indoor 7-Scenes [61] dataset to further assess the generalization capability of our method. 7-Scenes is composed of dense point clouds captured by an RGB-D sensor, and thus provides an alternative environment with different keypoint distributions, in both 2D images and 3D point clouds. We perform evaluation on the official test splits released by the Cambridge and 7-Scenes datasets. We provide detailed information about training data generation using MegaDepth in the supplementary.

5.2   Experimental Setup

Keypoint Detection. For MegaDepth and Cambridge, we use respectively SIFT [41] and SuperPoint [20], preserving the same keypoint detector used to reconstruct their 3D models. For 7-Scenes, we use both SIFT and SuperPoint to extract keypoints for both 2D images and 3D point cloud given RGB-D images.

Retrieval Pairs. We use ground truth to sample retrieval pairs that have at least 35% visual overlap in MegaDepth to ensure enough matches are present during training, as well as to isolate the side-effect of retrieval performance during ablations. For evaluation and comparison to state-of-the-art localization methods, we follow [52] and use their *top-10* pairs retrieved using NetVLAD [1] on Cambridge and DenseVLAD [68] on 7-Scenes.

Matching Baselines. We consider BPnPNet [10] as our geometric-based matching baseline. For a fair comparison, we re-train BPnPNet using our training data. Our visual-based matching baselines use SIFT [41] and SuperPoint [20] (SP) as keypoint descriptors. To match visual descriptors, we use nearest neighbor search [46] with mutual consistency by default and SuperGlue [51] (SG).

Localization Pipeline. Following the state-of-the-art structure-based localization, *e.g.*, HLoc [50], we first obtain up to $k = 10$ retrieval pairs between a query and database images. Then we establish per-pair 2D to 3D matches using either a geometric-based or a visual-based matching model, and then merge results from k pairs based on their matching scores to estimate camera poses. For fairness, all matching baselines use identical retrieval pairs and identical settings for the PnP+RANSAC solver [32].

Evaluation Metrics. For MegaDepth, we follow BPnPNet [10] to report the pose error quantiles at 25/50/75% for the translation and rotation (°) errors as evaluation metrics. However, as the scale unit of MegaDepth is undetermined and

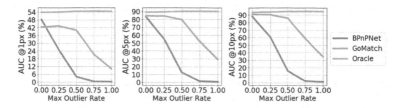

Fig. 4. Influence of keypoint outlier rate. In contrast to prior work BPnPnet [10], GoMatch is significantly more robust against keypoint outliers thanks to the more powerful attention-based architecture as well as our novel formulation of matching bearing vectors instead of cross-modal features.

varies between scenes, the translation errors are not consistent between scenes. Therefore, we propose a new metric based on pixel-level reprojection errors that preserves scene consistency. For each query, we project its inlier 3D keypoints using the predicted and the ground-truth poses. We then report the area under the cumulative curve (AUC) of the mean reprojection error up to 1/5/10px, inspired by the pose error based AUC metric used in [52,64]. We report the commonly used median translation (m) and rotation ($°$) errors [13,35,56] per-scene on Cambridge and 7-Scenes.

5.3 Ablations

We perform ablation studies with MegaDepth's [39] test split, where all retrieval pairs have guaranteed 35% co-visibility, to focus purely on matching performance. In addition, we study the effect of using a single co-visible reference view ($k = 1$) as a minimal setting, as well as multiple views, e.g., $k = 10$, following the common practice in hierarchical structure-based localization [52,56]. To better understand the new AUC metric, we also present an **Oracle** that uses ground truth matches as its prediction. It is used to show the upper-bound performance that can be achieved using our metric and generated data.

Sensitivity to Keypoint Outliers. In a real-world localization setting, the detected query image keypoints will often be noisy and will not have a direct correspondence in the 3D point cloud. Keypoint matching methods thus need to be able to cope with outliers. We first study whether our baseline has this capability by manually increasing the maximum outlier rate, ranging from 0 to 1. The outlier rate is computed as the number of keypoints without a match divided by the total number of keypoints, taking the maximum between 2D and 3D. For all other experiments, we do not control keypoint the outlier rate to properly mimic realistic conditions. As shown in Fig. 4, the Oracle stays round 55/90/94% (AUC@1/5/10px). The large error at 1px is due to our match generation process (*c.f.* supplementary for a detailed discussion). BPnPNet [10] slightly outperforms GoMatch at 1px threshold, being similarly accurate to us at 5/10px thresholds in the absence of outliers. However, as the ratio of outliers increases, the performance of BPnPNet drastically drops, while GoMatch gracefully handles outliers,

Table 2. GoMatch ablation. *Top:* We present Oracle for reference and re-trained BPnPNet [10] as our baseline. *Middle:* We study how the 3D representation (Repr.) and architectural changes influences the performance. Using bearing vector (BVs) instead of 3D coordinates (Coords) as representation and introducing feature attention (Att) are the most crucial factors to the performance improvement. Together with further benefits from the outlier rejection (OR) component and sharing the query and database keypoint feature encoders leads us to the full GoMatch model (*Bottom*). All results rely on a singe retrieval image unless stated otherwise, *e.g.*, $k = 10$.

Model	3D Repr.	Share Encoder	Att	OR	Rotation (°) Quantile@25/50/75% (↓)	Translation	Reproj. AUC (%) @1/5/10px (↑)
Oracle					0.03/0.06/0.10	0.00/0.00/0.01	54.58/90.37/94.87
BPnPNet	Coords	✗	✗	✗	15.17/31.05/59.78	1.67/3.14/5.31	0.34/0.83/1.21
BPnPNet ($k = 10$)	Coords	✗	✗	✗	16.03/33.27/63.90	1.59/3.24/5.80	0.56/1.08/1.50
Variants	BVs	✗	✗	✗	12.19/27.68/58.22	1.26/2.8/5.14	0.37/1.48/2.18
	BVs	✓	✗	✗	9.16/22.62/53.20	0.98/2.38/4.72	0.85/3.09/4.36
	BVs	✓	✓	✗	0.55/8.08/29.34	0.05/0.84/3.34	9.13/25.71/31.65
	BVs	✗	✓	✓	0.38/7.46/31.75	0.04/0.83/3.73	10.22/28.17/33.69
	Coords	✗	✓	✓	4.09/23.56/63.21	0.37/2.53/5.93	3.81/13.54/17.46
GoMatch	BVs	✓	✓	✓	0.36/6.97/29.85	0.03/0.69/3.38	10.30/29.08/34.79
GoMatch($k = 10$)	BVs	✓	✓	✓	**0.15/0.95/13.00**	**0.01/0.09/1.55**	**15.14/42.39/51.24**

i.e., GoMatch is always above 80% at 5/10px up to 50% of outliers. This experiment confirms that GoMatch is significantly more robust to outliers compared to BPnPNet. This outlier robustness is achieved through careful modifications to the network architecture and 3D point representation, both validated by a thorough performance analysis presented in the next sections.

Architecture-Level Analysis. In Table 2 (*Top*), we present the Oracle and BPnPNet [10] re-trained on our data for a direct comparison with GoMatch. This is paired with additional variants, progressively transitioning from BPnPNet to GoMatch. We found that shared encoding brings performance gains up to 0.48/1.61/2.18 AUC percentage points. Adding feature attention on top leads to a significant improvement of 8.28/22.62/27.29 AUC percentage points. By further adding the outlier rejection increases the AUC by 1.17/3.37/3.14% points. We conclude that these network components yield 9.93/27.6/32.61% points of improvements in terms of AUC scores when using bearing vectors the representation.

Representation-Level Analysis. Using 3D coordinates (Coords) instead of bearing vectors (BVs), even with attention and outlier rejection, hinders performance dramatically by 6.49/15.54/17.33% points. If we only change the representation from Coords to BVs, without attention nor outlier rejection, the improvement is merely 0.31/1.29/1.9% points. Therefore, we verify the bearing vector representation is as important as the architectural changes, and both contribute towards keypoint outlier resilience. By modifying both architecture and repre-

Table 3. Comparison to existing localization baselines. We consider end-to-end (E2E) methods and structure-based methods that either matches visual descriptors (VM) or geometries (GM). We report median translation and angular error for each landmark and combined storage requirements for operating on all landmarks. *No Desc. Maint.* is checked if a method does not require descriptor updates in the long run. *Privacy* is checked if a method is resilient to existing known privacy attacks.

	Method	Storage (MB)	No Desc. Maint.	Privacy	King's College	Old Hospital	Shop Facade	St. Mary's Church
					Median Pose Error (m, °) (↓)			
E2E	PoseNet [35]	200	✓	✓	1.92/5.40	2.31/5.38	1.46/8.08	2.65/8.48
	DSAC++ [6]	828	✓	✓	0.18/0.30	0.20/0.30	0.06/0.30	0.13/0.40
	MSPN [4]	-	✓	✓	1.73/3.65	2.55/4.05	2.92/7.49	2.67/6.18
	MS-Transformer [60]	71.1	✓	✓	0.83/1.47	1.81/2.39	0.86/3.07	1.62/3.99
VM	HybridSC [13]	3.13	✗	?	0.81/0.59	0.75/1.01	0.19/0.54	0.50/0.49
	Active Search [53]	812.7	✗	✗	0.42/0.55	0.44/1.01	0.12/0.40	0.19/0.54
	HLoc [50](w.SP [20])	3214.84	✗	✗	0.16/0.38	0.33/1.04	0.07/0.54	0.16/0.54
	HLoc(w.SP+SG [51])	3214.84	✗	✗	**0.12/0.20**	**0.15/0.30**	**0.04/0.20**	**0.07/0.21**
GM	BPnPNet [10]	48.15	✓	✓	26.73/106.99	24.8/162.99	7.53/107.17	11.11/49.74
	GoMatch	48.15	✓	✓	0.25/0.64	2.83/8.14	0.48/4.77	3.35/9.94

sentation, GoMatch outperforms the re-trained BPnPNet by 9.96/28.25/33.58 AUC percentage points.

Utilizing Multiple Co-visible Images. As shown in Table 2, when using $k = 10$ co-visible views, both methods improved their result: BPnPNet by a small margin and GoMatch by a large margin of 4.84/13.31/16.45 AUC percentage points. We thus use $k = 10$ for all of the following experiments.

5.4   Comparison to Localization Baselines

Following the discussion in Sect. 2, we comprehensively compare GoMatch with other established baselines by looking beyond localization performance, and considering as well the storage footprint, resiliency to privacy attacks, and descriptor maintenance. As shown in Table 3, HLoc with SuperPoint and SuperGlue is the most accurate method but also has the highest storage requirements while being vulnerable to privacy attacks. Using HLoc with a newly developed descriptor method will require the map to be updated. In end-to-end methods, DSAC++ is the most accurate method while being resilient to privacy attacks as it does not need to transmit visual descriptors. However, as it requires 4 model versions trained per-scene, it requires 828 MB storage to work under 4 scenes compared to our 48.12 MB. HybridSC as the most storage-efficient method keeps only 1.5% if its original points via compression. However, it is unclear whether the privacy issue still remains for this method since it still relies on full visual descriptors to perform matching. Notice, compressing scene structure can be theoretically combined with GoMatch to lower our storage requirements, which we leave as future work to design suitable scene compression techniques for geometric-base matching. On the whole, GoMatch and MS-Transformer both properly balance those three aspects showing benefits in storage, privacy and absence of descriptor maintenance, and are competitive in accuracy. Compared to its visual-descriptor

Table 4. Generalization study on 7-Scenes. GoMatch generalizes between different scene types and detector types and outperforming BPnPNet and PoseNet.

	Method	Storage (MB)	No Desc. Maint.	Privacy	Chess	Fire	Heads	Office	Pumpkin	Kitchen	Stairs
					Median Pose Error (m, °) (↓)						
E2E	PoseNet [35]	350	✓	✓	0.32/8.12	0.47/14.4	0.29/12.0	0.48/7.68	0.47/8.42	0.59/8.64	0.47/13.8
	DSAC++ [6]	1449	✓	✓	**0.02/0.50**	**0.02/0.90**	**0.01**/0.80	**0.03/0.70**	**0.04/1.10**	**0.04/1.10**	0.09/2.60
	MSPN [4]	-	✓	✓	0.09/4.76	0.29/10.5	0.16/13.1	0.16/6.8	0.19/5.5	0.21/6.61	0.31/11.63
	MS-Transformer [60]	71.1	✓	✓	0.11/4.66	0.24/9.6	0.14/12.19	0.17/5.66	0.18/4.44	0.17/5.94	0.26/8.45
VM	Active Search [53]	-	✗	✗	0.04/1.96	0.03/1.53	0.02/1.45	0.09/3.61	0.08/3.10	0.07/3.37	**0.03**/2.22
	HLoc [50](w.SIFT [41])	2923	✗	✗	0.03/1.13	0.03/1.08	0.02/2.19	0.05/1.42	0.07/1.80	0.06/1.84	0.18/4.41
	HLoc(w.SP [20])	22977	✗	✗	0.03/1.28	0.03/1.3	0.02/1.99	0.04/1.31	0.06/1.63	0.06/1.73	0.07/1.91
	HLoc(w.SP+SG [51])	22977	✗	✗	**0.02/0.85**	**0.02/0.94**	**0.01/0.75**	0.03/0.92	0.05/1.30	**0.04**/1.40	0.05/**1.47**
GM	BPnPNet [10](SIFT [41])	302	✓	✓	1.29/43.82	1.48/51.82	0.93/55.13	2.61/59.06	2.15/39.85	2.15/43.00	2.98/60.27
	BPnPNet (SP [20])	397	✓	✓	1.25/43.9	1.42/45.09	0.8/50.05	2.33/14.54	1.71/31.81	1.68/33.91	2.1/55.78
	GoMatch (SIFT)	302	✓	✓	0.04/1.65	0.13/3.86	0.09/5.17	0.11/2.48	0.16/3.32	0.13/2.84	0.89/21.12
	GoMatch (SP)	397	✓	✓	0.04/1.56	0.12/3.71	0.05/3.43	0.07/1.76	0.28/5.65	0.14/3.03	0.58/13.12

SuperPoint counterpart, GoMatch requires only 1.5% of the capacity to store same scene. GoMatch reduces the average pose errors by (10.67 m, 95.7°) compared to our only prior geometric-based matching work, significantly reducing the accuracy gap to state-of-the-art methods. We hope this inspires researchers to pursue this line of work.

5.5 Generalization

As our final experiment, we study the generalization capability of our method in terms of localization in different types of scenes, e.g., indoor and outdoor, and matching keypoints obtained using different detectors. According to our results in Table 4, similar to our previous experiments, we outperform BPnPNet by a large margin achieving (1.43 m, 34.7°) lower average median pose errors. Except for GoMatch with SIFT keypoints which produces a relatively large 21.12° median rotation error in Stairs, we are only slightly worse than our visual-based matching baselines with SIFT and SuperPoint. Yet, we require only 10/1.7% of the storage that is required by SIFT/SuperPoint to store maps. We also largely outperform PoseNet [35] in all metrics for all scenes except for the relatively lower translation error in Stairs scene, i.e., (0.47 m vs 0.58 m). Furthermore, we achieve better pose than MS-Transformer in the majority of scenes, at the expense of a higher storage requirement. The results clearly verify that GoMatch trained on outdoor scenes (MegaDepth) generalizes smoothly to indoor scenes (7-Scenes), being agnostic to scene types. Similarly, we also confirm that GoMatch trained with SIFT keypoints generalizes well to SuperPoint keypoints, being agnostic to detector types.

6 Conclusion

We present GoMatch, a novel sparse keypoint matching method for visual localization that relies only on geometrical information and that carefully balances common practical challenges of large-scale localization, namely: localization performance, storage demands, privacy and descriptor maintenance (or lack thereof). From all these, the last three are often overlooked. Through a rigorous architecture design process, GoMatch dramatically surpasses its prior work in handling outliers, enabling it for real-world localization. Compared to localization pipelines using visual descriptor-based matching, GoMatch allows localization with a minimal 3D scene representation, requiring as little as 1.5/1.7% to store the same scene. Geometric-based matching brings localization pipelines to a new level of scalability that opens the door for localizing in much larger environments. We see our work as a starting point for this new direction and we look forward to inspire other researchers to pursue more accurate and reliable geometric-based visual localization in the future.

Acknowledgments. This research was partially funded by the Humboldt Foundation through the Sofja Kovalevskaya Award.

References

1. Arandjelovic, R., Gronat, P., Torii, A., Pajdla, T., Sivic, J.: NetVLAD: CNN architecture for weakly supervised place recognition. In: IEEE Conference on Computer Vision and Pattern Recognition (CVPR) (2016)
2. Balntas, V., Li, S., Prisacariu, V.: RelocNet: continuous metric learning relocalisation using neural nets. In: Ferrari, V., Hebert, M., Sminchisescu, C., Weiss, Y. (eds.) Computer Vision – ECCV 2018. LNCS, vol. 11218, pp. 782–799. Springer, Cham (2018). https://doi.org/10.1007/978-3-030-01264-9_46
3. Bhowmik, A., Gumhold, S., Rother, C., Brachmann, E.: Reinforced feature points: optimizing feature detection and description for a high-level task. In: IEEE Conference on Computer Vision and Pattern Recognition (CVPR), pp. 4948–4957 (2020)
4. Blanton, H., Greenwell, C., Workman, S., Jacobs, N.: Extending absolute pose regression to multiple scenes. In: Proceedings of the IEEE/CVF Conference on Computer Vision and Pattern Recognition (CVPR) Workshops (2020)
5. Brachmann, E., et al.: DSAC - differentiable RANSAC for camera localization. In: IEEE Conference on Computer Vision and Pattern Recognition (CVPR) (2017)
6. Brachmann, E., Rother, C.: Learning less is more - 6D camera localization via 3D surface regression. In: IEEE Conference on Computer Vision and Pattern Recognition (CVPR) (2018)
7. Brachmann, E., Rother, C.: Expert sample consensus applied to camera relocalization. In: IEEE Conference on Computer Vision and Pattern Recognition (CVPR), pp. 7525–7534 (2019)
8. Brachmann, E., Rother, C.: Neural-guided RANSAC: learning where to sample model hypotheses. In: IEEE International Conference on Computer Vision (ICCV), pp. 4322–4331 (2019)
9. Brown, M., Windridge, D., Guillemaut, J.-Y.: Globally optimal 2D-3D registration from points or lines without correspondences. In: Proceedings of the IEEE International Conference on Computer Vision (ICCV) (2015)
10. Campbell, D., Liu, L., Gould, S.: Solving the blind perspective-n-point problem end-to-end with robust differentiable geometric optimization. In: Vedaldi, A., Bischof, H., Brox, T., Frahm, J.-M. (eds.) ECCV 2020. LNCS, vol. 12347, pp. 244–261. Springer, Cham (2020). https://doi.org/10.1007/978-3-030-58536-5_15

11. Campbell, D., Petersson, L., Kneip, L., Li, H.: Globally-optimal inlier set maximisation for simultaneous camera pose and feature correspondence. In: Proceedings of the IEEE International Conference on Computer Vision (ICCV) (2017)
12. Campbell, D., Petersson, L., Kneip, L., Li, H., Gould, S.: The alignment of the spheres: globally-optimal spherical mixture alignment for camera pose estimation. In: Proceedings of the IEEE/CVF Conference on Computer Vision and Pattern Recognition (CVPR) (2019)
13. Camposeco, F., Cohen, A., Pollefeys, M., Sattler, T.: Hybrid scene compression for visual localization. In: Proceedings of the IEEE/CVF Conference on Computer Vision and Pattern Recognition (CVPR) (2019)
14. Cao, S., Snavely, N.: Minimal scene descriptions from structure from motion models. In: Proceedings of the IEEE Conference on Computer Vision and Pattern Recognition (CVPR) (2014)
15. Cavallari, T., Bertinetto, L., Mukhoti, J., Torr, P., Golodetz, S.: Let's take this online: adapting scene coordinate regression network predictions for online RGB-D camera relocalisation. In: 2019 International Conference on 3D Vision (3DV), pp. 564–573 (2019)
16. Chelani, K., Kahl, F., Sattler, T.: How privacy-preserving are line clouds? Recovering scene details from 3D lines. In: IEEE Conference on Computer Vision and Pattern Recognition (CVPR), pp. 15668–15678 (2021)
17. Cheng, W., Lin, W., Chen, K., Zhang, X.: Cascaded parallel filtering for memory-efficient image-based localization. In: Proceedings of the IEEE/CVF International Conference on Computer Vision (ICCV) (2019)
18. Cuturi, M.: Sinkhorn distances: lightspeed computation of optimal transport. In: Burges, C.J., Bottou, L., Welling, M., Ghahramani, Z., Weinberger, K.Q. (eds.) Advances in Neural Information Processing Systems, vol. 26. Curran Associates Inc. (2013)
19. David, P., Dementhon, D., Duraiswami, R., Samet, H.: SoftPOSIT: simultaneous pose and correspondence determination. Int. J. Comput. Vis. $59(3)$, 259–284 (2004)
20. DeTone, D., Malisiewicz, T., Rabinovich, A.: SuperPoint: self-supervised interest point detection and description. In: CVPR Workshops, pp. 224–236 (2018)
21. Ding, M., Wang, Z., Sun, J., Shi, J., Luo, P.: CamNet: coarse-to-fine retrieval for camera re-localization. In: IEEE International Conference on Computer Vision (ICCV), pp. 2871–2880 (2019)
22. Dosovitskiy, A., Brox, T.: Generating images with perceptual similarity metrics based on deep networks. In: Lee, D., Sugiyama, M., Luxburg, U., Guyon, I., Garnett, R. (eds.) Advances in Neural Information Processing Systems, vol. 29. Curran Associates Inc. (2016)
23. Dosovitskiy, A., Brox, T.: Inverting visual representations with convolutional networks. In: IEEE Conference on Computer Vision and Pattern Recognition (CVPR), pp. 4829–4837 (2016)
24. Dusmanu, M., Miksik, O., Schonberger, J.L., Pollefeys, M.: Cross-descriptor visual localization and mapping. In: IEEE International Conference on Computer Vision (ICCV), pp. 6058–6067 (2021)
25. Dusmanu, M., et al.: D2-Net: a trainable CNN for joint detection and description of local features. In: IEEE Conference on Computer Vision and Pattern Recognition (CVPR) (2019)
26. Dusmanu, M., Schönberger, J.L., Sinha, S.N., Pollefeys, M.: Privacy-preserving image features via adversarial affine subspace embeddings. In: IEEE Conference on Computer Vision and Pattern Recognition (CVPR) (2020)

27. Gao, X.-S., Hou, X.-R., Tang, J., Cheng, H.-F.: Complete solution classification for the perspective-three-point problem. IEEE Trans. Pattern Anal. Mach. Intell. **25**(8), 930–943 (2003)
28. Geppert, M., Larsson, V., Speciale, P., Schönberger, J.L., Pollefeys, M.: Privacy preserving structure-from-motion. In: Vedaldi, A., Bischof, H., Brox, T., Frahm, J.-M. (eds.) ECCV 2020. LNCS, vol. 12346, pp. 333–350. Springer, Cham (2020). https://doi.org/10.1007/978-3-030-58452-8_20
29. Geppert, M., Larsson, V., Speciale, P., Schonberger, J.L., Pollefeys, M.: Privacy preserving localization and mapping from uncalibrated cameras. In: IEEE Conference on Computer Vision and Pattern Recognition (CVPR), pp. 1809–1819 (2021)
30. Germain, H., Bourmaud, G., Lepetit, V.: S2DNet: learning accurate correspondences for sparse-to-dense feature matching. In: European Conference on Computer Vision (ECCV) (2020)
31. Huang, S., Gojcic, Z., Usvyatsov, M., Wieser, A., Schindler, K.: PREDATOR: registration of 3D point clouds with low overlap. In: Proceedings of the IEEE/CVF Conference on Computer Vision and Pattern Recognition (CVPR), pp. 4267–4276 (2021)
32. Ke, T., Roumeliotis, S.I.: An efficient algebraic solution to the perspective-three-point problem. In: Proceedings of the IEEE Conference on Computer Vision and Pattern Recognition (CVPR) (2017)
33. Kendall, A., Cipolla, R.: Modelling uncertainty in deep learning for camera relocalization. In: IEEE International Conference on Robotics and Automation (ICRA) (2016)
34. Kendall, A., Cipolla, R.: Geometric loss functions for camera pose regression with deep learning. In: IEEE Conference on Computer Vision and Pattern Recognition (CVPR) (2017)
35. Kendall, A., Grimes, M., Cipolla, R.: PoseNet: a convolutional network for real-time 6-DoF camera relocalization. In: IEEE International Conference on Computer Vision (ICCV) (2015)
36. Kneip, L., Scaramuzza, D., Siegwart, R.: A novel parametrization of the perspective-three-point problem for a direct computation of absolute camera position and orientation. In: IEEE Conference on Computer Vision and Pattern Recognition (CVPR) (2011)
37. Laskar, Z., Melekhov, I., Kalia, S., Kannala, J.: Camera relocalization by computing pairwise relative poses using convolutional neural network. In: IEEE International Conference on Computer Vision (ICCV) Workshops (2017)
38. Li, X., Wang, S., Zhao, Y., Verbeek, J., Kannala, J.: Hierarchical scene coordinate classification and regression for visual localization. In: IEEE Conference on Computer Vision and Pattern Recognition (CVPR), pp. 11983–11992 (2020)
39. Li, Z., Snavely, N.: MegaDepth: learning single-view depth prediction from internet photos. In: IEEE Conference on Computer Vision and Pattern Recognition (CVPR) (2018)
40. Liu, L., Campbell, D., Li, H., Zhou, D., Song, X., Yang, R.: Learning 2D-3D correspondences to solve the blind perspective-n-point problem (2020)
41. Lowe, D.G.: Distinctive image features from scale-invariant keypoints. Int. J. Comput. Vis. **60**(2), 91–110 (2004)
42. Luo, Z., et al.: ASLFeat: learning local features of accurate shape and localization. In: IEEE Conference on Computer Vision and Pattern Recognition (CVPR), pp. 6589–6598 (2020)

43. Mera-Trujillo, M., Smith, B., Fragoso, V.: Efficient scene compression for visual-based localization. In: 2020 International Conference on 3D Vision (3DV), pp. 1–10 (2020)
44. Yi, K.M., Trulls, E., Ono, Y., Lepetit, V., Salzmann, M., Fua, P.: Learning to find good correspondences. In: IEEE Conference on Computer Vision and Pattern Recognition (CVPR), pp. 2666–2674 (2018)
45. Moreno-Noguer, F., Lepetit, V., Fua, P.: Pose priors for simultaneously solving alignment and correspondence. In: Forsyth, D., Torr, P., Zisserman, A. (eds.) ECCV 2008. LNCS, vol. 5303, pp. 405–418. Springer, Heidelberg (2008). https://doi.org/10.1007/978-3-540-88688-4_30
46. Muja, M., Lowe, D.G.: Scalable nearest neighbor algorithms for high dimensional data. IEEE Trans. Pattern Anal. Mach. Intell. **36**(11), 2227–2240 (2014)
47. Ng, T., et al.: NinjaDesc: content-concealing visual descriptors via adversarial learning. In: IEEE Conference on Computer Vision and Pattern Recognition (CVPR), pp. 12797–12807 (2022)
48. Pittaluga, F., Koppal, S.J., Kang, S.B., Sinha, S.N.: Revealing scenes by inverting structure from motion reconstructions. In: IEEE Conference on Computer Vision and Pattern Recognition (CVPR), pp. 145–154 (2019)
49. Radwan, N., Valada, A., Burgard, W.: VLocNet++: deep multitask learning for semantic visual localization and odometry. IEEE Robot. Autom. Lett. **3**(4), 4407–4414 (2018)
50. Sarlin, P.-E., Cadena, C., Siegwart, R., Dymczyk, M.: From coarse to fine: robust hierarchical localization at large scale. In: IEEE Conference on Computer Vision and Pattern Recognition (CVPR) (2019)
51. Sarlin, P.-E., DeTone, D., Malisiewicz, T., Rabinovich, A.: SuperGlue: learning feature matching with graph neural networks. In: IEEE Conference on Computer Vision and Pattern Recognition (CVPR), pp. 4938–4947 (2020)
52. Sarlin, P.-E., et al.: Back to the feature: learning robust camera localization from pixels to pose. In: IEEE Conference on Computer Vision and Pattern Recognition (CVPR), pp. 3247–3257 (2021)
53. Sattler, T., Leibe, B., Kobbelt, L.: Efficient & effective prioritized matching for large-scale image-based localization. IEEE Trans. Pattern Anal. Mach. Intell. **39**(9), 1744–1756 (2017)
54. Sattler, T., et al.: Benchmarking 6DoF outdoor visual localization in changing conditions. In: IEEE Conference on Computer Vision and Pattern Recognition (CVPR), pp. 8601–8610 (2018)
55. Sattler, T., et al.: Are large-scale 3D models really necessary for accurate visual localization? In: IEEE Conference on Computer Vision and Pattern Recognition (CVPR) (2017)
56. Sattler, T., Zhou, Q., Pollefeys, M., Leal-Taixe, L.: Understanding the limitations of CNN-based absolute camera pose regression. In: IEEE Conference on Computer Vision and Pattern Recognition (CVPR) (2019)
57. Schönberger, J.L., Frahm, J.-M.: Structure-from-motion revisited. In: IEEE Conference on Computer Vision and Pattern Recognition (CVPR) (2016)
58. Schönberger, J.L., Pollefeys, M., Geiger, A., Sattler, T.: Semantic visual localization. In: IEEE Conference on Computer Vision and Pattern Recognition (CVPR) (2018)
59. Schönberger, J.L., Zheng, E., Frahm, J.-M., Pollefeys, M.: Pixelwise view selection for unstructured multi-view stereo. In: Leibe, B., Matas, J., Sebe, N., Welling, M. (eds.) ECCV 2016. LNCS, vol. 9907, pp. 501–518. Springer, Cham (2016). https://doi.org/10.1007/978-3-319-46487-9_31

60. Shavit, Y., Ferens, R., Keller, Y.: Learning multi-scene absolute pose regression with transformers. In: Proceedings of the IEEE/CVF International Conference on Computer Vision (ICCV), pp. 2733–2742 (2021)
61. Shotton, J., Glocker, B., Zach, C., Izadi, S., Criminisi, A., Fitzgibbon, A.: Scene coordinate regression forests for camera relocalization in RGB-D images. In: IEEE Conference on Computer Vision and Pattern Recognition (CVPR), pp. 2930–2937 (2013)
62. Sinkhorn, R., Knopp, P.: Concerning nonnegative matrices and doubly stochastic matrices. Pac. J. Math. **21**(2), 343–348 (1967)
63. Speciale, P., Schonberger, J.L., Kang, S.B., Sinha, S.N., Pollefeys, M.: Privacy preserving image-based localization. In: IEEE Conference on Computer Vision and Pattern Recognition (CVPR), pp. 5493–5503 (2019)
64. Sun, J., Shen, Z., Wang, Y., Bao, H., Zhou, X.: LoFTR: detector-free local feature matching with transformers. In: IEEE Conference on Computer Vision and Pattern Recognition (CVPR), pp. 8922–8931 (2021)
65. Sun, W., Jiang, W., Trulls, E., Tagliasacchi, A., Yi, K.M.: ACNe: attentive context normalization for robust permutation-equivariant learning. In: Proceedings of the IEEE/CVF Conference on Computer Vision and Pattern Recognition (CVPR) (2020)
66. Taira, H., et al.: InLoc: indoor visual localization with dense matching and view synthesis. In: IEEE Conference on Computer Vision and Pattern Recognition (CVPR) (2018)
67. Toft, C., et al.: Long-term visual localization revisited. IEEE Trans. Pattern Anal. Mach. Intell. **44**(4), 2074–2088 (2022)
68. Torii, A., Arandjelovic, R., Sivic, J., Okutomi, M., Pajdla, T.: 24/7 place recognition by view synthesis. In: IEEE Conference on Computer Vision and Pattern Recognition (CVPR), pp. 1808–1817 (2015)
69. Tran, N.-T., et al.: On-device scalable image-based localization via prioritized cascade search and fast one-many RANSAC. IEEE Trans. Image Process. **28**(4), 1675–1690 (2019)
70. Vaswani, A., et al.: Attention is all you need. In: Guyon, I., et al. (eds.) Advances in Neural Information Processing Systems, vol. 30. Curran Associates Inc. (2017)
71. Walch, F., Hazirbas, C., Leal-Taixe, L., Sattler, T., Hilsenbeck, S., Cremers, D.: Image-based localization using LSTMs for structured feature correlation. In: IEEE International Conference on Computer Vision (ICCV) (2017)
72. Wang, Q., Zhou, X., Hariharan, B., Snavely, N.: Learning feature descriptors using camera pose supervision. In: Vedaldi, A., Bischof, H., Brox, T., Frahm, J.-M. (eds.) ECCV 2020. LNCS, vol. 12346, pp. 757–774. Springer, Cham (2020). https://doi.org/10.1007/978-3-030-58452-8_44
73. Yang, L., Bai, Z., Tang, C., Li, H., Furukawa, Y., Tan, P.: SANet: scene agnostic network for camera localization. In: IEEE Conference on Computer Vision and Pattern Recognition (CVPR), pp. 42–51 (2019)
74. Zhang, J., et al.: Learning two-view correspondences and geometry using order-aware network. In: Proceedings of the IEEE/CVF International Conference on Computer Vision (ICCV) (2019)
75. Zhou, Q., Sattler, T., Pollefeys, M., Leal-Taixe, L.: To learn or not to learn: visual localization from essential matrices. In: IEEE International Conference on Robotics and Automation (ICRA), pp. 3319–3326. IEEE (2020)

SWFormer: Sparse Window Transformer for 3D Object Detection in Point Clouds

Pei Sun[✉], Mingxing Tan, Weiyue Wang, Chenxi Liu, Fei Xia, Zhaoqi Leng, and Dragomir Anguelov

Waymo LLC, Palo Alto, USA
{peis,tanmingxing,weiyuewang,cxliu,feixia,lengzhaoqi,
dragomir}@waymo.com

Abstract. 3D object detection in point clouds is a core component for modern robotics and autonomous driving systems. A key challenge in 3D object detection comes from the inherent *sparse* nature of point occupancy within the 3D scene. In this paper, we propose Sparse Window Transformer (*SWFormer*), a scalable and accurate model for 3D object detection, which can take full advantage of the sparsity of point clouds. Built upon the idea of window-based Transformers, SWFormer converts 3D points into sparse voxels and windows, and then processes these variable-length sparse windows efficiently using a bucketing scheme. In addition to self-attention within each spatial window, our SWFormer also captures cross-window correlation with multi-scale feature fusion and window shifting operations. To further address the unique challenge of detecting 3D objects accurately from sparse features, we propose a new voxel diffusion technique. Experimental results on the Waymo Open Dataset show our SWFormer achieves state-of-the-art *73.36* L2 mAPH on vehicle and pedestrian for 3D object detection on the official test set, outperforming all previous single-stage and two-stage models, while being much more efficient.

1 Introduction

3D point cloud representation learning is critical for autonomous driving, especially for core tasks like 3D object detection. The challenges of learning from 3D point clouds mainly come from two aspects. The first aspect is that 3D points are sparsely distributed in the 3D space due to the nature of LiDAR sensors. This forces 3D models to be different from dense models in natural language processing (where words in a sentence are dense) or image understanding (where pixels in an image are dense). The second aspect is that both the number of points in a point cloud frame and the point cloud sensing region are increasing along with the improvement of the LiDAR sensor hardware. Some of the latest commercial LiDARs can sense up to 250 m [14] and 300 m [41] in all directions around the vehicle, leading to a large range of point clouds.

Supplementary Information The online version contains supplementary material available at https://doi.org/10.1007/978-3-031-20080-9_25.

To address these challenges, previous works have proposed many methods that can be roughly organized as five categories. **PointNet** [27,29,35] based method treats 3D point clouds as unordered sets and encodes them with MLPs and max pooling. Hierarchical structure is introduced to deal with the large input space and to better capture local information. These methods usually have inferior representation capacity compared with more recent methods. **PointPillars**-style methods [17] divide the space into grids of fixed sizes to convert the sparse 3D problem to a dense 2D problem. This method scales quadratically with the range, making it hard to scale with the advancement of LiDAR hardwares. **Sparse submanifold convolutions** [13,33,37] based method can handle the sparse input efficiently. Usually these methods use small 3 × 3 convolution kernels which cannot connect features that are sparsely disconnected without adding normal sparse convolution and striding. This weakness limits its representation capacity. Another weakness of this method is their need for heavily optimized custom ops to be efficient on the modern GPUs and incompatibility with matmul optimized accelerators such as TPUs. **Range image** is a compact representation of point cloud. Multi-view methods [2,37,40,47] run dense convolutions in this view to extract features and fuse with BEV features learned in the PointPillars-style to improve 3D representation learning. It is hard to regress 3D objects directly from the range image due to its lack of 3D information encoding in the dense 2D perspective convolutions. To tackle this weakness, graph-style kernels [4,11] replace convolutions to make use of the range information in range images to capture 3D information which greatly improves the accuracy but is still inferior to the state of the art. **Transformer** [38] is designed to process sequences of data. The challenge in applying it to a point cloud is to solve the quadratic complexity on the number of inputs. Recent methods tackle this problem by attending to neighboring points [26], neighboring voxels [22] or voxels in fixed windows [10]. A generic and efficient transformer-only model without limitations like limited receptive field, irregular memory access pattern, and lack of scalability is still to be designed.

In this paper, we adapt window-based Transformers to 3D point clouds. The Transformer [38] architecture has been hugely successful in modeling language sequences and image patches. In particular, on 2D images, Swin Transformer [21] proposed to partition images into windows and merge context information in a hierarchical manner. Our *Sparse Window Transformer (SWFormer)* builds upon similar ideas, but with several key adaptations for sparse windows. Our first adaption is to add a bucketing-based window partition for sparse windows. Although each window has the same spatial size, such as a 10 × 10 voxel grid, the number of non-empty voxels in each window can vary significantly, so we group these windows into buckets with different effective sequence lengths. Our second adaptation is to limit the expensive window shifting. Swin Transformer [21] uses window shifting once per Transformer layer to connect features between windows and increases receptive fields, but this shifting operation is expensive in the sparse world as it needs to re-order all the sparse features with gather operations. Moreover, it is extremely slow on matmul optimized accelerators such as TPUs. To address this issue, SWFormer employs a new hierarchical backbone architecture, where each SWFormer block has many Transformer layers but only one shifting operation, as shown in Fig. 3. It relies on multi-scale features to achieve large receptive fields for context information, and a multi-scale fusion network to effectively combine these features. The model uses additional custom downsample and upsample algorithms to properly handle the sparse features during feature fusion.

Our innovation continues from the backbone into the 3D object detection head. Existing 3D object detection methods [4,12,17,22,33,37,40,43,47,48] can mostly be viewed as either anchor based methods with implicit or explicit anchors or DETR [3] based methods [24]. The detection performance is closely related with the distribution of the difference between anchor and groundtruth. Methods with inaccurate anchors [4,22] have poor performance in detecting large objects such as vehicles though they can have reasonable performance on pedestrians. One way to solve this problem is to have a two-stage model to refine the boxes [22,33] which greatly improves the detection accuracy. CenterNet-style detection methods [12,37,43] strive to define anchors in the center of the groundtruth boxes only which enforces distributions of closer to zero mean and smaller variance. However, when detecting objects directly from sparse features (e.g. features from PointNet, Submanifold convolutions, sparse Transformers), there are not necessarily features close to the object centers. To alleviate this issue, [37] applies normal sparse convolutions to insert points in the convolution output; [10] scatters the sparse features to a dense BEV grid and runs dense convolutions to expand features to missing positions. These methods are expensive. In this paper, we propose a voxel diffusion module to address this issue efficiently in a scalable way by segmenting and diffusing foreground voxels to their nearby regions as described in Sect. 3.4.

Extensive experiments are conducted on the challenging Waymo Open Dataset [36] to show state of the art results of SWFormer on 3D object detection. We summarize our contributions as follows:

- We propose a hierarchical Sparse Window Transformer (SWFormer) backbone for 3D representation learning. Its flexible receptive fields and multi-scale features make it suitable for different self-driving tasks like object detection and semantic segmentation.
- We propose a generic voxel diffusion module to address the unique challenge of anchor placement in 3D object detection from sparse features.
- We conduct extensive experiments on Waymo Open Dataset [36] to demonstrate the state of the art performance of our SWFormer model.

2   Related Work

2.1   3D Object Detection

As one of the most important tasks in autonomous driving, 3D object detection has been extensively studied in prior works. Early works like PointNet [27] and

PointNet++ [29] directly apply multilayer perceptions on individual points, but it is difficult to scale them to large point clouds with good accuracy. The current mainstream 3D object detectors often convert point clouds into bird eye view 3D [48] or 2D voxels [17] (2D voxels are also referred as pillars), where each voxel aggregates the information from points it contains. In this way, regular 2D or 3D convolutional neural networks can be applied to process these bird-eye-view representations. The pseudo image of voxels also makes it easier to reuse the rich research advancements in 2D object detection, such as two-stage or anchor-based detection heads [43]. The downside is that the pseudo image of voxels grows cubically/quadratically with the voxelization granularity and detection range, not to mention that many of the voxels are effectively empty. Therefore, another type of approach is to perform 3D object detection without voxelization. This includes methods that detect objects from the perspective view [4,11,23], or lookup nearest neighbors for each point [25]. However, the detection accuracy is typically inferior to the voxelization route.

To have the best of both worlds, recent approaches [33,37,42] start to explore multi-view approaches and make use of *sparse* convolutions on the *voxelized* point cloud. For example, the recent range sparse net (RSN [37]) adopts a two-step approach, where the first step performs class-specific segmentation on the range image view, and the second step applies sparse 3D convolutions on the voxel view for specific classes. However, submanifold sparse convolutions cannot connect features that are sparsely disconnected without adding normal sparse convolutions and striding, and they often require heavily optimized customized ops to be efficient on modern accelerators.

Our work aims to learn the 3D representations from sparse point clouds without using any dense or sparse convolutions. Instead, we resort to a hierarchical Transformer to achieve our goal.

2.2   Transformers

Transformers [38] have shown great success in natural language processing [7]. Recently, researchers have brought this architecture to computer vision [1,6, 30,39]. ViT [8] partitions images into patches, which greatly advanced the use of Transformers for image classification. Swin Transformer [21] further demonstrated better ways to fuse contextual information through window shifting and hierarchy, and also generalized to other tasks such as segmentation and detection.

Interestingly, Transformers are naturally suitable for sparse point clouds, because they can take any length of sequences as inputs and do not require dense 2D/3D image representations. Therefore, recent works have attempted to adopt Transformers for 3D representation learning, but they are primary developed for object scans and indoor applications [9,24,26,44]. Voxel Transformer [22] is the submanifold sparse convolution [13] counterpart in the Transformer world, by replacing the convolution kernel with attention. Its irregular memory access pattern is computationally inefficient, and its accuracy is worse than state of the art methods. Recently, SST [10] proposes a single-stride transformer for 3D object detection and achieved impressive results on Waymo Open Datasets especially for pedestrian object detection. However, due to its single stride nature, SST has a limited receptive field and thus has difficulty dealing with large objects, making it ineffective in important tasks like large vehicle detection, large object segmentation (e.g. buildings), lane detection, and trajactory prediction. It needs to scatter features to a dense BEV grid to run several dense convolutions which limits its scalability. It is also computationally expensive as it needs to run many layers of transformers on the high resolution feature map which limits its applications in realtime systems.

Our work is inspired by window-based Transformers (e.g., SwinTransformer [21]) in the sense that we also adopt the hierarchical window-based Transformer backbone, but to address the unique challenges of 3D sparse point clouds, we propose several novel techniques such as the improved SWFormer blocks, multi-scale feature fusion, and voxel diffusion.

3   Sparse Window Transformer

3.1   Overall Architecture

SWFormer is a pure Transformer-based model without any convolutions. Figure 1 shows the overall network architecture: given a sequence of point cloud frames as inputs, each point is augmented with per-frame voxel features [17] and an auxiliary frame timestamp offset [37]. It uses dynamic voxelization [47] and a point net [17,27] based feature embedding net to get sparse voxel features. Note, our voxels are also referred as pillars in other works [17]. These sparse voxels are then processed by a hierarchical sparse window Transformer network described in Sect. 3.2. The resulting multi-scale features are then fused with a Transformer based feature fusion blocks. To address the unique challenge of detecting 3D boxes from sparse features, we first segment the foreground voxels and then apply a voxel diffusion module to expand foreground voxels to neighboring locations with pseudo voxels. In the end, we apply a center net [37,43,46] style detection head to regress 3D boxes.

3.2   Hierarchical Sparse Window Transformer Encoder

A key concept of our SWFormer is the *sparse window* in the birds eye view. After points are converted to a grid of 2D voxels on bird eye view, the voxel grid is further partitioned into a list of non-overlapping windows with fixed size $H \times W$ (e.g., 10×10), similar to Swin Transformer [21]; however, since points are often sparse, many voxels are empty with no valid points. Therefore, the number of non-empty voxels in each window may vary from 0 to HW. As we will explain later, all non-empty voxels within the same window will be flattened to a single variable-length sequence and fed into Transformer layers. In practice, these variable-length sequences prevent us from batch training, causing lower training efficiency. To solve this issue, we borrow a widely used ideas from natural language processing [7,38] and recent works [10], which group these sparse

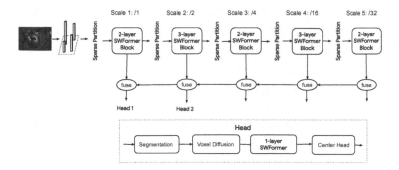

Fig. 1. Overview of SWFormer model architecture. Given a sparse point cloud, we first perform voxelization to generate a grid of 2D voxels. These voxels are then processed with a 5-scale sequence of hierarchical SWFormer blocks (Fig. 3), with strides $\{1, 2, 4, 16, 32\}$. The output features are combined with a multi-scale feature fusion network (Sect. 3.3). The fused features are fed to a head, which performs foreground segmentation and voxel diffusion (Sect. 3.4), and computes center net style classification and box regression loss (Sect. 3.5). Different object classes (e.g. vehicles and pedestrians) may use a separate head on different feature scales.

windows into different buckets based on their sequence lengths. Concretely, we divide sparse windows into at most k buckets $\{B_0, B_1, ..., B_k\}$, where windows in B_i are always padded to a maximum sequence length of $HW/2^i$. All padded tokens are masked in Transformer layers.

Based on the aforementioned sparse windows, our encoder adopts hierarchical Transformers to process the inputs and produce a list of multi-scale BEV features. As shown in Fig. 1, each scale starts with a sparse window partition layer followed by a multi-layer SWFormer block.

Sparse Window Partition: We divide the BEV voxels into non-overlapping windows with fixed size $H \times W$, which are then grouped into buckets $\{B_0, B_1, ..., B_k\}$. For each bucket B_i, we flatten all voxels within the same window into a sequence and zero-pad the sequence length to $HW/2^i$. These sequences are then batched and fed to the Transformer blocks, where the self-attention shares the keys and values for all query voxels coming from the same window [21]. Since SWFormer processes inputs in a hierarchical fashion with multiple feature scales, we need to apply strided window partitions at the beginning of each scale. The strided window partition is similar to traditional strided convolutions, except that it always picks the closest voxel to the center of the window with deterministic rules to break ties. Notably, no max or average pooling operations are applied because they are not friendly to sparse implementations. Figure 2 illustrates an example of a stride-4 window partition.

Sparse Window Transformer Block: Transformer [38] is inherently suitable for sparse point clouds, as it does not require the dense 2D/3D inputs as in convolutional networks; unfortunately, due to the quadratic complexity of self-attention with respect to the input sequence length, it is prohibitively expensive

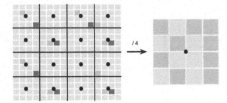

Fig. 2. Strided Sparse Window Partition. Left shows a grid of 16 × 16 BEV voxels, where grey voxels are empty and others are non-empty. Right shows the results of stride-4 window partition, leading to a grid of 4 × 4 voxels. For each striding window, it picks the nearest neighbor non-empty voxel feature (light green) from the center (black dot) with any deterministic rule to break ties; if all voxels are empty in the striding window, then the corresponding voxel after striding is also empty. Best viewed in color.

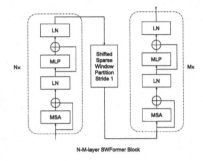

Fig. 3. Sparse Window Transformer Block. Given a sequence of sparse features, it first applies a multi-head self-attention (MSA) on all valid voxel within the same window, followed by a MLP and layer norm. After repeating the Transformer layer N times, it performs a shifted sparse window partition to re-generate the sparse windows, and then process the shifted windows with another M Transformer layers. If N and M are the same, we name it as N-layer SWFormer block for simplicity.

to feed the whole point cloud (with millions of points) or voxel features (with tens of thousands valid voxels) as a single input sequence to Transformer. In this paper, we adopt the idea of Swin Transformer [21]: the sparse BEV voxels are first partitioned into windows, and Transformer is applied to each window separately. To increase the receptive field and connect the features across windows, SwinTransformer uses a window shifting technique to re-partition the window for every layer of Transformer. However, as we are operating on sparse voxel features, such shift-window operation is memory-read/write intensive, especially for matrix-optimized accelerators like TPUs. To alleviate this problem, we propose to limit the shift-window operation to once per stride rather than per layer. Figure 3 shows the detailed architecture of a SWFormer block: it largely follows the same style of SwinTransformer to perform self-attention within a local window, except it only performs shift-window operation once in the middle.

Formally, our SWFormer block can be described as follows:

$$z^0 = [x;\ \text{mask}_z] + \text{PE}_z \tag{1}$$

$$\hat{z}^l = \text{LN}\left(z^{l-1} + \text{MSA}(z^{l-1})\right) \qquad\qquad l = 1...N$$

$$z^l = \text{LN}\left(\hat{z}^l + \text{MLP}(\hat{z}^l)\right) \qquad\qquad l = 1...N$$

$$u^0 = [\text{shift-window}(z^N);\ \text{mask}_u] + \text{PE}_u$$

$$\hat{u}^l = \text{LN}\left(u^{l-1} + \text{MSA}(u^{l-1})\right) \qquad\qquad l = 1...M$$

$$u^l = \text{LN}\left(\hat{u}^l + \text{MLP}(\hat{u}^l)\right) \qquad\qquad l = 1...M \tag{2}$$

where x is the input features after sparse window partition, mask_z is the mask for input padding, PE_z is the positional encoding. The process contains two stages: (1) the first stage applies N Transformer layers to z^0 and output z^N. Each Transformer layer consists of a standard multi-head self-attention (MSA) and multilayer perceptron (MLP), but slightly different from the standard version, here we adopt the post-norm scheme where layer norm (LN) is added after MSA and MLP. For simplicity, we use the standard sine/cosine absolute positional encoding in this paper. (2) The second stage first applies window-shift to z^N, and adds the updated mask_u and positional encoding PE_u based on z^N; afterwards, M Transformer layers are added to process u^0 and generate the final output u^M. Notably, each SWFormer block has $N + M$ Transformer layers but only one window-shift operation.

By restricting window-shift operations, our SWFormer block is more efficient than the conventional Swin Transformer; however, it also limits the receptive field, since each Transformer layer is only applied to a small window. To address this challenge, SWFormer is designed as a hierarchical network with multiple scales, where the strides are gradually increased: for simplicity, this paper uses strides $\{1, 2, 4, 16, 32\}$ for the five scales. For each scale, we always keep the window size fixed (e.g., 10×10); however, as the later scales have larger strides, the same window in later scales will cover much larger area. As an example, for the last scale with stride 32, a 10×10 window would cover 320×320 area on the original BEV voxel grid, and a single window-shift would connect all features within an area as large as 480×480.

3.3   Multi Scale Feature Fusion

Inspired by feature pyramid network (FPN [19]), SWFormer adopts Transformer-based multi-scale feature network to effectively combine all features from the hierarchical Transformer encoder. Figure 4 shows the overall architecture of the feature network: given a list of encoder features $\{P_0, P_1, ..P_5\}$, it iteratively fuses (P_{i+1}, P_i) from large-stride P_5 to small-stride P_0. Formally, our feature fusion process can be described as:

$$\hat{P}_5 = P_5 \tag{3}$$

$$\hat{P}_i = \text{SWFormer}(\text{Concat}(P_i, \text{Upsample}(\hat{P}_{i+1}))) \qquad i = 0, ..., 4 \tag{4}$$

Starting from the last feature map P_5, we first upsample it to have the same stride as P_4 such that they can be concatenated into a single feature map; afterwards, we simple apply a 1-layer SWFormer block to process the concatenated feature and generate the new $\hat{P}_4$. The process is iterated until all fused features $\{\hat{P}_0, ..., \hat{P}_5\}$ have been generated, which have the same strides as $\{P_0, ..., P_5\}$ features. The fused features are further used in voxel diffusion and box regression as described in the following sections.

One challenge in sparse upsamping is that one cannot naively duplicate the feature to all upsampled locations (like commonly done in dense upsampling), which will cause unnecessary excessive feature duplication and significantly reduce the sparsity. In this paper, we restrict features in P_{i+1} to only duplicate to locations that have non-empty features in P_i, as shown in Fig. 4. In this way, we can ensure $\hat{P}_i$ has the same sparsity as P_i.

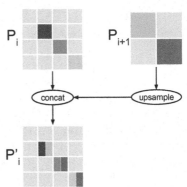

Fig. 4. Feature Fusion. Feature P_{i+1} is upsampled and concatenated with P_i to generate P'_i and the final P_i. During upsampling, we only duplicate P_{i+1} features to locations that are non-empty in P_i.

3.4 Voxel Diffusion

To detect 3D objects from sparse voxel features, a unique challenge is that there might be no valid voxel feature near object centers which are the best positions to place implicit [43] or explicit anchors [31]. Prior works have attempted to resolve this issue by: 1) second-stage box refinement [33], 2) sparse convolutions [37] or coordinate refinement [26] that can expand features to empty voxels close to the object centers, 3) scattering sparse voxel features to dense and applying dense convolutions [10]. In this paper, we propose a novel *voxel diffusion* module to effectively and efficiently address this challenge.

Voxel diffusion is based on two simple ideas: First, we segment all foreground voxels by jointly performing foreground/background segmentation, thus effectively filtering out the majority of background voxels. Second, we expand all foreground voxels by zero-initializing their features into neighboring locations with a simple $k \times k$ max pooling operations on the dense BEV grid, where k is the detection head specific diffusion factor to control the magnitude of expansion. The diffused voxel features are further connected and processed with a few Transformer layers. Combining these two ideas, we can simultaneously keep voxel features sparse (by filtering out background voxels) and features filled (by voxel diffusion) for voxels closer to the object center. Figure 5 illustrates an example of voxel diffusion.

Our foreground segmentation is jointly trained with object detection. Specifically, for each voxel, we assign a binary groundtruth label: 0 (background, voxel does not overlap with any objects) and 1 (foreground, voxel overlaps with at

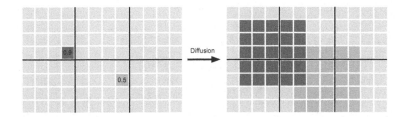

Fig. 5. Voxel Diffusion. After foreground segmentation, each voxel receives a segmentation score $s \in [0,1]$. All voxels with scores greater than a threshold $\gamma = 0.05$ are scattered to a dense BEV grid, and then we apply a $k \times k$ max pooling on the dense BEV grid to expand valid voxel features to their neighboring locations where k is set to 5 in this example. (Left) before diffusion, there are only two foreground voxels with segmentation scores $\{0.5, 0.9\}$ greater than γ; (Right) after voxel diffusion, 47 voxels become valid. Best viewed in color.

least one object). The foreground segmentation is trained with a two-class focal loss [20] for each object class c:

$$L_{\text{seg}}^c = \frac{1}{N} \sum_i L_i \tag{5}$$

where N is the total number of valid voxels and L_i is the focal loss for voxel i. At inference time, we keep voxels as foreground if their foreground scores are greater than a threshold γ.

3.5   Box Regression

SWFormer follows [37] to use a modified CenterNet [12,37,43,46] head to regress boxes from voxel features. The heatmap loss is computed as a penalty-reduced focal loss [20,46] per object class.

$$L_{\text{hm}}^c = -\frac{1}{N} \sum_i \{(1 - \tilde{h}_i)^\alpha \log(\tilde{h}_i) I_{h_i > 1-\epsilon} + (1 - h_i)^\beta \tilde{h}_i^\alpha \log(1 - \tilde{h}_i) I_{h_i \leq 1-\epsilon}\}, \tag{6}$$

where $\tilde{h}_i$ and h_i are the predicted and ground truth heatmap values for object class c respectively at voxel i. N is the number of boxes in class c. We use $\epsilon = 1e - 3$, $\alpha = 2$ and $\beta = 4$ in all experiments, following [18,37,46]. SWFormer parameterize 3D boxes as $\boldsymbol{b} = \{d_x, d_y, d_z, l, w, h, \theta\}$ where d_x, d_y, d_z are the box center offsets relative to the voxel centers. l, w, h, θ are box length, width, height and box heading. We follow [37] to apply a bin loss [35] to regress heading θ, smooth L1 to regress other box parameters, and an IoU loss [45] to improve overall box accuracy on the voxels with ground truth heatmap values above a threshold δ_1.

$$L^c_{\theta_i} = L_{bin}(\theta_i, \tilde{\theta}_i), \tag{7}$$

$$L^c_{b_i \backslash \theta_i} = \text{SmoothL1}(b_i \backslash \theta_i - \tilde{b}_i \backslash \tilde{\theta}_i), \tag{8}$$

$$L^c_{\text{box}} = \frac{1}{N} \sum_i (L_{\theta_i} + L_{b_i \backslash \theta_i} + L_{\text{iou}_i}) I_{h_i > \delta_1}, \tag{9}$$

where $\tilde{b}_i$, b_i are the predicted and ground truth box parameters respectively, $\tilde{\theta}_i$, θ_i are the predicted and ground truth box heading respectively.

The net is trained end to end with the total loss defined as

$$L = \sum_c (\lambda_1 L^c_{\text{seg}} + \lambda_2 L^c_{\text{hm}} + L^c_{\text{box}}) \tag{10}$$

When decoding prediction boxes, we first filter voxels with heatmap less than a threshold δ_2, then run max pool on the heatmap to select boxes corresponding to the local heatmap maximas without any non-maximum-suppression.

4   Experiments

We describe the SWFormer implementation details, and demonstrate its efficiency and accuracy in multiple experiments. Ablation studies are conducted to understand the importance of various design choices.

4.1   Waymo Open Dataset

Our experiments are primary based on the challenging Waymo Open Dataset (WOD) [36], which has been adopted in many recent state of the art 3D detection methods [10,28,33,37,43]. The dataset contains 1150 scenes, split into 798 training, 202 validation, and 150 test. Each scene has about 200 frames, where each frame captures the full 360° around the ego-vehicle. The dataset has one long range LiDAR with range capped at 75 m, four near range LiDARs and five cameras. SWFormer uses all five LiDARs in the experiments.

4.2   Implementation Details

We normalize intensity and elongation in the raw point cloud with the tanh function. The dynamic voxelization uses 0.32 m voxel size in x, y and infinite size in z. During training, we ignore all ground truth boxes with fewer than five points inside. The voxel feature embedding net has two layers of MLPs with channel size of 128. All of the transformer layers have channel size of 128, 8 heads, and inner MLP ratio of 2. We also use stochastic depth [15] with survival probability 0.6. The segmentation cutoff γ in Sect. 3.4 is set to 0.05. The heatmap threshold δ_1, δ_2 are set to 0.2, 0.1 respectively for both vehicle and pedestrian heads. For training efficiency, we cap the number of regression targets in each frame by 1024 for vehicle and 800 for pedestrian sorted by ground truth heatmap values. λ_1, λ_2 are set to 200 and 10 in Eq. 10.

Data Augmentation. We have adopted the several popular 3D data augmentation techniques described in [5] during training: randomly rotating the world by yaws uniformly chosen from $[-\pi, \pi]$ with probability 0.74, randomly flipping the world along y-axis with probability 0.5, randomly scaling the world with scaling factor uniformly chosen within $[0.95, 1.05)$, randomly dropping points with probability of 0.05.

Training and Inference. The SWFormer models are trained end-to-end with 32 TPUv3 cores using the Adam optimizer [16] for a total number of 128 epochs with an initial learning rate set to 1e−3. We apply cosine learning rate decay and 8 epoch warmup with initial warmup learning rate set to 5e−4.

4.3   Main Results

We measured the detection results using the official WOD detection metrics: BEV and 3D average precision (AP), heading error weighted BEV, and 3D average precision (APH) for L1 (easy) and L2 (hard) difficulty levels [36]. The official metrics used to rank in the leaderboard uses IoU cutoff of 0.7 for vehicle, 0.5 for pedestrian. We report additional AP results at IoU of 0.8 for vehicle, 0.6 for pedestrian. Large vehicles that have max dimension greater than 7 m are also reported. Table 1 reports the main results on validation set, Table 2 reports additional results for high IoU and large vehicles on the validation set, and Table 3 shows the test set results by submitting our predictions to the official test server. Results from methods with test time augmentation or ensemble are not included.

As shown in Table 1, SWFormer achieves new state-of-the-art results for vehicle detection on the WOD *validation set*: it has 1.5 APH/L2 higher than the prior best single-stage model RSN [37]. SWFormer even outperforms the prior best performing two-stage method PVRCNN++ [34] by 0.42 APH/L2. Importantly, SWFormer performs very well at detecting large vehicles, 6.35 AP/L2 higher than the prior art of RSN [37] as shown in Table 2. SWFormer slightly outperforms the state of the art single stage method SST_3f [10] by 0.12 APH/L2. Notably, the single frame single stage SWFormer_1f also outperforms all prior single frame methods.

We have compiled the model with XLA [32] and ran inference for the 15th frame in scene 8907419590259234067_1960_000_1980_000 that has 68 vehicles and 69 pedestrians on a Nvidia T4 GPU with fused transformer kernels. The latency is 20 ms, more efficient than the popular realtime detector PointPillars [17] which takes about 100 ms on the same GPU with our own implementation.

Table 3 shows vehicle and pedestrian detection result comparison with published results on the WOD *test set*, which shows SWFormeroutperforms all previous single-stage or two-stage methods on the official ranking method mAPH/L2.

Table 1. WOD *validation set* results. † is from [37]. Top methods are highlighted. Top one-frame (cyan), single-stage (blue) are colored. TS: two-stage. BEV: BEV L1 AP.

Method	TS	AP/APH Vehicle			AP/APH Pedestrian		
		3D L1	3D L2	BEV	3D L1	3D L2	BEV
PVRCNN++ [34]	✓	79.3/78.8	70.6/70.2	-	81.8/76.3	73.2/68.0	-
VoTr-TSD[22]	✓	75.0/74.3	65.9/65.3	-	-	-	-
SST_TS_3f [10]	✓	78.7/78.2	70.0/69.6	-	**83.8/80.1**	**75.9/72.4**	-
CenterPoint_TS [43]	✓	76.6/76.1	68.9/68.4	-	79.0/73.4	71.0/65.8	-
PointPillars [17] †	✗	63.3/62.7	55.2/54.7	82.5	68.9/56.6	60.0/49.1	76.0
MVF++_1f [28]	✗	74.6/-	-	87.6	78.0/-	-	83.3
RSN_1f [37]	✗	75.1/74.6	66.0/65.5	88.5	77.8/72.7	68.3/63.7	83.4
RSN_3f [37]	✗	78.4/78.1	69.5/69.1	91.3	79.4/76.2	69.9/67.0	85.0
SST_1f [10]	✗	74.2/73.8	65.5/65.1	-	78.7/69.6	70.0/61.7	-
SST_3f [10]	✗	77.0/76.6	68.5/68.1	-	82.4/78.0	75.1/70.9	
SWFormer_1f (Ours)	✗	77.8/77.3	69.2/68.8	91.7	80.9/72.7	72.5/64.9	86.1
SWFormer_3f (Ours)	✗	**79.4/78.9**	**71.1/70.6**	**92.6**	82.9/79.0	74.8/71.1	87.5

Table 2. Additional WOD *validation set* results. Top methods are highlighted.

Method	Vehicle L1 AP			Pedestrian L1 AP
	3D IoU = 0.8	BEV Large	3D Large	3D IoU = 0.6
MVF++_1f [28]	43.3	-	-	56.0
RSN_3f [37]	46.4	53.1	45.2	-
SWFormer_3f (Ours)	**47.5**	**60.1**	**51.5**	**62.1**

Table 3. WOD *test set* results. † is from [37]. Top methods are highlighted. mAPH/L2 is the official ranking metric on the WOD leaderboard. TS is short for two-stage.

Method	TS	mAPH	Vehicle AP/APH 3D		Pedestrian AP/APH 3D	
		L2	L1	L2	L1	L2
CenterPoint [43]	✓	69.1	80.20/79.70	72.20/71.80	78.30/72.10	72.20/66.40
SST_TS_3f [10]	✓	72.94	80.99/80.62	73.08/72.74	83.05/79.38	76.65/73.14
PVRCNN++ [34]	✓	71.24	81.62/81.20	73.86/73.47	80.41/74.99	74.12/69.00
P.Pillars [17] †	✗	55.10	68.60/68.10	60.50/60.10	68.00/55.50	61.40/50.10
RSN_3f [37]	✗	69.70	80.70/80.30	71.90/71.60	78.90/75.60	70.70/67.80
SWFormer_3f (Ours)	✗	**73.36**	82.89/82.49	75.02/74.65	82.13/78.13	75.87/72.07

4.4 Ablation Study

Voxel diffusion is one of the primary contributions of this paper. We study its impacts by varying the diffusion window size k introduced in Sect. 3.4. The result in Table 4 shows the significance of voxel diffusion. Disabling voxel diffusion (i.e. setting $k = 1$) results in 6.37 and 3.22 3D AP drop compared with $k = 9$ on

Table 4. Impact of Voxel Diffusion. Compared to the baseline (window size = 1), our voxel diffusion improves accuracy, especially with large diffusion window size.

Diffusion Window Size	1	3	5	9
Vehicle 3D AP/L1	72.13	78.07	78.58	78.50
Pedestrian 3D AP/L1	79.23	82.28	82.44	82.45
Vehicle BEV AP/L1	82.42	91.19	92.09	92.03
Pedestrian BEV AP/L1	83.65	87.01	87.15	87.47

Table 5. Impact of Multi-Scale and Window Shifting. Compared to single scale, multi-scale have much better accuracy. Window shifting is also important for performance.

	Number of Scales				Window Shift	
	1	2	3	5	✗	✓
Vehicle 3D AP/L1	74.96	77.68	78.88	79.36	76.74	79.36
Pedestrian 3D AP/L1	81.24	82.39	82.19	82.91	81.19	82.91
Vehicle BEV AP/L1	89.55	91.83	92.23	92.60	90.74	92.60
Pedestrian BEV AP/L1	86.48	87.30	87.13	87.54	86.46	87.54

vehicle and pedestrian detection respectively. Increasing k can slightly improve the detection accuracy especially on vehicle.

Multi-scale feature improves the model accuracy as shown in Table 5 especially going from one scale to two scales. The impact is larger on vehicle detection (+2.72 3D AP) than pedestrian detection (+1.15 3D AP). The 3-scale model has pretty close accuracy as the full 5-scale model. In practice, we can trade-off between accuracy and latency by adjusting the number of scales. Note that some autonomous driving tasks such as lane detection, behavior prediction require larger receptive field. The success of training a deep five-scale SWFormer model shows its potential in those tasks.

Window shifting is introduced in SwinTransformer [21] to connect the features among windows. We have limited its usage to one per scale. What happens if we completely remove it? Table 5 shows clear accuracy drop especially on vehicles if the window-shift operations are removed from the SWFormer blocks. This meets our intuition that it is important to keep one window shift operation per scale to make sure every voxel gets the similar receptive field in all directions.

5   Conclusion

This paper presents *SWFormer*, a scalable and accurate sparse window transformer-only model, to effectively learn 3D point cloud representations for object detection. Built upon window-based Transformers, it addresses the unique challenges brought by the sparse 3D point clouds, and proposes a bucketing-based multi-scale Transformer neural network. SWFormer takes full advantage of the sparsity of point clouds, and can effectively processes sparse windows of point clouds using pure Transformer layers without any convolutions. It also proposes a novel voxel diffusion module to further detect 3D objects from sparse features. Experiments show state-of-the-art results on the challenging Waymo Open Dataset.

References

1. Bello, I., Zoph, B., Vaswani, A., Shlens, J., Le, Q.V.: Attention augmented convolutional networks. In: Proceedings of the IEEE/CVF International Conference on Computer Vision, pp. 3286–3295 (2019)
2. Bewley, A., Sun, P., Mensink, T., Anguelov, D., Sminchisescu, C.: Range conditioned dilated convolutions for scale invariant 3D object detection. In: Conference on Robot Learning (2020)
3. Carion, N., Massa, F., Synnaeve, G., Usunier, N., Kirillov, A., Zagoruyko, S.: End-to-end object detection with transformers. In: Vedaldi, A., Bischof, H., Brox, T., Frahm, J.-M. (eds.) ECCV 2020. LNCS, vol. 12346, pp. 213–229. Springer, Cham (2020). https://doi.org/10.1007/978-3-030-58452-8_13
4. Chai, Y., et al.: To the point: efficient 3D object detection in the range image with graph convolution kernels. In: Proceedings of the IEEE/CVF Conference on Computer Vision and Pattern Recognition, pp. 16000–16009 (2021)
5. Cheng, S., et al.: Improving 3D object detection through progressive population based augmentation. In: Vedaldi, A., Bischof, H., Brox, T., Frahm, J.-M. (eds.) ECCV 2020. LNCS, vol. 12366, pp. 279–294. Springer, Cham (2020). https://doi.org/10.1007/978-3-030-58589-1_17
6. Dai, Z., Liu, H., Le, Q., Tan, M.: CoatNet: marrying convolution and attention for all data sizes. In: Advances in Neural Information Processing Systems, vol. 34 (2021)
7. Devlin, J., Chang, M.W., Lee, K., Toutanova, K.: BERT: pre-training of deep bidirectional transformers for language understanding. arXiv preprint arXiv:1810.04805 (2018)
8. Dosovitskiy, A., et al.: An image is worth 16 × 16 words: transformers for image recognition at scale. arXiv preprint arXiv:2010.11929 (2020)
9. Engel, N., Belagiannis, V., Dietmayer, K.: Point transformer. IEEE Access **9**, 134826–134840 (2021)
10. Fan, L., et al.: Embracing single stride 3D object detector with sparse transformer. arXiv preprint arXiv:2112.06375 (2021)
11. Fan, L., Xiong, X., Wang, F., Wang, N., Zhang, Z.: RangeDet: in defense of range view for lidar-based 3D object detection. In: Proceedings of the IEEE/CVF International Conference on Computer Vision, pp. 2918–2927 (2021)
12. Ge, R., et al.: AFDet: anchor free one stage 3D object detection. arXiv preprint arXiv:2006.12671 (2020)
13. Graham, B., van der Maaten, L.: Submanifold sparse convolutional networks. arXiv preprint arXiv:1706.01307 (2017)
14. Guizilini, V., Ambrus, R., Pillai, S., Raventos, A., Gaidon, A.: 3D packing for self-supervised monocular depth estimation. In: IEEE Conference on Computer Vision and Pattern Recognition (CVPR) (2020)

15. Huang, G., Sun, Yu., Liu, Z., Sedra, D., Weinberger, K.Q.: Deep networks with stochastic depth. In: Leibe, B., Matas, J., Sebe, N., Welling, M. (eds.) ECCV 2016. LNCS, vol. 9908, pp. 646–661. Springer, Cham (2016). https://doi.org/10.1007/978-3-319-46493-0_39

16. Kingma, D.P., Ba, J.: Adam: a method for stochastic optimization. arXiv preprint arXiv:1412.6980 (2014)

17. Lang, A.H., Vora, S., Caesar, H., Zhou, L., Yang, J., Beijbom, O.: PointPillars: fast encoders for object detection from point clouds. In: CVPR (2019)

18. Law, H., Deng, J.: CornerNet: detecting objects as paired keypoints. In: Proceedings of the European Conference on Computer Vision (ECCV), pp. 734–750 (2018)

19. Lin, T.Y., Dollár, P., Girshick, R., He, K., Hariharan, B., Belongie, S.: Feature pyramid networks for object detection. In: Proceedings of the IEEE Conference on Computer Vision and Pattern Recognition, pp. 2117–2125 (2017)

20. Lin, T.Y., Goyal, P., Girshick, R., He, K., Dollár, P.: Focal loss for dense object detection. In: Proceedings of the IEEE International Conference on Computer Vision, pp. 2980–2988 (2017)

21. Liu, Z., et al.: Swin transformer: hierarchical vision transformer using shifted windows. In: CVPR (2021)

22. Mao, J., et al.: Voxel transformer for 3D object detection. In: Proceedings of the IEEE/CVF International Conference on Computer Vision, pp. 3164–3173 (2021)

23. Meyer, G.P., Laddha, A., Kee, E., Vallespi-Gonzalez, C., Wellington, C.K.: LaserNet: an efficient probabilistic 3D object detector for autonomous driving. In: Proceedings of the IEEE/CVF Conference on Computer Vision and Pattern Recognition, pp. 12677–12686 (2019)

24. Misra, I., Girdhar, R., Joulin, A.: An end-to-end transformer model for 3D object detection. In: Proceedings of the IEEE/CVF International Conference on Computer Vision, pp. 2906–2917 (2021)

25. Ngiam, J., et al.: StarNet: targeted computation for object detection in point clouds. arXiv preprint arXiv:1908.11069 (2019)

26. Pan, X., Xia, Z., Song, S., Li, L.E., Huang, G.: 3D object detection with pointformer. In: Proceedings of the IEEE/CVF Conference on Computer Vision and Pattern Recognition, pp. 7463–7472 (2021)

27. Qi, C.R., Su, H., Mo, K., Guibas, L.J.: PointNet: deep learning on point sets for 3D classification and segmentation. In: CVPR (2017)

28. Qi, C.R., et al.: Offboard 3D object detection from point cloud sequences. In: Proceedings of the IEEE/CVF Conference on Computer Vision and Pattern Recognition, pp. 6134–6144 (2021)

29. Qi, C.R., Yi, L., Su, H., Guibas, L.J.: PointNet++: deep hierarchical feature learning on point sets in a metric space. In: NeurIPS (2017)

30. Ramachandran, P., Parmar, N., Vaswani, A., Bello, I., Levskaya, A., Shlens, J.: Stand-alone self-attention in vision models. In: Advances in Neural Information Processing Systems, vol. 32 (2019)

31. Ren, S., He, K., Girshick, R., Sun, J.: Faster R-CNN: towards real-time object detection with region proposal networks. IEEE Trans. Pattern Anal. Mach. Intell. **39**(6), 1137–1149 (2016)

32. Sabne, A.: XLA: compiling machine learning for peak performance (2020)

33. Shi, S., et al.: PV-RCNN: point-voxel feature set abstraction for 3D object detection. In: CVPR (2020)

34. Shi, S., et al.: PV-RCNN++: point-voxel feature set abstraction with local vector representation for 3D object detection. arXiv preprint arXiv:2102.00463 (2021)

35. Shi, S., Wang, X., Li, H.: PointRCNN: 3D object proposal generation and detection from point cloud. In: CVPR (2019)
36. Sun, P., et al.: Scalability in perception for autonomous driving: Waymo open dataset. In: CVPR (2020)
37. Sun, P., et al.: RSN: range sparse net for efficient, accurate lidar 3d object detection. In: Proceedings of the IEEE/CVF Conference on Computer Vision and Pattern Recognition, pp. 5725–5734 (2021)
38. Vaswani, A., et al.: Attention is all you need. In: NeurIPS (2017)
39. Wang, X., Girshick, R., Gupta, A., He, K.: Non-local neural networks. In: Proceedings of the IEEE Conference on Computer Vision and Pattern Recognition, pp. 7794–7803 (2018)
40. Wang, Y., et al.: Pillar-based object detection for autonomous driving. In: Vedaldi, A., Bischof, H., Brox, T., Frahm, J.-M. (eds.) ECCV 2020. LNCS, vol. 12367, pp. 18–34. Springer, Cham (2020). https://doi.org/10.1007/978-3-030-58542-6_2
41. Waymo: Waymo's 5th generation driver. https://blog.waymo.com/2020/03/introducing-5th-generation-waymo-driver.html
42. Yan, Y., Mao, Y., Li, B.: Second: sparsely embedded convolutional detection. Sensors (2018)
43. Yin, T., Zhou, X., Krahenbuhl, P.: Center-based 3D object detection and tracking. In: Proceedings of the IEEE/CVF Conference on Computer Vision and Pattern Recognition, pp. 11784–11793 (2021)
44. Zhao, H., Jiang, L., Jia, J., Torr, P.H., Koltun, V.: Point transformer. In: Proceedings of the IEEE/CVF International Conference on Computer Vision, pp. 16259–16268 (2021)
45. Zhou, D., et al.: IoU loss for 2D/3D object detection (2019)
46. Zhou, X., Wang, D., Krähenbühl, P.: Objects as points. arXiv preprint arXiv:1904.07850 (2019)
47. Zhou, Y., et al.: End-to-end multi-view fusion for 3D object detection in lidar point clouds. In: CORL (2019)
48. Zhou, Y., Tuzel, O.: VoxelNet: end-to-end learning for point cloud based 3d object detection. In: CVPR (2018)

PCR-CG: Point Cloud Registration via Deep Explicit Color and Geometry

Yu Zhang[1]([✉]), Junle Yu[2], Xiaolin Huang[1], Wenhui Zhou[2], and Ji Hou[3]

[1] Shanghai Jiaotong University, Shanghai, China
zhangyu606@gmail.com
[2] Hangzhou Dianzi University, Hangzhou, China
[3] TUM, Beijing, China

Abstract. In this paper, we introduce PCR-CG: a novel 3D point cloud registration module explicitly embedding the color signals into geometry representation. Different from the previous SOTA methods that used only geometry representation, our module is specifically designed to effectively correlate color and geometry for the point cloud registration task. Our key contribution is a 2D-3D cross-modality learning algorithm that embeds the features learned from color signals to the geometry representation. With our designed 2D-3D projection module, the pixel features in a square region centered at correspondences perceived from images are effectively correlated with point cloud representations. In this way, the overlap regions can be inferred not only from point cloud but also from the texture appearances. Adding color is non-trivial. We compare against a variety of baselines designed for adding color to 3D, such as exhaustively adding per-pixel features or RGB values in an implicit manner. We leverage Predator as our baseline method and incorporate our module into it. Our experimental results indicate a significant improvement on the 3DLoMatch benchmark. With the help of our module, we achieve a significant improvement of 6.5% registration recall with 5000 sampled points over our baseline method. To validate the effectiveness of 2D features on 3D, we ablate different 2D pre-trained networks and show a positive correlation between the pre-trained weights and task performance. Our study reveals a significant advantage of correlating explicit deep color features to the point cloud in the registration task.

1 Introduction

With commodity depth sensors commonly available, such as Kinect series, a variety of RGB-D datasets are created [3,11,41,47]. With recent breakthroughs in deep learning and the increasing prominence of RGB-D data, the computer vision community has made a tremendous progress on analyzing point cloud [33] and images [17,18]. Recently, we have observed a rapid progress in cross-modality

---

Supplementary Information The online version contains supplementary material available at https://doi.org/10.1007/978-3-031-20080-9_26.

Fig. 1. We seek to align two point clouds in RGB-D data. To better leverage color, we propose PCR-CG, a 2D-3D projection module that explicitly lifts 2D deep color features to 3D geometry representation. A pair of RGB-D frames are used as input, where each RGB-D frame is composed of a color image and a depth frame. 3D geometry is represented by the point cloud that is generated from depth frame. We leverage a pre-trained 2D network to predict correspondences between frames and extract regional features from color images. The 2D regional features are further lifted to 3D via our proposed 2D-3D projection module in an explicit manner.

learning between geometry and colors [7,9,21,25,26,42]. However, prior work mainly focused on high-level semantic scene understanding tasks, such as semantic/instance segmentation [12,24] and object detection [31]. Compared to high-level tasks, cross-modality learning between color and geometry is less explored in low-level tasks, such as point cloud registration. In this paper, we discuss correlating RGB priors for aligning two partial point clouds (Fig. 1).

Point cloud registration has been speedily developed because of its wide applications [2,5,14,23,46]; its 2D counter-part has been developed even earlier and achieved great success [29] in many systems, such as visual SLAM [43]. Mainstream methods adopt a first-correspondences-then-transformation manner, namely estimating transformations between two frames based on these correspondence matching. In this context, correspondence-matching-based methods [29,37,48] have showed appealing results in the 2D domain. However, current deep learning based methods in 3D merely use geometry as the only input. Therefore, exploring to combine deep RGB features is valuable and of great importance to the point cloud registration task. In this manner, a variety of existing 2D approaches and pre-trained models can also be further leveraged in 3D point cloud registration task.

Finding correspondences is essential for calculating the transformation matrix between two frames, and correspondences only appear in the overlap region. In this context, estimating the overlap region of two frames is critical for point cloud registration. Intuitively, we can identify the overlap regions not only from geometric inputs like point cloud, but also from color signals like images. Given this observation, we propose to embed color signals into point cloud representation, so as to effectively predict 3D correspondences for the registration task. To this end, we propose PCR-CG, a novel module that explicitly embeds RGB priors into the geometry representation for the point cloud registration.

In our work, we build upon the successful Predator [23], following the standard point cloud registration pipeline, namely first finding correspondences and then using RANSAC to estimate the rotation and translation matrices between two frames of point clouds. To enable the usage of RGB values from captured RGB-D data, our approach introduces three steps. First, a 2D pre-trained neural network [37] is used to predict pixel correspondences between pure RGB frames. Based on the correspondences, we extract square regions centered at each correspondence pixel. Furthermore, the 2D pre-trained neural network summarizes the features from pixels in each region. We investigate the effectiveness of 2D pre-trained features in the 3D task by trying different 2D pre-trained weights, such as ImageNet and Pri3D [21] pre-trained models. We note that the 2D models are pre-trained on different datasets. In this context, the transfer ability of the 2D part shows promising results. In this manner, we are able to take advantage of massive existing 2D pre-trained models. Secondly, we propose a 2D-3D projection module to explicitly project the 2D features to the 3D point cloud region by region (centered at each correspondence pixel), according to the camera intrinsic and transformation matrix. We exhaustively explore the possible designs, e.g., implicitly concatenating per-pixel features to each point. Finally, we demonstrate that the design of explicitly projecting the deep color features in overlap-aware regions surpass implicit manner in our ablation studies.

Following Predator [23], we evaluate our work on 3DMatch and the more competitive and difficult 3DLoMatch [23] benchmark. In both benchmarks, we observe significant improvements in our proposed color and geometry learning strategy. Our approach outperforms the state-of-the-art method by a large margin of registration recall on the 3DLoMatch benchmark.

In summary, the contributions of our work are three-fold:

- We introduce a novel 2D-3D projection module that explicitly embeds the 2D color into the point cloud for registration task.
- We experimentally show that our method outperforms the baseline by a significant gap of 6.5% registration recall with 5000 sampled points on the more challenging 3DLoMatch benchmark.
- We conduct empirical studies and show the transfer ability of 2D pre-trained weights for 3D point cloud registration tasks.

2 Related Work

Advancements in deep learning enable fast development in many high-level and low-level tasks. In this section, we firstly review point cloud and image registration tasks, and then discuss a few additional relevant works in the area of multi-modal learning across color and geometry.

Point Cloud Registration. Point Cloud Registration plays an important role in the computer vision community. Most successful methods in this field start with a low-level task, namely correspondence matching. A transformation matrix can then be estimated from the predicted correspondences. Correspondences matching have been investigated even before deep learning era. Traditional machine learning methods and hand-crafted descriptors, such as ICP [4,8] and SIFT [28], have drawn great attention back then. Color ICP [30] leverages both color and geometry to align two partial point clouds, but with traditional machine learning optimizations. And the field is moving even faster since deep learning era. Leveraging the powerful deep learning features to learn rotation-invariant descriptors [6,10] for correspondences that are further fed into RANSAC for registration is the most successful story nowadays. Following the same pipeline, Predator [23] achieves the state-of-the-art results and first proposes to solve the registration problem on low-overlap frames. CoFiNet [46] proposes a coarse-to-fine manner on the point cloud to speed up the inference. GeoTransformer [34] leverages transformer on geometry to boost the point cloud registration. However, these prior work only use geometry as the single-source input. In this paper, we build upon their framework and propose an effective module that explicitly fuses the overlap regions learned from 2D color signals. BYOC [15] transfers the visual signals to train a geometric encoder. UnsupervisedR&R [14] uses differentiable rendering to enforce photometric and geometric consistency. Previous methods focus on self- or unsupervised learning on color signals. Our approach on the other hand discusses effectively making full use of RGB-D data as inputs.

Image Registration. As the counterpart of 3D point cloud registration, 2D image registration contributes significantly to the computer vision community. It enables many high-level applications, such as 3D Reconstruction and visual SLAM [39,40]. Compared to point cloud registration, image registration uses only color input [35,38] and takes advantage of many existing pre-trained 2D network, such as ResNet with ImageNet pre-trained weights. The success of 2D image registration shows the possibility of learning registration from pixel input. Besides, the motivation of taking advantage of massive existing 2D pre-trained models suggests incorporating 2D signals into 3D registration task. In this work, we explore how to effectively use 2D signals on 3D registration task.

2D-3D Multi-modal Learning. Joint learning from color and geometry signals has been researched in many high-level tasks, such as in both 2D and 3D scene understanding [12,19,21,22,26,27,31]. 3D-SIS [19] proposes to implicitly leverage the color signal for 3D instance segmentation and detection tasks. RevalNet [20] adopts the similar idea of implicitly fusing color and geometry for 3D instance completion task. ImVoteNet [31] adds a 2D detector in addition to VoteNet [32] to explicitly use 2D color input. 3D-to-2D Distillation [27] presents a method to fuse 3D features for 2D semantic segmentation tasks. BPNet [22] uses a bidirectional projection module to mutually learn 2D-3D signals for both 2D and 3D semantic segmentation tasks. Besides scene understanding tasks, 2D-3D learning is also explored in representation learning. Pri3D [21] proposes to learn 2D representation in a pre-training paradigm for 2D scene understanding. P4Contrast [26] learns 3D representation from a novel 2D-3D loss for 3D scene

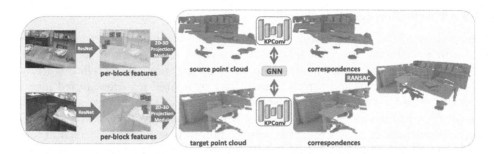

Fig. 2. PCR-CG Pipeline. The pipeline is composed of a 3D network, a 2D network and a 2D-3D projection module. Both 3D geometry and 2D images are taken as input and used to jointly learn features for detecting correspondences. The 2D network takes RGB images as input and extracts per-region features. A 2D-3D Projection Module is used to lift 2D pixel features into 3D point cloud. The concatenated features are fed into 3D network for finding correspondences. Due to our 2D-3D projection module, the 3D supervision can pass gradients back to the 2D network, and, therefore, yield an end-to-end training.

understanding. Image2Point [45] boosts 3D point cloud understanding with 2D image pre-trained models. However, most of the previous research focus on high-level semantic tasks. In this paper, we discuss the color-geometry learning in the point cloud registration task focusing on the low-level domain, i.e., predicting correspondences for point cloud registration. Additionally, we study the transfer ability of 2D pre-trained networks in the 3D registration task.

3   Methods

3.1   Data Representation

In our method, we use point cloud to represent the geometry input. At the same time, RGB images are the input to a pre-trained 2D network.

Geometry Data. Each training sample contains a pair of non-aligned RGB-D frames. The transformation matrix that aligns them is used as the ground truth. We use point cloud lifted by depth frame as geometric input and predict the correspondences between them. For pre-computing the ground truth of correspondences, we transform one point cloud to the other, according to the aforementioned transformation matrix. Then, correspondences are found by a nearest neighbor search within a threshold in the Euclidean space.

Color Data. We evaluate our method in RGB-D datasets, namely 3DMatch and 3DLoMatch. In these datasets, each point cloud is fused by 50 consecutive depth frames. The RGB images and depth images are in pairs. Therefore, each point cloud is also associated with 50 RGB frames. We pick up the first and the last RGB images for training and validation. Each RGB image is resized to the resolution of 240×320 in pixels. Notably, we do not need ground truth for 2D data, as the 2D network is pre-trained on other data.

3.2   Projection Module

Insertion of the Projection Module. Before entering into our method, we have to revisit Predator [23]. In Predator, a point cloud is input to a 3D neural network. In the encoder, attention modules are used to correlate features obtained from source and target frames. The correlated features are fed into a decoder. The final layer outputs a score for each point to indicate its likelihood on overlapped regions. Per-point features from the final layer are used for finding correspondences. Next, correspondences are ranked based on the scores, and top-k correspondences' features are fed into RANSAC. Finally, RANSAC consumes the features of selected correspondences to further estimate the transformation matrix between the source and target frames. In this context, our module is directly inserted at the beginning of the 3D network without interfering the rest of the pipeline. The overview of the pipeline is illustrated in Fig. 2.

Lifting 2D to 3D. To train on both color and geometry inputs, we propose a novel module that embeds deep color features into 3D representations. Our module PCR-CG takes the features extracted from RGB images and lifts them to 3D. The 3D network consumes a pair of point clouds, while our 2D-3D projection module takes the corresponding pairs of RGB images. To concatenate the features of 2D pixels into 3D points, we project XYZ coordinates of each point cloud onto its associated image planes. In our setup, we select the first and the last RBG images among 50 consecutive RGB-D frames that are used to generate the point cloud. Since each point cloud is tied to two color views, we average the feature vectors sampled from the overlapped regions. In the end, we append the feature vectors from 2D pixels to 3D points. We illustrate this projection procedure in Fig. 3. The 3D network remains the same as Predator [23] and we adjust input dimensions of the first layer. The combined features are fed into the KPConv encoder and are crossed at the bottleneck part via attention modules, which is identical to Predator [23].

2D Pre-trained Networks. We empirically find appending RGB values to 3D points brings less gain. Similar results are observed in ImVoteNet [31] and 3DMV [12], and we also confirm this in the low-level task. Therefore, we propose to lift deep color features rather than RGB values. In our module, the 2D network is a standard ResUNet-50 backbone. We choose ResUNet since its encoder weights can be initialized by most popular 2D pre-trained models, such as ImageNet, Pri3D [21] and SuperGlue [37]. In this manner, we can easily change to different pre-trained networks. In ablation studies, we indicate that different 2D pre-trained weights have a significant influence on the 3D results.

Frame Selection. Each point cloud is fused by 50 consecutive depth frames. We propose to use the first and last frames considering the performance and efficiency. Regarding the number of selected frames, we present the color coverage in Fig. 4. We show an increasing registration recall with more views in the ablation study.

Implicit vs. Explicit Projection. Implicit projection lifts the features of every pixel, while the other projects features of some certain pixels in an explicit man-

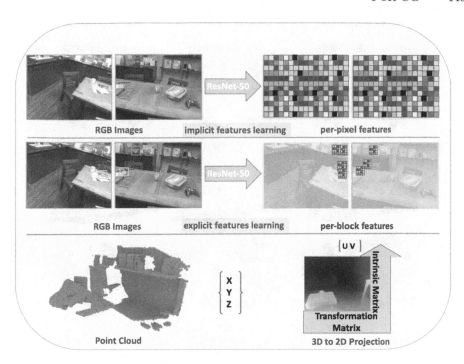

Fig. 3. PCR-CG: 2D-3D Projection Module. We introduce a novel 2D-3D Projection Module to lift 2D color features into 3D. The module takes the transformation matrix and depth map to project regional features to 3D point cloud.

ner. In our design, we use a pre-trained 2D network, i.e., SuperGlue [37], to predict the correspondences between the source and target RGB frames. Then, we project features extracted from the regions around the correspondences. In this manner, the regions are lifted explicitly to 3D, which indicates a rough overlap estimated from color signals. We experimentally demonstrate the advantages of explicit projection in the ablation study.

4   Experimental Results

In this section, we show experimental results and ablation studies regarding the proposed 2D-3D projection module. We focus on indoor data, namely *3DMatch* and *3DLoMatch*. In the main result, different numbers of points are sampled for registration in RANSAC. Additionally, we conduct ablation studies, such as different projections and 2D pre-trained weights in Sect. 4.1.

Experiments Setup. For training, we use the SGD optimizer with learning rate 0.005 and a batch size of 1. We use the exponential learning scheduler, and the learning rate is decreased by a factor of 0.95 in every epoch. During the test, we use open3D for feature matching and RANSAC. For 2D networks, we

One View Projection   **Two View Projection**   **Three View Projection**

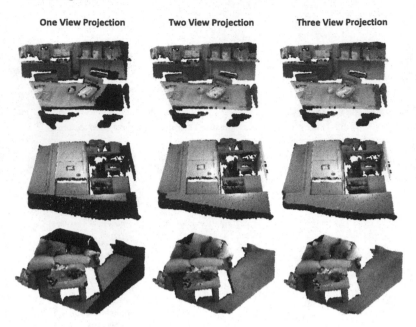

Fig. 4. Non-black points take 2D features; black points indicate no features taken from 2D. We observe not every point can be associated with the color features with one image; with two views, most points have the coverage of projected color features. However, adding the third view does not significantly improve cover coverage. Therefore, we choose two views as a default setup.

use ResUNet-50 to extract per-pixel features. KPConv [44] is used as the 3D Backbone.

Metrics. We mainly compare the results on four metrics, namely Registration Recall (RR), Feature Matching Recall (FMR), Relative Rotation Error (RRE), and Relative Translation Error (RTE). RR is the main metric we compare on and is most reliable, representing the fraction of pairs of point cloud, for which the correct transformation parameters are found after correspondence matching and RANSAC. Similar to Predator, we also report FMR, defined as the fraction of pairs that has at least 5% inlier matches. RTE and RRE measure the deviations from the ground truth pose. More specifically, RTE is computed by the differences between two frames by L1 norm; RRE is the drifted degrees between two frames registered by predicted transformation. Please refer to supplementary materials for detailed explanations and mathematical definitions.

3DLoMatch. We show results on 3DLoMatch in Table 1. In 3DLoMatch, each pair of frames has at most 30% overlaps, and therefore it is a more challenging benchmark. We compare our method with SOTA methods in terms of RR and FMR. We show our method outperforms previous algorithms, including the most recent CoFiNet [46] on different numbers of sampled points. More specifically, PCR-CG surpasses our baseline Predator by a large margin, especially with less

Table 1. Results on *3DMatch* and *3DLoMatch*. Our holistic approach combining explicit deep color and geometric features results in significantly improved results over previous approaches including the most recent CoFiNet. PCR-CG surpasses our baseline Predator [23] by a large margin. Note that our approach uses the same backbone and pipeline as Predator and does not include the coarse-to-fine technique compared to CoFiNet [46]. Pri3D pre-trained model and two-view projection (explicit) are used for our approach.

# Sampled points	3DMatch					3DLoMatch				
	5000	2500	1000	500	250	5000	2500	1000	500	250
Feature Matching Recall(%) ↑										
3DSN [16]	95.0	94.3	92.9	90.1	82.9	63.6	61.7	53.6	45.2	34.2
FCGF [10]	97.4	97.3	97.0	96.7	96.6	76.6	75.4	74.2	71.7	67.3
D3Feat [6]	95.6	95.4	94.5	94.1	93.1	67.3	66.7	67.0	66.7	66.5
SpinNet [1]	97.4	97.0	96.4	96.7	94.8	75.5	75.1	74.2	69.0	62.7
Predator [23]	96.6	96.6	96.5	96.3	96.5	78.6	77.4	76.3	75.7	75.3
CoFiNet [46]	**98.1**	**98.3**	**98.1**	**98.2**	**98.3**	**83.1**	**83.5**	**83.3**	<u>83.1</u>	<u>82.6</u>
Ours – PCR-CG	97.4	<u>97.5</u>	<u>97.7</u>	<u>97.3</u>	<u>97.6</u>	<u>80.4</u>	<u>82.2</u>	<u>82.6</u>	**83.2**	**82.8**
Registration Recall(%) ↑										
3DSN [16]	78.4	76.2	71.4	67.6	50.8	33.0	29.0	23.3	17.0	11.0
FCGF [10]	85.1	84.7	83.3	81.6	71.4	40.1	41.7	38.2	35.4	26.8
D3Feat [6]	81.6	84.5	83.4	82.4	77.9	37.2	42.7	46.9	43.8	39.1
SpinNet [1]	88.8	88.0	84.5	79.0	69.2	58.2	56.7	49.8	41.0	26.7
Predator [23]	89.0	<u>89.9</u>	**90.6**	<u>88.5</u>	86.6	59.8	61.2	62.4	60.8	58.1
CoFiNet [46]	<u>89.3</u>	88.9	88.4	87.4	**87.0**	**67.5**	<u>66.2</u>	<u>64.2</u>	<u>63.1</u>	<u>61.0</u>
Ours – PCR-CG	**89.4**	**90.7**	<u>90.0</u>	**88.7**	<u>86.8</u>	<u>66.3</u>	**67.2**	**69.0**	**68.5**	**65.0**

sampled points, e.g., +7.7% on RR and +7.5% on FMR respectively with 500 sampled points. In Table 2, our approach outperforms previous methods also on Relative Rotation and Translation Errors. Besides the quantitative results, we show qualitative results in 3DLoMatch benchmark in Fig. 6.

3DMatch. We additionally report numbers on 3DMatch benchmark, where the overlap between two frames is at least 30%. Compared to 3DLoMatch, 3DMatch is easier and saturated. In Table 1, our proposed method outperforms our baseline Predator in both RR and FMR in most cases. Our method surpasses all the other methods, including the most recent CoFiNet, except for 5000 sampled points in FMR and 1000 sampled points in RR, where we achieve the second best number. In Table 2, our method also achieves SOTA results on Relative Rotation Error and Relative Translation Error (Fig. 5).

Predator   CoFiNet   Ours: PCR-CG   Ground Truth

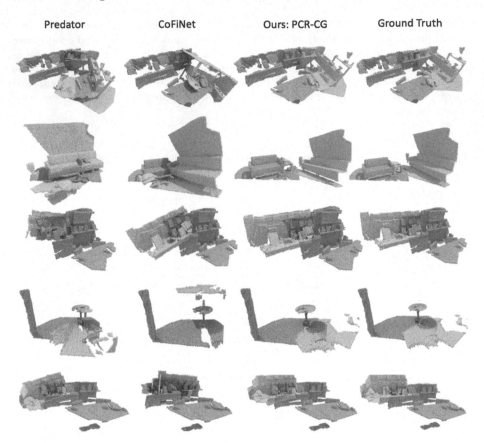

Fig. 5. Qualitative Comparisons on *3DLoMatch*. With the help of our proposed 2D-3D projection module, PCR-CG outperforms SOTA methods, such as our baseline Predator.

4.1 Ablation Study

In this section, we ablate the different designs of projecting 2D to 3D for point cloud registration task. We prove that our design of explicitly leveraging the color signals achieves the best result. Furthermore, we show the significant influence of the 2D pre-trained network and the frame selection on the final 3D registration results. We conduct our ablation experiments in *3DLoMatch* benchmark.

Frame Selection and Color Coverage. In 3DLoMatch benchmark, each point cloud is fused by 50 consecutive frames. To ensure 100% color coverage, 50 frames must be all used for each point cloud. However, 50 times forward and backward passes are time-consuming. To ensure the color coverage as well as efficiency, we propose to use the first and last frame to back-project pixel features into 3D geometry. The visuals in Fig. 4 demonstrate that there are approximately 30% points that are not covered with one frame. With two views, most points are

Input   Color ICP   Ours: PCR-CG   Ground Truth

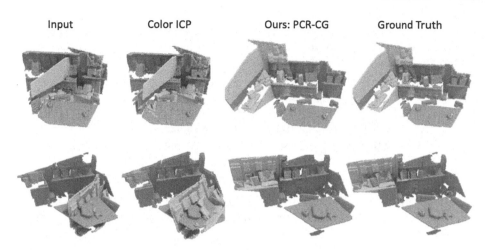

Fig. 6. Qualitative Comparisons on *3DLoMatch*. Compared to ColorICP [30], our method is more robust to initialization, especially in the case of large transformation and low overlaps such as in 3DLoMatch.

covered. With three views, it only slightly improves the color coverage. Quantitatively, the registration recall confirms the observation. To provide in-depth analysis of how much influence it has in terms of the number of views, we adjust the numbers of images used in the training and test. In Table 7, we can clearly see the signal that using more views leads to an increasing registration recall, which proves that the proposed 2D-3D Projection Module contributes significantly to the 3D registration task.

Deep Color Features vs. RGBs. We compare our method to ColorICP [30] in Table 3 to show the effectiveness of deep color features. Similar to ICP, ColorICP also requires a good pose initialization. With original pose initialization that has a large transformation, both ICP and ColorICP failed to align two point clouds. With improved poses estimated by our method as initialization, both show marginal improvements. This observation demonstrates the importance of our method by embedding deep rather than shallow color features into geometry. Similarly, we use SIFT estimated from RGB images to register their point clouds. This result indicates the same conclusion and is showed in Table 5.

2D Pre-trained Networks. PCR-CG lifts the 2D features into 3D. Therefore, massive existing 2D pre-trained models can be used. In Table 4, we show the influence of 2D representation on 3D results. We ablate on 2D models, such as ImageNet [13] and Pri3D [21] pre-trained weights. With 2D pre-trained weights, we achieve better 3D results compared to random initialization (Scratch). In general, we notice the trend that our method can achieve better registration recall numbers with more powerful 2D pre-trained models.

Table 2. Relative Rotation Errors (RRE) and Relative Translation Errors (RTE) with 5,000 sampled points on 3DMatch and 3DLoMatch benchmarks. Our approach achieves the best in RTE, and the second best in RRE.

	3DMatch		3DLoMatch	
	RRE (°)	RTE (m)	RRE (°)	RTE (m)
3DSN [16]	2.199	0.071	3.528	0.103
FCGF [10]	**1.949**	0.066	3.146	0.100
D3Feat [6]	2.161	0.067	3.361	0.103
Predator [23]	2.029	0.064	3.048	0.093
CoFiNet [46]	2.002	0.064	3.271	0.090
Ours – PCR-CG	1.993	**0.061**	**3.002**	**0.087**

Table 3. Registration Recall on *3DMatch* and *3DLoMatch*. Our method outperforms ICP and ColorICP on both benchmarks by large margins and more robust to the bad pose initialization.

	Original initial pose		Improved initial pose	
	3DMatch	3DLoMatch	3DMatch	3DLoMatch
ICP [36]	4.20	1.40	91.0	68.5
ColorICP [30]	4.90	1.50	**91.4**	**68.8**
PCR-CG	**90.7**	**68.2**	–	–

Table 4. Ablation study on different 2D pre-trained models. We observe a clear correlation between 2D pre-trained weights and 3D results when explicitly lifting deep color features. Using 2D pre-trained weights indicates higher registration recalls. Two-view project is used. Note that all 2D models are pre-trained on other data, thus showing a strong transfer ability in our method.

	2D Backbone	Registration Recall (%)				
		5000	2500	1000	500	250
PCR-CG	Scratch	66.1	67.2	68.2	68.3	64.7
PCR-CG	ImageNet	66.3	**67.9**	68.9	66.1	65.0
PCR-CG	Pri3D	**66.3**	67.2	**69.0**	**68.5**	**65.0**

Table 5. We utilize OpenCV SIFT-DLT [28] to calculate relative image pose and corresponding registration recall on 3DLoMatch benchmark.

	3DLoMatch	3DMatch
SIFT-DLT	0.4	0.9

Table 6. Ablation study on window sizes in 3DLoMatch. We empirically found 11×11 window size shows the best performance. Two-view projection is used. SuperGlue [37] is used to find correspondences and Pri3D [21] pre-trained model is used for feature extraction.

	Window size	Registration Recall (%)				
		5000	2500	1000	500	250
PCR-CG	3×3	63.1	64.0	65.1	64.6	60.7
PCR-CG	7×7	64.7	66.4	67.1	65.8	62.6
PCR-CG	11×11	**66.3**	**67.2**	**69.0**	**68.5**	**65.0**
PCR-CG	17×17	64.1	65.7	66.2	65.6	62.1

Table 7. Ablation study on color coverage. We show an increasing registration recall with more views used. SuperGlue [37] is used to find correspondences and Pri3D [21] pre-trained model is used for feature extraction.

	Views	Registration Recall (%)				
		5000	2500	1000	500	250
PCR-CG	1	64.4	67.0	66.6	66.4	64.3
PCR-CG	2	66.3	67.2	69.0	68.5	65.0
PCR-CG	3	**66.7**	**67.9**	**69.1**	**68.7**	**65.1**

Window Size. We ablate different window sizes for extracting deep color features, and empirically find window size 11×11 achieves the best performance (see Table 6).

Implicit vs. Explicit Projection. Adding color to 3D is non-trival. As aforementioned, we explore different ways of projecting 2D into 3D. Implicit one projects all the pixel values/features onto 3D, while explicit one leverages the 2D overlap information to project features region by region. We experimentally show that our design outperforms the rest. In Table 8, we show different combinations of 2D pre-trained weights and projections. In general, projecting deep color features such as Pri3D outperforms SIFT features and RGB values. In addition, we show that explicit projection outperforms implicit projection.

Different Baselines. We adopt the same backbone and pipeline as Predator. However, our module is not specifically tied to Predator. Notably, our module is agnostic to methods, and it is easy to be plugged into any frameworks operating on RGB-D data. In Table 9, we demonstrate that our module also brings a significant improvement on CoFiNet baseline, i.e., +3.5% Registration Recall at 5,000 sampled points.

Table 8. Ablation study on projections. RGB means simply appending RGB colors to point cloud. SIFT refers to projecting SIFT features onto points. Pri3D uses pre-trained weights to extract per-pixel features and projects them onto points. Similarly, SuperGlue/ImageNet refers to projecting SuperGlue/ImageNet pre-trained features. We show projecting deep color features outperforms SIFT and RGB values with the same projection. Implicit manner projects features of every pixel onto 3D, while explicit one projects features based on correspondences estimated by SuperGlue. We demonstrate the explicit projection surpasses the implicit one. Two-view projection is used in the experiments.

Method	Features	Projection	Registration Recall (%)				
			5000	2500	1000	500	250
PCR-CG	RGB	Implicit	60.5	63.0	63.6	62.3	59.4
PCR-CG	RGB	Explicit	60.4	63.1	63.5	62.8	59.9
PCR-CG	SIFT	Implicit	63.1	65.1	65.5	64.9	61.4
PCR-CG	SIFT	Explicit	64.8	67.0	67.1	66.5	63.9
PCR-CG	SuperGlue	Explicit	64.0	65.0	65.0	65.0	60.8
PCR-CG	ImageNet	Implicit	63.2	65.4	65.7	64.9	61.1
PCR-CG	ImageNet	Explicit	66.3	**67.9**	68.9	66.1	65.0
PCR-CG	Pri3D	Implicit	63.4	65.4	66.0	65.2	61.4
PCR-CG	Pri3D	Explicit	**66.3**	67.2	**69.0**	**68.5**	**65.0**

Table 9. Registration Recall based on CoFiNet on 3DLoMatch benchmark. We can notice a clear gap of plugging in our module compared to CoFiNet baseline. In this ablation experiment, our implementation is built upon the officially released code of CoFiNet. Thus, we re-train the official released code for a fair comparison. Pri3D pre-trained model and two-view projection (explicit) are used.

Baseline method	Registration Recall (%)				
	5000	2500	1000	500	250
CoFiNet	67.5	66.2	64.2	63.1	61.0
CoFiNet (re-train)	64.4	64.2	63.1	62.1	59.8
CoFiNet + PCR-CG	**67.9**	**67.0**	**65.4**	**64.2**	**62.2**

5　Conclusion

In this work, we correlate color and geometry for point cloud registration. To fully leverage RGB-D data, we propose a novel 2D-3D projection module to explicitly lift 2D features into 3D. Our module enables the usage of massive existing 2D pre-trained networks in 3D registration tasks. We hope our research can inspire the community to pay more attention on joint learning with color and geometry on various computer vision applications.

Acknowledgments. This work is supported by the Joint Funds of Zhejiang NSFC (LTY22F020001) and Open Research Fund of State Key Laboratory of Transient Optics and Photonics. Yu Zhang is the corresponding author.

References

1. Ao, S., Hu, Q., Yang, B., Markham, A., Guo, Y.: SpinNet: learning a general surface descriptor for 3D point cloud registration. In: CVPR, pp. 11753–11762 (2021)
2. Aoki, Y., Goforth, H., Srivatsan, R.A., Lucey, S.: PointNetLK: robust & efficient point cloud registration using pointnet. In: CVPR, pp. 7163–7172 (2019)
3. Armeni, I., et al.: 3D semantic parsing of large-scale indoor spaces. In: ICCV (2016)
4. Arun, K.S., Huang, T.S., Blostein, S.D.: Least-squares fitting of two 3-D point sets. TPAMI **5**, 698–700 (1987)
5. Bai, X., et al.: PointDSC: robust point cloud registration using deep spatial consistency. In: CVPR, pp. 15859–15869 (2021)
6. Bai, X., Luo, Z., Zhou, L., Fu, H., Quan, L., Tai, C.L.: D3Feat: joint learning of dense detection and description of 3D local features. In: CVPR, pp. 6359–6367 (2020)
7. Balntas, V., Doumanoglou, A., Sahin, C., Sock, J., Kouskouridas, R., Kim, T.K.: Pose guided RGBD feature learning for 3D object pose estimation. In: CVPR, pp. 3856–3864 (2017)
8. Besl, P.J., McKay, N.D.: Method for registration of 3-D shapes. In: Sensor Fusion IV: Control Paradigms and Data Structures, vol. 1611, pp. 586–606. International Society for Optics and Photonics (1992)
9. Chang, A., et al.: Matterport3D: learning from RGB-D data in indoor environments. arXiv preprint arXiv:1709.06158 (2017)
10. Choy, C., Park, J., Koltun, V.: Fully convolutional geometric features. In: CVPR, pp. 8958–8966 (2019)
11. Dai, A., Chang, A.X., Savva, M., Halber, M., Funkhouser, T., Nießner, M.: ScanNet: richly-annotated 3D reconstructions of indoor scenes. In: CVPR (2017)
12. Dai, A., Nießner, M.: 3DMV: joint 3D-multi-view prediction for 3D semantic scene segmentation. In: ECCV, pp. 452–468 (2018)
13. Deng, J., Dong, W., Socher, R., Li, L.J., Li, K., Fei-Fei, L.: ImageNet: a large-scale hierarchical image database. In: CVPR (2009)
14. El Banani, M., Gao, L., Johnson, J.: UnsupervisedR&R: unsupervised point cloud registration via differentiable rendering. In: CVPR, pp. 7129–7139 (2021)
15. El Banani, M., Johnson, J.: Bootstrap your own correspondences. In: ICCV, pp. 6433–6442 (2021)
16. Gojcic, Z., Zhou, C., Wegner, J.D., Wieser, A.: The perfect match: 3D point cloud matching with smoothed densities. In: CVPR, pp. 5545–5554 (2019)
17. He, K., Gkioxari, G., Dollár, P., Girshick, R.: Mask R-CNN. In: ICCV (2017)
18. He, K., Zhang, X., Ren, S., Sun, J.: Deep residual learning for image recognition. In: CVPR (2016)
19. Hou, J., Dai, A., Nießner, M.: 3D-SIS: 3D semantic instance segmentation of RGB-D scans. In: CVPR (2019)
20. Hou, J., Dai, A., Nießner, M.: RevealNet: seeing behind objects in RGB-D scans. In: CVPR (2020)
21. Hou, J., Xie, S., Graham, B., Dai, A., Nießner, M.: Pri3D: can 3D priors help 2D representation learning? In: Proceedings of the IEEE/CVF International Conference on Computer Vision, pp. 5693–5702 (2021)

22. Hu, W., Zhao, H., Jiang, L., Jia, J., Wong, T.T.: Bidirectional projection network for cross dimension scene understanding. In: CVPR, pp. 14373–14382 (2021)
23. Huang, S., Gojcic, Z., Usvyatsov, M., Wieser, A., Schindler, K.: PREDATOR: Registration of 3D point clouds with low overlap. In: CVPR, pp. 4267–4276 (2021)
24. Lahoud, J., Ghanem, B., Pollefeys, M., Oswald, M.R.: 3D instance segmentation via multi-task metric learning. In: ICCV (2019)
25. Liu, Y., Fan, Q., Zhang, S., Dong, H., Funkhouser, T., Yi, L.: Contrastive multi-modal fusion with tupleinfonce. In: CVPR, pp. 754–763 (2021)
26. Liu, Y., Yi, L., Zhang, S., Fan, Q., Funkhouser, T., Dong, H.: P4contrast: contrastive learning with pairs of point-pixel pairs for RGB-D scene understanding. arXiv preprint arXiv:2012.13089 (2020)
27. Liu, Z., Qi, X., Fu, C.W.: 3D-to-2D distillation for indoor scene parsing. In: CVPR, pp. 4464–4474 (2021)
28. Lowe, D.G.: Distinctive image features from scale-invariant keypoints. IJCV **60**(2), 91–110 (2004)
29. Niethammer, M., Kwitt, R., Vialard, F.X.: Metric learning for image registration. In: ICCV, pp. 8463–8472 (2019)
30. Park, J., Zhou, Q.Y., Koltun, V.: Colored point cloud registration revisited. In: ICCV, pp. 143–152 (2017)
31. Qi, C.R., Chen, X., Litany, O., Guibas, L.J.: ImVoteNet: boosting 3D object detection in point clouds with image votes. In: CVPR (2020)
32. Qi, C.R., Litany, O., He, K., Guibas, L.J.: Deep Hough voting for 3D object detection in point clouds. In: ICCV, pp. 9277–9286 (2019)
33. Qi, C.R., Su, H., Mo, K., Guibas, L.J.: PointNet: deep learning on point sets for 3D classification and segmentation. In: CVPR (2017)
34. Qin, Z., Yu, H., Wang, C., Guo, Y., Peng, Y., Xu, K.: Geometric transformer for fast and robust point cloud registration. In: CVPR, pp. 11143–11152 (2022)
35. Revaud, J., et al.: R2D2: repeatable and reliable detector and descriptor. arXiv preprint arXiv:1906.06195 (2019)
36. Rusinkiewicz, S., Levoy, M.: Efficient variants of the ICP algorithm. In: Proceedings Third International Conference on 3-D Digital Imaging and Modeling, pp. 145–152. IEEE (2001)
37. Sarlin, P.E., DeTone, D., Malisiewicz, T., Rabinovich, A.: SuperGlue: learning feature matching with graph neural networks. In: CVPR (2020)
38. Sarlin, P.E., DeTone, D., Malisiewicz, T., Rabinovich, A.: SuperGlue: learning feature matching with graph neural networks. In: CVPR, pp. 4938–4947 (2020)
39. Schönberger, J.L., Frahm, J.M.: Structure-from-motion revisited. In: CVPR (2016)
40. Schönberger, J.L., Zheng, E., Frahm, J.-M., Pollefeys, M.: Pixelwise view selection for unstructured multi-view stereo. In: Leibe, B., Matas, J., Sebe, N., Welling, M. (eds.) ECCV 2016. LNCS, vol. 9907, pp. 501–518. Springer, Cham (2016). https://doi.org/10.1007/978-3-319-46487-9_31
41. Song, S., Xiao, J.: Sliding shapes for 3D object detection in depth images. In: Fleet, D., Pajdla, T., Schiele, B., Tuytelaars, T. (eds.) ECCV 2014. LNCS, vol. 8694, pp. 634–651. Springer, Cham (2014). https://doi.org/10.1007/978-3-319-10599-4_41
42. Srinivasan, P.P., Wang, T., Sreelal, A., Ramamoorthi, R., Ng, R.: Learning to synthesize a 4D RGBD light field from a single image. In: CVPR, pp. 2243–2251 (2017)
43. Stückler, J., Gutt, A., Behnke, S.: Combining the strengths of sparse interest point and dense image registration for RGB-D odometry. In: ISR/Robotik; International Symposium on Robotics, pp. 1–6. VDE (2014)

44. Thomas, H., Qi, C.R., Deschaud, J.E., Marcotegui, B., Goulette, F., Guibas, L.J.: KPConv: flexible and deformable convolution for point clouds. In: CVPR (2019)
45. Xu, C., et al.: Image2Point: 3D point-cloud understanding with 2D image pre-trained models (2021)
46. Yu, H., Li, F., Saleh, M., Busam, B., Ilic, S.: CofiNet: reliable coarse-to-fine correspondences for robust pointcloud registration. In: NeurIPS, vol. 34 (2021)
47. Zeng, A., Song, S., Nießner, M., Fisher, M., Xiao, J., Funkhouser, T.: 3DMatch: learning local geometric descriptors from RGB-D reconstructions. In: CVPR (2017)
48. Zhou, Q., Sattler, T., Leal-Taixe, L.: Patch2Pix: epipolar-guided pixel-level correspondences. In: ICCV, pp. 4669–4678 (2021)

GLAMD: Global and Local Attention Mask Distillation for Object Detectors

Younho Jang[1], Wheemyung Shin[1], Jinbeom Kim[2], Simon Woo[2(✉)], and Sung-Ho Bae[1(✉)]

[1] Kyung Hee University, Seoul, South Korea
{2014104142,wheemi,shbae}@khu.ac.kr
[2] Sungkyunkwan University, Seoul, South Korea
{kjinb1212,swoo}@g.skku.edu

Abstract. Knowledge distillation (KD) is a well-known model compression strategy to improve models' performance with fewer parameters. However, recent KD approaches for object detection have faced two limitations. First, they distill nearby foreground regions, ignoring potentially useful background information. Second, they only consider global contexts, thereby the student model can hardly learn local details from the teacher model. To overcome such challenging issues, we propose a novel knowledge distillation method, GLAMD, distilling both global and local knowledge from the teacher. We divide the feature maps into several patches and apply an attention mechanism for both the entire feature area and each patch to extract the global context as well as local details simultaneously. Our method outperforms the state-of-the-art methods with 40.8 AP on COCO2017 dataset, which is 3.4 AP higher than the student model (ResNet50 based Faster R-CNN) and 0.7 AP higher than the previous global attention-based distillation method.

Keywords: Knowledge distillation · Object detection

1 Introduction

Recent advancements in deep convolutional neural networks have achieved remarkable success in various applications, especially for visual tasks such as image classification [11,29,34] and object detection [2,10,17,18,24–27,31]. With their high performance, current deep-learning-based methods have been integrated and deployed for a wide range of real-world applications such as CCTV surveillance, autonomous driving, and unmanned store. Although recent deep

---

Y. Jang and W. Shin—Equal contribution.

Supplementary Information The online version contains supplementary material available at https://doi.org/10.1007/978-3-031-20080-9_27.

(a) Original   (b) Global attention   (c) Ours

Fig. 1. Visualization of the attention masks generated by (b) Zhang *et al.* [36], and (c) GLAMD (Ours). Zhang *et al.* [36] focus only on a single small region, ignoring the other important regions. On the other hand, our attention mask successfully represents the other important local regions (people, bikes, etc.).

learning models have demonstrated promising results, deploying deep-learning-based applications on mobile or edge devices is still challenging. This is because of limited computing resources on devices. To address this issue, model compression techniques such as weight pruning [9,15], model quantization [14], and Knowledge Distillation (KD) [13] have been introduced.

In particular, KD is one of the most promising methods for reducing the parameters of deep Convolutional Neural Networks (CNN) models while effectively achieving high performance. The KD method is formalized by Hinton *et al.* [13] which uses the prediction logits of a large and cumbersome teacher model to train a lightweight student model. Hence, the soft labels from the teacher model can help the student model to mimic the teacher model's decision, producing improved performance with the small number of parameters in the student model.

However, most distillation methods [13,22,28,30,32] developed for classification are not suitable for object detection tasks because of the class imbalance problem in object detection and the absence of localization knowledge in the previous KD methods. For instance, hint learning [28] is proposed to distill the teacher model's intermediate feature maps, however it does not transfer the teacher's classification and localization information of bounding boxes. To solve this issue, Chen *et al.* [3] introduce a method of distilling feature, classification, and localization information for object detectors. Nevertheless, the method in [3] still does not effectively distill the teacher's information due to the imbalance between foreground and background. To reduce overwhelmingly large background data and further distill only from the informative foreground regions, Wang *et al.* [33] propose the mask-based feature distillation method that filters out the background regions based on ground truth. This method still has the problem of providing uniform weights to target regions regardless of the importance. Hence Zhang *et al.* [36] propose to apply an attention mechanism on a global feature map to generate a mask with soft weights, where the mask allows to deliver knowledge from the selective regions with high importance.

However, we find that considering only global feature contexts can lose important knowledge in the teacher's features because of the following two major drawbacks. First, they mainly consider the foreground regions while hardly providing attention to background regions. Ignoring the background area is not ideal because there can be valuable knowledge in the background for object detection [8]. Therefore, the key enhancement for improving distillation performance in object detection tasks is carefully selecting informative regions from both background and foreground, effectively balancing and leveraging all information from them. Second, since the global mask-based methods only focus on a few global contexts of the entire features, some important local details that are evenly distributed across the entire regions can be ignored. For example, Zhang *et al.* [36] apply the softmax function on the global area to generate a mask that provides substantial weights to a single foreground object and barely provides attention to the other objects and background regions, as shown in Fig. 1(b).

To overcome the aforementioned limitations, we propose GLAMD, Global and Local Attention Mask Distillation for object detector, a novel patch-based attention mechanism that considers the both global contexts and local details of the teacher's features. GLAMD creates global and local attention masks by applying an attention mechanism to global features and local features divided by patches. The generated mask is then applied to the intermediate features, classification output, and regression output to distill the teacher's knowledge more efficiently.

Figure 1 illustrates the attention masks generated by the previous global attention method [36] and our patch-based attention method. Compared to the global attention mask that focuses only on one person in Fig. 1(b), the local-patch mask generated by our method in Fig. 1(c) covers other informative objects such as people and a bike. Since the mask is generated by applying an attention mechanism at the both global and local levels, we call the proposed mask Global and Local Attention Mask (GLAM) in this work. With the proposed GLAM, our method jointly considers the detailed information from the background and foreground. As a result, ResNet50 based Faster R-CNN with GLAMD achieves 40.8 AP on COCO2017 dataset [19], which is a 3.4 AP improvement over the baseline and 0.7 AP higher than the previous global attention mask method [36]. Our main contributions are summarized as follows: (1) we propose an attention-based distillation method that effectively incorporates a local perspective to overcome the limitation of the global attention mask that focuses on small areas of the image; and (2) we present quantitative and qualitative results and ablation studies of our distillation method on various object detection models, including two-stage, one-stage, and anchor-free detectors in the COCO dataset, achieving the state-of-the-art performance.

2   Related Work

2.1   Object Detection

Recently, object detection models have been developed as two-stage detectors [2,10,27] as well as one-stage detectors [16,18,25,26]. First, two-stage detectors, such as Faster-RCNN [27], utilize the region proposal network (RPN) and refinement procedure of bounding boxes. While two-stage detectors retain a high detection accuracy, their computational complexity precludes them from being used for real-time detection. In comparison to two-stage detectors, one-stage detectors such as RetinaNet [18] have lower latency since they extract bounding boxes straight from the feature map.

These anchor-based models achieve successful results in object detection by using predefined anchors. However, predefined anchors bring a huge number of outputs, resulting in substantial computational costs. Anchor-free models [31, 37] have been proposed to further reduce the computational cost by directly predicting critical bounding box information. As a result, anchor-free models are lighter than anchor-based models. Nevertheless, the detection performance of these models is proportional to their model size. Due to the models' enormous computational complexity, deploying detection models to mobile devices with low computing and storage capacity has been challenging. Therefore, model compression techniques such as weight pruning, model quantization, and knowledge distillation have been proposed to address such issues.

2.2   Knowledge Distillation

KD is a compression method for enhancing the small student model performance by using output from the large teacher model. As a result, extracting useful information from the teacher in the distillation process has become critical. In general, there are three different distillation approaches: response-based [13], feature-based [1, 12, 28, 35], and relation-based [20, 22, 30, 32]. The response-based distillation by Hinton et al. [13] selects the teacher's softmax logits and teaches the student by transferring the dark knowledge of the teacher. The feature-based distillation by Romero et al. [28] attempts to improve the performance of the student network by matching the teacher's intermediate features to the student's features. The relation-based distillation by Park et al. [22] uses information from several sample images in a mini-batch to calculate distance and angle relationships among the features.

However, there is still an issue with applying the aforementioned distillation approaches to object detection models since each local region contributes differently to student models' training. To address this issue, previous research employs a selective distillation method focusing on training-relevant local regions by applying masks. Wang et al. [33] focus on the area of the anchor boxes with a larger IoU with ground-truth than the flexible thresholds. Dai et al. [5] propose a distillation mask focusing on discriminative instances by calculating differences between the outputs of the teacher and the student. On the other hand, Zhang et al. [36] design a soft mask by extracting intermediate feature attention that focuses on the backbone network's concentrated regions. However, as networks often provide overwhelmingly large attention weights to a small region, the existing global softmax attention masks tend to neglect other critical regions. Therefore, we propose generating an attention mask for each local patch, which can focus on other significant regions that contain local knowledge to further improve the performance.

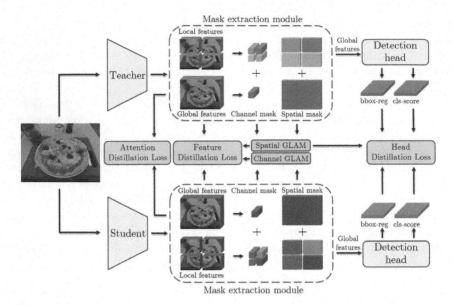

Fig. 2. The overall architecture of the proposed GLAMD. Local features are created by dividing the global features, which are the network's output with fixed-size patches. We then generate attention masks by taking average and the softmax function in channel and spatial directions. The proposed GLAM is generated by combining masks of the teacher and student. Finally, GLAM is applied in distillation losses.

2.3   Local Patch Mechanism

Recently, local patches-based methods are widely employed in various tasks, such as image classification [7,21] and object detection [6]. Dosovitskiy *et al.* [7] propose a transformer-based image classification model, namely ViT, which divides a single input image into several fixed-sized local patches and feeds them into the transformer module. Also, Liu *et al.* [21] design a hierarchical network with multiple stages that divides a local window into numerous sub-patches to calculate its attention. Their approach captures the interactions between the local windows by shifting the sub-patches over the network. Ding *et al.* [6] propose an approach to divide low-level features into local patches and then apply patch-wise channel attention to easily detect small objects that have been difficult to find in a global image. These approaches above effectively employ local patches from the input images, improving the overall network performance by recognizing local regions where the global context can hardly represent. Therefore, to overcome the limitation of the previous global mask-based distillation methods, we propose a novel mask-based distillation with local patches, which effectively distills both global and local knowledge.

3   Methods

Previous research [36] selectively distills features by applying global attention masks. However, [36] tends to distill only a small feature region because the global attention mask highlights a single spot, ignoring other multiple local details. To address this issue, we propose a novel mask that reflects the global and local characteristics of the features. It also can be used for feature and head distillation, as shown in Fig. 2.

3.1   Global and Local Attention Mask (GLAM)

In this section, we describe the global and local attention masks (GLAM), a core component of the proposed GLAMD. The attention methods used in GLAM are channel and spatial attention methods denoted as M_c and M_s, respectively. To obtain the channel attention masks, the spatial-wise average of the absolute feature elements $|x_{i,j}|$ is used in a softmax operation in the channel dimension as follows:

$$M_c(x) = HW \cdot \sigma \left(\frac{\frac{1}{HW} \cdot \sum_{i=1}^{H} \sum_{j=1}^{W} (|x_{i,j}|)}{\tau} \right), \tag{1}$$

where τ and $\sigma(\cdot)$ indicate a temperature parameter and a softmax operation, respectively, and H and W are the height and width of the input feature, respectively. Similarly, to obtain the spatial attention masks, the channel-wise average of the absolute feature elements $|x_k|$ is used in a softmax operation in the width and height dimensions as follows:

$$M_s(x) = C \cdot \sigma \left(\frac{\frac{1}{C} \cdot \sum_{k=1}^{C} (|x_k|)}{\tau} \right), \tag{2}$$

where C is the channel of the input feature.

To generate our proposed GLAM which considers local and global perspectives, we split each output feature of Feature Pyramid Network (FPN) into N local features $f_n \in \mathbb{R}^{p \times p \times C}$, where p is the predetermined patch size and $n \in \{1, 2, ..., N\}$. Then, the local channel mask L_c and local spatial mask L_s are formulated as follows:

$$L_{c,n} = M_c(f_n^{\mathcal{T}}) + M_c(f_n^{\mathcal{S}}), \quad L_c = \psi \left(L_{c,1}, L_{c,2}, ..., L_{c,N} \right), \tag{3}$$

$$L_{s,n} = M_s(f_n^{\mathcal{T}}) + M_s(f_n^{\mathcal{S}}), \quad L_s = \psi \left(L_{s,1}, L_{s,2}, ..., L_{s,N} \right), \tag{4}$$

where $\mathcal{T}$ and $\mathcal{S}$ indicate the teacher and student, respectively, and ψ denotes the concatenation operation. Similarly, given a global feature $F \in \mathbb{R}^{H \times W \times C}$, the global channel mask G_c and global spatial mask G_s are computed as follows:

$$G_c = M_c(F^{\mathcal{T}}) + M_c(F^{\mathcal{S}}), \quad G_s = M_s(F^{\mathcal{T}}) + M_s(F^{\mathcal{S}}). \tag{5}$$

By merging the local and global masks, our final channel and spatial attention masks, denoted as T_c and T_s, respectively, are constructed as follows:

$$T_c = \frac{1}{2} \cdot (L_c + G_c), \quad T_s = \frac{1}{2} \cdot (L_s + G_s). \tag{6}$$

3.2   Feature Distillation

Typically, the teacher's features are more informative than the student's features. Therefore, we distill the intermediate features extracted from the FPN to increase the student's performance. The feature in each stage is multiplied with the corresponding channel and spatial attention masks to selectively distill the area of interest. That is, our feature distillation loss is defined as follows:

$$\mathcal{L}_{feat} = \sum_{l=1}^{L} \left(\sum_{k=1}^{C} \sum_{i=1}^{H} \sum_{j=1}^{W} \left(F_{lkij}^{\mathcal{T}} - \phi_{adapt}(F_{lkij}^{\mathcal{S}}) \right)^2 \cdot T_{s,l} \cdot T_{c,l} \right)^{\frac{1}{2}}, \tag{7}$$

where L is the number of FPN stages and the function ϕ_{adapt} is the 1×1 convolutional adaptation layer that matches the student's feature size to that of the teacher's feature. And, $T_{s,l}$ and $T_{c,l}$ mean spatial and channel masks of the l-th stage, respectively.

   In addition, we distill the attention features to encourage the student in producing more effective GLAM. Hence, the extraction process of the channel and spatial attention feature can be formulated as $A_c(x) = \frac{1}{C} \cdot \sum_{k=1}^{C} x_k$ and $A_s(x) = \frac{1}{HW} \cdot \sum_{i=1}^{H} \sum_{j=1}^{W} x_{ij}$. Then, the channel attention loss is calculated by distilling both global and local channel attention features in our work. In particular, global and local spatial attention features are considered to be equivalent, as local features are formed by dividing global features into the spatial domain. As a result, in contrast to channel attention loss, spatial attention loss utilizes only global spatial attention features. Therefore, our proposed channel attention loss $\mathcal{L}_{cat}$ and spatial attention loss $\mathcal{L}_{sat}$ can be expressed as follows:

$$\mathcal{L}_{cat} = \frac{1}{2} \cdot \left(\left\| A_c(F^{\mathcal{S}}) - A_c(F^{\mathcal{T}}) \right\|_2 + \frac{1}{N} \cdot \sum_{n=1}^{N} \left\| A_c(f_n^{\mathcal{S}}) - A_c(f_n^{\mathcal{T}}) \right\|_2 \right), \tag{8}$$

$$\mathcal{L}_{sat} = \left\| A_s(F^{\mathcal{S}}) - A_s(F^{\mathcal{T}}) \right\|_2. \tag{9}$$

Finally, the overall feature attention loss is formulated by the sum of the channel and spatial attention losses, as follows:

$$\mathcal{L}_{at} = \mathcal{L}_{cat} + \mathcal{L}_{sat}. \tag{10}$$

3.3   Head Distillation

The response-based distillation encourages the student's outputs to mimic the teacher's. However, due to the imbalance between the foreground and background in object detection tasks, directly distilling the teacher's head outputs can cause a detrimental effect on the student's performance. Therefore, in this work, we apply spatial attention masks while performing the response-based distillation. Especially, we use the spatial attention masks from the same FPN stage in Eq. 6 to conduct the masked head distillation. The classification head loss $\mathcal{L}_{cls-head}$ can be defined as follows:

$$\mathcal{L}_{cls-head} = \sum_{l=1}^{L}\sum_{k=1}^{C}\sum_{i=1}^{H}\sum_{j=1}^{W}\mathcal{L}_{BCE}\left(z_{lkij}^{S}, z_{lkij}^{T}\right) \cdot T_{s,l}, \qquad (11)$$

where z^{S} and z^{T} represent the outputs of the student and the teacher classification head, respectively, and $\mathcal{L}_{BCE}$ represents the binary-cross-entropy loss.

According to Chen et al. [3], certain unbounded outputs of the teacher can provide incorrect guidance to the student model. To avoid the aforementioned issue, we distill the localization head using IoU loss, one of the bounded loss functions. For the localization head distillation, we use IoU loss to formulate the localization head loss as follows:

$$\mathcal{L}_{loc-head} = \sum_{l=1}^{L}\sum_{k=1}^{C}\sum_{i=1}^{H}\sum_{j=1}^{W}\mathcal{L}_{IoU}\left(r_{lkij}^{S}, r_{lkij}^{T}\right) \cdot T_{s,l}, \qquad (12)$$

where r is the localization head output.

3.4   Overall Loss Function

We form appropriate distillation losses using the outputs of the modules in the detector and construct an overall loss by taking weighted sum with the standard classification and localization losses for the object detection task, denoted as $\mathcal{L}_{task}$. Our overall loss is defined as follows:

$$\mathcal{L} = \mathcal{L}_{task} + \alpha\mathcal{L}_{feat} + \beta\mathcal{L}_{at} + \gamma(\mathcal{L}_{cls-head} + \mathcal{L}_{loc-head}), \qquad (13)$$

where α, β, and γ are the balancing hyper-parameters with the distillation loss and the task loss.

4   Experiment

4.1   Experiments Settings

To demonstrate the effectiveness of our method, we evaluate our method on various object detection models and compare the results with other KD methods [28,33,36,38]. All experiments are implemented using the mmdetection

Table 1. The generalization ability of our GLAMD in various object detectors.

Method	Scheduler	AP	AP_{50}	AP_{75}	AP_S	AP_M	AP_L
Faster-ResNet50 (Student)	1×	37.4	58.1	40.4	21.2	41.0	48.1
Faster-ResNext101 (Teacher)	3×	43.1	63.6	47.2	26.5	46.9	56.0
GLAMD (Ours)	1×	**40.8**	**61.4**	**44.3**	**23.2**	**45.0**	**53.2**
Cascade-ResNet50 (Student)	1×	40.3	58.6	44.0	22.5	43.8	52.9
Cascade-ResNext101 (Teacher)	3×	44.5	63.2	48.5	25.5	48.1	58.4
GLAMD (Ours)	1×	**43.0**	**61.5**	**46.8**	**24.1**	**47.3**	**56.8**
Mask-ResNet50 (Student)	1×	38.2	58.8	41.4	21.9	40.9	49.5
Mask-ResNext101 (Teacher)	2×	42.7	62.9	47.1	23.8	46.5	56.7
GLAMD (Ours)	1×	**40.2**	**61.1**	**43.7**	**23.0**	**44.3**	**52.6**
RetinaNet-ResNet50 (Student)	1×	36.5	55.4	39.1	20.4	40.3	48.1
RetinaNet-ResNext101 (Teacher)	3×	41.6	61.4	44.3	23.9	45.5	54.5
GLAMD (Ours)	1×	**40.0**	**59.5**	**42.5**	**22.8**	**44.0**	**53.4**
GFL-ResNet50 (Student)	1×	40.2	58.4	43.3	23.3	44.0	52.2
GFL-ResNet101 (Teacher)	2×	44.9	63.1	49.0	28.0	49.1	57.2
GLAMD (Ours)	1×	**43.0**	**61.0**	**46.5**	**26.4**	**47.4**	**55.2**
ATSS-ResNet50 (Student)	1×	39.4	57.6	42.8	23.6	42.9	50.3
ATSS-ResNet101 (Teacher)	1×	41.5	59.9	45.2	24.2	45.9	53.3
GLAMD (Ours)	1×	**41.0**	**59.1**	**44.3**	**23.8**	**45.1**	**52.9**
FCOS-ResNet50 (Student)	1×	36.6	56.0	38.8	21.0	40.6	47.0
FCOS-ResNet101 (Teacher)	1×	39.1	58.3	42.1	22.7	43.3	50.3
GLAMD (Ours)	1×	**38.6**	**58.1**	**41.2**	**22.8**	**42.5**	**49.3**

library [4] with PyTorch framework [23] on the COCO dataset [19]. We train our model with 120k training images and test with 5k validation images from the COCO dataset. All the performances are evaluated in average precision (AP). We use 4 RTX3090 GPUs during training and use the batch size of 16.

For all experiments, student models are trained under 1× scheduler, the default setting of the mmdetection, to train 12 epochs on the COCO dataset. We start training with a warm-up strategy during the first 2,000 iterations and perform a learning rate decay, which divides the learning rate by 10 at the 8-th and 11-th epochs. We use the SGD optimizer to train the detection model, and set the learning rate to 0.02 in Faster R-CNN and 0.01 in the rest of the models. Also, the weight decay and momentum are set to 1e-4 and 0.9, respectively. We set the hyper-parameters in Eq. 13 to $\{\alpha = 4 \times 10^{-4}, \beta = 2 \times 10^{-2}, \gamma = 1 \times 10^{-1}, \tau = 1 \times 10^{-1}\}$ for single-stage detectors and $\{\alpha = 7 \times 10^{-5}, \beta = 4 \times 10^{-3}, \gamma = 1 \times 10^{-1}, \tau = 5 \times 10^{-1}\}$ for two-stage detectors.

4.2 Results on Different Detection Frameworks

We evaluate the generalization ability of our proposed GLAMD on multiple detection architectures, including two-stage [2,10,27], one-stage [16,18], and

Table 2. Comparison with various object detection KD methods.

Method	Scheduler	AP	AP_{50}	AP_{75}	AP_S	AP_M	AP_L
RetinaNet-ResNet50 (Student)	1×	36.5	55.4	39.1	20.4	40.3	48.1
RetinaNet-ResNext101 (Teacher)	3×	41.6	61.4	44.3	23.9	45.5	54.5
Hint learning [28]	1×	37.1	56.5	39.2	21.4	40.7	48.8
Wang et al. [33]	1×	38.4	57.5	41.1	20.8	42.0	51.9
Zhang et al. [36]	1×	39.0	58.1	41.8	22.3	42.9	51.7
FRS [38]	1×	39.3	58.7	41.9	21.4	43.1	52.3
GLAMD (Ours)	1×	**40.0**	**59.5**	**42.5**	**22.8**	**44.0**	**53.4**
Faster-ResNet50 (Student)	1×	37.4	58.1	40.4	21.2	41.0	48.1
Faster-ResNext101 (Teacher)	3×	43.1	63.6	47.2	26.5	46.9	56.0
Hint learning [28]	1×	38.7	59.7	41.8	23.1	42.0	50.9
Wang et al. [33]	1×	39.5	59.9	43.2	21.7	43.4	**53.2**
Zhang et al. [36]	1×	40.1	60.8	43.4	22.9	44.1	53.1
FRS [38]	1×	40.3	**61.8**	43.9	**23.3**	44.3	52.4
GLAMD (Ours)	1×	**40.8**	61.4	**44.3**	23.2	**45.0**	53.2
Cascade-ResNet50 (Student)	1×	40.3	58.6	44.0	22.5	43.8	52.9
Cascade-ResNext101 (Teacher)	3×	44.5	63.2	48.5	25.5	48.1	58.4
Hint learning [28]	1×	40.6	59.4	44.4	22.9	44.1	53.8
Wang et al. [33]	1×	41.7	60.6	45.6	23.3	45.2	55.9
Zhang et al. [36]	1×	42.4	60.9	46.2	23.4	46.2	56.1
FRS [38]	1×	42.7	61.3	46.7	**24.4**	46.3	56.2
GLAMD (Ours)	1×	**43.0**	**61.5**	**46.8**	24.1	**47.3**	**56.8**

anchor-free [31,37] detectors. For all the detectors, we use ResNext101 [34] or ResNet101 [11] as backbones of teachers and ResNet50 as backbones of students, respectively. As shown in Table 1, our proposed method achieves significant gains in terms of AP on all types of detection architectures. On average, our method obtains 3.2 and 2.7 AP boosts, outperforming the baseline one-stage and two-stage detectors, respectively. For anchor-free detectors (ATSS and FCOS), our method obtains APs of 41.0 and 38.6 that are comparable to the teacher models. Such results demonstrate that our method is effective in various detectors.

4.3 Comparison with Other KD Methods

To compare the results of our method with other KD methods, we evaluate our method and recent KD methods on both one-stage (RetinaNet [18]) and two-stage detectors (Faster R-CNN [27] and Cascade R-CNN [2]). The comparison results with other KD methods are provided in Table 2. As shown in Table 2, our approach outperforms all previous KD methods in distillation performance. In particular, the results achieved by ours are 1.0, 0.7, and 0.6 AP higher than the results from the global attention-based method [36], respectively. Also, our method outperforms the recent distillation method FRS [38]. It clearly shows

Table 3. Ablation study for the contribution of each module in GLAMD. "Feat", "Cls Head", and "Loc Head" indicate each distillation loss used in our model. "GLAM" indicates applying our mask (GLAM) to distillation losses.

Feat	GLAM	Cls Head	Loc Head	AP	AP_{50}	AP_{75}	AP_S	AP_M	AP_L
✗	✗	✗	✗	36.5	55.4	39.1	20.4	40.3	48.1
✓	✗	✗	✗	37.1	56.5	39.2	21.4	40.7	48.8
✓	✓	✗	✗	39.5	58.9	42.0	23.2	43.5	52.0
✓	✓	✓	✗	39.7	59.2	42.4	**23.5**	**44.1**	52.5
✓	✓	✗	✓	39.6	58.9	42.3	22.1	43.6	51.9
✓	✓	✓	✓	**40.0**	**59.5**	**42.5**	22.8	44.0	**53.4**

Table 4. Experimental results for comparing performance change according to different types of attention masks.

Local	Global	AP	AP_S	AP_M	AP_L
✗	✗	38.7	22.7	42.5	51.8
✓	✗	39.8	**23.3**	44.0	53.0
✗	✓	38.9	22.4	42.8	52.0
✓	✓	**40.0**	22.8	**44.0**	**53.4**

that local knowledge extracted by our method effectively enhances the overall distillation performance.

4.4   Ablation Study

We conduct four different ablation studies to further explore the properties of our proposed method.

Modules in GLAMD. To verify the effect of each module in Eq. 13, we evaluate the detection performance with and without each of them in GLAMD. The result of the ablation study is presented in Table 3. Our method achieves 0.2 and 0.1 AP improvements on the classification head and regression head, respectively. When we conduct distillation from both classification and regression heads together, our method achieves 0.5 AP improvement. These results show that each part of the distillation loss in our method contributes to the performance gain, and fully utilizing our losses in the form of Eq. 12 can improve the final AP performance in a complementary manner.

Effectiveness of Local Attention Mask Distillation. Due to the biased distribution of the global attention mask, KD with the global feature attention tends to distill knowledge from a single large object. On the other hand, we hypothesize that the local feature attention can extract knowledge from small objects as well. To analyze the effectiveness of each attention mask, we perform

Table 5. Performance under different settings of the patch size p.

p	3	5	7	9	11
AP	39.7	39.7	**40.0**	39.8	39.7

Table 6. Results of three different loss functions used in $\mathcal{L}_{loc-head}$.

Loss	L_1	MSE	Smooth-L_1	**IoU**
AP	39.9	39.8	39.8	**40.0**

distillation with local or global attention masks individually. As shown in Table 4, local attention achieves higher AP than global attention, especially with significantly improved AP for small objects. Although the global attention result is worse than the local attention, it is noteworthy to observe that detection performance further increases by using global attention and local attention together. These results indicate that the local attention mask proposed by our GLAMD is complementary to the global attention mask to improve the performance further.

Effect of Local Patch Size. The primary parameter affecting local attention is the patch size. To evaluate the influence of the patch size, we alter the patch size in $[3, 5, 7, 9, 11]$. As shown in Table 5, the performance in AP tends to increase when the patch size decreases until the patch size of 7. This is because attention masks generated from small patches are suitable for representing fine-grained features, yet extremely tiny patches are incapable of capturing the underlying local structure. More efficient theoretical ways to determine the optimal p can be further investigated as future work.

Comparison of Different Localization Head Distillation Loss. We also study the impact of different types of loss functions used in Eq. 12. To verify the effectiveness of the bounded regression loss in Eq. 12, We compare the distillation performance of various loss functions including IoU loss, L1 loss, MSE loss, and smooth-L1 loss. As shown in Table 6, IoU loss produces the best result among the other losses.

4.5   Qualitative Analysis and Visualizations

The visualizations of the global attention mask generated by [36] and our mask generated by GLAMD are shown in Fig. 3. We observe that our mask encompasses various critical regions that the global attention mask overlooks. This property of our mask results in two significant enhancements in terms of mask distribution: (1) It captures the fine-grained details from various objects. For instance, our mask pays attention to a kid in Fig. 3(a) and another polar bear in Fig. 3(b) which are considered as the background in global attention; (2) It extracts structural information such as edges and lines from objects. In Fig. 3(e), our mask provides weight to the edges of the tent and car, demonstrating that it extracts crucial clues from the local objects for solving the challenging object detection tasks.

Next, Fig. 4 qualitatively compares the results produced by a model with our method and a baseline student model without KD. The results show that our

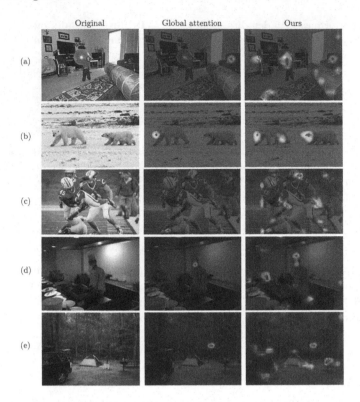

Fig. 3. Visualization of masks on COCO2017 samples. The original images are shown in the first column. Global attention masks [36] and our masks are shown in the second and the third columns, respectively.

Fig. 4. Qualitative analysis on COCO2017. The results are produced by a model without KD (baseline) and a model distilled with GLAMD. The orange boxes in (a), (c), and (d) indicate undetected objects of the baseline detector, and the box in (b) shows a wrongly detected object.

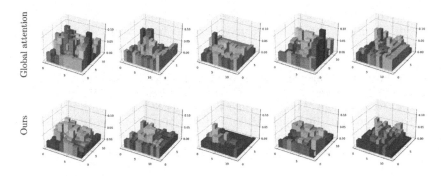

Fig. 5. Visualizations of the L1 distances between the local features of teacher and student. The distance maps in the top row are produced by a model trained with a global attention mask method and the distance maps in the bottom row are produced by a model trained with GLAMD.

method improves the detection performance by taking advantage of GLAM. As shown in Fig. 4(a) and (c), small objects neglected by the baseline model are detected after applying GLAMD, demonstrating that it is effective at enhancing the student model's capability to extract local information. Additionally, our method strengthens the student's ability to distinguish occluded objects by distilling knowledge about the object's edge, shown in Fig. 4(b) and (d).

4.6 Feature Similarity

We visualize patch-wise distance maps in Fig. 5. For the visualization, we calculate the L1 distance between the features of the teacher and the student. Next, we average the distance values in each patch to generate the distance maps. As shown in Fig. 5, the distance is much lower in every patch with GLAMD than with a global attention mask method. This means that our method encourages students to mimic the teacher's feature map more closely across all local regions owing to the local attention masks.

5 Conclusions

In this paper, we propose GLAMD, a novel mask-based KD method for object detection that effectively applies global and local attention mechanisms to extract local details and background knowledge. To obtain local details, we divide the input features into several patches and apply attention mechanisms to each patch. Our method enables the extraction of more useful background information as well as fine-grained details from a variety of objects, resulting in much improved distillation performance. We demonstrate GLAMD's effectiveness with the various detection frameworks, outperforming other KD methods. Additionally, we conduct an extensive ablation study and analysis, showing that distilling local knowledge from various regions is crucial in object detection tasks.

We expect that our work provides a turning point of conventional KD methods for object detection that focus exclusively on global knowledge to develop into more effective approaches that consider local knowledge as well.

Acknowledgments. This work was partially supported by the Institute of Information and Communications Technology Planning and Evaluation (IITP) grant funded by the Korea Government (MSIT) (Artificial Intelligence Innovation Hub) under Grant 2021-0-02068, and partially supported by Institute of Information & communications Technology Planning & Evaluation (IITP) grant funded by the Korea government (MSIT) (No.2019-0-00421, AI Graduate School Support Program (Sungkyunkwan University)

References

1. Ahn, S., Hu, S.X., Damianou, A., Lawrence, N.D., Dai, Z.: Variational information distillation for knowledge transfer. In: Proceedings of the IEEE/CVF Conference on Computer Vision and Pattern Recognition, pp. 9163–9171 (2019)
2. Cai, Z., Vasconcelos, N.: Cascade R-CNN: high quality object detection and instance segmentation. IEEE Trans. Pattern Anal. Mach. Intell. **43**(5), 1483–1498 (2019)
3. Chen, G., Choi, W., Yu, X., Han, T., Chandraker, M.: Learning efficient object detection models with knowledge distillation. In: Advances in Neural Information Processing Systems, vol. 30 (2017)
4. Chen, K., et al.: MMDetection: Open MMLab detection toolbox and benchmark. arXiv preprint arXiv:1906.07155 (2019)
5. Dai, X., et al.: General instance distillation for object detection. In: Proceedings of the IEEE/CVF Conference on Computer Vision and Pattern Recognition (CVPR), pp. 7842–7851 (2021)
6. Ding, L., Tang, H., Bruzzone, L.: LANet: local attention embedding to improve the semantic segmentation of remote sensing images. IEEE Trans. Geosci. Remote Sens. **59**(1), 426–435 (2020)
7. Dosovitskiy, A., et al.: An image is worth 16×16 words: transformers for image recognition at scale. arXiv preprint arXiv:2010.11929 (2020)
8. Guo, J., et al.: Distilling object detectors via decoupled features. In: Proceedings of the IEEE/CVF Conference on Computer Vision and Pattern Recognition, pp. 2154–2164 (2021)
9. Guo, Y., Yao, A., Chen, Y.: Dynamic network surgery for efficient DNNs. In: Advances in Neural Information Processing Systems, vol. 29 (2016)
10. He, K., Gkioxari, G., Dollár, P., Girshick, R.: Mask R-CNN. In: Proceedings of the IEEE International Conference on Computer Vision, pp. 2961–2969 (2017)
11. He, K., Zhang, X., Ren, S., Sun, J.: Deep residual learning for image recognition. In: Proceedings of the IEEE Conference on Computer Vision and Pattern Recognition, pp. 770–778 (2016)
12. Heo, B., Kim, J., Yun, S., Park, H., Kwak, N., Choi, J.Y.: A comprehensive overhaul of feature distillation. In: Proceedings of the IEEE/CVF International Conference on Computer Vision, pp. 1921–1930 (2019)
13. Hinton, G., Vinyals, O., Dean, J., et al.: Distilling the knowledge in a neural network. arXiv preprint arXiv:1503.02531, vol. 2, no. 7 (2015)

14. Jacob, B., et al.: Quantization and training of neural networks for efficient integer-arithmetic-only inference. In: Proceedings of the IEEE Conference on Computer Vision and Pattern Recognition, pp. 2704–2713 (2018)

15. Li, H., Kadav, A., Durdanovic, I., Samet, H., Graf, H.P.: Pruning filters for efficient convnets. arXiv preprint arXiv:1608.08710 (2016)

16. Li, X., et al.: Generalized focal loss: learning qualified and distributed bounding boxes for dense object detection. In: Advances in Neural Information Processing Systems, vol. 33, pp. 21002–21012 (2020)

17. Lin, T.Y., Dollár, P., Girshick, R., He, K., Hariharan, B., Belongie, S.: Feature pyramid networks for object detection. In: Proceedings of the IEEE Conference on Computer Vision and Pattern Recognition, pp. 2117–2125 (2017)

18. Lin, T.Y., Goyal, P., Girshick, R., He, K., Dollár, P.: Focal loss for dense object detection. In: Proceedings of the IEEE International Conference on Computer Vision, pp. 2980–2988 (2017)

19. Lin, T.-Y., et al.: Microsoft COCO: common objects in context. In: Fleet, D., Pajdla, T., Schiele, B., Tuytelaars, T. (eds.) ECCV 2014. LNCS, vol. 8693, pp. 740–755. Springer, Cham (2014). https://doi.org/10.1007/978-3-319-10602-1_48

20. Liu, Y., et al.: Knowledge distillation via instance relationship graph. In: Proceedings of the IEEE/CVF Conference on Computer Vision and Pattern Recognition, pp. 7096–7104 (2019)

21. Liu, Z., et al.: Swin transformer: hierarchical vision transformer using shifted windows. In: Proceedings of the IEEE/CVF International Conference on Computer Vision, pp. 10012–10022 (2021)

22. Park, W., Kim, D., Lu, Y., Cho, M.: Relational knowledge distillation. In: Proceedings of the IEEE/CVF Conference on Computer Vision and Pattern Recognition, pp. 3967–3976 (2019)

23. Paszke, A., et al.: PyTorch: an imperative style, high-performance deep learning library. In: Advances in Neural Information Processing Systems, vol. 32 (2019)

24. Redmon, J., Divvala, S., Girshick, R., Farhadi, A.: You only look once: unified, real-time object detection. In: Proceedings of the IEEE Conference on Computer Vision and Pattern Recognition, pp. 779–788 (2016)

25. Redmon, J., Farhadi, A.: YOLO9000: better, faster, stronger. In: Proceedings of the IEEE Conference on Computer Vision and Pattern Recognition, pp. 7263–7271 (2017)

26. Redmon, J., Farhadi, A.: YOLOv3: an incremental improvement. arXiv preprint arXiv:1804.02767 (2018)

27. Ren, S., He, K., Girshick, R., Sun, J.: Faster R-CNN: towards real-time object detection with region proposal networks. In: Advances in Neural Information Processing Systems, vol. 28 (2015)

28. Romero, A., Ballas, N., Kahou, S.E., Chassang, A., Gatta, C., Bengio, Y.: FitNets: hints for thin deep nets. arXiv preprint arXiv:1412.6550 (2014)

29. Simonyan, K., Zisserman, A.: Very deep convolutional networks for large-scale image recognition. arXiv preprint arXiv:1409.1556 (2014)

30. Tian, Y., Krishnan, D., Isola, P.: Contrastive representation distillation. arXiv preprint arXiv:1910.10699 (2019)

31. Tian, Z., Shen, C., Chen, H., He, T.: FCOS: fully convolutional one-stage object detection. In: Proceedings of the IEEE/CVF International Conference on Computer Vision, pp. 9627–9636 (2019)

32. Tung, F., Mori, G.: Similarity-preserving knowledge distillation. In: Proceedings of the IEEE/CVF International Conference on Computer Vision, pp. 1365–1374 (2019)

33. Wang, T., Yuan, L., Zhang, X., Feng, J.: Distilling object detectors with fine-grained feature imitation. In: Proceedings of the IEEE/CVF Conference on Computer Vision and Pattern Recognition (CVPR) (2019)
34. Xie, S., Girshick, R., Dollár, P., Tu, Z., He, K.: Aggregated residual transformations for deep neural networks. In: Proceedings of the IEEE Conference on Computer Vision and Pattern Recognition, pp. 1492–1500 (2017)
35. Yim, J., Joo, D., Bae, J., Kim, J.: A gift from knowledge distillation: fast optimization, network minimization and transfer learning. In: Proceedings of the IEEE Conference on Computer Vision and Pattern Recognition, pp. 4133–4141 (2017)
36. Zhang, L., Ma, K.: Improve object detection with feature-based knowledge distillation: towards accurate and efficient detectors. In: International Conference on Learning Representations (2020)
37. Zhang, S., Chi, C., Yao, Y., Lei, Z., Li, S.Z.: Bridging the gap between anchor-based and anchor-free detection via adaptive training sample selection. In: Proceedings of the IEEE/CVF Conference on Computer Vision and Pattern Recognition, pp. 9759–9768 (2020)
38. Zhixing, D., et al.: Distilling object detectors with feature richness. In: Advances in Neural Information Processing Systems, vol. 34 (2021)

FCAF3D: Fully Convolutional Anchor-Free 3D Object Detection

Danila Rukhovich[✉], Anna Vorontsova, and Anton Konushin

Samsung AI Center, Moscow, Russia
{d.rukhovich,a.vorontsova,a.konushin}@samsung.com

Abstract. Recently, promising applications in robotics and augmented reality have attracted considerable attention to 3D object detection from point clouds. In this paper, we present FCAF3D—a first-in-class fully convolutional anchor-free indoor 3D object detection method. It is a simple yet effective method that uses a voxel representation of a point cloud and processes voxels with sparse convolutions. FCAF3D can handle large-scale scenes with minimal runtime through a single fully convolutional feed-forward pass. Existing 3D object detection methods make prior assumptions on the geometry of objects, and we argue that it limits their generalization ability. To eliminate prior assumptions, we propose a novel parametrization of oriented bounding boxes that allows obtaining better results in a purely data-driven way. The proposed method achieves state-of-the-art 3D object detection results in terms of mAP@0.5 on ScanNet V2 (**+4.5**), SUN RGB-D (**+3.5**), and S3DIS (**+20.5**) datasets. The code and models are available at https://github.com/samsunglabs/fcaf3d.

Keywords: 3D object detection · Anchor-free object detection · Sparse convolutional networks

1 Introduction

3D object detection from point clouds aims at simultaneous localization and recognition of 3D objects given a 3D point set. As a core technique for 3D scene understanding, it is widely applied in autonomous driving, robotics, and AR.

While 2D methods [26,32] work with dense fixed-size arrays, 3D methods are challenged by irregular unstructured 3D data of arbitrary volume. Consequently, the 2D data processing techniques are not directly applicable for 3D object detection, so 3D object detection methods [10,19,22] employ inventive approaches to 3D data processing.

Convolutional 3D object detection methods have scalability issues: large-scale scenes either require an impractical amount of computational resources or take

Supplementary Information The online version contains supplementary material available at https://doi.org/10.1007/978-3-031-20080-9_28.

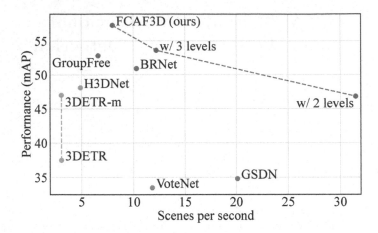

Fig. 1. mAP@0.5 scores on ScanNet against scenes per second. FCAF3D modifications (marked red) have different number of backbone feature levels. For each existing method, there is a FCAF3D modification surpassing this method in both detection accuracy and inference speed. (Color figure online)

too much time to process. Other methods opt for voxel data representation and employ sparse convolutions; however, these methods solve scalability problems at the cost of detection accuracy. In other words, there is no 3D object detection method that provides precise estimates *and* scales well (Fig. 1).

Besides being scalable and accurate, an ideal 3D object detection method should handle objects of arbitrary shapes and sizes without additional hacks and hand-tuned hyperparameters. We argue that prior assumptions on 3D object bounding boxes (e.g. aspect ratios or absolute sizes) restrict generalization and increase the number of hyperparameters and trainable parameters.

On the contrary, we do not want to rely on prior assumptions. We propose an anchor-free method that does not impose priors on objects and addresses 3D object detection with a purely data-driven approach. Moreover, we introduce a novel oriented bounding box (OBB) parametrization inspired by a Mobius strip that reduces the number of hyperparameters. To prove the effectiveness of our parametrization, we conduct experiments on SUN RGB-D with several 3D object detection methods and report improved results for all these methods.

In this paper, we present FCAF3D—a simple, effective, and scalable method for detecting 3D objects from point clouds. We evaluate the proposed method on ScanNet [7], SUN RGB-D [25], and S3DIS [1], demonstrating the solid superiority over the previous state-of-the-art on all benchmarks. On SUN RGB-D and ScanNet, our method surpasses other methods by at least 3.5% mAP@0.5. On S3DIS, FCAF3D outperforms the competitors by a huge margin.

Overall, our contribution is three-fold:

1. To our knowledge, we propose a first-in-class fully convolutional anchor-free 3D object detection method (FCAF3D) for indoor scenes.

2. We present a novel OBB parametrization and prove it to boost the accuracy of several existing 3D object detection methods on SUN RGB-D.
3. Our method significantly outperforms the previous state-of-the-art on challenging large-scale indoor ScanNet, SUN RGB-D, and S3DIS datasets in terms of mAP while being faster on inference.

2   Related Work

Recent 3D object detection methods are designed to be either indoor or outdoor. Indoor and outdoor methods have been developing almost independently, applying domain-specific data processing techniques. Many modern outdoor methods [13,30,35] project 3D points onto a bird-eye-view plane, thus reducing the task of 3D object detection to 2D object detection. Naturally, these methods take advantage of the fast-evolving algorithms for 2D object detection. Given a bird-eye-view projection, [14] processes it in a fully convolutional manner, while [31] exploits 2D anchor-free approach. Unfortunately, the approaches that proved to be effective for both 2D object detection and 3D outdoor object detection cannot be trivially adapted to indoor, as it would require an impracticable amount of memory and computing resources. To address performance issues, different 3D data processing strategies have been proposed. Currently, three approaches dominate the field of 3D object detection - voting-based, transformer-based, and 3D convolutional. Below we discuss each of these approaches in detail; we also provide a brief overview of anchor-free methods.

Voting-Based Methods. VoteNet [22] was the first method that introduced points voting for 3D object detection. VoteNet processes 3D points with PointNet [23], assigns a group of points to each object candidate according to their voted center, and computes object features from each point group. Among the numerous successors of VoteNet, the major progress is associated with advanced grouping and voting strategies applied to the PointNet features. BRNet [4] refines voting results with the representative points from the vote centers, which improves capturing the fine local structural features. MLCVNet [29] introduces three context modules into the voting and classifying stages of VoteNet to encode contextual information at different levels. H3DNet [33] improves the point group generation procedure by predicting a hybrid set of geometric primitives. VENet [28] incorporates an attention mechanism and introduces a vote weighting module trained via a novel vote attraction loss.

All VoteNet-like voting-based methods are limited by design. First, they show poor scalability: as their performance depends on the amount of input data, they tend to slow down if given larger scenes. Moreover, many voting-based methods implement voting and grouping strategies as custom layers, making it difficult to reproduce or debug these methods or port them to mobile devices.

Transformer-Based Methods. The recently emerged transformer-based methods use end-to-end learning and forward pass on inference instead of heuristics and optimization, which makes them less domain-specific. GroupFree [16] replaces VoteNet head with a transformer module, updating object query locations iteratively and ensembling intermediate detection results. 3DETR [19] was the first method of 3D object detection implemented as an end-to-end trainable transformer. However, more advanced transformer-based methods still experience scalability issues similar to early voting-based methods. Differently, our method is fully-convolutional, thus being faster and significantly easier to implement than both voting-based and transformer-based methods.

3D Convolutional Methods. Voxel representation allows handling cubically growing sparse 3D data efficiently. Voxel-based 3D object detection methods [12,18] convert points into voxels and process them with 3D convolutional networks. However, dense volumetric features still consume much memory, and 3D convolutions are computationally expensive. Overall, processing large scenes requires a lot of resources and cannot be done within a single pass.

GSDN [10] tackles performance issues with sparse 3D convolutions. It has encoder-decoder architecture, with both encoder and decoder parts built from sparse 3D convolutional blocks. Compared to the standard convolutional voting-based and transformer-based approaches, GSDN is significantly more memory-efficient and scales to large scenes without sacrificing point density. The major weakness of GSDN is its accuracy: this method is comparable to VoteNet in terms of quality, being significantly inferior to the current state-of-the-art [16].

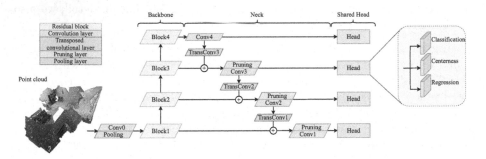

Fig. 2. The general scheme of the proposed FCAF3D. All convolutions and transposed convolutions are three-dimensional and sparse. This design allows processing the input point cloud in a single forward pass.

GSDN uses 15 aspect ratios for 3D object bounding boxes as anchors. If GSDN is trained in an anchor-free setting with a single aspect ratio, the accuracy decreases by 12%. Unlike GSDN, our method is anchor-free while taking advantage of sparse 3D convolutions.

RGB-Based Anchor-Free Object Detection. In 2D object detection, anchor-free methods are solid competitors for the standard anchor-based methods. FCOS [26] addresses 2D object detection in a per-pixel prediction manner and shows a robust improvement over its anchor-based predecessor RetinaNet

[15]. FCOS3D [27] trivially adapts FCOS by adding extra targets for monocular 3D object detection. ImVoxelNet [24] solves the same problem with an FCOS-like head built from standard (non-sparse) 3D convolutional blocks. We adapt the ideas from mentioned anchor-free methods to process sparse irregular data.

3 Proposed Method

Following the standard 3D detection problem statement, FCAF3D accepts N_{pts} RGB-colored points and outputs a set of 3D object bounding boxes. The FCAF3D architecture consists of a backbone, a neck, and a head (depicted in Fig. 2).

While designing FCAF3D, we aim for scalability, so we opt for a GSDN-like sparse convolutional network. For better generalization, we reduce the number of hyperparameters in this network that need to be manually tuned; specifically, we simplify sparsity pruning in the neck. Furthermore, we introduce an anchor-free head with a simple multi-level location assignment. Finally, we discuss the limitations of existing 3D bounding box parametrizations and propose a novel parametrization that improves both accuracy and generalization ability.

3.1 Sparse Neural Network

Backbone. The backbone in FCAF3D is a sparse modification of ResNet [11] where all 2D convolutions are replaced with sparse 3D convolutions. The family of sparse high-dimensional versions of ResNet was first introduced in [5]; for brevity, we refer to them as to HDResNet.

Neck. Our neck is a simplified GSDN decoder. Features on each level are processed with one sparse transposed 3D convolution and one sparse 3D convolution. Each transposed sparse 3D convolution with a kernel size of 2 might increase the number of non-zero values by 2^3 times. To prevent rapid memory growth, GSDN uses the *pruning* layer that filters input with a probability mask.

In GSDN, feature level-wise probabilities are calculated with an additional convolutional scoring layer. This layer is trained with a special loss encouraging consistency between the predicted sparsity and anchors. Specifically, voxel sparsity is set to be positive if any of the subsequent anchors associated with the current voxel is positive. However, using this loss may be suboptimal, as distant voxels of an object might get assigned with a low probability.

For simplicity, we remove the scoring layer with the corresponding loss and use probabilities from the classification layer in the head instead. We do not tune the probability threshold but keep at most N_{vox} voxels to control the sparsity level, where N_{vox} equals the number of input points N_{pts}. We claim this to be a simple yet elegant way to prevent sparsity growth since reusing the same hyperparameter makes the process more transparent and consistent.

Head. The anchor-free FCAF3D head consists of three parallel sparse convolutional layers with weights shared across feature levels. For each location $(\hat{x}, \hat{y}, \hat{z})$, these layers output classification probabilities $\hat{p}$, bounding box regression parameters $\boldsymbol{\delta}$, and centerness $\hat{c}$, respectively. This design is similar to the simple and light-weight head of FCOS [26] but adapted to 3D data.

Multi-level Location Assignment. During training, FCAF3D outputs locations $\{r_i = (\hat{x}_i, \hat{y}_i, \hat{z}_i, k_i)\}$. For a given set of boxes $\{b_j\}$, we define a function $\mu(r)$ that matches a location r with a corresponding box b (if any). Here, $k \in \{1, 2, 3, 4\}$ is the feature level index. The assignment strategy used in FCOS [26] and ImVoxelNet [24] is suboptimal, and its alterations are widely explored in 2D object detection [9,32]. We propose a simplified strategy for sparse data that does not require tuning dataset-specific hyperparameters.

For a box b, let $R_k(b)$ denote the locations inside b at the k-th feature level. We consider the levels with more than N_{loc} locations:

$$\mathcal{K}(b) := \{k : |R_k(b)| > N_{\text{loc}}\}.$$

We select the largest index $k(b)$ from $\mathcal{K}(b)$ if $\mathcal{K}(b) \neq \emptyset$ and set $k(b)$ to 1 otherwise, obtaining a correspondence between a box b and a location $r \in R_{k(b)}(b)$. Finally, for each location r, we select the corresponding box with the least volume:

$$\mu(r) = \underset{b: \; r \in R_{k(b)}(b)}{\arg\min} \; V(b).$$

Finally, we filter locations via *center sampling* [26], considering only the points near the bounding box center as positive matches (Sect. 5.4).

Through assignment, some locations $\{(\hat{x}, \hat{y}, \hat{z})\}$ are matched with ground truth bounding boxes $b_{\hat{x}, \hat{y}, \hat{z}}$. Accordingly, these locations get associated with ground truth labels $p_{\hat{x}, \hat{y}, \hat{z}}$ and 3D centerness values $c_{\hat{x}, \hat{y}, \hat{z}}$. During inference, the scores $\hat{p}$ are multiplied by 3D centerness $\hat{c}$ just before NMS as proposed in [24].

Loss Function. The overall loss function is formulated as follows:

$$L = \frac{1}{N_{\text{pos}}} \sum_{\hat{x}, \hat{y}, \hat{z}} (L_{\text{cls}}(\hat{p}, p) + \mathbb{1}_{\{p_{\hat{x}, \hat{y}, \hat{z}} \neq 0\}} L_{\text{reg}}(\hat{b}, b) + \mathbb{1}_{\{p_{\hat{x}, \hat{y}, \hat{z}} \neq 0\}} L_{\text{cntr}}(\hat{c}, c)). \quad (1)$$

Here, the number of matched locations N_{pos} is $\sum_{\hat{x}, \hat{y}, \hat{z}} \mathbb{1}_{\{p_{\hat{x}, \hat{y}, \hat{z}} \neq 0\}}$. Classification loss L_{cls} is a focal loss, regression loss L_{reg} is IoU, and centerness loss L_{cntr} is binary cross-entropy. For each loss, predicted values are denoted with a hat.

3.2   Bounding Box Parametrization

The 3D object bounding boxes can be axis-aligned (AABB) or oriented (OBB). An AABB can be described as $b^{\text{AABB}} = (x, y, z, w, l, h)$, while the definition of an OBB includes a *heading angle* θ: $b^{\text{OBB}} = (x, y, z, w, l, h, \theta)$. In both formulas, x, y, z denote the coordinates of the center of a bounding box, while w, l, h are its width, length, and height, respectively.

AABB Parametrization. For AABBs, we follow the parametrization proposed in [24]. Specifically, for a ground truth AABB (x, y, z, w, l, h) and a location $(\hat{x}, \hat{y}, \hat{z})$, δ can be formulated as a 6-tuple:

$$\delta_1 = x + \frac{w}{2} - \hat{x}, \; \delta_2 = \hat{x} - x + \frac{w}{2}, \; \delta_3 = y + \frac{l}{2} - \hat{y},$$
$$\delta_4 = \hat{y} - y + \frac{l}{2}, \; \delta_5 = z + \frac{h}{2} - \hat{z}, \; \delta_6 = \hat{z} - z + \frac{h}{2}. \tag{2}$$

The predicted AABB $\hat{b}$ can be trivially obtained from δ.

Heading Angle Estimation. All state-of-the-art 3D object detection methods from point clouds address the heading angle estimation task as classification followed by regression. The heading angle is classified into bins; then, the precise heading angle is regressed within a bin. For indoor scenes, the range from 0 to 2π is typically divided into 12 equal bins [19,21,22,33]. For outdoor scenes, there are usually only two bins [13,30], as the objects on the road can be either parallel or perpendicular to the road.

When a heading angle bin is chosen, the heading angle value is estimated through regression. VoteNet and other voting-based methods estimate the value of θ directly. Outdoor methods explore more elaborate approaches, e.g. predicting the values of trigonometric functions. For instance, SMOKE [17] estimates $\sin\theta$ and $\cos\theta$ and uses the predicted values to recover the heading angle.

Figure 3 depicts indoor objects where the heading angle is unambiguous. Accordingly, ground truth angle annotations can be chosen randomly for these objects, making heading angle bin classification meaningless. To avoid penalizing the correct predictions that do not coincide with annotations, we use

Fig. 3. Examples of objects with an ambiguous heading angle.

rotated IoU loss, as its value is the same for all possible choices of heading angle. Thus, we propose OBB parametrization that considers the rotation ambiguity.

Proposed Mobius OBB Parametrization. Considering the OBB with parameters $(x, y, z, w, l, h, \theta)$, let us denote $q = \frac{w}{l}$. If x, y, z, $w + l$, h are fixed, it turns out that the OBBs with

$$(q, \theta), \; \left(\frac{1}{q}, \theta + \frac{\pi}{2}\right), \; (q, \theta + \pi), \; \left(\frac{1}{q}, \theta + \frac{3\pi}{2}\right) \tag{3}$$

define the same bounding box. We notice that the set of (q, θ), where $\theta \in (0, 2\pi]$, $q \in (0, +\inf)$ is topologically equivalent to a Mobius strip [20] up to this equivalence relation. Hence, we can reformulate the task of estimating (q, θ) as a task of predicting a point on a Mobius strip. A natural way to embed a Mobius strip being a two-dimensional manifold to Euclidean space is the following:

$$(q, \theta) \mapsto (\ln(q)\sin(2\theta), \ln(q)\cos(2\theta), \sin(4\theta), \cos(4\theta)). \tag{4}$$

It is easy to verify that 4 points from Eq. 3 are mapped into a single point in Euclidean space (see Supplementary for details). However, the experiments reveal that predicting only $\ln(q)\sin(2\theta)$ and $\ln(q)\cos(2\theta)$ provides better results than predicting all four values. Thereby, we opt for a *pseudo* embedding of a Mobius strip to $\mathbb{R}^2$. We call it *pseudo* since it maps the entire center circle of a Mobius strip defined by $\ln(q) = 0$ to $(0,0)$. Accordingly, we cannot distinguish points with $\ln q = 0$. However, $\ln(q) = 0$ implies strict equality of w and l, which is rare in real-world scenarios. Moreover, the choice of an angle has a minor effect on the IoU if $w = l$; thereby, we ignore this rare case for the sake of detection accuracy and simplicity of the method. Overall, we obtain a novel OBB parametrization:

$$\delta_7 = \ln\frac{w}{l}\sin(2\theta), \quad \delta_8 = \ln\frac{w}{l}\cos(2\theta). \tag{5}$$

In the standard parametrization 2, $\hat{\boldsymbol{b}}$ is trivially derived from $\boldsymbol{\delta}$. In the proposed parametrization, w, l, θ are non-trivial and can be obtained as follows:

$$w = \frac{sq}{1+q}, \quad l = \frac{s}{1+q}, \quad \theta = \frac{1}{2}\arctan\frac{\delta_7}{\delta_8}, \tag{6}$$

where ratio $q = e^{\sqrt{\delta_7^2 + \delta_8^2}}$ and size $s = \delta_1 + \delta_2 + \delta_3 + \delta_4$.

4   Experiments

4.1   Datasets

We evaluate our method on three 3D object detection benchmarks: ScanNet V2 [7], SUN RGB-D [25], and S3DIS [1]. For all datasets, we use mean average precision (mAP) under IoU thresholds of 0.25 and 0.5 as a metric.

ScanNet. The ScanNet dataset contains 1513 reconstructed 3D indoor scans with per-point instance and semantic labels of 18 object categories. Given this annotation, we calculate AABBs via the standard approach [22]. The training subset is comprised of 1201 scans, while 312 scans are left for validation.

SUN RGB-D. SUN RGB-D is a monocular 3D scene understanding dataset containing more than 10,000 indoor RGB-D images. The annotation consists of per-point semantic labels and OBBs of 37 object categories. As proposed in [22], we run experiments with objects of the 10 most common categories. The training and validation splits contain 5285 and 5050 point clouds, respectively.

S3DIS. Stanford Large-Scale 3D Indoor Spaces dataset contains 3D scans of 272 rooms from 6 buildings, with 3D instance and semantic annotation. Following [10], we evaluate our method on furniture categories. AABBs are derived from 3D semantics. We use the official split, where 68 rooms from *Area 5* are intended for validation, while the remaining 204 rooms comprise the training subset.

4.2   Implementation Details

Hyperparameters. For all datasets, we use the same hyperparameters except for the following. First, the size of output classification layer equals the number of object categories, which is 18, 10, and 5 for ScanNet, SUN RGB-D, and S3DIS. Second, SUN RGB-D contains OBBs, so we predict additional targets δ_7 and δ_8 for this dataset; note that the loss function is not affected. Last, ScanNet, SUN RGB-D, and S3DIS contain different numbers of scenes, so we repeat each scene 10, 3, and 13 times per epoch, respectively.

Similar to GSDN [10], we use the sparse 3D modification of ResNet34 named HDResNet34 as a backbone. The neck and the head use the outputs of the backbone at all feature levels. In initial point cloud voxelization, we set the voxel size to 0.01 m and the number of points N_{pts} to 100,000. Respectively, N_{vox} equals to 100,000. Both ATSS [32] and FCOS [26] set N_{loc} to 3^2 for 2D object detection. Accordingly, we select a feature level so bounding box covers at least $N_{loc} = 3^3$ locations. We select 18 locations by center sampling. The NMS IoU threshold is 0.5.

Training. We implement FCAF3D using the MMdetection3D [6] framework. The training procedure follows the default MMdetection [3] scheme: training takes 12 epochs and the learning rate decreases on the 8th and the 11th epochs. We employ the Adam optimizer with an initial learning rate of 0.001 and weight decay of 0.0001. All models are trained on two NVidia V100 with a batch size of 8. Evaluation and performance tests are run on a single NVidia GTX1080Ti.

Table 1. Results of FCAF3D and existing indoor 3D object detection methods that accept point clouds. The best metric values are marked bold. FCAF3D outperforms previous state-of-the-art methods: GroupFree (on ScanNet and SUN RGB-D) and GSDN (on S3DIS). The reported metric value is the best one across 25 trials; the average value is given in brackets.

Method	Presented at	ScanNet		SUN RGB-D		S3DIS	
		mAP@0.25	mAP@0.5	mAP@0.25	mAP@0.5	mAP@0.25	mAP@0.5
VoteNet [22]	ICCV'19	58.6	33.5	57.7	-	-	-
3D-MPA [8]	CVPR'20	64.2	49.2	-	-	-	-
HGNet [2]	CVPR'20	61.3	34.4	61.6	-	-	-
MLCVNet [29]	CVPR'20	64.5	41.4	59.8	-	-	-
GSDN [10]	ECCV'20	62.8	34.8	-	-	47.8	25.1
H3DNet [33]	ECCV'20	67.2	48.1	60.1	39.0	-	-
BRNet [4]	CVPR'21	66.1	50.9	61.1	43.7	-	-
3DETR [19]	ICCV'21	65.0	47.0	59.1	32.7	-	-
VENet [28]	ICCV'21	67.7	-	62.5	39.2	-	-
GroupFree [16]	ICCV'21	69.1 (68.6)	52.8 (51.8)	63.0 (62.6)	45.2 (44.4)	-	-
FCAF3D	-	**71.5** (70.7)	**57.3** (56.0)	**64.2** (63.8)	**48.9** (48.2)	**66.7** (64.9)	**45.9** (43.8)

Evaluation. We follow the evaluation protocol introduced in [16]. Both training and evaluation are randomized, as the input N_{pts} are randomly sampled from the point cloud. To obtain statistically significant results, we run training 5 times and test each trained model 5 times independently. We report both the best and average metrics across 5×5 trials: this allows comparing FCAF3D to the 3D object detection methods that report either a single best or an average value.

5   Results

5.1   Comparison with State-of-the-Art Methods

We compare FCAF3D with previous state-of-the-arts on three indoor benchmarks in Table 1. As one might observe, FCAF3D achieves the best results on all benchmarks. The performance gap is especially tangible in terms of mAP@0.5: our method surpasses previous state-of-the-art by 4.5% on ScanNet and 3.7% on SUN RGB-D. On S3DIS, FCAF3D outperforms weak state-of-the-art by a huge margin. Overall, the proposed method is consistently better than existing methods, setting a new state-of-the-art for indoor 3D object detection. The examples of ScanNet, SUN RGB-D, and S3DIS point clouds with predicted bounding boxes are depicted in Fig. 4, 5, 6.

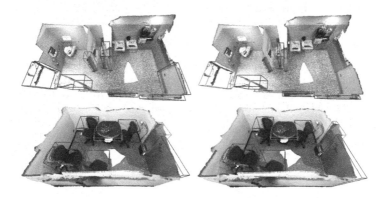

Fig. 4. The point cloud from ScanNet with AABBs. The color of a bounding box denotes the object category. Left: estimated with FCAF3D, right: ground truth. (Color figure online)

Fig. 5. The point cloud from SUN RGB-D with OBBs. The color of a bounding box denotes the object category. Left: estimated with FCAF3D, right: ground truth. (Color figure online)

5.2   Object Geometry Priors

To study geometry priors, we train and evaluate existing methods with proposed modifications. We experiment with 3D object detection methods accepting data of different modalities: point clouds, RGB images, or both, to see whether the effect is data-specific or universal. VoteNet and ImVoteNet have the same head and are trained with the same losses. Among them, there are 4 prior losses: size classification loss, size regression loss, direction classification loss, and direction regression loss. Both classification losses correspond to targets parametrized using priors (per-category mean object sizes and a set of angle bins). Similar to FCAF3D, we replace the aforementioned losses with a rotated IoU loss with Mobius parametrization 5. To give a complete picture, we also try a *sin-cos* parametrization used in the outdoor 3D object detection method SMOKE [17].

The rotated IoU loss decreases the number of trainable parameters and hyperparameters, including geometry priors and loss weights. This loss has already been used in outdoor 3D object detection [34]. Recently, [6] reported results of VoteNet trained with axis-aligned IoU loss on ScanNet.

Table 2 shows that replacing the standard parametrization with Mobius one boosts VoteNet and ImVoteNet mAP@0.5 by approximately 4%. ImVoxelNet does not use a classification+regression scheme to estimate heading angle but predicts its value directly in a single step. Since the original ImVoxelNet uses the rotated IoU loss, we do not need to remove redundant losses, only to change the parametrization. Again, the Mobius parametrization helps to obtain the best results, even though the superiority is minor.

Fig. 6. The point cloud from S3DIS with AABBs. The color of a bounding box denotes the object category. Left: estimated with FCAF3D, right: ground truth. (Color figure online)

5.3 Comparison to GSDN

For a fair comparison, we test our method against GSDN in the most similar scenario. We use a voxel size of 0.05m, ensuring we do not benefit from using more detailed and informative spatial information; the voxel sizes at different feature levels are also of the same sizes (0.2, 0.4, 0.8, 1.6).

As shown in Table 3, the best results are obtained by the original *accurate* FCAF3D with the HDResNet34 backbone, the voxel size of 0.01m, and the default stride of the first convolution of 2: in this setting, FCAF3D outperforms GSDN by a huge margin (mAP@0.25 of 70.7 against 62.8, mAP@0.5 of 56.0 against 34.8). With the same stride of 1, the same voxel size and the same voxel sizes at feature levels, FCAF3D slightly outperforms GSDN in mAP@0.25 (64.2 against 62.8), having a notable gain in mAP@0.5 (46.2 against 34.8).

The *balanced* FCAF3D with a lighter backbone with three feature levels, the voxel size of 0.05m, and the stride of 1 outperforms GSDN in *both accuracy and speed*. Overall, we argue that FCAF3D addresses the 3D object detection in a more efficient way and thus should be preferred.

Moreover, we address the speed issues with the most lightweight HDRes-Net34:2 backbone with two feature levels. The *fast* FCAF3D modification with HDResNet34:2 processes 30 scenes per second, while GSDN is able to handle only 20 scenes. While improving the inference speed, we maintain the superior accuracy: with the voxel size of 0.02m, FCAF3D with a HDResNet34:2 backbone still outperforms GSDN in both mAP@0.25 and mAP@0.5.

Finally, it can be observed that mAP@0.5 drops dramatically by 12% if GSDN is trained in an anchor-free setting (which is equivalent to using one anchor). In other words, GSDN demonstrates a poor performance without

Table 2. Results of several 3D object detection methods that accept inputs of different modalities, with different OBB parametrization on SUN RGB-D. The FCAF3D metric value is the best across 25 trials; the average value is given in brackets. For other methods, we report results from the original papers and also the results obtained through our experiments with MMdetection3D-based re-implementations (marked as Reimpl). PC stands for point cloud.

Method	Input	mAP@0.25	mAP@0.5
VoteNet [22]	PC	57.7	-
Reimpl. [6]		59.1	35.8
Reimpl. w/ IoU loss			
w/ naive param.		61.1 (60.3)	38.4 (37.7)
w/ *sin-cos* param.		60.7 (59.8)	37.1 (36.4)
w/ Mobius param.		**61.1** (60.5)	**40.4** (39.5)
ImVoteNet [21]	RGB +PC	63.4	-
Reimpl. [6]		64.0	37.8
Reimpl. w/IoU loss			
w/naive param.		64.2 (63.9)	39.1 (38.3)
w/*sin-cos* param.		64.6 (64.0)	39.9 (37.8)
w/Mobius param.		**64.6** (64.1)	**40.8** (39.8)
ImVoxelNet [24]	RGB	40.7	-
w/naive param.		41.3 (40.4)	13.8 (13.0)
w/*sin-cos* param.		41.3 (40.5)	13.2 (12.8)
w/Mobius param.		**41.5** (40.6)	**14.6** (14.0)
FCAF3D	PC		
w/naive param.		63.8 (63.5)	46.8 (46.2)
w/*sin-cos* param.		63.9 (63.6)	48.2 (47.3)
w/Mobius param.		**64.2** (63.8)	**48.9** (48.2)

domain-specific guidance in the form of anchors; hence, we claim this method to be inflexible and non-generalizable.

5.4 Ablation Study

In this section, we discuss the FCAF3D design choices and investigate how they affect metrics when applied independently in ablation studies. We run experiments with varying voxel size, the number of points in a point cloud N_{pts}, the number of locations selected by center sampling, and with and without centerness. The results of ablation studies are aggregated in Table 4 for all benchmarks.

Voxel Size. Expectedly, with an increasing voxel size, accuracy goes down. We try voxels of 0.03, 0.02, and 0.01 m. We do not experiment with smaller values since inference would take too much time. We attribute the notable gap in mAP

Table 3. Results of fully convolutional 3D object detection methods that accept point clouds on ScanNet. The FCAF3D results better than the results of the original GSDN (with anchors) are marked bold. The all-best results are underlined.

Method	Backbone	Voxel size [m]	Stride	Feature level voxel sizes [m]	Scenes per sec.	mAP	
						0.25	0.5
GSDN [10]	HDResNet34	0.05	1	0.2, 0.4, 0.8, 1.6	20.1	62.8	34.8
w/o anchors		0.05	1		20.4	56.3	22.7
FCAF3D		0.05	1		17.0	**64.2**	**46.2**
FCAF3D *(accurate)*	HDResNet34	0.01	2	0.08, 0.16, 0.32, 0.64	8.0	<u>**70.7**</u>	<u>**56.0**</u>
FCAF3D *(balanced)*	HDResNet34:3	0.05	1	0.2, 0.4, 0.8	**22.9**	**62.9**	**43.9**
FCAF3D *(fast)*	HDResNet34:2	0.02	2	0.16, 0.32	<u>**31.5**</u>	**63.1**	**46.8**

between voxel sizes of 0.01 and 0.02 m to the presence of *almost flat* objects, such as doors, pictures, and whiteboards. Namely, with a voxel size of 2 cm, the head would output locations with 16 cm tolerance, but the *almost flat* objects could be less than 16 cm by one of the dimensions. Accordingly, we observe a decrease in accuracy for larger voxel sizes.

Number of Points. Similar to 2D images, subsampled point clouds are sometimes referred to as *low-resolution* ones. Accordingly, they contain less information than their *high-resolution* versions. As can be expected, the fewer the points, the lower is detection accuracy. In this series of experiments, we sample 20k, 40k, and 100k points from the entire point cloud, and the obtained metric values revealed a clear dependency between the number of points and mAP. We do not consider larger N_{pts} values to be on a par with the existing methods (specifically, GSDN [10] uses all points in a point cloud, GroupFree [16] samples 50k points, VoteNet [22] selects 40k points for ScanNet and 20k for SUN RGB-D). We use $N_{vox} = N_{pts}$ to guide pruning in the neck. When N_{vox} exceeds 100k, the inference time increases due to growing sparsity in the neck, while the accuracy improvement is negligible. So we restrict our grid search for N_{pts} with 100k and use it as a default value regarding the obtained results.

Centerness. Using centerness improves mAP for the ScanNet and SUN RGB-D datasets. For S3DIS, the results are controversial: the better mAP@0.5 is balanced with a minor decrease of mAP@0.25. Nevertheless, we analyze the results altogether, so we can consider centerness a helpful feature with a small positive effect on the mAP, almost reaching 1% of mAP@0.5 on ScanNet.

Center Sampling. Finally, we study the number of locations selected in center sampling. We select 9 locations, as proposed in FCOS [26], the entire set of 27 locations, as in ImVoxelNet [24], and 18 locations. The latter appeared to be the best choice according to mAP on all the benchmarks.

Table 4. Results of ablation studies on the voxel size, the number of points (which equals the number of voxels N_{vox} in pruning), centerness, and center sampling in FCAF3D. The better options are marked bold (actually, these are the default options used to obtain the results in Table 1 above). The reported metric value is the best across 25 trials; the average value is given in brackets.

Ablating parameter	Value	ScanNet		SUN RGB-D		S3DIS	
		mAP@0.25	mAP@0.5	mAP@0.25	mAP@0.5	mAP@0.25	mAP@0.5
Voxel size	**0.01**	71.5 (**70.7**)	57.3 (**56.0**)	64.2 (**63.8**)	48.9 (**48.2**)	66.7 (**64.9**)	45.9 (**43.8**)
	0.02	66.3 (65.8)	49.4 (48.6)	62.3 (62.0)	46.3 (45.5)	61.0 (58.5)	43.8 (38.5)
	0.03	59.6 (59.2)	42.6 (41.6)	60.4 (59.7)	41.6 (41.0)	55.4 (53.3)	38.6 (35.0)
Number of points	20k	69.0 (68.1)	52.8 (52.0)	63.0 (62.5)	46.9 (46.5)	60.1 (58.8)	45.1 (40.1)
	40k	67.6 (66.7)	53.6 (52.2)	63.4 (63.1)	47.2 (46.6)	63.7 (61.2)	44.8 (42.2)
	100k	71.5 (**70.7**)	57.3 (**56.0**)	64.2 (**63.8**)	48.9 (**48.2**)	66.7 (**64.9**)	45.9 (**43.8**)
Centerness	No	71.0 (70.4)	56.1 (55.1)	63.8 (63.3)	48.2 (47.5)	67.9 (**65.5**)	46.0 (43.5)
	Yes	71.5 (**70.7**)	57.3 (**56.0**)	64.2 (**63.8**)	48.9 (**48.2**)	66.7 (64.9)	45.9 (**43.8**)
Center sampling	9	70.6 (70.1)	55.7 (55.0)	63.8 (63.3)	48.6 (48.2)	66.5 (63.6)	44.4 (42.5)
	18	71.5 (**70.7**)	57.3 (**56.0**)	64.2 (**63.8**)	48.9 (**48.2**)	66.7 (**64.9**)	45.9 (**43.8**)
	27	70.2 (69.7)	55.7 (54.1)	64.3 (63.8)	48.7 (47.9)	65.1 (63.2)	43.6 (41.7)

6 Conclusion

We presented FCAF3D, a first-in-class fully convolutional anchor-free 3D object detection method for indoor scenes. Our method significantly outperforms the previous state-of-the-art on the challenging indoor SUN RGB-D, ScanNet, and S3DIS benchmarks in terms of both mAP and inference speed. We also proposed a novel oriented bounding box parametrization and showed that it improves accuracy for several 3D object detection methods. Moreover, the proposed parametrization allows avoiding any prior assumptions about objects, thus reducing the number of hyperparameters. Overall, FCAF3D with our bounding box parametrization is accurate, scalable, and generalizable at the same time.

References

1. Armeni, I., et al.: 3D semantic parsing of large-scale indoor spaces. In: Proceedings of the IEEE Conference on Computer Vision and Pattern Recognition, pp. 1534–1543 (2016)
2. Chen, J., Lei, B., Song, Q., Ying, H., Chen, D.Z., Wu, J.: A hierarchical graph network for 3D object detection on point clouds. In: Proceedings of the IEEE/CVF Conference on Computer Vision and Pattern Recognition, pp. 392–401 (2020)
3. Chen, K., et al.: MMDetection: open MMLab detection toolbox and benchmark. arXiv preprint arXiv:1906.07155 (2019)
4. Cheng, B., Sheng, L., Shi, S., Yang, M., Xu, D.: Back-tracing representative points for voting-based 3D object detection in point clouds. In: Proceedings of the IEEE/CVF Conference on Computer Vision and Pattern Recognition, pp. 8963–8972 (2021)

5. Choy, C., Gwak, J., Savarese, S.: 4D spatio-temporal convnets: Minkowski convolutional neural networks. In: Proceedings of the IEEE Conference on Computer Vision and Pattern Recognition, pp. 3075–3084 (2019)
6. Contributors, M.: MMDetection3D: OpenMMLab next-generation platform for general 3D object detection (2020). https://github.com/open-mmlab/mmdetection3d
7. Dai, A., Chang, A.X., Savva, M., Halber, M., Funkhouser, T., Nießner, M.: ScanNet: richly-annotated 3D reconstructions of indoor scenes. In: Proceedings of the IEEE Conference on Computer Vision and Pattern Recognition, pp. 5828–5839 (2017)
8. Engelmann, F., Bokeloh, M., Fathi, A., Leibe, B., Nießner, M.: 3D-MPA: multi-proposal aggregation for 3D semantic instance segmentation. In: Proceedings of the IEEE/CVF Conference on Computer Vision and Pattern Recognition, pp. 9031–9040 (2020)
9. Ge, Z., Liu, S., Li, Z., Yoshie, O., Sun, J.: OTA: optimal transport assignment for object detection. In: Proceedings of the IEEE/CVF Conference on Computer Vision and Pattern Recognition, pp. 303–312 (2021)
10. Gwak, J.Y., Choy, C., Savarese, S.: Generative sparse detection networks for 3D single-shot object detection. In: Vedaldi, A., Bischof, H., Brox, T., Frahm, J.-M. (eds.) ECCV 2020. LNCS, vol. 12349, pp. 297–313. Springer, Cham (2020). https://doi.org/10.1007/978-3-030-58548-8_18
11. He, K., Zhang, X., Ren, S., Sun, J.: Deep residual learning for image recognition. In: Proceedings of the IEEE Conference on Computer Vision and Pattern Recognition, pp. 770–778 (2016)
12. Hou, J., Dai, A., Nießner, M.: 3D-SIS: 3D semantic instance segmentation of RGB-D scans. In: Proceedings of the IEEE/CVF Conference on Computer Vision and Pattern Recognition, pp. 4421–4430 (2019)
13. Lang, A.H., Vora, S., Caesar, H., Zhou, L., Yang, J., Beijbom, O.: PointPillars: fast encoders for object detection from point clouds. In: Proceedings of the IEEE/CVF Conference on Computer Vision and Pattern Recognition, pp. 12697–12705 (2019)
14. Li, B.: 3D fully convolutional network for vehicle detection in point cloud. In: 2017 IEEE/RSJ International Conference on Intelligent Robots and Systems (IROS), pp. 1513–1518. IEEE (2017)
15. Lin, T.Y., Goyal, P., Girshick, R., He, K., Dollár, P.: Focal loss for dense object detection. In: Proceedings of the IEEE International Conference on Computer Vision, pp. 2980–2988 (2017)
16. Liu, Z., Zhang, Z., Cao, Y., Hu, H., Tong, X.: Group-free 3D object detection via transformers. In: Proceedings of the IEEE/CVF International Conference on Computer Vision (ICCV), pp. 2949–2958 (2021)
17. Liu, Z., Wu, Z., Tóth, R.: Smoke: single-stage monocular 3D object detection via keypoint estimation. In: Proceedings of the IEEE/CVF Conference on Computer Vision and Pattern Recognition Workshops, pp. 996–997 (2020)
18. Maturana, D., Scherer, S.: VoxNet: a 3D convolutional neural network for real-time object recognition. In: 2015 IEEE/RSJ International Conference on Intelligent Robots and Systems (IROS), pp. 922–928. IEEE (2015)
19. Misra, I., Girdhar, R., Joulin, A.: An end-to-end transformer model for 3D object detection. In: Proceedings of the IEEE/CVF International Conference on Computer Vision, pp. 2906–2917 (2021)
20. Munkres, J.R.: Topology (2000)

21. Qi, C.R., Chen, X., Litany, O., Guibas, L.J.: ImvoteNet: boosting 3D object detection in point clouds with image votes. In: Proceedings of the IEEE/CVF Conference on Computer Vision and Pattern Recognition, pp. 4404–4413 (2020)
22. Qi, C.R., Litany, O., He, K., Guibas, L.J.: Deep Hough voting for 3D object detection in point clouds. In: Proceedings of the IEEE/CVF International Conference on Computer Vision, pp. 9277–9286 (2019)
23. Qi, C.R., Su, H., Mo, K., Guibas, L.J.: PointNet: deep learning on point sets for 3D classification and segmentation. In: Proceedings of the IEEE Conference on Computer Vision and Pattern Recognition, pp. 652–660 (2017)
24. Rukhovich, D., Vorontsova, A., Konushin, A.: ImVoxelNet: image to voxels projection for monocular and multi-view general-purpose 3D object detection. arXiv preprint arXiv:2106.01178 (2021)
25. Song, S., Lichtenberg, S.P., Xiao, J.: Sun RGB-D: a RGB-D scene understanding benchmark suite. In: Proceedings of the IEEE Conference on Computer Vision and Pattern Recognition, pp. 567–576 (2015)
26. Tian, Z., Shen, C., Chen, H., He, T.: FCOS: fully convolutional one-stage object detection. In: Proceedings of the IEEE/CVF International Conference on Computer Vision, pp. 9627–9636 (2019)
27. Wang, T., Zhu, X., Pang, J., Lin, D.: FCOS3D: fully convolutional one-stage monocular 3D object detection. arXiv preprint arXiv:2104.10956 (2021)
28. Xie, Q., et al.: VENet: voting enhancement network for 3D object detection. In: Proceedings of the IEEE/CVF International Conference on Computer Vision, pp. 3712–3721 (2021)
29. Xie, Q., et al.: MLCVNet: multi-level context VoteNet for 3D object detection. In: Proceedings of the IEEE/CVF Conference on Computer Vision and Pattern Recognition, pp. 10447–10456 (2020)
30. Yan, Y., Mao, Y., Li, B.: Second: sparsely embedded convolutional detection. Sensors **18**(10), 3337 (2018)
31. Yin, T., Zhou, X., Krahenbuhl, P.: Center-based 3D object detection and tracking. In: Proceedings of the IEEE/CVF Conference on Computer Vision and Pattern Recognition, pp. 11784–11793 (2021)
32. Zhang, S., Chi, C., Yao, Y., Lei, Z., Li, S.Z.: Bridging the gap between anchor-based and anchor-free detection via adaptive training sample selection. In: Proceedings of the IEEE/CVF Conference on Computer Vision and Pattern Recognition, pp. 9759–9768 (2020)
33. Zhang, Z., Sun, B., Yang, H., Huang, Q.: H3DNet: 3D object detection using hybrid geometric primitives. In: Vedaldi, A., Bischof, H., Brox, T., Frahm, J.-M. (eds.) ECCV 2020. LNCS, vol. 12357, pp. 311–329. Springer, Cham (2020). https://doi.org/10.1007/978-3-030-58610-2_19
34. Zhou, D., et al.: IoU loss for 2D/3D object detection. In: 2019 International Conference on 3D Vision (3DV), pp. 85–94. IEEE (2019)
35. Zhou, Y., Tuzel, O.: VoxelNet: end-to-end learning for point cloud based 3D object detection. In: Proceedings of the IEEE Conference on Computer Vision and Pattern Recognition, pp. 4490–4499 (2018)

Video Anomaly Detection by Solving Decoupled Spatio-Temporal Jigsaw Puzzles

Guodong Wang[1,2], Yunhong Wang[2], Jie Qin[3], Dongming Zhang[4],
Xiuguo Bao[4], and Di Huang[1,2(✉)] ⓘ

[1] SKLSDE, Beihang University, Beijing, China
wanggd@buaa.edu.cn
[2] SCSE, Beihang University, Beijing, China
{yhwang,dhuang}@buaa.edu.cn
[3] CCST, NUAA, Nanjing, China
zhdm@cert.org.cn
[4] CNCERT/CC, Beijing, China

Abstract. Video Anomaly Detection (VAD) is an important topic in computer vision. Motivated by the recent advances in self-supervised learning, this paper addresses VAD by solving an intuitive yet challenging pretext task, *i.e.*, spatio-temporal jigsaw puzzles, which is cast as a multi-label fine-grained classification problem. Our method exhibits several advantages over existing works: 1) the spatio-temporal jigsaw puzzles are decoupled in terms of spatial and temporal dimensions, responsible for capturing highly discriminative appearance and motion features, respectively; 2) full permutations are used to provide abundant jigsaw puzzles covering various difficulty levels, allowing the network to distinguish subtle spatio-temporal differences between normal and abnormal events; and 3) the pretext task is tackled in an end-to-end manner without relying on any pre-trained models. Our method outperforms state-of-the-art counterparts on three public benchmarks. Especially on ShanghaiTech Campus, the result is superior to reconstruction and prediction-based methods by a large margin.

Keywords: Video anomaly detection · Spatio-temporal jigsaw puzzles · Multi-label classification

1 Introduction

Video anomaly detection (VAD) refers to the task of detecting unexpected events that deviate from the normal patterns of familiar ones. Recently, it has become a very important task in the community of computer vision and pattern recognition with the exponential increase of video data captured from various scenarios.

Supplementary Information The online version contains supplementary material available at https://doi.org/10.1007/978-3-031-20080-9_29.

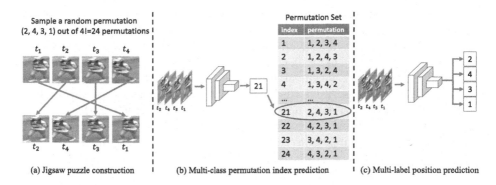

Fig. 1. Multi-class index classification *vs.* multi-label position classification. (a) Jigsaw puzzle construction. We permute the original sequence based on a randomly selected permutation from all possible ones. (b) Multi-class permutation index prediction. Traditional methods [24,26,41] take a permutation as one class out of $4! = 24$ classes. (c) Multi-label permutation position prediction (**ours**). We directly output multiple predictions, indicating the absolute position in the original sequence for each frame.

VAD is rather challenging as abnormal events are infrequent in real world and unbounded in category, jointly making typical supervised methods inapplicable due to the unavailability of balanced normal and abnormal samples for training. Therefore, VAD is generally performed in a one-class learning manner where only normal data are given [13,29,30].

In this regime, a series of VAD approaches [12,16,27,29,34,40,56,59] have been proposed, among which reconstruction and prediction based methods are two representative paradigms in the context of deep learning. Reconstruction based methods [16,40] build models, *e.g.*, autoencoders and generative adversarial networks (GAN), to recover input frames, and examples with high reconstruction errors are identified as anomalies at test time. In consideration of the temporal coherence, prediction based methods render missing frames *e.g.*, middle frames [59] or future frames [29,56], according to motion continuity. The difference between the predicted frame and its corresponding ground-truth suggests the probability of anomaly occurring.

The two types of methods above report promising performance; however, as stated in [16,39,62], they aim at high-quality pixel generation, and even though the networks are only trained to perfectly match normal examples, their inherent generalization abilities still make the anomalies well reconstructed or predicted, especially for static objects, *e.g.*, a stopped car in a pedestrian area. To address this, some follow-up studies attempt to boost the accuracy through incorporating memory modules [16,43], modeling optical flows [29], redesigning specific architectures [56], *etc.*

More recently, self-supervised learning has opened another avenue for VAD with significantly improved results. Different from the unsupervised generative solutions, self-supervised learning based methods explore supervisory signals for learning representations from unlabeled data [13,53], and current investigations mainly differ in the design of pretext tasks. Wang *et al.* [53] propose an instance discrimination task to establish subcategories of normality as clusters and examples far away from the cluster centers are determined as anomalies. Georgescu *et al.* [13] deliver an advancement by a model jointly considering multiple pretext tasks including discriminating arrow of time and motion regularity, middle frame reconstruction and knowledge distillation. Nevertheless, their pretext tasks are basically defined as binary classification problems, making them not so competent at learning highly discriminative features to distinguish *subtle spatiotemporal differences* between normal and abnormal events. Additionally, these methods [13,53] depend on the networks pre-trained on large-scale datasets, *e.g.*, ImageNet [47] and Kinetics-400 [23].

To circumvent the shortcomings aforementioned, in this paper, we propose a simple yet effective self-supervised learning method for VAD, through tackling an intuitive but challenging pretext task, *i.e.*, spatio-temporal jigsaw puzzles. We hypothesize that successfully solving such puzzles requires the network to understand the very detailed spatial and temporal coherence of video frames by learning powerful spatio-temporal representations, which are critical to VAD. To this end, we take into account full possible permutations, rather than a subset produced by a heuristic permutation selection algorithm [41], to increase the difficulty of jigsaw puzzles with the aim of offering fine-grained supervisory signals for discriminative features. Based on the observation that anomalous events usually involve abnormal appearances and abnormal motions, we decouple spatio-temporal jigsaw puzzles in terms of spatial and temporal dimensions, responsible for modeling appearance and motion patterns, respectively, which technically facilitates optimization compared to solving 3D jigsaw puzzles [2]. To be specific, we first randomly select a permutation from $n!$ possible permutations, where n is the number of elements in the sequence. With this permutation, we then spatially shuffle patches within frames to construct spatial jigsaw puzzles or temporally shuffle a sequence of consecutive frames to build temporal ones. The training objective is to recover an original sequence from its spatially or temporally permuted version. Unlike existing methods for learning general visual representations [24,26,41] which treat jigsaw puzzle solving as a multi-class classification problem where each permutation corresponds to a class (Fig. 1(b)), we cast it as a multi-label learning problem (Fig. 1(c)), allowing the method to be extendable to more advanced jigsaw puzzles with more pieces and free from significantly increased memory consumption. During inference, the confidence of the prediction with respect to unshuffled frames or images serves as the regularity score for anomaly detection. Abnormal events are expected to have lower confidence scores because they are unseen in training.

Compared to prior work on self-supervised VAD [13,53], the advantages of our method are three-fold. **First**, we dramatically simplify the self-supervised learning framework by solving only a single pretext task, which is decoupled into the spatial and temporal jigsaw puzzles, corresponding to modeling normal appearance and motion patterns, respectively. **Second**, full possible permutations are employed to produce large-scale learning samples of a high diversity, allowing the network to capture subtle spatio-temporal anomalies from the pretext task. To ensure computational efficiency, we formulate puzzle solving as a multi-label learning problem, accommodating a factorial of number of variations. **Third**, our method is free from any pre-trained networks, because solving the challenging pretext itself helps to learn rich and discriminative spatio-temporal representations. It achieves state-of-the-art results on three public benchmarks, especially on the ShanghaiTech Campus dataset [35].

2 Related Work

Video Anomaly Detection. While early studies [1,3,9] advocate manually-designed appearance and motion features for VAD, recent methods leverage the powerful representation capabilities of deep neural networks to automatically learn features from video events and deliver better performance. Most VAD methods follow the way of per-pixel generation, with reconstruction based and prediction based ones being the two important lines. Reconstruction based methods [11,18,34] learn to recover input frames or clips, while prediction based methods learn to predict missing frames, such as future frame prediction [12,29,33] or middle frame completion [27,59]. The combination of reconstruction and prediction as a hybrid solution is also explored in [38,58,61]. These methods aim at high-quality pixel generation during training and examples with large reconstruction or prediction errors are identified as anomalies. However, these networks often exhibit strong generalization abilities on anomalies (even though they are unseen in training), leading to decent reconstruction or prediction quality. The use of memory mechanisms [16,43] or multi-modal data (*e.g.*, optical flows [30,40] and RGB differences [6]) suppresses the generalization ability to some extent but the improvement is far from perfect given the additional computation and memory consumption.

Self-supervised Learning. Self-supervised learning (SSL) is a generic learning framework which seeks supervisory signals from data only. It can be broadly categorized into constructing pretext tasks and conducting constrastive learning. **Pretext tasks.** For images, pretext tasks typically include solving jigsaw puzzles [41], coloring images [60], and predicting relative patches [10] or image rotations [15], *etc*. For videos, a series of methods additionally exploit temporal information exclusive to videos based on verifying correct frame order [37], sorting frame order [26] or clip order [57], predicting playback speed [5] or arrow of time [45,54], *etc*. Among the pretext tasks, jigsaw puzzle is widely explored and proves effective in learning visual representation, but related methods fail to leverage all possible permutations, which scales factorially with the input length. Cruz *et al.* [48] avoid such a factorial complexity by directly predicting the permutation matrix that shuffles the original data. **Contrastive learning.** It is another prevalent self-supervised learning paradigm in which each instance is regarded as a category. Motivated by the success of self-supervised image representation learning such as SimCLR [8] and MoCo [19], many extensions [31,42]

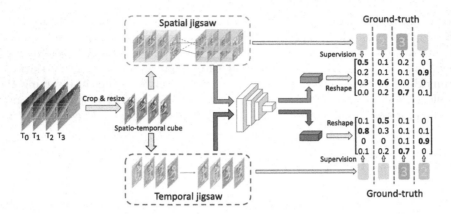

Fig. 2. Method overview. We devise a pretext task including temporal and spatial jigsaw puzzles, for self-supervised learning spatio-temporal representations. Based on the object-centric spatio-temporal cubes, we create jigsaw puzzles by performing temporal and spatial shuffling. The network comprises a shared 3D convolution backbone followed by two disjoint heads to predict the permutation used for shuffling frames in time and patches in space, respectively. Each column of a matrix denotes the prediction of an entry in the permutation.

of constrastive learning are proposed to adapt image-based methods to the video domain.

SSL in VAD. While these self-supervised methods prove very effective in generic representation learning, benefiting bundles of downstream recognition and detection tasks [8,19,31,42], the efforts that exploit SSL for VAD are very few. SSL based VAD methods capture spatio-temporal representations by either conducting constrastive learning or solving pretext tasks, diverging from per-pixel reconstruction or prediction based methods. Wang *et al.* [53] learn spatio-temporal representations via a contrastive learning framework with a cluster attention mechanism. However, it requires a large number of training samples and customized data augmentation strategies. Georgescu *et al.* [13] train a 3D convolutional neural network jointly on three self-supervised proxy tasks and knowledge distillation for VAD. These proxy tasks are easy to solve, preventing the network from learning highly discriminative representations for VAD.

In this work, we design a more challenging pretext task, *i.e.*, solving spatio-temporal jigsaw puzzles. Though solving jigsaw puzzles as a pretext task has been investigated for SSL by shuffling spatial layout [41], temporal order [26] or their combination [24], they mostly formulate it as a multi-class classification task, therein each type of permutation corresponds to one class. The representations learned from the pretext tasks prove very effective evaluated in a series of downstream tasks, *e.g.*, image retrieval and action recognition; however, its potential on VAD remains unexplored. A straightforward solution is directly applying these methods [26,41] to learn representations of normal events for

VAD. Nevertheless, this simple adaptation is sub-optimal since they only focus on modeling either appearances or motions while abnormal appearances and abnormal motions intertwine with each other in anomalous events in videos. Kim *et al.* [24] manage to solve space-time cubic puzzles, however, the multi-class formulation restricts itself to more advanced jigsaw puzzles (in fact they only leverage four-piece jigsaw puzzles), leading to inferior performance, shown in Table 2. Though Ahsan *et al.* [2] consider directly solving 3D spatio-temporal jigsaw puzzles, we empirically find that its performance is not as good as expected due to the extreme difficulty of solving 3D jigsaw puzzles. For example, a cube compressing 7 frames with 3×3 grid results in $7! \times (3 \times 3)! = 1,828,915,200$ possibles permutations. Therefore, we decompose the 3D spatio-temporal jigsaw puzzles into spatial and temporal jigsaw puzzles, corresponding to learning appearance and motion patterns, respectively.

3   Method

3.1   Overview

Figure 2 shows the pipeline of the proposed method, in which a sequence of four frames is used as an example for easy illustration. The method contains three steps: object-centric cube extraction, puzzle construction, and puzzle solving. We first employ an off-the-shelf object detector [46] to extract all objects in the frames and stack the objects along the time dimension to construct object-centric cubes. For each cube, we further apply spatial or temporal shuffling to construct the corresponding spatial or temporal jigsaw puzzle. Finally, a convolutional neural network, acting as a jigsaw solver, attempts to recover the original sequence from its spatially or temporally permuted version. The proposed method is equivalent to solving a multi-label classification problem and is trained in an end-to-end manner.

It is noteworthy that we **do not** use any optical flows or pre-trained models (except for the object detector). The spatial and temporal permutations are only applied in training, allowing fast inference with a single forward pass.

3.2   Fine-Grained Decoupled Jigsaw Puzzles

In self-supervised learning, it is crucial to prepare neither ambiguous nor easy self-labeled data [41]. Based on the observation [26,41] that networks can learn richer spatio-temporal representations from a more difficult pretext, we introduce full permutations for fine-grained jigsaw puzzle construction with the aim of capturing subtle spatial and temporal differences.

We first extract a large number of objects of interest by applying a YOLOv3 detector [46] pre-trained on MS-COCO [28] frame by frame, therein we only keep the localization information and discard the classification labels. For each object detected in the frame i, we construct an object-centric spatio-temporal cube by simply stacking patches cropped from its temporally adjacent frames

500 G. Wang et al.

$\{i - t, ..., i - 1, i, i + 1, ...i + t\}$ using the same bounding box and location. We rescale all the extracted patches into a fixed size, *e.g.*, 64×64. Based on the extracted object-centric spatio-temporal cubes, we prepare training samples by constructing spatial or temporal jigsaw puzzles.

Spatial Jigsaw. Following [41], for each frame, we start by decomposing it into $n \times n$ equal-sized patches which are then randomly shuffled. We make all the frames in the cube share the same permutation meanwhile keep them in the chronological order. Different from [41] that separately passes each patch into the network, we directly take as input the frames after spatial shuffling, which are of the same size with the original frame, *i.e.*, 64×64 in our setting.

Temporal Jigsaw. To construct temporal jigsaw puzzles, we shuffle a sequence of l frames without disorganizing the spatial content. Jenni *et al.* [22] reveal that the most effective pretext tasks for powerful video representation learning are those that can be solved by observing the largest number of frames. For instance, motion irregularity [13] can be easily detected by just comparing the first two frames, in contrast to observing the total number of frames to solve our temporal jigsaw puzzles, which is crucial for learning more discriminative representations of motion patterns. Note that we do not temporally shuffle the frame sequence containing only static contents since it is impossible to infer its temporal order by simply observing visual cues.

3.3   Multi-label Supervision

Our jigsaw solving task is essentially a permutation prediction problem. Recall that, to make the task more challenging for learning discriminative representations, we employ the full permutations to produce fine-grained jigsaw puzzles. Different from typical methods [24,26,41] that formulate jigsaw puzzle solving as multi-class classification, therein each permutation is a class, we cast jigsaw puzzle solving as a multi-label classification problem and attempt to directly predict the absolute position of each frame or the location of each patch. For each frame in the temporally shuffled sequence, we predict the correct position in the original sequence, while for each patch in the spatially shuffled frame, we predict the correct location in the original splitting grid. The strategy reduces the complexity $\mathcal{O}(l!)$ to $\mathcal{O}(l^2)$, and it can thus be easily extended to input frames of longer sequences or finer grid-splits with negligible memory consumption.

   We adopt the mixed training strategy where a training mini-batch consists of two disjoint sets: Q_s and Q_t, denoting the sets of spatial and temporal jigsaw puzzles, respectively. Thus, the mini-batch has a total of $|Q_t| + |Q_s|$ samples. It is worth noting that the two solvers (heads) are only responsible for their own puzzle types, *i.e.*, we do not rely on the temporal solver to deal with spatial jigsaw puzzles to avoid ambiguity and vice versa. Algorithm 1 provides more details for constructing puzzles in mini-batches.

We optimize the network using the cross-entropy (CE) loss. For a jigsaw puzzle p, its loss is computed as Eq. (1).

$$L_p = \begin{cases} \frac{1}{l} \sum_{i=1}^{l} CE(t_i, \hat{t}_i), & p \in Q_t \\ \frac{1}{n^2} \sum_{j=1}^{n^2} CE(s_j, \hat{s}_j), & p \in Q_s \end{cases}, \tag{1}$$

where t_i and $\hat{t}_i$ are the ground-truth and predicted positions of a frame in the original sequence, respectively, and s_j and $\hat{s}_i$ are the ground-truth and predicted locations of a patch in the original splitting grid, respectively.

Algorithm 1: Puzzle construction in mini-batches

Input: object-centric spatio-temporal cubes C, ratio r, frame length l, number of patches n^2, threshold ζ.

Output: sets of jigsaw puzzles: Q_t, Q_s.

1 $Q_t \leftarrow \varnothing, Q_s \leftarrow \varnothing$
2 $P^t \leftarrow$ all permutations $[P_1^t, P_2^t, ..., P_{l!}^t]$
3 $P^s \leftarrow$ all permutations $[P_1^s, P_2^s, ..., P_{(n^2)!}^s]$
4 **for** c in C **do**
5 $\quad$ $p \leftarrow \mathcal{U}_{float}[0, 1]$ // uniform sampling
6 $\quad$ **if** $p \le r$ **then**
7 $\quad\quad$ **if** $p \le \zeta$ **then**
8 $\quad\quad\quad$ $i \leftarrow 1$
9 $\quad\quad$ **else**
10 $\quad\quad\quad$ $i \leftarrow \mathcal{U}_{int}[1, (n^2)!]$
11 $\quad\quad$ **end**
12 $\quad\quad$ $q \leftarrow$ SpatiallyShuffle(c, P_i^s)
13 $\quad\quad$ $Q_s \leftarrow Q_s \cup \{q\}$
14 $\quad$ **else**
15 $\quad\quad$ $j \leftarrow \mathcal{U}_{int}[1, l!]$
16 $\quad\quad$ $q \leftarrow$ TemporallyShuffle(c, P_j^t)
17 $\quad\quad$ $Q_t \leftarrow Q_t \cup \{q\}$
18 $\quad$ **end**
19 **end**

3.4   VAD Inference

Following the same protocol of object detection in training, for each object in frame i, we construct the corresponding object-centric cube by cropping the bounding boxes from its temporally adjacent frames $\{i-t, ..., i-1, i, i+1, ...i+t\}$. During inference, we reuse the built-in jigsaw solvers to obtain the regularity scores. We pass the object-centric cubes without performing spatial or temporal shuffling and obtain two matrices, M_s and M_t, corresponding to spatial and temporal permutation predictions, respectively.

Intuitively, the diagonal entries of the matrices of normal events are larger than those of abnormal ones, as the network is only trained to recover the original normal sequences. We thus simply take the minimum prediction score of a sequence as its regularity, as in Eq. (3).

$$\begin{cases} r_s = \min(\text{diag}(M_s)) \\ r_t = \min(\text{diag}(M_t)) \end{cases}, \tag{2}$$

where $\text{diag}(\cdot)$ extracts the matrix diagonal, M_s and M_t are predicted by the spatial or temporal jigsaw solver, and r_s and r_t indicate the object-level regularity scores, respectively. We select the minimum score along the diagonal of the matrix as the resulting object-level regularity score, since an example is likely anomalous as long as one frame or patch is wrongly predicted, in accordance with fine-grained multi-label supervision in training. Similarly, we obtain the frame-level regularity score R_s (R_d) by simply selecting the minimum object-level regularity score in the frame. Similar to [13], we also apply a 3D mean filter to create a smooth anomaly score map. Following [29,56,58], we normalize the irregularity scores of all frames in each video:

$$\begin{cases} R_s = \dfrac{R_s - \min(R_s)}{\max(R_s) - \min(R_s)} \\ R_t = \dfrac{R_t - \min(R_t)}{\max(R_t) - \min(R_t)} \end{cases}. \tag{3}$$

The final frame-level regularity score R (Eq. (4)) is the weighted average of R_s and R_t, followed by a temporal 1-D Gaussian filter.

$$R = w * R_s + (1 - w) * R_t. \tag{4}$$

4   Experiments

4.1   Datasets

We present the experimental results on three popular benchmarks, namely UCSD Ped2 [36], CUHK Avenue [32], ShanghaiTech Campus [35].

UCSD Ped2 [36]. Ped2 contains 16 training videos and 12 test videos captured by a fixed camera. Example objects are pedestrians, bikes, and vehicles. Each video has a resolution of 240 × 360 pixels in gray scale.

CUHK Avenue [32]. Avenue consists of 16 training videos and 21 test videos, respectively. It includes a total number of 47 abnormal events with throwing bag and moving toward/away from the camera being example anomalies. Each video has a resolution of 360 × 640 RGB pixels.

ShanghaiTech Campus (STC) [35]. It contains 330 training videos and 107 test videos covering 13 different scenes, making it more challenging than the other two datasets. Example anomalous events include car invading and person chasing. Each video has a resolution of 480×856 RGB pixels.

4.2 Implementation Details

Since we train our network only on the object-centric cubes, the first stage of our method is object detection. For fair comparison, we follow [13] to adopt the same implementation[1] of YOLOv3 [46] and use the same configurations to filter out the detected objects with low confidence. We set the confidence thresholds to 0.5, 0.8, and 0.8 for Ped2, Avenue and STC, respectively. The confidence thresholds are shared during training/test for each dataset. The input to the network is a tensor of $l \times 64 \times 64 \times 3$ where l is the length of the sequence. The difficulty levels of spatial and temporal jigsaw puzzles are adjusted by varying n and l, respectively. We obtain the optimal results with $l = 9$ on STC and $l = 7$ on Ped2 and Avenue, and $n = 3$ for all the three datasets. We empirically set $r = 0.5$ ($|Q_t| = |Q_s|$) and $w = 0.5$ throughout all the experiments, indicating the equivalent importance of spatial and temporal branches. Considering that Avenue and Ped2 are relatively small compared to the scale of spatial jigsaw puzzles ($9! = 362,800$), we do not perform spatial shuffling with the probability $\zeta = 1e - 4$ (Line 7 in Algorithm 1).

Our framework is implemented using the PyTorch library [44] and trained in an end-to-end manner. We adopt the Adam optimizer with $\beta_1 = 0.9, \beta_2 = 0.999$. The learning rate is $1e-4$. We train the network for 100 epochs on Avenue and STC and 50 epochs on UCSD Ped2, and set the batch size as 192.

4.3 Evaluation Metric

Following the widely-adopted evaluation metric used in VAD community [12,16, 29,30,53,59], we report the frame-level area under the curve (AUC) of Receiver Operation Characteristic (ROC) with respect to the ground-truth annotations by varying the threshold. Specifically, we concatenate all the frames in dataset and then compute the overall frame-level AUC, *i.e.*, micro-averaged AUROC [14].

4.4 Experimental Results

Table 1 shows the comparison results with different types of state-of-the-art approaches, where we can observe that our method delivers very impressive performance on all the three benchmarks. On the challenging STC, our method outperforms reconstruction-based, prediction-based, and hybrid methods by significant margins. For example, our method achieves 84.3% while the best accuracy of previous generative methods is 77.7% by CT-D2GAN [56]. This suggests

---

[1] https://github.com/wizyoung/YOLOv3_TensorFlow.

Table 1. Comparison with state-of-the-art methods in terms of micro-AUROC (%). The best and second-best results are bold and underlined, respectively. * denotes that micro-AUROC is reported. SSL is short for self-supervised learning.

Type	Method	Ped2	Avenue	STC
Reconstruction	Conv-AE [18]	90.0	70.2	–
	StackRNN [35]	92.2	81.7	68.0
	Mem-AE [16]	94.1	83.3	71.2
	AM-Corr [40]	96.2	86.9	–
	MNAD-Recon. [43]	90.2	82.8	69.8
	ClusterAE [6]	96.5	86.0	73.3
	VEC [59]	97.3	90.2	74.8
	LNRA (Patch based) [4]	94.8	84.9	72.5
	LNRA (Skip frame based) [4]	96.5	84.7	76.0
	I3D-Recons.	–	69.3 –	69.4
Prediction	Frame-Pred. [29]	95.4	85.1	72.8
	BMAN [27]	96.6	90.0	76.2
	Multipath-Pred. [52]	96.3	88.3	76.6
	MNAD-Pred. [43]	97.0	88.5	70.5
	CT-D2GAN [56]	97.2	85.9	77.7
	Bi-Prediction [7]	96.6	87.8	–
Hybrid	ST-CAE [61]	91.2	80.9	–
	MPED-RNN [38]	–	–	73.4
	AnoPCN [58]	96.8	86.2	73.6
	IntegradAE [50]	96.3	85.1	73.0
	HF^2-VAD [30]	**99.3**	91.1	76.2
Others	SCL [32]	–	80.9	–
	DeepOC [55]	96.9	86.6	–
	CAE-SVM* [21]	94.3	87.4	78.7
	Scene-Aware [49]	–	89.6	74.7
SSL	CAC [53]	–	87.0	79.3
	SS-MTL* [13]	97.5	<u>91.5</u>	<u>82.4</u>
	Ours	<u>99.0</u>	**92.2**	**84.3**

the superiority of self-supervised learning which captures discriminative representations of normal events by solving pretext tasks, bypassing the requirement for per-pixel generation. Additionally, compared to the VAD methods [13,53] leveraging self-supervised learning, we still achieve the best performance, boosting the second-best method [13] by 1.9%. We attribute it to the design of our challenging pretext task, *i.e.*, solving fine-grained spatio-temporal jigsaw puzzles with full permutations, which helps to learn discriminative representations.

Note that we only use the VAD training set to train our network and do not use an extra model for either knowledge distillation [13] or transfer learning [53]. On Avenue and UCSD Ped2, we also deliver very competitive performance, indicating that our method is robust to datasets of different scales.

5   Ablation Study

To understand the factors that contribute to the anomaly detection performance, we conduct ablation studies on STC and Avenue considering four key factors that control the puzzle difficulty: a) number of permutations; b) number of frames/patches; c) types of puzzles; and d) other pretexts beyond jigsaw solving. We also discuss the reliance on the object detector.

Table 2. Results of various numbers of permutations on STC and Avenue in terms of AUROC (%). T and S represent the number of permutations for temporal and spatial jigsaw puzzle construction, respectively. Here, $l = 7$ and $n^2 = 9$.

Exp. ID	Method	T	S	Avenue	STC
A1	Baseline (Multi-class)	504	504	84.6	76.8
A2		5040	504	85.3	77.6
A3		504	5040	87.0	78.1
A4		5040	5040	87.5	78.5
A5	Ours (Multi-label)	504	504	87.1	79.7
A6		5040	504	87.5	81.2
A7		504	5040	88.6	79.8
A8		5040	5040	89.5	82.0
A9		5040	362880	**92.2**	**83.2**

Number of Permutations. We constrain the number of permutations used to construct puzzles by selecting the subsets of full permutations using a Hamming distance based selection algorithm [41]. We first build a baseline that follows the typical solution for solving puzzles, which considers a permutation as a class. During inference, the regularity scores are the probabilities of the spatio-temporal cubes not being spatially or temporally permuted. From Table 2, both the baseline method and our method achieve improved results with a large number of permutations for both spatial and temporal puzzles, since the networks need to capture more discriminative representations to perceive subtle differences among jigsaw puzzles. Moreover, our method consistently outperforms the baseline for the same number of permutations. One possible reason is that the baseline attempts to discriminate jigsaw puzzles by different permutations, while we aim to predict the correct position of each frame/patch in the permutation in

Table 3. Results of different numbers of frames/patches on STC and Avenue in terms of AUROC (%). l and n^2 denote the number of frames in an object-centric cube and the number of patches in the frames, respectively.

Exp. ID	l	n^2	Avenue	STC
B1	5	4	89.7	79.3
B2	7	4	90.2	80.2
B3	7	9	**92.2**	83.2
B4	9	4	88.6	81.1
B5	9	9	89.2	**84.3**
B6	9	16	87.9	80.4

a more detailed way. Moreover, for advanced puzzles with more pieces, the baseline model fails due to memory limitation. In contrast, thanks to the multi-label classification formulation, our method can handle finer-grained puzzles with full permutations in a memory-friendly way, achieving the best (A9).

Number of Frames/Patches. With full permutations considered for puzzle construction, we next examine the effects of the number of frames (l) in the temporal dimension and the number of patches (n^2) in the spatial dimension. We do not try a larger l ($l > 9$) as the object would go beyond the boundary of the spatio-temporal cube. From Table 3, we can observe a trend of performance improvement when we increase l and n^2 in a certain range. The observation is consistent with human beings who need more efforts to solve puzzles with more pieces. However, when we increase l and n^2 further, the performance deteriorates. The reason lies in that the network is difficult to optimize especially on the spatial jigsaw puzzles, as each patch is very small (16×16 pixels for $n^2 = 16$ in our setting) and thus causes ambiguity.

Types of Puzzles. Finally, we investigate the effects of solving spatial and temporal jigsaw puzzles for VAD. To this end, we design four alternative configurations based on when and which jigsaw puzzles are activated. Here, we set $l = 7$ and $l = 9$ for Avenue and STC, respectively; $n^2 = 9$ for both. Our method benefits more from solving spatial and temporal jigsaw puzzles in the training phase. For example, C3 indicates simultaneously solving spatial and temporal jigsaw puzzles during training, while C1 represents solving temporal jigsaw puzzles only. We activate the temporal solver only during testing for C1 and C3. In other words, the only difference between C1 and C3 is the training goal, *i.e.*, multi-task *vs.* single-task. Our method clearly benefits from multi-task learning and achieves better performance 82.7% *vs.* 78.6% on STC. However, when only one type of puzzle is activated either during training or testing, the results are always worse than our complete version, namely C5. The observations are intuitive that anomalous events are caused by abnormal appearances and/or motions. Therefore, it is beneficial to include both types of jigsaw puzzles to detect both types of anomalies.

Table 4. Results of different pretexts for VAD on STC in terms of AUROC (%).

Exp. ID	Spatial	Temporal	STC
D1	Rotation	Arrow of time	72.9
D2	Rotation	Temporal order verification	74.8
D3	Translation	Arrow of time	73.0
D4	Translation	Temporal order verification	75.6
D5	Translation	Jigsaw (ours)	81.1
D6	Jigsaw (ours)	Temporal order verification	78.3
D7	Jigsaw (ours)	Jigsaw (ours)	**84.3**

Table 5. Results of different jigsaw puzzles. T and S are short for "temporal" and "spatial", respectively.

Exp. ID	Train		Test		Avenue	STC
	T	S	T	S		
C1	✓	–	✓	–	78.9	78.6
C2	–	✓	–	✓	86.7	76.0
C3	✓	✓	✓		86.9	82.7
C4	✓	✓		✓	89.0	79.8
C5	✓	✓	✓	✓	**92.2**	**84.3**

Table 6. Results on RetroTrucks in terms of AUROC (%).

Method	RetroTrucks
Frame-Pred. [29]	60.6
Mem-AE [16]	63.6
I3D [17]	71.2
I3D + GCN [17]	71.5
Ours	**72.8**

Other Pretexts Beyond Jigsaw Solving. We design other alternative pretext tasks considering the spatial dimension (*e.g.*, rotation prediction [25] and translation prediction [20]) and the temporal dimension (*e.g.*, arrow of time prediction [54] and temporal order verification [37]). Our method achieves the best performance in Table 4. It gives evidence that a proper design of the pretext task enabling fine-grained discrimination is essential for VAD. Compared to other pretexts, ours sets a more challenging task which requires the model to perceive every patch within a frame and every frame within a clip.

Object Detector. Although we mainly focus on object-level anomaly detection, our method can also be applied at frame level. To this end, we remove the object detector and report the results on the RetroTrucks dataset [17]. For fair comparison with [17], we train an I3D [51] network to predict the absolute position of the original sequence, since we observe that activating the temporal branch only is sufficient. Our method achieves the best performance in Table 6, even outperforming [17] that incorporates object interaction reasoning (Table 5).

6   Conclusion

In this work, we present a simple yet effective self-supervised learning framework for VAD through solving a challenging pretext task, *i.e.*, spatio-temporal jigsaw puzzles, which are decoupled into spatial and temporal jigsaw puzzles for easy optimization. We emphasize that a challenging pretext task is key to learning discriminative spatio-temporal representations. To this end, we perform full permutations to generate a rich set of spatial and temporal jigsaw puzzles with varying degrees of difficulty, which allows the network to discriminate subtle spatio-temporal differences between normal and abnormal events. We reformulate the pretext task as a multi-label fine-grained classification problem, which is addressed in an efficient and end-to-end manner. Experiments show that our method achieves state-of-the-art on three popular benchmarks.

Acknowledgment. This work is partly supported by the National Natural Science Foundation of China (62022011, U20B2069), the Research Program of State Key Laboratory of Software Development Environment (SKLSDE-2021ZX-04), and the Fundamental Research Funds for the Central Universities.

References

1. Adam, A., Rivlin, E., Shimshoni, I., Reinitz, D.: Robust real-time unusual event detection using multiple fixed-location monitors. IEEE TPAMI **30**(3), 555–560 (2008)
2. Ahsan, U., Madhok, R., Essa, I.: Video jigsaw: unsupervised learning of spatiotemporal context for video action recognition. In: WACV (2019)
3. Antić, B., Ommer, B.: Video parsing for abnormality detection. In: ICCV (2011)
4. Astrid, M., Zaheer, M.Z., Lee, J.Y., Lee, S.I.: Learning not to reconstruct anomalies. In: BMVC (2021)
5. Benaim, S., et al.: SpeedNet: learning the speediness in videos. In: CVPR (2020)
6. Chang, Y., Tu, Z., Xie, W., Yuan, J.: Clustering driven deep autoencoder for video anomaly detection. In: Vedaldi, A., Bischof, H., Brox, T., Frahm, J.-M. (eds.) ECCV 2020. LNCS, vol. 12360, pp. 329–345. Springer, Cham (2020). https://doi.org/10.1007/978-3-030-58555-6_20
7. Chen, D., Wang, P., Yue, L., Zhang, Y., Jia, T.: Anomaly detection in surveillance video based on bidirectional prediction. IVC **98**, 103915 (2020)
8. Chen, T., Kornblith, S., Norouzi, M., Hinton, G.: A simple framework for contrastive learning of visual representations. In: ICML (2020)
9. Cong, Y., Yuan, J., Liu, J.: Abnormal event detection in crowded scenes using sparse representation. PR **46**(7), 1851–1864 (2013)
10. Doersch, C., Gupta, A., Efros, A.A.: Unsupervised visual representation learning by context prediction. In: ICCV (2015)
11. Fan, Y., Wen, G., Li, D., Qiu, S., Levine, M.D., Xiao, F.: Video anomaly detection and localization via gaussian mixture fully convolutional variational autoencoder. CVIU **195**, 102920 (2020)
12. Feng, X., Song, D., Chen, Y., Chen, Z., Ni, J., Chen, H.: Convolutional transformer based dual discriminator general adversarial networks for video anomaly detection. In: ACM MM (2021)

13. Georgescu, M.I., Barbalau, A., Ionescu, R.T., Khan, F.S., Popescu, M., Shah, M.: Anomaly detection in video via self-supervised and multi-task learning. In: CVPR (2021)

14. Georgescu, M.I., Ionescu, R.T., Khan, F.S., Popescu, M., Shah, M.: A background-agnostic framework with adversarial training for abnormal event detection in video. arXiv preprint arXiv:2008.12328 (2020)

15. Gidaris, S., Singh, P., Komodakis, N.: Unsupervised representation learning by predicting image rotations. In: ICLR (2018)

16. Gong, D., et al.: Memorizing normality to detect anomaly: memory-augmented deep autoencoder for unsupervised anomaly detection. In: ICCV (2019)

17. Haresh, S., Kumar, S., Zia, M.Z., Tran, Q.H.: Towards anomaly detection in dash-cam videos. In: IV (2020)

18. Hasan, M., Choi, J., Neumann, J., Roy-Chowdhury, A.K., Davis, L.S.: Learning temporal regularity in video sequences. In: CVPR (2016)

19. He, K., Fan, H., Wu, Y., Xie, S., Girshick, R.: Momentum contrast for unsupervised visual representation learning. In: CVPR (2020)

20. Hendrycks, D., Mazeika, M., Kadavath, S., Song, D.: Using self-supervised learning can improve model robustness and uncertainty. In: NeurIPS (2019)

21. Ionescu, R.T., Khan, F.S., Georgescu, M.I., Shao, L.: Object-centric auto-encoders and dummy anomalies for abnormal event detection in video. In: CVPR (2019)

22. Jenni, S., Meishvili, G., Favaro, P.: Video representation learning by recognizing temporal transformations. In: Vedaldi, A., Bischof, H., Brox, T., Frahm, J.-M. (eds.) ECCV 2020. LNCS, vol. 12373, pp. 425–442. Springer, Cham (2020). https://doi.org/10.1007/978-3-030-58604-1_26

23. Kay, W., et al.: The kinetics human action video dataset. arXiv preprint arXiv:1705.06950 (2017)

24. Kim, D., Cho, D., Kweon, I.S.: Self-supervised video representation learning with space-time cubic puzzles. In: AAAI (2019)

25. Komodakis, N., Gidaris, S.: Unsupervised representation learning by predicting image rotations. In: ICLR (2018)

26. Lee, H.Y., Huang, J.B., Singh, M., Yang, M.H.: Unsupervised representation learning by sorting sequences. In: ICCV (2017)

27. Lee, S., Kim, H.G., Ro, Y.M.: BMAN: bidirectional multi-scale aggregation networks for abnormal event detection. IEEE TIP **29**, 2395–2408 (2019)

28. Lin, T.-Y., et al.: Microsoft COCO: Common Objects in Context. In: Fleet, D., Pajdla, T., Schiele, B., Tuytelaars, T. (eds.) ECCV 2014. LNCS, vol. 8693, pp. 740–755. Springer, Cham (2014). https://doi.org/10.1007/978-3-319-10602-1_48

29. Liu, W., Luo, W., Lian, D., Gao, S.: Future frame prediction for anomaly detection-a new baseline. In: CVPR (2018)

30. Liu, Z., Nie, Y., Long, C., Zhang, Q., Li, G.: A hybrid video anomaly detection framework via memory-augmented flow reconstruction and flow-guided frame prediction. In: ICCV (2021)

31. Lorre, G., Rabarisoa, J., Orcesi, A., Ainouz, S., Canu, S.: Temporal contrastive pretraining for video action recognition. In: WACV (2020)

32. Lu, C., Shi, J., Jia, J.: Abnormal event detection at 150 fps in MATLAB. In: ICCV (2013)

33. Lu, Y., Kumar, K.M., shahabeddin Nabavi, S., Wang, Y.: Future frame prediction using convolutional VRNN for anomaly detection. In: AVSS (2019)

34. Luo, W., Liu, W., Gao, S.: Remembering history with convolutional LSTM for anomaly detection. In: ICME (2017)

35. Luo, W., Liu, W., Gao, S.: A revisit of sparse coding based anomaly detection in stacked RNN framework. In: ICCV (2017)
36. Mahadevan, V., Li, W., Bhalodia, V., Vasconcelos, N.: Anomaly detection in crowded scenes. In: CVPR (2010)
37. Misra, I., Zitnick, C.L., Hebert, M.: Shuffle and learn: unsupervised learning using temporal order verification. In: Leibe, B., Matas, J., Sebe, N., Welling, M. (eds.) ECCV 2016. LNCS, vol. 9905, pp. 527–544. Springer, Cham (2016). https://doi. org/10.1007/978-3-319-46448-0_32
38. Morais, R., Le, V., Tran, T., Saha, B., Mansour, M., Venkatesh, S.: Learning regularity in skeleton trajectories for anomaly detection in videos. In: CVPR (2019)
39. Munawar, A., Vinayavekhin, P., De Magistris, G.: Limiting the reconstruction capability of generative neural network using negative learning. In: MLSP (2017)
40. Nguyen, T.N., Meunier, J.: Anomaly detection in video sequence with appearance-motion correspondence. In: ICCV (2019)
41. Noroozi, M., Favaro, P.: Unsupervised learning of visual representations by solving jigsaw puzzles. In: Leibe, B., Matas, J., Sebe, N., Welling, M. (eds.) ECCV 2016. LNCS, vol. 9910, pp. 69–84. Springer, Cham (2016). https://doi.org/10.1007/978-3-319-46466-4_5
42. Pan, T., Song, Y., Yang, T., Jiang, W., Liu, W.: VideoMoCo: contrastive video representation learning with temporally adversarial examples. In: CVPR (2021)
43. Park, H., Noh, J., Ham, B.: Learning memory-guided normality for anomaly detection. In: CVPR (2020)
44. Paszke, A., et al.: Automatic differentiation in PyTorch (2017)
45. Pickup, L.C., et al.: Seeing the arrow of time. In: CVPR (2014)
46. Redmon, J., Farhadi, A.: YOLOv3: an incremental improvement. arXiv preprint arXiv:1804.02767 (2018)
47. Russakovsky, O., et al.: ImageNet large scale visual recognition challenge. IJCV **115**(3), 211–252 (2015)
48. Santa Cruz, R., Fernando, B., Cherian, A., Gould, S.: Visual permutation learning. IEEE TPAMI **41**(12), 3100–3114 (2018)
49. Sun, C., Jia, Y., Hu, Y., Wu, Y.: Scene-aware context reasoning for unsupervised abnormal event detection in videos. In: ACM MM (2020)
50. Tang, Y., Zhao, L., Zhang, S., Gong, C., Li, G., Yang, J.: Integrating prediction and reconstruction for anomaly detection. PRL **129**, 123–130 (2020)
51. Wang, X., Girshick, R., Gupta, A., He, K.: Non-local neural networks. In: CVPR (2018)
52. Wang, X., Che, Z., Jiang, B., Xiao, N., Yang, K., Tang, J., Ye, J., Wang, J., Qi, Q.: Robust unsupervised video anomaly detection by multipath frame prediction. IEEE TNNLS **33**, 2301–2312 (2021)
53. Wang, Z., Zou, Y., Zhang, Z.: Cluster attention contrast for video anomaly detection. In: ACM MM (2020)
54. Wei, D., Lim, J.J., Zisserman, A., Freeman, W.T.: Learning and using the arrow of time. In: CVPR (2018)
55. Wu, P., Liu, J., Shen, F.: A deep one-class neural network for anomalous event detection in complex scenes. IEEE TNNLS **31**(7), 2609–2622 (2019)
56. Xinyang Feng, Dongjin Song, Y.C.Z.C.J.N.H.C.: Convolutional transformer based dual discriminator generative adversarial networks for video anomaly detection. In: ACM MM (2021)
57. Xu, D., Xiao, J., Zhao, Z., Shao, J., Xie, D., Zhuang, Y.: Self-supervised spatiotemporal learning via video clip order prediction. In: CVPR (2019)

58. Ye, M., Peng, X., Gan, W., Wu, W., Qiao, Y.: AnoPCN: video anomaly detection via deep predictive coding network. In: ACM MM (2019)
59. Yu, G., et al.: Cloze test helps: effective video anomaly detection via learning to complete video events. In: ACM MM (2020)
60. Zhang, R., Isola, P., Efros, A.A.: Colorful image colorization. In: Leibe, B., Matas, J., Sebe, N., Welling, M. (eds.) ECCV 2016. LNCS, vol. 9907, pp. 649–666. Springer, Cham (2016). https://doi.org/10.1007/978-3-319-46487-9_40
61. Zhao, Y., Deng, B., Shen, C., Liu, Y., Lu, H., Hua, X.S.: Spatio-temporal autoencoder for video anomaly detection. In: ACM MM (2017)
62. Zong, B., et al.: Deep autoencoding gaussian mixture model for unsupervised anomaly detection. In: ICLR (2018)

Class-Agnostic Object Detection
with Multi-modal Transformer

Muhammad Maaz[1]([✉]), Hanoona Rasheed[1], Salman Khan[1,2],
Fahad Shahbaz Khan[1,3], Rao Muhammad Anwer[1,4], and Ming-Hsuan Yang[5,6,7]

[1] Mohamed bin Zayed University of AI, Abu Dhabi, UAE
muhammad.maaz@mbzuai.ac.ae
[2] Australian National University, Canberra, Australia
[3] Linköping University, Linkoping, Sweden
[4] Aalto University, Espoo, Finland
[5] University of California, Merced, Merced, USA
[6] Yonsei University, Seoul, South Korea
[7] Google Research, Mountain View, USA

Abstract. What constitutes an object? This has been a long-standing
question in computer vision. Towards this goal, numerous learning-free
and learning-based approaches have been developed to score *objectness*.
However, they generally do not scale well across new domains and novel
objects. In this paper, we advocate that existing methods lack a top-down
supervision signal governed by human-understandable semantics. For the
first time in literature, we demonstrate that Multi-modal Vision Transformers (MViT) trained with aligned image-text pairs can effectively
bridge this gap. Our extensive experiments across various domains and
novel objects show the state-of-the-art performance of MViTs to localize
generic objects in images. Based on the observation that existing MViTs
do not include multi-scale feature processing and usually require longer
training schedules, we develop an efficient MViT architecture using multi-
scale deformable attention and late vision-language fusion. We show the
significance of MViT proposals in a diverse range of applications including open-world object detection, salient and camouflage object detection,
supervised and self-supervised detection tasks. Further, MViTs can adaptively generate proposals given a specific language query and thus offer
enhanced interactability. Code: https://git.io/J1HPY.

Keywords: Object detection · Class-agnostic · Vision transformers

1 Introduction

The recent years have witnessed significant advances in object detection (OD)
[42] based on developments of large-scale annotated datasets and carefully

---

M. Maaz and H. Rasheed—Equal contribution.

Supplementary Information The online version contains supplementary material
available at https://doi.org/10.1007/978-3-031-20080-9_30.

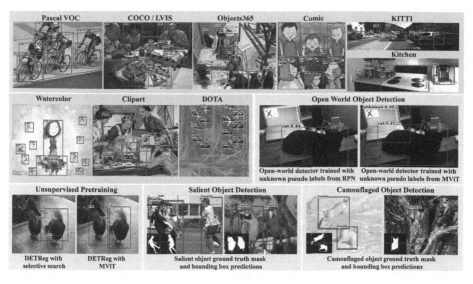

Fig. 1. We show that Multi-modal Vision Transformers (MViTs) excel at Class-agnostic OD across multiple domains: natural images [14,17,18,40], satellite images [72], sketches, cartoons and paintings [26] (gray background). The MViTs perform well on diverse datasets (with many classes *e.g.,* LVIS, Object365) using intuitive natural language text queries (*e.g.,* all objects). Further, class-agnostic detectors (MViTs) can be applied to several downstream applications (pearl background). In Open-world OD [28], unknown pseudo-labels generated using MDETR [29] can improve novelty detection. For unsupervised object localization, replacing Selective Search proposals [64] in DETReg [3] pretraining with only top-30 MViT proposals leads to improved localization. For Salient and Camouflaged OD, task specific text queries can help perform competitively against fully supervised models without any task specific tuning. Overall, MViTs achieve the state-of-the-art results on various downstream applications. (Color figure online)

designed deep learning models. Notably, efforts have been made to tackle more difficult cases such as universal OD [67], long-tailed object distribution modeling [19], open-vocabulary [78] and open-world OD [28]. In contrast, little progress has been made towards a seemingly simpler task of class-agnostic OD [1] in recent years. In the era of fully trainable pipelines, class-agnostic OD is still often approached using typical bottom-up approaches such as Selective Search [64], EdgeBox [84], DeepMask [49] and MCG [52].

Despite being an apparently simpler problem in terms of the two-way classification space, the class-agnostic OD task is indeed challenging from the representation learning perspective. The main challenge is to model the vast diversity of *all* valid object classes and delineate such a diverse group from the *background* class which itself has vague semantic definition [2]. Our experiments indicate that this intrinsic complexity of the task makes it difficult to design fully trainable class-agnostic OD models that can work across domains and for novel unseen objects. Although the bottom-up approaches offer proposals for generic objects, they come at the cost of a prohibitively large number of candidate boxes, low-precision, lack of semantic understanding and slow processing, making them less scalable to generic operation in the wild. More recently, self-supervised learning frameworks – based on both ViTs [3,11] and CNNs [73,74] – have focused on promoting better localization of generic objects, however they still show modest performance on class-agnostic OD [3]. Our intuition is that *top-down supervisory signals* are necessary to resolve the ambiguous nature of class-agnostic OD task, which is precisely what is missing from the aforementioned approaches.

In this paper, we bring out the capacity of recent Multi-modal Vision Transformers (MViTs) to propose generic class-agnostic OD across different domains. The high-level information provided by the language descriptions helps learn fairly generalizable properties of universal object categories. In turn, the MViTs perform exceptionally well compared to uni-modal object detectors trained for generic object detection as well as the typical bottom-up object proposal generation schemes. Due to the multi-modal nature of these models, we design language-driven queries to discover valid objects in a human-understandable format that can be adapted to explore varied aspects of the object semantic space. With the state-of-the-art performance, an ensuing question is to explore the root cause of such generalization for the '*concept of objects*' embedded in MViTs. Through a series of systematic experiments, we find that it is the language skeleton/structure (rather than the lexicon itself) that defines this strong understanding of generic object definition within MViT models. As an interesting example, when the MViT is trained without actual captions, but just the bounding boxes corresponding to a natural language description, the model still demonstrates strong class-agnostic OD generalization. These insights on the interactive class-agnostic OD mechanism can be deployed in several *downstream* tasks such as novel object discovery, saliency detection, self-supervised learning and open-world detection. The main highlights of this work include:

- We demonstrate the state-of-the-art performance of pre-trained MViTs [20,29] towards class-agnostic OD via a set of human-understandable natural language queries. We also develop an efficient and flexible MViT model, *Multiscale Attention ViT with Late fusion* (MAVL), which performs better in locating generic objects as compared to existing MViTs (Sects. 2 and 3).
- We benchmark generalization of MViT based OD models on diverse domains *e.g.,* natural images, sketches, cartoons, satellite images, paintings and show their favorable performance compared to existing class-agnostic OD models (bottom-up approaches, CNN and ViT based uni-modal pipelines) (Sect. 3).
- Our class-agnostic detectors can benefit various down-stream applications: Open-world OD, Salient OD, Camouflaged OD and Self-supervised learning. Furthermore, when these proposals are combined with RPN proposals in two-stage detectors, it can lead to overall performance improvements due to their rich top-down semantic understanding of the image content (Sect. 4).
- Through an extensive set of systematic experiments, we analyze the factors that majorly contribute to the improved performance of MViTs (Sect. 5).

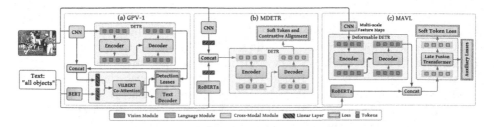

Fig. 2. Architecture overview of MViTs used in this work – GPV-1 [20], MDETR [29] and MAVL (ours). GPV-1 takes image along with a task description as input and outputs relevant region boxes and text. MDETR uses soft token prediction and contrastive alignment in latent space for cross-conceptualization using aligned image-text pairs. MAVL utilizes multi-scale image features with multi-scale deformable attention module (MSDA), and uses late-fusion strategy for vision-language fusion.

2   Multi-modal ViTs

In this work, we bring out the generalization capacity of Multi-modal ViTs (MViT) to tackle generic OD. The capability of relating natural language with visual features helps MViTs to generalize to novel concepts, achieving state-of-the-art results on class-agnostic OD using human-understandable text queries (e.g., 'all objects/entities'). Before a detailed analysis, we provide background on MViTs and propose Multiscale Attention ViT with Late fusion (MAVL).

(a) **GPV:** Gupta *et al.* proposed GPV-I [20], a unified architecture for multi-task learning, where the task is inferred from the text prompt. It takes an image and a task description as input and outputs text with the corresponding bounding boxes. This model uses pretrained BERT [12] to encode the text, concatenates it with the region descriptors from DETR [5] and passes it to ViLBERT [44] co-attention layers for cross-modal conceptualization. It predicts relevance scores for each predicted bounding box indicating the importance of the region for the prompted task. An output text decoder conditioned on the relevance scores is used for better cross-modal understanding (Fig. 2(a)). GPV is trained on data from five different vision-language tasks.

(b) **MDETR:** Kamath *et al.* [29] proposed a modulated transformer trained to detect objects in an image conditioned on a text query. In MDETR, visual and text features are extracted from a convolutional backbone (*e.g.,* ResNet-101 [23] or EfficientNet [63]) and a language model (RoBERTa [43]) respectively. These features are then concatenated and passed to the DETR [5] model for detection (Fig. 2(b)). MDETR uses soft token prediction and contrastive alignment in latent space for addressing text-conditioned object detection. In soft token prediction, a uniform probability distribution is predicted over all text tokens for each detected object. In contrastive alignment, the embedded object queries from decoder are aligned with the text representation from encoder. This multi-modal alignment makes the object embeddings closer to the corresponding text embeddings in feature space. The model is pre-trained with 1.3M image-text pairs and achieves the state-of-the-art results on various vision-language downstream tasks including VQA, referring expression and phrase grounding.

(c) **MAVL:** We develop a new multimodal architecture called Multi-scale Attention ViT with Late fusion (MAVL) that improves the class-agnostic OD performance of MDETR using multi-scale spatial context and deformable attention making it efficient to train. Figure 2(c) shows our overall design. Below, we highlight the main features of MAVL:

- *Multi-scale Deformable Attention (MSDA).* MDETR [29] finds it challenging to scale to high-resolution feature maps due to a fixed self-attention design. Further, it operates on a specified spatial scale which can be suboptimal for small objects. Our design calculates attention at multiple scales to incorporate better contextual information. However, multiple scales can increase the computational cost, therefore we use Deformable Attention proposed in [83] that employs multi-scale feature processing and dynamically attends to relevant pixel locations for context aggregation. Specifically, it samples a small set of keys around a reference (query) image location. The sparse key sampling in MSDA achieves linear complexity with respect to the size of the image feature maps.

- *Late Multi-modal Fusion.* MSDA module utilizes the spatial structure of an image to sparsely sample keys for each query point. Following the MDETR strategy of concatenating text embeddings with flattened features would destroy the spatial structure of an image. Hence, we fuse text in MAVL model after the images are processed through the Def-DETR encoder-decoder architecture using a *late fusion* mechanism. Specifically, the object query representations from the deformable decoder are concatenated with the text embeddings, and passed through a series of six transformer self-attention (SA) blocks. This design choice is inspired by the recent vision-language fusion works [44,60–62]. Using the training procedure of [5], the output head is applied after each SA block and the total loss is calculated by adding all auxiliary losses. We note that no explicit contrastive alignment of object query representation and encoded text is required in our approach. Our experiments show fast convergence (only *half* iterations) and competitive performance of MAVL against MDETR (Tables 1, 2).

- *Implementation Details.* Similar to MDETR [29], we train MAVL on approx. 1.3M aligned image-text pairs, using images from Flickr30k [51], MS-COCO (2014) [40] and Visual Genome (VG) [32]. The corresponding annotations are taken from Flickr entities, RefCOCO/+/g referring expression [30], VG regions and GQA [25]. In the onward discussion, we refer to this dataset as *Large-scale Modulated Detection* (LMDet)dataset. All MDETR and MAVL models are trained with ImageNet-1K [55] pre-trained ResNet-101 [23]. Our MAVL *converges in 20 epochs* (MDETR requires 40 epochs) on LMDet using the same hyper-parameters as in MDETR. See Appendix A.1 for more details.

Table 1. Class-agnostic OD results of MViTs in comparison with bottom-up approaches (row 3–5) and uni-modal detectors (row 6–8) trained to localize generic objects. Bottom row shows gain of MAVL over the best uni-modal method. In general, MViTs achieve state-of-the-art performance using intuitive text queries (details in Sect. 4.1).

Dataset → Model ↓	Pascal-VOC AP50	R50	COCO AP50	R50	KITTI AP50	R50	Objects365 AP50	R50	LVIS AP50	R50
Edge Boxes	0.08	7.14	0.09	5.16	0.09	6.58	0.07	3.27	0.05	3.00
Selective Search	0.32	21.4	0.27	12.7	0.03	4.85	0.38	10.7	0.24	9.31
Deep Mask	5.92	40.4	2.16	19.2	1.33	15.5	1.31	14.5	0.51	8.17
Faster-RCNN	42.9	85.8	26.4	58.7	23.5	53.2	24.8	54.6	8.91	35.6
RetinaNet	43.2	86.6	24.6	59.1	30.4	57.6	24.3	54.8	8.57	35.7
Def-DETR	30.1	81.0	20.0	53.5	23.7	55.0	17.0	45.9	6.60	30.7
GPV-I	61.9	91.1	38.0	64.4	43.0	64.4	25.6	50.2	9.18	27.5
MDETR	66.0	90.1	40.7	62.2	46.7	**67.2**	30.4	54.0	10.7	32.8
MAVL (Ours)	**68.6**	**91.3**	**43.6**	**65.0**	**48.2**	63.5	**33.2**	**57.9**	**11.7**	**37.0**
	+25.4	+4.7	+19.0	+5.9	+17.8	+5.9	+8.4	+3.1	+2.8	+1.3

3 Multi-modal ViTs as Generic Detectors

The class-agnostic OD seeks to differentiate between generic objects and background in images. This task involves learning the notion of *objectness*. Existing approaches typically explore low-level visual cues (i.e. superpixels, edges, etc.) or directly learn the mapping between images and generic object locations using fully trainable pipelines learned with bounding box annotations [3,27,64,84]. We note that these procedures lack high-level semantic information necessary to relate objects across diverse scenes to derive a comprehensive and general notion of universal objects. In this work, We explore the class-agnostic OD capacity of MViTs trained using aligned image-text pairs (Sect. 2). We observe these models can produce high quality object proposals by using intuitive text queries like 'all objects' and 'all entities'. This demonstrates their capability to relate natural language with visual concepts to model generic objectness, enabling them to discover novel categories and generalize across different domains while offering human interaction with intelligible text queries.

3.1 Class-agnostic Object Detection

Settings: Table 1 shows the object proposal generation performance of MViTs with the typical bottom-up approaches and the end-to-end supervised deep learning methods on five challenging natural image OD datasets (Pascal VOC [14], MS COCO [40], KITTI [17], Objects365 [56] and LVIS [19]). The bottom-up

Table 2. Class-agnostic OD performance of MViTs in comparison with RetinaNet [39] on several out-of-domain datasets. MViTs show consistently good results on all datasets. †Proposals on DOTA [72] are generated by multi-scale inference (see Sect. A.2).

Dataset →	Kitchen		Clipart		Comic		Watercolor		DOTA†	
Model ↓	AP50	R50	AP50	R50	AP50	R50	AP50	R50	AP50	R50
RetinaNet	35.3	89.5	27.0	90.0	33.1	86.1	47.8	91.9	0.72	15.6
GPV-1	24.5	84.8	35.1	86.1	42.3	83.6	50.3	89.5	0.55	9.33
MDETR	38.4	**91.4**	44.9	90.7	55.8	**89.5**	63.6	94.3	1.94	21.8
MAVL (Ours)	**45.4**	91.0	**50.6**	**92.9**	**57.7**	89.2	**63.8**	**95.6**	**2.86**	**24.2**

approaches considered for comparison include EdgeBoxes [84], Selective Search [64] and DeepMask [49] while Faster-RCNN [54], RetinaNet [39] and Deformable-DETR [83] are selected from the deep-learning based methods due to the state-of-the-art performance in class-aware OD. The MViTs considered are GPV-I [20] and MDETR [29] alongside our proposed MAVL (see Sect. 2 for details).

For fairness, all the uni-modal detectors considered for evaluation are trained with ResNet-101 backbone using box-level supervision on LMDet dataset. Faster-RCNN and RetinaNet follow the standard Detectron2 [70] training setting with FPN at 1× schedule. The combined detections from the text queries in Table 3 are used for evaluating MViTs (see Sect. 4.1 and Appendix A.2 for details). Moreover, images used in the evaluation *do not* have any overlap with LMDet.

Results: We report both average precision (AP) and Recall at IoU threshold of 0.5 using the top-50 boxes from each method. Overall, the detectors trained in class-agnostic fashion perform reasonably well on all datasets, surpassing the bottom-up methods by a large margin. Furthermore, the MViTs perform better than the uni-modal approaches with the use of simple human understandable natural language text queries. This performance shows MViTs' strong understanding of language content obtained from the pretrained NLP model (BERT [12], RoBERTa [43]) along with the aligned image-text pairs used in pretraining.

For MViTs, interestingly a relatively small number of boxes match the quality achieved by a much larger proposal set from competing methods. Figure 3a shows the recall obtained by varying the number of top object proposals for all methods on two datasets. MViTs achieve competitive recall with only top-10 proposals.

3.2   How Well MViTs Generalize?

Generalization to New Domains: We extend our analysis from natural image datasets (Sect. 3.1) to rule out if MViT representations are biased towards natural images, for which these models are originally trained on. To this end, we evaluate on universal OD datasets [67] belonging to five different domains (Table 2). The studied domains include indoor kitchen scenes [18], cartoon images, watercolor drawings, clipart, comics [26] and satellite/aerial images (DOTA dataset) [72]. The experiments follow the same setting as in Sect. 3.1. These results indicate the generalization capability of MViTs in comparison to the best proposal generation methods earlier evaluated in Table 1 (RetinaNet trained for class-agnostic OD).

Generalization to Rare/Novel Classes: With the notion of objectness, humans are capable of identifying novel and rare objects, although they may not recognize their specific category. Similarly, scalabiltiy to rare and novel classes is a desired quality of an object detector. To analyze this, the class-agnostic OD mechanism of MAVL is evaluated on rare categories from Open-Images [34] versus frequent categories and compared with Deformable DETR and Deep Mask trained for class agnostic OD. Figure 3b indicate state-of-the-art recall on rare categories such as *lynx, humidifier,* and *armadillo* with as few as zero training instance. Overall, we note the model generalizes well to rare/unseen categories.

4   Applications and Use-cases

The high-quality class-agnostic object proposals obtained from MViTs can be helpful towards several downstream applications, as we demonstrate next.

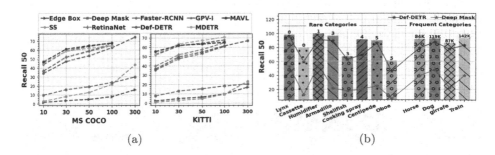

(a)   (b)

Fig. 3. (a) Effect of using different number of top-ranked boxes on multiple class-agnostic OD methods. The MViTs exhibits good recall even with only top-10 proposals. (b) MAVL class-agnostic OD performance on rarely and frequently occurring categories in LMDet. Rare categories are selected from Open Images [34]. The MAVL recall rates (represented by the bars) are compared with those of Def-DETR [83] and DeepMask [49] (represented by the lines). The numbers on top of the bars indicate the total occurrences of the category in LMDet captions. The MViT achieves good recall even for the classes with no or very few occurrences in the training dataset.

4.1 Enhanced Interactability

We have observed that MViTs can generate high quality object proposals with intuitive human understandable queries such as 'all objects'. This motivates us to explore the language semantic space of such models to construct a set of queries that can well capture the generic concept of objectness. We filter words from captions in LMDet that are semantically close to the word 'object' in the linguistic feature space. We then utilize these words to construct intuitive text queries such as 'all objects', 'all entities', 'all visible entities and objects', and 'all obscure entities and objects', for exploiting the class-agnostic OD performance of MViTs. The detections from the individual text queries are combined, filtered with class-agnostic non-maximum suppression (NMS) to remove duplicate detections, and top-N boxes are selected for evaluation. We use N = 50 in all of our experiments.

Table 3. Using different intuitive text queries with MAVL. Combining detections from multiple queries captures varying aspects of objectness.

Dataset →	Pascal-VOC		COCO		KITTI	
Text Query ↓	AP50	R50	AP50	R50	AP50	R50
all objects	51.3	85.5	33.3	58.4	40.2	64.0
all entities	65.2	88.4	34.6	54.6	41.9	59.5
all visible entities & objects	63.3	89.0	37.9	61.6	42.0	63.0
all obscure entities & objects	59.5	86.6	35.2	59.1	42.4	63.5
all small objects	40.0	83.9	28.9	58.9	40.4	65.2
combined detections (CD)	63.7	91.0	42.0	**65.0**	48.2	**63.5**
CD w/o 'all small objects'	**68.6**	**91.3**	**43.6**	65.0	45.8	61.6

Task Specific Queries: The detection of small and irregular sized objects has remained a long-standing challenge. In our case, the flexible nature of MViTs facilitates using a range of human-understandable text queries. The queries can be chosen that best describe the special requirements needed in a given detection task. We demonstrate certain scenarios of how this feature can be exploited for better predictions. Figure 4a (left) shows an interesting case of how the text query 'all little objects' improves recall for small objects as compared to a

(a)   (b)

Fig. 4. (a) MAVL recall for small (S), medium (M) and large (L) objects across three datasets. The use of specific query ('all little objects') increases recall of small objects across different datasets (*left*). Targeted detections by the relevant text queries (*right*). (b) Visualizations of ORE [28] unknown detections when trained with RPN versus MAVL unknown pseudo-labels (*top*). Class-agnostic OD of DETReg [3] when trained using Selective Search (SS) [64] versus MAVL proposals (*bottom*).

Table 4. MViT proposals are used for pseudo-labelling of unknowns in ORE [28]. MAVL represents the model trained on a filtered dataset generated by *removing* all captions from LMDet listing any of the 60 unknown categories evaluated in ORE. The results indicate a notable improvement in unknown detection.

Task ID	Task 1		Task 2				Task 3				Task 4		
Pseudo-label for Unknown	mAP	R50	mAP			R50	mAP			R50	mAP		
	Current Known	Unknown	Previous Known	Current Known	Both	Unknown	Previous Known	Current Known	Both	Unknown	Previous Known	Current Known	Both
RPN	63.4	14.4	58.3	30.8	45.1	11.3	43.3	23.4	36.7	14.8	37.2	20.7	33.1
MAVL*	64.0	**50.1**	61.6	30.8	46.2	**49.5**	43.8	22.7	36.8	**50.9**	36.2	20.6	32.3

rather general text query. Similarly, Fig. 4a (right) indicates how the use of special queries like 'all long objects' helps improve the detection of irregular shaped objects (without any dataset specific fine-tuning!).

4.2   Open-World Object Detection

The open-world setting assumes a realistic paradigm where a model can experience *unknown objects* during training and inference [4,13,28,65]. The goal is to identify unknowns and incrementally learn about them as and when new annotations are provided about a subset of unknowns. This stands in contrast to generic OD where models are trained to label unknown objects as background and only focus on the known objects. Here, we explore how a generic class-agnostic OD model can help with the open-world task to identify unknowns. As a case study, we apply our approach to a recent open-world detector (ORE) [28].

- *ORE Setting:* The authors distribute the 80 COCO [40] classes in four incremental learning tasks where 20 classes have been added to the known categories in each subsequent task. At each stage, the model must learn from the given subset of 20 newly introduced known classes, should not forget the previous known classes and must be able to detect unknown classes whose labelled examples have not been provided so far as the unknowns. ORE uses Faster-RCNN [54] as the base detector, with contrastive clustering in latent space and an energy-based classification head for unknown detection. It utilizes example-replay strategy [66] for alleviating forgetting, when progressively learning the unknown categories once their labels become available.
- *Unknown Pseudo-labels with MViTs:* ORE exploits the two-stage mechanism of Faster-RCNN [54] and uses proposals from the class-agnostic region proposal network (RPN) for pseudo-labelling of unknowns. The foreground object proposals with high objectness score which do not overlap with any ground-truth are labelled as unknowns. We note that since RPN is only trained on the objects of interest, its detections are overly sparse and lead to a low recall for unknowns. The pipeline therefore lacks a good proposal set that generalizes to *novel objects*. We propose a variant of ORE, by using class-agnostic proposals for unknown object categories obtained from MAVL. For a fair comparison, the MViT is trained on a filtered dataset,

generated by explicitly removing all captions from LMDet that contain any unknown category, leaving 0.76M image-text pairs (see Appendix A.4 for further details). The results in Table 4 and Fig. 4b indicate significant improvements in unknown detection. See Fig. 10 in Appendix C for more qualitative results.

4.3   Pretraining for Class-Aware Object Detection

The recent progress in self-supervised learning (SSL) [6,21,46,79] has minimized the need for large *labelled* datasets to achieve good performance on downstream tasks. These techniques encode the global image representation and achieve competitive generalization on various downstream tasks. How-

Table 5. Effect of using MAVL proposals for pretraining of DETReg [3] instead of Selective Search [64] proposals.

Dataset→	Pascal-VOC 10%			Pascal-VOC 100%		
Model ↓	AP	AP50	AP75	AP	AP50	AP75
DETReg - SS	51.4	72.2	56.6	63.5	83.3	70.3
DETReg - MAVL	**58.8**	**80.5**	**65.7**	**64.5**	**84.2**	**71.3**

ever, these methods are suboptimal for class-aware OD, where the classification needs to be performed at local image patches (i.e. bounding boxes). Several recent efforts have been reported to address this challenge. ReSim [73] and DetCo [74] only pretrain the backbone to encode local and global representations. Whereas, DETReg [3] pretrains both the backbone and detection network using off-the-shelf proposals from selective search [64] and achieves improvement over the previous methods.

However, the proposals from heuristic selective search method, used in DETReg pretraining, are overly noisy and contain redundant boxes. We show that replacing these noisy pseudo-labels with MViT proposals can improve the downstream performance on OD task (Table 5). Following DETReg, we select top-30 proposals from MAVL and pretrain the model for 50 epochs on ImageNet [55] dataset, followed by fine-tuning on 10% and 100% data from Pascal VOC [14] for 150 and 100 epochs respectively. The results show an absolute gain of ∼7 and ∼1 in AP in the two respective cases.

Table 6. Proposals from MAVL are evaluated against state-of-the-art SOD and COD approaches. The **general**[†] represents 'all objects' text query.

Dataset →		DUT-OMRON		ECSSD	
Model ↓	Text Query	AP50	R50	AP50	R50
CPD [71]	-	64.5	77.4	87.1	92.7
PoolNet [41]	-	66.5	78.8	87.4	93.1
MAVL	General[†]	67.0	89.1	84.5	95.7
MAVL	Task specific[††]	75.5	93.3	85.7	96.1

(a) Salient OD (SOD). Here task specific[††] query combines proposals from 'all salient objects' and 'all foreground objects' text queries.

Dataset →		CHAMELEON		CAMO		COD10K	
Model ↓	Text Query	AP50	R50	AP50	R50	AP50	R50
SINET-V2 [15]	-	67.3	76.7	56.5	77.2	44.4	66.6
MAVL	General[†]	30.2	53.3	46.5	75.4	39.6	67.8
MAVL	Task specific[††]	36.2	61.1	48.0	78.3	42.0	69.1

(b) Camouflaged OD (COD) on three datasets. Here task specific[††] query combines proposals from 'all camouflaged objects' and 'all disguised objects' text queries.

4.4 Salient Object Detection

Given the generalized class-agnostic performance of MViTs on multiple domains, we evaluate their ability to distinguish between salient and non-salient parts of an image. We exploit the interactive nature of MViTs by passing specific queries to detect the salient objects. To this end, MAVL proposals generated with queries like 'all salient objects' are compared with PoolNet [41] and CPD [71] models that are specifically trained for predicting saliency maps. We evaluate the models on the DUT-OMRON [77] and ECSSD [57] datasets. These datasets are only used for MViT evaluation and are not used during training. Since MViTs generate bounding boxes, we convert the saliency ground-truths and the saliency maps predicted by CPD and PoolNet to bounding boxes using connected components labelling [69]. In the case of DUT-OMRON, the provided ground-truth bounding boxes are used by computing an average across the five human annotations.

Table 6a indicates the effectiveness of MAVL in detecting the foreground salient objects. It is also interesting to note how the task specific[††] query (e.g., 'all salient/foreground objects') provides better prediction of salient parts of the image in comparison to a more generic[†] query like 'all objects' (Fig. 5a). See Appendix D.5 and Fig. 11 in Appendix C for additional details.

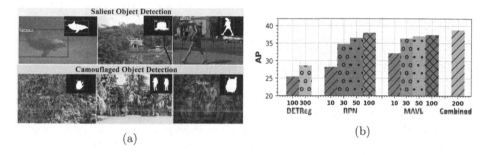

(a)   (b)

Fig. 5. (a) Qualitative results of Salient (Top) and Camouflaged OD (Bottom). The ground-truth masks and boxes are shown on top right of the images. (b) Complimentary effect of using off-the-shelf proposals from MAVL in Faster RCNN [54] trained on COCO [40], indicated as 'combined' (*i.e.*, RPN + MAVL). The x-axis shows the number of proposals. MAVL generates good quality proposals, which perform well even with small proposal set sizes and demonstrate complimentary advantage to RPN.

4.5 Camouflaged Object Detection

Camouflaged object detection (COD) involves identifying objects that are *seamlessly* embedded in their background. The objects have a similar texture to their surroundings and are difficult to locate as compared to salient or generic objects. Here, we explore the interactive OD capacity of MViTs on COD task by evaluating the performance of MAVL against the state-of-the-art model (SINET-V2 [15]) on CHAMELEON [59], CAMO [35] and COD10K [16] datasets (Table 6b).

Similar to salient OD setting, we convert camouflage ground-truth masks and masks predicted by SINET-V2 to bounding boxes using connected components labelling [69]. However, the available bounding box ground-truths have been used for COD10K dataset. We note favorable performance of MAVL proposals, although the model is not specifically trained on camouflaged objects (Fig. 5a). This affirms the generality of MAVL proposals. See Appendix D.6 and Fig. 11.

4.6   Improving Two-Stage Object Detection

The class-agnostic object proposals from MViTs have strong understanding of semantics and can be deployed along with the region proposal network (RPN) [54]. We observe an improvement in accuracy when off-the-shelf MAVL proposals are combined with RPN proposals in Faster RCNN [54] during inference (Fig. 5b). This indicates the complimentary nature of these proposals that is based on a rich top-down perception of the image content.

Figure 5b shows the results of replacing RPN proposals in Faster RCNN with DETReg [3] and MAVL proposals. The results indicate that the supervised proposal generation methods (RPN and MAVL) perform well compared to the unsupervised method (DETReg). However, off-the-shelf MAVL proposals show better performance than RPN when using a small proposal set (e.g., 10 proposals). Combining RPN and MAVL proposals improves the overall detection accuracy.

5   What Makes MViTs a Generic Detector?

Our empirical analysis shows the state-of-the-art performance of MViTs towards class-agnostic OD across different domains (Sect. 3) which positively impacts a number of downstream applications (Sect. 4). Having established this, we conduct a series of systematic experiments to explore the contributing factors for representational learning of the general 'objectness measure' in MViTs. Specifically, we identify the role of supervision and multi-modal learning as crucial factors.

5.1   On the Importance of Supervision

We consider two recent unsupervised learning models, DETReg [3] and UP-DETR [11]. DETReg trains Deformable DETR [83] to localize objects in class-agnostic fashion, with bounding box pseudo-labels from an off-the-shelf region proposal method (Selective Search

Table 7. MAVL proposals perform well compared to unsupervised methods (UP-DETR [11] and DETReg [3]) and supervised uni-modal method (Def-DETR [83]).

Dataset → Model ↓	Supervision	Pascal-VOC		COCO		KITTI	
		AP50	R50	AP50	R50	AP50	R50
UP-DETR	unsupervised	0.56	16.6	0.19	6.56	0.01	0.65
DETReg	self-supervised	2.58	45.7	2.04	26.0	0.01	2.48
Def-DETR	box-level	30.1	81.0	20.0	53.5	23.7	55.0
MAVL	box + text	68.6	91.3	43.6	65.0	48.2	63.5

[64]). Meanwhile, UP-DETR performs unsupervised pretraining on random query patches in an image for class-agnostic OD. Both the unsupervised models, DETReg and UP-DETR, are trained on uni-modal (Deformable DETR [83]) trained on LMDet in class-agnostic fashion, to evaluate the performance contributed by language supervision. We note that the image-level supervision with only box labels improves the performance in comparison with unsupervised methods. However, the use of caption texts aligned with input images proves to be vital and improves the performance approximately by *two* times, highlighting the importance of multi-modal supervision.

5.2 How Much Does Language Contribute?

Given the importance of multi-modal supervision towards better performance, we find it pertinent to explore the benefit solely from the language supervision. We conduct an ablation study on MDETR and MAVL, by removing all textual inputs corresponding to captions, but keeping intact the structure introduced by

Table 8. Effect of removing language branch from MViTs keeping the data loader structure intact. The performance is not affected largely as the language structure is still intact (boxes from caption are seen together).

Dataset→		Pascal-VOC		COCO		KITTI	
Model ↓	Lang.	AP50	R50	AP50	R50	AP50	R50
MDETR	✓	63.9	88.0	38.1	58.5	42.5	60.9
MAVL	✓	65.0	89.1	39.3	62.0	39.0	61.0
MDETR	✗	59.7	86.4	33.4	57.9	36.9	55.0
MAVL	✗	61.6	86.7	34.4	58.3	36.5	58.9

language *i.e.*, learning to localize boxes corresponding to a caption for each image in an iteration (without any language branch). Both MDETR and MAVL are trained on LMDet containing aligned image-text pairs. Here, the structure in which the information is fed during training is of high importance to us. Each image may have multiple captions, and hence it may be seen multiple times in the same iteration, but with varying contexts. The experimental setup removes all captions during training and evaluations, however keeps the described data loader structure intact, thus having approximately 1.3M iterations in an epoch. All models use ResNet-101 backbone and are evaluated after 10 epochs for ablation (instead of total 20 epochs). Table 8 indicate that visual branch plays a vital role, however the importance of language cannot be ruled out since the boxes related to a caption are still seen together. We analyze the importance of this implicit language structure next.

Ablation on Language Structure: The above experimental results reveal that removal of textual information does not significantly affect model performance. However, a further ablation on the structure introduced by language is required for the completeness of this evaluation. As such, we conduct ablations at five levels using Deformable DETR [83], as shown in Table 9. First, all the annotations in LMDet are combined at image level by concatenating the bounding boxes of all captions corresponding to an image (Setting-1). This removes any prior information introduced by the language structure. Then, class-agnostic NMS is applied at a threshold of 0.9 to filter boxes that have high overlaps (Setting-2). To imitate the repetitive pattern introduced during training, bounding box annotations corresponding to an image are randomly sampled and grouped (Setting-3).

The number of samples in a combination is kept close to the average number of boxes in image-text pairs in original MAVL training (~6 boxes). Finally, a longer training schedule is used in the same setting to replicate a scenario closer to the original MAVL training (Setting-4). These four settings are then compared with a model that is trained

Table 9. Experimental analysis to explore the contribution of language by removing all textual inputs, but maintaining the structure introduced by captions. Experiments are performed on Def-DETR [83] using LMDet.

Experiment	Language Structure	Pascal-VOC AP50	Pascal-VOC R50	MSCOCO AP50	MSCOCO R50	KITTI AP50	KITTI R50
Setting-1	×	16.2	74.5	10.7	47.0	19.4	57.3
Setting-2	×	30.1	81.0	20.0	53.5	23.7	55.0
Setting-3	×	33.8	82.5	19.3	55.8	21.2	52.7
Setting-4	×	35.1	82.7	21.2	56.3	21.5	58.5
Setting-5	✓	**61.6**	**86.7**	**34.4**	**58.3**	**36.5**	**58.9**

without any captions, but maintains the structure introduced by language (Setting-5, same as Table 8 last row). This analysis indicates that language structure has significant impact in learning a general notion of objectness. With the use of aligned image-text pairs, additional contextual information is provided to the model. As objects generally tend to co-occur with other objects and certain scenes, such contexual association can be exploited for visual understanding [47]. Use of captions that describe a scene conveys such a notion of co-occurring objects and their mutual relationships, indicating that the structure introduced by language provides rich semantic and spatial context. Consistent with our findings, other recent efforts also indicate strong generalization achieved using the context encoded within natural language [53,78,80,82].

6   Conclusion

This paper demonstrates intriguing performance of MViTs, trained only on natural images, for generic OD across a diverse set of domains. We systematically study the main reasons for this generalization, and note that the language structure available in image-caption pairs used to train MViTs plays a key role. Based on these insights, we develop a more flexible and efficient MViT for off-the-shelf class-agnostic OD, that can be instantiated with different text queries to generate desired proposal sets. Furthermore, we show various use-cases where class-agnostic proposals can be used to improve performance *e.g.,* open-world OD, camouflaged and salient OD, supervised and self-supervised OD.

Acknowledgements. Ming-Hsuan Yang is supported by the NSF CAREER grant 1149783. Fahad Shahbaz Khan is supported by the VR starting grant (2016-05543).

References

1. Alexe, B., Deselaers, T., Ferrari, V.: What is an object? In: Proceedings of the IEEE/CVF Conference on Computer Vision and Pattern Recognition, pp. 73–80. IEEE (2010)
2. Alexe, B., Deselaers, T., Ferrari, V.: Measuring the objectness of image windows. IEEE Trans. Pattern Anal. Mach. Intell. **34**(11), 2189–2202 (2012)
3. Bar, A.,et al.: DETReg: unsupervised Pretraining with region priors for object detection. In: Proceedings of the IEEE/CVF Conference on Computer Vision and Pattern Recognition (2022)
4. Bendale, A., Boult, T.: Towards open world recognition. In: Proceedings of the IEEE/CVF Conference on Computer Vision and Pattern Recognition, pp. 1893–1902 (2015)
5. Carion, N., Massa, F., Synnaeve, G., Usunier, N., Kirillov, A., Zagoruyko, S.: End-to-end object detection with transformers. In: Vedaldi, A., Bischof, H., Brox, T., Frahm, J.-M. (eds.) ECCV 2020. LNCS, vol. 12346, pp. 213–229. Springer, Cham (2020). https://doi.org/10.1007/978-3-030-58452-8_13
6. Caron, M., Misra, I., Mairal, J., Goyal, P., Bojanowski, P., Joulin, A.: Unsupervised learning of visual features by contrasting cluster assignments. In: Advances in Neural Information Processing Systems (2020)
7. Caron, M., et al.: Emerging properties in self-supervised vision transformers. arXiv preprint arXiv:2104.14294 (2021)
8. Chen, T., Kornblith, S., Norouzi, M., Hinton, G.: A simple framework for contrastive learning of visual representations. In: International Conference on Machine Learning, pp. 1597–1607. PMLR (2020)
9. Chen, Y.C., et al.: UNITER: UNiversal image-TExt representation learning. In: Vedaldi, A., Bischof, H., Brox, T., Frahm, J.-M. (eds.) ECCV 2020. LNCS, vol. 12375, pp. 104–120. Springer, Cham (2020). https://doi.org/10.1007/978-3-030-58577-8_7
10. Cheng, M.M., Zhang, Z., Lin, W.Y., Torr, P.: BING: binarized normed gradients for objectness estimation at 300fps. In: Proceedings of the IEEE/CVF Conference on Computer Vision and Pattern Recognition, pp. 3286–3293 (2014)
11. Dai, Z., Cai, B., Lin, Y., Chen, J.: UP-DETR: unsupervised pre-training for object detection with transformers. In: Proceedings of the IEEE/CVF Conference on Computer Vision and Pattern Recognition, pp. 1601–1610 (2021)
12. Devlin, J., Chang, M.W., Lee, K., Toutanova, K.: BERT: pre-training of deep bidirectional transformers for language understanding. In: NAACL (2019)
13. Dhamija, A., Gunther, M., Ventura, J., Boult, T.: The overlooked elephant of object detection: open set. In: Proceedings of the IEEE/CVF Winter Conference on Applications of Computer Vision, pp. 1021–1030 (2020)
14. Everingham, M., Van Gool, L., Williams, C.K., Winn, J., Zisserman, A.: The pascal visual object classes (VOC) challenge. Int. J. Comput. Vision **88**(2), 303–338 (2010). https://doi.org/10.1007/s11263-009-0275-4
15. Fan, D.P., Ji, G.P., Cheng, M.M., Shao, L.: Concealed object detection. IEEE Trans. Pattern Anal. Mach. Intell. **44**, 6024–6042 (2021)
16. Fan, D.P., Ji, G.P., Sun, G., Cheng, M.M., Shen, J., Shao, L.: Camouflaged object detection. In: Proceedings of the IEEE/CVF Conference on Computer Vision and Pattern Recognition, pp. 2777–2787 (2020)
17. Geiger, A., Lenz, P., Urtasun, R.: Are we ready for autonomous driving? The KITTI vision benchmark suite. In: Proceedings of the IEEE/CVF Conference on Computer Vision and Pattern Recognition, pp. 3354–3361. IEEE (2012)

18. Georgakis, G., Reza, M.A., Mousavian, A., Le, P.H., Košecká, J.: multiview RGB-D dataset for object instance detection. In: CoRR, pp. 426–434. IEEE (2016)
19. Gupta, A., Dollar, P., Girshick, R.: LVIS: a dataset for large vocabulary instance segmentation. In: Proceedings of the IEEE/CVF Conference on Computer Vision and Pattern Recognition, pp. 5356–5364 (2019)
20. Gupta, T., Kamath, A., Kembhavi, A., Hoiem, D.: Towards general purpose vision systems. In: Proceedings of the IEEE/CVF Conference on Computer Vision and Pattern Recognition, pp. 16399–16409 (2022)
21. He, K., Fan, H., Wu, Y., Xie, S., Girshick, R.: Momentum contrast for unsupervised visual representation learning. In: Proceedings of the IEEE/CVF Conference on Computer Vision and Pattern Recognition, pp. 9729–9738 (2020)
22. He, K., Gkioxari, G., Dollár, P., Girshick, R.: Mask R-CNN. In: Proceedings of the IEEE/CVF Conference on Computer Vision and Pattern Recognition, pp. 2961–2969 (2017)
23. He, K., Zhang, X., Ren, S., Sun, J.: Deep residual learning for image recognition. In: Proceedings of the IEEE/CVF Conference on Computer Vision and Pattern Recognition, pp. 770–778 (2016)
24. Honnibal, M., Montani, I.: spaCy: industrial-strength natural language processing in python (2020)
25. Hudson, D.A., Manning, C.D.: GQA: a new dataset for real-world visual reasoning and compositional question answering. In: Proceedings of the IEEE/CVF Conference on Computer Vision and Pattern Recognition, pp. 6700–6709 (2019)
26. Inoue, N., Furuta, R., Yamasaki, T., Aizawa, K.: Cross-domain weakly-supervised object detection through progressive domain adaptation. In: Proceedings of the IEEE/CVF Conference on Computer Vision and Pattern Recognition, pp. 5001–5009 (2018)
27. Jaiswal, A., Wu, Y., Natarajan, P., Natarajan, P.: Class-agnostic object detection. In: Proceedings of the IEEE/CVF Winter Conference on Applications of Computer Vision. pp. 919–928 (2021)
28. Joseph, K., Khan, S., Khan, F.S., Balasubramanian, V.N.: Towards open world object detection. In: Proceedings of the IEEE/CVF Conference on Computer Vision and Pattern Recognition, pp. 5830–5840 (2021)
29. Kamath, A., Singh, M., LeCun, Y., Synnaeve, G., Misra, I., Carion, N.: MDETR-modulated detection for end-to-end multi-modal understanding. In: Proceedings of the IEEE/CVF International Conference on Computer Vision. pp. 1780–1790 (2021)
30. Kazemzadeh, S., Ordonez, V., Matten, M., Berg, T.: Referitgame: Referring to objects in photographs of natural scenes. In: Conference on Empirical Methods in Natural Language Processing
31. Kim, D., Lin, T.Y., Angelova, A., Kweon, I.S., Kuo, W.: Learning open-world object proposals without learning to classify. arOXiv preprint arXiv:2108.06753 (2021)
32. Krishna, R., et al.: Visual genome: connecting language and vision using crowd-sourced dense image annotations. Int. J. Comput. Vision **123**(1), 32–73 (2017). https://doi.org/10.1007/S11263-016-0981-7
33. Kuo, W., Hariharan, B., Malik, J.: DeepBox: learning objectness with convolutional networks. In: Proceedings of the IEEE/CVF Conference on Computer Vision and Pattern Recognition,pp. 2479–2487 (2015)
34. Kuznetsova, A.: The open images dataset v4. IJCV **128**(7), 1956–1981 (2020). https://doi.org/10.1007/s11263-020-01316-z

35. Le, T.N., Nguyen, T.V., Nie, Z., Tran, M.T., Sugimoto, A.: Anabranch network for camouflaged object segmentation. Comput. Vis. Image Underst. **184**, 45–56 (2019)
36. Li, L.H., Yatskar, M., Yin, D., Hsieh, C.J., Chang, K.W.: VisualBERT: a simple and performant baseline for vision and language. arXiv preprint arXiv:1908.03557 (2019)
37. Li, X., et al.: Oscar: object-semantics aligned pre-training for vision-language tasks. In: Vedaldi, A., Bischof, H., Brox, T., Frahm, J.-M. (eds.) ECCV 2020. LNCS, vol. 12375, pp. 121–137. Springer, Cham (2020). https://doi.org/10.1007/978-3-030-58577-8_8
38. Lin, T.Y., Dollár, P., Girshick, R., He, K., Hariharan, B., Belongie, S.: Feature pyramid networks for object detection. In: Proceedings of the IEEE/CVF Conference on Computer Vision and Pattern Recognition,pp. 2117–2125 (2017)
39. Lin, T.Y., Goyal, P., Girshick, R., He, K., Dollár, P.: Focal loss for dense object detection. In: Proceedings of the IEEE/CVF Conference on Computer Vision and Pattern Recognition, pp. 2980–2988 (2017)
40. Lin, T.-Y., et al.: Microsoft COCO: common objects in context. In: Fleet, D., Pajdla, T., Schiele, B., Tuytelaars, T. (eds.) ECCV 2014. LNCS, vol. 8693, pp. 740–755. Springer, Cham (2014). https://doi.org/10.1007/978-3-319-10602-1_48
41. Liu, J.J., Hou, Q., Cheng, M.M., Feng, J., Jiang, J.: A simple pooling-based design for real-time salient object detection. In: Proceedings of the IEEE/CVF Conference on Computer Vision and Pattern Recognition, pp. 3917–3926 (2019)
42. Liu, L., et al.: Deep learning for generic object detection: a survey. Int. J. Comput. Vision **128**(2), 261–318 (2020). https://doi.org/10.1007/s11263-019-01247-4
43. Liu, Y., et al.: RoBERTa: a robustly optimized BERT pretraining approach. arXiv preprint arXiv:1907.11692 (2019)
44. Lu, J., Batra, D., Parikh, D., Lee, S.: ViLBERT: pretraining task-agnostic visiolinguistic representations for vision-and-language tasks. In: Advances in Neural Information Processing Systems (2019)
45. Lu, J., Goswami, V., Rohrbach, M., Parikh, D., Lee, S.: 12-in-1: multi-task vision and language representation learning. In: Proceedings of the IEEE/CVF Conference on Computer Vision and Pattern Recognition, pp. 10437–10446 (2020)
46. Misra, I., Maaten, L.V.D.: Self-supervised learning of pretext-invariant representations. In: Proceedings of the IEEE/CVF Conference on Computer Vision and Pattern Recognition, pp. 6707–6717 (2020)
47. Oliva, A., Torralba, A.: The role of context in object recognition. Trends Cogn. Sci. **11**(12), 520–527 (2007)
48. Peyré, G., Cuturi, M.: Computational Optimal Transport (2020)
49. Pinheiro, P.O., Collobert, R., Dollár, P.: Learning to segment object candidates. In: Advances in Neural Information Processing Systems (2015)
50. Pinheiro, P.O., Lin, T.-Y., Collobert, R., Dollár, P.: Learning to refine object segments. In: Leibe, B., Matas, J., Sebe, N., Welling, M. (eds.) ECCV 2016. LNCS, vol. 9905, pp. 75–91. Springer, Cham (2016). https://doi.org/10.1007/978-3-319-46448-0_5
51. Plummer, B.A., Wang, L., Cervantes, C.M., Caicedo, J.C., Hockenmaier, J., Lazebnik, S.: Flickr30k entities: collecting region-to-phrase correspondences for richer image-to-sentence models. In: Proceedings of the IEEE/CVF Conference on Computer Vision and Pattern Recognition, pp. 2641–2649 (2015)
52. Pont-Tuset, J., Arbelaez, P., Barron, J.T., Marques, F., Malik, J.: Multiscale combinatorial grouping for image segmentation and object proposal generation. IEEE Trans. Pattern Anal. Mach. Intell. **39**(1), 128–140 (2016)

53. Radford, A., et al.: Learning transferable visual models from natural language supervision. In: International Conference on Machine Learning (2021)
54. Ren, S., He, K., Girshick, R., Sun, J.: Faster R-CNN: towards real-time object detection with region proposal networks. Adv. Neural. Inf. Process. Syst. **28**, 91–99 (2015)
55. Russakovsky, O., et al.: ImageNet large scale visual recognition challenge. Int. J. Comput. Vision **115**(3), 211–252 (2015). https://doi.org/10.1007/s11263-015-0816-y
56. Shao, S., et al.: Objects365: a large-scale, high-quality dataset for object detection. In: Proceedings of the IEEE/CVF International Conference on Computer Vision, pp. 8430–8439 (2019)
57. Shi, J., Yan, Q., Xu, L., Jia, J.: Hierarchical image saliency detection on extended CSSD. IEEE Trans. Pattern Anal. Mach. Intell. **38**(4), 717–729 (2015)
58. Siméoni, O., et al.: Localizing objects with self-supervised transformers and no labels. In: British Machine Vision Conference (2021)
59. Skurowski, P., Abdulameer, H., Błaszczyk, J., Depta, T., Kornacki, A., Kozieł, P.: Animal camouflage analysis: Chameleon database. Unpublished Manuscript **2**(6), 7 (2018)
60. Su, W., et al.: VL-BERT: pre-training of generic visual-linguistic representations. In: International Conference on Learning Representations (2019)
61. Sun, C., Myers, A., Vondrick, C., Murphy, K., Schmid, C.: VideoBERT: a joint model for video and language representation learning. In: Proceedings of the IEEE/CVF Conference on Computer Vision and Pattern Recognition, pp. 7464–7473 (2019)
62. Tan, H., Bansal, M.: LXMERT: learning cross-modality encoder representations from transformers. In: Conference on Empirical Methods in Natural Language Processing (2019)
63. Tan, M., Le, Q.: EfficientNet: rethinking model scaling for convolutional neural networks. In: International Conference on Machine Learning, pp. 6105–6114. PMLR (2019)
64. Uijlings, J.R., Van De Sande, K.E., Gevers, T., Smeulders, A.W.: Selective search for object recognition. Int. J. Comput. Vision **104**(2), 154–171 (2013). https://doi.org/10.1007/s11263-013-0620-5
65. Wang, W., Feiszli, M., Wang, H., Tran, D.: Unidentified video objects: a benchmark for dense, open-world segmentation. arXiv preprint arXiv:2104.04691 (2021)
66. Wang, X., Huang, T.E., Darrell, T., Gonzalez, J.E., Yu, F.: Frustratingly simple few-shot object detection. arXiv preprint arXiv:2003.06957 (2020)
67. Wang, X., Cai, Z., Gao, D., Vasconcelos, N.: Towards universal object detection by domain attention. In: Proceedings of the IEEE/CVF Conference on Computer Vision and Pattern Recognition, pp. 7289–7298 (2019)
68. Wightman, R.: PyTorch image models (2019). https://github.com/rwightman/pytorch-image-models. https://doi.org/10.5281/zenodo.4414861
69. Wu, K., Otoo, E., Shoshani, A.: Optimizing connected component labeling algorithms. In: Medical Imaging 2005: Image Processing, vol. 5747, pp. 1965–1976. International Society for Optics and Photonics (2005)
70. Wu, Y., Kirillov, A., Massa, F., Lo, W.Y., Girshick, R.: Detectron2 (2019). https://github.com/facebookresearch/detectron2
71. Wu, Z., Su, L., Huang, Q.: Cascaded partial decoder for fast and accurate salient object detection. In: Proceedings of the IEEE/CVF Conference on Computer Vision and Pattern Recognition, pp. 3907–3916 (2019)

72. Xia, G.S., et al.: DOTA: a large-scale dataset for object detection in aerial images. In: Proceedings of the IEEE/CVF Conference on Computer Vision and Pattern Recognition, pp. 3974–3983 (2018)
73. Xiao, T., Reed, C.J., Wang, X., Keutzer, K., Darrell, T.: Region similarity representation learning. In: Proceedings of the IEEE/CVF International Conference on Computer Vision (2021)
74. Xie, E., et al.: DetCo: unsupervised contrastive learning for object detection. In: Proceedings of the IEEE/CVF Conference on Computer Vision and Pattern Recognition, pp. 8392–8401 (2021)
75. Xie, Q., Luong, M.T., Hovy, E., Le, Q.V.: Self-training with noisy student improves imageNet classification. In: Proceedings of the IEEE/CVF Conference on Computer Vision and Pattern Recognition, pp. 10687–10698 (2020)
76. Yan, K., Wang, X., Lu, L., Summers, R.M.: DeepLesion: automated mining of large-scale lesion annotations and universal lesion detection with deep learning. J. Med. Imaging 5(3), 036501 (2018)
77. Yang, C., Zhang, L., Lu, H., Ruan, X., Yang, M.H.: Saliency detection via graph-based manifold ranking. In: Proceedings of the IEEE/CVF Conference on Computer Vision and Pattern Recognition, pp. 3166–3173 (2013)
78. Zareian, A., Rosa, K.D., Hu, D.H., Chang, S.F.: Open-vocabulary object detection using captions. In: Proceedings of the IEEE/CVF Conference on Computer Vision and Pattern Recognition, pp. 14393–14402 (2021)
79. Zbontar, J., Jing, L., Misra, I., LeCun, Y., Deny, S.: Barlow twins: self-supervised learning via redundancy reduction. In: International Conference on Machine Learning (2021)
80. Zhang, M., Tseng, C., Kreiman, G.: Putting visual object recognition in context. In: Proceedings of the IEEE/CVF Conference on Computer Vision and Pattern Recognition, pp. 12985–12994 (2020)
81. Zhang, Z., et al.: BING++: a fast high quality object proposal generator at 100fps. In: IEEE Transactions on Pattern Analysis and Machine Intelligence, vol. 40, pp. 1209–1223 (2018)
82. Zhou, M., et al.: UC2: universal cross-lingual cross-modal vision-and-language pre-training. In: Proceedings of the IEEE/CVF Conference on Computer Vision and Pattern Recognition, pp. 4155–4165 (2021)
83. Zhu, X., Su, W., Lu, L., Li, B., Wang, X., Dai, J.: Deformable DETR: deformable transformers for end-to-end object detection. In: International Conference on Learning Representations (2021)
84. Zitnick, C.L., Dollár, P.: Edge boxes: locating object proposals from edges. In: Fleet, D., Pajdla, T., Schiele, B., Tuytelaars, T. (eds.) ECCV 2014. LNCS, vol. 8693, pp. 391–405. Springer, Cham (2014). https://doi.org/10.1007/978-3-319-10602-1_26

Enhancing Multi-modal Features Using Local Self-attention for 3D Object Detection

Hao Li[1], Zehan Zhang[1,2], Xian Zhao[1], Yulong Wang[1], Yuxi Shen[1],
Shiliang Pu[1(✉)], and Hui Mao[1]

[1] Hikvision Research Institute, Hangzhou, China
{lihao85,zhangzehan,zhaoxian,wangyulong13,shenyuxi,
pushiliang.hri,maohui}@hikvision.com
[2] Shanghai Jiao Tong University, Shanghai, China

Abstract. LiDAR and Camera sensors have complementary properties: LiDAR senses accurate positioning, while camera provides rich texture and color information. Fusing these two modalities can intuitively improve the performance of 3D detection. Most multi-modal fusion methods use networks to extract features of LiDAR and camera modality respectively, then simply add or concancate them together. We argue that these two kinds of signals are completely different, so it is not proper to combine these two heterogeneous features directly. In this paper, we propose EMMF-Det to do multi-modal fusion leveraging range and camera images. EMMF-Det uses self-attention mechanism to do feature re-weighting on these two modalities interactively, which can enchance the features with color, texture and localiztion information provided by LiDAR and camera signals. On the Waymo Open Dataset, EMMF-Det acheives the state-of-the-art performance. Besides this, evaluation on self-built dataset further proves the effectiveness of our method.

Keywords: 3D detection · Self-attention · Range images · Multi-modal fusion

1 Introduction

Recently, 3D object detection has attracted more and more attention due to its importance in autonomous driving. In the 3D object detection task, the network predicts 3D objects using multiple kinds of signals. Among them, LiDAR signal is sparse and provides accurate location information of objects. Different from LiDAR signal, camera signal is compact and provides rich texture and color information. It is intuitive to leverage these signals to improve 3D detection performance.

From the Fig. 1, we can observe that the road conditions are complicated in real world. Even human eyes cannot identify objects from background only using LiDAR representation. If relying too much on LiDAR signal, the model will produce a number of wrong detection results. To take the Human Visual System's

Fig. 1. Visualization of some instances in autonomous driving scenes. The yellow circle is a person while the red one is actually a camera mounted on a pole. It is difficult for even the human being to distinguish the category of objects only relying on LiDAR representation. This is mainly because that only the shape and relative position of objects is not enough to distinguish them from background. Therefore, color and texture information are very important for the 3D detection tasks. (Color figure online)

characteristics into account, texture and color information play a important role in recognizing and locating objects. This raises an interesting question: *Can we integrate the texture and color information from camera images with LiDAR points to make LiDAR representation of objects more differentiated?* The answer is yes, however, it is a non-trival work for two reasons. In the one respect, camera image and LiDAR representation are two heterogenous signals that have different characteristics. There exists a big domain gap between them. In the other respect, camera images record the color, texture information that are sensitive to occlusion. Previous works mostly use 2D/3D CNN to extract LiDAR features and camera features and concatenate them together on the bird's-eye view (BEV) or the point-wise view. However, these methods only establish a simple correspondence between LiDAR features and camera image features and concatenate the multi-modal features naively. The two main issues mentioned above remain unsolved. The success of transformer in Natural Language Processing (NLP) attracts the attention of the vision community. Transformer establishes the topology graph between discrete tokens and aggregates the features according to the attention coefficients. Benefiting from the self-attention mechanism, transformer is a suitable alternative to fuse multi-modal features that have a large domain gap. However, directly calculating self-attention on the whole 3D scene is computationally demanding. Therefore, we design a fusion method using local self-attention to enhance the LiDAR features with camera feature. The other advantage of local self-attention is that it can alleviate the point misalignment caused by occlusion. And we call the resulting 3D detector EMMF-Det.

EMMF-Det uses range images and camera images as input. This is mainly because range image is a compact and regular LiDAR signal that can be processed by 2D convolutions like camera image. To process the range image, we apply a 2D encoder-decorder network to extract high-level point-wise feature. Prior works also have the similar idea to process range images for 3D detection [10,24] and segmentation [29] tasks. For the camera images, we adopt the pretrained UniverseNet-50 [39] followed by a feature pyramid network (FPN) [25] to generate a group of camera image features that consists of high-level features at different scales. After obtaining the LiDAR features and camera features, we use the self-attention mechanism of transformers to integrate the LiDAR features and camera feature. To be specific, we first divide the whole 3D scene into local regions and calculate the local attention matrices for LiDAR and camera modalities. Then we swap the attention matrices and use camera (LiDAR) attention matrix to do feature-reweighting on the LiDAR (camera) features. In this way, color, texture information from local region are utilized to enhance the LiDAR feature.

Besides the multi-modal fusion module design, we find that the performances of most existing multi-modal fusion methods are limited by the lack of data augmentations used in LiDAR-only methods, especially copy paste. In the proposed EMMF-Det, we introduce two practical data augmentation strategies during training to complement this shortage. One is the multi-modal copy-paste that adds some groundtruths to range images and camera images simultaneously. Besides, we find that laser has poor reflectivity on transparent materials or objects with black color. Hence we randomly corrupt the points in range images during training, to enable LiDAR features more robust.

In summary, our contributions are summarized as follow:

- We propose a multi-modal feature fusion framework EMMF-Det, which uses a local transformer fusion module to do feature re-weighting on the multi-modal features locally.
- We explore the characteristics of LiDAR signal and introduce two effective multi-modal data augmentation strategies to improve the 3D detection performance.
- We evaluate our method on the Waymo Open Dataset and self-built dataset. EMMF-Det achieves state-of-the-art results in range-view-based methods on the Waymo Open Dataset, and the experiment results on self-built dataset further prove the effectiveness of our method.

2 Related Work

2.1 Lidar-Only 3D Object Detection

Lidar-only 3D object detection methods aim to predict 3D object boxes using LiDAR returns. They can be divided into voxel-based, point-based, and range-view-based methods based on different representations. Voxel-based methods [13,17,18,21,38,48,48,51,53,58,62,63] use voxelization to encode unordered points into voxels, which can be processed by 3D convolutions. In these methods, VoxelNet [63] is an end-to-end 3D detection network, which uses voxels as input. Second [51] uses sparse 3D convolution to accelerate VoxelNet. PointPillar [18] uses pillars that can be seen as a variant of voxels to encode points. Point-based [13,36,37,50,52] methods take raw point cloud as input. Among these methods, PointRCNN [37] is a two-stage 3D detection framework using

PointNet++ [34] to extract features from points. PV-RCNN [36] uses a RoIgrid pooling layer to improve the quality of 3D proposals generated by the voxel CNN. Recently, some methods [1,10,23,24,41] use range-view as input to extract 3D features. RangeIoUDet [24] uses 2D convolution to process range images and inherits the RPN module from PointPillars. In [1], the authors propose a range conditioned pyramid to alleviate the scale variation in range images. [41] designs a Range Sparse Net using sparse convolutions to process the foreground features. However, during training, RSN needs to train each category separately, which makes it impractical.

Voxel-based and Point-based methods use 3D convolution layers as the backbone to achieve high performance. But 3D convolution is difficult to optimize on practical chips. This is the reason why most onboard algorithms are still dominated by methods like pointpillars, which use 2D convolutional layers as the backbone. Our approach EMMF-Det achieves SOTA performance only using 2D convolutional layers, which is efficient and easy to deploy. Compared with other range-view-based methods, our method also has obvious advantages on performance.

2.2   Multi-modal Fusion 3D Object Detection

Multi-modal fusion 3D object detection uses multiple modalities information to predict the 3D object bounding boxes. Existing multi-modal fusion methods can be divided into early and late fusion. As for late fusion methods, F-ConvNet [50] and F-PointNet [33] directly do 3D detection in frustum, which is projected by 2D bounding box. AVOD [16] and MV3D [6] perform multi-modal fusion for 3D proposals using the ROI-pooling layer. MVP [55] proposes to use 2D detection to generate dense 3D virtual points to augment an otherwise sparse 3D point-cloud. In summary, late-fusion methods fuse the 2D detection or segmentation results with the 3D detector, relying heavily on the 2D tasks. If the 2D models fails during the inference, it will hurt the performance seriously. Instead of late fusion, more and more researchers focus on early fusion, leveraging 2D and 3D features simultaneously. Existing early fusion methods can be divided into two categories according to the form of feature alignment. One family of early fusion methods [22,56] construct camera feature maps and LiDAR feature maps separately and concatenate the multi-modal features on the BEV). However, it is not proper to do fusion on the BEV directly because the field of view (FOV) of cameras is totally different from BEV. So the cross-view transformation will cause feature blurring during the fusion, so 3D-CVF [56] proposes the auto-calibration, which projects multi-modal features to a smooth BEV map. The other family [40,44,45] fuses the multi-modal features by the point-wise manner, which uses each point in the point cloud as the medium to concatenate the multi-modal features point by point. MVX-Net [40] extracts the multi-modal features separately and fuses them in point cloud coordinates system. Pointpainting concatenates the 2D segmentation scores with original LiDAR to enrich the information. EPNet [15] proposes an adaptive fusion module to combine LiDAR features and RGB features point by point. However, it is not easy to combine these two heterogenous signals together without loss. Our proposed EMMF-Det utilizes self-attention to aggregate the multi-modal features by applying feature re-weighting in the local region to improve the performance of LiDAR-only 3D detection methods.

2.3 Transformer in 3D Vision

Recently, the success of transformer [43] in NLP attracts the attention of vision community and inspires a lot of works to investigate the power of attention in visual recognition [8, 26, 42, 59]. Recently, several works have investigated using transformer in 3D perception tasks. In [12, 60], authors design self-attention networks for scene segmentation, object part segmentation and object classification. [2, 27, 31, 35] introduce the self-attention layers to learn point cloud representation, aiming to improve the performance of existing 3D detection models. In [30], 3DETR is proposed to use an end-to-end transformer framework for 3D object detection, which can be seen as a variant of DETR [3]. Transfuser [32] proposes to integrate image and LiDAR representation using transformers in strategy prediction task. In [49], DETR3D is proposed to use multi-view images to predict 3D bounding boxes. SST [9] uses a single-stride sparse transformer module to process point clouds and achieves the SOTA performance on the open dataset. To our best knowledge, our proposed method, EMMF-Det, is the first work to use transformer to fuse multi-modal features in the 3D detection task.

3   Methods

This section presents the details of our proposed method EMMF-Det, which is a multi-modal fusion 3D detector. EMMF-Det consists of four components. In Sect. 3.1, we design an one-stage 3D detector as our baseline; In Sect. 3.2, we describe the details of processing 2D features; In Sect. 3.3, a novel fusion strategy based on transformer is introduced for multi-modal fusion.

3.1   LiDAR Detector Pipeline

Range image is a compact, regular LiDAR signal that can be processed by 2D convolution like camera images. Inspired by some prior range-based detection and segmentation works [23, 24, 29], we apply a 2D encoder-decorder network to extract high-level point-wise features using range images. The encoder-decorder network is a symmetric architecture, which has four down-sampling blocks and four up-sampling blocks. Benefitting from the symmetric architecture and correspondence between range image and LiDAR points, we can obtain point-wise LiDAR high-dimensional features, which are suitable for our multi-modal fusion framework. The projection from LiDAR points to range images can be calculated by Eq. 1.

$$
\begin{pmatrix} u_r \\ v_r \end{pmatrix} = \begin{pmatrix} \frac{1}{2}[1 - arctan(y_l, x_l)\pi^{-1}] \times w \\ [1 - (arcsin(z_l, r) + f_{down})f^{-1}] \times h \end{pmatrix} \tag{1}
$$

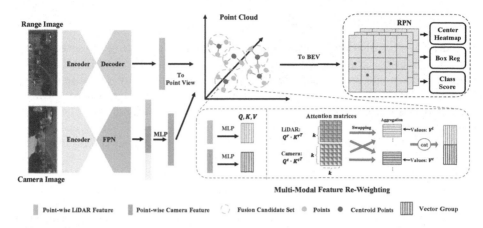

Fig. 2. The overall architecture of our proposed EMMF-Det. In the left part, we use a 2D FCN to extract point-wise LiDAR features from range images, and a 2D detection network with FPN to extract camera image features at three scales. Then we project the LiDAR features and camera features onto point cloud and perform multi-modal fusion using local self-attention. The details of multi-modal fusion module are described in Sect. 3.3. Finally, we scatter the point-wise features to a BEV map and use an anchor-free detector to predict the 3D bounding boxes.

where (x_l, y_l, z_l) represents the point coordinates in the LiDAR coordinate system. (u_r, v_r) is the pixel coordinates in the range image. $r = \sqrt{x_l^2 + y_l^2 + z_l^2}$ is the range value. w and h symbolize the width and height of the range image. $f = f_{up} + f_{down}$ is the vertical field-of-view of the LiDAR sensor, where f_{up} and f_{down} represent the distance below and above the ground plane respectively.

Given N points, we can obtain the point-wise features f_i^l with high dimensions (64 dims). The pointwise features can be projected to the x-y plane to generate the BEV features. Similar with other anchor-free 3D detection methods [46,47,54], we design a 2D FCN to process the BEV features to predict a keypoint heatmap. Each peak in the heatmap represents a ground truth center. As for the regression head for size, rotation and location of objects, we use the features stored at the peak to regress the location refinement $o \in \mathbb{R}^2$ in map view, height-above-ground $h_g \in \mathbb{R}$, 3D box size $s \in \mathbb{R}$ and a yaw rotation angle $\{\sin(x), \cos(x)\} \in \mathbb{R}^2$. Using these information, we can predict the full state information of 3D objects.

The above range-view-based model is a single-stage 3D detector that only uses 2D convolutions and achieves superior performance compared to other range-view-based methods. However, only using the location information encoded by LiDAR features is not enough to compete with SOTA methods. So we use the attention mechanism to fuse camera images and range images to further improve the performance.

3.2 Camera Feature Pipeline

In parallel to the 3D detection pipeline, we introduce an existing 2D detector and use the 2D features generated by FPN to incorporate with the LiDAR feature. Here we choose the pretrained UniverseNet-50 [39] followed by a feature pyramid network (FPN) [25] to generate a group of RGB features that consists of high-level features at different scales (8×, 16×, 32× downsampling from the original size) for each image.

To fuse the LiDAR features and camera features, we project the LiDAR point onto the image at first by the equation [11,28]:

$$\alpha[u_c, v_c, 1]^T = K(Rp + t) \tag{2}$$

where (u_c, v_c) is the pixel coordinate in the camera image and p denotes the point coordinates (x_l, y_l, z_l). K is the intrinsic calibration matrix of camera. R and t are the rotation and translation vector from LiDAR coordinates to the camera coordinates. However, the high-level features we obtain have different resolution from the original image. So we need to divide projected pixels coordinates by the downsampling scale factor and round them to integer. Through this way, we can collect the three scales point-wise camera features for N points. To align with the LiDAR point features, we concatenate the three scales camera features together and use a MLP to reduce the dimension to 64, so the point-wise camera features $f_i^c \in \mathbb{R}^{1 \times 64}, i \in \{1, 2, ..., N\}$ can be obtained.

3.3 Feature Re-Weighting Using Self-attention

Once obtaining features $(f_i^l, f_i^c), i \in \{1, 2, ..., N\}$ for N points from two modalities, most multi-modal fusion methods will concatenate or add them together. We argue that it is not very proper to do this. LiDAR signals and camera signals are heterogeneous signals that have a large domain gap. By the characteristics of Human Visual System, color and texture information can help to distinguish the objects from background, while range information helps to locate the objects. So our key idea is to exploit the self-attention mechanism from transformers to incorporate the texture, color information with range information to improve the 3D detection performance.

Fusion Candidate Sets. Transformer takes a sequence consisting of discrete tokens as input. Unlike the tokens used in Natural Language Processing (NLP), we use each LiDAR point as one token in 3D detection. However, directly calculating self-attention on the whole scene in 3D vision tasks will takes up a lot of memory. So we propose to split the whole point cloud into small point sets, defined as fusion candidate sets, and compute the self-attention in the local region. The advantages are: first, caculating self-attention in the local region can reduce the computational complexity; second, local texture features and colors are more meaningful to distinguish the boundary of objects.

One remaining issues is that how to generate local partition of a point cloud. Given N input points $\{p_1, p_2, ..., p_N\}$ with $p_i \in \mathbb{R}^{1 \times 3}$, we first use farthest point sampling (FPS) [34] to choose N' points $\{p_{c_1}, p_{c_2}, ..., p_{c_{N'}}\}$ with $p_{c_i} \in \mathbb{R}^{1 \times 3}$ as the set of centroids. For centroid point p_{c_i}, we apply k-nearest neighbor algorithm to select k points in the neignborhood of p_{c_i} and denote these points as set Ω_i. Through this, we have divided the point cloud into N' partitions, which are k-nearest neighbor sets.

Feature Re-Weighting Layer. Following [43], we denote the $\mathbf{Q}, \mathbf{K}, \mathbf{V}$ as queries, keys and values separately. Given the LiDAR feature set $\{f_1^l, f_2^l, ..., f_n^l\}$, $f_i^l \in \mathbb{R}^{1 \times 64}$ and camera feature set $\{f_1^c, f_2^c, ..., f_n^c\}$, $f_i^c \in \mathbb{R}^{1 \times 64}$ for k input points. $\mathbf{Q}, \mathbf{K}, \mathbf{V}$ for fusion candidate set Ω_i can be generated by the linear transformations of the multi-modal points features . Then the attention matrices of Ω_i can be caculated via matrix dot-product operations:

$$\mathbf{A}_i^{mod} = (\alpha_i^{mod})_{m,n} = \mathbf{Q}_i^{mod} \cdot \mathbf{K}_i^{mod \top}$$
$$m, n \in 1, ..., k, \ mod \in \{l, c\} \tag{3}$$

where $\mathbf{A}_i^{mod}$ is the attention matrix of k points. l and c denote the LiDAR modality and camera modality separately.

For points set Ω_i, we calculate the attention matrices $(\mathbf{A}_i^l, \mathbf{A}_i^c)$ in LiDAR and camera modality separately. α_i^l in matrix $\mathbf{A}_i^l$ represents the attention coefficients that are mostly determined by location information in LiDAR signal. α_i^c in matrix $\mathbf{A}_i^c$ represents the attention coefficients that are mostly determined by texture, color information in camera signal. These two attention matrices $(\mathbf{A}_i^l, \mathbf{A}_i^c)$ help to build the topology graph for fusion candidate set Ω_i. After obtaining attention matrices $(\mathbf{A}_i^l, \mathbf{A}_i^c)$, we propose to do feature re-weighting on the LiDAR point features by aggregating the value vector $\mathbf{V}_i^l$ with attention matrix $\mathbf{A}_i^c$. By this way, the correlation of LiDAR points in local region can be enhanced by the texture and color information provided by camera image. Coupled with the attention matrix $\mathbf{A}_i^l$ from its own modality, we can get the final output features $\mathbf{F}_i^l$ for LiDAR modality. In turn, we can also use attention matrix $\mathbf{A}_i^l$ from LiDAR modality to enhance the camera features $\mathbf{V}_i^c$. The whole process be described as follows:

$$\mathbf{F}_i^{mod} = \text{softmax}(\frac{\mathbf{A}_i^l/2 + \mathbf{A}_i^c/2}{\sqrt{d_k}}) \cdot \mathbf{V}_i^{mod} \tag{4}$$

where the d_k is the dimension of querys and keys. We adapt this equation from [43], which proposes the transformer for the first time. The attention matrices $(\mathbf{A}_i^l, \mathbf{A}_i^c)$ from two modalities represent the attention coefficients among points in the fusion candidate sets. The operation of attention swapping introduces attention matrix from one modality to do feature re-weighting on the other modality.

After processing with two feature re-weighting layers, we can get the output features $\{\tilde{\mathbf{F}}_i^l, \tilde{\mathbf{F}}_i^c\}, i \in \{1, ..., N'\}$ for set Ω_i. The point-wise features in set $\tilde{\mathbf{F}}_i^{mod}$

Fig. 3. Examples of multi-modalities copy paste data augmentation. The left one is the visualization of LiDAR point. The right one is the visualization of camera images. The cyclist in the yellow is pasted on by Eq. 5 and Eq. 6 (Color figure online).

are fused in the local region. Then we pick out the point-wise features from two modalities and concatenate them point-by-point. Note that, some points may appear multiple times in different sets, so we use average pooling to de-duplicate the features of these points. Finally, we use the point-wise features after fusion as the input to the RPN head.

Our proposed feature re-weighting layer using local self-attention enhances the LiDAR features with texture and color information provided by camera images. The enhanced features improve the performance of range-view-based detector in Sect. 3.1, and help it to achieve state-of-the-art performance.

3.4   Data Augmentation

Multi-modalities Copy Paste. In LiDAR-only methods, GT-Paste augmentation is a widely used data augmentation strategy. In EMMF-Det, we extend the copy-paste strategy into multi-modalities. First, we generate a database containing the labels of all ground truths and their associated point cloud data, image patches. Then during training, we randomly select some ground truths from this database and introduce them into the current training scene, both in LiDAR points and RGB images. To avoid physically impossible outcomes, we perform a collision test in both LiDAR points and camera images, and remove any ground truths that collide with other objects. For the camera modality, if we directly replace the corresponding area of original training image I_i with associated image patch p from I_j, generated image $\tilde{I}_i$ will look very different from authentic images in terms of co-occurrences of color or layout. We propose to use a linear combination of pixels instead of "copy-paste". The linear combination of pixels [19,20,57] can be described as follow:

$$\tilde{I}_i = \mathbf{M}_p \odot I_j + (1 - \mathbf{M}_p) \odot I_i \tag{5}$$

where $\mathbf{M}_p$ is a mask with the same size as the image I_j. The value of p area in mask $\mathbf{M}_p$ obeys 2D Gaussian distribution in Eq. 6, and other area in $\mathbf{M}_p$ is filled with zero values.

$$\mathbf{M}_p = \begin{cases} e^{-\frac{(x-x_0)^2}{(w/2)^2} - \frac{(y-y_0)^2}{(h/2)^2}}, & (x,y) \in p \\ 0, & otherwise \end{cases} \tag{6}$$

where (x, y) is the coordinates in image coordinates system. w and h are the width and height of patch p. In the Fig. 3, we present some augmented examples.

Noise Jitter for Range Image. According to the properties of LiDAR sensor, the laser has poor reflectivity when it encounters transparent materials or objects with black color. To address this issue, we propose a data augmentation method for corrupting range images, which has been used in the 2D vision community [5, 7] and has not been explored in 3D vision. EMMF-Det uses range images as input. We randomly generate some patches of variable size on the range image and replace the point cloud data in these patches with zero values. By adding data corruption, we train a network to learn robust representation for LiDAR signals.

4 Experiments

Here we first describe the implementation details of EMMF-Det in Sect. 4.1. Then we compare with the SOTA methods on Waymo Open Dataset and our actual operation scenario dataset in Sect. 4.2 and Sect. 4.3. We also conduct extensive ablation studies to analyze the effectiveness of different components in Sect. 4.4.

4.1 Implementation Details

Network Details. The overall framework is shown in Fig. 2. The 2D FCN part in Sect. 3.1 uses four blocks to downsample the features by a factor of 8 and another four blocks to recover the features to the original size. All blocks apply a series of dilated convolutions to extract multi-scale features. For the anchor-free head, we follow the settings in CenterPoint [54]. In the feature re-weighting layer, we use the hyperparameters $k = 8$ to search candidate fusion set Ω for Waymo Open Dataset and self-built dataset. The choice of N_c is mainly determined by k and the number of points in the point cloud. Here we empirically set $10,240$ for Waymo Open Dataset and $2,048$ for self-built dataset when k equals 8.

Training and Inference Details. We train the network for 30 epochs on 8 T V100 GPUs using the ADAM optimizer with batch size 16. For the learning rate, we use a one-cycle learning rate policy with max learning rate 0.003, weight decay 0.01, and momentum 0.85 to 0.95. During the inference stage, we keep the top 500 predictions and use NMS with IoU threshold 0.5 and score threshold 0.1.

Table 1. Performance comparison on Waymo validation set. The AP/APH results for Level 1 and Level 2 are shown in the table below. Note that all methods we compared with only use one frame LiDAR signal as input. †: implemented by ourselves using open source code. ⋆: from [9]. ‡: design two model for vehicle and pedestrian seperately. ∗: use IoU prediction module in [61]. Some papers only provide evaluation results on one category, so we use '−' instead of those that are not provided. The best result is marked in red, and the second result is marked in blue.

Method	Input	Vehicle (AP/APH)		Ped (AP/APH)		All (AP/APH)	
		L1	L2	L1	L2	L1	L2
Two-stage							
PV-RCNN† [36]	Point cloud	75.2 74.6	66.4 65.9	65.9 58.1	58.2 51.1	70.6 66.4	62.3 58.5
Single-stage							
MVF [62]	Point cloud	62.9 –	– –	65.3 –	– –	64.1 –	– –
PointPillars [18]	Point cloud	56.5 –	– –	59.3 –	– –	57.9 –	– –
Pillar-based [48]	Point cloud	69.8 –	– –	72.5 –	– –	71.2 –	– –
SECOND† [51]	Point cloud	70.3 69.8	62.6 62.1	62.1 52.9	54.0 45.9	66.2 61.4	58.3 54.0
CenterPoint-pillar⋆ [54]	Point cloud	74.6 74.1	66.3 65.8	71.5 59.6	64.1 53.2	73.1 66.9	65.2 59.5
CenterPoint-voxel⋆ [54]	Point cloud	74.8 74.2	66.7 66.2	75.8 69.6	68.3 62.4	75.3 71.9	67.5 64.3
SST [9]	Point cloud	74.2 73.8	65.5 65.1	78.7 69.5	70.0 61.6	76.5 71.7	67.8 63.4
AFDetV2-Lite⋆ [14]	Point cloud	77.6 77.1	69.7 69.2	80.2 74.6	72.2 67.00	78.9 75.9	71.0 68.1
PointAugmenting [45]	Point cloud, cam	67.4 –	62.7 –	75.4 –	70.6 –	71.4 –	66.7 –
RCS [1]	Range	69.6 69.2	– –	– –	– –	– –	– –
RSN ‡ [41]	Range	74.6 –	– 65.5	77.8 –	– 63.7	76.2 –	– 64.6
RangeDet [10]	Range	72.9 –	– –	75.9 –	– –	74.4 –	– –
RangeIoUDet [24]	Range	72.2 –	– –	60.4 –	– –	66.3 –	– –
PPC-EdgeConv [4]	Range	65.2 –	– 56.7	73.9 –	– 59.6	69.6 –	– 58.2
PPC-EdgeConv-Cam [4]	Range, cam	– –	– –	75.5 –	– 61.5	– –	– –
EMMF-Det	Range, cam	76.2 75.5	67.8 67.3	77.5 69.1	69.8 61.9	76.9 72.3	68.8 64.6
EMMF-Det∗	Range, cam	77.1 76.7	69.1 68.4	80.5 74.7	72.6 65.9	78.8 75.7	70.9 67.2

4.2   3D Detection on Waymo Dataset

Waymo dataset is one of the most popular 3D detection datasets, which contains totally 798 scenes for training and 202 scenes for validation. Each pair of sample consists of one frame of LiDAR return and five frames of camera images. These five camera images only cover the 250 degree range in total compared with the LiDAR which covers 360 degree range. To address this issue, we use LiDAR-only model to complete the prediction result.

Waymo uses (Average precision) AP and APH which incorporates heading information as the metric. We compare our method with many SOTA 3D detection methods, including the most popular one-stage 3D detector CenterPoint [54], two-stage 3D detector PV-RCNN [36], transformer based method SST [9], the latest multimodal detection method pointaugmenting [45] and some methods [1,4,10,24] using range images as input. For fair comparison, the results provided in this table only use single frame LiDAR as input. Table 1 shows the performance of our method on the validation set. Since some works only train their models on vehicle or pedstrian and the results reported in their papers arev not complete, we use their open-source codes to reproduce on all categories. The reproduced accuracy of PV-RCNN is 4.0 points better than results reported in

Table 2. Performance comparison on self-built dataset. † : implemented by ourselves using open source code. The best result is marked in red, and the second result is marked in blue.

Method	Model	Car		Bus		Pedestrian		Cyclist		Tricycle		Mean	
		Easy	Hard	Easy	Hard	Easy	Hard	Easy	Hard	Easy	Hard	Easy	Hard
Two-stage													
PV-RCNN† [6]	3D conv	98.6	95.3	84.2	72.9	53.6	45.9	77.3	72.3	73.3	61.5	77.3	69.6
Single-stage													
MVX-Net† [40]	3D conv	96.9	96.4	72.1	63.8	56.2	46.8	79.6	73.8	64.7	58.7	73.9	67.9
SECOND† [51]	3D conv	98.5	95.3	83.8	72.8	50.0	42.9	76.6	70.1	64.8	57.3	71.3	67.7
CenterPoint† [54]	3D conv	99.0	95.1	85.1	76.1	53.1	44.3	79.7	72.2	68.4	64.7	77.1	70.5
PointPillars† [18]	2D conv	96.4	95.2	80.3	66.4	47.6	39.6	71.3	64.9	58.9	51.0	70.9	63.4
RangeIoUDet† [24]	2D conv	98.9	96.2	82.7	70.0	52.3	44.2	76.0	69.6	66.7	59.5	75.3	67.9
EMMF-Det	2D conv	99.4	96.7	87.2	78.4	58.9	51.3	82.9	76.8	72.3	66.1	80.1	73.9

original paper. CenterPoint only reports the APH on Level2 difficulty, so we use the results of the latest published paper SST [9] as a reference. Compared with RSN [41], our method performs better on vehicle but worse on pedestrian's APH. However, it designs two networks and trains two categories seperately, while we only uses one network. Inspired by AFDetV2 [14], we integrate the IoU module [61] with EMMF-Det and achieves 77.1 L1 AP on vehicle and 80.5 L1 AP on pedestrian. Compared with all other 3D detection methods, it can be observed that EMMF-Det outperforms on the vehicle class. And compared with other range-view-based methods, the performance of EMMF-Det is significantly ahead.

4.3   3D Detection on Self-built Lidar-Vision Dataset

We also evaluate our proposed method on the self-built dataset. This dataset is collected by a HESAI Pandar40 LiDAR sensor and a front-view camera. There are 18,000 samples collected for training, 3,000 samples for validation and 3,000 samples for testing in total. We label these samples with five categories including: car, bus, pedestrian, cyclist and tricycle. The 3D detection performance is measured by the average precision (AP) with 40 recall positions. The IoU threshold for vehicle category is set as 0.7. For other non-vehicle categiories, the IoU threshold is set as 0.5. Furthermore, we use the pixel height of the box on the camera image to measure the difficulty of bounding boxes.

Table 2 shows the performance of our method on the test set of self-built dataset. We adopt the open-source code to reproduce the SOTA methods on our dataset. For each method, we adjust the parameters based on our dataset and report the best accuracies. From the Table 2, we can observe that our model boost the performance on all categories significantly. The results can prove that our proposed EMMF-Det still has a good performance even if the LiDAR sensor is changed.

Table 3. Quantitative performance comparison on Waymo validation set of using Multi-Modal Feature Re-Weighting. (averaged by 5 trials)

Method	Vehicle (AP/APH)		Ped (AP/APH)		All (AP/APH)	
	L1	L2	L1	L2	L1	L2
Range-based-method	70.7	70.1	62.3	61.8	74.7	65.5	66.2	58.4	72.7	67.8	64.3	60.1
+ Naive Fusion	71.1	71.0	63.1	62.6	75.4	66.1	66.5	59.1	73.3	68.5	64.8	60.8
+ Feature Re-Weighting	**72.2**	**71.8**	**65.0**	**64.7**	**76.3**	**67.1**	**67.8**	**60.7**	**74.3**	**69.5**	**66.4**	**62.7**

Table 4. Quantitative performance comparison of different choices of k on Waymo validation set. (averaged by 5 trials)

Method	Vehicle (AP/APH)		Ped (AP/APH)		All (AP/APH)	
	L1	L2	L1	L2	L1	L2
$k = 8$	**72.2**	**71.8**	**65.0**	**64.7**	**76.3**	67.1	67.8	**60.7**	**74.3**	**69.5**	**66.4**	**62.7**
$k = 16$	71.6	71.4	64.2	63.6	76.1	**67.2**	**68.0**	60.5	73.9	69.3	66.1	62.1

4.4 Ablation Studies

In this section, we present ablation studies on Waymo Open Dataset to better understand how each component affects the performance. Unless specified, we train the model for 30 epochs with 20% training samples and evaluate on the entire validation set for the reason that training with whole Waymo dataset is computationally demanding.

Effectiveness of Feature Re-Weighting. In Table 3, we compare the performance with model without feature re-weighting. 'Range-based-method' denotes the 3D detector only using range images as input. 'naive fusion' denotes the method directly concatenating the multi-modal features together to improve the range image features with camera image features. 'Feature re-weighting' denotes the method using self-attention to do feature re-weighting mentioned in Sect. 3.3. It can be observed that our proposed feature re-weighting is a effective fusion method for range and camera images.

Effectiveness of k in Fusion Candiate Set. For the hyperparameter k in fusion candidate set, we refer to the *ball query* operation in pointnet++ [34] and empirically try several choices of k. The comparisons are illustrated in Table 4. When k is set as 8, the model achieves the best performance. If we set k too large, the performance becomes poor. This is partly because redundant points in the set Ω will have a negative impact on the localization of objects. However, the improvment is robust to the hyperparameter k. Whether K is set as 8 or 16, the performance is still better than directly concancating multi-modal features.

Effectiveness of Data Augmentations. To further improve our proposed EMMF-Det, we introduce two data augmentation strategies. One is multi-modal

Table 5. Comparison of using different augmentation strategies. * denotes using 'linear combination of pixels' instead of 'copy paste' in camera modality. (averaged by 5 trials)

Method	Vehicle (AP/APH)		Ped (AP/APH)		All (AP/APH)	
	L1	L2	L1	L2	L1	L2
+ wo copy-paste	70.5 | 70.2	62.8 | 61.7	72.1 | 63.9	65.1 | 58.0	71.3 | 67.1	64.0 | 59.9
+ multi-modal copy-paste	71.2 | 70.8	63.3 | 62.8	74.6 | 65.0	66.2 | 59.6	73.0 | 67.8	64.8 | 61.2
+ multi-modal copy-paste*	71.8 | 71.2	63.8 | 63.2	74.7 | 65.5	66.8 | 60.0	73.3 | 68.4	65.3 | 61.6
+ noise jitter	**72.2** | **71.8**	**65.0** | **64.7**	**76.3** | **67.1**	**67.8** | **60.7**	**74.3** | **69.5**	**66.4** | **62.7**

copy-paste, and the other is noise jitter for range images. In the Table 5, 'multi-modal copy-paste' means directly pasting the image patches on the original images in camera modality, while 'multi-modal copy-paste*' denotes using linear combination of pixels instead. It can be observed that multi-modal copy-paste strategy improve the performance over the baseline. If we use linear combination of pixels, the performance can be further improved. Noise jitter for range images enables the model to learn robust features. The improvement in Table 5 further supports our motivation of introducing certain disturbances during training.

5   Conclusion and Discussion

In this paper, we propose the EMMF-Det, which is a novel multi-modal fusion 3D detector using range images and camera images as input. EMMF-Det uses a one-stage anchor-free 3D detector as the baseline, and fuse the LiDAR features with the camera features to further improve the performance. To enhance the LiDAR features with the texture, color information provided by camera images, multi-modal feature re-weighting layer is designed for local fusion within the points/pixels neighborhood. Furthermore, we introduce two effective data augmentation strategies including multi-modal copy-paste and noise jitter for range images based on the properties of LiDAR and camera signal. Experiments evaluated on several 3D detection benchmarks demonstrate the effectiveness of our method.

Limitation of Range-View-Based Methods. EMMF-Det uses range images as input, which are raw signal scaned by mechanical LiDAR. The results and conclusions are under the premise that Waymo and self-built dataset both are collected by mechanical LiDAR. If the dataset is collected by solid-state LiDAR, there will be information loss during the transformation from point cloud to range image. We will explore and try to solve this problem in future work.

Acknowledgement. Supported by National key R&D Program of China (Grant No.2020AAA010400x).

References

1. Bewley, A., Sun, P., Mensink, T., Anguelov, D., Sminchisescu, C.: Range conditioned dilated convolutions for scale invariant 3D object detection. arXiv preprint arXiv:2005.09927 (2020)
2. Bhattacharyya, P., Huang, C., Czarnecki, K.: Self-attention based context-aware 3D object detection. arXiv e-prints, p. arXiv-2101 (2021)
3. Carion, N., Massa, F., Synnaeve, G., Usunier, N., Kirillov, A., Zagoruyko, S.: End-to-end object detection with transformers. In: Vedaldi, A., Bischof, H., Brox, T., Frahm, J.-M. (eds.) ECCV 2020. LNCS, vol. 12346, pp. 213–229. Springer, Cham (2020). https://doi.org/10.1007/978-3-030-58452-8_13
4. Chai, Y., et al.: To the point: efficient 3D object detection in the range image with graph convolution kernels. In: Proceedings of the IEEE/CVF Conference on Computer Vision and Pattern Recognition, pp. 16000–16009 (2021)
5. Chen, P., Liu, S., Zhao, H., Jia, J.: GridMask data augmentation. arXiv preprint arXiv:2001.04086 (2020)
6. Chen, X., Ma, H., Wan, J., Li, B., Xia, T.: Multi-view 3D object detection network for autonomous driving. In: Proceedings of the IEEE Conference on Computer Vision and Pattern Recognition, pp. 1907–1915 (2017)
7. DeVries, T., Taylor, G.W.: Improved regularization of convolutional neural networks with cutout. arXiv preprint arXiv:1708.04552 (2017)
8. Dosovitskiy, A., et al.: An image is worth 16×16 words: transformers for image recognition at scale. arXiv preprint arXiv:2010.11929 (2020)
9. Fan, L., et al.: Embracing single stride 3D object detector with sparse transformer. arXiv preprint arXiv:2112.06375 (2021)
10. Fan, L., Xiong, X., Wang, F., Wang, N., Zhang, Z.: RangeDet: in defense of range view for LiDAR-based 3D object detection. arXiv preprint arXiv:2103.10039 (2021)
11. Geiger, A., Lenz, P., Stiller, C., Urtasun, R.: Vision meets robotics: the KITTI dataset. Int. J. Robot. Res. **32**(11), 1231–1237 (2013)
12. Guo, M.H., Cai, J.X., Liu, Z.N., Mu, T.J., Martin, R.R., Hu, S.M.: PCT: point cloud transformer. Comput. Vis. Media **7**(2), 187–199 (2021). https://doi.org/10.1007/s41095-021-0229-5
13. He, C., Zeng, H., Huang, J., Hua, X.S., Zhang, L.: Structure aware single-stage 3D object detection from point cloud. In: Proceedings of the IEEE/CVF Conference on Computer Vision and Pattern Recognition, pp. 11873–11882 (2020)
14. Hu, Y., Ding, Z., Ge, R., Shao, W., Huang, L., Li, K., Liu, Q.: AFDetV2: rethinking the necessity of the second stage for object detection from point clouds. In: Proceedings of the AAAI Conference on Artificial Intelligence, vol. 36, pp. 969–979 (2022)
15. Huang, T., Liu, Z., Chen, X., Bai, X.: EPNet: enhancing point features with image semantics for 3D object detection. In: Vedaldi, A., Bischof, H., Brox, T., Frahm, J.-M. (eds.) ECCV 2020. LNCS, vol. 12360, pp. 35–52. Springer, Cham (2020). https://doi.org/10.1007/978-3-030-58555-6_3
16. Ku, J., Mozifian, M., Lee, J., Harakeh, A., Waslander, S.L.: Joint 3D proposal generation and object detection from view aggregation. In: 2018 IEEE/RSJ International Conference on Intelligent Robots and Systems (IROS), pp. 1–8. IEEE (2018)
17. Kuang, H., Wang, B., An, J., Zhang, M., Zhang, Z.: Voxel-FPN: Multi-scale voxel feature aggregation for 3D object detection from LIDAR point clouds. Sensors **20**(3), 704 (2020)

18. Lang, A.H., Vora, S., Caesar, H., Zhou, L., Yang, J., Beijbom, O.: PointPillars: fast encoders for object detection from point clouds. In: Proceedings of the IEEE/CVF Conference on Computer Vision and Pattern Recognition, pp. 12697–12705 (2019)
19. Li, H., Zhang, X., Sun, R., Xiong, H., Tian, Q.: Center-wise local image mixture for contrastive representation learning. arXiv preprint arXiv:2011.02697 (2020)
20. Li, H., Zhang, X., Tian, Q., Xiong, H.: Attribute mix: semantic data augmentation for fine grained recognition. In: 2020 IEEE International Conference on Visual Communications and Image Processing (VCIP), pp. 243–246. IEEE (2020)
21. Li, P., Shi, J., Shen, S.: Joint spatial-temporal optimization for stereo 3D object tracking. In: Proceedings of the IEEE/CVF Conference on Computer Vision and Pattern Recognition, pp. 6877–6886 (2020)
22. Liang, M., Yang, B., Chen, Y., Hu, R., Urtasun, R.: Multi-task multi-sensor fusion for 3D object detection. In: Proceedings of the IEEE/CVF Conference on Computer Vision and Pattern Recognition, pp. 7345–7353 (2019)
23. Liang, Z., Zhang, M., Zhang, Z., Zhao, X., Pu, S.: RangeRCNN: towards fast and accurate 3D object detection with range image representation. arXiv preprint arXiv:2009.00206 (2020)
24. Liang, Z., Zhang, Z., Zhang, M., Zhao, X., Pu, S.: RangeIoUDET: range image based real-time 3D object detector optimized by intersection over union. In: Proceedings of the IEEE/CVF Conference on Computer Vision and Pattern Recognition, pp. 7140–7149 (2021)
25. Lin, T.Y., Dollár, P., Girshick, R., He, K., Hariharan, B., Belongie, S.: Feature pyramid networks for object detection. In: Proceedings of the IEEE Conference on Computer Vision and Pattern Recognition, pp. 2117–2125 (2017)
26. Liu, Z., et al.: Swin transformer: hierarchical vision transformer using shifted windows. In: Proceedings of the IEEE/CVF International Conference on Computer Vision, pp. 10012–10022 (2021)
27. Mao, J., et al.: Voxel transformer for 3D object detection. In: Proceedings of the IEEE/CVF International Conference on Computer Vision, pp. 3164–3173 (2021)
28. Meyer, G.P., Charland, J., Hegde, D., Laddha, A., Vallespi-Gonzalez, C.: Sensor fusion for joint 3D object detection and semantic segmentation. In: Proceedings of the IEEE/CVF Conference on Computer Vision and Pattern Recognition Workshops (2019)
29. Milioto, A., Vizzo, I., Behley, J., Stachniss, C.: RangeNet++: Fast and accurate LiDAR semantic segmentation. In: 2019 IEEE/RSJ International Conference on Intelligent Robots and Systems (IROS), pp. 4213–4220. IEEE (2019)
30. Misra, I., Girdhar, R., Joulin, A.: An end-to-end transformer model for 3D object detection. In: Proceedings of the IEEE/CVF International Conference on Computer Vision, pp. 2906–2917 (2021)
31. Pan, X., Xia, Z., Song, S., Li, L.E., Huang, G.: 3D object detection with point-former. In: Proceedings of the IEEE/CVF Conference on Computer Vision and Pattern Recognition, pp. 7463–7472 (2021)
32. Prakash, A., Chitta, K., Geiger, A.: Multi-modal fusion transformer for end-to-end autonomous driving. In: Proceedings of the IEEE/CVF Conference on Computer Vision and Pattern Recognition, pp. 7077–7087 (2021)
33. Qi, C.R., Liu, W., Wu, C., Su, H., Guibas, L.J.: Frustum pointNets for 3D object detection from RGB-D data. In: Proceedings of the IEEE Conference on Computer Vision and Pattern Recognition, pp. 918–927 (2018)
34. Qi, C.R., Yi, L., Su, H., Guibas, L.J.: PointNet++: deep hierarchical feature learning on point sets in a metric space. arXiv preprint arXiv:1706.02413 (2017)

35. Sheng, H., et al.: Improving 3D object detection with channel-wise transformer. In: Proceedings of the IEEE/CVF International Conference on Computer Vision, pp. 2743–2752 (2021)
36. Shi, S., et al.: PV-RCNN: point-voxel feature set abstraction for 3D object detection. In: Proceedings of the IEEE/CVF Conference on Computer Vision and Pattern Recognition, pp. 10529–10538 (2020)
37. Shi, S., Wang, X., Li, H.: PointRCNN: 3D object proposal generation and detection from point cloud. In: Proceedings of the IEEE/CVF Conference on Computer Vision and Pattern Recognition. pp. 770–779 (2019)
38. Shi, S., et al.: From points to parts: 3d object detection from point cloud with part-aware and part-aggregation network. IEEE Trans. Pattern Anal. Mach. Intell. **43**(8), 2647–2664 (2020)
39. Shinya, Y.: USB: universal-scale object detection benchmark. arXiv:2103.14027 (2021)
40. Sindagi, V.A., Zhou, Y., Tuzel, O.: MVX-Net: multimodal VoxelNet for 3D object detection. In: 2019 International Conference on Robotics and Automation (ICRA), pp. 7276–7282. IEEE (2019)
41. Sun, P., et al.: RSN: range sparse net for efficient, accurate lidar 3D object detection. In: Proceedings of the IEEE/CVF Conference on Computer Vision and Pattern Recognition, pp. 5725–5734 (2021)
42. Touvron, H., Cord, M., Douze, M., Massa, F., Sablayrolles, A., Jégou, H.: Training data-efficient image transformers & distillation through attention. In: International Conference on Machine Learning, pp. 10347–10357. PMLR (2021)
43. Vaswani, A., et al.: Attention is all you need. In: Advances in Neural Information Processing Systems, pp. 5998–6008 (2017)
44. Vora, S., Lang, A.H., Helou, B., Beijbom, O.: PointPainting: sequential fusion for 3D object detection. In: Proceedings of the IEEE/CVF Conference on Computer Vision and Pattern Recognition, pp. 4604–4612 (2020)
45. Wang, C., Ma, C., Zhu, M., Yang, X.: PointAugmenting: cross-modal augmentation for 3D object detection. In: Proceedings of the IEEE/CVF Conference on Computer Vision and Pattern Recognition, pp. 11794–11803 (2021)
46. Wang, G., Tian, B., Ai, Y., Xu, T., Chen, L., Cao, D.: CenterNet3D: an anchor free object detector for autonomous driving. arXiv preprint arXiv:2007.07214 (2020)
47. Wang, Q., Chen, J., Deng, J., Zhang, X.: 3D-CenterNet: 3D object detection network for point clouds with center estimation priority. Pattern Recogn. **115**, 107884 (2021)
48. Wang, Y., et al.: Pillar-based object detection for autonomous driving. In: Vedaldi, A., Bischof, H., Brox, T., Frahm, J.-M. (eds.) ECCV 2020, Part XXII. LNCS, vol. 12367, pp. 18–34. Springer, Cham (2020). https://doi.org/10.1007/978-3-030-58542-6_2
49. Wang, Y., Guizilini, V., Zhang, T., Wang, Y., Zhao, H., Solomon, J.M.: DETR3D: 3D object detection from multi-view images via 3D-to-2D queries. In: The Conference on Robot Learning (CoRL) (2021)
50. Wang, Z., Jia, K.: Frustum convnet: sliding frustums to aggregate local pointwise features for amodal 3D object detection. In: 2019 IEEE/RSJ International Conference on Intelligent Robots and Systems (IROS), pp. 1742–1749. IEEE (2019)
51. Yan, Y., Mao, Y., Li, B.: SECOND: sparsely embedded convolutional detection. Sensors **18**(10), 3337 (2018)
52. Yang, Z., Sun, Y., Liu, S., Shen, X., Jia, J.: STD: sparse-to-dense 3D object detector for point cloud. In: Proceedings of the IEEE/CVF International Conference on Computer Vision, pp. 1951–1960 (2019)

53. Ye, M., Xu, S., Cao, T.: HVNet: hybrid voxel network for lidar based 3D object detection. In: Proceedings of the IEEE/CVF Conference on Computer Vision and Pattern Recognition, pp. 1631–1640 (2020)
54. Yin, T., Zhou, X., Krahenbuhl, P.: Center-based 3D object detection and tracking. In: Proceedings of the IEEE/CVF Conference on Computer Vision and Pattern Recognition, pp. 11784–11793 (2021)
55. Yin, T., Zhou, X., Krähenbühl, P.: Multimodal virtual point 3D detection. In: NeurIPS (2021)
56. Yoo, J.H., Kim, Y., Kim, J., Choi, J.W.: 3D-CVF: generating joint camera and lidar features using cross-view spatial feature fusion for 3D object detection. In: Vedaldi, A., Bischof, H., Brox, T., Frahm, J.-M. (eds.) ECCV 2020, Part XXVII. LNCS, vol. 12372, pp. 720–736. Springer, Cham (2020). https://doi.org/10.1007/978-3-030-58583-9_43
57. Zhang, H., Cisse, M., Dauphin, Y.N., Lopez-Paz, D.: Mixup: beyond empirical risk minimization. arXiv preprint arXiv:1710.09412 (2017)
58. Zhang, Z., et al.: ATF-3D: Semi-supervised 3D object detection with adaptive thresholds filtering based on confidence and distance. IEEE Robot. Autom. Lett. **7**, 10573–10580 (2022)
59. Zhao, H., Jia, J., Koltun, V.: Exploring self-attention for image recognition. In: Proceedings of the IEEE/CVF Conference on Computer Vision and Pattern Recognition, pp. 10076–10085 (2020)
60. Zhao, H., Jiang, L., Jia, J., Torr, P.H., Koltun, V.: Point transformer. In: Proceedings of the IEEE/CVF International Conference on Computer Vision, pp. 16259–16268 (2021)
61. Zheng, W., Tang, W., Chen, S., Jiang, L., Fu, C.W.: CIA-SSD: confident IoU-aware single-stage object detector from point cloud. In: Proceedings of the AAAI conference on artificial intelligence, vol. 35, pp. 3555–3562 (2021)
62. Zhou, Y., et al.: End-to-end multi-view fusion for 3D object detection in lidar point clouds. In: Conference on Robot Learning, pp. 923–932. PMLR (2020)
63. Zhou, Y., Tuzel, O.: VoxelNet: end-to-end learning for point cloud based 3D object detection. In: Proceedings of the IEEE Conference on Computer Vision and Pattern Recognition, pp. 4490–4499 (2018)

Object Detection as Probabilistic Set Prediction

Georg Hess[1,2][✉] [iD], Christoffer Petersson[1,2], and Lennart Svensson[1] [iD]

[1] Chalmers University of Technology, Gothenburg, Sweden
georghe@chalmers.se
[2] Zenseact, Gothenburg, Sweden

Abstract. Accurate uncertainty estimates are essential for deploying deep object detectors in safety-critical systems. The development and evaluation of probabilistic object detectors have been hindered by shortcomings in existing performance measures, which tend to involve arbitrary thresholds or limit the detector's choice of distributions. In this work, we propose to view object detection as a set prediction task where detectors predict the distribution over the set of objects. Using the negative log-likelihood for random finite sets, we present a proper scoring rule for evaluating and training probabilistic object detectors. The proposed method can be applied to existing probabilistic detectors, is free from thresholds, and enables fair comparison between architectures. Three different types of detectors are evaluated on the COCO dataset. Our results indicate that the training of existing detectors is optimized toward non-probabilistic metrics. We hope to encourage the development of new object detectors that can accurately estimate their own uncertainty.

Keywords: Probabilistic object detection · Random finite sets · Proper scoring rules · Uncertainty estimation

1 Introduction

Accurately locating and classifying a set of objects has a range of applications, such as autonomous driving, transportation, surveillance, scene analysis, and image captioning. Common approaches for solving this rely on a deep object detector which provides a set of detections containing bounding box parameters, semantic class and classification confidence. However, as pointed out in previous works [3,5,11,15,28] most state-of-the-art networks lack the ability to assess their own regression confidence and fail to provide a complete uncertainty description. As an effect, this can limit the performance in downstream tasks such as multi-object tracking, sensor fusion, or decision making, ultimately hindering humans to establish trust in the deep learning agent.

Supplementary Information The online version contains supplementary material available at https://doi.org/10.1007/978-3-031-20080-9_32.

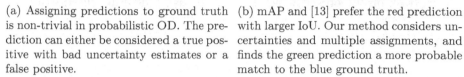

(a) Assigning predictions to ground truth is non-trivial in probabilistic OD. The prediction can either be considered a true positive with bad uncertainty estimates or a false positive.

(b) mAP and [13] prefer the red prediction with larger IoU. Our method considers uncertainties and multiple assignments, and finds the green prediction a more probable match to the blue ground truth.

Fig. 1. Predictions (red and green) and ground truth (blue), highlighting the object detection assignment problem. Ellipses represent spatial uncertainty. (Color figure online)

There are many strategies to evaluate predictive uncertainties in the deep learning regime. Broadly speaking, a distribution should perform well on two criteria: calibration and sharpness. For a distribution to be well calibrated, it should not be over- or under-confident, but reflect the true confidence in its predictions. Sharpness instead promotes concentrated and, consequently, informative distributions [9]. Both these properties can be measured simultaneously by using a proper scoring rule such as negative log-likelihood [10]. Proper scoring rules assess the quality of predictive uncertainties and are minimized only when the prediction is equivalent to the distribution that generated the ground truth observations [10]. Besides measuring calibration and sharpness, proper scoring rules enable a theoretically sound ranking of different predictive distributions.

Evaluating the quality of predictive uncertainties in object detection (OD) is a non-trivial task. First, any measure has to jointly consider the performance in terms of ability to detect, correctly classify and accurately locate objects. Second, as we do not know the correspondence between predictions and ground truth objects, any analysis is colored by the selected assignment rules. As an example, the prediction in Fig. 1a can be considered either a correct detection with bad uncertainty predictions or a false positive. Having multiple predictions makes the assignment even harder, as shown in Fig. 1b. The most common measure in OD, mAP, uses handcrafted assignment rules based on IoU and class confidence and fails to consider predicted uncertainties. The probability-based detection quality (PDQ) [11] tries to address these issues, but is limited to Gaussian distributions for regression. More recently, the lack of proper scoring rules for evaluating probabilistic object detection was pointed out by [13], also proving that PDQ is not a proper scoring rule. However, while they use proper scoring rules for the different subtasks, such as the energy score for regression and the Brier score for classification, predictions are assigned to targets using ad hoc IoU-based rules which ignore regression uncertainties. As highlighted earlier, these types of assignment rules have a large influence on the reported performance, do not yield proper scoring rules, and make it harder to draw conclusions about model performance.

In this paper, we propose to use random finite sets (RFS) to model the probabilistic object detection task. Object detection is often seen as a set prediction task, and we extend this perspective to probabilistic object detection (PrOD). We describe the set of objects in a given image by a single random variable, and the task of our object detection networks is to describe the distribution of that variable. This simple change of perspective enables us to use the negative log-likelihood to evaluate the uncertainty estimates of our detections, which gives rise to the first proper scoring rule for object detection. Our framework explicitly models the assignment problem, is general enough to be applied to any type of distribution, enables easy ranking between different algorithms, and can be decomposed to highlight different types of errors (detection, regression and classification). Our key contributions are the following.

- We propose to view the set of objects in an image as a single stochastic variable. By applying the negative log-likelihood (NLL) to a distribution over sets, we present the first proper scoring rule for object detection.
- We show how to apply the random finite set framework to object detection by interpreting the detector output as parameters of multi-Bernoulli (MB) and Poisson multi-Bernoulli (PMB) densities. Further, we present how to efficiently calculate and interpret the NLL of the MB and PMB densities.
- Using our proposed scoring rule, we evaluate one-stage, two-stage, and set-based detectors on the popular MS COCO dataset, and showcase their strengths and shortcomings using the decomposability of PMB-NLL.
- Further, we leverage the fact that the proposed method is differentiable and fine-tune the detectors to optimize PMB-NLL directly. Our results show that this helps detectors to reduce the number of false and duplicate detections.

2 Related Work

Quantifying uncertainties with deep neural networks has been a long-standing challenge. We aim to provide a brief overview here, as to motivate the importance of our work. Interested readers are referred to [1,5,8] for details.

Types of Uncertainties. In computer vision, uncertainties are generally divided into two categories: aleatoric and epistemic [15]. The first category refers to noise inherent to the data, which can originate from sensor noise, class ambiguities, label noise and such, and cannot be reduced with more data. Epistemic uncertainties are due to uncertainties in model parameters, and can, in principle, be eliminated given enough data. In this work, we do not aim to disentangle the two types, but consider overall predictive uncertainty [26].

Uncertainty Estimation. Most approaches for quantifying uncertainties in object detection either apply Monte Carlo dropout [12,21,33], deep ensembles [6,19] or direct modeling [14,16,36]. Unfortunately, uncertainty estimates are often overlooked when evaluating probabilistic detectors, while methods that do evaluate their uncertainties use a range of different performance measures, making comparison challenging. The lack in standard performance measures has also been pointed out as a main obstacle for uncertainty estimation [1,5,28].

Evaluating Uncertainty. As the commonly used performance measure mAP fails to consider spatial uncertainties and is insensitive to badly calibrated classification, several methods trying to address these issues have been suggested. The Probability-based Detection Quality (PDQ) [11] evaluates both spatial and semantic uncertainties, but is limited to Gaussian spatial uncertainties, requires practitioners to select confidence thresholds, and has been shown by [13] to not be a proper scoring rule, thereby introducing biases into its ranking of detectors. The authors of [13] promote the use of proper scoring rules for object detection. However, their approach disregards the spatial uncertainty information when assigning predictions to targets, requires confidence thresholds, and does not provide clear recommendations on model ranking.

Set Prediction. While object detection inherently can be seen as a set prediction task, this has been made more explicit by a range of set-based detectors [2,27,35,37]. These detectors highlight the assignment problem, i.e., how to assign predictions to ground truth elements when calculating losses or metrics. In this work, we extend this perspective to probabilistic object detection by modeling the problem using distributions over random finite sets. This paradigm is applicable to any type of detector, set-based or not, and naturally models and solves the assignment problem.

Random Finite Sets. Random finite sets have been used extensively in the model-based multi-object tracking community [7,20,30,32]. The RFS framework has proven useful for modeling potentially detected and undetected objects as it captures uncertainties in the cardinality of present objects and their individual properties. However, these algorithms are often evaluated without taking their uncertainties into account. Recently, the authors of [24] suggested the use of negative log-likelihood for probabilistic evaluation of model-based multi-object trackers and presented an efficient approximation of the NLL. Our work shows how to interpret parameters of existing deep object detectors as RFSs and uses [24] to calculate our proper scoring rule. Unlike the custom designed and low-dimensional regression problems explored in [24], we apply this method to a large scale dataset, jointly evaluating detection, classification, and regression.

3   Probabilistic Modeling for Object Detection

Object detection is a set prediction task, where, given an image $\boldsymbol{X}$, the aim is to predict the set of corresponding objects $\mathbb{Y}$ present in said image. Here, the number of objects n in the set $\mathbb{Y} = \{y_1, y_2, \ldots, y_n\}$ is unknown beforehand. Further, for each object $y_i = (c_i, b_i)$, we do not know which class $c_i \in \{1, \ldots, C\}$ it belongs to, nor where its bounding box $b_i \in \mathbb{R}^4$ is located in the image. In supervised learning, we aim to learn a model that, given the image $\boldsymbol{X}$, predicts a set of $\hat{n}$ objects $\hat{\mathbb{Y}} = \{\hat{y}_1, \hat{y}_2, \cdots, \hat{y}_{\hat{n}}\}$ which is close to the ground truth label $\mathbb{Y}$ in some sense. For probabilistic object detection, we further want an uncertainty description for the number of objects and their individual properties.

In this work, we evaluate probabilistic object detectors by seeing the set of objects $\mathbb{Y}$ as a single random variable. The task for our networks is to predict the distribution of this set $f(\mathbb{Y}|\boldsymbol{X})$. This is a natural and general probabilistic extension to the set prediction perspective, as a distribution over sets can capture the varying cardinality and uncertainty in properties for individual objects. Using this novel perspective, all predictions for a single image are evaluated together by applying the negative log-likelihood

$$\mathrm{NLL}((\mathbb{Y}, \boldsymbol{X}), f) = -\log(f(\mathbb{Y}|\boldsymbol{X})). \tag{1}$$

This can be compared to existing methods where classification and regression are treated separately and evaluated conditioned on an ad hoc assignment rule [13], or network performance is measured using non-proper scoring rules [11].

To use the negative log-likelihood in practice, we need our deep object detectors to predict distributions $f(\mathbb{Y}|\boldsymbol{X})$. We propose to use random finite sets (RFSs) and the Poisson multi-Bernoulli (PMB) distribution and demonstrate how the PMB parameters are naturally obtained from the output of standard probabilistic deep object detectors. Further, using the results of [24], we show how to efficiently calculate and decompose the negative log-likelihood of $f(\mathbb{Y}|\boldsymbol{X})$ into detection, classification and regression errors.

Notation: Scalars and vectors are denoted by lowercase or uppercase letters with no special typesetting x, matrices by uppercase boldface letters $\boldsymbol{X}$, and sets by uppercase blackboard-bold letters $\mathbb{X}$. We define $\mathbb{N}_a = \{i \in \mathbb{N} | i \leq a\}, a \in \mathbb{N}$.

3.1   Modeling Detections with Random Finite Sets

We need a way to describe the distribution over $\mathbb{Y}$ using deep neural networks. Interestingly, existing probabilistic detectors already contain the parameters needed. To this end, we propose to model $\mathbb{Y}$ with random finite sets. Random finite sets are described using a multi-object density $f(\mathbb{Y})$, which means that sampling from $f(\mathbb{Y})$ yields finite sets of objects with varying cardinality, where objects consist of a class and a bounding box. We should note that RFSs are not the only way to describe a distribution over $\mathbb{Y}$. However, we will show that our method has multiple properties suitable for object detection and advantages such as being compatible with existing architectures.

Fig. 2. Four sampled sets (left) from a Bernoulli RFS (right) with existence probability $r = 0.75$. The RFS can model the absence of objects, as well as semantic and spatial uncertainties. The image is only included for context.

Bernoulli RFS. One of the simplest RFSs is the Bernoulli RFS, commonly used for modeling single potential objects in the multi-target tracking community [7,29]. Here, we use it to model each individual detected object, and its density is

$$f_{\mathrm{B}}(\mathbb{Y}) = \begin{cases} 1 - r & \text{if } \mathbb{Y} = \emptyset, \\ rp(y) & \text{if } \mathbb{Y} = \{y\}, \\ 0 & \text{if } |\mathbb{Y}| > 1, \end{cases} \tag{2}$$

where $p(y)$ is the single-object density. For instance, assuming the class and bounding box to be independent, $p(y) = p_{\mathrm{cls}}(c)p_{\mathrm{reg}}(b)$ contains the class distribution $p_{\mathrm{cls}}(c)$ and some density describing the object's spatial distribution $p_{\mathrm{reg}}(b)$. Further, $r \in [0, 1]$ is the probability of existence, which is the probability that the Bernoulli RFS yields an object when sampling from it. Note that a Bernoulli RFS can account for at most one object since the likelihood is zero for any set with cardinality greater than one.

The parameters of $p(y)$ are already present in probabilistic detectors. Depending on the architecture, we can interpret r as objectness and predicted it directly, or, find it as the sum of probabilities assigned to foreground classes and let $p_{\mathrm{cls}}(c)$ be the class distribution conditioned on existence. Note that $f_{\mathrm{B}}(\emptyset) = 1 - r$ is the probability that the object is not present, which we may think of as the event where the prediction is background. An example of a Bernoulli RFS prediction and corresponding samples is shown in Fig. 2.

Multi-Bernoulli RFS. Generally, the number of objects in an image can vary greatly. Modeling many potential objects can be achieved by taking the union of multiple Bernoulli RFSs [7], resulting in a multi-Bernoulli (MB) RFS. In other words, individual predictions made by a detector are interpreted as parameters of individual Bernoulli RFSs, and by taking their union we combine them into a single random variable. Unlike a Bernoulli RFS, an MB RFS can be used to model the set of potentially detected objects for an entire image.

Formally, let $\mathbb{X}_1, \ldots, \mathbb{X}_m$ be m independent Bernoulli RFSs with the densities $f_{\mathrm{B}_1}(\mathbb{X}_1), \ldots, f_{\mathrm{B}_m}(\mathbb{X}_m)$, existence probabilities $r_1, \ldots, r_m$, and single-object densities $p_1(x), \ldots, p_m(x)$. Then $\mathbb{X} = \cup_{i=1}^m \mathbb{X}_i$ is an MB RFS with multi-object density

$$f_{\mathrm{MB}}(\mathbb{X}) = \sum_{\uplus_{i=1}^m \mathbb{X}_i = \mathbb{X}} \prod_{j=1}^m f_{\mathrm{B}_j}(\mathbb{X}_j), \tag{3}$$

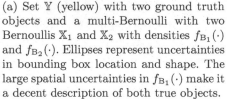

(a) Set $\mathbb{Y}$ (yellow) with two ground truth objects and a multi-Bernoulli with two Bernoullis $\mathbb{X}_1$ and $\mathbb{X}_2$ with densities $f_{\mathrm{B}_1}(\cdot)$ and $f_{\mathrm{B}_2}(\cdot)$. Ellipses represent uncertainties in bounding box location and shape. The large spatial uncertainties in $f_{\mathrm{B}_1}(\cdot)$ make it a decent description of both true objects.

(b) Visualization of the four potential assignments, ordered in decreasing likelihood. In the bottom row, both ground truth objects have been assigned to $\mathbb{X}_1$ and $\mathbb{X}_2$ respectively. As $f_{\mathrm{B}_1}(\mathbb{Y}) = f_{\mathrm{B}_2}(\mathbb{Y}) = 0$ for sets with cardinality larger than one, both these assignments have a likelihood of zero.

Fig. 3. Visualization of likelihood evaluation for a multi-Bernoulli RFS.

where $\sum_{\uplus_{i=1}^m \mathbb{X}_i = \mathbb{X}}$ denotes the sum over all disjoint sets whose union is $\mathbb{X}$. In other words, when evaluating the multi-object density $f_{\mathrm{MB}}(\mathbb{Y})$ of a set $\mathbb{Y}$ we sum the multi-object densities of all possible assignments between elements in $\mathbb{Y}$ and Bernoulli components in f_{MB}.

We illustrate this concept with an example. Consider an image containing two objects $\mathbb{Y} = \{y_1, y_2\}, y_i = (c_i, b_i)$ and two predictions, as shown in Fig. 3. Each prediction consists of a class distribution and a spatial pdf. We let these parameterize the densities $f_{\mathrm{B}_1}(\cdot)$, $f_{\mathrm{B}_2}(\cdot)$ of two separate Bernoulli RFS, whereas the multi-object density $f_{\mathrm{MB}}(\mathbb{Y})$ of their union is the MB RFS used to describe all objects in the image. When evaluating the likelihood $f_{\mathrm{MB}}(\mathbb{Y})$ using (3), we sum the four ways to assign ground truth objects to the Bernoulli RFSs

$$
\begin{aligned}
f_{\mathrm{MB}}(\mathbb{Y}) = {} & f_{\mathrm{B}_1}(\{y_1\}) f_{\mathrm{B}_2}(\{y_2\}) f_{\mathrm{B}_1}(\{y_2\}) f_{\mathrm{B}_2}(\{y_1\}) \\
& + f_{\mathrm{B}_1}(\{y_1, y_2\}) f_{\mathrm{B}_2}(\emptyset) + f_{\mathrm{B}_1}(\emptyset) f_{\mathrm{B}_2}(\{y_1, y_2\}),
\end{aligned}
\tag{4}
$$

where each individual assignment is visualized in Fig. 3b. As $f_{\mathrm{B}_1}(\cdot)$ and $f_{\mathrm{B}_2}(\cdot)$ both evaluate to zero for sets with more than one element, the last two assignments have a likelihood of zero, and we are left with two terms

$$
\begin{aligned}
f_{\mathrm{MB}}(\mathbb{Y}) = {} & r_1 p_{1,\mathrm{cls}}(c_1) p_{1,\mathrm{reg}}(b_1) \cdot r_2 p_{2,\mathrm{cls}}(c_2) p_{2,\mathrm{reg}}(b_2) \\
& + r_1 p_{1,\mathrm{cls}}(c_2) p_{1,\mathrm{reg}}(b_2) \cdot r_2 p_{2,\mathrm{cls}}(c_1) p_{2,\mathrm{reg}}(b_1).
\end{aligned}
\tag{5}
$$

In contrast to existing methods with handcrafted assignment rules [11,13, 18], the assignment problem is modeled explicitly and rigorously by the RFS framework. The intuition behind considering all possible assignments is that we cannot know the correspondence between ground truths and predictions. In cases with overlapping boxes, predictions may have large IoU with multiple objects, making the assignment highly ambiguous. Further, for PrOD, large uncertainties can make it even harder to pair predictions to true objects.

3.2   Proper Scoring Rule for Object Detection

A scoring rule measures the quality of predictive uncertainty in terms of sharpness and calibration [10]. It does so by assigning a numerical value $S(p_\theta, (\mathbf{x}, \mathbf{y}))$ to a predicted distribution $p_\theta(\mathbf{y}|\mathbf{x})$, given that some event $(\mathbf{x}, \mathbf{y}) \sim p^*(\mathbf{y}|\mathbf{x})p(\mathbf{x})$ materialized, where a lower number indicates better quality. A scoring rule is further known to be strictly proper if it is minimized only when p_θ is equal to the distribution p^* that generated the observed event. For OD this translates to the predictive distribution being the same as the distribution from which the annotations have been generated. The noise present in a perfect prediction p_θ should in other words be equal to the noise in the annotations. These properties make proper scoring rules suitable for evaluating and ranking different predictions.

Negative log-likelihood (NLL) is a local proper scoring rule used to evaluate the quality of predictive distributions for both regression and classification. Local refers to the fact that the predicted distribution is only evaluated at the event that materialized [4]. If we let $\mathbb{Y}$ denote the set of ground truth objects present in the current image and let $f_{\mathrm{MB}}(\mathbb{X})$ be the multi-object density of an MB RFS produced by some model, then

$$\mathrm{NLL}(\mathbb{Y}, f_{\mathrm{MB}}) = -\log f_{\mathrm{MB}}(\mathbb{Y}) = -\log \left(\sum_{\uplus_{i=1}^m \mathbb{Y}_i = \mathbb{Y}} \prod_{j=1}^m f_{\mathrm{B}_j}(\mathbb{Y}_j) \right). \qquad (6)$$

As discussed in the previous section, to evaluate the likelihood of an MB RFS density $f_{\mathrm{MB}}(\mathbb{Y})$, we consider all possible assignments. As the number of predictions m, or the cardinality of the ground truth set $|\mathbb{Y}|$ grows, the number of assignments grows super-exponentially, making the NLL computation intractable. However, recently it was shown how to efficiently approximate the NLL of certain RFS densities, including the MB density [24]. Assuming that the ground truth objects, as well as the individual Bernoulli components, are somewhat separated, only a few assignments have a substantial contribution to the overall likelihood. Referring back to the example from Fig. 3, we can see that mainly the first assignment contributed to the sum of likelihoods. Thus, we approximate the NLL by only considering the most likely assignments. We find these assignments efficiently by solving an optimal assignment problem

$$\min_A \quad \sum_k \sum_l C_{k,l} A_{k,l} \qquad (7a)$$

$$\text{s.t.} \quad \sum_{k=1}^{m+|\mathbb{Y}|} A_{k,l} = 1, \sum_{l=1}^{|\mathbb{Y}|} A_{k,l} \le 1, \qquad (7b)$$

$$C_{k,l} = -\log \left(\frac{p_k(y_l)}{1-r_k} r_k \right), \qquad (7c)$$

where C is a cost matrix and its derivation can be found in Appendix A. In (7c), both the cost of assigning the object l to prediction k, $p_k(y_l)r_k$, and the alternative of not assigning the prediction to anything, $1 - r_k$, are considered jointly.

The assignment matrix A describes the pairing between predictions and ground-truth objects, where ground truth object y_l is assigned to the k-th component of the MB i.f.f. $[A]_{k,l} = 1$. Murty's algorithm [22,23] efficiently computes the Q lowest cost associations $A_1^*, \cdots, A_Q^*$ to this assignment problem. We obtain

$$\text{NLL}(\mathbb{Y}, f_{\text{MB}}) \approx -\log \left(\sum_{q=1}^{Q} \prod_{k=1}^{m} f_{B_k}(\mathbb{Y}_k(A_q^*)) \right), \tag{8}$$

where $\mathbb{Y}_k(A_q^*) = \{y_j \in \mathbb{Y} | [A_q^*]_{k,j} = 1\}$, i.e., $\mathbb{Y}_k$ contains the ground truth y_j if y_j was assigned to Bernoulli component k, otherwise it is the empty set. Comparing this expression to (6), only Q terms have to be calculated. During our experiments, we use $Q = 25$ as we find that the approximation does not change considerably when using additional assignments.

3.3   Modeling All Objects

Using only a MB RFS to describe the objects in an image can be problematic as it assumes that the number of predictions is greater than or equal to the number of objects present. For an algorithm providing too few detections, multiple objects are assigned to the same Bernoulli in (3), resulting in the MB likelihood being zero and an infinite NLL. Fortunately, there are RFSs that can model an arbitrary number of objects. Within model-based multi-object tracking, the Poisson Point Process (PPP) is used to model undetected objects [7], and we show here how to use it for OD to ensure a finite NLL. The PPP is then combined with the detections, yielding the Poisson multi-Bernoulli (PMB) RFS. Importantly, we also establish a technique to obtain the PPP directly from the output of our deep object detectors.

Poisson Point Process. Intuitively speaking, the PPP is intended to capture objects that are not properly detected. By complementing the detections in the MB, we model both the detected and undetected objects in an image. In contrast to the MB, the cardinality of a PPP is Poisson distributed which gives it a non-zero probability for any set cardinality. Thus we avoid the issue of infinite NLL due to lack of detections. The multi-object density of a PPP is

$$f_{\text{PPP}}(\mathbb{X}) = \exp\left(-\bar{\lambda}\right) \prod_{x \in \mathbb{X}} \lambda(x), \tag{9}$$

where $\lambda(\cdot)$ is the intensity function and $\bar{\lambda} = \int \lambda(x') dx'$ is the expected cardinality of the set. The intensity function is expected to describe the properties of poorly detected objects, e.g., partially occluded objects, far-away objects, or even classes of objects that are inherently harder to detect. The intensity function is similar to a density function, but its integral does not have to sum to one.

Poisson Multi-Bernoulli RFS. With models for both detected and undetected objects, we have to combine them to a single model for all objects. To this end, we propose to use a Poisson multi-Bernoulli (PMB) RFS, which is the union of a PPP and an MB RFS. The PMB RFS also arises naturally as the posterior density of all objects after a single measurement update, when using standard models in model-based target tracking [7,32].

The multi-object density of a PMB is

$$f_{\text{PMB}}(\mathbb{X}) = \sum_{\mathbb{X}^U \uplus \mathbb{X}^D = \mathbb{X}} f_{\text{PPP}}(\mathbb{X}^U) f_{\text{MB}}(\mathbb{X}^D), \tag{10}$$

were $\mathbb{X}^U \uplus \mathbb{X}^D$ refers to summing over all possible ways of partitioning $\mathbb{X}$ into two disjoint sets, one being the set of undetected objects $\mathbb{X}^U$ and the other one being the set of detected objects $\mathbb{X}^D$. When evaluating the likelihood of a set $\mathbb{Y}$ this translates to, for each object in $\mathbb{Y}$, considering it to be detected and assigning it to a Bernoulli following (3), or it being undetected and assigning it to the PPP.

Selecting the PPP Intensity. To use the PMB in object detection, we must describe the PPP intensity function $\lambda(\cdot)$. During this work, we explored various ways of learning $\lambda(\cdot)$ from data, e.g., estimating the parameters of a uniform intensity function or describing $\lambda(\cdot)$ as a constant mixture model. However, the method we found to work best for the detectors considered in our experiments, is to create $\lambda(\cdot)$ from low confidence predictions. In practice, we parameterize the intensity function as the unnormalized mixture of low confidence predictions where the mixture weights are the existence probabilities

$$\lambda(x) = \sum_i r_i p_i(x). \tag{11}$$

Specifically, we remove all predictions from the MB RFS, whose existence probabilities are $r < 0.1$, and instead use them to construct the intensity function using (11). The theoretical motivation for this change is that the Kullback-Leibler divergence between a Bernoulli RFS with existence probability $r < 0.1$ and a PPP with intensity function $\lambda(x) = rp(x)$ is small [31]. The proposed PMB density should therefore be a good approximation to the MB density that we had before, but this minor adjustment is sufficient to avoid issues with infinite NLL.

NLL Evaluation. For evaluating the NLL of a PMB RFS, we use the same approach as for the MB and consider only the Q most likely assignments. The cost matrix from (7c) used in the optimization is extended to

$$C_{k,l} = \begin{cases} -\log\left(\frac{p_k(y_l)}{1-r_k} r_k\right), & \text{if } k \leq |\mathbb{Y}| \\ -\log \lambda(y_l), & \text{if } k = l + |\mathbb{Y}| \\ \infty, & \text{otherwise,} \end{cases} \tag{12}$$

which translates to appending a diagonal matrix of size $|\mathbb{Y}| \times |\mathbb{Y}|$ to the original cost matrix. The NLL from (8) is extended as

$$\text{NLL}(\mathbb{Y}, f_{\text{PMB}}) \approx \int \lambda(y')\mathrm{d}y' - \log\Big(\sum_{q=1}^{Q} \prod_{y \in \mathbb{Y}^{\text{U}}(\boldsymbol{A}_q^*)} \lambda(y) \prod_{k=1}^{m} f_{\text{B}_k}(\mathbb{Y}_k(\boldsymbol{A}_q^*))\Big), \quad (13)$$

where we define $\mathbb{Y}^{\text{U}}(\boldsymbol{A}_q^*) = \mathbb{Y} \setminus \cup_{i=1}^{m} \mathbb{Y}_i(\boldsymbol{A}_q^*)$, i.e., $\mathbb{Y}^U$ contains all the ground truth elements matched to the PPP.

NLL Decomposition. Often the most likely assignment yields a good approximation to the NLL. For $Q = 1$, the NLL can be decomposed into four parts and expressed in terms of assignments

$$\text{NLL}(\mathbb{Y}, f_{\text{PMB}}) \approx \min_{\gamma \in \Gamma} - \underbrace{\sum_{(i,j) \in \gamma} \log\big(r_i p_{i,\text{cls}}(c_j)\big)}_{\text{Classification}} - \underbrace{\sum_{(i,j) \in \gamma} \log\big(p_{i,\text{reg}}(b_j)\big)}_{\text{Regression}} \quad (14)$$

$$- \underbrace{\sum_{i \in \mathbb{F}(\gamma)} \log(1 - r_i)}_{\text{False detections}} + \underbrace{\int \lambda(y')\mathrm{d}y' - \sum_{j \in \mathbb{M}(\gamma)} \log\lambda(y_j)}_{\text{Missed objects}},$$

where Γ is the set of all possible assignment sets, $(i, j) \in \gamma$ means that prediction i has been assigned to ground truth j, and $\mathbb{F}(\gamma) = \{i \in \mathbb{N}_m | \nexists j : (i, j) \in \gamma\}$ is the set of indices of the Bernoullis not matched to any ground-truth, i.e. false positives. Note that we assume the classification and regression distributions are independent $p_i(x) = p_{i,\text{cls}}(\cdot)p_{i,\text{reg}}(\cdot)$ for this decomposition. Further, we define $\mathbb{M}(\gamma) = \{j \in \mathbb{N}_{|\mathbb{Y}|} | \nexists i : (i, j) \in \gamma\}$ as the set of indices of ground-truths not matched to any Bernoulli component, i.e., missed objects. This decomposition enables further insight into the types of errors made by an algorithm, e.g., instead of treating all false positives equally as in [11], we take their existence probability into account for deciding how much to penalize an algorithm.

4　Experiments

For our experiments, we evaluate three existing object detection models: DETR [2], RetinaNet [17], and Faster-RCNN [25], all using ResNet50 backbones. These are chosen to represent a set-based, one-stage, and two-stage detector, which highlights that the RFS framework is applicable regardless of architecture. All these models are publicly available through the Detectron2 [34] object detection framework, with hyperparameters[1] optimized to produce competitive detection results for the COCO dataset [18]. Further, the models have previously been retrofitted with variance networks to estimate their spatial uncertainty [13]. Due

---

[1] Hyperparameters are used as is unless stated otherwise.

Table 1. mAP, PMB-NLL and PDQ with/without threshold for three detectors on the COCO validation set. * detections excluded due to ∞ NLL.

Detector	Loss	PMB-NLL ↓	mAP ↑	PDQ@F1 ↑	PDQ@0.0 ↑
DETR	ES	**120.33**	**0.407**	0.262	**0.033**
	NLL	152.13	0.376	0.113	0.014
	MB-NLL	124.20	0.389	**0.271**	0.023
RetinaNet	ES	127.66	**0.362**	0.228	**0.028**
	NLL	126.86	0.351	0.185	0.021
	MB-NLL	**121.02**	0.361	**0.251**	0.023
Faster-RCNN	ES*	140.53	**0.373**	0.281	**0.087**
	NLL*	139.08	0.371	**0.282**	**0.087**
	MB-NLL	**117.77**	0.326	0.199	0.024

to hardware limitations, models in [13] used a smaller batch size and adjusted learning rates, resulting in decreased mAP compared to numbers reported by Detectron2. For fair comparison, we use the same hyperparameters as [13], but note that increasing the batch size can improve mAP for all models.

The models are also fine-tuned with MB-NLL (8) as loss function. During training, the aim is to detect all objects, hence the PPP for undetected objects is ignored. We also found training to be more stable when the number of assignments Q is set to one. Further, when calculating the assignment costs for matching, ignoring spatial uncertainties improved training stability. That is, in (7c), we use the L2 distance instead of $\log(p_{k,\mathrm{reg}})$. This can be thought of as learning the spatial uncertainty given the predicted mean of the bounding box.

For evaluation, the $Q = 25$ assignments with the highest likelihood are used to approximate the PMB-NLL, as larger values for Q do not affect the approximation for any of the models considered. In contrast to training, the matching cost is used as described in (12). Further, following the COCO standard, models are limited to 100 predictions and no confidence threshold is used. DETR is designed to provide exactly 100 predictions, while we apply NMS and keep the 100 top-scoring predictions for RetinaNet and Faster-RCNN. For all models, bounding boxes are parameterized by their top-left and bottom-right coordinates $[x_1, y_1, x_2, y_2]$. While the pre-trained models from [13] used a Gaussian distribution for regression, we found that using a Laplace distribution results in considerably lower NLL for both training and evaluation, across all models.

Evaluating Object Detection with Proper Scoring Rule. We report mAP, PDQ [11] and PMB-NLL in Table 1 and the decomposed results following (14) are shown in Table 2, with additional analysis in the supplementary material. For models with loss ES (energy score) and NLL, please refer to [13] for their details. PDQ is reported both when thresholding prediction confidences at the detectors' optimal F1-score and without any thresholding. The decomposition in Table 2 is

Table 2. Decomposed PMB-NLL on COCO validation set. Numbers are given as [mean per image]/[mean per prediction]. FP = NLL of unmatched predictions. PPP match + PPP rate = missed objects. *detections excluded due to ∞ NLL.

Detector	Loss	Regression ↓	Classification ↓	FP ↓	PPP match ↓	PPP rate ↓
DETR	ES	82.3/**12.3**	3.79/0.57	17.6/0.71	15.6/**23.3**	1.46
	NLL	124.7/17.5	3.57/**0.50**	18.4/**0.59**	5.0/23.8	1.52
	MB-NLL	93.3/14.6	3.26/0.51	3.1/0.99	24.8/25.4	0.18
RetinaNet	ES	103.1/14.4	7.95/1.11	10.1/**0.22**	4.3/23.8	2.87
	NLL	105.0/14.5	7.87/1.09	9.8/**0.22**	2.3/**20.7**	2.91
	MB-NLL	79.9/**13.9**	4.00/**0.70**	2.6/0.44	34.1/21.1	0.98
F-RCNN	ES*	105.5/15.1	8.23/1.18	12.9/0.57	14.0/37.1	0.43
	NLL*	104.7/15.0	8.23/1.18	13.2/0.58	13.5/36.1	0.43
	MB-NLL	62.0/**12.3**	4.94/**0.98**	3.3/**0.36**	46.8/**20.4**	1.30

calculated for the assignment with the lowest NLL and shown averaged per image and per assigned objects. For instance, the DETR ES regression term 82.3/12.3 is read as, on average the regression distribution of *all* matched predictions contributes with 82.3 to the overall NLL. For a *single* matched prediction, it contributes with 12.3 to the total NLL on average.

We can see from Table 1 that optimizing the networks toward MB-NLL rather than the NLL formulation used in [13] consistently gives lower PMB-NLL at evaluation. With the exception of Faster-RCNN, this lower PMB-NLL is achieved without sacrificing mAP performance. We can also note that mAP does not indicate quality of predictive uncertainty. For instance, Faster-RCNN trained with the energy score achieves competitive performance in terms of mAP, but its uncertainty estimates result in the second worse PMB-NLL among the models. Further, although PDQ is described as a threshold-free performance measure, it is sensitive to false positive detections regardless of their confidence, as predictions with low and high confidence receive the same penalty by PDQ. When including low confidence predictions (PDQ@0.0), the reported PDQ results become hard to distinguish between detectors. For PMB-NLL, FP penalties are instead proportional to the predicted existence probabilities.

Inspecting the decomposition of PMB-NLL in Table 2 gives further insights into the strengths and weaknesses of the detectors. Models that have not been trained with MB-NLL, show high penalties for producing many false positives. This is exemplified in Fig. 4, where the model trained with MB-NLL produces a single prediction per object, and fewer false detections. Rather than producing multiple plausible predictions per object, where each prediction has low spatial uncertainty, they are compiled into a single hypothesis with slightly larger uncertainty. More examples of this are available in the Appendix. We theorize that the ES and NLL training is optimized toward mAP evaluation, where low confidence predictions are not penalized as heavily, and that the MB-NLL loss instead encourages models to produce plausible set predictions. Comparing across architectures, we can see from FP penalties that RetinaNet generally assigns lower

Fig. 4. Ground truth (left), predictions from DETR ES (middle) and DETR MB-NLL (right). Predictions with a score less than 0.1 not shown. Models not trained with MB-NLL tend to produce many false positive detections.

existence probabilities to its incorrect predictions compared to DETR. For the matched predictions, DETR instead has the strongest classification performance, indicating that DETR generally has higher existence probabilities for its predictions, regardless of them being assigned to a ground truth or not.

The example in Fig. 4 also underlines important advantages with our evaluation. For the person in the image, DETR ES has one prediction with good regression but low confidence (in turquoise with 0.4), and one confident (in white with 0.96) with bad regression. Depending on which prediction is assigned to the true object, the error is either related to classification or regression. As highlighted previously, confidence thresholds are in practice needed by PDQ and used explicitly in other methods [13]. Thus, existing methods only consider the confident prediction and report large regression errors. In contrast, PMB-NLL evaluates both possibilities and seamlessly weighs their contribution based on their individual likelihood, where the most likely assignment is in fact the one with lower existence probability.

Further, it is interesting to study the balance between matched predictions, and ground truth objects matched to the PPP. For Faster-RCNN trained with MB-NLL, many objects are assigned to the PPP. However, its PPP is a reasonably good description of the missed objects, resulting in a total PMB-NLL which is lower than the other models. For an application where a high recall level is desirable, the RetinaNet ES model might be a better choice, at the cost of worse regression and classification performance.

5   Conclusions

We propose the use of random finite sets for probabilistic object detection. Instead of predicting a set of objects $\mathbb{X}$, we ask our models to predict the distribution over the set of objects $f(\mathbb{X})$. Using a distribution over sets enables us to evaluate model performance for the true set of objects $\mathbb{Y}$ by applying the proper scoring rule negative log-likelihood $-\log(f(\mathbb{Y}))$. Our proposed method is general enough to be applied to detectors with any type of regression or classification distribution. It handles the assignments between predictions and objects automatically and can be decomposed into different error types. We evaluate three types of detectors using our new scoring rule and highlight their strengths and weaknesses. Our method enables fair comparison between probabilistic object detectors and we hope this will encourage the creation of novel architectures that aim for accurate uncertainty estimates rather than just accurate means. Future directions include how to better optimize networks toward our scoring rule and exploring further scoring rules within the random finite set framework.

Acknowledgements. This work was partially supported by the Wallenberg AI, Autonomous Systems and Software Program (WASP) funded by the Knut and Alice Wallenberg Foundation. Computational resources were provided by the Swedish National Infrastructure for Computing at C3SE and NSC, partially funded by the Swedish Research Council, grant agreement no. 2018-05973.

References

1. Abdar, M., et al.: A review of uncertainty quantification in deep learning: techniques, applications and challenges. Inf. Fusion **76**, 243–297 (2021)
2. Carion, N., Massa, F., Synnaeve, G., Usunier, N., Kirillov, A., Zagoruyko, S.: End-to-end object detection with transformers. In: Vedaldi, A., Bischof, H., Brox, T., Frahm, J.-M. (eds.) ECCV 2020. LNCS, vol. 12346, pp. 213–229. Springer, Cham (2020). https://doi.org/10.1007/978-3-030-58452-8_13
3. Choi, J., Chun, D., Kim, H., Lee, H.J.: Gaussian YOLOv3: an accurate and fast object detector using localization uncertainty for autonomous driving. In: Proceedings of the IEEE/CVF International Conference on Computer Vision, pp. 502–511 (2019)
4. Dawid, A.P., Musio, M.: Theory and applications of proper scoring rules. Metron **72**(2), 169–183 (2014). https://doi.org/10.1007/s40300-014-0039-y
5. Feng, D., Harakeh, A., Waslander, S.L., Dietmayer, K.: A review and comparative study on probabilistic object detection in autonomous driving. IEEE Trans. Intell. Transp. Syst. **23**, 9961–9980 (2021)
6. Feng, D., Wei, X., Rosenbaum, L., Maki, A., Dietmayer, K.: Deep active learning for efficient training of a LiDAR 3D object detector. In: 2019 IEEE Intelligent Vehicles Symposium (IV), pp. 667–674. IEEE (2019)
7. García-Fernández, Á.F., Williams, J.L., Granström, K., Svensson, L.: Poisson multi-Bernoulli mixture filter: direct derivation and implementation. IEEE Trans. Aerosp. Electron. Syst. **54**(4), 1883–1901 (2018)
8. Gawlikowski, J., et al.: A survey of uncertainty in deep neural networks. arXiv preprint arXiv:2107.03342 (2021)
9. Gneiting, T., Balabdaoui, F., Raftery, A.E.: Probabilistic forecasts, calibration and sharpness. J. Roy. Stat. Soc.: Ser. B (Stat. Methodol.) **69**(2), 243–268 (2007)
10. Gneiting, T., Raftery, A.E.: Strictly proper scoring rules, prediction, and estimation. J. Am. Stat. Assoc. **102**(477), 359–378 (2007)
11. Hall, D., et al.: Probabilistic object detection: definition and evaluation. In: Proceedings of the IEEE/CVF Winter Conference on Applications of Computer Vision, pp. 1031–1040 (2020)
12. Harakeh, A., Smart, M., Waslander, S.L.: BayesOD: a Bayesian approach for uncertainty estimation in deep object detectors. In: 2020 IEEE International Conference on Robotics and Automation (ICRA), pp. 87–93. IEEE (2020)

13. Harakeh, A., Waslander, S.L.: Estimating and evaluating regression predictive uncertainty in deep object detectors. In: International Conference on Learning Representations (2021)
14. He, Y., Wang, J.: Deep mixture density network for probabilistic object detection. In: 2020 IEEE/RSJ International Conference on Intelligent Robots and Systems (IROS), pp. 10550–10555. IEEE (2020)
15. Kendall, A., Gal, Y.: What uncertainties do we need in Bayesian deep learning for computer vision? In: Advances in Neural Information Processing Systems, vol. 30 (2017)
16. Lee, Y., Hwang, J.W., Kim, H.I., Yun, K., Kwon, Y.: Localization uncertainty estimation for anchor-free object detection. arXiv preprint arXiv:2006.15607 (2020)
17. Lin, T.Y., Goyal, P., Girshick, R., He, K., Dollár, P.: Focal loss for dense object detection. In: Proceedings of the IEEE International Conference on Computer Vision, pp. 2980–2988 (2017)
18. Lin, T.-Y., et al.: Microsoft COCO: common objects in context. In: Fleet, D., Pajdla, T., Schiele, B., Tuytelaars, T. (eds.) ECCV 2014. LNCS, vol. 8693, pp. 740–755. Springer, Cham (2014). https://doi.org/10.1007/978-3-319-10602-1_48
19. Lyu, Z., Gutierrez, N., Rajguru, A., Beksi, W.J.: Probabilistic object detection via deep ensembles. In: Bartoli, A., Fusiello, A. (eds.) ECCV 2020. LNCS, vol. 12540, pp. 67–75. Springer, Cham (2020). https://doi.org/10.1007/978-3-030-65414-6_7
20. Mahler, R.P.: Advances in Statistical Multisource-Multitarget Information Fusion. Artech House, Norwood (2014)
21. Miller, D., Nicholson, L., Dayoub, F., Sünderhauf, N.: Dropout sampling for robust object detection in open-set conditions. In: 2018 IEEE International Conference on Robotics and Automation (ICRA), pp. 3243–3249. IEEE (2018)
22. Motro, M., Ghosh, J.: Scaling data association for hypothesis-oriented MHT. In: 2019 22th International Conference on Information Fusion (FUSION), pp. 1–8. IEEE (2019)
23. Murty, K.G.: An algorithm for ranking all the assignments in order of increasing cost. Oper. Res. **16**(3), 682–687 (1968)
24. Pinto, J., Xia, Y., Svensson, L., Wymeersch, H.: An uncertainty-aware performance measure for multi-object tracking. IEEE Signal Process. Lett. **28**, 1689–1693 (2021)
25. Ren, S., He, K., Girshick, R., Sun, J.: Faster R-CNN: towards real-time object detection with region proposal networks. In: Advances in Neural Information Processing Systems, vol. 28 (2015)
26. Skafte, N., Jørgensen, M., Hauberg, S.R.: Reliable training and estimation of variance networks. In: Advances in Neural Information Processing Systems, vol. 32 (2019)
27. Sun, Z., Cao, S., Yang, Y., Kitani, K.M.: Rethinking transformer-based set prediction for object detection. In: Proceedings of the IEEE/CVF International Conference on Computer Vision, pp. 3611–3620 (2021)
28. Valdenegro-Toro, M.: I find your lack of uncertainty in computer vision disturbing. In: Proceedings of the IEEE/CVF Conference on Computer Vision and Pattern Recognition, pp. 1263–1272 (2021)
29. Vo, B., Vo, B., Hoang, H.G.: An efficient implementation of the generalized labeled multi-Bernoulli filter. IEEE Trans. Signal Process. **65**(8), 1975–1987 (2017)
30. Vo, B.T., Vo, B.N.: Labeled random finite sets and multi-object conjugate priors. IEEE Trans. Signal Process. **61**(13), 3460–3475 (2013)
31. Williams, J.L.: Hybrid poisson and multi-Bernoulli filters. In: 2012 15th International Conference on Information Fusion, pp. 1103–1110. IEEE (2012)

32. Williams, J.L.: Marginal multi-Bernoulli filters: RFS derivation of MHT, JIPDA, and association-based MeMBer. IEEE Trans. Aerosp. Electron. Syst. **51**(3), 1664–1687 (2015)
33. Wirges, S., Reith-Braun, M., Lauer, M., Stiller, C.: Capturing object detection uncertainty in multi-layer grid maps. In: 2019 IEEE Intelligent Vehicles Symposium (IV), pp. 1520–1526. IEEE (2019)
34. Wu, Y., Kirillov, A., Massa, F., Lo, W.Y., Girshick, R.: Detectron2 (2019). https://github.com/facebookresearch/detectron2
35. Zhang, Y., Hare, J., Prugel-Bennett, A.: Deep set prediction networks. In: Advances in Neural Information Processing Systems, vol. 32 (2019)
36. Zhou, X., Koltun, V., Krähenbühl, P.: Probabilistic two-stage detection. arXiv preprint arXiv:2103.07461 (2021)
37. Zhu, X., Su, W., Lu, L., Li, B., Wang, X., Dai, J.: Deformable DETR: deformable transformers for end-to-end object detection. In: International Conference on Learning Representations (2021)

Weakly-Supervised Temporal Action Detection for Fine-Grained Videos with Hierarchical Atomic Actions

Zhi Li[1]([⊠]) [iD], Lu He[2], and Huijuan Xu[3]

[1] University of California, Berkeley, USA
zhili@berkeley.edu
[2] Tencent America, Palo Alto, USA
lhluhe@tencent.com
[3] Pennsylvania State University, University Park, USA
hkx5063@psu.edu

Abstract. Action understanding has evolved into the era of fine granularity, as most human behaviors in real life have only minor differences. To detect these fine-grained actions accurately in a label-efficient way, we tackle the problem of weakly-supervised fine-grained temporal action detection in videos for the first time. Without the careful design to capture subtle differences between fine-grained actions, previous weakly-supervised models for general action detection cannot perform well in the fine-grained setting. We propose to model actions as the combinations of reusable atomic actions which are automatically discovered from data through self-supervised clustering, in order to capture the commonality and individuality of fine-grained actions. The learnt atomic actions, represented by visual concepts, are further mapped to fine and coarse action labels leveraging the semantic label hierarchy. Our approach constructs a visual representation hierarchy of four levels: clip level, atomic action level, fine action class level and coarse action class level, with supervision at each level. Extensive experiments on two large-scale fine-grained video datasets, FineAction and FineGym, show the benefit of our proposed weakly-supervised model for fine-grained action detection, and it achieves state-of-the-art results.

Keywords: Fine-grained · Weakly-supervised · Temporal action detection · Atomic actions

1 Introduction

Early video benchmarks [2,16] mostly contain actions with distinct movement. Recent works have evolved into fine-grained action understanding [23,39], which is closer to the distribution of actions in real life. These fine-grained actions are either visually similar actions, e.g., *mop floor* and *sweep floor*, or actions from

---

Supplementary Information The online version contains supplementary material available at https://doi.org/10.1007/978-3-031-20080-9_33.

Action 1: Clear pike circle backward to handstand

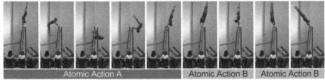

Action 2: Clear pike circle backward with 0.5 turn to handstand

Action 3: Clear pike circle backward with 1 turn to handstand

Fig. 1. Fine-grained action examples from FineGym dataset [39] with atomic action decomposition. The three actions all share the same atomic action A (*clear pike circle backward to handstand*), but differ in the ending phase of the action. Action 1 only contains atomic action A. Action 2 has another atomic action B (*0.5 turn*) following A, and action 3 has atomic action B repeated twice after A

continuously recorded instructional videos. Designing algorithms to detect fine-grained actions could potentially assist people in acquiring new skills, since people usually learn from continuous instructional videos, and correctly segmented action steps could benefit their learning process. Fine-grained action detection algorithms are also needed on home assistance devices to better perceive actions happening in home and take appropriate actions to assist people.

For temporal action detection, data annotation in the form of start and end frames suffers from high annotation cost due to the large volume of videos, and annotation consistency issue among various annotators. These problems are even more severe in fine-grained videos, because the distinction between fine-grained actions is not so obvious, and the time granularity of action annotation is also more refined. To alleviate these problems and conduct label-efficient temporal action detection in fine-grained videos, we propose to tackle weakly-supervised action detection with only video-level action labels and without temporal annotations of when the actions take place, for the first time in fine-grained videos.

Traditional weakly-supervised action detection models are mostly based on Multiple Instance Learning (MIL) [14]. The core of these MIL-based models is video-level action classification, and video segments having high classification activation are selected as detected action segments. Fine-grained videos, however, introduce extra challenges in MIL, as fine-grained actions are visually similar and the differences only manifest in small details (examples are shown in Fig. 1). As a result, classification itself is much more difficult in fine-grained tasks [23,39].

Prior works [10,15,20] on action detection decompose human's behaviours into a series of atomic building blocks inspired by human's cognition of actions. Following this idea, we model fine-grained action details through the lens of **Atomic Actions**, defined as short temporal parts representing a single semantically meaningful component of an action, to benefit their classification. This is inspired by the observation that visually similar fine-grained actions often share common atomic actions and only differ in the key atomic segments. For example, as shown in Fig. 1, when comparing the three fine-grained actions, *clear pike circle backward to handstand, clear pike circle backward with 0.5 turn to handstand,* and *clear pike circle backward with 1 turn to handstand,* we humans perceive their differences by looking at the last atomic action. However, the boundaries of atomic actions are not explicitly labeled, and are very hard to obtain even if we want to label them.

Inspired by **Visual Concept** in fine-grained image understanding [5,12,13], we propose to automatically discover these atomic actions in the feature level, which are hard to be defined in advance by humans. This is different from prior works defining atomic building blocks ahead of time [10,15,20]. We leverage self-supervised clustering to discover temporal visual concepts from video clip features. We then use visual concepts to represent atomic actions and model a fine-grained action as a composition of atomic actions. Specifically, MIL classifier weights are used to select visual concepts for each fine-grained action. Visual concepts capture fine details, and can in turn facilitate the MIL training.

The MIL classification relies on the most discriminative part of the action and thus is prone to detecting only the discriminative segment as target action. To learn the commonality among fine-grained actions and detect complete action, we incorporate coarse-to-fine label hierarchy often available in fine-grained videos to regularize the commonality between actions in the feature space. Concretely, we aggregate fine-level visual concepts to obtain coarse-level visual concept representations, and connect them with the coarse-level labels' supervision.

In summary, we propose a Hierarchical Atomic Action Network (HAAN) to model the commonality and individuality of fine-grained actions in the MIL framework to conduct weakly-supervised fine-grained temporal action detection[1]. The contributions of this paper include:

1. We are the first to tackle the weakly-supervised fine-grained temporal action detection problem, and benchmark previous weakly-supervised approaches for general action detection on fine-grained datasets.
2. Propose a self-supervised learning approach to discover visual concepts for building atomic actions, which promotes the learning of fine action details.
3. Leverage coarse-to-fine semantic label relationship to construct a hierarchical visual concept system to encourage learning commonality among fine actions.

---

[1] Code is available at https://github.com/lizhi1104/HAAN.git.

4. Conduct extensive experiments for the HAAN model on two large-scale fine-grained video datasets: FineAction and FineGym, and achieve state-of-the-art results.

2   Related Work

2.1   Weakly-Supervised Temporal Action Detection

Labeling an action's start and end points in video frames is a labor-intensive task. Thus the weakly-supervised approach, which drastically reduces annotation requirements, becomes an important research topic. Under weakly-supervised setting, detection models are trained with only video-level action labels, without temporal annotations of the action's start and end points. Previous research mostly involved the Multiple Instance Learning (MIL) [3,8,14] process. MIL leverages classification signals to help action detection: given a video-level action label, some parts of the video must contain the specific action, and the key is to figure out which parts. To solve that, MIL conducts classification for the whole video, during which it carefully selects some parts of the video with high activation scores as action segments. Typically the selection method can be either k-max pooling [25,30,34,40,44], or attention-based pooling [22,31,44,46].

On top of the basic MIL classifier, previous researchers also explored adding different regularization losses, constraints or temporal property modeling to boost the action detection performance. Nguyen et al. [31] added a sparsity loss to the attention weights in order to predict accurate action segments. Paul et al. [34] proposed a co-activity similarity loss to enforce similarity between features of the same action. Shou et al. [40] added a contrastive loss to help action boundary prediction. And Ma et al. [25] introduced a class-agnostic actionness score, which leverages context to help focus on the parts that contain actions.

None of these prior works, however, tackled fine-grained actions. Two widely used benchmarks, THUMOS-14 [16] and ActivityNet-1.2 [2], do not consistently contain fine-grained actions, either. Sun et al. [43] mentioned fine-grained actions in weakly-supervised setting, but their definition of fine-grained actions is closer to the granularity of THUMOS-14 and ActivityNet-1.2, and they require extra supervision from web images. To the best of our knowledge, we are the first to tackle weakly-supervised action detection task for fine-grained actions.

2.2   Fine-Grained Temporal Action Detection

Fine-grained action detection has become an increasingly important research topic recently. Several fine-grained action datasets have been proposed, such as MPII [38], Salad 50 [42], MERL Shopping [41], GTEA [9], EPIC-KITCHENS-100 [7], FineGym [39], and FineAction [23]. Small differences between fine-grained action categories post extra challenges for action detection. As a result, it is not uncommon to see that models designed for general action detection perform much worse on fine-grained datasets [23,39].

Previous works explored different methods to model fine-grained action details. Mac et al. [26] applied deformable convolution to extract local spatio-temporal features in order to obtain fine-grained motion details. Piergiovanni and Ryoo [35] leveraged temporal structures to detect actions. Mavroudi et al.'s work [28] involved learning a dictionary for action primitives. These primitives capture fine-grained action details, and inspired our work in the use of atomic actions. The most relevant to our work is [32], which decomposed the detection task into two steps on coarse and fine levels respectively. This inspired our hierarchical modeling of visual concepts. All these prior works require full supervision of action start/end point annotations.

Some previous works' settings are close to weakly-supervised setting, but still require extra supervision other than just the set of actions, such as the order of actions [11,37]. This research is set to address weakly-supervised action detection for fine-grained videos with only the set of actions available.

2.3   Atomic Actions and Visual Concepts

The concept of atomic actions naturally arises when researchers analyze humans' cognitive perception of actions. Gaidon et al. [10] used a histogram of features representing atomic actions to conduct action detection. Similarly, Lillo et al. [20] modeled human activities as smaller individual components. Recently, Ji et al. [15] decomposed an action event into atomic spatial-temporal scene graphs, aiming to understand actions as sequences of atomic interactions with the surrounding environments.

Visual concept, on the other hand, is often related to promoting models' interpretability. Chen et al. [6] showed that InfoGAN encodes disentangled visual concepts such as pose, emotion, and hairstyle. Whitney et al. [45] learned symbolic representations from video frames. Kim et al. [18] analyzed how each visual concept of the input image affects the classification prediction. Ghorbani et al. [12] proposed a method that automatically recovers visual concepts and determines their importance without user's input. Chen et al. [5] proposed to model prototypical parts in image recognition and combine those parts in final predictions. Those prototypical parts can be viewed as visual concepts.

Visual concepts are typically obtained via unsupervised learning [12,13]. Given that atomic actions are not directly annotated, these works inspire us to use visual concepts to model atomic actions. In the image field, visual concepts usually correspond to small patches of the image for a single subject [5]. In our work, we extend this concept to temporal visual concepts in videos.

3   Method

We first introduce the notations. Given a set of videos with C categories, each video contains M action segments (M can be different for different videos). The mth action segment is described by its class label $a_m \in \{1, \cdots, C\}$ and its start/end timestamp $(Start_m, End_m)$. Under the weakly-supervised action

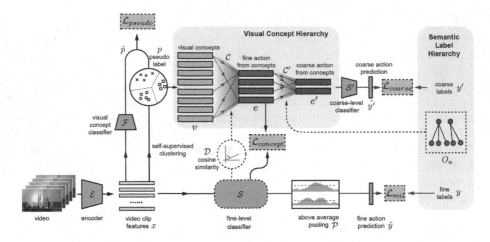

Fig. 2. An overview of our HAAN model. It contains a fine-grained action MIL classifier $\mathcal{S}$ trained with $\mathcal{L}_{mil}$. To capture fine-grained details, HAAN leverages self-supervised clustering ($\mathcal{L}_{pseudo}$) to learn visual concepts which represent atomic actions. In order to model each fine-grained action as a composition of atomic actions, we connect visual concept v with the MIL classifier $\mathcal{S}$ based on a distance function $\mathcal{D}$. The model learns to compose visual concepts into fine-grained actions through $\mathcal{L}_{concept}$. In addition, we use the coarse-to-fine semantic label hierarchy (represented by O_u) to further compose fine-grained actions into coarse-grained actions, and train it with $\mathcal{L}_{coarse}$

detection setting, for each video we only have access to the set of action labels $Set(a_1, \cdots, a_M)$ at training time. The number of action segments M, the order of action segments, and their temporal timestamps are not available. In other words, the annotation for each video can be represented by a multi-hot encoding label vector $y = \{y^1, \cdots, y^C\} \in \{0,1\}^C$, where each entry is a binary indicator representing whether the video contains the corresponding action. The goal is to detect the start and end points $(Start_m, End_m)$ for every action. Figure 2 is an overview of the HAAN model.

3.1   Multiple Instance Learning

Multiple Instance Learning (MIL) is widely used in previous non fine-grained weakly-supervised action detection models. The idea is quite straightforward: given the multi-hot video-level action label $y \in \{0,1\}^C$, we know that the video contains specific actions. In order to detect which parts (a.k.a. instances) correspond to that action, MIL uses the signal from action classification loss. The model aggregates information along the temporal axis to obtain a global representation for the whole video, and is trained with classification loss. During this process, the parts that contribute the most to video-level class prediction are selected as target actions.

Following prior work [24,25,30,34,40,44], we divide a long video into T short video clips. Then we use feature encoder $\mathcal{E}$ to extract clip level features $\{x_1, \cdots, x_T\}$, where each $x_i \in R^d$ is the d-dimensional feature vector for i^{th} clip. A classifier $\mathcal{S}$ then predicts a score for each clip: $s_i = \mathcal{S}(x_i) \in R^C, 1 \leq i \leq T$. After that, a pooling method $\mathcal{P}$ aggregates scores from all clips $s = \{s_1, s_2, \cdots, s_T\} \in R^{T \times C}$ into a global action label prediction $\hat{y} = \mathcal{P}(s) \in R^C$. $\hat{y}$ is then compared with y via standard classification loss.

Previous works explored different pooling methods $\mathcal{P}$ including k-max pooling [25,30,34,40,44] and attention-based pooling [22,31,44,46]. In our paper, we filter the scores $\{s_1, s_2, \cdots, s_T\}$ with the mean $\bar{s}$ of all the scores as threshold, and take the average of the scores above the mean. Concretely, for each action class j $(1 \leq j \leq C)$:

$$\hat{y^j} = \frac{1}{\sum\limits_{i=1}^{T} \mathbf{1}(s_i^j \geq \overline{s^j})} \sum_{i=1}^{T} \mathbf{1}(s_i^j \geq \overline{s^j}) \cdot s_i^j \tag{1}$$

where $\overline{s^j}$ is the mean of scores of class j for all T clips. The aggregated video-level prediction logit $\hat{y^j}$ is then used in the binary cross entropy (BCE) MIL loss with logits.

$$\mathcal{L}_{mil} = BCE(\hat{y^j}, y^j) \tag{2}$$

3.2   Visual Concept Learning

To capture fine-grained temporal details, we introduce self-supervised clustering to discover visual concepts from video features. Before each epoch, we collect features of all clips in the whole training data, and then conduct K-means clustering [27] on the whole feature pool to obtain N clusters. This generates a pseudo label p_i for each video clip i, $p_i \in \{1, \cdots, N\}$ is assigned by the clustering algorithm.

Pseudo label is then used to train a visual concept classifier $\mathcal{F}$. Visual concept classifier $\mathcal{F}$ maps the shared features x_i to a predicted cluster logit, $\hat{p}_i = \mathcal{F}(x_i) \in R^N$. The model then trains $\hat{p}_i$ with cross entropy (CE) loss.

$$\mathcal{L}_{pseudo} = CE(\hat{p}_i, p_i) \tag{3}$$

In addition, pseudo label p_i is used to extract visual concepts from the video's features. To obtain the representation v_n of the nth visual concept, we pool the features of clips whose pseudo label is equal to n.

$$v_n = \frac{1}{\sum\limits_{i=1}^{T} \mathbf{1}(p_i = n)} \sum_{i=1}^{T} \mathbf{1}(p_i = n) \cdot x_i \tag{4}$$

The above equation holds if at least one clip is labeled as cluster n. If no clip corresponds to cluster n in this video, we set $v_n = \vec{0}$.

Each visual concept represents a specific atomic action, and each fine-grained action can be modeled as a set of atomic actions. We connect the MIL classifier

$\mathcal{S}$ to visual concepts $v = \{v_1, \cdots, v_N\}$ to learn the composition relationship between fine-grained actions and atomic actions. Given that the MIL classifier $\mathcal{S}$ maps clip features x to their action prediction scores s, the last layer's weights w in clip-level classifier S naturally define class prototypes. Since visual concepts v can also be viewed as an aggregated feature of clips, we propose to reinterpret the linear classifier weights w on clip features x as a nearest neighbor classifier on visual concepts v, to find relevant visual concepts for each fine-grained action. Specifically, we measure the relationship between fine classes and visual concepts through a distance function $\mathcal{D}$. $\mathcal{D}$ calculates the feature distance between visual concepts v and the classification weights w in MIL classifier $\mathcal{S}$.

$$d_n^j = \mathcal{D}(v_n, w^j) \tag{5}$$

Intuitively, d_n^j should be small if the jth fine-grained action consists of the atomic action represented by the nth visual concept v_n. We use cosine similarity in the distance function $\mathcal{D}$.

For each action j in the video, we calculate $\mathcal{D}^j$, the distances between w_j and all visual concepts, and then select the top k visual concepts with the smallest distance (d_n^j), denoted as the set $TopK(\mathcal{D}^j)$. These k visual concepts are then considered as atomic actions for fine action j. Thus we can generate fine-grained action j's representation e^j using these selected visual concepts' representation via a composition function $\mathcal{C}$.

$$e^j = \mathcal{C}(\{v_n | n \in TopK(\mathcal{D}^j)\}) \tag{6}$$

Average pooling is used in the composition function $\mathcal{C}$. We then enforce the fine-grained action representation e^j to be close to the class prototype w^j by minimizing their distance measured by $\mathcal{D}$:

$$\mathcal{L}_{concept} = \mathcal{D}(e^j, w^j) \tag{7}$$

$\mathcal{L}_{concept}$ is calculated only when the video contains fine action j.

3.3   Coarse-to-Fine Semantic Hierarchy

Due to the fine granularity in the label space, many actions are very close to each other with only minor differences. Based on the commonality between actions, fine-grained actions can usually be grouped into a few coarse-grained hyper-categories, forming a semantic hierarchy. Actions within the same coarse category are visually more similar to each other, when compared to actions from different coarse categories (e.g., *cut hair* is visually closer to *brush hair* than *play tennis*). This semantic label hierarchy thus implies a useful prior of the feature distribution that helps visual concept learning.

In Sect. 3.2 we obtain the action representation e^j composed by visual concepts through composition function $\mathcal{C}$. This formula models a hierarchical relationship between visual concepts and fine-grained actions. Similarly, a fine-to-coarse composition function $\mathcal{C}'$ can also be used to model the semantic relationship between fine-grained and coarse-grained actions. Specifically, for the uth

coarse-grained category O_u containing a set of fine-grained classes, we compose the features of the fine-grained actions in O_u to obtain the coarse-grained action representation e'_u:

$$e'_u = C'(\ \{e^j | j \in O_u\}\ ) \tag{8}$$

After obtaining coarse-grained action representation e'_u, we use the coarse-grained action label y' to train a coarse-grained action classifier S' with binary cross entropy (BCE) loss with logits:

$$\mathcal{L}_{coarse} = BCE(S'(e'_u), y') \tag{9}$$

We combine these four losses to form the total loss L used at training time, with λ as weights.

$$\mathcal{L} = \lambda_1 \mathcal{L}_{mil} + \lambda_2 \mathcal{L}_{pseudo} + \lambda_3 \mathcal{L}_{concept} + \lambda_4 \mathcal{L}_{coarse} \tag{10}$$

3.4   Inference

The inference process contains two steps. The first step is action classification. We run the MIL classifier S to obtain classification scores s_i for each clip. Then for each action class j, we take the top k clips which contain the highest activation scores for that class and average their scores. Then we threshold the average score to predict whether the video contains that action class or not.

The second step is action detection. For each positive action class j, we calculate a threshold based on the class activation score sequence $s^j = \{s_1^j, s_2^j, \cdots, s_T^j\}$:

$$thresh^j = Mean(s^j) + \alpha(Max(s^j) - Min(s^j)) \tag{11}$$

Clips with scores above the threshold $thresh^j$ are detected as actions, and we connect adjacent positive action clips to generate action segments.

4   Experiments

We test our model on two fine-grained video datasets, FineAction [23] and FineGym [39]. In this section, we first introduce datasets and evaluation metrics. We also present implementation details. Then we discuss the main experiment results, followed by ablation studies on each of our components. In addition, we analyze the proposed visual concept learning with some qualitative results.

4.1   Datasets and Evaluation Metrics

FineAction [23] combines three existing datasets, YouTube8M [1], Kinetics400 [4], FCVID [17], and adds more videos crawled from the Internet. It has 8,440 videos with 57,752 action segments in the training set and 4,174 videos with 24,236 action segments in the validation set. The dataset contains a wide range of video contents including sports, household activities, personal care, etc. Fine-Action contains a three-level coarse-to-fine label hierarchy in its annotations. The three label levels contain 4, 14, 106 categories respectively and temporal annotations are available for every action label. The results reported by [23] is trained on the training set and tested on the validation set, so we follow the same setup. In addition to the 106-category fine-grained labels, we use the middle-level labels (14 classes) as the coarse-level labels in HAAN model.

For fair comparison in this dataset, we use the same evaluation metrics as in the FineAction dataset paper [23]. Specifically, mean average precision (mAP) at temporal IoU thresholds from 0.5 to 0.95 with an interval of 0.05 is reported, as well as mAP@0.5, 0.75, 0.95.

FineGym [39] is a dataset of gymnastics videos with three levels of annotations: *Events*, *Sets* and *Elements*. An *event* is a program routine of a player performing a whole set of actions. Within each *event*, actions are temporally annotated. Each action has two levels of labels, *sets* (coarse) and *elements* (fine). Two types of action detection can be done in FineGym: *event* detection within a video, and *element* detection within an *event*. The latter one is a fine-grained action detection task, thus we use it to conduct our experiments. Our experiments use FineGym-99, which has 14 coarse labels and 99 fine labels.

We find that the data split introduced in the original FineGym paper [39] is not suitable for action detection experiments, because under that data split, actions in the training set and the validation set can come from the same video. As a result, 18% of the validation videos are actually seen by the model during training. To avoid the data leakage which can lead to unrealistically high results during testing, we propose a new train-val data split in FineGym using an iterative sampling approach with corresponding ratio control.

The training-to-validation sample ratio in the original split of FineGym is 75 to 25. In the iterative sampling approach, our goal is to also select 75% of the total samples as training samples, and at the same time maintain the 75-to-25 ratio in each action class as much as possible. Since each video in FineGym might contain more than one action class, we follow the greedy search idea to generate the new data split. We first add a minimum number of videos to both training and validation sets so that both of them contain all action classes. Then we find the action class with the least per-class sample ratio in the training set, and sample a video containing that class into the training set. We repeat this process until each action class in the training set contains at least 75% samples in that class. We run the sampling algorithm for 100 times, and pick the resulting data split whose sample distribution is the closest to our criterion with the approximate 75-to-25 ratios in both overall and per-class sample distribution. The new data split contains 3,775 videos with 26,866 action segments in the training set, and 1,193 videos with 7,975 action segments in the validation set. The training-to-validation sample ratios of each action class range from 75% to 81%.

Average mAP at temporal IoU thresholds from 0.1 to 0.5 with an interval of 0.05 is reported in this data split, as well as mAP@0.1, 0.2, 0.3, 0.4, 0.5.

Table 1. Results on FineAction dataset. The avg.mAP refers to the average of mAPs at temporal IoU thresholds ranging from 0.5 to 0.95 with an interval of 0.05. The fully-supervised BMN model [21]'s results are from [23]. We run previous weakly-supervised models [19,25,29,33,34] using publicly available code. Ablation studies of our HAAN model with different losses enabled are also presented

Methods		mAP@ τ			avg.mAP
		0.5	0.75	0.95	
Prior	BMN (fully-supervised) (2019) [21]	14.44	8.92	3.12	9.25
	W-TALC (2018) [34]	6.18	3.15	0.83	3.45
	RefineLoc (2021) [33]	5.93	2.55	0.96	3.02
	WTAL-UM (2021) [19]	6.65	3.23	0.95	3.64
	ASL (2021) [25]	6.79	2.68	0.81	3.30
	D2-Net (2021) [29]	6.75	3.02	0.82	3.35
Ours	$\mathcal{L}_{mil}$	5.74	2.29	0.39	2.72
	$\mathcal{L}_{mil} + \mathcal{L}_{pseudo}$	6.40	2.73	0.61	3.18
	$\mathcal{L}_{mil} + \mathcal{L}_{pseudo} + \mathcal{L}_{concept}$	6.57	3.27	0.83	3.57
	$\mathcal{L}_{mil} + \mathcal{L}_{pseudo} + \mathcal{L}_{concept} + \mathcal{L}_{coarse}$	**7.05**	**3.95**	**1.14**	**4.10**

4.2 Implementation Details

Our model is implemented in PyTorch. We use two fully connected layers on top of the two-stream Inception3D (I3D) backbone [4] with RGB and Optical Flow inputs to form the feature encoder $\mathcal{E}$, following the standard practice in weakly-supervised temporal action detection, e.g. [31]. We use one fully connected layer for MIL classifier $\mathcal{S}$, and two fully connected layers for self-supervised visual concept classifier $\mathcal{F}$. The number of visual concepts N is set as 500, and each class retains top $k = 5$ relevant visual concepts. Fine-to-coarse composition function $\mathcal{C}'$ is max pooling for FineAction and mean pooling for FineGym. We use Adam optimizer with learning rate $\beta = 3 \times 10^{-5}$. The weights for each loss are: $\lambda_1 = 1, \lambda_2 = 0.001, \lambda_3 = 0.01, \lambda_4 = 1$. The α in Eq. 11 is -0.8 for FineAction and 0.1 for FineGym.

4.3 Main Results

We compare our HAAN model to previous weakly-supervised temporal action detection models [19,25,29,33,34], and results on the two datasets are shown in Tables 1, 2. Results of fully-supervised models (BMN or SSN) are also listed as reference. In FineGym dataset, we re-run the fully-supervised algorithm SSN [48] on the new data split, and the new results shown in Table 2 are worse than the results reported in FineGym paper [39] as expected, because the original data split has train-test video data leakage problem. Overall, fully-supervised models also struggle on both datasets with low performance, demonstrating the difficulty of temporal action detection on fine-grained datasets.

Our HAAN model outperforms the best weakly-supervised detection model WTAL-UM [19] by 12% on FineAction and 25% on FineGym in average mAP relatively. We also find that more advanced weakly models ASL [25] and RefineLoc [33] are not superior to the older weakly model W-TALC [34] in fine-grained

Table 2. Results on FineGym dataset. The fully-supervised SSN model's results are reported on the new data split. We also run previous weakly-supervised models [19, 25,29,33,34] using publicly available code. Ablation results of our HAAN model with different losses enabled are also presented

Methods		mAP@ τ					avg.mAP
		0.1	0.2	0.3	0.4	0.5	
Prior	SSN (fully-supervised) (2017) [48]	20.23	19.29	17.12	14.38	11.45	16.61
	W-TALC (2018) [34]	8.85	7.32	6.24	4.95	3.15	6.03
	RefineLoc (2021) [33]	6.67	4.63	4.15	3.86	3.72	4.54
	WTAL-UM (2021) [19]	9.45	8.63	5.10	4.34	3.05	6.11
	ASL (2021) [25]	9.33	7.92	5.45	3.67	2.24	5.74
	D2-Net (2021) [29]	9.46	8.67	5.21	4.22	2.65	6.04
Ours	$\mathcal{L}_{mil}$	7.78	7.23	5.92	4.12	2.98	5.61
	$\mathcal{L}_{mil} + \mathcal{L}_{pseudo}$	8.56	7.50	5.83	4.60	3.45	6.09
	$\mathcal{L}_{mil} + \mathcal{L}_{pseudo} + \mathcal{L}_{concept}$	9.36	8.28	6.99	5.25	3.91	6.95
	$\mathcal{L}_{mil} + \mathcal{L}_{pseudo} + \mathcal{L}_{concept} + \mathcal{L}_{coarse}$	**10.79**	**9.62**	**7.65**	**6.16**	**4.16**	**7.67**

Table 3. mAP@0.5 results for different clustering methods on FineAction dataset using the HAAN model version with $\mathcal{L}_{mil} + \mathcal{L}_{pseudo}$ supervision

Methods	Number of clusters			
	250	500	750	1000
GMM [36]	6.15	6.14	6.20	6.36
Birch [47]	6.25	6.31	6.19	6.31
K-means [27]	6.31	6.40	6.25	6.26

videos. This again indicates the big difference between fine-grained action datasets and general action datasets. Models that perform well on THUMOS-14 and ActivityNet-1.2 may not perform well on fine-grained video datasets.

Results in Table 1 are reported on the validation set of FineAction. We also submit our HAAN model's predictions on the withheld test set to the FineAction competition leaderboard[2], and get the average mAP of 4.48 on the test set with hidden labels, which is close to the average mAP of 4.10 on the validation set.

For ablation study, we also include four different versions of our model with different losses enabled in Tables 1 and 2. It shows that each component in our HAAN model has a considerable contribution to the detection performance.

4.4 Visual Concept Learning Analysis

We use K-means clustering to obtain visual concepts, and then build connections with fine-grained action classes by minimizing the cosine distance between visual concepts and the MIL classifier's weights. Here we show the ablation results of different clustering methods and distance calculations in visual concept learning.

---

[2] https://competitions.codalab.org/competitions/32363.

Table 4. Results of different distance calculations on FineAction dataset using the HAAN model version with $\mathcal{L}_{mil} + \mathcal{L}_{pseudo} + \mathcal{L}_{concept}$ supervision

Method	mAP@0.5	mAP@0.75	mAP@0.95	avg.mAP
Euclidean	5.92	3.03	0.81	3.26
Cosine	6.57	3.27	0.83	3.57

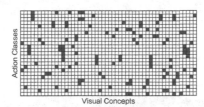

Fig. 3. Visualization of relevant visual concepts for each fine-grained action class in the *Uneven Bars* event from FineGym dataset

For the clustering method to generate pseudo labels, we explore Gaussian Mixture Model (GMM) [36] and Birch [47] in addition to K-means, and test on different numbers of clusters. The HAAN model version with $\mathcal{L}_{mil} + \mathcal{L}_{pseudo}$ supervision is used in this ablation to better reflect the effect of different clustering methods. The ablated mAP@0.5 results on FineAction dataset are shown in Table 3. Among all the clustering methods, K-means with 500 clusters achieves the best result.

To build connection between visual concepts and fine-grained action classes, distance metric is used, e.g. in the mapping function $\mathcal{D}$ (Eq. 5) between visual concepts and fine-grained actions, and the auxiliary loss function for fine-grained action representation learning based on visual concepts (Eq. 7). We experiment with Euclidean distance and cosine similarity in the HAAN model version with $\mathcal{L}_{mil} + \mathcal{L}_{pseudo} + \mathcal{L}_{concept}$ supervision, and ablation results are shown in Table 4. Cosine similarity outperforms Euclidean distance generally in our model.

4.5 Qualitative Results

Our model assumes that fine-grained actions share common visual concepts (a.k.a. atomic actions) and vary in certain visual concepts. Figure 3 shows the visual concepts that each fine-grained action class is most related to in the *Uneven Bars* event from FineGym dataset. The appearance pattern of visual concepts indeed demonstrates that there exists visual concepts that are shared by actions, and every action can be represented by a unique combination of visual concepts.

To better understand what the visual concepts are, we plot some examples of visual concepts in Fig. 4, and the specific atomic action label below each visual concept (Visual concept A, B, C) is generated from our observation for illustration purpose. Each visual concept represents an atomic action. Visual

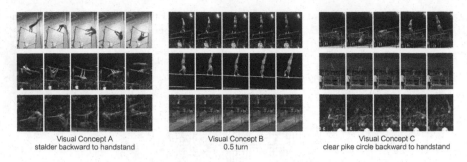

Visual Concept A
stalder backward to handstand

Visual Concept B
0.5 turn

Visual Concept C
clear pike circle backward to handstand

Fig. 4. Three example visual concepts learned in our model representing atomic actions

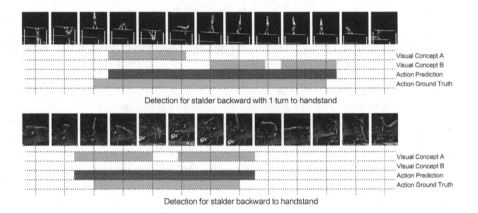

Visual Concept A
Visual Concept B
Action Prediction
Action Ground Truth

Detection for stalder backward with 1 turn to handstand

Visual Concept A
Visual Concept B
Action Prediction
Action Ground Truth

Detection for stalder backward to handstand

Fig. 5. Two example action detections from our HAAN model. Visual concepts A and B correspond to those visualized in Fig. 4

concept A represents atomic action *stalder backward to handstand* where the athlete starts from handstand phase, circles around the bar with legs wide apart, and moves backward to handstand. Visual concept B represents atomic action *0.5 turn* on handstand. Visual concept C represents *clear pike circle backward to handstand* with two legs together. Visual concepts A and C differ in whether the athlete's legs are wide apart or together in the circle. Also, visual concept B can occur following visual concept A to form action *stalder backward with 0.5/1 turn to handstand*, or following visual concept C to form action *clear pike circle backward with 0.5/1 turn to handstand*.

Our model also learns to compose visual concepts into fine-grained actions. As shown in Fig. 5, our model successfully detects the sequence of visual concept A followed by two visual concepts B as fine-grained action *stalder backward with 1 turn to handstand*, and the sequence of only visual concepts A as fine-grained action *stalder backward to handstand*.

5   Conclusion

We propose Hierarchical Atomic Action Network (HAAN) to address weakly-supervised temporal action detection in fine-grained videos for the first time. HAAN automatically discovers the visual concepts to capture the fine-grained action details, utilizing clustering-based self-supervised learning and the coarse-to-fine action label hierarchy. Experiment results demonstrate that HAAN outperforms state-of-the-art weakly-supervised methods on two large-scale fine-grained video datasets, FineAction and FineGym.

References

1. Abu-El-Haija, S., et al.: YouTube-8M: a large-scale video classification benchmark. arXiv preprint arXiv:1609.08675 (2016)
2. Caba Heilbron, F., Escorcia, V., Ghanem, B., Carlos Niebles, J.: Activitynet: a large-scale video benchmark for human activity understanding. In: Proceedings of the IEEE Conference on Computer Vision and Pattern Recognition, pp. 961–970 (2015)
3. Carbonneau, M.A., Cheplygina, V., Granger, E., Gagnon, G.: Multiple instance learning: a survey of problem characteristics and applications. Pattern Recogn. **77**, 329–353 (2018)
4. Carreira, J., Zisserman, A.: Quo vadis, action recognition? A new model and the kinetics dataset. In: Proceedings of the IEEE Conference on Computer Vision and Pattern Recognition, pp. 6299–6308 (2017)
5. Chen, C., Li, O., Tao, D., Barnett, A., Rudin, C., Su, J.K.: This looks like that: deep learning for interpretable image recognition. In: Advances in Neural Information Processing Systems, vol. 32 (2019)
6. Chen, X., Duan, Y., Houthooft, R., Schulman, J., Sutskever, I., Abbeel, P.: Infogan: interpretable representation learning by information maximizing generative adversarial nets. In: Proceedings of the 30th International Conference on Neural Information Processing Systems, pp. 2180–2188 (2016)
7. Damen, D., et al.: Rescaling egocentric vision: collection, pipeline and challenges for epic-kitchens-100. Int. J. Comput. Vision **130**(1), 33–55 (2022)
8. Dietterich, T.G., Lathrop, R.H., Lozano-Pérez, T.: Solving the multiple instance problem with axis-parallel rectangles. Artif. Intell. **89**(1), 31–71 (1997)
9. Fathi, A., Ren, X., Rehg, J.M.: Learning to recognize objects in egocentric activities. In: CVPR 2011, pp. 3281–3288. IEEE (2011)
10. Gaidon, A., Harchaoui, Z., Schmid, C.: Temporal localization of actions with actoms. IEEE Trans. Pattern Anal. Mach. Intell. **35**(11), 2782–2795 (2013)
11. Ghoddoosian, R., Sayed, S., Athitsos, V.: Hierarchical modeling for task recognition and action segmentation in weakly-labeled instructional videos. In: Proceedings of the IEEE/CVF Winter Conference on Applications of Computer Vision, pp. 1922–1932 (2022)
12. Ghorbani, A., Wexler, J., Kim, B.: Automating interpretability: discovering and testing visual concepts learned by neural networks. arXiv abs/1902.03129 (2019)
13. Higgins, I., et al.: Scan: learning hierarchical compositional visual concepts. arXiv preprint arXiv:1707.03389 (2017)

14. Ilse, M., Tomczak, J., Welling, M.: Attention-based deep multiple instance learning. In: Dy, J., Krause, A. (eds.) Proceedings of the 35th International Conference on Machine Learning. Proceedings of Machine Learning Research, vol. 80, pp. 2127–2136. PMLR (2018)

15. Ji, J., Krishna, R., Fei-Fei, L., Niebles, J.C.: Action genome: actions as compositions of spatio-temporal scene graphs. In: Proceedings of the IEEE/CVF Conference on Computer Vision and Pattern Recognition, pp. 10236–10247 (2020)

16. Jiang, Y.G., et al.: Thumos challenge: action recognition with a large number of classes (2014)

17. Jiang, Y.G., Wu, Z., Wang, J., Xue, X., Chang, S.F.: Exploiting feature and class relationships in video categorization with regularized deep neural networks. IEEE Trans. Pattern Anal. Mach. Intell. **40**(2), 352–364 (2018)

18. Kim, B., Wattenberg, M., Gilmer, J., Cai, C., Wexler, J., Viegas, F., et al.: Interpretability beyond feature attribution: quantitative testing with concept activation vectors (TCAV). In: International Conference on Machine Learning, pp. 2668–2677. PMLR (2018)

19. Lee, P., Wang, J., Lu, Y., Byun, H.: Weakly-supervised temporal action localization by uncertainty modeling. In: AAAI Conference on Artificial Intelligence, vol. 2 (2021)

20. Lillo, I., Soto, A., Carlos Niebles, J.: Discriminative hierarchical modeling of spatiotemporally composable human activities. In: Proceedings of the IEEE Conference on Computer Vision and Pattern Recognition, pp. 812–819 (2014)

21. Lin, T., Liu, X., Li, X., Ding, E., Wen, S.: BMN: boundary-matching network for temporal action proposal generation. In: Proceedings of the IEEE/CVF International Conference on Computer Vision, pp. 3889–3898 (2019)

22. Liu, D., Jiang, T., Wang, Y.: Completeness modeling and context separation for weakly supervised temporal action localization. In: Proceedings of the IEEE/CVF Conference on Computer Vision and Pattern Recognition, pp. 1298–1307 (2019)

23. Liu, Y., Wang, L., Ma, X., Wang, Y., Qiao, Y.: Fineaction: a fine-grained video dataset for temporal action localization. arXiv preprint arXiv:2105.11107 (2021)

24. Luo, Z., et al.: Weakly-supervised action localization with expectation-maximization multi-instance learning. In: Vedaldi, A., Bischof, H., Brox, T., Frahm, J.-M. (eds.) ECCV 2020. LNCS, vol. 12374, pp. 729–745. Springer, Cham (2020). https://doi.org/10.1007/978-3-030-58526-6_43

25. Ma, J., Gorti, S.K., Volkovs, M., Yu, G.: Weakly supervised action selection learning in video. In: Proceedings of the IEEE/CVF Conference on Computer Vision and Pattern Recognition, pp. 7587–7596 (2021)

26. Mac, K.N.C., Joshi, D., Yeh, R.A., Xiong, J., Feris, R.S., Do, M.N.: Learning motion in feature space: locally-consistent deformable convolution networks for fine-grained action detection. In: Proceedings of the IEEE/CVF International Conference on Computer Vision, pp. 6282–6291 (2019)

27. MacQueen, J.: Classification and analysis of multivariate observations. In: 5th Berkeley Symposium on Mathematical Statistics and Probability, pp. 281–297 (1967)

28. Mavroudi, E., Bhaskara, D., Sefati, S., Ali, H., Vidal, R.: End-to-end fine-grained action segmentation and recognition using conditional random field models and discriminative sparse coding. In: 2018 IEEE Winter Conference on Applications of Computer Vision (WACV), pp. 1558–1567. IEEE (2018)

29. Narayan, S., Cholakkal, H., Hayat, M., Khan, F.S., Yang, M.H., Shao, L.: D2-Net: weakly-supervised action localization via discriminative embeddings and denoised

activations. In: Proceedings of the IEEE/CVF International Conference on Computer Vision, pp. 13608–13617 (2021)

30. Narayan, S., Cholakkal, H., Khan, F.S., Shao, L.: 3C-Net: category count and center loss for weakly-supervised action localization. In: Proceedings of the IEEE/CVF International Conference on Computer Vision, pp. 8679–8687 (2019)

31. Nguyen, P., Liu, T., Prasad, G., Han, B.: Weakly supervised action localization by sparse temporal pooling network. In: Proceedings of the IEEE Conference on Computer Vision and Pattern Recognition, pp. 6752–6761 (2018)

32. Ni, B., Paramathayalan, V.R., Moulin, P.: Multiple granularity analysis for fine-grained action detection. In: Proceedings of the IEEE Conference on Computer Vision and Pattern Recognition, pp. 756–763 (2014)

33. Pardo, A., Alwassel, H., Caba, F., Thabet, A., Ghanem, B.: Refineloc: iterative refinement for weakly-supervised action localization. In: Proceedings of the IEEE/CVF Winter Conference on Applications of Computer Vision, pp. 3319–3328 (2021)

34. Paul, S., Roy, S., Roy-Chowdhury, A.K.: W-TALC: weakly-supervised temporal activity localization and classification. In: Proceedings of the European Conference on Computer Vision (ECCV), pp. 563–579 (2018)

35. Piergiovanni, A.J., Ryoo, M.S.: Fine-grained activity recognition in baseball videos. In: 2018 IEEE/CVF Conference on Computer Vision and Pattern Recognition Workshops (CVPRW), pp. 1821–18218 (2018)

36. Reynolds, D.A.: Gaussian mixture models. Encyclopedia Biometrics **741**, 659–663 (2009)

37. Richard, A., Kuehne, H., Gall, J.: Weakly supervised action learning with RNN based fine-to-coarse modeling. In: Proceedings of the IEEE Conference on Computer Vision and Pattern Recognition, pp. 754–763 (2017)

38. Rohrbach, M., Amin, S., Andriluka, M., Schiele, B.: A database for fine grained activity detection of cooking activities. In: 2012 IEEE Conference on Computer Vision and Pattern Recognition, pp. 1194–1201. IEEE (2012)

39. Shao, D., Zhao, Y., Dai, B., Lin, D.: Finegym: a hierarchical video dataset for fine-grained action understanding. In: Proceedings of the IEEE/CVF Conference on Computer Vision and Pattern Recognition, pp. 2616–2625 (2020)

40. Shou, Z., Gao, H., Zhang, L., Miyazawa, K., Chang, S.F.: Autoloc: weakly-supervised temporal action localization in untrimmed videos. In: Proceedings of the European Conference on Computer Vision (ECCV), pp. 154–171 (2018)

41. Singh, B., Marks, T.K., Jones, M., Tuzel, O., Shao, M.: A multi-stream bi-directional recurrent neural network for fine-grained action detection. In: Proceedings of the IEEE Conference on Computer Vision and Pattern Recognition, pp. 1961–1970 (2016)

42. Stein, S., McKenna, S.J.: Combining embedded accelerometers with computer vision for recognizing food preparation activities. In: Proceedings of the 2013 ACM International Joint Conference on Pervasive and Ubiquitous Computing, pp. 729–738 (2013)

43. Sun, C., Shetty, S., Sukthankar, R., Nevatia, R.: Temporal localization of fine-grained actions in videos by domain transfer from web images. In: Proceedings of the 23rd ACM International Conference on Multimedia, pp. 371–380 (2015)

44. Wang, L., Xiong, Y., Lin, D., Van Gool, L.: Untrimmednets for weakly supervised action recognition and detection. In: Proceedings of the IEEE Conference on Computer Vision and Pattern Recognition, pp. 4325–4334 (2017)

45. Whitney, W.F., Chang, M., Kulkarni, T., Tenenbaum, J.B.: Understanding visual concepts with continuation learning. arXiv preprint arXiv:1602.06822 (2016)

46. Yuan, Y., Lyu, Y., Shen, X., Tsang, I., Yeung, D.Y.: Marginalized average atten-tional network for weakly-supervised learning. In: ICLR 2019-Seventh International Conference on Learning Representations (2019)
47. Zhang, T., Ramakrishnan, R., Livny, M.: Birch: an efficient data clustering method for very large databases. ACM SIGMOD Rec. **25**(2), 103–114 (1996)
48. Zhao, Y., Xiong, Y., Wang, L., Wu, Z., Tang, X., Lin, D.: Temporal action detec-tion with structured segment networks. In: Proceedings of the IEEE International Conference on Computer Vision, pp. 2914–2923 (2017)

Neural Correspondence Field for Object Pose Estimation

Lin Huang[1], Tomas Hodan[2(✉)], Lingni Ma[2], Linguang Zhang[2], Luan Tran[2],
Christopher Twigg[2], Po-Chen Wu[2], Junsong Yuan[1], Cem Keskin[2],
and Robert Wang[2]

[1] University at Buffalo, Buffalo, USA
[2] Reality Labs at Meta, Seattle, USA
tom.hodan@gmail.com

Abstract. We propose a method for estimating the 6DoF pose of a rigid
object with an available 3D model from a single RGB image. Unlike
classical correspondence-based methods which predict 3D object coordinates at pixels of the input image, the proposed method predicts 3D
object coordinates at 3D query points sampled in the camera frustum.
The move from pixels to 3D points, which is inspired by recent PIFu-
style methods for 3D reconstruction, enables reasoning about the whole
object, including its (self-)occluded parts. For a 3D query point associated with a pixel-aligned image feature, we train a fully-connected
neural network to predict: (i) the corresponding 3D object coordinates,
and (ii) the signed distance to the object surface, with the first defined
only for query points in the surface vicinity. We call the mapping realized by this network as *Neural Correspondence Field*. The object pose is
then robustly estimated from the predicted 3D-3D correspondences by
the Kabsch-RANSAC algorithm. The proposed method achieves state-
of-the-art results on three BOP datasets and is shown superior especially in challenging cases with occlusion. The project website is at:
linhuang17.github.io/NCF.

1 Introduction

Estimating the 6DoF pose of a rigid object is a fundamental computer vision
problem with great importance to application fields such as augmented reality
and robotic manipulation. In recent years, the problem has received considerable
attention and the state of the art has improved substantially, yet there remain
challenges to address, particularly around robustness to object occlusion [24,25].

Recent PIFu-style methods for 3D reconstruction from an RGB image [28,
37,66,67,84] rely on 3D implicit representations and demonstrate the ability to
learn and incorporate strong priors about the invisible scene parts. For example,
PIFu [66] is able to faithfully reconstruct a 3D model of the whole human body,
and DRDF [37] is able to reconstruct a 3D model of the whole indoor scene,

---

L. Huang—Work done during Lin Huang's internship with Reality Labs at Meta.

S. Avidan et al. (Eds.): ECCV 2022, LNCS 13670, pp. 585–603, 2022.
https://doi.org/10.1007/978-3-031-20080-9_34

RGB input   Predicted 3D-3D correspondences   Estimated pose

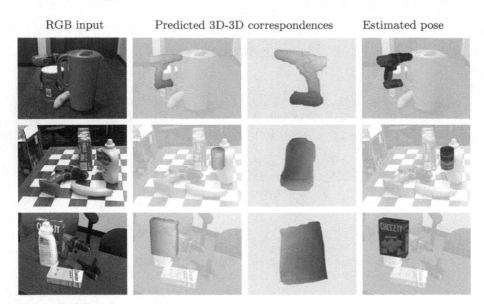

Fig. 1. An overview of the proposed method. The object pose is estimated from 3D-3D correspondences established by predicting 3D object coordinates at 3D query points densely sampled in the camera frustum. For efficient selection of reliable correspondences nearby the object surface, the method predicts for each query point also the signed distance to the surface. The middle columns show two views of a mesh that is reconstructed by Marching Cubes [45] from the predicted signed distances and colored with the predicted 3D object coordinates (the mesh is reconstructed only for visualization purposes, not when estimating the object pose). The 3D CAD model, which is assumed available for each object, is shown in the estimated pose on the right.

including parts hidden behind a couch. Inspired by these results, we propose a 6DoF object pose estimation method based on a 3D implicit representation and analyze its performance specifically in challenging cases with occlusion (Fig. 1).

Similarly to PIFu [66], the proposed method makes predictions for 3D query points that are sampled in the camera frustum and associated with pixel-aligned image features. PIFu predicts color and occupancy, *i.e.*, a binary signal that indicates whether a query point is inside or outside the object. Instead, the proposed method predicts (i) the corresponding 3D object coordinates, and (ii) the signed distance to the object surface, with the first defined only for query points in the surface vicinity, *i.e.*, points for which the predicted signed distance is below a threshold. The 6DoF object pose is then robustly estimated from the predicted 3D-3D correspondences between 3D query points and the predicted 3D object coordinates by the Kabsch algorithm [31] in combination with RANSAC [16].

Classical methods for 6DoF object pose estimation [5,9,23,59,61,63,73,83] rely on 2D-3D correspondences established between pixels of the input image and the 3D object model, and estimate the pose by the PnP-RANSAC algorithm [39]. The proposed method predicts 3D object coordinates for 3D query points instead of pixels. This enables reasoning about the whole object surface, including self-occluded parts and parts occluded by other objects. In Sect. 5, we show that the proposed method noticeably outperforms a baseline method that relies on the classical 2D-3D correspondences. Besides, we show that the proposed method outperforms all existing methods with the same training and evaluation setup (*i.e.*, RGB-only and without any iterative refinement of pose estimates) on datasets YCB-V, LM-O, and LM from the BOP benchmark [24,25].

This work makes the following contributions:

1. The first method for 6DoF object pose estimation which demonstrates the effectiveness of a 3D implicit representation in solving this problem.
2. Neural Correspondence Field (NCF), a learned 3D implicit representation defined by a mapping from the camera space to the object model space, is used to establish 3D-3D correspondences from a single RGB image.
3. The proposed method noticeably outperforms a baseline based on 2D-3D correspondences and achieves state-of-the-art results on three BOP datasets.

2   Related Work

6DoF Object Pose Estimation. Early methods for 6DoF object pose estimation assumed a grayscale or RGB input image and relied on local image features [9,46] or template matching [7]. After the introduction of Kinect-like sensors, methods based on RGB-D template matching [21,26], point-pair features [15,22,78], 3D local features [19], and learning-based methods [5,35,72] demonstrated superior performance over RGB-only counterparts. Recent methods are based on convolutional neural networks (CNNs) and focus primarily on estimating the pose from RGB images. In the 2020 edition of the BOP challenge [25], CNN-based methods finally caught up with methods based on point-pair features which were dominating previous editions of the challenge. A popular approach adopted by the CNN-based methods is to establish 2D-3D correspondences by predicting 3D object coordinates at densely sampled pixels, and robustly estimate the object pose by the PnP-RANSAC algorithm [23,30,41,59,79,83]. In Sect. 5, we show that our proposed method outperforms a baseline method that follows the 2D-3D correspondence approach and shares implementation of the common parts with the proposed method. Methods establishing the correspondences in the opposite direction, *i.e.*, by predicting the 2D projections of a fixed set of 3D keypoints pre-selected for each object model, have also been proposed [27,54,60,61,63,73,76]. Other approaches localize the objects with 2D bounding boxes, and for each box predict the pose by regression [38,40,47,80] or classification into discrete viewpoints [10,33,71]. However, in the case of occlusion, estimating accurate 2D bounding boxes covering the whole object, including the invisible parts, is problematic [33].

Shape Reconstruction with Implicit Representations. Recent works have shown that a 3D shape can be modeled by a continuous and differentiable implicit representation realized by a fully-connected neural network. Examples of such representations include signed distance fields (SDF) [1,2,17,57,69], which map a 3D query point to the signed distance from the surface, and binary occupancy fields [8,42,48], which map a 3D query point to the occupancy value. Following the success of implicit representations, GraspingField [32] extends the idea to reconstructing hands grasping objects. Instead of learning a single SDF, the method learns one SDF for hand and one for object, which allows to directly enforce physical constraints such as no interpenetration and proper contact.

For image-based reconstruction, Texture fields [55] learn textured 3D models by mapping a shape feature, an image feature, and a 3D point to color. OccNet [48] proposes to condition occupancy prediction on an image feature extracted by a CNN. DISN [81] improves this technique by combining local patch features with a global image feature to estimate SDF for 3D query points. PIFu [66], which is closely related to our work, first extracts an image feature map by an hourglass CNN and then applies a fully-connected neural network to map a pixel-aligned feature with the depth of a 3D query point to occupancy. The follow-up work, PIFuHD [67], recovers more detailed geometry by leveraging the surface normal map and multi-resolution volumes. PIFu and PIFuHD focus on human digitization. As for many other methods, experiments are done on images with cleanly segmented foreground. Recently, NeRF-like methods reported impressive results in scene modeling [44,50,53,70,82]. These methods typically require multi-view images with known camera calibration. For an in-depth discussion, we refer to the survey in [74]. In this work, we focus on a single input image and reconstruct known objects in unknown poses that we aim to recover.

Learning Dense Correspondences. One of the pioneering works that learns dense correspondences is proposed in [68] for camera relocalization, and extended for pose estimation of specific rigid objects in [5,6,49]. These methods predict 3D scene/object coordinates at each pixel of the input image by a random forest. Later methods predict the coordinates by a CNN [23,30,41,59,83]. NOCS [79] defines normalized object coordinates for category-level object pose estimation. Besides correspondences for object pose estimation, DensePose [18] densely regresses part-specific UV coordinates for human pose estimation. CSE [51] extends the idea to predict correspondences for deformable object categories by regressing Laplace-Beltrami basis and is extended to model articulated shapes in [36]. These methods focus on learning mapping from pixels to 3D coordinates. DIF-Net [12] jointly learns the shape embedding of an object category and 3D-3D correspondences with respect to a template. Similarly, NPMs [56] learns a 3D deformation field to model deformable shapes. Recent methods [58,62,77] model deformable shapes by learning radiance and deformation fields. None of these methods aims to recover the pose from images.

3   Preliminaries

Notations. An RGB image is denoted by $I : \mathbb{R}^2 \mapsto \mathbb{R}^3$ and can be mapped to a feature map $F : \mathbb{R}^2 \mapsto \mathbb{R}^K$ with K channels by an hourglass neural network [52, 66]. A 3D point $\mathbf{x} = [x, y, z]^\top \in \mathbb{R}^3$ in the camera coordinate frame can be projected to a pixel $[u, v]^\top \in \mathbb{R}^2$ by the projection function $\pi(\mathbf{x}) : \mathbb{R}^3 \mapsto \mathbb{R}^2$. Without loss of generality, we use a pinhole camera model with the projection function defined as: $\pi(\mathbf{x}) = [x f_x / z + c_x, \, y f_y / z + c_y]^\top$, where f_x, f_y is the focal length and (c_x, c_y) is the principal point.

A 6DoF object pose is defined as a rigid transformation $(R, \mathbf{t})$, where $R \in \mathbb{SO}(3)$ is a 3D rotation matrix and $\mathbf{t} \in \mathbb{R}^3$ is a 3D translation vector. A 3D point $\mathbf{y}$ in the model coordinate frame (also referred to as *3D object coordinates* [5]) is transformed to a 3D point $\mathbf{x}$ in the camera coordinate frame as: $\mathbf{x} = R\mathbf{y} + \mathbf{t}$.

Signed Distance Function (SDF) [11,57]. In the proposed method, the object surface is represented implicitly with a signed distance function, $\psi(\mathbf{x}) : \mathbb{R}^3 \mapsto \mathbb{R}$, which maps a 3D point $\mathbf{x}$ to the signed distance between $\mathbf{x}$ and the object surface. The signed distance is zero on the object surface, positive if $\mathbf{x}$ is outside the object and negative if $\mathbf{x}$ is inside.

Kabsch Algorithm [31]. Given $N \geq 3$ pairs of corresponding 3D points $X = \{\mathbf{x}_i\}_N$ and $Y = \{\mathbf{y}_i\}_N$, the Kabsch algorithm finds a rigid transformation that aligns the corresponding 3D points by minimizing the following least squares:

$$R^\star, \mathbf{t}^\star = \arg\min_{R,\mathbf{t}} \sum_i^N \|R\mathbf{y}_i + \mathbf{t} - \mathbf{x}_i\|_2. \tag{1}$$

The 3D rotation is solved via SVD of the covariance matrix: $USV^\top = \mathrm{Cov}(X - \mathbf{c}_X, Y - \mathbf{c}_Y)$, $R^\star = VU^\top$, where $\mathbf{c}_X$ and $\mathbf{c}_Y$ are centroids of the point sets X and Y respectively. To ensure right-handed coordinate system, the signs of the last column of matrix V are flipped if $\det(R^\star) = -1$ [31]. The 3D translation is then calculated as: $\mathbf{t}^\star = \mathbf{c}_X - R^\star \mathbf{c}_Y$. In the proposed method, we combine the Kabsch algorithm with a RANSAC-style fitting scheme [16] to estimate the object pose from 3D-3D correspondences.

PIFu [66]. The PIFu method reconstructs 3D models of humans from segmented single/multi-view RGB images. For the single-view inference, the method first obtains a feature map F with an hourglass neural network. Then it applies a fully-connected neural network, $f_{\mathrm{PIFu}}(F(\pi(\mathbf{x})), \mathbf{x}_z) = o$, to map a pixel-aligned feature $F(\pi(\mathbf{x}))$ and the depth $\mathbf{x}_z$ of a 3D query point $\mathbf{x}$ to the occupancy $o \in [0, 1]$ (1 means the 3D point is inside the model and 0 means it is outside).

4   The Proposed Method

This section describes the proposed method for estimating the 6DoF object pose from an RGB image. The image is assumed to show a single target object, potentially with clutter, occlusion, and diverse lighting and background. In addition, the 3D object model, camera intrinsic parameters, and a large set of training images annotated with ground-truth object poses are assumed available.

The proposed method consists of two stages: (1) prediction of 3D-3D correspondences between the camera coordinate frame and the model coordinate frame (Sect. 4.1), and (2) fitting the 6DoF object pose to the predicted correspondences using the Kabsch-RANSAC algorithm (Sect. 4.2).

4.1   Predicting Dense 3D-3D Correspondences

Neural Correspondence Field (NCF). The 3D-3D correspondences are established using NCF defined as a mapping from the pixel-aligned feature $F(\pi(\mathbf{x}))$ and the depth $\mathbf{x}_z$ of a 3D query point $\mathbf{x}$ in the camera frame to the corresponding 3D point $\mathbf{y}$ in the model frame and its signed distance s (see also Fig. 2):

$$f_{\mathrm{NCF}} : \mathbb{R}^K \times \mathbb{R} \mapsto \mathbb{R}^3 \times \mathbb{R} \quad \text{as} \quad f_{\mathrm{NCF}}\big(F(\pi(\mathbf{x})), \mathbf{x}_z; \boldsymbol{\theta}\big) = (\mathbf{y}, s), \tag{2}$$

where $\boldsymbol{\theta}$ are parameters of a fully-connected neural network f_{NCF} that realizes the mapping. In our experiments, f_{NCF} has the same architecture as the fully-connected network in PIFu [66], except the output dimension is 4 and tanh is used as an activation function in the last layer, as in [57]. The feature extractor F is realized by the hourglass neural network from PIFu and is applied to the input image remapped to a reference pinhole camera (arbitrarily chosen). The remapping is important to keep the depth $\mathbf{x}_z$ in accord with the image feature $F(\pi(\mathbf{x}))$ across images captured by cameras with different focal lengths.

Compared to PIFu, NCF additionally predicts the corresponding 3D point $\mathbf{y}$, which enables establishing 3D-3D correspondences that are used for object pose fitting. Besides, NCF predicts the signed distance instead of the binary occupancy. This enables efficient selection of near-surface correspondences by thresholding the signed distances. Using near-surface correspondences increases pose fitting accuracy as learning correspondences from images with diverse background becomes ill-posed for 3D points far from the surface. Since the 3D object model is available, the signed distance s could be calculated from the predicted 3D point $\mathbf{y}$. However, we chose to predict the signed distance explicitly to speed up the method at both training and test time (predicting the value explicitly takes virtually no extra time nor resources).

Training. With parameters of the hourglass network F denoted as $\boldsymbol{\eta}$ and parameters of the NCF network f_{NCF} denoted as $\boldsymbol{\theta}$, the two networks are trained jointly by solving the following optimization problem:

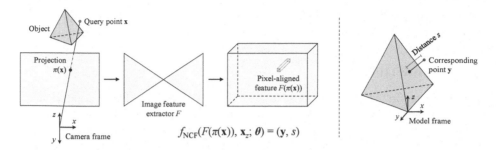

Fig. 2. Neural Correspondence Field is a mapping learned by a fully-connected neural network f_{NCF} with parameters $\boldsymbol{\theta}$. The input of the network is (i) an image feature $F(\pi(\mathbf{x}))$ extracted at the 2D projection $\pi(\mathbf{x})$ of a 3D query point $\mathbf{x}$ sampled in the camera frustum, and (ii) the depth $\mathbf{x}_z$ of $\mathbf{x}$. The output is (i) the corresponding 3D point $\mathbf{y}$ in the model frame, and (ii) the signed distance s between $\mathbf{y}$ and the object surface. The point $\mathbf{y}$ is defined only if $|s|$ is below a fixed clamping threshold δ.

$$\eta^\star, \boldsymbol{\theta}^\star = \arg\min_{\eta,\theta} L_{\mathbf{y}} + \lambda L_s, \tag{3}$$

where $L_{\mathbf{y}}$ and L_s are regression losses on the 3D point $\mathbf{y}$ and the signed distance s, respectively. The scalar λ is a balancing weight. Assuming N 3D points sampled in the camera frustum per image, the losses are defined as:

$$L_{\mathbf{y}} = \min_{(\bar{R},\bar{\mathbf{t}})\in S} \frac{1}{N} \sum_i \mathbb{1}\left(\left|\psi\left(\bar{\mathbf{y}}_i\right)\right| < \delta\right) H\left(\bar{R}\mathbf{y}_i + \bar{\mathbf{t}}, \mathbf{x}_i\right), \tag{4}$$

$$L_s = \frac{1}{N} \sum_i \left|\text{clamp}\left(\psi(\bar{\mathbf{y}}_i), \delta\right) - \text{clamp}\left(s, \delta\right)\right|, \tag{5}$$

where $(\bar{R}, \bar{\mathbf{t}})$ is a ground-truth pose, $\bar{\mathbf{y}}_i = \bar{R}^{-1}(\mathbf{x}_i - \bar{\mathbf{t}})$ is the ground-truth corresponding 3D point, and δ is a clamping parameter controlling the distance from the surface over which we expect to maintain a metric SDF, as in [57]. The indicator function $\mathbb{1}(\cdot)$ selects points within the clamping distance, and H is the Huber loss [29]. To handle symmetric objects, we adopt the approach from NOCS [79] which uses a pre-defined set of symmetry transformations (continuous symmetries are discretized) to get a set S of possible ground-truth poses.

Sampling 3D Query Points. Given a training image and the ground-truth object pose, the 3D object model is first transformed to the camera frame to assist with sampling of the query points. As the training images may show the object in diverse scenes, we found it crucial to focus the training on the object by sampling the query points more densely around the object surface. In our experiments, we first sample three types of points: 12500 points nearby the surface, 1000 points inside the bounding sphere of the model, and 1000 points inside the camera frustum. From these points, we sample 2500 points inside the model and 2500 points outside. Note that this sampling strategy is invariant to occlusion, which forces the network f_{NCF} to learn the complete object surface.

At test time, with no knowledge of the object pose, the points are sampled at centers of voxels that fill up the camera frustum in a specified depth range.

4.2   Pose Fitting

To estimate the 6DoF object pose at test time, a set of 3D-3D correspondences, $C = \{(\mathbf{x}_i, \mathbf{y}_i)\}_M$ with $M \geq 3$, is established by linking each 3D query point $\mathbf{x}$ with the predicted 3D point $\mathbf{y}$ for which the predicted signed distance s is below the threshold δ. The object pose is then estimated from C by a RANSAC-style fitting scheme [16], which iteratively proposes a pose hypothesis by sampling a random triplet of 3D-3D correspondences from C and calculating the pose from the triplet by the Kabsch algorithm detailed in Sect. 3. The quality of a pose hypothesis $(R, \mathbf{t})$ is measured by the number of inliers, $i.e.$, the number of correspondences $(\mathbf{x}, \mathbf{y}) \in C$ for which $\|R\mathbf{y} + \mathbf{t} - \mathbf{x}\|_2$ is below a fixed threshold τ. In the presented experiments, a fixed number of pose hypotheses is generated for each test image, and the final pose estimate is given by the hypothesis of the highest quality which is further refined by the Kabsch algorithm applied to all inliers. Note that the pose is not estimated at training time as the pose estimate is not involved in the training loss calculation.

Since we assume that a single instance of the object of interest is present in the input image, the set C is assumed to contain only correspondences originating from the single object instance, while being potentially contaminated with outlier correspondences caused by errors in prediction. The method could be extended to handle multiple instances of the same object, $e.g.$, by using the Progressive-X multi-instance fitting scheme [4], as in EPOS [23].

5   Experiments

This section analyzes the proposed method for 6DoF object pose estimation and compares its performance with the state-of-the-art methods from the BOP Challenge 2020 [25]. To demonstrate the advantage of predicting dense 3D-3D correspondences, the proposed method is also compared with a baseline that relies on classical 2D-3D correspondences.

5.1   2D-3D Baseline Method

Many state-of-the-art methods for 6DoF object pose estimation build on 2D-3D correspondence estimation [5,23,41,59,79,83]. While these methods are included in overall evaluation, we also design a directly comparable baseline that uses the same architecture of the feature extractor F and of the subsequent fully-connected network as the proposed method described in Sect. 4. However, unlike the fully-connected network f_{NCF} which takes a pixel-aligned feature $F(\pi(\mathbf{x}))$ and the depth $\mathbf{x}_z$ of a 3D query point $\mathbf{x}$ and outputs the corresponding 3D coordinates $\mathbf{y}$ and the signed distance s, the baseline method relies on a network f_{BL} which takes only a pixel-aligned feature $F(\mathbf{p})$ at a pixel $\mathbf{p}$ and outputs the corresponding 3D coordinates $\mathbf{y}$ and the probability $q \in [0, 1]$ that the object is present at $\mathbf{p}$: $f_{\mathrm{BL}} : \mathbb{R}^K \mapsto \mathbb{R}^3 \times \mathbb{R}$ as $f_{\mathrm{BL}}(F(\mathbf{p}); \boldsymbol{\theta}) = (\mathbf{y}, q)$. The baseline method is trained by solving the following optimization problem:

$$\boldsymbol{\eta}^\star, \boldsymbol{\theta}^\star = \arg\min_{\eta, \theta} L_\mathbf{y} + \lambda L_q \tag{6}$$

$$= \arg\min_{\eta, \theta} \min_{(\bar{R}, \bar{\mathbf{t}}) \in S} \frac{1}{U} \sum_i \bar{q}_i H\left(\bar{R}\mathbf{y}_i + \bar{\mathbf{t}}, \mathbf{x}_i\right) + \lambda \frac{1}{U} \sum_i E\left(q_i, \bar{q}_i\right), \tag{7}$$

where U is the number of pixels, E is the softmax cross entropy loss, $\bar{q}$ is given by the ground-truth object mask, and $\bar{\mathbf{y}}$ are the ground-truth 3D coordinates. At test time, 2D-3D correspondences are established at pixels with $q > 0.5$ and used to fit the object pose with the PnP-RANSAC algorithm [39]. In RANSAC, a 2D-3D correspondence $(\mathbf{p}, \mathbf{y})$ is considered an inlier $w.r.t.$ a pose hypothesis $(R, \mathbf{t})$ if $\|\mathbf{p} - \pi(R\mathbf{y} + \mathbf{t})\|_2$ is below a fixed threshold τ_{2D}.

We experiment with two variants of the baseline: "Baseline-visib" defines $\bar{q} = 1$ for the visible foreground pixels, and "Baseline-full" defines $\bar{q} = 1$ for all pixels in the object silhouette, even if occluded by other objects.

5.2 Experimental Setup

Evaluation Protocol. We follow the evaluation protocol of the BOP Challenge 2020 [25]. In short, a method is evaluated on the 6DoF object localization problem, and the error of an estimated pose $w.r.t.$ the ground-truth pose is calculated by three pose-error functions: Visible Surface Discrepancy (VSD) which treats indistinguishable poses as equivalent by considering only the visible object part, Maximum Symmetry-Aware Surface Distance (MSSD) which considers a set of pre-identified global object symmetries and measures the surface deviation in 3D, and Maximum Symmetry-Aware Projection Distance (MSPD) which considers the object symmetries and measures the perceivable deviation. An estimated pose is considered correct $w.r.t.$ a pose-error function e, if $e < \theta_e$, where $e \in \{\mathrm{VSD}, \mathrm{MSSD}, \mathrm{MSPD}\}$ and θ_e is the threshold of correctness. The fraction of annotated object instances for which a correct pose is estimated is referred to as Recall. The Average Recall $w.r.t.$ a function e, denoted as AR_e, is defined as the average of the Recall rates calculated for multiple settings of the threshold θ_e and also for multiple settings of a misalignment tolerance τ in the case of VSD. The overall accuracy of a method is measured by the Average Recall: $\mathrm{AR} = (\mathrm{AR}_{\mathrm{VSD}} + \mathrm{AR}_{\mathrm{MSSD}} + \mathrm{AR}_{\mathrm{MSPD}})/3$.

The BOP Challenge 2020 considers the problem of 6DoF localization of a varying number of instances of a varying number of objects from a single image. To evaluate the proposed method, which was designed to handle a single instance of a single object, we consider only BOP datasets where images show up to one instance of each object. On images that show single instances of multiple objects, we evaluate the proposed method multiple times, each time estimating the pose of a single object instance using the neural networks trained for that object.

Datasets. The experiments are conducted on the BOP 2020 [25] version of three datasets: LM [21], LM-O [5], and YCB-V [80]. The datasets include color 3D object models and RGB-D images of VGA resolution annotated with ground-truth 6DoF object poses (only the RGB channels are used in this work). LM contains 15 texture-less objects with discriminative color, shape, and size. Every object is associated with a set of 200 test images, each showing one annotated object instance under significant clutter and no or mild occlusion. LM-O provides ground-truth annotation for instances of eight LM objects in one of the test sets, which introduces challenging test cases with various levels of occlusion. YCB-V includes 21 objects that are both textured and texture-less, 900 test images showing the objects with occasional occlusions and limited clutter, and 113K real and 80K OpenGL-rendered training images. Each of these datasets is also associated with 50K physically-based rendered (PBR) images generated by BlenderProc [13,14] and provided by the BOP organizers. The datasets provide also sets of object symmetry transformations that are used in Eq. 5 and 7.

Training. We report results achieved by the proposed and the baseline methods trained on the synthetic PBR images. On the YCB-V dataset, for which real training images are available, we report also results achieved by the proposed method trained on both real and synthetic PBR images. To reduce the domain gap between the synthetic training and real test images, the training images are augmented by randomly adjusting contrast, brightness, sharpness, and color, as in [38]. The feature extractor F and networks f_{NCF} and f_{BL} are initialized with random weights. The networks are optimized by RMSProp [75] with the batch size of 4 training images, learning rate of 0.0001, no learning rate drop, and the balancing weight λ set to 1. On LM and LM-O, the optimization is run for 220 epochs. On YCB-V, the optimization is run for 300 epochs on synthetic PBR images, and then for extra 150 epochs on PBR and real images (we report scores before and after the extra epochs). Special neural networks are trained for each object, while all hyper-parameters are fixed across all objects and datasets.

Method Parameters. The architecture of neural networks is adopted from PIFu [66]. Specifically, the feature extractor F is a stacked hourglass network with the output stride of 4 and output channel of 256. Networks f_{NCF} and f_{BL} have four hidden fully-connected layers with 1024, 512, 256 and 128 neurons and with skip connections from F. Unless stated otherwise, the clamping distance $\delta = 5$ mm, the inlier threshold $\tau_{3D} = 20$ mm, the inlier threshold for the baseline method $\tau_{2D} = 4$ px, and the RANSAC-based pose fitting in the proposed and the baseline method is run for a fixed number of 200 iterations. The sampling step of 3D query points at test time is 10 mm (in all three axes) and the near and far planes of the camera frustum, in which the points are sampled, is determined by the range of object distances annotated in the test images (the BOP benchmark explicitly allows using this information at test time). We converged to these settings by experimenting with different parameter values and optimizing the performance of both the proposed and the baseline method.

Table 1. Average Recall (AR) scores on datasets YCB-V and LM-O from BOP 2020 [25]. The 2nd to 5th columns show the training and test setup: image channels used at training (*Train*), type of training images (*Train type: pbr* for physically-based rendered images, *syn* for synthetic images which include not only *pbr* images, *real* for real images), image channels used at test (*Test*), and type of iterative pose refinement used at test time (*Refine: icp* for a depth-based Iterative Closest Point algorithm, *rc* for a color-based render-and-compare refinement). While *pbr* training images are included in both datasets, *real* training images are only in YCB-V – training setups *pbr* and *pbr+real* are therefore equivalent on LM-O, which leads to several duplicate scores in the table. Top scores among methods with the same training and test setup are **bold**. The time is the average time to estimate poses of all objects in an image [s].

Method	Train	..type	Test	Refine	YCB-V	..time	LM-O	..time
NCF (ours)	rgb	pbr	rgb	–	**67.3**	1.09	**63.2**	4.33
Baseline-full	rgb	pbr	rgb	–	37.1	0.74	33.9	0.81
Baseline-visib	rgb	pbr	rgb	–	31.9	0.71	31.6	0.79
EPOS [23]	rgb	pbr	rgb	–	49.9	0.76	54.7	0.47
CDPNv2 [41]	rgb	pbr	rgb	–	39.0	0.45	62.4	0.16
NCF (ours)	rgb	pbr+real	rgb	–	**77.5**	1.09	**63.2**	4.33
leaping 2D-6D [43]	rgb	pbr+real	rgb	–	54.3	0.13	52.5	0.94
CDPNv2 [41]	rgb	pbr+real	rgb	–	53.2	0.14	62.4	0.16
Pix2Pose [59]	rgb	pbr+real	rgb	–	45.7	1.03	36.3	1.31
CosyPose [38]	rgb	pbr+real	rgbd	rc+icp	86.1	2.74	71.4	8.29
CosyPose [38]	rgb	pbr+real	rgb	rc	82.1	0.24	63.3	0.55
Pix2Pose [59]	rgb	pbr+real	rgbd	icp	78.0	2.59	58.8	5.19
FFB6D [20]	rgbd	pbr	rgbd	–	75.8	0.20	68.7	0.19
König-Hybrid [34]	rgb	syn+real	rgbd	icp	70.1	2.48	63.1	0.45
CDPNv2 [41]	rgb	pbr+real	rgbd	icp	61.9	0.64	63.0	0.51
CosyPose [38]	rgb	pbr	rgb	rc	57.4	0.34	63.3	0.55
CDPNv2 [41]	rgb	pbr	rgbd	icp	53.2	1.03	63.0	0.51
Félix&Neves [64,65]	rgbd	syn+real	rgbd	icp	51.0	54.51	39.4	61.99
AAE [71]	rgb	syn+real	rgbd	icp	50.5	1.58	23.7	1.20
Vidal et al. [78]	–	–	d	icp	45.0	3.72	58.2	4.00
CDPN [41]	rgb	syn+real	rgb	–	42.2	0.30	37.4	0.33
Drost-3D-Only [15]	–	–	d	icp	34.4	6.27	52.7	15.95

In the presented experiments, the signed distance $\psi(\mathbf{y})$ is measured from the query point $\mathbf{x}$ to the closest point on the model surface along the projection ray (*i.e.*, a ray passing through the camera center and $\mathbf{x}$), not to the closest point in 3D as in the conventional SDF [57]. However, our additional experiments suggest the two definitions yield comparable performance.

5.3   Main Results

Accuracy. Table 1 compares the proposed method (NCF) with participants of the BOP Challenge 2020 and with the baseline method described in Sect. 5.1. On the YCB-V dataset, NCF trained on the synthetic PBR images outperforms all competitors which also rely only on RGB images and which do not apply

Table 2. Per-object AR scores on datasets LM-O [5], LM [21], and YCB-V [80]. Objects with symmetries are marked by the prime symbol (').

Method	LM-O								LM													
	1	5	6	8	9	10'	11'	12	1	2	3'	4	5	6	7	8	9	10'	11'	12	13	14
NCF	**58**	**83**	**55**	**83**	**75**	**11**	**66**	**70**	**74**	**92**	**72**	**89**	**91**	**83**	**63**	**92**	**73**	**73**	**73**	**74**	**90**	**85**
BL-full	23	53	31	62	38	0	12	40	35	72	45	66	47	47	36	61	45	7	19	49	68	64
BL-visib	25	48	18	46	37	1	27	45	34	69	55	57	48	45	40	54	35	10	29	51	61	47

Method	YCB-V																					
	15	1'	2	3	4	5	6	7	8	9	10	11	12	13'	14	15	16'	17	18'	19'	20'	21'
NCF	**83**	**67**	**81**	**83**	**57**	**77**	**72**	**76**	**75**	**51**	**85**	**84**	**72**	**8**	**61**	**84**	**36**	**63**	**41**	**60**	**62**	**49**
BL-full	57	54	53	66	40	55	6	26	15	31	20	75	36	1	53	60	2	31	18	2	1	0
BL-visib	64	57	40	45	24	52	10	23	32	17	24	55	37	2	40	60	0	25	32	3	0	0

any iterative refinement to the pose estimates. NCF achieves 17.4% absolute improvement over EPOS [23] and 28.3% over CDPNv2 [41], which are trained on the same set of PBR images, and 13.0% and up over [41,43,59], which are trained on PBR and real images. Training on the additional real images improves the AR score of NCF further to 77.5. Although with smaller margins, NCF outperforms these competitors also on the LM-O dataset. All higher scores reported on the two datasets are achieved by methods that use the depth image or iteratively refine the estimates by ICP or a render-and-compare technique (*c.f.*, [25] for details). On the LM dataset [21] (not in Table 1, see BOP leaderboard [25]), NCF achieves 81.0 AR and is close the overall leading method which achivcs 81.4 AR and is based on point-pair features [15] extracted from depth images.

Table 1 also shows scores of the two variants of the baseline method. NCF achieves significant improvements over both variants, reaching almost double AR scores. As shown in Table 2, NCF outperforms the baseline on all objects from the three datasets. Some of the most noticeable differences are on YCB-V objects 19, 20, and 21. The baseline method struggles due to symmetries of these objects, even though it adopts a very similar symmetry-aware loss as NCF, which performs well on these objects. Qualitative results are in Fig. 4.

Speed. NCF takes 1.09 and 4.33 s on average to estimate poses of all objects in a test image from YCB-V and LM-O respectively (with a single Nvidia V100 GPU; 3–6 objects are in YCB-V images and 7–8 in LM-O images). As discussed in Sect. 5.4, the processing time can be decreased with sparser query point sampling or with less RANSAC iterations, both yielding only a moderate drop in AR score. Besides, NCF can be readily used for object tracking, where the exhaustive scanning of the frustum could be replaced by sampling a limited number of query points around the model in the pose estimated in the previous frame. This would require a lower number of query points and therefore faster processing.

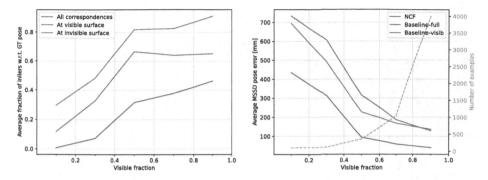

Fig. 3. Performance w.r.t. visible object fraction. Left: The average fraction of established 3D-3D correspondences that are inliers *w.r.t.* the ground-truth pose (*i.e.*, the error of predicted 3D object coordinates is less than a threshold $\tau_{3D} = 20\,\text{mm}$). The set of all correspondences is not the union of correspondences at the visible and invisible surface, hence the red curve is not in between the other two – see text for details. Right: The average MSSD error [25] of object poses estimated by the proposed method (NCF) and the baselines. The average values in both plots are calculated over test examples split into five bins based on the visible fraction of the object silhouette.

5.4   Ablation Studies

Performance Under Occlusion. First, we study the impact of different occlusion levels on the quality of predicted 3D-3D correspondences, using the visibility information from [25]. This analysis is conducted on datasets YCB-V and LM-O which include partially occluded examples. The quality of correspondences is measured by the fraction of inliers, which is the key metric determining the success of RANSAC [16]. A correspondence $(\mathbf{x}, \mathbf{y})$ is considered an inlier if $\|\bar{R}\mathbf{y} + \bar{\mathbf{t}} - \mathbf{x}\|_2 < \tau_{3D} = 20\,\text{mm}$, where $\mathbf{x}$ is a 3D query point in the camera coordinates, $\mathbf{y}$ is the predicted 3D point in the model coordinates, and $(\bar{R}, \bar{\mathbf{t}})$ is the ground-truth object pose. Figure 3 (left) shows the average inlier fraction for test examples split into five bins based on the object visibility. Already with around 40% visibility (*i.e.*, 60% occlusion), the established correspondences (red curve) include 20% inliers, which is typically sufficient for fitting a good pose with 200 RANSAC iterations.[1] To separately analyze the quality of correspondences established around the visible and invisible surface, we first select a subset of correspondences established at query points that are in the vicinity of the object surface in the ground-truth pose. This subset is then split into correspondences at the visible surface (green curve in Fig. 3, left) and at the invisible surface (blue curve). Although the inlier percentage is higher for correspondences at the visible surface, correspondences at the invisible surface keep up, demonstrating the ability of the proposed method to reason about the whole object.

---

[1] The number of required RANSAC iterations is given by $\log(1-p)/\log(1-w^n)$, where p is the desired probability of success, w is the fraction of inliers, and n is the minimal set size [16]. In the discussed case, $p = 0.8$ yields $\log(1 - 0.8)/\log(1 - 0.2^3) \approx 200$.

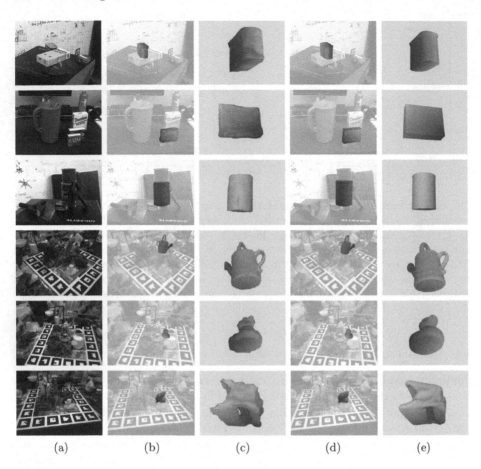

(a)   (b)   (c)   (d)   (e)

Fig. 4. Qualitative results on YCB-V and LM-O: (a) An RGB input. (b) A mesh model reconstructed by Marching Cubes [45] from the signed distances predicted at 3D query points in the camera frustum. Mesh vertices are colored with the predicted 3D object coordinates. Note that the mesh is reconstructed only for visualization, not when estimating the object pose. (c) The reconstructed mesh from a novel view. (d) GT mesh colored with GT 3D object coordinates. (e) GT mesh in the view from (c).

Next, Fig. 3 (right) shows the impact of occlusion on the average MSSD error [25] of object poses estimated by the proposed method and the baselines. The proposed method (NCF) clearly outperforms the baselines at all occlusion levels and keeps the average error below 10 cm up to around 50% occlusion.

Density of 3D Query Points. The scores discussed so far were obtained with 3D query points sampled with the step of 10 mm, $i.e.$, the points are at the centers of $10 \times 10 \times 10$ mm voxels that fill up the camera frustum. On YCB-V, this sampling step yields $230,383$ query points, 0.85 s average image processing time and 66.8 AR (with 100 RANSAC iterations). Reducing the step size to

5 mm yields $1,852,690$ points and 3.95 s, while only slightly improved accuracy of 67.0 AR. Enlarging the step size to 20 mm yields $28,232$ points, improves the time to 0.63 s, and still achieves competitive accuracy of 66.2 AR. These results suggest that the method is relatively insensitive to the sampling density.

Number of Pose Fitting Iterations. We further investigate the effect of the number of RANSAC iterations on the accuracy and speed. On the YCB-V dataset, reducing the number of iterations from 200 to 50 and 10 decreases the AR score from 67.3 to 66.7 and 65.1, and improves the average processing time from 1.09 to 0.77 and 0.68 s, respectively. On the other hand, increasing the number of iterations from 200 to 500 yields the same AR score and higher average processing time of 1.67 s. Note that in the presented experiments we run both Kabsch-RANSAC and $P n P$-RANSAC algorithms for a fixed number of iterations. Further improvements in speed could be achieved by applying an early stopping criterion, which is typically based on the number of inliers $w.r.t.$ the so-far-the-best pose hypothesis [3, 16].

6   Conclusion

We have proposed the first method for 6DoF object pose estimation based on a 3D implicit representation, which we call Neural Correspondence Field (NCF). The proposed method noticeably outperforms a baseline, which adopts a popular 2D-3D correspondence approach, and also all comparable methods on the YCB-V, LM-O, and LM datasets. Ablation studies and qualitative results demonstrate the ability of NCF to learn and incorporate priors about the whole object surface, which is important for handling challenging cases with occlusion.

References

1. Atzmon, M., Lipman, Y.: SAL: sign agnostic learning of shapes from raw data. In: CVPR (2020)
2. Atzmon, M., Lipman, Y.: SALD: sign agnostic learning with derivatives. In: ICLR (2021)
3. Baráth, D., Matas, J.: Graph-cut RANSAC. In: CVPR (2018)
4. Baráth, D., Matas, J.: Progressive-X: efficient, anytime, multi-model fitting algorithm. In: ICCV (2019)
5. Brachmann, E., Krull, A., Michel, F., Gumhold, S., Shotton, J., Rother, C.: Learning 6D object pose estimation using 3D object coordinates. In: Fleet, D., Pajdla, T., Schiele, B., Tuytelaars, T. (eds.) ECCV 2014. LNCS, vol. 8690, pp. 536–551. Springer, Cham (2014). https://doi.org/10.1007/978-3-319-10605-2_35
6. Brachmann, E., Michel, F., Krull, A., Yang, M.Y., Gumhold, S., Rother, C.: Uncertainty-driven 6D pose estimation of objects and scenes from a single RGB image. In: CVPR (2016)
7. Brunelli, R.: Template Matching Techniques in Computer Vision: Theory and Practice. Wiley, Hoboken (2009)
8. Chen, Z., Zhang, H.: Learning implicit fields for generative shape modeling. In: CVPR (2019)

9. Collet, A., Martinez, M., Srinivasa, S.S.: The MOPED framework: object recognition and pose estimation for manipulation. IJRR **30**, 1284–1306 (2011)
10. Corona, E., Kundu, K., Fidler, S.: Pose estimation for objects with rotational symmetry. In: IROS (2018)
11. Curless, B., Levoy, M.: A volumetric method for building complex models from range images. In: SIGGRAPH (1996)
12. Deng, Y., Yang, J., Tong, X.: Deformed implicit field: modeling 3D shapes with learned dense correspondence. In: CVPR (2021)
13. Denninger, M., et al.: BlenderProc: reducing the reality gap with photorealistic rendering. In: RSS Workshops (2020)
14. Denninger, M., et al.: BlenderProc. arXiv preprint arXiv:1911.01911 (2019)
15. Drost, B., Ulrich, M., Navab, N., Ilic, S.: Model globally, match locally: efficient and robust 3D object recognition. In: CVPR (2010)
16. Fischler, M.A., Bolles, R.C.: Random sample consensus: a paradigm for model fitting with applications to image analysis and automated cartography. Commun. ACM **24**, 381–395 (1981)
17. Gropp, A., Yariv, L., Haim, N., Atzmon, M., Lipman, Y.: Implicit geometric regularization for learning shapes. In: ICML (2020)
18. Güler, R.A., Neverova, N., Kokkinos, I.: DensePose: dense human pose estimation in the wild. In: CVPR (2018)
19. Guo, Y., Bennamoun, M., Sohel, F., Lu, M., Wan, J., Kwok, N.M.: A comprehensive performance evaluation of 3D local feature descriptors. IJCV **116**, 66–89 (2016)
20. He, Y., Huang, H., Fan, H., Chen, Q., Sun, J.: FFB6D: a full flow bidirectional fusion network for 6d pose estimation. In: CVPR (2021)
21. Hinterstoisser, S., et al.: Model based training, detection and pose estimation of texture-less 3D objects in heavily cluttered scenes. In: Lee, K.M., Matsushita, Y., Rehg, J.M., Hu, Z. (eds.) ACCV 2012. LNCS, vol. 7724, pp. 548–562. Springer, Heidelberg (2013). https://doi.org/10.1007/978-3-642-37331-2_42
22. Hinterstoisser, S., Lepetit, V., Rajkumar, N., Konolige, K.: Going further with point pair features. In: Leibe, B., Matas, J., Sebe, N., Welling, M. (eds.) ECCV 2016. LNCS, vol. 9907, pp. 834–848. Springer, Cham (2016). https://doi.org/10.1007/978-3-319-46487-9_51
23. Hodaň, T., Baráth, D., Matas, J.: EPOS: estimating 6D pose of objects with symmetries. In: CVPR (2020)
24. Hodaň, T., et al.: BOP: benchmark for 6D object pose estimation. In: Ferrari, V., Hebert, M., Sminchisescu, C., Weiss, Y. (eds.) ECCV 2018. LNCS, vol. 11214, pp. 19–35. Springer, Cham (2018). https://doi.org/10.1007/978-3-030-01249-6_2
25. Hodaň, T., et al.: BOP challenge 2020 on 6D object localization. In: Bartoli, A., Fusiello, A. (eds.) ECCV 2020. LNCS, vol. 12536, pp. 577–594. Springer, Cham (2020). https://doi.org/10.1007/978-3-030-66096-3_39
26. Hodaň, T., Zabulis, X., Lourakis, M., Obdržálek, Š., Matas, J.: Detection and fine 3D pose estimation of texture-less objects in RGB-D images. In: IROS (2015)
27. Hu, Y., Hugonot, J., Fua, P., Salzmann, M.: Segmentation-driven 6D object pose estimation. In: CVPR (2019)
28. Huang, Z., Xu, Y., Lassner, C., Li, H., Tung, T.: ARCH: animatable reconstruction of clothed humans. In: CVPR (2020)
29. Huber, P.J.: Robust estimation of a location parameter. In: Kotz, S., Johnson, N.L. (eds.) Breakthroughs in Statistics. Springer Series in Statistics, pp. 492–512. Springer, New York (1992). https://doi.org/10.1007/978-1-4612-4380-9_35

30. Hosseini Jafari, O., Mustikovela, S.K., Pertsch, K., Brachmann, E., Rother, C.: iPose: instance-aware 6D pose estimation of partly occluded objects. In: Jawahar, C.V., Li, H., Mori, G., Schindler, K. (eds.) ACCV 2018. LNCS, vol. 11363, pp. 477–492. Springer, Cham (2019). https://doi.org/10.1007/978-3-030-20893-6_30

31. Kabsch, W.: A discussion of the solution for the best rotation to relate two sets of vectors. Acta Crystallogr. Sect. A **34**, 827–828 (1978)

32. Karunratanakul, K., Yang, J., Zhang, Y., Black, M.J., Muandet, K., Tang, S.: Grasping field: Learning implicit representations for human grasps. In: 3DV (2020)

33. Kehl, W., Manhardt, F., Tombari, F., Ilic, S., Navab, N.: SSD-6D: making RGB-based 3D detection and 6D pose estimation great again. In: ICCV (2017)

34. König, R., Drost, B.: A hybrid approach for 6DoF pose estimation. In: Bartoli, A., Fusiello, A. (eds.) ECCV 2020. LNCS, vol. 12536, pp. 700–706. Springer, Cham (2020). https://doi.org/10.1007/978-3-030-66096-3_46

35. Krull, A., Brachmann, E., Michel, F., Ying Yang, M., Gumhold, S., Rother, C.: Learning analysis-by-synthesis for 6D pose estimation in RGB-D images. In: ICCV (2015)

36. Kulkarni, N., Gupta, A., Fouhey, D.F., Tulsiani, S.: Articulation-aware canonical surface mapping. In: CVPR (2020)

37. Kulkarni, N., Johnson, J., Fouhey, D.F.: What's behind the couch? Directed ray distance functions (DRDF) for 3D scene reconstruction. arXiv e-prints (2021)

38. Labbé, Y., Carpentier, J., Aubry, M., Sivic, J.: CosyPose: consistent multi-view multi-object 6D pose estimation. In: Vedaldi, A., Bischof, H., Brox, T., Frahm, J.-M. (eds.) ECCV 2020. LNCS, vol. 12362, pp. 574–591. Springer, Cham (2020). https://doi.org/10.1007/978-3-030-58520-4_34

39. Lepetit, V., Moreno-Noguer, F., Fua, P.: EPnP: an accurate O(n) solution to the PnP problem. IJCV **81**, 155–166 (2009)

40. Li, C., Bai, J., Hager, G.D.: A unified framework for multi-view multi-class object pose estimation. In: Ferrari, V., Hebert, M., Sminchisescu, C., Weiss, Y. (eds.) ECCV 2018. LNCS, vol. 11220, pp. 263–281. Springer, Cham (2018). https://doi.org/10.1007/978-3-030-01270-0_16

41. Li, Z., Wang, G., Ji, X.: CDPN: coordinates-based disentangled pose network for real-time RGB-based 6-DoF object pose estimation. In: ICCV (2019)

42. Liu, F., Tran, L., Liu, X.: Fully understanding generic objects: modeling, segmentation, and reconstruction. In: CVPR (2021)

43. Liu, J., Zou, Z., Ye, X., Tan, X., Ding, E., Xu, F., Yu, X.: Leaping from 2D detection to efficient 6DoF object pose estimation. In: Bartoli, A., Fusiello, A. (eds.) ECCV 2020. LNCS, vol. 12536, pp. 707–714. Springer, Cham (2020). https://doi.org/10.1007/978-3-030-66096-3_47

44. Lombardi, S., Simon, T., Saragih, J., Schwartz, G., Lehrmann, A., Sheikh, Y.: Neural volumes: Learning dynamic renderable volumes from images. TOG (2019)

45. Lorensen, W.E., Cline, H.E.: Marching cubes: a high resolution 3D surface construction algorithm. In: SIGGRAPH (1987)

46. Lowe, D.G., et al.: Object recognition from local scale-invariant features. In: ICCV (1999)

47. Manhardt, F., Arroyo, D.M., Rupprecht, C., Busam, B., Navab, N., Tombari, F.: Explaining the ambiguity of object detection and 6D pose from visual data. In: ICCV (2019)

48. Mescheder, L., Oechsle, M., Niemeyer, M., Nowozin, S., Geiger, A.: Occupancy networks: learning 3D reconstruction in function space. In: CVPR (2019)

49. Michel, F., et al.: Global hypothesis generation for 6D object pose estimation. In: CVPR (2017)

50. Mildenhall, B., Srinivasan, P.P., Tancik, M., Barron, J.T., Ramamoorthi, R., Ng, R.: NeRF: representing scenes as neural radiance fields for view synthesis. In: Vedaldi, A., Bischof, H., Brox, T., Frahm, J.-M. (eds.) ECCV 2020. LNCS, vol. 12346, pp. 405–421. Springer, Cham (2020). https://doi.org/10.1007/978-3-030-58452-8_24

51. Neverova, N., Novotny, D., Khalidov, V., Szafraniec, M., Labatut, P., Vedaldi, A.: Continuous surface embeddings. In: NeurIPS (2020)

52. Newell, A., Yang, K., Deng, J.: Stacked hourglass networks for human pose estimation. In: Leibe, B., Matas, J., Sebe, N., Welling, M. (eds.) ECCV 2016. LNCS, vol. 9912, pp. 483–499. Springer, Cham (2016). https://doi.org/10.1007/978-3-319-46484-8_29

53. Niemeyer, M., Mescheder, L., Oechsle, M., Geiger, A.: Differentiable volumetric rendering: learning implicit 3D representations without 3D supervision. In: CVPR (2020)

54. Oberweger, M., Rad, M., Lepetit, V.: Making deep heatmaps robust to partial occlusions for 3D object pose estimation. In: Ferrari, V., Hebert, M., Sminchisescu, C., Weiss, Y. (eds.) ECCV 2018. LNCS, vol. 11219, pp. 125–141. Springer, Cham (2018). https://doi.org/10.1007/978-3-030-01267-0_8

55. Oechsle, M., Mescheder, L., Niemeyer, M., Strauss, T., Geiger, A.: Texture fields: learning texture representations in function space. In: ICCV (2019)

56. Palafox, P., Božič, A., Thies, J., Nießner, M., Dai, A.: NPMS: neural parametric models for 3D deformable shapes. In: ICCV (2021)

57. Park, J.J., Florence, P., Straub, J., Newcombe, R., Lovegrove, S.: DeepSDF: learning continuous signed distance functions for shape representation. In: CVPR (2019)

58. Park, K., et al.: Nerfies: deformable neural radiance fields. In: ICCV (2021)

59. Park, K., Patten, T., Vincze, M.: Pix2Pose: pixel-wise coordinate regression of objects for 6D pose estimation. In: ICCV (2019)

60. Pavlakos, G., Zhou, X., Chan, A., Derpanis, K.G., Daniilidis, K.: 6-DoF object pose from semantic keypoints. In: ICRA (2017)

61. Peng, S., Liu, Y., Huang, Q., Zhou, X., Bao, H.: PVNet: pixel-wise voting network for 6DoF pose estimation. In: CVPR (2019)

62. Pumarola, A., Corona, E., Pons-Moll, G., Moreno-Noguer, F.: D-NeRF: neural radiance fields for dynamic scenes. In: CVPR (2020)

63. Rad, M., Lepetit, V.: BB8: a scalable, accurate, robust to partial occlusion method for predicting the 3D poses of challenging objects without using depth. In: ICCV (2017)

64. Raposo, C., Barreto, J.P.: Using 2 point+normal sets for fast registration of point clouds with small overlap. In: ICRA (2017)

65. Rodrigues, P., Antunes, M., Raposo, C., Marques, P., Fonseca, F., Barreto, J.: Deep segmentation leverages geometric pose estimation in computer-aided total knee arthroplasty. Healthc. Technol. Lett. **6**, 226–230 (2019)

66. Saito, S., Huang, Z., Natsume, R., Morishima, S., Kanazawa, A., Li, H.: PiFu: pixel-aligned implicit function for high-resolution clothed human digitization. In: ICCV (2019)

67. Saito, S., Simon, T., Saragih, J., Joo, H.: PiFuHD: multi-level pixel-aligned implicit function for high-resolution 3D human digitization. In: CVPR (2020)

68. Shotton, J., Glocker, B., Zach, C., Izadi, S., Criminisi, A., Fitzgibbon, A.: Scene coordinate regression forests for camera relocalization in RGB-D images. In: CVPR (2013)

69. Sitzmann, V., Chan, E., Tucker, R., Snavely, N., Wetzstein, G.: MetaSDF: meta-learning signed distance functions. In: NeurIPS (2020)

70. Sitzmann, V., Zollhöfer, M., Wetzstein, G.: Scene representation networks: continuous 3D-structure-aware neural scene representations. In: NeurIPS (2019)
71. Sundermeyer, M., Marton, Z.C., Durner, M., Triebel, R.: Augmented autoencoders: implicit 3D orientation learning for 6D object detection. IJCV **128**, 714–729 (2019)
72. Tejani, A., Tang, D., Kouskouridas, R., Kim, T.-K.: Latent-class hough forests for 3D object detection and pose estimation. In: Fleet, D., Pajdla, T., Schiele, B., Tuytelaars, T. (eds.) ECCV 2014. LNCS, vol. 8694, pp. 462–477. Springer, Cham (2014). https://doi.org/10.1007/978-3-319-10599-4_30
73. Tekin, B., Sinha, S.N., Fua, P.: Real-time seamless single shot 6D object pose prediction. In: CVPR (2018)
74. Tewari, A., et al.: Advances in neural rendering. In: Computer Graphics Forum (2022)
75. Tieleman, T., Hinton, G.: RMSProp: divide the gradient by a running average of its recent magnitude. COURSERA: Neural Netw. Mach. Learn. (2012)
76. Tremblay, J., To, T., Sundaralingam, B., Xiang, Y., Fox, D., Birchfield, S.: Deep object pose estimation for semantic robotic grasping of household objects. CoRL (2018)
77. Tretschk, E., Tewari, A., Golyanik, V., Zollhöfer, M., Lassner, C., Theobalt, C.: Non-rigid neural radiance fields: reconstruction and novel view synthesis of a dynamic scene from monocular video. In: ICCV (2021)
78. Vidal, J., Lin, C.Y., Lladó, X., Martí, R.: A method for 6D pose estimation of free-form rigid objects using point pair features on range data. Sensors **18**, 2678 (2018)
79. Wang, H., Sridhar, S., Huang, J., Valentin, J., Song, S., Guibas, L.J.: Normalized object coordinate space for category-level 6d object pose and size estimation. In: CVPR (2019)
80. Xiang, Y., Schmidt, T., Narayanan, V., Fox, D.: PoseCNN: a convolutional neural network for 6D object pose estimation in cluttered scenes. In: RSS (2018)
81. Xu, Q., Wang, W., Ceylan, D., Mech, R., Neumann, U.: DISN: deep implicit surface network for high-quality single view 3D reconstruction. In: Advances in Neural Information Processing Systems (2019)
82. Yariv, L., et al.: Multiview neural surface reconstruction by disentangling geometry and appearance. In: NeurIPS (2020)
83. Zakharov, S., Shugurov, I., Ilic, S.: DPOD: 6D pose object detector and refiner. In: ICCV (2019)
84. Zheng, Z., Yu, T., Liu, Y., Dai, Q.: PaMIR: parametric model-conditioned implicit representation for image-based human reconstruction. TPAMI **44**, 3170–3184 (2021)

On Label Granularity and Object Localization

Elijah Cole[1(✉)], Kimberly Wilber[2], Grant Van Horn[3], Xuan Yang[2],
Marco Fornoni[2], Pietro Perona[1], Serge Belongie[4], Andrew Howard[2],
and Oisin Mac Aodha[5]

[1] Caltech, Pasadena, USA
ecole@caltech.edu
[2] Google, Mountain View, USA
[3] Cornell University, Ithaca, USA
[4] University of Copenhagen, Copenhagen, Denmark
[5] University of Edinburgh, Edinburgh, UK

Abstract. Weakly supervised object localization (WSOL) aims to learn representations that encode object location using only image-level category labels. However, many objects can be labeled at different levels of granularity. Is it an animal, a bird, or a great horned owl? Which image-level labels should we use? In this paper we study the role of label granularity in WSOL. To facilitate this investigation we introduce iNatLoc500, a new large-scale fine-grained benchmark dataset for WSOL. Surprisingly, we find that choosing the right training label granularity provides a much larger performance boost than choosing the best WSOL algorithm. We also show that changing the label granularity can significantly improve data efficiency.

1 Introduction

For many problems in computer vision, it is not enough to know *what* is in an image, we also need to know *where* it is. Examples can be found in many domains, including ecological conservation [20], autonomous driving [55], and medical image analysis [30]. The most popular paradigm for locating objects in images is object *detection*, which aims to predict a bounding box for every instance of every category of interest. Object *localization* is special case of detection where each image is assumed to contain exactly one object instance of interest, and the category of that object is known.

Standard approaches to object detection and localization require bounding boxes for training, which are expensive to collect at scale [37]. Weakly supervised object localization (WSOL) methods aim to sidestep this obstacle by learning to localize objects using only image-level labels at training time. The potential reduction in annotation cost which could result from effective weakly supervised methods has stimulated significant interest in WSOL over the last few years [60].

Supplementary Information The online version contains supplementary material available at https://doi.org/10.1007/978-3-031-20080-9_35.

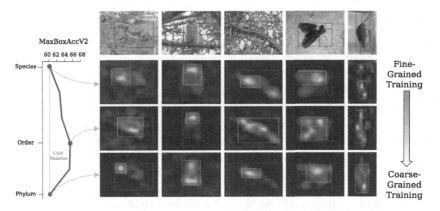

Fig. 1. Label granularity is a critical but understudied factor in weakly supervised object localization (WSOL). We show five hand-picked examples from our iNatLoc500 dataset. Below each image we show class activation maps (CAMs) [63] derived from training a classifier at different granularity levels, with ground truth bounding boxes (red) and WSOL-based bounding boxes (yellow) superimposed. Conventional training does not consider label granularity and can lead to inferior localization performance (red line). Better WSOL results can be achieved by training with coarse (i.e. "order") labels, as opposed to fine-grained (i.e. "species") ones. (Color figure online)

In this paper we explore the role of label granularity in WSOL. The *granularity* of a category is the degree to which it is specific, which can vary from coarse-grained (e.g. "animal") to fine-grained (e.g. "great horned owl") [54]. When we work with benchmark datasets in computer vision, we often take the given level of label granularity for granted. However, it is usually possible to make those labels more general or more specific. It is worth asking whether the label granularity we are given is the best one to use for a certain task. Label granularity matters for WSOL because the first step in most WSOL algorithms is to train a classifier using image-level category labels. By choosing a label granularity we are choosing which training images are grouped into categories. This affects the discriminative features learned by the classifier and ultimately determines the bounding box predictions. Is it possible to improve WSOL performance by controlling label granularity? (Fig. 1).

Unfortunately, it is difficult to explore label granularity in WSOL due to the limitations of existing datasets. The field of WSOL largely relies on CUB [52] and ImageNet [41]. CUB has a consistent label hierarchy (i.e. one that can be used to measure label granularity), but it is small (∼6k training images) and homogeneous (only bird categories). ImageNet is large and diverse, but lacks a consistent label hierarchy (see Sect. 4.2). Furthermore, [12] recently found that many purported algorithmic advances in WSOL over the last few years – which were based on these two datasets – perform no better than baselines when they are evaluated fairly. This calls for the development of more diverse and challenging benchmarks for WSOL.

Our primary contributions are as follows:

1. We explore the effect of label granularity on WSOL, and show that training at coarser levels of granularity leads to surprisingly large performance gains across many different WSOL methods compared to conventional training e.g. +5.1 MaxBoxAccV2 for CAM and +6.6 MaxBoxAccV2 for CutMix (see Fig. 3).
2. We demonstrate that training on coarse labels is more data efficient than conventional training. For instance, training at a coarser level achieves the same performance as conventional CAM with ∼ 15× fewer labels (see Fig. 4).
3. We introduce the iNaturalist Localization 500 (iNatLoc500) dataset, which consists of 138k images for weakly supervised training and 25k images with manually verified bounding boxes for validation and testing. iNatLoc500 covers 500 diverse categories with a consistent hierarchical label space.

2 Related Work

Here we primarily focus on literature related to WSOL. See [60] for a broader overview of related techniques such as weakly supervised object detection [6,7,47].

Weakly Supervised Object Localization. The goal of WSOL is to determine the location of single objects in images using only image-level labels at training time. Early attempts at WSOL explored a variety of different approaches, such as adapting boosting-based methods [34], framing the problem as multiple instance learning [19,21], and applying latent deformable part-based formulations [36].

Some foundational work in deep learning investigated the degree to which object localization comes "for free" when training supervised CNNs for image classification tasks [35,59,63]. In particular, the Class Activation Mapping (CAM) method of [63] showed that CNNs can capture some object location information even when they are trained using only image-level class labels. This inspired a large body of work (e.g. [13,26,27,45,61,62]) that attempted to address some of the shortcomings of CAM, e.g. by preventing the underlying model from only focusing on the most discriminative parts of an object [58] or increasing the spatial resolution of its outputs [10,43].

Recently, [12] showed that when state-of-the-art WSOL methods are fairly compared (e.g. by controlling for the backbone architecture and operating thresholds), they are no better than the standard CAM [63] baseline. Thus, despite its simplicity, CAM is still a surprisingly effective baseline for WSOL. Subsequent work has explored further techniques for improving CAM-based methods [2,28] and alternative approaches for estimating model coefficients [24].

Task Granularity and Localization. Despite the considerable interest in WSOL in recent years, many open questions remain. Examples include the effect of label granularity (e.g. coarse-grained labels like "bird" vs. fine-grained labels indicating the specific species of bird) and the effect of training set size. In the context of supervised object detection, [51] showed that *coarsening* category labels at training time can improve the localization performance of *object detectors*. It is unclear if the same phenomenon holds for WSOL. [53] explored the impact of label granularity for object detection on the OpenImages [29] dataset and observed a small performance improvement when training on finer labels. In the semi-supervised detection setting, [57] trained object detectors on OpenImages and ImageNet using both coarse-grained bounding box annotations and fine-grained image-level labels. [49] also explored semi-supervised detection with an approach that generates object proposals across multiple hierarchical levels. Unlike our work, these detection-based methods require bounding box information at training time. In addition, the label hierarchies for datasets like ImageNet and OpenImages are not necessarily good proxies for visual similarity or concept granularity (see Sect. 4.2).

For WSOL, [27] showed that aggregating class attribution maps at coarser hierarchical levels (e.g. "dog") results in more spatial coverage of the objects of interest, whereas maps for finer-scale concepts (e.g. "Afghan hound") only focus on subparts of the object. However, their analysis does not explore the impact of training at different granularity levels. It is also worth noting that their aggregation method only improves performance on CUB. Regarding data quantity, [12] studied the number of supervised examples used to tune the hyperparameters of CAM, but did not consider the impact of the number of examples used to train the image classifier.

Though not directly related to our work, we note that label granularity has been studied in many contexts other than object localization, including action recognition [44], knowledge tracing [14], animal face alignment [25], and fashion attribute recognition [22]. In the context of image classification, prior work has tackled topics like analyzing the emergence of hierarchical structure in trained classifiers [5], identifying patterns in visual concept generalization [42], and training finer-grained image classifiers using only coarse-grained labels [40,46,48,56].

Datasets for Object Localization. Early work in WSOL (e.g. [19,32,34]) focused on relatively simple and small-scale datasets such as Caltech4 [18], the Weizmann Horse Database [8], or subsets of PASCAL-VOC [17]. With the rise of deep learning-based methods, CUB [52] and ImageNet [16,41] became the standard benchmarks for this task. CUB [52] consists of images of 200 different categories of birds, where each image contains a single bird instance. ImageNet [16,41] contains 1000 diverse categories and has significantly more images than CUB (>1M compared to ~6k). [12] proposed OpenImages30k, a 100-category localization-focused subset of the OpenImages V5 dataset [29]. An overview of these datasets is presented in Table 1.

These existing datasets are valuable, but they have shortcomings. CUB is small and homogeneous (only birds). OpenImages30k, as presented in [12], is not actually evaluated as a bounding box localization task. It is instead a per-pixel foreground object segmentation task where the ground truth also features some "ignore" regions that are excluded from the evaluation. Finally, while both OpenImages30k and ImageNet have label hierarchies, they do not reflect concept granularity in a consistent way. As a result, it is difficult to use them to better understand the relationship between concept granularity and localization. We discuss these issues in greater detail in Sect. 4.2. To address these shortcomings we introduce iNatLoc500, a new WSOL dataset composed of images from 500 fine-grained visual categories and equipped with a consistent label hierarchy.

Table 1. Comparison of datasets for WSOL. The vast majority of WSOL papers use only CUB and ImageNet. The OpenImages30k dataset was introduced by [12], which also defines the splits we use for CUB and ImageNet. For each split we provide the minimum, maximum, and mean number of images per category, along with the total number of images in the split. Means are rounded to the nearest integer. The properties of these four datasets are discussed in detail in Sect. 4.2.

Dataset	# Cat.	train-weaksup (D_w)				train-fullsup (D_f)				test (D_{test})			
		Min	Max	Mean	Total	Min	Max	Mean	Total	Min	Max	Mean	Total
CUB [52]	200	29	30	30	6k	3	6	5	1k	11	30	29	5.8k
ImageNet [16]	1000	732	1300	1281	1.28M	10	10	10	10k	10	10	10	10k
OpenImages30k [3,12]	100	230	300	298	30k	25	25	25	2.5k	50	50	50	5k
iNatLoc500	500	149	307	276	138k	25	25	25	12.5k	25	25	25	12.5k

3 Background

3.1 Weakly Supervised Object Localization (WSOL)

We begin by formalizing the WSOL setting. Let D_w be a set of *weakly labeled* images, i.e. $D_w = \{(x_i, y_i)\}_{i=1}^{N_w}$ where $x_i \in \mathbb{R}^{H \times W \times 3}$ is an image and $y_i \in \{1, \ldots, C\}$ is an image-level label corresponding to one of C categories. Let D_f be a set of *fully labeled* images, i.e. $D_f = \{(x_i, y_i, \mathbf{b}_i)\}_{i=1}^{N_f}$ where x_i and y_i are defined as before and $\mathbf{b}_i \in \mathbb{R}^4$ is a bounding box for an instance of category y_i. In practice $N_w \gg N_f$. WSOL approaches typically comprise three steps:

(1) Train. Use D_w to train an image classifier $h_\theta : \mathbb{R}^{H \times W \times 3} \rightarrow [0,1]^C$ by solving

$$\hat{\theta}(D_w) = \operatorname{argmin}_\theta \frac{1}{|D_w|} \sum_{(x_i, y_i) \in D_w} \mathcal{L}(h_\theta(x_i), y_i)$$

where $\mathcal{L}$ is some training loss and θ represents the parameters of h. Different WSOL methods are primarily distinguished by the loss functions and training protocols they use to train h.

(2) Localize. For each $(x_i, y_i, \mathbf{b}_i) \in D_f$, predict a bounding box

$$\hat{\mathbf{b}}_i = g(x_i, y_i | h_{\hat{\theta}(D_w)})$$

according to some procedure $g : \mathbb{R}^{H \times W \times 3} \times \{1, \ldots, C\} \rightarrow \mathbb{R}^4$. Typically g is a simple sequence of image processing operations applied to the feature maps of the trained classifier $h_{\hat{\theta}(D_w)}$.

(3) Evaluate. Let E denote a suitable WSOL error metric which compares the predicted boxes $\{\hat{\mathbf{b}}_i\}_{i=1}^{N_f}$ against the ground-truth boxes $\{\mathbf{b}_i\}_{i=1}^{N_f}$. Use the validation error $E(D_f | D_w)$ for model selection and hyperparameter tuning and then use a held-out test set D_{test} (which is fully labeled like D_f) to measure test error $E(D_{\text{test}} | D_w)$. See [12] for a discussion of WSOL performance metrics.

The Role of Low-Shot Supervised Localization. Without the fully labeled images D_f, the WSOL problem becomes ill-posed [12]. Since WSOL therefore requires at least a small number of bounding box annotations for validation, it is natural to ask how WSOL compares to few-shot object localization? For our purposes, we define few-shot object localization methods as those which use only D_f for training and validation. Under this definition, the few-shot methods (which use only D_f) actually require strictly *less* data than WSOL (which requires both D_w and D_f). Since WSOL and few-shot object localization are practical alternatives, it is important to consider them together as in [12].

3.2 Label Hierarchies and Label Granularity

We define a *label hierarchy* (on a label set L) to be a directed rooted tree H whose leaf nodes (i.e. nodes $v \in H$ with no children) correspond to the labels in L. Edges in H represent "is-a" relationships, so a directed edge from $u \in H$ to $v \in H$ means that v (e.g. "bird") is a kind of u (e.g. "animal"). We overload L to refer to the label set and to the corresponding set of nodes in H. Let r denote the root node of H and let $d(u, v)$ denote the number of edges on the path from $u \in H$ to $v \in H$.

Coarsening a Label. Because there is a unique path from the root node r to any leaf node $\ell \in L$, we can "coarsen" the label ℓ in a well-defined way by merging it with its parent node. We define the *coarsening operator* $c_k : H \to H$, which takes any node in the label hierarchy and returns the node which is k edges closer to the root. Thus, $c_0(\ell) = \ell$, $c_1(\ell)$ is the parent of ℓ, $c_2(\ell)$ is the grandparent of ℓ, and so on, with $c_k(\ell) = r$ for all $k \geq d(r, \ell)$.

Coarsening a Dataset. We can describe a general "coarsened" version of $D_w = \{(x_i, y_i)\}_{i=1}^{N_w}$ as $D_w^{\mathbf{k}} = \{(x_i, c_{k_i}(y_i))\}_{i=1}^{N_w}$ where $\mathbf{k} = (k_1, \dots, k_{|D_w|})$. If we allow the entries of $\mathbf{k}$ to be chosen completely independently, then we can encounter problems e.g. images with multiple valid labels. To prevent these cases, we require $\mathbf{k}$ to be chosen such that $c_{k_i}(y_i) \in H$ is not a descendant of $c_{k_j}(y_j) \in H$ for any $i, j \in \{1, \dots, N_w\}$.

Problem Statement. We can now formalize our key questions: How does $\mathbf{k}$ affect $E(D_{\text{test}}|D_w^{\mathbf{k}})$? Are there choices of $\mathbf{k}$ such that $E(D_{\text{test}}|D_w^{\mathbf{k}}) < E(D_{\text{test}}|D_w)$?

4   The iNatLoc500 Dataset

In this section we introduce the iNaturalist Localization 500 (iNatLoc500) dataset, a large-scale fine-grained dataset for weakly supervised object localization. We first detail the process of building the dataset and cleaning the localization annotations. We then discuss the key properties of the dataset and highlight the advantages of iNatLoc500 compared to three WSOL datasets that are currently commonly used (CUB, ImageNet, and OpenImages30k).

iNatLoc500 has three parts: `train-weaksup` (D_w), `train-fullsup` (D_f), and `test` (D_{test}). Each image in the weakly supervised training set (D_w) has one image-level category label. Each image in the fully supervised validation set (D_f) and test set (D_{test}) has one image-level category label *and* one bounding box

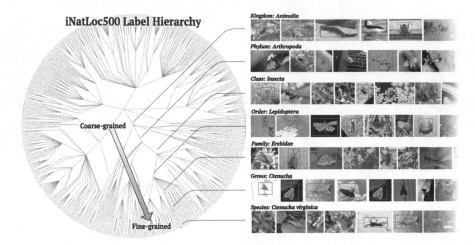

Fig. 2. Sample images from iNatLoc500 at different levels of the label hierarchy, from coarse ("kingdom") to fine ("species"). Random images from coarse levels of the hierarchy tend to be much more varied than random images ones from finer levels.

annotation. All bounding boxes have been manually validated. Split statistics are presented in Table 1 and sample images from the dataset can be found in Fig. 2. The dataset is publicly available.[1]

4.1   Dataset Construction

The iNatLoc500 dataset is derived from two existing datasets: iNat17 [51] and iNat21 [50]. Both datasets contain images of plants and animals collected by the citizen science platform iNaturalist [1]. iNat21 is much larger than iNat17 (2.7M images, 10k species vs. 675k images, 5k species), but iNat17 has crowdsourced bounding box annotations. We draw from iNat21 for D_w and we draw from iNat17 for D_f and D_{test}.

Full details on the process of constructing iNatLoc500 can be found in the supplementary material, but we note two important design choices here. First, iNat17 did not collect bounding boxes for plant categories because it is often unclear how to draw bounding boxes for plants. Consequently, iNatLoc500 does not contain any plant categories. Second, we set very high quality standards for the bounding boxes. Five computer vision researchers manually reviewed $\sim$ 65k images to ensure the quality of the bounding boxes for D_f and D_{test}, of which only 51% met our quality standards. Explicit quality criteria and examples of removed images can be found in the supplementary material.

4.2   Dataset Properties

iNatLoc500 is fine-grained, large-scale, and visually diverse. Moreover, iNat-Loc500 has a consistent label hierarchy which serves as a reliable proxy for

---

[1] https://github.com/visipedia/inat_loc/.

label granularity. We now discuss the importance of each of these properties and contrast iNatLoc500 with existing WSOL datasets.

Fine-Grained Categories. Each category in iNatLoc500 corresponds to a different species, and the differences between species can be so subtle as to require expert-level knowledge [51]. While there are challenging images in ImageNet and OpenImages30k, most of the categories are coarse-grained i.e. relatively few pairs of categories are highly visually similar. For instance, the reptile categories in OpenImages30k (`lizard`, `snake`, `frog`, `crocodile`) are typically easy to distinguish. In iNatLoc-500 there are 107 reptile species, some of which are highly similar (e.g. `Chihuahuan spotted whiptail` vs. `Common spotted whiptail`).

Consistent Label Hierarchy. The label hierarchy for iNatLoc500 consists of the following seven tiers, ordered from coarsest to finest: kingdom, phylum, class, order, family, genus, and species. All of the species in iNatLoc500 are animals, so the "kingdom" tier only has one node (`Animalia`), which is the root node of the label hierarchy. Every species lies at the same distance from the root. The iNatLoc500 label hierarchy is *consistent* in the sense that all nodes at a given level of the hierarchy correspond to concepts with similar levels of specificity. This means that depth in the label hierarchy measures label granularity. The label hierarchy for CUB is also consistent. However, the taxonomies that underlie ImageNet and OpenImages30k are considerably more arbitrary. For instance, in OpenImages30k some categories are far from the root of the label hierarchy (e.g. `entity/vehicle/land_vehicle/car/limousine` or `entity/animal/mammal/carnivore/fox`) while others are close to the root (e.g. `entity/bicycle_wheel` or `entity/human_ear`) despite the fact that there is no obvious difference in concept specificity.

Unambiguous Label Semantics. The categories in iNatLoc500 are well-defined in the sense that (for most species) there is little room for debate about what "counts" as an instance of that species. While the distinctions between species can be quite subtle, each species is a well-defined category. CUB shares this advantage for the most part, but ImageNet and OpenImages30k do not. For instance, OpenImages30k contains the categories `wine` and `bottle`. To which category does a bottle of wine belong? (In fact, we find bottles of wine in both categories.) ImageNet is known to have similar issues with ambiguous and overlapping category definitions [4].

Visual Diversity. Like ImageNet and OpenImages30k, iNatLoc500 has a category set which exhibits a high degree of visual diversity. CUB is much more homogeneous, consisting of only birds. Combined with its consistent label hierarchy, the visual diversity of iNatLoc500 enables future work on e.g. how localization ability generalizes across categories as a function of taxonomic distance.

Large Scale. iNatLoc500 is a large-scale dataset, both in terms of the number of categories and the number of training images. CUB and OpenImages30k are considerably smaller on both counts. Large training sets are valuable because they simplify supervised learning. Large training sets also enable research on self-supervised representation learning, which has received little attention thus far in WSOL. We provide a summary of the key dataset statistics in Table 1.

5   Experiments

In this section we present WSOL results on iNatLoc500 as well as existing benchmark datasets. We also consider few-shot learning baselines based on segmentation and detection architectures. Finally, we use the unique properties of iNatLoc500 to study how label granularity affects localization performance and data efficiency. A summary of the different WSOL datasets can be found in Table 1.

5.1   Implementation Details

Performance Metrics. All WSOL performance numbers in this paper are MaxBoxAccV2, which is defined in [12]. The only exceptions are the results for OpenImages30k in Table 2, which are given in PxAP as defined in [12].

Fixed-Granularity Training. In Sect. 5.3 we probe the effect of granularity on WSOL by training on "coarsened" versions of D_w. In the notation of Sect. 3.2, these can be written $D_w^{k \cdot 1}$ for $k = 1, 2, \ldots$, where 1 denotes the "all ones" vector. This corresponds to merging all leaves with their parent k times. We then run the entire WSOL pipeline from scratch to compute $E(D_{\text{test}}|D_w^{k \cdot 1})$ for each k. To the best of our knowledge this is compatible with all existing WSOL methods.

Fixed-Granularity CAM Aggregation. We also consider a second method for using label hierarchy information to improve WSOL, inspired by [27]. Just like traditional CAM, the first step is to train an image classifier using the standard (most fine-grained) label set. However, instead of returning only the CAM for the species labeled in the input image, we return a CAM for each species in the same genus/family/.../phylum and average them. This "aggregated" CAM is then evaluated as normal. We abbreviate this method as CAM-Agg.

Hyperparameter Search for WSOL Methods. Each time we train a WSOL method we re-tune the learning rate over the set $\{10^{-1}, 10^{-2}, 10^{-3}, 10^{-4}, 10^{-5}\}$ and choose the one that leads to the best MaxBoxAccV2 performance on the fully supervised validation set D_f. We then report the MaxBoxAccV2 performance for the selected model on D_{test}. We leave all other hyperparameters fixed. Full training details can be found in the supplementary material.

Non-WSOL Methods. We provide results for the baselines proposed in [12] (Center, FSL-Seg), as well as a new few-shot detection baseline (FSL-Det). "Center" is a naive baseline that simply assumes a centered Gaussian activation map for all images. "FSL-Seg" is a supervised baseline that is trained on the D_f split of each dataset. The architecture is based on models for saliency mask prediction [33]. Finally, we introduce "FSL-Det", a few-shot detection baseline for WSOL that is also trained on D_f. It uses Faster-RCNN [39] with the same backbone as other methods (i.e. ImageNet-pretrained ResNet-50 [23]). Full implementation details can be found in the supplementary material.

5.2   Baseline Results

We follow [12] and evaluate six recent WSOL methods and two non-WSOL methods (Center and FSL-Seg) on iNatLoc500. The results can be found in Table 2.

Table 2. Comparison of WSOL methods. Numbers are `MaxBoxAccV2` for ImageNet, CUB, and iNatLoc500 and `PxAP` for OpenImages30k. All results use an ImageNet-pretrained ResNet-50 [23] backbone with an input resolution of 224 × 224. WSOL numbers for ImageNet, CUB, and OpenImages30k are the updated results from [11]. WSOL numbers for iNatLoc500 are our own, as are the numbers for the baselines (Center, FSL-Seg, FSL-Det). FSL baselines use 10 images/class for ImageNet, 5 images/class for CUB, 25 images/class for OpenImages30k, and 25 images/class for iNatLoc500. We do not report FSL-Det for OpenImages30k because the evaluation protocol for that dataset requires segmentation masks.

Method	ImageNet	CUB	OpenImages30k	iNatLoc500
CAM [63]	63.7	63.0	58.5	60.2
HaS [45]	63.4	64.7	55.9	60.0
ACoL [61]	62.3	66.5	57.3	55.3
SPG [62]	63.3	60.4	56.7	60.7
ADL [13]	63.7	58.4	55.2	58.9
CutMix [58]	63.3	62.8	57.7	60.1
Center	53.4	56.8	46.0	42.8
FSL-Seg	68.7	89.4	75.2	78.6
FSL-Det	70.4	95.4	–	83.6

We focus our observations on ImageNet, CUB, and iNatLoc500 since OpenImages30k is evaluated using a different task and evaluation metric. We first note that our findings on iNatLoc500 reinforce the main results from [12], namely that (a) none of the WSOL methods performs substantially better than CAM and (b) FSL-Seg significantly outperforms all WSOL methods. Second, if we consider the performance gap between CAM and the Center baseline, we see that simple centered boxes are not as successful on iNatLoc500 (-17.2 `MaxBoxAccV2`) as they are on CUB (-6.2 `MaxBoxAccV2`) and ImageNet (-10.3 `MaxBoxAccV2`). This indicates that iNatLoc500 is a more challenging dataset for benchmarking WSOL. Finally, we provide results for our few-shot detection baseline (FSL-Det). For ImageNet, CUB, and iNatLoc500 we find that FSL-Det is a stronger baseline than FSL-Seg. Like FSL-Seg, FSL-Det directly trains on the boxes in D_f, whereas the WSOL methods only use those boxes to tune their hyperparameters. However, FSL-Det sets a new ceiling for localization performance on these datasets, indicating that current WSOL methods have considerable room for improvement.

5.3   Label Granularity and Localization Performance

iNatLoc500 is equipped with a consistent label hierarchy which allows us to directly study the relationship between label granularity and localization performance. The traditional approach to WSOL on iNatLoc500 would begin by training a classifier on the *species-level* labels, i.e. the finest level in the label hierarchy. However, our hypothesis is that training at the most fine-grained level may not lead to the best localization performance. To study this, we use the fixed-granularity training method discussed in Sect. 5.1. In particular, we "re-label" D_w at each level of the label hierarchy using successively coarser categories. We then use each of these re-labeled datasets to train and evaluate different WSOL methods. The results in Fig. 3(left) show that coarsening the labels of D_w can significantly boost WSOL performance (e.g. up to +5.1 `MaxBoxAccV2` for CAM). The numerical values plotted in Fig. 3(left) can be found in the supplementary materials. Note that it would be difficult to draw similar conclusions by studying ImageNet or OpenImages30k because their label hierarchies do not measure how fine-grained different categories are – see Sect. 4.2 for a discussion. Our conceptually simple coarsening approach results in large performance improvements across five different WSOL methods, without any modifications to the model architectures or training losses.

Coarse Training Beyond iNatLoc500. Figure 3(left) shows that coarse training significantly improves WSOL performance on iNatLoc500. We study the effect of coarse training on FGVC-Aircraft [31], CUB [52], and ImageNet [16] in the supplementary material. As expected, FGVC-Aircraft and CUB (which have consistent label hierarchies) both benefit from coarse training while ImageNet (which lacks a consistent label hierarchy) does not.

Localization Performance vs. Classification Performance. In Fig. 3(right) we show the image classification performance for each WSOL method in Fig. 3(left) at each granularity level. We see that classification performance and WSOL performance are not necessarily correlated. WSOL performance increases before decreasing at the coarsest level of granularity. Classification performance increases with label coarsening, even at the coarsest level of granularity.

An Alternative Method for Incorporating Label Granularity. We also present the performance of CAM-Agg, an alternative method for incorporating granularity information in WSOL (see Sect. 5.1). In our experiments, CAM-Agg underperforms vanilla CAM at every granularity level. As a point of comparison, [27] finds that CAM-Agg is better than CAM for CUB but worse than CAM for ImageNet. Our findings suggest that training the model with coarse categories leads to much better localization performance when compared to aggregating the localization outputs for multiple similar fine-grained categories.

5.4   Label Granularity and Data Efficiency

Most WSOL work makes D_w as large as possible by default, so there has been little attention paid to how the size of D_w trades off against localization performance. In this section we analyze the performance of CAM-based WSOL as a function of the size of D_w. We are particularly interested in how label granularity interacts with data efficiency. To study this question, we first pick a granularity level and generate subsampled versions of D_w by choosing, uniformly at random, 50, 100, or 200 images from each category. Note that the size of each subsampled version of D_w depends on the granularity level. For instance, if the categories are the 317 genera, then 50 images per category is $50 \times 317 = 15,850$, compared to $50 \times 61 = 3,050$ images if the categories are the 61 orders. We present

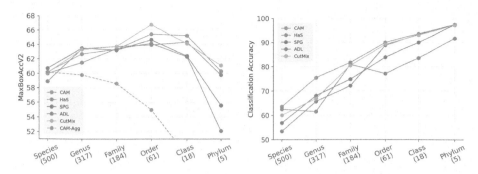

Fig. 3. Effect of label granularity of D_w on WSOL performance (left) and classification accuracy (right) for iNatLoc500. The number of categories at each tier is given in parentheses. **(Left)** Localization performance suffers when the category labels are either too fine (e.g. Species) or too coarse (e.g. Phylum). The results on the very left of the plot are the same as those in Table 2. Note that ACoL is excluded due to poor performance – we suspect it requires more epochs of training than the standard protocol allows for iNatLoc500. We also show results for CAM-Agg (Sect. 5.1), an alternative method for aggregating hierarchy information in WSOL. **(Right)** Each WSOL method trains the image classifier in a different way, but classification accuracy generally increases as the labels become more coarse. Naturally it is easier to distinguish between coarser categories, but it is interesting to note that classification performance is excellent at the phylum level, despite poor localization performance.

WSOL results for four granularity levels in Fig. 4. We find that by training at a coarser level, we can obtain better performance with fewer labels. All of the square markers above the dashed line in Fig. 4 correspond to cases where we can achieve better performance than the standard species level CAM approach using fewer labels. To take one example, by training at the family level we can match the performance of the standard CAM approach by training with 50 images per family (9200 images), a training set reduction of ∼15×.

6   Discussion

Why Does Performance Increase as We Coarsen the Labels? In Fig. 3(left) we see that five different WSOL algorithms perform better as we coarsen the labels in D_w, up until the coarsest level when performance drops. What accounts for this behavior? Our analysis of CAM in Fig. 5 provides some clues. Fig. 5(left) shows that the area of the predicted box tends to be larger than the area of the ground truth box, and that their ratio *decreases* towards unity as we coarsen the labels (black curve). That is, the predicted box size gets closer to the true box size as we coarsen the labels. This casts doubt on a common intuition (which as far as we know has not been empirically investigated before now) that WSOL methods predict smaller boxes for more fine-grained categories [27].

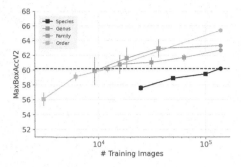

Fig. 4. Effect of the number of training images (N_w) on CAM performance for iNat-Loc500. The dashed line corresponds to the performance of species-level CAM with the entirety of D_w. Each color corresponds to a different label granularity for D_w. Circles at the right of the graph indicate performance using all of D_w. Squares represent subsampled datasets which use a fixed number of images per category: 50, 100, or 200. All squares have error bars indicating the standard deviation over 5 runs with different randomly sampled subsets of D_w. (Color figure online)

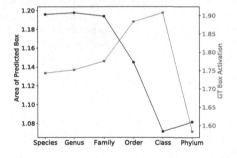
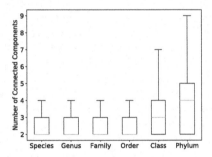

Fig. 5. Analysis of CAM-based WSOL on the D_f split of iNatLoc500. **(Left)** *Black*: Ratio of the area of the predicted box to the area of the ground truth box. *Red*: Ratio of the activation inside the ground truth box to the activation of background pixels. Both curves show medians over the 12.5k images in D_f at each granularity level. **(Right)** Number of connected components in the binarized activation maps at each granularity level. Each box plot shows the distribution over the 12.5k images in D_f. See the supplementary material for full details on the construction of these plots. (Color figure online)

Why Does Performance Drop at the Coarsest Level of Granularity? In Fig. 5(left) we see that as we coarsen the labels the concentration of *activation* in the ground truth box *increases* before collapsing at the coarsest level (red curve). Figure 5(right) shows that the activation maps become highly fragmented at coarser levels. Taken together, these two findings suggest that at the coarsest level the activation maps tend to focus more on global image characteristics (e.g. land vs. water) than the properties of the foreground object. Note that these features are still useful for image classification, as is shown in Fig. 3(right).

Limitations. The iNatLoc500 dataset has several limitations. First, it contains only animal categories. These categories are highly diverse, but they are not representative of all visual domains. Second, it is possible that there are errors in the image-level labels provided by the iNaturalist community, though this is expected to be rare as each image has been labeled by multiple people [50]. Third, many real fine-grained problems have a long-tailed class distribution but, like other localization datasets, iNatLoc500 is approximately balanced (at the species level). Finally, there is a conceptual limitation in our experiments: the use of a single granularity level across the entire dataset. In fact, it is likely that different images are best treated at different granularity levels. Our work does not address this important topic which we leave for future work.

iNatLoc500 Can Be Used to Investigate Numerous Research Agendas Beyond Traditional WSOL. For example, D_w was designed to be large enough for self-supervised learning, which has received surprisingly little attention in the WSOL community [9]. We are also interested in using iNatLoc500 to study whether self-supervised learning methods can be improved by using WSOL methods to select crops [38], especially in the context of fine-grained data [15]. For the object detection community, the clean boxes in iNatLoc500 can (i) serve as a test set for object detectors trained on the noisy iNat17 boxes, (ii) be used to study the problem of learning multi-instance detectors from one box per image, and (iii) be used to analyze the role of label granularity in object detection. Finally, we have seen that hierarchical reasoning can significantly improve localization performance. In the future, we aim to explore methods for automatically determining the most appropriate level of coarseness required for generating representations that best encode object location.

7 Conclusion

We have shown that substantial improvements in WSOL performance can be achieved by modulating the granularity of the training labels, and that coarser-grained training leads to more data-efficient WSOL. We also presented iNatLoc500, a new large-scale fine-grained dataset for WSOL. Despite the gains in performance from coarse-level training, iNatLoc500 remains a challenging localization task which we hope will motivate additional progress in WSOL.

Acknowledgements. We thank the iNaturalist community for sharing images and species annotations. This work was supported by the Caltech Resnick Sustainability Institute, an NSF Graduate Research Fellowship (grant number DGE1745301), and the Pioneer Centre for AI (DNRF grant number P1).

References

1. iNaturalist. www.inaturalist.org. Accessed 7 Mar 2022
2. Bae, W., Noh, J., Kim, G.: Rethinking class activation mapping for weakly supervised object localization. In: Vedaldi, A., Bischof, H., Brox, T., Frahm, J.-M. (eds.) ECCV 2020. LNCS, vol. 12360, pp. 618–634. Springer, Cham (2020). https://doi.org/10.1007/978-3-030-58555-6_37

3. Benenson, R., Popov, S., Ferrari, V.: Large-scale interactive object segmentation with human annotators. In: CVPR (2019)
4. Beyer, L., Hénaff, O.J., Kolesnikov, A., Zhai, X., van den Oord, A.: Are we done with ImageNet? arXiv:2006.07159 (2020)
5. Bilal, A., Jourabloo, A., Ye, M., Liu, X., Ren, L.: Do convolutional neural networks learn class hierarchy? IEEE Trans. Visual Comput. Graphics **24**(1), 152–162 (2017)
6. Bilen, H., Pedersoli, M., Tuytelaars, T.: Weakly supervised object detection with convex clustering. In: CVPR (2015)
7. Bilen, H., Vedaldi, A.: Weakly supervised deep detection networks. In: CVPR (2016)
8. Borenstein, E., Ullman, S.: Class-specific, top-down segmentation. In: Heyden, A., Sparr, G., Nielsen, M., Johansen, P. (eds.) ECCV 2002. LNCS, vol. 2351, pp. 109–122. Springer, Heidelberg (2002). https://doi.org/10.1007/3-540-47967-8_8
9. Caron, M., et al.: Emerging properties in self-supervised vision transformers. In: ICCV (2021)
10. Chattopadhay, A., Sarkar, A., Howlader, P., Balasubramanian, V.N.: Grad-CAM++: generalized gradient-based visual explanations for deep convolutional networks. In: WACV (2018)
11. Choe, J., Oh, S.J., Chun, S., Akata, Z., Shim, H.: Evaluation for weakly supervised object localization: protocol, metrics, and datasets. arXiv:2007.04178 (2020)
12. Choe, J., Oh, S.J., Lee, S., Chun, S., Akata, Z., Shim, H.: Evaluating weakly supervised object localization methods right. In: CVPR (2020)
13. Choe, J., Shim, H.: Attention-based dropout layer for weakly supervised object localization. In: CVPR (2019)
14. Choi, Y., et al.: EdNet: a large-scale hierarchical dataset in education. In: Bittencourt, I.I., Cukurova, M., Muldner, K., Luckin, R., Millán, E. (eds.) AIED 2020. LNCS (LNAI), vol. 12164, pp. 69–73. Springer, Cham (2020). https://doi.org/10.1007/978-3-030-52240-7_13
15. Cole, E., Yang, X., Wilber, K., Mac Aodha, O., Belongie, S.: When does contrastive visual representation learning work? In: CVPR (2022)
16. Deng, J., Dong, W., Socher, R., Li, L.J., Li, K., Fei-Fei, L.: ImageNet: a large-scale hierarchical image database. In: CVPR (2009)
17. Everingham, M., Van Gool, L., Williams, C.K., Winn, J., Zisserman, A.: The pascal visual object classes (VOC) challenge. IJCV **88**, 303–338 (2010)
18. Fergus, R., Perona, P., Zisserman, A.: Object class recognition by unsupervised scale-invariant learning. In: CVPR (2003)
19. Galleguillos, C., Babenko, B., Rabinovich, A., Belongie, S.: Weakly supervised object localization with stable segmentations. In: Forsyth, D., Torr, P., Zisserman, A. (eds.) ECCV 2008. LNCS, vol. 5302, pp. 193–207. Springer, Heidelberg (2008). https://doi.org/10.1007/978-3-540-88682-2_16
20. van Gemert, J.C., Verschoor, C.R., Mettes, P., Epema, K., Koh, L.P., Wich, S.: Nature conservation drones for automatic localization and counting of animals. In: Agapito, L., Bronstein, M.M., Rother, C. (eds.) ECCV 2014. LNCS, vol. 8925, pp. 255–270. Springer, Cham (2015). https://doi.org/10.1007/978-3-319-16178-5_17
21. Gokberk Cinbis, R., Verbeek, J., Schmid, C.: Multi-fold mil training for weakly supervised object localization. In: CVPR (2014)
22. Guo, S., et al.: The iMaterialist fashion attribute dataset. In: Proceedings of the IEEE/CVF International Conference on Computer Vision Workshops, p. 0 (2019)
23. He, K., Zhang, X., Ren, S., Sun, J.: Deep residual learning for image recognition. In: CVPR (2016)

24. Jung, H., Oh, Y.: Towards better explanations of class activation mapping. In: ICCV (2021)
25. Khan, M.H., et al.: AnimalWeb: a large-scale hierarchical dataset of annotated animal faces. In: Proceedings of the IEEE/CVF Conference on Computer Vision and Pattern Recognition, pp. 6939–6948 (2020)
26. Ki, M., Uh, Y., Lee, W., Byun, H.: In-sample contrastive learning and consistent attention for weakly supervised object localization. In: ACCV (2020)
27. Kim, J.M., Choe, J., Akata, Z., Oh, S.J.: Keep calm and improve visual feature attribution. In: ICCV (2021)
28. Kim, J., Choe, J., Yun, S., Kwak, N.: Normalization matters in weakly supervised object localization. In: ICCV (2021)
29. Kuznetsova, A., et al.: The open images dataset V4. IJCV **128**, 1956–1981 (2020)
30. Li, Z., Dong, M., Wen, S., Hu, X., Zhou, P., Zeng, Z.: CLU-CNNs: object detection for medical images. Neurocomputing **350**, 53–59 (2019)
31. Maji, S., Kannala, J., Rahtu, E., Blaschko, M., Vedaldi, A.: Fine-grained visual classification of aircraft. Technical report (2013)
32. Nguyen, M.H., Torresani, L., De La Torre, F., Rother, C.: Weakly supervised discriminative localization and classification: a joint learning process. In: ICCV (2009)
33. Oh, S.J., Benenson, R., Khoreva, A., Akata, Z., Fritz, M., Schiele, B.: Exploiting saliency for object segmentation from image level labels. In: CVPR (2017)
34. Opelt, A., Pinz, A.: Object localization with boosting and weak supervision for generic object recognition. In: Kalviainen, H., Parkkinen, J., Kaarna, A. (eds.) SCIA 2005. LNCS, vol. 3540, pp. 862–871. Springer, Heidelberg (2005). https://doi.org/10.1007/11499145_87
35. Oquab, M., Bottou, L., Laptev, I., Sivic, J.: Is object localization for free?-Weakly-supervised learning with convolutional neural networks. In: CVPR (2015)
36. Pandey, M., Lazebnik, S.: Scene recognition and weakly supervised object localization with deformable part-based models. In: ICCV (2011)
37. Papadopoulos, D.P., Uijlings, J.R., Keller, F., Ferrari, V.: Extreme clicking for efficient object annotation. In: ICCV (2017)
38. Peng, X., Wang, K., Zhu, Z., Wang, M., You, Y.: Crafting better contrastive views for Siamese representation learning. In: Proceedings of the IEEE/CVF Conference on Computer Vision and Pattern Recognition, pp. 16031–16040 (2022)
39. Ren, S., He, K., Girshick, R., Sun, J.: Faster R-CNN: towards real-time object detection with region proposal networks. In: NeurIPS (2015)
40. Robinson, J., Jegelka, S., Sra, S.: Strength from weakness: fast learning using weak supervision. In: ICML (2020)
41. Russakovsky, O., et al.: ImageNet large scale visual recognition challenge. IJCV **115**, 211–252 (2015)
42. Sariyildiz, M.B., Kalantidis, Y., Larlus, D., Alahari, K.: Concept generalization in visual representation learning. In: ICCV (2021)
43. Selvaraju, R.R., Cogswell, M., Das, A., Vedantam, R., Parikh, D., Batra, D.: Grad-CAM: visual explanations from deep networks via gradient-based localization. In: ICCV (2017)
44. Shao, D., Zhao, Y., Dai, B., Lin, D.: FineGym: a hierarchical video dataset for fine-grained action understanding. In: Proceedings of the IEEE/CVF Conference on Computer Vision and Pattern Recognition, pp. 2616–2625 (2020)
45. Singh, K.K., Lee, Y.J.: Hide-and-seek: forcing a network to be meticulous for weakly-supervised object and action localization. In: ICCV (2017)
46. Taherkhani, F., Kazemi, H., Dabouei, A., Dawson, J., Nasrabadi, N.M.: A weakly supervised fine label classifier enhanced by coarse supervision. In: ICCV (2019)

47. Tang, P., Wang, X., Bai, X., Liu, W.: Multiple instance detection network with online instance classifier refinement. In: CVPR (2017)
48. Touvron, H., Sablayrolles, A., Douze, M., Cord, M., Jégou, H.: Grafit: learning fine-grained image representations with coarse labels. In: ICCV (2021)
49. Uijlings, J., Popov, S., Ferrari, V.: Revisiting knowledge transfer for training object class detectors. In: CVPR (2018)
50. Van Horn, G., Cole, E., Beery, S., Wilber, K., Belongie, S., Mac Aodha, O.: Benchmarking representation learning for natural world image collections. In: CVPR (2021)
51. Van Horn, G., et al.: The iNaturalist species classification and detection dataset. In: CVPR (2018)
52. Wah, C., Branson, S., Welinder, P., Perona, P., Belongie, S.: The Caltech-UCSD Birds-200-2011 Dataset. Technical report, CNS-TR-2011-001. California Institute of Technology (2011)
53. Wang, R., Mahajan, D., Ramanathan, V.: What leads to generalization of object proposals? In: Bartoli, A., Fusiello, A. (eds.) ECCV 2020. LNCS, vol. 12536, pp. 464–478. Springer, Cham (2020). https://doi.org/10.1007/978-3-030-66096-3_32
54. Wei, X.S., et al.: Fine-grained image analysis with deep learning: a survey. PAMI **PP**, 1 (2021)
55. Wu, B., Iandola, F., Jin, P.H., Keutzer, K.: SqueezeDet: unified, small, low power fully convolutional neural networks for real-time object detection for autonomous driving. In: CVPR Workshops (2017)
56. Xu, Y., Qian, Q., Li, H., Jin, R., Hu, J.: Weakly supervised representation learning with coarse labels. In: ICCV (2021)
57. Yang, H., Wu, H., Chen, H.: Detecting 11K classes: large scale object detection without fine-grained bounding boxes. In: ICCV (2019)
58. Yun, S., Han, D., Oh, S.J., Chun, S., Choe, J., Yoo, Y.: CutMix: regularization strategy to train strong classifiers with localizable features. In: ICCV (2019)
59. Zeiler, M.D., Fergus, R.: Visualizing and understanding convolutional networks. In: Fleet, D., Pajdla, T., Schiele, B., Tuytelaars, T. (eds.) ECCV 2014. LNCS, vol. 8689, pp. 818–833. Springer, Cham (2014). https://doi.org/10.1007/978-3-319-10590-1_53
60. Zhang, D., Han, J., Cheng, G., Yang, M.H.: Weakly supervised object localization and detection: a survey. PAMI **44**, 5866–5885 (2021)
61. Zhang, X., Wei, Y., Feng, J., Yang, Y., Huang, T.S.: Adversarial complementary learning for weakly supervised object localization. In: CVPR (2018)
62. Zhang, X., Wei, Y., Kang, G., Yang, Y., Huang, T.: Self-produced guidance for weakly-supervised object localization. In: Ferrari, V., Hebert, M., Sminchisescu, C., Weiss, Y. (eds.) ECCV 2018. LNCS, vol. 11216, pp. 610–625. Springer, Cham (2018). https://doi.org/10.1007/978-3-030-01258-8_37
63. Zhou, B., Khosla, A., Lapedriza, A., Oliva, A., Torralba, A.: Learning deep features for discriminative localization. In: CVPR (2016)

OIMNet++: Prototypical Normalization and Localization-Aware Learning for Person Search

Sanghoon Lee[1], Youngmin Oh[1], Donghyeon Baek[1], Junghyup Lee[1], and Bumsub Ham[1,2(✉)]

[1] Yonsei University, Seoul, South Korea
bumsub.ham@yonsei.ac.kr
[2] Korea Institute of Science and Technology (KIST), Seoul, South Korea
https://cvlab.yonsei.ac.kr/projects/OIMNetPlus

Abstract. We address the task of person search, that is, localizing and re-identifying query persons from a set of raw scene images. Recent approaches are typically built upon OIMNet, a pioneer work on person search, that learns joint person representations for performing both detection and person re-identification (reID) tasks. To obtain the representations, they extract features from pedestrian proposals, and then project them on a unit hypersphere with L2 normalization. These methods also incorporate all positive proposals, that sufficiently overlap with the ground truth, equally to learn person representations for reID. We have found that 1) the L2 normalization without considering feature distributions degenerates the discriminative power of person representations, and 2) positive proposals often also depict background clutter and person overlaps, which could encode noisy features to person representations. In this paper, we introduce OIMNet++ that addresses the aforementioned limitations. To this end, we introduce a novel normalization layer, dubbed ProtoNorm, that calibrates features from pedestrian proposals, while considering a long-tail distribution of person IDs, enabling L2 normalized person representations to be discriminative. We also propose a localization-aware feature learning scheme that encourages better-aligned proposals to contribute more in learning discriminative representations. Experimental results and analysis on standard person search benchmarks demonstrate the effectiveness of OIMNet++.

1 Introduction

Person search aims at jointly localizing and re-identifying a query person from a set of raw scene images [36,42]. Different from person re-identification (reID) [39, 41], person search incorporates pedestrian detection in a unified framework, facilitating retrieving query persons without hand-labelled [22] or auto-detected [18, 40] pedestrian bounding boxes during inference. This provides a wide range of

---

Supplementary Information The online version contains supplementary material available at https://doi.org/10.1007/978-3-031-20080-9_36.

applications, particularly where the bounding boxes are expensive to obtain, including large-scale surveillance and pedestrian analysis. Person search is extremely challenging, since it inherits problems from both pedestrian detection (*e.g.*, background clutter and scale variations) and person reID (*e.g.*, large intra-class variations).

Recent approaches to person search focus on extracting person representations that are eligible to handle both detection and reID tasks [3,7,16,37]. They typically build on top of OIMNet [36], a pioneer work on person search. OIMNet and its variants leverage a 2D object detection framework [28], and obtain person features from pedestrian proposals. The obtained feature representations are further projected onto a unit hypersphere by applying L2 normalization. These approaches also leverage the OIM loss [36] that employs a lookup table (LUT) consisting of features that describe each ID in a training set, and exploits them as supervisory signals to guide learning discriminative features. While these methods have allowed significant advances for person search, there are two main limitations. First, L2 normalization is effective only when the person representations are roughly centered around zero. Moreover, the person representations are encouraged to have similar variances (*e.g.*, unit variance) across channel dimensions over a whole training set. This is because it promotes each channel to contribute equally in determining a decision boundary, while preventing a small set of channels from dominating the decision boundary. Current person search methods implicitly assume that features obtained from pedestrian proposals have zero-mean and unit variance, *i.e.*, standardized. Accordingly, they project the features onto a unit hypersphere using L2 normalization, without explicit constraints, which rather degenerates the discriminative power of person representations (Fig. 1(b)). A standard way of alleviating this problem is to *shift and scaling* the feature distribution using BatchNorm [14]. However, we have observed that the standardization using BatchNorm is not able to offer satisfactory results. This is mainly due to the extreme class imbalance across person IDs, which is largely inevitable in training person search networks. Specifically, human trajectory patterns are highly diverse across person IDs, and the extent of a person's exposure to cameras in public is difficult to model [6]. Person search datasets obtained from real-world environments thus contain person images whose ID labels are extremely imbalanced, forming a long-tail distribution across person IDs. As BatchNorm calibrates the feature distribution with input features directly, it is easily biased towards dominant IDs. This restrains the discriminative power of features on a unit hypersphere (Fig. 1(c)). Second, the OIM loss updates each feature in the LUT using an exponential moving average with a fixed momentum. Each object proposal contributes equally when updating the corresponding feature in the LUT, regardless of the localization accuracy w.r.t the ground truth. This is suboptimal in that not all object proposals are equally discriminative, as they are often misaligned during training. Namely, the OIM loss ignores the fact that reID relies on detection during training; better localized object proposals could contribute more to learning discriminative features for reID.

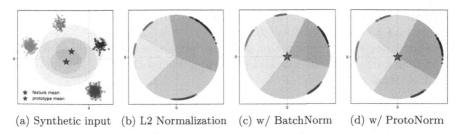

(a) Synthetic input   (b) L2 Normalization   (c) w/ BatchNorm   (d) w/ ProtoNorm

Fig. 1. We visualize in (a) synthetic 2D features in circles, where each color represents an ID label. We represent mean obtained from input features and ID prototypes with stars colored in red and yellow, respectively. Note that pink and green features are sampled 4× more. The features are clearly not zero-centered with unit variance. In this case, simply applying L2 normalization degenerates the discriminative power, as shown in (b), where background colors indicate decision boundaries. Adopting a feature standardization with feature mean and variance, *i.e.*, in a BatchNorm-fashion, prior to L2 normalization, alleviates this problem in (c). However, this does not consider a sample distribution across IDs to calibrate the feature distribution. The distribution is thus biased towards majority IDs, which weakens the inter-class separability. Instead, calibrating feature distribution using ID prototypes with ProtoNorm provides highly discriminative L2-normalized features in (d), where each ID is assigned similar angular space. (Best viewed by zooming in with color.) (Color figure online)

In this paper, we present a simple but highly effective approach to person search, dubbed OIMNet++, built upon OIMNet [36]. We introduce two modifications of OIMNet that offer significant performance gains over the vanilla one. First, we propose a novel normalization layer, ProtoNorm, to obtain discriminative person representations on a hypersphere. ProtoNorm exploits prototypical features for individual person IDs to calibrate feature distributions, such that the distributions are less biased towards dominant IDs (Fig. 1(d)). This enhances the intra-class compactness for majority IDs, as well as the inter-class separability for minority ones. Second, we propose a localization-aware OIM loss (LOIM) that adaptively updates each feature in the LUT w.r.t the localization accuracy of each object proposal during training. As better localized object bounding boxes translate to less noisy features, *e.g.*, with less background clutter and person overlaps, we encourage better-aligned proposals to incorporate more to construct the LUT. In this way, we can train a network with more discriminative features as guidance. By employing ProtoNorm and the LOIM loss to a vanilla OIMNet [36], we establish OIMNet++, setting a new state of the art on standard benchmarks for person search, including CUHK-SYSU [36] and PRW [42]. The main contributions of our work can be summarized as follows:

- We introduce a simple yet effective normalization layer, ProtoNorm, to learn discriminative person representations for person search. ProtoNorm alleviates the class imbalance problem in person search, while retaining the effectiveness of BatchNorm.
- We propose a novel LOIM loss that assigns larger degree of update to better aligned object proposals. This allows to compose the LUT with less noisy

features, better guiding the discriminative feature learning for person search, compared with the OIM loss [36].

- We set a new state of the art on standard person search benchmarks [36,42] and demonstrate the effectiveness of our approach with extensive experiments and ablation studies.

2   Related Work

2.1   Person Search

Many approaches attempt to decompose person search into pedestrian detection and person reID tasks. Current person search methods can be categorized into two groups. The first line of works [2,8,10,17] design a two-step method that performs pedestrian detection to obtain cropped person images, which are then sequentially fed into a person reID network to extract person representations. These methods further employ auxiliary modules to enhance the discriminative power of person representations. For example, they exploit an off-the-shelf instance segmentation network [20] to focus more on foreground regions [2], design a multi-layer feature aggregation module [17], or take a query image as an additional input with a siamese network [8]. While these methods have achieved remarkable performances for person search, they require a heavy computational cost, due to the separate feature extractors, and prohibit joint optimization between detection and reID tasks. Another line of works [3,7,16,37] formulate person search as a joint feature learning problem, and optimize person search models with multi-task objectives in an end-to-end manner. Given an input image, they extract joint features for detection and reID tasks, enabling an efficient pipeline. A main challenge in training these models is known to be the contradictory objectives between detection and reID; pedestrian detection tries to extract the commonness across different person IDs, while reID focuses on the uniqueness [2,3]. To address this problem, recent works propose to disentangle person representations into detection- and reID-related features [3], stop gradient flows in certain layers of a network [16], or extract reID features prior to detection [37]. Similar to ours, the work of [16] proposes to adaptively update features in the LUT, while considering the hardest negative example. This, however, still ignores the localization accuracy, when adjusting momentum values for the updates. All the aforementioned person search approaches also ignore the class imbalance problem across person IDs and the corresponding detrimental effect in learning discriminative person representations.

2.2   Feature Normalization

The seminal work of [14] introduces a BatchNorm layer, where intermediate features of deep networks are standardized, followed by applying an affine transform. This improves the generalization capability of a network and stabilizes the training process. BatchNorm has become an indispensable component of modern deep neural networks [12,31]. While many variants have been proposed for

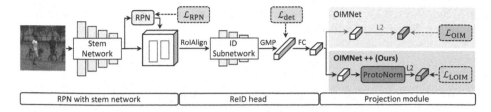

Fig. 2. An overview of OIMNet++. Similar to OIMNet [36], OIMNet++ mainly consists of three parts: An RPN with a stem network, a reID head, and a projection module. The main differences between OIMNet++ (bottom) and OIMNet (top) are the projection module and the training loss. We incorporate a ProtoNorm layer to explicitly standardize features prior to L2 normalization, while considering the class imbalance problem in person search. We also exploit the LOIM loss that leverages localization accuracies of object proposals to learn discriminative features. See text for details.

various applications [1, 13, 19, 30, 32, 34, 35, 38], there are no attempts to leverage normalization methods for person search, to our knowledge. Thus, we mainly describe representative works in the context of person reID, which is closely related to person search.

The work of [25] has shown that adding a BatchNorm layer right before a final classifier boosts performance by a large margin, especially when computing distances with L2 normalized person representations. As will be shown in our experiments, this simple normalization scheme also notably improves the performance of person search methods, establishing a strong baseline. However, we have found that a vanilla BatchNorm might be susceptible to the presence of class imbalance, since statistics are dominated by majority IDs. To address this issue, ProtoNorm incorporates minority IDs to calibrate feature distributions. This standardizes features better than BatchNorm, outperforming the strong baseline. Recently, the works of [4, 15, 44] propose to exploit both InstanceNorm [32] and BatchNorm in order to alleviate the influence of identity-irrelevant features. Although these methods achieve a better generalization ability, especially in a cross-domain setting, they still ignore the class imbalance across person IDs, when calibrating feature distributions. This suggests that our ProtoNorm further boosts the performance in a complementary way, providing more accurate feature distributions for InstanceNorm and BatchNorm. Instead of combining different normalization layers, the work of [45] adopts multiple BatchNorm layers. It computes the mini-batch statistics separately for each camera to reduce the distribution gap across different cameras. Instead of standardizing features for each ID, we exploit a single set of statistics based on prototypical features for individual person IDs for standardization.

3   Method

We show in Fig. 2 an overview of our approach. Following the previous works [3, 7, 16, 43], we build OIMNet++ upon OIMNet [36]. In this section, we briefly review

OIMNet (Sect. 3.1), and provide a detailed description of OIMNet++ (Sect. 3.2), including ProtoNorm and the LOIM loss.

3.1   OIMNet

Network. OIMNet [36] mainly consists of three components: A region proposal network (RPN) with a stem network, a reID head, and a projection module. Given an input image, it employs the RPN to generate pedestrian proposals with feature maps obtained from the stem network. These proposals form candidates to be matched with a query person. While features obtained from a stem network are able to discriminate between persons and background, they are not able to discriminate between person IDs. Thus, OIMNet further employs a reID head, consisting of an identification subnetwork with a global max pooling (GMP) layer, followed by a fully-connected (FC) layer, to refine the features from object proposals. The projection module further projects the features on a unit hypersphere with L2 normalization. At test time, OIMNet computes distances between L2-normalized features for query and gallery persons for matching.

Loss. OIMNet is trained with the following loss:

$$\mathcal{L} = \lambda_{\mathrm{RPN}}\mathcal{L}_{\mathrm{RPN}} + \lambda_{\mathrm{det}}\mathcal{L}_{\mathrm{det}} + \mathcal{L}_{\mathrm{OIM}}, \tag{1}$$

where $\mathcal{L}_{\mathrm{RPN}}$, $\mathcal{L}_{\mathrm{det}}$, and $\mathcal{L}_{\mathrm{OIM}}$ are RPN, detection, and OIM losses, respectively, and λ_{RPN} and λ_{det} are balancing parameters for corresponding terms. The RPN and detection losses consist of binary classification and offset regression terms, for anchors and proposals, respectively. They facilitate OIMNet to perform pedestrian detection.

On the other hand, to learn discriminative person representations for reID, OIMNet employs the OIM loss [36]. It leverages a LUT that stores features representing labelled IDs in a training set. We denote by $\mathbf{v}_l \in \mathbb{R}^D$, $l \in \{1, \cdots, L\}$ an L2-normalized feature within the LUT representing the l-th ID, where L is the number of labelled IDs and D is the channel dimension. Meanwhile, there are also pedestrian instances without corresponding ID labels. These instances form a set of unlabelled IDs that can be regarded as negatives for the labelled ones. The OIM loss also leverages a circular queue to store features obtained from the unlabelled IDs for training. Let us denote by $\mathbf{u}_q \in \mathbb{R}^D$, $q \in \{1, \cdots, Q\}$ an L2-normalized q-th feature within the queue, where Q is the queue size. Given an L2-normalized feature $\mathbf{x}_t \in \mathbb{R}^D$, with the t-th ID label, the OIM loss is formally defined by

$$\mathcal{L}_{\mathrm{OIM}} = \mathbb{E}_{\mathbf{x}}[-\log p_t], \tag{2}$$

where

$$p_t = \frac{\exp(\mathbf{v}_t^\top \mathbf{x}_t / \tau)}{\sum_{i=1}^{L} \exp(\mathbf{v}_i^\top \mathbf{x}_t / \tau) + \sum_{j=1}^{Q} \exp(\mathbf{u}_j^\top \mathbf{x}_t / \tau)}, \tag{3}$$

and τ is a temperature value. Namely, this term encourages an input feature to be embedded near to the corresponding ID feature within the LUT, while being

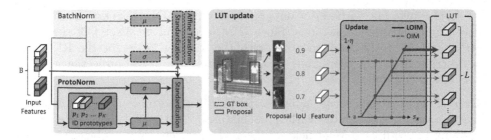

Fig. 3. Left: A comparison between BatchNorm [14] and ProtoNorm. BatchNorm computes feature statistics with input features directly. On the other hand, ProtoNorm aggregates multiple features with the same ID into a single prototype. ProtoNorm then computes mean and variance based on the prototype features, alleviating the bias towards dominant IDs. **Right:** LUT update scheme within the LOIM loss. The vanilla OIM loss assigns equal momentum values for all positive proposals, regardless of the localization qualities. The LOIM loss, instead, assigns an adaptive momentum value to each proposal w.r.t. its IoU with the ground truth. Thicker arrows indicate larger degree of updates to the LUT. See text for details.

distant from negative ones within the LUT and the circular queue. The OIM loss subsequently updates $\mathbf{v}_t$ with a fixed momentum η as follows:

$$\mathbf{v}_t \leftarrow \eta\mathbf{v}_t + (1 - \eta)\mathbf{x}_t. \tag{4}$$

Note that $\mathbf{v}_t$ is L2 normalized after every update. The OIM loss stabilizes a training process, even with a large number of person IDs, and allows to leverage unlabelled IDs for learning discriminative person representations.

3.2 OIMNet++

While OIMNet [36] has allowed significant advances for person search, there are two main limitations. First, performing L2 normalization without considering the feature distribution could be problematic, especially when features are not well standardized. In this case, L2 normalization rather degenerates the discriminative power of the features on a unit hypersphere. Note that we can employ a BatchNorm [14] layer, prior to L2 normalization, that explicitly standardizes features to be zero-centered with a unit variance. As will be shown in our experiments, this improves the performance of OIMNet drastically. However, current person search datasets [36,42] form a long-tail distribution across ID labels, making BatchNorm a suboptimal choice for standardization. This weakens the intra-class compactness for majority IDs and the inter-class separability for minority ones (Fig. 1(c)). Second, during training, the RPN outputs pedestrian proposals that are often misaligned. On the one hand, small misalignments are acceptable, making the reID head robust to misalignment at test time. Large misalignments caused by person overlaps or mis-detections (Fig. 3), on the other hand, distract discriminative feature learning. The OIM loss simply assumes that all proposals could contribute equally to learning discriminative features, and updates the LUT with a fixed momentum, as in (4).

In the following, we describe our approach, dubbed OIMNet++, that addresses the aforementioned limitations. Since OIMNet++ and OIMNet [36] share the RPN and the reID head, together with the training losses for the RPN and pedestrian detection, we mainly describe ProtoNorm in the projection module and the LOIM loss in detail.

ProtoNorm. BatchNorm calibrates feature distributions using channel-wise feature statistics computed with input features directly. This makes the distributions susceptible to frequencies of ID labels, and thus they are biased towards frequent IDs. Instead of directly calibrating the distributions, we propose to exploit mini-batch statistics over prototypical features for individual person IDs. Specifically, to obtain the prototypical feature for a particular ID, we average features for the corresponding ID within a mini-batch. We provide in Fig. 3 an illustration of ProtoNorm and BatchNorm.

Concretely, let us denote a set of features, $\boldsymbol{X} = \{\mathbf{x}^1, \cdots, \mathbf{x}^B\}$, where B is the mini-batch size, along with corresponding set of ID labels $Y = \{y^1, \cdots, y^B\}$, where $y^i \in \{1, \cdots, L\}$. We denote by $\boldsymbol{X}^i(d)$ the d-th channel element within the i-th feature $\mathbf{x}^i$. We first obtain a prototypical feature representing t-th ID, denoted by $\mathbf{p}_t \in \mathbb{R}^D$, as follows:

$$\mathbf{p}_t(d) = \frac{\sum_{b=1}^{B} \boldsymbol{X}^b(d) \mathbb{1}[y^b = t]}{\sum_{b=1}^{B} \mathbb{1}[y^b = t]}, \tag{5}$$

where $\mathbb{1}[\cdot]$ is an indicator function whose value is 1 when the argument is true, and 0 otherwise. With the prototypical features, $\mathbf{p}_t$, in hand, we compute mean and variance vectors of input features $\boldsymbol{X}$, denoted by $\boldsymbol{\mu} \in \mathbb{R}^D$ and $\boldsymbol{\sigma} \in \mathbb{R}^D$, respectively, as follows:

$$\boldsymbol{\mu}(d) = \frac{1}{K} \sum_{k=1}^{K} \mathbf{p}_k(d) \quad \text{and} \quad \boldsymbol{\sigma}(d) = \sqrt{\frac{1}{B} \sum_{b=1}^{B} (\boldsymbol{X}^b(d) - \boldsymbol{\mu}(d))^2}, \tag{6}$$

where K is the number of unique IDs in the set of ID labels Y. We then standardize the features as $\frac{\boldsymbol{X}^b(d) - \boldsymbol{\mu}(d)}{\boldsymbol{\sigma}(d)}$[1]. Instead of using input features directly, exploiting prototypical features in ProtoNorm offers standardization with mean and variance that are less biased towards dominant IDs. ProtoNorm adopts a weighted summation of the input features, where the weight can be represented as $\frac{1}{K \sum_{b=1}^{B} \mathbb{1}[y^b = t]}$ for the t-th ID, and is inversely proportional to an occurrence of an ID. Namely, ProtoNorm adaptively assigns larger weight values to minority ID features, while setting to smaller ones for majority IDs. This steers the mean towards minority IDs, encouraging inter-class separateness for L2-normalized

---

[1] We could apply a learnable affine transform after standardization, similar to Batch-Norm. We have empirically found that affine parameters for scaling and offset converge to constant (but not zero) and zero values, respectively. This suggests that the effect of the affine transform is canceled out by L2 normalization, and thus we omit the transform when ProtoNorm is followed by L2 normalization.

person representations. Note that we may apply the weighting method in an image level to address the class imbalance problem across person IDs, *e.g.*, using a class-balanced mini-batch sampling technique [25]. This is, however, not scalable to person search, as each image depicts different number of person instances.

Similar to BatchNorm, we track running mean and variance during training and exploit them as estimates for a global distribution of prototypical features at test time. This assumes that mean and variance sampled from the global distribution are less biased towards dominant IDs, enables calibrating the feature distribution without ID labels at test time.

LOIM Loss. The OIM loss [36] encourages involving positive proposals, that overlap with a ground truth more than a pre-defined threshold, equally in learning discriminative features. Since not all proposals are equally created, they should contribute to feature learning differently. The features in the LUT should thus be chosen more carefully. Specifically, the LUT should accept discriminative features only for the update, while discarding noisy ones. However, estimating the degree of noise within a feature obtained from a proposal is ambiguous. Previous works [2,43] have relied on an auxiliary supervision obtained from, *e.g.*, an off-the-shelf pose estimator [9], or an instance segmentation network [20]. They are computationally expensive, and require additional datasets for training. Intersection-of-union (IoU) between a proposal and its ground-truth bounding box, on the other hand, serves as a good indicator for estimating extent of noise within the proposal. Namely, a proposal with a large IoU score tightly covers a person-of-interest, with less background clutter and person overlaps. Note that ground-truth bounding boxes are already available in person search datasets, suggesting that leveraging IoU scores does not require additional labelling effort. To implement this idea, we exploit the IoU score of each proposal to update features in the LUT. We assign small momentum values for proposals with large IoU scores, as these proposals are able to provide less noisy features. Let us denote by $s_\mathbf{x} \in [0,1]$ the IoU score between a proposal and its ground-truth bounding box. Concretely, we update the features within the LUT as follows:

$$\mathbf{v}_t \leftarrow (1 - c_\mathbf{x})\mathbf{v}_t + c_\mathbf{x}\mathbf{x}_t, \tag{7}$$

where $c_\mathbf{x}$ computes an adaptive momentum, defined using the IoU score, as follows:

$$c_\mathbf{x} = \mathrm{clip}(s_\mathbf{x}, 0, 1 - \epsilon). \tag{8}$$

$\mathrm{clip}(\cdot, 0, 1 - \epsilon)$ is a clipping function with lower and upper bounds set to 0 and $1 - \epsilon$, respectively, and ϵ is a hyperparameter. We simply set ϵ to 0.1 to prevent perfectly-aligned proposals (*i.e.*, $s_\mathbf{x} = 1$) from totally overriding the corresponding feature after the LUT update. The LOIM loss is defined by $\mathcal{L}_{\mathrm{LOIM}} = \mathbb{E}_\mathbf{x}[-\log p_t]$, whereas $\mathbf{v}_t$ is updated with the adaptive momentum, as in (7). By leveraging IoU scores to define momentum values, noisy features are discouraged to form the LUT, better guiding discriminative feature learning. This also encourages a network to favor extracting better-localized features at test time.

4   Experiments

4.1   Implementation Details

Network. Following the previous works [3,7,16,43], we exploit ResNet50 [12] pretrained on ImageNet [29] as our backbone network. Concretely, we split ResNet50 at `conv4-6` layer, and establish a stem network and an identification subnetwork with preceding and succeeding layers, respectively. We employ RoIAlign [11] to crop 14×14 proposal feature maps obtained from the stem network, and set the channel dimension of person representations, D, to 256, following OIMNet [36]. We leverage the circular queue with size, Q, 5000 and 500 for CUHK-SYSU [36] and PRW [42], respectively. Note that we exploit feature maps obtained from `conv5-3` of ResNet50 only as inputs to the RoIAlign layer, rather than fusing multi-level features in a pyramid fashion [23].

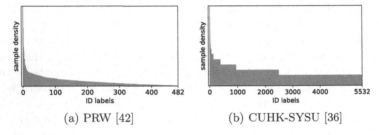

(a) PRW [42]   (b) CUHK-SYSU [36]

Fig. 4. Density of training samples across ID labels in PRW [42] and CUHK-SYSU [36] datasets. Since human trajectory patterns in public are highly diverse across persons [6], person IDs, collected from a real-world environment, are extremely imbalanced, forming a long-tail distribution.

Dataset. We use two standard benchmarks for training and evaluation: 1) The PRW dataset [42] is collected using 6 cameras in a university. It includes $11,816$ images with $4,310$ pedestrian bounding boxes, which are labelled to 932 IDs. We adopt the train/test splits provided by the authors, and use $5,704$ images containing 482 IDs for training. There are $2,057$ query images with 450 different IDs, whereas a gallery set contains $6,112$ images. For each query image, we use the whole gallery set for evaluation. 2) The CUHK-SYSU dataset [36] is collected from urban scenes and movie clips. It is composed of $18,184$ images that contain $96,143$ pedestrian bounding boxes with $8,432$ labelled IDs. We use official train/test splits provided by the authors. Concretely, we use $11,206$ images with $5,532$ IDs for training, $6,978$ gallery images with $2,900$ query person instances for testing. Following the standard protocol [36], we sample 100 gallery images for each query person during evaluation. For both datasets, we adjust input images to the size of $900 \times 1,500$ for training and testing. We visualize in Fig. 4 the distributions for the number of training samples across ID labels.

Training. We use the same training strategy and hyperparameter setting as the ones in [3]. Specifically, we train our model for 20 epochs for both the PRW [42]

Table 1. Quantitative comparison with the state of the art for person search. We report mAP (%) and rank-1 accuracy (%) on CUHK-SYSU [36] and PRW [42] datasets. For each category of person search methods, numbers in bold indicate the best and underscored ones indicate the second best. R50 and DC are abbreviations for ResNet50 [12] and deformable convolution [5], respectively. We report our average scores over 4 runs with standard deviations in parentheses.

	Method	Backbone	CUHK-SYSU [36]		PRW [42]	
			mAP	rank-1	mAP	rank-1
Two-step	MGTS [2]	R50	83.0	83.7	32.6	72.1
	RDLR [10]	R50	93.0	94.2	42.9	70.2
	IGPN [8]	R50	90.3	91.4	**47.2**	87.0
	TCTS [33]	R50	**93.9**	**95.1**	46.8	**87.5**
End-to-end	OIM [36]	R50	75.5	78.7	21.3	49.4
	NPSM [24]	R50	77.9	81.2	24.2	53.1
	QEEPS [26]	R50	88.9	89.1	37.1	76.7
	NAE+ [3]	R50	92.1	92.9	44.0	81.1
	BINet [7]	R50	90.0	90.7	45.3	81.7
	PGA [16]	R50	90.2	91.8	42.5	83.5
	AlignPS [37]	R50	**93.1**	93.4	45.9	81.9
	OIMNet++ (Ours)	R50	**93.1** (0.24)	**93.9** (0.30)	46.8 (0.51)	**83.9** (0.59)
	PGA* [16]	R50-Dilation	92.3	**94.7**	44.2	**85.2**
	AlignPS+ [37]	R50-DC [5]	**94.0**	94.5	46.1	82.1
	OIMNet+++ (Ours)	R50-ProtoNorm	93.1 (0.21)	94.1 (0.25)	**47.7** (0.19)	84.8 (0.20)

and CUHK-SYSU [36] datasets, and set the batch size to 5. We employ a warm-up strategy, gradually increasing a learning rate to 0.003 during the first epoch, which is divided by 10 at the 16th epoch. We assign the same balancing parameter for each term in the training objective, *i.e.*, $\lambda_{RPN} = 1$ and $\lambda_{det} = 1$, and set the temperature value τ to 0.33. We set the momentum value η to 0.5 for training a network with the OIM loss. We train our model using PyTorch [27] end-to-end, which takes about 5 and 10 h for PRW and CUHK-SYSU datasets, respectively, with a Titan RTX GPU.

4.2 Comparison with the State of the Art

We provide in Table 1 a quantitative comparison between our method with the state of the art [2,3,7,8,10,16,24,26,33,36,37] for person search. For fair comparison, we categorize person search methods into two-step [2,8,10,33] and end-to-end [3,7,16,24,26,36,37] approaches. The end-to-end approaches are further split into two groups according to the backbone network.

Overall, we can see from the experimental results that OIMNet++ provides highly discriminative person representations for person search. In particular, OIMNet++ shows high mAP scores. This indicates that our model is able to offer retrieval results with less false positives, *i.e.*, matches that are not likely to be a

Table 2. Ablative analysis of our approach. We measure the mAP (%) and rank-1 accuracy (%) on PRW [42] using person representations obtained from detected and annotated bounding boxes to evaluate search and reID performances separately. BN and PN indicates BatchNorm [14] and ProtoNorm, respectively. Numbers in bold indicate the best performance and the underscored ones indicate the second best. All results are obtained by averaging scores over 4 runs.

BN	PN	$\mathcal{L}_{\mathrm{OIM}}$	$\mathcal{L}_{\mathrm{LOIM}}$	Search		ReID	
				mAP	rank-1	mAP	rank-1
		✓		42.0	80.5	44.3	82.6
✓		✓		44.3	81.5	46.6	83.2
	✓	✓		_46.3_	82.7	_48.4_	84.6
✓			✓	45.1	_82.9_	47.4	_84.7_
	✓		✓	**46.8**	**83.9**	**49.0**	**86.2**

false alarm. Among the end-to-end approaches that adopt vanilla ResNet50 [12] as a backbone network, OIMNet++ achieves the state-of-the-art performance. Note that OIMNet++ even outperforms PGA [16] that requires additional parameters and computational overhead at test time due to an auxiliary attention module.

Recent works [16,37] modify a backbone network to further boost the performance. For example, PGA* [16] provides a variant by reducing the dilation rate of a conv5 block in ResNet50 from 2 to 1 to obtain features of high resolution. AlignPS+ [37] additionally exploits deformable convolutions from conv3 to conv5 blocks within ResNet50. Similarly, we replace BatchNorm layers within a conv5 block with ProtoNorm for OIMNet+++. In this case, we apply a learnable affine transformation after ProtoNorm layers within ResNet50, as in BatchNorm. Note that our modification, compared to other ones for PGA [16] and AlignPS [37], does not require additional computational overheads or parameters at test time. This places our model at a disadvantage, but we can see from the results in the last row of Table 1 that OIMNet+++ shows the person search performances comparable with competitive approaches, even including two-step ones [2,8,10,33].

4.3 Discussion

Ablation Study. We provide in Table 2 an ablation study of our approach using different combinations of components and losses. We measure mAP (%) and rank-1 accuracy (%) on the test set of PRW [42]. To better evaluate the discriminative power of person representations, we also measure the reID performance using annotated bounding boxes. We can see from the first and second rows that a person search model trained with the OIM loss only shows the

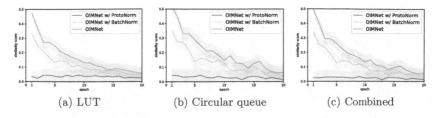

(a) LUT   (b) Circular queue   (c) Combined

Fig. 5. We plot average cosine similarity scores between features in (a) the LUT, (b) the circular queue, and a (c) concatenation of the two, over training epochs on the PRW dataset [42]. To better demonstrate the advantages of normalization operators, we train all models with the OIM loss. We also illustrate the standard deviation in transparent colors. (Best viewed in color.) (Color figure online)

worst performance[2], and incorporating a BatchNorm layer can boost the performance significantly. This suggests that applying the L2 normalization to person representations without standardization techniques degenerates the discriminative power. By replacing BatchNorm with our ProtoNorm in the third row, we can achieve additional performance gains. This demonstrates the effectiveness of ProtoNorm calibrating feature distributions while explicitly considering the class imbalance problem in person search. The results coincide with our finding in the toy experiment illustrated in Fig. 1, confirming once more the importance of a class-unbiased standardization scheme prior to projecting features on a unit hypersphere. We can observe from the second and fourth rows that the LOIM loss boosts the performance drastically. This suggests that selectively updating LUT features with the localization accuracy in the LOIM loss helps learning more discriminative representations than the OIM loss. Lastly, jointly exploiting ProtoNorm and the LOIM loss in the last row shows the best performance, and the two components complement each other.

Inter-class Separability. To demonstrate the effectiveness of ProtoNorm, we compute cosine similarity scores between features in the LUT, the circular queue, and both. We average the scores for all possible pairs and show in Fig. 5 the results over training epochs. We compare the results between three variants of OIMNet [36]; a vanilla OIMNet, and OIMNets equipped with BatchNorm and ProtoNorm. The variants are trained using the OIM loss. Low similarity scores indicate that the features in the LUT or the circular queue for different IDs encode different information, suggesting a strong inter-class separability. We can observe that employing BatchNorm offers better results in terms of the inter-class separability, compared to the vanilla model, which also demonstrates the importance of calibrating the feature distribution prior to L2 normalizations. We

---

[2] The model in the first row is exactly same as the original OIMNet [36], apart from the RoIAlign module in ours. Note that re-implementing OIMNet using common practices in recent works [3,16,21] (an improved learning rate scheduler, larger batch size, and the RoIAlign module) performs significantly better than the original OIMNet shown in Table 1. Similar findings are also reported in [3,21].

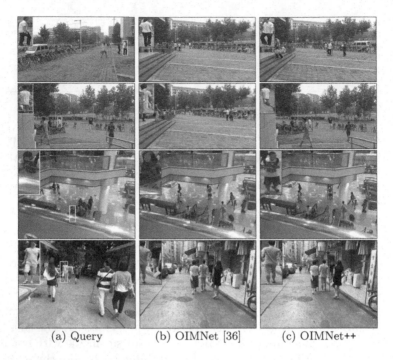

(a) Query   (b) OIMNet [36]   (c) OIMNet++

Fig. 6. Qualitative comparison between OIMNet [36] and OIMNet++. For each query image (left), we visualize top-1 search results, where red and green boxes indicate failure and correct cases, respectively. The first two rows are from PRW [42], and the remaining ones are from CUHK-SYSU [36]. For each image, we magnify the person-of-interest at the top-left corner for a better visualization. (Color figure online)

can also see that ProtoNorm obtaining feature statistics less biased towards dominant IDs provides lower similarity scores then BatchNorm, even when trained with a small number of epochs, encouraging more inter-class separability. Moreover, the average distances do not deviate from the initial point severely with ProtoNorm, suggesting that ProtoNorm also stabilizes training process.

Qualitative Analysis. We provide in Fig. 6 the visual comparisons between retrieval results for OIMNet [36] and OIMNet++ on PRW [42] and CUHK-SYSU [36]. We can see that OIMNet++ provides person representations that capture subtle discriminative cues, *e.g.*, hair and glasses (first row), as ProtoNorm in OIMNet++ enhances the inter-class separability. We can also observe the effectiveness of the LOIM loss. For example, OIMNet++ is more robust to occlusions (second and third row) and person overlaps (fourth row), since the LOIM loss favors pedestrian proposals with better localization accuracies to train with features in the LUT.

5   Conclusion

We have introduced OIMNet++ for person search that addresses the limitations of existing methods. To this end, we have presented a novel normalization scheme, dubbed ProtoNorm, that provides better statistics for feature standardization, even under the extreme class imbalance across person IDs. We have also introduced the LOIM loss that exploits the localization accuracy of each proposal to learn more discriminative representations. Finally, we have demonstrated the effectiveness of each component with extensive ablation studies, and have shown that OIMNet++ outperforms other person search methods on the standard person search benchmarks by a large margin.

Acknowledgements. This work was partly supported by Institute of Information & communications Technology Planning & Evaluation (IITP) grant funded by the Korea government (MSIT) (No. RS-2022-00143524, Development of Fundamental Technology and Integrated Solution for Next-Generation Automatic Artificial Intelligence System, and No. 2021-0-02068, Artificial Intelligence Innovation Hub), the Yonsei Signature Research Cluster Program of 2022 (2022-22-0002), and the KIST Institutional Program (Project No. 2E31051-21-203).

References

1. Ba, J.L., Kiros, J.R., Hinton, G.E.: Layer normalization. arXiv preprint arXiv:1607.06450 (2016)
2. Chen, D., Zhang, S., Ouyang, W., Yang, J., Tai, Y.: Person search via a mask-guided two-stream CNN model. In: Ferrari, V., Hebert, M., Sminchisescu, C., Weiss, Y. (eds.) ECCV 2018. LNCS, vol. 11211, pp. 764–781. Springer, Cham (2018). https://doi.org/10.1007/978-3-030-01234-2_45
3. Chen, D., Zhang, S., Yang, J., Schiele, B.: Norm-aware embedding for efficient person search. In: CVPR (2020)
4. Choi, S., Kim, T., Jeong, M., Park, H., Kim, C.: Meta batch-instance normalization for generalizable person re-identification. In: CVPR (2021)
5. Dai, J., et al.: Deformable convolutional networks. In: ICCV (2017)
6. De Montjoye, Y.A., Hidalgo, C.A., Verleysen, M., Blondel, V.D.: Unique in the crowd: the privacy bounds of human mobility. Sci. Rep. **3**(1), 1–5 (2013)
7. Dong, W., Zhang, Z., Song, C., Tan, T.: Bi-directional interaction network for person search. In: CVPR (2020)
8. Dong, W., Zhang, Z., Song, C., Tan, T.: Instance guided proposal network for person search. In: CVPR (2020)
9. Fang, H.S., Xie, S., Tai, Y.W., Lu, C.: RMPE: regional multi-person pose estimation. In: ICCV (2017)
10. Han, C., et al.: Re-ID driven localization refinement for person search. In: CVPR (2019)
11. He, K., Gkioxari, G., Dollár, P., Girshick, R.: Mask R-CNN. In: ICCV (2017)
12. He, K., Zhang, X., Ren, S., Sun, J.: Deep residual learning for image recognition. In: CVPR (2016)
13. Ioffe, S.: Batch renormalization: towards reducing minibatch dependence in batch-normalized models. In: NeurIPS (2017)

14. Ioffe, S., Szegedy, C.: Batch normalization: accelerating deep network training by reducing internal covariate shift. In: ICML (2015)
15. Jin, X., Lan, C., Zeng, W., Chen, Z., Zhang, L.: Style normalization and restitution for generalizable person re-identification. In: CVPR (2020)
16. Kim, H., Joung, S., Kim, I.J., Sohn, K.: Prototype-guided saliency feature learning for person search. In: CVPR (2021)
17. Lan, X., Zhu, X., Gong, S.: Person search by multi-scale matching. In: Ferrari, V., Hebert, M., Sminchisescu, C., Weiss, Y. (eds.) ECCV 2018. LNCS, vol. 11205, pp. 553–569. Springer, Cham (2018). https://doi.org/10.1007/978-3-030-01246-5_33
18. Li, W., Zhao, R., Xiao, T., Wang, X.: DeepReID: deep filter pairing neural network for person re-identification. In: CVPR (2014)
19. Li, X., Sun, W., Wu, T.: Attentive normalization. In: Vedaldi, A., Bischof, H., Brox, T., Frahm, J.-M. (eds.) ECCV 2020. LNCS, vol. 12362, pp. 70–87. Springer, Cham (2020). https://doi.org/10.1007/978-3-030-58520-4_5
20. Li, Y., Qi, H., Dai, J., Ji, X., Wei, Y.: Fully convolutional instance-aware semantic segmentation. In: CVPR (2017)
21. Li, Z., Miao, D.: Sequential end-to-end network for efficient person search. In: AAAI (2021)
22. Liao, S., Hu, Y., Zhu, X., Li, S.Z.: Person re-identification by local maximal occurrence representation and metric learning. In: CVPR (2015)
23. Lin, T.Y., Dollár, P., Girshick, R., He, K., Hariharan, B., Belongie, S.: Feature pyramid networks for object detection. In: CVPR (2017)
24. Liu, H., et al.: Neural person search machines. In: ICCV (2017)
25. Luo, H., Gu, Y., Liao, X., Lai, S., Jiang, W.: Bag of tricks and a strong baseline for deep person re-identification. In: CVPR Workshops (2019)
26. Munjal, B., Amin, S., Tombari, F., Galasso, F.: Query-guided end-to-end person search. In: CVPR (2019)
27. Paszke, A., et al.: Automatic differentiation in PyTorch (2017)
28. Ren, S., He, K., Girshick, R., Sun, J.: Faster R-CNN: towards real-time object detection with region proposal networks. In: NeurIPS (2015)
29. Russakovsky, O., et al.: ImageNet large scale visual recognition challenge. IJCV 115, 211–252 (2015)
30. Shao, W., et al.: SSN: learning sparse switchable normalization via SparsestMax. In: CVPR (2019)
31. Szegedy, C., Vanhoucke, V., Ioffe, S., Shlens, J., Wojna, Z.: Rethinking the inception architecture for computer vision. In: CVPR (2016)
32. Ulyanov, D., Vedaldi, A., Lempitsky, V.: Instance normalization: the missing ingredient for fast stylization. arXiv preprint arXiv:1607.08022 (2016)
33. Wang, C., Ma, B., Chang, H., Shan, S., Chen, X.: TCTS: a task-consistent two-stage framework for person search. In: CVPR (2020)
34. Wang, G., Peng, J., Luo, P., Wang, X., Lin, L.: Batch Kalman normalization: towards training deep neural networks with micro-batches. arXiv preprint arXiv:1802.03133 (2018)
35. Wu, Y., He, K.: Group normalization. In: Ferrari, V., Hebert, M., Sminchisescu, C., Weiss, Y. (eds.) ECCV 2018. LNCS, vol. 11217, pp. 3–19. Springer, Cham (2018). https://doi.org/10.1007/978-3-030-01261-8_1
36. Xiao, T., Li, S., Wang, B., Lin, L., Wang, X.: Joint detection and identification feature learning for person search. In: CVPR (2017)
37. Yan, Y., et al.: Anchor-free person search. In: CVPR (2021)
38. Yao, Z., Cao, Y., Zheng, S., Huang, G., Lin, S.: Cross-iteration batch normalization. In: CVPR (2021)

39. Ye, M., Shen, J., Lin, G., Xiang, T., Shao, L., Hoi, S.C.: Deep learning for person re-identification: a survey and outlook. IEEE TPAMI **44**, 2872–2893 (2021)
40. Zheng, L., Shen, L., Tian, L., Wang, S., Wang, J., Tian, Q.: Scalable person re-identification: a benchmark. In: ICCV (2015)
41. Zheng, L., Yang, Y., Hauptmann, A.G.: Person re-identification: past, present and future. arXiv preprint arXiv:1610.02984 (2016)
42. Zheng, L., Zhang, H., Sun, S., Chandraker, M., Yang, Y., Tian, Q.: Person re-identification in the wild. In: CVPR (2017)
43. Zhong, Y., Wang, X., Zhang, S.: Robust partial matching for person search in the wild. In: CVPR (2020)
44. Zhou, K., Yang, Y., Cavallaro, A., Xiang, T.: Omni-scale feature learning for person re-identification. In: ICCV (2019)
45. Zhuang, Z., et al.: Rethinking the distribution gap of person re-identification with camera-based batch normalization. In: Vedaldi, A., Bischof, H., Brox, T., Frahm, J.-M. (eds.) ECCV 2020. LNCS, vol. 12357, pp. 140–157. Springer, Cham (2020). https://doi.org/10.1007/978-3-030-58610-2_9

Out-of-Distribution Identification: Let Detector Tell Which I Am Not Sure

Ruoqi Li[1], Chongyang Zhang[1,2(✉)], Hao Zhou[1], Chao Shi[1], and Yan Luo[1]

[1] School of Electronic Information and Electrical Engineering, Shanghai Jiao Tong University, Shanghai 200240, China
{nilponi,sunny_zhang,zhouhao_0039,shichaostone,luoyan_bb}@sjtu.edu.cn
[2] MoE Key Lab of Artificial Intelligence, AI Institute, Shanghai Jiao Tong University, Shanghai 200240, China

Abstract. The superior performance of object detectors is often established under the condition that the test samples are in the same distribution as the training data. However, in most practical applications, out-of-distribution (OOD) instances are inevitable and usually lead to detection uncertainty. In this work, the Feature structured OOD-IDentification (FOOD-ID) model is proposed to reduce the uncertainty of detection results by identifying the OOD instances. Instead of outputting each detection result directly, FOOD-ID uses a likelihood-based measuring mechanism to identify whether the feature satisfies the corresponding class distribution and outputs the OOD results separately. Specifically, the clustering-oriented feature structuration is firstly developed using class-specified prototypes and Attractive-Repulsive loss for more discriminative feature representation and more compact distribution. With the structured features space, the density distribution of all training categories is estimated based on a class-conditional normalizing flow, which is then used for the OOD identification in the test stage. The proposed FOOD-ID can be easily applied to various object detectors including anchor-based frameworks and anchor-free frameworks. Extensive experiments on the PASCAL VOC-IO dataset and an industrial defect dataset demonstrate that FOOD-ID achieves satisfactory OOD identification performance, with which the certainty of detection results is improved significantly.

Keywords: Out-of-distribution · Identification · Object detection

1 Introduction

Over the last decade, the success of object detection has boosted widespread applications in various fields. However, their superior performance often relies on the assumption that test instances and training instances are in the same distribution [10,33]. When encountering out-of-distribution (OOD) inputs, the detector may make some seemingly stupid mistakes as shown in Fig. 1. The sheep is mistakenly classified as a dog and the cow is mistakenly classified as

S. Avidan et al. (Eds.): ECCV 2022, LNCS 13670, pp. 638–654, 2022.
https://doi.org/10.1007/978-3-031-20080-9_37

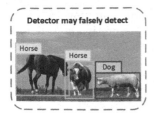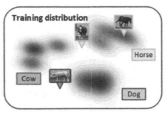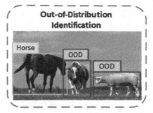

Fig. 1. The object detectors may falsely detect two types of OOD objects, including unknown-category objects and confusing-category objects. Our proposed FOOD-ID can perform OOD identification to improve detection certainty.

a horse. The former belongs to the unknown-category objects, which do not appear in the training set but are mistakenly detected and classified as a known class. The latter belongs to confusing-category objects, although it is a known class object, it is misclassified into another known class since it is located in low-probability distribution regions. The above drawback limits the deployment of object detectors in safety-critical applications, in which the detection results should be with high certainty to avoid high risks.

The phenomenon is more obvious in industrial automatic production. To avoid immeasurable risks, each unqualified product needs to be detected by a defect detector. However, it is difficult to balance the miss rate and false rate well because few or zero misses tend to bring more false positives. We observe that most of the false detections are made by the reason that their features are out of training distribution, which makes the detection results high uncertainty. Thus, identifying whether each detected object is OOD or not, can reduce the detection uncertainty, and then the false rate can be decreased effectively. At the same time, rather than simply suppressing such OOD false detections, they need to be output separately for further confirmation by humans.

Most existing object detectors follow the in-distribution (IND) assumption and can not identify OOD objects. Recently, some methods [21,24,27,38,43,49] leverage an independent classifier to recognize OOD image input, preventing them from entering downstream tasks. However, OOD objects and their combination with IND object detection are rarely explored. Besides, Open set detection methods [4,29,31] are dedicated to simultaneously performing known-category object detection and new unknown-category object recognition. However, apart from unknown-category instances, OOD objects also include confusing-category objects such as the cow that is mistakenly detected as a horse in Fig. 1.

To address the above challenges, we propose FOOD-ID, a unified model capable of object detection and OOD identification. Specifically, FOOD-ID adds a dynamic prototype branch to the detector head, which can dynamically store and update the multi-scale feature prototypes of training categories. The clustering-oriented feature structuration is developed by class-specified prototypes and Attractive-Repulsive loss for discriminative feature representation and compact distribution. With the structured feature space, the density distribution of all categories is estimated based on a class-conditional normalizing flow (CCNF). At test time, the log-likelihood of each detected object feature in the distribution of all categories will be predicted by the trained CCNF, based on which OOD identification is performed. With OOD identification, the detector is able to express uncertainty by picking out the OOD objects which have a higher error probability, and then the certainty of detection can be improved significantly.

Our contributions can be summarized as follows:

1. We propose FOOD-ID, a unified model capable of object detection and out-of-distribution identification.
2. We propose the clustering-oriented feature structuration developed by class-specific prototypes and Attractive-Repulsive loss. Furthermore, we adopt a class-conditional normalizing flow for feature distribution modeling, which can be used to estimate the likelihood and identify OOD objects.
3. We conduct experiments on various object detection frameworks and datasets. FOOD-ID achieves satisfactory OOD identification performance and improves the certainty of detection results.

2   Related Work

2.1   In-Distribution Object Detection

In recent years, object detectors have achieved rapid development from anchor-based frameworks [12,13,25,26,37,39] to recent anchor-free frameworks [7,19, 42,48]. Continuous breakthroughs in accuracy and speed have allowed them to be widely deployed in various applications. Object detectors are trained to detect objects of known classes labeled in the training set, and perform detection based on the assumption that test inputs satisfy the training distribution. The ideal in-distribution setting ignores the existence of OOD inputs, which will often encounter in practical applications. In this case, it is difficult for the detector to make confident and correct predictions of these OOD objects due to a lack of knowledge, resulting in large uncertainty in detection results. The above flaws limit their deployment in safety-critical real-world applications.

2.2   Out-of-Distribution Detection

OOD detection aims to detect OOD inputs in advance and prevent them from entering downstream tasks, e.g. localization or segmentation. Recent works improve OOD detection by using the ODIN score [16,24], Mahalanobis distance [21], energy score [27], ensemble [43,47], flows [1,49] and generative models [38]. However, the above studies usually focus on image classification, simply classifying the input as IND or OOD image, and rarely explore OOD objects in more complex object detection tasks. Recently, the work VOS [6] has begun to investigate the integration of OOD detection into object detection, but their focus on OOD objects is still on all detections on unknown categories from other datasets. VOS synthesizes outliers by sampling and trains the head to classify OOD in a supervised way. While our FOOD-ID is only based on IND samples and does not rely on OOD supervision. Open set detection requires correctly classifying known classes and labeling other classes that are not in the training set as unknown. Various discriminative [2,46] and generative models [11,32,34,36] have been proposed to improve open set recognition. Although most studies still focus on image classification, some studies have paid attention to suppressing open set false positives in object detection. MC Dropout-based [29], Gaussian Mixture Model [31] and distance-based methods [30] are used to extract model uncertainty and reject open-set error. Unlike the above studies, the OOD objects we target do not necessarily belong to an independent new unknown-category, but can also be confusing-category objects that are located in low-probability regions of known class distribution. In addition, we do not wish to simply suppress OOD detections, but rather perform OOD identification across all detections, and output OOD separately for human experts to utilize.

2.3   Uncertainty Estimation in Object Detection

The key to performing OOD identification is that model needs the ability to estimate its epistemic uncertainty, which is the uncertainty caused by the model's lack of knowledge [17]. Sampling-based methods (such as Bayesian-based [9], ensemble-based [20] and test-time augmentation [44]) are often used in regression, but they are difficult to apply in object detection due to time consumption. Recently proposed non-sampling uncertainty estimation methods (such as Gaussian yolov3 [3], Gaussian FCOS [22], GFLv2 [23]) measure uncertainty in terms of variance by modeling the localization output as a distribution rather than a deterministic value. The above methods pay more attention to the uncertainty of localization to achieve accurate bounding box regression to improve detection performance. However, they are still based on the IND assumption and do not consider OOD inputs. Instead, we focus on the uncertainty in the detection results of OOD objects due to the model's lack of knowledge. Our proposed method adopts a sampling-free manner, and can be used as a plug-in to enhance object detection frameworks.

3   Method

3.1   Problem Statement

We consider a object detection model M_C which is trained with the training set D, which contains C known categories $\mathcal{K} = \{1, 2, \ldots, C\} \subset N_+$. On the one hand, the detection model M_C needs to perform the correct classification and localization of IND objects x_{IND}, which include known objects that satisfy a high-probability distribution of known classes $\mathcal{K}$ in the training set D. On the other hand, the M_C needs to identify OOD objects x_{OOD}, including confusing-category and unknown-category objects. The former are located in low-probability regions of known class distribution. The latter do not belong to a known class $\mathcal{K}$ in the training set D.

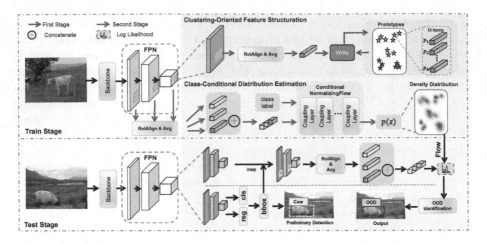

Fig. 2. Overview of the proposed FOOD-ID.

3.2   Overview

We propose Feature structured OOD-IDentification (FOOD-ID), a unified model for object detection and OOD identification. Figure 2 overviews the training and testing procedures for FOOD-ID. In the first training stage, all labeled ground-truth bounding boxes are mapped to Feature Pyramid Networks (FPN) and their multi-scale features are extracted by the RoIAlign layer and Average Pooling layer. Then the features are used to dynamically update the prototypes of the corresponding class. The Attractive-Repulsive loss is added to the detector to form a more discriminative feature space (detailed in Sect. 3.3). In the second training stage, both class labels and ground-truth features extracted by the trained detector are input to the class-conditional normalizing flow to model the density distribution of the feature space (detailed in Sect. 3.4). In the testing stage, the detector firstly obtains preliminary detection results and maps them to FPN for feature extraction. Each object feature is then fed into the trained normalizing flow to estimate the log-likelihood of satisfying each class distribution. Objects with a high likelihood class that is different from the original detected class or objects with high entropy are identified as OOD objects, while for other IND objects, the original detection results are output (detailed in Sect. 3.5).

3.3   Clustering-Oriented Feature Structuration

The clustering-oriented feature structuration is developed for more discriminative feature representation and more compact distribution. The feature structuration requires centralization and compactification. For centralization, we introduce a dynamic prototype branch to dynamically update class prototypes to form prototype-centric feature clusters. For compactification, the Attractive-Repulsive loss are proposed to attract features to corresponding prototypes and encourage different class prototypes mutually repulsive.

The dynamic prototype branch is introduced to dynamically store and update class prototypes as cluster centers for feature centralization. Suppose there are a total of C classes in the training set, and feature maps of S scales are extracted through FPN, and M prototype features are stored for each class on each scale, that is, a total of $C \times S \times M$ prototypes are stored in the branch. During training, the ground-truth bounding boxes in the training set are respectively mapped to the S scale feature maps extracted by FPN, and then the ground-truth object features are extracted by the RoIAlign layer and Average Pooling layer. Inspired by the memory network [28,35,41,45], we adopt a similar memory update strategy for prototypes. When K object features q^K of class c on the scale j are extracted, they are used to update the corresponding M prototypes p^M.

First, calculate the cosine similarity of K object features and M prototype features as update weight $w^{k,m}$, as follows:

$$w^{k,m} = \text{softmax}((p^m)^T q^k) \tag{1}$$

Then for each prototype p^m, select the most similar object features U_m to update p^m using the following formula, where $f(\cdot)$ is the L_2 normalization.

$$p^m = f(p^m + \sum_{k \in U_m} w'^{k,m} q^k) \tag{2}$$

$$w'^{k,m} = \frac{w^{k,m}}{\max_{k' \in U_m} w^{k',m}} \tag{3}$$

Then, the Attractive-Repulsive loss is introduced to facilitate feature compactification. The attractive loss encourages the object feature to be close to its most similar prototype of the corresponding class, which is calculated as the L_2 distance between the object feature q^k and its closest positive class prototype p^{pos}.

$$\mathcal{L}_{attractive} = \sum_k^K \|q^k - p^{pos}\|_2 \tag{4}$$

$$pos = \underset{m \in M_c}{\text{argmax}} \, w^{k,m} \tag{5}$$

While the repulsive loss encourages prototypes of different classes to be more dispersed and is calculated as formula (6). The first term is the L_2 distance between the object feature q^k and its closest p^{pos} prototype in class c. While the second term is the distance between the object feature q^k and its closest negative prototype p^{neg} in other classes, where α is a parameter used to control the gap between the two distances, which is set to 1 in the experiment.

$$\mathcal{L}_{repulsive} = \sum_k^K [\|q^k - p^{pos}\|_2 - \|q^k - p^{neg}\|_2 + \alpha]_+ \tag{6}$$

$$neg = \underset{m \in M_{c'}, c' \neq c}{\text{argmax}} \, w^{k,m} \tag{7}$$

So the loss function of the detector includes the classification loss $\mathcal{L}_{cls}$ and the localization loss $\mathcal{L}_{loc}$ of the original head, as well as the Attractive-Repulsive loss $\mathcal{L}_{AR}$ with the balance parameters η and λ, which are empirically set to 0.5.

$$\mathcal{L}_{AR} = \eta \mathcal{L}_{attractive} + (1 - \eta) \mathcal{L}_{repulsive} \tag{8}$$

$$\mathcal{L}_{detector} = \mathcal{L}_{cls} + \mathcal{L}_{loc} + \lambda\mathcal{L}_{AR} \tag{9}$$

Note that to ensure high-quality prototypes, the dynamic prototype branch will start updating only when the model has sufficient detection capabilities (i.e. after training for long enough epochs). After at least one epoch of storage of all ground-truth object features in the training set, the AR loss is added.

3.4   Class-Conditional Distribution Estimation

Then we model the distribution of the structured feature space based on class-conditional normalizing flow (CCNF). Normalizing flows are a class of generative probabilistic models, first proposed by Dinh et al. [5]. These models can fit arbitrary density distributions $q(x)$ by a simple base density $q(z)$ and a invertible mapping $g : X \to Z$. Then, the log-likelihood of any $x \in X$ can be estimated as follows:

$$\log q(x, \theta) = \log q(z) + \log |det J_x| \tag{10}$$

where the latent variable z is usually assumed to satisfy a standard multivariate Gaussian prior $(z \sim \mathcal{N}(0, \mathbb{I}))$ [5] and $J_x = \nabla_x g(x, \theta)$ is the Jacobian matrix of a invertible flow model $(z = g(x, \theta))$ with trainable parameter θ.

In order to model the distribution of all categories in the structured feature space in a unified manner, we introduce class information to achieve better feature distinction. Similar to [1], we assume the latent variable z satisfy a Gaussian mixture model with class-dependent mean μ_y and a unit covariance matrix $\mathbb{I}$ as follows, where y is the class label.

$$q(Z|Y) = N(\mu_y, \mathbb{I}) \quad and \quad q(z) = \textstyle\sum_y p(y)\mathcal{N}(\mu_y, \mathbb{I}) \tag{11}$$

We utilize the Information Bottleneck(IB)-based loss function [1] to train the class-conditional normalizing flow, where the trade-off parameter β balances the two terms.

$$\mathcal{L}_{CCNF} = \mathcal{L}_X - \beta\mathcal{L}_Y \tag{12}$$

The $\mathcal{L}_X$ term represents the mutual information term $I(X, Z)$, which is approximated by the empirical mean of the negative log-likelihood of the unconditional normalizing flow over a training dataset. Note that the input is a noisy version $X' = X + \mathcal{E}$, where $\mathcal{E} \sim \mathcal{N}(0, \sigma^2\mathbb{I}) = p(\mathcal{E})$ to artificially introduce a minimal amount of information loss. The $\mathcal{L}_X$ term encourages the normalizing flow to ignore class information and become an accurate likelihood model.

$$\mathcal{L}_X = \mathbb{E}_{p(X), p(\mathcal{E})}[- \log q(x + \varepsilon)] \tag{13}$$

While the $\mathcal{L}_Y$ term represents the mutual information term $I(X, Y)$, which is defined as the empirical mean of the log-posterior in a training set $\{x_i, y_i, \varepsilon_i\}_{i=1}^N$ of size N as follows. This term encourages each pair $g_\theta(x + \varepsilon)$ to be drawn to the correct cluster center μ_y while the cluster centers $(\mu_{Y \neq y})$ of the other classes are repulsed, which ensures accurate classification.

$$\mathcal{L}_Y = \frac{1}{N} \sum_{i=1}^N \log \frac{\mathcal{N}(g_\theta(x_i + \varepsilon_i); \mu_{y_i}, \mathbb{I})p(y_i)}{\sum_{y'} \mathcal{N}(g_\theta(x_i + \varepsilon_i); \mu_{y'}, \mathbb{I})p(y')} \tag{14}$$

We construct the CCNF based on invertible neural networks composed of several affine coupling layers [5]. We first extract multi-scale features from all ground-truth objects in the training set via the trained dynamic prototype branch and concatenate them together. Then all object features and class labels are input to the CCNF for training based on Formula (12). As a result, the trained CCNF can perform effective density estimation and class distinction.

3.5   Likelihood-Based Out-of-Distribution Identification

At test time, the classification branch and localization branch of the detector firstly obtain preliminary detection results, and the detection boxes are mapped to FPN and then object features are extracted through the dynamic prototype branch. Then the log-likelihood of each object feature in the distribution of all categories will be predicted by the trained CCNF as follows:

$$\log p(x) = \log \sum_y \exp(\frac{\|z-\mu_y\|_2^2}{2}) + \log|det J_x| \tag{15}$$

Likewise, the entropy of the likelihoods is calculated as follows:

$$H(x) = -\sum_x p(x) \log p(x) \tag{16}$$

Compared with the original predicted class, objects with a different maximum likelihood class will be regarded as OOD directly. Otherwise, we further adopt entropy as the uncertainty score and identify objects with entropy greater than a threshold. The former case means that the object features are more in line with the distribution of another category rather than the detected category, which corresponds to the misclassification of confusing-category objects. The latter case means that the object feature achieve similar likelihood across all categories, which correspond to unknown-category objects. While for other IND objects, the original detection results are output.

4   Experiments

4.1   Experimental Setup

Datasets. For a given dataset D containing a total of N categories, we first divide it into the training set D_{train} and test set D_{test} by stratified sampling. We select the instances in D_{train} that only contain $C(C < N)$ known classes objects as the model's training dataset D_C, which is achieved by deleting all images in D_{train} that contain unknown $N - C$ classes objects. During testing, the original test dataset D_{test} with N categories is used. To evaluate the performance of methods on both general object detection tasks and specific object detection tasks, we tested the following datasets:

PASCAL VOC-IO [8]: The dataset PASCAL VOC contains a total of 20 categories. We select the first $C = 15$ categories as known categories, pick out the data that only contain these C categories in the original training set as the training set D_C, and use the original test set D_{test} containing 20 categories as the test to construct PASCAL VOC-IO.

Crack Defect: We build Crack Defect dataset to detect crack defects in the junction of reed tubes, and it contains four main categories, namely, *crack*, *deformation*, *bubble*, and *stain*. Only the categories of *crack* need to be detected for product screening. *Deformation*, *bubble*, and *stain* are all qualified products that are easily mistakenly detected as *crack* in practice. Crack Defect is constructed by selecting the instances that only contain the categories of crack as the training set D_C, and using the test set D_{test} containing all categories.

Metrics. We categorize the raw detections outputs of the object detector into correct detections D_C, OOD false detections D_{OF}, and remaining false detections. A detection box is considered as D_C if it is located and classified correctly (has an IoU greater than 0.5 with a ground-truth box of the predicted class). A detection box is considered as D_{OF} if it is correctly located but misclassified (has an IoU greater than 0.5 with a ground-truth box of a class different from the predicted class). The remaining false detections are usually background detections or duplicate detections. We tested the following metrics to evaluate the distinction between D_C and D_{OF}:

ROC: Receiver Operating Characteristic (ROC) curve represents the trade-off between true positive rate (TPR) and false positive rate (FPR) when changing the uncertainty threshold θ in OOD identification. TPR represents the proportion of D_{OF} that are correctly identified and FPR represents the proportion of D_C that are misidentified as OOD. And the area under the ROC curve (AUC) is also calculated to represent the overall performance.

$$TPR(\theta) = \frac{|D_{OF} > \theta|}{|D_{OF}|} \quad FPR(\theta) = \frac{|D_C > \theta|}{|D_C|} \quad (17)$$

TPR@FPR: We report TPR at 5%, 10% and 20% FPR respectively. These operating points evaluate the identification rate of D_{OF} under a low misidentification of D_C, which corresponds to the ability to identify OOD with the lowest possible miss-rate in the application.

Precision: We calculated the precision before and after OOD identification respectively. The precision before OOD identification is calculated as the proportion of D_C in all raw detection results. After taking 10% of all detected results as OOD, all detection results are divided into IND set and OOD set. The precision of the former is the proportion of Dc in the IND set, and the precision of the latter is the proportion of D_{OF} in the OOD set.

4.2   Main Results

We test on three representative object detectors separately: FCOS [42], an anchor-free one-stage detector; RetinaNet [25], an anchor-based one-stage detector; and Faster RCNN [39], an anchor-based two-stage detector. For each object

Table 1. The OOD identification performance measured by AUC and TPR@FPR metrics across both datasets and three detectors.

Method	PASCAL VOC-IO				Crack defect			
	AUC	TPR@			AUC	TPR@		
		5%FPR	10%FPR	20%FPR		5%FPR	10%FPR	20%FPR
FCOS								
Baseline-Score	0.830	43.5	59.0	73.6	0.865	51.8	68.1	80.3
Baseline-Entropy	0.861	53.0	64.7	77.4	0.882	56.9	70.2	81.4
FOOD-ID-Proto	0.899	64.3	72.8	82.7	0.906	68.3	76.0	84.5
FOOD-ID-CCNF	**0.913**	**70.1**	**80.1**	**88.0**	**0.921**	**73.4**	**82.7**	**90.3**
RetinaNet								
Baseline-Score	0.900	53.5	72.7	84.9	0.923	62.7	79.9	90.2
Baseline-Entropy	0.903	60.4	72.3	83.2	0.900	59.4	71.1	82.4
FOOD-ID-Proto	0.919	69.5	79.0	87.7	0.936	75.2	83.4	90.8
FOOD-ID-CCNF	**0.928**	**76.5**	**85.3**	**91.2**	**0.942**	**80.5**	**88.5**	**93.6**
Faster RCNN								
Baseline-Score	0.840	35.5	54.7	71.6	0.872	49.1	64.3	78.4
Baseline-Entropy	0.843	45.4	61.4	74.7	0.881	50.2	65.9	81.0
FOOD-ID-Proto	0.861	50.2	67.8	78.1	0.887	56.7	72.2	82.7
FOOD-ID-CCNF	**0.866**	**57.7**	**68.1**	**79.7**	**0.908**	**63.4**	**75.6**	**85.2**

detector, we train the model and test it under a certain model detection threshold. After obtaining the detection results, we compare the performance of OOD identification based on the following methods:

Baseline-Score: The confidence score of the detector is used as the criterion for uncertainty estimation, low score means high uncertainty [4,15,29].

Baseline-Entropy: The entropy of the confidence scores for all classes of the detector is used for uncertainty estimation, high entropy means high uncertainty [14,18,40].

FOOD-ID-Proto: Based on the dynamic prototype branch, the distance from the detected object feature to the nearest prototype of the predicted category is used as the uncertainty score, large distance means high uncertainty.

FOOD-ID-CCNF: Based on the trained CCNF, we leverage both likelihood and entropy to measure the uncertainty. As described in Sect. 3.5, compared to the original predicted class, objects with a different maximum likelihood class will be regarded as OOD directly. Otherwise, we further adopt entropy as the uncertainty score to identify OOD objects.

As shown in Table 1, the two methods we proposed achieve advanced performance on OOD identification, which is maintained across three object detectors and two datasets. Especially under a very low misidentify rate of D_C, FOOD-ID can achieve significantly better D_{OF} identification performance than baseline methods. It can be noted that FOOD-ID-CCNF outperforms FOOD-ID-Proto, because the former can accurately model the training feature distribution and

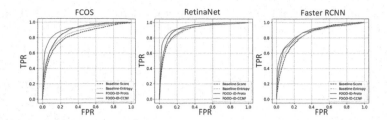

Fig. 3. The OOD identification performance measured by ROC metric on PASCAL VOC-IO dataset.

Table 2. The precision of detection results before and after excluding 10% of the detection results as OOD with OOD identification on PASCAL VOC-IO dataset.

Method	FCOS			RetinaNet			Faster RCNN		
	Before	After		Before	After		Before	After	
	IND Set	IND Set	OOD Set	IND Set	IND Set	OOD Set	IND Set	IND Set	OOD Set
Baseline-Score	0.797	0.827	0.234	0.738	0.772	0.268	0.759	0.785	0.167
Baseline-Entropy		0.830	0.358		0.773	0.369		0.782	0.273
FOOD-ID-Proto		0.831	0.367		0.789	0.437		0.789	0.260
FOOD-ID-CCNF		**0.836**	**0.414**		**0.791**	**0.540**		**0.792**	**0.335**

estimate exact likelihood, while the latter only measures the distance to the class closest prototype. The complete ROC curve on PASCAL VOC-IO is shown in Fig. 3. Meanwhile, as shown in the Table 2, the raw detection results are divided into IND set and OOD set through ood identification. For the IND set, the precision of detection results is significantly improved, which means that OOD identification improves the certainty of detection. For the OOD set, it is a more challenging task with the interference of background false positives. FOOD-ID-CCNF can achieve advanced precision in both IND set and OOD set.

4.3 Ablation Study

FOOD-ID is mainly composed of clustering-oriented feature structuration and class-conditional distributed estimation. We investigate the impact of each component on the overall performance of the model.

The Benefit of Feature Structuration. To explore the need for feature structuration, we conduct extra experiments on detectors trained without feature structuration. We still use the dynamic prototype branch to extract ground-truth object features but do not train with Attractive-Repulsive loss. The same conditional normalizing flow model is then used to model the feature distribution and perform OOD identification at test time. The OOD identification results are shown in Table 3. It can be seen that in the absence of AR loss, the ability to identify OOD is severely degraded after passing the same distribution modeling

Table 3. The OOD identification performance with or without Attractive-Repulsive (AR) loss on PASCAL VOC-IO dataset.

Method	FCOS				RetinaNet				Faster RCNN			
	AUC	TPR@			AUC	TPR@			AUC	TPR@		
		5%FPR	10%FPR	20%FPR		5%FPR	10%FPR	20%FPR		5%FPR	10%FPR	20%FPR
FOOD-ID-Proto w/o ARloss	0.705	16.1	26.9	43.1	0.704	18.8	32.3	47.2	0.687	16.1	25.7	41.1
FOOD-ID-Proto w ARloss	0.899	64.3	72.8	82.7	0.919	69.5	79.0	87.7	0.861	50.2	67.8	78.1
FOOD-ID-CCNF w/o ARloss	0.888	69.1	75.1	83.6	0.921	73.9	82.6	89.9	0.857	54.5	65.3	76.3
FOOD-ID-CCNF w ARloss	**0.913**	**70.1**	**80.1**	**88.0**	**0.928**	**76.5**	**85.3**	**91.2**	**0.866**	**57.7**	**68.1**	**79.7**

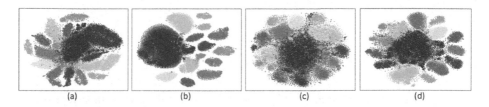

(a)   (b)   (c)   (d)

Fig. 4. Visualization of the detector feature distribution and the corresponding normalizing flow latent variable distribution with or without AR loss on PASCAL VOC-IO dataset. (a) Detector feature distribution without AR loss. (b) Detector feature distribution with AR loss. (c) Latent variable distribution without AR loss. (d) Latent variable distribution with AR loss. (Color figure online)

model. Thus, feature structuration facilitates subsequent accurate distribution modeling and class distinction.

We visualize the ground-truth features of the PASCAL VOC-IO training set extracted by the dynamic prototype branch applied to FCOS with or without AR loss by t-SNE in Fig. 4, where the same color dots represent the features of the same class. It can be seen intuitively that the feature distribution with AR loss is more structural and discriminative. It is achieved by utilizing dynamic prototypes as cluster centers for centralization and AR loss for compactification.

The Benefit of Class-Conditional Distribution Estimation. To explore the benefit of class-conditional distribution estimation, we compare the impact of distribution modeling using class-conditional normalizing flow and unconditional normalizing flow (UNF) on OOD identification performance. The former adopts the CCNF we describe in Subsect. 3.4. The latter adopts a series of UNFs to individually model the distribution of each class of features. The UNFs are trained with the objective of minimizing the log-likelihood in formula (10), assuming that the distribution of the latent variables z satisfies a multivariate Gaussian distribution [5].

The performance of OOD identification on the same detection model using different flow models is shown in Table 4. It can be seen that class-conditional distribution estimation has a clear advantage over unconditional distribution estimation in terms of OOD identification. The latter case can only access the features of a single category with ignorance of other category information, resulting in a weak feature discrimination ability because the features of different categories are not conditionally independent.

Table 4. The performance of OOD identification under distribution modeling using class-conditional normalizing flow (CCNF) and unconditional normalizing flow (UNF) on PASCAL VOC-IO dataset.

Method	FCOS				RetinaNet				Faster RCNN			
	AUC	TPR@			AUC	TPR@			AUC	TPR@		
		5%FPR	10%FPR	20%FPR		5%FPR	10%FPR	20%FPR		5%FPR	10%FPR	20%FPR
UNF	0.881	65.6	71.4	78.9	0.885	60.3	70.9	82.9	0.830	39.2	54.8	72.6
CCNF	**0.913**	**70.1**	**80.1**	**88.0**	**0.928**	**76.5**	**85.3**	**91.2**	**0.866**	**57.7**	**68.1**	**79.7**

The Trade-Off Between Density Estimation and Class Distinction. To explore the trade-off between density estimation and class distinction in the class-conditional distribution estimation, we experiment with different values of the balance parameter β in the loss function of the CCNF. The OOD identification results of different β with FOOD-ID-CCNF applied to FCOS are shown in Table 5. We also visualize the distribution of latent variables for CCNF trained with different β on PASCAL VOC-IO training set by t-SNE, as shown in Fig. 5.

Table 5. The OOD identification results under different β on PASCAL VOC-IO dataset.

β	AUC	TPR@5%FPR	TPR@10%FPR	TPR@20%FPR
0.0	0.500	4.9	9.8	19.8
0.5	0.911	69.9	78.1	86.6
1.0	**0.913**	**70.1**	**80.1**	**88.0**
2.0	0.912	68.6	80.0	87.4
10.0	0.912	68.1	78.0	87.3

The β trades off density estimation and class distinction. Smaller β encourages more accurate density estimation, at the cost of losing class distinction. When β is equal to 0, it will degenerate into a density model that does not consider class conditions, resulting in a lack of OOD identification ability. When β increases, the flow can achieve more efficient classification, but it is more difficult to accurately estimate the density within the class. We take $\beta = 1$ to achieve a balance.

4.4   Visualization

Figure 6 shows the comparison of the detection results of FOOD-ID and the original detector on two datasets. FOOD-ID demonstrates advanced OOD identification capabilities. It also can be noted that it is difficult to identify OOD

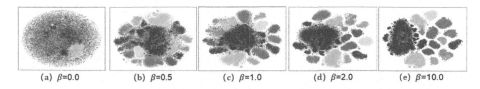

(a) β=0.0   (b) β=0.5   (c) β=1.0   (d) β=2.0   (e) β=10.0

Fig. 5. Visualization of the distribution of latent variables with different β values on PASCAL VOC-IO dataset.

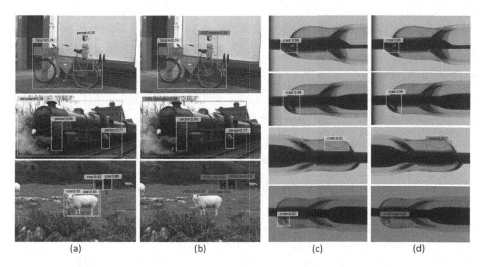

(a)   (b)   (c)   (d)

Fig. 6. Visualization of detection results. (a) Original detections on PASCAL VOC-IO dataset. (b) FOOD-ID detections on PASCAL VOC-IO dataset. (c) Original detections on Crack Defect dataset. (d) FOOD-ID detections on Crack Defect dataset.

by confidence score of original detector, because OOD usually has a non-low confidence score.

5   Conclusions

Out-of-distribution inputs limit the deployment of in-distribution object detectors in safety-critical real-world applications. In this paper, we propose a unified model FOOD-ID capable of object detection and out-of-distribution identification. FOOD-ID develops the clustering-oriented feature structuration by class-specific prototypes and Attractive-Repulsive loss. Furthermore, a class-conditional normalizing flow is adopted to model the feature distribution and estimate likelihood at test time. FOOD-ID achieves satisfactory OOD identification performance and improves the certainty of detection results.

Acknowledgement. This work was supported in part by the National Natural Science Fund of China (61971281), the National Key R&D Program of China (2021YFD1400104), the Shanghai Municipal Science and Technology Major Project (2021SHZDZX0102), and the Science and Technology Commission of Shanghai Municipality (18DZ2270700).

References

1. Ardizzone, L., Mackowiak, R., Rother, C., Kothe, U.: Training normalizing flows with the information bottleneck for competitive generative classification. arXiv:Learning (2020)
2. Bendale, A., Boult, T.E.: Towards open set deep networks. In: 2016 IEEE Conference on Computer Vision and Pattern Recognition (CVPR), pp. 1563–1572 (2016)
3. Choi, J., Chun, D., Kim, H., Lee, H.J.: Gaussian YOLOv3: an accurate and fast object detector using localization uncertainty for autonomous driving. In: 2019 IEEE/CVF International Conference on Computer Vision (ICCV), pp. 502–511 (2019)
4. Dhamija, A., Günther, M., Ventura, J., Boult, T.: The overlooked elephant of object detection: open set, pp. 1010–1019 (2020). https://doi.org/10.1109/WACV45572.2020.9093355
5. Dinh, L., Sohl-Dickstein, J., Bengio, S.: Density estimation using real NVP. ArXiv abs/1605.08803 (2017)
6. Du, X., Wang, Z., Cai, M., Li, S.: VOS: learning what you don't know by virtual outlier synthesis. In: International Conference on Learning Representations (2022). https://openreview.net/forum?id=TW7d65uYu5M
7. Duan, K., Bai, S., Xie, L., Qi, H., Huang, Q., Tian, Q.: CenterNet: keypoint triplets for object detection. In: 2019 IEEE/CVF International Conference on Computer Vision (ICCV), pp. 6568–6577 (2019)
8. Everingham, M., Gool, L.V., Williams, C.K.I., Winn, J., Zisserman, A.: The pascal visual object classes (VOC) challenge. Int. J. Comput. Vis. **88**(2), 303–338 (2010)
9. Gal, Y., Ghahramani, Z.: Dropout as a Bayesian approximation: Representing model uncertainty in deep learning. ArXiv abs/1506.02142 (2016)
10. Gawlikowski, J., et al.: A survey of uncertainty in deep neural networks. ArXiv abs/2107.03342 (2021)
11. Ge, Z., Demyanov, S., Chen, Z., Garnavi, R.: Generative OpenMax for multi-class open set classification. ArXiv abs/1707.07418 (2017)
12. Girshick, R.B.: Fast R-CNN. In: 2015 IEEE International Conference on Computer Vision (ICCV), pp. 1440–1448 (2015)
13. Girshick, R.B., Donahue, J., Darrell, T., Malik, J.: Rich feature hierarchies for accurate object detection and semantic segmentation. In: 2014 IEEE Conference on Computer Vision and Pattern Recognition, pp. 580–587 (2014)
14. Harakeh, A., Smart, M., Waslander, S.L.: BayesOD: a Bayesian approach for uncertainty estimation in deep object detectors. In: 2020 IEEE International Conference on Robotics and Automation (ICRA), pp. 87–93. IEEE (2020)
15. Hendrycks, D., Gimpel, K.: A baseline for detecting misclassified and out-of-distribution examples in neural networks. arXiv preprint arXiv:1610.02136 (2016)
16. Hsu, Y.C., Shen, Y., Jin, H., Kira, Z.: Generalized ODIN: detecting out-of-distribution image without learning from out-of-distribution data. In: 2020 IEEE/CVF Conference on Computer Vision and Pattern Recognition (CVPR), pp. 10948–10957 (2020)

17. Hüllermeier, E., Waegeman, W.: Aleatoric and epistemic uncertainty in machine learning: an introduction to concepts and methods. Mach. Learn. **110**, 457–506 (2021)
18. Kaur, R., Jha, S., Roy, A., Park, S., Sokolsky, O., Lee, I.: Detecting OODs as datapoints with high uncertainty. arXiv preprint arXiv:2108.06380 (2021)
19. Kong, T., Sun, F., Liu, H., Jiang, Y., Li, L., Shi, J.: FoveaBox: Beyound anchor-based object detection. IEEE Trans. Image Process. **29**, 7389–7398 (2020)
20. Lakshminarayanan, B., Pritzel, A., Blundell, C.: Simple and scalable predictive uncertainty estimation using deep ensembles. In: NIPS (2017)
21. Lee, K., Lee, K., Lee, H., Shin, J.: A simple unified framework for detecting out-of-distribution samples and adversarial attacks. In: NeurIPS (2018)
22. Lee, Y., won Hwang, J., Kim, H., Yun, K., Park, J.: Localization uncertainty estimation for anchor-free object detection. ArXiv abs/2006.15607 (2020)
23. Li, X., Wang, W., Hu, X., Li, J., Tang, J., Yang, J.: Generalized focal loss V2: learning reliable localization quality estimation for dense object detection. In: 2021 IEEE/CVF Conference on Computer Vision and Pattern Recognition (CVPR), pp. 11627–11636 (2021)
24. Liang, S., Li, Y., Srikant, R.: Enhancing the reliability of out-of-distribution image detection in neural networks. arXiv:Learning (2018)
25. Lin, T.Y., Goyal, P., Girshick, R.B., He, K., Dollár, P.: Focal loss for dense object detection. IEEE Trans. Pattern Anal. Mach. Intell. **42**, 318–327 (2020)
26. Liu, W., et al.: SSD: single shot MultiBox detector. In: Leibe, B., Matas, J., Sebe, N., Welling, M. (eds.) ECCV 2016. LNCS, vol. 9905, pp. 21–37. Springer, Cham (2016). https://doi.org/10.1007/978-3-319-46448-0_2
27. Liu, W., Wang, X., Owens, J.D., Li, Y.: Energy-based out-of-distribution detection. ArXiv abs/2010.03759 (2020)
28. Miller, A., Fisch, A., Dodge, J., Karimi, A.H., Bordes, A., Weston, J.: Key-value memory networks for directly reading documents. arXiv preprint arXiv:1606.03126 (2016)
29. Miller, D., Nicholson, L., Dayoub, F., Sünderhauf, N.: Dropout sampling for robust object detection in open-set conditions. In: 2018 IEEE International Conference on Robotics and Automation (ICRA), pp. 1–7 (2018)
30. Miller, D., Sünderhauf, N., Milford, M., Dayoub, F.: Class anchor clustering: a loss for distance-based open set recognition. In: 2021 IEEE Winter Conference on Applications of Computer Vision (WACV), pp. 3569–3577 (2021)
31. Miller, D., Sunderhauf, N., Milford, M., Dayoub, F.: Uncertainty for identifying open-set errors in visual object detection. IEEE Robot. Autom. Lett. **7**, 215–222 (2022)
32. Neal, L., Olson, M., Fern, X., Wong, W.-K., Li, F.: Open set learning with counterfactual images. In: Ferrari, V., Hebert, M., Sminchisescu, C., Weiss, Y. (eds.) ECCV 2018. LNCS, vol. 11210, pp. 620–635. Springer, Cham (2018). https://doi.org/10.1007/978-3-030-01231-1_38
33. Ovadia, Y., et al.: Can you trust your model's uncertainty? Evaluating predictive uncertainty under dataset shift. In: NeurIPS (2019)
34. Oza, P., Patel, V.M.: C2AE: class conditioned auto-encoder for open-set recognition. In: 2019 IEEE/CVF Conference on Computer Vision and Pattern Recognition (CVPR), pp. 2302–2311 (2019)
35. Park, H., Noh, J., Ham, B.: Learning memory-guided normality for anomaly detection. In: Proceedings of the IEEE/CVF Conference on Computer Vision and Pattern Recognition, pp. 14372–14381 (2020)

36. Perera, P., et al.: Generative-discriminative feature representations for open-set recognition. In: 2020 IEEE/CVF Conference on Computer Vision and Pattern Recognition (CVPR), pp. 11811–11820 (2020)
37. Redmon, J., Divvala, S.K., Girshick, R.B., Farhadi, A.: You only look once: unified, real-time object detection. In: 2016 IEEE Conference on Computer Vision and Pattern Recognition (CVPR), pp. 779–788 (2016)
38. Ren, J., et al.: Likelihood ratios for out-of-distribution detection. In: NeurIPS (2019)
39. Ren, S., He, K., Girshick, R.B., Sun, J.: Faster R-CNN: towards real-time object detection with region proposal networks. IEEE Trans. Pattern Anal. Mach. Intell. **39**, 1137–1149 (2015)
40. Steinhardt, J., Liang, P.S.: Unsupervised risk estimation using only conditional independence structure. In: Advances in Neural Information Processing Systems, vol. 29 (2016)
41. Sukhbaatar, S., Weston, J., Fergus, R., et al.: End-to-end memory networks. In: Advances in Neural Information Processing Systems, vol. 28 (2015)
42. Tian, Z., Shen, C., Chen, H., He, T.: FCOS: fully convolutional one-stage object detection. In: 2019 IEEE/CVF International Conference on Computer Vision (ICCV), pp. 9626–9635 (2019)
43. Vyas, A., Jammalamadaka, N., Zhu, X., Das, D., Kaul, B., Willke, T.L.: Out-of-distribution detection using an ensemble of self supervised leave-out classifiers. In: Ferrari, V., Hebert, M., Sminchisescu, C., Weiss, Y. (eds.) ECCV 2018. LNCS, vol. 11212, pp. 560–574. Springer, Cham (2018). https://doi.org/10.1007/978-3-030-01237-3_34
44. Wang, G., Li, W., Aertsen, M., Deprest, J.A., Ourselin, S., Vercauteren, T.K.M.: Aleatoric uncertainty estimation with test-time augmentation for medical image segmentation with convolutional neural networks. Neurocomputing **335**, 34–45 (2019)
45. Weston, J., Chopra, S., Bordes, A.: Memory networks. arXiv preprint arXiv:1410.3916 (2014)
46. Yoshihashi, R., Shao, W., Kawakami, R., You, S., Iida, M., Naemura, T.: Classification-reconstruction learning for open-set recognition. In: 2019 IEEE/CVF Conference on Computer Vision and Pattern Recognition (CVPR), pp. 4011–4020 (2019)
47. Yu, Q., Aizawa, K.: Unsupervised out-of-distribution detection by maximum classifier discrepancy. In: 2019 IEEE/CVF International Conference on Computer Vision (ICCV), pp. 9517–9525 (2019)
48. Zhu, C., He, Y., Savvides, M.: Feature selective anchor-free module for single-shot object detection. In: 2019 IEEE/CVF Conference on Computer Vision and Pattern Recognition (CVPR), pp. 840–849 (2019)
49. Zisselman, E., Tamar, A.: Deep residual flow for out of distribution detection. In: 2020 IEEE/CVF Conference on Computer Vision and Pattern Recognition (CVPR), pp. 13991–14000 (2020)

Learning with Free Object Segments
for Long-Tailed Instance Segmentation

Cheng Zhang$^{(\boxtimes)}$, Tai-Yu Pan, Tianle Chen, Jike Zhong, Wenjin Fu,
and Wei-Lun Chao

The Ohio State University, Columbus, OH 43210, USA
zhang.7804@osu.edu

Abstract. One fundamental challenge in building an instance segmentation model for a large number of classes in complex scenes is the lack of training examples, especially for rare objects. In this paper, we explore the possibility to increase the training examples without laborious data collection and annotation. We find that an abundance of instance segments can potentially be obtained freely from object-centric images, according to two insights: (i) an object-centric image usually contains one salient object in a simple background; (ii) objects from the same class often share similar appearances or similar contrasts to the background. Motivated by these insights, we propose a simple and scalable framework FREESEG for extracting and leveraging these "free" object foreground segments to facilitate model training in long-tailed instance segmentation. Concretely, we investigate the similarity among object-centric images of the same class to propose candidate segments of foreground instances, followed by a novel ranking of segment quality. The resulting high-quality object segments can then be used to augment the existing long-tailed datasets, e.g., by copying and pasting the segments onto the original training images. Extensive experiments show that FREESEG yields substantial improvements on top of strong baselines and achieves state-of-the-art accuracy for segmenting rare object categories. Our code is publicly available at https://github.com/czhang0528/FreeSeg.

1 Introduction

Object detection and instance segmentation are fundamental building blocks for many high-impact real-world applications (e.g., autonomous driving). Recent years have witnessed an unprecedented breakthrough in both of them, thanks to deep neural networks [12,14,31] and large-scale datasets for common objects (e.g., persons and cars) [10,24,61]. Yet, when it comes to rare, less commonly seen objects (e.g., an unusual traffic sign), there is a drastic performance drop due to insufficient training examples [13,37,57]. This challenge has attracted significant attention lately in how to learn an object detection or instance segmentation model given labeled data of a "long-tailed" distribution across classes [60].

Supplementary Information The online version contains supplementary material available at https://doi.org/10.1007/978-3-031-20080-9_38.

Fig. 1. Illustration of our approach FREESEG. We sample two rare classes, *ferret* (left) and *heron* (right) from LVIS v1 [13], and retrieve object-centric images (the upper row of each class) from the ImageNet dataset [35]. We then show the discovered object segments (middle) and binary masks (bottom) by FREESEG. The abundant object segments have diverse appearances and poses and can be effectively used to improve the instance segmentation.

Specifically, a number of works have been dedicated to developing new training algorithms, objectives, or model architectures [13,17,22,26,42,43,46,47,49,50].

In this paper, we explore a drastically different approach. *We investigate the possibility of obtaining more labeled instances (i.e., instance segments of objects) at a minimal cost, especially for rare objects.* We build upon the recent observation in [54]—many objects do not appear frequently enough in complex scenes but are found frequently alone in object-centric images—to acquire an abundance of object-centric images (*e.g.,* ImageNet [9] or Google images) for rare classes. Zhang *et al.* [54] have shown that, even with only pseudo bounding boxes for these images, they can already improve the detector effectively.

We take one key step further to leverage the underlying properties of object-centric images to create high-quality instance labels that can facilitate both detection and segmentation model training. In general, object-centric images usually contain one salient object in a relatively simple background than scene-centric images like those in MSCOCO [24]. Moreover, objects of the same class usually share similar appearances, shapes, contrasts, or more abstractly, common parts to the background [33] (see Fig. 1 for an example). These properties open up the opportunity to discover object segments almost *freely* from object-centric images of the same class—by exploring their common salient regions.

To this end, we propose a framework named FREESEG (Free Object Segments) to take advantage of these properties. We first extract the common foreground regions from object-centric images of the same class. This can be done, for example, by off-the-shelf co-segmentation models [55]. While not perfect, sometimes missing the true objects or including backgrounds, these extracted regions have surprisingly captured a decent portion of objects with tight segmentation masks. Nevertheless, directly using all of these regions, mixed with false positive and noisy segments, would inevitably introduce a great amount of noise to the downstream tasks. To address this, we propose a novel segment ranking approach to mine the most reliable and high-confident object masks. After all, we aim for a set of high-quality instance segments from object-centric images, not to segment all the object-centric images well.

How can we leverage these high-quality instance segments from object-centric images? One naive way is to directly train the instance segmentation model on the object-centric images, using these segments as supervision. Nevertheless, the fact that these objects mostly show up alone in simple backgrounds makes them somewhat too simple for the model. We, therefore, choose to place these object segments in the context of complex scene-centric images, via simple copy-paste augmentation [11]. Unlike [11], which merely pastes human-annotated segments from one image to another to increase the *context diversity*, our FREESEG approach brings the best of abundant free object segments to increase the *appearance diversity*, especially for rare object categories.

We evaluate FREESEG on the long-tailed LVIS benchmark [13]. FREESEG leads to a massive improvement in segmenting rare object instances by effectively increasing the labeled training data for them. Moreover, FREESEG is detached from the model training phase and is thus model-agnostic. Namely, it can potentially benefit all kinds of instance segmentation model architectures. FREESEG is also compatible with existing efforts on long-tailed object detection and segmentation to achieve further gains.

In summary, our FREESEG framework opens up a novel direction that brings the best of discovering pixel-level supervision in object-centric images to facilitate long-tailed instance segmentation. Our **main contributions** are:

- We demonstrate the possibility to increase the number of training examples for instance segmentation without laborious pixel-level data collection and annotation.
- We propose a simple and scalable pipeline for discovering, extracting, and leveraging free object foreground segments to facilitate long-tailed instance segmentation.
- Our FREESEG framework shows promising gains on the challenging LVIS dataset and demonstrates a strong compatibility with existing works.

2   Related Work

Long-Tailed Object Detection and Instance Segmentation. Most existing works tackle the problem of "long-tailed" distributions in the model training phase, by developing training objectives or algorithms [17,19,22,30,47–49,56]. They usually first pre-train the models in a conventional way, using data from all or just the head classes, and then fine-tunes them on the entire long-tailed dataset using either re-sampling [5,13,38] or cost-sensitive learning [16,42,43,46]. Instead of directly learning a model from long-tailed data, another thread of works investigate data augmentation techniques to improve the performance of long-tailed object detection and instance segmentation [11,28,53,54]. For example, Simple Copy-Paste [11] augments the training data in the image space using the original long-tailed dataset. FASA [53] enhances class-wise features using a Gaussian prior. DLWL [28] and MosaicOS [54] extensively leverage extra data sources from YFCC-100M [44], ImageNet [9] or Internet to augment the long-tailed LVIS dataset [13].

Our work follows the second thread on learning with additional weakly-supervised or unsupervised data, similar to the recently proposed MosaicOS framework [54]. We, however, further develop an effective way to obtain high-quality instance segments from object-centric images, while MosaicOS merely learns with pseudo bounding box annotations. Since collecting pixel-level annotations is more challenging and prone to error, we develop a novel ranking mechanism such that only the high-quality segments will be used for model training. Moreover, by copying and pasting the segments into the context of scene-centric images, our method can further bridge the domain gap between different data sources. Overall, we view our approach as a critical leap upon [11,54] that can significantly improve long-tailed instance segmentation by largely increasing the training segments of rare objects.

Image-Based Foreground Object Segmentation. There are a variety of techniques that we can potentially leverage to extract the foreground object segments from object-centric images without laborious annotations. Representative methods include image (co-)saliency detection [8,18], unsupervised/weakly-supervised object segmentation [32], attention [3], instance localization [36,58], and image co-segmentation [7,33,55]. The purpose of our work is thus not to propose a new way or compare to those methods, but to investigate approaches that are more effective and efficient for the large-scale long-tailed setting. In this paper, we mainly focus on one potential solution for segmenting foreground objects: image co-segmentation. Aiming at jointly segmenting the common foreground regions from a group of images, co-segmentation is very useful in many semantic labeling tasks [4,7] and is a direct fit to the object-centric images we collect. Existing image co-segmentation models are usually trained and evaluated on relatively small-scale benchmarks such as MSRC [39], Internet [34], iCoseg [2], PASCAL-VOC [10], etc. Our work is almost the first attempt to test the generalizability of existing, pre-trained co-segmentation models on a much larger-scale setting that contains more than $1,000$ categories; each category consists of hundreds or thousands of object-centric images with various appearances and poses. As will be shown in the experimental results and analyses, our framework can effectively utilize the off-the-shelf image co-segmentation models.

3   Approach

Our FREESEG (Free Object Segments) framework for data augmentation is fairly simple and scalable for large-vocabulary and long-tailed instance segmentation. Figure 2 illustrates the overall pipeline, which consists of three major steps: (i) segment generation and refinement, (ii) segment ranking, and (iii) data synthesis for model training.

3.1   Generating Object Segments

We assume that we can obtain a sufficient amount of object-centric images for each class of interest. As discussed in [54], this is mostly doable. We can take advantage of existing image classification datasets like ImageNet [9] or leverage image search engine (*e.g.*, Google Images).

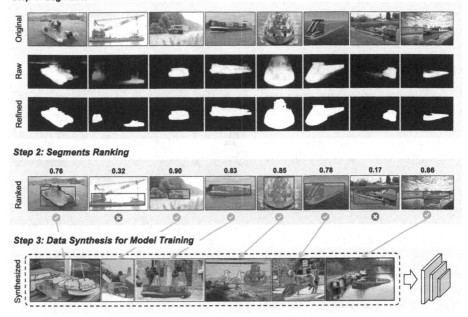

Fig. 2. Illustration of the FREESEG **pipeline.** We show a rare class *Barge* in LVIS v1 [13] as the example. We first perform image co-segmentation on top of the object-centric images of *Barge* (outside LVIS v1) to obtain raw object segments, followed by segments refinement. The segments are then scored by a learned ranker (the green boxes in step 2) such that only the high-quality ones would be used for augmenting data for model training. Finally, we randomly paste the selected object segments (red) onto the original scene-centric images of LVIS v1 to improve the long-tailed instance segmentation. Green segments indicate the original objects in scene-centric images. (Color figure online)

Raw Segments Generation. Given object-centric images of the same class, *which usually share similar appearances or contrasts to the background*, we apply image co-segmentation techniques [33,55] to extract their common foreground regions. Without loss of generality, we use the state-of-the-art image co-segmentation algorithms, Spatial and Semantic Modulation (SSM) [55]. The outputs of SSM are raw segments in gray scales for each image, as shown in Fig. 2 (see Sect. 4.1 for more details). Please be referred to Sect. 2 for other potential algorithms for this stage.

Post-Processing for Segment Refinement. To turn the raw, grayscale segmentation map into a binary one that can be used to train a segmentation model, we threshold the map. As the suitable threshold value may vary across images and classes, we apply a Gaussian filter followed by dynamic thresholding, *i.e.*, Li thresholding [20,21], which minimizes the cross-entropy between the foreground and the background to find the optimal threshold to distinguish them. To further improve the resulting binary map, we apply erosion and dilation to smooth the boundary. Finally, we then remove small, likely false positive segments by only keeping the largest connected component in the binary map. Figure 2 (Step 1) gives an illustration. Please also see supplementary materials for more details.

3.2 Learning to Rank the Segments

While the post-processing step has greatly improved the binary masks and made them look more like the true object masks, they may occasionally miss the target objects (*i.e.*, the objects of the image labels) or include background pixels. This is not surprising: we apply image co-segmentation class-by-class to only explore the within-class similarity. Some co-occurring objects (*e.g.*, persons for unicycles) thus may be miss-identified as the target objects; some target objects that are too small may be dominated by other objects.

At first glance, this seems to paint a grim picture. However, as mentioned in Sect. 1, our ultimate goal is to *obtain a set of high-quality instance segments from object-centric images, not to segment all the object-centric images well.* Therefore, in the second stage, we develop a novel approach to rank the object segments for each class. Specifically, we aim to select images whose masks truly cover the target objects and are as tight as possible to them.

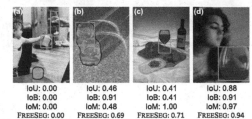

IoU: 0.00   IoU: 0.46   IoU: 0.41   IoU: 0.88
IoB: 0.00   IoB: 0.91   IoB: 0.41   IoB: 0.91
IoM: 0.00   IoM: 0.48   IoM: 1.00   IoM: 0.97
FREESEG: 0.00 FREESEG: 0.69 FREESEG: 0.71 FREESEG: 0.94

Fig. 3. Comparison of metrics for ranking segments. We show four examples of the class *wine glasses*. The red masks are by our method; green boxes are by LORE. In (a) and (d), IoU ranks the segments well, when the box locations are precise. However, in (b), the poor box location leads to a small IoU, even if the segment is precise. In (c), IoU fails due to the specific shape of *wine glasses*, even if the segment is precise. FREESEG score is able to take all the above into account to faithfully rank segments. (Color figure online)

Ranking by Learning a Classifier. Given an object segment obtained from co-segmentation, how can we determine if the segment truly covers the target object? Here, we take one intuition: *if a segment covers the target object, then by removing it from the image, an image classifier[1] will unlikely classify the manipulated image correctly.* This idea has indeed been used in [54] to discover pseudo bounding boxes given only image labels. More specifically, the authors developed "localization by region removal (LORE)", which sequentially removes bounding box regions from an image till the image classifier fails to predict the right class. Those removed bounding boxes are then treated as pseudo bounding boxes for the target object class.

We thus adopt the idea of LORE to rank our object segments. But instead of removing the discovered segments and checking the classifier's failure, we

---

[1] We have image labels for object-centric images, and thus we can train an image classifier upon them.

directly compare our object segments to the bounding boxes selected by LORE. *In essence, if the LORE boxes and our segments are highly overlapped, then the segments are considered high-quality.*

Ranking Metrics. Arguably the most common way to characterize the overlap/agreement between two masks/boxes is intersection over union (IoU), which simply treats all contents in a box or mask as foreground. However, this metric is not suitable in our case for the following reasons: (i) both boxes and segments may be noisy, and simply measuring the IoU between them fails to rank good segments when the boxes are poor; (ii) object shapes are not always convex, and thus IoU may underestimate the agreement. As shown in Fig. 3, IoU fails to recall true positives.

We therefore propose the FREESEG score to rank the segments. We make one mild assumption: either the object box or the segment is trustable, and introduce two metrics: intersection over bounding box (IoB) and intersection over mask (IoM). While they share the same numerator with intersection over union (IoU), they have different denominators. IoM implies that the bounding box is precise and measures how much portion of the mask is inside the box, and vice versa for IoB. We take both into account by averaging them as our FREESEG score. As shown in Fig. 4, it effectively keeps the good segments in the pool.

Drop Rate by the Classifier. We introduce another metric for ranking the segment or, more precisely, its corresponding object-centric image. The rationale is, if an object does not clearly show up in an image (*e.g.*, occluded or of small sizes), then the obtained segment is unlikely accurate. To this end, we leverage the image classifier trained for LORE, and compute the drop rate—the classifier's relative confidence drop for the target class, before and after LORE box removal. Let $s(c)$ and $s'(c)$ denote the classifier's confidence of the target class c before and after LORE box removal

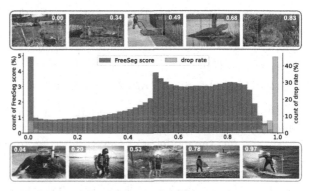

Fig. 4. Ranking the object segments. We apply the FREESEG score and the drop rate to select high-quality segments/images. We show the LORE boxes in green and discovered segments in red. In the top images of the class *alligator*, FREESEG scores on the upper right corner of images imply the alignment between the segments and the box locations. In the bottom images of the class *wet suit*, drop rates on the upper left corner of images indicate the quality of object-centric images (the larger, the better). These metrics are shown to be effective to rank the segments/images. For both metrics, we simply set a threshold 0.5 to discard low-confidence segments and images. (Color figure online)

from the image, the drop rate is $\frac{s(c)-s'(c)}{s(c)}$. The drop rate indicates how easily,

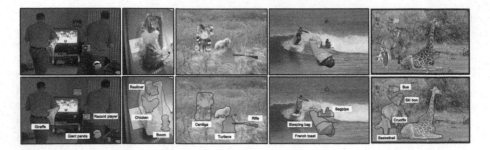

Fig. 5. Synthesized examples via FREESEG. We generate object segments from object-centric images and randomly paste them onto scene-centric images. Red masks indicate pasted segments by FREESEG; green masks indicate original objects in scene-centric images. Please see supplementary materials for more examples. (Color figure online)

by removing LORE's localized target objects, would the classifier's confidence reduce. The larger the drop is, the easier the localization of target objects is, and thus the higher-quality the object-centric image is. See Fig. 4 for an illustration on the drop rate.

Ranking the Segments. We use both the FREESEG score and the drop rate to rank the object-centric images and their co-segmentation segments. We keep those with both scores larger than 0.5 as the high-quality segments.

3.3 Putting the Segments in the Context

We now describe how we leverage the discovered high-quality instance segments to facilitate segmentation model training. As discussed in Sect. 1, instead of directly training the model with the segments on top of object-centric images, we choose to synthesize more scene-centric alike examples by pasting the segments into labeled scene-centric images (*e.g.*, those in LVIS v1 [13]). We adopt the idea of simple copy-paste augmentation [11] for this purpose. Specifically, we randomly (i) sample several object-centric images, (ii) re-scale and horizontally flip the object segments, and (iii) paste them onto the scene-centric images from the original training set (see Sect. 4.1 for details). The resulting synthesized images (see Fig. 5) then can be used to improve model training.

4 Experiments

4.1 Setup

Dataset and Evaluation Metrics. We validate our approach on the LVIS v1 instance segmentation benchmark [13]. (See the supplementary materials for the results on COCO-LT [47].) The dataset contains 1,203 entry-level object categories with around 2 million high-quality instance annotations. The training

Table 1. Statistics of LVIS training data and the augmented data by FREESEG. Collected: # of all images collected from ImageNet-22K and Google Images. Selected via FREESEG: # of remaining images selected by segments ranking. Note that our data curation process is quite straightforward and fully automated.

# of samples	ImageNet	Google Images	Total
Original instance	–	–	1,270K
Original image	–	–	100K
Collected	1,242K	588K	1,830K
Selected via FREESEG	662K	304K	966K

set contains $100,170$ images for all the classes; the validation set contains $19,809$ images for $1,035$ classes. The categories follow a long-tailed distribution and are divided into three groups based on the number of training images: rare (1–10 images), common (11–100 images), and frequent (>100 images). *We report our results on the validation set by convention.* We adopt the standard mean average precision (AP) metric [13], which sets the cap of detected objects per image to 300. We denote the AP for rare, common, and frequent classes as AP_r, AP_c, and AP_f, respectively. We also report AP for bounding boxes (*i.e.*, AP^b), predicted by the same instance segmentation models. Following [13,51], we set the score threshold to 1×10^{-4} during testing. No test-time augmentation is used.

Object-Centric Data Sources. We follow [54] to search images in ImageNet-22K [9] and Google Images [1]. Specifically, we use the unique WordNet synset ID [25] to match the categories between ImageNet-22K and LVIS v1. We are able to match 997 LVIS classes and retrieve $1,242,180$ images from ImageNet. Because ImageNet images are nearly balanced by design, with around 1K images/class, the imbalance situation in LVIS can be largely reduced. In addition, we retrieve images via Google by querying with class names provided by LVIS. Such a search returns hundreds of iconic images and we take top 500 for each of the $1,203$ classes. Overall, for the rarest class (one image in LVIS), the increase factor is larger than 500 times. Please see the supplementary material for more details.

Image Co-segmentation Algorithm. We adopt the state-of-the-art image co-segmentation algorithm Spatial and Semantic Modulation (SSM) [55] to discover raw segments of objects from the object-centric images. SSM designs a spatial and semantic modulated deep network to jointly learn the structural and semantic information from the objects in the same class. The checkpoint of released SSM model is pre-trained on COCO-SEG dataset [45] with a VGG16 backbone [40]. We directly apply the model on all the object-centric images for each category without bells and whistles.

Learning an Object Segments Ranker. As mentioned in Sect. 3.2, we train a 1203-way classifier with a ResNet-50 backbone [15], using all the object-centric images, to rank the candidate segments within each class. We use a batch size 256 and follow the standard training schedule. The classifier achieves 85% Top-

1 accuracy on the training images. We use the idea of "localization by region removal" (LORE) [54] to detect the bounding boxes of objects. Table 1 shows the statistics of the augmented data before and after the ranking via FREESEG.

Base Models for Instance Segmentation. We mainly evaluate the performance of FREESEG using two base models for instance segmentation, *i.e.*, Mask R-CNN [14] and MosaicOS [54], implemented with [51]. Both models use ResNet [15], which is pre-trained on ImageNet [35], with a Feature Pyramid Network (FPN) [23] as the backbone. The base Mask R-CNN model is trained with the LVIS v1 training set with *repeated factor sampling* and follows the standard training procedure in [13] (1× scheduler).

MosaicOS [54] is one of the state-of-the-art models[2], which is further pre-trained with balanced object-centric images from ImageNet-22K and Google Images. However, MosaicOS mainly focuses on improving long-tailed object detection with pseudo-labeled bounding boxes. As will be shown in the experimental results, FREESEG can notably boost the performance upon MosaicOS with the same image resources. Furthermore, such an improvement can not be achieved by the vanilla simple copy-paste [11] using the training data from LVIS alone, especially for rare object categories.

Details of Object Segments Pasting. We follow the pasting mechanism in [11] to randomly pick examples from LVIS training set as the background images. We then paste segments from N random object-centric images at different locations of each background image, where N is in $[1, 6]$[3]. For LVIS images, we follow the standard data augmentation policy in [13] and [51]. For binary masks originally on LVIS images, we remove pixel annotations if the objects are occluded by the pasted ones in the front. Please see the supplementary material for more details.

Training and Optimization. Given the base instance segmentation model, we first fine-tune the model for 90K iterations with FREESEG segments, using all the loss terms in Mask R-CNN. We fine-tune all the parameters except the batch-norm layers in the backbone. We then fine-tune the model again for another 90K iterations using the original LVIS training images. The rationale of training with multiple stages is to prevent the augmented instances from dominating the training process (see Table 1 for statistics) and it is shown to be effective in [54]. Both fine-tuning steps are trained with stochastic gradient descent with a batch size of 8, momentum of 0.9, weight decay of 10^{-4}, and learning rate of 2×10^{-4}. All models are trained with four NVIDIA A6000 GPUs.

4.2   Main Results on Instance Segmentation

State-of-the-Art Comparison. We compare to the state-of-the-art methods for long-tailed instance segmentation in Table 2. The proposed FREESEG method

---

[2] We note that FREESEG is detector-agnostic and is thus complementary to and compatible with other models [29,41,59] that incorporate external images like [54].

[3] The median number of instances per image in LVIS dataset is 6.

Table 2. State-of-the-art comparison on LVIS v1 instance segmentation. FREESEG are initialized with MosaicOS [54] as the base model. 2×: Seesaw applies a stronger 2× training schedule while other methods are with 1× schedule. ⋆: with post-processing calibration introduced by [27].

Backbone	Method	AP	AP_r	AP_c	AP_f	AP^b
ResNet-50 FPN	RFS [13]	22.58	12.30	21.28	28.55	23.25
	BaGS [22]	23.10	13.10	22.50	28.20	25.76
	Forest R-CNN [50]	23.20	14.20	22.70	27.70	24.60
	RIO [5]	23.70	15.20	22.50	28.80	24.10
	EQL v2 [42]	23.70	14.90	22.80	28.60	24.20
	FASA [53]	24.10	17.30	22.90	28.50	–
	DisAlign [56]	24.30	8.50	26.30	28.10	23.90
	Seesaw [46]$^{2\times}$	26.40	19.60	26.10	29.80	27.40
	MosaicOS [54]	24.45	18.17	23.00	28.83	25.05
	w/ FREESEG	25.19	*20.23*	23.80	28.92	25.98
	MosaicOS [54] ⋆	26.76	23.86	25.82	29.10	27.77
	w/ FREESEG ⋆	27.34	*25.11*	26.29	29.49	28.47
ResNet-101 FPN	RFS [13]	24.82	15.18	23.71	30.31	25.45
	FASA [53]	26.30	19.10	25.40	30.60	–
	Seesaw [46]$^{2\times}$	28.10	20.00	28.00	31.90	28.90
	MosaicOS [54]	26.73	20.52	25.78	30.53	27.41
	w/ FREESEG	27.54	*23.00*	26.48	30.72	28.63
	MosaicOS [54] ⋆	29.03	26.38	28.15	31.19	29.96
	w/ FREESEG ⋆	29.72	*28.69*	28.67	31.34	31.11
ResNeXt-101 FPN	RFS [13]	26.67	17.60	25.58	31.89	27.35
	MosaicOS [54]	28.29	21.75	27.22	32.35	28.85
	w/ FREESEG	28.86	*23.34*	27.77	32.49	29.98
	MosaicOS [54] ⋆	29.81	25.73	28.92	32.59	30.56
	w/ FREESEG ⋆	30.37	*26.43*	29.63	32.92	31.81

achieves comparable or even better results, especially for rare object categories. For example, FREESEG outperforms all the other methods except Seesaw loss [46], which is implemented with a different framework [6] and trained with a stronger scheduler. (We provide further comparisons in this aspect in the supplementary.)

Backbone Agnostic. Beyond ResNet-50, we further evaluate FREESEG with stronger backbone model architectures: ResNet-101 [15] and ResNeXt-101 [52], following the same training pipeline as ResNet-50. FREESEG achieves notably

Table 3. Ablation study on object segments ranking. We evaluate the performance of the model trained with and without the segments ranking mechanism by FREESEG. Results demonstrate the importance of ranking the object segments.

Method	Random	Ranking	#Image	AP	AP_r	AP_c	AP_f
MosaicOS [54]				24.45	18.17	23.00	28.83
			1,830K	24.87	19.13	23.55	28.86
w/ FREESEG	✓		966K	24.50	18.68	23.18	28.52
		✓	966K	**25.19**	**20.23**	**23.80**	**28.92**

Table 4. Analysis on different object segments ranking metrics. The proposed FREESEG score can take different scenarios into account thus achieves better results.

Method	Ranking metrics	AP	AP_r	AP_c	AP_f
MosaicOS [54]	–	24.45	18.17	23.00	28.83
w/ FREESEG	IoU	24.74	19.04	23.58	28.53
	IoB	24.69	18.41	23.58	28.70
	IoM	24.56	18.62	23.14	28.74
	FREESEG	**25.19**	**20.23**	**23.80**	**28.92**

gains over MosaicOS [54], justifying that FREESEG can benefit different instance segmentation models and architectures.

Compatibility with Existing Methods. We further apply post-processing calibration [27] on top of the model trained with FREESEG. Results are shown in Table 2 (FREESEG ⋆) and the improvements are consistent. More surprisingly, FREESEG can boost the performance of rare classes to be similar to common classes. This indicates that by introducing more while not so perfect training instances, FREESEG dramatically overcomes the long-tailed problem.

4.3 Detailed Analyses and Ablation Studies

Does Segment Ranking Help? The quality of the segments is important because inferior pixel-level annotations for instance segmentation may contain certain noise (cf. Sect. 1). Such an issue will be amplified for rare categories when the training examples are long-tailed. Here we conduct experiments with and without ranking object segments. As shown in Table 1, we are able to collect 1, 830K segments from ImageNet-22k and Google Images, while only half of them are left after filtering with FREESEG. Table 3 shows the results. While both versions outperform the baseline models, segment ranking does help more (row 4 *vs.* row 2 in Table 3), suggesting that the quality of pixel labels is more important than the quantity for instance segmentation.

We notice that filtering by ranking gives higher quality but fewer masks. To further understand the effect of quality and quantity of object segments on the

Table 5. Ablation study on segments filtering by drop rate.

Method	Drop rate	#Image	AP	AP_r	AP_c	AP_f
MosaicOS [54]			24.45	18.17	23.00	28.83
w/ FREESEG	✗	1,134K	24.81	19.37	23.62	28.54
	✓	966K	**25.19**	**20.23**	**23.80**	**28.92**

Table 6. Importance of the context. Segments Pasting [11]: ✗ indicates directly training the instance segmentation model on the object-centric images, using FREESEG segments as supervision.

Method	Segments pasting	AP	AP_r	AP_c	AP_f
MosaicOS [54]		24.45	18.17	23.00	28.83
w/ FREESEG	✗	24.78	18.85	23.40	28.90
	✓	**25.19**	**20.23**	**23.80**	**28.92**

accuracy of FREESEG, we randomly sample the original co-segmentation masks such that the remaining ones are of the same quantity as those *selected by our ranking method*. We see a bigger gain by our ranking method (row 4 *vs.* row 3 in Table 3), justifying its effectiveness in selecting high-quality masks.

Ranking Metrics. We show both quantitative and qualitative comparisons of different ranking metrics for filtering noisy segments in Table 4 and Fig. 3. FREESEG score can take different scenarios into account and successfully select confident segments from noisy ones. This verifies that the quality of the segments is the key and that the proposed FREESEG pipeline effectively does the job.

Effect of Segments Filtering by Drop Rate. Table 5 reports results with and without segments filtering with drop rate (cf. Sect. 3.2). By jointly using drop rate and FREESEG score, our method achieves better results by using fewer and cleaner object segments for training.

Importance of the Context. We investigate training the instance segmentation model directly with the object-centric images without pasting FREESEG segments to LVIS images. The results are shown in Table 6. As expected, we see that the performance is worse than the proposed FREESEG framework, in which we apply copy-paste augmentation to put the object instances into the context of original training images. This demonstrates the fact that there exists a gap between the contexts of two different image resources, which could limit the improvement on the main task.

Additional Results. Please see supplementary materials, including the results with other evaluation metrics and datasets, the analysis of multi-stage training, effects of different data sources, **qualitative results**, etc.

Table 7. Comparison of pasting ground truth (GT) object segments and FREESEG. The base models are trained with ResNet-50 and FPN. †: models from [54].

Method	GT	FREESEG	AP	AP_r	AP_c	AP_f	AP^b
Mask R-CNN [13]†			22.58	12.30	21.28	28.55	23.25
	✓		24.06	17.00	22.62	28.77	24.91
		✓	24.28	17.68	22.79	28.83	25.13
	✓	✓	24.74	*18.80*	23.38	28.86	25.51
MosaicOS [54]†			24.45	18.17	23.00	28.83	25.05
	✓		24.57	18.63	23.31	28.59	25.52
		✓	25.19	20.23	23.80	28.92	25.98
	✓	✓	25.36	*20.72*	24.00	28.92	26.00

4.4 Comparison to Pasting Ground-Truth Segments

Ghiasi *et al.* [11] show that copying and pasting human-annotated segments from one image to another as augmentation can improve instance segmentation with richer *context diversity*. They employ a much larger batch size and longer scheduler with another strong augmentation, large-scale jittering [11]. However, in this work, we focus on enriching *appearance diversity* for objects with abundant free segments from object-centric images. We, therefore, conduct a detailed comparison between pasting ground truth and FREESEG object segments. We follow the pasting mechanism in Sect. 4.1 but use ground truths segments instead. That is, we randomly pick two images from the LVIS training set, apply the same data augmentation policy following the standard instance segmentation model (*i.e.*, resizing shortest edge and random horizontal flip), and then *paste random numbers of instances from one image onto the other image*.

We show results in Table 7. We validate FREESEG on two base models and compare to the results of using ground truth segments for augmentation. FREESEG achieves consistent gains against the baseline models and, more importantly, outperforms those with copy-paste augmentation using only ground truth segments. This demonstrates that with ample images that can be acquired easily online, even noisy labels without any human efforts could significantly improve long-tailed instance segmentation. We also note that FREESEG is more effective when the baseline is already re-balanced (*e.g.*, MosaicOS in Table 7 bottom and Table 2), while GT-only can hardly improve upon it due to the lack of training examples. Furthermore, by learning with copy-paste from both sources, the gain can be even larger on both base models. These observations demonstrate that, besides context diversity, the appearance diversity of objects is also the key to improve segmentation.

5   Conclusion

Our main contribution and novelty are the insight that object segments emerge freely from object-centric images, and they effectively benefit the challenging long-tailed instance segmentation problem. We propose a scalable framework FREESEG to realize this idea. We show that, with the underlying properties of object-centric images, simple co-segmentation with proper ranking can result in high-quality instance segments to largely increase the labeled training instances.

We believe that the prospect of leveraging ample data without human labeling has enormous future potential. We note that there are several ways to realize this insight, and [55] is just an instantiation but turns out to be very useful: it is worth mentioning that co-segmentation has never been used to enhance instance segmentation. Further, our pipeline is clean and conceptually simple, clearly indicating where future improvement can be made (*e.g.*, segment discovery, extraction, leveraging). We expect our approach to serve as a strong baseline for this direction: for future work to build upon and take advantage of.

Acknowledgments. This research is supported in part by grants from the National Science Foundation (IIS-2107077, OAC-2118240, OAC-2112606), the OSU CCTS pilot grant, and Cisco Systems, Inc. We are thankful for the generous support of the computational resources by the Ohio Supercomputer Center and AWS Cloud Credits for Research.

References

1. Google Images. https://www.google.com/imghp?hl=EN
2. Batra, D., Kowdle, A., Parikh, D., Luo, J., Chen, T.: iCoseg: interactive co-segmentation with intelligent scribble guidance. In: CVPR (2010)
3. Caron, M., et al.: Emerging properties in self-supervised vision transformers. In: ICCV (2021)
4. Cech, J., Matas, J., Perdoch, M.: Efficient sequential correspondence selection by cosegmentation. IEEE Trans. Pattern Anal. Mach. Intell. (TPAMI) **32**(9), 1568–1581 (2010)
5. Chang, N., Yu, Z., Wang, Y.X., Anandkumar, A., Fidler, S., Alvarez, J.M.: Image-level or object-level? A tale of two resampling strategies for long-tailed detection. In: ICML (2021)
6. Chen, K., et al.: MMDetection: open MMLab detection toolbox and benchmark. arXiv preprint arXiv:1906.07155 (2019)
7. Chen, Y.C., Lin, Y.Y., Yang, M.H., Huang, J.B.: Show, match and segment: joint weakly supervised learning of semantic matching and object co-segmentation. IEEE Trans. Pattern Anal. Mach. Intell. (TPAMI) (2020)
8. Cheng, M.M., Mitra, N.J., Huang, X., Torr, P.H., Hu, S.M.: Global contrast based salient region detection. IEEE Trans. Pattern Anal. Mach. Intell. (TPAMI) **37**(3), 569–582 (2014)
9. Deng, J., Dong, W., Socher, R., Li, L.J., Li, K., Fei-Fei, L.: ImageNet: a large-scale hierarchical image database. In: CVPR (2009)

10. Everingham, M., Van Gool, L., Williams, C.K., Winn, J., Zisserman, A.: The PASCAL visual object classes (VOC) challenge. Int. J. Comput. Vis. (IJCV) **88**(2), 303–338 (2010)
11. Ghiasi, G., et al.: Simple copy-paste is a strong data augmentation method for instance segmentation. In: CVPR (2021)
12. Girshick, R., Donahue, J., Darrell, T., Malik, J.: Rich feature hierarchies for accurate object detection and semantic segmentation. In: CVPR (2014)
13. Gupta, A., Dollar, P., Girshick, R.: LVIS: a dataset for large vocabulary instance segmentation. In: CVPR (2019)
14. He, K., Gkioxari, G., Dollár, P., Girshick, R.: Mask R-CNN. In: ICCV (2017)
15. He, K., Zhang, X., Ren, S., Sun, J.: Deep residual learning for image recognition. In: CVPR (2016)
16. Hsieh, T.I., Robb, E., Chen, H.T., Huang, J.B.: DropLoss for long-tail instance segmentation. In: AAAI (2021)
17. Hu, X., Jiang, Y., Tang, K., Chen, J., Miao, C., Zhang, H.: Learning to segment the tail. In: CVPR (2020)
18. Itti, L., Koch, C., Niebur, E.: A model of saliency-based visual attention for rapid scene analysis. IEEE Trans. Pattern Anal. Mach. Intell. (TPAMI) **20**(11), 1254–1259 (1998)
19. Kang, B., et al.: Decoupling representation and classifier for long-tailed recognition. In: ICLR (2020)
20. Li, C., Tam, P.K.S.: An iterative algorithm for minimum cross entropy thresholding. Pattern Recogn. Lett. (PRL) **19**(8), 771–776 (1998)
21. Li, C.H., Lee, C.: Minimum cross entropy thresholding. Pattern Recogn. **26**(4), 617–625 (1993)
22. Li, Y., et al.: Overcoming classifier imbalance for long-tail object detection with balanced group softmax. In: CVPR (2020)
23. Lin, T.Y., Dollár, P., Girshick, R., He, K., Hariharan, B., Belongie, S.: Feature pyramid networks for object detection. In: CVPR (2017)
24. Lin, T.-Y., et al.: Microsoft COCO: common objects in context. In: Fleet, D., Pajdla, T., Schiele, B., Tuytelaars, T. (eds.) ECCV 2014. LNCS, vol. 8693, pp. 740–755. Springer, Cham (2014). https://doi.org/10.1007/978-3-319-10602-1_48
25. Miller, G.A.: WordNet: a lexical database for English. Commun. ACM **38**(11), 39–41 (1995)
26. Oksuz, K., Cam, B.C., Kalkan, S., Akbas, E.: Imbalance problems in object detection: a review. IEEE Trans. Pattern Anal. Mach. Intell. (TPAMI) (2020)
27. Pan, T.Y., et al.: On model calibration for long-tailed object detection and instance segmentation. In: NeurIPS (2021)
28. Ramanathan, V., Wang, R., Mahajan, D.: DLWL: improving detection for lowshot classes with weakly labelled data. In: CVPR (2020)
29. Redmon, J., Farhadi, A.: YOLO9000: better, faster, stronger. In: CVPR (2017)
30. Ren, J., et al.: Balanced meta-softmax for long-tailed visual recognition. In: NeurIPS (2020)
31. Ren, S., He, K., Girshick, R., Sun, J.: Faster R-CNN: towards real-time object detection with region proposal networks. IEEE Trans. Pattern Anal. Mach. Intell. (TPAMI) **39**(6), 1137–1149 (2016)
32. Rother, C., Kolmogorov, V., Blake, A.: "GrabCut" interactive foreground extraction using iterated graph cuts. ACM Trans. Graph. (TOG) **23**(3), 309–314 (2004)
33. Rother, C., Minka, T., Blake, A., Kolmogorov, V.: Cosegmentation of image pairs by histogram matching-incorporating a global constraint into MRFs. In: CVPR (2006)

34. Rubinstein, M., Joulin, A., Kopf, J., Liu, C.: Unsupervised joint object discovery and segmentation in internet images. In: CVPR (2013)
35. Russakovsky, O., et al.: ImageNet large scale visual recognition challenge. IJCV **115**(3), 211–252 (2015)
36. Selvaraju, R.R., Cogswell, M., Das, A., Vedantam, R., Parikh, D., Batra, D.: Grad-CAM: visual explanations from deep networks via gradient-based localization. In: ICCV (2017)
37. Shao, S., et al.: Objects365: a large-scale, high-quality dataset for object detection. In: ICCV (2019)
38. Shen, L., Lin, Z., Huang, Q.: Relay backpropagation for effective learning of deep convolutional neural networks. In: Leibe, B., Matas, J., Sebe, N., Welling, M. (eds.) ECCV 2016. LNCS, vol. 9911, pp. 467–482. Springer, Cham (2016). https://doi. org/10.1007/978-3-319-46478-7_29
39. Shotton, J., Winn, J., Rother, C., Criminisi, A.: *TextonBoost*: joint appearance, shape and context modeling for multi-class object recognition and segmentation. In: Leonardis, A., Bischof, H., Pinz, A. (eds.) ECCV 2006. LNCS, vol. 3951, pp. 1–15. Springer, Heidelberg (2006). https://doi.org/10.1007/11744023_1
40. Simonyan, K., Zisserman, A.: Very deep convolutional networks for large-scale image recognition. arXiv preprint arXiv:1409.1556 (2014)
41. Sohn, K., Zhang, Z., Li, C.L., Zhang, H., Lee, C.Y., Pfister, T.: A simple semi-supervised learning framework for object detection. arXiv preprint arXiv:2005.04757 (2020)
42. Tan, J., Lu, X., Zhang, G., Yin, C., Li, Q.: Equalization loss v2: a new gradient balance approach for long-tailed object detection. In: CVPR (2021)
43. Tan, J., et al.: Equalization loss for long-tailed object recognition. In: CVPR (2020)
44. Thomee, B., et al.: YFCC100M: the new data in multimedia research. Commun. ACM **59**(2), 64–73 (2016)
45. Wang, C., Zha, Z.J., Liu, D., Xie, H.: Robust deep co-saliency detection with group semantic. In: AAAI (2019)
46. Wang, J., et al.: Seesaw loss for long-tailed instance segmentation. In: CVPR (2021)
47. Wang, T., et al.: The Devil is in classification: a simple framework for long-tail instance segmentation. In: ECCV (2020)
48. Wang, T., Zhu, Y., Zhao, C., Zeng, W., Wang, J., Tang, M.: Adaptive class suppression loss for long-tail object detection. In: CVPR (2021)
49. Wang, X., Huang, T.E., Darrell, T., Gonzalez, J.E., Yu, F.: Frustratingly simple few-shot object detection. In: ICML (2020)
50. Wu, J., Song, L., Wang, T., Zhang, Q., Yuan, J.: Forest R-CNN: large-vocabulary long-tailed object detection and instance segmentation. In: ACM MM (2020)
51. Wu, Y., Kirillov, A., Massa, F., Lo, W.Y., Girshick, R.: Detectron2. https://github. com/facebookresearch/detectron2 (2019)
52. Xie, S., Girshick, R., Dollár, P., Tu, Z., He, K.: Aggregated residual transformations for deep neural networks. In: CVPR (2017)
53. Zang, Y., Huang, C., Loy, C.C.: FASA: feature augmentation and sampling adaptation for long-tailed instance segmentation. In: ICCV (2021)
54. Zhang, C., et al.: MosaicOS: a simple and effective use of object-centric images for long-tailed object detection. In: ICCV (2021)
55. Zhang, K., Chen, J., Liu, B., Liu, Q.: Deep object co-segmentation via spatial-semantic network modulation. In: AAAI (2020)
56. Zhang, S., Li, Z., Yan, S., He, X., Sun, J.: Distribution alignment: a unified framework for long-tail visual recognition. In: CVPR (2021)

57. Zhang, Y., Kang, B., Hooi, B., Yan, S., Feng, J.: Deep long-tailed learning: a survey. arXiv preprint arXiv:2110.04596 (2021)
58. Zhou, B., Khosla, A., Lapedriza, A., Oliva, A., Torralba, A.: Learning deep features for discriminative localization. In: CVPR (2016)
59. Zhou, X., Girdhar, R., Joulin, A., Krähenbühl, P., Misra, I.: Detecting twenty-thousand classes using image-level supervision. In: ECCV (2022)
60. Zhu, X., Anguelov, D., Ramanan, D.: Capturing long-tail distributions of object subcategories. In: CVPR (2014)
61. Zou, Z., Shi, Z., Guo, Y., Ye, J.: Object detection in 20 years: a survey. arXiv preprint arXiv:1905.05055 (2019)

Autoregressive Uncertainty Modeling for 3D Bounding Box Prediction

YuXuan Liu[1,2]([✉]), Nikhil Mishra[1,2], Maximilian Sieb[1], Yide Shentu[1,2], Pieter Abbeel[1,2], and Xi Chen[1]

[1] Covariant, Emeryville, USA
[2] UC Berkeley, Berkeley, USA
yuxuanliu@berkeley.edu

Abstract. 3D bounding boxes are a widespread intermediate representation in many computer vision applications. However, predicting them is a challenging task, largely due to partial observability, which motivates the need for a strong sense of uncertainty. While many recent methods have explored better architectures for consuming sparse and unstructured point cloud data, we hypothesize that there is room for improvement in the modeling of the output distribution and explore how this can be achieved using an autoregressive prediction head. Additionally, we release a simulated dataset, COB-3D, which highlights new types of ambiguity that arise in real-world robotics applications, where 3D bounding box prediction has largely been underexplored. We propose methods for leveraging our autoregressive model to make high confidence predictions and meaningful uncertainty measures, achieving strong results on SUN-RGBD, Scannet, KITTI, and our new dataset (Code and dataset are available at bbox.yuxuanliu.com.).

Keywords: 3D bounding boxes · 3D bounding box estimation · 3D object detection · Autoregressive models · Uncertainty modeling

1 Introduction

Predicting 3D bounding boxes is a core part of the computer vision stack in many real world applications, including autonomous driving, robotics, and augmented reality. The inputs to a 3D bounding box predictor usually consist of an RGB image and a point cloud; the latter is typically obtained from a 3D sensor such as LIDAR or stereo depth cameras. These 3D sensing modalities have their own idiosyncrasies: LIDAR tends to be accurate but very sparse, and stereo depth can be both sparse and noisy. When combined with the fact that objects are only seen from one perspective, the bounding-box prediction problem is fundamentally underspecified: the available information is not sufficient to unambiguously perform the task.

Supplementary Information The online version contains supplementary material available at https://doi.org/10.1007/978-3-031-20080-9_39.

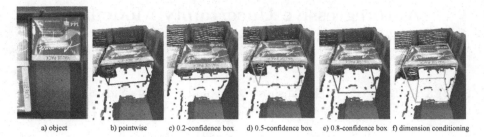

a) object   b) pointwise   c) 0.2-confidence box   d) 0.5-confidence box   e) 0.8-confidence box   f) dimension conditioning

Fig. 1. a) In this scene from a real-world robotics application, how tall is the object highlighted in red? b) A pointwise model could output only one box prediction with no notion of uncertainty c)–e) Predictions from our confidence box method. Notice that the predicted box expands in the direction of uncertainty as we increase the confidence requirement. f) Our dimension conditioning method can leverage additional information to make more accurate predictions.

Imagine that a robot is going to grasp an object and manipulate it—understanding the uncertainty over the size can have a profound impact on what the robot decides to do next. For example, if it uses the predicted bounding box to avoid collisions during motion planning, then we may want to be conservative and err on the larger side. However, if it is trying to pack the items into a shipment, then having accurate dimensions may also be important.

Consider the scene depicted in Fig. 1, which we observed in a real-world robotics application. From the image of the object in a), it is fairly easy to gauge the width and length of the indicated object, but how tall is it? The object could be as deep as the bin, or it could be a stack of two identical objects, or even a thin object – but from the available information, it is impossible to say for sure. Formulating bounding box prediction as a regression problem results in a model that can only make a "pointwise" prediction – even in the face of ambiguity, we will only get a single predicted bounding box, shown in b).

A sufficiently expressive bounding-box model should be able to output the entire range of plausible bounding box hypotheses and make different predictions for different confidence requirements. A 0.5-confidence box d) must contain the object 50% of the time while a 0.8-confidence box e) will expand in the direction of uncertainty to contain the object 80% of the time. Moreover, such a model could leverage additional information, such as known dimensions of an object, to make even more accurate predictions, as shown in f).

Setting aside partial observability, the prediction space has complexities that require care in the design of a bounding-box estimator. Making accurate predictions requires the estimator to reason about rotations, which has been observed to be notoriously difficult for neural networks to predict and model uncertainty over [5,16,29]. Many existing methods sidestep this problem by constraining their predictions to allow rotation about a single axis or no rotations at all. This can be sufficient for some applications but has shortcomings for the general case.

A common thread that links these challenges together is the necessity to reason about uncertainty. This has been largely underexplored in existing work, but we hypothesize that it is critical to improving 3D bounding box estimators and expanding their usability in applications of interest. We propose to tackle this problem by predicting a more expressive probability distribution that explicitly accounts for the relationships between different box parameters. Using a technique that has proven effective in other domains, we propose to model 3D bounding boxes autoregressively: that is, to predict each box component sequentially, conditioned on the previous ones. This allows us to model multimodal uncertainty due to incomplete information, make high confidence predictions in the face of uncertainty, and seamlessly relax the orientation constraints that are popular in existing methods. To summarize our contributions:

1. We propose an autoregressive formulation to 3D bounding box prediction that can model complex, multimodal uncertainty. We show how this formulation can gracefully scale to predict complete 3D orientations, rather than the 0- or 1-D alternatives that are common in prior work.
2. We propose a method to make high confidence predictions in ambiguous scenarios and estimate useful measures of uncertainty.
3. We introduce a simulated dataset of robotics scenes that illustrates why capturing uncertainty is important for 3D bounding box prediction, as well as the benefits and challenges of predicting full 3D rotations.
4. We show that our formulation applies to both traditional 3D bounding box estimation and 3D object detection, achieving competitive results on popular indoor and autonomous driving datasets in addition to our dataset.

2   Related Work

3D Bounding-Box Estimation: Early work on 3D bounding box prediction [14,19] assumes that object detection or segmentation has already been performed, and the bounding box predictor solely needs to identify a single 3D bounding box within a filtered point cloud. In this paper, we refer to this task as *3D bounding-box estimation*. Much of this work focused on developing architectures to easily consume point cloud data, which often can be sparse and/or unstructured when obtained from real-world data.

3D Object Detection: Recently, a number of methods [9,13,17,20–22,27] have explored how to jointly perform object detection and 3D bounding box estimation, rather than treating them as two explicit steps. This task is known as *3D object detection* and is quickly gaining popularity over the decoupled detection and estimation tasks. The main focus is on how to take the network architectures that have proven successful at the estimation task (which have strong inductive biases for operating on point clouds), and combine them with the architectures commonly used for the 2D object detection method (which are usually based on region proposals).

Uncertainty Modeling in Object Detection: Uncertainty modeling has been studied in the context of 2D and 3D Object Detection [6,8,11,12,28]. In many cases, these methods will use independent distributions, such as Gaussian or Laplace, to model uncertainty over box parameters such as corners, dimensions, and centers [1,7,11]. While these distributions may capture some uncertainty for simple box parameterizations, they don't capture correlations across parameters and have yet to be proven on full 3D rotations.

Autoregressive Models: Deep autoregressive models are frequently employed across a variety of domains. In deep learning, they first gained popularity for generative modeling of images [15,25,26], since they can model long-range dependencies to ensure that pixels later in the autoregressive ordering are sampled consistently with the ones sampled earlier. In addition to being applied to other high-dimensional data such as audio [15], they have also been shown to offer precise predictions even for much lower-dimensional data, such as robot joint angles or motor torques [10].

3   Autoregressive 3D Bounding Box Prediction

3D bounding box estimation is typically formulated as a regression problem over the dimensions $d = (d_x, d_y, d_z)$, center $c = (c_x, c_y, c_z)$, and rotation $R = (\psi, \theta, \phi)$ of a bounding box, given some perceptual features h computed from the scene, e.g. from an image and point cloud. Prior work has explored various parametrizations and loss functions, but a notable salient feature to observe is that they all predict a *pointwise* estimate of the bounding box: the model simply outputs all of the box parameters at once. In 3D object detection, such regression is typically applied to every box within a set of candidates (or *anchors*), and fits into a larger cascade that includes classifying which anchors are relevant and filtering out unnecessary or duplicate anchors. In practice, this formulation can be greatly limiting, especially in the face of partial observability or symmetry.

3.1   Autoregressive Modeling

We propose to tackle this problem by autoregressively modeling the components of a 3D bounding box. That is, for some ordering of the components (e.g. dimensions → center → orientation, or any permutation thereof), such a predictor will sequentially predict each component conditioned on the previous ones. In theory, the particular autoregressive ordering should not matter; empirically, we find that dimensions → center → orientation was effective, so we use this ordering for our model. Having dimension as first in the autoregressive ordering also enables us to condition on dimensions when they are known which can be effective at improving the prediction accuracy.

We discretize the box parameters rather than predicting continuous values, which is a well-known technique that allows the model to easily express multimodal distributions [25]. For rotations, we chose Euler angles since each dimension has a fixed range and does not to be normalized. To make discrete dimension

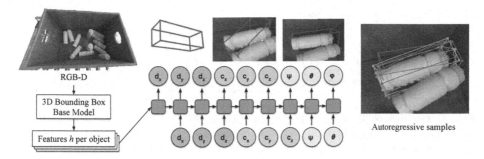

Fig. 2. We compute per-object features h using a base model from RGB-D input. Then, we autoregressively sample dimensions, center, and rotations, each step conditioned on the previous one. We can express uncertainty through samples, such as the rotational symmetry of the bottle, whereas pointwise models could only make a single prediction.

and center predictions, we normalize those parameters so that they can fit within a fixed set of discrete bins. We normalize dimensions by some scale s so that most values of d/s are within the range $[0, 1]$, and offset the centers by c_0 so that most normalized centers $(c - c_0)/s$ are within the range $[-1, 1]$. We use 512 bins for each dimension and adjust the bin range to achieve on average ≥ 0.99 IOU with the quantized box and $<0.1\%$ overflow or underflow due to quantization (Fig. 2).

From RGB-D inputs we extract a fixed-dimensional feature vector h for each object. For each parameter $b = (d_x, d_y, d_z, c_x, c_y, c_z, \psi, \theta, \phi)$ in the autoregressive ordering, we model $p(b_i|b_1, \ldots, b_{i-1}, h)$ using a MLP with 2–3 hidden layers. This autoregressive model is then trained using maximum likelihood:

$$\log p(b|h) = \sum_{i=1}^{9} \log p(b_i|b_1, \ldots, b_{i-1}, h) \tag{1}$$

3.2 Model Architectures

Our autoregressive prediction scheme can be applied to any type of 3D bounding box predictor. In this section, we discuss how it might be applied in two different contexts: 3D object detection and 3D bounding box estimation.

Autoregressive 3D Object Detection. FCAF3D [20] is a state-of-the-art 3D object detection method that was heavily engineered to exploit sparse and unstructured point clouds. Given a colored point cloud, it applies a specialized feature extractor consisting of sparse 3D convolutions, and then proposes 3D bounding boxes following a popular single-stage detector, FCOS [24].

Autoregressive FCAF3D: We can make FCAF3D autoregressive by adding a head and training this head with maximum likelihood in addition to the FCAF3D loss $L_F(h, y)$ (Fig. 3). We found that the pointwise box prediction was useful to

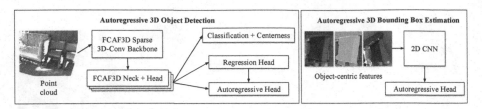

Fig. 3. For indoor 3D Object Detection, we use FCAF3D as a base model with an autoregressive head for bounding box prediction. For 3D Bounding Box Estimation we take object-centric features from a 2D object detector and pass them into a 2D CNN for autoregressive bounding box prediction.

condition the autoregressive prediction and estimate the scaling normalization factor $s = \max\{d'_x, d'_y, d'_z\}$, where d' is the pointwise dimension prediction of FCAF3D. Bounding box centers c are normalized by the output locations c_0 of the sparse convolutions and scaled by the same s: $(c - c_0)/s$. Since 3D object detection datasets have at most one degree of freedom for rotation, we predict only one θ parameter for box rotation.

To optimize the autoregressive prediction for higher IOU, we sample boxes $b \sim p(b|h)$ and maximize the IOUs of the samples with the ground truth box y. For this optimization, we use the conditional expectation b' where $b'_i = \mathbb{E}[b_i|b_1, \ldots, b_{i-1}, h]$ (since b' is differentiable) to maximize $IOU(b', y)$. Altogether, we train autoregressive FCAF3D using the combined loss:

$$L(h, y) = L_F(h, y) - \log p(b|h) + \mathbb{E}_{b \sim p(b|h)}[1 - IOU(b', y)] \qquad (2)$$

Autoregressive PV-RCNN: Lidar-based object detection networks, such as PV-RCNN [22], typically have different architectures and inductive biases than indoor detection models. However, we show that our autoregressive box parameterization is agnostic to the underlying architecture by applying it to PV-RCNN. We propose Autoregressive PV-RCNN by extending the proposal refinement head to be autoregressive, modeling the residual Δr^α as discrete autoregressive $p(\Delta r^\alpha|h)$. Then, we add $-\log p(\Delta r^\alpha|h)$ to the total training loss.

Autoregressive 3D Bounding Box Estimation. 3D Bounding Box Estimation assumes that object detection has already been performed in 2D, and we simply need to predict a 3D bounding box for each detected object. To highlight that our autoregressive prediction scheme can be applied to any bounding box predictor, we chose a model architecture that is substantially different from FCAF3D. For each detected object, we take an object-centric crop of the point cloud, normals, and object mask as input to a 2D-CNN, producing a fixed feature vector h per object. This h is used as features for our autoregressive parameterization $p(b|h)$. See Appendix A for more details on the architecture.

To normalize the input and box parameters, we scale by the range of the first and third quartiles of each point cloud dimension $s = Q_3 - Q_1$, and recenter by the mean of the quartiles $c_0 = \frac{Q_1 + Q_3}{2}$. For full SO(3) rotations, we found there were many box parameters that could represent the same box; for example, a box with $d = (1, 2, 3)$ is equivalent to a box with $d' = (2, 1, 3)$ and a 90° rotation. To account for this, we find all the box parameters $B = \{b^{(1)}, ..., b^{(m)}\}$ that represent the same box and supervise on all of them:

$$L(h, B) = -\frac{1}{|B|} \sum_{b^{(i)} \in B} \log(b^{(i)}|h) \qquad (3)$$

4   Applying Autoregressive 3D Bounding Box Models

Given a trained autoregressive bounding-box model, how do we actually obtain predictions from it? There can be a few different options, depending on how the downstream application plans to use the predictions.

4.1   Beam Search

In many applications, we want to simply obtain the most likely 3D bounding box given the input observation. That is, we find the box $b^* = \arg\max_b p(b|h)$ which is most likely under the model. Finding b^* exactly can be computationally expensive, but we can approximate it using *beam search*, a technique that has proven especially popular for autoregressive models in natural language applications [3]. Beam search allows us to estimate the mode of the distribution learned by the model and serves as an effective pointwise prediction.

4.2   Quantile and Confidence Boxes

In applications such as robotics and autonomous driving, 3D bounding boxes are often used to estimate object extents and avoid collisions. To that end, we often care that an object o is fully contained in the estimated box b. For a given confidence requirement p, we define a confidence box b_p as a box that contains the true object o with probability at least p: $\mathbb{P}(o \subseteq b_p) \geq p$. We'll show how to use an autoregressive bounding box model for confidence box predictions.

Suppose we draw multiple samples K from our model. If a point $x \in \mathbb{R}^3$ is contained in many boxes, then it's likely that point is actually part of the object. Conversely, a point that is only contained in a few sampled boxes is not likely to be part of the object. We can formalize this intuition as the occupancy measure

$$O(x) = \mathbb{P}(x \in b) = \mathbb{E}_{b \sim p(b|h)}[\mathbb{1}\{x \in b\}] \approx \frac{1}{K} \sum_{i=1}^{K} \mathbb{1}\{x \in b^{(i)}\} \qquad (4)$$

which can be approximated using samples $b^{(1)}, \ldots, b^{(K)} \sim p(b|h)$ from our model.

To find regions that are very likely to be part of an object, consider the set of all points that have occupancy greater than q:

$$Q(q) = \{x : O(x) > q\} \qquad (5)$$

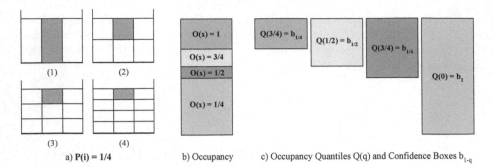

Fig. 4. Consider a scenario where we are estimating the bounding box of a tightly packed bin of stacked boxes. a) There is not enough visual information to estimate the object height, however, we know that the object could have heights H/i for $i \in \{1, 2, 3, 4\}$ with equal probability. b) We compute the occupancy $O(x)$ for different regions. c) We visualize occupancy quantiles $Q(q)$ which correspond to confidence boxes b_{1-q}. Notice that as the confidence requirement increases, the size of the box increases to ensure we can contain the true object.

which we'll refer to as the *occupancy quantile*. The minimum volume bounding box over the occupancy quantile is the *quantile box*:

$$b_q = \arg \min_{b:Q(q) \subseteq b} \mathrm{vol}(b) \tag{6}$$

Under some conditions, we can show that quantile boxes are confidence boxes.

Theorem 1. *A quantile box with quantile q is a confidence box with confidence $p = 1 - q$ when $p(b|h)$ is an ordered object distribution.*

$p(b|h)$ is an ordered object distribution if for any two distinct boxes b_i, b_j in the sample space of $p(b|h)$, one box must be contained within the other, $b_i \subset b_j$ or $b_j \subset b_i$. Empirically we find that quantile boxes are good approximations for confidence boxes even when $p(b|h)$ is not an ordered object distribution. See Fig. 4 for a visualization of occupancy and confidence boxes.

Quantile boxes provide an efficient way to make confidence box predictions with an autoregressive model. We can use the autoregressive distribution to estimate occupancy using supervision from 3D box labels (without requiring meshes for direct occupancy supervision). Occupancy quantiles provide a fast approach for confidence box estimation on ordered object distributions and a good confidence box approximation for general object distributions. Appendix B has the full proof of Theorem 1 and the details of our fast quantile box algorithm.

4.3 Uncertainty Measure

Uncertainty estimation is an important application of bounding box estimation. When the 3D extent of an object is unknown or not fully observed, it can be valuable if a model can also indicate that its predictions are uncertain. For instance, a robot may choose to manipulate that uncertain object more slowly to avoid collisions, or an autonomous vehicle may be more cautious around a moving object of unknown size.

A pointwise predictor can accomplish this by predicting both a mean μ and variance σ^2 for each box parameter, maximizing a $\mathcal{N}(\mu, \sigma^2)$ likelihood [7]. However, the spread of the distribution is measured independently for each box parameter which doesn't measure the spread of the overall box distribution well.

With an autoregressive box parameterization, we can measure uncertainty in the space of boxes using quantile boxes. Let b_α and b_β be two quantile boxes with different quantiles. If we consider these boxes as confidence boxes, we can interpret (b_α, b_β) as a confidence interval or the spread of the box distribution. With this intuition, we can measure uncertainty using the IOU of different quantile boxes $U_{\alpha,\beta} = 1 - IOU(b_\alpha, b_\beta)$. This $U_{\alpha,\beta}$ effectively measures the span of the distribution in units of relative volume.

4.4 Dimension Conditioning

For some robotics applications, such as object manipulation in industrial settings, we are often presented with Stock-Keeping Unit, or SKU, information beforehand. In these scenarios, the dimensions of each SKU are provided, and the prediction task essentially boils down to correctly assigning the dimensions to a detected object instance, and predicting the pose of the 3D bounding box.

The autoregressive nature of our model allows for conveniently conditioning on the dimensions of each bounding box. However, we don't know which object in the scene corresponds to which SKU dimensions. How can we leverage dimension information from multiple SKUs without object-SKU correspondence? Our autoregressive model provides an elegant solution using conditioning and likelihood evaluation.

Given $\{d^{(1)}, ..., d^{(k)}\}$ known SKU dimensions, we can make a bounding box prediction using this information by maximizing:

$$b^* = \arg\max_b \{ \max_{d^{(1)}, ..., d^{(k)}} p(b|d^{(i)}, h) \} \tag{7}$$

We can find the optimal b^* by using beam search conditioned on each of the d_i and returning the box with the highest likelihood. Figure 1 shows an illustrative example of how dimension conditioning can be used to greatly increase the fidelity of the predicted 3D bounding boxes.

5 Experiments

We designed our experiments to answer the following questions:

1. How does an autoregressive bounding box predictor perform compared to a pointwise predictor, across a variety of domains and model architectures?
2. How meaningful are the uncertainty estimates from an autoregressive model? Are quantile boxes confidence boxes for general object distributions?

5.1   Datasets

To demonstrate the flexibility of our method, we conducted experiments on a diverse set of indoor, outdoor, and industrial datasets:

SUN-RGBD [23] is a real-world dataset containing monocular images and point clouds captured from a stereo depth camera. It features a large variety of indoor scenes and is one of the most popular benchmarks in 3D object detection. The box labels only include one rotational degree of freedom θ.

Scannet [2] is a dataset of indoor 3D reconstructions. There are 18 classes and box labels are axis-aligned (no rotation). We train on 1201 scenes and evaluate on 312 validation scenes.

KITTI [4] is a widely popular 3D detection dataset for autonomous driving. Objects in KITTI have one degree of rotational freedom θ, and we report evaluation results on the validation split.

COB-3D. *Common Objects in Bins 3D* is a simulated dataset rendered by Theory Studios to explore a qualitatively different set of challenges than the ones exhibited in popular datasets in the literature. We are releasing nearly 7000 scenes that aim to emulate industrial order-picking environments with each scene consisting of a bin containing a variety of items. There are two main themes we chose to highlight: first, the objects are in a greater range of orientations than any other 3D-bounding-box dataset. In particular, a model that performs well must reason about complete 3D rotations, whereas the state-of-the-art methods on SUN-RGBD only need to predict one rotational degree of freedom. Secondly, it exhibits many types of ambiguity including rotation symmetry, occlusion reasoning in cluttered scenes, and tightly-pack bins with unobserved dimensions. See Appendix C for full details on this dataset including visual examples.

5.2   Evaluation

To evaluate 3D-bounding-box predictions, *intersection-over-union*, or IoU, is commonly used to compare the similarity between two boxes. 3D object detection uses mean average precision, or mAP, to measure how well a detector trades off precision and recall. IoU is used to determine whether a prediction is close enough to a ground-truth box to constitute a true positive. For 3D bounding-box estimation, detection has already happened, so we simply measure the mean IoU between the prediction and ground-truth, averaged across objects.

Unlike 2D detection, many applications that use 3D bounding boxes especially care about underestimation more than overestimation: if the predicted bounding box is too large, that is generally a less costly error than if it is too small. In the latter case, there are parts of the object that are outside the bounding box, which may result in collisions in robotics or autonomous driving setting.

To help quantify this error asymmetry, we consider a new similarity functions, the *intersection-over-ground-truth* (IoG). IoG measure what fraction of the ground truth box is contained within the predicted box; when IoG is 1, the ground truth box is fully contained in the predicted box. With IoG and IoU, we

Table 1. 3D Object Detection results on SUN-RGBD, Scannet, and KITTI

Dataset	Method	IoU			IoG		
		$AP_{0.25}$	$AP_{0.50}$	AP_{all}	$AP_{0.25}$	$AP_{0.50}$	AP_{all}
SUN-RGBD	FCAF3D	63.8	48.2	37.42	64.72	59.82	48.75
	3DETR	59.52	32.17	31.13	63.00	53.33	44.08
	VoteNet	60.71	38.98	30.25	62.81	54.58	43.62
	ImVoteNet	**64.24**	39.38	31.12	**67.00**	57.41	45.78
	Beam Search	62.94	47.03	38.15	64.75	58.50	47.17
	Quantile 0.1	61.21	30.94	31.06	65.89	**64.34**	**60.08**
	Quantile 0.4	63.46	48.41	38.43	65.34	61.68	51.76
	Quantile 0.45	63.47	**48.64**	**38.55**	65.19	61.03	50.36
	Quantile 0.5	63.30	47.70	38.50	64.99	59.83	48.44
Scannet	FCAF3D	68.53	**53.87**	43.32	72.05	67.63	60.66
	3DETR	64.09	47.16	39.57	68.62	59.17	49.82
	Beam Search	**69.06**	53.67	**43.85**	71.46	66.10	59.13
	Quantile 0.1	67.10	43.13	34.17	72.23	**70.01**	**66.73**
	Quantile 0.2	68.03	48.68	38.27	**72.30**	69.68	65.43
	Quantile 0.4	68.73	52.98	42.76	72.08	67.74	61.98
KITTI		AP IoU Hard Split			AP IoG Hard Split		
	Method	Car	Ped.	Cycl.	Car	Ped.	Cycl.
	PVRCNN	**82.37**	53.12	68.69	91.86	67.08	73.14
	Beam Search	**82.37**	52.28	**69.13**	91.84	66.96	73.40
	Quantile 0.1	59.75	39.26	58.38	**96.02**	**71.85**	**76.09**
	Quantile 0.4	81.98	**54.15**	68.45	93.98	70.63	74.08
	Quantile 0.5	82.32	53.78	69.03	91.84	68.14	73.52

have a more complete understanding of the types of errors that a bounding-box predictor is making. For the detection task, we compute mAP separately using IoU and IoG, and for the estimation task, we compute the mean IoG along with the mean IoU.

5.3   3D Object Detection

To evaluate the autoregressive box parameterization for 3D Object Detection, we evaluate Autoregressive FCAF3D and Autoregressive PV-RCNN introduced in Sect. 3.2. Table 1 shows the comparison between autoregressive models and baselines on SUN-RGBD, Scannet, and KITTI. We find that beam search generally matches the baseline performance, if not exceeding performance on IoU AP_{all}.

As for quantile boxes, we find that lower quantiles result in higher IoG mAP which suggests that the predicted boxes are more likely to contain the ground truth box. This is consistent with our claim from Theorem 1 since lower quantiles correspond to higher confidence boxes and must contain the true object with higher probability. We find that quantile boxes 0.4–0.5 strike the best balance between IoU and IoG, achieving better mAP than baselines in most cases. This flexible quantile parameter enables applications to trade off bounding box accuracy as measured by IoU with containment probability as measured by IoG. For instance, an autonomous vehicle may use a lower quantile to mitigate the risk of collisions at the cost of some bounding box accuracy.

5.4   3D Bounding Box Estimation

We evaluate the bounding box estimation on COB-3D using the model architecture described in Sect. 3.2. To compare the effectiveness of our autoregressive parameterization, we train the same model architecture with different box parameterizations and losses. All models receive the same 2D detection results and features as input and must make 3D bounding box predictions for each detected object. We consider 4 baseline parameterizations for this task inspired by various works in the literature:

L1 Regression: In this parameterization, the model outputs 9 real values for each of the 9 box parameters: $b = (d_x, d_y, d_z, c_x, c_y, c_z, \psi, \theta, \phi)$. The model predicts dimensions and centers in coordinates normalized around the object's point cloud. This model is trained using a L1 loss over the normalized box parameters $L(b, g) = ||b - g||_1$, where g is the ground truth box [13].

Gaussian: For this baseline, the model outputs 18 real values for the mean, μ, and log-variance, $\log \sigma^2$, of 9 Gaussian distributions $\mathcal{N}(\mu, \sigma)$ over the box parameters b [7,11]. Predicting the variance enables the model to output uncertainty over different box parameters, independently of each other. We train this model using maximum likelihood: $L(\mu, \log \sigma^2, g) = -\sum_i \log \mathcal{N}(g_i; \mu_i, \sigma_i)$.

Discrete: In some prior works, box parameters are predicted as discrete bins but not in an autoregressive manner [18]. To evaluate this parameterization and ablate the necessity of autoregressive predictions, we predict each box parameter *independently* as discrete bins: $\log p(b|h) = \sum_{i=1}^{9} \log p(b_i|h)$

4-Point: This baseline outputs 12 real values for four 3D corner points $(p_0, p_1, p_2, p_3) \in \mathbb{R}^3$, constituting a 3D bounding box [11,12]. We ensure that the 3D bounding box is orthogonal by applying the Gram-Schmidt process on the basis vectors $(p_1 - p_0, p_2 - p_0, p_3 - p_0)$. We use an L1-loss on the difference between the predicted points and the points of the ground truth 3D bounding box. Since there are many permutations of valid 4-point corners of a bounding box, we supervise on the permutation that induces the minimum loss.

Metrics. To make reasoning about the trade-off between IoG and IoU more quantifiable, we report the F1-score equivalent for this use case, i.e., $F1_{score} = \frac{2(IoU*IoG)}{IoU+IoG}$. We further report metrics on the dimension & pose errors, which are computed as follows:

Table 2. Results of the proposed method & baselines on our dataset. We also show results for conditioning our method on ground truth dimensions

	IoU	IoG	F1	$err_{dim}[m]$	$err_{quat}[rad]$	$err_{center}[m]$
L1 Regression	0.4219	0.6113	0.4992	0.0436	0.4667	0.0138
Discrete	0.5232	0.6282	0.5709	0.0339	0.2926	**0.0105**
Gaussian	0.3169	0.5304	0.3967	0.0450	0.5154	0.0119
4-Point	0.5688	0.7113	0.6321	0.0332	0.1999	0.0132
Beam Search	**0.6296**	0.7877	0.6999	**0.0287**	**0.1598**	0.0109
Quantile 0.1	0.3821	**0.9723**	0.5486	0.0986	0.1762	0.0123
Quantile 0.4	0.5949	0.8871	0.7122	0.0377	0.1640	0.0110
Quantile 0.5	0.6275	0.8295	**0.7126**	0.0318	0.1657	0.0110
Conditioning	0.6709	0.7899	0.7215	0.0086	0.1674	0.0096

○ $err_{dim} = \mathrm{sum}(|\mathbf{d} - \mathbf{d}_{gt}|)$, where we compute the error across all possible permutations and then choose the one with the smallest error.

○ $err_{quat} = 2\arccos(|\langle \mathbf{q}, \mathbf{q}_{gt}\rangle|)$, where $\mathbf{q}$ represents the rotational part of the pose as a quaternion. We compute the error across all possible symmetries and choose the one with the smallest error.

○ $err_{center} = ||\mathbf{c} - \mathbf{c}_{gt}||_2$, where $\mathbf{c}$ is the 3D-center of the bounding box.

Results. Table 2 shows how our autoregressive methods compare to the baseline parameterizations. We find that *Beam Search* achieves the best IoU, dimension & rotation error. As for the *Quantile* methods, we find that lower quantiles achieve higher IoG while sacrificing IoU and dimension error. *Quantile 0.5* offers the best tradeoff in terms of overall performance, achieving higher IoG with similar IoU and dimension error compared to *Beam Search*. Baseline models that predict box parameters directly generally performed worse since those models cannot properly capture multimodal correlations across the box parameters. The *Discrete* baseline performs the best in terms of center error, but we can see that the best autoregressive methods are only a few millimeters worse. For bounding box predictions with full rotations in SO(3), we find that an autoregressive bounding box parameterization can effectively model rotation uncertainty, achieving the lowest rotation error. We can also see that conditioning the model on known dimensions of the items in the scene increases performance in all relevant metrics (besides IoG), most notably in IoU & dimension error. Note that the dimension error is non-zero because the model is given the dimensions as an unordered set, and still needs to predict the association of each dimension tuple to the corresponding item in the scene.

5.5 Quantile and Confidence Boxes

In Sect. 4.2 we introduced quantile boxes as a fast approximation for confidence boxes. We showed that when $p(b|h)$ is an ordered object distribution, a quantile

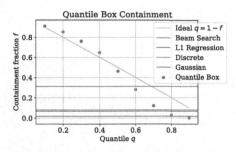

Fig. 5. We compare fraction of predicted boxes that contain ground truth boxes f with different quantiles q and find that q-quantile boxes contain approximately $f \approx 1 - q$ fraction of ground truth boxes.

Table 3. We compare Quantile Uncertainty Measure $U_{0.2,0.8}$ with Gaussian dimension variance G, and find that $U_{0.2,0.8}$ a better predictor of ground-truth IoU compared to G as measured by ROC AUC. $U_{0.2,0.8}$ is also better correlated with ground-truth IoU compared to G as measured by Spearman r_s

Method	ROC AUC	Spearman r_s
Gaussian	0.731	−0.530
Quantile 0.2	0.897	**−0.865**
Quantile 0.5	0.878	−0.789
Quantile 0.8	**0.967**	−0.850

box with quantile q is equivalent to a confidence box with $p = 1 - q$ and should contain the true object with probability p.

While it's hard to ensure that real world objects follow an ordered distribution, we can empirically evaluate whether q confidence boxes contain the ground truth object $1 - q$ fraction of the time. To test our hypothesis, we predict quantile boxes with different q and calculate the fraction of predictions f with IoG > 0.95. In Fig. 5, we can see that $f \approx 1 - q$ and follows a generally linear relationship. This suggests that even for general object distributions, quantile boxes can be an effective approximation for confidence boxes.

5.6   Uncertainty Measures

In Sect. 4.3, we introduced the uncertainty measure using quantile boxes $U_{\alpha,\beta} = 1 - IoU(b_\alpha, b_\beta)$ as a measure of the span of the confidence box interval. To evaluate the effectiveness of this uncertainty measure, we calculate the ROC AUC of using $U_{0.2,0.8}$ to predict when the IoU of the predicted box b with the ground truth box g is less than 0.25. We also measure the correlation between ground truth IoU and uncertainty using the Spearman's rank correlation r_s. We compare $U_{0.2,0.8}$ on different quantile boxes against Gaussian dimension variance $G = \frac{\sigma_{d_x} \sigma_{d_y} \sigma_{d_z}}{\mu_{d_x} \mu_{d_y} \mu_{d_z}}$ on the Gaussian baseline. Table 3 shows that quantile uncertainty $U_{0.2,0.8}$ can be a better uncertainty measure than G.

6   Discussion

We introduced an autoregressive formulation to 3D bounding prediction that greatly expands the ability of existing architectures to express uncertainty. We showed that it can be applied to both the 3D object detection and 3D bounding-box estimation settings, and explored different ways to extract bounding box predictions from such autoregressive models. In particular, we showed how the uncertainty expressed by these models can make high confidence predictions and meaningful uncertainty estimates. We introduced a dataset that requires predicting bounding boxes with full 3D rotations, and showed that our model naturally handles this task as well. While autoregressive models are just one class of distributionally expressive models, they are not the only option for more expressive bounding box modeling. We hope that future lines of work will continue to build upon the method, dataset, and benchmarks we introduced in this paper.

A   Model Architecture and Training

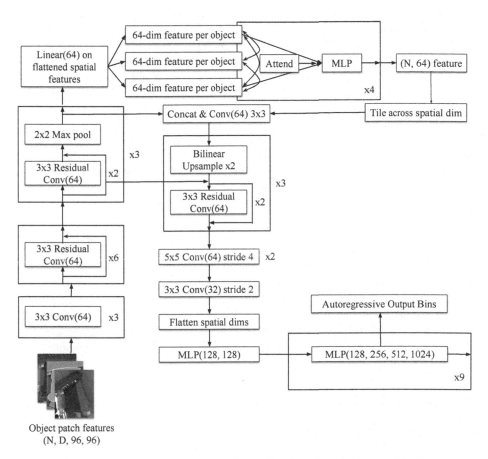

Fig. 6. Overview of Autoregressive Bounding Box Estimation architecture

A.1   Autoregressive 3D Bounding Box Estimation

For bounding box estimation, our model operates on 2D detection patch outputs of size 96×96. We take the 2D bounding box from object-detection to crop and resize the following features for each object: 3D point cloud, depth uncertainty score, normals, instance mask, amodal instance mask (which includes the occluded regions of the object). We normalize each point p in the point cloud with the 0.25 (Q_1) and 0.75 (Q_3) quantiles per dimension using $\frac{p-c_0}{s}$ for $c_0 = \frac{Q_1+Q_3}{2}$, $s = Q_3 - Q_1$. We omitted RGB since we found it wasn't necessary for training and improved generalization.

We stack each 2D feature along the channel dimension and embed the features using a 2D Resnet U-Net. The features from the top of the U-Net are used in a series of self-attention modules across embeddings from all objects in a scene so that information can be shared across objects. The resulting features from self-attention are tiled across the spatial dimension before the downward pass of the U-Net. Finally, the features from the highest spatial resolution of the U-Net are passed into several strided-convs, flattened, and projected to a 128-dimension feature h per object. Figure 6 shows the overview of our model architecture.

For the autoregressive layers, we use 9 MLPs with hidden layers (128, 256, 512, 1024). For baselines, we keep the same architecture through h and use different sized MLPs depending on the box parameterization. We train using Adam with learning rate 1e−5 with a batch size of 24 scenes per step with varying number of objects per scene. We train for 10000 steps or until convergence.

A.2   Autoregressive 3D Object Detection

For Autoregressive FCAF3D, we add 7 autoregressive MLPs with hidden dimensions (128, 256, 512). All other parameters of FCAF3D are the same and we train the same hyperparameters as the released code for 30 epochs. For the baseline FCAF3D, we trained the author-released model for 30 epochs on 8 gpus. We found that the benchmarked numbers for $AP_{0.25}$ and $AP_{0.50}$ were slightly lower than the reported ones in the original paper, so in our table, we use the reported average AP across trials from the original paper. AP_{all} was calculated in a similar way as in MS-COCO by averaging AP for iou thresholds over $0.05, 0.10, 0.15, ..., 0.95$.

B   Quantile Box

B.1   Proof of Quantile-Confidence Box

Proof Sketch: Let $P(b)$ be a distribution over an ordered set of boxes where for any two distinct boxes b_1, b_2 in the sample space, one must be contained in the other, $b_1 \subset b_2$ or $b_2 \subset b_1$. We'll show that a quantile box b_q is a confidence box with $p = 1 - q$ by 1) constructing a confidence box b_p for any given q, 2) showing that any $x \in b_p$ must have $O(x) > q$, and 3) therefore $b_p \subseteq Q(q) \subseteq b_q$ so the quantile box is a confidence box.

1) Confidence Box: For any $p = 1 - q$, we'll show how to construct a confidence box b_p. Using the ordered object distribution property of $P(b)$, we can define ordering as containment $b_1 < b_2 \equiv b_1 \subset b_2$. This ordering defines an inverse cdf:

$$F^{-1}(p) = \inf\{x : P(b \leq x) \geq p\} \tag{8}$$

Let $b_p = F^{-1}(1 - q)$ be the inverse cdf of p; by definition b_p is a confidence box with confidence p since $P(b \leq b_p) = P(b \subseteq b_p) \geq p$

2) Occupancy Of b_p: We'll show that any $x \in b_p$ satisfies $O(x) > 1 - p$. First we'll prove that that $P(b \geq b_p) > 1 - p$. Let $b_0 = \inf\{b : b < b_p\}$, the smallest box that is strictly contained in b_p. (If no such b_0 exists, then b_p must be the smallest box in the distribution order such that $P(b \geq b_p) = 1$ and $P(b \geq b_p) > 1 - p$ for $p \neq 0$)

Since b_p is the inverse cdf of p, we know that $P(b \leq b_0) < p$, otherwise b_0 would be the inverse cdf of p (i.e. $b_0 = b_p$ a contradiction). It follows that

$$P(b \geq b_p) = P(b > b_0) \tag{9}$$
$$= 1 - P(b \leq b_0) \tag{10}$$
$$> 1 - p \tag{11}$$

Now consider any point $x \in b_p$:

$$O(x) = P(x \in b) \tag{12}$$

$$= \int_b \mathbb{1}\{x \in b\}p(b)db \tag{13}$$

$$\geq \int_{b \geq b_p} \mathbb{1}\{x \in b\}p(b)db \tag{14}$$

$$= \int_{b \geq b_p} p(b)db \tag{15}$$

$$= P(b \geq b_p) \tag{16}$$
$$> 1 - p \tag{17}$$

where (14) follows from the nonegativity of $\mathbb{1}\{x \in b\}p(b)$. (15) follows from $x \in b_p$, $b_p \subseteq b$ which implies $x \in b$.

3) Quantile-Confidence Box: Since any $x \in b_p$ satisfies $O(x) > 1 - p$, it follows that $b_p \subseteq Q(1 - p)$, where $Q(q) = \{x : O(x) > q\}$ is the occupancy quantile with quantile q. The quantile box by construction must contain the occupancy quantile $Q(q) \subseteq b_q$, therefore we have $b_p \subseteq Q(1 - p) \subseteq b_q$, and

$$P(b \subseteq b_q) \geq P(b \subseteq b_p) \tag{18}$$
$$\geq p \tag{19}$$

So b_q is a confidence box with confidence requirement p.

Algorithm 1: Quantile Box Algorithm

Given: quantile q, box distribution $P(b|h)$, numbers of box samples k, number of point samples m

Sample $b^{(1)}, ..., b^{(k)} \sim P(b|h)$ boxes

For each $b^{(i)}$, sample m random points within $b^{(i)}$, adding all points to a set T

For all $x \in T$, estimate $O(x) = \frac{1}{k}\sum_i^k \mathbb{1}\{x \in b^{(i)}\}$

Construct the occupancy quantile $Q(q) = \{x \in T : O(x) > q\}$

for $b^{(1)}, ..., b^{(k)}$ **do**
> Let R_i be the rotation of $b^{(i)}$
> Compute the volume of the $Q(q)$ bounding box under R_i,
> $v_i = \prod_{a \in x,y,z}(\max_{x \in Q(q)}(R_i^{-1}x)_a - \min_{x \in Q(q)}(R_i^{-1}x)_a)$

Find the minimum volume box $i^* = \arg\min_i v_i$

Let $s_a = \max_{x \in Q(q)}(R_{i^*}^{-1}x)_a$, $t_a = \min_{x \in Q(q)}(R_{i^*}^{-1}x)_a$

Return box $b = (d, c, R_{i^*})$ with dimensions $d = (t_x - s_x, t_y - s_y, t_z - s_z)$ and center $c = R_{i^*}(s_x + d_x/2, s_y + d_y/2, s_z + d_z/2)$

B.2   Quantile Box Algorithm

We propose a fast quantile box Algorithm 1 that runs in polynomial time and is easily batchable on GPU. We use a finite sample of k boxes to approximate the occupancy and a sample of km points to approximate the occupancy quantile $Q(q)$. To find the minimum volume box, we assume that one of the sampled box rotations will be close to the optimal quantile box rotation. We take the sampled rotations and calculate the rotation-axis-aligned bounding box volume for the occupancy quantile. The minimum volume rotation is selected for the quantile box and corresponding dimension/center calculated accordingly.

Empirically we find that $k = 64$, $m = 4^3$ provides a good trade-off of variance and inference time. We can efficiently batch all operations on GPU, and find that quantile box inference for 15 objects takes no more than 10 ms on a NVIDIA 1080TI.

C   Dataset

Our dataset consists of almost 7000 simulated scenes of common objects in bins. See Fig. 7 for examples. Each scene consists of the following data:

- **RGB** image of shape (H, W, 3)
- **Depth** map of shape (H, W)
- **Intrinsic Matrix** of the camera (3, 3)
- **Normals Map** of shape (H, W, 3)
- **Instance Masks** of shape (N, H, W) where N is the number of objects
- **Amodal Instance masks** of shape (N, H, W) which includes the occluded regions of the object
- **3D Bounding Box** of each object (N, 9) as determined by dimensions, center, and rotation.

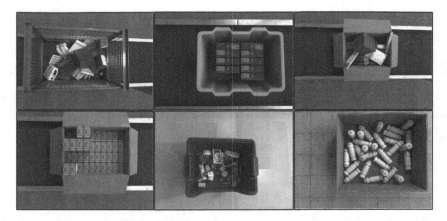

Fig. 7. Examples of scenes from our dataset

D   Visualizations

In this section, we show various qualitative comparisons and visualization of our method (Figs. 8, 9, 10 and 11).

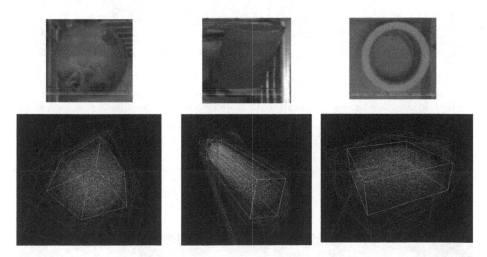

Fig. 8. Visualization of our model predictions on objects with rotational symmetry. The blue boxes show various samples from our model. The orange point cloud is the occupancy quantile. The white box is the quantile box. (Color figure online)

Fig. 9. Visualization of our dimension conditioning method. The model is able to lever-age the conditioning information to accurately predict the correct pose & dimension for each object's 3D bounding box. The prediction is shown in red-blue-green and the ground truth in turquoise-yellow-pink. Left: image of the scene. Middle: vanilla beam search. Right: beam search with dimension conditioning. (Color figure online)

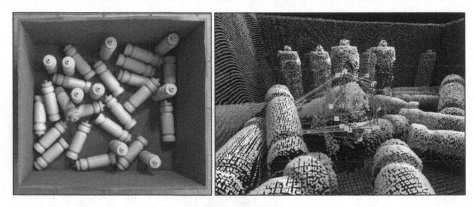

Fig. 10. Visualization of bounding box samples from our autoregressive model on a rotationally symmetric water bottle. Our model is able to sample different modes for symmetric objects whereas a deterministic model would only be able to predict a single mode.

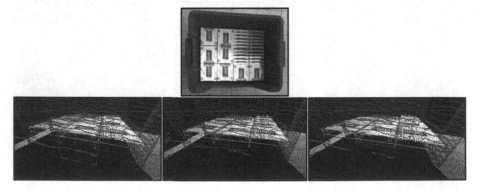

Fig. 11. Visualization of bounding box predictions with different quantiles. We can see that lower quantiles lead to larger boxes in the direction of uncertainty. Top: image of the scene. Left: quantile 0.1 Middle: quantile 0.3. Right: quantile 0.5.

References

1. Choi, J., Chun, D., Kim, H., Lee, H.J.: Gaussian YOLOv3: an accurate and fast object detector using localization uncertainty for autonomous driving. In: 2019 IEEE/CVF International Conference on Computer Vision (ICCV), pp. 502–511 (2019)
2. Dai, A., Chang, A.X., Savva, M., Halber, M., Funkhouser, T., Nießner, M.: Scan-Net: richly-annotated 3D reconstructions of indoor scenes. In: Proceedings of the Computer Vision and Pattern Recognition (CVPR). IEEE (2017)
3. Freitag, M., Al-Onaizan, Y.: Beam search strategies for neural machine translation. In: Proceedings of the First Workshop on Neural Machine Translation, pp. 56–60. Association for Computational Linguistics, Vancouver, August 2017. https://doi.org/10.18653/v1/W17-3207. https://aclanthology.org/W17-3207
4. Geiger, A., Lenz, P., Stiller, C., Urtasun, R.: Vision meets robotics: the KITTI dataset. Int. J. Robot. Res. (IJRR) (2013)
5. Gilitschenski, I., Sahoo, R., Schwarting, W., Amini, A., Karaman, S., Rus, D.: Deep orientation uncertainty learning based on a Bingham loss. In: International Conference on Learning Representations (2020). https://openreview.net/forum?id=ryloogSKDS
6. Hall, D., et al.: Probabilistic object detection: definition and evaluation, November 2018
7. He, Y., Zhu, C., Wang, J., Savvides, M., Zhang, X.: Bounding box regression with uncertainty for accurate object detection. In: Proceedings of the ieee/cvf conference on computer vision and pattern recognition. pp. 2888–2897 (2019)
8. Li, X., et al.: Generalized focal loss: learning qualified and distributed bounding boxes for dense object detection. In: Larochelle, H., Ranzato, M., Hadsell, R., Balcan, M.F., Lin, H. (eds.) Advances in Neural Information Processing Systems, vol. 33, pp. 21002–21012. Curran Associates, Inc. (2020). https://proceedings.neurips.cc/paper/2020/file/f0bda020d2470f2e74990a07a607ebd9-Paper.pdf
9. Liu, Z., Zhang, Z., Cao, Y., Hu, H., Tong, X.: Group-free 3D object detection via transformers. In: Proceedings of the IEEE/CVF International Conference on Computer Vision, pp. 2949–2958 (2021)
10. Metz, L., Ibarz, J., Jaitly, N., Davidson, J.: Discrete sequential prediction of continuous actions for deep RL. arXiv preprint arXiv:1705.05035 (2017)
11. Meyer, G.P., Laddha, A., Kee, E., Vallespi-Gonzalez, C., Wellington, C.K.: Laser-Net: an efficient probabilistic 3D object detector for autonomous driving. In: CVPR, pp. 12677–12686. Computer Vision Foundation/IEEE (2019). https://dblp.uni-trier.de/db/conf/cvpr/cvpr2019.html
12. Meyer, G.P., Thakurdesai, N.: Learning an uncertainty-aware object detector for autonomous driving. In: 2020 IEEE/RSJ International Conference on Intelligent Robots and Systems (IROS), pp. 10521–10527 (2020)
13. Misra, I., Girdhar, R., Joulin, A.: An end-to-end transformer model for 3D object detection. In: Proceedings of the IEEE/CVF International Conference on Computer Vision, pp. 2906–2917 (2021)
14. Mousavian, A., Anguelov, D., Flynn, J., Kosecka, J.: 3D bounding box estimation using deep learning and geometry. In: Proceedings of the IEEE Conference on Computer Vision and Pattern Recognition, pp. 7074–7082 (2017)
15. van den Oord, A., et al.: WaveNet: a generative model for raw audio. arXiv preprint arXiv:1609.03499 (2016)

16. Peretroukhin, V., Giamou, M., Rosen, D.M., Greene, W.N., Roy, N., Kelly, J.: A smooth representation of SO(3) for deep rotation learning with uncertainty. In: Proceedings of Robotics: Science and Systems (RSS 2020), 12–16 July 2020 (2020)

17. Qi, C.R., Chen, X., Litany, O., Guibas, L.J.: ImVoteNet: boosting 3D object detection in point clouds with image votes. In: IEEE Conference on Computer Vision and Pattern Recognition (CVPR) (2020)

18. Qi, C.R., Litany, O., He, K., Guibas, L.J.: Deep Hough voting for 3D object detection in point clouds. In: ICCV, pp. 9276–9285. IEEE (2019). https://dblp.uni-trier.de/db/conf/iccv/iccv2019.html

19. Qi, C.R., Liu, W., Wu, C., Su, H., Guibas, L.J.: Frustum PointNets for 3D object detection from RGB-D data. In: Proceedings of the IEEE Conference on Computer Vision and Pattern Recognition, pp. 918–927 (2018)

20. Rukhovich, D., Vorontsova, A., Konushin, A.: FCAF3D: fully convolutional anchor-free 3D object detection. arXiv preprint arXiv:2112.00322 (2021)

21. Shi, S., Wang, X., Li, H.P., et al.: 3D object proposal generation and detection from point cloud. In: Proceedings of the IEEE Conference on Computer Vision and Pattern Recognition, Long Beach, CA, USA, pp. 16–20 (2019)

22. Shi, S., et al.: PV-RCNN: point-voxel feature set abstraction for 3D object detection. In: 2020 IEEE/CVF Conference on Computer Vision and Pattern Recognition, CVPR 2020, Seattle, WA, USA, 13–19 June 2020, pp. 10526–10535. Computer Vision Foundation/IEEE (2020). https://doi.org/10.1109/CVPR42600.2020.01054. https://openaccess.thecvf.com/content_CVPR_2020/html/Shi_PV-RCNN_Point-Voxel_Feature_Set_Abstraction_for_3D_Object_Detection_CVPR_2020_paper.html

23. Song, S., Lichtenberg, S.P., Xiao, J.: SUN RGB-D: A RGB-D scene understanding benchmark suite. In: Proceedings of the IEEE Conference on Computer Vision and Pattern Recognition, pp. 567–576 (2015)

24. Tian, Z., Shen, C., Chen, H., He, T.: FCOS: fully convolutional one-stage object detection. In: Proceedings of the IEEE/CVF International Conference on Computer Vision, pp. 9627–9636 (2019)

25. Van Oord, A., Kalchbrenner, N., Kavukcuoglu, K.: Pixel recurrent neural networks. In: International Conference on Machine Learning, pp. 1747–1756. PMLR (2016)

26. Vaswani, A., et al.: Attention is all you need. In: Advances in Neural Information Processing Systems 30 (2017)

27. Xie, Q., et al.: MLCVNet: multi-level context VoteNet for 3D object detection. In: Proceedings of the IEEE/CVF Conference on Computer Vision and Pattern Recognition (CVPR), June 2020

28. Zhong, Y., Zhu, M., Peng, H.: Uncertainty-aware voxel based 3D object detection and tracking with von-Mises loss. ArXiv abs/2011.02553 (2020)

29. Zhou, Y., Barnes, C., Lu, J., Yang, J., Li, H.: On the continuity of rotation representations in neural networks. In: 2019 IEEE/CVF Conference on Computer Vision and Pattern Recognition (CVPR), pp. 5738–5746 (2019)

3D Random Occlusion and Multi-layer Projection for Deep Multi-camera Pedestrian Localization

Rui Qiu[1,2], Ming Xu[1,2(✉)], Yuyao Yan[1], Jeremy S. Smith[2], and Xi Yang[1]

[1] School of Advanced Technology, Xi'an Jiaotong-Liverpool University,
Suzhou 215123, China
{ming.xu,xi.yang01}@xjtlu.edu.cn
[2] Department of Electrical Engineering and Electronics, University of Liverpool,
Liverpool L69 3BX, UK
{rui.qiu,j.s.smith}@liverpool.ac.uk

Abstract. Although deep-learning based methods for monocular pedestrian detection have made great progress, they are still vulnerable to heavy occlusions. Using multi-view information fusion is a potential solution but has limited applications, due to the lack of annotated training samples in existing multi-view datasets, which increases the risk of overfitting. To address this problem, a data augmentation method is proposed to randomly generate 3D cylinder occlusions, on the ground plane, which are of the average size of pedestrians and projected to multiple views, to relieve the impact of overfitting in the training. Moreover, the feature map of each view is projected to multiple parallel planes at different heights, by using homographies, which allows the CNNs to fully utilize the features across the height of each pedestrian to infer the locations of pedestrians on the ground plane. The proposed 3DROM method has a greatly improved performance in comparison with the state-of-the-art deep-learning based methods for multi-view pedestrian detection. Code is available at https://github.com/xjtlu-cvlab/3DROM.

Keywords: Multi-view detection · Deep learning · Data augmentation · Perspective transformations

1 Introduction

Pedestrian detection plays an important role in the fields of tracking, person re-identification and crowd counting. In recent years, deep-learning based object detection methods have made significant progress in pedestrian detection. However, these deep monocular methods are not robust enough to detect heavily occluded pedestrians or localise partially occluded pedestrians on the ground. The solution to this problem lies in multi-view pedestrian detection. Compared with single-view pedestrian detection, multi-view methods can detect heavily occluded pedestrians more effectively and accurately [9].

S. Avidan et al. (Eds.): ECCV 2022, LNCS 13670, pp. 695–710, 2022.
https://doi.org/10.1007/978-3-031-20080-9_40

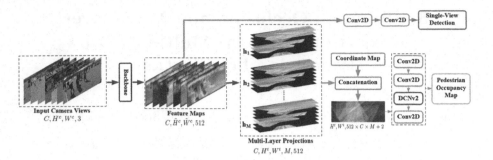

Fig. 1. The structure of 3DROM. h_1, h_2, ..., h_M represent the multi-layer projections at different heights.

Deep-learning based multi-camera detection methods need to be trained on sufficient annotated samples to achieve the desired performance. However, the limited ground truth data available in existing multi-view video datasets makes it difficult for the network to achieve the best performance in training, which limits deep learning methods from being widely used in multi-view pedestrian detection. The reason behind this is that the annotation of a multi-view pedestrian dataset is a tedious and time-consuming process. For example, with the help of an annotation tool specifically designed for multi-view datasets, it took a trained annotator an average of 10 min to annotate one frame with 7 views for the WILDTRACK dataset [3,6]. On the other hand, although monocular data augmentation methods, such as flipping, random cropping and Random Erasing [28], can relieve overfitting and improve the robustness of the networks to occlusion, these methods violate the homographic constraint among multiple views and cannot be used for multi-view pedestrian detection methods.

In this paper, on the basis of the MVDet framework [12], a data augmentation method is proposed to address this problem, in which occlusion boxes are randomly but consistently added to multiple camera views in the training. In this method, the ground-plane area of interest (AOI) is discretized into a grid of locations; 3D cylinders, of the average size of pedestrians, are placed at randomly selected locations on the ground plane and projected into each of the multiple camera views as filled rectangles. It reduces the risk of overfitting in the training and improves the robustness of pedestrian detection with heavy occlusions. In addition, the feature maps are projected to multiple planes parallel to the ground plane and at different heights. The multi-layer projection allows the different features (feet, torso and head) of each pedestrian to be projected to the same location in the top view but at different heights. This allows the features across the height of that pedestrian to be fully utilised in comparison with the ground-plane feature projection in MVDet. This proposed algorithm is referred to as 3DROM. A schematic diagram of the system architecture is shown in Fig. 1.

The contributions of this paper are twofold: (1) A data augmentation method is proposed for deep multi-view pedestrian detection, in which 3D random occlusions are generated and back-projected to multiple camera views. It can be used to prevent overfitting and improve the detection performance with a limited number of multi-view training samples. To the best of our knowledge, this method is used for deep multi-view pedestrian detection for the first time. (2) A multi-layer projection method for the single-view feature maps is used to fully utilize the pedestrians' features across a range of heights. The locations of pedestrians can be inferred from the multi-height features, rather than only the ground-plane features, of the pedestrians.

2   Related Work

2.1   Multi-view Pedestrian Detection

A recent survey on multi-view pedestrian detection can be found in [18]. The state-of-the-art methods in this field can be categorised into top-down approach and bottom-up approach. The top-down approach divides the ground plane into a grid. Each location in this grid is thought of as the location of a potential pedestrian and is back-projected to individual views for finding the optimal match between foregrounds and a generative model. The bottom-up approach projects the foregrounds from the individual views to a reference view and analyses the overlaid foreground projections to determine the locations of pedestrians.

Top-Down Approach. Fleuret et al. [9] estimated a probabilistic occupancy map through a generative model that represents each pedestrian as a filled rectangle of the average size of pedestrians. The occupancy probability was updated iteratively for finding the locations of the rectangles which cover more foreground pixels in all the views. On the basis of this point of view, Alahi et al. [4] formulated multi-view pedestrian detection as a linear inverse problem; Peng et al. [17] modelled pedestrians and their occlusion relationships by using a multi-view Bayesian network; Yan et al. [25] used a non-iterative logic minimization method to reduce false-positive detections. Chavdarova and Fleuret [7] proposed an end-to-end multi-view pedestrian detection network. They back-projected each ground-plane location to individual views and created a rectangle box at the corresponding positions. A CNN was used to extract features within these rectangles and infer the locations of pedestrians by using Multi-Layer Perception. Baqué et al. [5] proposed a method which combines CNNs and a Conditional Random Field. The CNN in the discriminative model extracts pedestrian features from individual views and uses Gaussian Mixture networks to classify the body parts as pedestrian features. Meanwhile, a generative model is used to model the occlusion relationships among pedestrians. The locations where the discriminative model fits the generative model well are thought of as the locations of pedestrians.

Bottom-Up Approach. Khan and Shah [14,15] projected the foreground likelihood maps of individual views to a reference view using multi-plane homographies. Areas with heavily overlaid foregrounds are thought of as the locations of pedestrians. However, the foreground projections of different pedestrians may overlap, which leads to false positive detections. Eshel and Moses [8] projected the individual views to the head plane and detected pedestrians at the locations where the intensities projected from different views are pixelwise correlated. Ge and Collins [10] modelled each pedestrian as a cylinder and used Gibbs sampling to find the locations of pedestrians. Utasi and Benedek [22] also used cylinders in the 3D space to model the foreground silhouettes, which was enhanced by pixel-level leg and head features, and determined the pedestrians' locations by using a 3D Bayesian Marked Point Process model. Xu et al. [24] detected pedestrians in individual views using Faster RCNN [19] and projected the foot points of the bounding boxes of the pedestrians to the ground plane. They clustered the projected foot points to determine the locations of pedestrians in the top view. Hou et al. proposed MVDet [12], an anchor-free end-to-end pedestrian detection network. This system uses ResNet18 [11] as the backbone to extract feature maps from individual views. The feature maps from multiple views are projected to the ground plane and concatenated there. Then a ground-plane classifier predicts the locations of pedestrians. This feature projection method is similar to that proposed by Zhang and Chan [26,27] for multi-camera crowd counting. On the basis of the MVDet framework, Song et al. [21] proposed the SHOT algorithm which projects the feature map of each individual view to multiple parallel planes. The multi-plane feature maps projected from the same view were weighted and summed into one feature map. Such feature maps from the multiple views are concatenated to predict a pedestrian occupancy map on the ground. When the multi-height feature maps were summed into a single feature map, it causes an information loss; whilst such multi-height feature maps are concatenated with no information loss in the 3DROM algorithm, which leads to an improved performance.

2.2 Data Augmentation

In deep-learning based methods, data augmentation methods are widely used to increase the number of training samples and improve the robustness by applying various transformations to existing samples [11,16,20]. One of these methods is to directly apply an image processing operation, such as flipping, folding, rotating, adding noise and Random Erasing, to existing samples. Random Erasing [28] overwrites each pixel in a randomly selected region of an image with a random colour. This method can be applied to the training of deep-learning based algorithms for image classification, person re-identification and object detection tasks. It improves the robustness of an algorithm to occlusion and reduces the risk of overfitting the samples in the training. In addition, Wang et al. [23] proposed a method for generating samples with occlusion and deformation using adversarial networks. These generated samples can improve the accuracy and robustness of Faster R-CNN in the detection of deformed or occluded objects. However, both methods are currently used in monocular detection only and cannot work well for deep end-to-end multi-view pedestrian detection without considering the geometrical relationship among multiple views.

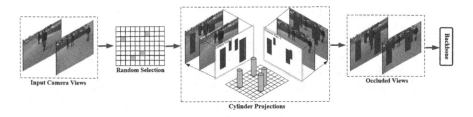

Fig. 2. A schematic diagram of the 3D Random Occlusion method.

3   Methodology

The motivation of our work is to address the performance improvement on deep multi-view pedestrian detection networks with a limited number of training samples. Robust pedestrian detection requires efficient network training with limited samples and an effective fusion method for multi-view features. We focus on reducing the risk of overfitting during the training and improving the utilization of the feature maps across multiple views to improve the detection performance in the MVDet framework.

3.1   Notations and Homography Estimation

Let C be the number of the cameras in a multi-view pedestrian dataset. The size of input image I_c, from camera view c ($c \in [1, C]$), is $H^c \times W^c$. (u^c, v^c) represents an image coordinate in view c. The size of the feature map F_c, extracted from camera view c, is $\widetilde{H}^c \times \widetilde{W}^c$. $H^t \times W^t$ is the size of the top view image. Assume the area of interest (AOI) on the ground plane is discretized into a grid of G locations. Let $\mathbf{X}_i$ be the coordinate of the i-th location ($i \in [1, G]$). Let S denote the set of the index numbers for the grid locations that have been selected to place the 3D occlusions.

Planar homography is the relationship between a pair of captured images of the same plane. Let $\mathbf{u}$ and $\mathbf{X}$ be the homogeneous image coordinates of the same point on a plane in camera view c and the top view. They are associated by the homography matrix $\mathbf{H}^{c,t}$ for that plane as follow:

$$\mathbf{X} \cong \mathbf{H}^{c,t}\mathbf{u}. \tag{1}$$

A 3×4 projection matrix can be calculated by using the intrinsic and extrinsic parameters of camera c: $\mathbf{M} = [\mathbf{m}_1, \mathbf{m}_2, \mathbf{m}_3, \mathbf{m}_4]$. The homography matrix, from the top view t to camera view c, for the ground plane is:

$$\mathbf{H}_0^{t,c} = (\mathbf{H}_0^{c,t})^{-1} = [\mathbf{m}_1, \mathbf{m}_2, \mathbf{m}_4]. \tag{2}$$

The homography matrix, from the top view t to camera view c, for the plane parallel to the ground plane and at a height of h can be written as:

$$\mathbf{H}_h^{t,c} = [\mathbf{m}_1, \mathbf{m}_2, h\mathbf{m}_3 + \mathbf{m}_4] = \mathbf{H}_0^{t,c} + [\mathbf{0} \mid h\mathbf{m}_3], \tag{3}$$

where $[\mathbf{0}]$ is a 3×2 zero matrix.

3.2   3D Random Occlusion

Compared with single-view detection, multi-view pedestrian detection requires the use of geometric constraints to establish the correspondence among multiple views. Monocular data augmentation methods, such as flipping, cropping, rotation and Random Erasing, may affect the performance of multi-view detection algorithms, since they violate the homography constraint. Therefore, Algorithm 1 was developed as a 3D data augmentation method for the training of multi-view pedestrian detection algorithms.

The 3D Random Occlusion algorithm is based on the input camera views in the training, as shown in Algorithm 1. The process of 3D Random Occlusion is illustrated in Fig. 2. The ground plane is discretized into a grid of locations. The i-th location ($i \in [1, G]$) in the top view is associated with its corresponding location (u_i^c, v_i^c) in camera view c ($c \in [1, C]$) through the ground-plane homography $\mathbf{H}_0^{t,c}$. A 3D cylinder placed at the ith location on the ground plane is back-projected to a filled rectangle r_i^c sitting at location (u_i^c, v_i^c) in camera view c. The rectangle is designed to have the average height H_i^c and width W_i^c of the pedestrians standing at the ith location. H_i^c is calculated as follows: the i-th location in the top view is projected back to camera view c using the homographies, $\mathbf{H}_0^{t,c}$ and $\mathbf{H}_{h_a}^{t,c}$, for the planes at the heights of 0 cm and 180 cm; The vertical distance between the two projected points in view c is H_i^c; the average width $W_i^c = \alpha H_i^c$, where α is a constant ratio.

The inputs of Algorithm 1 are the images $I = \{I_1, I_2, \cdots, I_c\}$ from multiple camera views, the number of occlusions n per frame and the occlusion probability p of each frame to be selected to add 3D random occlusions. The n locations in the top view are selected to generate filled rectangles at the corresponding locations in all the views. To ensure that the occlusions are not too close to each other, the ground distance between each selected location and other cylinder occlusions must be greater than a threshold $d = 1$ meter. The selected locations are projected to all the views, by using homographies $\mathbf{H}_0^{t,c}$ and $\mathbf{H}_{h_a}^{t,c}$, to generate the filled rectangles with a constant pixel value Ω.

3.3   The Multi-layer Projection of Feature Maps

Within the MVDet framework, the feature map F_c of view c is projected to the ground plane by using a homography transformation. The feature map in the output of the backbone network does not have the same size as the input image I_c of view c. However, it is resized to the same size afterwards. Therefore, the projected feature map $F_h^{c,t}$ from view c to the top view can be written as:

$$F_h^{c,t} = \mathbf{H}_h^{c,t}(F_c), \tag{4}$$

for a plane parallel to the ground and at a height of h.

The feature map on the ground plane is compromised when pedestrians' feet are occluded or their feet are off the ground. This may affect the model to infer the locations of the pedestrians. In [14], foreground likelihood maps are projected to multiple planes parallel to the ground plane and at different heights, which can significantly reduce detection errors. The foreground likelihood map, which indicates how likely a pixel in an image belongs to foregrounds, is similar to the feature map in MVDet. We assume that each pedestrian occupies a specific location in the top view. The multi-layer projection of the feature maps of multiple views can provide the comprehensive feature information for any pedestrian standing at that location. Compared with the ground-plane projection used in MVDet, the top view CNN is able to infer the locations of pedestrians from a wider range of features.

Algorithm 1: 3D Random Occlusion at one frame

Input   : Input image $I = \{I_1, I_2, \cdots, I_c\}$;
The number of occlusions n per frame;
Occlusion probability p;
Output: Occluded image $I^* = \{I_1^*, I_2^*, \cdots, I_c^*\}$.

1   $S = \phi$;
2   $I^* = I$;
3   $p_1 = \text{Rand}(0,\ 1)$;
4   **if** $p_1 > p$ **then**
5   **return** I^*.
6   **else**
7     $i = 0$;
8   **while** $i < n$ **do**
9       $k = \text{Rand}(1,\ G)$;
10   **if** $\forall l \in S, \|\boldsymbol{X}_k - \boldsymbol{X}_l\|_2 < d$ **then**
11   **goto** 9;
12   **else**
13   **for** *camera view* $c = 1$ *to* C **do**
14        $(\mathbf{H}_0^{t,c}\boldsymbol{X}_k, \mathbf{H}_{h_a}^{t,c}\boldsymbol{X}_k) \Rightarrow (u_k^c, v_k^c, H_k^c, W_k^c)$;
15   **for** $u = u_k^c - W_k^c/2$ *to* $u_k^c + W_k^c/2$ **do**
16   **for** $v = v_k^c$ *to* $v_k^c + H_k^c$ **do**
17          $I_c^*(u, v) = \Omega$;
18       $S = S \cup \{k\}$;
19       $i = i + 1$
20   **return** I^*;

The multi-layer feature projection is illustrated in Fig. 3(a) and (b). The projected features (or silhouette) of a pedestrian is like the shadow of that pedestrian. When the features of a pedestrian are projected from multiple views to a specific plane, they intersect at the body parts of that pedestrian at the height of that plane. By using multi-plane feature projection, the features across the height of each pedestrian can be utilized. An example of the multi-layer feature projection is shown in Fig. 3(c)–(g).

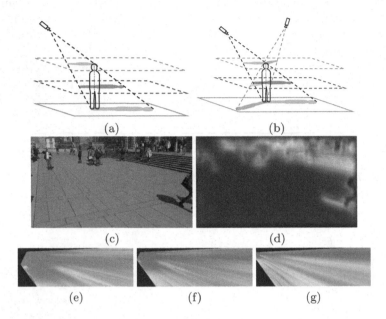

Fig. 3. The multi-layer projections: (a) from a single camera view, (b) from two camera views, and an example of the WILDTRACK dataset, where (c) is the original image of a camera view, (d) is its feature map, and (e)–(g) are the projected feature maps at the heights of 0 cm, 90 cm and 180 cm, respectively.

The projected feature maps and the ground-plane coordinate map are concatenated for the inference of pedestrian locations. The concatenated feature maps are denoted as:

$$F = \{F_h^{c,t}, c \in [1, C], h \in \{h_1, h_2, \ldots, h_M\}\}. \tag{5}$$

where M is the number of the parallel planes used for feature map projection.

Since the feature maps are projected to the top view with geometric deformation, a layer of DCNv2 [29] is added to the top view CNN to handle the geometric deformation in the projected feature maps. The DCNv2 layer is a complementary component used with the multi-layer projection in 3DROM.

3.4 Loss Function

The loss function is the same with that of the MVDet [12]. The network output is an occupancy probability map $\tilde{g}$. A Gaussian kernel $f(\cdot)$ is used to blur the ground-truth pedestrian occupancy map g. The loss of the top view L_t is the Euclidean distance between them:

$$L_t = \|\tilde{g} - f(g)\|_2. \tag{6}$$

The loss function of the single view detection in camera view c is:

$$L_{single}^c = \|\tilde{s}_{head}^c - f(s_{head}^c)\|_2 + \|\tilde{s}_{foot}^c - f(s_{foot}^c)\|_2, \tag{7}$$

where $\tilde{s}_{head}^c$ and $\tilde{s}_{foot}^c$ are the single-view likelihood maps for heads and feet, respectively; s_{head}^c and s_{foot}^c are the ground-truth location maps for heads and feet, respectively.

The overall loss for training 3DROM combines the single view loss L_{single} and the top view loss L_t. It can be written as:

$$L_{overall} = L_t + \frac{1}{C}\sum_{c=1}^{C} L_{single}^c. \tag{8}$$

4 Experimental Results

4.1 Experiment Setup

The proposed method has been evaluated on the EPFL WILDTRACK [3,6], MultiviewX [1,12] and EPFL Terrace datasets [2]. These three public video datasets have been widely used to evaluate multi-view pedestrian detection algorithms. Table 1 shows the detailed information of these datasets.

Table 1. Datasets used for performance evaluation.

Dataset	Input resolution	Feature resolution	Training frames	Testing frames	AOI $(m \times m)$	Top view grid size	Number of 3D occlusions
WILDTRACK	1920×1080	270×480	360	40	12×36	120×360	25
MultiviewX	1920×1080	270×480	360	40	16×25	160×250	25
Terrace	360×288	360×288	300	200	5.3×5	220×150	20

The proposed 3DROM method is based on the MVDet framework. Therefore, most of the network parameters were set to the same values as those in MVDet. ResNet-18 was used as the backbone network without using a pre-trained model. The kernel of DCNv2 used in location regression in the top view was set to a size of 2×2. The setup of the input image size, the feature map size, the top view grid size and the number of 3D random occlusions for each dataset are shown in Table 1. The 3D random occlusions were added to each frame before the images were input to the backbone in the training.

For the training and testing on all the three datasets, the number of projection layers was set to $M = 5$. The feature maps were projected to 5 parallel planes at the heights of $0\,cm$, $15\,cm$, $30\,cm$, $60\,cm$ and $90\,cm$, respectively. The batch size was set to 1. The occlusion probability p was set to 100%. All experiments were carried out using one RTX-3090 GPU.

Fig. 4. The detection results at frame 3225 of the EPFL Terrace dataset: from left to right, camera views C0, C1, C2, C3 and the top view. Each detected pedestrian is represented by a distinguished colour consistent across different views. The red rectangle on the ground is the AOI. The field of view of each camera is shown in the top view. (Color figure online)

4.2   Qualitative Performance Evaluation

The performance of 3DROM on three datasets is demonstrated in the qualitative evaluation. Figure 4 shows the detection results at frame 3225 of the EPFL Terrace dataset with four camera views. The red rectangle on the ground shows the AOI region. The pedestrians outside the AOI were ignored in the detection and evaluation. The camera positions labelled in the top view are approximate ones. The colour points in the top view represent the detected pedestrians. Meanwhile, the colour of each point in the top view is consistent with the colour of the bounding boxes of the same pedestrian in all the camera views. As can be seen in Fig. 4, the pedestrian in the pink bounding box is completely occluded in C0, partially occluded in C1 and C2, and out of the field of view in C3. The 3DROM method can still infer the location of this pedestrian using limited pedestrian features, which demonstrates its strong detection capability in heavy occlusion.

Figure 5 shows the detection results at frame 1960 of the EPFL WILD-TRACK dataset with seven camera views. The pedestrians stand in a group at the centre of the square and are occluded by each other. The 3DROM algorithm combines the feature information in the multi-view and multi-layer feature projections. These pedestrians are detected correctly by 3DROM.

Fig. 5. The detection results at frame 1960 of the EPFL WILDTRACK dataset: (top row) from left to right, camera views C1, C2, C3 and C4; (bottom row) camera views C5, C6, C7 and the top view.

Fig. 6. The detection results at frame 399 on the MultiviewX dataset: (top row) from left to right, camera views C1, C2 and C3; (bottom row) camera views C4, C5, C6 and the top view.

Figure 6 shows the detection results at frame 399 of the MultiviewX dataset with six camera views. A large number of pedestrians are standing very close to the border of the AOI in the top view with limited feature information. The use of multi-layer feature projection and 3D Random Occlusion in the training allows the 3DROM algorithm to detect such pedestrians accurately.

4.3 Quantitative Evaluation

The proposed method was evaluated using performance metrics Multiple Object Detection Accuracy (MODA) [13], Multiple Object Detection Precision (MODP) [13], Precision (Prec.) and Recall, which are widely used for multi-view pedestrian detection. The Hungarian algorithm was used to match the detected pedestrians and ground-truth pedestrians. A distance threshold $r = 0.5$m on the ground plane was used in the matching.

The proposed method was compared with several state-of-the-art deep-learning based methods such as RCNN-2D/3D [24], POM-CNN [9], DeepMCD [7], Deep Occlusion [5], MVDet [12] and SHOT [21], as shown in Table 2 in which "Eval." indicates who made the evaluation. The MODA of the 3DROM method is increased to 93.5%, 95.0%, and 94.8% in the evaluation on the WILDTRACK, MultiviewX, and Terrace datasets, respectively. Compared with the baseline algorithm MVDet that uses single-layer projections, the 3DROM increases the MODA by 5.3%, 11.1%, and 7.6%, respectively. Compared with the algorithm SHOT that partly uses multi-layer projections, the 3DROM increases the MODA by 3.3%, 6.7% and 7.7%, respectively. Meanwhile, the 3DROM achieves the best performance in almost all the four performance metrics.

Ablation Study. In order to evaluate the contributions of each component in our model, an ablation study was carried out. The results are shown in Table 3, in which M denotes the multi-layer projection and R represents 3D Random Occlusion. As seen from the result, whichever component is added on the baseline MVDet, the performance can have a significant boost in all three datasets. When

Table 2. Performance comparisons of deep multiview pedestrian detection.

Methods	Eval.	MODA	MODP	Prec.	Recall
MultiviewX Dataset					
RCNN-2D/3D [24]	[12]	0.187	0.464	0.635	0.439
DeepMCD [7]	[12]	0.700	0.730	0.857	0.833
Deep Occlusion [5]	[12]	0.752	0.547	0.978	0.802
MVDet [12]	[12]	0.839	0.796	0.968	0.867
SHOT [21]	[21]	0.883	0.820	0.966	0.915
3DROM	ours	**0.950**	**0.849**	**0.990**	**0.961**
EPFL WILDTRACK Dataset					
RCNN-2D/3D [24]	[5]	0.113	0.184	0.68	0.43
POM-CNN [5]	[5]	0.232	0.305	0.75	0.55
DeepMCD [7]	[5]	0.678	0.642	0.85	0.82
Deep Occlusion [5]	[5]	0.741	0.538	0.95	0.80
MVDet [12]	[12]	0.882	0.757	0.947	0.936
SHOT [21]	[21]	0.902	**0.765**	0.961	0.940
3DROM	ours	**0.935**	0.759	**0.972**	**0.962**
EPFL Terrace Dataset					
RCNN-2D/3D [24]	[5]	-0.11	0.28	0.39	0.50
POM-CNN [5]	[5]	0.58	0.46	0.80	0.78
Deep Occlusion [5]	[5]	0.71	0.48	0.88	0.82
MVDet [12]	ours	0.872	0.700	0.982	0.888
SHOT [21]	ours	0.871	0.703	0.989	0.881
3DROM	ours	**0.948**	**0.705**	**0.997**	**0.951**

Table 3. Ablation study of 3DROM.

Methods	MultiviewX Dataset				WILDTRACK Dataset				Terrace Dataset			
	MODA	MODP	Prec.	Recall	MODA	MODP	Prec.	Recall	MODA	MODP	Prec.	Recall
MVDet	0.839	0.796	0.968	0.867	0.882	0.757	0.947	0.936	0.872	0.700	0.982	0.888
MVDet+M	0.900	0.837	0.975	0.924	0.912	**0.769**	0.959	0.953	0.894	0.689	0.983	0.911
MVDet+R	0.898	0.830	0.986	0.912	0.923	0.768	0.964	0.959	0.915	**0.709**	0.994	0.920
3DROM	**0.950**	**0.849**	**0.990**	**0.961**	**0.935**	0.759	**0.972**	**0.962**	**0.948**	0.705	**0.997**	**0.951**

both components are used in 3DROM, the models are driven to find more robust features across multiple views, and multi-layer projection can provide sufficient features. These two components do not conflict but work better together.

Choice of Projection Layers. To illustrate the benefits of using five-layer feature projections, a validation study was carried out on the Terrace dataset. As reported in Table 4, when more than one layer is used in the feature map projection, MODA increases with the number of the projection layers. The experiments show that the feature projection, by using the planes below the waist height (100 cm), leads to better results than that using the planes equidistantly selected between 0 cm and the average pedestrian height 180 cm. This can be interpreted as follows: as can be seen in Fig. 3(a) and (b), in comparison with the ground-plane projection, the feature projection of a pedestrian on a higher plane tends to move towards the underlying camera in the top view, which projects the features, for the pedestrians who are outside of the AOI, into the AOI of the top view. Therefore, by using a projection plane at the pedestrians' heights, the features, extracted from the distant pedestrians, disturb the pedestrian detection within the AOI. The use of the projection planes below the waist is a good trade-off between the benefits of using multiple planes and the side effects.

Table 4. Validation of the number of projection layers (with 3D Random Occlusion applied).

Layers	Heights (cm)	MODA	MODP	Prec.	Recall
1	0	0.915	0.709	0.994	0.920
2	0, 180	0.867	0.688	0.972	0.893
	0, 60	0.934	0.708	0.996	0.937
3	0, 90, 180	0.892	0.700	0.973	0.918
	0, 60, 90	0.936	0.710	**0.997**	0.938
4	0, 60, 120, 180	0.902	0.697	0.988	0.912
	0, 30, 60, 90	0.943	**0.712**	0.996	0.946
5	0, 45, 90, 135, 180	0.901	0.682	0.966	0.934
	0, 15, 30, 60, 90	**0.948**	0.705	**0.997**	**0.951**

Validation of 3D Random Occlusion. To investigate the role of the frequency to use 3D Random Occlusion, we tried different values of the occlusion probability p for using 3D Random Occlusion. As reported in Table 5, MODA increases with p and reaches the maximum value when $p = 100\%$ in all three

Table 5. Validation of the occlusion probability (with 5-layer projection applied).

p	MultiviewX Dataset				WILDTRACK Dataset				Terrace Dataset			
	MODA	MODP	Prec.	Recall	MODA	MODP	Prec.	Recall	MODA	MODP	Prec.	Recall
0%	0.900	0.837	0.975	0.924	0.882	0.757	0.947	0.936	0.894	0.689	0.983	0.911
30%	0.927	**0.852**	**0.991**	0.936	0.920	0.757	**0.975**	0.944	0.924	0.697	0.982	0.941
50%	0.934	0.851	0.978	0.956	0.923	0.748	0.961	0.962	0.941	0.694	0.983	**0.957**
70%	0.941	0.846	0.984	0.956	0.928	0.742	0.967	0.960	0.944	**0.706**	0.994	0.949
100%	**0.950**	0.849	0.990	**0.961**	**0.935**	**0.759**	0.972	**0.962**	**0.948**	0.705	**0.997**	0.951

Table 6. A comparison of data augmentation schemes (with 5-layer projection applied).

Methods	MultiviewX Dataset				WILDTRACK Dataset				Terrace Dataset			
	MODA	MODP	Prec.	Recall	MODA	MODP	Prec.	Recall	MODA	MODP	Prec.	Recall
w/o Augmentation	0.900	0.837	0.975	0.924	0.882	0.757	0.947	0.936	0.894	0.689	0.983	0.911
Random Erasing	0.927	0.847	0.983	0.943	0.920	**0.766**	0.953	**0.967**	0.923	0.692	0.980	0.943
3DROM	**0.950**	**0.849**	**0.990**	**0.961**	**0.935**	0.759	**0.972**	0.962	**0.948**	**0.705**	**0.997**	**0.951**

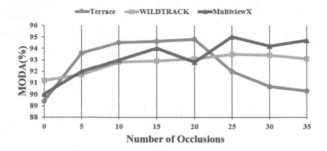

Fig. 7. Parameter validation on the number of occlusions.

datasets. We further compared the 3D Random Occlusion with the related Random Erasing method which was applied to each camera view independently. In this experiment, the optimal settings of Random Erasing [28] proposed by the authors were used. In Table 6, The MODA decreases after 3D Random Occlusion is replaced by Random Erasing in all three datasets. This experiment shows the 3D Random Occlusion method can simulate the effect of Random Erasing in 3D space and is specifically designed for multi-view detection.

Figure 7 shows the validation of the number of 3D random occlusions. When occlusions are too few, the risk of overfitting increases in the training. On the other hand, too many occlusions will cover most pedestrians so that the network cannot learn effective features well. The most appropriate number of occlusions used in training correlates with the average number of pedestrians per frame and the density of pedestrians. Since the WILDTRACK and MultiviewX datasets contain more pedestrians than the Terrace, this number is greater.

5   Conclusions and Future Work

In this paper, we have proposed 3DROM for deep multiview pedestrian detection, which is based on the MVDet framework. 3D Random Occlusion provides extra training samples to the multi-view pedestrian detection network to improve the robustness in occlusion and prevent overfitting. In addition, by learning the multi-layer feature information, 3DROM can fully utilize the limited feature information from each camera view and improve pedestrian detection performance. The greatly improved performance of the 3DROM has been demonstrated in comparison with state-of-the-art methods. Future work is to find a more efficient way to fuse large-scale features and improve the across-dataset generalizability in deep-learning based multi-view pedestrian detection.

Acknowledgments. This work was supported by National Natural Science Foundation of China (NSFC) under Grant 60975082 and Xi'an Jiaotong-Liverpool University under Grant RDF-17-01-33, RDF-19-01-21 and FOSA2106045.

References

1. MultiviewX. https://github.com/hou-yz/MVDet
2. Terrace. https://www.epfl.ch/labs/cvlab/data-pom-index-php/
3. WILDTRACK. https://www.epfl.ch/labs/cvlab/data/data-wildtrack/
4. Alahi, A., Jacques, L., Boursier, Y., Vandergheynst, P.: Sparsity driven people localization with a heterogeneous network of cameras. J. Math. Imaging Vis. **41**(1), 39–58 (2011)
5. Baqué, P., Fleuret, F., Fua, P.: Deep occlusion reasoning for multi-camera multi-target detection. In: Proceedings of the IEEE International Conference on Computer Vision, pp. 271–279 (2017)
6. Chavdarova, T., et al.: WILDTRACK: a multi-camera HD dataset for dense unscripted pedestrian detection. In: Proceedings of the IEEE Conference on Computer Vision and Pattern Recognition, pp. 5030–5039 (2018)
7. Chavdarova, T., Fleuret, F.: Deep multi-camera people detection. In: 2017 16th IEEE International Conference on Machine Learning and Applications (ICMLA), pp. 848–853. IEEE (2017)
8. Eshel, R., Moses, Y.: Tracking in a dense crowd using multiple cameras. Int. J. Comput. Vis. **88**(1), 129–143 (2010)
9. Fleuret, F., Berclaz, J., Lengagne, R., Fua, P.: Multicamera people tracking with a probabilistic occupancy map. IEEE Trans. Pattern Anal. Mach. Intell. **30**(2), 267–282 (2007)
10. Ge, W., Collins, R.T.: Crowd detection with a multiview sampler. In: Daniilidis, K., Maragos, P., Paragios, N. (eds.) ECCV 2010. LNCS, vol. 6315, pp. 324–337. Springer, Heidelberg (2010). https://doi.org/10.1007/978-3-642-15555-0_24
11. He, K., Zhang, X., Ren, S., Sun, J.: Deep residual learning for image recognition. In: Proceedings of the IEEE Conference on Computer Vision and Pattern Recognition, pp. 770–778 (2016)
12. Hou, Y., Zheng, L., Gould, S.: Multiview detection with feature perspective transformation. In: Vedaldi, A., Bischof, H., Brox, T., Frahm, J.-M. (eds.) ECCV 2020. LNCS, vol. 12352, pp. 1–18. Springer, Cham (2020). https://doi.org/10.1007/978-3-030-58571-6_1
13. Kasturi, R., et al.: Framework for performance evaluation of face, text, and vehicle detection and tracking in video: data, metrics, and protocol. IEEE Trans. Pattern Anal. Mach. Intell. **31**(2), 319–336 (2008)
14. Khan, S.M., Shah, M.: Tracking multiple occluding people by localizing on multiple scene planes. IEEE Trans. Pattern Anal. Mach. Intell. **31**(3), 505–519 (2009)
15. Khan, S.M., Shah, M.: A multiview approach to tracking people in crowded scenes using a planar homography constraint. In: Leonardis, A., Bischof, H., Pinz, A. (eds.) ECCV 2006. LNCS, vol. 3954, pp. 133–146. Springer, Heidelberg (2006). https://doi.org/10.1007/11744085_11

16. Krizhevsky, A., Sutskever, I., Hinton, G.E.: ImageNet classification with deep convolutional neural networks. In: Advances in Neural Information Processing Systems, vol. 25, pp. 1097–1105 (2012)

17. Peng, P., Tian, Y., Wang, Y., Li, J., Huang, T.: Robust multiple cameras pedestrian detection with multi-view Bayesian network. Pattern Recogn. 48(5), 1760–1772 (2015)

18. Qiu, R., Xu, M., Yan, Y., Smith, J.S.: A methodology review on multi-view pedestrian detection. In: Pedrycz, W., Chen, S.M. (eds.) Recent Advancements in Multi-View Data Analytics, pp. 317–339. Springer, Cham (2022). https://doi.org/10.1007/978-3-030-95239-6_12

19. Ren, S., He, K., Girshick, R., Sun, J.: Faster R-CNN: towards real-time object detection with region proposal networks. IEEE Trans. Pattern Anal. Mach. Intell. 39(6), 1137–1149 (2016)

20. Simonyan, K., Zisserman, A.: Very deep convolutional networks for large-scale image recognition. arXiv preprint arXiv:1409.1556 (2014)

21. Song, L., Wu, J., Yang, M., Zhang, Q., Li, Y., Yuan, J.: Stacked homography transformations for multi-view pedestrian detection. In: Proceedings of the IEEE/CVF International Conference on Computer Vision, pp. 6049–6057 (2021)

22. Utasi, Á., Benedek, C.: A Bayesian approach on people localization in multicamera systems. IEEE Trans. Circuits Syst. Video Technol. 23(1), 105–115 (2012)

23. Wang, X., Shrivastava, A., Gupta, A.: A-Fast-RCNN: hard positive generation via adversary for object detection. In: Proceedings of the IEEE Conference on Computer Vision and Pattern Recognition, pp. 2606–2615 (2017)

24. Xu, Y., Liu, X., Liu, Y., Zhu, S.: Multi-view people tracking via hierarchical trajectory composition. In: Proceedings of the IEEE Conference on Computer Vision and Pattern Recognition, pp. 4256–4265 (2016)

25. Yan, Y., Xu, M., Smith, J.S., Shen, M., Xi, J.: Multicamera pedestrian detection using logic minimization. Pattern Recogn. 112, 107703 (2021)

26. Zhang, Q., Chan, A.B.: Wide-area crowd counting via ground-plane density maps and multi-view fusion CNNs. In: Proceedings of the IEEE/CVF Conference on Computer Vision and Pattern Recognition, pp. 8297–8306 (2019)

27. Zhang, Q., Lin, W., Chan, A.B.: Cross-view cross-scene multi-view crowd counting. In: IEEE Conference on Computer Vision and Pattern Recognition, pp. 557–567 (2021)

28. Zhong, Z., Zheng, L., Kang, G., Li, S., Yang, Y.: Random erasing data augmentation. In: Proceedings of the AAAI Conference on Artificial Intelligence, vol. 34, pp. 13001–13008 (2020)

29. Zhu, X., Hu, H., Lin, S., Dai, J.: Deformable ConvNets v2: more deformable, better results. In: Proceedings of the IEEE/CVF Conference on Computer Vision and Pattern Recognition, pp. 9308–9316 (2019)

A Simple Single-Scale Vision Transformer for Object Detection and Instance Segmentation

Wuyang Chen[1(✉)], Xianzhi Du[2], Fan Yang[2], Lucas Beyer[2], Xiaohua Zhai[2], Tsung-Yi Lin[2], Huizhong Chen[2], Jing Li[2], Xiaodan Song[2], Zhangyang Wang[1], and Denny Zhou[2]

[1] University of Texas at Austin, Austin 78712, USA
{wuyang.chen,atlaswang}@utexas.edu
[2] Google, Mountain View, USA
{xianzhi,fyangf,lbeyer,xzhai,tsungyi,huizhongc,jingli,
xiaodansong,dennyzhou}@google.com

Abstract. This work presents a simple vision transformer design as a strong baseline for object localization and instance segmentation tasks. Transformers recently demonstrate competitive performance in image classification. To adopt ViT to object detection and dense prediction tasks, many works inherit the multistage design from convolutional networks and highly customized ViT architectures. Behind this design, the goal is to pursue a better trade-off between computational cost and effective aggregation of multiscale global contexts. However, existing works adopt the multistage architectural design as a black-box solution without a clear understanding of its true benefits. In this paper, we comprehensively study three architecture design choices on ViT – spatial reduction, doubled channels, and multiscale features – and demonstrate that a vanilla ViT architecture can fulfill this goal without handcrafting multiscale features, maintaining the original ViT design philosophy. We further complete a scaling rule to optimize our model's trade-off on accuracy and computation cost / model size. By leveraging a constant feature resolution and hidden size throughout the encoder blocks, we propose a simple and compact ViT architecture called Universal Vision Transformer (**UViT**) that achieves strong performance on COCO object detection and instance segmentation benchmark. Our code is available at https://github.com/tensorflow/models/tree/master/official/projects/uvit.

Keywords: Vision transformer · Self-attention · Object detection · Instance segmentation

---

W. Chen—Work done during the first author's research internship with Google.

Supplementary Information The online version contains supplementary material available at https://doi.org/10.1007/978-3-031-20080-9_41.

1   Introduction

Transformer [40], the de-facto standard architecture for natural language processing (NLP), recently has shown promising results on computer vision tasks. Vision Transformer (ViT) [16], an architecture consisting of a sequence of transformer encoder blocks, has achieved competitive performance compared to convolution neural networks (CNNs) [21,34] on the ImageNet classification task [15].

With the success on image classification, recent works extend transformers to more vision tasks, such as object detection [19,25,29], semantic segmentation [19, 25,29,43] and video action recognition [1,13]. Conventionally, CNN architectures adopt a multistage design with gradually enlarged receptive fields [21,34] via spatial reduction or dilated convolutions. These design choices are also naturally introduced to change vision transformer architectures [22,29,43], with two main purposes: 1) **support of multi-scale features**, since dense vision tasks require the visual understanding of objects of different scales and sizes; 2) **reduction of computation cost**, for the input images of dense vision tasks are often of high resolutions, and computation complexity of vanilla self-attention is quadratic to the sequence length. The motivation behind these changes is that, tokens of the original ViT are all of a fixed fine-grained scale throughout the encoder attention blocks, which are not adaptive to dense vision applications, and more importantly incur huge computation/memory overhead. Despite the success of recent works, it is still unclear if complex design conventions of CNNs are indeed necessary for ViT to achieve competitive performance on vision tasks, and how much benefit comes from each individual design.

In this work, we demonstrate that a vanilla ViT architecture, which we call Universal Vision Transformer (**UViT**), is sufficient for achieving competitive

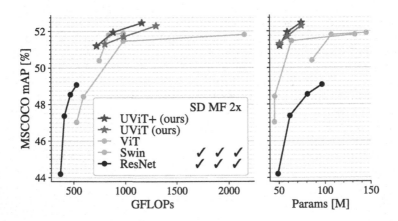

Fig. 1. Trade-off between mAP (COCO) and FLOPs (left)/number of parameters (right). We compare our UViT/UViT+ with Swin Transformer [29], ViT [45], and ResNet (18/50/101/152) [21], all adopting the same standard Cascade Mask RCNN framework [4]. Our UViT is compact, strong, and simple, avoid using any hierarchical design ("SD": spatial downsampling, "MF": multi-scale features, "2×": double channels).

results on the tasks of object detection and instance segmentation. Our hope is not "*to add*" any special layers to the ViT architecture (thus keeping ViT neat and simple), but instead to choose "*not to add*" complex designs that follow CNN structures (multi-scale, double channels, spatial reduction, whose compatibility with attention layers are not thoroughly verified). In other words, our goal is not to pursue a state-of-the-art performance, but to systematically study the principles in ViT architecture designs.

First, to **support multiscale features**, instead of re-designing ViT with a multistage fashion [22,29,43], our core motivation is that self-attention mechanism naturally encourages the learning of non-local information and makes the feature pyramid no longer necessary for ViTs on dense vision tasks. This leads us to design a simple yet strong UViT architecture: we only leverage constant feature resolution and hidden size throughout the encoder blocks, and extract a single-scale feature map. Second, to **reduce the computation cost**, we adopt window splits in attention layers. We observe that on large input images for detection and instance segmentation, global attentions in early layers are redundant and compact local attentions are both effective and efficient. This motivates us to progressively increase the window sizes as the attention layers become deeper, leading to the drop of self-attention's computation cost with preserved performance.

To support the above two purposes, we systematically study fundamental architecture design choices for UViTs on dense prediction tasks. It is worth noting that, although recent works try to analyze vision transformer's generalization [31], loss landscapes [9], and patterns of learned representations [32,39], they mostly focus on image classification tasks. On dense prediction tasks like object detection and instance segmentation, many transformer models [22,29,43] directly inherit architecture principles from CNNs, without validating the actual benefit of each individual design choice. In contrast, our simple solution is based on rigorous ablation studies on dense prediction tasks, which is for the first time. Moreover, we complete a comprehensive study of UViT's compound scaling rule on dense prediction tasks, providing a series of UViT configurations that improve the performance-efficiency trade-off with highly compact architectures (even fewer than 40M parameters on transformer backbone). Our proposed UViT architectures serve as a simple yet strong baseline on COCO object detection and instance segmentation.

We summarize our contributions as below:

- We systematically study the benefits of fundamental architecture designs for ViTs on dense prediction tasks, and propose a simple UViT design that shows strong performance without hand-crafting CNN-like feature pyramid design conventions into transformers.
- We discover a new compound scaling rule (depth, width, input size) for UViTs on dense vision tasks. We find a larger input size creates more room for improvement via model scaling, and a moderate depth (number of attention blocks) outperforms shallower or deeper ones.
- We reduce the computation cost via only attention windows. We observe that attention's receptive field is limited in early layers and compact local attentions are sufficient, while only deeper layers require global attentions.

– Experiments on COCO object detection and instance segmentation demonstrate that our UViT is simple yet a strong baseline for transformers on dense prediction tasks.

2   Related Works

2.1   CNN Backbones for Dense Prediction Problems

CNNs are now mainstream and standard deep network models for dense prediction tasks in computer vision, such as object detection and semantic segmentation. During decades of development, people summarized several high-level and fundamental design conventions: 1) deeper networks for more accurate function approximation [12,17,18,26]: ResNet [21], DenseNet [24]; 2) shallow widths in early layers for high feature resolutions, and wider widths in deeper layers for compressed features, which can deliver good performance-efficiency trade-off: Vgg [34], ResNet [21]; 3) enlarged receptive fields for learning long-term correlations: dilated convolution (Deeplab series [7]), deformable convolutions [14]; 4) hierarchical feature pyramids for learning across a wide range of object scales: FPN [27], ASPP [7], HRNet [41]. In short, the motivations behind these successful design solutions fall in two folds: 1) to support the semantic understanding of objects with diverse sizes and scales; 2) to maintain a balanced computation cost under large input sizes. These two motivations, or challenges, also exist in designing our UViT architectures when we are facing dense prediction tasks, for which we provide a comprehensive study in our work (Sect. 3.1).

2.2   ViT Backbones for Dense Prediction Problems

The first ViT work [16] adopted a transformer encoder on coarse non-overlapping image patches for image classification and requires large-scale training datasets (JFT [35], ImageNet-21K [15]) for pretraining. DeiT further introduce strong augmentations on both data-level and architecture-level to efficiently train ViT on ImageNet-1k [15]. Beyond image classification, more and more works try to design ViT backbones for dense prediction tasks. Initially people try to directly learn high-resolution features extracted by ViT backbone via extra interpolation or convolution layers [2,47]. Some works also leverage self-attention operations to replace partial or all convolution layers in CNNs [23,33,46]. More recent trends [11,19,29,42–44] start following design conventions in CNNs discussed above (Sect. 2.1) and customize ViT architectures to be CNN-like: tokens are progressively merged to downsample the feature resolutions with reduced computation cost, along with increased embedding sizes. Multi-scale feature maps are also collected from the ViT backbone. These ViT works can successfully achieve strong or state-of-the-art performance on object detection or semantic segmentation, but the architecture is again highly customized for vision problems and lose the potential for multi-modal learning in the future. More importantly, those CNN-like design conventions are directly inherited into ViTs without a clear understanding of each individual benefit, leading to empirical black-box designs. In contrast, the simple and neat solution we will provide is motivated by a complete study on ViT's architecture preference on dense prediction tasks (Sect. 3.1 and 3.2).

2.3 Inductive Bias of ViT Architecture

Since the architecture of vision transformers is still in its infant stage, there are few works that systematically study principles in ViT's model design and scaling rule. Initially, people leverage coarse tokenizations, constant feature resolution, and constant hidden size [16,38], while recently fine-grained tokens, spatial downsampling, and doubled channels are also becoming popular in ViT design [29,48]. They all achieve good performance, calling for an organized study on the benefits of different fundamental designs. In addition, different learning behaviors of self-attentions (compared with CNNs) make the scaling law of ViTs highly unclear. Recent works [32] revealed ViT generates more uniform receptive fields across layers, enabling the aggregation of global information in early layers. This is contradictory to CNNs which require deeper layers to help the learning of visual global information [8]. Attention scores of ViTs are also found to gradually become indistinguishable as the encoder goes deeper, leading to identical and redundant feature maps, and plateaued performance [48]. These observations all indicate that previously discovered design conventions and scaling laws for CNNs [21,37] may not be suitable for ViTs, thus calling for comprehensive studies on the new inductive bias of ViT's architecture on dense prediction tasks.

3   Methods

Our work targets designing a simple ViT model for dense prediction tasks, and trying to avoid hand-crafted customization on architectures. We will first explain our motivations with comprehensive ablation studies on individual design benefits in Sect. 3.1, and then elaborate the discovered principles of our UViT designs in Sect. 3.2.

3.1 Is a Simple ViT Design All You Need?

As discussed in Sect. 1, traditionally CNNs leverage resolution downsampling, doubled channels, and hierarchical pyramid structures, to support both multi-scale features and reduction of computation cost [7,21,27]. Although recent trends in designing ViTs also inherit these techniques, it is still unclear whether they are still beneficial to ViTs. Meanwhile, ViT [16], DeiT [38], and T2T-ViT [44] demonstrate that, at least for image classification, a constant feature resolution and hidden size can also achieve competitive performance. Without spatial downsampling, the computation cost of self-attention blocks can also be reduced by using attention window splits [3,29], i.e., to limit the spatial range of the query and the key when we calculate the dot product attention scores.

To better understand each individual technique and to systematically study the principles in ViT architecture designs, we provide a comprehensive study on the contributions of CNN-like design conventions to ViTs on dense prediction tasks.

Implementations: We conduct this study on the object detection task on COCO 2017 dataset. We leverage the standard Cascade Mask-RCNN detection framework [4,20], with a fixed input size as 640×640. All detection models are fine-tuned from an ImageNet pretrained initialization. More details can be found in Sect. 4.1.

Settings: We systematically study the benefit of spatial downsampling, multi-scale features, and doubled channels to the object detection performance of ViT. We start from a baseline ViT architecture close to the S16 model proposed in [16], which has 18 attention blocks, a hidden size of 384, and six heads for each self-attention layer. The first linear project layer embeds images into $\frac{1}{8}$-scale patches, i.e., the input feature resolution to the transformer encoder is $\frac{1}{8}$. The attention blocks will be grouped into three stages for one or a combination of two or three purposes below:

- Spatial downsampling: tokens will be merged between two consecutive stages to downsample the feature resolution. If the channel number is also doubled between stages, the tokens will be merged by a learned convolution with a stride as 2; otherwise, tokens will be merged by a 2D bi-linear interpolation.
- Multi-scale features: after each stage, features of a specific resolution will be output and fed into the detection FPN head. Multi-scale features of three target resolutions $(\frac{1}{8}, \frac{1}{16}, \frac{1}{32})$ will be collected from the encoder from early to deep attention layers.
- Doubled channels: after each of the first two stages, the token's hidden size will be doubled via a linear projection.

We study all combinations of the above three techniques, i.e. eight settings in total, and show the results in Fig. 2. Note that each dot in Fig. 2 indicates an individually designed and trained model. All models are of around 72 million parameters, and are trained and evaluated under the same 640×640 input size. Therefore, for vertically aligned dots, they share the same FLOPs, number of parameters, and input size, thus being fairly comparable. We control the FLOPs (x-axis) by changing the depths or attention windows allocated to different stages, see our supplement for more architecture details.

Observations

- Spatial Downsampling ("SD") does not seem to be beneficial. Our hypothesis is that, under the same FLOPs constraint, the self-attention layers already provide global features, and do not need to downsample the features to enlarge the receptive field.
- Multi-scale Features ("MF") can mitigate the poor performance from downsampling by leveraging early high-resolution features ("SD+MF"). However,

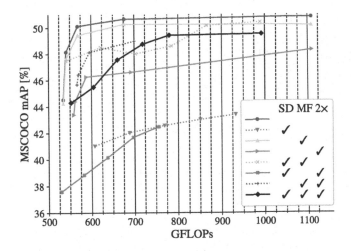

Fig. 2. The benefits of various commonly used CNN-inspired design changes to ViT: spatial downsampling ("SD"), multi-scale features ("MF"), and doubled channels ("2×"). With controlled number of parameters (72M) and input size (640×640), not using any of these designs and sticking to the original ViT model [16] performs the best in a wide range of FLOPs we explore.

the vanilla setting still outperforms this combination. We hypothesize that high-resolution features are extracted too early in the encoder; in contrast, tokens in vanilla ViTs are able to learn fine-grained details throughout the encoder blocks.

– Doubled channels ("2×") plus multi-scale features ("MF") may potentially seem competitive. However, ViT does not show strong inductive bias on "deeper compressed features with more embedding dimension". This observation is also aligned with findings in [32] that ViTs have highly similar representations throughout the model, indicating that we should not sacrifice embedding dimensions of early layers to compensate for deeper layers.

In summary, we did not find strong benefits by adopting CNN-like design conventions. Instead, A simple architecture solution of a constant feature resolution and hidden size could be a strong ViT baseline.

3.2   UViT: A Simple Yet Effective Solution

Based on our study in Sect. 3.1, we are motivated to simplify the ViT design for dense prediction tasks and provide a neat solution, as illustrated in Fig. 3. Taking 8×8 patches of input images, we learn the representation by using a constant token resolution of $\frac{1}{8}$ scale (the number of tokens remains the same) and a constant hidden size (the channel number will not be increased). A single-scale feature map will be fed into a detection or segmentation head. Meanwhile, attention windows [3] will be leveraged to reduce the computation cost.

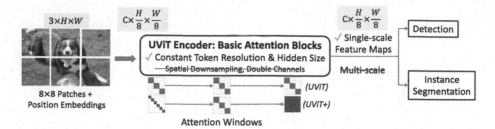

Fig. 3. We keep the architecture of our UViT neat: image patches (plus position embeddings) are processed by a stack of vanilla attention blocks with a constant resolution and hidden size. Single-scale feature maps as outputs are fed into head modules for detection or segmentation tasks. Constant (UViT, Sect. 3.2.1) or progressive (UViT+, Sect. 3.2.2) attention windows are introduced to reduce the computation cost. We demonstrate that this simple architecture is strong, without introducing design overhead from hierarchical spatial downsampling, doubled channels, and multi-scale feature pyramids.

The motivation behind our UViT design is not *"to add"* any layers to the ViT architecture, but instead to choose *"not to add"* complex designs. Our detailed study on input/model scaling will demonstrate that, a vanilla ViT architecture plus a better depth-width trade-off can achieve a high performance.

Though being simple, still we have two core questions to be determined in our design: (1) How to balance the UViT's depth, width, and input size to achieve the best performance-efficiency trade-off? (Sect. 3.2.1) (2) Which attention window strategy can effectively save the computation cost without sacrificing the performance? (Sect. 3.2.2)

3.2.1   A Compound Scaling Rule of UViTs

Previous works studied compound scaling rules for CNNs [37] and ViTs [45] on image classification. However, few works studied the scaling of ViTs on dense prediction tasks. To achieve the best performance-efficiency trade-off, we systematically study the compounding scaling of UViTs on three dimensions: input size, depth, and widths. We show our results in Fig. 4 and Fig. 5[1]. For all models (circle markers), we first train them on ImageNet-1k, then fine-tune them on the COCO detection task.

- Depth (number of attention blocks): we study different UViT models of depths selected from $\{12, 18, 24, 32, 40\}$.
- Input size: we study three levels of input sizes: 640×640, 768×768, 896×896, and 1024×1024.
- Width (i.e. hidden size, or output dimension of attention blocks): we will tune the width to further control different model sizes and computation costs to make different scaling rules fairly comparable.

---

[1] This compound scaling rule is studied in Sect. 3.2.1 before we study the attention window strategy in Sect. 3.2.2. Thus for all models in Fig. 4 and Fig. 5 we adopt the window scale as $\frac{1}{2}$, for fair comparisons.

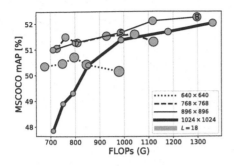 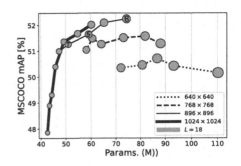

Fig. 4. Input scaling rule for UViT on COCO object detection. Given a fixed depth, an **input size of 896 × 896** (thin solid line) leaves more room for model scaling (by increasing the width) and is slightly better than 1024 × 1024 (thick solid line); and 640 × 640 (dashed line) or 768 × 768 (dotted line) are of worse performance-efficiency trade-off. Black capital letters "*T*", "*S*", and "*B*" annotate three final depth/width configurations of UViT variants we will propose (Table 2). Different sizes of markers represent the hidden sizes (widths).

Observations

- In general, UViT can achieve a strong mAP with a moderate computation cost (FLOPs) and a highly compact number of parameters (even fewer than 70M including the Cascaded FPN head).
- For input sizes (Fig. 4 by different line styles): large inputs generally create more room for models to further scale up. Across a wide range of model parameters and FLOPs, we find that the scaling under an 896 × 896 input size constantly outperforms smaller input sizes (which lead to severe model overfitting), and is also better than 1024×1024 in a comparable FLOPs range.
- For the model depths (Fig. 5), different depths in colors): we find that considering both FLOPs and the number of parameters, 18 blocks achieve better performance than 12/24/32/40 blocks. This indicates UViT needs a balanced trade-off between depth and width, instead of sacrificing depth for more width (e.g. 12 blocks) or sacrificing width for more depth (e.g. 40 blocks).

In summary, based on our final compound scaling rule, we propose our basic version of UViT as 18 attention blocks under 896 × 896 input size. See our supplement for more architecture details.

3.2.2 Attention Windows: A Progressive Strategy

In this section, we will show that a progressive attention window strategy can reduce UViT's computation cost while still preserving or even increasing the performance.

Early Attentions are Local Operators. Originally, self-attention [40] is a global operation: unlike convolution layers that share weights to local regions, any pair of tokens in the sequence will contribute to the feature aggregation, thus collecting global information to each token. In practice, however, self-attention in different layers may still have biases in regions they prefer to focus on.

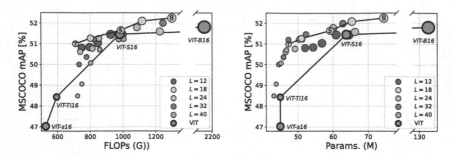

Fig. 5. Model scaling rule for UViT on COCO object detection. **18 attention blocks** (orange), which provide a balanced trade-off between depth and width, performs better than shallower or deeper UViTs. Black capital letters "*T*", "*S*", and "*B*" annotate three final depth/width configurations of UViT variants we will propose (Table 2). Different sizes of markers represent the hidden sizes (widths). (Color figure online)

To validate this assumption, we select a pretrained ViT-B16 model [16], and calculate the relative receptive field of each self-attention layer on COCO. Given a sequence feature of length L and the attention score s (after softmax) from a specific head, the relative receptive field r is defined as:

$$r = \frac{1}{L} \sum_{i=1}^{L} \frac{\sum_{j=1}^{L} s_{i,j} |i - j|}{\max(i, L - i)}, i, j = 1, \cdots, L, \tag{1}$$

where $\sum_{j=1}^{L} s_{i,j} = 1$ for $j = 1, \cdots, L$. This relative receptive filed takes into consideration the token's position and the furthest possible location a token can aggregate, and indicates the spatial focus of the self-attention layer.

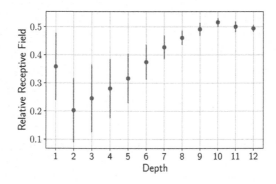

Fig. 6. Relative attention's receptive field of a ImageNet pretrained ViT-B16 [16] along depth (indices of attention blocks), on the COCO dataset. Error bars are standard deviations across different attention heads.

We collect the averages and standard deviations across different attention heads. As shown in Fig. 6, we can see that tokens in early attention layers, although having the potential to aggregate long-range features, weight more on their neighbor tokens and thus act like a "local operator". As the attention layers stack deeper, the receptive field increases, transiting the self-attention to a global operation. This inspires us that, if we explicitly limit the attention range of early layers, we may save the computation cost but still preserve the capability of self-attentions.

Attention Window Improves UViT's Efficiency. Motivated by Fig. 6, we want to study the most effective attention window strategy. Specifically, we need principled answers to two design questions:

1) *How small a window size can early attention layers endure?* To answer this question, we start the attention blocks with square windows with different small scales: $\{\frac{1}{16}, \frac{1}{8}, \frac{1}{4}\}$ of height or width a sequence's 2D shape[2].
2) *Do deeper layers require global attention, or some local attentions are also sufficient?* To compare with global attentions (window size as 1), we will also try small attention windows (window size of $\frac{1}{2}$ scale) in deeper layers.

To represent an attention window strategy that "progressively increases window scales from $\frac{1}{4}$ to $\frac{1}{2}$ to 1", we use a simple annotation "$[4^{-1}] \times 14 \to [2^{-1}] \times 2 \to [1] \times 2$", indicating that there are 14 attention blocks assigned with $\frac{1}{4}$-scale windows, then two attention blocks assigned with $\frac{1}{2}$-scale windows, and finally two attention blocks assigned with 1-scale windows. When comparing different window strategies, we make sure all strategies have the same number of parameters and share the similar computation cost for fair comparisons. We also include four more baselines of constant attention window scale across all attention blocks: global attention, and also windows of $\frac{1}{4} \sim \frac{1}{2}$ scale. We show our results in Table 1, and summarize observations below:

- With smaller constant window scale ($\frac{1}{2}/\frac{1}{3}/\frac{1}{4}$), we save more computation cost with slight sacrifice in mAP.
- Adopting constant global attentions throughout the whole encoder blocks (window size as 1, first row) is largely redundant, which contributes marginal benefits but suffers from a huge computation cost.
- Early attentions can use smaller windows like $\frac{1}{4}$-scale, but over-shrank window sizes ($\frac{1}{16}, \frac{1}{8}$) can impair the capability of self-attentions (3rd, 4th rows).
- Deeper layers still require global attentions to preserve the final performance (last two rows).
- A properly designed window strategy (5th row) can outperform vanilla solutions (1st, 2nd row) with a reduced computation cost.

In conclusion, we set the window scale of our basic version (UViT, Sect. 3.2.1) as constant 2^{-1}, and proposed an improved version of our model, dubbed "UViT+" with the attention window strategy adopted as "$[4^{-1}] \times 14 \to [2^{-1}] \times 2 \to [1] \times 2$".

---

[2] For example, if the input sequence has $(896/8) \times (896/8) = 112 \times 112$ tokens, a window of scale $\frac{1}{16}$ will contain $7 \times 7 = 49$ elements. Similar ideas for $\frac{1}{8}$ and $\frac{1}{4}$.

Table 1. Over-shrank window sizes in early layers are harmful, and global attention windows in deep layers are vital to the final performance. Fractions in brackets indicate attention window scales (relative to sequence feature sizes), and the multiplier indicates the number of attention blocks allocated to an attention window scale (18 blocks in total). Standard Deviations of three random runs are shown in parentheses.

[window_scale] × #layers	GFLOPs	AP_{val}	Img/s
$[1] \times 18$	2961.9	52.4 (0.09)	3.5
$[2^{-1}] \times 18$	1298.7	52.3 (0.17)	10.5
$[16^{-1}] \times 4 \rightarrow [8^{-1}] \times 4 \rightarrow [4^{-1}] \times 4 \rightarrow [2^{-1}] \times 4 \rightarrow [1] \times 2$	1154.3	52.0 (0.15)	11.5
$[8^{-1}] \times 9 \rightarrow [4^{-1}] \times 4 \rightarrow [2^{-1}] \times 3 \rightarrow [1] \times 2$	1131.2	52.2 (0.21)	12.7
$[4^{-1}] \times 14 \rightarrow [2^{-1}] \times 2 \rightarrow [1] \times 2$	1160.1	52.5 (0.11)	12.3
$[4^{-1}] \times 6 \rightarrow [2^{-1}] \times 12$	1160.1	52.2 (0.12)	12.5

4   Final Results

We conduct our experiments on COCO [28] object detection and instance segmentation to show our final performance.

4.1   Implementations

We implement our model and training in TensorFlow and Keras. Experiments are conducted on TPUs. Before fine-tuning on object detection or instance segmentation, we follow the DeiT [38] training settings to pretrain our UViTs on ImageNet-1k with a 224 × 224 input size and a batch size of 1024. We follow the convention in [16]: during ImageNet pretraining the kernel size of the first linear projection layer is 16 × 16. During fine-tuning, we will use a more fine-grained 8 × 8 patch size for the dense sampling purpose. The kernel weight of the first linear project layer will be interpolated from 16 × 16 to 8 × 8, and the position embedding will also be elongated by interpolation. We also report the throughput ("Img/s"), which measures the latency of UViTs by feeding one image per TPU core.

4.2   Architectures and ImageNet Pretraining

We propose three variants of our UViT variants. The architecture configurations of our model variants are listed in Table 2, and are also annotated in Fig. 4 and Fig. 5 ("T", "S", "B" in black). The number of heads is fixed as six, and the expansion ratio of each FFN (feed-forward network) layer if fixed as four in all experiments. As discussed in Sect. 3.2.2, the attention window strategy will be "$[4^{-1}] \times 14 \rightarrow [2^{-1}] \times 2 \rightarrow [1] \times 2$".

Table 2. Architecture variants of our UViT with ImageNet [15] Pretraining Performance.

Name	Depth	Hidden size	Params. (M)	GFLOPs	Top-1	Img/s
UViT-T	18	222	13.5	2.5	76.0%	170.2
UViT-S	18	288	21.7	4.0	78.9%	145.4
UViT-B	18	384	32.8	6.9	81.3%	134.2

Table 3. Two-stage object detection and instance segmentation results on COCO 2017. We compare employing different backbones with Cascade Mask R-CNN on single model without test-time augmentation. UViT sets a constant window scale as 3^{-1}, and UViT+ adopts the attention window strategy as "$[4^{-1}] \times 14 \to [2^{-1}] \times 2 \to [1] \times 2$". We also reproduced the performance of ResNet under the same settings.

Backbone	Resolution	GFLOPs	Params. (M)	AP_{val}	AP_{val}^{mask}	Img/s
ResNet-18	896×896	370.4	48.9	44.2	38.5	–
ResNet-50	896×896	408.8	61.9	47.4	40.8	–
Swin-T [29]	480~800×1333	745	86	50.5	43.7	15.3
Shuffle-T [25]	480~800×1333	746	86	50.8	44.1	–
UViT-T (ours)	896×896	801.4	51.0	**51.3**	43.6	11.8
UViT-T+ (ours)	896×896	720.2	51.0	51.2	**43.9**	14.2
ResNet-101	896×896	468.2	81.0	48.5	41.8	–
Swin-S [29]	480~800×1333	838	107	51.8	44.7	12.0
Shuffle-S [25]	480~800×1333	844	107	**51.9**	**44.9**	–
UViT-S (ours)	896×896	986.8	59.2	51.7	44.1	11.1
UViT-S+ (ours)	896×896	882.2	59.2	**51.9**	44.5	12.5
ResNet-152	896×896	527.7	96.7	49.1	42.1	–
Swin-B [29]	480~800×1333	982	145	51.9	45	11.6
Shuffle-B [25]	480~800×1333	989	145	52.2	45.3	–
GCNet [5]	–	1041	–	51.8	44.7	–
UViT-B (ours)	896×896	1298.7	74.4	52.3	44.3	10.5
UViT-B+ (ours)	896×896	1160.1	74.4	**52.5**	44.8	12.3
UViT-B+ (ours) w/ self-training	896×896	1160.1	74.4	**53.9**	**46.1**	12.3

4.3 COCO Detection and Instance Segmentation

Settings. Object detection experiments are conducted on COCO 2017 [28], which contains 118K training and 5K validation images. We consider the popular Cascade Mask-RCNN detection framework [4,20], and leverage multi-scale training [6,36] (resizing the input to 896 × 896), AdamW optimizer [30] (with an initial learning rate as 3×10^{-3}), weight decay as 1×10^{-4}, and a batch size of 256. Similar above, the thoughput ("Img/s") measures the latency of UViTs with one COCO image per TPU core.

From Table 3 we can see that on different levels of model variants, our UViTs are highly compact. Compared with both CNNs and other ViT works, our UViT achieves strong results with much better efficiency: with similar GFLOPs, UViT uses a much fewer number of parameters (at least **44.9%** parameter reduction compared with Swin [29]). To make this comparison clean, we did not adopt any system-level techniques [29] to boost the performance[3]. As we did not leverage any CNN-like hierarchical pyramid structures, the results of our simple and neat solution suggest that, the original design philosophy of ViT [16] is a strong baseline without any hand-crafted architecture customization. We also show the mAP-efficiency trade-off curve in Fig. 1. Besides, we also adopt our UViT-B backbone with the Mask-RCNN [20] framework, and achieve 50.5 AP_{val} with 1026.1 GFLOPs.

Additionally, we adopt self-training on top of our largest model (UViT-B) to evaluate the performance gain by leveraging unlabeled data, similar as [49]. We use ImageNet-1K without labels as the unlabeled set, and a pretrained UViT-B model as the teacher model to generate pseudo-labels. All predicted boxes with confidence scores larger than 0.5 are kept, together with their corresponding masks. For UViT-B with self-training, the student model is initialized from the same weights of the teacher model. The ratio of labeled data to pseudo-labeled data is 1:1 in each batch. Apart from increasing training steps by 2× for each epoch, all other hyperparameters remain unchanged. We can see from the last row in Table 3 that self-training significantly improves box AP and mask AP by 1.4% and 1.3%, respectively.

5   Conclusion

We present a simple, single-scale vision transformer backbone that can serve as a strong baseline for object detection and semantic segmentation. Our novelty is not "to add" any special layers to ViT, but instead to choose "not to add" complex designs, with strong motivations and clear experimental supports. ViT is proposed for image classification. To adapt ViT to dense vision tasks, recent works choose "to add" more CNN-like designs (multi-scale, double channels, spatial reduction). But these add-ons mainly follow the success of CNNs, and their compatibility with attention layers is not verified. However, our detailed study shows that CNN-like designs are not prerequisites for ViT, and a vanilla ViT architecture plus a better scaling rule (depth, width, input size) and a progressive attention widow strategy can indeed achieve a high detection performance. Our proposed UViT architectures achieve strong performance on both COCO object detection and instance segmentation. Our uniform design has the potential of supporting multi-modal/multi-task learning and vision-language problems. Most importantly, we hope our work could bring the attention to the community that ViTs may require careful and special architecture design on dense prediction tasks, instead of directly adopting CNN design conventions in black-box.

---

[3] As we adopt the popular Cascade Mask-RCNN detection framework [4,20], some previous detection works [10,36] may not be directly compared.

References

1. Arnab, A., Dehghani, M., Heigold, G., Sun, C., Lucic, M., Schmid, C.: Vivit: a video vision transformer. ArXiv abs/2103.15691 (2021)
2. Beal, J., Kim, E., Tzeng, E., Park, D.H., Zhai, A., Kislyuk, D.: Toward transformer-based object detection. arXiv preprint arXiv:2012.09958 (2020)
3. Beltagy, I., Peters, M.E., Cohan, A.: Longformer: the long-document transformer. arXiv preprint arXiv:2004.05150 (2020)
4. Cai, Z., Vasconcelos, N.: Cascade r-cnn: delving into high quality object detection. In: Proceedings of the IEEE Conference on Computer Vision and Pattern Recognition, pp. 6154–6162 (2018)
5. Cao, Y., Xu, J., Lin, S., Wei, F., Hu, H.: Global context networks. IEEE Trans. Pattern Anal. Mach. Intell. (2020)
6. Carion, N., Massa, F., Synnaeve, G., Usunier, N., Kirillov, A., Zagoruyko, S.: End-to-end object detection with transformers. In: Vedaldi, A., Bischof, H., Brox, T., Frahm, J.-M. (eds.) ECCV 2020. LNCS, vol. 12346, pp. 213–229. Springer, Cham (2020). https://doi.org/10.1007/978-3-030-58452-8_13
7. Chen, L.C., Papandreou, G., Schroff, F., Adam, H.: Rethinking atrous convolution for semantic image segmentation. arXiv preprint arXiv:1706.05587 (2017)
8. Chen, L.C., Zhu, Y., Papandreou, G., Schroff, F., Adam, H.: Encoder-decoder with atrous separable convolution for semantic image segmentation. In: Proceedings of the European Conference on Computer Vision (ECCV), pp. 801–818 (2018)
9. Chen, X., Hsieh, C.J., Gong, B.: When vision transformers outperform resnets without pretraining or strong data augmentations. arXiv preprint arXiv:2106.01548 (2021)
10. Chen, Y., Zhang, Z., Cao, Y., Wang, L., Lin, S., Hu, H.: Reppoints v2: verification meets regression for object detection. Adv. Neural Inf. Process. Syst. **33**, 5621–5631 (2020)
11. Chu, X., Zhang, B., Tian, Z., Wei, X., Xia, H.: Do we really need explicit position encodings for vision transformers? arXiv e-prints, pp arXiv 2102 (2021)
12. Cohen, N, Sharir, O., Shashua, A.: On the expressive power of deep learning: a tensor analysis. In: Conference on Learning Theory, pp. 698–728. PMLR (2016)
13. Crotts, A.P.S.: Vatt/columbia microlensing survey of m31 and the galaxy. arXiv: Astrophysics (1996)
14. Dai, J., Qi, H., Xiong, Y., Li, Y., Zhang, G., Hu, H., Wei, Y.: Deformable convolutional networks. In: Proceedings of the IEEE International Conference on Computer Vision, pp. 764–773 (2017)
15. Deng, J., Dong, W., Socher, R., Li, L.J., Li, K., Fei-Fei, L.: Imagenet: a large-scale hierarchical image database. In: 2009 IEEE Conference on Computer Vision and Pattern Recognition, pp. 248–255. IEEE (2009)
16. Dosovitskiy, A., et al.: An image is worth 16×16 words: transformers for image recognition at scale. arXiv preprint arXiv:2010.11929 (2020)
17. Elbrächter, D., Perekrestenko, D., Grohs, P., Bölcskei, H.: Deep neural network approximation theory. arXiv preprint arXiv:1901.02220 (2019)
18. Eldan, R., Shamir, O.: The power of depth for feedforward neural networks. In: Conference on Learning Theory, pp. 907–940. PMLR (2016)
19. Han, K., Xiao, A., Wu, E., Guo, J., Xu, C., Wang, Y.: Transformer in transformer. arXiv preprint arXiv:2103.00112 (2021)
20. He, K., Gkioxari, G., Dollár, P., Girshick, R.: Mask r-cnn. In: Proceedings of the IEEE International Conference on Computer Vision, pp. 2961–2969 (2017)

21. He, K., Zhang, X., Ren, S., Sun, J.: Deep residual learning for image recognition. In: Proceedings of the IEEE Conference on Computer Vision and Pattern Recognition, pp. 770–778 (2016)
22. Heo, B., Yun, S., Han, D., Chun, S., Choe, J., Oh, S.J.: Rethinking spatial dimensions of vision transformers. arXiv preprint arXiv:2103.16302 (2021)
23. Hu, H., Zhang, Z., Xie, Z., Lin, S.: Local relation networks for image recognition. In: Proceedings of the IEEE International Conference on Computer Vision, pp. 3464–3473 (2019)
24. Huang, G., Liu, Z., Van Der Maaten, L., Weinberger, K.Q.: Densely connected convolutional networks. In: Proceedings of the IEEE Conference on Computer Vision and Pattern Recognition, pp. 4700–4708 (2017)
25. Huang, Z., Ben, Y., Luo, G., Cheng, P., Yu, G., Fu, B.: Shuffle transformer: rethinking spatial shuffle for vision transformer. arXiv preprint arXiv:2106.03650 (2021)
26. Liang, S., Srikant, R.: Why deep neural networks for function approximation? arXiv preprint arXiv:1610.04161 (2016)
27. Lin, T.Y., Dollár, P., Girshick, R., He, K., Hariharan, B., Belongie, S.: Feature pyramid networks for object detection. In: Proceedings of the IEEE Conference on Computer Vision and Pattern Recognition, pp. 2117–2125 (2017)
28. Lin, T.-Y., et al.: Microsoft COCO: common objects in context. In: Fleet, D., Pajdla, T., Schiele, B., Tuytelaars, T. (eds.) ECCV 2014. LNCS, vol. 8693, pp. 740–755. Springer, Cham (2014). https://doi.org/10.1007/978-3-319-10602-1_48
29. Liu, Z., et al.: Swin transformer: hierarchical vision transformer using shifted windows. arXiv preprint arXiv:2103.14030 (2021)
30. Loshchilov, I., Hutter, F.: Decoupled weight decay regularization. arXiv preprint arXiv:1711.05101 (2017)
31. Naseer, M., Ranasinghe, K., Khan, S., Hayat, M., Khan, F.S., Yang, M.H.: Intriguing properties of vision transformers. arXiv preprint arXiv:2105.10497 (2021)
32. Raghu, M., Unterthiner, T., Kornblith, S., Zhang, C., Dosovitskiy, A.: Do vision transformers see like convolutional neural networks? arXiv preprint arXiv:2108.08810 (2021)
33. Ramachandran, P., Parmar, N., Vaswani, A., Bello, I., Levskaya, A., Shlens, J.: Stand-alone self-attention in vision models. arXiv preprint arXiv:1906.05909 (2019)
34. Simonyan, K., Zisserman, A.: Very deep convolutional networks for large-scale image recognition. arXiv preprint arXiv:1409.1556 (2014)
35. Sun, C., Shrivastava, A., Singh, S., Gupta, A.: Revisiting unreasonable effectiveness of data in deep learning era. In: Proceedings of the IEEE International Conference on Computer Vision, pp. 843–852 (2017)
36. Sun, P., et al.: Sparse r-cnn: End-to-end object detection with learnable proposals. In: Proceedings of the IEEE/CVF Conference on Computer Vision and Pattern Recognition, pp. 14454–14463 (2021)
37. Tan, M., Le, Q.V.: Efficientnet: rethinking model scaling for convolutional neural networks. arXiv preprint arXiv:1905.11946 (2019)
38. Touvron, H., Cord, M., Douze, M., Massa, F., Sablayrolles, A., Jégou, H.: Training data-efficient image transformers & distillation through attention. arXiv preprint arXiv:2012.12877 (2020)
39. Touvron, H., Cord, M., Sablayrolles, A., Synnaeve, G., Jégou, H.: Going deeper with image transformers. arXiv preprint arXiv:2103.17239 (2021)
40. Vaswani, A., et al.: Attention is all you need. Adv. Neural Inf. Process. Syst. **30**, 5998–6008 (2017)
41. Wang, J., et al.: Deep high-resolution representation learning for visual recognition. IEEE Trans. Pattern Anal. Mach. Intell. (2020)

42. Wang, W., et al.: Pyramid vision transformer: a versatile backbone for dense prediction without convolutions. arXiv preprint arXiv:2102.12122 (2021)
43. Xie, E., Wang, W., Yu, Z., Anandkumar, A., Alvarez, J.M., Luo, P.: Segformer: simple and efficient design for semantic segmentation with transformers. arXiv preprint arXiv:2105.15203 (2021)
44. Yuan, L., et al.: Tokens-to-token vit: training vision transformers from scratch on imagenet. arXiv preprint arXiv:2101.11986 (2021)
45. Zhai, X., Kolesnikov, A., Houlsby, N., Beyer, L.: Scaling vision transformers. In: Proceedings of the IEEE/CVF Conference on Computer Vision and Pattern Recognition, pp. 12104–12113 (2022)
46. Zhao, H., Jia, J., Koltun, V.: Exploring self-attention for image recognition. In: Proceedings of the IEEE/CVF Conference on Computer Vision and Pattern Recognition, pp. 10076–10085 (2020)
47. Zheng, S., et al.: Rethinking semantic segmentation from a sequence-to-sequence perspective with transformers. In: Proceedings of the IEEE/CVF Conference on Computer Vision and Pattern Recognition, pp. 6881–6890 (2021)
48. Zhou, D., et al.: Deepvit: towards deeper vision transformer. arXiv preprint arXiv:2103.11886 (2021)
49. Zoph, B., et al.: Rethinking pre-training and self-training. arXiv preprint arXiv:2006.06882 (2020)

Simple Open-Vocabulary Object Detection

Matthias Minderer[✉], Alexey Gritsenko, Austin Stone, Maxim Neumann,
Dirk Weissenborn, Alexey Dosovitskiy, Aravindh Mahendran, Anurag Arnab,
Mostafa Dehghani, Zhuoran Shen, Xiao Wang, Xiaohua Zhai, Thomas Kipf,
and Neil Houlsby

Google Research, Mountain View, USA
{mjlm,agritsenko}@google.com

Abstract. Combining simple architectures with large-scale pre-training
has led to massive improvements in image classification. For object
detection, pre-training and scaling approaches are less well established,
especially in the long-tailed and open-vocabulary setting, where training data is relatively scarce. In this paper, we propose a strong recipe
for transferring image-text models to open-vocabulary object detection. We use a standard Vision Transformer architecture with minimal modifications, contrastive image-text pre-training, and end-to-end
detection fine-tuning. Our analysis of the scaling properties of this
setup shows that increasing image-level pre-training and model size yield
consistent improvements on the downstream detection task. We provide the adaptation strategies and regularizations needed to attain very
strong performance on zero-shot text-conditioned and one-shot image-
conditioned object detection. Code and models are available on GitHub
github.com/google-research/scenic/tree/main/scenic/projects/owl_vit.

Keywords: Open-vocabulary detection · Transformer · Vision
transformer · Zero-shot detection · Image-conditioned detection ·
One-shot object detection · Contrastive learning · Image-text models ·
Foundation models · CLIP

1 Introduction

Object detection is a fundamental task in computer vision. Until recently, detection models were typically limited to a small, fixed set of semantic categories,
because obtaining localized training data with large or open label spaces is costly
and time-consuming. This has changed with the development of powerful language encoders and contrastive image-text training. These models learn a shared
representation of image and text from loosely aligned image-text pairs, which
are abundantly available on the web. By leveraging large amounts of image-text

---

M. Minderer and A. Gritsenko—Equal conceptual and technical contribution.

Supplementary Information The online version contains supplementary material
available at https://doi.org/10.1007/978-3-031-20080-9_42.

data, contrastive training has yielded major improvements in zero-shot classification performance and other language-based tasks [19,33,44].

Many recent works aim to transfer the language capabilities of these models to object detection [12,20,26,45,46]. These methods, for example, use distillation against embeddings of image crops [12], weak supervision with image-level labels [46], or self-training [26,45]. Here, we provide a simple architecture and end-to-end training recipe that achieves strong open-vocabulary detection without these methods, even on categories not seen during training.

We start with the Vision Transformer architecture [22], which has been shown to be highly scalable, and pre-train it contrastively on a large image-text dataset [19,44]. To transfer the model to detection, we make a minimal set of changes: We remove the final token pooling layer and instead attach a lightweight classification and box head to each transformer output token. Open-vocabulary classification is enabled by replacing the fixed classification layer weights with the class-name embeddings obtained from the text model [2] (Fig. 1). We fine-tune the pre-trained model on standard detection datasets using a bipartite matching loss [6]. Both the image and the text model are fine-tuned end-to-end.

We analyze the scaling properties of this approach and find that increasing model size and pre-training duration continue to yield improvements in detection performance beyond 20 billion image-text pairs. This is important since image-text pairs, in contrast to detection data, are abundant and allow further scaling.

A key feature of our model is its simplicity and modularity. Since the image and text components of our model are not fused, our model is agnostic to the source of query representations. We can therefore use our model without modification as a one-shot detection learner simply by querying it with image-derived embeddings. One-shot object detection is the challenging problem of detecting novel objects solely based on a query image patch showing the object [4,16,31]. The image-conditioned one-shot ability is a powerful extension to text-conditioned detection because it allows detecting objects that are difficult to describe through text (yet easy to capture in an image), such as specialized technical parts. Despite using a generic architecture not specialized for this problem, we improve the state of the art for one-shot detection on *unseen* COCO categories (held out during training) from 26.0 to 41.8 AP50, an improvement of 72%.

For open-vocabulary text-conditioned detection, our model achieves 34.6% AP overall and 31.2% AP_{rare} on unseen classes on the LVIS dataset.

In summary, we make the following contributions:

1. A simple and strong recipe for transferring image-level pre-training to open-vocabulary object detection.
2. State-of-the-art one-shot (image conditional) detection by a large margin.
3. A detailed scaling and ablation study to justify our design.

We believe our model will serve as a strong baseline that can be easily implemented in various frameworks, and as a flexible starting point for future research on tasks requiring open-vocabulary localization. We call our method *Vision Transformer for Open-World Localization*, or **OWL-ViT** for short.

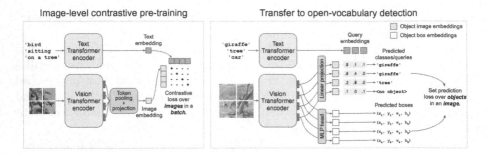

Fig. 1. Overview of our method. *Left:* We first pre-train an image and text encoder contrastively using image-text pairs, similar to CLIP [33], ALIGN [19], and LiT [44]. *Right:* We then transfer the pre-trained encoders to open-vocabulary object detection by removing token pooling and attaching light-weight object classification and localization heads directly to the image encoder output tokens. To achieve open-vocabulary detection, query strings are embedded with the text encoder and used for classification. The model is fine-tuned on standard detection datasets. At inference time, we can use text-derived embeddings for open-vocabulary detection, or image-derived embeddings for few-shot image-conditioned detection.

2   Related Work

Contrastive Vision-Language Pre-training. The idea of embedding images and text into a shared space has been used to achieve "zero-shot" generalization for a long time [10,36,40]. Thanks to innovations in contrastive losses and better architectures, recent models can learn consistent visual and language representations from web-derived image and text pairs without the need for explicit human annotations. This vastly increases the available training data and has led to large improvements on zero-shot classification benchmarks [19,32,33,44]. While any of the recent image-text models are compatible with our approach, our model and dataset are most similar to LiT [44] and ALIGN [19].

Closed-Vocabulary Object Detection. Object detection models have been traditionally formulated for closed-vocabulary settings. Initially, "one-stage" and "two-stage" detectors, such as SSD [28] and Faster-RCNN [34] respectively, proliferated. More recently, DETR [6] showed that object detection can be framed as a set prediction problem, trained with bipartite matching, and achieve competitive results. Notably, such architectures do not require region proposal generation or non-maximum suppression. Follow-up works have proposed more efficient variants of DETR [37,41,48], including architectures without a "decoder-stage" [9]. Our work also simplifies DETR, in that we do not use a decoder. Compared to [9], which uses additional "detection" tokens, we further simplify the model by predicting one object instance directly from each image token.

Long-Tailed and Open-Vocabulary Object Detection. To go beyond a closed vocabulary, fixed classification layers can be replaced by language embeddings to create open-vocabulary detectors [2]. Open-vocabulary object detection has recently seen much progress from combining contrastively trained image-text models and classic object detectors [12,20,26,42,45,46]. The main challenge in this task is how to transfer the image-level representations of the image-text backbone to detection despite the scarcity of localized annotations for rare classes. Making efficient use of the image-text pre-training is crucial since it allows for scaling without the need for expensive human annotations. Various approaches have been proposed. **ViLD** [12] distills embeddings obtained by applying CLIP or ALIGN to cropped image regions from a class-agnostic region proposal network (RPN). The RPN, however, limits generalization performance on novel objects, which is exacerbated by ViLD's two-step distillation-training process. Multistage training is also used by **RegionCLIP**, which generates pseudo-labels on captioning data, followed by region-text contrastive pre-training, and transfer to detection. In contrast, our method fine-tunes both image and text models end-to-end on publicly available detection datasets, which simplifies training and improves generalization to unseen classes. **MDETR** [20] and **GLIP** [26] use a single text query for the whole image and formulate detection as the phrase grounding problem. This limits the number of object categories that can be processed per forward pass. Our architecture is simpler and more flexible in that it performs no image-text fusion and can handle multiple independent text or image-derived queries. **OVR-CNN** [42] is most similar to our approach in that it fine-tunes an image-text model to detection on a limited vocabulary and relies on image-text pre-training for generalization to an open vocabulary. However, we differ in all modelling and loss function choices. We use ViT [22] instead of their ResNet [15], a DETR-like model instead of their Faster RCNN [34] and image-text pre-training as in LiT [44] instead of their PixelBERT [18] and visual grounding loss. Orthogonal to our approach, **Detic** [46] improves long-tail detection performance with weak supervision by training only the classification head on examples where only image-level annotations are available.

We note that in our definition of *open-vocabulary* detection, object categories may overlap between detection training and testing. When we specifically refer to detecting categories for which no localized instances were seen during training, we use the term *zero-shot*.

Image-Conditioned Detection. Related to open-vocabulary detection is the task of image-conditioned detection, which refers to the ability to detect objects matching a single *query image* which shows an object of the category in question [4,7,16,31]. This task is also called *one-shot object detection* because the query image is essentially a single training example. Image-based querying allows open-world detection when even the *name* of the object is unknown, e.g. for unique objects or specialized technical parts. Our model can perform this task without modifications by simply using image-derived instead of text-derived embeddings as queries. Recent prior works on this problem have focused mainly on architectural innovations, for example using sophisticated forms of cross-attention between the query and target image [7,16]. Our approach instead relies on a simple but large model and extensive image-text pre-training.

3   Method

Our goal is to create a simple and scalable open-vocabulary object detector. We focus on standard Transformer-based models because of their scalability [22] and success in closed-vocabulary detection [6]. We present a two-stage recipe:

1. Contrastively pre-train image and text encoders on large-scale image-text data.
2. Add detection heads and fine-tune on medium-sized detection data.

The model can then be queried in different ways to perform open-vocabulary or few-shot detection.

3.1   Model

Architecture. Our model uses a standard Vision Transformer as the image encoder and a similar Transformer architecture as the text encoder (Fig. 1). To adapt the image encoder for detection, we remove the token pooling and final projection layer, and instead linearly project each output token representation to obtain per-object image embeddings for classification (Fig. 1, right). The maximum number of predicted objects is therefore equal to the number of tokens (sequence length) of the image encoder. This is not a bottleneck in practice since the sequence length of our models is at least 576 (ViT-B/32 at input size 768×768), which is larger than the maximum number of instances in today's datasets (e.g., 294 instances for LVIS [13]). Box coordinates are obtained by passing token representations through a small MLP. Our setup resembles DETR [6], but is simplified by removing the decoder.

Open-Vocabulary Object Detection. For open-vocabulary classification of detected objects, we follow prior work and use text embeddings, rather than learned class embeddings, in the output layer of the classification head [2]. The text embeddings, which we call *queries*, are obtained by passing category names or other textual object descriptions through the text encoder. The task of the model then becomes to predict, for each object, a bounding box and a probability with which each query applies to the object. Queries can be different for each image. In effect, each image therefore has its own discriminative label space, which is defined by a set of text strings. This approach subsumes classical closed-vocabulary object detection as the special case in which the complete set of object category names is used as query set for each image.

In contrast to several other methods [20,26], we do not combine all queries for an image into a single token sequence. Instead, each query consists of a separate token sequence which represents an individual object description, and is individually processed by the text encoder. In addition, our architecture includes no fusion between image and text encoders. Although early fusion seems intuitively beneficial, it dramatically reduces inference efficiency because encoding a query requires a forward pass through the entire image model and needs to be repeated for each image/query combination. In our setup, we can compute query embeddings independently of the image, allowing us to use thousands of queries per image, many more than is possible with early fusion [26].

One-or Few-Shot Transfer. Our setup does not require query embeddings to be of textual origin. Since there is no fusion between image and text encoders, we can supply image- instead of text-derived embeddings as queries to the classification head without modifying the model. By using embeddings of prototypical object images as queries, our model can thus perform image-conditioned one-shot object detection. Using image embeddings as queries allows detection of objects which would be hard to describe in text.

3.2   Training

Image-Level Contrastive Pre-training. We pre-train the image and text encoder contrastively using the same image-text dataset and loss as in [44] (Fig. 1, left). We train both encoders from scratch with random initialization with a contrastive loss on the image and text representations. For the image representation, we use multihead attention pooling (MAP) [25,43] to aggregate token representation. The text representation is obtained from the final end-of-sequence (EOS) token of the text encoder. Alternatively, we use publicly available pre-trained CLIP models [33] (details in Appendix A.3).

An advantage of our encoder-only architecture is that nearly all of the model's parameters (image and text encoder) can benefit from image-level pre-training. The detection-specific heads contain at most 1.1% (depending on the model size) of the parameters of the model.

Training the Detector. Fine-tuning of pre-trained models for *classification* is a well-studied problem. Classifiers, especially large Transformers, require carefully tuned regularization and data augmentation to perform well. Recipes for classifier training are now well established in the literature [3,38,39]. Here, we aim to provide a similar fine-tuning recipe for *open-vocabulary detection*.

The general detection training procedure of our model is almost identical to that for closed-vocabulary detectors, except that we provide the set of object category names as queries for each image. The classification head therefore outputs logits over the per-image label space defined by the queries, rather than a fixed global label space.

We use the bipartite matching loss introduced by DETR [6], but adapt it to long-tailed/open-vocabulary detection as follows. Due to the effort required for annotating detection datasets exhaustively, datasets with large numbers of classes are annotated in a federated manner [13,24]. Such datasets have non-disjoint label spaces, which means that each object can have multiple labels. We therefore use focal sigmoid cross-entropy [48] instead of softmax cross-entropy as the classification loss. Further, since not all object categories are annotated in every image, federated datasets provide both positive (present) and negative (known to be absent) annotations for each image. During training, for a given image, we use all its positive and negative annotations as queries. Additionally, we randomly sample categories in proportion to their frequency in the data and add them as "pseudo-negatives" to have at least 50 negatives per image [47].

Even the largest federated detection datasets contain only $\approx 10^6$ images, which is small in contrast to the billions of image-level weak labels which exist for pre-training [19,29,33,43]. It is known that large Transformers trained on datasets of this size (such as ImageNet-1k) require carefully-tuned regularization and data augmentation to perform well [3,38,39]. We found the same to be true for detection training and provide a detailed breakdown of the augmentations and regularizations required to achieve very high performance with large Transformers in Sect. 4.6.

4   Experiments

4.1   Model Details

For the image model, we use standard Vision Transformers [22]. We follow the nomenclature from [22] for model size, patch size, and Transformer vs. hybrid architectures. For example, B/32 refers to ViT-Base with patch size 32, while R50+H/32 refers to a hybrid ResNet50 + ViT-Huge with stride 32.

For the text model, we use a Transformer architecture similar to the image model. Unless otherwise noted, we use a text model with 12 layers, 512 hidden size (D), 2048 MLP size and 8 heads (this is smaller than B).

Image and text models are first pre-trained on the image level and then fine-tuned on object-level annotations. Pre-training is performed from scratch as in LiT [44] (uu in their notation) on their dataset of 3.6 billion image-text pairs.

After pre-training, token pooling is removed and detection heads are added (see Sect. 3.1 and Fig. 1). The model predicts one box for each output token. We add a bias to the predicted box coordinates such that each box is by default centered on the image patch that corresponds to the token from which this box is predicted when arranging the token sequence as a 2D grid. The model therefore predicts the difference from that default location, similar to how Region Proposal Networks [34] predict offsets with respect to pre-defined anchors. Although there is no strict correspondence between image patches and tokens representations later in the Transformer network, biasing box predictions in this way speeds up training and improves final performance (Sect. 4.6).

We use an image size of 224 × 224 in most models for pre-training (see Appendix A.3) and larger sizes for detection fine-tuning and evaluation (specified in Table 1). To change model input size after pre-training, we resize the image position embeddings with linear interpolation. Models are fine-tuned at a batch size of 256 for at most 140'000 steps (fewer for larger models). We implement our model using JAX [5] and the *Scenic* library [8].

4.2 Detection Data

Due to the open-vocabulary design of our model, we can easily combine datasets with different label spaces by replacing integer labels with class name strings. For object-level training, we use publicly available detection datasets with a total of around 2 million images (OpenImages V4 (OI) [24], Objects 365 (O365) [35], and/or Visual Genome (VG) [23], as indicated). Evaluation is performed on the COCO [27], LVIS [13], and O365. For dataset details, see Appendix A.2.

Since OI, VG, O365 and the image-level pre-training data contain images that are also in COCO / LVIS, we use a strict deduplication procedure to remove any COCO or LVIS test and validation images from all datasets we use for training (see Appendix A.2 for details). Unless otherwise noted, we mix OI and VG randomly at a ratio of 70% to 30% for detection training in our experiments. In Table 1, as indicated, we use either LVIS base training (for comparability to prior work), or O365 and VG at a ratio of 80% to 20%. We use a range of image and label augmentations, which we discuss in Sect. 4.6.

4.3 Open-Vocabulary Detection Performance

We use LVIS v1.0 val [13] as our main benchmark since this dataset has a long tail of rare categories and is therefore well-suited to measure open-vocabulary performance. For evaluation, we use all category names as query for each image, i.e. 1203 queries per image for LVIS. Class predictions are ensembled over seven prompt templates as described in Sect. 4.6. Some LVIS categories appear in the datasets we use for training. To measure performance on unseen categories, we therefore remove from our training data all box annotations with labels that match any of the LVIS "rare" categories. The AP_{rare}^{LVIS} metric therefore measures the "zero-shot" performance of our model in the sense that the model has not seen localized annotations for these categories (Fig. 2).

Table 1 shows LVIS results for our models and a range of prior work. We compare to open-vocabulary models that do not train on the full LVIS dataset. Results obtained by training on parts of LVIS (e.g. "base" categories [12]) are shown in gray. Our method is highly competitive across architecture sizes in both open-vocabulary (AP^{LVIS}) and zero-shot (AP_{rare}^{LVIS}) scenarios. Our best model achieves 31.2% AP_{rare}^{LVIS} and uses a publicly available CLIP backbone.

For comparison to prior work, we also provide results on MS-COCO 2017 and Objects 365. For these evaluations, we train models on OI+VG instead

Table 1. Open-vocabulary and zero-shot performance on LVIS v1.0 val. For our models, we remove annotations matching LVIS rare category names from all detection training datasets, such that AP_{rare}^{LVIS} measures zero-shot performance. Gray numbers indicate models trained on the LVIS frequent and common ("base") annotations. For reference, ViT-B/32 is comparable to ResNet50 in inference compute (139.6 vs 141.5 GFLOPs). For our models, we report the mean performance over three fine-tuning runs. Results for COCO and O365 are provided in Appendix A.8.

	Method	Backbone	Image-level	Object-level	Res.	AP^{LVIS}	AP_{rare}^{LVIS}
LVIS base training:							
1	ViLD-ens [12]	ResNet50	CLIP	LVIS base	1024	25.5	16.6
2	ViLD-ens [12]	EffNet-b7	ALIGN	LVIS base	1024	29.3	26.3
3	Reg. CLIP [45]	R50-C4	CC3M	LVIS base	?	28.2	17.1
4	Reg. CLIP [45]	R50x4-C4	CC3M	LVIS base	?	32.3	22.0
5	OWL-ViT (ours)	ViT-H/14	LiT	LVIS base	840	35.3	23.3
6	OWL-ViT (ours)	ViT-L/14	CLIP	LVIS base	840	34.7	25.6
Unrestricted open-vocabulary training:							
7	GLIP [26]	Swin-T	Cap4M	O365, GoldG,	?	17.2	10.1
8	GLIP [26]	Swin-L	CC12M, SBU	OI, O365, VG,	?	26.9	17.1
9	OWL-ViT (ours)	ViT-B/32	LiT	O365, VG	768	23.3	19.7
11	OWL-ViT (ours)	R26+B/32	LiT	O365, VG	768	25.7	21.6
10	OWL-ViT (ours)	ViT-B/16	LiT	O365, VG	768	26.7	23.6
12	OWL-ViT (ours)	ViT-L/16	LiT	O365, VG	768	30.9	28.8
13	OWL-ViT (ours)	ViT-H/14	LiT	O365, VG	840	33.6	30.6
14	OWL-ViT (ours)	ViT-B/32	CLIP	O365, VG	768	22.1	18.9
15	OWL-ViT (ours)	ViT-B/16	CLIP	O365, VG	768	27.2	20.6
16	OWL-ViT (ours)	ViT-L/14	CLIP	O365, VG	840	34.6	31.2

of O365+VG, to measure generalization. However, most COCO and O365 categories are present in the training data and we do not remove them, since they constitute a large fraction of the available annotations. Our COCO and O365 results are therefore not "zero-shot", but test the open-vocabulary transfer ability of our model. Our best model (CLIP L/14; see Table 1) achieves 43.5% AP^{COCO}; a version of the model trained without O365 achieves 15.8% AP^{O365} (further results in Appendix A.8).

4.4   Few-Shot Image-Conditioned Detection Performance

As described in Sect. 3.1, our model can perform one- or few-shot object detection simply be replacing text-derived query embeddings with image-derived query embeddings. In few-shot detection, we are given a query image with a box around an example object. The goal is to detect objects of the same category as the example in new target images. To get the query embedding, we first run inference on the query image and select a predicted detection which has high box overlap

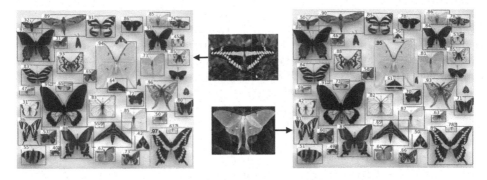

Fig. 2. Example of one-shot image-conditioned detection. Images in the middle are used as queries; the respective detections on the target image are shown on the left and right. In both cases, the highest score is given to instances of the species matching the query. In contrast, text-based querying (not shown) detects the correct species only for the top example ("swallowtail butterfly") but not for the bottom ("luna moth").

with the query box (after some filtering; see Appendix A.7 for details). We then use the image embedding of that prediction as query on the test images.

For evaluation on this task, we follow the procedure described in [16]: During detection training, we hold out some COCO categories to evaluate on, and in addition all synonymous and semantically descendant categories that appear in our detection training data. We do not modify the image-text pre-training stage.

Despite not being designed specifically for this task, our model strongly outperforms the best task-specific prior work by a margin of 72% across the four COCO splits as shown in Table 2. Unlike prior work, our model does not entangle query image and target image features during inference, which enables us to run our models on thousands of different image embeddings simultaneously and efficiently, enhancing its practicality.

To move beyond a single query example (one-shot) to few-shot predictions, we can simply average image embeddings for multiple query examples for each category. This leads to further significant improvements (Table 2, bottom row).

4.5   Scaling of Image-Level Pre-training

After establishing that our method achieves strong open-vocabulary, zero-shot, and image-conditioned detection performance, we next analyze its scaling properties and design choices. We focus on image-level pre-training in this section. In Sect. 4.6, we will describe the fine-tuning methods that are necessary for successful transfer of the pre-trained model to detection.

To understand how image-level pre-training relates to final detection performance, we systematically explored the dimensions of pre-training duration, model size, and model architecture. For every configuration, we pre-trained and then fine-tuned several models across a range of learning rates and weight

Table 2. One- and few-shot image-conditioned detection performance on COCO AP50. Our method (R50+H/32 architecture) strongly outperforms prior work and also shows marked improvements as the number of conditioning queries is increased to $k = 10$. COCO category splits as in [16]. Because the evaluation is stochastic, for our results, we report the average across 3 runs.

	Method	Split 1	Split 2	Split 3	Split 4	Mean
Seen	SiamMask [30]	38.9	37.1	37.8	36.6	37.6
	CoAE [16]	42.2	40.2	39.9	41.3	40.9
	AIT [7]	**50.1**	47.2	45.8	46.9	47.5
	OWL-ViT (ours)	49.9	**49.1**	**49.2**	48.2	**49.1**
	OWL-ViT ($k = 10$; ours)	54.1	55.3	56.2	54.9	55.1
Unseen	SiamMask [30]	15.3	17.6	17.4	17.0	16.8
	CoAE [16]	23.4	23.6	20.5	20.4	22.0
	AIT [7]	26.0	26.4	22.3	22.6	24.3
	OWL-ViT (ours)	**43.6**	**41.3**	**40.2**	**41.9**	**41.8**
	OWL-ViT ($k = 10$; ours)	49.3	51.1	42.4	44.5	46.8

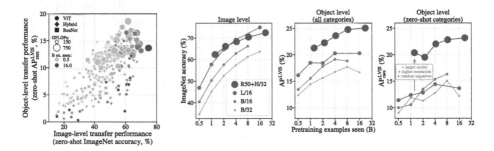

Fig. 3. Image-level pre-training transfers to detection. *Left:* Overview of the relationship between image-level performance (zero-shot ImageNet accuracy after pretraining) and object-level performance (AP_{rare}^{LVIS} after detection fine-tuning) of contrastively trained image-text models. Each dot represents one pre-training configuration and its best detection performance across a range of learning rates and weight decays. Configurations vary in encoder architecture (ViT/Hybrid/ResNet), model size (in order of detection inference compute: R50, B/32, R26+B/32, R101, L/32, B/16, H/32, R50+H/32, L/16), and pre-training duration (billions of examples seen including repetitions; 3.6B unique examples). High image-level performance is necessary, but not sufficient, for high object-level performance (Pearson's $r = 0.73$; in contrast, image-level transfer performance correlates better with pre-training-task performance: $r = 0.98$). *Right:* Across model sizes, longer image-level pre-training translates to higher object-level performance. Further gains on detection are possible by scaling up fine-tuning.

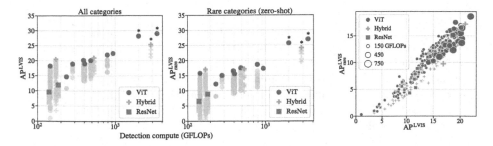

Fig. 4. Effect of model architecture on detection performance. *Left:* Hybrid architectures are more efficient than pure transformers for small models. As the model size increases (in terms of detection inference FLOPs), pure ViTs scale better than hybrids both in overall and zero-shot performance. Pure ResNets perform poorly in our setup. Colored markers indicate the best model of a given size across all explored hyperparameters; light gray markers indicate the suboptimal hyperparameters. Asterisks ($*$) indicate models trained with random negative labels. *Right:* Architecture also influences which aspects of the task a model learns: Pure ViTs perform systematically better at zero-shot detection (AP_{rare}^{LVIS}) than hybrid architectures at a given overall object-level performance (AP^{LVIS}). We speculate that ViTs are biased towards learning semantic generalization, whereas ResNets/Hybrids are biased towards learning localization of known classes. This difference diminishes as model size and performance increases.

decays, since the optimal settings of these parameters vary by configuration (see Appendix A.3 for a list of covered settings).

We first consider how well image-level pre-training transfers to detection in general. Figure 3 shows the relationship between image-level performance (zero-shot ImageNet accuracy) and object-level performance (zero-shot AP_{rare}^{LVIS}) for all architecture, size, and pre-training-duration configurations covered by our study (the best result across learning rates and weight decays is shown). We find that, while the best object-level models typically also have good image-level performance, the reverse is not true: many models that do well to the image-level task transfer poorly to detection. In other words, high image-level performance is necessary, but not sufficient, for strong transfer to detection.

Which factors contribute to strong transfer? Prior work on classification found that pre-training and model size must be scaled *together* to achieve optimal transfer – over-training small models on large data can even lead to reduced performance [21]. We find this effect to be even stronger for transfer to detection. As the amount of pre-training is increased, detection performance increases at first but then peaks, while image-level performance continues to increase (Fig. 3, right). However, the positive trend of detection performance with pre-training can be extended by increasing model size and improving detection fine-tuning (Fig. 3, right, R50+H/32).

Given that increasing model size improves performance, an important question is which architectures have the most favorable scaling properties. For classification, Transformer-based architectures have been found to be more efficient in terms of pre-training compute than ResNets, and hybrid ResNet-Transformer architectures to be the most efficient, at least at smaller computational budgets [22]. In addition, ResNets were found to be better when little pre-training data is available, but were overtaken by Transformers as available data increases [22,38]. We performed a similar analysis for detection. Using detection inference compute as the measure of model size, and choosing the best hyperparameters and pre-training duration for each size, we found that hybrid models tend to be more efficient than pure ViTs at small model sizes, while ResNets perform poorly in our setup (Fig. 4). However, for large models, pure ViTs overtake hybrids. To start explaining this difference, we compared overall and zero-shot detection performance and found a clear dissociation between hybrids and pure Transformers (at least at small model sizes; Fig. 4, right). This perhaps indicates that Transformers are more biased than hybrid architectures towards learning semantic generalization (necessary for high zero-shot performance), which might be beneficial when large-scale pre-training is possible. Overall, our findings go beyond those for classification and suggest that further scaling efforts should focus on pure Transformer architectures.

4.6   How to Unlock Pre-training Potential for Detection

In Sect. 4.5, we found that strong image-level performance is necessary, but not sufficient, for strong detection performance. We will now describe our recipe for obtaining strong open-vocabulary detection performance after image-level pre-training. Ultimately, all components of our recipe aim at reducing overfitting on the relatively small number of available detection annotations, and the small semantic label space covered by the annotations. Our approach relies on (i) measures to stabilize optimization, (ii) careful use of the available detection training data, and (iii) a range of data augmentations. We discuss these ablations in detail below, where numbers in italic (e.g. *(15)*) refer to individual ablation experiments in Table 3. Importantly, the optimal recipe for zero-shot performance (AP_{rare}^{LVIS}) does not necessarily maximize in-distribution performance (AP^{OI}). We discuss this finding and further ablations in Appendix A.9.

Stabilizing Optimization. The goal of fine-tuning is to learn from the available detection data without destroying the representations learned during pre-training. To this end, we take the following measures. First, we **reduce the learning rate of the text encoder** to 2×10^{-6} (i.e. 100× smaller than the image encoder learning rate) during fine-tuning *(3)*. This reduces overfitting, possibly by preventing the text encoder from "forgetting" the semantics learned during pre-training while fine-tuning on the small space of detection labels. Interestingly, freezing the text encoder completely yields poor results. Second, we **bias predicted box coordinates** *(11)* to be centred at the position of the corresponding token on the 2D grid, as described in Sect. 3.1. This speeds up learning and improves final performance, presumably by breaking symmetry during the bipartite matching used in the loss. Third, for larger models, we use **stochastic**

Table 3. Ablation study of the main methodological improvements necessary for successful transfer of image-text models to detection. For simplicity, difference in AP to the *baseline* is shown. Except for the experiment retraining LVIS rare labels (last row), all differences are expected to be negative. To reduce variance, all results are averaged across two replicates. All ablations were carried out for the ViT-R26+B/32 model, and unless otherwise specified used a 70K step training schedule.

Ablation	AP^{LVIS}	AP^{LVIS}_{rare}	AP^{COCO}	AP^{OI}
Baseline	21.0	18.9	30.9	54.1
(1) Only use VG for training	−14.5	−14.0	−23.6	−38.3
(2) Only use OI for training	−6.9	−5.7	−4.2	0.3
(3) Same LR for image and text encoders	−3.0	−8.5	−0.5	0.4
(4) No prompt ensembling at inference	−2.8	−5.5	−5.9	−0.1
(5) No prompts (train or inference)	−1.2	−1.3	−0.6	−6.3
(6) No random negatives	−1.0	−2.8	−0.4	1.0
(7) No mosaics	−2.3	−1.5	−1.7	−0.7
(8) No mosaics, train 2× longer	−2.9	−2.8	−1.8	−0.7
(9) No mosaics, train 3× longer	−3.4	−3.6	−1.8	−0.8
(10) Do not merge overlapping instances	−0.8	−1.3	−0.6	−0.7
(11) No location bias in box predictor	−1.2	−1.1	−1.3	−1.0
(12) Do not filter out *any* cropped boxes	−0.1	0.0	0.1	−0.1
(13) Filter out *all* cropped boxes	−0.1	−0.6	0.1	0.2
(14) Do not remove OI crowd instances	0.0	0.7	−0.4	3.0
(15) Do not remove LVIS rare labels	0.1	0.2	−0.1	1.1

depth regularisation [1,17] with probability of 0.1 on both the image and text encoders, and **shorter training schedules** (Sect. A.3).

Careful Use of Available Detection Data. As our ablations show (Table 3), the amount of detection training data is a limiting factor for the performance of our models. Therefore, we **combine multiple datasets** – OI+VG for most models in our study *(1–2)*, and O365+VG for the largest models as indicated in Table 1. Further, we take care to keep the available annotations free of noise: We **remove "group" annotations and "not exhaustively annotated" categories** *(14)* from datasets indicating such annotations (e.g. OI). These annotations provide conflicting supervision to the model because it cannot learn (except through memorization) which annotations are exhaustive and which are not. Removing them improves performance of larger models. In addition, we **remove partial boxes left by random crop augmentation**, since these can also provide conflicting supervision if most of an object was actually cropped out. Retaining instances with at least 60% of their original area leads to better results than retaining all *(12)* or only uncropped *(13)* instances.

Augmentations. Finally, we enrich the available detection labels through augmentation of both images and queries. On the images, we use **random cropping** (removing partially cropped boxes as described above). Additionally, we use **image scale augmentation** similar to "large scale jitter" [11]. However, instead of simply resizing and padding images, we tile several downscaled images into one large "mosaic" image. We randomly sample single images, 2×2 grids, and 3×3 grids with probabilities 0.5, 0.33, and 0.17, respectively *(7–9)*. To augment the queries (category names), we use **random prompts** during training, and **ensemble predictions over several prompts** for evaluation *(4–5)*. We use the 80 CLIP prompts for training and ensemble over the 7 "best" CLIP prompts (as defined in [33]) during evaluation. Finally, we randomly sample **pseudo-negative labels** for each image until there are at least 50 negative labels [47]. Further implementation details are provided in Appendix A.5 and A.6.

5   Conclusion

We presented a simple recipe for transferring contrastively trained image-text models to detection. Our method achieves zero-shot detection results competitive with much more complex approaches on the challenging LVIS benchmark and outperforms existing methods on image-conditioned detection by a large margin. Our results suggest that pre-training on billions of image-text examples confers strong generalization ability that can be transferred to detection even if only relatively limited object-level data are available (millions of examples). In our analyses we disentangle the determinants of successful transfer of image-level representations to detection, and show that pre-training simple, scalable architectures on more data leads to strong zero-shot detection performance, mirroring previous observations for image classification tasks. We hope that our model will serve as a strong starting point for further research on open-world detection .

Acknowledgements.. We would like to thank Sunayana Rane and Rianne van den Berg for help with the DETR implementation, Lucas Beyer for the data deduplication code, and Yi Tay for useful advice.

A   Appendix

The appendix provides additional examples, results and methodological details. For remaining questions, please refer to the code at github.com/google-research/scenic/tree/main/scenic/projects/owl_vit.

A.1   Qualitative Examples

(See Figs. 5 and 6).

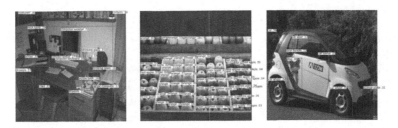

Fig. 5. Text conditioning examples. Prompts: "an image of a {}", where {} is replaced with one of bookshelf, desk lamp, computer keyboard, binder, pc computer, computer mouse, computer monitor, chair, drawers, drinking glass, ipod, pink book, yellow book, curtains, red apple, banana, green apple, orange, grapefruit, potato, for sale sign, car wheel, car door, car mirror, gas tank, frog, head lights, license plate, door handle, tail lights.

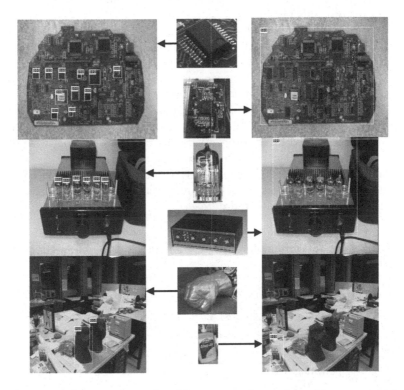

Fig. 6. Image conditioning examples. The center column shows the query patches and the outer columns show the detections along with the similarity score.

A.2 Detection Datasets

Five datasets with object detection annotations were used for fine-tuning and evaluation in this work. Table 4 shows relevant statistics for each of these datasets:

MS-COCO (COCO) [27]: The Microsoft Common Objects in Context dataset is a medium-scale object detection dataset. It has about 900k bounding box annotations for 80 object categories, with about 7.3 annotations per image. It is one of the most used object detection datasets, and its images are often used within other datasets (including VG and LVIS). This work uses the 2017 train, validation and test splits.

Visual Genome (VG) [23] contains dense annotations for objects, regions, object attributes, and their relationships within each image. VG is based on COCO images, which are re-annotated with free-text annotations for an average of 35 objects per image. All entities are canonicalized to WordNet synsets. We only use object annotations from this dataset, and do not train models using the attribute, relationship or region annotations.

Objects 365 (O365) [35] is a large-scale object detection dataset with 365 object categories. The version we use has over 10M bounding boxes with about 15.8 object annotations per image.

LVIS [13]: The Large Vocabulary Instance Segmentation dataset has over a thousand object categories, following a long-tail distribution with some categories having only a few examples. Similarly to VG, LVIS uses the same images as in COCO, re-annotated with a larger number of object categories. In contrast to COCO and O365, LVIS is a federated dataset, which means that only a subset of categories is annotated in each image. Annotations therefore include positive and negative object labels for objects that are present and categories that are not present, respectively. In addition, LVIS categories are not pairwise disjoint, such that the same object can belong to several categories.

OpenImages V4 (OI) [24] is currently the largest public object detection dataset with about 14.6 bounding box annotations (about 8 annotations per image). Like LVIS, it is a federated dataset.

Table 4. Statistics of object detection datasets used in this work.

Name	Train	Val	Test	Categories
MS-COCO 2017 [27]	118k	5k	40.1k	80
Visual Genome [23]	84.5k	21.6k	–	–
Objects 365 [35]	608.5k	30k	–	365
LVIS [13]	100k	19.8k	19.8k	1203
OpenImages V4 [24]	1.7M	41.6k	125k	601

De-duplication. Our detection models are typically fine-tuned on a combination of OpenImages V4 (OI) and Visual Genome (VG) datasets and evaluated on MS-COCO 2017 (COCO) and LVIS. In several experiments our models are additionally trained on Objects 365 (O365). We never train on COCO and LVIS datasets, but the public versions of our training datasets contain some of the same images as the COCO and LVIS validation sets. To ensure that our models see no validation images during training, we filter out images from OI, VG and O365 train splits that also appear in LVIS and COCO validation and tests splits following a procedure identical to [21]. De-duplication statistics are given in Table 5.

Table 5. Train dataset de-duplication statistics. 'Examples' refers to images and 'instances' refers to bounding boxes.

Name	Original		Duplicates		Remaining	
	Examples	Instances	Examples	Instances	Examples	Instances
OpenImages V4	1.7M	14.6M	948	6.4k	1.7M	14.6M
Visual Genome	86.5k	2M	6.7k	156k	79.8K	1.9M
Objects 365	608.6k	9.2M	147	2.4k	608.5k	9.2M

A.3   Hyper-parameters

Table 6 provides an exhaustive overview of the hyper-parameter settings used for our main experiments. Beyond this, we

- used cosine learning rate decay;
- used focal loss with $\alpha = 0.3$ and $\gamma = 2.0$;
- set equal weights for the bounding box, gIoU and classification losses [6];
- used the Adam optimizer with $\beta_1 = 0.9$, $\beta_2 = 0.999$;
- used per-example global norm gradient clipping (see Sect. A.9);
- limited the text encoder input length to 16 tokens for both LIT and CLIP-based models.

CLIP-Based Models. The visual encoder of the publicly available CLIP models provides, in addition to the image embedding features, a class token. In order to evaluate whether the information in the class token is useful for detection fine-tuning, we explored to either drop this token, or to merge it into other feature map tokens by multiplying it with them. We found that multiplying the class token with the feature map tokens, followed by layer norm, worked best for the majority of architectures, so we use this approach throughout. Other hyper-parameters used in the fine-tuning of CLIP models are shown in Table 6.

Table 6. List of hyperparameters used for all models shown in the paper. Asterisks (∗) indicate parameters varied in sweeps. MAP and GAP indicate the use of multihead attention pooling and global average pooling for image-level representation aggregation. Where two numbers are given for the droplayer rate, the first is for the image encoder and the second for the text encoder.

Model	Training duration	Batch size	Learning rate	Weight decay	Image size	Pool type	Training steps	Batch size	Learning rate	Weight decay	Droplayer rate	Image size	Training datasets	Dataset proportions	Mosaic proportions	Random negatives
		Image-level pre-training									Detection fine-tuning					
CLIP-based OWL-ViT models from Table 1:																
B/32							140k	256	5×10^{-5}	0	.2/.1	768	O365, VG	.8/.2	.4/.3/.3	yes
B/16							140k	256	5×10^{-5}	0	.2/.1	768	O365, VG	.8/.2	.4/.3/.3	yes
L/14							70k	256	2×10^{-5}	0	.2/.1	840	O365, VG	.8/.2	.4/.3/.3	yes
LiT-based OWL-ViT models from Table 1:																
B/32	16B	16k	3×10^{-4}	1×10^{-5}	224	MAP	140k	256	2×10^{-4}	0	0.0	768	O365, VG	.8/.2	.4/.3/.3	yes
B/16	8B	16k	3×10^{-4}	1×10^{-5}	224	MAP	140k	256	2×10^{-4}	0	0.0	768	O365, VG	.8/.2	.4/.3/.3	yes
R26+B/32	16B	16k	3×10^{-4}	1×10^{-5}	288	MAP	140k	256	2×10^{-4}	0	0.0	768	O365, VG	.8/.2	.4/.3/.3	yes
L/16	16B	16k	3×10^{-4}	1×10^{-5}	224	MAP	70k	256	5×10^{-5}	0	0.0	768	O365, VG	.8/.2	.4/.3/.3	yes
H/14	12B	16k	3×10^{-4}	1×10^{-5}	224	MAP	70k	256	5×10^{-5}	0	.1/.0	840	O365, VG	.8/.2	.4/.3/.3	yes
Model used for one-shot detection (Table 2):																
R50+H/32	24B	12k	7×10^{-4}	1×10^{-5}	224	GAP	28k	256	2×10^{-4}	0	0.1	960	OI, O365, VG	.4/.4/.2	.5/.33/.17	yes
Baseline models for the ablation study (Tables 3 and A5):																
B/32	2B	16k	3×10^{-4}	1×10^{-5}	224	MAP	70k	256	2×10^{-4}	0	0.0	768	OI, VG	.7/.3	.5/.33/.17	yes
R26+B/32	8B	16k	3×10^{-4}	1×10^{-5}	288	MAP	70k	256	2×10^{-4}	0	0.0	768	OI, VG	.7/.3	.5/.33/.17	yes
Models used in the scaling study (Figures 3 and 4):																
∗	∗	16k	∗	∗	∗	MAP	140k	256	∗	0	0.0	768	OI, VG	.7/.3	.5/.33/.17	no
R50+H/32	∗	12k	7×10^{-4}	1×10^{-5}	224	GAP	28k	256	2×10^{-4}	0	0.0	960	OI, VG	.7/.3	.5/.33/.17	yes

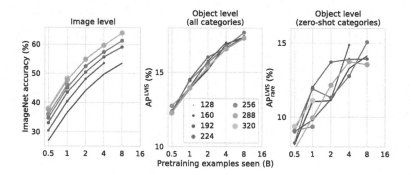

Fig. 7. Effect of image size used during image-level pre-training on zero-shot classification and detection performance shown for the ViT-B/32 architecture.

A.4   Pre-Training Image Resolution

We investigated the effect of the image size used during image-text pre-training, on zero-shot classification and detection performance (Fig. 7). To reduce clutter the results are shown for the ViT-B/32 architecture only, but the observed trends extend to other architectures, including Hybrid Transformers. The use of larger images during pre-training consistently benefits zero-shot classifica-

Fig. 8. Example training images. Ground-truth boxes are indicated in red. From left to right, a single image, a 2 × 2 mosaic, and a 3 × 3 mosaic are shown. Non-square images are padded at the bottom and right (gray color). (Color figure online)

tion, but makes no significant difference for the detection performance. We thus default to the commonly used 224 × 224 resolution for pre-training. We used 288 × 288 for some of our experiments with Hybrid Transformer models.

A.5   Random Negatives

Our models are trained on federated datasets. In such datasets, not all categories are exhaustively annotated in every image. Instead, each image comes with a number of labeled bounding boxes (making up the set of *positive* categories), and a list of categories that are known to be absent from the image (i.e., *negative* categories). For all other categories, their presence in the image unknown. Since the number of negative labels can be small, prior work has found it beneficial to randomly sample "pseudo-negative" labels for each image and add them to the annotations [47]. We follow the same approach and add randomly sampled pseudo-negatives to the real negatives of each image until there are at least 50 negative categories. In contrast to [47], we sample categories in proportion to their frequency in the full dataset (i.e. a weighted combination of OI, VG, and potentially O365). We exclude categories from the sample that are among the positives for the given image.

A.6   Image Scale Augmentation

To improve invariance of detection models to object size, prior work found it beneficial to use strong random jittering of the image scale during training [11]. We use a similar approach, but follow a two-stage strategy that minimizes image padding.

First, we randomly crop each training image. The sampling procedure is constrained to produce crops with an aspect ratio between 0.75 and 1.33, and an area between 33% and 100% of the original image. Bounding box annotations are retained if at least 60% of the box area is within the post-crop image area. After cropping, images are padded to a square aspect ratio by appending gray pixels at the bottom or right edge.

Second, we assemble multiple images into grids ("mosaics") of varying sizes, to further increase the range of image scales seen by the model. We randomly sample single images, 2×2 mosaics, and a 3×3 mosaics, with probabilities 0.5, 0.33, and 0.17, respectively, unless otherwise noted (Fig. 8). This procedure allows us to use widely varying images scales while avoiding excessive padding and/or the need for variable model input size during training.

A.7   One-shot (Image-Conditioned) Detection Details

Extracting Image Embeddings to Use as Queries. We are given a query image patch Q for which we would like to detect similar patches in a new target image, I. We first run inference on the image from which patch Q was selected, and extract an *image embedding* from our model's class head in the region of Q. In general, our model predicts many overlapping bounding boxes, some of which will have high overlap with Q. Each predicted bounding box b_i has a corresponding class head feature z_i. Due to our DETR-style bipartite matching loss, our model will generally predict a single *foreground* embedding for the object in Q and many *background* embeddings adjacent to it which should be ignored. Since all the background embeddings are similar to each other and different from the single foreground embedding, to find the foreground embedding, we search for the most *dissimilar* class embedding within the group of class embeddings whose corresponding box has IoU > 0.65 with Q. We score a class embedding z_i's similarity to other class embeddings as $f(z_i) = \sum_{j=0}^{N-1} z_i \cdot z_j^T$. Therefore, we use the most dissimilar class embedding $\operatorname{argmin}_{z_i} f(z_i)$ as our query feature when running inference on I. In about 10% of the cases, there are no predicted boxes with IoU > 0.65 with Q. In these cases we fall back to using the embedding for the text query `"an image of an object"`.

Image-Conditioned Evaluation Protocol. We follow the evaluation protocol of [16]. During evaluation, we present the model with a target image containing at least one instance of a held-out MS-COCO category and a query image patch containing the same held-out category. Both the target image and the query patch are drawn from the validation set. We report the AP50 of the detections in the target image. Note that unlike typical object detection, it is assumed that there is at least one instance of the query image category within the target image. Like prior work, we use Mask-RCNN [14] to filter out query patches which are too small or do not show the query object clearly. During detection training, we took care to hold out all categories related to any category in the held-out split. We removed annotations for any label which matched a held-out label or was a descendant of a held-out label (for example, the label "girl" is a descendant label of "person"). Beyond this we also manually removed any label which was similar to a held-out category. We will publish all held-out labels with the release of our code.

A.8   Detection Results on COCO and O365

We present additional evaluation results on the COCO and O365 datasets in Table 7. These results show the open-vocabulary generalization ability of our approach. Although we do not train these models directly on COCO or O365 (unless otherwise noted), our training datasets contain object categories overlapping with COCO and O365, so these results are not "zero-shot" according to our definition. The breadth of evaluation setups in the literature makes direct comparison to existing methods difficult. We strove to note the differences relevant for a fair comparison in Table 7.

Table 7. Open-vocabulary detection performance on COCO and O365 datasets. The results show the open-vocabulary generalization ability of our models to datasets that were not used for training. Results for models trained on the target dataset are shown in gray. Most of our models shown here were not trained directly on COCO or O365 (they are different from the models in Table 1). However, we did not remove COCO or O365 object categories from the training data, so these numbers are not "zero-shot". For our models, we report the mean performance over three fine-tuning runs.

Method	Backbone	Image-level	Object-level	Res.	AP^{COCO}	$AP50^{COCO}$	AP^{O365}	$AP50^{O365}$
ViLD [12]	ResNet50	CLIP	LVIS base	1024	36.6	55.6	11.8	18.2
Reg. CLIP [45]	R50-C4	CC3M	COCO base	?	–	50.4	–	–
Reg. CLIP [45]	R50x4-C4	CC3M	COCO base	?	–	55.7	–	–
GLIP [26]	Swin-T	Cap4M	O365, GoldG,	?	46.7	–	–	–
GLIP [26]	Swin-L	CC12M, SBU	OI, O365, VG,	?	49.8	–	–	–
Detic [46]	R50-C4	CLIP, COCO-Cap	COCO base	1333	–	45.0	–	–
Detic [46]	Swin-B	CLIP, I21K	LVIS base	869	–	–	21.5	–
OWL-ViT (ours)	ViT-B/32	CLIP	OI, VG	768	28.1	44.7	–	–
OWL-ViT (ours)	ViT-B/16	CLIP	OI, VG	768	31.7	49.2	–	–
OWL-ViT (ours)	ViT-L/14	CLIP	O365, VG	840	43.5	64.7	–	–
OWL-ViT (ours)	ViT-B/32	LiT	OI, VG	768	28.0	44.4	9.4	15.2
OWL-ViT (ours)	ViT-B/16	LiT	OI, VG	768	30.3	47.4	10.7	17.0
OWL-ViT (ours)	R26+B/32	LiT	OI, VG	768	30.7	47.2	11.1	17.4
OWL-ViT (ours)	ViT-L/16	LiT	OI, VG	672	34.7	53.9	13.7	21.6
OWL-ViT (ours)	ViT-H/14	LiT	OI, VG	840	36.0	55.3	15.5	24.0
OWL-ViT (ours)	ViT-H/14	LiT	O365, VG	840	42.2	64.5	–	–

A.9   Extended Ablation Study

Table 8 extends the ablation results provided in Table tab:ablations of the main text. It uses the same training and evaluation protocol as outlined in Table 3, but goes further in the range of settings and architectures (ViT-B/32 and ViT-R26+B/32) considered in the study. We discuss the additional ablations below.

Dataset Ratios. In the majority of our experiments we use OI and VG datasets for training. In the ablation study presented in the main text (Table 3), we

Table 8. Additional ablations. VG(obj) and VG(reg) respectively refer to Visual Genome object and region annotations.

Ablation	ViT-B/32				ViT-R26+B/32			
	AP^{LVIS}	AP^{LVIS}_{rare}	AP^{COCO}	AP^{OI}	AP^{LVIS}	AP^{LVIS}_{rare}	AP^{COCO}	AP^{OI}
Baseline	15.7	14.1	24.1	48.5	21.0	18.9	30.9	54.1
Dataset ratio. Baseline uses OI:VG(obj) = 7:3								
OI:VG(obj) = 2:8	−1.9	−2.7	−2.4	−4.8	−4.2	−4.1	−4.7	−4.8
OI:VG(obj) = 3:7	−1.0	−1.9	−1.2	−3.1	−3.0	−3.0	−3.3	−2.9
OI:VG(obj) = 4:6	−0.6	−1.8	−0.4	−1.7	−2.2	−3.6	−2.2	−1.5
OI:VG(obj) = 5:5	0.0	−0.5	0.1	−0.6	−1.0	−1.1	−1.0	−1.1
OI:VG(obj) = 6:4	0.1	−0.6	0.1	−0.3	−0.3	−1.4	−0.4	−0.2
OI:VG(obj) = 8:2	−0.7	−0.9	−0.6	−0.1	−0.4	−0.3	0.2	0.4
OI:VG(obj) = 9:1	−1.8	−1.1	−1.6	0.1	−1.8	−1.8	−1.1	0.3
OI:VG(obj, reg) = 7:3	−0.6	0.0	−0.9	−3.3	−1.2	−0.5	−0.8	−3.6
OI:VG(reg) = 7:3	−2.1	−1.4	−2.3	−2.5	−2.9	−2.3	−2.2	−2.2
Only OI	−4.9	−3.2	−3.5	−0.5	−6.9	−5.7	−4.2	0.3
Only VG(obj)	−8.0	−8.4	−14.2	−28.5	−14.5	−14.0	−23.6	−38.3
Gradient clipping. Baseline uses per-example clipping and per-example normalization								
Global clip, global norm	−1.0	−2.0	−1.4	−4.9	−2.3	−2.9	−2.8	−5.4
Global clip, per-ex. norm	−4.0	−2.6	−5.3	−4.7	−5.0	−5.0	−5.7	−5.7
Instance merging. Baseline merges instance that overlap with IoU $\geq$ 0.9								
No merging	−0.8	−1.2	−0.3	−1.2	−0.8	−1.3	−0.6	−0.7
IoU $\geq$ 0.7	0.2	0.3	−0.2	0.1	0.2	0.2	0.0	0.6
IoU $\geq$ 0.8	0.0	0.4	0.0	0.4	0.0	−1.3	0.1	0.4
IoU $\geq$ 0.95	−0.1	−0.1	0.0	−0.7	−0.5	−1.3	−0.2	−0.5
Text encoder learning rate. Baseline uses image LR 2×10^{-4} and text LR 2×10^{-6}								
LR 2×10^{-3}	−5.1	−10.3	−0.8	−0.6	−7.1	−14.1	−1.4	−0.5
LR 2×10^{-4}	−2.3	−6.7	−0.7	0.2	−3.0	−8.5	−0.5	0.4
LR 2×10^{-5}	−1.1	−3.8	−0.5	0.6	−1.2	−3.2	−0.4	0.9
Do not fine-tune text enc	−1.8	−1.2	−1.9	−0.7	−1.5	−2.3	−0.6	1.2
Cropped box filtering. Baseline retains boxes with $\geq$ 60% of their original area								
No box area filtering	−0.1	−0.3	−0.2	−0.2	−0.1	0.0	0.1	−0.1
$\geq$ 20% area	−0.3	−1.7	0.0	−0.3	−0.2	−0.8	−0.2	−0.1
$\geq$ 40% area	0.1	0.0	0.0	0.2	0.1	0.9	0.1	−0.2
Only full boxes	−0.2	−0.9	−0.3	−0.2	−0.1	−0.6	0.1	0.2
Mosaics. Baseline uses 1-to-3-size mosaics at ratio 0.5:0.33:0.17								
1–2 @ 2:1	−0.4	−1.1	−0.1	0.4	−0.5	0.3	−0.5	0.0
1–4 @ 4:3:2:1	0.1	0.3	0.0	−0.3	0.0	−0.8	0.1	−0.3
No mosaics	−1.4	−1.6	−1.5	−0.4	−2.3	−1.5	−1.7	−0.7
No mosaics, 2x train sched.	−1.0	−1.8	−0.3	1.2	−2.9	−2.8	−1.8	−0.7
No mosaics, 3x train sched.	−1.2	−3.4	0.3	1.1	−3.4	−3.6	−1.8	−0.8
Prompting. Baseline uses train prompting for OI and test ensemble (ens.) prompting								
Train: none; test: none	0.0	−0.1	0.8	−10.2	−1.2	−1.3	−0.6	−6.3
Train: none; test: ens	−2.6	−2.2	−7.3	−11.1	−4.5	−5.0	−10.0	−6.6
Train: OI+VG; test: ens	0.8	1.3	0.9	−0.1	−0.7	−0.7	−0.4	−0.2
Train: VG; test: ens	−0.8	−1.1	−2.9	−7.8	−3.1	−4.0	−7.8	−5.6
Other. Baseline uses location bias, samples 50 random negatives and removes LVIS rare labels								
No location bias	−2.8	−2.9	−3.7	−2.6	−1.2	−1.1	−1.3	−1.0
No random negatives	−1.2	−3.7	−0.8	−0.4	−1.0	−2.8	−0.4	1.0
Keep LVIS rare	0.1	0.9	0.0	0.7	0.1	0.2	−0.1	1.1

showed that having more training data (i.e. training on both VG and OI) improves zero-shot performance. Here, we further explored the optimal ratio in which these datasets should be mixed and found that a 7:3 = OI:VG ratio worked best. Note that this overweighs VG significantly compared to the relative size of these datasets. Overweighing VG might be beneficial because VG has a larger label space than OI, such that each VG example provides more valuable semantic supervision than each OI example.

We also tested the relative value of VG "object" and "region" annotations. In VG, "region" annotations provide free-text descriptions of whole image regions, as opposed to the standard single-object annotations. Interestingly, we found that training on the region annotations hurts the generalization ability of our models, so we do not use them for training.

Loss Normalization and Gradient Clipping. In its official implementation, DETR [6] uses *local* (i.e. per-device) loss normalization and is thus sensitive to the (local) batch size. We found this to be an important detail in practice, which can significantly affect performance. We explored whether normalizing the box, gIoU and classification losses by the number of instances in the image or the number of instances in the entire batch performed better. Our experiments show that per-example normalization performs best, but only *when combined with per-example gradient clipping*, i.e. when clipping the gradient norm to 1.0 for each example individually, before accumulating gradients across the batch. We found that per-example clipping improves training stability, leads to overall lower losses and allows for training models with larger batch sizes.

Instance Merging. Federated datasets such as OI have non-disjoint label spaces, which means that several labels can apply to the same object, either due to (near-)synonymous labels (e.g. "Jug" and "Mug"), or due to non-disjoint concepts (e.g. "Toy" and "Elephant" labels both apply to a toy elephant). Due to the annotation procedure, in which a single label is considered at a time, one object can therefore be annotated with several similar (but not identical) bounding boxes. We found it helpful to merge such instances into a single multi-label instance. Multi-label annotations are consistent with the non-disjoint nature of federated annotations and we speculate that this provides more efficient supervision to the models, since it trains each token to predict a single box for all appropriate labels. Without this instance merging, the model would be required to predict individual boxes for each label applying to an object, which clearly cannot generalize to the countless possible object labels.

To merge overlapping instances we use a randomized iterative procedure with the following steps for each image:

1. Pick the two instances with the largest bounding box overlap.
2. If their intersection over union (IoU) is above a given threshold:
   2.1 Merge their labels.
   2.2 Randomly pick one of the original bounding boxes as the merged instance bounding box.

The picked instances are then removed and the procedure is repeated until no instances with a high enough IoU are left. Having explored multiple IoU thresholds, we note that not merging instances with highly similar bounding boxes is clearly worse than merging them; and that a moderately high threshold of 0.7–0.9 works best in practice.

Learning Rates. In Table 3 we show that using the same learning rate for the image and text encoders is clearly sub-optimal, and that it is necessary to training the text encoder with a lower learning rate. This may help to prevent catastrophic forgetting of the wide knowledge the model acquired during the contrastive pre-training stage. Here we explore a range of text encoder learning rates and demonstrate that the learning rate for the text encoder needs to be much lower (e.g. 100×) than that of the image encoder to get good zero-shot transfer (AP_{rare}^{LVIS}). However, freezing the text encoder completely (learning rate 0) does not work well either. AP^{OI}, which measure in-distribution performance, behaves in the opposite way. While using the same learning rate for the image and text encoders results in a big drop in AP_{rare}^{LVIS}, it increases AP^{OI}. This demonstrates that the optimal recipe for zero-shot transfer (AP_{rare}^{LVIS}) does not necessarily maximize in-distribution performance (AP^{OI}).

Cropped Bounding Box Filtering. We use random image crop augmentation when training our models. Upon manual inspection of the resulting images and bounding boxes we noticed a frequent occurrence of instances with degenerate bounding boxes that no longer matched their original instance label (e.g. a bounding box around a hand with label "Person" resulting from cropping most of the person out of the image). To reduce the chance of our models overfitting due to having to memorize such instances, we remove object annotations if a large fraction of their box area falls outside of the random crop area. The optimal area threshold lies between 40% and 60%, and that neither keeping all boxes, nor keeping only uncropped boxes, performs as well (Tables 3 and A.9).

Mosaics. As described in Appendix A.6, we perform image scale augmentation by tiling multiple small images into one large "mosaic". We explored mosaic sizes up to 4×4, and found that while using only 2×2 mosaics in addition to single images is clearly worse than also including larger mosaics, for the considered resolutions and patch sizes the benefits of using larger mosaics (i.e. smaller mosaic tiles) saturates with the inclusion of 3×3 or 4×4 mosaics. We have not performed extensive sweeps of the mosaic ratios, and for mosaics with grid sizes from 1×1 (i.e. a single image) to $M \times M$ we use a heuristic of sampling $k \times k$ girds with probability $\frac{2 \cdot (M-k+1)}{M \cdot (1+M)}$, such that smaller mosaics are sampled more frequently than the larger mosaics proportionally to the mosaic size.

Prompting. For generating text queries, similar to prior work, we augment object category names with prompt templates such as `"a photo of a {}"`

(where {} is replaced by the category name) to reduce the distribution shift between image-level pre-training and detection fine-tuning. We use the prompt templates proposed by CLIP [33]. During training, we randomly sample from the list of 80 CLIP prompt templates such that, within an image, every instance of a category has the same prompt, but prompt templates differ between categories and across images. During testing, we evaluate the model for each of the "7 best" CLIP prompts and ensemble the resulting predicted probabilities by averaging them. The results in Table 8 show that not using any prompting does not perform well, especially on the in-distribution AP^{OI} metric. Perhaps unsurprisingly, test-time prompt ensembling works better in cases when random prompting was also used during training. In some cases, prompting can have different effects on different model architectures. For example, applying random prompt augmentation to the VG dataset tends to improve performance of the B/32 model, but worsens that of the R26+B/32 model. We speculate that this variability is due to the relatively small number of prompt templates; expanding the list of prompt templates might provide more consistent benefits. We thus only use train-time random prompting for the OI dataset, where it yields consistent benefits.

Location Bias. As discussed in the main text, biasing box predictions to the location of the corresponding image patch improves training speed and final performance. The gain is especially large for the pure Transformer architecture (ViT-B/32 in Table 8), where removing the bias reduces performance by almost 3 points on AP^{LVIS} and AP^{LVIS}_{rare}, whereas the hybrid R26+B/32 drops by only slightly more than 1 point. We therefore speculate that the spatial inductive bias of the convolutional component of the hybrid serves a similar function as the location bias.

References

1. Arnab, A., Dehghani, M., Heigold, G., Sun, C., Lučić, M., Schmid, C.: ViViT: a video vision transformer. In: ICCV, pp. 6836–6846 (2021)
2. Bansal, A., Sikka, K., Sharma, G., Chellappa, R., Divakaran, A.: Zero-shot object detection. In: Ferrari, V., Hebert, M., Sminchisescu, C., Weiss, Y. (eds.) ECCV 2018. LNCS, vol. 11205, pp. 397–414. Springer, Cham (2018). https://doi.org/10.1007/978-3-030-01246-5_24
3. Bello, I., et al.: Revisiting ResNets: improved training and scaling strategies. In: NeurIPS, vol. 34 (2021)
4. Biswas, S.K., Milanfar, P.: One shot detection with laplacian object and fast matrix cosine similarity. IEEE Trans. Pattern Anal. Mach. Intell. **38**(3), 546–562 (2016)
5. Bradbury, J., et al.: JAX: composable transformations of Python+NumPy programs (2018). http://github.com/google/jax
6. Carion, N., Massa, F., Synnaeve, G., Usunier, N., Kirillov, A., Zagoruyko, S.: End-to-end object detection with transformers. In: Vedaldi, A., Bischof, H., Brox, T., Frahm, J.-M. (eds.) ECCV 2020. LNCS, vol. 12346, pp. 213–229. Springer, Cham (2020). https://doi.org/10.1007/978-3-030-58452-8_13
7. Chen, D.J., Hsieh, H.Y., Liu, T.L.: Adaptive image transformer for one-shot object detection. In: CVPR, pp. 12242–12251 (2021)

8. Dehghani, M., Gritsenko, A.A., Arnab, A., Minderer, M., Tay, Y.: SCENIC: a JAX library for computer vision research and beyond. arXiv preprint arXiv:2110.11403 (2021)

9. Fang, Y., et al.: You only look at one sequence: rethinking transformer in vision through object detection. In: NeurIPS, vol. 34 (2021)

10. Frome, A., et al.: Devise: a deep visual-semantic embedding model. In: NeurIPS. vol. 26 (2013)

11. Ghiasi, G., et al.: Simple copy-paste is a strong data augmentation method for instance segmentation. In: CVPR, pp. 2918–2928 (2021)

12. Gu, X., Lin, T.Y., Kuo, W., Cui, Y.: Open-vocabulary object detection via vision and language knowledge distillation. arXiv preprint arXiv:2104.13921 (2021)

13. Gupta, A., Dollar, P., Girshick, R.: LVIS: a dataset for large vocabulary instance segmentation. In: CVPR (2019)

14. He, K., Gkioxari, G., Dollar, P., Girshick, R.: Mask R-CNN. In: ICCV (2017)

15. He, K., Zhang, X., Ren, S., Sun, J.: Deep residual learning for image recognition. In: CVPR (2016)

16. Hsieh, T.I., Lo, Y.C., Chen, H.T., Liu, T.L.: One-shot object detection with co-attention and co-excitation. In: NeurIPS, vol. 32. Curran Associates, Inc. (2019)

17. Huang, G., Sun, Yu., Liu, Z., Sedra, D., Weinberger, K.Q.: Deep networks with stochastic depth. In: Leibe, B., Matas, J., Sebe, N., Welling, M. (eds.) ECCV 2016. LNCS, vol. 9908, pp. 646–661. Springer, Cham (2016). https://doi.org/10.1007/978-3-319-46493-0_39

18. Huang, Z., Zeng, Z., Liu, B., Fu, D., Fu, J.: Pixel-BERT: aligning image pixels with text by deep multi-modal transformers. arXiv preprint arXiv:2004.00849 (2020)

19. Jia, C., et al.: Scaling up visual and vision-language representation learning with noisy text supervision. In: ICML, vol. 139, pp. 4904–4916. PMLR (2021)

20. Kamath, A., Singh, M., LeCun, Y., Synnaeve, G., Misra, I., Carion, N.: MDETR - modulated detection for end-to-end multi-modal understanding. In: ICCV, pp. 1780–1790 (2021)

21. Kolesnikov, A., et al.: Big Transfer (BiT): general visual representation learning. In: Vedaldi, A., Bischof, H., Brox, T., Frahm, J.-M. (eds.) ECCV 2020. LNCS, vol. 12350, pp. 491–507. Springer, Cham (2020). https://doi.org/10.1007/978-3-030-58558-7_29

22. Kolesnikov, A., et al.: An image is worth 16×16 words: transformers for image recognition at scale. In: ICLR (2021)

23. Krishna, R., et al.: Visual genome: connecting language and vision using crowd-sourced dense image annotations. Int. J. Comput. Vision 123(1), 32–73 (2017)

24. Kuznetsova, A.: The open images dataset V4. Int. J. Comput. Vision 128(7), 1956–1981 (2020)

25. Lee, J., Lee, Y., Kim, J., Kosiorek, A.R., Choi, S., Teh, Y.W.: Set transformer: a framework for attention-based permutation-invariant neural networks. In: ICML, Proceedings of Machine Learning Research, vol. 97, pp. 3744–3753. PMLR (2019)

26. Li, L.H., et al.: Grounded language-image pre-training. arXiv preprint arXiv:2112.03857 (2021)

27. Lin, T.-Y., et al.: Microsoft COCO: common objects in context. In: Fleet, D., Pajdla, T., Schiele, B., Tuytelaars, T. (eds.) ECCV 2014. LNCS, vol. 8693, pp. 740–755. Springer, Cham (2014). https://doi.org/10.1007/978-3-319-10602-1_48

28. Liu, W., et al.: SSD: single shot multibox detector. In: Leibe, B., Matas, J., Sebe, N., Welling, M. (eds.) ECCV 2016. LNCS, vol. 9905, pp. 21–37. Springer, Cham (2016). https://doi.org/10.1007/978-3-319-46448-0_2

29. Mahajan, D.: Exploring the limits of weakly supervised pretraining. In: Ferrari, V., Hebert, M., Sminchisescu, C., Weiss, Y. (eds.) ECCV 2018. LNCS, vol. 11206, pp. 185–201. Springer, Cham (2018). https://doi.org/10.1007/978-3-030-01216-8_12

30. Michaelis, C., Ustyuzhaninov, I., Bethge, M., Ecker, A.S.: One-shot instance segmentation. arXiv preprint arXiv:1811.11507 (2018)

31. Osokin, A., Sumin, D., Lomakin, V.: OS2D: one-stage one-shot object detection by matching anchor features. In: Vedaldi, A., Bischof, H., Brox, T., Frahm, J.-M. (eds.) ECCV 2020. LNCS, vol. 12360, pp. 635–652. Springer, Cham (2020). https://doi.org/10.1007/978-3-030-58555-6_38

32. Pham, H., et al.: Combined scaling for zero-shot transfer learning. arXiv preprint arXiv:2111.10050 (2021)

33. Radford, A., et al.: Learning transferable visual models from natural language supervision. In: ICML, 18–24 July 2021, vol. 139, pp. 8748–8763. PMLR (2021)

34. Ren, S., He, K., Girshick, R., Sun, J.: Faster R-CNN: towards real-time object detection with region proposal networks. In: NeurIPS, vol. 28. Curran Associates, Inc. (2015)

35. Shao, S., et al.: Objects365: a large-scale, high-quality dataset for object detection. In: ICCV, pp. 8429–8438 (2019)

36. Socher, R., Ganjoo, M., Manning, C.D., Ng, A.: Zero-shot learning through cross-modal transfer. In: NeurIPS, vol. 26 (2013)

37. Song, H., et al.: ViDT: an efficient and effective fully transformer-based object detector. In: ICLR (2022)

38. Steiner, A., Kolesnikov, A., Zhai, X., Wightman, R., Uszkoreit, J., Beyer, L.: How to train your ViT? data, augmentation, and regularization in vision transformers. arXiv preprint arXiv:2106.10270 (2021)

39. Touvron, H., Cord, M., Douze, M., Massa, F., Sablayrolles, A., Jegou, H.: Training data-efficient image transformers and distillation through attention. In: ICML, vol. 139, pp. 10347–10357 (2021)

40. Xian, Y., Lampert, C.H., Schiele, B., Akata, Z.: Zero-shot learning-a comprehensive evaluation of the good, the bad and the ugly. IEEE Trans. Pattern Anal. Mach. Intell. 41(9), 2251–2265 (2018)

41. Yao, Z., Ai, J., Li, B., Zhang, C.: Efficient detr: improving end-to-end object detector with dense prior. arXiv preprint arXiv:2104.01318 (2021)

42. Zareian, A., Rosa, K.D., Hu, D.H., Chang, S.F.: Open-vocabulary object detection using captions. In: CVPR, pp. 14393–14402 (2021)

43. Zhai, X., Kolesnikov, A., Houlsby, N., Beyer, L.: Scaling vision transformers. arXiv preprint arXiv:2106.04560 (2021)

44. Zhai, X., et al.: LiT: zero-shot transfer with locked-image text tuning. arXiv preprint arXiv:2111.07991 (2021)

45. Zhong, Y., et al.: RegionCLIP: region-based language-image pretraining. arXiv preprint arXiv:2112.09106 (2021)

46. Zhou, X., Girdhar, R., Joulin, A., Krähenbühl, P., Misra, I.: Detecting twenty-thousand classes using image-level supervision. In: arXiv preprint arXiv:2201.02605 (2021)

47. Zhou, X., Koltun, V., Krähenbühl, P.: Probabilistic two-stage detection. arXiv preprint arXiv:2103.07461 (2021)

48. Zhu, X., Su, W., Lu, L., Li, B., Wang, X., Dai, J.: Deformable DETR: deformable transformers for end-to-end object detection. In: ICLR (2021)

Author Index

Printed in the United States
by Baker & Taylor Publisher Services